TRADITIONS & ENCOUNTERS

A Brief Global History

Second Edition

Jerry H. Bentley
University of Hawai`i

Herbert F. Ziegler
University of Hawai`i

Heather E. Streets Salter
Washington State University

with additional materials
Chemeketa Community College

Boston Burr Ridge, IL Dubuque, IA New York San Francisco St. Louis
Bangkok Bogotá Caracas Lisbon London Madrid
Mexico City Milan New Delhi Seoul Singapore Sydney Taipei Toronto

The McGraw-Hill Companies

Traditions & Encounters: A Brief Global History, Second Edition
with additional materials
Chemeketa Community College

This book is a McGraw-Hill Learning Solutions textbook and contains select material from *Traditions and Encounters: A Brief Global History*, Second Edition by Jerry Bentley, Herbert Ziegler, and Heather Streets Salter. Copyright © 2010 by The McGraw-Hill Companies, Inc. Reprinted with permission of the publisher. Many custom published texts are modified versions or adaptations of our best-selling textbooks. Some adaptations are printed in black and white to keep prices at a minimum, while others are in color.

2 3 4 5 6 7 8 9 0 WDD WDD 12 11 10

ISBN-13: 978-0-07-747222-1
ISBN-10: 0-07-747222-5

Learning Solutions Manager: Danielle Meier
Production Editor: Lynn Nagel
Cover Photo: Statue © 2010 Royalty-Free/CORBIS
Printer/Binder: Quad/Graphics

Brief Table of Contents

Table of Contents

15 STATES AND SOCIETIES OF SUB-SAHARAN AFRICA 283

16 CHRISTIAN WESTERN EUROPE DURING THE MIDDLE AGES 299

17 WORLDS APART: THE AMERICAS AND OCEANIA 323

18 REACHING OUT: CROSS-CULTURAL INTERACTIONS 343

THE ORIGINS OF GLOBAL INTERDEPENDENCE, 1500–1800 364

26 The Making of Industrial Society 515

27 The Americas in the Age of Independence 535

28 The Building of Global Empires 555

PART VII

CONTEMPORARY GLOBAL REALIGNMENTS 580

29 The Great War: The World in Upheaval 583

Section Taken From

Mitchell, Taking Sides: Clashing Views in World History 2nd Editoin

PRIMARY SOURCES FROM THE PAST

A BRIEF NOTE ON USAGE

This book qualifies dates as B.C.E. ("Before the Common Era") or C.E. ("Common Era"). In practice, B.C.E. refers to the same epoch as B.C. ("Before Christ"), and C.E. refers to the same epoch as A.D. (*Anno Domini,* a Latin term meaning "in the year of the Lord"). As historical study becomes a global, multicultural enterprise, however, scholars increasingly prefer terminology that does not apply the standards of one society to all the others. Thus reference in this book to B.C.E. and C.E. reflects emerging scholarly convention concerning the qualification of historical dates.

Measurements of length and distance appear here according to the metric system, followed by their English-system equivalents in parentheses.

The book transliterates Chinese names and terms into English according to the *pinyin* system, which has largely displaced the more cumbersome Wade-Giles system. Transliteration of names and terms from other languages follows contemporary scholarly conventions.

Preface

HOW IS IT POSSIBLE TO MAKE SENSE OF THE ENTIRE HUMAN PAST?

World history is about people. But it is easy to lose people in the telling of history. *Traditions and Encounters: A Brief Global History* is not merely a recounting of the facts of history. Rather, we wanted to tell the story of people in history, the traditions they embraced and the encounters with other cultures that brought about inevitable change.

It is the interaction of these traditions and encounters that provides the key to making sense of our past. Human communities furthered themselves not by remaining isolated, but by interacting with others and exploring the benefits and risks of reaching out. The vitality of history—and its interpretation—lies in understanding the nature of individual traditions and the scope of encounters that punctuated every significant event in human history.

Traditions & Encounters

TELLING THE STORY OF PEOPLE

Traditions & Encounters: A Brief Global History provides a global vision of history that grows increasingly meaningful in a shrinking world. The theme of ***traditions*** draws attention to the formation, maintenance, and sometimes collapse of individual societies. Because the world's peoples have also interacted regularly with one another since the earliest days of human history, the theme of ***encounters*** directs attention to communications, interactions, networks, and exchanges that have linked individual societies to their neighbors and others in the larger world.

The themes of traditions and encounters are at the heart of every chapter in the text. They provide a lens through which to interpret the affairs of humankind and the pressures that continue to shape history. All aspects of the text support these themes—from the organization of chapters, engaging stories of the world's peoples, to the robust map program and critical-thinking features.

Organization: Seven Eras of Global History

We discuss the world's development through time by organizing it into seven eras of global history. These eras, treated successively in the seven parts of this book, represent coherent epochs that form the larger architecture of world history as we see it. Every region of the world is discussed in each of the seven eras. The eras owe their coherence in large part to the networks of transportation, communication, and exchange that have linked peoples of different societies at different times in the past. This structure allows us to make cross-cultural comparisons that help frame world history for students to put events in a perspective that renders them more understandable.

FEATURES THAT ENRICH THE HISTORY EXPERIENCE

This text contains a carefully selected range of tools to enhance student comprehension and interest. These tools are crafted to underscore the vital theme of "traditions and encounters," encourage critical thinking, and reinforce the global view of the course. Among these tools are several new and remodeled features that strengthen these objectives further.

- **Revised Part Openers.** Seven newly designed part openers begin with an introduction that outlines the themes running through all the chapters in that part. This information creates a strong framework for understanding the details of individual chapters. New part-opening maps preview the cultures and regions discussed in a given era.

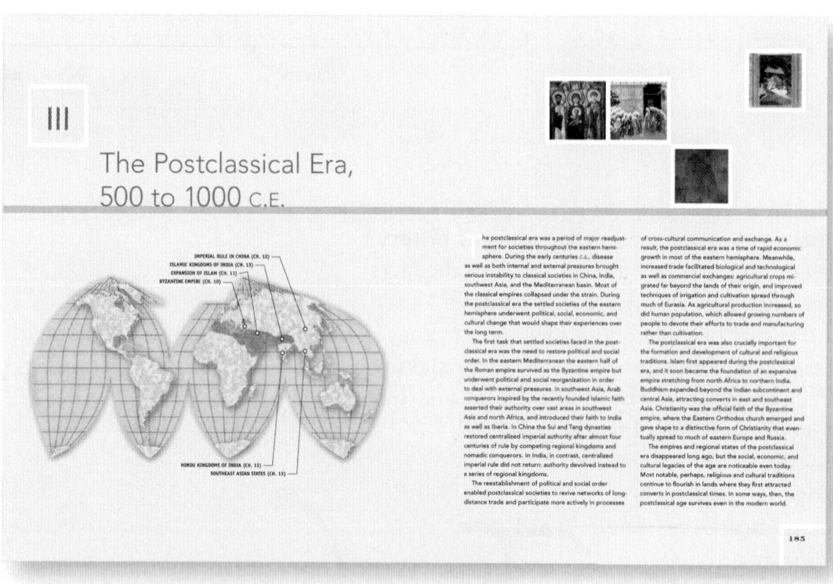

III

The Postclassical Era, 500 to 1000 C.E.

The postclassical era was a period of major readjustment for societies throughout the eastern hemisphere. During the early centuries C.E., disease as well as both internal and external pressures brought serious instability to classical societies in China, India, southwest Asia, and the Mediterranean basin. Most of the classical empires collapsed under the strain. During the postclassical era the settled societies of the eastern hemisphere underwent political, social, economic, and cultural change that would shape their experiences over the long term.

The first task that settled societies faced in the postclassical era was the need to restore political and social order. In the eastern Mediterranean the eastern half of the Roman empire survived as the Byzantine empire but underwent political and social reorganization in order to deal with external pressures. In southwest Asia, Arab conquerors inspired by the recently founded Islamic faith asserted their authority over vast areas in southwest Asia and north Africa, and introduced their faith to India as well as Iberia. In China the Sui and Tang dynasties restored centralized imperial authority after almost four centuries of rule by competing regional kingdoms and nomadic conquerors. In India, in contrast, centralized imperial rule did not return: authority devolved instead to a series of regional kingdoms.

The reestablishment of political and social order enabled postclassical societies to revive networks of long-distance trade and participate more actively in processes of cross-cultural communication and exchange. As a result, the postclassical era was a time of rapid economic growth in most of the eastern hemisphere. Meanwhile, increased trade facilitated biological and technological as well as commercial exchanges: agricultural crops migrated far beyond the lands of their origin, and improved techniques of irrigation and cultivation spread through much of Eurasia. As agricultural production increased, so did human population, which allowed growing numbers of people to devote their efforts to trade and manufacturing rather than cultivation.

The postclassical era was also crucially important for the formation and development of cultural and religious traditions. Islam first appeared during the postclassical era, and it soon became the foundation of an expansive empire stretching from north Africa to northern India. Buddhism expanded beyond the Indian subcontinent and central Asia, attracting converts in east and southeast Asia. Christianity was the official faith of the Byzantine empire, where the Eastern Orthodox church emerged and gave shape to a distinctive form of Christianity that eventually spread to much of eastern Europe and Russia.

The empires and regional states of the postclassical era disappeared long ago, but the social, economic, and cultural legacies of the age are noticeable even today. Most notable, perhaps, religious and cultural traditions continue to flourish in lands where they first attracted converts in postclassical times. In some ways, then, the postclassical age survives even in the modern world.

185

- **Chapter-opening Vignettes** draw the reader into the larger story and allow students to remember that world history is really about people.
- **New Part Closers.** The last chapter of each era now concludes with an interpretive summary called "Bringing It All Together." This feature encourages the student to assimilate material from all chapters in the era and to apply the broader theme of traditions and encounters.

SOURCES FROM THE PAST

Socrates' View of Death

In one of his earliest dialogues, the Apology, *Plato offered an account of Socrates' defense of himself during his trial before a jury of Athenian citizens. After the jury had convicted him and condemned him to death, Socrates reflected on the nature of death and reemphasized his commitment to virtue rather than to wealth or fame.*

And if we reflect in another way we shall see that we may well hope that death is a good thing. For the state of death is one of two things: either the dead man wholly ceases to be and loses all sensation; or, according to the common belief, it is a change and a migration of the soul unto another place. And if death is the absence of all sensation, like the sleep of one whose slumbers are unbroken by any dreams, it will be a wonderful gain. For if a man had to select that night in which he slept so soundly that he did not even see any dreams, and had to compare with it all the other nights and days of his life, and then had to say how many days and nights in his life he had slept better and more pleasantly than this night, I think that a private person, nay, even the great king of Persia himself, would find them easy to count, compared with the others. If that is the nature of death, I for one count it a gain. For then it appears that eternity is nothing more than a single night.

But if death is a journey to another place, and the common belief be true, that all who have died dwell there, what good could be greater than this, my judges? Would a journey not be worth taking if at the end of it, in the other world, we should be released from the self-styled judges of this world, and should find the true judges who are said to sit in judgment below? . . . It would be an infinite happiness to converse with them, and to live with them, and to examine them. Assuredly there they do not put men to death for doing that. For besides the other ways in which they are happier than we are, they are immortal, at least if the common belief be true.

And you too, judges, must face death with a good courage, and believe this as a truth, that no evil can happen to a good man, either in life, or after death. His fortunes are not neglected by the gods, and what has come to me today has not come by chance. I am persuaded that it is better for me to die now, and to be released from trouble. . . . And so I am hardly angry with my accusers, or with those who have condemned me to die. Yet it was not with this mind that they accused me and condemned me, but rather they meant to do me an injury. Only to that extent do I find fault with them.

Yet I have one request to make of them. When my sons grow up, visit them with punishment, my friends, and vex them in the same way that I have vexed you if they seem to you to care for riches or for anything other than virtue: and if they think that they are something when they are nothing at all, reproach them as I have reproached you for not caring for what they should and for thinking that they are great men when in fact they are worthless. And if you will do this, I myself and my sons will have received our deserts at your hands. But now the time has come, and we must go hence: I to die, and you to live. Whether life or death is better is known to God, and to God only.

- How does Socrates' understanding of personal morality and its rewards compare and contrast with the Zoroastrian, Buddhist, and Hindu views discussed in earlier chapters?

SOURCE: F. J. Church, trans. *The Trial and Death of Socrates*, 2nd ed. London: Macmillan, 1886, pp. 76–78. (Translation slightly modified.)

- **Sources from the Past.** Found in every chapter, "Sources from the Past" boxes bring the past to life by spotlighting significant primary source documents relevant to the chapter, such as poems, journal accounts, religious writings, and letters. We place the documents in context and explain their significance, and thought-provoking questions prompt readers to contextualize and think critically about key issues raised in the document. For this edition, we carefully reviewed our existing selections and replaced ten of them with compelling new choices.

- **New Map Program.** The entire map program has been revised for clarity, greater detail, and more topographical information. Maps now include newly written captions and critical-thinking questions that draw attention to the geographical dimensions of historical developments.
- **New Study Terms.** A list of important terms (with page references) has been added to the end of each chapter.

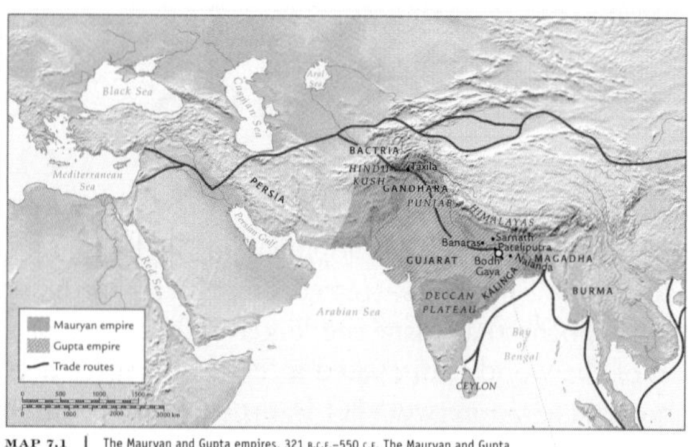

MAP 7.1 | The Mauryan and Gupta empires, 321 B.C.E.–550 C.E. The Mauryan and Gupta dynasties both originated in the kingdom of Magadha. ***Why was this region so important in ancient India? What advantages did it offer for purposes of trade and communication with other regions?***

- **New "Thinking About" Questions.** Each chapter presents two new critical thinking questions—one on "traditions" and one on "encounters"—to further reinforce the underlying themes of the text.
- **Chronology.** Found in each chapter, the chronology box lists the most important dates and events discussed in the chapter. These revised timelines have been relocated to the third page of each chapter for easier access.
- **New Photos and Illustrations.** The second edition has nearly 100 new illustrations and photographs. Many photo and illustration captions now include critical-thinking questions to link the text's illustrations to the chapter discussion.
- **Expanded Pronunciation Guide.** This expanded guide appears along the bottom of pages and helps readers with unfamiliar names and terms. The pronunciations can also be found in the text's glossary.
- **Links for Primary Source Investigator (PSI).** Links to our customized online archive of primary source documents and images can be found throughout the book in the chapter margins.
- **Summary.** Clearly written chapter-ending summaries remind students of the highlights in each chapter.
- **New Study Terms.** A list of important study terms recaps important concepts and people from each chapter.
- **For Further Reading.** Fully updated in the second edition, these annotated lists of references that end each chapter provide readers with a starting point for research assignments or their own study.

THINKING ABOUT

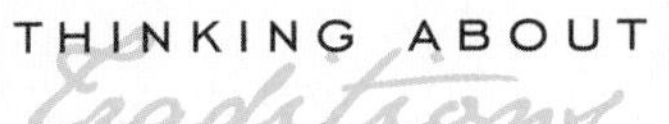

TRADITIONS IN STATES AND SOCIETIES IN SUB-SAHARAN AFRICA. Geographical barriers posed many difficulties for cross-cultural interaction between sub-Saharan African societies and other societies in north Africa and Eurasia. In what ways did the relative isolation imposed by these barriers contribute to the persistence of distinctly sub-Saharan traditions regarding religion, culture, and community organization in this period?

Changes for the Second Edition

In preparing this second edition of *Traditions & Encounters: A Brief Global History,* we have revised, updated, and reorganized the text to stay current with recent world historical scholarship and to remain true to the goals of a brief textbook.

Significant modifications to the second edition include:

- **New Chapter 16, "Christian Western Europe during the Middle Ages."** By combining elements of former chapters 14 and 17, we strengthen the book's story about Christianity and place Europe in a world perspective. This change provides coverage that is broader, deeper, and more focused.
- **New Chapter 33, "The Cold War and the End of Empires."** By combining elements of former chapters 34 and 35, we strategically join the discussion of two contemporaneous issues that affected one another: the relationship between the cold war and its effect on the empires.
- **Expanded Chapter 34, "A World without Borders."** This concluding chapter provides a more timely discussion of the contemporary world with added coverage of the Middle East and a broader discussion of globalization in the context of world history.
- **A Briefer Text.** Many instructors told us that brevity was one of the most important aspects of this text. Following their lead, and implementing the changes described above, we have succeeded in making the second edition even shorter by one chapter with 34 instead of 35 chapters.
- **New Sources from the Past.** Primary source documents highlight individual voices from the human past. We carefully reviewed our existing Sources from the Past selections, which appear in each chapter, and updated ten of them with compelling new selections.

WHAT'S NEW IN EACH CHAPTER?

Other notable chapter changes and revisions include the following:

In Every Chapter...	New and expanded critical thinking features including: Thinking about Traditions and Thinking about Encounters questions; photo and figure captions with probing questions; new map program with visual pointers and questions; new photos; study terms.
Chapter 1	Revised discussion of the Hebrew patriarch Abraham, and an expanded section on early Jewish communities. New Sources from the Past selection: the Sumerian flood story in *The Epic of Gilgamesh.*
Chapter 2	Revised discussion of early economic specialization and trade in Nile societies.
Chapter 4	Revised discussion of Olmec society and trade.
Chapter 7	New Sources from the Past: "The Teachings of Buddha."
Chapter 9	New chapter ending summary.
Chapter 12	Revised discussion of early Japan.
Chapter 15	Expanded discussion of Bantu migrations. New Sources from the Past selection: "Ibn Battuta on Muslim Society at Mogadishu."
Chapter 16	New discussions of the establishment of regional states in early Europe; the Franks and the temporary revival of empire; serfs and the growth of an agricultural economy; and the conversion of western Europe to Christianity. Expanded discussion of the Crusades. New chapter ending summary.
Chapter 18	New chapter ending summary.
Chapter 20	New Sources from the Past selection: Galileo Galilei, "Letter to the Grand Duchess Christina."
Chapter 21	Revised description and question for the primary source from the past: "First Impressions of Spanish Forces." Expanded discussion of tobacco farming in North America.
Chapter 22	New discussion of African-American music.
Chapter 24	New Sources from the Past selection: Sultan Selim I, "Letter to Shah Ismail of Persia."
Chapter 26	New Sources from the Past selection: "Testimony for the Factory Act of 1833: Working Conditions in England."
Chapter 27	Expanded discussion of the annexation of New Mexico.
Chapter 29	Expanded discussion on the Armenian massacre and the influenza pandemic of 1918.
Chapter 30	New Sources from the Past selection: *Mein Kampf.*
Chapter 31	New Sources from the Past selection: Mohandas Gandhi.
Chapter 33	New discussion on apartheid in South Africa. Expanded discussion on decolonization and global cold war. New Sources from the Past selection: "National Security Council Paper Number 68."
Chapter 34	Expanded chapter on globalization. New discussions on Consumption and Cultural Interaction and The Age of Access.

SUPPLEMENTS

Primary Source Investigator Online

McGraw-Hill's Primary Source Investigator (PSI), available online at www.mhhe.com/psi, is designed to support and enrich the text discussion in *Traditions & Encounters: A Brief Global History.* PSI gives instructors and students access to more than 700 primary and secondary sources including documents, images, maps, and videos. Students can use these resources to formulate and defend their arguments as well as further their understanding of the topics discussed in each chapter. All assets are indexed alphabetically as well as by type, subject, place, and time period, allowing students and instructors to locate resources quickly and easily.

STUDENT RESOURCES IN PSI

Primary Source Documents: Newly updated for this edition of *Traditions & Encounters,* this database includes items from a wide range of contemporary accounts. Each document is accompanied by a detailed description and a series of critical thinking questions that draw students into the content and engage them in thoughtful analysis. Sources include private papers, government documents, and publications.

Images: This extensive collection includes photographs of artifacts and buildings as well as contemporary paintings, engravings, and drawings. Each image is also accompanied by a description and critical thinking question.

Interactive Maps: Each map's legend is interactive, allowing students to see historical change over time and compare various factors in the order of their choice.

Research and Writing Center: The PSI Research and Writing Center provides a wide range of resources to assist you in writing papers, conducting research, and organizing your efforts to achieve success in college. Divided into four sections, the Writing Center provides tips regarding achieving success in college, tools for conducting research and formatting your materials, avoiding plagiarism, and writing an effective paper.

INSTRUCTOR RESOURCES IN PSI

Faculty Guide: The Faculty Guide provides easy reference to all learning assets, both in the text and on PSI, available to teachers and students. Each chapter is accompanied by a rich list of resources, including **PowerPoint slides, image bank, outline maps, book maps,** and **test bank questions,** all keyed to the chapter. In addition to assets, the Faculty Guide also includes a chapter overview, a list of themes, lecture strategies, discussion suggestions, suggestions for further reading, and chapter-specific film recommendations.

ADDITIONAL RESOURCES FOR STUDENTS

- **The Online Learning Center (OLC) for Students** at www.mhhe.com/bentleybrief2e provides students with a wide range of tools that will help them test their understanding of the book. It includes chapter overviews, interactive maps, multiple choice and essay quizzes, matching and identification games, as well as primary source indexes for further research.
- Two **After the Fact Interactive** units are available for use with *Traditions & Encounters:* "After the Fact Interactive: Tracing the Silk Roads" for volume 1 (ISBN 0-07-281843-3) and "After the Fact Interactive: Envisioning the Atlantic World" for volume 2 (ISBN 0-07-281844-1). These rich, visually appealing modules on CD-ROM allow students to be apprentice historians, examining a variety of multimedia primary source material and constructing arguments based on their research.

ADDITIONAL RESOURCES FOR INSTRUCTORS

- The **Online Learning Center (OLC) for Instructors** at www.mhhe.com/bentleybrief2e contains several instructor tools, including a link to the Teacher's Edition of Primary Source Investigator (www.mhhe.com/psi) and PowerPoint presentations for each chapter. The instructor side of the OLC is password protected to prevent tampering. Please contact your local McGraw-Hill sales representative for details.
- A **Computerized Test Bank,** McGraw-Hill's EZ Test, allows you to quickly create a customized test using the publisher's supplied test banks or your own questions. You

decide the number, type, and order of test questions with a few simple clicks. EZ Test runs on your computer without a connection to the Internet.

- **Videos** on topics in world history are available through the Films for Humanities and Sciences collection. Contact your local McGraw-Hill sales representative for further information.
- **Classroom Performance System (CPS).** The Classroom Performance System brings ultimate interactivity to *Traditions & Encounters: A Brief Global History.* CPS is a wireless polling system that gives you immediate feedback from every student in the class. Use CPS to ask questions during your lecture that have been prepared by McGraw-Hill or enter your own questions. A complete CPS Tutorial is available at www.einstruction.com.

This text is available as an eTextbook at *www.CourseSmart.com.* At CourseSmart your students can take advantage of significant savings off the cost of a print textbook, reduce their impact on the environment, and gain access to powerful Web tools for learning. CourseSmart eTextbooks can be viewed online. The eTextbooks allow students to do full text searches, add highlighting and notes, and share notes with classmates. CourseSmart has the largest selection of eTextbooks available anywhere. Visit *www.CourseSmart.com* to learn more and to try a sample chapter.

McGraw-Hill Higher Education. Connect. Learn. Succeed.

McGraw-Hill Higher Education's mission is to help prepare students for the world that awaits them. With textbooks, e-books, and other digital instructional content, as well as experiential learning and assignment/assessment platforms, McGraw-Hill enables instructors to connect with their students more closely. In turn, students can learn to their full potential and, thus, succeed academically now and in the real world. Learn more at www.mhhe.com.

Acknowledgments

Many individuals have contributed to this book, and the authors take pleasure in recording deep thanks for all the comments, criticism, advice, and suggestions that helped to improve the work. Special thanks to the editorial and production teams at McGraw-Hill: Chris Freitag, Matthew Busbridge, Thom Holmes, Lisa Pinto, Brett Coker, Cassandra Chu, Kim Adams, and Sheryl Rose, who provided crucial support by helping the authors work through difficult issues and solving the innumerable problems of content, style, organization, and design that arise in any project to produce a history of the world.

Academic Reviewers

This edition continues to reflect many discerning suggestions made by instructors of the world history course. We would like to acknowledge the contributions of the following reviewers who suggested many of the changes implemented here in the second edition:

Wayne Ackerson
Salisbury University

Patrick Albano
Fairmont State University

Gene Barnett
Calhoun Community College

Kathryn Braund
Auburn University

David Brosius
Air Force Academy/USAFA

Samuel Brunk
University of Texas, El Paso

Robert Carriedo,
US Air Force Academy/USAFA

Patricia Colman
Moorpark College

Kevin Dougherty
University of Southern Mississippi

Tim Dowling
Virginia Military Institute

Christopher Drennan
Clinton Community College

Shawn Dry
Oakland Community College

Sarah Franklin
University of Southern Mississippi

Ernie Grieshaber
Minnesota State University-Mankato

Theodore Kallman
San Joaquin Delta Community College

David Katz
Mohawk Valley Community College

Richard Kennedy
Mount Olive College

Janine Lanza
Wayne State University

David Massey
Bunker Hill Community College

Anne Osborne
Rider University, Lawrenceville, NJ

Charles Parker
Saint Louis University

Brian Plummer
Asuza Pacific University

William Rodner
Tidewater Community College

Pamela Sayre
Henry Ford Community College

David Schmidt
Bethel College

Jerry Sheppard
Mount Olive College

Kyle Smith
Grand Valley State University

Michael Snodgrass
Indiana University Purdue University Indianapolis

Paul Steeves
Stetson University

Elisaveta Todorova
University of Cincinnati

Judith Walden
College of the Ozarks

Kathleen Warnes
Grand Valley State University

Kurt Werthmuller
Azusa Pacific University

Sherri West
Brookdale Community College

Kenneth Wilburn
East Carolina University

Jeffrey Wilson
University of New Orleans

William Zogby
Mohawk Valley Community College

We are also grateful to the valued reviewers who contributed to the creation of the first edition of the text. Their ideas and comments continue to inform the planning of subsequent editions:

Heather J. Abdelnur
Blackburn College

Wayne Ackerson
Salisbury University

William H. Alexander
Norfolk State University

Michael Balyo
Chemeketa Community College

Diane Barefoot
Caldwell Community College, Watauga Campus

Gene Barnett
Calhoun Community College

John Boswell
San Antonio College

W. H. Bragg
Georgia College and State University

Robert Brown
UNC Pembroke

Gayle Brunelle
California State University, Fullerton

Marybeth Carlson
University of Dayton

Kay J. Carr
Southern Illinois University

Jon Davidann
Hawaii Pacific University

Mitch Driebe
Andrew College

Shawn Dry
Oakland Community College

Shannon Duffy
Loyola University of New Orleans

Robert J. Flynn
Portland Community College

Deanna D. Forsman
North Hennepin Community College

Kristine Frederickson
Brigham Young University

James Fuller
University of Indianapolis

Jessie Ruth Gaston
California State University, Sacramento

George W. Gawrych
Baylor University

Deborah Gerish
Emporia State University

Gary G. Gibbs
Roanoke College

Candace Gregory
California State University, Sacramento

Jillian Hartley
Arkansas Northeastern College

Gregory Havrilcsak
The University of Michigan, Flint

John K. Hayden
Southwest Oklahoma State University

About the Authors

JERRY H. BENTLEY is professor of history at the University of Hawai`i and editor of the *Journal of World History.* He has written extensively on the cultural history of early modern Europe and on cross-cultural interactions in world history. His research on the religious, moral, and political writings of the Renaissance led to the publication of *Humanists and Holy Writ: New Testament Scholarship in the Renaissance* (1983) and *Politics and Culture in Renaissance Naples* (1987). His more recent research has concentrated on global history and particularly on processes of cross-cultural interaction. His book *Old World Encounters: Cross-Cultural Contacts and Exchanges in Pre-Modern Times* (1993) studies processes of cultural exchange and religious conversion before modern times, and his pamphlet *Shapes of World History in Twentieth-Century Scholarship* (1996) discusses the historiography of world history. His current interests include processes of cross-cultural interaction and cultural exchange in modern times.

HERBERT F. ZIEGLER is an associate professor of history at the University of Hawai`i. He has taught world history since 1980 and currently serves as director of the world history program at the University of Hawai`i. He also serves as book review editor of the *Journal of World History.* His interest in twentieth-century European social and political history led to the publication of *Nazi Germany's New Aristocracy* (1990). He is at present working on a study that explores from a global point of view the demographic trends of the past ten thousand years, along with their concomitant technological, economic, and social developments. His other current research project focuses on the application of complexity theory to a comparative study of societies and their internal dynamics.

HEATHER E. STREETS-SALTER is an associate professor of history at Washington State University, where she teaches world history at the graduate and undergraduate levels. She has been teaching at WSU since 1998 and is the director of the WSU history department's world history Ph.D. program. Streets-Salter was also co-editor of *World History Connected: the ejournal of Learning and Teaching* from 2003 to 2008. Recent publications include *Martial Races: The Military, Race, and Masculinity in British Imperial Culture, 1857–1914* (2004). She is currently researching nineteenth- and twentieth-century imperialism as a global phenomenon rather than as a strictly national issue. Her next book will explore the connections between French Indochina, the Dutch East Indies, and British Malaya as a way of demonstrating that the various national empires learned from, imitated, and stayed in contact with one another.

TRADITIONS & ENCOUNTERS

I

The Early Complex Societies, 3500 to 500 B.C.E.

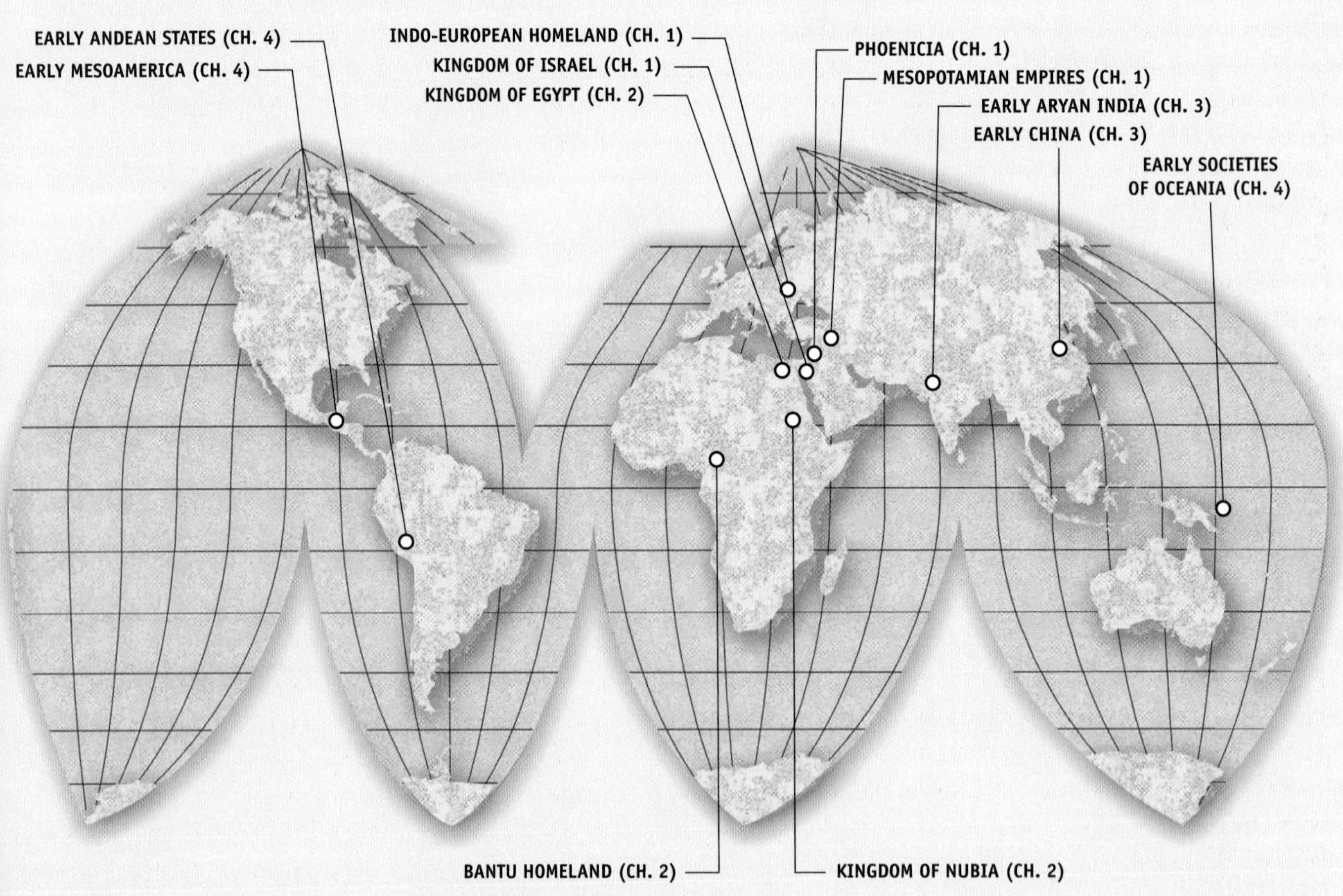

About 12,000 years ago, humans crossed an important threshold when they began to experiment with agriculture. It quickly became clear that cultivation of crops provided a larger and more reliable food supply than foraging. Groups that turned to agriculture experienced rapid population growth, and they settled into permanent communities. Some of these developed into cities and became the world's first complex societies.

The term *complex society* refers to a form of large-scale social organization in which productive agricultural economies produced surplus food. That surplus allowed some people to devote their time to specialized tasks, other than food production, and to congregate in urban settlements. During the centuries from 3500 to 500 B.C.E., complex societies arose independently in several regions of the world, including Mesopotamia, Egypt, northern India, China, Mesoamerica, and the central Andean region of South America. Each established political authorities, built states with formal governmental institutions, collected surplus agricultural production in the form of taxes or tribute, and redistributed wealth. Complex societies also traded with other peoples, and they often sought to extend their authority to surrounding territories.

Complex societies were able to generate and preserve much more wealth than smaller societies. When bequeathed to heirs and held within particular families, this accumulated wealth became the foundation for social distinctions. These societies developed different kinds of social distinctions, but all recognized several classes of people, including ruling elites, common people, and slaves.

All early complex societies also created sophisticated cultural traditions. Most of them either invented or borrowed a system of writing, which quickly came to be used to construct traditions of literature, learning, and reflection. All the complex societies organized systems of formal education that introduced intellectual elites to skills such as writing and astronomical observation deemed necessary for their societies' survival. In addition, all of these societies explored the nature of humanity, the world, and the gods.

Although all the early complex societies shared some common features, each nevertheless developed distinct cultural, political, social, and economic traditions of its own. These distinctions were based, at least initially, on geographical differences and the differing availability of resources. For instance, the absence or presence of large supplies of freshwater, of river or ocean transport, of mountains or desert, or of large draft animals or domesticable plants helped structure the shape of early economic activities, cultural beliefs, and state structures. As a result, early complex societies in different parts of the world grew into a variety of rich and unique cultures.

At the same time, none of the early complex societies developed their distinct cultures in complete isolation. Indeed, each interacted with neighboring peoples, with whom they traded valuable items, fought, married, and borrowed ideas about government, philosophy, or religion. In many ways, these encounters were crucial to the development of early complex societies. Because of this, it seems clear that, even in the earliest complex societies, connections between peoples were an important part of the human story.

The Foundations of Complex Societies

1

y far, the most familiar individual of ancient Mesopotamian society was a man named Gilgamesh. According to historical sources, Gilgamesh was the fifth king of the city of Uruk. He ruled about 2750 B.C.E., and he led his community in its conflicts with Kish, a nearby city that was the principal rival of Uruk.

Gilgamesh was a figure of Mesopotamian mythology and folklore as well as history. He was the subject of numerous poems and legends, and Mesopotamian bards made him the central figure in a cycle of stories known collectively as the *Epic of Gilgamesh.* As a figure of legend, Gilgamesh became the greatest hero figure of ancient Mesopotamia. According to the stories, the gods granted Gilgamesh a perfect body and endowed him with superhuman strength and courage. The legends declare that he constructed the massive city walls of Uruk as well as several of the city's magnificent temples to Mesopotamian deities.

The stories that make up the *Epic of Gilgamesh* recount the adventures of this hero and his cherished friend Enkidu as they sought fame. They killed an evil monster, rescued Uruk from a ravaging bull, and matched wits with the gods. In spite of their heroic deeds, Enkidu offended the gods and fell under a sentence of death. His loss profoundly affected Gilgamesh, who sought for some means to cheat death and gain eternal life. He eventually found a magical plant that had the power to confer immortality, but a serpent stole the plant and carried it away, forcing Gilgamesh to recognize that death is the ultimate fate of all human beings. Thus, while focusing on the activities of Gilgamesh and Enkidu, the stories explored themes of friendship, loyalty, ambition, fear of death, and longing for immortality. In doing so they reflected the interests and concerns of the complex, urban-based society that had recently emerged in Mesopotamia.

The *Epic of Gilgamesh*
www.mhhe.com/bentleybrief2e

Yet such interests and concerns had their foundation deep in the human past. By the time Mesopotamian society emerged, our own species of human, *Homo sapiens,* had existed for about two hundred thousand years. These humans, who themselves descended from earlier hominids, were already accomplished problem solvers and thinkers long before urban societies developed. In fact, early human communities were responsible for laying the social, economic, and cultural foundations on which their descendants built increasingly complex societies—especially through the domestication of plants and animals and by establishing agricultural economies.

Indeed, productive agricultural economies supported the development of the first known complex societies during the

❮ A wall relief from an Assyrian palace of the eighth century B.C.E. depicts Gilgamesh as a heroic figure holding a lion.

Uruk (OO-rook)
hominid (HAW-mih-nihd)

CHRONOLOGY

4 million–1 million years ago	Era of first hominids, *Australopithecus*
2.5 million–200,000 years ago	Era of *Homo erectus*
200,000 years ago	Early evolution of *Homo sapiens*
40,000 years ago	First appearance of *Homo sapiens sapiens*
10,000–8000 B.C.E.	Early experimentation with agriculture
4000–3500 B.C.E.	Appearance of cities in southwest Asia
3200–2350 B.C.E.	Era of Sumerian dominance in Mesopotamia
3000 B.C.E.–1000 C.E.	Era of Indo-European migrations
2350–1600 B.C.E.	Era of Babylonian dominance in Mesopotamia
2334–2315 B.C.E.	Reign of Sargon of Akkad
1792–1750 B.C.E.	Reign of Hammurabi
1450–1200 B.C.E.	Era of Hittite dominance in Anatolia
1000–612 B.C.E.	Era of Assyrian dominance in Mesopotamia
1000–970 B.C.E.	Reign of Israelite king David
970–930 B.C.E.	Reign of Israelite king Solomon
722 B.C.E.	Assyrian conquest of the kingdom of Israel
605–562 B.C.E.	Reign of Nebuchadnezzar
600–550 B.C.E.	New Babylonian empire
586 B.C.E.	New Babylonian conquest of the kingdom of Judah

fourth millennium B.C.E. Such societies, in which sizable numbers of people lived in cities and extended their political, social, economic, and cultural influence over large regions, emerged first in southwest Asia, particularly in Mesopotamia. As these complex societies developed and grew, people found that they needed to resolve disputes that inevitably arose as individual and group interests conflicted. In Mesopotamia, settled agricultural peoples in search of order recognized political authorities and built states. The establishment of states in turn encouraged the creation of empires, as some states sought to extend their power by imposing their rule on neighboring lands.

Apart from stimulating the establishment of states, urban society in Mesopotamia also promoted the emergence of social classes, thus giving rise to increasingly complex social and economic structures. Cities fostered specialized labor, and the efficient production of high-quality goods in turn stimulated trade. Furthermore, early Mesopotamia developed distinctive cultural traditions as Mesopotamians invented a system of writing and supported organized religions.

Mesopotamian and other peoples regularly interacted with one another, which helped further the geographic reach of Mesopotamian society. Some Indo-European peoples also had direct dealings with their Mesopotamian contemporaries, with effects crucial for both Indo-European and Mesopotamian societies. Other Indo-European peoples never heard of Mesopotamia, but they employed Mesopotamian inventions such as wheels and metallurgy when undertaking extensive migrations that profoundly influenced historical development throughout much of Eurasia from western Europe to India and beyond. Even in the earliest days of city life, the world was the site of frequent and intense interaction between peoples of different societies.

THE TRANSITION TO AGRICULTURE

Between twelve and six thousand years ago, humans crossed a critical threshold of immense significance for the species, and the earth more generally, when they began to domesticate plants and animals. That transition to agriculture led to a population explosion, which enabled human communities to establish themselves in far greater numbers around the world than ever before. Agriculture also led to new forms of social organization, which ultimately resulted in the birth of the world's first urban centers.

The Paleolithic Era

Spread of the earliest humans
www.mhhe.com/bentleybrief2e

HOMO SAPIENS *Homo sapiens* ("consciously thinking human")—the direct ancestor of our own subspecies, *Homo sapiens sapiens*—evolved about two hundred thousand years ago from a hominid ancestry that originated in east Africa about four to five million years ago. *Homo sapiens* possessed larger brains and greater intelligence than earlier hominids—a feature that enabled them to adapt to widely varying environmental conditions and to displace earlier hominid species. More than one hundred thousand years ago, communities of *Homo sapiens* began to spread throughout the temperate lands of the eastern hemisphere. Using their intelligence to make warm clothes and shelters, *Homo sapiens* soon established communities in progressively colder regions. Then, between sixty and fifteen thousand years ago, *Homo sapiens* took advantage of land bridges exposed by lowered sea levels and spread to Indonesia, New Guinea, Australia, and, finally, the Americas. Thus by about fifteen thousand years ago, communities of *Homo sapiens* had appeared in almost every habitable region of the world.

For most of human existence—indeed, from the evolution of the first hominids until about twelve thousand years ago—our ancestors foraged for their food. In other words, they hunted wild animals or gathered edible products of naturally growing plants. That reliance on foraging characterized what historians and archaeologists call the *paleolithic era,* or the "old stone age."

The conditions of foraging economies decisively influenced all dimensions of the human experience during the paleolithic era. For instance, because of constant mobility in the search for food, a foraging economy virtually prohibits individuals from accumulating private property and basing social distinctions on wealth. In the absence of accumulated wealth, hunters and gatherers of paleolithic times probably lived a relatively egalitarian existence. Some scholars believe that this relative social equality also extended to relations between the sexes, because all members of a paleolithic group made important contributions to the survival of the community. Although meat from the hunt (provided by men) was the most highly prized item in the paleolithic diet, plant foods (provided by women) were essential to survival and sustained communities when the hunt did not succeed. Because of the thorough interdependence of the sexes from the viewpoint of food production, paleolithic society probably did not encourage the domination of one sex by the other.

The Neolithic Era

Between twelve and six thousand years ago, human communities in a variety of locations underwent profound economic, social, and political changes when they began to experiment with the domestication of plants and animals. Scientists refer to this period as the *neolithic era,* or "new stone age," because of the polished stone tools associated with peoples who relied on cultivation for subsistence.

Neolithic peoples sought to ensure themselves of more regular food supplies by encouraging the growth of edible crops and bringing wild animals into dependence on human keepers. Many scholars believe that women most likely began the systematic care of plants. As the principal gatherers in foraging communities, women in neolithic societies probably began to nurture plants instead of simply collecting available foods in the wild. Meanwhile, instead of just stalking game with the intention of killing it for meat, neolithic men began to capture animals and domesticate them by providing for their needs and supervising their breeding. Over a period of decades and centuries, these practices gradually led to the formation of agricultural economies.

Homo sapiens (HOH-moh SAY-pyans)
Homo sapiens sapiens (HOH-moh SAY-pyans SAY-pyans)
paleolithic (pey-lee-oh-LITH-ik)
neolithic (nee-uh-LITH-ik)

THE EARLY SPREAD OF AGRICULTURE The transition to agriculture—including both the cultivation of crops and the domestication of animals—emerged independently in several parts of the world. The earliest evidence of agricultural activity discovered so far dates to the era after 9000 B.C.E. in southwest Asia (modern-day Iraq, Syria, and Turkey). Between 9000 and 7000 B.C.E., agriculture also emerged among African peoples inhabiting the southeastern margin of the Sahara desert (modern-day Sudan), and then among the peoples of sub-Saharan west Africa (in the vicinity of modern Nigeria) between 8000 and 6000 B.C.E. In east Asia, residents of the Yangzi River valley began to cultivate crops as early as 6500 B.C.E., and their neighbors to the north in the Yellow River valley did the same after 5500 B.C.E. In southeast Asia the cultivation of crops dates from an indeterminate but very early time, probably 3000 B.C.E. or earlier. In the western hemisphere, inhabitants of Mesoamerica (central Mexico) cultivated plants as early as 4000 B.C.E., and residents of the central Andean region of South America (modern Peru) followed suit after 3000 B.C.E. It is also possible that the Amazon River valley was yet another site of independently invented agriculture.

Once established, agriculture spread rapidly. As a result, foods originally cultivated in only one region also spread widely, as merchants, migrants, or other travelers carried knowledge of these foods to agricultural lands that previously had relied on different crops. However, agriculture did not spread rapidly because it was easier than foraging. On the contrary, agriculture involved long hours of hard physical labor—clearing land, preparing fields, planting seeds, pulling weeds, and harvesting crops—and thus probably required more work than paleolithic foraging. Yet agriculture had its own appeal in that it made possible the production of abundant food supplies, which in turn allowed human populations to grow to unprecedented levels. For example, historians estimate that before agriculture, about 10,000 B.C.E., the earth's human population was about four million. By 500 B.C.E., after agriculture had spread to most world regions, the human population had risen to about one hundred million.

THE DEVELOPMENT OF SOCIAL DISTINCTIONS Such rapidly increasing populations encouraged neolithic peoples to adopt new forms of social organization. Because they devoted their time to cultivation rather than to foraging, neolithic peoples did not continue the migratory life of their paleolithic predecessors but, rather, settled near their fields in permanent villages. Most people in neolithic villages cultivated crops or kept animals, and many even continued to hunt and forage for wild plants. But a surplus of food enabled some individuals to concentrate their time and talents on enterprises that had nothing to do with the production of food, especially pottery making, metallurgy, and textile production. Moreover, the concentration of people into permanent settlements and the increasing specialization of labor provided the first opportunity for individuals to accumulate considerable wealth. The institutionalization of privately owned landed property—which occurred at an uncertain date after the introduction of agriculture—enhanced the significance of accumulated wealth. Because land was (and remains) the ultimate source of wealth in any agricultural society, ownership of land carried enormous economic power. When especially successful individuals managed to consolidate wealth in their families' hands and kept it there for several generations, clearly defined social classes emerged.

ÇATAL HÜYÜK Within four thousand years of its introduction, agriculture had dramatically transformed the face of the earth. Human beings multiplied prodigiously, congregated in densely populated quarters, placed the surrounding lands under cultivation, and domesticated several species of animals. Besides altering the physical appearance of the earth, agriculture transformed the lives of human beings. Even a modest neolithic village dwarfed a paleolithic band of a few dozen hunters and gatherers. In larger villages and towns, with their populations of several thousand people, their specialized labor, and

Çatal Hüyük (chat-l-hoo-yook)

their craft industries, social relationships became more complex than would have been conceivable during paleolithic times.

Excavations carried out at Çatal Hüyük, one of the best-known neolithic settlements, have helped confirm that view. Located in south-central Anatolia (modern Turkey), Çatal Hüyük grew from a small village to a bustling town of five thousand inhabitants between its settlement in 7250 B.C.E. and its abandonment in 5400 B.C.E. Archaeological evidence indicates that because the site was close to large obsidian deposits, Çatal Hüyük became a center for production and trade in obsidian tools. The wealth generated from such trade in turn allowed increasing specialization of labor, so that residents eventually manufactured and traded pots, textiles, leather, beads, and jewelry at the site. Gradually, dense populations, specialized labor, and complex social relations such as those that developed at Çatal Hüyük gave rise to an altogether new form of social organization—the city.

THE QUEST FOR ORDER

The earliest known cities grew out of agricultural villages and towns in the valleys of the Tigris and Euphrates rivers in Mesopotamia (modern-day Iraq). During the fourth millennium B.C.E., human population increased rapidly in the area, which in turn presented inhabitants with the challenge of keeping order in a large-scale society. Over time, by experimentation and adaptation, they created states and governmental machinery that brought political and social order to their territories. Moreover, effective political and military organization enabled them to build regional empires and extend their authority to neighboring peoples.

Mesopotamia: "The Land between the Rivers"

The place-name *Mesopotamia* comes from two Greek words meaning "the land between the rivers." Mesopotamia receives little rainfall, but the Tigris and the Euphrates brought large volumes of freshwater to the region. Early cultivators realized that by tapping these

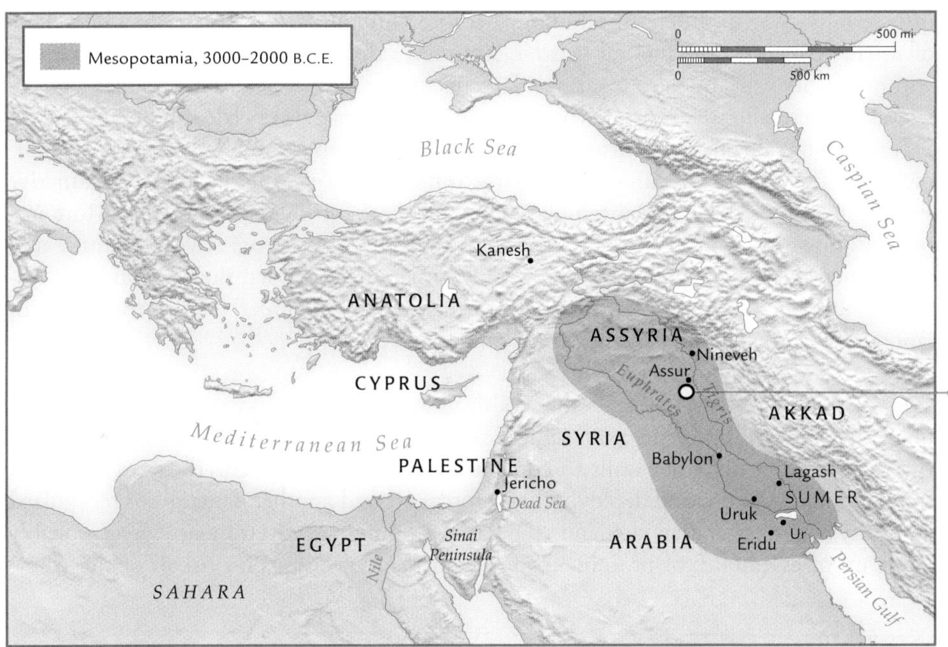

MAP 1.1 | Early Mesopotamia, 3000–2000 B.C.E. Note the locations of Mesopotamian cities in relation to the Tigris and Euphrates rivers. ***In what ways were the rivers important for Mesopotamian society?***

rivers, building reservoirs, and digging canals, they could irrigate fields of barley, wheat, and peas. Small-scale irrigation began in Mesopotamia soon after 6000 B.C.E.

SUMER Artificial irrigation led to increased food supplies, which in turn supported a rapidly increasing human population and attracted migrants from other regions. Human numbers grew especially fast in the land of Sumer in the southern half of Mesopotamia. By about 5000 B.C.E. the Sumerians were constructing elaborate irrigation networks that helped them realize abundant agricultural harvests. By 3000 B.C.E. the population of Sumer approached one hundred thousand—an unprecedented concentration of people in ancient times—and the Sumerians were the dominant people of Mesopotamia.

SEMITIC MIGRANTS While supporting a growing population, the wealth of Sumer also attracted migrants from other regions. Most of the new arrivals were Semitic peoples—so called because they spoke tongues in the Semitic family of languages, including Akkadian, Aramaic, Hebrew, and Phoenician. Semitic peoples were nomadic herders who went to Mesopotamia from the Arabian and Syrian deserts to the south and west. They often intermarried with the Sumerians, and they largely adapted to Sumerian ways.

PSI img The remains of Ur www.mhhe.com/bentleybrief2e

SUMERIAN CITY-STATES Beginning about 4000 B.C.E., as human numbers increased in southern Mesopotamia, the Sumerians built the world's first cities. These cities differed markedly from the neolithic villages that preceded them. Unlike the earlier settlements, the Sumerian cities were centers of political and military authority, and their jurisdiction extended into the surrounding regions. Moreover, bustling marketplaces that drew buyers and sellers from near and far turned the cities into economic centers as well. Finally, the cities also served as cultural centers where priests maintained organized religions and scribes developed traditions of writing and formal education. For almost a millenium, from 3200 to 2350 B.C.E., a dozen Sumerian cities—Eridu, Ur, Uruk, Lagash, Nippur, Kish, and others—dominated public affairs in Mesopotamia.

These cities all experienced internal and external pressures that prompted them to establish states—formal governmental institutions that wielded authority throughout their territories. Internally, the cities needed recognized authorities to maintain order and ensure that inhabitants cooperated on community projects. With their expanding populations, the cities also needed to prevent conflicts between urban residents from escalating into serious civic disorder. In addition, because agriculture was crucial to the welfare of urban residents, the cities all became city-states: they not only controlled public life within the city walls but also oversaw affairs in surrounding agricultural regions.

While preserving the peace, recognized authorities were also needed to organize work on projects of value to the entire community. Palaces, temples, and defensive walls dominated all the Sumerian cities. Particularly impressive were the ziggurats—distinctive stepped pyramids that housed temples and altars to the principal local deity. More important, however, were the irrigation systems that supported productive agriculture and urban society. As their population grew, the Sumerians expanded their networks of reservoirs and canals, whose construction and maintenance required untold thousands of laborers and provided precious water for Sumerian crops.

SUMERIAN KINGS As the wealth of Sumerian cities grew, they began to face increasing external problems from raiders outside the cities. The cities responded to that threat by building defensive walls and organizing military forces. Thus the need to recruit, train, equip, maintain, and deploy military forces created another demand for recognized authority. To answer that demand, the earliest Sumerian governments were probably made up of assemblies of prominent men who made decisions on behalf of the whole

Sumerians (soo-MEHR-ee-uhns)
Semitic (suh-MIHT-ihk)
ziggurats (ZIG-uh-rahts)

SUMERIAN ZIGGURAT. | The massive temple of the moon god Nanna-Suen (sometimes known as Sin) dominated the Sumerian city of Ur. Constructing temples of this size required a huge investment of resources and thousands of laborers. ***How might commoners have viewed such massive structures?***

community. By about 3000 B.C.E., however, most Sumerian cities were ruled by individual kings who claimed absolute authority within their realms. By 2500 B.C.E. city-states ruled by kings dominated public life in Sumer.

The Course of Empire

Conflicts between city-states often led to war between ambitious or aggrieved kings. However, after 2350 B.C.E. a series of conquerors sought to put an end to these constant conflicts by building empires that supervised the affairs of numerous subject cities and peoples.

SARGON OF AKKAD The first of these conquerors was Sargon of Akkad. A talented administrator and brilliant warrior, Sargon (2370–2315 B.C.E.) began his career as a minister to the king of Kish. About 2334 B.C.E. he organized a coup against the king, recruited an army, and went on the offensive against the Sumerian city-states. He conquered the cities one by one, destroyed their defensive walls, and placed them under his own governors and administrators. Sargon financed his empire by seizing control of trade routes and taxing the goods that traveled along them, which allowed him to transform his capital at Akkad into the wealthiest and most powerful city in the world. At the high point of his reign, his empire embraced all of Mesopotamia, and his armies had ventured as far afield as the Mediterranean and the Black Sea.

By about 2150 B.C.E. Sargon's empire had collapsed in the midst of rebellion from within and invasion from outsiders. Yet the memory of his deeds, recorded in legends and histories as well as in his own works of propaganda, inspired later conquerors to follow his example. Most prominent of these later conquerors was the Babylonian Hammurabi

Hammurabi (hahm-uh-RAH-bee)

HAMMURABI'S LAWS. | This handsome basalt stele shows Hammurabi receiving his royal authority from the sun god, Shamash. Some four thousand lines of Hammurabi's laws are inscribed below. ***Why would it have been important to emphasize Hammurabi's connection to divinity?***

(reigned 1792–1750 B.C.E.), who styled himself "king of the four quarters of the world." Hammurabi improved on Sargon's administrative techniques by relying on centralized bureaucratic rule and regular taxation rather than on suppression and plunder.

HAMMURABI'S LAWS By these means Hammurabi developed a more efficient and predictable government than his predecessors and also spread its costs more evenly over the population. Hammurabi also sought to maintain his empire by providing it with a code of law, which became the most extensive and complete Mesopotamian law code up to that point. In the prologue to his laws, Hammurabi proclaimed that the gods had chosen him "to promote the welfare of the people, . . . to cause justice to prevail in the land, to destroy the wicked and evil, [so] that the strong might not oppress the weak, to rise like the sun over the people, and to light up the land." Hammurabi's laws established high standards of behavior and stern punishments for violators. They prescribed death penalties for murder, theft, fraud, false accusations, sheltering of runaway slaves, failure to obey royal orders, adultery, and incest. Civil laws regulated prices, wages, commercial dealings, marital relationships, and the conditions of slavery.

The code relied heavily on the principle that offenders should suffer punishments resembling their violations. However, the code did not treat all social classes equally and demanded lesser punishments for those of higher classes who committed crimes against those of lower classes. In addition, local judges did not always follow the prescriptions of Hammurabi's code: indeed, they frequently relied on their own judgment when deciding cases that came before them. Nevertheless, Hammurabi's laws established a set of common standards that lent some degree of cultural unity to the far-flung Babylonian empire.

Eventually, the wealth of the Babylonian empire attracted invaders. Foremost among them were the Hittites, who had built a powerful empire in Anatolia (modern-day Turkey). By about 1595 B.C.E. the Babylonian empire had crumbled before Hittite assaults. For several centuries after the fall of Babylon, southwest Asia was a land of considerable turmoil, as regional states competed for power and position while migrants and invaders struggled to establish footholds for themselves in Mesopotamia and neighboring regions.

PSI img Drawing of Khorsabad, an Assyrian city www.mhhe.com/bentleybrief2e

THE ASSYRIAN EMPIRE Imperial rule returned to Mesopotamia with the Assyrians, a people from northern Mesopotamia who had built a compact state in the Tigris River valley during the nineteenth century B.C.E. Taking advantage of their location on trade routes running both north-south and east-west, the Assyrians built flourishing cities at Assur and Nineveh. They built a powerful and intimidating army by organizing their forces into standardized units and placing them under the command of professional officers chosen on the basis of merit and skill. They supplemented infantry with cavalry forces and light, swift, horse-drawn chariots, which they borrowed from the Hittites. These chariots were devastating instruments of war that allowed archers to attack their enemies from rapidly moving platforms.

Many states jockeyed for power following the collapse of the Babylonian empire, but after about 1300 B.C.E. the Assyrians gradually extended their authority to much of south-

Assyrians (uh-SEER-ee-uhns)

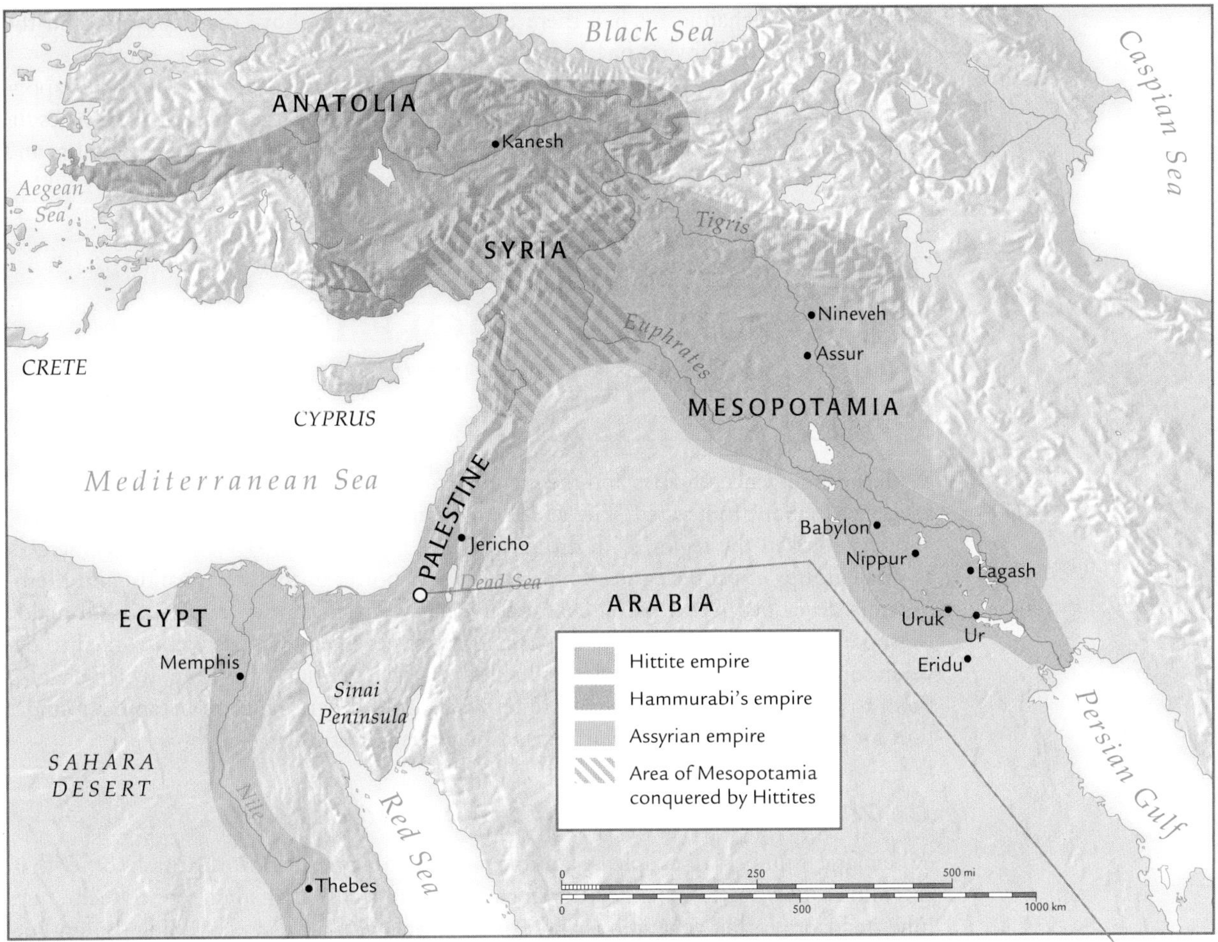

MAP 1.2 | Mesopotamian empires, 1800–600 B.C.E. Mesopotamian empires facilitated interactions between peoples from different societies. Consider the various land, river, and sea routes by which peoples of Mesopotamia, Anatolia, and Egypt were able to communicate with one another in the second and first millennia B.C.E.

The distinctive shape of the Assyrian empire closely correlates to areas that could be irrigated by large rivers.

west Asia. At its high point, during the eighth and seventh centuries B.C.E., the Assyrian empire embraced not only Mesopotamia but also Syria, Palestine, much of Anatolia, and most of Egypt.

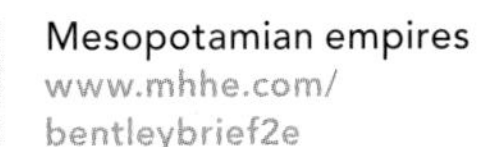

Mesopotamian empires
www.mhhe.com/bentleybrief2e

Like most other Mesopotamian peoples, the Assyrians relied on the administrative techniques pioneered by their Babylonian predecessors, and they followed laws much like those enshrined in the code of Hammurabi. They also preserved a great deal of Mesopotamian literature in huge libraries maintained at their large and lavish courts. Yet Assyrian domination was extremely unpopular and proved impossible to maintain. In 612 B.C.E. a combination of internal unrest and external assault brought the empire down.

THE NEW BABYLONIAN EMPIRE For half a century, from 600 to 550 B.C.E., Babylon once again dominated Mesopotamia during the New Babylonian empire, sometimes called the Chaldean empire. King Nebuchadnezzar (reigned 605–562 B.C.E.) lavished wealth and resources on his capital city. Babylon occupied some 850 hectares (more than 2,100 acres), and the city's defensive walls were reportedly so thick that a four-horse chariot could turn around on top of them. Within the walls there were enormous palaces and 1,179 temples, some of them faced with gold and decorated with thousands of statues. When one of the king's wives longed for flowering shrubs from her mountain

Nebuchadnezzar (neb-uh-kud-NEZ-er)

homeland, Nebuchadnezzar had them planted in terraces above the city walls, and the hanging gardens of Babylon have symbolized the city's luxuriousness ever since.

By this time, however, peoples beyond Mesopotamia had acquired advanced weapons and were experimenting with techniques of administering large territories. As a result, in the mid–sixth century B.C.E. Mesopotamians largely lost control of their affairs, and foreign conquerors absorbed them into their own empires.

The Formation of a Complex Society and Sophisticated Cultural Traditions

With the emergence of cities and the congregation of dense populations in urban spaces, specialized labor proliferated. The Mesopotamian economy became increasingly diverse, and trade linked the region with distant peoples. Clearly defined social classes emerged, as small groups of people concentrated wealth and power in their own hands, and Mesopotamia developed into a patriarchal society that vested authority largely in adult males. Mesopotamians also allocated some of their resources to individuals who worked to develop sophisticated cultural traditions, including the invention of writing, which enabled them to record information for future retrieval. Indeed, writing soon became a foundation for education, science, literature, and religious reflection.

Economic Specialization and Trade

When large numbers of people began to congregate in cities and work at tasks other than agriculture, they vastly expanded the stock of human skills. Craftsmen refined techniques inherited from earlier generations and experimented with new ways of doing things. Pottery making, textile manufacture, woodworking, leather production, brick making, stonecutting, and masonry all became distinct occupations in the world's earliest cities.

BRONZE METALLURGY Metallurgical innovations ranked among the most important developments that came about because of specialized labor. About 3500 B.C.E. experimentation with copper metallurgy led to the invention of bronze when Mesopotamian metalworkers learned to alloy copper with tin. Unlike pure copper, bronze is both hard and strong, and it quickly became the preferred metal for military weaponry as craftsmen turned out swords, spears, axes, shields, and armor made of the recently invented metal. And although bronze was expensive, over a long period Mesopotamian farmers also began to use bronze knives and bronze-tipped plows instead of tools made of bone, wood, stone, or obsidian.

IRON METALLURGY After about 1000 B.C.E. Mesopotamian craftsmen began to manufacture effective tools and weapons with iron as well as bronze. Whereas early experimentation with iron metallurgy resulted in products that were too brittle for heavy-duty uses, by about 1300 B.C.E. craftsmen from Hittite society in Anatolia (discussed later in this chapter) developed techniques of forging exceptionally strong iron tools and weapons. As knowledge of those techniques spread, Assyrian conquerors made particularly effective use of them by forging iron weapons to build their empire. Iron also had the advantage of being less expensive than bronze, which quickly made it the metal of choice for weapons and tools.

THE WHEEL Other craftsmen focused on devising efficient means of transportation based on wheeled vehicles and sailing ships, both of which facilitated long-distance trade. Sumerians first invented the wheel in about 3500 B.C.E., and they were building wheeled carts by 3000 B.C.E. Wheeled carts and wagons enabled people to haul heavy

Sumerian Shipbuilding. | A silver model of a boat discovered in a royal tomb at Ur throws light on Sumerian transportation of grain and other goods on the rivers, canals, and marshes of southern Mesopotamia about 2700 B.C.E.

loads of bulk goods over much longer distances than human porters or draft animals could manage. The wheel rapidly diffused from Sumer to neighboring lands, and within a few centuries it had become a standard means of overland transportation.

SHIPBUILDING Sumerians also experimented with technologies of maritime transportation. By 3500 B.C.E. they had built watercraft that allowed them to venture into the Persian Gulf and beyond. By 2300 B.C.E. they were trading regularly with merchants of Harappan society in the Indus River valley of northern India (discussed in chapter 3), which they reached by sailing through the Persian Gulf and the Arabian Sea. During the time of the Babylonian empire, Mesopotamians traded extensively with peoples in all directions: they imported silver from Anatolia, cedarwood from Lebanon, copper from Arabia, gold from Egypt, tin from Persia, lapis lazuli from Afghanistan, and semiprecious stones from northern India.

The Emergence of a Stratified Patriarchal Society

With their increasingly specialized labor and long-distance trade, cities provided many more opportunities for the accumulation of wealth than ever before. As a result, social distinctions in Mesopotamia became much more sharply defined than those in neolithic villages.

SOCIAL CLASSES In early Mesopotamia the ruling classes originally consisted of kings and nobles who were elected to their positions because of their valor and success as warriors. However, royal status soon became hereditary, as kings arranged for their sons to succeed them. Nobles were mostly members of royal families and other close supporters of the kings and thus controlled significant wealth and power. Members of the ruling class displayed their high status through large-scale construction projects and by lavishly decorating their capital cities.

TEMPLE COMMUNITIES Closely allied with the ruling elites were priests and priestesses, many of whom were younger relatives of the rulers. The principal role of the priestly elites was to intervene with the gods to ensure good fortune for their communities. In exchange for those services, priests and priestesses lived in temple communities and received offerings of food, drink, and clothing from city inhabitants. Temples also generated income from the vast tracts of land that they owned and large workshops that they maintained. Because of their wealth, temples provided comfortable livings for their inhabitants, and they also served the needs of the larger community. For instance, temples functioned as banks where individuals could store wealth, and they helped underwrite trading ventures to

COMMONERS IN MESOPOTAMIA. | Gypsum carving of an elderly couple from the city of Nippur about 2500 B.C.E. ***How does this figure give us insight into daily life among the Sumerians?***

distant lands. They also helped those in need by taking in orphans, supplying grain in times of famine, and providing ransoms for community members captured in battle.

Apart from the ruling and priestly elites, Mesopotamian society included less privileged classes of free commoners, dependent clients, and slaves. Free commoners mostly worked as peasant cultivators in the countryside on land owned by their families, although some also worked in the cities as builders, craftsmen, or professionals. Dependent clients possessed no property and usually worked as agricultural laborers on estates owned by others. Free commoners and dependent clients all paid taxes—usually in the form of surplus agricultural production—that supported the ruling classes, military forces, and temple communities. In addition, free commoners and dependent clients were subject to conscription by ruling authorities to provide labor services for large-scale construction projects such as roads, city walls, irrigation systems, temples, and public buildings.

SLAVES Slaves came from three main sources: prisoners of war, convicted criminals, and heavily indebted individuals who sold themselves into slavery to satisfy their obligations. Some slaves worked as agricultural laborers on the estates of nobles or temple communities, but most were domestic servants in wealthy households. Many masters granted slaves their freedom, often with a financial bequest, after several years of good service.

In addition to recognizing differences of rank, wealth, and social status, Mesopotamians built a patriarchal society that vested authority over public and private affairs in adult men. Men made most of the important decisions within households and dominated public life as well. In effect, men ruled as kings, and decisions about policies and public affairs rested almost entirely in their hands.

GENDER ROLES Hammurabi's laws throw considerable light on sex and gender relations in ancient Mesopotamia. The laws recognized men as heads of their households and entrusted all major family decisions to their judgment. Men even had the power to sell their wives and children into slavery to satisfy their debts. In the interests of protecting the reputations of husbands and the legitimacy of offspring, the laws prescribed death by drowning as the punishment for adulterous wives, as well as for their partners, while permitting men to engage in consensual sexual relations with concubines, slaves, or prostitutes without penalty.

In spite of their subordinate legal status, women made their influence felt in Mesopotamian society. At ruling courts women sometimes advised kings and their governments. A few women wielded great power as high priestesses who managed the enormous estates belonging to their temples. Others obtained a formal education and worked as scribes—literate individuals who prepared administrative and legal documents for governments and private parties. Women also pursued careers as midwives, shopkeepers, brewers, bakers, tavern keepers, and textile manufacturers.

During the second millennium B.C.E., however, Mesopotamian men progressively tightened their control over the social and sexual behavior of women. To protect family fortunes and guarantee the legitimacy of heirs, Mesopotamians insisted on the virginity of brides at marriage, and they forbade casual socializing between married women and men outside their family. By 1500 B.C.E. and probably even earlier, married women in Mesopotamian cities had begun to wear veils when they ventured beyond their own households in order to discourage the attention of men from other families. This concern to control women's social and sexual behavior spread throughout much of southwest Asia and the Mediterranean basin, where it reinforced patriarchal social structures.

The Development of Written Cultural Traditions

The world's earliest known writing came from Mesopotamia. Sumerians invented a system of writing about the middle of the fourth millennium B.C.E. to keep track of commercial transactions and tax collections. They first experimented with pictographs representing animals, agricultural products, and trade items that figured prominently in tax and

SOURCES FROM THE PAST

The Flood Story from the *Epic of Gilgamesh*

The Epic of Gilgamesh *is the oldest surviving epic poem in history, dating from about 2500* B.C.E. *As part of his adventures, Gilgamesh seeks the secret of immortality from a wise man named Ut-napishtim. During the visit, Ut-napishtim tells him how the god Ea alerted him to a plot by the gods to destroy humankind by a massive flood. Here, Ut-napishtim recounts the story to Gilgamesh.*

The *Epic of Gilgamesh*
www.mhhe.com/
bentleybrief2e

This is the message:
"Man of Shuruppak, son of Ubara-Tutu,*
Dismantle your house, build a boat.
Leave possessions, search out living things.
Reject chattels+ and save lives!
Put aboard the seed of all living things, into the boat.
The boat that you are to build
Shall have her dimensions in proportion,
Her width and length should be in harmony,
Roof her like the Apsu."**
I realized and spoke to my master Ea,
"I have paid attention to the words that you spoke in this way,
My master, and I shall act upon them. . . .
I loaded her with everything there was,
Loaded her with all the silver,
Loaded her with all the gold
Loaded her with all the seed of living things, all of them.
I put on board the boat all my kith and kin.
Put on board cattle from open country, wild beasts from open country, all kinds of craftsmen. . . .
That hour arrived; . . .
I saw the shape of the storm,
The storm was terrifying to see.
I went aboard the boat and closed the door. . . .
For six days and seven nights
The wind blew, flood and tempest overwhelmed the land;
When the seventh day arrived the tempest, flood and onslaught
Which had struggled like a woman in labor, blew themselves out.
The sea became calm, the wind grew quiet, the flood held back.
[S]ilence reigned, for all mankind had returned to clay. . . .
The boat came to rest on Mount Nimush.++ . . .
When the seventh day arrived,
I put out and released a dove.
The dove went; it came back,
For no perching place was visible to it; and it turned round.
I put out and released a swallow.
The swallow went; it came back,
For no perching place was visible to it, and it turned round.
I put out and released a raven.
The raven went, and saw the waters receding.
And it ate, preened, lifted its tail and did not turn round.

*This refers to Ut-napishtim
+ Property
** The realm of freshwater under the earth
++ A mountain in modern Iraq

■ Discuss the similarities between the flood story above and the story of Noah's Ark from the Old Testament. Why are these stories so similar?

SOURCE: Thomas Sanders et al. *Encounters in World History: Sources and Themes from the Global Past,* Vol. I. Boston: McGraw-Hill, 2006, pp. 40–41.

commercial transactions. By 3100 B.C.E. conventional signs representing specific words had spread throughout Mesopotamia.

A writing system that depends on pictures is useful for purposes such as keeping records, but it is a cumbersome way to communicate abstract ideas. Beginning about 2900 B.C.E. the Sumerians developed a more flexible system of writing that used graphic symbols to represent sounds, syllables, and ideas as well as physical objects. By combining pictographs and other symbols, the Sumerians created a powerful writing system.

CUNEIFORM WRITING When writing, a Sumerian scribe used a stylus fashioned from a reed to impress symbols on wet clay. Because the stylus left lines and wedge-shaped marks, Sumerian writing is known as *cuneiform,* a term that comes from two Latin words meaning "wedge-shaped." When dried in the sun or baked in an oven, the clay hardened and preserved a permanent record of the scribe's message. Babylonians, Assyrians, and other peoples later adapted the Sumerians' script to their own languages, and the tradition of cuneiform writing continued for more than three thousand years.

Though originally invented for purposes of keeping records, writing clearly had potential that went far beyond the purely practical matter of storing information. Mesopotamians relied on writing to communicate complex ideas about the world, the gods, human beings, and their relationships with one another. Indeed, writing made possible the emergence of a distinctive cultural tradition that shaped Mesopotamian values for almost three millennia.

ASTRONOMY AND MATHEMATICS Literacy led to a rapid expansion of knowledge. Mesopotamian scholars devoted themselves to the study of astronomy and mathematics—both important sciences for agricultural societies. Knowledge of astronomy helped them prepare accurate calendars, which in turn enabled them to chart the rhythms of the seasons and determine the appropriate times for planting and harvesting crops. They used their mathematical skills to survey agricultural lands and allocate them to the proper owners or tenants. Some Mesopotamian conventions persist to the present day: Mesopotamian scientists divided the year into twelve months, for example, and they divided the hour into sixty minutes, each composed of sixty seconds.

THE EPIC OF GILGAMESH Mesopotamians also used writing to communicate abstract ideas, investigate intellectual problems, and reflect on human beings and their place in the world. Best known of the reflective literature from Mesopotamia is the *Epic of Gilgamesh,* completed after 2000 B.C.E. In recounting the experiences of Gilgamesh and Enkidu, the epic explored themes of friendship, relations between humans and the gods, and especially the meaning of life and death. The stories of Gilgamesh and Enkidu resonated so widely that for some two thousand years—from the time of the Sumerian city-states to the fall of the Assyrian empire—they were the principal vehicles for Mesopotamian reflections on moral issues.

The Broader Influence of Mesopotamian Society

While building cities and regional states, Mesopotamians deeply influenced the development and experiences of peoples living far beyond their own lands. Often their wealth and power attracted the attention of neighboring peoples. Sometimes Mesopotamians projected their power to foreign lands and imposed their ways by force. Occasionally migrants left Mesopotamia and carried their inherited traditions to new lands. Mesopotamian influence did not completely transform other peoples and turn them into carbon copies of Mesopotamians. On the contrary, other peoples adopted Mesopotamian ways selectively and adapted them to their own needs and interests. Yet the broader impact of Mesopotamian society shows that, even in early times, complex agricultural societies organized around cities had strong potential to influence the development of distant human communities.

Hebrews, Israelites, and Jews

The best-known cases of early Mesopotamian influence involved Hebrews, Israelites, and Jews, who preserved memories of their historical experiences in an extensive collection of sacred writings. Hebrews were speakers of the ancient Hebrew language. Israelites formed a branch of Hebrews who settled in Palestine (modern-day Israel) after 1300 B.C.E. Jews descended from southern Israelites who inhabited the kingdom of Judah. For more than two thousand years, Hebrews, Israelites, and Jews interacted constantly with Mesopotamians and other peoples as well, with profound consequences for the development of their own societies.

THE EARLY HEBREWS The earliest Hebrews were pastoral nomads who inhabited lands between Mesopotamia and Egypt during the second millennium B.C.E. As Mesopotamia prospered, some of the Hebrews settled in the region's cities. According to the Hebrew scriptures (the Old Testament of the Christian Bible), the Hebrew patriarch Abraham came from the Sumerian city of Ur, but he migrated to northern Mesopotamia about 1850 B.C.E. Abraham's descendants continued to recognize many of the deities, values, and customs common to Mesopotamian peoples. Hebrew law, for example, borrowed heavily from Hammurabi's code. The Hebrews also told the story of a devastating flood that had destroyed all early human society, which was a variation on similar flood stories related from the earliest days of Sumerian society. One early version of the story made its way into the *Epic of Gilgamesh.* The Hebrews altered the story and adapted it to their own interests and purposes, but their familiarity with the flood story shows that they participated fully in the larger society of Mesopotamia.

MIGRATIONS AND SETTLEMENT IN PALESTINE According to their scriptures, some Hebrews migrated from Palestine to Egypt during the eighteenth century B.C.E. About 1300 B.C.E., however, this branch of the Hebrews departed under the leadership of Moses and returned to Palestine. Organized into a loose federation of twelve tribes, those Hebrews, known as the Israelites, fought bitterly with other inhabitants of Palestine and carved out a territory for themselves. Eventually the Israelites abandoned their inherited tribal structure in favor of a Mesopotamian-style monarchy that brought all their twelve tribes under unified rule. During the reigns of King David (1000–970 B.C.E.) and King Solomon (970–930 B.C.E.), Israelites dominated the territory between Syria and the Sinai peninsula. They built an elaborate and cosmopolitan capital city at Jerusalem and entered into diplomatic and commercial relations with Mesopotamians, Egyptians, and Arabian peoples. Like other peoples of southwest Asia, the Israelites made use of iron technology to strengthen their military forces and produce tough agricultural implements.

MOSES AND MONOTHEISM After the time of Moses, however, the religious beliefs of the Israelites developed along increasingly distinctive lines. Whereas the early Hebrews had recognized many of the same gods as their Mesopotamian neighbors, Moses embraced monotheism: he taught that there was only one god, known as Yahweh, who was a supremely powerful deity, the creator and sustainer of the world. Yahweh expected his followers to worship him alone, and he demanded that they observe high moral and ethical standards. In the Ten Commandments, a set of religious and ethical principles that Moses announced to the Israelites, Yahweh warned his followers against destructive and antisocial behavior such as lying, theft, adultery, and murder. Between about 1000 and 400 B.C.E., the Israelites' religious leaders compiled their teachings in a set of holy scriptures known as the Torah (Hebrew for "doctrine" or "teaching"), which laid down Yahweh's laws and outlined his role in creating the world and guiding human affairs. The Torah taught that Yahweh would reward those who obeyed his will and punish those who did not.

ASSYRIAN AND BABYLONIAN CONQUESTS The Israelites placed increasing emphasis on devotion to Yahweh as they experienced a series of political and military setbacks. Following King Solomon's reign, tribal tensions led to the division of the community into a large kingdom of Israel in the north and a smaller kingdom of Judah in the land known as Judea to the south. In 722 B.C.E. Assyrian forces conquered the northern kingdom and deported many of its inhabitants to other regions, causing many of the deported to lose their identity as Israelites. In 586 B.C.E., the New Babylonian empire toppled the kingdom of Judah and destroyed Jerusalem, forcing many residents into exile. Unlike their cousins to the north, however, most of these Israelites maintained

monotheism (mah-noh-THEE-iz'm)
Yahweh (YAH-way)

their religious identity, and many of the deportees eventually returned to Judea, where they became known as Jews.

Ironically, perhaps, the Israelites' devotion to Yahweh intensified during this era of turmoil. Between the ninth and sixth centuries B.C.E., a series of prophets urged the Israelites to rededicate themselves to their faith and obey Yahweh's commandments. Failure to do so, they warned, would be punished by Yahweh in the form of conquest by foreigners. Many Israelites took the Assyrian and Babylonian conquests as proof that the prophets accurately represented Yahweh's mind and will.

The exiles who returned to Judea after the Babylonian conquest did not abandon hope for a state of their own, and even organized several small Jewish states as tributaries to the larger empires that dominated the area. But the returnees also built a distinctive religious community based on their conviction that they had a special relationship with Yahweh. This conviction enabled the Jews to maintain a strong sense of identity as a people distinct from others, even as they participated fully in the development of a larger complex society in southwest Asia. Over the longer term, Jewish monotheism, scriptures, and moral concerns also profoundly influenced the development of Christianity and Islam.

The Phoenicians

PSI img Phoenician artifacts
www.mhhe.com/bentleybrief2e

PHOENICIAN TRADE NETWORKS North of the Israelites' kingdom in Palestine, the Phoenicians occupied a narrow coastal plain between the Mediterranean Sea and the Lebanon Mountains. They spoke a Semitic language, referring to themselves as Canaanites and their land as Canaan. (The term *Phoenician* comes from early Greek references.) Sometime after 3000 B.C.E., the Phoenicians established a series of city-states ruled by local kings, the most important of which were Tyre, Sidon, Beirut, and Byblos. Though not a numerous or militarily powerful people, the Phoenicians influenced societies throughout the Mediterranean basin because of their trade and communication networks. Their meager lands did not permit development of a large agricultural society, so after about 2500 B.C.E. the Phoenicians turned increasingly to industry and trade. Although the Phoenicians traded overland, they were also excellent sailors, and they built the best ships of their times. Between 1200 and 800 B.C.E., they dominated Mediterranean trade. They established commercial colonies in Rhodes, Cyprus, Sicily, Sardinia, Spain, and north Africa. They sailed far and wide in search of raw materials, which took them well beyond the Mediterranean: Phoenician merchant ships visited the Canary Islands, coastal ports in Portugal and France, and even the distant British Isles, and adventurous Phoenician mariners made exploratory voyages to the Azores Islands and down the west coast of Africa as far as the Gulf of Guinea.

ALPHABETIC WRITING Like the Hebrews, the Phoenicians largely adapted Mesopotamian cultural traditions to their own needs. Their gods, for example, were mostly adapted from Mesopotamian gods. The Phoenicians also creatively adapted the Mesopotamian practice of writing by experimenting with simpler alternatives to cuneiform. By 1500 B.C.E. Phoenician scribes had devised an early alphabetic script consisting of twenty-two symbols representing consonants (the Phoenician alphabet had no symbols for vowels). Learning twenty-two letters and building words with them was much easier than memorizing the hundreds of symbols employed in cuneiform. Because alphabetic writing required much less investment in education than did cuneiform writing, more people were able to become literate than ever before.

Alphabetic writing spread widely as the Phoenicians traveled and traded throughout the Mediterranean basin. About the ninth century

THINKING ABOUT *Traditions*

TRADITIONS IN EARLY COMPLEX SOCIETIES. In the period between 3500 and 500 B.C.E., peoples such as the Sumerians, Assyrians, Hittites, and Phoenicians independently developed distinctive characteristics in terms of architecture, economic pursuits, and technology. What were some of the defining characteristics that marked these societies as different from one another, and why might these differences have arisen? Think carefully here about geographical location, the presence or absence of plants and animals, and the availability of resources.

Phoenicians (fi-NEE-shins)

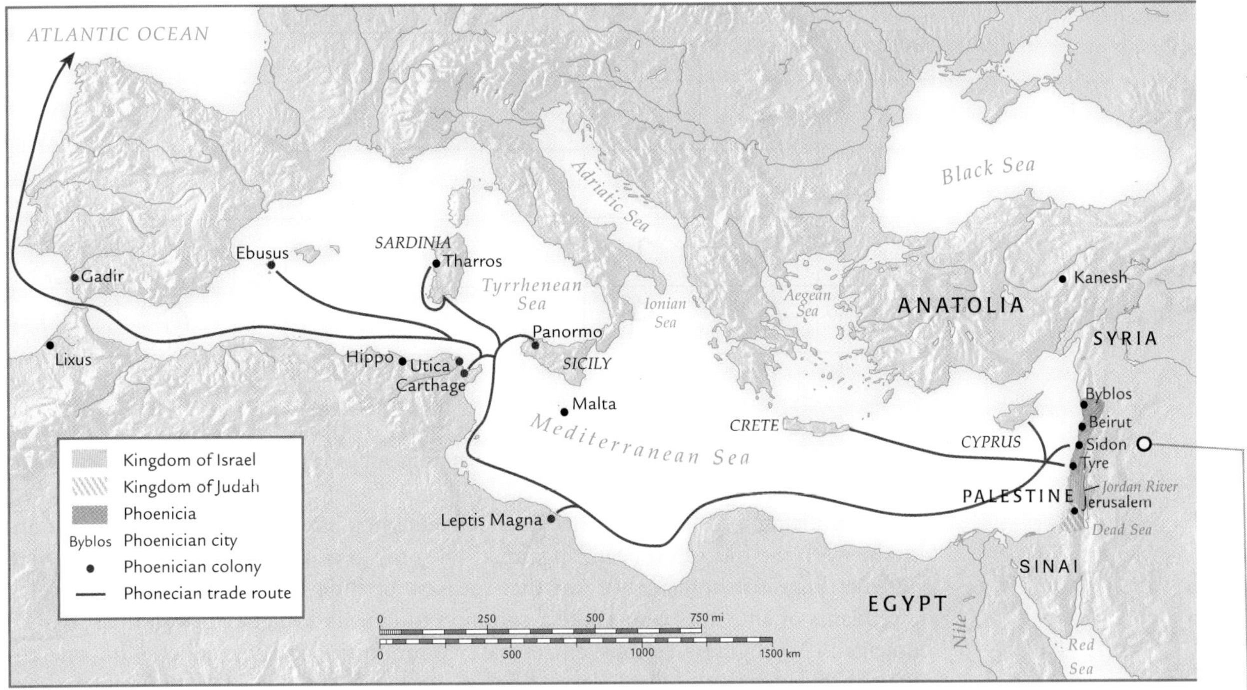

MAP 1.3 | Israel and Phoenicia, 1500–600 B.C.E. Note the location of Israel and Phoenicia with respect to Mesopotamia, Egypt, and the Mediterranean Sea. ***How might geographic location have influenced communications and exchanges between Israel, Phoenicia, and other lands of the region?***

The coastal position of Phoenician cities was conducive to trade by sea.

B.C.E., for example, Greeks modified the Phoenician alphabet and added symbols representing vowels. Romans later adapted the Greek alphabet to their own language and passed it along to their cultural heirs in Europe. In later centuries alphabetic writing spread to central Asia, south Asia, and southeast Asia, and ultimately throughout most of the world.

The Indo-European Migrations

After 3000 B.C.E. Mesopotamia was a prosperous, productive region where peoples from many different communities mixed and mingled. But Mesopotamia was only one region in a much larger world of interaction and exchange. Mesopotamians and their neighbors all dealt frequently with peoples from regions far beyond southwest Asia. Among the most influential of these peoples in the third and second millennia B.C.E. were those who spoke various Indo-European languages. Their migrations throughout much of Eurasia profoundly influenced historical development in both southwest Asia and the larger world.

Indo-European Origins

INDO-EUROPEAN LANGUAGES During the eighteenth and nineteenth centuries, linguists noticed that many languages of Europe, southwest Asia, and India featured remarkable similarities in vocabulary and grammatical structure. Ancient languages displaying these similarities included Sanskrit (the sacred language of ancient India), Old Persian, Greek, and Latin. Because of the geographic regions where these tongues are found, scholars refer to them as Indo-European languages. Major subgroups of the Indo-European family of languages include Indo-Iranian, Greek, Balto-Slavic, Germanic,

Phoenician, Greek, Hebrew, and Roman letters.

NORTH SEMITIC			GREEK		ETRUSCAN	LATIN	
EARLY PHOENICIAN	EARLY HEBREW	PHOENICIAN	EARLY	CLASSICAL	EARLY	EARLY	CLASSICAL
𐤀	𐤀	𐤀	Α	Α	𐌀	A	A
𐤁	𐤁	𐤁	Β	Β	𐌁		B
𐤂	𐤂	𐤂	Γ	Γ	𐌂		C
𐤃	𐤃	𐤃	Δ	Δ	𐌃	D	D

Italic, and Celtic. English belongs to the Germanic subgroup of the Indo-European family of languages.

After noticing linguistic similarities, scholars sought a way to explain the close relationship between the Indo-European languages. The only persuasive explanation for the high degree of linguistic coincidence was that speakers of Indo-European languages were all descendants of ancestors who spoke a common tongue and migrated from their original homeland. As migrants established separate communities and lost touch with one another, their languages evolved along different lines, adding new words, pronunciations, and spellings but retaining the basic grammatical structure of their original speech.

THE INDO-EUROPEAN HOMELAND The original homeland of Indo-European speakers was probably the steppe region of modern-day Ukraine and southern Russia, where the earliest of them built a society between about 4500 and 2500 B.C.E. A central feature of Indo-European society was the domestication of wild horses from the Eurasian steppe about 4000 B.C.E. Horses were initially used for food and soon thereafter for riding as well. When Sumerian knowledge of bronze metallurgy spread to the Indo-European homeland about 3000 B.C.E., Indo-European speakers devised ways to hitch horses to carts, wagons, and chariots. The possession of domesticated horses vastly magnified the power of the Indo-Europeans. Horses enabled them to develop transportation technologies that were much faster and more efficient than other alternatives. Furthermore, because of their strength and speed, horses provided Indo-European speakers with a tremendous military advantage over peoples they encountered. It is perhaps significant that many groups of Indo-European speakers considered themselves superior to other peoples: the terms *Aryan, Iran,* and *Eire* (the official name of the modern Republic of Ireland) all derive from the Indo-European word *aryo,* meaning "nobleman" or "lord."

Indo-European Expansion and Its Effects

THE NATURE OF INDO-EUROPEAN MIGRATION Horses also provided Indo-European speakers with a means of expanding far beyond their original homeland. As they flourished in southern Russia, Indo-European speakers experienced a population explosion, which prompted some of them to move into the sparsely inhabited eastern steppe or even beyond the grasslands altogether. The earliest Indo-European migrations began about 3000 B.C.E. and continued until about 1000 B.C.E. Like early movements of other peoples, these were not mass migrations so much as gradual and incremental processes that resulted in the spread of Indo-European languages and ethnic communities, as small groups of people established settlements in new lands, which then became foundations for further expansion.

THE HITTITES The most influential Indo-European migrants in ancient times were the Hittites. About 1900 B.C.E. the Hittites migrated to the central plain of Anatolia, where they imposed their language and rule on the region's inhabitants. During the

TABLE 1.1 Similarities in Vocabulary Indicating Close Relationships between Select Indo-European Languages

English	German	Spanish	Greek	Latin	Sanskrit
father	vater	padre	pater	pater	pitar
one	ein	uno	hen	unus	ekam
fire	feuer	fuego	pyr	ignis	agnis
field	feld	campo	agros	ager	ajras
sun	sone	sol	helios	sol	surya
king	könig	rey	basileus	rex	raja
god	gott	dios	theos	deus	devas

seventeenth and sixteenth centuries B.C.E., they built a powerful kingdom and established close relations with Mesopotamian peoples. They traded with Babylonians and Assyrians, adapted cuneiform writing to their Indo-European language, and accepted many Mesopotamian deities into their own pantheon. In 1595 B.C.E. the Hittites toppled the mighty Babylonian empire of Mesopotamia, and for several centuries thereafter they were the dominant power in southwest Asia. Between 1450 and 1200 B.C.E. their authority extended to eastern Anatolia, northern Mesopotamia, and Syria down to Phoenicia. After 1200 B.C.E. the unified Hittite state dissolved, but a Hittite identity survived, along with the Hittite language, throughout the era of the Assyrian empire and beyond.

WAR CHARIOTS The Hittites were responsible for two technological innovations—the construction of light, horse-drawn war chariots and the refinement of iron metallurgy—that greatly strengthened their own society and influenced other peoples throughout much of the ancient world. The Hittites' speedy chariots were crucial in their campaign to establish a state in Anatolia. Following the Hittites' example, Mesopotamians soon added chariot teams to their own armies, and Assyrians made especially effective use of chariots in building their empire. Indeed, chariot warfare was so effective—and its techniques spread so widely—that charioteers became the elite strike forces in armies throughout much of the ancient world from Rome to China.

IRON METALLURGY After about 1300 B.C.E. the Hittites also refined the technology of iron metallurgy, which enabled them to produce effective weapons cheaply and in large quantities. Hittite methods of iron production diffused rapidly and eventually spread throughout all of Eurasia. (Peoples of sub-Saharan Africa independently invented iron metallurgy.) Hittites were not the original inventors either of horse-drawn chariots or of iron metallurgy: in both cases they built on Mesopotamian precedents. But in both cases they clearly improved on existing technologies and introduced innovations that other peoples readily adopted.

INDO-EUROPEAN MIGRATIONS TO THE WEST AND EAST While the Hittites were building a state in Anatolia, other Indo-European speakers migrated from the steppe to different regions. Some went east into central Asia, venturing as far as the Tarim Basin (now western China) by 2000 B.C.E. Meanwhile, other Indo-European migrants moved west. One wave of migration took Indo-European speakers into Greece after 2200 B.C.E., with their descendants

ENCOUNTERS IN EARLY COMPLEX SOCIETIES. Despite important differences between the early complex societies, it is nevertheless clear that significant interaction occurred among them. What were the mechanisms by which such interaction occurred (i.e., trade, transport), and what evidence do scholars have that these early societies influenced one another?

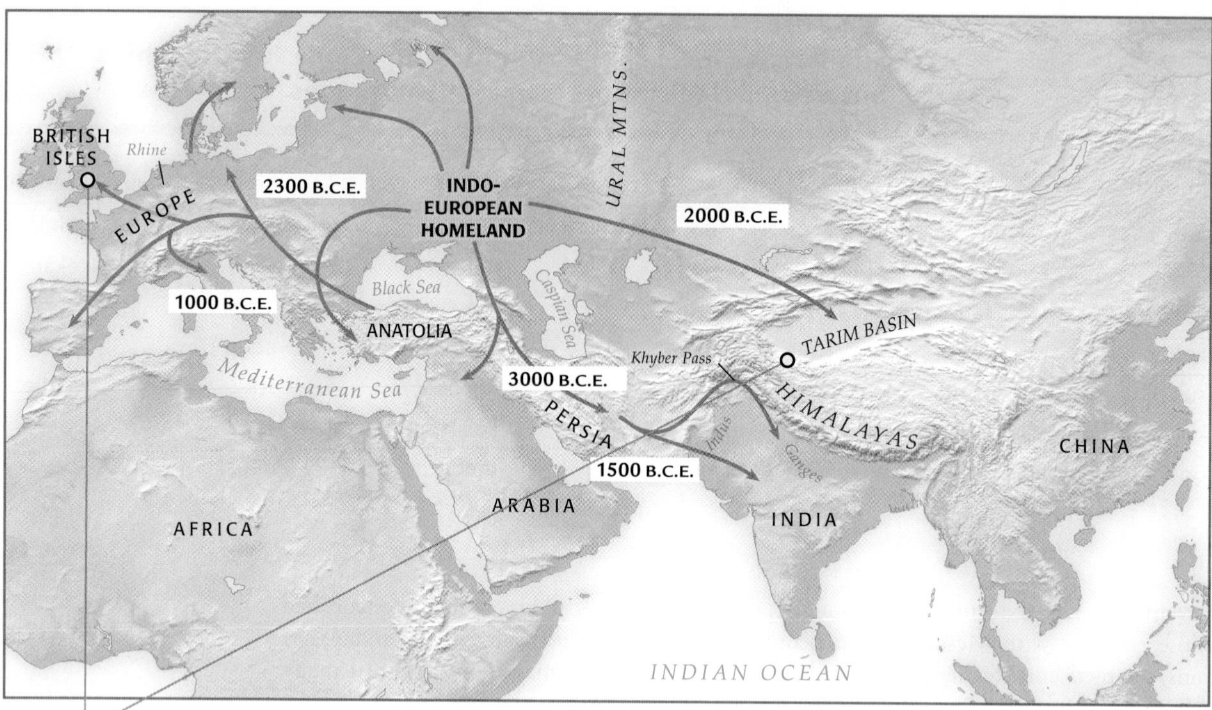

The distance between the British Isles and the Tarim Basin is about 4000 miles.

MAP 1.4 | Indo-European migrations, 3000–1000 B.C.E. Consider the vast distances over which Indo-European migrants established communities. ***Would it have been possible for speakers of Indo-European languages to spread so widely without the aid of domesticated horses?***

moving into central Italy by 1000 B.C.E. Another migratory wave established an Indo-European presence farther to the west. By 2300 B.C.E. some Indo-European speakers had made their way from southern Russia into central Europe (modern Germany and Austria), by 1200 B.C.E. to western Europe (modern France), and shortly thereafter to the British Isles, the Baltic region, and the Iberian peninsula. Yet another, later, wave of migrations established an Indo-European presence in Iran and India. About 1500 B.C.E. the Medes and the Persians migrated into the Iranian plateau, while the Aryans began filtering into northern India. As in earlier migrations, Indo-European migrants borrowed from, influenced, and mixed with the settled peoples they discovered and in so doing shaped future historical developments in each area.

Aryans (AYR-ee-uhns)

SUMMARY

Building on neolithic foundations, Mesopotamian peoples constructed societies much more complex, powerful, and influential than those of their predecessors. Through their city-states, kingdoms, and regional empires, Mesopotamians created formal institutions of government that extended the authority of ruling elites to all corners of their states, and they occasionally mobilized forces that projected their power to distant lands. They generated several distinct social classes. Specialized labor fueled productive economies and encouraged the establishment of long-distance trade networks. They devised systems of writing, which enabled them to develop sophisticated cultural traditions. They deeply influenced other peoples, such as the Hebrews and the Phoenicians, throughout southwest Asia and the eastern Mediterranean basin. They had frequent dealings also with Indo-European peoples. Although Indo-European society emerged far to the north of Mesopotamia, speakers of Indo-European languages migrated widely and established societies throughout much of Eurasia. Sometimes they drew inspiration from Mesopotamian practices, and sometimes they developed their own practices that influenced Mesopotamians and others as well. Thus, already in remote antiquity, the various peoples of the world profoundly influenced one another through cross-cultural interaction and exchange.

STUDY TERMS

Aryans (24)
Assyrians (12)
bronze (14)
chariot (23)
cuneiform (17)
Gilgamesh (17)
Hammurabi (11)
Hebrews (18)
Hittites (22)
Homo sapiens (7)
Indo-European migrations (21)
Israelites (18)
Mesopotamia (9)
monotheism (19)
neolithic era (7)
New Babylonian empire (13)
paleolithic era (7)
Phoenician (20)
Sargon of Akkad (11)
Sumerians (10)
wheel (14)
Yahweh (19)

FOR FURTHER READING

Elizabeth Wayland Barber. *Women's Work: The First 20,000 Years.* New York, 1994. Fascinating study of ancient textiles, which the author argues was a craft industry dominated by women from the earliest times.

David Christian. *Maps of Time: An Introduction to Big History.* Berkeley, 2004. A brilliant study that considers human history in the context of natural history since the big bang.

Jared Diamond. *The Third Chimpanzee: Evolution and the Future of the Human Animal.* New York, 1992. An insightful guide to human evolution and its significance for human behavior.

Andrew George, trans. *The Epic of Gilgamesh.* London, 1999. A careful study and fresh translation of the best-known Mesopotamian literary work prepared on the basis of recently discovered texts.

J. P. Mallory. *In Search of the Indo-Europeans: Language, Archaeology, and Myth.* London, 1989. Carefully reviews modern theories about early Indo-European speakers in light of both the linguistic and the archaeological evidence.

Marc van de Mieroop. *A History of the Ancient Near East, ca 3000–323 B.C.* Oxford, 2004. A concise and readable history of ancient Mesopotamia and neighboring societies.

Hans J. Nissen. *The Early History of the Ancient Near East, 9000–2000 B.C.* Trans. by E. Lutzeier. Chicago, 1988. A brilliant synthesis of scholarship on the development of cities and complex society in Mesopotamia and neighboring regions.

James B. Pritchard, ed. *Ancient Near Eastern Texts Relating to the Old Testament.* 2 vols. 3rd ed. Princeton, 1975. Important collection of primary sources in translation, emphasizing parallels between the ancient Hebrews and other peoples.

Michael Roaf. *Cultural Atlas of Mesopotamia and the Ancient Near East.* New York, 1990. Richly illustrated volume with well-informed essays on all dimensions of Mesopotamian history.

Bruce D. Smith. *The Emergence of Agriculture.* New York, 1995. Concentrates on the initial domestication of plant and animal species in world regions where agriculture developed.

Early African Societies and the Bantu Migrations

2

EARLY AGRICULTURAL SOCIETY IN AFRICA

Climatic Change and the Development of Agriculture in Africa

Egypt and Nubia: "Gifts of the Nile"

The Unification of Egypt

Turmoil and Empire

THE FORMATION OF COMPLEX SOCIETIES AND SOPHISTICATED CULTURAL TRADITIONS

The Emergence of Cities and Stratified Societies

Economic Specialization and Trade

Early Writing in the Nile Valley

The Development of Organized Religious Traditions

BANTU MIGRATIONS AND EARLY AGRICULTURAL SOCIETIES OF SUB-SAHARAN AFRICA

The Dynamics of Bantu Expansion

Early Agricultural Societies of Sub-Saharan Africa

For almost three thousand years, Egyptian embalmers preserved the bodies of deceased individuals through a process of mummification. Egyptian records rarely mention the techniques of mummification, but the Greek historian Herodotus traveled in Egypt about 450 B.C.E. and briefly explained the craft. The embalmer first used a metal hook to draw the brain of the deceased out through a nostril, then removed the internal organs through an incision made alongside the abdomen, washed them in palm wine, and sealed them with preservatives in stone vessels. Next, the embalmer washed the body, filled it with spices and aromatics, and covered it for about two months with natron, a naturally occurring salt substance. When the natron had extracted all moisture from the body, the embalmer cleansed it again and wrapped it with strips of fine linen covered with resin. Adorned with jewelry, the preserved body then went into a coffin bearing a painting or a sculpted likeness of the deceased. .

Canopic Coffinette of Tutankhamon www.mhhe.com/bentleybrief2e

Careful preservation of the body was only a part of the funerary ritual for prominent Egyptians. Ruling elites, wealthy individuals, and sometimes common people as well laid their deceased to rest in expensive tombs equipped with furniture, tools, weapons, and ornaments that the departed would need in their next lives. Relatives periodically brought food and wine to nourish the deceased in their new dimension of existence.

Egyptian funerary customs were reflections of a prosperous agricultural society. Food offerings consisted mostly of local agricultural products, and scenes painted on tomb walls often depicted workers preparing fields or cultivating crops. Moreover, bountiful harvests explained the accumulation of wealth that supported elaborate funerary practices, and they also enabled some individuals to devote their efforts to specialized tasks such as embalming. Agriculture even influenced religious beliefs. Many Egyptians believed fervently in a life beyond the grave, and they likened the human experience of life and death to the agricultural cycle in which crops grow, die, and come to life again in another season.

❮ Excavations surrounding the pyramids, as seen from the air.

As Mesopotamians built a productive agricultural society in southwest Asia and as Indo-European peoples introduced domesticated horses to much of Eurasia, cultivation and herding also transformed African societies. African agriculture first took root in the Sudan, then moved into the Nile River valley and also to most parts of sub-Saharan Africa. Agriculture flourished

Nubia (NOO-bee-uh)

CHRONOLOGY

9000 B.C.E.	Origins of Sudanic herding
7500 B.C.E.	Origins of Sudanic cultivation
3100 B.C.E.	Unification of Egypt
3100–2660 B.C.E.	Archaic Period of Egyptian history
2660–2160 B.C.E.	Egyptian Old Kingdom
2600–2500 B.C.E.	Era of pyramid building in Egypt
2500–1450 B.C.E.	Early kingdom of Kush with capital at Kerma
2040–1640 B.C.E.	Egyptian Middle Kingdom
2000 B.C.E.	Beginnings of Bantu migrations
1550–1070 B.C.E.	Egyptian New Kingdom
1479–1425 B.C.E.	Reign of Pharaoh Tuthmosis III
1473–1458 B.C.E.	Reign of Queen Hatshepsut (coruler with Tuthmosis III)
1353–1335 B.C.E.	Reign of Pharaoh Amenhotep IV (Akhenaten)
900 B.C.E.	Invention of iron metallurgy in sub-Saharan Africa
760 B.C.E.	Conquest of Egypt by King Kashta of Kush

particularly in the fertile Nile valley, and abundant harvests soon supported fast-growing populations. That agricultural bounty underwrote the development of Egypt, the most prosperous and powerful of the early agricultural societies in Africa, and also of Nubia, Egypt's neighbor to the south.

Distinctive Egyptian and Nubian societies began to take shape in the valley of the Nile River during the late fourth millennium B.C.E., shortly after the emergence of complex society in Mesopotamia. Like their Mesopotamian counterparts, Egyptians and Nubians drew on agricultural surpluses to organize formal states, support specialized laborers, and develop distinctive cultural traditions. Also like Mesopotamians, Egyptian and Nubian residents of the Nile valley had regular dealings with peoples from other societies. They drew inspiration for political and social organization both from Mesopotamia and from their African neighbors to the south. In addition, they both traded with and competed against Mesopotamians, Phoenicians, Africans, and others, which resulted in increasing connections with other societies as well as intermittent military conflict.

Indeed, like their counterparts in Mesopotamia, Egyptian and Nubian societies developed from their earliest days in a larger world of interaction and exchange. Just as the peoples of southwest Asia influenced one another, so inhabitants of the Nile valley mixed and mingled with peoples from the eastern Mediterranean, southwest Asia, and sub-Saharan Africa. Just as Indo-European peoples migrated to new lands and established communities that transformed much of Eurasia, so Bantu peoples migrated from their original homeland in west Africa and established settlements that brought profound change to much of sub-Saharan Africa. By no means were Egypt and Nubia isolated centers of social development. Instead, they were only a small part of a much larger world of interacting societies.

EARLY AGRICULTURAL SOCIETY IN AFRICA

Egypt was the most prominent of early African societies, but it was by no means the only agricultural society, or even the only complex, city-based society of ancient Africa. On the contrary, Egypt emerged alongside Nubia and other agricultural societies in sub-Saharan Africa. Indeed, agricultural crops and domesticated animals reached Egypt from sub-Saharan Africa by way of Nubia as well as from southwest Asia. Favorable geographic conditions enabled Egyptians to build an especially productive agricultural economy that supported a powerful state, while Nubia became home to a somewhat less prosperous but nonetheless sophisticated society. After taking shape as distinctive societies, Egypt had regular dealings with both eastern Mediterranean and southwest Asian peoples, and Nubia linked Egypt and the eastern Mediterranean basin with the peoples and societies of sub-Saharan Africa.

Bantu (BAHN-too)

Climatic Change and the Development of Agriculture in Africa

African agriculture emerged in the context of gradual but momentous changes in climatic conditions. About 10,000 B.C.E., after the end of the last ice age, the area now occupied by the Sahara desert was mostly a grassy steppe with numerous lakes, rivers, and streams. Indeed, climatic and geographic conditions were similar to those of the Sudan—a region of savanna and grassland that stretches across the African continent between the Sahara to the north and the tropical rain forest to the south.

EARLY SUDANIC AGRICULTURE After about 9000 B.C.E., peoples of the eastern Sudan domesticated cattle and became nomadic herders but also continued to collect wild grains. After 7500 B.C.E. they established permanent settlements and began to cultivate sorghum. Meanwhile, after about 8000 B.C.E., inhabitants of the western Sudan began to cultivate yams in the region between the Niger and Congo rivers. Sudanic agriculture became increasingly diverse over the following centuries: sheep and goats arrived from southwest Asia after 7000 B.C.E., and Sudanic peoples began to cultivate gourds, watermelons, and cotton after 6500 B.C.E.

Agricultural productivity—and the need for order—led Sudanic peoples to organize small-scale states. By about 5000 B.C.E. many Sudanic peoples had formed small monarchies ruled by kings who were viewed as divine or semidivine beings. Sudanic peoples also developed religious beliefs that reflected their agricultural society. They recognized a single divine force as the source of good and evil, and they associated it with rain—a matter of concern for any agricultural society.

CLIMATIC CHANGE After 5000 B.C.E. the northern half of Africa became much hotter and drier than before. The Sahara desert in particular became increasingly arid and uninhabitable. This process of desiccation drove both humans and animals to regions that offered reliable sources of water such as lakes and rivers. One of those regions was the valley of the Nile River, the principal source of water flowing through north Africa.

THE NILE RIVER VALLEY Fed by rain and snow in the mountains of east Africa, the Nile, which is the world's longest river, courses some 6,695 kilometers (4,160 miles) from its source at Lake Victoria to its outlet through the delta to the Mediterranean Sea. Each spring, rain and melting snow swell the river, which surges north through the Sudan and Egypt. Until the completion of the high dam at Aswan in 1968, every year the Nile flooded the plains downstream. When the waters receded, they left behind a layer of rich, fertile muck, and those alluvial deposits supported a remarkably productive agricultural economy throughout the Nile River valley.

Egypt and Nubia: "Gifts of the Nile"

Herodotus & Egypt
www.mhhe.com/
bentleybrief2e

Agriculture transformed the entire Nile River valley, with effects that were most dramatic in Egypt. In ancient times, Egypt referred not to the territory embraced by the modern state of Egypt but, rather, to the ribbon of land bordering the lower third of the Nile between the Mediterranean and the river's first cataract (an unnavigable stretch of rapids and waterfalls) near Aswan. Egypt enjoyed a much larger floodplain than most of the land to the south known as Nubia, the middle stretches of the Nile valley between the river's first and sixth cataracts. As the Sahara became increasingly arid, cultivators flocked to the Nile valley and established societies that depended on intensive agriculture. Because of their broad floodplains, Egyptians were able to take better advantage of the Nile's annual floods than their neighbors to the south, and they turned Egypt into an especially productive agricultural region that was capable of supporting a much larger population than were Nubian lands. Because of its prosperity, the Greek historian Herodotus proclaimed Egypt the "gift of the Nile."

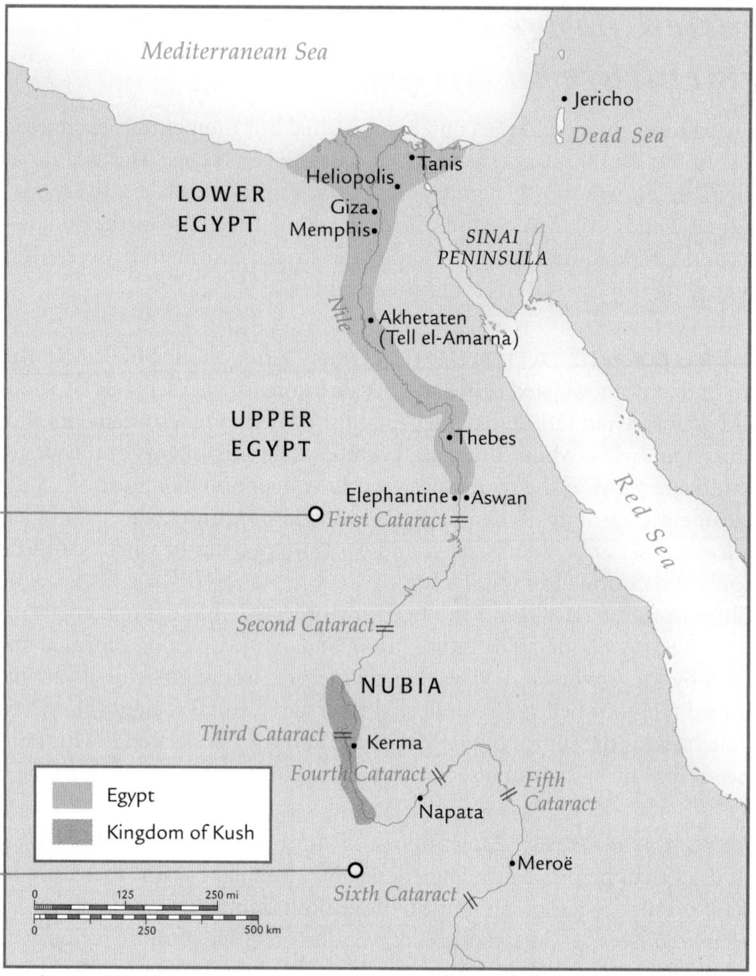

The region between the first and sixth cataracts was known as Nubia.

MAP 2.1 | The Nile valley, 3000–2000 B.C.E. Note the difference in size between the kingdom of Egypt and the kingdom of Kush. ***What geographical conditions favored the establishment of large states north of the first cataract of the Nile River?***

Counting livestock, a model from a tomb
www.mhhe.com/bentleybrief2e

EARLY AGRICULTURE IN THE NILE VALLEY Geography ensured that Egypt and Nubia would come under the influence of both sub-Saharan Africa and the eastern Mediterranean basin, since the Nile River links the two regions. About 10,000 B.C.E. migrants from the Red Sea hills in northern Ethiopia traveled down the Nile valley and introduced to Egypt and Nubia the practice of collecting wild grains as well as their language, which became the language of ancient Egypt. After 5000 B.C.E., as the African climate grew hotter and drier, Sudanic peoples moved down the Nile, introducing Egypt and Nubia to crops such as gourds and watermelons and domesticated animals such as cattle and donkeys. About the same time, wheat and barley reached Egypt and Nubia from Mesopotamia by traveling up the Nile from the Mediterranean.

Both Egyptians and Nubians relied heavily on agriculture at least by 5000 B.C.E. Egyptian cultivators went into the floodplains in the late summer, after the recession of the Nile's annual flood, sowed their seeds without extensive preparation of the soil, allowed their crops to mature during the cool months of the year, and harvested them during the winter and early spring. With less-extensive floodplains, Nubians relied more on prepared fields and irrigation by waters diverted from the Nile. As in Mesopotamia, high agricultural productivity led to a rapid increase in population throughout the Nile valley. Demographic pressures soon forced Egyptians in particular to develop more intense and sophisticated methods of agriculture as cultivators found it necessary to move beyond the Nile's immediate floodplains to areas that required careful preparation and irrigation. By

4000 B.C.E. agricultural villages dotted the Nile's shores from the Mediterranean in the north to the river's fourth cataract in the south. As in Mesopotamia, dense human population in Egypt and Nubia brought a need for formal organization of public affairs. Although geographical barriers in the form of seas and desert meant that neither area faced external dangers to the extent that Mesopotamia did, the two areas still needed to maintain order and organize community projects. As a result, both Egyptians and Nubians created states and recognized official authorities.

The earliest Egyptian and Nubian states were small kingdoms much like those instituted in the Sudan after 5000 B.C.E. Indeed, it is likely that the notion of divine or semidivine rulers reached Egypt and Nubia from the eastern and central Sudan. In any case, small kingdoms appeared first in southern Egypt and Nubia after 4000 B.C.E., and by 3300 B.C.E. small local kingdoms organized public life throughout Egypt as well as Nubia.

EARLY AGRICULTURE IN EGYPT. | A painting from the tomb of a priest who lived about the fifteenth century B.C.E. depicts agricultural workers plowing and sowing crops in southern Egypt.

The Unification of Egypt

MENES By 3500 B.C.E. political and economic competition fueled numerous skirmishes and small-scale wars between the Nile kingdoms. Some kingdoms overcame their neighbors and gradually expanded until they controlled sizable territories. About 3100 B.C.E. Egyptian rulers drew on the considerable agricultural and demographic advantages of Egypt's large population and broad floodplains to forge all the territory between the Nile delta and the river's first cataract into a powerful and unified kingdom. Tradition holds that unified rule came to Egypt in the person of a conqueror named Menes (sometimes identified with an early Egyptian ruler called Narmer). Menes was an ambitious minor official from southern Egypt (known as Upper Egypt, since the Nile flows north) who rose to power and extended his authority north and into the delta (known as Lower Egypt). According to tradition, Menes founded the city of Memphis, near modern Cairo, which stood at the junction of Upper and Lower Egypt. Memphis served as Menes' capital and eventually became the cultural as well as the political center of ancient Egypt.

Menes and his successors built a centralized state ruled by the pharaoh, the Egyptian king. The early pharaohs claimed to be gods living on the earth in human form, the owners and absolute rulers of all the land. In that respect, they continued the tradition of divine kingship inherited from the early agricultural societies of the Sudan. Over time, Egyptians viewed rulers as offspring of Amon, a sun god. They considered the ruling pharaoh a human sun overseeing affairs on the earth, just as Amon was the sun supervising the larger cosmos, and they believed that after his death the pharaoh actually merged with Amon.

Diagram of the pyramids
www.mhhe.com/bentleybrief2e

THE ARCHAIC PERIOD AND THE OLD KINGDOM The power of the pharaohs was greatest during the first millennium of Egyptian history—the eras known as the Archaic Period (3100–2660 B.C.E.) and the Old Kingdom (2660–2160 B.C.E.). The most enduring symbols of their authority and divine status are the massive pyramids constructed during the Old Kingdom as royal tombs, most of them during the century from 2600 to 2500 B.C.E. These enormous monuments stand today at Giza, near Cairo, as testimony to the pharaohs' ability to marshal Egyptian resources. The largest is the pyramid of Khufu (also known as Cheops), which involved the precise cutting and fitting of 2.3 million limestone blocks weighing up to 15 tons, with an average weight of 2.5 tons. Scholars estimate that construction of Khufu's pyramid required the services of some eighty-four thousand laborers working eighty days per year for twenty years.

RELATIONS BETWEEN EGYPT AND NUBIA Even after the emergence of the strong pharaonic state, the fortunes of Egypt and Nubia remained closely intertwined. Egyptians had strong interests in Nubia for both political and commercial

Menes (mee-neez)

reasons: they were wary of Nubian kingdoms that might threaten Upper Egypt, and they desired products such as gold, ivory, ebony, and precious stones that were available only from southern lands. Meanwhile, Nubians had equally strong interests in Egypt: they wanted to protect their independence from their large and powerful neighbor to the north, and they sought to profit by controlling trade down the Nile.

THE EARLY KINGDOM OF KUSH Tensions led to frequent violence between Egypt and Nubia throughout the Archaic Period and the Old Kingdom. Indeed, Egypt dominated Lower Nubia (the land between the first and second cataracts of the Nile) for more than half a millennium, from about 3000 to 2400 B.C.E. This Egyptian presence in the north forced Nubian leaders to concentrate their efforts at political organization farther to the south in Upper Nubia. By about 2500 B.C.E. they had established a powerful kingdom, called Kush, with a capital at Kerma, about 700 kilometers (435 miles) south of Aswan. Though not as powerful as united Egypt, the kingdom of Kush became a formidable and wealthy state in its own right.

In spite of constant tension and frequent hostilities, Egypt and Nubia remained connected in many ways. About 2300 B.C.E., for example, the Egyptian explorer Harkhuf made four expeditions to Nubia. He returned from one of his trips with a caravan of some three hundred donkeys bearing exotic products from tropical Africa, as well as a dancing dwarf, and his cargo stimulated Egyptian desire for trade with southern lands. Meanwhile, by the end of the Old Kingdom, Nubian mercenaries had become quite prominent in Egyptian armies. In fact, they often married Egyptian women and assimilated into Egyptian society.

Turmoil and Empire

THE MIDDLE KINGDOM Toward the end of the Old Kingdom, high agricultural productivity made several regions of Egypt so prosperous and powerful that they were able to ignore the pharaohs and pursue their own interests. As a result, the central state declined and eventually disappeared altogether during a long period of upheaval and unrest (2160–2040 B.C.E.). Pharaonic authority returned with the establishment of the Middle Kingdom (2040–1640 B.C.E.). Pharaohs of the Middle Kingdom were not as powerful as their predecessors of the Old Kingdom, but they effectively stabilized Egypt and supervised relations with neighboring lands.

THE HYKSOS Gradually, however, Egypt came under the pressure of foreign peoples from southwest Asia, particularly a Semitic people whom Egyptians called the Hyksos ("foreign rulers"). Little information survives about the Hyksos, but it is clear that they were horse-riding nomads. Indeed, their horse-drawn chariots, which they learned about from Hittites and Mesopotamians, provided them with a significant military advantage over Egyptian forces. They enjoyed an advantage also in their weaponry: the Hyksos used bronze weapons and bronze-tipped arrows, whereas Egyptians relied mostly on wooden weapons and arrows with stone heads. About 1674 B.C.E. the Hyksos captured Memphis and levied tribute throughout Egypt.

Hyksos rule provoked a strong reaction especially in Upper Egypt, where disgruntled nobles organized revolts against the foreigners. They adopted horses and chariots for their own military forces. They also equipped their troops with bronze weapons. Working from Thebes and later from Memphis, Egyptian leaders gradually pushed the Hyksos out of the Nile delta and founded a powerful state known as the New Kingdom (1550–1070 B.C.E.).

Pharaohs of the New Kingdom presided over a prosperous and productive society. Agricultural surpluses supported a population of perhaps four million people as well as an army and an elaborate bureaucracy that divided responsibilities among different offices.

Kush (kuhsh)

Hyksos (HICK-sohs)

SOURCES FROM THE PAST

Harkhuf's Expeditions to Nubia

Many Egyptians wrote brief autobiographies that they or their descendants had carved into their tombs. One of the most famous autobiographies from the Old Kingdom is that of Harkhuf, a royal official who became governor of Upper Egypt before 2300 B.C.E. The inscriptions in his tomb mention his four expeditions to Nubia to seek valuable items and report on political conditions there. The inscriptions also include the text of a letter from the boy-pharaoh Neferkare expressing his appreciation for Harkhuf's fourth expedition and his desire to see the dancing dwarf that Harkhuf had brought back from Nubia.

The majesty of [Pharaoh] Mernere, my lord, sent me together with my father . . . to [the Upper Nubian kingdom of] Yam to open the way to that country. I did it in seven months; I brought from it all kinds of beautiful and rare gifts, and was praised for it greatly.

His majesty sent me a second time alone. . . . I came down [the Nile] bringing gifts from that country in great quantity, the likes of which had never before been brought back to this land [Egypt]. . . .

Then his majesty sent me a third time to Yam. . . . I came down with three hundred donkeys laden with incense, ebony, . . . panther skins, elephant's tusks, throw sticks, and all sorts of good products.

[The letter of Pharaoh Neferkare to Harkhuf:] Notice has been taken of this dispatch of yours which you made for the King of the Palace, to let one know that you have come down in safety from Yam with the army that was with you. You have said in this dispatch of yours that you have brought all kinds of great and beautiful gifts. . . . You have said in this dispatch of yours that you have brought a pygmy of the god's dances from the land of the horizon-dwellers [the region of Nubia southeast of Egypt], like the pygmy whom the [royal official] Bawerded brought from Punt [Ethiopia and Somalia] in the time of King Isesi. You have said to my majesty that his like has never been brought by anyone who [visited] Yam previously.

Truly you know how to do what your lord loves and praises. Truly you spend day and night planning to do what your lord loves, praises, and commands. His majesty will provide you many worthy honors for the benefit of your son's son for all time, so that all people will say, when they hear what my majesty did for you: "Does anything equal what was done for the sole companion Harkhuf when he came down from Yam, on account of the vigilance he showed in doing what his lord loved, praised, and commanded?"

Come north to the residence at once! Hurry and bring with you this pygmy whom you brought from the land of the horizon-dwellers live, hale, and healthy, for the dances of the god, to gladden the heart, to delight the heart of King Neferkare who lives forever! When he goes down with you into the ship, get worthy men to be around him on deck, lest he fall into the water! When he lies down at night, get worthy men to lie around him in his tent. Inspect ten times at night! My majesty desires to see this pygmy more than the gifts of the mineland [the Sinai peninsula] and of Punt!

When you arrive at the residence and this pygmy is with you live, hale, and healthy, my majesty will do great things for you, more than was done for the [royal official] Bawerded in the time of King Isesi, in accordance with my majesty's wish to see this pygmy. Orders have been brought to the chief of the new towns and the companion, overseer of priests to command that supplies be furnished from what is under the charge of each from every storage depot and every temple that has not been exempted.

■ How does Harkhuf's autobiography illuminate early Egyptian interest in Nubia and the processes by which Egyptians of the Old Kingdom developed knowledge about Nubia?

SOURCE: Miriam Lichtheim, ed. *Ancient Egyptian Literature.* 3 vols. Berkeley: University of California Press, 1973, 1:25–27.

EGYPTIAN IMPERIALISM Pharaohs of the New Kingdom also worked to extend Egyptian authority well beyond the Nile valley and the delta. After expelling the Hyksos, they sought to prevent new invasions by seizing control of regions that might pose threats in the future. Most vigorous of the New Kingdom pharaohs was Tuthmosis III

Tuthmosis (tuh-MOE-sis)

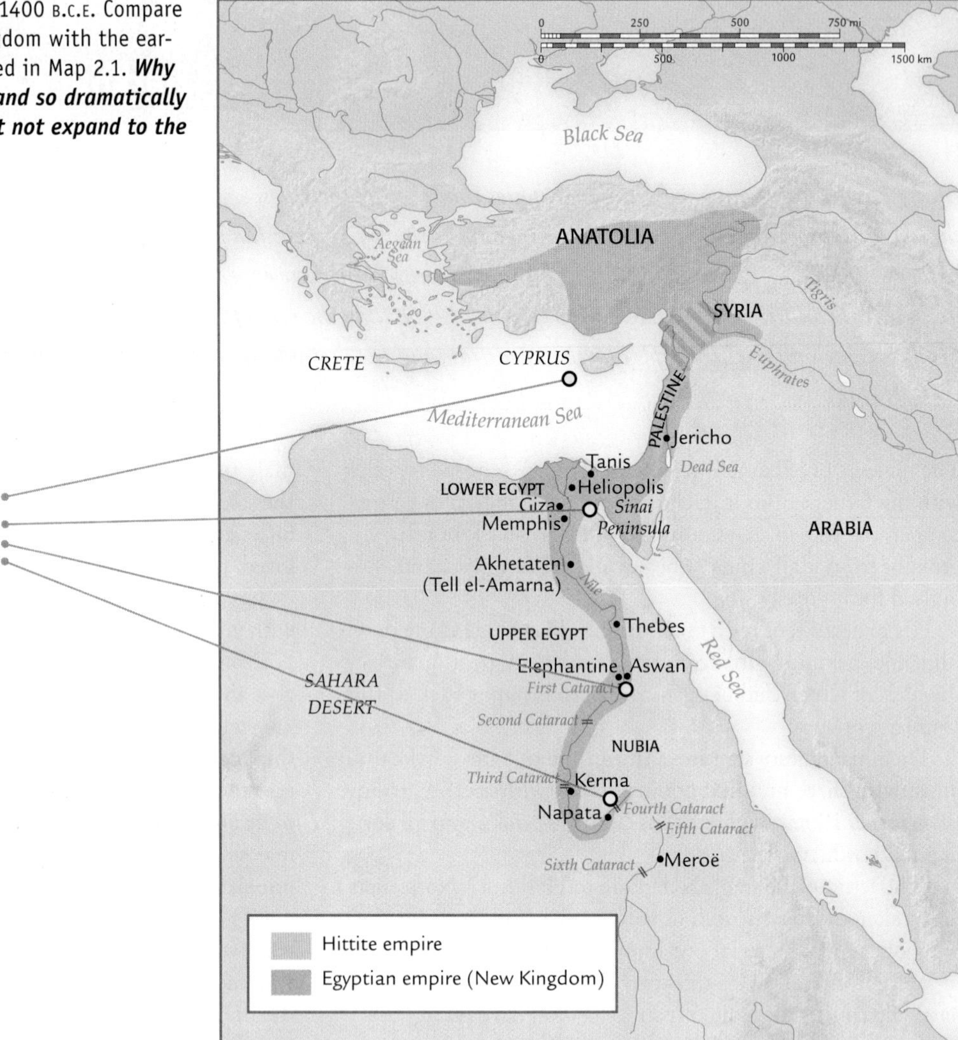

MAP 2.2 | Imperial Egypt, 1400 B.C.E. Compare the territory ruled by the New Kingdom with the earlier kingdom of Egypt as represented in Map 2.1. ***Why was the New Kingdom able to expand so dramatically to the north and south? Why did it not expand to the east and west also?***

Areas of Egyptian expansion during the New Kingdom

(reigned 1479–1425 B.C.E.). After seventeen campaigns that he personally led to Palestine and Syria, Tuthmosis dominated the coastal regions of the eastern Mediterranean as well as north Africa. Rulers of the New Kingdom also turned their attention to the south and restored Egyptian dominance in Nubia. Thus for half a millennium Egypt was an imperial power throughout much of the eastern Mediterranean basin and southwest Asia as well as most of the Nile River valley.

After the New Kingdom, Egypt entered a long period of political and military decline. Just as Hyksos rule provoked a reaction in Egypt, so Egyptian rule provoked reactions in the regions subdued by pharaonic armies. Local resistance drove Egyptian forces out of Nubia and southwest Asia; then Kushite and Assyrian armies invaded Egypt itself.

THE REVIVED KINGDOM OF KUSH By 1100 B.C.E. Egyptian forces were in full retreat from Nubia, and in the tenth century B.C.E. Nubian leaders organized a new kingdom of Kush with a capital at Napata, located just below the Nile's fourth cataract. By the eighth century B.C.E., rulers of this revived kingdom of Kush were powerful enough to invade Egypt. King Kashta conquered Thebes about 760 B.C.E. and founded a Kushite dynasty that ruled Egypt for almost a century. Kashta's successors consolidated Kushite authority in Upper Egypt, claimed the title of pharaoh, and eventually extended their rule to the Nile delta and beyond.

Meanwhile, as Kushites pushed into Egypt from the south, Assyrian armies equipped with iron weapons bore down from the north. During the mid–seventh century B.C.E.,

NUBIAN TRIBUTE TO EGYPT. | A wall painting from the tomb of an Egyptian imperial official in Nubia depicts a delegation of Nubians bringing tribute in the forms of exotic beasts, animal skins, and rings of gold. ***What kinds of products are the delegates bringing, and why?***

while building their vast empire, the Assyrians invaded Egypt, campaigned as far south as Thebes, drove out the Kushites, and subjected Egypt to Assyrian rule. After the mid–sixth century B.C.E., like Mesopotamia, Egypt fell to a series of foreign conquerors who built vast empires throughout southwest Asia and the eastern Mediterranean region.

THE FORMATION OF COMPLEX SOCIETIES AND SOPHISTICATED CULTURAL TRADITIONS

As in Mesopotamia, cities and the congregation of dense populations encouraged the emergence of specialized labor in the early agricultural societies of Africa. Clearly defined social classes emerged throughout the Nile valley, and both Egypt and Nubian lands built patriarchal societies that placed authority largely in the hands of adult males. The Egyptian economy was especially productive, and because of both its prosperity and its geographic location, Egypt figured as a center of trade, linking lands in southwest Asia, the eastern Mediterranean, and sub-Saharan Africa. Meanwhile, like southwest Asia, the Nile valley was a site of sophisticated cultural development. Writing systems appeared in both Egypt and Nubia, and writing soon became a principal medium of literary expression and religious reflection as well as a means for preserving governmental records and commercial information.

The Emergence of Cities and Stratified Societies

CITIES OF THE NILE VALLEY Cities were not as prominent in early societies of the Nile River valley as they were in ancient Mesopotamia. Nevertheless, several major cities emerged and guided affairs in both Egypt and Nubia. In Egypt, Memphis, Thebes, Heliopolis, and Tanis all became important political, administrative, or cultural

Social Stratification in Egyptian Society. | Building pyramids and other large structures involved heavy work, especially by the less privileged classes. Here an Egyptian manuscript painting produced about 1000 B.C.E. depicts a supervisor overseeing a group of laborers as they drag a sled loaded with building blocks.

centers. In Nubia, Kerma, Napata, and Meroë all took their turn as political capitals between about 2500 B.C.E. and 100 C.E.

Limestone relief of Akhenaten & Nefertiti
www.mhhe.com/bentleybrief2e

SOCIAL CLASSES In Egypt and Nubia alike, ancient cities were centers of considerable accumulated wealth, which encouraged the development of social distinctions and hierarchies. Like the Mesopotamians, ancient Egyptians recognized a series of well-defined social classes. Egyptian peasants and slaves played roles in society similar to those of their Mesopotamian counterparts: they supplied the hard labor that made complex agricultural society possible. The organization of the ruling classes, however, differed considerably between Mesopotamia and Egypt. Instead of a series of urban kings, as in Mesopotamia, Egyptians recognized the pharaoh as a supreme central ruler. In addition, rather than depending on nobles who owed their positions to their birth, Egypt relied on professional military forces and an elaborate bureaucracy of administrators and tax collectors who served the central government. Thus, in Egypt much more than in Mesopotamia, individuals of common birth could attain high positions in society through government service.

Surviving information illuminates Egyptian society much better than Nubian, but it is clear that Nubia also was the site of a complex, hierarchical society in ancient times. Indeed, cemeteries associated with Nubian cities clearly reveal social and economic distinctions. Tombs of wealthy and powerful individuals were often elaborate structures—comfortable dwelling places tastefully decorated with paintings and filled with expensive goods such as gold jewelry, gems, fine furniture, and abundant supplies of food. In contrast, graves of commoners were much simpler, although they usually contained jewelry, pottery, personal ornaments, and other goods to accompany the departed.

PATRIARCHAL SOCIETY Like their Mesopotamian counterparts, both Egyptian and Nubian peoples built patriarchal societies that vested authority over public and private affairs in their men. With rare exceptions men were the rulers in both Egyptian and Nubian private as well as public life, and decisions about government policies rested mostly in men's hands.

Yet women made their influence felt in ancient Egyptian and Nubian societies much more than in contemporary Mesopotamia. In Egypt, women of the royal family sometimes served as regents for young rulers. In one notable case, a woman took power as pharaoh herself: Queen Hatshepsut (reigned 1473–1458 B.C.E.) served as coruler with her stepson Tuthmosis III. However, the notion of a female ruler may have been unsettling to many Egyptians. In what seems to have been an effort to present her in unthreatening guise, a monumental statue of Queen Hatshepsut depicts her wearing the stylized beard traditionally associated with the pharaohs. In Nubia, in contrast, there is abundant evidence of many women rulers in the kingdom of Kush. Some ruled in their own right, others reigned jointly with male kings, and many governed also in the capacity of regents. Meanwhile, other women wielded considerable power as priestesses in the numerous religious cults observed in Egypt and Nubia. A few women also obtained a formal education and worked as scribes.

THINKING ABOUT *Traditions*

TRADITIONS IN EARLY AFRICAN SOCIETIES. Egyptian kingdoms flourished along the Nile River as a result of the fertile alluvial soils that made agriculture so productive. What were some of the distinctive styles of ruling, monument building, and religious worship in this prosperous agricultural society, and why might they have developed differently than in Nubia?

Economic Specialization and Trade

With the formation of complex, city-based societies, peoples of the Nile valley were able to draw on a rapidly expanding stock of human skills. Bronze metallurgy made its way from Mesopotamia to both Egypt and Nubia, and by 1000 B.C.E. Sudanic peoples independently developed a technology of iron production that eventually spread to most parts of sub-Saharan Africa. Pottery, textile manufacture, woodworking, leather production, stonecutting, and masonry all became distinct occupations in cities throughout the Nile valley. Specialized labor and the invention of efficient transportation technologies encouraged the development of trade networks that linked the Nile valley to a much larger world.

BRONZE METALLURGY Nile societies were much slower than their Mesopotamian counterparts to adopt metal tools and weapons. Whereas the production of bronze flourished in Mesopotamia by 3000 B.C.E., use of bronze implements became widespread in Egypt only after the seventeenth century B.C.E., when the Hyksos relied on bronze weapons to impose their authority on the Nile delta. Although Egyptians equipped their own forces with bronze weapons after expelling the Hyksos, the high cost of copper and tin kept bronze out of the hands of most people. Indeed, bronze was considered so valuable that officers weighed the bronze tools issued to workers at royal tombs to ensure that craftsmen did not shave slivers off them for personal uses.

IRON METALLURGY Bronze was even less prominent in Nubian societies than in Egypt. During the centuries after 1000 B.C.E., however, the southern Nile societies made up for their lack of bronze with the emergence of large-scale iron production. Furnaces churned out iron implements both in Nubia and in west Africa at least by 500 B.C.E. Meroë in particular became a site of large-scale iron production. Indeed, archaeologists who excavated Meroë in the early twentieth century C.E. found enormous mounds of slag still remaining from ancient times.

TRANSPORTATION Nile craftsmen also worked from the early days of agricultural society to devise efficient means of transportation. Before 3500 B.C.E. Egyptians already traveled up and down the Nile with ease. Because the Nile flows north, boats could ride the currents from Upper to Lower Egypt. Meanwhile, prevailing winds blow almost year-round from the north, so that by raising a sail, boats could easily make their way upriver from Lower to Upper Egypt. Soon after 3000 B.C.E. Egyptians sailed beyond the Nile into the Mediterranean, and by about 2000 B.C.E. they had also thoroughly explored the waters of the Red Sea, the Gulf of Aden, and the western portion of the Arabian Sea. Egyptians also made use of Mesopotamian-style wheeled vehicles for local transport as well as donkey caravans for overland transport.

In Nubia, navigation on the Nile was less convenient than in Egypt because unnavigable cataracts made it necessary to transport goods overland before continuing on the

Hatshepsut (hat-SHEP-soot)

Egyptian River Transport. | A wooden model found in a tomb shows how Egyptians traveled up and down the Nile River. Produced about 2000 B.C.E., this sculpture depicts a relatively small boat with a mast, sail, rudder, and poles to push the vessel through shallow waters. Many wall and tomb paintings confirm the accuracy of this model. ***Why is the figure in front trying to gauge the water's depth?***

river. Moreover, sailing ships heading upriver could not negotiate a long stretch of the Nile around the fourth cataract because winds blow the same direction that currents flow. As a result, Nubian societies had to rely more than Egyptians on overland transport by wheeled vehicles and donkey caravan.

TRADE NETWORKS In both Egypt and Nubia, specialized labor and efficient means of transportation encouraged the development of long-distance trade. By the time of the Old Kingdom, trade flowed regularly between Egypt and Nubia. Exotic African goods such as ivory, ebony, leopard skins, ostrich feathers, gemstones, gold, and slaves went down the Nile in exchange for pottery, wine, honey, and finished products from Egypt. Among the most prized Egyptian exports were fine linen textiles woven from the flax that flourished in the Nile valley as well as high-quality decorative and ornamental objects such as boxes, furniture, and jewelry produced by skilled artisans.

Egyptian merchants looked north as well as south. They traded with Mesopotamians as early as 3500 B.C.E., and after 3000 B.C.E. they were active throughout the eastern Mediterranean basin. Since Egypt has very few trees, Egyptian ships regularly imported huge loads from Lebanon. Pharaohs especially prized aromatic cedar for their tombs, and one record from about 2600 B.C.E. mentions an expedition of forty ships hauling cedar logs. In exchange for cedar, Egyptians offered gold, silver, linen textiles, leather goods, and dried foods such as lentils.

After the establishment of the New Kingdom, Egyptians also traded through the Red Sea and the Gulf of Aden with an east African land they called Punt—probably modern-day Somalia and Ethiopia. From Punt they imported gold, ebony, ivory, cattle, aromatics, and slaves. Thus, as in southwest Asia, specialization of labor and efficient technologies of transportation not only quickened the economies of complex societies in Egypt and Nubia but also encouraged their interaction with peoples of distant lands.

Early Writing in the Nile Valley

HIEROGLYPHIC WRITING Writing appeared in Egypt at least by 3200 B.C.E., possibly as a result of Mesopotamian influence. As in Mesopotamia, the earliest Egyptian writing was pictographic, but Egyptians soon supplemented their pictographs with symbols representing sounds and ideas. Early Greek visitors to Egypt marveled at the large and handsome pictographs that adorned Egyptian monuments and buildings. Since the symbols were particularly prominent on temples, the visitors called them hieroglyphs, from two Greek words meaning "holy inscriptions." Hieroglyphic writing also survives on sheets of papyrus, a paper-like material fashioned from the insides of papyrus reeds, which flourish along the Nile River. The hot, dry climate of Egypt has preserved large numbers of papyrus texts bearing administrative and commercial records as well as literary and religious texts.

Although striking and dramatic, hieroglyphs were also somewhat cumbersome. Egyptians went to the trouble of using hieroglyphs for formal writing and monumental inscriptions, but for everyday affairs they commonly relied on the hieratic ("priestly") script, a simplified, cursive form of hieroglyphs. Hieratic appeared in the early centuries of the third millennium B.C.E., and Egyptians made extensive use of the script for more than three thousand years, from about 2600 B.C.E. to 600 C.E. Hieratic largely disappeared after the middle of the first millennium C.E., when Egyptians adapted the Greek alphabet to their own language and developed alphabetic scripts known as the demotic ("popular") and Coptic ("Egyptian") scripts.

MEROITIC WRITING Nubian peoples spoke their own languages, but all early writing in Nubia was Egyptian hieroglyphic writing. Indeed, over the centuries, Egypt wielded great cultural influence in Nubia, especially during times when Egyptian political and military influence was strong in southern lands. After about the fifth century B.C.E., however, Egyptian cultural influence declined noticeably in Nubia. After the transfer of the Kushite capital from Napata to Meroë, Nubian scribes even devised an alphabetic script for the Meroitic language. They borrowed Egyptian hieroglyphs but used them to represent sounds rather than ideas and so created a flexible writing system. Many Meroitic inscriptions survive, both on monuments and on papyrus. However, although scholars have ascertained the sound values of the alphabet, the Meroitic language itself is so different from other known languages that no one has been able to decipher Meroitic texts.

The Development of Organized Religious Traditions

AMON AND RE Like their counterparts in other world regions, Egyptians and Nubians believed that deities played prominent roles in the world and that proper cultivation of the gods was an important community responsibility. The principal gods revered in ancient Egypt were Amon and Re. Amon was originally a local Theban deity associated with the sun, creation, fertility, and reproductive forces, and Re was a sun god worshiped at Heliopolis. During the Old Kingdom and the Middle Kingdom, priests increasingly associated the two gods with each other and honored them in the combined cult of Amon-Re. At Heliopolis a massive temple complex supported priests who tended to the cult of Amon-Re and studied the heavens for astronomical purposes. When Egypt became an imperial power during the New Kingdom, some devotees suggested that Amon-Re might even be a universal god who presided over all the earth.

hieroglyphics (heye-ruh-GLIPH-iks)
hieratic (hahy-uh-RAT-tik)
Amon-Re (AH-mohn RAY)

The Cult of Osiris. Osiris (seated at right) receives a recently deceased individual, while attendants weigh the heart of another individual against a feather. This illustration comes from a papyrus copy of the *Book of the Dead* that was buried with a royal mummy.

PSI img Egyptian *Book of the Dead* www.mhhe.com/bentleybrief2e

ATEN AND MONOTHEISM For a brief period the cult of Amon-Re faced a monotheistic challenge from the god Aten, another deity associated with the sun. Aten's champion was Pharaoh Amenhotep IV (reigned 1353–1335 B.C.E.), who changed his name to Akhenaten in honor of his preferred deity. Akhenaten considered Aten the world's "sole god, like whom there is no other." This faith represented one of the world's earliest expressions of monotheism—the belief that a single god rules over all creation. As long as Akhenaten lived, the cult of Aten flourished. But when the pharaoh died, traditional priests mounted a fierce counterattack, restored the cult of Amon-Re to privileged status, and nearly annihilated the worship and even the memory of Aten.

MUMMIFICATION Whereas Mesopotamians believed with Gilgamesh that death brought an end to an individual's existence, many Egyptians believed that death was not an end so much as a transition to a new dimension of existence. The yearning for immortality helps to explain the Egyptian practice of mummifying the dead. During the Old Kingdom, Egyptians believed that only the ruling elites would survive the grave, so they mummified only pharaohs and their close relatives. During the Middle and New Kingdoms, however, Egyptians came to think of eternal life as a condition available to normal mortals as well as members of the ruling classes. Mummification never became general practice in Egypt, but with or without preservation of the body, a variety of religious cults promised to lead individuals of all classes to immortality.

CULT OF OSIRIS The cult of Osiris attracted particularly strong popular interest. According to the myths surrounding the cult, Osiris's evil brother Seth murdered him and scattered his dismembered parts throughout the land, but the victim's loyal wife, Isis, retrieved his parts and gave her husband a proper burial. Impressed by her devotion, the gods restored Osiris to life as god of the underworld, the dwelling place of the departed.

Egyptians also associated Osiris with immortality and honored him through a religious cult that demanded observance of high moral standards. Following their deaths, individual souls faced the judgment of Osiris, who had their hearts weighed against a feather symbolizing justice. Those with heavy hearts carrying a burden of evil and guilt did not merit immortality, whereas those of pure heart and honorable deeds gained the gift of eternal life. Thus Osiris's cult held out hope of eternal reward for those who behaved according to high moral standards.

NUBIAN RELIGIOUS BELIEFS Nubian peoples observed their own religious traditions, but very little written information survives to throw light on their religious beliefs. The most prominent of the Nubian deities was the lion-god Apedemak,

Akhenaton (ahk-eh-NAH-ton)

often depicted with a bow and arrows, who served as war god for the kingdom of Kush. Another deity, Sebiumeker, was a creator god and divine guardian of his human devotees. Alongside native traditions, Egyptian religious cults were quite prominent in Nubia, especially after the aggressive pharaohs of the New Kingdom imposed Egyptian rule on the southern lands. Nubian peoples did not mummify the remains of their deceased, but they built pyramids similar to those of Egypt, although smaller, and they embraced several Egyptian gods. Amon was the preeminent Egyptian deity in Nubia as in Egypt itself. Osiris was also popular in Nubia, where he sometimes appeared in association with the native deity Sebiumeker. However, Egyptian gods did not displace native gods so much as they joined them in the Nubian pantheon. Indeed, Nubians often identified Egyptian gods with their own deities or endowed the foreign gods with traits important in Nubian society.

THINKING ABOUT *Encounters*

ENCOUNTERS IN EARLY AFRICAN SOCIETIES. Egyptian and Nubian kingdoms were positioned in such a way that they provided crucial links between the Mediterranean basin on the one hand and sub-Saharan Africa on the other. In what ways did trade and contact with distant regions shape Egyptian and Nubian ideas about religion, written expression, technology, and agriculture?

Bantu Migrations and Early Agricultural Societies of Sub-Saharan Africa

Like their counterparts in southwest Asia, Egyptian and Nubian societies participated in a much larger world of interaction and exchange. Mesopotamian societies developed under the strong influences of long-distance trade, diffusions of technological innovations, the spread of cultural traditions, and the far-flung migrations of Semitic and Indo-European peoples. Similarly, quite apart from their dealings with southwest Asian and Mediterranean peoples, Egyptian and Nubian societies developed in the context of widespread interaction and exchange in sub-Saharan Africa. The most prominent processes unfolding in sub-Saharan Africa during ancient times were the migrations of Bantu-speaking peoples and the establishment of agricultural societies in regions where Bantu speakers settled. Just as Sudanic agriculture spread to the Nile valley and provided an economic foundation for the development of Egyptian and Nubian societies, it also spread to most other regions of Africa south of the Sahara and supported the emergence of distinctive agricultural societies.

The Dynamics of Bantu Expansion

THE BANTU Among the most influential peoples of sub-Saharan Africa in ancient times were those who spoke Bantu languages. The original Bantu language was one of many related tongues in the larger Niger-Congo family of languages widely spoken in west Africa after 4000 B.C.E. The earliest Bantu speakers inhabited a region embracing the eastern part of modern Nigeria and the southern part of modern Cameroon. Members of this community referred to themselves as *bantu* (meaning "persons" or "people"). The earliest Bantu speakers settled mostly along the banks of rivers, which they navigated in canoes, and in open areas of the region's forests. They cultivated yams and oil palms, and in later centuries they added millet and sorghum. They also kept goats and raised guinea fowl. They lived in clan-based villages headed by chiefs who conducted religious rituals and represented their communities in dealings with neighboring villages. They traded regularly with hunting and gathering peoples who inhabited the tropical forests. Bantu cultivators provided these forest peoples with pottery and stone axes in exchange for meat, honey, and other forest products.

Sebiumeker (sehb-ih-meh-kur)

MAP 2.3 | Bantu migrations, 2000 B.C.E.–1000 C.E. Note that Bantu migrations proceeded to the south and east of the original homeland of Bantu-speaking peoples. ***To what extent do technological considerations help to explain the extent of the Bantu migrations? Why did Bantu-speaking peoples not migrate also to the north and west of their homeland?***

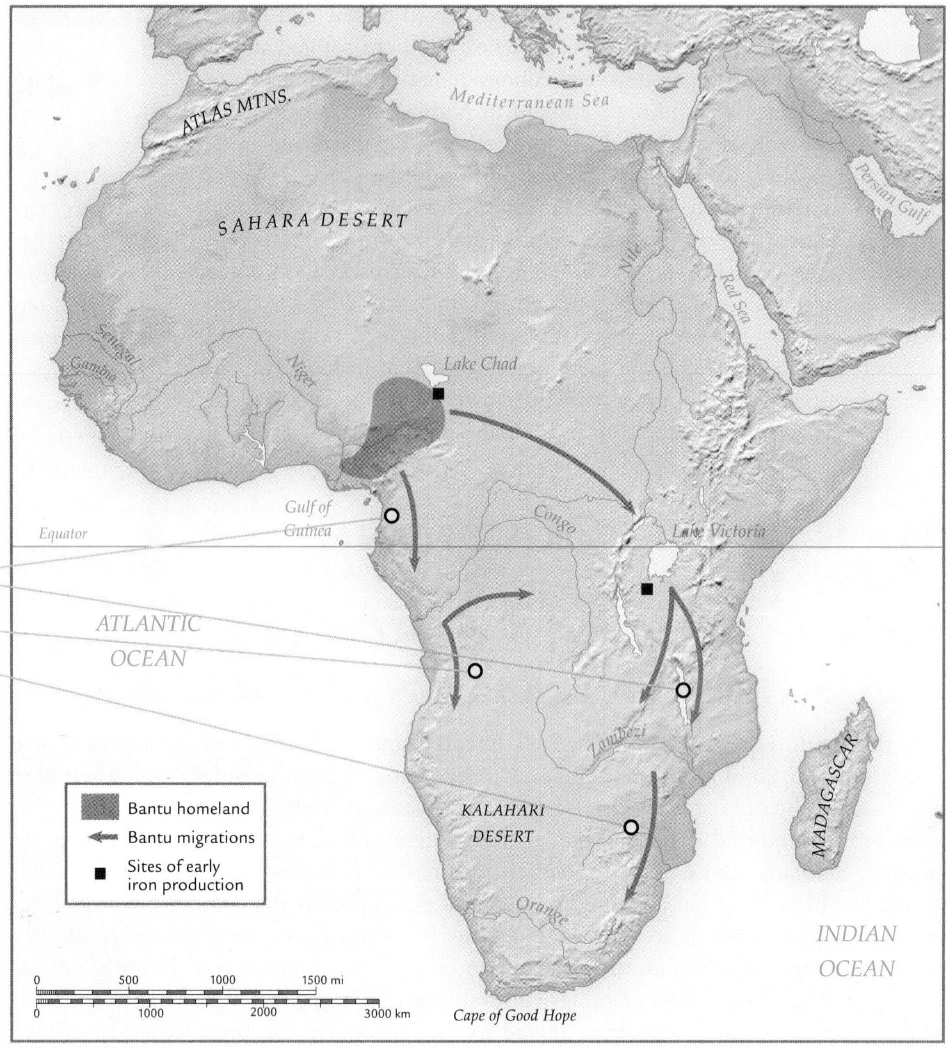

Agriculture spread to sub-Saharan Africa with the Bantu migrations.

BANTU MIGRATIONS Unlike most of their neighbors, the Bantu displayed an early readiness to migrate to new territories. By 3000 B.C.E. they were slowly spreading south into the west African forest, and after 2000 B.C.E. they expanded rapidly to the south toward the Congo River basin and east toward the Great Lakes, absorbing local populations of hunting, gathering, and fishing peoples into their own agricultural societies. Over the centuries, as some groups of Bantu speakers settled and others moved on to new territories, their languages differentiated into more than five hundred distinct but related tongues. (Today more than ninety million people speak Bantu languages, which collectively constitute the most prominent family of languages in sub-Saharan Africa.) Like the Indo-European migrations discussed in chapter 1, the Bantu migrations were not mass movements of peoples. Instead, they were intermittent and incremental processes that resulted in the gradual spread of Bantu languages and ethnic communities, as small groups moved to new territories and established settlements, which then became foundations for further expansion. By 1000 C.E. Bantu-speaking peoples occupied most of Africa south of the equator.

The precise motives of the early Bantu migrants are unknown, but it seems likely that population pressures drove the migrations. When settlements grew uncomfortably large and placed strains on available resources, small groups left their parent communities and moved to new territories. As they moved, Bantu migrants placed pressures on the forest dwellers, sometimes clashing with them over land resources but often intermarrying and absorbing them into Bantu agricultural society.

IRON AND MIGRATION After about 1000 B.C.E., the pace of Bantu migrations quickened, as Bantu peoples began to produce iron tools and weapons. Iron tools enabled Bantu cultivators to clear land and expand the zone of agriculture more effectively than before, while iron weapons strengthened the hand of Bantu groups against adversaries and competitors for land or other resources. Thus iron metallurgy supported rapid population growth among the Bantu while also lending increased momentum to their continuing migrations.

Early Agricultural Societies of Sub-Saharan Africa

Several smaller migrations took place alongside the spread of Bantu peoples in sub-Saharan Africa. Between 3500 and 1000 B.C.E., southern Kushite herders pushed into parts of east Africa (modern-day Kenya and Tanzania), while Sudanese cultivators and herders moved into the upper reaches of the Nile River (now southern Sudan and northern Uganda). Meanwhile, Mande-speaking peoples who cultivated African rice established communities along the Atlantic estuaries of west Africa, and other peoples speaking Niger-Congo languages spread the cultivation of okra from forest regions throughout much of west Africa.

SPREAD OF AGRICULTURE Among the most important effects of Bantu and other migrations was the establishment of agricultural societies throughout most of sub-Saharan Africa. Between 1000 and 500 B.C.E., cultivators extended the cultivation of yams and grains deep into east and south Africa (modern-day Kenya, Malawi, Mozambique, Zimbabwe, and South Africa), while herders introduced sheep and cattle to the region. About the same time, Bantu and other peoples speaking Niger-Congo languages spread the intensive cultivation of yams, oil palms, millet, and sorghum throughout west and central Africa while also introducing sheep, pigs, and cattle to the region. By the late centuries B.C.E., agriculture had reached almost all of sub-Saharan Africa except for densely forested regions and deserts.

As cultivation and herding spread throughout sub-Saharan Africa, agricultural peoples built distinctive societies and cultural traditions. Most Bantu and other peoples lived in communities of a few hundred individuals led by chiefs. Many peoples recognized groups known as age sets, or age grades, consisting of individuals born within a few years of one another. Members of each age set jointly assumed responsibility for tasks appropriate to their levels of strength, energy, maturity, and experience. During their early years, for example, members of an age set might perform light public chores. At maturity, members jointly underwent elaborate initiation rites that introduced them to adult society. Older men cultivated fields and provided military service, and women tended to domestic chores and sometimes traded at markets. In later years, members of age sets served as community leaders and military officers.

AFRICAN CULTIVATORS African cultivators and herders also developed distinctive cultural and religious traditions. Both Sudanic and Niger-Congo peoples (including Bantu speakers), for example, held monotheistic religious beliefs by 5000 B.C.E. Sudanic peoples recognized a single, impersonal divine force that they regarded as the source of both good and evil. They believed that this divine force could take the form of individual spirits, and they often addressed the divine force through prayers to intermediary spirits. The divine force itself, however, was ultimately responsible for rewards and punishments meted out to human beings. For their part, Niger-Congo peoples recognized a single god originally called Nyamba who created the world and established the principles that would govern its development, then stepped back and allowed the world to proceed on its own. Individuals did not generally address this distant creator god directly but, rather, offered their prayers to ancestor spirits and local territorial spirits believed to inhabit the world and influence the fortunes of living humans. Proper attention to these spirits would ensure them good fortune, they believed, whereas their neglect would bring punishment or adversity from disgruntled spirits.

Individual communities frequently borrowed religious elements from other communities and adapted their beliefs to changing circumstances or fresh understandings of the world. Migrations of Bantu and other peoples in particular resulted in a great deal of cultural mixing and mingling, and religious beliefs often spread to new communities in the wake of population movements. After 1000 B.C.E., for example, as they encountered Sudanic peoples and their reverence of a single divine force that was the source of good and evil, many Bantu peoples associated the god Nyamba with goodness. As a result, this formerly distant creator god took on a new moral dimension that brought him closer to the lives of individuals. Thus changing religious beliefs sometimes reflected widespread interactions among African societies.

SUMMARY

Like other world regions, Africa was a land in which peoples of different societies regularly traded, communicated, and interacted with one another from ancient times. African agriculture and herding first emerged in the Sudan, then spread both to the Nile River valley and to arable lands throughout sub-Saharan Africa. Agricultural crops and domesticated animals from southwest Asia soon made their way into the Nile valley. With its broad floodplains, Egypt became an especially productive land, while Nubia supported a smaller but flourishing society. Throughout the Nile valley, abundant agricultural surpluses supported dense populations and the construction of prosperous societies with sophisticated cultural traditions. Elsewhere in sub-Saharan Africa, populations were less dense, but the migrations of Bantu and other peoples facilitated the spread of agriculture, and later iron metallurgy as well, throughout most of the region. Meanwhile, the Nile River served as a route of trade and communication linking Egypt and the Mediterranean basin to the north with the Sudan and sub-Saharan Africa to the south. Only in the context of migration, trade, communication, and interaction is it possible to understand the early development of African societies.

STUDY TERMS

Akhenaton (40)
Amon-Re (39)
Archaic Period (31)
Aten (40)
Bantu (28)
Bantu migrations (42)
cult of Osiris (40)
Egypt (29)
Hatshepsut (37)
hieratic script (39)
hieroglyphics (39)
Hyksos (32)
Kush (32)
Menes (31)
Meroitic writing (39)
Middle Kingdom (32)
mummification (27)
New Kingdom (32)
Nile River (29)
Nubia (27)
Old Kingdom (31)
pharaoh (31)
pyramids (31)
Sebiumeker (41)
Tuthmosis III (33)

FOR FURTHER READING

Cyril Aldred. *The Egyptians.* Rev. ed. New York, 1984. A popular, well-illustrated, and reliable survey of ancient Egyptian history.

Christopher Ehret. *An African Classical Age: Eastern and Southern Africa in World History, 1000 B.C. to A.D. 400.* Charlottesville, Va., 1998. A pathbreaking volume focusing on eastern and southern Africa and drawing on both linguistic and archaeological evidence.

———. *The Civilizations of Africa: A History to 1800.* Charlottesville, Va., 2001. An important contribution that views Africa in the context of world history.

Zahi Hawass. *Silent Images: Women in Pharaonic Egypt.* New York, 2000. A prominent archaeologist draws on both textual and artifactual evidence in throwing light on women's experiences in ancient Egypt.

Miriam Lichtheim, ed. *Ancient Egyptian Literature.* 3 vols. Berkeley, 1973–80. An important collection of primary sources in translation that reflects the results of recent scholarship.

Roderick James McIntosh. *The Peoples of the Middle Niger: The Island of Gold.* Oxford, 1998. Fascinating volume emphasizing the environmental context of west African history.

Jan Vansina. *Paths in the Rainforests: Toward a History of Political Tradition in Equatorial Africa.* Madison, 1990. A brilliant synthesis concentrating on central Africa by one of the world's foremost historians of Africa.

Derek A. Welsby. *The Kingdom of Kush: The Napatan and Meroitic Empires.* London, 1996. Draws on both written and archaeological sources in tracing the development of ancient Nubia and charting its relationship with Egypt.

Early Societies in South and East Asia

3

For a god, Indra was a very rambunctious fellow. According to the stories told about him by the Aryans, Indra had few if any peers in fighting, feasting, or drinking. The Aryans were a herding people who spoke an Indo-European language and who migrated to south Asia in large numbers after 1500 B.C.E. In the early days of their migrations they took Indra as their chief deity. The Aryans told dozens of stories about Indra and sang hundreds of hymns in his honor. One favorite story described how Indra brought rain to the earth by killing a dragon who lived in the sky and hoarded water in the clouds. When the dragon fell to earth, its weight caused such turmoil in the atmosphere that it rained enough to fill seven rivers in northern India. Those rivers, in turn, brought life-giving waters to inhabitants of the region.

A warrior such as Indra was a useful god for the Aryans, because as they migrated into south Asia they came into frequent conflict with Dravidian peoples already living there. For a thousand years and more, Aryans looked on the rowdy, raucous war god as a ready source of inspiration as they sought to build a society in an already occupied land.

In ancient China, heroic figures were quite different. Legends tell stories of heroes who invented agriculture, domesticated animals, taught people to marry and live in families, created music, introduced the calendar, and instructed people in the arts and crafts. Most dashing of those heroes was a sage-king named Yu, who helped lay the foundations of Chinese society by rescuing China from the devastating floodwaters of the Yellow River. Rather than dam the river as his predecessors had done, Yu dredged it and dug canals parallel to the river to allow the floodwaters to flow harmlessly out to sea.

The legends say that Yu worked on the river for thirteen years without ever returning home. Once, he passed by the gate to his home and heard his wife and children crying out of loneliness, but he continued on his way rather than interrupt his flood-control work. Because he tamed the Yellow River, Yu became a popular hero, and poets praised the man who protected fields and villages from deadly and destructive floods. By exalting Yu as an exemplar of virtue, Chinese moralists promoted the values of social harmony and selfless, dedicated work that the sage-king represented.

❮ Sandstone bust of a distinguished man, perhaps a priest-king, from Mohenjo-daro.

Archaeological excavations show that China was a site of paleolithic communities as early as four hundred thousand years ago. In south Asia, humans appeared at least two hundred thousand years ago, long before the Aryans introduced Indra to south Asia. Yet, as in Mesopotamia and Egypt, population

Yu (yoo)

CHRONOLOGY

SOUTH ASIA	
8000–7000 B.C.E.	Beginnings of agriculture in south Asia
2500–2000 B.C.E.	High point of Harappan society
1900 B.C.E.	Beginning of Harappan decline
1500 B.C.E.	Beginning of Aryan migration to India
1500–500 B.C.E.	Vedic age
1400–900 B.C.E.	Composition of the *Rig Veda*
1000 B.C.E.	Early Aryan migrations into the Ganges River valley
1000 B.C.E.	Emergence of *varna* distinctions
1000–500 B.C.E.	Formation of regional kingdoms in northern India
800–400 B.C.E.	Composition of the principal Upanishads
750 B.C.E.	Establishment of first Aryan cities in the Ganges valley
500 B.C.E.	Aryan migrations to the Deccan Plateau
EAST ASIA	
2200–1766 B.C.E.	Xia dynasty
1766–1122 B.C.E.	Shang dynasty
1122–256 B.C.E.	Zhou dynasty
403–221 B.C.E.	Period of the Warring States

pressures in both east and south Asia induced human groups to begin experimenting with agriculture. By 7000 B.C.E. agriculture had taken root in India's Indus River valley, and by 3000 B.C.E. it had spread throughout much of the Indian subcontinent. In roughly the same period, between 7000 and 5000 B.C.E., people in China's Yangzi River valley domesticated and became dependent on rice, while people farther north in the Yellow River valley learned to cultivate and depend on millet.

In both south and east Asia, agricultural surpluses encouraged the growth of complex societies. Indeed, people in both locations developed bustling cities. By 3000 B.C.E. people in India's Indus River valley built south Asia's first cities in what has come to be known as *Harappan* society. Harappan society collapsed about 1500 B.C.E., just as Aryans moved into India in large numbers, which created a period of turmoil and conflict. Eventually, however, Aryan peoples interacted and intermarried with the indigenous Dravidians, and that combination led to the development of a distinctive society and a rich cultural tradition. In China, three dynastic states based in the Yellow River valley brought much of China under their authority during the second millennium B.C.E. In the process they forged many local communities into a larger Chinese society. At the same time, all three dynasties had frequent dealings with neighboring peoples to the west, who linked China to other societies and brought knowledge and technologies from afar. As in early Mesopotamia and Egypt, then, complex society in both south and east Asia promoted the development of distinctive social and cultural traditions in the context of cross-cultural interaction and exchange.

HARAPPAN SOCIETY

Like societies in Mesopotamia and Egypt, the earliest urban society in south Asia was built by Dravidian peoples in the valley of a river, the Indus, whose waters were available for irrigation of crops. This society—called Harappan society after one of its two chief cities—thrived between about 3000 B.C.E. and 1900 B.C.E. As it fell into decline over the next four hundred years, Indo-European migrants from the northwest began to settle in south Asia. Although Indo-Europeans initially clashed with the indigenous Dravidians, over time the two groups mixed and became indistinguishable from each other. In the process, they created a unique social and religious order that helped shape south Asian society until modern times.

Although scholars know that cities were evolving in the Indus region by 3000 B.C.E., it is impossible to follow the development of Harappan society in detail. One reason is that many of the earliest Harappan physical remains lie below the existing water table and thus are inaccessible to archaeologists. Another reason is the lack of deciphered written records, because scholars have so far been unable to understand

Dravidian (drah-VIHD-een)
Harappan (huh-RUHP-puhn)

the complex pictographic Harappan script. As a result, our understanding of Harappan society depends entirely on the study of accessible material remains.

THE INDUS RIVER If the Greek historian Herodotus had known of Harappan society, he might have called it "the gift of the Indus." Like the Nile, the Indus draws its waters from rain and melting snow in towering mountains—in this case, the Hindu Kush and the Himalayas. As the waters reach the lowlands, the Indus deposits huge quantities of silt on its banks. Although the Indus periodically caused extensive destruction from flooding, it did make agricultural society possible in northern India. Early cultivators sowed their crops along its banks in September, after the flood receded, and harvested their crops the following spring.

As in Mesopotamia and Egypt, agricultural surpluses in India vastly increased the food supply, stimulated population growth, and supported the establishment of cities and specialized labor. Between 3000 and 2500 B.C.E., the agricultural surplus of the Indus valley fed two large cities, Harappa and Mohenjo-daro, as well as subordinate cities and a vast agricultural hinterland. Harappan society embraced much of modern-day Pakistan and a large part of northern India as well—a territory of about 1.3 million square kilometers (502,000 square miles)—and thus was considerably larger than either Mesopotamian or Egyptian society.

HARAPPA AND MOHENJO-DARO No evidence survives concerning the Harappan political system, although archaeological excavations do not suggest a royal or imperial authority. However, both Harappa and Mohenjo-daro had city walls, a fortified citadel, and a large granary, suggesting that they served as centers of political authority and sites for the collection and redistribution of taxes paid in the form of grain. The two cities represented a considerable investment of human labor and other resources: both featured marketplaces, temples, public buildings, extensive residential districts, and broad streets laid out on a carefully planned grid.

Mohenjo-daro statue of a bearded man
www.mhhe.com/bentleybrief2e

The two cities clearly established the patterns that shaped the larger society: weights, measures, architectural styles, and even brick sizes were consistent throughout the land. This standardization no doubt reflects the prominence of Harappa and Mohenjo-daro as powerful and wealthy cities whose influence touched all parts of Harappan society, as well as the degree to which the Indus River facilitated trade, travel, and communication among the far-flung regions of Harappan society.

SPECIALIZED LABOR AND TRADE Like other complex societies in ancient times, Harappa engaged in trade, both domestic and foreign. Pottery, tools, and decorative items produced in Harappa and Mohenjo-daro found their way to all corners of the Indus valley, while the cities imported precious metals and stones from neighboring peoples in Persia and the Hindu Kush mountains. During the period about 2300 to 1750 B.C.E., they also traded with Mesopotamians, mostly via ships that followed the coastline of the Arabian Sea between the mouth of the Indus River and the Persian Gulf.

Harappan Society and Culture

SOCIAL DISTINCTIONS Like societies in Mesopotamia and Egypt, Harappan society generated considerable wealth. Excavations at Mohenjo-daro show that at its high point, from about 2500 to 2000 B.C.E., the city was a thriving economic center with a population of about forty thousand. The wealth of Harappan society, like that in Mesopotamia and Egypt, encouraged the formation of social distinctions. It is clear from Harappan dwellings that rich and poor lived in very different styles. In Mohenjo-daro, for example, many people lived in one-room tenements in barracks-like structures, but there were also individual houses of two and three stories with a dozen rooms and an interior

Plan for a Mohenjo-daro house
www.mhhe.com/bentleybrief2e

Indus (IN-duhs)

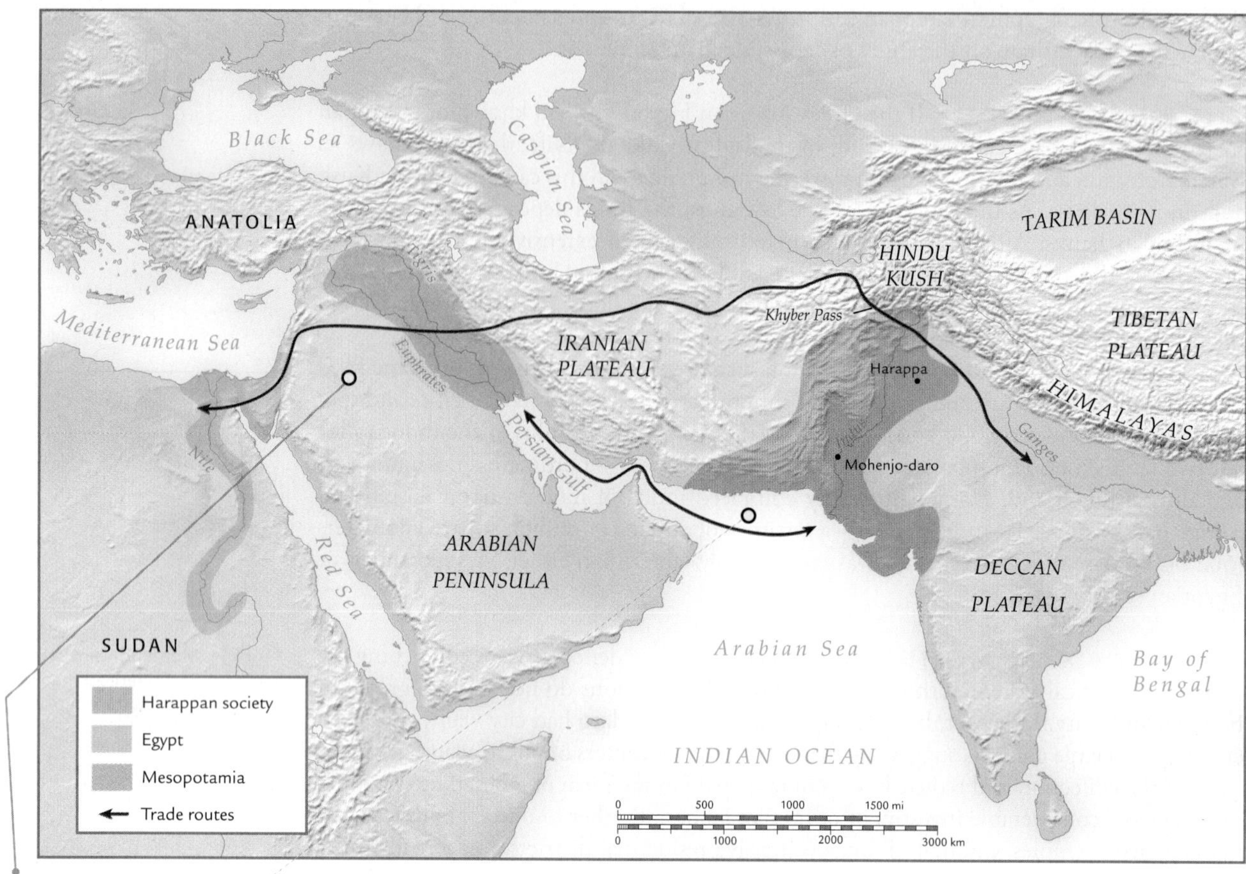

Harappans traded with distant societies by land and sea.

MAP 3.1 | Harappan society and its neighbors, ca. 2000 B.C.E. Compare Harappan society with its Mesopotamian and Egyptian contemporaries with respect to size. ***What conditions would have been necessary to enable trade to flow between the Indus River valley and Mesopotamia?***

courtyard, as well as a few even larger houses. Almost all houses had private bathrooms with showers and toilets that drained into city sewage systems, which themselves were among the most sophisticated of the ancient world.

In the absence of deciphered writing, Harappan beliefs and values are very difficult to interpret. Even without written texts, however, material remains shed some tantalizing light on Harappan society. Like other early agricultural societies, Harappans venerated gods and goddesses they associated with creation and procreation. They recognized a mother goddess and a horned fertility god, and they held trees and animals sacred because of their associations with vital forces. In fact, many scholars believe that some Harappan deities survived the collapse of the larger society and later found places in the Hindu pantheon, because they have noticed striking similarities between Harappan and Hindu deities—especially those associated with fertility and procreation.

HARAPPAN DECLINE Sometime after 1900 B.C.E. Harappan society entered a period of decline. A primary cause was ecological degradation: in clearing the land for cultivation and firewood, Harappans deforested the Indus valley. In the process, they facilitated soil erosion and desertification. Over a period of half a millennium or more, most of the Indus valley became a desert: agriculture is possible there today only with the aid of artificial irrigation. These climatic and ecological changes reduced agricultural yields, and Harappan society faced a subsistence crisis during the centuries after 1900 B.C.E. By about 1700 B.C.E. the populations of Harappa and Mohenjo-daro had abandoned the cities, and by 1500 B.C.E. even the smaller Harappan cities had almost entirely collapsed.

MOHENJO-DARO. | This aerial view of the excavations at Mohenjo-daro illustrates the careful planning and precise layout of the city. ***What does the layout of this city reveal about the lifestyle of the people who lived there?***

THE INDO-EUROPEAN MIGRATIONS AND EARLY ARYAN INDIA

During the second millennium B.C.E., just as Harappan society declined, bands of foreigners filtered into the Indian subcontinent via the Hindu Kush mountains and settled throughout the Indus valley and beyond. Most prominent were nomadic and pastoral peoples speaking Indo-European languages who called themselves Aryans ("noble people"). By about 1500 B.C.E. they had begun to establish small herding and agricultural communities throughout northern India.

Their migrations took place over several centuries and thus did not constitute an invasion or a military campaign. Even so, it is clear that Indo-European migrants clashed with Dravidians and other peoples already settled in India. However, in the centuries after 1500 B.C.E., Dravidian and Indo-European peoples increasingly intermingled, in the process laying the social and cultural foundations that would influence Indian society to the present day.

The Aryans and India

THE EARLY ARYANS When they entered India, the Aryans depended heavily on a pastoral economy. They especially prized their horses and herds of cattle. Horses were quite valuable because of their expense and rarity: horses do not breed well in India,

Aryan (AIR-ee-uhn)

so it was necessary for Aryans to replenish their stock by importing animals from central Asia. Like their Indo-European cousins to the north, the Aryans harnessed horses to carts, and they also hitched them to chariots for use in warfare. Meanwhile, cattle became the principal measure of wealth in early Aryan society. The Aryans consumed both dairy products and beef, and they often calculated prices in terms of cattle.

THE VEDAS The early Aryans did not use writing but instead preserved extensive collections of religious and literary works by transmitting them orally from one generation to another in their sacred language, Sanskrit. The earliest of these orally transmitted works were the *Vedas,* which were collections of hymns, songs, prayers, and rituals honoring the various gods of the Aryans. There are four *Vedas,* the earliest and most important of which is the *Rig Veda,* a collection of 1,028 hymns addressed to Aryan gods. Although it was compiled between about 1400 and 900 B.C.E., Aryan priests committed the *Rig Veda* to writing only in about 600 B.C.E.

While the *Vedas* represent a priestly perspective on affairs because of their function in transmitting religious knowledge, they also shed considerable light on early Aryan society in India. Indeed, in view of their importance as historical sources, scholars refer to Indian history during the millennium between 1500 and 500 B.C.E. as the Vedic age.

THE VEDIC AGE The *Vedas* reflect a boisterous society in which the Aryans clashed repeatedly with the Dravidians and other peoples—referred to in the texts as *dasas,* meaning "enemies" or "subject peoples"—already living in India. The *Vedas* identify Indra, the Aryan war god and military hero, as one who ravaged citadels, smashed dams, and destroyed forts the way age consumes cloth garments. These characterizations suggest that competition over land and resources fueled intermittent conflict between Aryan and Dravidian peoples. The Aryans also fought ferociously among themselves. They did not have a state or common government but, rather, formed hundreds of chiefdoms organized around herding communities and agricultural villages. Because of their close proximity, this practice encouraged competition for resources and created enormous potential for conflict.

ARYAN MIGRATIONS IN INDIA During the early centuries of the Vedic age, Aryan groups settled in the Punjab, the upper Indus River valley that straddles the modern-day border between northern India and Pakistan. After 1000 B.C.E. they began to settle in the area between the Himalayan foothills and the Ganges River, where they learned to make iron tools and to practice agriculture. Agricultural surpluses encouraged larger populations and more complex social organization, and by about 750 B.C.E., Aryans had established the first small cities in the Ganges River valley. Population growth also encouraged further migration. Thus, by 500 B.C.E. Aryan groups had migrated as far south as the northern Deccan, a plateau region in the southern cone of the Indian subcontinent about 1,500 kilometers (950 miles) south of the Punjab.

As they settled into permanent communities and began to rely more on agriculture than on herding, the Aryans gradually lost the tribal political organization they had brought into India and instead evolved more formal political institutions. Indeed, between 1000 and 500 B.C.E., tribal chiefdoms increasingly developed into regional kingdoms, and for centuries these became the most common form of political organization on the subcontinent.

Origins of the Caste System

Although the Aryans did not build large imperial states, they did construct a well-defined social order. In fact, in some ways their social hierarchy served to maintain the order and stability that states and political structures guaranteed in other societies. The Aryan social structure, known today as the caste system, rested on sharp hereditary distinctions between individuals and groups, according to their occupations and roles in society.

Vedas (VAY-duhs)

CASTE AND VARNA Caste identities developed gradually as the Aryans established settlements throughout India. Initially, increased interaction with Dravidian peoples probably prompted Aryans to base social distinctions on either Aryan or Dravidian ancestry. In part, those distinctions may have arisen from differences in complexion between the Aryans, who referred to themselves as "wheat-colored," and the darker-skinned Dravidians. Indeed, the Aryan term *varna,* which refers to the major social classes, comes from the Sanskrit word meaning "color." However, over time Aryans and Dravidians mixed, mingled, interacted, and intermarried to the point that distinguishing between them was impossible.

After about 1000 B.C.E. the Aryans increasingly recognized four main *varnas: brahmins* (priests), *kshatriyas* (warriors and aristocrats), *vaishyas* (cultivators, artisans, and merchants), and *shudras* (landless peasants and serfs). Some centuries later, probably about the end of the Vedic age, they added the category of the *untouchables*—people who performed dirty or unpleasant tasks, such as butchering animals or handling dead bodies, and who theoretically became so polluted from their work that their very touch could defile individuals of higher status.

Brahmins
www.mhhe.com/
bentleybrief2e

SUBCASTES AND JATI Until about the sixth century B.C.E., the four *varnas* described Vedic society reasonably well. Because they did not live in cities and did not yet pursue many specialized occupations, the Aryans had little need for a more complicated social order. Over the longer term, however, a much more elaborate scheme of social classification emerged. As Vedic society became more complex and generated increasingly specialized occupations, the caste system served as the umbrella for a complicated hierarchy of subcastes known as *jati,* which were hereditary categories largely determined by occupation. By the eighteenth and nineteenth centuries C.E., in its most fully articulated form, the system featured several thousand *jati,* which prescribed individuals' roles in society in minute detail.

Castes and subcastes deeply influenced the lives of individual Indians through much of history. Members of a *jati* ate with one another and intermarried, and they cared for those who became ill or fell on hard times. Elaborate rules dictated forms of address and specific behavior appropriate for communication between members of different castes and subcastes. Violation of *jati* rules could result in expulsion from the larger group. That penalty was serious, since an outcast individual could not function well and sometimes could not even survive when shunned by members of the larger society.

CASTE AND SOCIAL MOBILITY The caste system never functioned in an absolutely rigid or inflexible manner but, rather, operated so as to accommodate social change. Individuals sometimes prospered on the basis of their own initiative, or else they could fall on hard times and move down in the social hierarchy. More often, however, social mobility came about as members of *jati* improved their condition collectively. Achieving upward mobility was not an easy matter—it often entailed moving to a new area, or at least taking on a new line of work—but the possibility of improving individual or group status helped to dissipate social tensions. In addition, the caste system enabled foreign peoples to find a place in Indian society by allowing newcomers to organize into well-defined groups that eventually came to adopt caste identities.

By the end of the Vedic age, caste distinctions had become central institutions in Aryan India. Whereas in other lands states and empires maintained public order, in India the caste system served as a principal foundation of social stability. Individuals have often identified more closely with their *jati* than with their cities or states, and castes have played a large role in maintaining social discipline in India.

ARYAN SWORD. | This bronze sword manufactured by Aryan craftsmen was a much stronger and more effective weapon than those available to Harappan defenders.

varna (VUHR-nuh)
brahmins (BRAH-minz)
kshatriyas (SHUHT-ree-uhs)
vaishyas (VEYESH-yuhs)
shudras (SHOO-druhs)

THE LAWBOOK OF MANU While building an elaborate social hierarchy on the foundations of caste and *varna* distinctions, the Aryans also constructed a strongly patriarchal social order on the basis of gender distinctions. At the time of their migrations into India, men already dominated Aryan society. All priests, warriors, and tribal chiefs were men, and the Aryans recognized descent through the male line. Women influenced affairs within their own families but enjoyed no public authority. As the Aryans settled in agricultural communities throughout India, they maintained this thoroughly patriarchal society. Only males could inherit property, unless a family had no male heirs, and only men could preside over family rituals that honored departed ancestors.

A text from about the first century B.C.E., called the *Lawbook of Manu,* illustrates the patriarchal ideologies that helped structure Indian society. Although composed after the Vedic age, the *Lawbook of Manu* reflected the society constructed earlier under Aryan influence. The author advised men to treat women with honor and respect, but he insisted that women remain subject to the guidance of the principal men in their lives. The *Lawbook* also specified that the most important duties of women were to bear children and maintain wholesome homes for their families.

RELIGION IN THE VEDIC AGE

As the caste system emerged and helped to organize Indian society, distinctive cultural and religious traditions also took shape. The Aryans entered India with traditions and beliefs that met the needs of a mobile and often violent society. As they spread throughout India and mixed with the Dravidians, however, the Aryans encountered new religious ideas they considered intriguing and persuasive. The resulting fusion of Aryan traditions with Dravidian beliefs and values laid the foundation for Hinduism, a faith immensely popular in India and parts of southeast Asia for more than two millennia.

Aryan Religion

ARYAN WOMAN AND CHILD. | This greenish blue schist carving illustrates the devotion of a mother to her child.

As in Mesopotamia, Egypt, and other lands, religious values in India reflected the larger society. For example, during the early centuries following the Aryan migrations, the focus on Indra the war god testified to the instability and turbulence of early Vedic society. Also important to those early beliefs was the proper performance of ritual sacrifices. Through sacrifices, Aryans hoped to win the favor of the gods to ensure military success, large families, long life, and abundant herds of cattle. But those rewards required constant attention to religious ritual: proper honor for the gods called for households to have brahmins perform no fewer than five sacrifices per day—a time-consuming and expensive obligation.

SPIRITUALITY As the centuries passed, many Aryans became dissatisfied with the sacrificial cults of the Vedas, which increasingly seemed like sterile rituals rather than a genuine means of communicating with the gods. Beginning about 800 B.C.E. many thoughtful individuals left their villages and retreated to the forests of the Ganges valley, where they lived as hermits and reflected on the relationships between human beings, the world, and the gods. These mystics drew considerable inspiration from the religious beliefs of Dravidian peoples, who often worshiped nature spirits that they associated with fertility and the generation of new life. Dravidians also believed that human souls took on new physical forms after the deaths of their bodily hosts. The notion that souls could experience transmigration and reincarnation—that an individual soul could depart one body at death and become associated with another body through a new birth—intrigued thoughtful people and encouraged them to try to understand the principles that governed the fate of souls. As a result, a remarkable tradition of religious speculation emerged.

The Blending of Aryan and Dravidian Values

This tradition achieved its fullest development in a body of works known as the *Upanishads,* which began to appear late in the Vedic age, about 800 to 400 B.C.E. The word *upanishad* literally means "a sitting in front of," and it refers to the practice of disciples gathering before a sage for discussion of religious issues. The Upanishads often took the form of dialogues that explored the *Vedas* and the religious issues that they raised.

BRAHMAN, THE UNIVERSAL SOUL The Upanishads taught that each person participates in a larger cosmic order and forms a small part of a universal soul, known as *Brahman.* Whereas the physical world is a theater of change, instability, and illusion, Brahman is an eternal, unchanging, permanent foundation for all things that exist—hence the only genuine reality. The authors of the Upanishads believed that individual souls were born into the physical world, not once, but many times: they believed that souls appeared most often as humans, but sometimes as animals, and possibly even occasionally as plants or other vegetable matter.

TEACHINGS OF THE UPANISHADS The Upanishads developed several specific doctrines that helped to explain this line of thought. One was the doctrine of *samsara,* which held that upon death, individual souls go temporarily to the World of the Fathers and then return to earth in a new incarnation. Another was the doctrine of *karma,* which accounted for the specific incarnations that souls experienced. According to this doctrine, individuals who lived virtuous lives and fulfilled all their duties could expect rebirth into a purer and more honorable existence—for example, into a higher and more distinguished caste. Those who accumulated a heavy burden of karma, however, would suffer in a future incarnation by being reborn into a difficult existence, or perhaps even into the body of an animal or an insect.

The Upanishads also encouraged the cultivation of personal integrity—a self-knowledge that would incline individuals naturally toward both ethical behavior and union with Brahman. In addition, they taught respect for all living things, animal as well as human. Animal bodies, after all, might well hold incarnations of unfortunate souls suffering the effects of a heavy debt of karma. A vegetarian diet thus became a common feature of the ascetic regime.

Yet even under the best of circumstances, the cycle of rebirth involved a certain amount of pain and suffering. The authors of the Upanishads sought to escape the cycle altogether and attain the state of *moksha,* which they characterized as a deep, dreamless sleep that came with permanent liberation from physical incarnation. This goal was difficult to reach, since it entailed severing all ties to the physical world and identifying with the ultimate reality of Brahman, the universal soul. The two principal means to the goal were asceticism and meditation, which could help individuals purge themselves of desire for the comforts of the physical world.

RELIGION AND VEDIC SOCIETY Just as the Aryan focus on Indra reflected early Aryan society, so the religious views of the Upanishads dovetailed with the social order of the late Vedic age. Indeed, the doctrines of samsara and karma certainly reinforced the Vedic social order: they explained why individuals were born into their castes, and they encouraged individuals to observe their caste duties in hopes of enjoying a more comfortable and honorable incarnation in the future. However, these doctrines were not simply cynical means of controlling Vedic society. Indeed, the sages who gave voice to these doctrines were conscientiously attempting to deal with meaningful spiritual and intellectual problems. Like Greek philosophers, Christian theologians, and many others, the authors of the Upanishads sought ultimate truth and certain knowledge in an ideal world that transcends our own.

Upanishads (oo-pah-NIH-shuhds)
samsara (suhm-SAH-ruh)
karma (KAHR-mah)
moksha (MOHK-shuh)

Political Organization in Early China

As in the Indus River valley of India, fertile river valleys in China allowed villages and towns to flourish along their banks. The most important of these valleys were those of the Yellow and Yangzi rivers, which supported settlements of agriculturalists after about 7000 B.C.E. By the late years of the third millennium B.C.E., these small settlements began to give way to much larger regional states. Among the most notable were those of the Xia, Shang, and Zhou dynasties, which progressively brought much of China under their authority and laid a political foundation for the development of a distinctive Chinese society.

THE YELLOW RIVER Like the Indus, the Yellow River is boisterous and unpredictable. It rises in the mountains bordering the high plateau of Tibet, and it courses almost 4,700 kilometers (2,920 miles) before emptying into the Yellow Sea. It takes its name, Huang He, meaning "Yellow River," from the vast quantities of light-colored soil that it picks up along its route. So much soil becomes suspended in the Yellow River that the water turns yellow. The soil gradually builds up, raising the river bed and forcing the water out of its established path, periodically unleashing tremendous floods. The Yellow River has caused so much destruction that it has earned the nickname "China's Sorrow." Despite the periodic damage caused by the Yellow River, however, the soil it deposits is extremely fertile and easy to work, so even before the introduction of metal tools, cultivators using wooden implements could bring in generous harvests. As in India, agricultural surpluses resulted in increased population, which eventually gave rise to complex societies.

Chinese legends speak of three ancient dynasties—the Xia, the Shang, and the Zhou—that arose before the Qin and Han dynasties brought China under unified rule in the third century B.C.E. These dynasties were hereditary states that extended their control over progressively larger regions, although none of them embraced all the territory claimed by later Chinese dynasties.

The Xia and Shang Dynasties

THE XIA DYNASTY The Xia dynasty emerged about 2200 B.C.E. and was one of the earliest to organize public life in China on a large scale. Ancient legends credit the dynasty's founder, the sage-king Yu, with the organization of effective flood-control projects on the Yellow River: thus here, as in Mesopotamia and Egypt, the need to organize large-scale public works projects helped to establish recognized authorities and formal political institutions. Although no information survives about the political institutions of the Xia, the dynasty's rulers probably exercised power throughout the middle Yellow River valley by controlling the leaders of individual villages. By extending formal control over this region, the Xia dynasty established a precedent for hereditary monarchical rule in China.

THE SHANG DYNASTY According to the legends, the last Xia king was an oppressive despot who lost his realm to the founder of the Shang dynasty. In fact, the Xia state probably gave way gradually before the Shang, which arose in a region to the south and east of the Xia realm. Tradition assigns the Shang dynasty to the period 1766 to 1122 B.C.E., and archaeological discoveries have largely confirmed those dates. Because the Shang dynasty left written records as well as mate-

THINKING ABOUT *Traditions*

TRADITIONS IN EARLY SOCIETIES IN SOUTH AND EAST ASIA. In the period between 3000 and 500 B.C.E., sophisticated, stratified, and wealthy states developed in both China and India. Although each society shared concerns with morality and ethics, their approaches to religion and social organization were quite distinct. Think carefully about these differences in approach, and try to explain how such differences might have arisen.

Yangzi (YAHNG-zuh)
Xia (shyah)

MAP 3.2 | The Xia, Shang, and Zhou dynasties, 2200–256 B.C.E. Note that the three dynasties extended their territorial reach through time. ***How might technological considerations explain the increasing size of early Chinese states?***

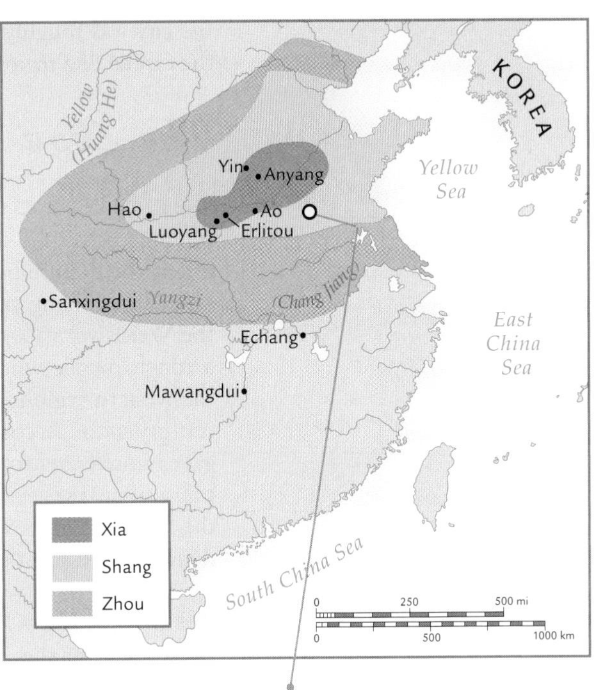

Note the many cities that served as capitals

rial remains, the basic features of early Chinese society come into much clearer focus than they did during the Xia.

BRONZE METALLURGY AND CHARIOTS

Technology helps to explain the rise and success of the Shang dynasty. Bronze metallurgy transformed Chinese society during Shang times and indeed may well have enabled Shang rulers to displace the Xia dynasty. Bronze metallurgy—together with horses, horse-drawn chariots, and other wheeled vehicles—came to China with Indo-European migrants from southwest Asia. Although the Xia dynasty already made limited use of bronze tools and weapons, Shang ruling elites managed to monopolize the production of bronze in the Yellow River valley. Thus, control over bronze production strengthened Shang forces against those of the Xia, and they had little difficulty imposing their rule on agricultural villages and extending their influence throughout much of the Yellow River valley.

Shang kings extended their rule to a large portion of northeastern China centered on the modern-day province of Henan. Like state builders in other parts of the world, the kings claimed a generous portion of the surplus agricultural production from the regions they controlled and then used that surplus to support military forces, political allies, and others who could help them maintain their rule.

SHANG POLITICAL ORGANIZATION

The Shang state rested on a vast network of walled towns whose local rulers recognized the authority of the Shang kings. During the course of the dynasty, Shang kings may have controlled one thousand or more towns. According to tradition, the Shang capital moved six times during the course of the dynasty. Though originally chosen for political and military reasons, in each case the capital also became an important social, economic, and cultural center—the site not only of administration and military command but also of bronze foundries, arts, crafts, trade, and religious observances.

King Tang, first ruler of the Shang
www.mhhe.com/bentleybrief2e

THE SHANG CAPITAL AT YIN

Excavations have revealed much about the workings of the Shang dynasty. One remarkable site is Yin, near modern Anyang, which was the Shang capital during the last two or three centuries of the dynasty. Archaeologists working at Yin have identified a complex of royal palaces, archives with written documents, several residential neighborhoods, two large bronze foundries, several workshops used by craftsmen, and scattered burial grounds. Eleven large and lavish tombs constructed for Shang kings have received particular attention. The graves included thousands of objects—chariots, weapons, bronze goods, pottery, carvings, and sacrificial victims, including dogs, horses, and scores of human beings intended to serve the deceased royals in another existence. One tomb alone contained skeletons of more than three hundred sacrificial victims who joined the Shang king in death.

A ritual wine vessel from the Shang Dynasty
www.mhhe.com/bentleybrief2e

The Xia and Shang dynasties were not the only states that developed in ancient China, although legendary and historical accounts paid special attention to them because of their location in the Yellow River valley, where the first Chinese imperial states rose in later times. Indeed, archaeological excavations are making it clear that similar states dominated other regions at the same time the Xia and the Shang ruled the Yellow River valley. Recent excavations, for example, have unearthed evidence of a very large city at Sanxingdui in modern-day Sichuan province (southwestern China). Occupied about 1700 to 1000 B.C.E., the city was roughly contemporaneous with the Shang dynasty, and it probably served as the capital of a regional kingdom.

The Zhou Dynasty

THE RISE OF THE ZHOU Although little information survives to illustrate the principles of law, justice, and administration by which Shang rulers maintained order, the picture becomes more clear in the practices of the Zhou dynasty, which succeeded the Shang as the preeminent political authority in northern China. Dwelling in the Wei River valley of northwestern China (modern Shaanxi province), the Zhou were a tough people who battled Shang forces and eventually won recognition as kings of the western regions. But the ambitions of the two dynasties collided in the late twelfth century B.C.E. According to Zhou accounts, the last Shang king was a criminal fool who gave himself over to wine, women, tyranny, and greed. As a result, many of the towns and political districts subject to the Shang transferred their loyalties to the Zhou, who toppled the Shang king's government in 1122 B.C.E. and replaced it with their own state. The new dynasty ruled most of northern and central China, at least nominally, until 256 B.C.E.

THE MANDATE OF HEAVEN In justifying the deposition of the Shang, spokesmen for the Zhou dynasty articulated a set of principles that influenced Chinese thinking about government and political legitimacy until the twentieth century. The Zhou theory of politics rested on the assumption that heavenly powers granted the right to govern—"the mandate of heaven"—to an especially deserving individual known as the son of heaven. The ruler had the duty to govern conscientiously, to observe high standards of honor and justice, and to maintain order and harmony within his realm. As long as he did so, the heavenly powers would approve of his work, the cosmos would enjoy stability, and the ruling dynasty would retain its mandate to govern. If a ruler failed in his duties, however, chaos and suffering would afflict his realm, the cosmos would fall out of balance, and the displeased heavenly powers would withdraw the mandate to rule and transfer it to a more deserving candidate. On the basis of that reasoning, spokesmen for the new dynasty explained the fall of the Shang and the transfer of the mandate of heaven to the Zhou.

POLITICAL ORGANIZATION The Zhou state was much larger than the Shang. In fact, it was so extensive that a single central court could not rule the entire land effectively. As a result, Zhou rulers relied on a decentralized administration: they entrusted power, authority, and responsibility to subordinates who in return owed allegiance, tribute, and military support to the central government. During the early days of the dynasty, that system worked reasonably well. Gradually, however, subordinates established their own bases of power, which allowed them to become more independent of the Zhou dynasty. In addition, iron production spread rapidly across China in the first millennium B.C.E., and Zhou subordinates took advantage of the technology to outfit their own forces with weapons to resist the central government.

DECLINE OF THE ZHOU After the early eighth century B.C.E., Zhou rule deteriorated as nomadic invaders forced the royal court from their capital at Hao. Although the dynasty survived, it never regained its authority, and competing states fought ferociously with one another in hopes of establishing themselves as leaders of a new political order. So violent were the last centuries of the Zhou dynasty that they are known as the Period of the Warring States (403–221 B.C.E.). The Zhou dynasty officially ended in 256 B.C.E. when the last king abdicated his position under pressure from his ambitious subordinate, the king of Qin. Only with the establishment of the Qin dynasty in 221 B.C.E. did effective central government return to China.

Zhou (JOH)
Qin (Chin)

Society and Family in Ancient China

Bronze Vessel. | The delicate design of this bronze wine vessel displays the high level of craftsmanship during the late Shang dynasty. ***Why did the elite classes prefer objects made of bronze?***

In China, as in India, the introduction of agriculture enabled individuals to accumulate wealth and preserve it within their families. Social distinctions began to appear during neolithic times, and after the establishment of the Xia, Shang, and Zhou dynasties the distinctions became even sharper. Throughout China the patriarchal family emerged as the institution that most directly influenced individuals' lives and their roles in the larger society.

The Social Order

RULING ELITES Already during the Xia dynasty, but especially under the Shang and the early Zhou, the royal family and allied noble families occupied the most honored positions in Chinese society. They resided in large, palatial compounds made of pounded earth, and they lived on the agricultural surplus and taxes delivered by their subjects. One of the hallmarks of these elites was their conspicuous consumption of bronze, which was far too expensive for most people to afford. Indeed, ruling elites controlled much of the bronze weaponry that existed in northern China and also supplied their households with elaborately decorated cast-bronze utensils and vessels. Ruling elites consumed bronze in such staggering quantities that the tomb of Yi of Zeng, a provincial governor of the late Zhou dynasty, contained a collection of bronze weapons and decorative objects that weighed almost eleven tons.

A privileged class of hereditary aristocrats rose from the military allies of Shang and Zhou rulers. These aristocrats possessed extensive landholdings, and their standard of living was much more refined than that of the commoners and slaves who worked their fields and served their needs. They were served by a small class of free artisans and craftsmen, including bronzesmiths, jewelers, jade workers, and silk manufacturers, who enjoyed a reasonably comfortable existence because of aristocratic patronage.

PEASANTS Far less comfortable was a large class of semiservile peasants who populated the Chinese countryside. They owned no land but provided agricultural, military, and labor services for their lords in exchange for plots to cultivate, security, and a portion of the harvest. They lived like their neolithic predecessors in small, partially subterranean houses excavated to a depth of about one meter (three feet) and protected from the elements by thatched walls and roofs. Women's duties included mostly indoor activities such as wine making, weaving, and cultivation of silkworms, whereas men spent most of their time outside working in the fields, hunting, and fishing.

SLAVES Finally, there was a sizable class of slaves, most of whom were enemy warriors captured during battles between the many competing states of ancient China. Slaves performed hard labor, such as the clearing of new fields or the building of city walls, that required a large workforce.

Family and Patriarchy

Throughout human history the family has served as the principal institution for the socialization of children and the preservation of cultural traditions. In China the extended family emerged as a particularly influential institution during neolithic times, and it continued to play a prominent role in shaping both private and public affairs after the appearance of the Xia, Shang, and Zhou states. Indeed, the early dynasties ruled their territories largely through family and kinship groups.

SOURCES FROM THE PAST

Peasants' Protest

Peasants in ancient China mostly did not own land. Instead, they worked as tenants on plots allotted to them by royal or aristocratic owners, who took sizable portions of the harvest for their own uses. In the following poem from the Book of Songs, *a collection of verses dating from Zhou times, peasants liken their lords to rodents, protest the bite lords take from the peasants' agricultural production, and threaten to abandon the lords' lands for a neighboring state where conditions are better.*

Large rats! Large rats!
Do not eat our millet.
Three years have we had to do with you.
And you have not been willing to show any regard for us.
We will leave you,
And go to that happy land.
Happy land! Happy land!
There shall we find our place.
Large rats! Large rats!
Do not eat our wheat.
Three years have we had to do with you.
And you have not been willing to show any kindness to us.
We will leave you,
And go to that happy state.
Happy state! Happy state!
There shall we find ourselves aright.
Large rats! Large rats!
Do not eat our springing grain!
Three years have we had to do with you,
And you have not been willing to think of our toil.
We will leave you,
And go to those happy borders.
Happy borders! Happy borders!
Who will there make us always to groan?

■ **How might you go about judging the extent to which these verses throw reliable light on class relations in ancient China?**

SOURCE: James Legge, trans. *The Chinese Classics,* 5 vols. London: Henry Frowde, 1893, 4:171–72.

VENERATION OF ANCESTORS One reason for the pronounced influence of the Chinese family was the veneration of ancestors, a practice with roots in neolithic times. This practice was based on the belief that dead ancestors had the power to support and protect their surviving families, but only if their descendants displayed proper respect and ministered to the spirits' needs. A family could expect to prosper only if all its members—dead as well as living—worked cooperatively toward common interests. Thus, the family became an institution linking departed generations to the living and helped build a strong ethic of family solidarity.

PATRIARCHAL SOCIETY In the absence of organized religion or official priesthood in ancient China, the patriarchal head of the family presided at ceremonies honoring ancestors' spirits. As mediator between the family's dead and living members, the family patriarch possessed tremendous authority. Indeed, Chinese society vested authority principally in elderly males who headed their households. And, like its counterparts in other regions, Chinese patriarchy intensified with the emergence of large states. During neolithic times Chinese men wielded public authority, but they won their rights to it by virtue of the female line of their descent. Gradually, however, Chinese society lost its matrilineal character. By the later Shang and Zhou dynasties, women lived increasingly in the shadow of men, and even queens and empresses were honored only as a result of being associated with their illustrious husbands.

patriarch (PAY-tree-ahrk)

Early Chinese Writing and Cultural Development

Early Chinese myths and legends explained the origins of the world, the human race, agriculture, and the various arts and crafts. But Chinese thinkers saw no need to organize those ideas into systematic religious traditions. Although they often spoke of an impersonal heavenly power, they did not recognize a personal supreme deity who intervened in human affairs or took special interest in human behavior. Nor did ancient China support a large class of priests like those of Mesopotamia, Egypt, and India. As a result, it was family patriarchs who represented the interests of living generations to the spirits of departed ancestors.

In that environment, writing served as the foundation for a distinctive secular cultural tradition in ancient China. Surviving evidence suggests that writing came into extensive use during the Shang dynasty. As in other lands, writing in east Asia quickly became an indispensable tool of government as well as a means of expressing ideas and offering reflections on human beings and their world.

THINKING ABOUT *Encounters*

ENCOUNTERS IN EARLY SOCIETIES IN SOUTH AND EAST ASIA. Both Chinese and Indian (Aryan) societies developed in the context of interactions with peoples outside their own territories or social groupings: in China with nomads to the north and west, and in India with indigenous Dravidian peoples. How did these interactions influence the development of Chinese and Indian trade, social structure, or culture?

Oracle Bones and Early Chinese Writing

In Mesopotamia and India, merchants pioneered the use of writing. In China, however, the earliest known writing served the interests of rulers rather than traders. Writing in China goes back at least to the early part of the second millennium B.C.E. Surviving records indicate that scribes at the Shang royal court kept written accounts of important events on strips of bamboo or pieces of silk. Unfortunately, almost all those materials have perished, along with their messages. Yet one medium employed by ancient Chinese scribes has survived the ravages of time. Recognized just over a century ago, inscriptions on oracle bones have thrown tremendous light both on the Shang dynasty and on the early stages of Chinese writing.

Shang oracle bone
www.mhhe.com/bentleybrief2e

ORACLE BONES Oracle bones were the principal instruments used by fortune-tellers in ancient China. Diviners inscribed a question on a specially prepared broad bone—such as the shoulder blade of a sheep—and then subjected it to heat. When heated, the bone developed networks of splits and cracks. The fortune-teller then studied the patterns and determined the answer to the question inscribed on the bone. Often the diviner recorded the answer on the bone, and later scribes occasionally added further information about the events that actually came to pass.

Most of the oracle bones have come from royal archives, and the questions posed on them clearly reveal the day-to-day concerns of the Shang royal court. Will the season's harvest be abundant or poor? Will the queen bear a son or a daughter? Taken together, bits of information preserved on the oracle bones have allowed historians to piece together an understanding of the political and social order of Shang times.

Even more important, the oracle bones offer the earliest glimpse into the tradition of Chinese

CHINESE ORACLE BONE. | Oracle bone from Shang times with an inscribed question and cracks caused by exposure of the bone to heat.

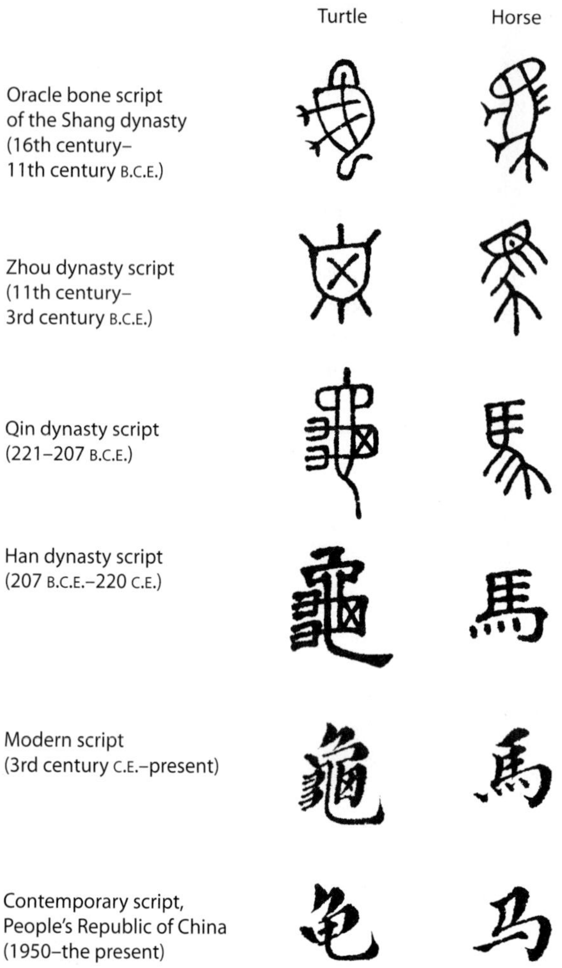

Turtle Horse

Oracle bone script of the Shang dynasty (16th century–11th century B.C.E.)

Zhou dynasty script (11th century–3rd century B.C.E.)

Qin dynasty script (221–207 B.C.E.)

Han dynasty script (207 B.C.E.–220 C.E.)

Modern script (3rd century C.E.–present)

Contemporary script, People's Republic of China (1950–the present)

CHINESE WRITING. | The evolution of Chinese characters from the Shang dynasty to the present. ***In what ways did the characters above change over time?***

writing. The earliest form of Chinese writing, like Sumerian and Egyptian writing, was the pictograph—a conventional or stylized representation of an object. The characters used in contemporary Chinese writing are direct descendants of those used in Shang times. Scholars have identified more than two thousand characters inscribed on oracle bones, most of which have a modern counterpart. Over the centuries, written Chinese characters have undergone considerable modification: generally speaking, they have become more stylized, conventional, and abstract. Yet the affinities between Shang and later Chinese written characters are apparent at a glance.

The political interests of the Shang kings may have accounted for the origin of Chinese writing, but once established, the technology was available for other uses. Because Shang writing survives only on oracle bones and a small number of bronze inscriptions, however, evidence for the expanded uses of writing comes only from the Zhou dynasty and later times.

ZHOU LITERATURE Indeed, the Zhou dynasty produced books of poetry and history, manuals of divination and ritual, and essays dealing with moral, religious, philosophical, and political themes. Best known of these works are the reflections of Confucius and other late Zhou thinkers (discussed in chapter 6), which served as the intellectual foundation of classical Chinese society. But many works won recognition in Zhou society, including the popular *Book of Changes* (a manual instructing diviners in the art of foretelling the future), the *Book of History* (a collection of documents that justified the Zhou state), the *Book of Etiquette* (a manual in the arts of polite behavior), and—most notable of all—the *Book of Songs* (a collection of verses).

Unfortunately, most other Zhou writings have perished. One important reason for this is that when the imperial house of Qin ended the chaos of the Period of the Warring States and brought all of China under tightly centralized rule in 221 B.C.E., the victorious emperor ordered the destruction of all writings that did not have some immediate utilitarian value. Only a few items escaped, hidden away for a decade or more until scholars and writers could once again work without fear of persecution. These few survivors represent the earliest development of Chinese literature and moral thought.

ANCIENT CHINA AND THE LARGER WORLD

High mountain ranges, forbidding deserts, and turbulent seas stood between China and other early societies of the eastern hemisphere. These geographic features did not entirely prevent communication between China and other lands, but they hindered the establishment of direct long-distance trade relations such as those linking Mesopotamia with Harappan India or those between the Phoenicians and other peoples of the Mediterranean basin. Nevertheless, like other early societies, ancient China developed in the context of a larger world of interaction and exchange. Trade, migration, and the expansion of Chinese agricultural society all ensured that peoples of the various east Asian and central Asian societies would have regular dealings with one another. Chinese cultivators had particularly intense relations—sometimes friendly and sometimes hostile—with their neighbors to the north, the west, and the south.

Relations with Nomadic Peoples of Central Asia

STEPPE NOMADS From the valley of the Yellow River, Chinese agriculture spread to the north and west. As this expansion occurred, Chinese cultivators encountered nomadic peoples who had built pastoral societies in the grassy steppes of central Asia. These lands were too arid to sustain large agricultural societies, but their grasses supported large herds of livestock. By 2200 B.C.E. these nomads were already experienced horseback riders, had learned the technology of bronze metallurgy, and had introduced large numbers of heavy wagons into the steppes. After about 1000 B.C.E. several clusters of nomadic peoples organized powerful herding societies on the Eurasian steppes.

NOMADIC SOCIETY Nomadic peoples did little farming but instead concentrated on herding their animals, driving them to regions where they could find food and water. Because nomadic peoples ranged widely over the grassy steppes of central Asia, they served as links between agricultural societies to the east and west. They were prominent intermediaries in trade networks spanning central Asia. They also brought knowledge of bronze metallurgy and horse-drawn chariots from southwest Asia. Nomadic peoples depended on agricultural societies for grains and finished products, such as textiles and metal goods, which they could not readily produce for themselves. In exchange for those products, they offered horses, which flourished on the steppes, and their services as links to other societies. Yet the Chinese and nomadic peoples always had tense relations. Indeed, they often engaged in bitter wars, and nomadic raids posed a constant threat to the northern and western regions of China.

The Southern Expansion of Chinese Society

THE YANGZI VALLEY Chinese influence spread to the south as well as to the north and west. There was no immediate barrier to cultivation in the south: indeed, the valley of the Yangzi River supports even more intensive agriculture than is possible in the Yellow River basin. In fact, the moist, subtropical climate of southern China lent itself readily to the cultivation of rice: ancient cultivators sometimes raised two crops of rice per year.

But intensive cultivation of rice depended on the construction and maintenance of an elaborate irrigation system that allowed cultivators to flood their paddies and release the waters at the appropriate time. The Shang and Zhou states provided sources of authority that could supervise a complex irrigation system, and harvests in southern China—along with the population—increased dramatically during the second and first millennia B.C.E.

THE STATE OF CHU Agricultural surpluses and growing populations led to the emergence of cities, states, and complex societies in the Yangzi as well as the Yellow River valley. During the late Zhou dynasty, the powerful state of Chu, situated in the central region of the Yangzi, governed its affairs autonomously and challenged the Zhou for supremacy. By the end of the Zhou dynasty, Chu and other states in southern China were in regular communication with their counterparts in the Yellow River valley.

CHINESE AGRICULTURE. | Terraced rice paddies in the river valleys of southern China have long produced abundant harvests. ***What is the advantage of terraces in agriculture?***

They adopted Chinese political and social traditions as well as Chinese writing, and they built societies closely resembling those of the Yellow River valley. As a result, although only the northern portions of the Yangzi River valley fell under the authority of the Shang and Zhou states, by the end of the Zhou dynasty all of southern China formed part of an emerging larger Chinese society.

SUMMARY

Agricultural peoples in south and east Asia built complex societies that in broad outline were much like those to the west. Particularly in the valleys of the Yellow River, the Yangzi River, and the Indus River, early Chinese and Indian cultivators organized states, developed social distinctions, and established sophisticated cultural traditions. Their languages, writing, beliefs, and values differed considerably from one another and from those of their contemporaries in other societies, and these cultural elements lent distinctiveness to both Chinese and Indian society. Moreover, inhabitants of both ancient China and India managed to trade and communicate with peoples of other societies. As a result, wheat cultivation, bronze and iron metallurgy, horse-drawn chariots, and wheeled vehicles all made their way from southwest Asia in ancient times. Thus, in south and east Asia, as in other parts of the eastern hemisphere, agriculture demonstrated its potential to provide a foundation for large-scale social organization and to support interaction and exchange between peoples of different societies.

STUDY TERMS

Aryans (51)
Brahman (55)
brahmins (53)
caste (52)
Dravidian (48)
Harappan (48)
Indus River (49)
jati (53)
karma (55)
kshatriyas (53)
mandate of heaven (58)
moksha (55)
oracle bones (61)
Qin (58)
samsara (55)
Shang dynasty (56)
shudras (53)
untouchables (53)
Upanishads (54)
vaishyas (53)
varna (53)
Vedas (52)
Vedic age (52)
Xia dynasty (56)
Yangzi (56)
Yellow River (56)
Yu (47)
Zhou dynasty (58)

FOR FURTHER READING

F. R. Allchin. *The Archaeology of Early Historic South Asia: The Emergence of Cities and States.* Cambridge, 1995. A collection of scholarly essays on the roles of cities and states in ancient India.

Cyril Birch, ed. *Anthology of Chinese Literature.* 2 vols. New York, 1965. Collection of primary sources in translation.

Nicola di Cosmo. *Ancient China and Its Enemies: The Rise of Nomadic Power in East Asian History.* Cambridge, 2002. An insightful study analyzing the emergence of pastoral nomadism and relations between Chinese cultivators and nomadic peoples in ancient times.

David N. Keightley, ed. *The Origins of Chinese Civilization.* Berkeley, 1983. An important collection of scholarly articles dealing with all aspects of early Chinese society.

Jonathan Mark Kenoyer. *Ancient Cities of the Indus Valley Civilization.* Oxford, 1998. A well-illustrated volume that synthesizes recent archaeological and linguistic scholarship on Harappan society.

J. P. Mallory. *In Search of the Indo-Europeans: Language, Archaeology, and Myth.* London, 1989. Carefully reviews modern theories about early Indo-European speakers in light of both the linguistic and the archaeological evidence.

Juan Mascaró, trans. *The Upanishads.* London, 1965. A superb English version of selected Upanishads by a gifted translator.

Shereen Ratnagar. *Encounters: The Westerly Trade of the Harappan Civilization.* Delhi, 1981. Relies on archaeological discoveries in examining commercial relations between Harappan society and Mesopotamia.

Jessica Rawson. *Ancient China: Art and Archaeology.* New York, 1980. An outstanding and well-illustrated volume with especially strong treatment of archaeological discoveries.

Robert L. Thorp. *China in the Early Bronze Age: Shang Civilization.* Philadelphia, 2006. Authoritative synthesis of archaeological studies that places the Shang dynasty in its historical context.

Early Societies in the Americas and Oceania

4

EARLY SOCIETIES OF MESOAMERICA

The Olmecs

Heirs of the Olmecs: The Maya

Maya Society and Religion

Heirs of the Olmecs: Teotihuacan

EARLY SOCIETIES OF SOUTH AMERICA

Early Andean Society and the Chavín Cult

Early Andean States: Mochica

EARLY SOCIETIES OF OCEANIA

Early Societies in Australia and New Guinea

The Peopling of the Pacific Islands

n early September of the year 683 C.E., a Maya man named Chan Bahlum grasped a sharp obsidian knife and cut three deep slits into the skin of his penis. He inserted into each slit a strip of paper made from beaten tree bark so as to encourage a continuing flow of blood. His younger brother Kan Xul performed a similar rite, and other members of his family also drew blood from their own bodies.

The bloodletting observances of September 683 C.E. were political and religious rituals, acts of deep piety performed as Chan Bahlum presided over funeral services for his recently deceased father, Pacal, king of the Maya city of Palenque in the Yucatan peninsula. The Maya believed that the shedding of royal blood was essential to the world's survival. Thus, as Chan Bahlum prepared to succeed his father as king of Palenque, he let his blood flow copiously.

Throughout Mesoamerica, Maya and other peoples performed similar rituals for a millennium and more. Maya rulers and their family members regularly spilled their own blood. Men commonly drew blood from the penis, like Chan Bahlum, and women often drew from the tongue. Both sexes occasionally drew blood also from the earlobes, lips, or cheeks, and they sometimes increased the flow by pulling long, thick cords through their wounds.

According to Maya priests, the gods had shed their own blood to water the earth and nourish crops of maize, and they expected human beings to honor them by imitating their sacrifice. By spilling human blood the Maya hoped to please the gods and ensure that life-giving waters would bring bountiful harvests to their fields. By inflicting painful wounds not just on their enemies but on their own bodies as well, the Maya demonstrated their conviction that bloodletting rituals were essential to the coming of rain and the survival of their agricultural society.

This agricultural society was the product of a distinctive tradition. Human groups migrated to the Americas and Oceania long after they had established communities throughout most of the eastern hemisphere, but long before any people began to experiment with agriculture. Their migrations took place during ice ages, when glaciers locked up much of the earth's water, causing sea levels all over the world to decline precipitously—sometimes by as much as 300 meters (984 feet). For thousands of years, temporary land bridges joined regions that both before and after the ice ages were separated by the seas. One land bridge linked Siberia with Alaska. Another

❮ In this Mayan mural from Bonampak in modern Mexico, war captives prepare to be sacrificed by their captors.

Maya (MY-uh)

Yucatan (yoo-kah-TAN)

CHRONOLOGY

AMERICAS	
13,000 B.C.E.	Human migration to North America from Siberia
8000–7000 B.C.E.	Origins of agriculture in Mesoamerica
4000 B.C.E.	Origins of maize cultivation in Mesoamerica
3000 B.C.E.	Origins of agriculture in South America
1200–100 B.C.E.	Olmec society
1000–300 B.C.E.	Chavín cult
200 B.C.E.–750 C.E.	Teotihuacan society
300–1100 C.E.	Maya society
300–700 C.E.	Mochica society
OCEANIA	
60,000 B.C.E.	Human migration to Australia and New Guinea
3000 B.C.E.	Origins of agriculture in New Guinea
3000 B.C.E.	Austronesian migrations to New Guinea
1500–500 B.C.E.	Lapita society
1500 B.C.E.–700 C.E.	Austronesian migrations to Pacific islands

joined the continent of Australia to the island of New Guinea. Human groups took advantage of those bridges by migrating to new lands.

When the earth's temperature rose and the glaciers melted, beginning about eighteen thousand years ago, the waters returned and flooded low-lying lands around the world. Eventually, the seas once again divided Asia from America by the body of water known as the Bering Strait, and they also separated Australia and New Guinea. By that time, however, human communities had become well established in each of those areas.

The return of high waters did not put an end to human migrations. Human groups fanned out from Alaska and ventured to all corners of North, Central, and South America. Beginning about 3000 B.C.E. coastal peoples of southeast Asia built large sailing canoes and established human settlements in the previously uninhabited islands of the Pacific Ocean. By about 700 C.E. human beings had established communities in almost every habitable part of the world.

Although they were separated by large bodies of water, by no means did human migrants to the Americas and Oceania lead completely isolated lives. On the contrary, there were frequent and sometimes regular interactions between peoples of different societies within the Americas and within Oceania. It is likely that at least fleeting encounters took place as well between peoples of the eastern and western hemispheres, although very little evidence survives to throw light on the nature of those encounters in early times. Yet even as they dealt with peoples of other societies, the first inhabitants of the Americas and Oceania also established distinctive societies of their own.

Despite their different origins and their distinctive political, social, and cultural traditions, peoples of the Americas and Oceania built societies that in some ways resembled those of the eastern hemisphere. Human communities independently discovered agriculture in several regions of North America and South America, and migrants introduced cultivation to the inhabited Pacific islands as well. With agriculture came increasing populations, settlement in towns, specialized labor, formal political authorities, hierarchical social orders, long-distance trade, and organized religious traditions. The Americas also generated large, densely populated societies featuring cities, monumental public works, imperial states, and sometimes traditions of writing as well. Thus, like their counterparts in the eastern hemisphere, the earliest societies of the Americas and Oceania reflected a common human tendency toward the development of increasingly complex social forms.

Early Societies of Mesoamerica

Much is unclear about the early population of the Americas by human communities. Several archaeological excavations suggest that at least a few human groups had made their way to the Americas by 15,000 B.C.E. or earlier, although it is not clear whether they arrived by land or by water. However, it is clear that large-scale migration to the Americas began after 13,000 B.C.E., as humans made their way in large numbers across the Bering land bridge. Once in the Americas, humans quickly populated all habitable regions of the western hemisphere. By 9500 B.C.E. they had reached the southernmost part of South America, more than 17,000 kilometers (10,566 miles) from the Bering land bridge.

The earliest human inhabitants of the Americas lived exclusively by hunting and gathering. Beginning about 8000 B.C.E., however, large game animals became scarce, partly because they did not adapt well to the rapidly warming climate and partly because of overhunting by expanding human communities. By 7500 B.C.E. many species of large animals in the Americas were well on the road to extinction. To survive, some human communities supplemented the foods they gathered with fish and small game. Others turned to agriculture, and they gave rise to the first complex societies in the Americas.

The Olmecs

EARLY AGRICULTURE IN MESOAMERICA By 8000 to 7000 B.C.E. the peoples of Mesoamerica—the region from the central portion of modern Mexico to Honduras and El Salvador—had begun to experiment with the cultivation of beans, chili peppers, avocados, squashes, and gourds. By 4000 B.C.E. they had discovered the agricultural potential of maize, which soon became the staple food of the region. Later they added tomatoes to the crops they cultivated. Agricultural villages appeared soon after 3000 B.C.E., and by 2000 B.C.E. agriculture had spread throughout Mesoamerica.

Early Mesoamerican peoples had a diet rich in cultivated foods, but most large animals of the western hemisphere were not susceptible to domestication. For that reason, Mesoamericans were unable to harness animal energy as did the peoples of the eastern hemisphere. As a result, human laborers prepared fields for cultivation, and human porters carried trade goods on their backs. Mesoamericans had no need for wheeled vehicles, which would have been useful only if draft animals had been available to pull them.

CEREMONIAL CENTERS Toward the end of the second millennium B.C.E., the tempo of Mesoamerican life quickened as elaborate ceremonial centers with monumental pyramids, temples, and palaces arose alongside the agricultural villages. These were not cities like those that existed in the eastern hemisphere, because only members of the ruling elite, priests, and those who tended to their needs were permanent residents. Instead, most people lived in surrounding villages and gathered in the ceremonial centers only on special occasions or on market days.

OLMECS: THE "RUBBER PEOPLE" The earliest known ceremonial centers of the ancient Americas appeared on the coast of the Gulf of Mexico, near the modern Mexican city of Veracruz, and they served as the nerve center of the Olmecs, the first complex society of the Americas. Historians and archaeologists have systematically studied Olmec society only since the 1940s, and many questions about them remain unanswered. Even their proper name is unknown: the term *Olmec* (meaning "rubber people") did not come from the ancient people themselves but derives instead from the rubber trees that flourish in the region they inhabited. Nevertheless, some of the basic features of Olmec society have become reasonably clear, and it is certain that Olmec cultural traditions influenced all complex societies of Mesoamerica until the arrival of European peoples in the sixteenth century C.E.

The first Olmec ceremonial center arose about 1200 B.C.E. on the site of the modern town of San Lorenzo, and it served as their capital for some four hundred years. When the influence of San Lorenzo waned, leadership passed to new ceremonial centers at La Venta (800–400 B.C.E.) and Tres Zapotes (400–100 B.C.E.). These sites defined the heartland of Olmec society, where agriculture produced rich harvests. The entire region receives

Mesoamerica (mez-oh-uh-MER-i-kuh)

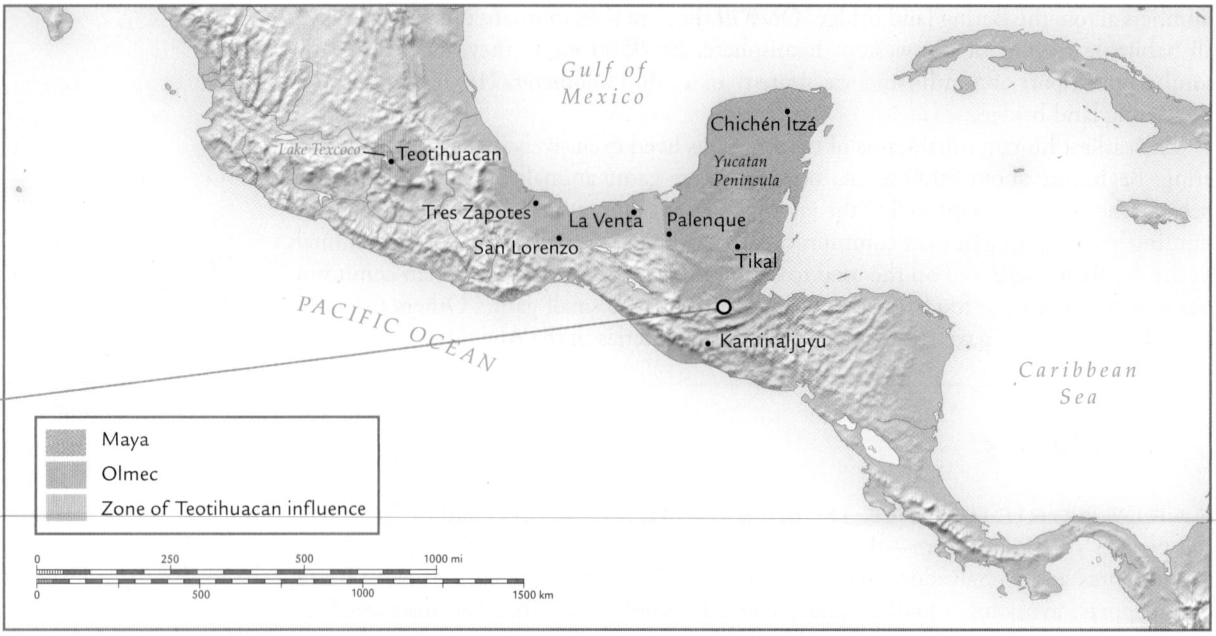

Note how much larger Maya society was than Teotihuacan or the earlier Olmec society.

MAP 4.1 | Early Mesoamerican societies, 1200 B.C.E.–1100 C.E. Describe the different geographical settings of the early Mesoamerican societies represented here. Consider the extent to which geographical and environmental conditions influenced the historical development and daily life of these societies.

abundant rainfall; so, like the Harappans, the Olmecs constructed elaborate drainage systems to divert waters that otherwise might have flooded their fields or destroyed their settlements.

Olmec altar from La Venta
www.mhhe.com/bentleybrief2e

OLMEC SOCIETY Olmec society was probably authoritarian in nature. Common subjects delivered a portion of their harvests for the maintenance of the elite classes living in the ceremonial centers and provided labor for large-scale construction projects. Indeed, untold thousands of laborers were required to build the temples, pyramids, altars, sculptures, and tombs that characterized each Olmec ceremonial center.

Common subjects also provided appropriate artistic adornment for the elites in Olmec capitals. The most distinctive artistic creations of the Olmecs were colossal human heads—possibly likenesses of rulers—sculpted from basalt rock. The largest of these sculptures stands 3 meters (almost 10 feet) tall and weighs some twenty tons. In the absence of draft animals and wheels, human laborers had to move rocks to the ceremonial centers. The largest sculptures required the services of about one thousand laborers.

TRADE IN JADE AND OBSIDIAN Olmec influence extended to much of the central and southern regions of modern Mexico and beyond to modern Guatemala and El Salvador. The Olmecs spread their influence partly by military force, but trade was a prominent link between the Olmec heartland and the other regions of Mesoamerica. Indeed, the Olmecs obtained both jade and obsidian—used for decorative objects and for cutting tools, respectively—from distant regions in the interior of Mesoamerica.

Among the many mysteries surrounding the Olmecs, one of the most perplexing concerns the decline and fall of their society. The Olmecs systematically destroyed their ceremonial centers at both San Lorenzo and La Venta and then deserted the sites. Archaeologists study-

La Venta (lah BEHN-tah)
Tres Zapotes (TRACE-zah-POE-tace)

ing those sites found statues broken and buried, monuments defaced, and the capitals themselves burned. Although intruders may have ravaged the ceremonial centers, many scholars believe that the Olmecs deliberately destroyed their capitals, perhaps because of civil conflicts or doubts about the effectiveness and legitimacy of the ruling classes. In any case, Olmec society collapsed and disappeared by about 100 B.C.E.

OLMEC COLOSSAL HEAD. | This particular head was carved from basalt rock between 1000 and 600 B.C.E. and discovered at La Venta. Olmecs carved similar heads for their ceremonial centers at San Lorenzo and Tres Zapotes. ***In the absence of wheeled vehicles, how could human laborers have moved these enormous sculptures?***

Heirs of the Olmecs: The Maya

During the thousand years following the Olmecs' disappearance about 100 B.C.E., complex societies arose in several Mesoamerican regions and carried on many of the legacies of the Olmecs. Human population grew dramatically, and ceremonial centers cropped up at sites far removed from the Olmec heartland. Some of them evolved into genuine cities that attracted large populations of permanent residents and encouraged increasing specialization of labor. Networks of long-distance trade linked the new urban centers and extended their influence to all parts of Mesoamerica. Within the cities themselves, priests devised written languages and compiled a body of astronomical knowledge. In short, Mesoamerican societies developed in a manner roughly parallel to that of their counterparts in the eastern hemisphere.

THE MAYA The earliest heirs of the Olmecs were the Maya, who created a remarkable society in the region now occupied by southern Mexico, Guatemala, Belize, Honduras, and El Salvador. Although Maya society originally appeared in the fertile Guatemalan highlands beginning in the third century B.C.E., after the fourth century C.E. it flourished mostly in the poorly drained Mesoamerican lowlands, where thin, tropical soils quickly lost their fertility. To enhance the agricultural potential of their region, the Maya built terraces designed to trap silt carried by the numerous rivers passing through the lowlands. By artificially retaining rich earth, they dramatically increased the agricultural productivity of their lands. They harvested maize in abundance, and they also cultivated cotton, from which they wove fine textiles highly prized both in their own society and by trading partners in other parts of Mesoamerica. Maya cultivators also raised cacao, the large bean that is the source of chocolate. Cacao was a precious commodity consumed mostly by nobles in Maya society. They whisked powdered cacao into water to create a stimulating beverage, and they sometimes even ate the bitter cacao beans as snacks. The product was so valuable that the Maya used cacao beans as money.

Drawing of a Maya fortress city
www.mhhe.com/bentleybrief2e

TIKAL The Maya organized themselves politically into scores of small city-kingdoms. From about 300 to 900 C.E., the Maya built more than eighty large ceremonial centers in the lowlands—all with pyramids, palaces, and temples—as well as numerous smaller settlements. Some of the larger centers attracted dense populations and evolved into genuine cities. Foremost among them was Tikal, the most important Maya political center between the fourth and ninth centuries C.E. At its height, roughly 600 to 800 C.E., Tikal was a wealthy and bustling city with a population approaching forty thousand. It boasted enormous paved plazas and scores of temples, pyramids, palaces, and public buildings. The Temple of the Giant Jaguar, a stepped pyramid rising sharply to a height of 47 meters (154 feet), dominated the skyline and represented Tikal's control over the surrounding region, which had a population of about five hundred thousand.

MAYA WARFARE The Maya kingdoms fought constantly with one another. Victors generally destroyed the peoples they defeated and took over their ceremonial centers, but the purpose of Maya warfare was not so much to kill enemies as to capture them in hand-to-hand combat on the battlefield. Warriors won enormous prestige when they brought back important captives from neighboring kingdoms. Ultimately, most captives ended their lives either as slaves or as sacrificial victims to Maya gods. High-ranking captives

Tikal (tee-KAHL)

in particular often underwent ritual torture and sacrifice in public ceremonies on important occasions.

MAYA TEMPLE OF THE GIANT JAGUAR. | This temple, built in the city of Tikal, served as the funerary pyramid for Lord Cacao, a prominent Maya ruler of the late sixth and early seventh centuries C.E. ***What kind of message might a monument of this size have been trying to convey?***

CHICHÉN ITZÁ Bitter conflicts between small kingdoms were a source of constant tension in Maya society. Only about the ninth century C.E. did the state of Chichén Itzá in the northern Yucatan peninsula seek to construct a larger society by integrating captives into their own society instead of killing them. Some captives refused the opportunity and went to their deaths as proud warriors, but many agreed to recognize the authority of Chichén Itzá. Between the ninth and eleventh centuries C.E., Chichén Itzá organized a loose empire that brought a measure of political stability to the northern Yucatan.

MAYA DECLINE By about 800 B.C.E., however, most Maya populations had begun to desert their cities. Within a century Maya society was in full decline everywhere except the northern Yucatan, where Chichén Itzá continued to flourish. Historians have suggested many possible causes of the decline, including invasion, internal dissension and civil war, failure of the system of water control, ecological problems caused by destruction of the forests, the spread of epidemic diseases, and natural catastrophes such as earthquakes. Possibly several problems combined to destroy Maya society. It is likely that debilitating civil conflict and excessive siltation of agricultural terraces caused particularly difficult problems for the Maya. In any case, the population declined, the people abandoned their cities, and long-distance trade came to a halt. Meanwhile, the tropical jungles of the lowlands encroached on human settlements and gradually smothered the cities, temples, pyramids, and monuments of a once-vibrant society.

Maya Society and Religion

In addition to kings and ruling families, Maya society included a large class of priests who maintained an elaborate calendar and transmitted knowledge of writing, astronomy, and mathematics. A hereditary nobility owned most land and cooperated with the kings and the priests by organizing military forces and participating in religious rituals. Maya merchants also came from the ruling and noble classes, because they served not only as traders but also as ambassadors to neighboring lands and allied peoples. Maya society also generated several other distinct social classes. Professional architects and sculptors oversaw construction of large monuments and public buildings. Artisans specialized in the production of pottery, tools, and cotton textiles. Finally, large classes of peasants and slaves fed the entire society and provided physical labor for the construction of cities and monuments.

Building on the achievements of their Olmec predecessors, Maya priests studied astronomy and mathematics, and they devised both a sophisticated calendar and an elaborate system of writing. They understood the movements of heavenly bodies well enough to plot planetary cycles and to predict eclipses of the sun and the moon. They invented the concept of zero and used a symbol to represent zero mathematically, which facilitated their manipulation of large numbers. By combining their astronomical and mathematical observations, Maya priests calculated the length of the solar year at 365.242 days—about seventeen seconds shorter than the figure reached by modern astronomers.

THE MAYA CALENDAR Maya priests constructed the most elaborate calendar of the ancient Americas, which reflected a powerful urge to identify meaningful cycles of time. The Maya calendar interwove two kinds of year: a solar year of 365 days governed the agricultural cycle, and a ritual year of 260 days governed daily affairs by organizing time into twenty "months" of 13 days apiece. The Maya believed that each day derived certain specific characteristics from its position in both the solar and the ritual calendar and that the combined attributes of each day would determine the fortune of activities undertaken on that day. It took fifty-two years for the two calendars to work through all possible combinations of days and return simultaneously to their respective starting points. Maya priests carefully studied the various opportunities and dangers that would come together on a given day in hopes that they could determine which activities were safe to initiate. The Maya attributed especially great significance to the fifty-two-year periods in which the two calendars ran. They believed that the end of a cycle would bring monumental changes and that ultimately the world would end after one such cycle.

MAYA WRITING The Maya also expanded on the Olmec tradition of written inscriptions. In doing so they created the most flexible and sophisticated of all the early American systems of writing. The Maya script contained both ideographic elements (like Chinese characters) and symbols for syllables. Scholars have begun to decipher this script only since the 1960s, and it has become clear that writing was just as important to the Maya as it was to early complex societies in the eastern hemisphere. Most Maya writing survives today in the form of inscriptions on temples and monuments, because sixteenth-century Spanish conquerors and missionaries destroyed untold numbers of books in hopes of undermining native religious beliefs. Today only four books of the ancient Maya survive, all dealing with astronomical and calendrical matters.

MAYA RELIGIOUS THOUGHT Surviving inscriptions and other writings shed considerable light on Maya religious and cultural traditions. The *Popol Vuh,* a Maya creation myth, taught that the gods had created human beings out of maize and water, the ingredients that became human flesh and blood. Thus Maya religious thought reflected the fundamental role of agriculture in their society, much like religious thought in early complex societies of the eastern hemisphere. Maya priests also taught that the gods kept the world going and maintained the agricultural cycle in exchange for honors and sacrifices performed for them by human beings.

Maya Stone Relief Sculpture. In this relief, a Maya king from Yaxchilán (between Tikal and Palenque in the southern Yucatan peninsula) holds a torch over a woman from the royal family as she draws a thorn-studded rope through a hole in her tongue, so as to shed her blood in honor of the Maya gods.

BLOODLETTING RITUALS The most important of those sacrifices involved the shedding of human blood, which the Maya believed would prompt the gods to send rain to water their crops of maize. Some bloodletting rituals centered on war captives. Before sacrificing the victims by decapitation, their captors cut off the ends of their fingers or lacerated their bodies so as to cause a copious flow of blood in honor of the gods. Yet the Maya also frequently and voluntarily shed their own blood as a means of displaying reverence to their gods.

THE MAYA BALL GAME Apart from the calendar and sacrificial rituals, the Maya also inherited a distinctive ball game from the Olmecs. The game usually involved teams of two to four members apiece. Its object was for players to score points by propelling a rubber ball through a ring or onto a marker without using their hands. The Maya used a solid rubber ball about 20 centimeters (8 inches) in diameter, which was both heavy and hard. Players needed great dexterity and skill to maneuver it accurately using only their feet, legs, hips, torso, shoulders, or elbows. The game was extremely popular: almost all Maya ceremonial centers, towns, and cities had stone-paved courts on which players performed publicly.

Mayan ball court
www.mhhe.com/bentleybrief2e

The Maya played the ball game for several reasons. Sometimes individuals competed for sporting purposes, and sometimes the game was used as a ritual that honored the conclusion of treaties. High-ranking captives often engaged in forced public competition in which the stakes were their very lives: losers became sacrificial victims and faced torture and execution immediately following the match. Alongside some ball courts were skull racks that bore the decapitated heads of losing players. Thus Maya concerns to please the gods by shedding human blood extended even to the realm of sport.

Popol Vuh (paw-pawl vuh)

SOURCES FROM THE PAST

The *Popol Vuh* on the Creation of Human Beings

The* Popol Vuh *outlines traditional Maya views on the creation of the world and human beings. The version of the work that survives today dates from the mid–sixteenth century, but it reflects beliefs of a much earlier era. According to the* Popol Vuh, *the gods wanted to create intelligent beings that would recognize and praise them. Three times they tried to fashion such beings out of animals, mud, and wood, but without success. Then they decided to use maize and water as their ingredients.

And here is the beginning of the conception of humans, and of the search for the ingredients of the human body. So they spoke, the [gods] Bearer, Begetter, the Makers, Modelers named Sovereign Plumed Serpent:

"The dawn has approached, preparations have been made, and morning has come for the provider, nurturer, born in the light, begotten in the light. Morning has come for humankind, for the people of the face of the earth," they said. It all came together as they went on thinking in the darkness, in the night, as they searched and they sifted, they thought and they wondered.

And here their thoughts came out in clear light. They sought and discovered what was needed for human flesh. . . . Broken Place, Bitter Water Place is the name: the yellow corn, white corn came from there. . . .

And these were the ingredients for the flesh of the human work, the human design, and the water was for the blood. It became human blood, and corn was also used by the Bearer, Begetter. . . .

And then the yellow corn and white corn were ground, and Xmucane did the grinding nine times. Corn was used, along with the water she rinsed her hands with, for the creation of grease; it became human fat when it was worked by the Bearer, Begetter, Sovereign Plumed Serpent, as they are called. . . .

It was staples alone that made up their flesh.

These are the names of the first people who were made and modeled.

This is the first person: Jaguar Quitze.

And now the second: Jaguar Night.

And now the third: Mahucutah.

And the fourth: True Jaguar.

And these are the names of our first mother-fathers. They were simply made and modeled, it is said; they had no mother and no father. We have named the men by themselves. No woman gave birth to them, nor were they begotten by the builder, sculptor, Bearer, Begetter. By sacrifice alone, by genius alone they were made, they were modeled by the Maker, Modeler, Bearer, Begetter, Sovereign Plumed Serpent. And when they came to fruition, they came out human:

They talked and they made words.

They looked and they listened.

They walked, they worked. . . .

And then their wives and women came into being. Again, the same gods thought of it. It was as if they were asleep when they received them, truly beautiful women were there with Jaguar Quitze, Jaguar Night, Mahucutah, and True Jaguar. With their women there they became wider awake. Right away they were happy at heart again, because of their wives.

Celebrated Seahouse is the name of the wife of Jaguar Quitze.

Prawn House is the name of the wife of Jaguar Night.

Hummingbird House is the name of the wife of Mahucutah.

Macaw House is the name of the wife of True Jaguar.

So these are the names of their wives, who became ladies of rank, giving birth to the people of the tribes, small and great.

■ **Discuss the extent to which this account of human creation reflects the influences on Maya society of both agriculture and the untamed natural world.**

SOURCE: Dennis Tedlock, trans. *Popol Vuh: The Definitive Edition of the Mayan Book of the Dawn of Life and the Glories of Gods and Kings.* New York: Simon and Schuster, 1985, pp. 163–65, 167.

Heirs of the Olmecs: Teotihuacan

While the Maya flourished in the Mesoamerican lowlands, a different society arose to the north in the highlands of Mexico. For most of human history, the valley of central Mexico, situated some two kilometers (more than a mile) above sea level, was the site of several large lakes fed by the waters coming off the surrounding mountains. Although

TEOTIHUACAN. | Aerial view of Teotihuacan, looking toward the Pyramid of the Moon (top center) from the Pyramid of the Sun (bottom left). Shops and residences occupied the spaces surrounding the main street and the pyramids.

environmental changes have caused most of the lakes to disappear, in earlier times their abundant supplies of freshwater, fish, and waterfowl attracted human settlers.

The earliest settlers in the valley of Mexico channeled some of the waters from the mountain streams into their fields and established a productive agricultural society. The earliest center of this society was the large and bustling city of Teotihuacan, located about 50 kilometers (31 miles) northeast of modern Mexico City.

THE CITY OF TEOTIHUACAN Teotihuacan was probably a large agricultural village by 500 B.C.E., but by the end of the millennium its population approached fifty thousand. By the year 100 C.E., the city's two most prominent monuments, the colossal pyramids of the sun and the moon, dominated the skyline. The Pyramid of the Sun is the largest single structure in Mesoamerica. It occupies nearly as much space as the pyramid of Khufu in Egypt, though it stands only half as tall. At its high point, about 400 to 600 C.E., Teotihuacan was home to almost two hundred thousand inhabitants, a thriving metropolis with scores of temples, several palatial residences, neighborhoods with small apartments for the masses, busy markets, and hundreds of workshops for artisans and craftsmen.

PSI img Detail from Teotihuacan www.mhhe.com/bentleybrief2e

The organization of a large urban population, along with the hinterland that supported it, required a recognized source of authority. Unfortunately, scholars have little information about the character of that authority, since books and written records from the city did not survive. Yet paintings and murals suggest that Teotihuacan was a theocracy of sorts. Priests figure prominently in the works of art, and scholars interpret many figures as representations of deities.

THE SOCIETY OF TEOTIHUACAN Apart from rulers and priests, Teotihuacan's population included cultivators, artisans, and merchants. Artisans of Teotihuacan were especially famous for their obsidian tools and fine orange pottery. Professional merchants traded the products of Teotihuacan throughout Mesoamerica, from the region of modern Guatemala City in the south to Durango and beyond in the north.

Until about 500 C.E. there was little sign of military organization in Teotihuacan. The city did not have defensive walls, and works of art rarely depicted warriors. Yet the influence of Teotihuacan extended to much of modern Mexico and beyond. Apparently, the city's influence derived less from military might than from its ability to produce fine manufactured goods that appealed to consumers in distant markets.

Teotihuacan (tay-oh-tee-wa-KAHN)

THINKING ABOUT *Traditions*

TRADITIONS IN EARLY SOCIETIES IN THE AMERICAS AND OCEANIA. As a result of geographical distance across vast expanses of ocean, the earliest complex societies in both the Americas and Oceania developed in complete isolation from those in Africa and Eurasia. In what ways did this isolation lead to unique social, political, cultural, or economic formations? In what ways did societies in the Americas and Oceania develop similarly to those in Africa and Eurasia in spite of such isolation?

CULTURAL TRADITIONS Like the Maya, the residents of Teotihuacan built on cultural foundations established by the Olmecs. They played the ball game, adapted the Olmec calendar to their own uses, and expanded the Olmecs' graphic symbols into a complete system of writing. Unfortunately, because their books have all perished, it is impossible to know exactly how they viewed the world and their place in it. Works of art suggest that they recognized an earth god and a rain god, and it is certain that they carried out human sacrifices during their religious rituals.

DECLINE OF TEOTIHUACAN Teotihuacan began to experience increasing military pressure from other peoples about 500 C.E. About the middle of the eighth century, invaders sacked and burned the city, destroying its books and monuments. After that catastrophe most residents deserted Teotihuacan, and the city slowly fell into ruin.

EARLY SOCIETIES OF SOUTH AMERICA

By about 12,000 B.C.E. hunting and gathering peoples had made their way across the narrow isthmus of Central America and into South America. Those who migrated into the region of the northern and central Andes mountains hunted deer, llama, alpaca, and other large animals. Both the mountainous highlands and the coastal regions below benefited from a cool and moist climate that provided natural harvests of squashes, gourds, and wild potatoes. Beginning about 8000 B.C.E., however, the climate of this whole region became increasingly warm and dry, and the changes placed pressure on natural food supplies. To maintain their numbers, the human communities of the region began to experiment with agriculture. Here, as elsewhere, agriculture encouraged population growth, the establishment of villages and cities, the building of states, and the elaboration of organized cultural traditions. During the centuries after 1000 B.C.E., the central Andean region generated complex societies parallel to those of Mesoamerica.

Early Andean Society and the Chavín Cult

Although they were exact contemporaries, early Mesoamerican and Andean societies developed largely independently. Geography discouraged the establishment of communications between the Andean region and Mesoamerica because neither society possessed abundant pack animals or a technology to facilitate long-distance transportation. Although some agricultural products and technologies diffused slowly from one area to the other, neither the Andes mountains nor the lowlands of modern Panama and Nicaragua offered an attractive highway linking the two regions.

Geography made even communications within the central Andean region difficult. Deep valleys crease the western flank of the Andes mountains as rivers drain waters from the highlands to the Pacific Ocean, so transportation and communication between the valleys have always been very difficult. Nevertheless, powerful Andean states sometimes overcame the difficulties and influenced human affairs over a broad geographical range.

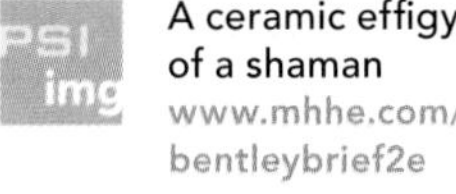
A ceramic effigy of a shaman www.mhhe.com/bentleybrief2e

Most of the early Andean heartland came under cultivation between 2500 and 2000 B.C.E. The coastal regions probably developed complex societies first, since cultivators there experienced abundant harvests as a result of crops such as beans, peanuts, and sweet potatoes, and supplemented them with the rich marine life of the Pacific Ocean. Settlements likely appeared somewhat later in the Andean highlands, but it is clear that potatoes were being cultivated in the region after about 2000 B.C.E. By 1800 B.C.E. peoples in all the Andean regions had begun to fashion distinctive styles of pottery and to build temples and pyramids in large ceremonial centers.

MAP 4.2 | Early societies of Andean South America, 1000 B.C.E.–700 C.E. The early societies of Andean South America occupied long, narrow territories between the Andes Mountains and the Pacific Ocean. ***Why did these societies not occupy territories to the east?***

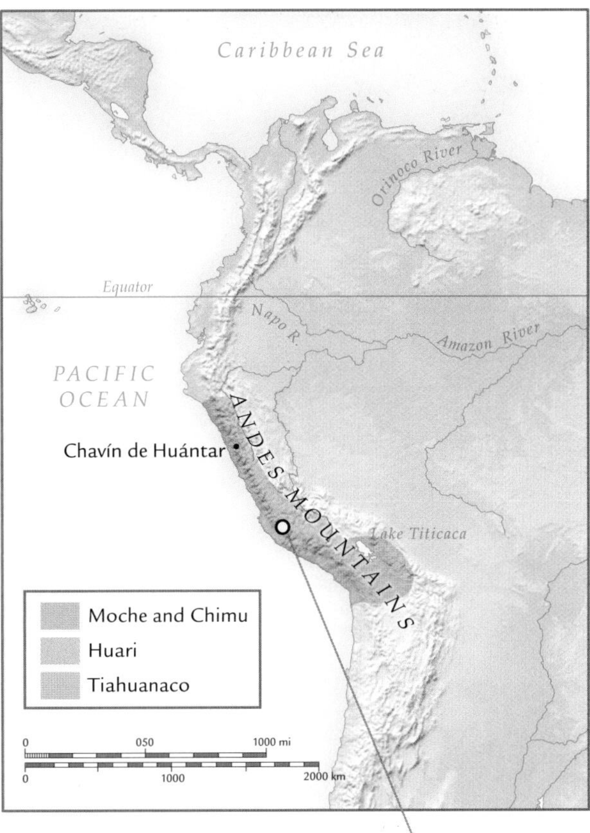

Early Andean societies had to cope with extremely mountainous territories.

THE CHAVÍN CULT Shortly after the year 1000 B.C.E., a new religion appeared in the central Andes. The Chavín cult, which enjoyed enormous popularity during the period 900 to 800 B.C.E., spread through most of the territory occupied by modern Peru and then vanished about 300 B.C.E. Although scholars do not understand the precise significance of the cult, it is clear that Andean society became increasingly complex during this period. Weavers devised techniques of producing elaborate, intricately patterned cotton textiles. Artisans manufactured large, light, and strong fishnets from cotton string. Craftsmen experimented with minerals and discovered techniques of gold, silver, and copper metallurgy and used them to make jewelry as well as small tools.

EARLY CITIES There is no evidence to suggest that Chavín cultural and religious beliefs led to the establishment of a state or any organized political order. Indeed, they probably inspired the building of ceremonial centers rather than the making of true cities. As the population increased and society became more complex, however, cities began to appear shortly after the disappearance of the Chavín cult. Beginning about 200 B.C.E. large cities emerged at the modern-day sites of Huari, Pucara, and Tiahuanaco. Each of these early Andean cities had a population exceeding ten thousand, and each also featured large public buildings, ceremonial plazas, and extensive residential districts.

Early Andean States: Mochica

Along with cities there appeared regional states. The earliest Andean states arose in the many valleys on the western side of the mountains. These states emerged when conquerors unified the valleys and organized them into integrated societies. They coordinated the building of irrigation systems so that the lower valleys could support intensive agriculture, and they established trade and exchange networks that tied the highlands, the central valleys, and the coastal regions together. Each region contributed its own products to the larger economy of the valley: from the highlands came potatoes, llama meat, and alpaca wool; the central valleys supplied maize, beans, and squashes; and the coasts provided sweet potatoes, fish, and cotton.

THE MOCHICA STATE Because early Andean societies did not make use of writing, their beliefs, values, and ways of life remain largely hidden. Surviving fortifications as well as art suggest that early Andean states relied heavily on arms to introduce order and maintain stability within their realms. In addition, art from the early Andean state of Mochica—which dominated the coasts and valleys of northern Peru from about 300 to 700 C.E.—offers a detailed and expressive depiction of early Andean society in all its variety. Most Mochica art survives in the form of pottery vessels, many of which depict individuals' heads or represent the major gods and various subordinate deities and demons. Most interesting, perhaps, are those that illustrate scenes in the everyday life of the Mochica people: warriors leading captives bound by ropes, women working in a textile factory under the careful eye of a supervisor, and beggars looking for handouts on a busy street. Even in the absence of writing, Mochica artists left abundant evidence of a complex society with considerable specialization of labor.

Moche corn goddess
www.mhhe.com/bentleybrief2e

MOCHICA ARTWORK. Many Mochica pots portray human figures and often depict distinctive characteristics of individuals or typical scenes from daily life. This pot represents two women helping a man who consumed a little too much maize beer.

Mochica was only one of several large states that dominated the central Andean region during the first millennium C.E. Although they integrated the regional economies of the various Andean valleys, none of these early states was able to impose order on the entire region or even to dominate a portion of it for very long. The exceedingly difficult geographical barriers posed by the Andes mountains presented challenges that ancient technology and social organization simply could not meet. As a result, at the end of the first millennium C.E., Andean society exhibited regional differences much sharper than those of Mesoamerica and early complex societies in the eastern hemisphere.

Early Societies of Oceania

Human migrants entered Australia and New Guinea at least 60,000 years ago, and possibly earlier than that. They arrived in watercraft—probably canoes fitted with sails—but because of the low sea levels of that era, the migrants did not have to cross large stretches of open ocean. These earliest inhabitants of Oceania also migrated—perhaps over land when sea levels were still low—to the Bismarcks, the Solomons, and other small island groups near New Guinea. Beginning about 5,000 years ago, seafaring peoples from southeast Asia settled the northern coast of New Guinea and then ventured farther and established communities in the island groups of the western Pacific Ocean. By the middle centuries of the first millennium C.E., their descendants had established communities in all the habitable islands of the Pacific Ocean.

Early Societies in Australia and New Guinea

Human migrants reached Australia and New Guinea long before any people had begun to cultivate crops or keep herds of domesticated animals. As a result, the earliest inhabitants of Australia and New Guinea lived by hunting and gathering. Once rising seas covered the land bridge connecting Australia and New Guinea about 10,000 years ago, however, human societies in each area followed radically different paths. While the aboriginal peoples of Australia continued as hunting and gathering societies, in New Guinea communities turned to agriculture: beginning about 3000 B.C.E. the cultivation of root crops such as yams and taro and the keeping of pigs and chickens spread rapidly throughout the island.

EARLY HUNTING AND GATHERING SOCIETIES IN AUSTRALIA

Like hunting and gathering peoples elsewhere, the aboriginal Australians lived in small, mobile communities that undertook seasonal migrations in search of food. Over the centuries, they learned to exploit the resources of the various ecological regions of Australia. Plant foods, including fruits, berries, roots, nuts, seeds, shoots, and green leaves, constituted the bulk of their diet. To supplement their plant-based diet, they used axes, spears, clubs, nets, lassos, snares, and boomerangs to bring down animals ranging in size from rats to giant kangaroos, which grew to a height of 3 meters (almost 10 feet), and to catch fish, waterfowl, and small birds.

AUSTRONESIAN PEOPLES In New Guinea, seafaring peoples from southeast Asia introduced agriculture to the island about 5,000 years ago when they began to establish trading and settlement communities on the northern coast. These sail-

Mochica (moh-CHEE-kah)

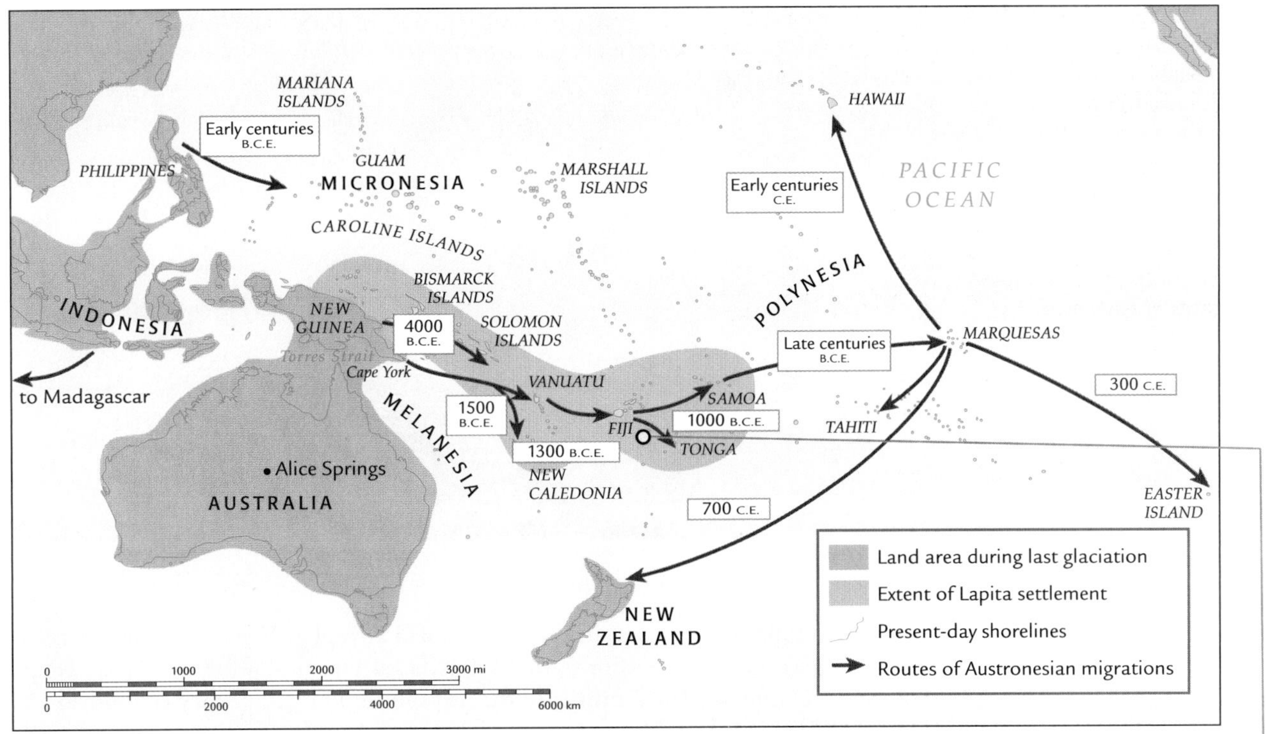

MAP 4.3 | Early societies of Oceania, 1500 B.C.E.–700 C.E. Notice the routes that Austronesian migrants followed. ***What technologies enabled Austronesian peoples to travel so widely and to maintain an extensive communication and exchange network in the western and central regions of the Pacific Ocean?***

Note how many centuries it took for humans to populate most of the islands in the Pacific Ocean.

ors spoke Austronesian languages (whose modern relatives include Malayan, Indonesian, and Polynesian) and were highly skilled in seafaring technologies. They sailed the open ocean in large canoes equipped with outriggers, which stabilized their craft and reduced the risks of long voyages. By paying close attention to winds, currents, stars, cloud formations, and other natural indicators, they learned how to find distant lands reliably and return home safely.

EARLY AGRICULTURE IN NEW GUINEA Austronesian seafarers came from societies that depended on the cultivation of root crops and the herding of animals. When they settled in New Guinea, they introduced yams, taro, pigs, and chickens to the island, and the indigenous peoples themselves soon followed suit. Within a few centuries agriculture and herding had spread to all parts of New Guinea. There, as in other lands, agriculture brought population growth and specialization of labor: after the change to agriculture, permanent settlements, pottery, and carefully crafted tools appeared throughout the island.

The Peopling of the Pacific Islands

AUSTRONESIAN MIGRATIONS TO POLYNESIA Austronesian-speaking peoples possessed a sophisticated maritime technology as well as agricultural expertise, and they established human settlements in the islands of the Pacific Ocean. Their outrigger canoes enabled them to sail safely over long distances of open ocean, and their food crops and domesticated animals enabled them to establish agricultural societies in the islands. Once they had established coastal settlements in New Guinea, Austronesian seafarers sailed easily to the Bismarck and Solomon islands east of New Guinea. From there they undertook exploratory voyages that led them to previously unpopulated islands.

Austronesian Migration. | Austronesian mariners sailed double-hulled voyaging canoes much like this one from Ra`iatea in the Society Islands, drawn in 1769 by an artist who accompanied Captain James Cook on his first voyage in the Pacific Ocean. ***What features allowed these canoes to travel across such huge expanses of open ocean?***

PSI img Stone heads, Easter Island www.mhhe.com/bentleybrief2e

By about 1500 B.C.E. Austronesian mariners had arrived at Vanuatu (formerly called New Hebrides) and New Caledonia, by 1300 B.C.E. at Fiji, and by 1000 B.C.E. at Tonga and Samoa. During the late centuries of the first millennium B.C.E., they established settlements in Tahiti and the Marquesas. From there they launched ventures that took them to the most remote outposts of Polynesia, which required them to sail over thousands of nautical miles of blue water. They reached the islands of Hawai`i in the early centuries C.E., Easter Island by 300 C.E., and the large islands of New Zealand by 700 C.E.

AUSTRONESIAN MIGRATIONS TO MICRONESIA AND MADAGASCAR While one branch of the Austronesian-speaking peoples populated the islands of Polynesia, other branches sailed in different directions. From the Philippines some ventured to the region of Micronesia, which includes small islands and atolls such as the Mariana, Caroline, and Marshall islands of the western Pacific. Others looked west from their homelands in Indonesia, sailed throughout the Indian Ocean, and became the first human settlers of the large island of Madagascar off the east African coast.

THE LAPITA PEOPLES The earliest Austronesian migrants to sail out into the blue water of the Pacific Ocean and establish human settlements in Pacific islands are known as the Lapita peoples. No one knows what they called themselves: the name Lapita comes from a beach in New Caledonia where some of the earliest recognizable Lapita artifacts came to the attention of archaeologists. It is clear, however, that between about 1500 and 500 B.C.E., Lapita peoples maintained communication and exchange networks throughout a large region extending about 4,500 kilometers (2,800 miles) from New Guinea and the Bismarck Archipelago to Samoa and Tonga.

Wherever they settled, Lapita peoples established agricultural villages where they raised pigs and chickens and introduced the suite of crops they inherited from their Austronesian ancestors. They supplemented their crops and domesticated animals with fish and seaweed from nearby waters, and they soon killed off most of the large land animals and birds that were suitable for human consumption. They left abundant evidence of their presence in the form of their distinctive pottery decorated with stamped geometric designs.

For about 1,000 years, Lapita peoples maintained extensive networks of trade and communication across vast stretches of open ocean. Their agricultural settlements were largely self-sufficient, but they placed high value on some objects from distant islands. Their pottery was a principal item of long-distance exchange, as was high-quality obsidian, which

Lapita (lah-PEE-tah)

they sometimes transported over thousands of kilometers, since it was available at only a few sites of Lapita settlement. Other trade items brought to light by archaeologists include shell jewelry and stone tools. Indeed, it is clear that, like their counterparts in other regions of the world, the earliest inhabitants of the Pacific islands maintained regular contacts with peoples well beyond their own societies.

THINKING ABOUT *Encounters*

ENCOUNTERS IN EARLY SOCIETIES IN THE AMERICAS AND OCEANIA. Although all of the early complex societies in the Americas and Oceania engaged in long-distance trade with neighboring societies, it seems clear that such interactions were more difficult to sustain over the long term than they were in the complex societies of Africa and Eurasia. What factors contributed to these difficulties? What might the existence of such interactions—despite such difficulties—tell us about early complex societies more generally?

CHIEFLY POLITICAL ORGANIZATION After about 500 B.C.E. Lapita trade networks fell into disuse, probably because the various Lapita settlements had grown large enough that they could supply their own needs. By the middle part of the first millennium B.C.E., Lapita and other Austronesian peoples had established hierarchical chiefdoms in the Pacific islands. Contests for power and influence between ambitious subordinates frequently caused tension and turmoil, but the possibility of migration offered an alternative to conflict. Indeed, the spread of Austronesian peoples throughout the Pacific islands came about partly because of population pressures and conflicts that encouraged small parties to seek fresh opportunities in more hospitable lands.

Over the longer term, descendants of Lapita peoples built strong, chiefly societies, particularly on large islands with relatively dense populations, such as those of the Tongan, Samoan, and Hawaiian groups. In Hawai`i, for example, militarily skilled chiefs cooperated closely with priests, administrators, soldiers, and servants in ruling their districts. Chiefs and their retinues claimed a portion of the agricultural surplus produced by their subjects, and they sometimes required subjects to deliver additional products, such as fish, birds, or timber. Chiefs and their administrators also vied with the ruling classes of neighboring districts, led public ritual observances, and oversaw irrigation systems that watered the taro plants that were crucial to the survival of Hawaiian society. Eventually, the chiefly and aristocratic classes became so entrenched and powerful that they regarded themselves as divine or semidivine, and the law of the land prohibited common subjects from even gazing directly at them.

SUMMARY

Very little writing survives to illuminate the historical development of early societies in the Americas and Oceania. Thus it is impossible to offer the sort of richly detailed account of their political organization, social structures, and cultural traditions that historians commonly provide for societies of the eastern hemisphere. Nevertheless, it is clear that migrations to the Americas and Oceania represented continuations of population movements that began with *Homo erectus* and early *Homo sapiens,* resulting eventually in the establishment of human communities in almost all habitable parts of the earth. Moreover, it is clear that the earliest inhabitants of the Americas and Oceania built productive and vibrant societies whose development roughly paralleled that of their counterparts in the eastern hemisphere. Many communities depended on an agricultural economy, and with their surplus production they supported dense populations, engaged in specialized labor, established formal political authorities, constructed hierarchical social orders, carried on long-distance trade, and formed distinctive cultural traditions. The early historical development of the Americas and Oceania demonstrates once again the tendency of agriculture to encourage human communities to construct ever more elaborate and complex forms of social organization.

STUDY TERMS

Austronesian peoples (78)
bloodletting rituals (73)
cacao (71)
Chavín cult (76)
Chichén Itzá (72)
colossal heads (71)
Lapita peoples (80)
La Venta (70)
maize (71)
Maya (71)
Maya ball game (73)
Mesoamerica (69)
Mochica (77)
Oceania (78)
Olmecs (69)
Popul Vuh (73)
San Lorenzo (70)
Temple of the Giant Jaguar (71)
Teotihuacan (74)
Tikal (71)
Tres Zapotes (70)
Yucatan (67)

FOR FURTHER READING

Robert McC. Adams. *The Evolution of Urban Society.* Chicago, 1966. Provocative analysis comparing the development of Mesopotamian and Mesoamerican societies by a leading archaeologist.

Ignacio Bernal. *Mexico before Cortez: Art, History, and Legend.* Trans. by W. Barnstone. Garden City, 1963. Judicious survey by a leading student of ancient Mesoamerica.

Geoffrey Blainey. *Triumph of the Nomads: A History of Aboriginal Australia.* Melbourne, 1975. A sympathetic account of Australia before European arrival, well informed by archaeological discoveries.

Michael D. Coe. *The Maya.* 4th ed. London, 1987. Well-illustrated popular account by one of the world's leading scholars of the Maya.

David Freidel, Linda Schele, and Joy Parker. *Maya Cosmos: Three Thousand Years on the Shaman's Path.* New York, 1993. Fascinating investigation of Maya conceptions of the world and their continuing influence in the present day.

K. R. Howe. *The Quest for Origins: Who First Discovered and Settled the Pacific Islands?* Honolulu, 2003. Reviews the numerous theories advanced to explain the arrival of human populations and the establishment of human societies in the remote islands of the Pacific Ocean.

Jesse D. Jennings, ed. *The Prehistory of Polynesia.* Cambridge, Mass., 1979. Brings together essays by prominent scholars on Polynesia before the arrival of Europeans in the Pacific Ocean.

Friedrich Katz. *The Ancient American Civilizations.* Trans. by K. M. L. Simpson. New York, 1972. Detailed survey that compares the experiences of Mesoamerica and Andean South America.

Charles C. Mann. *1491: New Revelations of the Americas before Columbus.* New York, 2006. Summarizes a great deal of archaeological research on the pre-Columbian Americas.

Michael E. Mosley. *The Incas and Their Ancestors: The Archaeology of Peru.* Rev. ed. London, 2001. A comprehensive survey of Andean history through the era of the Incas.

Linda Schele and Mary Ellen Miller. *The Blood of Kings: Dynasty and Ritual in Maya Art.* New York, 1986. A richly illustrated volume that explores Maya society through works of art and architecture as well as writing.

Dennis Tedlock, trans. *Popol Vuh: The Definitive Edition of the Mayan Book of the Dawn of Life and the Glories of Gods and Kings.* New York, 1985. The best translation of the *Popol Vuh,* with an excellent introduction.

Bringing It All Together

Part I The Early Complex Societies, 3500 to 500 B.C.E.

As we have seen in chapters 1–4, early complex societies—whether in Mesopotamia, Egypt, India, China, or the Americas—shared certain common features. This is because all of these societies were responding to similar pressures: in the areas where prosperous agricultural communities grew large enough to develop into cities, each sought to secure protection from outsiders, to establish and maintain internal order, and to ensure the maintenance of property and wealth among the groups who prospered most from settled urban life. The responses to these common pressures resulted, in each case, to the development of political authorities, warrior groups, class and social distinctions, religious and philosophical beliefs, and systems of education.

Furthermore, early complex societies interacted with neighboring peoples for purposes of trade, war, conquest, or intermarriage. Although these encounters with outsiders were more extensive and ranged over longer distances in early Mesopotamia, Egypt, India, and China than in either Mesoamerica, the Andes, or Oceania, they nevertheless made important contributions to all of the early complex societies. In some cases, as in early India, these interactions contributed to changes in the religious worldview of the Aryans; in others, as in early Egypt and Mesoamerica, they facilitated the exchange of luxury trade items over long distances. Indeed, material items, technologies, and ideas regularly flowed both into and out of the early complex societies. Thus, connections and encounters between peoples were important to the development of early complex societies from their beginnings.

While all of the early complex societies developed common features and responded to similar pressures, they obviously did not turn out exactly alike. Rather, each developed political structures, cultural beliefs, social customs, and economic systems that reflected unique local and regional conditions. For example, although each of the societies discussed in chapters 1–4 sought ways to maintain internal order and to conceptualize the meaning of life and death, the ways they did so were quite different: Indian society developed the caste system, Chinese society emphasized the importance of family and ancestor worship, and Mesoamerican societies sought to re-create the cycle of life through ritual sacrifice. Thus, despite important similarities between early complex societies, it is equally important to explore the rich variety of traditions that developed in response to the needs and pressures of urban agricultural life in distant parts of the world.

II

The Formation of Classical Societies, 500 B.C.E. to 500 C.E.

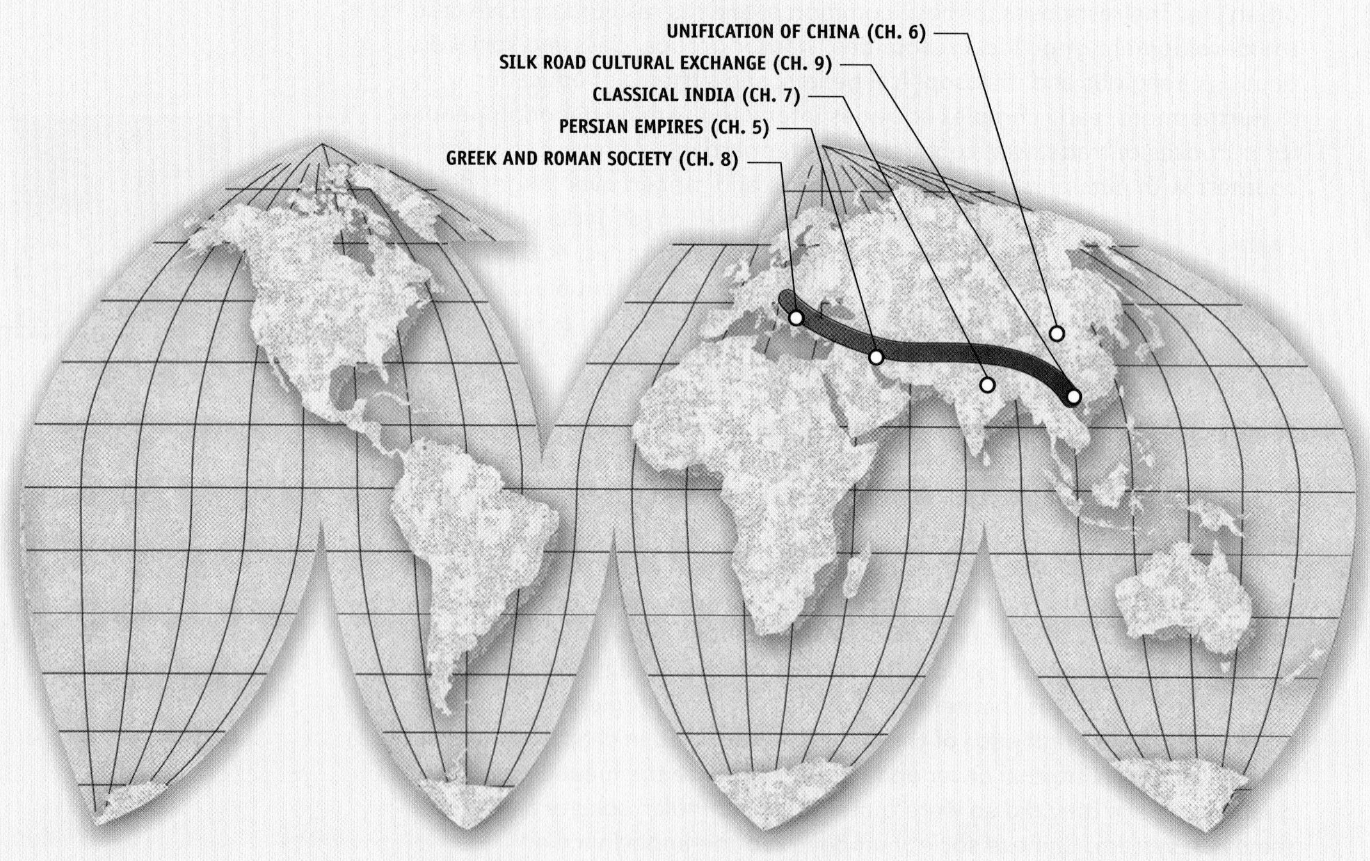

In the millennium between about 500 B.C.E. and 500 C.E., several early complex societies achieved particularly high degrees of internal organization, extended their authority over extremely large regions, and elaborated especially influential cultural traditions. Because their legacies have endured so long and have influenced the ways that literally billions of people have led their lives, historians often refer to them as classical societies.

Although the classical societies of Persia, China, India, and the Mediterranean differed from one another in many ways, they all shared several common challenges. One such challenge was that of administering vast territories without advanced technologies of transportation and communication. To meet that challenge, classical rulers standardized systems of governance, law, and taxation; built roads and transportation networks; and encouraged trade and communication between the sometimes far-flung regions under their authority. In some cases, rulers also encouraged the people under their influence to adopt particular religious, social, or cultural beliefs and practices as a way of promoting unity within their realms.

Most of the classical societies were also aggressively expansionist. As a result, their leaders were prepared to use powerful armies to conquer new areas, to fend off the advances of competing states, and to quell rebellion within their own territories. Indeed, one of the central problems most classical societies faced was how to balance the need to create loyalty and unity among their diverse subjects with the realities of authoritarian, foreign, and often unwanted rule. Heavy taxation and stiff labor requirements were particularly distasteful to many subjects of the classical societies, and these sometimes contributed to rebellions and civil wars that threatened the very survival of the societies themselves.

Another shared feature of all the classical societies was that each sponsored and maintained a vast system of roads and ports, which resulted in a dramatic increase in long-distance trade. This trade encouraged economic integration within and between societies, and various regions came to depend on one another for agricultural products and manufactured items. In fact, long-distance trade was such an important feature of the classical societies that a well-established network of land and sea routes, known collectively as the silk roads, linked lands as distant as China and Europe.

Finally, all the classical societies generated sophisticated cultural and religious traditions that offered guidance on moral, religious, political, and social issues. Because of the extensive trade networks that linked distant regions, many of these traditions spread along the trade routes and shaped peoples and cultures in societies far from their origin. Thus, even though each of the classical societies adopted outside traditions selectively, for most of the classical period cultural borrowing was more widespread than it had been in the period of the early complex societies.

Accelerated interaction also carried the seeds of disintegration because disease pathogens travelled the trade routes alongside people, goods, and ideas. In the second and third centuries C.E., epidemic diseases afflicted most societies along the silk roads, disrupting long-distance trade and creating severe social unrest. As a result, many societies turned inward and sacrificed long-distance connections for local and regional concerns.

Over the centuries since the height of their influence, many of the specific political, social, economic, and cultural features of the classical societies have disappeared. Yet their legacies deeply influenced future societies and in many ways continue to influence the lives of the world's peoples. Appreciation of the legacies of classical societies is thus crucial to understanding the world's historical development.

The Empires of Persia

5

he Greek historian Herodotus relished a good story, and he related many a tale about the Persian empire and its conflicts with other peoples, including Greeks. One story had to do with a struggle between Cyrus, leader of the expanding Persian realm, and Croesus, ruler of the powerful and wealthy kingdom of Lydia in southwestern Anatolia (modern Turkey). Croesus noted the growth of Persian influence with concern and asked the Greek oracle at Delphi whether to go to war against Cyrus. The oracle responded that an attack on Cyrus would destroy a great kingdom.

Overjoyed, Croesus lined up his allies and prepared for war. In 546 B.C.E. he provoked Cyrus to engage the formidable Lydian cavalry. The resulting battle was hard fought but inconclusive. Because winter was approaching, Croesus disbanded his troops and returned to his capital at Sardis, expecting Cyrus to retreat as well. But Cyrus was a vigorous and unpredictable warrior, and he pursued Croesus to Sardis. When he learned of the pursuit, Croesus hastily assembled an army to confront the invaders. Cyrus threw it into disarray, however, by advancing a group of warriors mounted on camels, which spooked the Lydian horses and sent them into headlong flight. Cyrus's army then surrounded Sardis and took the city after a siege of only two weeks. Croesus was taken captive and afterward became an advisor to Cyrus. Herodotus could not resist pointing out that events proved the Delphic oracle right: Croesus's attack on Cyrus did indeed lead to the destruction of a great kingdom—his own.

The victory over Lydia was a major turning point in the development of the Persian empire. Lydia had a reputation as a kingdom of fabulous wealth, partly because it conducted maritime trade with Greece, Egypt, and Phoenicia as well as overland trade with Mesopotamia and Persia. Lydian wealth and resources gave Cyrus tremendous momentum as he extended Persian authority to new lands and built the earliest of the vast imperial states of classical times.

Classical Persian society began to take shape during the sixth century B.C.E. when warriors conquered an enormous region from the Indus River to Egypt and southeastern Europe. Indeed, the very size of the Persian empire created political and administrative problems for its rulers. Once they solved those problems, however, a series of Persian-based empires governed much of the territory between India and the Mediterranean Sea for more than a millennium—from the mid–sixth century B.C.E. until the early seventh century C.E.—and brought centralized political organization to many distinct peoples living over vast geographic spaces.

❮ Gold plaque depicting a figure who was perhaps a priest in Achaemenid times.

Cyrus (SIGH-ruhs)
Croesus (CREE-suhs)

CHRONOLOGY

7th–6th centuries B.C.E. (?)	Life of Zarathustra
558–330 B.C.E.	Achaemenid dynasty
558–530 B.C.E.	Reign of Cyrus the Achaemenid
521–486 B.C.E.	Reign of Darius
334–330 B.C.E.	Invasion and conquest of the Achaemenid empire by Alexander of Macedon
323–83 B.C.E.	Seleucid dynasty
247 B.C.E–224 C.E.	Parthian dynasty
224–651 C.E.	Sasanid dynasty

In organizing their realm, Persian rulers relied heavily on Mesopotamian techniques of administration, but they also created institutions and administrative procedures of their own. In addition, they invested resources in the construction of roads and highways to improve communications and mobility across the empire. As a result of those efforts, central administrators were able to send instructions throughout the empire, dispatch armies in times of turmoil, and ensure that local officials would carry out imperial policies.

The organization of the vast territories embraced by the classical Persian empires had important social, economic, and cultural implications. Because high agricultural productivity allowed more people to work at tasks other than cultivation, classes of bureaucrats, administrators, priests, craftsmen, and merchants increased in number. Meanwhile, social extremes between the wealthy and the poor became more pronounced. In addition, good roads across the empire allowed Persian society to serve as a commercial and cultural bridge between Indian and Mediterranean societies. As a result, Persia became an important link in long-distance trade networks as well as a conduit for the exchange of philosophical and religious ideas. Indeed, Persian religious traditions inspired religious thinkers subject to Persian rule and deeply influenced Judaism, Christianity, and Islam.

The Rise and Fall of the Persian Empires

The empires of Persia arose in the arid land of Iran. For centuries Iran had developed under the shadow of the wealthier and more productive Mesopotamia to the west while absorbing migrations and invasions of nomadic peoples coming out of central Asia. During the sixth century B.C.E., rulers of the province of Persia in southwestern Iran embarked on a series of conquests that resulted in the formation of an enormous empire. For more than a millennium, four ruling dynasties—the Achaemenids (558–330 B.C.E.), the Seleucids (323–83 B.C.E.), the Parthians (247 B.C.E.–224 C.E.), and the Sasanids (224–651 C.E.)—maintained a continuous tradition of imperial rule in much of southwest Asia.

The Achaemenid Empire

Achaemenid and Seleucid empires
www.mhhe.com/bentleybrief2e

THE MEDES AND THE PERSIANS The origins of classical Persian society trace back to the late stages of Mesopotamian society. During the centuries before 1000 B.C.E., two closely related Indo-European peoples known as the Medes and the Persians migrated from central Asia to Persia, where they lived in loose subjection to the Babylonian and Assyrian empires. The Medes and the Persians shared many cultural traits with their distant cousins the Aryans, who had migrated into India. Like the Aryans, they were mostly pastoralists, although they also practiced a limited amount of agriculture. They also possessed considerable military power: like other Indo-Europeans, they were skilled equestrians and expert archers. They also organized themselves by clans rather than by states, although they did recognize leaders who collected taxes and delivered tribute to their Mesopotamian overlords.

CYRUS'S CONQUESTS When the Assyrian and Babylonian empires weakened in the sixth century B.C.E., the Medes and the Persians launched their first bid for empire in the person of Cyrus the

Achaemenid (ah-KEE-muh-nid)
Medes (meeds)

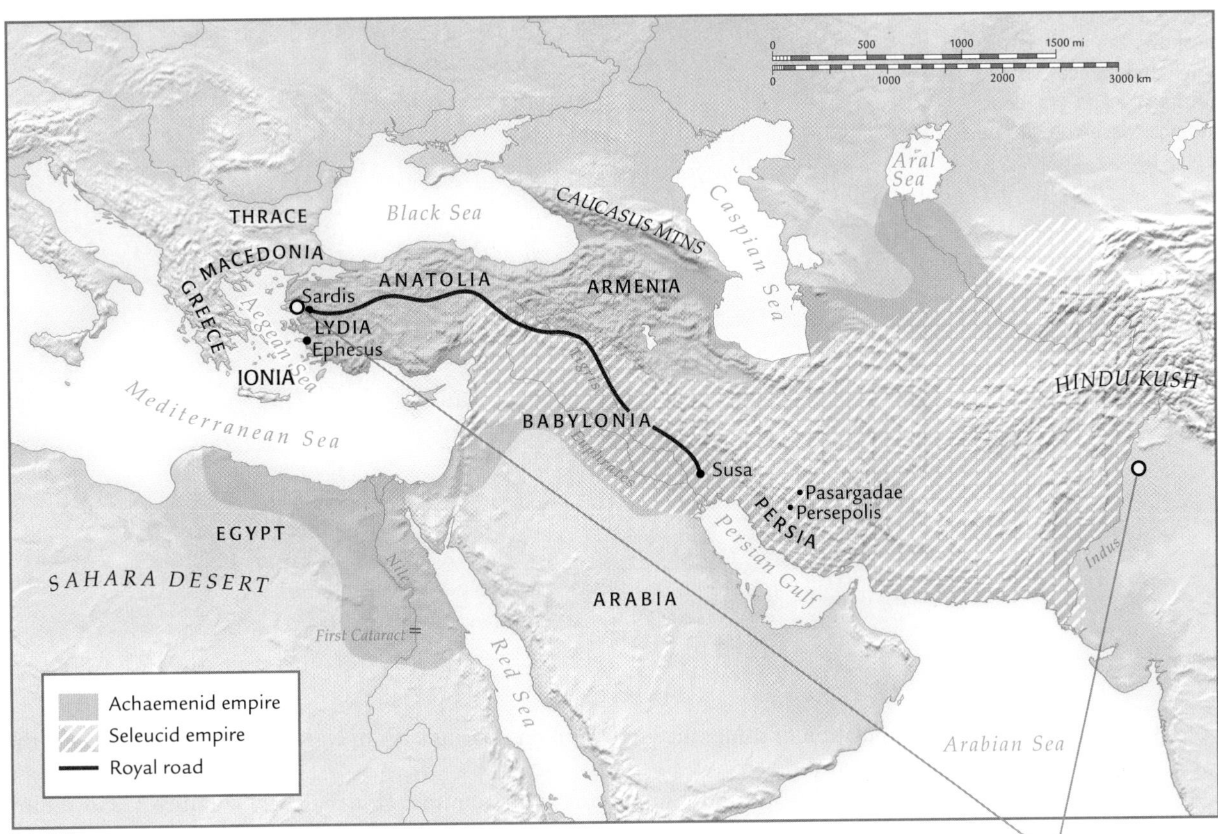

MAP 5.1 | The Achaemenid and Seleucid empires, 558–83 B.C.E. Compare the size of the Achaemenid empire to the earlier Mesopotamian and Egyptian empires discussed in chapters 1 and 2. ***What role did the Royal Road and other highways play in the maintenance of the Achaemenid empire?***

Darius's empire stretched 3,000 km from East to West.

Achaemenid (reigned 558–530 B.C.E.). Cyrus proved to be a tough, wily leader and an outstanding military strategist, whose conquests laid the foundation for the first Persian empire. In 558 B.C.E. Cyrus became king of the Persian tribes, which he ruled from his mountain fortress at Pasargadae. In 553 B.C.E. he initiated a rebellion against his Median overlord, whom he crushed within three years. By 548 B.C.E. he had brought all of Iran under his control, and he began to look for opportunities to expand. In 546 B.C.E., as we know, he conquered the powerful kingdom of Lydia in Anatolia. Between 545 B.C.E. and 539 B.C.E. he campaigned in central Asia and Bactria (modern Afghanistan). In a swift campaign of 539 B.C.E., he seized Babylonia, whose vassal states immediately recognized him as their lord. Within twenty years Cyrus went from minor regional king to ruler of an empire that stretched from India to the borders of Egypt. Had he lived long enough, Cyrus no doubt would have mounted a campaign against Egypt, the largest and wealthiest neighboring state outside his control. But in 530 B.C.E. he fell, mortally wounded, while protecting his northeastern frontier from nomadic raiders.

DARIUS Cyrus's empire survived and expanded during the reigns of his successors. His son Cambyses (reigned 530–522 B.C.E.) conquered Egypt in 525 B.C.E. His younger kinsman Darius (reigned 521–486 B.C.E.) then extended the empire both east and west. Indeed, Darius's armies pushed into northwestern India as far as the Indus River, absorbing the northern Indian kingdom of Gandhara, while also capturing Thrace, Macedonia, and the western coast of the Black Sea in southeastern Europe. By the late sixth century B.C.E., Darius presided over an empire stretching some 3,000 kilometers (1,865 miles) from the Indus River in the east to the Aegean Sea in the west and 1,500 kilometers (933 miles) from Armenia in the north to the first cataract of the Nile River in the south. With

Pasargadae (pah-SAR-gah-dee)

Ruins of Persepolis. This image shows the imperial reception hall and palaces. Try to imagine the size and grandeur of the buildings these columns supported.

a population of some thirty-five million, Darius's realm was by far the largest empire the world had yet seen.

Yet Darius was more important as an administrator than as a conqueror. Governing a far-flung empire of so many ethnic groups, languages, and traditions was a much more difficult challenge than conquering it. To maintain their empire, the Achaemenids needed to establish lines of communication with all parts of their realm and design institutions that would enable them to administer their territories efficiently. Their solutions not only made it possible for the Achaemenid empire to survive but also pioneered administrative techniques that would outlast their own dynasty and influence political life in southwestern Asia for centuries to come.

PSI img The palace at Persepolis www.mhhe.com/bentleybrief2e

PERSEPOLIS Soon after his rise to power, Darius began to centralize his administration. About 520 B.C.E. he started to build a new capital of astonishing magnificence at Persepolis. Darius intended Persepolis to serve not only as an administrative center but also as a monument to the Achaemenid dynasty. From the time of Darius to the end of the Achaemenid dynasty in 330 B.C.E., Persepolis served as the nerve center of the Persian empire—a resplendent capital bustling with advisors, ministers, diplomats, scribes, accountants, translators, and bureaucratic officers of all descriptions. Even today, massive columns and other ruins bespeak the grandeur of Darius's capital.

ACHAEMENID ADMINISTRATION: THE SATRAPIES The government of the Achaemenid empire depended on a finely tuned balance between central initiative and local administration. Like their Mesopotamian predecessors, the Achaemenids appointed governors to serve as agents of the central administration and oversee affairs in the various regions. Darius divided his realm into twenty-three administrative and taxation districts he called satrapies, with each governed by an official satrap. Yet the Achaemenids did not try to push direct rule on their subjects: although most satraps were Persian, the Achaemenids recruited local officials to fill almost all other administrative posts.

Cambyses (kam-BIE-sees)
Aegean (ih-GEE-an)
Persepolis (per-SEP-uh-lis)

The Achaemenid rulers employed two strategies to discourage distant satraps from allying with local groups or trying to become independent of Achaemenid authority. First, each satrapy had a contingent of military officers and tax collectors who served as checks on the satraps' power and independence. Second, the rulers created a new category of officials—essentially imperial spies—known as "the eyes and ears of the king." These agents traveled throughout the empire with their own military forces, conducting surprise audits of accounts and procedures in the provinces and collecting intelligence reports. Taken together, these two strategies helped prevent the vast Achaemenid empire from splitting into a series of independent kingdoms.

TAXATION AND LAW Darius also sought to improve administrative efficiency by regularizing tax levies and standardizing laws. Instead of exacting irregular tribute payments from subject lands as his predecessors had done, Darius instituted regular, formal tax levies. Each satrapy was now required to pay a set quantity of silver to the imperial court every year. To simplify the process, Darius issued standardized coins—a move that also fostered trade throughout his empire. Equally important, beginning in 520 B.C.E., Darius also sought to bring the many legal systems of his empire closer to a single standard. The point was not to abolish the existing laws of individual lands or peoples to impose a uniform law code on his entire empire. Rather, Darius wished to codify the laws of his subject peoples, modifying them when necessary to harmonize them with the legal principles observed in the empire as a whole.

ROADS AND COMMUNICATIONS Alongside administrative and legal policies, the Achaemenid rulers took other measures to knit their far-flung realm into a coherent whole. They built good roads across their realm, notably the Persian Royal Road, which stretched some 2,575 kilometers (1,600 miles) from the Aegean port of Ephesus to Sardis in Anatolia, through Mesopotamia along the Tigris River, to Susa in Iran, with an extension to Pasargadae and Persepolis. Caravans took some ninety days to travel this road, lodging at inns along the well-policed route.

The imperial government also organized a courier service and built 111 postal stations at intervals of 40 to 50 kilometers (25 to 30 miles) along the Royal Road. Each station kept a supply of fresh horses, enabling couriers to speed from one end of the Royal Road to the other in a week's time. The Achaemenids also improved existing routes between Mesopotamia and Egypt, and they built a new road between Persia and the Indus River to link the imperial center with the satrapy of Gandhara in northwestern India. In addition to improving communications, these roads facilitated trade, which helped to integrate the empire's various regions into a larger economy.

Decline and Fall of the Achaemenid Empire

THE ACHAEMENID COMMONWEALTH The Achaemenids' roads and administrative machinery enabled them to govern a vast empire and extend Persian influences throughout their territories. Persian concepts of law and justice administered by trained imperial officials linked peoples from the Mediterranean Sea to the Indus River in a larger Persian society. Political stability made it possible to undertake enormous public works projects such as the construction of *qanat* (underground canals), which led to enhanced agricultural production and population growth. Iron metallurgy spread to all parts of the empire, and by the end of the Achaemenid dynasty, iron tools were common in Persian agricultural communities. Peoples in the various regions of the Achaemenid empire maintained their ethnic identities, but all participated in a larger Persian commonwealth.

Eventually, however, difficulties between rulers and subject peoples undermined the integrity of the empire. Cyrus and Darius both consciously pursued a policy of toleration

satraps (SAY-traps)
qanat (kah-NAHT)

Stone Carving from Persepolis. | This carving shows an enthroned Darius (with his son Xerxes standing behind him) receiving a high court official, as incense burners perfume the air. ***What purpose might the formality of this reception have served?***

in administering their vast multicultural empire: they took great care to respect the values and cultural traditions of the peoples they ruled. In Mesopotamia, for example, they portrayed themselves not as Persian conquerors but, rather, as legitimate Babylonian rulers and representatives of Marduk, the patron deity of Babylon. Cyrus also won high praise from Jews in the Achaemenid empire, since he allowed them to return to Jerusalem and rebuild the temple that Babylonian conquerors had destroyed in 586 B.C.E.

PSI img Darius enthroned with Xerxes behind him www.mhhe.com/bentleybrief2e

Darius's successor, Xerxes (reigned 486–465 B.C.E.), retreated from this policy of toleration, however, flaunted his Persian identity, and sought to impose his own values on conquered lands. That policy caused enormous ill will, especially in Mesopotamia and Egypt, where peoples with their own cultural traditions resented Xerxes' pretensions. Although Xerxes successfully repressed rebellions against his rule in Mesopotamia and Egypt, resentment of Persian conquerors continued to fester, and it caused serious problems for the later Achaemenids.

THE PERSIAN WARS In fact, efforts to control their ethnic Greek subjects helped to bring about the collapse of the Achaemenid empire. Ethnic Greeks inhabited many of the cities in Anatolia—particularly in the region of Ionia on the Aegean coast of western Anatolia—and they maintained close economic and commercial ties with their cousins in the peninsula of Greece. The Ionian Greeks fell under Persian domination during the reign of Cyrus. They became restive under Darius's Persian governors who oversaw their affairs, and in 500 B.C.E. the Ionian cities rebelled, expelled or executed their governors, and asserted their independence. Their rebellion launched a series of conflicts known as the Persian Wars (500–479 B.C.E.).

The conflict between the Ionian Greeks and the Persians expanded considerably when the cities of peninsular Greece sent fleets to aid their kinsmen in Ionia. Darius managed to put down the rebellion and reassert Achaemenid authority, but he and his successors became entangled in a difficult and ultimately destructive effort to extend their authority to the Greek peninsula. Indeed, after some initial successes against the Greeks, the Persians suffered a rout at the battle of Marathon (490 B.C.E.), and they returned home without achieving their goals. Ten years later, in 480 B.C.E., a renewed Persian attempt to conquer the Greek cities ended in costly defeats for the Persians. Thereafter, for almost 150 years the Persian empire continued to spar intermittently with the Greek cities without achieving victory.

ALEXANDER OF MACEDON The standoff ended with the rise of Alexander of Macedon, often called Alexander the Great (discussed more fully in chapter 8). In 334 B.C.E. Alexander invaded Persia with an army of some forty-eight thousand tough, battle-hardened Macedonians. Though far smaller than the Persian army in numbers, the well-disciplined Macedonians carried heavier arms and employed more sophisticated military tactics than their opponents. As a result, they sliced through the Persian empire and dealt their adversaries a series of devastating defeats. In 331 B.C.E. Alexander shattered Achaemenid forces at the battle of Gaugamela, and within a year the empire founded by Cyrus had dissolved.

Alexander led his forces into Persepolis and proclaimed himself heir to the Achaemenid rulers. After a brief season of celebration, Alexander and his forces ignited a blaze—perhaps intentionally—that destroyed Persepolis. The conflagration was so great that when archaeologists first began to explore the ruins of Persepolis in the eighteenth century, they found layers of ash and charcoal up to 1 meter (3 feet) deep.

The Achaemenid empire had crumbled, but its legacy was by no means exhausted. Alexander portrayed himself in Persia and Egypt as a legitimate successor of the Achaemenids who observed their precedents and deserved their honors. He retained the Achaemenid administrative structure, and he even confirmed the appointments of many satraps and other officials. As it happened, Alexander had little time to enjoy his conquests, because he died in 323 B.C.E. after a brief effort to extend his empire to India. But the states that succeeded him—the Seleucid, Parthian, and Sasanid empires—continued to employ a basically Achaemenid structure of imperial administration.

ALEXANDER OF MACEDON. Tetradrachm of Kingdom of Thrace with head of deified Alexander the Great, struck under Lysimachos. *Photograph © 2010 Museum of Fine Arts, Boston.*

The Seleucid, Parthian, and Sasanid Empires

THE SELEUCIDS After Alexander died, his chief generals carved his empire into three large realms, which they divided among themselves. The choicest realm, which included most of the former Achaemenid empire, went to Seleucus (reigned 305–281 B.C.E.), who had commanded an elite corps of guards in Alexander's army. Like Alexander, Seleucus and his successors retained the Achaemenid systems of administration and taxation as well as the imperial roads and postal service. The Seleucids also founded new cities throughout the realm and attracted Greek colonists to occupy them. These new cities greatly stimulated trade and economic development both within the Seleucid empire and beyond.

As foreigners, the Seleucids faced opposition from native Persians. Satraps often revolted against Seleucid rule and tried to establish their independence. The Seleucids soon lost their holdings in northern India, and the seminomadic Parthians progressively took over Iran during the third century B.C.E. The Seleucids continued to rule a truncated empire until 83 B.C.E., when Roman conquerors put an end to their empire.

THE PARTHIANS Meanwhile, the Parthians established themselves as lords of a powerful empire based in Iran that they extended to Mesopotamia. The Parthians had occupied the region of eastern Iran around Khurasan since Achaemenid times. They retained many of the customs and traditions of nomadic peoples from the steppes of central Asia. They did not have a centralized government, for example, but organized themselves into a federation of clans. They were also skillful warriors, accustomed to defending themselves against constant threats from nomadic peoples farther east.

As they settled and turned increasingly to agriculture, the Parthians discovered that they could resist nomadic invasions better by feeding their horses on alfalfa during the winter. The alfalfa allowed the animals to grow much larger and stronger than the small horses and ponies of nomadic peoples who had to forage on the steppes in winter. The larger Parthian horses could then support heavily armed warriors outfitted with metal armor, which served as an effective shield against the arrows

THINKING ABOUT *Traditions*

TRADITIONS IN THE EMPIRES OF PERSIA. One of the problems of the Achaemenids, Seleucids, Parthians, and Sasanids was that some of the peoples each empire conquered strongly resented what they viewed as rule by foreigners. At times, such resentment contributed to the toppling of one empire for another. How did the Persian-based empires try to balance the imposition of their rule from above with the cultural and ethnic identities of the people they conquered, and why did this balance sometimes fail?

Macedon (MAS-ih-don)
Gaugamela (GAW-guh-mee-luh)
Seleucids (sih-LOO-sihds)

PARTHIAN SCULPTURE. Gold sculpture of a nomadic horseman discharging an arrow. This figurine dates from the fifth or fourth century B.C.E. and might well represent a Parthian.

A coin with Mithradates I
www.mhhe.com/
bentleybrief2e

of the steppe nomads. Indeed, few existing forces could stand up to Parthian heavy cavalry.

As early as the third century B.C.E., the Parthians began to wrest their independence from the Seleucids. The Parthian satrap revolted against his Seleucid overlord in 238 B.C.E., and during the following decades his successors gradually enlarged their holdings. Mithradates I, the Parthians' greatest conqueror, came to the throne about 171 B.C.E. and transformed his state into a mighty empire. By about 155 B.C.E. he had consolidated his hold on Iran and had also extended Parthian rule to Mesopotamia.

PARTHIAN GOVERNMENT The Parthians portrayed themselves as enemies of the foreign Seleucids and as restorers of rule in the Persian tradition. To some extent that characterization was accurate. The Parthians largely followed the example of the Achaemenids in structuring their empire: they governed through satraps, employed Achaemenid techniques of administration and taxation, and built a lavish capital city. But the Parthians also retained elements of their own steppe traditions. For example, they did not develop nearly as centralized a regime as the Achaemenids or the Seleucids but, rather, vested a great deal of authority and responsibility in their clan leaders. These men—who frequently served as satraps—could be troublesome, because they frequently rebelled against the imperial government from their regional bases.

For about three centuries the Parthians presided over a powerful empire between India and the Mediterranean. Beginning in the first century C.E., they faced pressure in the west from the expanding Roman empire. On three occasions in the second century C.E., Roman armies captured the Parthian capital at Ctesiphon. Combined with internal difficulties caused by rebellious satraps, Roman pressure contributed to the weakening of the Parthian state. During the early third century C.E., internal rebellion brought it down.

THE SASANIDS Once again, though, the tradition of imperial rule continued, this time under the Sasanids, who came from Persia and claimed direct descent from the Achaemenids. The Sasanids toppled the Parthians in 224 C.E. and ruled until 651 C.E., re-creating much of the splendor of the Achaemenid empire. From their cosmopolitan capital at Ctesiphon, the Sasanid "king of kings" provided strong rule from Parthia to Mesopotamia. Sasanid merchants traded actively with peoples to both the east and the west, and they introduced into Iran the cultivation of crops such as rice, sugarcane, citrus fruits, eggplant, and cotton that came west over the trade routes from India and China.

During the reign of Shapur I (239–272 C.E.), the Sasanids stabilized their western frontier and created a series of buffer states between themselves and the Roman empire. After Shapur, the Sasanids did not expand militarily but entered into a standoff relationship with the Kushan empire in the east and the Roman and Byzantine empires in the west. None of those large empires was strong enough to overcome the others, but they contested border areas and buffer states, sometimes engaging in lengthy and bitter disputes that sapped the energies of all involved.

These continual conflicts seriously weakened the Sasanid empire in particular. The empire came to an end in 651 C.E. when Arab warriors killed the last Sasanid ruler, overran his realm, and incorporated it into their rapidly expanding Islamic empire. Yet even conquest by external invaders did not end the legacy of classical Persia, since Arab conquerors adopted Persian administrative techniques and cultural traditions for their own use in building a new Islamic society.

Mithradates (mihth-rah-DAY-teez)
Ctesiphon (TES-uh-phon)
Sasanids (suh-SAH-nids)

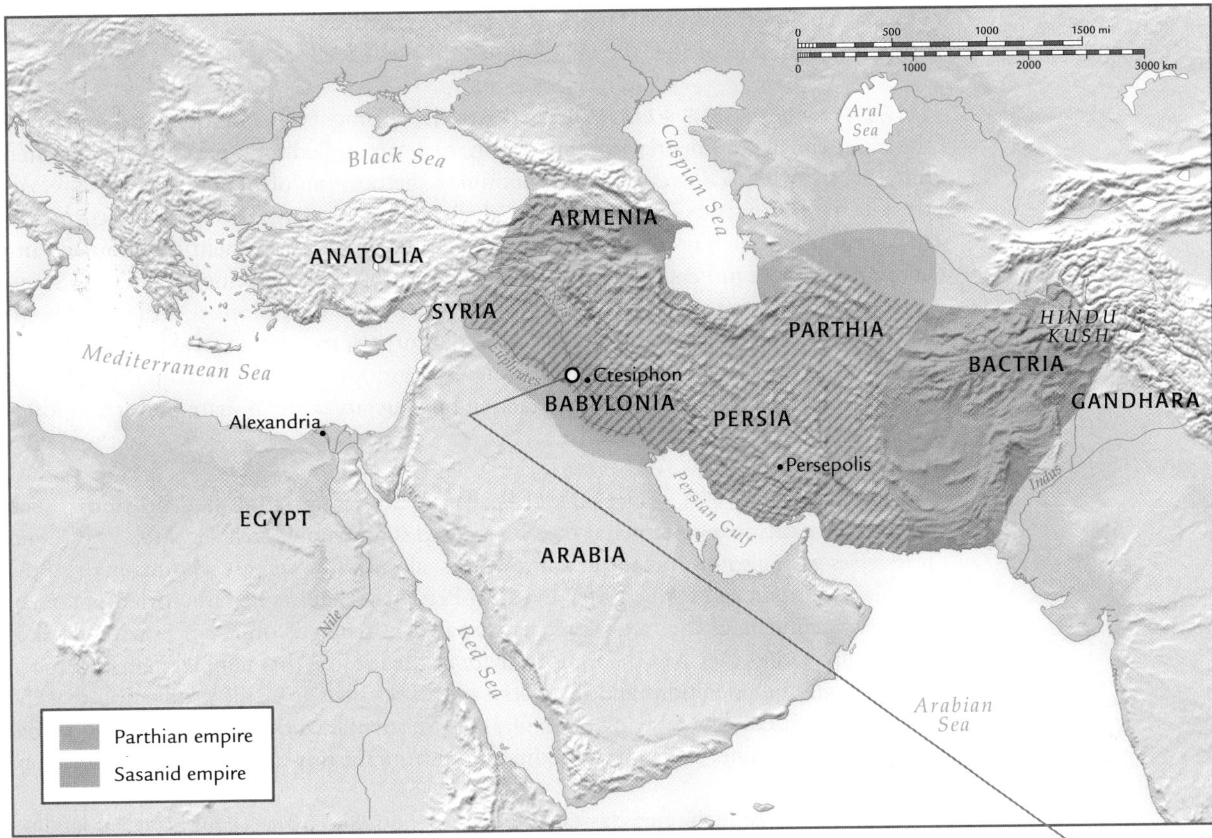

MAP 5.2 | The Parthian and Sasanid empires, 247 B.C.E.–651 C.E. Note the location of the Parthian and Sasanid empires between the Mediterranean Sea and northern India. ***What roles did these two empires play in facilitating or hindering communications between lands to their east and west?***

Ctesiphon was the capital of both the Parthian and Sasanid empires.

Imperial Society and Economy

Throughout the eastern hemisphere during the classical era, public life and social structure became much more complicated than they had been during the days of the early complex societies. Centralized imperial governments needed large numbers of administrative officials, which led to the emergence of educated classes of bureaucrats. Stable empires also enabled many individuals to engage in trade or other specialized labor. Some of these individuals accumulated vast wealth, which led to increased distance and tensions between rich and poor. Meanwhile, slavery became more common than in earlier times. The prominence of slavery had to do partly with the expansion of imperial states, which often enslaved conquered foes, but it also reflected the increasing gulf between rich and poor, which placed such great economic pressure on some individuals that they had to give up their freedom in order to survive. All these developments had implications for the social structures of classical societies in Persia as well as China, India, and the Mediterranean basin.

Social Development in Classical Persia

During the early days of the Achaemenid empire, Persian society reflected its nomadic steppe origins. When the Medes and the Persians migrated to Iran, their social structure was very similar to that of the Aryans in India, consisting primarily of warriors, priests, and peasants. Family and clan relationships were extremely important in the organization of Persian political and social affairs. Male warriors headed the clans, which retained much of their influence long after the establishment of the Achaemenid empire.

IMPERIAL BUREAUCRATS The development of a cosmopolitan empire and the requirements of imperial administration, however, called for a new class of educated bureaucrats, who to a large extent undermined the position of the old warrior elite. Although the bureaucrats did not directly challenge the patriarchal warriors, their crucial role in running the day-to-day affairs of the empire guaranteed them a prominent and comfortable place in Persian society. By the time of the later Achaemenids and the Seleucids, Persian cities were home to masses of administrators, tax collectors, and record keepers. The bureaucracy even included a substantial corps of translators, who facilitated communications among the empire's many linguistic groups. Imperial survival depended on these literate professionals, and high-ranking bureaucrats came to share power and influence with warriors and clan leaders.

FREE CLASSES The bulk of Persian society consisted of free individuals such as artisans, craftspeople, farmers, merchants, and low-ranking civil servants. Priests and priestesses were also prominent urban residents, along with servants who maintained the temple communities in which they lived. In Persian society, as in earlier Mesopotamian societies, members of the free classes participated in religious observances conducted at local temples, and they had the right to share in the income that temples generated from their agricultural operations and from craft industries such as textile production that the temples organized. The weaving of textiles was mostly the work of women, who received rations of grain, wine, beer, and sometimes meat from the imperial and temple workshops that employed them.

In the countryside the free classes included peasants who owned land as well as landless cultivators who worked on properties owned by the state, temple communities, or other individuals. Free residents of rural areas had the right to marry and move as they wished, and they could seek better opportunities in the cities or in military service. The Persian empires embraced a great deal of parched land that received little rainfall, and free residents of the countryside contributed much of the labor that went into the building and maintenance of irrigation systems. Most remarkable of those systems were underground canals known as *qanat,* which allowed cultivators to distribute water to fields without losing large quantities to evaporation through exposure to the sun and open air. Numerous *qanat* crisscrossed the Iranian plateau in the heartland of the Persian empire, where extreme scarcity of water justified the enormous investment of human labor required to build the canals.

SLAVES A large class of slaves also worked in both the cities and the countryside. Individuals passed into slavery by two main routes. Most were prisoners of war who became slaves as the price of survival. Other slaves came from the ranks of free subjects who accumulated debts that they could not satisfy. In the cities, for example, merchants, artisans, and craftsmen borrowed funds to purchase goods or open shops, while in the countryside small farmers facing competition from large-scale cultivators borrowed against their property and liberty to purchase tools, seed, or food. Failure to repay those debts in a timely fashion often forced the borrowers not only to forfeit their property but also to sell their children, their spouses, or themselves into slavery.

Economic Foundations of Classical Persia

Agriculture was the economic foundation of classical Persian society. Like other classical societies, Persia needed large agricultural surpluses to support military forces and administrative specialists as well as residents of cities who were artisans, crafts workers, and merchants rather than cultivators. The Persian empires embraced several regions of exceptional fertility—notably Mesopotamia, Egypt, Anatolia, and northern India—and they prospered by mobilizing the agricultural surpluses of those lands.

Staircase from Persepolis. | In this sculpture from Persepolis, Persian nobles dressed in fine cloaks and hats ascend the staircase leading to the imperial reception hall. ***What kinds of feelings might these sculptures have elicited from visitors to the reception hall?***

AGRICULTURAL PRODUCTION Barley and wheat were the grains cultivated most commonly in the Persian empires. Peas, lentils, mustard, garlic, onions, cucumbers, dates, apples, pomegranates, pears, and apricots supplemented the cereals in diets throughout Persian society, and beer and wine were the most common beverages. In most years agricultural production far exceeded the needs of cultivators, making sizable surpluses available for sale in the cities or for distribution to state servants through the imperial bureaucracy. Vast quantities of produce flowed into the imperial court from state-owned lands. Even though they are incomplete, surviving records show that in 500 B.C.E., during the middle period of Darius's reign, the imperial court received almost eight hundred thousand liters of grain, quite apart from vegetables, fruits, meat, poultry, fish, oil, beer, wine, and textiles. Officials distributed some of this produce to the imperial staff as wages in kind, but much of it also found its way into the enormous banquets that Darius organized for as many as ten thousand guests.

TRADE Agriculture was the foundation of the Persian economy, but long-distance trade grew rapidly during the course of the Persian empires and linked lands from India to Egypt in a vast commercial zone. Each region of the Persian empire contributed particular products to the imperial economy, from the gold and ivory of India to the semiprecious stones of Iran, and from the metals of Anatolia to the textiles and grain of Egypt. Several conditions promoted the growth of trade: the relative political stability maintained by the Persian empires, the general prosperity of the realm, the use of standardized coins, and the availability of good trade routes, including long-established routes, newly constructed highways such as the Persian Royal Road, and sea routes through the Red Sea, the Persian Gulf, and the Arabian Sea. Markets operated regularly in all the larger cities of the Persian empires, and the largest cities, such as Babylon, also were home to banks and companies that invested in commercial ventures.

Long-distance trade of this sort became especially prominent during the reigns of Alexander of Macedon and his Seleucid successors. The cities they established and the colonists they attracted stimulated trade throughout the whole region from the Mediterranean to northern India. Indeed, Greek migrants facilitated cultural as well as commercial exchanges by encouraging the mixing and mingling of religious faiths, art styles, and philosophical speculation throughout the Persian realm.

THINKING ABOUT *Encounters*

ENCOUNTERS IN THE EMPIRES OF PERSIA. Between the mid–sixth century B.C.E. and the early seventh century C.E., Persian-based empires ruled a variety of diverse peoples and territories between India and the Mediterranean Sea. What effects did these empires have on the movement of people and goods across their territories, and how did such movement alter or modify the ways people thought about themselves and others?

Religions of Salvation in Classical Persian Society

Cross-cultural influences were especially noticeable in the development of Persian religion. Persians came from the family of peoples who spoke Indo-European languages, and their earliest religion closely resembled that of the Aryans of India. During the classical era, however, the new faith of Zoroastrianism emerged and became widely popular in Iran and to a lesser extent also in the larger Persian empires. Zoroastrianism reflected the cosmopolitan society of the empires, and it profoundly influenced the beliefs and values of Judaism, Christianity, and Islam.

Zarathustra and His Faith

The earliest Persian religion recognized many of the same gods as the ancient Aryans, and their priests performed sacrifices similar to those conducted by the brahmins in India. Like the Aryans, the ancient Persians glorified strength and martial virtues, and the cults of both peoples sought principally to bring about a comfortable material existence for their practitioners.

ZARATHUSTRA During the classical era Persian religion underwent considerable change, as moral and religious thinkers sought to adapt their messages to the circumstances of a complex, cosmopolitan society. One result was Zoroastrianism, which emerged from the teachings of Zarathustra. Though Zarathustra was undoubtedly a historical person, little certain information survives about his life and career. It is not even clear when he lived, though most scholars date his life to the late seventh and early sixth centuries B.C.E. He came from an aristocratic family, and he probably was a priest who became disenchanted with the traditional religion. In any case, when he was about twenty years old, Zarathustra left his family and home in search of wisdom. After about ten years of travel, he experienced a series of visions and became convinced that the supreme god, whom he called Ahura Mazda (the "wise lord"), had chosen him to serve as his prophet and spread his message.

THE GATHAS Like his life, Zarathustra's doctrine remains largely unknown, since many of the earliest Zoroastrian teachings were not preserved in writing. Only during the Seleucid dynasty did Zoroastrian priests, known as *magi,* begin to preserve religious texts in writing, and only under the Sasanids did they compile their scriptures in a holy book known as the *Avesta.* Nevertheless, many of Zarathustra's own compositions survive because of the diligence by which magi preserved them through oral transmission. Known as the *Gathas,* Zarathustra's works were hymns that he composed in honor of the various deities that he recognized. Apart from the *Gathas,* ancient Zoroastrian literature included a wide variety of hymns, liturgical works, and treatises on moral and theological themes. Though some of these works survive, the arrival of Islam in the seventh century C.E. and the subsequent decline of Zoroastrianism resulted in the loss of most of the Avesta and later Zoroastrian works.

ZOROASTRIAN TEACHINGS Zarathustra and his followers were not strict monotheists. They recognized Ahura Mazda as a supreme deity and the creator of all good things, but Zarathustra also praised six lesser deities in the *Gathas.* Furthermore, he believed that Ahura Mazda engaged in a cosmic conflict with an independent adversary, an evil and malign spirit known as Angra Mainyu (the "destructive spirit" or "hostile spirit"). Following a struggle of some twelve thousand years, Zarathustra believed, Ahura Mazda and the forces of good would ultimately prevail, and Angra Mainyu and the principle of evil would disappear forever. At that time individual human souls would undergo judgment and would experience the rewards or punishments they deserved.

Zoroastrianism (zohr-oh-ASS-tree-ahn-iz'm)
Zarathustra (zar-uh-THOO-struh)
Gathas (GATH-uhs)

Zarathustra did not call for ascetic renunciation of the world in favor of a future heavenly existence. On the contrary, he considered the material world a blessing that reflected the benevolent nature of Ahura Mazda. His moral teachings allowed human beings to enjoy the world and its fruits—including wealth, sexual pleasure, and social prestige—as long as they did so in moderation and behaved honestly toward others. Zoroastrians have often summarized their moral teachings in the simple formula "good words, good thoughts, good deeds."

ZOROASTRIAN DIVINE IMAGE. | A gold clasp or button of the fifth century B.C.E. with the symbol of Ahura Mazda as a winged god.

POPULARITY OF ZOROASTRIANISM Zarathustra's teachings began to attract large numbers of followers during the sixth century B.C.E., particularly among Persian aristocrats and ruling elites. Wealthy patrons donated land and established endowments for the support of Zoroastrian temples. The Achaemenid era saw the emergence of a sizable priesthood, whose members conducted religious rituals, maintained a calendar, taught Zoroastrian values, and preserved Zoroastrian doctrine through oral transmission.

Beginning with Darius, the Achaemenid emperors closely associated themselves with Ahura Mazda and claimed divine sanction for their rule. Darius ordered stone inscriptions celebrating his achievements, and in those monuments he clearly revealed his devotion to Ahura Mazda and his opposition to the principle of evil. In one of his inscriptions, Darius praised Ahura Mazda as the great god who created the earth, the sky, and humanity and who moreover elevated Darius himself to the imperial honor. With the aid of imperial sponsorship, Zoroastrian temples cropped up throughout the Achaemenid realm. The faith was most popular in Iran, but it attracted sizable followings also in Mesopotamia, Anatolia, Egypt, and other parts of the Achaemenid empire even though there was no organized effort to spread it beyond its original homeland.

Shapur I with Ahura Mazda
www.mhhe.com/
bentleybrief2e

Religions of Salvation in a Cosmopolitan Society

The arrival of Alexander of Macedon inaugurated a difficult era for the Zoroastrian community. During his Persian campaign, Alexander's forces burned many temples and killed numerous magi. Because at that time the magi still transmitted Zoroastrian doctrines orally, an untold number of hymns and holy verses disappeared. The Zoroastrian faith survived, however, and the Parthians cultivated it to rally support against the Seleucids.

OFFICIALLY SPONSORED ZOROASTRIANISM During the Sasanid dynasty, however, Zoroastrianism experienced a revival. As self-proclaimed heirs to the Achaemenids, the Sasanids identified closely with Zoroastrianism and supported it zealously. Indeed, the Sasanids often persecuted other faiths if they seemed likely to become popular enough to challenge the supremacy of Zoroastrianism.

With generous imperial backing, the Zoroastrian faith and the magi flourished as never before. Theologians prepared written versions of the holy texts and collected them in the Avesta. They also explored points of doctrine and addressed difficult questions of morality and theology. Ordinary people flocked to Zoroastrian temples, where they prayed to Ahura Mazda and participated in rituals. The Zoroastrian faith faced severe difficulties in the seventh century C.E. when Islamic conquerors toppled the Sasanid empire. The conquerors did not outlaw the religion altogether, but they placed political and financial pressure on the magi and Zoroastrian temples. Some Zoroastrians fled their homeland and found refuge in India, where their descendants, known as Parsis ("Persians"), continue even today to observe Zoroastrian traditions. But most Zoroastrians remained in Iran and eventually converted to Islam. Only a few thousand faithful maintain a Zoroastrian community in modern-day Iran.

INFLUENCE OF ZOROASTRIANISM Meanwhile, even though Zoroastrianism ultimately declined in its homeland, the cosmopolitan character of the Persian realm offered it opportunities to influence other religious faiths. In particular, Jews living in Persia during Achaemenid times adopted several specific teachings of Zoroastrianism,

Parsis (pahr-SEES)

SOURCES FROM THE PAST

Zarathustra on Good and Evil

Like many other religious faiths of classical times, Zoroastrianism encouraged the faithful to observe high moral and ethical standards. In this hymn from the **Gathas*****, Zarathustra relates how Ahura Mazda and Angra Mainyu—representatives of good and evil, respectively—made choices about how to behave based on their fundamental natures. Human beings did likewise, according to Zarathustra, and ultimately all would experience the rewards and punishments that their choices merited.***

In the beginning, there were two Primal Spirits, Twins spontaneously active;
These are the Good and the Evil, in thought, and in word, and in deed:
Between these two, let the wise choose aright;
Be good, not base.

And when these Twin Spirits came together at first,
They established Life and Non-Life,
And so shall it be as long as the world shall last;
The worst existence shall be the lot of the followers of evil,
And the Good Mind shall be the reward of the followers of good.

Of these Twin Spirits, the Evil One chose to do the worst;
While the bountiful Holy Spirit of Goodness,
Clothing itself with the mossy heavens for a garment, chose the Truth;
And so will those who [seek to] please Ahura Mazda with righteous deeds, performed with faith in Truth. . . .

And when there cometh Divine Retribution for the Evil One,
Then at Thy command shall the Good Mind establish the Kingdom of Heaven, O Mazda,
For those who will deliver Untruth into the hands of Righteousness and Truth.

Then truly cometh the blow of destruction on Untruth,
And all those of good fame are garnered up in the Fair Abode,
The Fair Abode of the Good Mind, the Wise Lord, and of Truth!

O ye mortals, mark these commandments—
The commandments which the Wise Lord has given, for Happiness and for Pain;
Long punishment for the evil-doer, and bliss for the follower of Truth,
The joy of salvation for the Righteous ever afterwards!

What assumptions does Zarathustra make about human nature and the capacity of human beings to make morally good choices out of their own free will?

SOURCE: D. J. Irani. *The Divine Songs of Zarathustra.* London: George Allen & Unwin, 1924.

which later found their way into the faiths of Christianity and Islam as well. These teachings included the notion that an omnipotent and beneficent deity was responsible for all creation, the idea that a purely evil being worked against the creator god, the conviction that the forces of good will ultimately prevail over the forces of evil after a climactic struggle, the belief that human beings must strive to observe the highest moral standards, and the doctrine that individuals will undergo judgment, after which the morally upright will experience rewards in paradise while evildoers will suffer punishments in hell. These teachings, which have profoundly influenced Judaism, Christianity, and Islam, all derived ultimately from the faith of Zarathustra and his followers.

SUMMARY

The Achaemenid empire inaugurated a new era of world history. The Achaemenids borrowed military and administrative techniques devised earlier by Babylonian and Assyrian rulers, but they applied those techniques on a much larger scale than did any of their Mesopotamian predecessors. In doing so they conquered a vast empire and then governed its diverse lands and peoples with tolerable success for more than two centuries. The Achaemenids demonstrated how it was possible to build and maintain a massive imperial state, and their example inspired later efforts to establish similar large-scale imperial states based in Persia and other Eurasian lands as well. The Achaemenid and later Persian empires integrated much of the territory from the Mediterranean Sea to the Indus River into a commonwealth in which peoples of different regions and ethnic groups participated in a larger economy and society. By sponsoring regular and systematic interactions between peoples of different communities, the Persian empires wielded tremendous cultural as well as political, social, and economic influence. Indeed, Persian religious beliefs helped to shape moral and religious thought throughout much of southwest Asia and the Mediterranean basin. Zoroastrian teachings were particularly influential: although Zoroastrianism declined after the Sasanid dynasty, its doctrines decisively influenced the fundamental teachings of Judaism, Christianity, and Islam.

STUDY TERMS

Achaemenids (88)
Ahura Mazda (98)
Alexander of Macedon (92)
Avesta (98)
battle of Marathon (92)
Croesus (87)
Cyrus (87)
Darius (89)
Gathas (98)
magi (98)
Medes (88)
Mithradates I (94)
Parthians (93)
Pasargadae (89)
Persepolis (90)
Persian Royal Road (91)
Persian Wars (92)
Persians (95)
qanat (91)
Sasanids (94)
satraps (91)
Seleucids (93)
Shapur I (94)
Xerxes (92)
Zarathustra (98)

FOR FURTHER READING

Mary Boyce, ed. *Textual Sources for the Study of Zoroastrianism.* Totowa, N.J., 1984. Sources in translation with numerous explanatory comments by the author.

Maria Brosius. *Women in Ancient Persia, 559–331 B.C.* Oxford, 1996. Carefully examines both Persian and Greek sources for information about women and their role in Achaemenid society.

John Curtis and Nigel Tallos, eds. *Forgotten Empire: The World of Ancient Persia.* Berkeley, 2005. A lavishly illustrated collection of essays on various aspects of the Achaemenid Empire.

Muhammad A. Dandamaev and Vladimir G. Lukonin. *The Culture and Social Institutions of Ancient Iran.* Ed. by P. L. Kohl. Cambridge, 1989. Scholarly account that brings the results of Russian research to bear on the Achaemenid empire.

Richard C. Foltz. *Spirituality in the Land of the Noble: How Iran Shaped the World's Religions.* Oxford, 2004. Includes an accessible discussion of the Zoroastrian faith.

Richard N. Frye. *The Heritage of Central Asia: From Antiquity to the Turkish Expansion.* Princeton, 1996. Briefly sketches the history of various Iranian-speaking peoples in the steppes of central Asia as well as on the Iranian plateau.

Susan Sherwin-White and Amélie Kuhrt. *From Samarkhand to Sardis: A New Approach to the Seleucid Empire.* Berkeley, 1993. Detailed scholarly analysis of the Seleucid empire concentrating on political and economic matters.

Mark van de Mieroop. *A History of the Ancient Near East, ca. 3000–323 B.C.* Oxford, 2004. A concise and readable history that concludes with the Achaemenid Empire.

Mortimer Wheeler. *Flames over Persepolis.* New York, 1968. Deals with Alexander's conquest of the Achaemenid empire and especially the spread of Greek art styles throughout the Persian empire.

Robert C. Zaehner. *The Dawn and Twilight of Zoroastrianism.* London, 1961. An important interpretation of Zoroastrianism that concentrates on the Achaemenid and Sasanid periods.

The Unification of China

6

n the year 99 B.C.E., Chinese imperial officials sentenced the historian Sima Qian to punishment by castration. For just over a decade, Sima Qian had worked on a project that he had inherited from his father, a history of China from earliest times to his own day. That project brought Sima Qian high prominence at the imperial court. Thus, when he spoke in defense of a dishonored general, his views attracted widespread attention. The emperor reacted furiously when he learned that Sima Qian had publicly expressed opinions that contradicted the ruler's judgment and ordered the historian to undergo his humiliating punishment.

Human castration was by no means uncommon in premodern times. Thousands of boys and young men of undistinguished birth underwent voluntary castration in China and many other lands as well to pursue careers as eunuchs. Ruling elites often appointed eunuchs, rather than nobles, to sensitive posts because eunuchs did not sire families and so could not build power bases to challenge established authorities. As personal servants of ruling elites, eunuchs sometimes came to wield enormous power.

Castration was not an appealing alternative, however, to educated elites and other prominent individuals: indeed, Chinese men of honor normally avoided the penalty by taking their own lives. Yet Sima Qian chose to endure his punishment. In a letter to a friend he explained that suicide would mean that his work would go forever unwritten. To transmit his understanding of the Chinese past, then, Sima Qian opted to live and work in disgrace until his death about 90 B.C.E.

During his last years Sima Qian completed a massive work consisting of 130 chapters, most of which survive. He composed historical accounts of the emperors' reigns and biographical sketches of notable figures, including ministers, statesmen, generals, empresses, aristocrats, scholars, officials, merchants, and rebels. He even described the societies of neighboring peoples with whom the Chinese sometimes conducted trade and sometimes made war. As a result, Sima Qian's efforts still provide the best information available about the development of early imperial China.

A rich body of political and social thought prepared the way for the unification of China under the Qin and Han dynasties. Confucians, Daoists, Legalists, and others formed schools of thought and worked to bring political and social stability to China during the chaotic years of the late Zhou dynasty and the Period of the Warring States. Legalist ideas contributed directly to unification by

❮ The Han emperor discusses classical texts with Confucian scholars.

Qin (chin)

CHRONOLOGY

sixth century B.C.E. (?)	Laozi
551–479 B.C.E.	Confucius
403–221 B.C.E.	Period of the Warring States
390–338 B.C.E.	Shang Yang
372–289 B.C.E.	Mencius
298–238 B.C.E.	Xunzi
280–233 B.C.E.	Han Feizi
221–207 B.C.E.	Qin dynasty
206 B.C.E.–9 C.E.	Former Han dynasty
141–87 B.C.E.	Reign of Han Wudi
9–23 C.E.	Reign of Wang Mang
25–220 C.E.	Later Han dynasty

outlining means by which rulers could strengthen their states. The works of the Confucians and the Daoists were not directly concerned with unification, but both schools of thought profoundly influenced Chinese political and cultural traditions over the long term.

Rulers of the Qin and Han dynasties adopted Legalist principles and imposed centralized imperial rule on all of China. Like the Achaemenids of Persia, the Qin and Han emperors ruled through an elaborate bureaucracy, and they built roads that linked the various regions of China. They went further than the Persian emperors in their efforts to foster cultural unity in their realm. They imposed a common written language throughout China and established an educational system based on Confucian thought and values. For almost 450 years the Qin and Han dynasties guided the fortunes of China and established a strong precedent for centralized imperial rule.

Especially during the Han dynasty, political stability brought economic prosperity. High agricultural productivity supported the development of iron and silk industries, and Chinese goods found markets in central Asia, India, the Persian Empire, and even the Mediterranean basin. In spite of economic prosperity, however, later Han society experienced deep divisions between rich landowners and poor peasants. Those divisions eventually led to civil disorder and the emergence of political factions, which ultimately brought the Han dynasty to an end.

In Search of Political and Social Order

The late centuries of the Zhou dynasty led eventually to the chaos associated with the Period of the Warring States (403–221 B.C.E.). Yet the political turmoil of that period also resulted in a remarkable cultural flowering, because it forced thoughtful people to reflect on the proper roles of human beings in society. Some sought to identify principles that would restore political and social order. Others concerned themselves with a search for individual tranquility apart from society. Three schools of thought that emerged during those centuries of confusion and chaos—Confucianism, Daoism, and Legalism—exercised a particularly deep influence on Chinese political and cultural traditions.

Confucius and His School

CONFUCIUS The first Chinese thinker who addressed the problem of political and social order in a straightforward and self-conscious way was Kong Fuzi (551–479 B.C.E.)—"Master Philosopher Kong," as his disciples called him, or Confucius, as he is known in English. He came from an aristocratic family in the state of Lu in northern China, and for many years he sought an influential post at the Lu court. But Confucius was a strong-willed man who often did not get along well with others. He could be quite cantankerous: he was known to lodge bitter complaints, for

Zhou (joh)
Confucianism (kuhn-FEW-shuhn-iz'm)

example, if someone undercooked or overcooked his rice. Not surprisingly, then, he refused to compromise his beliefs in the interest of political expediency, and he insisted on observing principles that frequently clashed with state policy. As a result, Confucius was unable to obtain a high position at the Lu court. Confucius then sought employment with other courts in northern China but after a decade of travel found none willing to accept his services. In 484 B.C.E., bitterly disappointed, he returned to Lu, where he died five years later.

Although Confucius never realized his ambition, he left an enduring mark on Chinese society through his work as an educator and a political advisor. He attracted numerous disciples who aspired to political careers, and those disciples compiled the master's sayings and teachings in a book known as the *Analects*—a work that has profoundly influenced Chinese political and cultural traditions.

CONFUCIUS. | No contemporary portrait of Confucius survives, but artists have used their imaginations and depicted him in many ways over the years. This portrait of 1735 identifies Confucius as "the Sage and Teacher" and represents him in the distinctive dress of an eighteenth-century Confucian scholar-bureaucrat.

CONFUCIAN IDEAS Confucius's thought was fundamentally moral, ethical, and political in character. It was also thoroughly practical: Confucius did not address philosophical or religious questions but focused instead on the proper ordering of human relationships. In an age when bureaucratic institutions were not yet well developed, Confucius believed that the best way to promote good government was to fill official positions with individuals who were both well educated and extraordinarily conscientious. Thus Confucius concentrated on the formation of what he called *junzi*—"superior individuals"—who did not allow personal interests to influence their judgments.

In the absence of an established educational system and a formal curriculum, Confucius had his disciples study works of poetry and history that provided insight into human nature. He and his students carefully examined works produced during the Zhou dynasty, such as the *Book of Songs,* the *Book of History,* and the *Book of Rites,* concentrating especially on their practical value for prospective administrators. As a result of Confucius's influence, literary works of the Zhou dynasty became the core texts of the traditional Chinese education. For more than two thousand years, until the early twentieth century C.E., talented Chinese seeking government posts followed a program of study deriving from the one developed by Confucius in the fifth century B.C.E.

CONFUCIAN VALUES For Confucius, though, ideal government officials needed more than an advanced education: they also needed a strong sense of moral integrity and a capacity to deliver wise and fair judgments. Several qualities were particularly important to Confucius. One of them he called *ren,* by which he meant an attitude of kindness and benevolence or a sense of humanity. Confucius explained that individuals possessing *ren* were courteous, respectful, diligent, and loyal—characteristics desperately needed in government officials. Another quality of central importance was *li,* a sense of propriety, which called for individuals to behave appropriately: they should treat all other human beings with courtesy, while showing special respect and deference to elders or superiors. Yet another quality that Confucius emphasized was *xiao,* filial piety, which obliged children to respect their parents and other family elders, look after their welfare, support them in old age, and remember them along with other ancestors after their deaths.

li (LEE)
xiao (SHAYOH)

Confucius emphasized personal qualities such as *ren, li,* and *xiao* because he believed that individuals who possessed those traits would gain influence in the larger society and in the process would lead others by their example. Only through enlightened leadership by morally strong individuals, Confucius believed, was there any hope for the restoration of political and social order in China. Thus his goal was not simply the cultivation of personal morality for its own sake but also the creation of *junzi* who could bring order and stability to China.

Because Confucius expressed his thought in general terms, later disciples could adapt it to the particular problems of their times. Indeed, the flexibility of Confucian thought helps to account for its remarkable longevity and influence in China. Two later disciples of Confucius—Mencius and Xunzi—illustrate especially well the ways in which Confucian thought lent itself to adaptation.

MENCIUS Mencius (372–289 B.C.E.) was the most learned man of his age and the principal spokesman for the Confucian school. During the Period of the Warring States, he traveled widely throughout China as a political advisor. Mencius firmly believed that human nature was basically good; thus he placed special emphasis on the Confucian virtue of *ren* and advocated government by benevolence and humanity. This principle implied that rulers would levy light taxes, avoid wars, support education, and encourage harmony and cooperation. In his lifetime, Mencius's advice had little practical effect, and critics charged that his views about human nature were naïve. Over the long term, however, his ideas deeply influenced the Confucian tradition. Since about the tenth century C.E., many Chinese scholars have considered Mencius the most authoritative of Confucius's early expositors.

XUNZI Like Confucius and Mencius, Xunzi (298–238 B.C.E.) was a man of immense learning, but unlike his predecessors, he also served for many years as a government administrator. His practical experience encouraged him to develop a less optimistic view of human nature than Mencius's. Xunzi believed that human beings selfishly pursued their own interests and resisted making any voluntary contribution to the larger society. He considered strong social discipline the best means to bring order to society. Thus, whereas Mencius emphasized the Confucian quality of *ren,* Xunzi emphasized *li.* He advocated the establishment of clear, well-publicized standards of conduct that would set limits on the pursuit of individual interests and punish those who neglected their obligations to the larger society.

Like Confucius and Mencius, however, Xunzi also believed that it was possible to improve human beings and restore order to society. That fundamental optimism was a basic characteristic of Confucian thought. It explains the high value that Confucian thinkers placed on education and public behavior, and it accounts also for their activist approach to public affairs. Confucians involved themselves in society: they sought government positions and made conscientious efforts to solve political and social problems and to promote harmony in public life.

Daoism

Some contemporaries, however, regarded Confucian activism as little more than misspent energy. Among the most prominent of these critics were the Daoists. Like Confucianism, Daoism developed in response to the turbulence of the late Zhou dynasty and the Period of the Warring States. But unlike the Confucians, the Daoists considered it pointless to waste time on social activism. Instead, the Daoists devoted their energies to reflection and

junzi (juhn-zee)
Mencius (MEN-shi-us)
Xunzi (SHOON-dzuh)
Daoism (DOW-iz'm)

SOURCES FROM THE PAST

Confucius on Good Government

Confucius never composed formal writings, but his disciples collected his often pithy remarks into a work known as the Analects (Sayings). *Referred to as "the Master" in the following excerpts from the* Analects, *Confucius consistently argued that only good men possessing moral authority could rule effectively.*

The Master said, "He who exercises government by means of his virtue may be compared to the north polar star, which keeps its place, while all the stars turn toward it. . . ."

The Master said, "If the people be led by laws, and uniformity be imposed on them by punishments, they will try to avoid the punishment, but will have no sense of shame."

"If they be led by virtue, and uniformity be provided for them by the rules of propriety, they will have the sense of shame, and moreover will become good. . . ."

The duke Ai asked, saying, "What should be done in order to secure the submission of the people?" Confucius replied, "Advance the upright and set aside the crooked, and then the people will submit. Advance the crooked and set aside the upright, and then the people will not submit."

Ji Kang asked how to cause the people to reverence their ruler, to be faithful to him, and to go on to seek virtue. The Master said, "Let him preside over them with gravity; then they will reverence him. Let him be filial and kind to all; then they will be faithful to him. Let him advance the good and teach the incompetent; then they will eagerly seek to be virtuous. . . ."

Zigong asked about government. The Master said, "The requisites of government are that there be sufficiency of food, sufficiency of military equipment, and the confidence of the people in their ruler." Zigong said, "If it cannot be helped, and one of these must be dispensed with, which of the three should be foregone first?" "The military equipment," said the Master.

Zigong again asked, "If it cannot be helped, and one of the remaining two must be dispensed with, which of them should be foregone?" The Master answered, "Part with the food. From olden times, death has been the lot of all men; but if the people have no faith in their rulers, there is no standing for the state. . . ."

Ji Kang asked Confucius about government, saying, "What do you say to killing the unprincipled for the good of the principled?" Confucius replied, "Sir, in carrying on your government, why should you use killing at all? Let your evinced desires be for what is good, and the people will be good. The relation between superiors and inferiors is like that between the wind and the grass. The grass must bend when the wind blows across it. . . ."

The Master said, "When a prince's personal conduct is correct, his government is effective without the issuing of orders. If his personal conduct is not correct, he may issue orders, but they will not be followed."

■ **Compare Confucius's understanding of moral virtue with Zarathustra's notion of morality discussed in the previous chapter.**

SOURCE: James Legge, trans. *The Chinese Classics,* 7 vols. Oxford: Clarendon Press, 1893, 1:145, 146, 152, 254, 258–59, 266. (Translations slightly modified.)

introspection, in hopes that they could understand how to live in harmony with the natural principles that governed the world. The Daoists believed that, over time, this approach would bring harmony to society as a whole, as people ceased to meddle in affairs that they could not understand or control.

LAOZI AND THE DAODEJING According to Chinese tradition, the founder of Daoism was a sixth-century B.C.E. sage named Laozi. Although Laozi has been credited with composing the *Daodejing (Classic of the Way and of Virtue),* the basic exposition of Daoist beliefs, it is almost certain that the book acquired its definitive form over several centuries. After the *Daodejing,* the most important Daoist work was the *Zhuangzi,* named

Daodejing (DOW-DAY-JIHNG)
Zhuangzi (joo-wong-dz)

LAOZI. | A jade statue produced about the tenth century C.E. depicts the sage Laozi on an ox. Legends reported that Laozi rode a blue ox from China to central Asia when spreading his teachings. ***Why is Laozi depicted wearing common, simple clothing?***

after its author, the philosopher Zhuangzi (369–286 B.C.E.), which provided a well-reasoned compendium of Daoist views.

THE DAO Daoism represented an effort to understand the fundamental character of the world and nature. The central concept of Daoism is the elusive concept of *dao,* meaning "the way," or more specifically "the way of nature" or "the way of the cosmos." In the *Daodejing, dao* figures as the original force of the cosmos, an eternal principle that governs all the workings of the world. Yet the *Daodejing* envisioned *dao* as a supremely passive force and spoke of it mostly in negative terms: *dao* does nothing, and yet it accomplishes everything. *Dao* resembles water, which is soft and yielding, yet is also so powerful that it eventually erodes even the hardest rock placed in its path. *Dao* also resembles the cavity of a pot: although it is nothing more than an empty space, it makes the pot a useful tool.

Daoists believed that human beings should live in harmony with the passive and yielding nature of *dao.* To the Daoists, that meant retreating from the world of politics and administration. Ambition and activism had only brought the world to a state of chaos. The proper response to that situation was to cease frantic striving and live in as simple a manner as possible.

THE DOCTRINE OF WUWEI Thus early Daoists recognized as the chief moral virtue the trait of *wuwei*—disengagement from active involvement in worldly affairs. *Wuwei* required that individuals refrain from advanced education and personal striving, and that they live simply, unpretentiously, and in harmony with nature.

Wuwei also had implications for state and society: the less government, the better. Instead of expansive kingdoms, the *Daodejing* envisioned a world of tiny, self-sufficient communities where people had no desire to conquer their neighbors or even to trade or visit with them.

Although Daoist thought opposed the activism of Confucianism, in fact the Daoist encouragement of self-knowledge appealed strongly to many Confucians. And, since neither Confucianism nor Daoism was an exclusive faith, it was possible for individuals to study the Confucian curriculum and take administrative posts in the government while devoting their private hours to reflection on human nature and the place of humans in the larger world—to live as Confucians by day, as it were, and Daoists by night.

Legalism

Ultimately, neither Confucian activism nor Daoist retreat was able to solve the problems of the Period of the Warring States. Order returned to China only after the emergence of a third school of thought—that of the Legalists—which promoted a practical and ruthlessly efficient approach to statecraft. Unlike the Confucians, the Legalists did not concern themselves with ethics, morality, or propriety. Unlike the Daoists, the Legalists cared nothing about the place of human beings in nature. Instead, they devoted their attention exclusively to the state, which they sought to strengthen and expand at all costs.

SHANG YANG AND HAN FEIZI Legalist doctrine emerged from the insights of men who were active in Chinese political affairs during the late fourth century B.C.E. Most notable of them was Shang Yang (ca. 390–338 B.C.E.), who served as chief

wuwei (woo-WAY)

minister to the duke of the Qin state in western China. His policies survive in a work titled *The Book of Lord Shang.* Though a clever and efficient administrator, Shang Yang was despised because of his power and ruthlessness. Thus, when his patron died, Shang's enemies at court executed him, mutilated his body, and annihilated his family. Another Legalist theorist, Han Feizi (ca. 280–233 B.C.E.) also fell afoul of ambitious men at the Qin court. During his life, Han Feizi synthesized Legalist ideas in a collection of powerful and well-argued essays on statecraft. However, his enemies forced him to commit suicide by taking poison. Thus, the Legalist state itself consumed the two foremost exponents of Legalist doctrine.

TRADITIONS IN THE UNIFICATION OF CHINA. Although the Qin and Han dynasties built large empires that encompassed a variety of peoples and languages, they insisted on a cultural unity that emphasized the primacy of Chinese customs and traditions over other traditions. What measures did the two dynasties use to impose this cultural unity, and how successful were they?

LEGALIST DOCTRINE Shang Yang, Han Feizi, and other Legalists reasoned that the foundations of a state's strength were agriculture and armed forces. Since both lines of work directly advanced the interests of the state, Legalists sought to channel as many individuals as possible into cultivation or military service. Meanwhile, they discouraged others from pursuing what they believed were less useful careers as merchants, entrepreneurs, scholars, educators, philosophers, poets, or artists.

The Legalists expected to harness subjects' energy by means of clear and strict laws—hence the name "Legalist." Their faith in laws distinguished the Legalists clearly from the Confucians, who relied on education and example to induce individuals to behave appropriately. The Legalists believed that this was not enough: to persuade individuals to serve the needs of the state, they imposed a strict legal regimen that clearly outlined expectations and provided severe punishment for violators. They believed that if people feared to commit small crimes, they would hesitate all the more before committing great crimes. Thus Legalists imposed harsh penalties for even minor infractions: individuals could suffer amputation of their hands or feet, for example, for disposing of trash in the street. The Legalists also established the principle of collective responsibility before the law, whereby all members of a family or a community were liable to be punished along with the actual violator.

The Legalists' principles of government did not win them much popularity. Yet Legalist doctrine lent itself readily to practical application, and Legalist principles of government quickly produced remarkable results for rulers who adopted them. In fact, Legalist methods put an end to the Period of the Warring States and brought about the unification of China.

THE UNIFICATION OF CHINA

During the Period of the Warring States, rulers of several regional states adopted elements of the Legalist program. Legalist doctrines met the most enthusiastic response in the state of Qin, in western China, where Shang Yang and Han Feizi oversaw the implementation of Legalist policies. The Qin state soon dominated its neighbors and imposed centralized imperial rule throughout China. Qin rule survived for only a few years, but the succeeding Han dynasty followed the Qin example by governing China through a centralized imperial administration.

China under the Qin dynasty
www.mhhe.com/bentleybrief2e

The Qin Dynasty

THE KINGDOM OF QIN During the fourth and third centuries B.C.E., the Qin state underwent a remarkable round of economic, political, and military development. Shang Yang encouraged peasant cultivators to migrate to the sparsely populated state by granting them private plots. That policy dramatically boosted agricultural production

Han Feizi (hahn-fay-zi)

while it simultaneously weakened the economic position of the hereditary aristocratic classes. As a result, Qin rulers found fewer obstacles to establishing centralized, bureaucratic rule throughout their state. Meanwhile, they devoted their newfound wealth to the organization of a powerful army equipped with the most effective iron weapons available. During the third century B.C.E., Qin rulers attacked one state after another, absorbing each new conquest into their centralized structure, until finally they had brought China for the first time under the sway of a single state.

THE FIRST EMPEROR In 221 B.C.E., Qin Shihuangdi, the king of Qin (reigned 221–210 B.C.E.), proclaimed himself the First Emperor and decreed that his descendants would reign for thousands of generations. In fact, the dynasty lasted only fourteen years, dissolving in 207 B.C.E. because of civil insurrections. Yet the Qin dynasty had a significance out of proportion to its short life, because like the Achaemenid empire in Persia, the Qin dynasty established a tradition of centralized imperial rule that later rulers sought to emulate.

PSI img The Great Wall www.mhhe.com/bentleybrief2e

Like his ancestors in the kingdom of Qin, the First Emperor of China ignored the nobility and ruled his empire through a centralized bureaucracy. He governed from his capital at Xianyang, near the modern city of Xi'an. The remainder of China he divided into administrative provinces and districts, and he entrusted the implementation of his policies to officers of the central government who served at his pleasure. He disarmed regional military forces, and he built roads to facilitate communications and the movement of armies. He also drafted laborers by the hundreds of thousands to build a massive defensive barrier that was a precursor to the Great Wall of China.

RESISTANCE TO QIN POLICIES It is likely that many Chinese welcomed the political stability introduced by the Qin dynasty, but it did not win universal acceptance. Confucians, Daoists, and others launched a vigorous campaign of criticism. In an effort to reassert his authority, Qin Shihuangdi ordered execution for those who criticized his regime. In the year following this decree, for example, he sentenced some 460 scholars residing in the capital to be buried alive for their criticism of his regime. Qin Shihuangdi also demanded that all books of philosophy, ethics, history, and literature be burned. Although he spared some works on medicine, fortune-telling, and agriculture on the grounds that they had some utilitarian value, many classical literary or philosophical works were lost.

QIN CENTRALIZATION The First Emperor launched several initiatives that enhanced the unity of China. In keeping with his policy of centralization, he standardized the laws, currencies, weights, and measures of the various regions of China. Previously, regional states had organized their own legal and economic systems, which often hampered commerce and communications across state boundaries. Uniform coinage and legal standards encouraged the integration of China's various regions into a society more tightly knit than ever before. The roads and bridges that Qin Shihuangdi built throughout his realm, like those built in other classical societies, also encouraged economic integration because they facilitated interregional commerce.

STANDARDIZED SCRIPT Perhaps even more important than his legal and economic policies was the First Emperor's standardization of Chinese script. Before the Qin dynasty, regional Chinese scripts had developed along different lines and had become mutually unrecognizable. In hopes of ensuring better understanding and uniform application of his policies, Qin Shihuangdi mandated the use of a common script throughout his empire. The regions of China continued to use different spoken languages, as they do

Qin Shihuangdi (chin she-huang-dee)
Xianyang (SHYAHN-YAHNG)
Xi'an (shee-ahn)

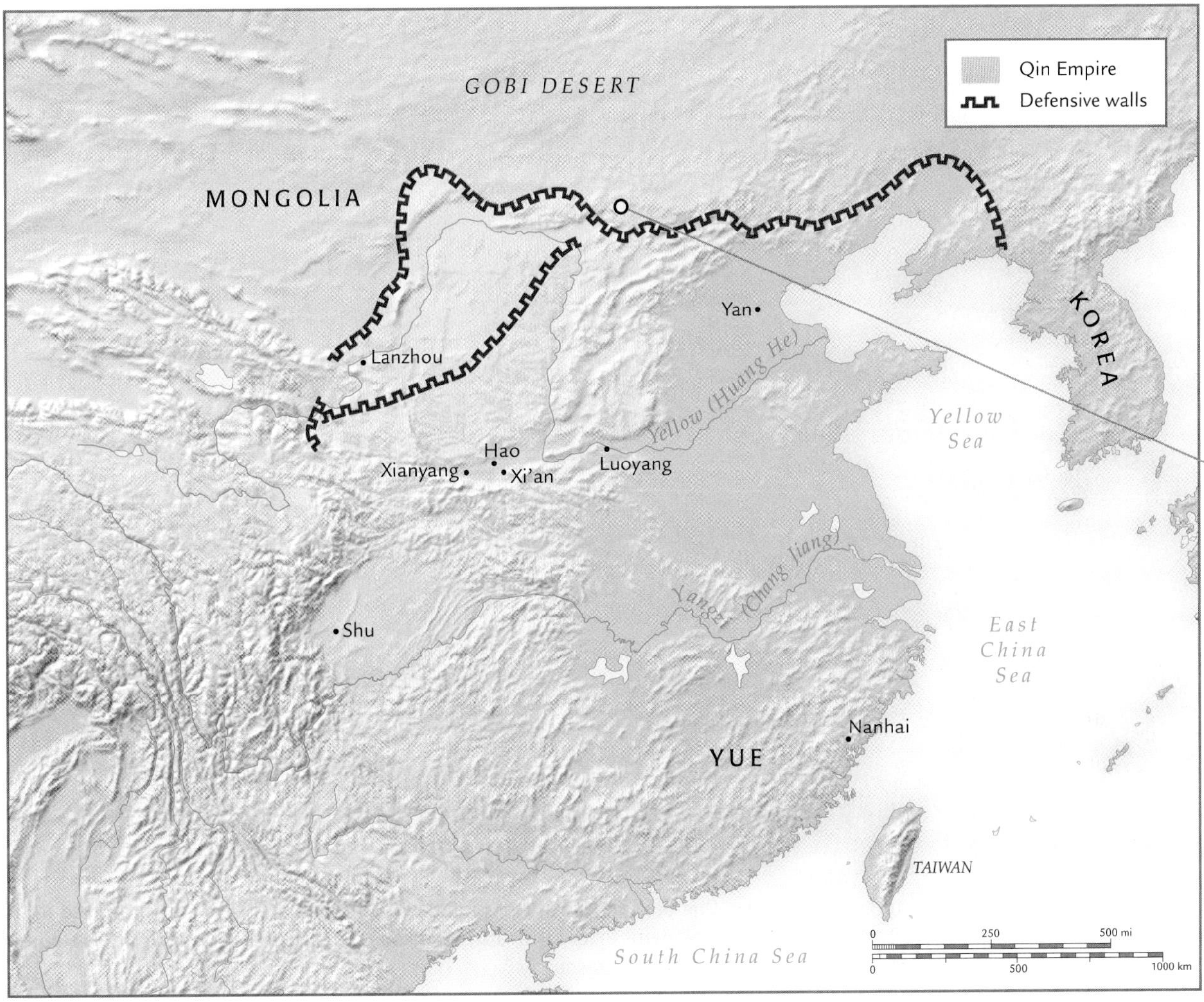

MAP 6.1 | China under the Qin dynasty, 221–207 B.C.E. Compare the size of Qin territories to those of earlier Chinese kingdoms depicted in Map 3.2. ***How is it possible to account for the greater reach of the Qin dynasty?***

These defensive walls were precursors to China's Great Wall, which was built during the Ming dynasty (1368–1644 C.E.)

today, but they wrote those languages with a common script—just as if Europeans spoke English, French, German, and other languages but wrote them all down in Latin. In China, speakers of different languages use the same written symbols, which enables them to communicate in writing across linguistic boundaries.

In spite of his ruthlessness, Qin Shihuangdi ranks as one of the most important figures in Chinese history. The First Emperor established a precedent for centralized imperial rule, which remained the norm in China until the early twentieth century. He also pointed China in the direction of political and cultural unity, and with some periods of interruption, China has remained politically and culturally unified to the present day.

Emperor Qin's tomb
www.mhhe.com/bentleybrief2e

TOMB OF THE FIRST EMPEROR Qin Shihuangdi died in 210 B.C.E. His final resting place was a lavish tomb constructed by some seven hundred thousand drafted laborers as a permanent monument to the First Emperor. Rare and expensive grave goods accompanied the emperor in burial, along with sacrificed slaves, concubines, and many of the craftsmen who designed and built the tomb. Qin Shihuangdi was laid to rest in an elaborate underground palace lined with bronze and protected by traps and crossbows rigged to fire at intruders. Buried in the vicinity of the tomb itself was an entire army of magnificently detailed life-size pottery figures to guard the emperor in death.

The terra-cotta army of Qin Shihuangdi protected his tomb, but it could not save his successors or his empire. The First Emperor had conscripted millions of laborers from

THE TOMB OF QIN SHIHUANGDI. | One detachment of the formidable, life-size, terra-cotta army buried in the vicinity of Qin Shihuangdi's tomb to protect the emperor after his death. ***What does the construction of such an elaborate tomb tell us about Qin Shihuangdi's ability to command resources?***

all parts of China to work on massive public works projects. Although these projects increased productivity and promoted the integration of China's various regions, they also generated tremendous ill will among the drafted laborers. Revolts began in the year after Qin Shihuangdi's death, and in 207 B.C.E. waves of rebels overwhelmed the Qin court, slaughtering government officials and burning state buildings. The Qin dynasty quickly dissolved in chaos.

The Early Han Dynasty

LIU BANG The bloody end of the Qin dynasty might well have ended the experiment with centralized imperial rule in China. However, centralized rule returned almost immediately, largely because of a determined commander named Liu Bang. Judging from the historian Sima Qian's account, Liu Bang was not a colorful or charismatic figure, but he was a persistent man and a methodical planner. He surrounded himself with brilliant advisors and enjoyed the unwavering loyalty of his troops. By 206 B.C.E. he had restored order throughout China and established himself at the head of a new dynasty.

Liu Bang called the new dynasty the Han, in honor of his native land. The Han dynasty turned out to be one of the longest and most influential in all of Chinese history. It lasted for more than four hundred years, from 206 B.C.E. to 220 C.E., although for a brief period (9–23 C.E.) a usurper temporarily displaced Han rule. Thus historians conventionally divide the dynasty into the Former Han (206 B.C.E.–9 C.E.) and the Later Han (25–220 C.E.).

The Han dynasty consolidated the tradition of centralized imperial rule that the Qin dynasty had pioneered. During the Former Han, emperors ruled from Chang'an, a cosmopolitan city near modern Xi'an that became the cultural capital of China. During the Later Han, the emperors moved their capital east to Luoyang, also a cosmopolitan city and second in importance only to Chang'an throughout much of Chinese history.

EARLY HAN POLICIES During the early days of the Han dynasty, Liu Bang attempted to follow a middle path between the decentralized political alliances of the Zhou dynasty and the tightly centralized state of the Qin to reap the advantages and avoid the excesses of both. On the one hand, he allotted large landholdings to members of the imperial family, in the expectation that they would provide a reliable network of support for his rule. On the other hand, he divided the empire into administrative districts governed by officials who served at the emperor's pleasure.

Liu Bang learned quickly that reliance on his family did not guarantee support for the emperor. In 200 B.C.E. an army of nomadic Xiongnu warriors besieged Liu Bang and almost captured him. He managed to escape—but without receiving the support he had expected from his family members. From that point forward, Liu Bang and his successors followed a policy of centralization. They reclaimed lands from family members, absorbed those lands into the imperial domain, and entrusted political responsibilities to an administrative bureaucracy. Thus, despite a brief flirtation with a decentralized government, the Han dynasty left as its principal political legacy a tradition of centralized imperial rule.

THE MARTIAL EMPEROR: HAN WUDI Much of the reason for the Han dynasty's success was the long reign of the dynasty's greatest and most energetic emperor, Han Wudi, the "Martial Emperor," who occupied the throne for fifty-four years, from 141 to 87 B.C.E. Han Wudi ruled his empire with vision and vigor. He pursued two policies in particular: administrative centralization and imperial expansion.

HAN CENTRALIZATION Domestically, Han Wudi worked strenuously to increase the authority and prestige of the central government. He built an enormous bureaucracy to administer his empire, and he relied on Legalist principles of government. He also continued the Qin policy of building roads and canals to facilitate trade and communication between China's regions. To finance the vast machinery of his government, he levied taxes on agriculture, trade, and craft industries, and he established imperial monopolies on the production of essential goods such as iron and salt. In building such an enormous governmental structure, Han Wudi faced a serious problem of recruitment. He needed thousands of reliable, intelligent, educated individuals to run his bureaucracy, but there was no institutionalized educational system in China that could provide a continuous supply of such people.

THE CONFUCIAN EDUCATIONAL SYSTEM Han Wudi addressed that problem in 124 B.C.E. by establishing an imperial university that prepared young men for government service. Personally, the Martial Emperor cared little for learning. In that respect he resembled all the other early Han emperors: Liu Bang once emptied his bladder in the distinctive cap worn by Confucian scholars in order to demonstrate his contempt for academic pursuits. Yet Han Wudi recognized that the success of his efforts at bureaucratic centralization would depend on a corps of educated officeholders. The imperial university took Confucianism—the only Chinese cultural tradition developed enough to provide rigorous intellectual discipline—as the basis for its curriculum. Ironically, then, although he relied on Legalist principles of government, Han Wudi ensured the long-term survival of the Confucian tradition by establishing it as the official imperial ideology.

Xiongnu (SHE-OONG-noo)

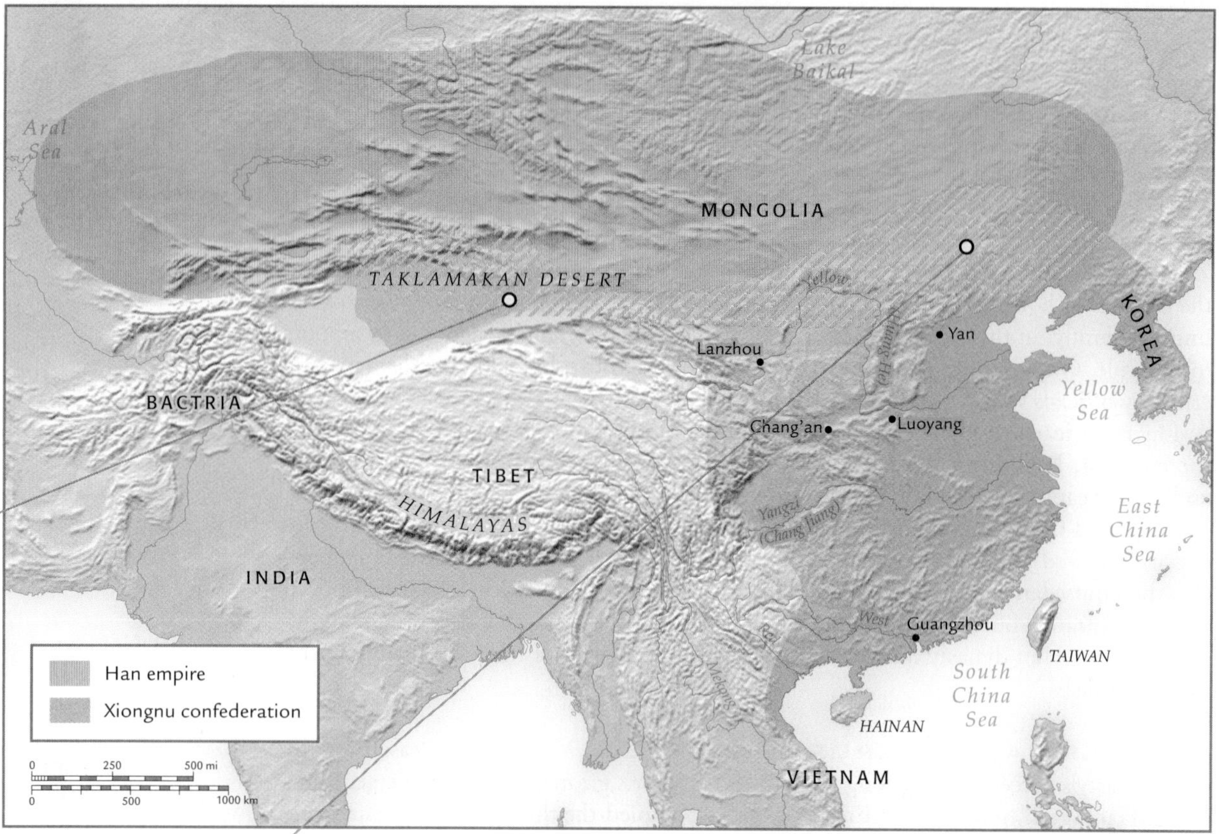

The Xiongnu frequently mounted raids into this border region.

MAP 6.2 | East Asia and central Asia at the time of Han Wudi, ca. 87 B.C.E. Note the indication in this map that Han authority extended to Korea and central Asia during the first century B.C.E. ***What strategic value did these regions hold for the Han dynasty?***

HAN IMPERIAL EXPANSION While he moved aggressively to centralize power and authority at home, Han Wudi pursued an equally vigorous foreign policy of imperial expansion. He invaded northern Vietnam and Korea, subjected them to Han rule, and brought them into the orbit of Chinese society. He ruled both lands through a Chinese-style government, and Confucian values followed the Han armies into the new colonies. Over the course of the centuries, the educational systems of both northern Vietnam and Korea drew their inspiration almost entirely from Confucianism.

The Xiongnu abduct Lady Wenji
www.mhhe.com/bentleybrief2e

Lady Wenji's scroll
www.mhhe.com/bentleybrief2e

THE XIONGNU The greatest foreign challenge that Han Wudi faced came from the Xiongnu, a nomadic people from the steppes of central Asia. Like most of the other nomadic peoples of central Asia, the Xiongnu were superb horsemen. Although their weaponry was not as sophisticated as that of the Chinese, their mobility offered the Xiongnu a distinct advantage. When they could not satisfy their needs through peaceful trade, they mounted sudden raids into villages or trading areas, where they commandeered supplies and then rapidly departed. Because they had no cities or settled places to defend, the Xiongnu could quickly disperse when confronted by a superior force.

During the reign of Maodun (210–174 B.C.E.), their most successful leader, the Xiongnu ruled a vast federation of nomadic peoples that stretched from the Aral Sea to the Yellow Sea. Maodun brought strict military discipline to the Xiongnu. According to Sima Qian, Maodun once instructed his forces to shoot their arrows at whatever target he himself selected. He aimed in succession at his favorite horse, one of his wives, and his father's best horse, and he summarily executed those who failed to discharge their arrows. When his forces reliably followed his orders, Maodun targeted his father, who immediately fell under a hail of arrows, leaving Maodun as the Xiongnu chief.

With its highly disciplined army, the Xiongnu empire was a source of concern to the Han emperors. During the early days of the dynasty, they attempted to pacify the Xiongnu by paying them tribute—providing them with food and finished goods in hopes that they would refrain from mounting raids in China—or by arranging marriages between the ruling houses of the two peoples in hopes of establishing peaceful diplomatic relations. Neither method succeeded for long.

THINKING ABOUT *Encounters*

ENCOUNTERS IN THE UNIFICATION OF CHINA. During the Han dynasty, the Han emperors successfully projected their influence across a wide swath of east and central Asia, including much of modern China as well as Korea, Vietnam, and the central Asian desert. In what ways did this influence encourage interaction between the various peoples of the realm?

HAN EXPANSION INTO CENTRAL ASIA Ultimately, Han Wudi decided to go on the offensive against the Xiongnu. He invaded central Asia with vast armies and brought much of the Xiongnu empire under Chinese military control. He pacified a long central Asian corridor extending almost to Bactria, which served as the lifeline of a trade network that linked much of the Eurasian landmass. He even planted colonies of Chinese cultivators in the oasis communities of central Asia. As a result of those efforts, the Xiongnu empire soon fell into disarray. For the moment, the Han state enjoyed uncontested hegemony in both east Asia and central Asia. Before long, however, economic and social problems within China brought serious problems for the Han dynasty itself.

FROM ECONOMIC PROSPERITY TO SOCIAL DISORDER

Already during the Xia, Shang, and Zhou dynasties, a productive agricultural economy supported the emergence of complex society in China. High agricultural productivity continued during the Qin and Han dynasties, and it supported the development of craft industries such as the forging of iron tools and the weaving of silk textiles. During the Han dynasty, however, China experienced serious social and economic problems as land became concentrated in the hands of a small, wealthy elite class. Social tensions generated banditry, rebellion, and even the temporary deposition of the Han state itself. Although Han rulers regained the throne, they presided over a much-weakened realm. By the early third century C.E., social and political problems brought the Han dynasty to an end.

Productivity and Prosperity during the Former Han

PATRIARCHAL SOCIAL ORDER The structure of Chinese society during the Qin and Han dynasties was very similar to that of the Zhou era. Patriarchal households averaged five inhabitants, although several generations of aristocratic families sometimes lived together in large compounds. During the Han dynasty, moralists sought to enhance the authority of patriarchal family heads by emphasizing the importance of filial piety and women's subordination to their menfolk. A widely read treatise titled *Admonitions for Women,* for example, emphasized humility, obedience, subservience, and devotion to their husbands as the virtues most appropriate for women. To Confucian moralists and government authorities alike, orderly, patriarchal families were the foundations of a stable society.

The vast majority of the Chinese population worked in the countryside cultivating grains and vegetables, which they harvested in larger quantities than ever before. The increased agricultural surplus allowed many Chinese to produce fine manufactured goods and to engage in trade.

IRON METALLURGY During the Han dynasty, the iron industry entered a period of rapid growth. Han artisans experimented with production techniques and learned to craft fine utensils for both domestic and military uses. Iron pots, stoves, knives, needles,

HAN-ERA ARISTOCRATIC HOUSE. | Clay model of an aristocratic house of the sort inhabited by a powerful clan during the Han dynasty. This model came from a tomb near the city of Guangzhou in southern China. *The Nelson-Atkins Museum of Art, Kansas City, Missouri. Purchase: William Rockhill Nelson Trust, 33-521.*

axes, hammers, saws, and other tools became standard fixtures in households that could not have afforded more expensive bronze utensils. The ready availability of iron also had important military implications. Craftsmen designed suits of iron armor to protect soldiers against arrows and blows, which helps to explain the success of Chinese armies against the Xiongnu and other nomadic peoples.

SILK TEXTILES Textile production—particularly sericulture, the manufacture of silk—became an especially important industry. The origins of sericulture date to the fourth millennium B.C.E., but only in Han times did sericulture expand from its original home in the Yellow River valley to most parts of China. Although silkworms inhabited much of Eurasia, Chinese silk was especially fine because of advanced sericulture techniques. Chinese producers bred their silkworms, fed them on finely chopped mulberry leaves, and carefully unraveled their cocoons so as to obtain long fibers of raw silk that they wove into light, strong, lustrous fabrics. (In other lands, producers relied on wild silkworms that ate a variety of leaves and chewed through their cocoons, leaving only short fibers that yielded lower-quality fabrics.) Chinese silk became a prized commodity in India, Persia, Mesopotamia, and even the distant Roman empire. Commerce in silk and other products led to the establishment of an intricate network of trade routes known collectively as the silk roads (discussed in chapter 9).

PAPER While expanding the iron and silk industries, Han craftsmen also invented paper. In earlier times Chinese scribes had written mostly on bamboo strips and silk fabrics, but about 100 C.E. Chinese craftsmen began to fashion hemp, bark, and textile fibers into sheets of paper. Although wealthy elites continued to read books written on silk rolls, paper soon became the preferred medium for most writing.

POPULATION GROWTH High agricultural productivity supported rapid demographic growth and general prosperity during the early part of the Han dynasty. Historians estimate that about 220 B.C.E., just after the founding of the Qin dynasty, the Chinese population was twenty million. By the year 9 C.E., at the end of the Former Han dynasty, it had tripled to sixty million. Meanwhile, taxes claimed only a small portion of production, yet state granaries bulged so much that their contents sometimes spoiled before they could be consumed.

Economic and Social Difficulties

In spite of general prosperity, China began to experience economic and social difficulties in the Former Han period. The military adventures and the central Asian policy of Han Wudi caused severe economic strain. To finance his ventures, Han Wudi raised taxes and confiscated land and personal property from wealthy individuals, sometimes on the pretext that they had violated imperial laws. Those measures discouraged investment in manufacturing and trading enterprises, which in turn had a dampening effect on the larger economy.

SOCIAL TENSIONS Distinctions between rich and poor hardened during the course of the Han dynasty. Wealthy individuals wore fine silk garments and ate rich foods, whereas the poor classes made do with rough hemp clothing and a diet of mostly grain. By the first century B.C.E., social and economic differences had generated serious tensions, and peasants in hard-pressed regions began to organize rebellions in hopes of gaining a larger share of Han society's resources.

LAND DISTRIBUTION A particularly difficult problem concerned the distribution of land. Economic problems forced many small landowners to sell their property under unfavorable conditions or even to forfeit it in exchange for cancellation of their

BURIAL SUIT. | In Han times the wealthiest classes enjoyed the privilege of being buried in suits of jade plaques sewn together with gold threads, like the burial dress of Liu Sheng, who died in 113 B.C.E. at Manzheng in Hebei Province. Legend held that jade prevented decomposition of the deceased's body. Scholars have estimated that a jade burial suit like this one required ten years' labor. ***What can such a suit tell us about the lives of the Chinese elite?***

debts. In extreme cases, individuals had to sell themselves and their families into slavery to satisfy their creditors. Owners of large estates not only increased the size of their holdings by absorbing the property of their less fortunate neighbors but also increased the efficiency of their operations by employing cheap labor.

By the end of the first century B.C.E., land had accumulated in the hands of a relatively small number of individuals who owned vast estates, while ever-increasing numbers of peasant cultivators led difficult lives with few prospects for improvement. Landless peasants became restive, and Chinese society faced growing problems of banditry and sporadic rebellion.

THE REIGN OF WANG MANG Tensions came to a head during the early first century C.E. when a powerful and respected Han minister named Wang Mang undertook a thoroughgoing program of reform. In 6 C.E. a two-year-old boy inherited the Han imperial throne. Because the boy was unable to govern, Wang Mang served as his regent. Many officials regarded Wang as more capable than members of the Han family and urged him to claim the imperial honor for himself. In 9 C.E. he did just that: announcing that the mandate of heaven had passed from the Han to his family, he seized the throne. Wang Mang then introduced a series of wide-ranging reforms that have prompted historians to refer to him as the "socialist emperor."

The most important reforms concerned landed property: Wang Mang limited the amount of land that a family could hold and ordered officials to break up large estates, redistribute them, and provide landless individuals with property to cultivate. Despite his good intentions, the socialist emperor attempted to impose his policy without adequate preparation and communication. The result was confusion: landlords resisted a policy that threatened their holdings, and even peasants found its application inconsistent and unsatisfactory. After several years of chaos, in 23 C.E. a coalition of disgruntled landlords and desperate peasants ended both his dynasty and his life.

The Later Han Dynasty

Within two years a recovered Han dynasty returned to power, but it ruled over a weakened realm. Nevertheless, during the early years of the Later Han, emperors ruled vigorously in the manner of Liu Bang and Han Wudi. They regained control of the centralized administration and reorganized the state bureaucracy. They also maintained the Chinese presence in central Asia, continued to keep the Xiongnu in submission, and exercised firm control over the silk roads.

However, the Later Han emperors did not seriously address the problem of land distribution that had helped to bring down the Former Han dynasty. The wealthy classes still lived in relative luxury while peasants worked under difficult conditions. The empire continued to suffer the effects of banditry and rebellions organized by desperate peasants with few opportunities to improve their lot.

COLLAPSE OF THE HAN DYNASTY In addition, the Later Han emperors were unable to prevent the development of factions at court that paralyzed the central government. Factions of imperial family members, Confucian scholar-bureaucrats, and court eunuchs sought to increase their influence, protect their own interests, and destroy their rivals. On several occasions relations between the various factions became so strained that they made war against one another. In 189 C.E., for example, a faction led by an imperial relative descended on the Han palace and slaughtered more than two thousand eunuchs in an effort to destroy them as a political force. In that respect the attack succeeded. From the unmeasured violence of the operation, however, it is clear that the Later Han dynasty had reached a point of internal weakness from which it could not easily recover. Indeed, early in the next century, the central government disintegrated, and for almost four centuries China remained divided into several large regional kingdoms.

SUMMARY

The Qin state lasted for a short fourteen years, but it opened a new era in Chinese history. Qin conquerors imposed unified rule on a series of politically independent kingdoms and launched an ambitious program to forge culturally distinct regions into a larger Chinese society. The Han dynasty endured for more than four centuries and largely completed the project of unifying China. Han rulers built a centralized bureaucracy that administered a unified empire, thus establishing a precedent for centralized imperial rule in China. They also entered into a close alliance with Confucian moralists who organized a system of advanced education that provided recruits for the imperial bureaucracy. Moreover, on the basis of a highly productive economy stimulated by technological innovations, Han rulers projected Chinese influence abroad to Korea, Vietnam, and central Asia. Thus, like classical societies in Persia, India, and the Mediterranean basin, Han China produced a set of distinctive political and cultural traditions that shaped Chinese and neighboring societies over the long term.

STUDY TERMS

Analects (105)
Confucianism (104)
Daodejing (107)
Daoism (106)
Former Han (112)
Han dynasty (112)
Han Wudi (113)
junzi (105)
Laozi (107)
Later Han (112)
Legalism (108)
li (105)
Liu Bang (112)
Maodun (114)
Mencius (106)
Qin (103)
Qin Shihuangdi (110)
ren (105)
Sima Qian (103)
Wang Mang (117)
wuwei (108)
xiao (105)
Xiongnu (113)
Xunzi (106)
Zhuangzi (107)

FOR FURTHER READING

Thomas J. Barfield. *The Perilous Frontier: Nomadic Empires and China.* Cambridge, Mass., 1989. A provocative analysis of the relations between Chinese and central Asian peoples.

Sebastian De Grazia, ed. *Masters of Chinese Political Thought from the Beginnings to the Han Dynasty.* New York, 1973. A valuable collection of primary sources in translation, all of them bearing on political themes.

Mark Elvin. *The Pattern of the Chinese Past.* Stanford, 1973. A remarkable analysis of Chinese history by an economic historian who brings a comparative perspective to his work.

Cho-yun Hsu. *Han Agriculture: The Formation of Early Chinese Agrarian Economy (206 B.C.–A.D. 220).* Seattle, 1980. Studies the development of intensive agriculture in Han China and provides English translations of more than two hundred documents illustrating the conditions of rural life.

Michael Loewe. *The Government of the Qin and Han Empires, 221 B.C.E.–220 C.E.* Indianapolis, Ind., 2006. A reliable survey by a leading scholar.

Victor H. Mair, trans. *Tao Te Ching: The Classic Book of Integrity and the Way.* New York, 1990. A fresh and lively translation of the Daoist classic *Daodejing,* based on recently discovered manuscripts.

Frederick W. Mote. *Intellectual Foundations of China.* 2nd ed. New York, 1989. A compact and concise introduction to the cultural history of classical China.

Michele Pirazzoli-t'Serstevens. *The Han Dynasty.* Trans. by J. Seligman. New York, 1982. An excellent and well-illustrated survey of Han China that draws on archaeological discoveries.

Benjamin I. Schwartz. *The World of Thought in Ancient China.* Cambridge, Mass., 1985. A synthesis of classical Chinese thought by a leading scholar.

Arthur Waley, trans. *The Analects of Confucius.* New York, 1938. An English version of Confucius's sayings by a gifted translator.

State, Society, and the Quest for Salvation in India

7

he earliest description of India by a foreigner came from the pen of a Greek ambassador named Megasthenes. As the diplomatic representative of the Seleucid emperor, Megasthenes lived in India for many years during the late fourth and early third centuries B.C.E., and he traveled throughout much of northern India. Although Megasthenes' book, the *Indika,* has long been lost, many quotations from it survive in Greek and Latin literature. These fragments clearly show that Megasthenes had great respect for the Indian land, people, and society.

Like travel writers of all times, Megasthenes included a certain amount of spurious information in his account of India. He wrote, for example, of ants the size of foxes that mined gold from the earth and fiercely defended their hoards from any humans who tried to steal them. Only by distracting them with slabs of meat, Megasthenes said, could humans safely make away with their treasure. He also reported races of monstrous human beings: some with no mouth who survived by breathing in the odors of fruits, flowers, and roots, others with the heads of dogs who communicated by barking.

Beyond the tall tales, Megasthenes offered a great deal of reliable information. He portrayed India as a fertile land that supported two harvests of grain per year. He described the capital of Pataliputra as a rectangle-shaped city situated along the Ganges River and surrounded by a moat and a massive timber wall with 570 towers and sixty-four gates. He mentioned large armies that used elephants as war animals. He pointed out the strongly hierarchical character of Indian society. He noted that two main schools of "philosophers" (Hindus and Buddhists) enjoyed special prominence as well as exemption from taxes, and he described the ascetic lifestyles and vegetarian diets followed by particularly devout individuals. In short, Megasthenes portrayed India as a wealthy land that supported a distinctive society with well-established cultural traditions.

❮ A painting produced in the sixth century C.E. in the Ajanta caves of central India depicts individuals of different castes, jati, *and ethnic groups in a crowd scene.*

In India as in Persia and China, the centuries after 500 B.C.E. witnessed the development of a classical society whose influence has persisted over the centuries. Its most prominent features were a well-defined social structure, which left individuals with few doubts about their position and role in society, and several popular religious traditions that helped to shape Indian beliefs and values. Two religions, Buddhism and Hinduism, also appealed strongly to peoples beyond the subcontinent.

For the most part, classical India fell under the sway of regional kingdoms rather than centralized empires. Yet the empires

CHRONOLOGY

563–483 B.C.E.	Life of Siddhartha Gautama, the Buddha
540–468 B.C.E.	Life of Vardhamana Mahavira
520 B.C.E.	Invasion of India by Darius of Persia
327 B.C.E.	Invasion of India by Alexander of Macedon
321–185 B.C.E.	Mauryan dynasty
321–297 B.C.E.	Reign of Chandragupta Maurya
268–232 B.C.E.	Reign of Ashoka Maurya
182 B.C.E.–1 C.E.	Bactrian rule in northern India
1–300 C.E.	Kushan empire in northern India and central Asia
78–103 C.E.	Reign of Kushan emperor Kanishka
320–550 C.E.	Gupta dynasty

that did arise were crucial for the consolidation of Indian cultural traditions, because they sponsored cultural leaders and promoted their ideals throughout the subcontinent and beyond. The spread of Buddhism is a case in point: imperial support helped the faith secure its position in India and attract converts in other lands. Thus, even in the absence of a continuous imperial tradition like that of Persia or China, the social and cultural traditions of classical India not only shaped the lives and experiences of the subcontinent's inhabitants but also influenced peoples in distant lands.

THE FORTUNES OF EMPIRE IN CLASSICAL INDIA

Following their migrations to India after 1500 B.C.E., the Aryans established a series of small kingdoms throughout the subcontinent. By the sixth century B.C.E., wars of expansion between these small kingdoms had resulted in the consolidation of several large regional kingdoms that dominated much of the subcontinent. Despite strenuous efforts, none of these kingdoms was able to establish hegemony over the others until the classical era, when the Mauryan and the Gupta dynasties founded centralized, imperial states that embraced much of India. However, neither empire survived long enough to establish centralized rule as a lasting feature of Indian political life.

The Mauryan Dynasty and the Temporary Unification of India

The unification of India came about partly as a result of intrusion from beyond the subcontinent. About 520 B.C.E. the Persian emperor Darius crossed the Hindu Kush Mountains, conquered parts of northwestern India, and made the kingdom of Gandhara in the northern Punjab (the northern part of modern-day Pakistan) a province of the Achaemenid empire. Almost two centuries later, in 327 B.C.E., after overrunning the Persian empire, Alexander of Macedon crossed the Indus River and crushed the states he found there. Alexander remained in India for only two years, and he did not make a deep impression on the Punjabi people. Yet his campaign had an important effect on Indian history, since he created a political vacuum in northwestern India by destroying the existing states and then withdrawing his forces.

KINGDOM OF MAGADHA Poised to fill the vacuum was the dynamic kingdom of Magadha, located in the central portion of the Ganges plain. By about 500 B.C.E. Magadha had emerged as the most important state in northeastern India. During the next two centuries, the kings of Magadha conquered the neighboring states and gained control of Indian commerce passing through the Ganges valley as well as overseas trade between India and Burma passing across the Bay of Bengal. The withdrawal of Alexander from the Punjab presented Magadha with a rare opportunity to expand.

CHANDRAGUPTA MAURYA During the late 320s B.C.E., an ambitious adventurer named Chandragupta Maurya exploited that opportunity and laid the foundation for the Mauryan empire, the first state to bring a centralized, unified government to most of the Indian subcontinent. Chandragupta

Chandragupta Maurya (chuhn-dra-GOOP-tah MORE-yuh)

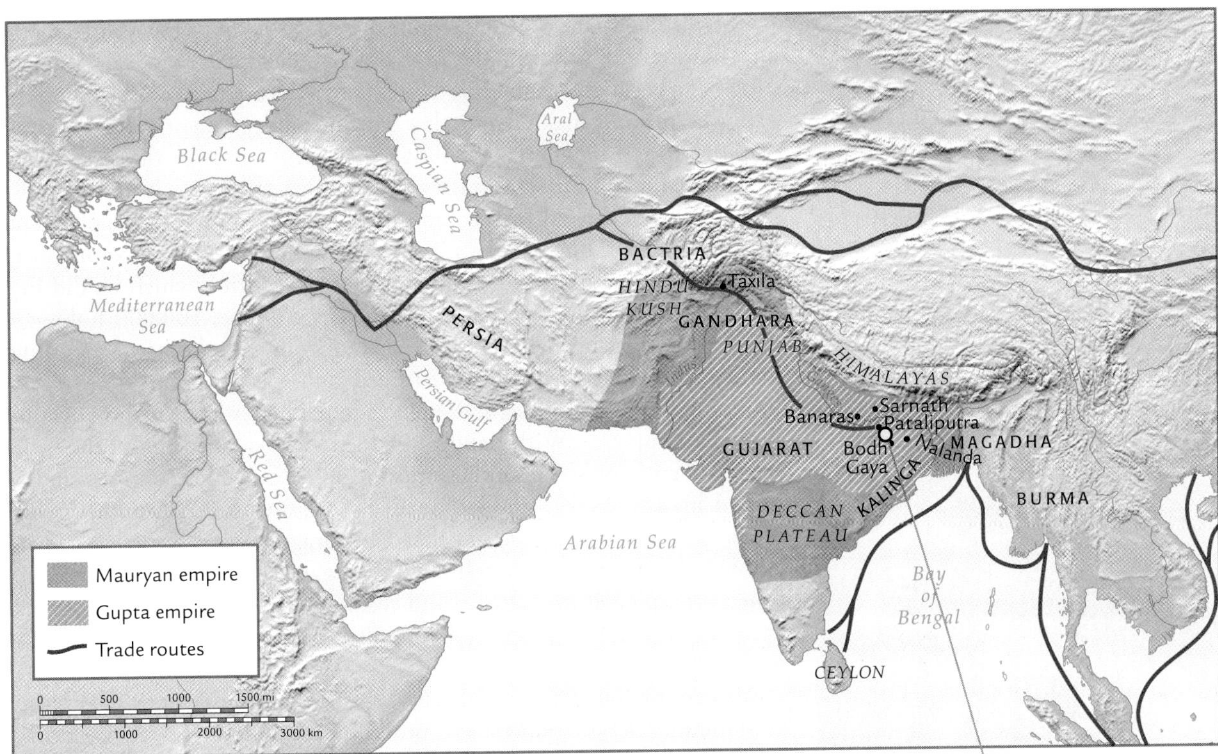

MAP 7.1 | The Mauryan and Gupta empires, 321 B.C.E.–550 C.E. The Mauryan and Gupta dynasties both originated in the kingdom of Magadha. ***Why was this region so important in ancient India? What advantages did it offer for purposes of trade and communication with other regions?***

Both the Mauryan and Gupta empires made their capital in Pataliputra, near the Ganges River.

began by seizing control of small, remote regions of Magadha and then worked his way gradually toward the center. By 321 B.C.E. he had overthrown the ruling dynasty and consolidated his hold on the kingdom. He then moved into the Punjab and brought northwestern India under his control. Next he ventured beyond the Indus River and conquered the Greek state in Bactria. By the end of the fourth century B.C.E., Chandragupta's empire embraced all of northern India from the Indus to the Ganges.

PSI map — Mauryan & Gupta empires www.mhhe.com/bentleybrief2e

CHANDRAGUPTA'S GOVERNMENT A careful and systematic advisor named Kautalya devised procedures for the governance of Chandragupta's realm. Some of Kautalya's advice survives in the ancient Indian political handbook known as the *Arthashastra.* The *Arthashastra* outlined methods of administering the empire, overseeing trade and agriculture, collecting taxes, maintaining order, conducting foreign relations, and waging war. Kautalya also advised Chandragupta to make abundant use of spies, even including prostitutes in his stable of informants. Like the emperors of Persia and China, Chandragupta and Kautalya built a bureaucratic administrative system that enabled them to implement policies throughout the state.

ASHOKA MAURYA Tradition holds that Chandragupta abdicated his throne to become a monk and led such an ascetic life that he starved himself to death. Whether that report is true or not, it is certain that his son succeeded him in 297 B.C.E. and added most of

Arthashastra (UHRR-th-sha-strah)
Kautalya (KAHT-ahl-yah)
Ashoka (ah-SHOW-kuh)

southern India to the growing empire. The high point of the Mauryan empire, however, came during the reign of Chandragupta's grandson Ashoka.

Ashoka began his reign (268–232 B.C.E.) as a conqueror. When he came to power, the only major region that remained independent of the Mauryan empire was the kingdom of Kalinga (modern Orissa) in the east-central part of the subcontinent. Kalinga was desirable territory for Ashoka because it controlled both land and sea trade routes between the Ganges plain and southern India. Thus Ashoka's first major undertaking as emperor was to conquer Kalinga and bring it under Mauryan control, which he did in a bloody campaign in 260 B.C.E. By Ashoka's estimate, 100,000 Kalingans died in the fighting, 150,000 were driven from their homes, and untold numbers of others perished in the ruined land.

STONE COLUMN FROM THE REIGN OF ASHOKA. As a symbol of his rule, Ashoka had this sculpture of four lions mounted atop a column about 20 meters (66 feet) tall. The lion capital is the official symbol of the modern Republic of India. ***Why might Ashoka have chosen the lion as a symbol of his rule?***

In spite of that campaign, Ashoka is much better known as a governor than as a conqueror. With Kalinga subdued, Ashoka ruled almost the entire subcontinent—only the southernmost region escaped his control—and he turned his attention to the responsible government of his realm. As heir to the administrative structure that Chandragupta and Kautalya had instituted, Ashoka ruled through a tightly organized bureaucracy. He established his capital at the fortified and cosmopolitan city of Pataliputra (near modern Patna), where a central administration developed policies for the whole empire. A central treasury oversaw the efficient collection of taxes—a hallmark of Kautalya's influence—which supported legions of officials, accountants, clerks, soldiers, and other imperial employees. Ashoka communicated his policies throughout his realm by inscribing edicts in natural stone formations or on pillars that he ordered erected. In those promulgations, known as the rock and pillar edicts, Ashoka issued imperial decrees, encouraged his subjects to observe Buddhist values, and expressed his intention to serve as a fair, just, and humane ruler.

As a result of Ashoka's policies, the various regions of India became well integrated, and the subcontinent benefited from both an expanding economy and a stable government. Ashoka encouraged the expansion of agriculture by building irrigation systems. He encouraged trade by building roads, most notably a highway of more than 1,600 kilometers (1,000 miles) linking Pataliputra with Taxila, the chief political and commercial center of northern India, which offered access to Bactria, Persia, and other points west. Ashoka also provided comforts for administrators, merchants, and other travelers by planting banyan trees to offer shade, digging wells, and establishing inns along the roads.

DECLINE OF THE MAURYAN EMPIRE Ashoka's policies did not long survive his rule, nor did his empire. Ashoka died in 232 B.C.E., and decline set in almost immediately. During its later years the Mauryan empire suffered from acute financial and economic difficulties. The empire depended on a strong army and a large corps of officials to administer imperial policy. Salaries for soldiers and bureaucrats were very expensive, and administrative costs soon outstripped the revenues that flowed into the central treasury. Because of their financial difficulties, the later Mauryan emperors were unable to hold the realm together. By about 185 B.C.E., almost fifty years after Ashoka's death, the Mauryan empire had disappeared.

The Emergence of Regional Kingdoms and the Revival of Empire

BACTRIAN RULE IN NORTHWESTERN INDIA Although the Mauryan empire came to an end, India did not crumble into anarchy. Instead, local rulers formed a series of kingdoms that brought order to large regions. Although regional

Pataliputra (pah-tal-ih-puh-trah)

kingdoms emerged throughout the subcontinent, historical records and archaeological excavations have thrown clearest light on developments in northern India. For almost two centuries after the collapse of the Mauryan empire, northwestern India fell under the rule of Greek-speaking conquerors from Bactria—Alexander of Macedon's imperial heirs who had mingled with local populations since establishing an independent Bactrian kingdom in the third century B.C.E. Bactria was a thriving commercial center linking lands from China in the east to the Mediterranean basin in the west, so Bactrian rule had the effect of promoting cross-cultural interaction and exchange in northern India. Large volumes of trade provided sources of revenue for the Bactrian rulers, and the city of Taxila flourished because of its strategic location on trade routes leading from northern India to Bactria.

THINKING ABOUT *Traditions*

TRADITIONS IN CLASSICAL INDIA. Although classical Indian society did not develop long-lasting imperial traditions like classical Persia and China, people throughout the subcontinent nevertheless developed other traditions that promoted both social unity and social order. In what ways did the caste system function to promote this unity and order, and how might it have encouraged a shared sense of identity in India?

THE KUSHAN EMPIRE Beginning in the late second century B.C.E., several groups of nomadic conquerors from central Asia attacked Bactria and eventually put an end to the Indo-Greek kingdom there. The most successful of those conquerors were the Kushans, who ruled a sizable empire embracing much of northern India and central Asia from about 1 to 300 C.E. Under Kanishka, the most prominent of the Kushan emperors (reigned 78–103 C.E.), the Kushan empire embraced modern-day Pakistan, Afghanistan, and northern India to Gujarat and the central part of the Ganges valley. Like the Indo-Greek Bactrians, the Kushans facilitated commerce between India and lands to the north. Indeed, the Kushan empire played a crucial role in the silk roads network (discussed in chapter 9) by pacifying much of the large region between Persia and China, thus making it possible for merchants to travel safely across long distances.

THE GUPTA DYNASTY In about 320 C.E., a new power—the Guptas—arose in the Ganges region and established a dynamic kingdom. Like the Mauryas, the Guptas based their state in Magadha, a crucial region because of its wealth, its dominance of the Ganges valley, and its role as intermediary between the various regions of the subcontinent. The empire was founded by Chandra Gupta (not related to Chandragupta Maurya), who forged alliances with powerful families in the Ganges region. His successors, Samudra Gupta (reigned 335–375 C.E.) and Chandra Gupta II (reigned 375–415 C.E.), took the former Mauryan capital of Pataliputra as their own, conquered many of the regional kingdoms of India, and established tributary alliances with others that elected not to fight. Only the Deccan Plateau and the southernmost part of the subcontinent remained outside the orbit of Gupta influence.

The Gupta empire was somewhat smaller in size than the Mauryan, and it also differed considerably in organization. Ashoka had insisted on knowing the details of regional affairs, which he closely monitored from his court at Pataliputra. The Guptas left local government and administration, and even the making of basic policy, in the hands of their allies in the various regions of their empire. Nevertheless, during the late fourth and early fifth centuries C.E., the Gupta dynasty brought stability and prosperity to much of the subcontinent.

GUPTA DECLINE The Guptas were eventually overcome, however, by the White Huns, a nomadic people from central Asia. For the first half of the fifth century, the Guptas repelled the Huns as they tried to invade across the Hindu Kush mountains from Bactria, but the defense cost them dearly in resources and eventually weakened their state. By the end of the fifth century, the Huns moved across the Hindu Kush almost at will and had established several kingdoms in northern and western India.

The Gupta dynasty continued in name only: regional governors progressively usurped imperial rights and powers, and contemporary documents do not even record the names of all the later Gupta emperors. Once again, imperial government survived only for a short term in India. Not until the establishment of the Mughal dynasty in the sixteenth

Gupta (GOOP-tah)

century C.E. did any state rule as much of India as the Mauryan and Gupta empires ruled. Memories of empire remained, to be sure, but for the most part large regional kingdoms dominated political life in India during the millennium between the Gupta and the Mughal dynasties.

Economic Development and Social Distinctions

After spreading through the subcontinent, Aryan migrants turned increasingly from herding to agriculture. Once they learned the techniques of iron metallurgy after about 1000 B.C.E., they used iron axes and tools to advance into previously inaccessible regions, notably the jungle-covered valley of the Ganges River. Agricultural surpluses from these fertile lands supported large-scale states such as the regional kingdoms and the Mauryan and Gupta empires that organized Indian public life. Agricultural surpluses also encouraged the emergence of towns, the growth of trade, and further development of the caste system.

Towns and Trade

After about 600 B.C.E. towns dotted the Indian countryside, especially in the northwestern corner of the subcontinent. These towns served the needs of a productive agricultural society by providing manufactured products for local consumption—pots, textiles, iron tools, and other metal utensils—as well as luxury goods such as jewelry destined for the wealthy and elite classes.

Flourishing towns maintained marketplaces and encouraged the development of trade. Within the subcontinent itself trade was most active along the Ganges River, although trade routes also passed through the Ganges delta east to Burma and down the east Indian coast to the Deccan and southern India. Roads built by Ashoka also facilitated overland commerce within the subcontinent.

LONG-DISTANCE TRADE Meanwhile, the volume of long-distance trade also grew as large imperial states in China, southwest Asia, and the Mediterranean basin provided a political foundation enabling merchants to deal with their counterparts in distant lands. From India, long-distance trade passed overland in two directions: through the Hindu Kush mountains and the Gandharan capital of Taxila to Persia and the Mediterranean basin, and across the silk roads of central Asia to markets in China. Cotton, aromatics, black pepper, pearls, and gems were the principal Indian exports, in exchange for which Indian merchants imported horses and bullion from western lands and silk from China.

TRADE IN THE INDIAN OCEAN BASIN During the Mauryan era merchants continued to use land routes, but they increasingly turned to the sea to transport their goods. Seaborne trade benefited especially from the rhythms of the monsoon winds that govern weather and the seasons in the Indian Ocean basin. During the spring and summer, the winds blow from the southwest, and during the fall and winter, they blow from the northeast. Once mariners recognized these rhythms, they could sail easily and safely before the wind to any part of the Indian Ocean basin.

As early as the fifth century B.C.E., Indian merchants had traveled to the islands of Indonesia and the southeast Asian mainland, where they exchanged pearls, cotton, black pepper, and Indian manufactured goods for spices and exotic local products. Many of those goods then traveled west through the Arabian Sea to the lands bordering the Persian Gulf and the Red Sea. Indian products also found markets in the Mediterranean basin. Indian pepper became so popular there that the Romans established direct commercial relations and built several trading settlements in southern India. Archaeologists in southern India have unearthed hoards of Roman coins that testify to the large volume of trade between classical India and Mediterranean lands.

Gupta-era Painting. Jewel-bedecked flying goddesses drop flowers on the earth from their perch in the heavens. Their gems and personal adornments reflect the tastes of upper-class women during the Gupta dynasty. This painting on a rock wall, produced about the sixth century C.E., survives in modern Sri Lanka.

Family Life and the Caste System

GENDER RELATIONS In the midst of urban growth and economic development, Indian moralists sought to promote stability by encouraging respect for strong patriarchal families and to promote the maintenance of a social order in which all members played well-defined roles. Although most people lived with members of their nuclear family, among the higher castes several generations of a family often lived in large compounds ruled by powerful patriarchs. Literary works suggest that women were largely subordinate to men. The two great Indian epics, the *Mahabharata* and the *Ramayana,* commonly portrayed women as weak-willed and emotional creatures and exalted wives who devoted themselves to their husbands.

During the early centuries C.E., patriarchal dominance became more pronounced in India. By the Gupta era child marriage was common: when girls were age eight or nine, their parents betrothed them to men in their twenties. Formal marriage took place just after the girls reached puberty. Wives often came to dominate domestic affairs in their households, but the practice of child marriage placed them under the control of older men and encouraged them to devote themselves to family matters rather than to public affairs in the larger society.

SOCIAL ORDER After their arrival in India, the Aryans recognized four main castes, or classes of people: *brahmins* (priests), *kshatriyas* (warriors and aristocrats), *vaishyas*

Mahabharata (mah-hah-BAH-'rah-tah)
Ramayana (rah-MAY-yuh-nah)
kshatriyas (kuh-SHAT-tree-uhs)

Buddhist Temple Sculpture. | Buddhist art often depicted individuals as models of proper social relationships. Here a sculpture from a Buddhist temple at Karli, produced about the first century C.E., represents an ideal Buddhist married couple. ***What does the position of the images imply about the ideal relationship between husband and wife?***

(peasants and merchants), and *shudras* (serfs). Brahmins in particular endorsed this social order, which brought them honor, prestige, and sometimes considerable wealth as well.

CASTES AND GUILDS However, as trade and industrial activity expanded, new groups of artisans, craftsmen, and merchants appeared, many of whom did not fit easily into the established structure. Individuals working in the same craft or trade usually joined together to form a guild, a corporate body that supervised prices and wages in a given industry and provided for the welfare of members and their families. Guild members lived in the same quarter of town, socialized with one another, intermarried, and cared for the group's widows, orphans, and needy.

In effect, the guilds functioned as subcastes based on occupation, known as *jati.* These *jati,* in turn, assumed much of the responsibility for maintaining social order in India. *Jati* regularly organized their own courts, through which they disciplined members, resolved differences, and regulated community affairs. Individuals who did not abide by group rules were liable to expulsion from the community. Thus Indian guilds and *jati* performed services that central governments provided in other lands. The tendency for individuals and their families to associate closely with others of the same occupation remained a prominent feature of Indian society well into modern times.

WEALTH AND THE SOCIAL ORDER Beyond encouraging further development of the caste system, economic development in the subcontinent also generated tremendous wealth, which posed a serious challenge to the social order that arose in India following the Aryan migrations. Traditional social theory accorded special honor to the brahmins and the kshatriyas because of the worthy lives they had led during previous incarnations and the heavy responsibilities they assumed as priests, warriors, and rulers during their current incarnations. Members of the vaishya and shudra castes, on the other hand, had the obligation to work as directed by the higher castes. During the centuries after 600 B.C.E., however, trade and industry brought prosperity to many vaishyas and even shudras, who sometimes became wealthier and more influential in society than their brahmin and kshatriya contemporaries.

Economic development and social change in classical India had profound implications for the established cultural as well as the social order. The beliefs, values, and rituals that were meaningful in early Aryan society—especially the ritual sacrifices offered by brahmins—seemed increasingly irrelevant during the centuries after 600 B.C.E. Along with emerging towns, growing trade, increasing wealth, and a developing social structure, classical India saw the appearance of new religions that addressed the needs of the changing times.

Religions of Salvation in Classical India

During the sixth and fifth centuries B.C.E., new religions and philosophies appealed to the interests of new social classes. Some of them tended toward atheistic materialism: members of the Charvaka sect, for example, believed that the gods were figments of the imagination, that brahmins were charlatans who enriched themselves by hoodwinking others, and that human beings came from dust and returned to dust like any other animal in the natural world. Others, such as the Jains, the Buddhists, and the Hindus, turned to intense spirituality as an alternative to the mechanical rituals of the brahmins.

vaishyas (VEYESH-yuhs)
shudras (SHOO-druhs)
Charvaka (CHAHR-vah-kuh)

Jainism and the Challenge to the Established Cultural Order

JAIN SCULPTURE. | Mahavira with one of his disciples. Representations of the early Jains often depicted them in the nude because of their ascetic way of life.

VARDHAMANA MAHAVIRA Among the most influential of the new religions was Jainism. Although Jainist doctrines first appeared during the seventh century B.C.E., they became popular only when the great teacher Vardhamana Mahavira turned to Jainism in the late sixth century B.C.E. Mahavira (the "great hero") was born in northern India about 540 B.C.E. to a prominent kshatriya family. According to the semilegendary accounts of his life, he left home at age thirty to seek salvation by escaping from the cycle of incarnation. For twelve years he led an ascetic life wandering throughout the Ganges valley, after which he gained enlightenment. He abandoned all his worldly goods, even his clothes, and taught an ascetic doctrine of detachment from the world. For the next thirty years, until his death about 468 B.C.E., he expounded his thought to a group of disciples who formed a monastic order to perpetuate and spread his message. These disciples referred to Mahavira as *Jina* (the "conqueror"), and borrowing from this title his followers referred to themselves as *Jains.*

Much of the inspiration for Jainist doctrine came from the Upanishads. Jains believed that everything in the universe—humans, animals, plants, the air, bodies of water, and even inanimate physical objects—possessed a soul. As long as they remained trapped in terrestrial bodies, these souls experienced both physical and psychological suffering. Only by purification from selfish behavior could souls gain release from their imprisonment and attain a state of bliss.

JAINIST ETHICS Individuals underwent purification by observing the principle of *ahimsa,* or nonviolence to other souls. Devout Jainist monks went to extremes to avoid harming the millions of souls they encountered each day. They swept the ground before them as they walked to avoid causing harm to insects; they strained their drinking water through cloth filters to remove tiny animals they might unwittingly consume; they followed an abstemious and strictly vegetarian diet; they even wore masks and avoided making sudden movements so that they would not bruise or otherwise disturb the tiny souls inhabiting the surrounding air.

Jainist ethics were so demanding that few people other than devout monks could hope to observe them closely. For certain groups, however, Jainism represented an attractive alternative to the traditional cults. Indeed, since Jains believed all creatures had souls that should be protected equally, Jains did not recognize human social hierarchies based on caste or *jati.* It is not surprising, then, that their faith became popular especially among members of lower castes, including merchants, scholars, and literary figures. These people provided substantial lay support for the Jainist monks and helped to maintain the ideal of ahimsa as a prominent concern of Indian ethics. Indeed, the doctrine of ahimsa has been an especially influential teaching over the long term, both in India and beyond. Quite apart from some two million Indian individuals who maintain Jainist traditions in the present day, many Buddhists and Hindus recognize ahimsa as a fundamental element of their beliefs, and prominent reformers of the twentieth century C.E. such as Mohandas K. Gandhi and Martin Luther King Jr. relied on the doctrine of ahimsa when promoting social reform by nonviolent means.

In spite of the moral respect it has commanded and the influence it has wielded through the centuries, however, Jainism has always been the faith of a small minority. It has simply

Jainism (JEYEN-iz'm)
Vardhamana (vahr-duh-MAH-nuh)
Upanishads (oo-pan-NIH-shuhds)
ahimsa (uh-HIM-suh)

been too difficult for most people to observe. A more popular and practical alternative to the brahmins' cults came in the form of Buddhism.

Early Buddhism

SIDDHARTHA GUATAMA Like Mahavira, the founder of Buddhism, Siddhartha Gautama, came from a kshatriya family but gave up his position and inheritance to seek salvation. He was born about 563 B.C.E. in a small tribal state governed by his father in the foothills of the Himalayas. According to early accounts, Gautama lived a pampered and sheltered life in palaces and parks, because his father had determined that Gautama would never know misery. He married his cousin and excelled in the program of studies that would prepare him to succeed his father as governor.

Eventually, however, Gautama became dissatisfied with his comfortable life. One day, according to an early legend, while riding toward a park in his chariot, Gautama saw a man made miserable by age and infirmity. When he asked for an explanation of this unsettling sight, Gautama learned from his chariot driver that all human beings grow old and weak. On later outings Gautama learned that disease and death were also inevitable features of the human condition. When he then came into contact with a monk traveling by foot, Gautama learned that some individuals withdraw from the active life of the world to lead holy lives. Inspired, Gautama determined to take up a similar life for himself in the hope that it would help him to understand the phenomenon of suffering.

GAUTAMA'S SEARCH FOR ENLIGHTENMENT About 534 B.C.E. Gautama left his wife and family and the comforts of home to lead the existence of a holy man. He wandered throughout the Ganges valley searching for spiritual enlightenment and an explanation for suffering. He sought enlightenment first by means of intense meditation and later through the rigors of extreme asceticism. None of those tactics satisfied him. Then, according to Buddhist legends, as he sat one day beneath a large bo tree in Bodh Gaya, southwest of Pataliputra, Gautama decided that he would remain exactly where he was until he understood the problem of suffering. For forty-nine days he sat in meditation as various demons tempted and threatened him to shake his resolution. On the forty-ninth day Gautama prevailed and received enlightenment: he understood both the problem of suffering and the means by which humans could eliminate it from the world. At that point, Gautama became the Buddha—the "enlightened one."

The standing Buddha
www.mhhe.com/
bentleybrief2e

THE BUDDHA AND HIS FOLLOWERS The Buddha publicly announced his doctrine for the first time about 528 B.C.E. at the Deer Park of Sarnath, near the Buddhist holy city of Banaras (modern Varanasi), in a sermon delivered to friends. Buddhists refer to this sermon as the "Turning of the Wheel of the Law" because it represented the beginning of the Buddha's quest to promulgate the law of righteousness. His teachings quickly attracted attention, and disciples came from all parts of the Ganges valley. He organized them into a community of monks who owned only their yellow robes and their begging bowls. For more than forty years, the Buddha led his disciples throughout much of northern India in hopes of bringing spiritual enlightenment to others.

BUDDHIST DOCTRINE: THE DHARMA The core of the Buddha's doctrine, known as the Four Noble Truths, teaches that all life involves suffering; that desire is the cause of suffering; that elimination of desire brings an end to suffering; and that a disciplined life conducted in accordance with the Noble Eightfold Path brings the elimination of desire. The Noble Eightfold Path calls for individuals to lead balanced and moderate lives, rejecting both devotion to luxury and to regimes of extreme asceticism.

Siddhartha Gautama (sih-DHAR-tuh GAHW-tah-mah)
Buddha (BOO-duh)

Specifically, the Noble Eightfold Path demands right belief, right resolve, right speech, right behavior, right occupation, right effort, right contemplation, and right meditation. Taken together, the teachings of the Four Noble Truths and the Noble Eightfold Path constitute the Buddhist *dharma*—the basic doctrine shared by Buddhists of all sects.

Ultimately, Buddhists believed that a lifestyle based on the Buddhist dharma would lead to personal salvation, which meant an escape from the cycle of incarnation and attainment of *nirvana,* a state of perfect spiritual independence. Like the Jains, the Buddhists sought to escape the cycle of incarnation without depending on the services of the brahmins. Like the Jains, too, they did not recognize social distinctions based on caste or *jati.* As a result, their message appealed strongly to members of lower castes. Yet, because it did not demand the rigorous asceticism of Jainism, Buddhism became far more popular, especially with merchants.

SCULPTURE OF THE BUDDHA. | A confident and serene Buddha preaches his first sermon after his enlightenment at the Deer Park of Sarnath. ***Why is the Buddha commonly depicted in this position?***

APPEAL OF BUDDHISM Apart from the social implications of the doctrine, there were several other reasons for the popularity of early Buddhism in India. One has to do with language. Following the example of the Buddha himself, early Buddhist monks and preachers avoided the use of Sanskrit, the literary language of the *Vedas* that the brahmins employed in their rituals, in favor of vernacular tongues that reached a much larger popular audience. Furthermore, early Buddhists recognized holy sites that served as focal points for devotion. Even in the early days of Buddhism, pilgrims flocked to Bodh Gaya, where Gautama received enlightenment, and the Deer Park of Sarnath, where as the Buddha he preached his first sermon. Also popular with the faithful were stupas—shrines housing relics of the Buddha and his first disciples that pilgrims venerated while meditating on Buddhist values.

Buddha with devotees
www.mhhe.com/bentleybrief2e

Yet another reason for the early popularity of Buddhism was the organization of the Buddhist movement. From the days of the Buddha himself, the most enthusiastic and highly motivated converts joined monastic communities where they dedicated their lives to the search for enlightenment and to preaching the Buddhist dharma to lay audiences. During the centuries following the Buddha's death, this monastic organization proved to be extremely efficient at spreading the Buddhist message and winning converts to the faith.

Buddhist statues at Sanchi
www.mhhe.com/bentleybrief2e

dharma (DHUHR-muh)
Buddhism (BOO-diz'm)
nirvana (ner-VAHN-nah)
stupas (STOO-pahs)

The Buddhist Stupa at Sanchi. | This stupa was originally built by Ashoka and enlarged in later times.

ASHOKA'S SUPPORT The early Buddhist movement also benefited from the official patronage and support of the Mauryan dynasty. The precise reason for Ashoka's conversion to Buddhism is unclear. Ashoka's own account, as preserved in one of his edicts, explains that the emperor adopted Buddhism about 260 B.C.E. after the war against Kalinga. Saddened by the violence of the war and the suffering of the Kalingans, Ashoka said that he decided to pursue his aims henceforth by means of virtue, benevolence, and humanity rather than arms. Quite apart from his sincere religious convictions, it is also likely that Ashoka found Buddhism appealing as a faith that could lend unity to his culturally diverse and far-flung realm. In any case, in honor of ahimsa, the doctrine of nonviolence, Ashoka banned animal sacrifices in Pataliputra, gave up his beloved hunting expeditions, and eliminated most meat dishes from the tables of his court. Ashoka rewarded Buddhists with grants of land, and he encouraged them to spread their faith throughout India. He built monasteries and stupas and made pilgrimages to the holy sites of Buddhism. Ashoka also sent missionaries to Bactria and Ceylon (modern Sri Lanka), thus inaugurating a process by which Buddhism attracted large followings in central Asia, east Asia, and southeast Asia.

Mahayana Buddhism

From its earliest days Buddhism attracted merchants, artisans, and others of low rank in the traditional Indian social order. Its appeal was due both to its disregard for social classes and to its concern for ethical behavior instead of complicated ceremonies. Yet, even though it vastly simplified religious observances, early Buddhism made heavy demands on individuals seeking to escape from the cycle of incarnation. A truly righteous existence involved considerable sacrifice: giving up personal property, forsaking the search for social standing, and resolutely detaching oneself from the charms of family and the world. Although perhaps more attractive than the religion of the *brahmins,* Buddhism did not promise to make life easy for its adherents.

DEVELOPMENT OF BUDDHISM Between the third century B.C.E. and the first century C.E., however, three new developments in Buddhist thought and practice reduced obligations of believers, opened new avenues to salvation, and brought explosive popularity to the faith. In the first place, whereas the Buddha had not considered himself divine, some of his later followers began to worship him as a god. Thus Buddhism acquired a devotional focus that helped converts channel their spiritual energies. In the second place, theologians articulated the notion of the *boddhisatva,* an enlightened being. Boddhisatvas were individuals who had reached spiritual perfection and merited the reward of nirvana, but who intentionally delayed their entry into nirvana to help others who were still struggling. Like Christian saints, boddhisatvas served as examples of spiritual excellence, and they provided a source of inspiration. Finally, Buddhist monasteries began to accept gifts from wealthy individuals and to regard the bequests as acts of generosity that merited salvation. Thus wealthy individuals could avoid the sacrifices demanded by early Buddhist teachings and still ensure their salvation.

BODDHISATVA CARVING. This carving dates from the second or third century C.E. It may represent Avalokitesvara, also known as the Lord of Compassion. Almost as perfect as the Buddha, Avalokitesvara had a reputation for protecting merchants and sailors, helping women conceive, and turning enemies into kindhearted friends.

THE SPREAD OF MAHAYANA BUDDHISM Because these innovations opened the road to salvation for large numbers of people, their proponents called their faith the *Mahayana* (the "greater vehicle," which could carry more people to salvation), as opposed to the *Hinayana* (the "lesser vehicle"), a pejorative term for the earlier and stricter doctrine known also as Theravada Buddhism. During the early centuries C.E., Mahayana Buddhism spread rapidly throughout India and attracted many converts. In later centuries Mahayana Buddhism became established also in central Asia, China, Japan, and Korea. The stricter Theravada faith did not disappear, but since the first century C.E. most of the world's Buddhists have practiced Mahayana Buddhism.

NALANDA Mahayana Buddhism flourished partly because of educational institutions that promoted the faith. During the Vedic era, Indian education was mostly an informal affair involving a sage and his students. When Jains and Buddhists organized monasteries, however, they began to establish educational institutions. Most monasteries provided basic education, and larger communities offered advanced instruction as well. Best known of all was the Buddhist monastery at Nalanda, founded during the Gupta dynasty in the Ganges River valley near Pataliputra. At Nalanda it was possible to study not only Buddhism but also the *Vedas,* Hindu philosophy, logic, mathematics, astronomy, and medicine. Nalanda soon became famous, and by the end of the Gupta dynasty, several thousand students may have been in residence there.

Buddhist priests in Sri Lanka and Cambodia
www.mhhe.com/bentleybrief2e

The Emergence of Popular Hinduism

As Buddhism generated new ideas and attracted widespread popular interest, Hinduism underwent a similar evolution that transformed it into a popular religion of salvation. Although drawing inspiration from the *Vedas* and the Upanishads, popular Hinduism increasingly departed from the older traditions of the brahmins to meet the needs of ordinary people.

THE BHAGAVAD GITA A short poetic work known as the *Bhagavad Gita* ("song of the lord") best illustrates both the expectations that Hinduism made of individuals and the promise of salvation that it held out to them. Scholars have dated the work at various points between 300 B.C.E. and 300 C.E., and it most likely underwent several rounds of revision before taking on its final form about 400 C.E. Yet it eloquently evokes the cultural climate of India between the Mauryan and the Gupta dynasties.

THINKING ABOUT *Encounters*

ENCOUNTERS IN CLASSICAL INDIA. Throughout the classical period, India was tied to vast overland trading networks linking it to central and east Asia, as well as ocean trading networks linking it to southeast and east Asia. How did the interactions promoted by these networks alter Indian society, and to what extent did these same networks allow for the diffusion of Indian cultural beliefs and practices?

boddhisatvas (BOH-dih-SAT-vuhs)
Mahayana (mah-huh-YAH-nah)
Hinayana (HEE-nah-yah-nuh)
Theravada (thehr-ah-VAH-dah)

SOURCES FROM THE PAST

The Teachings of the Buddha

According to the sources written about the Buddha (born Siddhartha Gautama) after his death, his first sermon addressed the problem of human suffering. According to the Buddha, human suffering was the result of attachment to life's passions, to the body, to health, to things, or to people. In order to alleviate suffering, then, the Buddha advised a practice of non-attachment. Eventually, the goal was to reach a state of nirvana, or extinguishment, in which the soul is released from the cycle of rebirth and suffering.

The world is full of suffering. Birth is suffering, old age is suffering, sickness and death are sufferings. To meet a man whom one hates is suffering. To be separated from a beloved one is suffering. To be vainly struggling to satisfy one's needs is suffering. In fact, life that is not free from desire and passion is always involved with distress. This is called the Truth of Suffering.

The cause of human suffering is undoubtedly found in the thirsts of the physical body and in the illusions of worldly passion. If these thirsts and illusions are traced to their source, they are found to be rooted in the intense desires of physical instincts. Thus, desire, having a strong will-to-live as its basis, seeks that which it feels desirable, even if it is sometimes death. This is called the Truth of the Cause of Suffering.

If desire, which lies at the root of all human passion, can be removed, then passion will die out and all human suffering will be ended. This is called the Truth of the Cessation of Suffering.

In order to enter into a state where there is no desire and no suffering, one must follow a certain Path. The stages of the Noble Eightfold Path are: Right Understanding, Right Purpose, Right Speech, Right Behavior, Right Livelihood, Right Effort, Right Mindfulness, and Right Concentration. This is called the Truth of the Noble Path to the Cessation of the Cause of Suffering.

People should keep these Truths clearly in mind, for the world is filled with suffering, and if anyone wishes to escape from suffering, he must sever the ties of worldly passion, which is the sole cause of suffering. The way of life which is free from all worldly passion and suffering can only be known through Enlightenment, and Enlightenment can only be attained through the discipline of the Noble Eightfold Path.

■ **Consider the teachings of the Buddha in comparison to popular Hinduism as it was expressed in the *Bhagavad Gita*. How did the lessons of the Buddha differ from those of the *Bhagavad Gita*, especially regarding the advisability of involving oneself in the affairs of day-to-day life?**

SOURCE: Thomas Sanders et al. *Encounters in World History: Sources and Themes from the Global Past,* Vol. I. Boston: McGraw-Hill, 2006, pp. 113–114.

Mahabharata map of important Hindu sites
www.mhhe.com/bentleybrief2e

The work is a self-contained episode of the *Mahabharata,* one of the great epic poems of India. It presents a dialogue between Arjuna, a kshatriya about to enter battle, and his charioteer Krishna, who was in fact a human incarnation of the god Vishnu. The immediate problem addressed in the work was Arjuna's reluctance to fight: the enemy included many of his friends and relatives, and even though he recognized the justice of his cause, he shrank from the conflict. In an effort to persuade the warrior to fight, Krishna presented Arjuna with several lines of argument. In the first place, he said, Arjuna must not worry about harming his friends and relatives, because the soul does not die with the human body, and Arjuna's weapons did not have the power to touch the soul.

Vishnu dreaming the universe
www.mhhe.com/bentleybrief2e

Krishna also held that Arjuna's caste imposed specific moral duties and social responsibilities on him. The duty of shudras was to serve, of vaishyas to work, of brahmins to learn the scriptures and seek wisdom. Similarly, Krishna argued, the duty of kshatriyas was to govern and fight. Indeed, Krishna went further and held that failure to fulfill caste duties was a grievous sin, whereas their observance brought spiritual benefits.

Finally, Krishna taught that Arjuna would attain everlasting peace if he devoted himself to the love, adoration, and service of Krishna himself. Arjuna should abandon his selfish and superficial personal concerns and surrender to the deeper wisdom of the god. As a reward, Arjuna would receive eternal salvation through unity with his god. Alongside understanding of the soul and caste duties, then, unquestioning faith and devotion would put Arjuna in the proper state of mind for the conflict by aligning his actions with divine wisdom and will. Krishna's teaching that faith would bring salvation helped inspire a tradition of ecstatic and unquestioning devotion in popular Hinduism.

HINDU ETHICS Hindu ethics thus differed considerably from those of earlier Indian moralists. The Upanishads had taught that only through renunciation and detachment from the world could individuals escape the cycle of incarnation. As represented in the *Bhagavad Gita,* however, Hindu ethical teachings also held out the promise of salvation to those who participated actively in the world and met their caste responsibilities. To be sure, Krishna taught that individuals should meet their responsibilities in detached fashion and that they should not strive for material reward or recognition. Rather, they should perform their duties faithfully, with no thought as to their consequences.

Other works by early Hindu moralists acknowledged even more openly than did the *Bhagavad Gita* that individuals could lead honorable lives in the world. Indeed, Hindu ethics commonly recognized four principal aims of human life: *dharma,* obedience to religious and moral laws; *artha,* the pursuit of economic well-being and honest prosperity; *kama,* the enjoyment of social, physical, and sexual pleasure; and *moksha,* the salvation of the soul. According to Hindu moral precepts, a proper balance of *dharma, artha,* and *kama* would help an individual to attain *moksha.*

As devotional Hinduism evolved and became increasingly distinct from the teachings of the Upanishads and the older traditions of the brahmins, it also enhanced its appeal to all segments of Indian society. Hinduism offered salvation to masses of people who, as a matter of practical necessity, had to lead active lives in the world and thus could not hope to achieve the detachment envisioned in the Upanishads.

POPULARITY OF HINDUISM Hinduism gradually displaced Buddhism as the most popular religion in India. Later Buddhist monks did not seek to communicate their message to the larger society in the zealous way of their predecessors but increasingly confined themselves to the comforts of monasteries richly endowed by wealthy patrons. Meanwhile, devotional Hinduism attracted political support and patronage, particularly from the Gupta emperors. The Guptas and their successors bestowed grants of land on Hindu *brahmins* and supported an educational system that promoted Hindu values. Just as Ashoka Maurya had advanced the cause of Buddhism, the Guptas and their successors later helped Hinduism become the dominant religious and cultural tradition in India. By about 1000 C.E., Buddhism had entered a noticeable decline in India, while Hinduism was growing in popularity. Within a few centuries devotional Hinduism and the more recently introduced faith of Islam almost completely eclipsed Buddhism in its homeland.

SUMMARY

In India, as in classical Persia and China, a robust agricultural economy supported the creation of large-scale states and interregional trade. Although an imperial state did not become a permanent feature of Indian political life, the peoples of the subcontinent maintained an orderly society based on the caste system and regional states. Indian cultural and religious traditions reflected the conditions of the larger society in which they developed. Mahayana Buddhism and devotional Hinduism in particular addressed the needs of the increasingly prominent lay classes, and the two faiths profoundly influenced the religious life of Asian peoples over the long term of history.

STUDY TERMS

ahimsa (129)
artha (135)
Arthashastra (123)
Ashoka (123)
Bhagavad Gita (133)
boddhisatva (133)
brahmin (127)
Buddhism (131)
Chandragupta Maurya (122)
dharma (131)
Four Noble Truths (130)
Gupta dynasty (125)
Hinayana Buddhism (133)
Jainism (129)
kama (135)
kshatriya (127)
Kushan empire (125)
Maghada (122)
Mahabharata (127)
Mahayana Buddhism (133)
Mauryan dynasty (122)
moksha (135)
nirvana (131)
Pataliputra (124)
shudra (128)
Siddhartha Gautama (130)
Theravada Buddhism (133)
vaishya (128)

FOR FURTHER READING

Roy C. Amore and Larry D. Shinn. *Lustful Maidens and Ascetic Kings.* New York, 1981. Translations of stories and moral tales from Hindu and Buddhist writings.

Jeannine Auboyer. *Daily Life in Ancient India.* Trans. by S. W. Taylor. New York, 1965. An excellent and well-researched, though somewhat dated, introduction to Indian social history during the classical era.

Edward Conze. *Buddhism: Its Essence and Development.* New York, 1959. Systematic account of Buddhism from a theological point of view.

William Theodore De Bary, ed. *Sources of Indian Tradition.* 2 vols. 2nd ed. New York, 1988. Important collection of sources in translation.

Xinru Liu. *Ancient India and Ancient China: Trade and Religious Exchanges, A.D. 1–600.* Delhi, 1988. Important study exploring the early spread of Buddhism from India to central Asia and China.

Juan Mascaró, trans. *The Bhagavad Gita.* Harmondsworth, 1962. Brilliant and evocative English version by a gifted translator.

Jean W. Sedlar. *India and the Greek World: A Study in the Transmission of Culture.* Totowa, N.J., 1980. Important study of relations between India and Greece, based on solid research.

Romila Thapar. *Ashoka and the Decline of the Mauryas.* London, 1961. The best scholarly study of Ashoka and his reign.

———. *Early India: From the Origins to A.D. 1300.* Berkeley, 2003. A fresh view by one of the leading scholars of early Indian history.

Stanley Wolpert. *A New History of India,* 7th ed. New York, 2004. A concise and readable survey of Indian history.

Mediterranean Society under the Greeks and the Romans

8

EARLY DEVELOPMENT OF GREEK SOCIETY
- Minoan and Mycenaean Societies
- The World of the Polis

GREECE AND THE LARGER WORLD
- Greek Colonization
- Conflict with Persia
- The Macedonians and the Coming of Empire
- The Hellenistic Empires

THE FRUITS OF TRADE: GREEK ECONOMY AND SOCIETY
- Trade and the Integration of the Mediterranean Basin
- Family and Society

THE CULTURAL LIFE OF CLASSICAL GREECE
- Rational Thought and Philosophy
- Popular Religion and Greek Drama
- Hellenistic Philosophy and Religion

ROME: FROM KINGDOM TO REPUBLIC
- The Etruscans and Rome
- The Roman Republic and Its Constitution
- The Expansion of the Republic

FROM REPUBLIC TO EMPIRE
- Imperial Expansion and Domestic Problems
- The Foundation of Empire
- Continuing Expansion and Integration of the Empire

ECONOMY AND SOCIETY IN THE ROMAN MEDITERRANEAN
- Trade and Urbanization
- Family and Society in Roman Times

THE COSMOPOLITAN MEDITERRANEAN
- Greek Philosophy and Religions of Salvation
- Judaism and Early Christianity

or a man who perhaps never existed, Homer has been a profoundly influential figure. According to tradition, Homer composed the two great epic poems of ancient Greece, the *Iliad* and the *Odyssey*. In fact, scholars now know that bards recited both poems for generations before Homer, and some believe that Homer was simply a convenient name for the otherwise anonymous scribes who committed the *Iliad* and the *Odyssey* to writing. Whether Homer ever really lived or not, the epics attributed to him deeply influenced the development of classical Greek thought and literature. The *Iliad* offered a Greek perspective on a campaign waged by a band of Greek warriors against the city of Troy in Anatolia during the twelfth century B.C.E. The *Odyssey* recounted the experiences of the Greek hero Odysseus as he sailed home after the Trojan War. The two works described scores of difficulties faced by Greek warriors, including battles, monsters, and conflicts among themselves. Between them, the two epics preserved a rich collection of stories that literary figures mined for more than a millennium.

The *Iliad* and the *Odyssey* also testify to the frequency and normality of travel, communication, and interaction in the Mediterranean basin during the second and first millennia B.C.E. Both works portray Greeks as expert and fearless seamen, almost as comfortable aboard their ships as on land, who did not hesitate to venture into the waters of what Homer called the "wine-dark sea." Homer lovingly described the sleek galleys in which Greek warriors raced across the waters, and he even had Odysseus construct a sailing ship single-handedly when he found himself shipwrecked on an island inhabited only by a goddess. The *Iliad* and the *Odyssey* make it clear that maritime links touched peoples throughout the Mediterranean basin in Homer's time and, further, that Greeks were among the most prominent seafarers of the age.

❮ Pericles organized the construction of numerous marble buildings, partly with funds collected from poleis belonging to the Delian League. Most notable of his projects was the Parthenon, a temple dedicated to the goddess Athena, which symbolizes the prosperity and grandeur of classical Athens.

The maritime links established by the Greeks lived on long after the decline of classical Greek society. Indeed, the Romans took advantage of those links and used them to build a powerful society that dominated the whole Mediterranean basin by the first century C.E. By that time, Roman citizens found themselves living in a cosmopolitan world in which Roman administrators oversaw affairs from Anatolia and Palestine in the east to Spain and Morocco in the west.

PSI img **Ship fresco from Akroti** www.mhhe.com/bentleybrief2e

Just as Homer's epics recall the world of the Greeks, the story of Paul of Tarsus reflects the cosmopolitan world of the

CHRONOLOGY

2200–1100 B.C.E.	Minoan society
1600–1100 B.C.E.	Mycenaean society
800–338 B.C.E.	Era of the classical Greek polis
509 B.C.E.	Establishment of the Roman republic
500–479 B.C.E.	Persian Wars
470–399 B.C.E.	Life of Socrates
443–429 B.C.E.	Pericles' leadership in Athens
431–404 B.C.E.	Peloponnesian War
430–347 B.C.E.	Life of Plato
384–322 B.C.E.	Life of Aristotle
359–336 B.C.E.	Reign of Philip II of Macedon
336–323 B.C.E.	Reign of Alexander of Macedon
264–146 B.C.E.	Roman expansion in the Mediterranean basin
106–43 B.C.E.	Life of Marcus Tullius Cicero
first century B.C.E.	Civil war in Rome
46–44 B.C.E.	Rule of Gaius Julius Caesar as dictator
31 B.C.E.–14 C.E.	Rule of Augustus
4 B.C.E.–early 30s C.E.	Life of Jesus of Nazareth
first century C.E.	Life of Paul of Tarsus
66–70 C.E.	Jewish War

Romans. Born in the first century C.E., Paul was a devout Jew from Anatolia who accepted the Christian teachings of Jesus of Nazareth. Paul was a principal figure in the development of Christianity to an independent religious faith, largely because of his zealous missionary efforts to attract converts from outside as well as within the Jewish community. While promoting his adopted faith in Jerusalem about 55 C.E., however, Paul was attacked by a crowd of his enemies who believed his views were a threat to Judaism. The disturbance was so severe that Roman authorities intervened to restore order.

Under normal circumstances, Roman authorities would have delivered Paul to the leaders of his own ethnic community, where he would be dealt with according to custom. But knowing that Jewish leaders would probably execute him, Paul asserted his rights as a Roman citizen to appeal his case in Rome. Paul had never been to Rome, but this Anatolian traveling in Palestine called on the laws of the imperial center to determine his fate. Paul traveled across the Mediterranean to Rome, but his appeal did not succeed. Tradition holds that he was executed by imperial authorities out of concern that Christianity was a threat to the peace and stability of the empire.

Under both the Greeks and the Romans, the Mediterranean basin became much more tightly integrated than before as both societies organized commercial exchange and sponsored interaction throughout the region. In fact, under Greek and then Roman supervision, the Mediterranean served not as a barrier but, rather, as a highway. Moreover, this highway carried more than soldiers, citizens, and goods: it also carried ideas. Indeed, Greek philosophy—which generated a remarkable body of moral thought and philosophical reflection—shaped the cultural foundations of the Roman republic and empire, as educated Roman thinkers drew inspiration from their neighbors to the east. Later, this highway carried the Christian religion to all corners of the Roman empire.

Yet Greek and Roman societies also differed substantially, both in organization and in outlook. Early in the classical era, the Greeks lived in independent, autonomous city-states. Only after the late third century B.C.E. did they play prominent roles in the large, centralized empire established by their neighbors to the north in Macedon. Until then, the Greeks had integrated the societies and economies of distant lands mainly through energetic commercial activity over the Mediterranean sea-lanes. In contrast to the Greeks, the Romans built an extensive, centralized land empire. At its high point the Roman empire dominated the entire Mediterranean basin and parts of southwest Asia as well as north Africa and much of continental Europe and Britain. In addition, whereas Greek authorities did not sponsor an evangelical religion, Christianity eventually became the official religion of the Roman empire, which allowed the new religion to spread much more effectively than before.

Early Development of Greek Society

During the third millennium B.C.E., the peoples of the Balkan region and the Greek peninsula increasingly met and mingled with peoples from different societies who traveled and traded in the Mediterranean basin. As a result, early inhabitants of the Greek peninsula built their societies under the influence of Mesopotamians, Egyptians, Phoenicians, and others active in the region. Beginning in the ninth century B.C.E., the Greeks organized a series of city-states, which served as the political context for the development of classical Greek society.

Minoan and Mycenaean Societies

KNOSSOS During the late third millennium B.C.E., a sophisticated society arose on the island of Crete. Scholars refer to it as Minoan society, after Minos, a legendary king of ancient Crete. Between 2000 and 1700 B.C.E., the inhabitants of Crete built a series of lavish palaces throughout the island, most notably the enormous complex at Knossos decorated with vivid frescoes depicting Minoans at work and play. These palaces were the nerve centers of Minoan society: they were residences of rulers, and they also served as storehouses where officials collected taxes in kind from local cultivators.

Between 2200 and 1450 B.C.E., Crete was a principal center of Mediterranean commerce. By 2200 B.C.E. Cretans were traveling aboard advanced sailing craft of Phoenician design. Minoan ships sailed to Greece, Anatolia, Phoenicia, and Egypt, where they exchanged Cretan wine, olive oil, and wool for grains, textiles, and manufactured goods. After 1600 B.C.E. Cretans established colonies on Cyprus and many islands in the Aegean Sea.

DECLINE OF MINOAN SOCIETY After 1700 B.C.E. Minoan society experienced a series of earthquakes, volcanic eruptions, and tidal waves. Between 1600 and 1450 B.C.E., Cretans embarked on a new round of palace building to replace structures destroyed by those natural catastrophes: they built luxurious complexes with indoor plumbing and drainage systems and even furnished some of them with flush toilets. After 1450 B.C.E., however, the wealth of Minoan society attracted a series of invaders, and by 1100 B.C.E. Crete had fallen under foreign domination. Yet Minoan traditions deeply influenced the inhabitants of nearby Greece.

MYCENAEAN SOCIETY Beginning about 2200 B.C.E. migratory Indo-European peoples filtered into the Greek peninsula. By 1600 B.C.E. they had begun to trade with Minoan merchants and visit Crete, where they learned about writing and large-scale construction. After 1450 B.C.E. they also built massive stone fortresses and palaces throughout the southern part of the Greek peninsula, known as the Peloponnesus. Because the fortified sites offered protection, they soon attracted settlers, who built small agricultural communities. Their society is known as Mycenaean, after Mycenae, one of their most important settlements.

CHAOS IN THE EASTERN MEDITERRANEAN From 1500 to 1100 B.C.E., the Mycenaeans expanded their influence beyond peninsular Greece. They largely overpowered Minoan society, and they took over the Cretan palaces. The Mycenaeans also established settlements in Anatolia, Sicily, and southern Italy. About 1200 B.C.E. the Mycenaeans engaged in a conflict with the city of Troy in Anatolia. This Trojan

Minoan (mih-NOH-uhn)

Mycenaean (meye-suh-NEE-uhn)

Peloponnesus (pell-uh-puh-NEE-suhs)

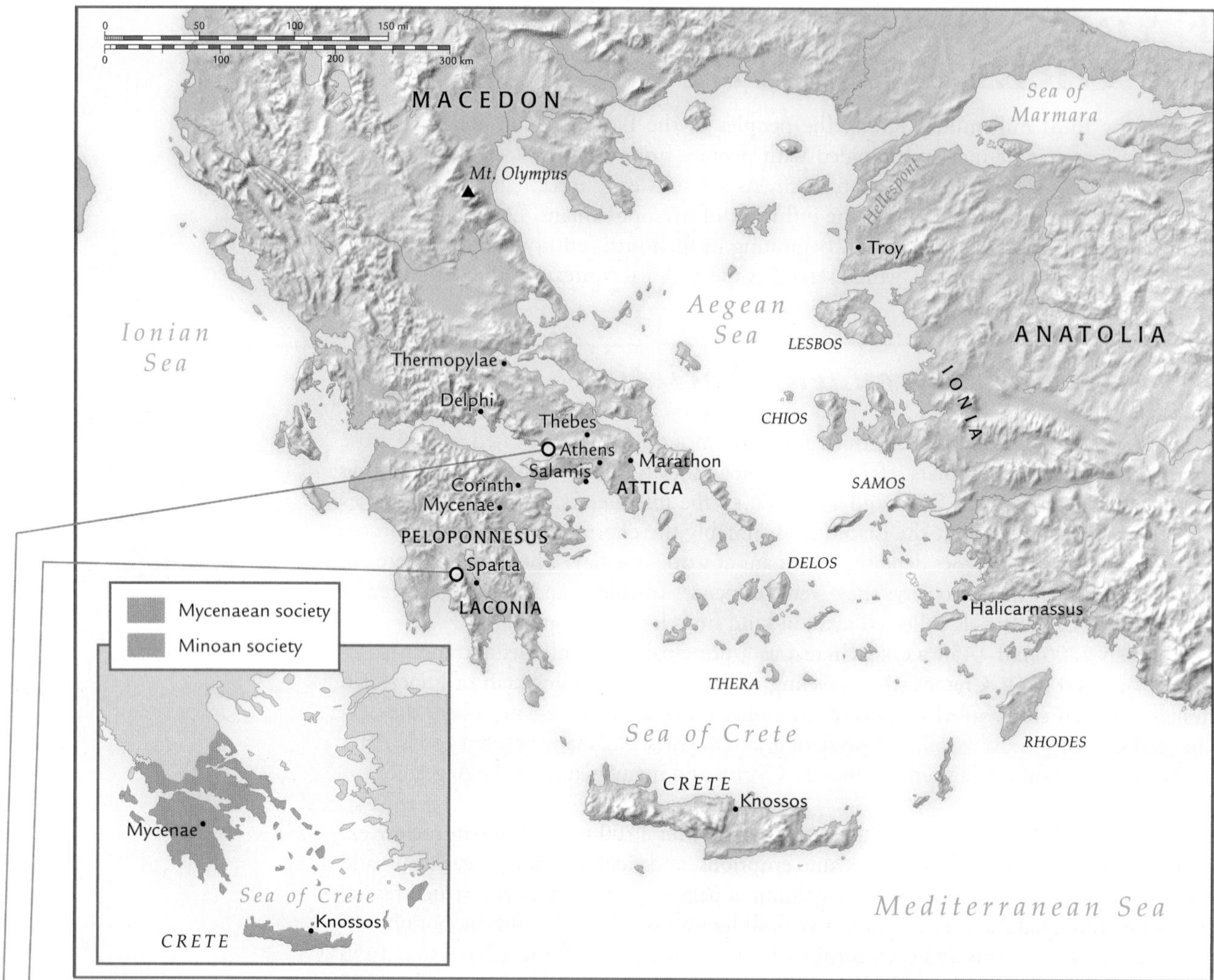

Sparta and Athens were the two main rival poleis in classical Greece.

MAP 8.1 | Classical Greece, 800–350 B.C.E. Note the mountainous topography of the Greek peninsula and western Anatolia. ***To what extent did geography encourage Greeks to venture into the Mediterranean Sea?***

War, which Homer recalled from a Greek perspective in his *Iliad,* coincided with invasions of foreign mariners in the Mycenaean homeland. Indeed, from 1100 to 800 B.C.E., chaos reigned throughout the eastern Mediterranean region. Invasions and civil disturbances made it impossible to maintain stable governments or even productive agricultural societies. Mycenaean palaces fell into ruin, the population sharply declined, and people abandoned most settlements.

The World of the Polis

In the absence of a centralized state or empire, local institutions took the lead in restoring political order in Greece after the decline of Mycenaean society. The most important institution was the *polis,* or city-state. Over time, many of these *poleis* (the plural of *polis*) became lively commercial centers. They took on an increasingly urban character and extended their authority over surrounding regions. By about 800 B.C.E. many poleis had become bustling city-states that functioned as the principal centers of Greek society. The most important of the poleis were Sparta and Athens, whose contrasting constitutions help to illustrate the variety of political styles in classical Greece.

polis (POH-lihs)

SPARTA Sparta was situated in a fertile region of the Greek peninsula, whose lands the Spartans exploited by forcing neighboring peoples to perform agricultural labor. These *helots,* or servants of the Spartan state, were not slaves, but neither were they free to leave the land. Their role in society was to keep Sparta supplied with food. By the sixth century B.C.E., the helots probably outnumbered the Spartan citizens by more than ten to one, which meant that the Spartans constantly had to guard against rebellion. As a result, the Spartans devoted most of their resources to maintaining a powerful and disciplined military machine.

PAINTED SPARTAN VESSEL. | This painted cup produced in Sparta about 550 B.C.E. depicts hunters attacking a boar. Spartans regarded hunting as an exercise that helped to sharpen fighting skills and aggressive instincts.

SPARTAN SOCIETY In theory, Spartan citizens were equal in status. To discourage the development of economic and social distinctions, Spartans observed an extraordinarily austere lifestyle. They did not wear jewelry or elaborate clothes, nor did they pamper themselves with luxuries or accumulate private wealth on a large scale. It is for good reason, then, that our adjective *spartan* refers to a lifestyle characterized by simplicity, frugality, and austerity.

Distinction among the ancient Spartans came by prowess, discipline, and military talent, which the Spartan educational system cultivated from an early age. All Spartans, men and women, underwent a rigorous regime of physical training. The sons of Spartan citizens left their homes at age seven and went to live in military barracks. At age twenty they began active military service, which they continued until retirement. Spartan women married when they reached age eighteen to twenty but did not live with their husbands. Only at about age thirty did men leave the barracks and set up a household with their wives and children. Although Spartan society had lost much of its ascetic rigor by the fourth century B.C.E., Spartan institutions nevertheless continued to reflect the larger society's commitment to military values.

ATHENS Whereas Sparta sought to impose order by military means, Athenians relieved social tensions by establishing a government based on democratic principles. Indeed, Athenians opened government offices to all citizens and broadened the base of political participation in classical Greece. Citizenship was by no means open to all residents, however: only free adult males from Athens played a role in public affairs, leaving foreigners, slaves, and women with no direct voice in government.

ATHENIAN SOCIETY During the seventh century B.C.E., the gap between rich and poor around Athens widened considerably as increased trade brought prosperity to wealthy landowners. By the early sixth century B.C.E., a large class of underprivileged people were unhappy enough to wage war against their wealthy neighbors. To avert civil war, an Athenian aristocrat named Solon devised a solution to class conflict in Attica, the region around Athens.

SOLON AND ATHENIAN DEMOCRACY Solon forged a compromise between the classes. He allowed aristocrats to keep their lands, but he cancelled debts, forbade debt slavery, and liberated those already enslaved for debt. Solon also provided representation for the common classes in the Athenian government by opening the councils of the polis to any citizen wealthy enough to devote time to public affairs. During the late sixth and fifth centuries B.C.E., these reforms went even further as Athenian leaders paid salaries to officeholders so financial hardship would not exclude anyone from service.

View of the Acropolis
www.mhhe.com/bentleybrief2e

PERICLES These reforms gradually transformed Athens into a democratic state. The high tide of Athenian democracy came under the leadership of the statesman Pericles, who became the most popular Athenian leader from 461 B.C.E. until his death in 429 B.C.E.

Pericles (PEH-rih-kleez)

Under the leadership of Pericles, Athens became the most sophisticated of the poleis, with a vibrant community of scientists, philosophers, poets, dramatists, artists, and architects.

GREECE AND THE LARGER WORLD

Classical Greece
www.mhhe.com/bentleybrief2e

As the poleis prospered, Greeks became increasingly prominent in the larger world of the Mediterranean basin. They established colonies along the shores of the Mediterranean Sea and the Black Sea, and they traded throughout the region. Eventually, their political and economic interests brought them into conflict with the expanding Persian empire. After a century of intermittent war, in the fourth century B.C.E. Alexander of Macedon toppled the Achaemenid empire and built an empire stretching from India to Egypt and Greece. His conquests created a vast zone of trade and communication that encouraged commercial and cultural exchange on an unprecedented scale.

Greek Colonization

To relieve population pressures in the rocky Greek peninsula, Greeks began to establish colonies in other parts of the Mediterranean basin. Between the mid–eighth and the late sixth centuries B.C.E., they founded more than four hundred colonies along the shores of the Mediterranean Sea and the Black Sea.

GREEK COLONIES The Greeks established their first colonies in the central Mediterranean during the early eighth century B.C.E. The most popular sites were Sicily and southern Italy, particularly the region around modern Naples, which was itself originally a Greek colony called Neapolis ("new polis"). These colonies provided merchants not only with fertile fields that yielded large agricultural surpluses but also with convenient access to the copper, zinc, tin, and iron ores of central Italy.

Some of the Greek colonies were very distant from the Greek poleis.

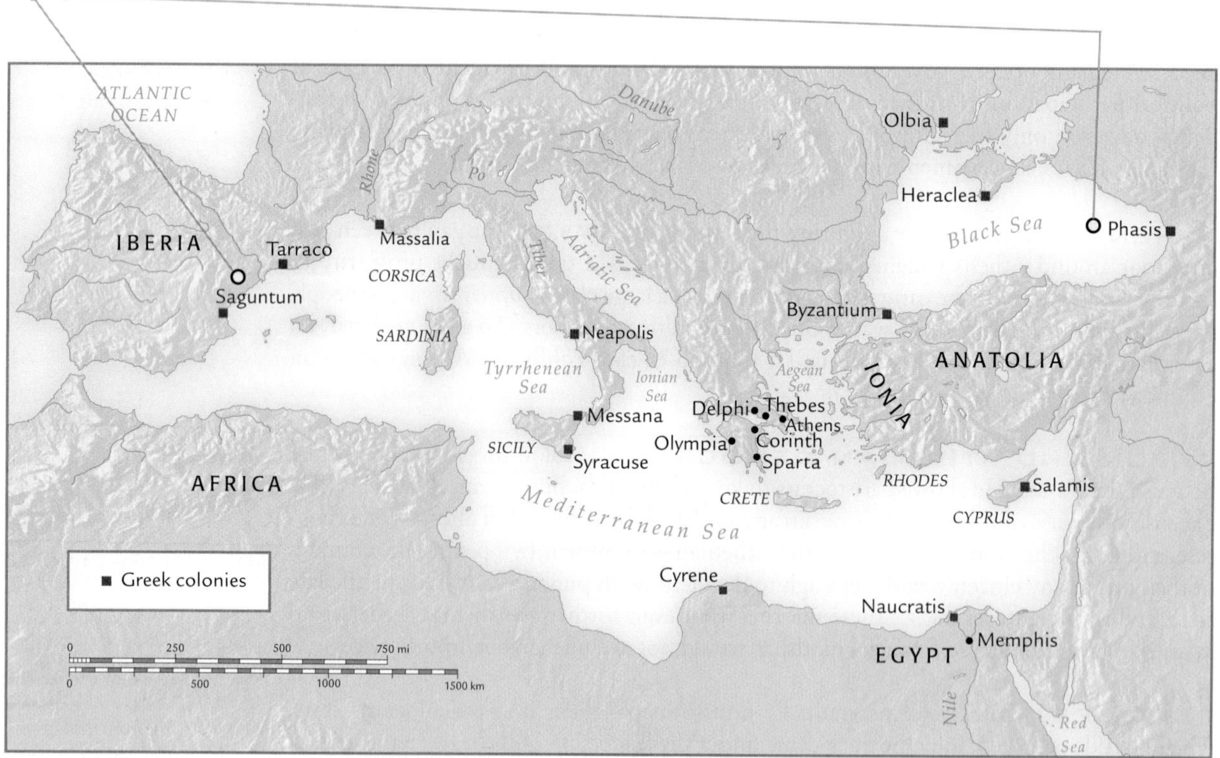

MAP 8.2 | Classical Greece and the Mediterranean basin, 800–500 B.C.E. All the Greek colonies were located on the coastlines of the Mediterranean Sea and the Black Sea. ***In what ways did the colonies serve as links between Greece and the larger Mediterranean region?***

During the eighth and seventh centuries B.C.E., Greeks ventured into the Black Sea in large numbers and established colonies all along its shores. These settlements offered merchants access to rich supplies of grain, fish, furs, timber, honey, wax, gold, and amber as well as slaves captured in southern Russia and transported to markets in the Mediterranean.

Unlike their counterparts in classical Persia, China, and India, the Greeks did not build a centralized imperial state. Instead, colonies relied on their own resources and charted their own courses. Nevertheless, Greek colonization sponsored more communication, interaction, and exchange than ever before among Mediterranean lands and peoples. From the early eighth century B.C.E., colonies facilitated trade between their own regions and the Greek poleis. At the same time, colonization spread Greek language as well as cultural and political traditions throughout the Mediterranean basin. Thus Greek colonization had important political and social effects throughout the Mediterranean basin.

Conflict with Persia

During the fifth century B.C.E., their links abroad brought the poleis of the Greek peninsula into direct conflict with the Persian empire in a long struggle known as the Persian Wars (500–479 B.C.E.). As the Persian emperors Cyrus and Darius tightened their grip on Anatolia, the Greek cities on the Ionian coast became increasingly restless. In 500 B.C.E. they revolted against Persian rule and expelled the Achaemenid administrators. In support of their fellow Greeks and commercial partners, the Athenians sent a fleet of ships to aid the Ionian effort.

THE PERSIAN WARS Despite Athenian assistance, Darius repressed the Ionian rebellion in 493 B.C.E. Three years later, he mounted a campaign against peninsular Greece to punish them for their interference. Although greatly outnumbered, the Athenians routed the Persian army at the battle of Marathon and then marched back to Athens in time to fight off the Persian fleet. In spite of success in individual battles, however, neither side could secure a definitive victory over the other, and for more than a century Greeks and Persians continued to skirmish intermittently without decisive results.

THE DELIAN LEAGUE Yet the Persian Wars did initiate serious conflict among the Greek poleis themselves. The cause was an alliance between the poleis known as the Delian League, which was formed to discourage further Persian actions in Greece. Because of its superior fleet, Athens became the leader of the alliance, benefiting greatly from the financial contributions of other poleis. However, once it was clear that the Persian threat no longer existed, the other poleis resented having to make contributions that seemed to benefit only the Athenians.

THE PELOPONNESIAN WAR Ultimately, the tensions resulted in a bitter civil conflict known as the Peloponnesian War (431–404 B.C.E.). Poleis divided into two armed camps under the leadership of Athens and Sparta, the principal contenders for hegemony in the Greek world. By 404 B.C.E. the Spartans and their allies had forced the Athenians to unconditional surrender. However, Sparta's victory soon generated new jealousies, and new conflicts quickly broke out between the poleis. Meanwhile, as internal struggles weakened the poleis, a formidable power took shape in the north.

The Macedonians and the Coming of Empire

THE KINGDOM OF MACEDON Until the fourth century B.C.E., the kingdom of Macedon was a frontier state north of peninsular Greece. During the reign of King Philip II (359–336 B.C.E.), however, Macedon became a powerful, unified state with

Achaemenid (uh-KEE-muh-nid)
Peloponnesian (pell-uh-puh-NEE-suhn)

an impressive military machine. When Philip had consolidated his hold on Macedon, he turned his attention to two larger prizes: Greece and the Persian empire. Greece proved relatively easy to conquer: the Peloponnesian War had poisoned the poleis against one another, which hampered organized resistance. Thus in 338 B.C.E., after a campaign of twelve years, Philip had all of Greece under his control.

ALEXANDER OF MACEDON Philip intended to use his conquest of Greece as a launching pad for an invasion of Persia but was prevented from doing so by an assassin who brought him down in 336 B.C.E. The invasion of Persia thus fell to his twenty-year-old son, Alexander of Macedon, often called Alexander the Great. Alexander soon assembled an army to invade the Persian empire. Alexander was a brilliant strategist and an inspired leader, and he inherited a well-equipped and highly spirited veteran force from his father. By 333 B.C.E. Alexander had subjected Ionia and Anatolia to his control; within another year he held Syria, Palestine, and Egypt; by 331 B.C.E. he controlled Mesopotamia and prepared to invade the Persian homeland. He took Pasargadae and burned the Achaemenid palace at Persepolis late in 331 B.C.E., and in 330 B.C.E. Alexander established himself as the new emperor of Persia.

ALEXANDER'S CONQUESTS By 327 B.C.E. Alexander had larger ambitions: he took his army into India but was forced to return home when his troops refused to proceed any farther. By 324 B.C.E. Alexander and his army had returned to Susa in Mesopotamia. In June of 323 B.C.E., however, after an extended round of feasting and drinking, he suddenly fell ill and died at age thirty-three. Thus, although Alexander proved to be a brilliant conqueror, he did not live long enough to develop a system of administration for his vast realm.

The Hellenistic Empires

Achaemenid & Seleucid Empires
www.mhhe.com/bentleybrief2e

When Alexander died, his generals divided the empire into three large states. Antigonus took Greece and Macedon, which his Antigonid successors ruled until replaced by the Romans in the second century B.C.E. Ptolemy took Egypt, which the Ptolemaic dynasty ruled until the Roman conquest of Egypt in 31 B.C.E. Seleucus took the largest portion, the former Achaemenid empire stretching from Bactria to Anatolia, which his successors ruled until the Parthians displaced them during the second century B.C.E.

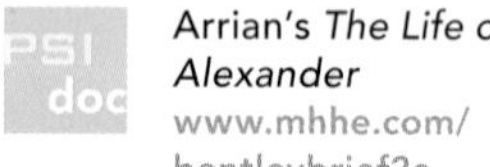

Arrian's *The Life of Alexander*
www.mhhe.com/bentleybrief2e

THE HELLENISTIC ERA Historians refer to the age of Alexander and his successors as the Hellenistic age—an era when Greek cultural traditions expanded their influence (*Hellas*) to a much larger world. Indeed, the Hellenistic empires governed cosmopolitan societies and sponsored interactions between peoples from Greece to India. Like imperial states in classical Persia, China, and India, the Hellenistic empires facilitated trade, and they made it possible for beliefs, values, and religions to spread over greater distances than ever before.

THE PTOLEMAIC EMPIRE All the Hellenistic empires benefited handsomely from the new order through the supervision of extensive trade networks and efficient tax collection. Yet perhaps the wealthiest of the Hellenistic empires was Ptolemaic Egypt. Greek and Macedonian overlords did not interfere in Egyptian society, contenting themselves with the efficient organization of agriculture, industry, and tax collection. They maintained the irrigation networks and monitored the cultivation of crops and the payment of taxes. They also established royal monopolies over the most lucrative industries, such as textiles, salt making, and the brewing of beer.

Antigonus (an-TIG-uh-nuhs)
Seleucid (sih-LOO-sid)
Ptolemaic (TAWL-oh-may-ihk)

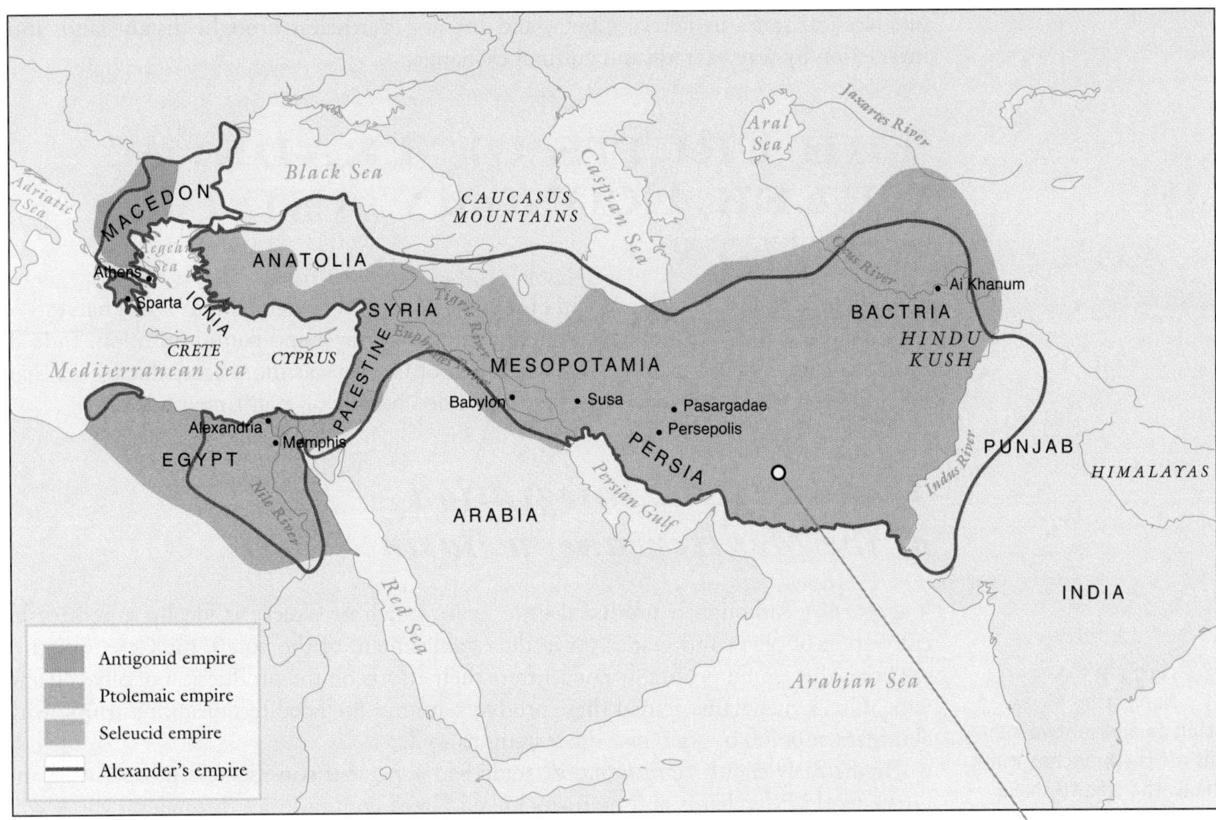

MAP 8.3 | Boundaries of Alexander's former empire and of the Hellenistic empires that succeeded it about the year 275 B.C.E. Notice the difference in size between the three Hellenistic empires. ***What would have been the economic and political advantages and disadvantages of each?***

The Seleucids were able to maintain control over such a large territory because of the many cities founded by Alexander of Macedon and his successors.

ALEXANDRIA Much of Egypt's wealth flowed to the Ptolemaic capital of Alexandria. Founded by Alexander at the mouth of the Nile, Alexandria served as the Ptolemies' administrative headquarters, but it became much more than a bureaucratic center. Alexandria's enormous harbor was able to accommodate 1,200 ships simultaneously, and the city soon became the most important port in the Mediterranean. Alongside Greeks, Macedonians, and Egyptians lived sizable communities of Phoenicians, Jews, Arabs, and Babylonians. The city was indeed an early megalopolis, where peoples of different ethnic, religious, and cultural traditions conducted their affairs. Under the Ptolemies, Alexandria also became the cultural capital of the Hellenistic world. It was the site of the famous Alexandrian Museum—a state-financed institute of higher learning where philosophical, literary, and scientific scholars carried on advanced research—and of the equally famous Alexandrian Library, which supported the scholarship sponsored by the museum and which, by the first century B.C.E., boasted a collection of more than seven hundred thousand works.

THE SELEUCID EMPIRE It was in the Seleucid realm, however, that Greek influence reached its greatest extent. The principal channels of that influence were the numerous cities that Alexander and his successors founded in the former Persian empire. Greek and Macedonian colonists flocked to these cities, where they created a Mediterranean-style urban society that left its mark on lands as distant as Bactria and India. Many Seleucids became familiar with Greek language, dress, literature, philosophy, art, and architecture. Emperor Ashoka of India himself had his edicts promulgated in Greek and Aramaic, the two most commonly used languages of the Hellenistic empires. Indeed, although the societies under Hellenistic domination did not lose their own customs, the Hellenistic empires, like classical states in Persia, China, and India, nevertheless brought distant lands into interaction by way of trade and cultural exchange.

The Fruits of Trade: Greek Economy and Society

The mountainous and rocky terrain of the Greek peninsula yielded only small harvests of grain, and the southern Balkan mountains hindered travel and communication. Indeed, until the construction of modern roads, much of Greece was more accessible by sea than by land. As a result, early Greek society depended heavily on maritime trade.

Trade and the Integration of the Mediterranean Basin

TRADE Although it produced little grain, much of Greece is ideally suited to the cultivation of olives and grapes. After the establishment of the poleis, the Greeks discovered that they could profitably concentrate their efforts on the production of olive oil and wine. Greek merchants traded these products around the Mediterranean, returning with abundant supplies of grain and other items as well.

By the early eighth century B.C.E., trade had generated considerable prosperity in the Greek world. Merchants and mariners linked Greek communities throughout the Mediterranean world—not only those in the Greek peninsula but also those in Anatolia, the Mediterranean islands, and the Black Sea region. These trade links contributed to a sense of a larger Greek community. Colonists recognized the same gods as their cousins in the Greek peninsula. They spoke Greek dialects, and they maintained commercial relationships with their native communities.

Greek Pottery Vessel. | Harvesting olives. In this painting on a vase, two men knock fruit off the branches while a third climbs the tree to shake the limbs, and another gathers olives from the ground.

THE OLYMPIC GAMES Greeks from all parts gathered periodically to participate in panhellenic festivals that reinforced their common bonds. Many of these festivals featured athletic, literary, or musical contests in which individuals sought to win glory for their polis. Best known of the panhellenic festivals were the Olympic Games. According to tradition, in 776 B.C.E. Greek communities from all parts of the Mediterranean sent their best athletes to the polis of Olympia to engage in contests of speed, strength, and skill. Events included footracing, long jump, boxing, wrestling, javelin tossing, and discus throwing. Winners of events received olive wreaths, and they became celebrated heroes in their home poleis. The ancient Olympic Games took place every four years for more than a millennium before quietly disappearing from Greek life. So, although they were not united politically, by the sixth century B.C.E. Greek communities had nevertheless established a sense of collective identity.

Family and Society

PATRIARCHAL SOCIETY With the establishment of poleis in the eighth century B.C.E., the nature of Greek family and society came into focus. Like urban societies in southwest Asia and Anatolia, the Greek poleis adopted strictly patriarchal family structures. Male family heads ruled their households, and fathers even had the right to decide whether to keep infants born to their wives. They could not legally kill infants, but they could abandon newborns in the mountains or the countryside, where they would soon die of exposure.

Greek women fell under the authority of their fathers, husbands, or sons. Upper-class Greek women spent most of their time in the family home and frequently wore veils when they ventured outside. In most of the poleis, women could not own landed property, but they sometimes operated small businesses such as shops and food stalls. The only public position open to Greek women was that of priestess of a religious cult. Sparta was something of a special case when it came to gender relations: there women participated in athletic contests, went about town by themselves, and sometimes even took up arms to defend the polis. Even in Sparta, however, men were family authorities, and men alone determined state policies.

Aristocratic families with extensive landholdings could afford to provide girls with a formal education, but in less privileged families all hands contributed to the welfare of the household. In rural families, men performed most of the outside work, while women took care of domestic chores and wove wool textiles. In artisan families living in the poleis, both men and women often participated in businesses and maintained stands or booths in the marketplace.

SLAVERY Throughout the Greek world, as in other classical societies, slavery was a prominent means of mobilizing labor. Slaves came from several different backgrounds. Some entered slavery because they could not pay their debts. Many were soldiers captured in war. A large number came from the peoples with whom the Greeks traded: slave markets at Black Sea ports sold seminomadic Scythians captured in Russia, and Egyptians provided African slaves.

Greek law regarded all slaves as the private chattel property of their owners, and the conditions of slaves' lives depended on the needs and the temperament of their owners. In general, however, slaves who possessed special skills fared better than unskilled slaves. A slave named Pasion, for example, worked first as a porter and then as a clerk at a prominent Athenian bank during the late fifth and early fourth centuries B.C.E. Ultimately, Pasion gained his freedom, took over management of the bank, outfitted five warships from his own pocket, and won a grant of Athenian citizenship.

The Cultural Life of Classical Greece

During the eighth and seventh centuries B.C.E., as Greek merchants ventured throughout the Mediterranean basin, they became acquainted with the sophisticated cultural traditions of Mesopotamia and Egypt. They learned astronomy, science, mathematics, medicine, and magic from the Babylonians as well as geometry, medicine, and divination from the Egyptians. They also drew inspiration from the myths, religious beliefs, art motifs, and architectural styles of Mesopotamia and Egypt. About 800 B.C.E. they adapted the Phoenician alphabet to their own language. To the Phoenicians' consonants they added symbols for vowels and thus created an exceptionally flexible system for representing human speech in written form.

During the fifth and fourth centuries B.C.E., the Greeks combined those borrowed cultural elements with their own intellectual interests to elaborate a rich cultural tradition that exercised enormous influence in the Mediterranean basin and western Europe. The most distinctive feature of classical Greek culture was the effort to construct a consistent system of philosophy based purely on human reason.

Pasion (pahs-ee-on)

Rational Thought and Philosophy

PSI doc "The *Apology* of Socrates" www.mhhe.com/bentleybrief2e

SOCRATES The pivotal figure in the development of philosophy was Socrates (470–399 B.C.E.), a thoughtful Athenian driven by a powerful urge to understand human beings in all their complexity. Socrates did not commit his thought to writing, but his disciple Plato later composed dialogues that represented Socrates' views. He suggested that honor was far more important than wealth, fame, or other superficial attributes. He scorned those who preferred public accolades to personal integrity, and he insisted on the need to reflect on the purposes and goals of life. "The unexamined life is not worth living," he held, implying that human beings had an obligation to strive for personal integrity, behave honorably toward others, and work toward the construction of a just society.

In elaborating those views, Socrates often subjected traditional ethical teachings to critical scrutiny. That outraged some of his fellow citizens, who brought him to trial on charges that he corrupted the Athenian youths who joined him in the marketplace to discuss moral and ethical issues. A jury of Athenian citizens decided that Socrates had indeed passed the bounds of propriety and condemned him to death. In 399 B.C.E. Socrates drank a potion of hemlock sap and died in the company of his friends.

PLATO Socrates' influence survived in the work of his most zealous disciple, Plato (430–347 B.C.E.), and in Plato's disciple Aristotle (384–322 B.C.E.). Inspired by his mentor's reflections, Plato elaborated a systematic philosophy of great subtlety. He presented his thought in a series of dialogues in which Socrates figured as the principal speaker. As time passed, Plato gradually formulated his thought into a systematic vision of the world and human society.

SOCRATES. | Tradition holds that Socrates was not a physically attractive man, but this statue emphasizes his sincerity and simplicity. *How does his clothing reinforce these aspects of his personality?*

The cornerstone of Plato's thought was his theory of Forms, or Ideas. It disturbed Plato that he could not gain satisfactory intellectual control over the world. The quality of virtue, for example, meant different things in different situations, as did honesty, courage, truth, and beauty. How was it possible, then, to understand virtue as an abstract quality? In seeking an answer to that question, Plato developed his belief that the world in which we live is not the world of genuine reality, but only a pale and imperfect reflection of the world of Forms or Ideas. The secrets of this world, Plato argued, were available only to philosophers—those who applied their rational faculties to the pursuit of wisdom.

Though abstract, Plato's thought had important political and social implications. In his dialogue the *Republic,* for example, Plato argued that since philosophers were in the best position to understand ultimate reality, they would also be the best rulers. In effect, Plato advocated an intellectual aristocracy: the philosophical elite would rule, and less intelligent classes would work at functions for which their talents best suited them.

ARISTOTLE During the generation after Plato, Aristotle elaborated a systematic philosophy that equaled Plato's work in its long-term influence. Unlike Plato, Aristotle believed that philosophers could rely on their senses to provide accurate information about the world and then depend on reason to sort out its mysteries. Aristotle explored the nature of reality in subtle metaphysical works, and he devised rigorous rules of logic in an effort to construct powerful and compelling arguments. His work provided such a coherent and comprehensive vision of the world that his later disciples called him "the master of those who know."

The Greek philosophers deeply influenced the development of European and Islamic cultural traditions. Until the seventeenth century C.E., most European philosophers regarded the Greeks as intellectual authorities. Christian and Islamic theologians alike went to great lengths to harmonize their religious convictions with the philosophical views of Plato and Aristotle. Thus, like philosophical and religious figures in other classical socie-

Socrates (SAHK-rah-teez)
Aristotle (AHR-ih-stot-uhl)

SOURCES FROM THE PAST

Socrates' View of Death

In one of his earliest dialogues, the Apology, *Plato offered an account of Socrates' defense of himself during his trial before a jury of Athenian citizens. After the jury had convicted him and condemned him to death, Socrates reflected on the nature of death and reemphasized his commitment to virtue rather than to wealth or fame.*

And if we reflect in another way we shall see that we may well hope that death is a good thing. For the state of death is one of two things: either the dead man wholly ceases to be and loses all sensation; or, according to the common belief, it is a change and a migration of the soul unto another place. And if death is the absence of all sensation, like the sleep of one whose slumbers are unbroken by any dreams, it will be a wonderful gain. For if a man had to select that night in which he slept so soundly that he did not even see any dreams, and had to compare with it all the other nights and days of his life, and then had to say how many days and nights in his life he had slept better and more pleasantly than this night, I think that a private person, nay, even the great king of Persia himself, would find them easy to count, compared with the others. If that is the nature of death, I for one count it a gain. For then it appears that eternity is nothing more than a single night.

But if death is a journey to another place, and the common belief be true, that all who have died dwell there, what good could be greater than this, my judges? Would a journey not be worth taking if at the end of it, in the other world, we should be released from the self-styled judges of this world, and should find the true judges who are said to sit in judgment below? . . . It would be an infinite happiness to converse with them, and to live with them, and to examine them. Assuredly there they do not put men to death for doing that. For besides the other ways in which they are happier than we are, they are immortal, at least if the common belief be true.

And you too, judges, must face death with a good courage, and believe this as a truth, that no evil can happen to a good man, either in life, or after death. His fortunes are not neglected by the gods, and what has come to me today has not come by chance. I am persuaded that it is better for me to die now, and to be released from trouble. . . . And so I am hardly angry with my accusers, or with those who have condemned me to die. Yet it was not with this mind that they accused me and condemned me, but rather they meant to do me an injury. Only to that extent do I find fault with them.

Yet I have one request to make of them. When my sons grow up, visit them with punishment, my friends, and vex them in the same way that I have vexed you if they seem to you to care for riches or for anything other than virtue: and if they think that they are something when they are nothing at all, reproach them as I have reproached you for not caring for what they should and for thinking that they are great men when in fact they are worthless. And if you will do this, I myself and my sons will have received our deserts at your hands. But now the time has come, and we must go hence: I to die, and you to live. Whether life or death is better is known to God, and to God only.

■ **How does Socrates' understanding of personal morality and its rewards compare and contrast with the Zoroastrian, Buddhist, and Hindu views discussed in earlier chapters?**

SOURCE: F. J. Church, trans. *The Trial and Death of Socrates,* 2nd ed. London: Macmillan, 1886, pp. 76–78. (Translation slightly modified.)

ties, Plato and Aristotle provided a powerful intellectual framework that shaped thought about the world and human affairs for two millennia and more.

Popular Religion and Greek Drama

DEITIES Because most Greeks of the classical era did not have an advanced education, they turned to traditions of popular culture and popular religion rather than philosophy to seek guidance for human behavior. The Greeks did not recognize a single, exclusive, all-powerful god. Rather, they believed that in the beginning there was the formless void of chaos out of which emerged the earth, the mother and creator of all things. The earth then generated the sky, and together they produced night, day, sun, moon, and

THINKING ABOUT *Traditions*

TRADITIONS IN MEDITERRANEAN SOCIETY UNDER THE GREEKS AND ROMANS. Both Greeks and Romans maintained multiple and consistent connections with a wide variety of peoples and places in the Classical period. Given such interaction, what cultural, political, and social institutions helped both Greeks and Romans maintain a sense of their own unique identities?

other natural phenomena. Struggles between the deities led to bitter heavenly battles, and ultimately Zeus, grandson of the earth and sky gods, emerged as paramount ruler of the divine realm. Zeus's heavenly court included scores of subordinate deities who had various responsibilities: the god Apollo promoted wisdom and justice, for example; the goddess Fortune brought unexpected opportunities and difficulties; and the Furies wreaked vengeance on those who violated divine law.

RELIGIOUS CULTS Like religious traditions in other lands, Greek myths sought to explain the world and the forces that shape it. They served also as foundations for religious cults based on individual poleis that contributed to a powerful sense of community in classical Greece. These religious cults varied widely: many conducted ritual observances in special places, for example, and some were open to only one sex. Before the fifth century B.C.E., many cults inspired emotional displays and spirited—sometimes frenzied—song and dance.

TRAGIC DRAMA During the fifth century B.C.E., however, as the poleis strengthened their grip on public and political life, the religious cults became progressively more tame. Instead of festivals, religious cults marked the year with the presentation of plays that examined relations between humans and the gods or reflected on ethics and morality. That transformation set the stage for the emergence of Greek dramatic literature, which sought to engage audiences in subtle reflection on complicated themes. The great tragedians—Aeschylus, Sophocles, and Euripides—whose lives spanned the fifth century B.C.E., explored the possibilities and limitations of human action. Comic dramatists such as Aristophanes also dealt with serious issues of human striving and responsible behavior by ridiculing the foibles of prominent public figures and calling attention to the absurd consequences of ill-considered action.

Hellenistic Philosophy and Religion

As the Hellenistic empires seized the political initiative in the Mediterranean basin and eclipsed the poleis, residents ceased to regard their polis as the focus of individual and religious loyalties. Instead, they increasingly looked toward cultural and religious alternatives that ministered to the needs and interests of individuals living in a cosmopolitan society.

THE HELLENISTIC PHILOSOPHERS The most popular Hellenistic philosophers—the Epicureans, the Skeptics, and the Stoics—addressed individual needs by searching for personal tranquility and serenity. Epicureans, for example, identified pleasure as the greatest good. By *pleasure* they meant not unbridled hedonism but, rather, a state of quiet satisfaction that would shield them from the pressures of the Hellenistic world. Skeptics refused to take strong positions on political, moral, and social issues because they doubted the possibility of certain knowledge. The most respected and influential of the Hellenistic philosophers, however, were the Stoics. Unlike the Epicureans and the Skeptics, the Stoics did not seek to withdraw from the pressures of the world. Rather, they taught that individuals had the duty to aid others and lead virtuous lives in harmony with reason and nature.

RELIGIONS OF SALVATION Whereas the philosophers' doctrines appealed to educated elites, religions of salvation spread across the trade routes of the Hellenistic empires and enjoyed surging popularity in Hellenistic society. Mystery religions promised eternal bliss for initiates who observed their rites and lived in accordance with their doctrines. Some of these faiths spread across the trade routes and found followers far from

Aeschylus (ES-kuh-luhs)
Epicureans (ehp-ih-KYOOR-eeuhns)
Stoics (STOH-ihks)

their homelands. The Egyptian cult of Osiris, for example, became extraordinarily popular because it promised salvation for those who led honorable lives. Cults from Persia, Mesopotamia, Anatolia, and Greece also attracted disciples throughout the Hellenistic world.

Many of the mystery religions involved the worship of a savior whose death and resurrection would lead the way to eternal salvation for devoted followers. Some philosophers and religious thinkers speculated that a single, universal god might rule the entire universe, and that this god had a plan for the salvation of all humankind. Like the Hellenistic philosophies, then, religions of salvation addressed the interests of individuals searching for security in a complex world. Indeed, those interests continued to be of concern to peoples in the Mediterranean basin long after political dominance passed from the Greek to the Italian peninsula.

Rome: From Kingdom to Republic

Founded in the eighth century B.C.E., the city of Rome was originally a small city-state ruled by a single king. In 509 B.C.E., however, the city's aristocrats deposed the king, ended the monarchy, and instituted a republic—a form of government in which delegates represent the interests of various constituencies. The Roman republic survived for more than five hundred years, and it was under the republican constitution that Rome came to establish itself as the dominant power in the Mediterranean basin.

The Etruscans and Rome

PSI img Capitoline wolf with Romulus & Remus www.mhhe.com/bentleybrief2e

ROMULUS AND REMUS According to legend, the city of Rome was founded by Romulus, who—along with his twin brother, Remus—was abandoned as a baby by an evil uncle near the flooded Tiber River. Before the infants could drown, a kindly she-wolf found them and nursed them to health. The boys grew strong and courageous, and in 753 B.C.E. Romulus founded the city and established himself as its first king.

Modern scholars do not tell so colorful a tale, but they do agree that bands of Indo-European migrants crossed the Alps and settled throughout the Italian peninsula beginning about 2000 B.C.E. Like their distant cousins in India, Greece, and northern Europe, these migrants blended with the neolithic inhabitants of the region, adopted agriculture, and established tribal federations. Sheepherders and small farmers occupied much of the Italian peninsula, including the future site of Rome. Bronze metallurgy appeared about 1800 B.C.E. and iron about 900 B.C.E.

THE ETRUSCANS The Etruscans, a dynamic people, dominated much of Italy between the eighth and fifth centuries B.C.E. The Etruscans probably migrated to Italy from Anatolia. They settled first in Tuscany, the region around modern Florence, but they soon controlled much of Italy. They built thriving cities and established political and economic alliances between their settlements. They manufactured high-quality bronze and iron goods, and they worked gold and silver into jewelry. They built a fleet and traded actively in the western Mediterranean. During the late sixth century B.C.E., however, the Etruscans encountered a series of challenges from other peoples, and their society began to decline.

THE KINGDOM OF ROME The Etruscans deeply influenced the early development of Rome. Like the Etruscan cities, Rome was a monarchy during the early days after its foundation, and several Roman kings were Etruscans. The kings ruled Rome through the seventh and sixth centuries B.C.E., and they provided the city with paved streets, public buildings, defensive walls, and large temples.

Romulus (ROM-yuh-luhs)
Remus (REE-muhs)
Etruscans (ih-TRUHS-kuhns)

Etruscan merchants drew a large volume of traffic to Rome, thanks partly to the city's geographical advantages. Rome enjoyed easy access to the Mediterranean by way of the Tiber River, but since it was not on the coast, it did not run the risk of invasion or attack from the sea. Already during the period of Etruscan dominance, trade routes from all parts of Italy converged on Rome. When Etruscan society declined, Rome was in a strong position to play a more prominent role both in Italy and in the larger Mediterranean world.

The Roman Republic and Its Constitution

ESTABLISHMENT OF THE REPUBLIC When the Roman nobility deposed the last Etruscan king and replaced him with a republic, they built the Roman forum at the heart of the city—a political and civic center filled with temples and public buildings where leading citizens tended to government business. They also instituted a republican constitution that entrusted executive responsibilities to two consuls who wielded civil and military power. Consuls were elected by an assembly dominated by the noble classes, known in Rome as the patricians, and they served one-year terms. The powerful Senate, whose members were mostly aristocrats with extensive political experience, advised the consuls and ratified all major decisions. When faced with crises, however, the Romans appointed an official, known as a dictator, who wielded absolute power for a term of six months. By providing for strong leadership during times of extraordinary difficulty, the republican constitution enabled Rome to maintain a reasonably stable society throughout most of the republic's history.

CONFLICTS BETWEEN PATRICIANS AND PLEBEIANS Because the consuls and the Senate both represented the interests of the patricians, there was constant tension between the wealthy classes and the common people, known as the plebeians. Indeed, during the early fifth century B.C.E., relations between the classes became so strained that the plebeians threatened to secede from Rome. To maintain the integrity of the Roman state, the patricians granted plebeians the right to elect officials, known as tribunes, who represented their interests in the Roman government. Originally plebeians chose two tribunes, but the number eventually rose to ten. Tribunes had the power to intervene in all political matters, and they possessed the right to veto measures that they judged unfair.

Although tensions between the classes never disappeared, during the fourth century B.C.E. plebeians became eligible to hold almost all state offices and gained the right to have one of the consuls come from their ranks. By the early third century, plebeian-dominated assemblies won the power to make decisions binding on all of Rome. Thus, like fifth-century Athens, republican Rome gradually broadened the base of political participation.

The Expansion of the Republic

Between the fourth and second centuries B.C.E., the people of Rome transformed their city from a small and vulnerable city-state to the center of an enormous empire. They began by consolidating their power in the Italian peninsula itself. Indeed, by the later fourth century they had emerged as the predominant power in the Italian peninsula. Roman success in the peninsula was partly a matter of military power and partly a matter of generous policies toward the peoples they conquered. Instead of ruling them as vanquished subjects, the Romans allowed conquered people to govern their internal affairs as long as they provided military support and did not enter into hostile alliances. In addition, conquered peoples were allowed to trade in Rome, to take Roman spouses, and even to gain Roman citizenship. These policies both provided Rome with essential support and eased the pain of conquest.

plebeians (plih-BEE-uhns)

RUINS OF THE ROMAN FORUM. | Political leaders conducted public affairs in the forum during the era of the republic.

EXPANSION IN THE MEDITERRANEAN With Italy under its control, Rome began to play a major role in the affairs of the larger Mediterranean basin and to experience conflicts with other Mediterranean powers. The principal power in the western Mediterranean during the fourth and third centuries B.C.E. was the city-state of Carthage, located near modern Tunis. Originally established as a Phoenician colony, Carthage enjoyed a strategic location that enabled it to trade actively throughout the Mediterranean. From the wealth generated by this commerce, Carthage became the dominant political power in north Africa (excluding Egypt), the southern part of the Iberian peninsula, and the western region of grain-rich Sicily as well. Meanwhile, the three Hellenistic empires that succeeded Alexander of Macedon continued to dominate the eastern Mediterranean.

THE PUNIC WARS Economic and political competition brought the Romans into conflict with Carthage first. Between 264 and 146 B.C.E., they fought three devastating conflicts known as the Punic Wars with the Carthaginians. The rivalry ended after Roman forces subjected Carthage to a long siege, conquered and burned the city, and forced some fifty thousand survivors into slavery. The Romans then annexed Carthaginian possessions in north Africa and Iberia—rich in grain, oil, wine, silver, and gold—and used those resources to finance continued imperial expansion.

Shortly after the beginning of the Carthaginian conflict, Rome became embroiled in conflicts with the Antigonids and the Seleucids in the eastern Mediterranean. Between 215 and 148 B.C.E., Rome fought five major wars, mostly in Macedon and Anatolia, against these opponents. As a result of these conflicts, Rome emerged as the preeminent power in the eastern as well as the western Mediterranean by the middle of the second century B.C.E.

FROM REPUBLIC TO EMPIRE

Imperial expansion brought wealth and power to Rome, but these brought problems as well as benefits. Unequal distribution of wealth aggravated class tensions and gave rise to conflict over political and social policies. Meanwhile, the need to administer conquered lands efficiently strained the capacities of the republican constitution. During the first century B.C.E. and the first century C.E., Roman civil and military leaders gradually dismantled

Carthage (KAHR-thihj)

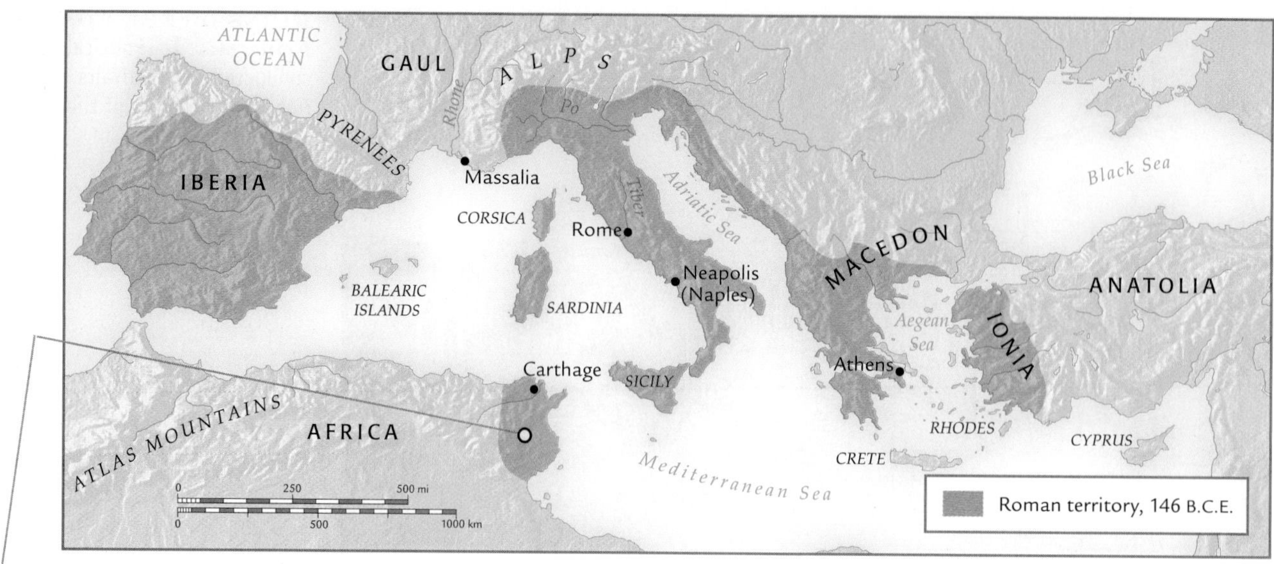

The conquest of Carthage in the second century B.C.E. helped finance further imperial expansion.

MAP 8.4 | Expansion of the Roman republic to 146 B.C.E. By the mid-second century B.C.E., the Roman republic controlled extensive territories outside Italy. ***In what ways did Roman expansion encourage interactions and exchanges throughout the Mediterranean region?***

the republican constitution and imposed a centralized imperial form of government on the city of Rome and its empire.

Imperial Expansion and Domestic Problems

In Rome, as in classical China and Greece, patterns of land distribution caused serious political and social tensions. Conquered lands fell largely into the hands of wealthy elites, who organized enormous plantations known as *latifundia.* Because they enjoyed economies of scale and often employed slave labor, owners of latifundia operated at lower costs than did owners of smaller holdings, who often had to sell out to their wealthier neighbors.

CIVIL WAR During the second and first centuries B.C.E., relations between the classes became so strained that they led to violent social conflict and civil war. Roman politicians and generals jockeyed for power in support of either social reform or the privileged position of the wealthy elites, with bloody results on both sides. By the middle of the first century B.C.E., it had become increasingly clear that the Roman republic was not suitable for a large and growing empire. In this chaotic context Gaius Julius Caesar inaugurated the process by which Rome replaced its republican constitution with a centralized imperial form of government.

The Foundation of Empire

Julius Caesar recognized the need for social reform and favored liberal policies that would ease the suffering of the poor. During the decade of the 60s B.C.E., he played an active role in Roman politics. He spent enormous sums of money sponsoring public spectacles—such as battles between gladiators and wild animals—which helped him build a reputation and win election to posts in the republican government. This activity kept him in the public eye and helped to publicize his interest in social reform. During the next decade Caesar led a Roman army to Gaul, which he conquered and brought into the still-growing Roman empire.

In 49 B.C.E. Caesar turned his army toward Rome itself after conservative leaders in the city sought to maneuver him out of power. By early 46 B.C.E. he had made himself master of the Roman state and named himself dictator—an office that he claimed for life rather

latifundia (lah-tee-FOON-dya)

than for the constitutional six-month term. Caesar then centralized military and political functions and brought them under his own control. He confiscated property from conservatives and distributed it to veterans of his armies and other supporters. He launched large-scale building projects in Rome as a way to provide employment for the urban poor. He also extended Roman citizenship to peoples in the imperial provinces.

JULIUS CAESAR. | This bust depicts a trim conqueror and a canny political leader.

AUGUSTUS Caesar never had the chance to consolidate his government, however, because in 44 B.C.E. members of the Roman elite stabbed him to death in the hopes of reestablishing the republic. Instead, they plunged Rome into thirteen more years of civil conflict. When the struggles ended, power belonged to Octavian, Caesar's nephew and adopted son. In a naval battle at Actium in Greece (31 B.C.E.), Octavian defeated his principal rival, Mark Antony, who had joined forces with Cleopatra, last of the Ptolemaic rulers of Egypt. Octavian then moved quickly to consolidate his rule. In 27 B.C.E. the Senate bestowed on him the title Augustus, a term with strong religious connotations suggesting the divine or semi-divine nature of its holder.

AUGUSTUS'S ADMINISTRATION Augustus's government was a monarchy disguised as a republic. He preserved traditional republican offices and forms of government and included members of the Roman elite in his government while at the same time fundamentally altering the nature of that government. He accumulated vast powers for himself and ultimately took responsibility for all important governmental functions. He reorganized the military system, creating a new standing army with commanders who owed allegiance directly to himself. He also was careful to place individuals loyal to him in all important positions. During his forty-five years of virtually unopposed rule, Augustus fashioned an imperial government that guided Roman affairs for the next three centuries.

Continuing Expansion and Integration of the Empire

During the two centuries following Augustus's rule, Roman armies conquered distant lands and integrated them into a larger economy and society. At its high point, during the early second century C.E., the Roman empire embraced much of Britain and continental Europe as well as a continuous belt of possessions surrounding the Mediterranean and extending to rich agricultural regions inland, including Mesopotamia.

Expansion of the Roman republic & empire
www.mhhe.com/bentleybrief2e

ROMAN ROADS Within the boundaries of the Roman empire itself, a long era of peace—known as the *pax romana,* or "Roman peace"—facilitated economic and political integration from the first to the middle of the third century C.E. Like their Persian, Chinese, Indian, and Hellenistic counterparts, the Romans integrated their empire by building networks of transportation and communication. Indeed, roads linked all parts of the Roman empire. One notable highway stretched more than 2,500 kilometers (1,554 miles) along the northeast imperial frontier from the Black Sea to the North Sea, parallel to the Danube and Rhine rivers. The roads permitted urgent travel and messages to proceed with remarkable speed: Tiberius, successor of Augustus as Roman emperor, once traveled 290 kilometers (180 miles) in a single day over Roman roads.

THINKING ABOUT *Encounters*

ENCOUNTERS IN MEDITERRANEAN SOCIETY UNDER THE GREEKS AND ROMANS. Both Greek and Roman society expanded well beyond their borders at the height of their respective influence in Mediterranean affairs. In what ways did Greek colonization and Roman empire-building facilitate and encourage the movement of goods, ideas, and people in the Mediterranean region?

ROMAN LAW As armies spread Roman influence throughout the Mediterranean, jurists also worked to construct a rational body of law that would apply to all peoples under Roman rule. During the late republic and especially during the empire, the jurists articulated standards of justice and gradually applied them throughout Roman territory. They established the principle that defendants were innocent until proven guilty, and they ensured that defendants had a right to challenge their accusers before a judge in a court of law. Like transportation and communication networks, Roman law helped to integrate the diverse

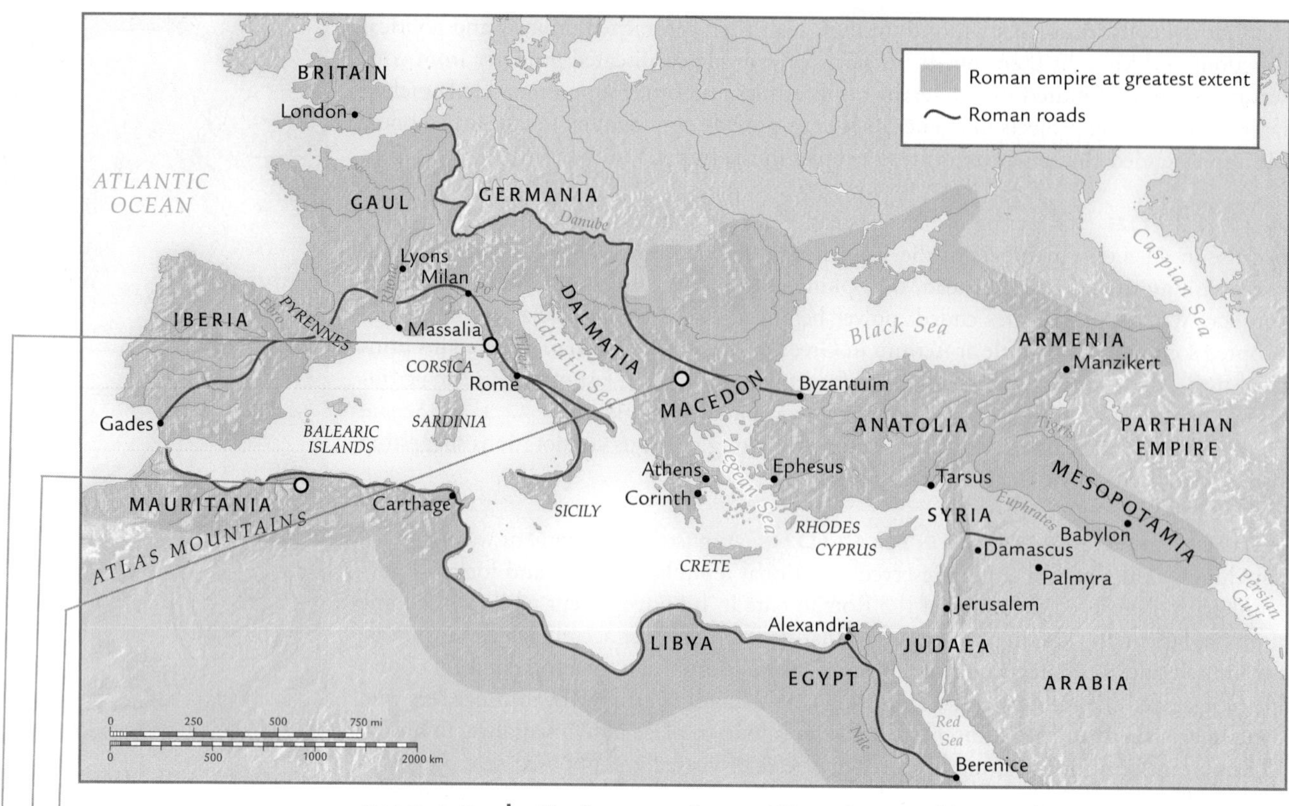

The Roman road system linked distant parts of the empire.

MAP 8.5 | The Roman empire, ca. 117 C.E. Compare this map of the Roman empire at its height with Map 8.4 showing territories controlled by the Roman republic almost two centuries earlier. ***How important was the Romans' extensive road network for the maintenance of their enormous empire?***

lands that made up the empire, and the principles of Roman law continued to shape Mediterranean and European society long after the empire had disappeared.

Economy and Society in the Roman Mediterranean

The rapid expansion of Roman influence and the imposition of Roman imperial rule brought economic and social changes to peoples throughout the Mediterranean basin. Good roads and the pax romana encouraged trade between regions. Existing cities benefited handsomely from the wealth generated by trade, and in the lands they conquered, the Romans founded new cities to serve as links between local regions and the larger Mediterranean economy. Meanwhile, like most other peoples of classical times, the Romans built a strictly patriarchal society and made extensive use of slave labor.

Trade and Urbanization

COMMERCIAL AGRICULTURE As the Roman empire became more integrated, agricultural production grew increasingly commercialized as well as specialized. Because it was possible to import grain at favorable prices from lands that routinely produced large surpluses, other regions could concentrate on the cultivation of fruits and vegetables or on the production of manufactured items. Greece, for example, concentrated on olives and vines, and Italy became a center for the production of pottery, glassware, and bronze goods.

MEDITERRANEAN TRADE Specialized production of agricultural commodities and manufactured goods set the stage for vigorous trade. Sea-lanes linked ports from Syria and Palestine to Spain and north Africa. Roman military and naval power kept the seas largely free of pirates so that sizable cargoes could move safely over long distances. Indeed, the Mediterranean became essentially a Roman lake, which the Romans called *mare nostrum* ("our sea").

THE CITY OF ROME Much of the profit from Mediterranean trade flowed to Rome, where it fueled remarkable urban development. In the first century C.E., some ten thousand statues and seven hundred pools decorated the city. The Roman state financed the construction of temples, bathhouses, public buildings, stadiums, and, perhaps most important of all, aqueducts—built with concrete invented by Roman engineers—that brought freshwater into the city from the neighboring mountains.

PSI img The Pont du Gard www.mhhe.com/bentleybrief2e

ROMAN CITIES AND THEIR ATTRACTIONS In addition to the spectacular growth of Rome, urban growth and development took place in cities all over the empire. And, as wealth concentrated in the cities, urban residents came to expect a variety of comforts not available in rural areas. Roman cities enjoyed abundant supplies of freshwater and elaborate sewage and plumbing systems. All sizable cities and even many smaller towns had public baths and often swimming pools and gymnasia as well. Enormous circuses, stadiums, and amphitheaters provided sites for the entertainment of the urban masses. Entertainment in stadiums often took forms now considered coarse and cruel—battles to the death between gladiators or between humans and wild animals—but urban populations flocked to such events, which they looked on as exciting diversions from daily routine. The Roman Colosseum, a magnificent marble stadium and sports arena opened in 80 C.E., provided seating for about fifty thousand spectators.

Family and Society in Roman Times

THE PATERFAMILIAS Roman law vested immense authority in male heads of families, known as the *paterfamilias*—"father of the family." Roman law gave the paterfamilias the authority to arrange marriages for his children, determine the work or duties they would perform, and punish them for offenses. He had rights also to sell them into slavery and even to execute them.

Although the paterfamilias was legally endowed with extraordinary powers, women usually supervised domestic affairs in Roman households, and by the time they reached middle age they generally wielded considerable influence within their families. Also, although Roman law placed strict limits on the ability of women to receive inheritances, clever individuals found ways to evade the law. During the third and second centuries B.C.E., women came to possess a great deal of property, and by the first century B.C.E., many women supervised the financial affairs of family businesses and wealthy estates.

SLAVERY Roman society made extensive use of slave labor: by the second century C.E., slaves may have represented as much as one-third of the population of the Roman empire. In the countryside they worked mostly on latifundia under extremely harsh conditions, often chained together in teams. In fact, discontent among rural slaves led to several large-scale revolts, especially during the second and first centuries B.C.E. During the most serious uprising, in 73 B.C.E., the escaped slave Spartacus assembled an army of seventy thousand rebellious slaves. The Roman army dispatched eight legions, comprising more than forty thousand well-equipped, veteran troops, to quell the revolt.

In the cities, conditions were much less difficult. Female slaves commonly worked as domestic servants while males toiled as servants, laborers, craftsmen, shopkeepers, or

nostrum (NAHS-truhm)
paterfamilias (PAH-tehr fah-MEE-lyas)
Spartacus (SPAHR-tah-cus)

business agents for their owners. As in Greece, slaves who had an education or possessed some particular talent had the potential to lead comfortable lives. In urban areas it was also common, though not mandatory, for masters to free slaves about the time they reached age thirty. Until freed, however, slaves remained under the strict authority of their masters, who had the right to sell them, arrange their family affairs, punish them, and even execute them for serious offenses.

THE COSMOPOLITAN MEDITERRANEAN

The integration of the Mediterranean basin had important effects not only for the trade and economy of the Roman empire but also for its cultural and religious traditions. Roads and communication networks favored the spread of new popular religions. Most important of these over the long run was Christianity, which became the official religion of the Roman empire and the predominant faith of the Mediterranean basin.

Greek Philosophy and Religions of Salvation

ROMAN DEITIES During the early days of their history, the Romans recognized many gods and goddesses, who they believed intervened directly in human affairs. Jupiter was the principal god, lord of the heavens, and Mars was the god of war, Ceres the goddess of grain, Janus the god who watched the threshold of individual houses, and Vesta the goddess of the hearth. In addition to those major deities, most Roman households honored tutelary deities, gods who looked after the welfare of individual families.

As the Romans expanded their political influence and built an empire, they encountered the religious and cultural traditions of other peoples. Often they adopted the deities of other peoples and used them for their own purposes. From the Etruscans, for example, they learned of Juno, the moon goddess, and Minerva, the goddess of wisdom, as well as certain religious practices, such as divination of the future through examination of the internal organs of ritually sacrificed animals.

GREEK INFLUENCE The Romans also drew deep inspiration from the Greek tradition of rational thought and philosophy, especially Stoicism. The Stoics' desire to identify a set of universal moral standards based on nature and reason appealed strongly to Roman intellectuals. Indeed, thinkers such as Marcus Tullius Cicero (106–43 B.C.E.) readily adopted Stoic values. His letters and treatises emphasized the individual's duty to live in accordance with nature and reason. He argued that the pursuit of justice was the individual's highest public duty, and he scorned those who sought to accumulate wealth or to become powerful through immoral, illegal, or unjust means. Through his speeches and especially his writings, Cicero helped to establish Stoicism as the most prominent school of moral philosophy in Rome.

RELIGIONS OF SALVATION Whereas educated thinkers drew inspiration from the Greeks, the masses found comfort in religions of salvation that established their presence throughout the Mediterranean basin and beyond. These religions became prominent features in Rome during the late republic as well as under the empire. Many originated in the far-flung realms of the empire, including the popular Anatolian cult of Mithras, the Anatolian cult of the mother goddess Cybele, and the Egyptian cult of the goddess Isis.

MITHRAISM The Mithraic religion provided divine sanction for human life and especially for purposeful moral behavior. It brought together a community that welcomed and nurtured like-minded individuals. Finally, it offered hope for individuals who conscientiously observed the cult's teachings by promising them ecstatic and mysterious union with

Cicero (SIHS-er-oh)

Mithras—who was strongly associated with military virtues such as strength, courage, and discipline—himself. During the late republic, Mithraic altars and temples appeared in military garrisons throughout the empire. During the early centuries C.E., administrators and merchants also became enchanted with Mithras, and his cult attracted followers among the male populations of all sizable communities and commercial centers in the Roman empire.

CULT OF ISIS The cult of Mithras did not admit women, but cults dedicated to the Anatolian mother goddess Cybele, the Egyptian goddess Isis, and other deities made a place for both men and women. Indeed, the cult of Isis may have been the most popular of all the Mediterranean religions of salvation before the rise of Christianity. Devotees built temples to Isis throughout the Roman empire, and they adored the Egyptian goddess as a benevolent and protective deity who nurtured her worshipers and helped them cope with the stresses of life in cosmopolitan society. Like the Mithraic religion, the cult of Isis and other religions of salvation attracted followers in Rome and other cities throughout the Mediterranean basin. The immense popularity of these religions of salvation provides a context that helps to explain the remarkable success of Christianity in the Roman empire.

ROMAN PANTHEON. Built between 118 and 125 C.E., the Pantheon in Rome was a temple honoring all gods, and it survives as one of the outstanding examples of Roman architecture. With a diameter of 43 meters (141 feet), the building's dome was the largest constructed until the twentieth century. ***What feelings might such a structure have evoked in worshipers?***

Judaism and Early Christianity

THE JEWS AND THE EMPIRE After the dissolution of the Jewish kingdom of David and Solomon in the early tenth century B.C.E., the Jewish people maintained their faith and their communities under various imperial regimes. At times, Jewish communities clashed with their imperial overlords, especially because monotheistic Jews refused to revere emperors as gods. As the Romans extended their empire in the eastern Mediterranean and brought the Jews in Palestine under their control, relations between the two became especially tense. Between 66 and 70 C.E., relations deteriorated to such a point that Palestinian Jews rose in rebellion against the Romans in what became known as the Jewish War.

JESUS OF NAZARETH The Jews were decisively defeated in the war, which prompted some Jews to found new sects that looked for saviors to deliver them from Roman rule so they could practice their faith without interference. The early Christians were one such sect. The Christians formed their community around Jesus of Nazareth, a charismatic Jewish teacher whom they recognized as their savior. Born about the year 4 B.C.E., Jesus grew up at a time of high tension between Roman overlords and their Jewish subjects. He was a peaceful man who taught devotion to God and love for fellow human beings. He attracted large crowds because of a reputation for wisdom and miraculous powers, especially the ability to heal the sick.

Yet Jesus alarmed the Romans because he also taught that "the kingdom of God is at hand." To Jesus, the kingdom of God was a spiritual realm in which God would gather those faithful to him. To Roman administrators, however, his message sounded like a threat to Roman rule in Palestine, especially since crowds routinely accompanied Jesus. In an effort to forestall a new round of rebellion, Roman administrators executed Jesus by fixing him to a cross in the early 30s C.E.

JESUS' EARLY FOLLOWERS Jesus' crucifixion did not put an end to his movement. Even after his execution Jesus' close followers strongly felt his presence and proclaimed that he had triumphed over death by rising from his grave. They called him "Christ," meaning "the anointed one," the savior who would bring individuals into the kingdom of God. They taught that he was the son of God and that his sacrifice served to offset the sins of those who had faith in him. They taught further that, like Jesus, the faithful would survive death and would experience eternal life in the spiritual kingdom of God. Following Jesus' teachings, the early Christians observed a demanding moral code and devoted themselves uncompromisingly to God. They also compiled a body of writings—accounts of Jesus' life, reports of his followers' works, and letters outlining Christian teachings—that gained recognition as the New Testament. Together with the Jews' Hebrew scriptures, which Christians referred to as the Old Testament, the New Testament became the holy book of Christianity.

PAUL OF TARSUS Jesus and his earliest followers were all Jews. Beginning about the middle of the first century C.E., however, some Christians avidly sought converts from non-Jewish communities in the Hellenistic world and the Roman empire. The principal figure in the expansion of Christianity beyond Judaism was Paul of Tarsus, a Jew from Anatolia who zealously preached his faith, especially in the Greek-speaking eastern region of the Roman empire. Paul taught a Christianity that attracted the urban masses in the same way as other religions of salvation that spread widely in the Roman empire. His doctrine called for individuals to observe high moral standards and to place their faith ahead of personal and family interests. His teaching also explained the world and human history as the results of God's purposeful activity so that it provided a framework of meaning for individuals' lives. Furthermore, Paul's doctrine promised a glorious future existence for those who conscientiously observed the faith.

EARLY CHRISTIAN COMMUNITIES Yet for two centuries after the crucifixion of Jesus, there was no central authority for the fledgling church. Rather, individual communities selected their own supervisors, known as *bishops,* who oversaw priests and governed their jurisdictions according to their own best understanding of Christian doctrine. As a result, until the emergence of Rome as the principal seat of church authority in the third century C.E., Christians held doctrinal views and followed practices that varied considerably from one community to the next. Some religious leaders taught that Jesus had literally risen from the dead and come back to life, for example, and others held that his resurrection was a spiritual rather than physical matter. Only gradually did believers agree to recognize certain texts as authoritative scripture—the New Testament—and adopt them as fundamental guides for Christian doctrine and practice.

THE GROWTH OF EARLY CHRISTIANITY Like the Jews from whose ranks they had sprung, the early Christians refused to honor the Roman state cults or revere the emperor as a god. As a result, Roman imperial authorities launched sporadic campaigns of persecution designed to eliminate Christianity as a threat to the empire. In spite of this repression, Christian numbers grew rapidly. During the first three centuries of the faith's existence, Christianity found its way to almost all parts of the Roman empire, and Christians established thriving communities throughout the Mediterranean basin and farther east in Mesopotamia and Iran. The remarkable growth of Christianity reflected the new faith's appeal particularly to the lower classes, urban populations, and women. Christianity accorded honor and dignity to individuals who did not enjoy high standing in Roman society, and it endowed them with a sense of spiritual freedom more meaningful than wealth, power, or social prominence. It taught the spiritual equality of the sexes and welcomed the contributions of both men and women. And it provided a promise of future glory for those who placed their faith in Jesus. Thus, although Christianity originated as a minor sect of Judaism, urban populations in the Roman empire embraced the new faith with such enthusiasm that by the third century C.E. it had become the most dynamic and influential religious faith in the Mediterranean basin.

SUMMARY

Under Greek and Roman influence, Mediterranean lands became a tightly integrated society. Although the Greeks did not build a centralized empire, they dotted the Mediterranean and Black Sea shorelines with their colonies, and their merchant fleets stimulated both commercial and cultural interactions between peoples of distant lands. Greek merchants, soldiers, and administrators also played prominent roles in the extensive empires of Alexander and the Hellenistic rulers, and they left a remarkably rich and enduring cultural legacy. Building in part on both the cultural and the economic legacies of the Greeks, the Romans proceeded to construct a republic, and then an empire, that eventually administered lands as distant as Mesopotamia and Britain. Highly organized trade networks enabled peoples throughout the empire to concentrate on specialized agricultural or industrial production. Popular religions spread widely and attracted enthusiastic converts. Like Confucianism and Buddhism in classical China and India, rational philosophy and Christianity became prominent sources of intellectual and religious authority in the classical Mediterranean and continued to influence cultural development in the Mediterranean, Europe, and southwest Asia over the long term.

STUDY TERMS

Alexander of Macedon (146)
Aristotle (150)
Athens (143)
Augustus (157)
Christians (161)
Cicero (160)
cult of Isis (161)
Delian League (145)
Epicureans (152)
Etruscans (153)
Jesus of Nazareth (161)
Jewish War (161)
Julius Caesar (156)
latifundia (156)
mare nostrum (159)
Minoan society (141)
Mithraism (160)
Mycenean society (141)
Olympic Games (148)
paterfamilias (159)
pax romana (157)
Peloponnesian War (145)
Persian Wars (145)
Plato (150)
plebians (154)
polis (142)
Ptolemaics (146)
Punic Wars (155)
Seleucids (147)
Senate (154)
Skeptics (152)
Socrates (150)
Sparta (143)
Stoics (152)

FOR FURTHER READING

Martin Bernal. *Black Athena: The Afroasiatic Roots of Classical Civilization.* 2 vols. to date. New Brunswick, 1987–. Provocative and controversial study arguing for Egyptian and Semitic influences on early Greek society.

Henry C. Boren. *Roman Society.* 2nd ed. Lexington, 1992. An authoritative synthesis that places social and economic history in its political context.

Keith R. Bradley. *Discovering the Roman Family: Studies in Roman Social History.* New York, 1991. A provocative analysis of Roman family life with illustrations from individual experiences.

Peter Brown. *The Rise of Western Christendom: Triumph and Diversity, A.D. 200–1000.* 2nd ed. Oxford, 2003. A landmark analysis of early Christian history that incorporates the findings of recent scholarship.

F. M. Cornford. *Before and after Socrates.* Cambridge, 1965. A short but brilliant synthesis of classical Greek philosophy.

M. I. Finley. *Ancient Slavery and Modern Ideology.* Expanded ed. Princeton, 1998. Presents a thoughtful analysis of Greek and Roman slavery in light of modern slavery and contemporary debates.

Frederick C. Grant, ed. *Hellenistic Religions: The Age of Syncretism.* Indianapolis, 1953. Fascinating collection of translated documents and texts that throw light on religious and philosophical beliefs of the Hellenistic era.

Michael Grant. *Cities of Vesuvius: Pompeii and Herculaneum.* London, 1971. Fascinating glimpse of Roman society as reconstructed by archaeologists working at sites destroyed by the eruption of Vesuvius in 79 C.E.

Naphtali Lewis and Meyer Reinhold, eds. *Roman Civilization: Selected Readings.* 2 vols. 3rd ed. New York, 1990. A rich collection of translated texts and documents that illuminate Roman history and society.

Sarah B. Pomeroy. *Goddesses, Whores, Wives, and Slaves: Women in Classical Antiquity.* New York, 1995. Outstanding study analyzing the status and role of women in classical Greece and Rome.

Cross-Cultural Exchanges on the Silk Roads

9

n the year 139 B.C.E., the Chinese emperor Han Wudi sent an envoy named Zhang Qian on a mission to lands west of China. The emperor's purpose was to find allies who could help combat the nomadic Xiongnu, who menaced the northern and western borders of the Han empire. From captives he had learned that other nomadic peoples in far western lands bore grudges against the Xiongnu, and he reasoned that they might ally with Han forces to pressure their common enemy.

The problem for Zhang Qian was that to communicate with potential allies against the Xiongnu, he had to pass directly through lands they controlled. Soon after Zhang Qian left Han territory, Xiongnu forces captured him. For ten years the Xiongnu held him in comfortable captivity: they allowed him to keep his personal servant, and they provided him with a Xiongnu wife, with whom he had a son. When suspicions about him subsided, however, Zhang Qian escaped with his family and servant. He even had the presence of mind to keep with him the yak tail that Han Wudi had given him as a sign of his ambassadorial status. He fled to the west and traveled as far as Bactria, but he did not succeed in lining up allies against the Xiongnu. While returning to China, Zhang Qian again fell into Xiongnu hands but managed to escape after one year's detention when the death of the Xiongnu leader led to a period of turmoil. In 126 B.C.E. Zhang Qian and his party returned to China and a warm welcome from Han Wudi.

Although his diplomatic efforts did not succeed, Zhang Qian's mission had far-reaching consequences. Apart from political and military intelligence about western lands and their peoples, Zhang Qian also brought back information of immense commercial value. While in Bactria about 128 B.C.E., he noticed Chinese goods—textiles and bamboo articles—offered for sale in local markets. Upon inquiry he learned that they had come from southwest China by way of Bengal. From that information he deduced the possibility of establishing trade relations between China and Bactria through India.

Han Wudi responded enthusiastically to this idea and dreamed of trading with peoples inhabiting lands west of China. From 102 to 98 B.C.E., he mounted an ambitious campaign that broke the power of the Xiongnu and pacified central Asia. His conquests simplified trade relations, since it became unnecessary to route commerce through India. The intelligence that Zhang Qian gathered during his travels thus contributed to the opening of the silk roads—the network of trade routes that linked lands as distant as China and the

‹ Tomb figure of a camel and a foreign rider. The majority of the silk road trade was handled by the nomadic peoples of central and western Asia.

Zhang Qian (jung-chen)

CHRONOLOGY

third century B.C.E.	Spread of Buddhism and Hinduism to southeast Asia
second century B.C.E.	Introduction of Buddhism to central Asia
139–126 B.C.E.	Travels of Zhang Qian in central Asia
first century B.C.E.	Introduction of Buddhism to China
second century C.E.	Spread of Christianity in the Mediterranean basin and southwest Asia
184 C.E.	Yellow Turban rebellion
216–272 C.E.	Life of Mani
220 C.E.	Collapse of the Han dynasty
284–305 C.E.	Reign of Diocletian
313–337 C.E.	Reign of Constantine
313 C.E.	Edict of Milan and the legalization of Christianity in the Roman empire
325 C.E.	Council of Nicaea
451 C.E.	Council of Chalcedon
476 C.E.	Collapse of the western Roman empire

Roman empire—and more generally to the establishment of relations between China and lands to the west.

China and other classical societies imposed political and military control over vast territories. They promoted trade and communication within their own empires, bringing regions that had previously been self-sufficient into a larger economy and society. They also fostered the spread of cultural, religious, and political traditions to distant regions, and they encouraged the construction of institutional frameworks that promoted the long-term survival of those traditions.

The classical societies established a broad zone of communication and exchange throughout much of the earth's eastern hemisphere. Trade networks crossed the deserts of central Asia and the depths of the Indian Ocean. Long-distance trade passed through much of Eurasia and north Africa, from China to the Mediterranean basin, and to parts of sub-Saharan Africa as well. That long-distance trade profoundly influenced the experiences of peoples and the development of societies throughout the eastern hemisphere. It brought wealth and access to foreign products, and it facilitated the spread of religious traditions beyond their original homelands. It also facilitated the transmission of disease. Indeed, the transmission of disease over the silk roads helped bring an end to the classical societies, since infectious and contagious diseases sparked devastating epidemics that caused political, social, and economic havoc. Long-distance trade thus had deep political, social, and cultural as well as economic and commercial implications for classical societies.

Long-Distance Trade and the Silk Roads Network

Ever since the earliest days of history, human communities have traded with one another, sometimes over long distances. Before classical times, however, long-distance trade was a risky venture. Ancient societies often policed their own realms effectively, but extensive regions were difficult to control. Trade passing between societies was therefore liable to interception by bandits or pirates. That risk increased the costs of long-distance transactions in ancient times.

During the classical era, two developments reduced the risks associated with travel and stimulated long-distance trade. First, rulers invested heavily in the construction of roads and bridges. They undertook these expensive projects primarily for military and administrative reasons, but roads also had the effect of encouraging trade within individual societies and facilitating exchanges between different societies. Second, classical societies pacified large stretches of Eurasia and north Africa. As a result, merchants did not face such great risk as in previous eras, the costs of long-distance trade dropped, and its volume rose dramatically.

Han Wudi (hahn-woo-dee)

Trade Networks of the Hellenistic Era

The tempo of long-distance trade increased noticeably during the Hellenistic era, partly because of the many colonies established by Alexander of Macedon and the Seleucid rulers in Persia and Bactria. Though originally populated by military forces and administrators, these settlements soon attracted Greek merchants and bankers who linked the recently conquered lands to the Mediterranean basin. The Seleucid rulers controlled land routes linking Bactria, which offered access to Indian markets, to Mediterranean ports in Syria and Palestine.

Like the Seleucids, the Ptolemies maintained land routes—in their case, routes going south from Egypt to the kingdom of Nubia and Meroë in east Africa—but they also paid close attention to sea-lanes and maritime trade. They ousted pirates from sea-lanes linking the Red Sea to the Arabian Sea and the Indian Ocean. They also built several new ports, the most important being Berenice on the Red Sea, while Alexandria served as their principal window on the Mediterranean.

THE MONSOON SYSTEM Even more important, perhaps, mariners from Ptolemaic Egypt learned from Arab and Indian seamen about the monsoon winds that governed sailing and shipping in the Indian Ocean. During the summer the winds blow regularly from the southwest, whereas in the winter they come from the northeast. Knowledge of these winds enabled mariners to sail safely and reliably to all parts of the Indian Ocean basin.

TRADE IN THE HELLENISTIC WORLD Establishment and maintenance of these trade routes was an expensive affair calling for substantial investment in military forces, construction, and bureaucracies to administer the commerce that passed over the routes. But the investment paid handsome dividends. Long-distance trade stimulated economic development within the Hellenistic realms themselves, bringing benefits to local economies throughout the empires. Moreover, Hellenistic rulers closely supervised foreign trade and levied taxes on it, thereby deriving income even from foreign products. Thus with official encouragement, a substantial trade developed throughout the Hellenistic world, from Bactria and India in the east to the Mediterranean basin in the west.

Indeed, maritime trade networks through the Indian Ocean linked not only the large classical societies of Eurasia and north Africa but also smaller societies in east Africa. During the late centuries B.C.E., the port of Rhapta (located near Dar es Salaam in Tanzania) emerged as the principal commercial center on the east African coast. With increasing trade, groups of professional merchants and entrepreneurs emerged at Rhapta, and coins came into general use on the east African coast. Merchants of Rhapta imported iron goods such as spears, axes, and knives from southern Arabia and the eastern Mediterranean region in exchange for ivory, rhinoceros horn, tortoise shell, and slaves obtained from interior regions.

The Silk Roads

The establishment of classical empires greatly expanded the scope of long-distance trade, as much of Eurasia and north Africa fell under the sway of one classical society or another. The Han empire maintained order in China and pacified much of central Asia, including a sizable corridor offering access to Bactria and western markets. The Parthian empire displaced the Seleucids in Persia and extended its authority to Mesopotamia. The Roman empire brought order to the Mediterranean basin. With the decline of the Mauryan dynasty, India lacked a strong imperial state, but the Kushan empire and other regional states provided stability and security, particularly in northern India, which favored long-distance trade.

The silk roads
www.mhhe.com/
bentleybrief2e

Ptolemaic (TAWL-oh-may-ihk)

OVERLAND TRADE ROUTES As the classical empires expanded, merchants and travelers created an extensive network of trade routes that linked much of Eurasia and north Africa. Historians refer to these routes collectively as the silk roads, since high-quality silk from China was one of the principal commodities exchanged over the roads. The overland silk roads took caravan trade from China to the Roman empire, thus linking the extreme ends of the Eurasian landmass. From the Han capital of Chang'an, the main silk road went west until it arrived at the Taklamakan desert, also known as the Tarim Basin. The silk road then split into two main branches that skirted the desert proper and passed through oasis towns that ringed it to the north and south. The branches came together at Kashgar (now known as Kashi, located in the westernmost corner of modern China). From there the reunited road went west to Bactria, where a branch forked off to offer access to Taxila and northern India, while the principal route continued across northern Iran. There it joined with roads to ports on the Caspian Sea and the Persian Gulf and proceeded to Palmyra (in modern Syria), where it met roads coming from Arabia and ports on the Red Sea. Continuing west, it terminated at the Mediterranean ports of Antioch (in modern Turkey) and Tyre (in modern Lebanon).

SEA-LANES AND MARITIME TRADE The silk roads also included a network of sea-lanes that sustained maritime commerce throughout much of the eastern hemisphere. From Guangzhou in southern China, sea-lanes through the South China Sea

Chang'an (chahng-ahn)
Tyre (tah-yer)

The silk roads connected cities as distant as Byzantium and Luoyang.

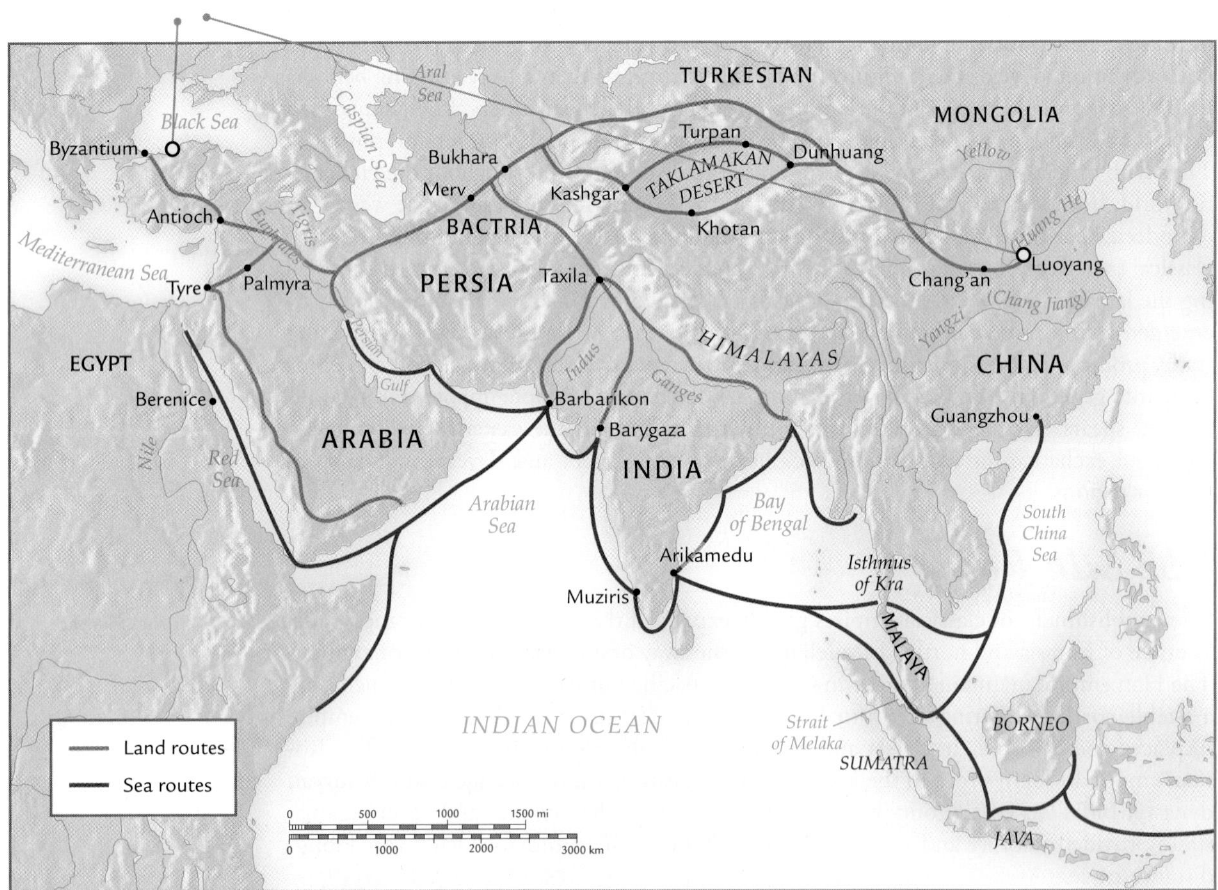

MAP 9.1 | The silk roads, 200 B.C.E.–300 C.E. Note the extent of the land and sea routes known collectively as the silk roads. ***Consider the political and economic conditions that would be necessary for regular travel and trade across the silk roads.***

Roman Glass Bowl. | During the first century B.C.E. Romans developed advanced glass-blowing techniques that enabled them to produce wares like this. ***What social group were bowls like these made for?***

Roman Coin. | This Roman coin, dated 189 C.E., depicts a merchant ship near the lighthouse at Alexandria. Ships like this regularly picked up pepper and cinnamon from India along with other cargoes.

linked the east Asian seaboard to the mainland and the islands of southeast Asia. Routes linking southeast Asia with Ceylon (modern Sri Lanka) and India were especially busy during classical times. From India, sea-lanes passed through the Arabian Sea to Persia and Arabia, and through the Persian Gulf and the Red Sea they offered access to land routes and the Mediterranean basin, which already possessed a well-developed network of trade routes.

"Battuta in China"
www.mhhe.com/bentleybrief2e

TRADE GOODS A wide variety of manufactured products and agricultural commodities traveled over the silk roads. Silk and spices traveled west from producers in southeast Asia, China, and India to consumers in central Asia, Iran, Arabia, and the Roman empire. Silk came mostly from China, and the fine spices—cloves, nutmeg, mace, and cardamom—all came from southeast Asia. Ginger came from China, cinnamon from China and southeast Asia, pepper from India, and sesame oil from India, Arabia, and southwest Asia. Spices were extremely important commodities in classical times because they had many more uses than they do in the modern world. They served not only as condiments and flavoring agents but also as drugs, anesthetics, aphrodisiacs, perfumes, aromatics, and magical potions. For the silk and spices they imported, western lands exchanged a variety of manufactured goods and other commodities, including horses and jade from central Asia and glassware, jewelry, textiles, and pottery from the Roman empire.

Zhang Qian was only one of many individuals who made very long journeys during classical times. Indeed, records indicate that merchants and diplomats from central Asia, China, India, southeast Asia, and the Roman empire traveled long distances in pursuit of trade and diplomacy. On a few occasions individuals even traveled across much or all of the eastern hemisphere between China and the Roman empire. A Chinese ambassador named Gang Ying embarked on a mission to distant western lands in 97 C.E. and proceeded as far as Mesopotamia before reports of the long and dangerous journey ahead persuaded him to return home. And Chinese sources reported the arrival in 166 C.E. of a delegation claiming to represent the Roman emperor Marcus Aurelius.

THE ORGANIZATION OF LONG-DISTANCE TRADE Individual merchants did not usually travel from one end of Eurasia to the other, either by land or by sea. Instead, they handled long-distance trade in stages. On the caravan routes between China and Bactria, for example, Chinese and central Asian nomadic peoples dominated trade. Farther west, however, the Parthians took advantage of their power and geographic position to control overland trade within their boundaries. Once merchandise reached Palmyra, it passed mostly into the hands of Roman subjects such as Greeks, Jews, and Armenians, who were especially active in the commercial life of the Mediterranean basin.

"The Geography of Strabo: The Roman Empire"
www.mhhe.com/bentleybrief2e

On the seas, the situation was similar: Malay and Indian mariners dominated trade in southeast Asian and south Chinese water, Persians and subjects of the Roman empire dominated the Arabian Sea, Parthians controlled the Persian Gulf, and the Roman empire dominated the Red Sea. Indeed, after Roman emperors absorbed Egypt in the first century C.E., their subjects carried on an especially brisk trade between India and the Mediterranean. The Greek geographer Strabo reported in the early first century C.E. that as many as 120 ships departed annually from the Red Sea for India. Meanwhile, since the mid-first century C.E., the Romans also had dominated both the eastern and the western regions of mare nostrum, the Mediterranean.

It is impossible to determine the quantity or the value of trade that passed over the silk roads in classical times, but it clearly made a deep impression on contemporaries. By the first century C.E., pepper, cinnamon, and other spices graced the tables of the wealthy classes in the Roman empire, where silk garments had become items of high fashion. Some Romans fretted that see-through silk attire would lead to moral decay, and others worried that hefty expenditures for luxury items would ruin the imperial economy. In both cases their anxieties testified to the powerful attraction of imported silks and spices for Roman consumers.

As it happened, long-distance trade more likely stimulated rather than threatened local economies. Yet long-distance trade did not occur in a vacuum. Commercial exchanges encouraged cultural and biological exchanges, some of which had large implications for classical societies.

Cultural and Biological Exchanges along the Silk Roads

The silk roads served as magnificent highways for merchants and their commodities, but others also took advantage of the opportunities they offered to travel in relative safety over long distances. Merchants, missionaries, and other travelers carried their beliefs, values, and religious convictions to distant lands: Buddhism, Hinduism, and Christianity all traveled the silk roads and attracted converts far from their original homelands. Meanwhile, invisible travelers such as disease pathogens also crossed the silk roads and touched off devastating epidemics when they found fresh populations to infect. Toward the end of the classical era, epidemic disease that was spread over the silk roads caused dramatic demographic decline, especially in China and the Mediterranean basin and to a lesser extent in other parts of Eurasia as well.

The Spread of Buddhism and Hinduism

By the third century B.C.E., Buddhism had become well established in northern India, and with the sponsorship of the emperor Ashoka the faith spread to Bactria and Ceylon. Buddhism was particularly successful in attracting merchants as converts. When they traveled, Buddhist merchants observed their faith among themselves and explained it to others. Gradually, Buddhism made its way along the silk roads to Iran, central Asia, China, and southeast Asia.

The Diamond Sutra
www.mhhe.com/bentleybrief2e

BUDDHISM IN CENTRAL ASIA Buddhism first established a presence in the oasis towns along the silk roads where merchants and their caravans found food, rest, lodging, and markets. The oases depended heavily on trade for their prosperity, and they allowed merchants to build monasteries and invite monks and scribes into their communities. Because they hosted travelers who came from different lands, spoke different

Buddhism (BOO-diz'm)

languages, and observed different religious practices, the oasis towns became cosmopolitan centers. As early as the second century B.C.E., many residents of the oases themselves adopted Buddhism, which was the most prominent faith of silk roads merchants for almost a millennium, from about 200 B.C.E. to 700 C.E.

BUDDHISM IN CHINA From the oasis communities Buddhism spread to the steppe lands of central Asia and to China via the nomadic peoples who visited the oases to trade. In the early centuries C.E., they increasingly responded to the appeal of Buddhism, and by the fourth century C.E., they had sponsored the spread of Buddhism throughout much of central Asia. Foreign merchants also brought their faith to China in about the first century B.C.E. Although the religion remained unpopular among native Chinese for several centuries, the presence of Buddhist monasteries and missionaries in China's major cities did attract some converts. Then, in about the fifth century C.E., the Chinese began to respond enthusiastically to Buddhism. Indeed, during the postclassical era Buddhism became the most popular religious faith throughout all of east Asia, including Japan and Korea as well as China.

BUDDHISM AND HINDUISM IN SOUTHEAST ASIA As Buddhism spread north from India into central Asia and China, both Buddhism and Hinduism also began to attract a following in southeast Asia. Once again, merchants traveling the silk roads—in this case the sea-lanes through the Indian Ocean—played prominent roles in spreading these faiths. By the first century C.E., clear signs of Indian cultural influence had appeared in many parts of southeast Asia. Many rulers converted to Buddhism, and others promoted the Hindu cults of Shiva and Vishnu. They built walled cities around lavish temples constructed in the Indian style, they adopted Sanskrit as a means of written communication, and they appointed Buddhist or Hindu advisors.

EARLY BUDDHIST SCULPTURE. | This sculpture from Bactria reflects the influence of Mediterranean and Greek artistic styles. This seated Buddha from the first or second century C.E. bears Caucasian features and wears Mediterranean-style dress.

The Spread of Christianity

Early Christians faced intermittent persecution from Roman officials. During the early centuries C.E., Roman authorities launched a series of campaigns to stamp out Christianity, because most Christians refused to observe the state cults that honored emperors as divine beings. Imperial officials also considered Christianity a menace to society because zealous missionaries attacked other religions and generated sometimes violent conflict. Nevertheless, Christian missionaries took full advantage of the Romans' magnificent network of roads and sea-lanes, which enabled them to carry their message throughout the Roman empire and the Mediterranean basin.

CHRISTIANITY IN THE MEDITERRANEAN BASIN During the second and third centuries C.E., countless missionaries worked zealously to attract converts. One of the more famous was Gregory the Wonderworker, a tireless missionary with a reputation for performing miracles, who popularized Christianity in central Anatolia during the mid-third century C.E. Contemporaries reported that Gregory not only preached Christian doctrine but also had access to impressive supernatural powers. Gregory and his fellow missionaries helped to make Christianity an enormously popular religion of salvation in the Roman empire. By the late third century C.E., in spite of continuing imperial opposition, devout Christian communities flourished throughout the Mediterranean basin in Anatolia, Syria, Palestine, Egypt, and north Africa as well as in Greece, Italy, Spain, and Gaul.

CHRISTIANITY IN SOUTHWEST ASIA The young faith also traveled the trade routes and found followers beyond the Mediterranean basin. By the second century C.E., sizable Christian communities flourished throughout Mesopotamia and Iran, and a few Christian churches had appeared as far away as India. Christians also attracted

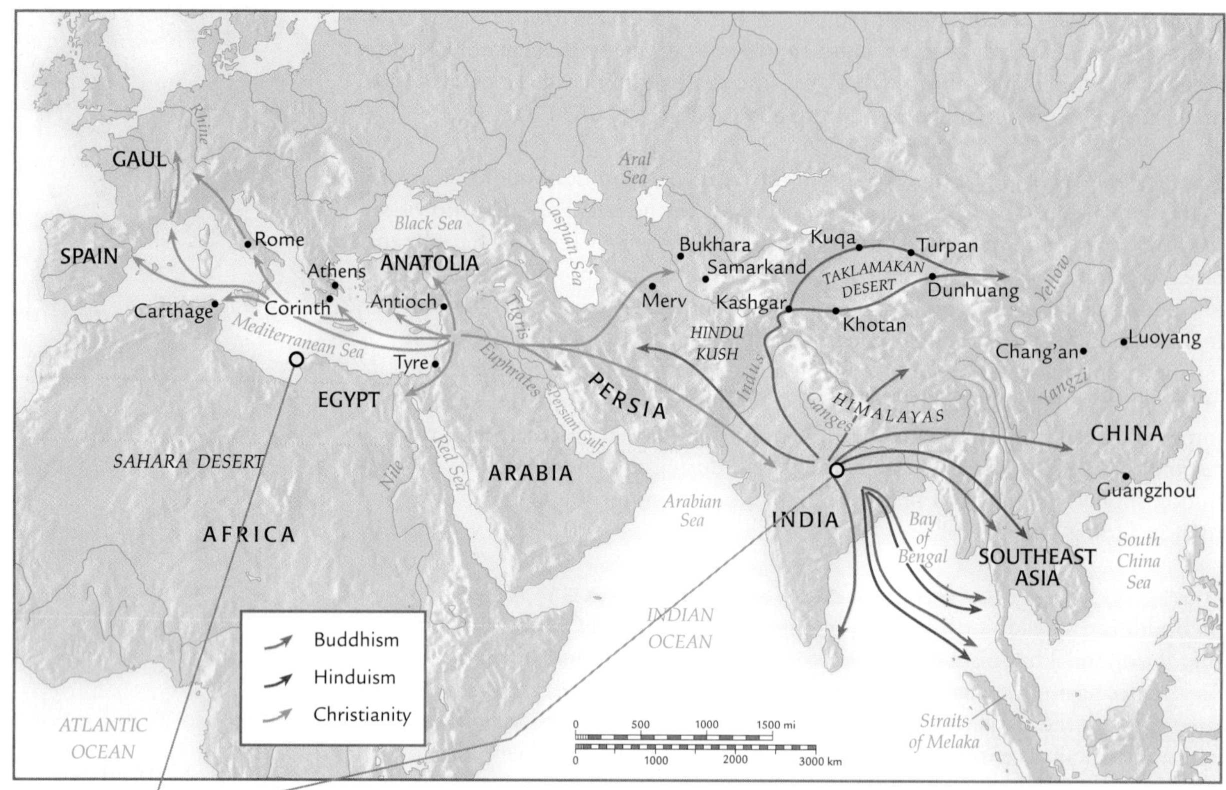

Christianity spread predominantly to the west, while Buddhism and Hinduism spread to the south and the east.

MAP 9.2 | The spread of Buddhism, Hinduism, and Christianity, 200 B.C.E.–400 C.E. Compare the routes taken by Buddhism, Hinduism, and Christianity with the routes followed by merchants on silk roads depicted on Map 9.1. ***How might you account for the similarities?***

large numbers of converts in southwest Asia and came to constitute—along with Jews and Zoroastrians—one of the major religious communities in the region.

Christian communities in Mesopotamia and Iran deeply influenced Christian practices in the Roman empire. To demonstrate utter loyalty to their faith, Christians in southwest Asia often followed strict ascetic regimes and sometimes even withdrew from family life and society. By the third century C.E., some Mediterranean Christians were so impressed by these practices that they began to live as hermits in isolated locations or to live exclusively among like-minded individuals who devoted their efforts to prayer and praise of God. Thus ascetic practices of Christians living in lands east of the Roman empire helped to inspire the formation of Christian monastic communities in the Mediterranean basin.

PSI img Nestorian stele www.mhhe.com/bentleybrief2e

After the fifth century C.E., Christian communities in southwest Asia and the Mediterranean basin increasingly went separate ways. Most of the faithful in southwest Asia became Nestorians—followers of the Greek theologian Nestorius, who lived during the early fifth century and emphasized the human as opposed to the divine nature of Jesus. Mediterranean church authorities rejected Nestorius's views, and many of his disciples departed for Mesopotamia and Iran. Although they had limited dealings with Mediterranean Christians, the Nestorians spread their faith east across the silk roads, and by the early seventh century they had established communities in central Asia, India, and China.

Zoroastrian (zohr-oh-ASS-tree-ahn)
Nestorian (neh-STOHR-eeuhn)

The Spread of Manichaeism

MANICHAEAN PAINTING. | A cave painting from about the seventh century C.E. depicts a group of devout Manichaean faithful, whose austere regimen called for them to dress in plain white garments and keep their hair uncut and untrimmed.

MANI AND MANICHAEISM The explosive spread of Manichaeism dramatically illustrated how missionary religions made effective use of the silk roads trading network. Manichaeism was the faith derived from the prophet Mani (216–272 C.E.), a devout Zoroastrian from Babylon in Mesopotamia who also drew deep inspiration from Christianity and Buddhism. Because of the intense interaction between peoples of different societies, Mani promoted a syncretic blend of Zoroastrian, Christian, and Buddhist elements as a religious faith that would serve the needs of a cosmopolitan world.

MANICHAEAN ETHICS Mani was a dualist: he viewed the world as the site of a cosmic struggle between the forces of light and darkness, good and evil. He urged his followers to reject worldly pleasures and to observe high ethical standards. Devout Manichaeans, known as "the elect," abstained from marriage, sexual relations, and personal comforts, dedicating themselves instead to prayer, fasting, and ritual observances. Less zealous Manichaeans, known as "hearers," led more conventional lives, but they followed a strict moral code and provided food and gifts to sustain the elect. Mani's doctrine had strong appeal because it offered a rational explanation for the presence of good and evil in the world while also providing a means for individuals to achieve personal salvation.

Mani was a fervent missionary and traveled widely to promote his faith. He also created a Manichaean church with its own services, rituals, hymns, and liturgies. His doctrine attracted converts first in Mesopotamia, and before Mani's death it had spread throughout the Sasanid empire and into the eastern Mediterranean region. In spite of its asceticism, Manichaeism appealed especially strongly to merchants, who adopted the faith as hearers and supported the Manichaean church. By the end of the third century C.E., Manichaean communities had appeared in all the large cities and trading centers of the Roman empire.

DECLINE OF MANICHAEISM Manichaeism soon came under tremendous pressure in both the Zoroastrian Sasanid state and the Roman empire. Mani himself died in chains as a prisoner of the Sasanid emperor, who saw Manichaeism as a threat to the public order. Authorities in the Roman empire also persecuted Manichaeans and largely exterminated the faith in the Mediterranean basin over the course of the fifth and sixth centuries. Yet Manichaeism survived in central Asia, where it attracted converts among nomadic Turkish peoples who traded with merchants from China, India, and southwest Asia. Like Buddhism, Hinduism, and Christianity, then, Manichaeism relied on the trade routes of classical times to extend its influence to new lands and peoples.

The Spread of Epidemic Disease

Like religious faiths, infectious and contagious diseases also spread along the trade routes of the classical world. Aided by long-distance travelers, pathogens had opportunities to spread beyond their original environments and attack populations with no inherited or acquired immunities to the diseases they caused. The resulting epidemics took a ferocious toll in human lives.

Manichaeism (man-ih-KEE-iz'm)
Sasanid (suh-SAH-nid)

EPIDEMIC DISEASES During the second and third centuries C.E., the Han and Roman empires suffered large-scale outbreaks of epidemic disease. The most destructive of these diseases were probably smallpox and measles, and epidemics of bubonic plague may also have erupted. All three diseases are devastating when they break out in populations without resistance, immunities, or medicines to combat them. As disease ravaged the two empires, Chinese and Roman populations declined sharply.

During the reign of Augustus, the population of the Roman empire stood at about sixty million people. During the second century C.E., epidemics reduced Roman population to forty-five million. Most devastating was an outbreak of smallpox that spread throughout the Mediterranean basin during the years 165 to 180 C.E. In combination with war and invasions, by 400 C.E. continuing outbreaks caused the population to decline even further, to about forty million. Whereas population in the eastern Mediterranean probably stabilized by the sixth century C.E., western Mediterranean lands experienced demographic stagnation until the tenth century.

Epidemics appeared slightly later in China than in the Mediterranean region. From fifty million people at the beginning of the millennium, Chinese population rose to sixty million in 200 C.E. As diseases found their way east, however, Chinese numbers fell back to fifty million by 400 C.E. and to forty-five million by 600 C.E. Thus by 600 C.E. both Mediterranean and Chinese populations had fallen by a quarter to a third from their high points during classical times.

EFFECTS OF EPIDEMIC DISEASES Demographic decline in turn brought economic and social change. Trade within the empires declined, and both the Chinese and the Roman economies contracted. Both economies also moved toward regional self-sufficiency: whereas previously the Chinese and Roman states had integrated the various regions of their empires into a larger network of trade and exchange, after about 200 C.E. they increasingly embraced several smaller regional economies that concentrated on their own needs instead of the larger imperial market. Indeed, epidemic disease contributed to serious instability in China after the collapse of the Han dynasty, and in weakening Mediterranean society, it helped bring about the decline and fall of the western Roman empire.

China after the Han Dynasty

By the time epidemic diseases struck China, internal political problems had already begun to weaken the Han dynasty. By the late second century C.E., Han authorities had largely lost their ability to maintain order. Early in the third century C.E., the central government dissolved, and a series of autonomous regional kingdoms took the place of the Han state. With the disappearance of the Han dynasty, China experienced significant cultural change, most notably an increasing interest in Buddhism.

ENCOUNTERS IN CROSS-CULTURAL EXCHANGES ON THE SILK ROADS. During the classical era, large empires and regional states maintained order across large portions of Eurasia and north Africa, which allowed long-distance trade to expand dramatically. In addition to material goods, what other kinds of exchanges did the maintenance of these trading routes encourage?

Internal Decay of the Han State

The Han dynasty collapsed largely because of internal problems that its rulers could not solve. One problem involved the development of factions within the ranks of the ruling elites. The desire of some elites to advance their own prospects in the imperial government at the cost of others led to constant infighting and backstabbing among the ruling elites, which reduced the effectiveness of the central government. An even more difficult problem had to do with the perennial issue of land and its equitable distribution. In the last two centuries of the Han dynasty, large landowners gained new influence in the government. They

SOURCES FROM THE PAST

St. Cyprian on Epidemic Disease in the Roman Empire

St. Cyprian, bishop of Carthage, was an outspoken proponent of Christianity during the early and middle decades of the third century C.E. When epidemic disease struck the Roman empire in 251 C.E., imperial authorities blamed the outbreak on Christians who refused to honor pagan gods. Cyprian refuted this charge in his treatise On Mortality, *which described the symptoms of epidemic disease and reflected on its significance for the Christian community.*

It serves as validation of the [Christian] faith when the bowels loosen and drain the body's strength, when fever generated in bone marrow causes sores to break out in the throat, when continuous vomiting roils the intestines, when blood-shot eyes burn, when the feet or other bodily parts are amputated because of infection by putrefying disease, when through weakness caused by injuries to the body either mobility is impeded, or hearing is impaired, or sight is obscured. It requires enormous greatness of heart to struggle with resolute mind against so many onslaughts of destruction and death. It requires great loftiness to stand firm amidst the ruins of the human race, not to concede defeat with those who have no hope in God, but rather to rejoice and embrace the gift of the times. With Christ as our judge, we should receive this gift as the reward of his faith, as we vigorously affirm our faith and, having suffered, advance toward Christ by Christ's narrow path. . . .

Many of us [Christians] are dying in this epidemic—that is, many of us are being liberated from the world. The epidemic is a pestilence for the Jews and the pagans and the enemies of Christ, but for the servants of God it is a welcome event. True, without any discrimination, the just are dying alongside the unjust, but you should not imagine that the evil and the good face a common destruction. The just are called to refreshment, while the unjust are herded off to punishment: the faithful receive protection, while the faithless receive retribution. We are unseeing and ungrateful for divine favors, beloved brethren, and we do not recognize what is granted to us. . . .

How suitable and essential it is that this plague and pestilence, which seems so terrible and ferocious, probes the justice of every individual and examines the minds of the human race to determine whether the healthy care for the ill, whether relatives diligently love their kin, whether masters show mercy to their languishing slaves, whether physicians do not abandon those seeking their aid, whether the ferocious diminish their violence, whether the greedy in the fear of death extinguish the raging flames of their insatiable avarice, whether the proud bend their necks, whether the shameless mitigate their audacity, whether the rich will loosen their purse strings and give something to others as their loved ones perish all around them and as they are about to die without heirs.

■ To what extent do you think St. Cyprian was effective in his efforts to bring inherited Christian teachings to bear on the unprecedented conditions he and his followers faced?

SOURCE: Wilhelm von Hartel, ed. *S. Thasci Caecili Cypriani opera omnia* in *Corpus scriptorum ecclesiasticorum latinorum.* Vienna, 1868, vol. 3, pp. 305–6. (Translation by Jerry H. Bentley.)

reduced their share of taxes and shifted the burden onto peasants. They even formed private armies to advance the interests of their class.

PEASANT REBELLION These developments provoked widespread unrest among peasants, who found themselves under increasing economic pressure with no means to influence the government. Pressures became particularly acute during the late second and third centuries when epidemics began to take their toll. In 184 C.E. peasant discontent fueled a large-scale uprising known as the Yellow Turban rebellion, so called because the rebels wore yellow headbands that represented the color of the Chinese earth and symbolized their peasant origins. Although quickly suppressed, the rebellion proved to be only the first in a series of insurrections that plagued the late Han dynasty.

COLLAPSE OF THE HAN DYNASTY Meanwhile, Han generals increasingly usurped political authority. By 190 C.E. the Han emperor had become a mere puppet, and the generals effectively ruled the regions controlled by their armies. They allied with wealthy landowners of their regions and established themselves as warlords who

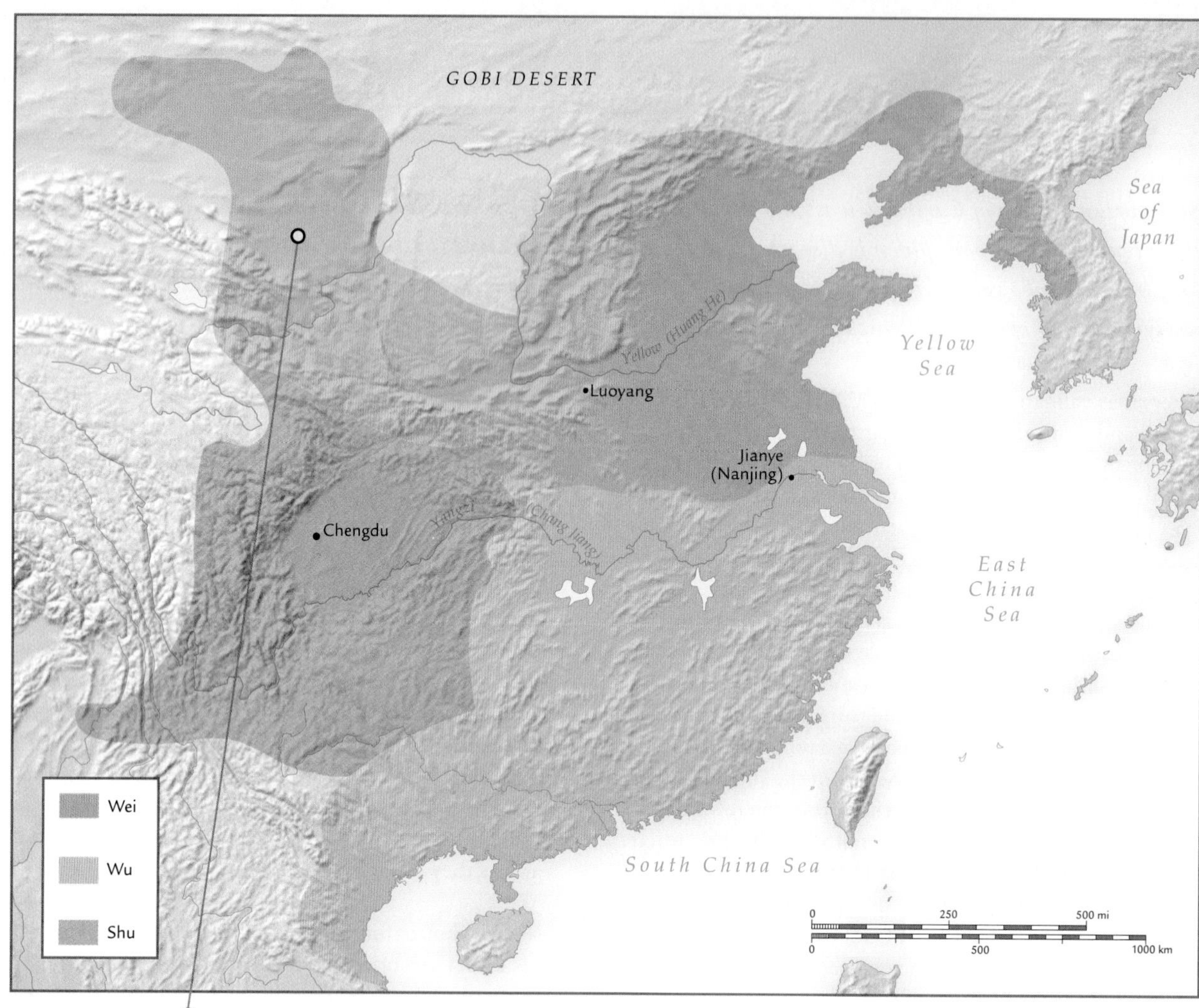

The Wei empire encompassed considerably less territory inhabited by northwestern nomadic groups than the Han empire had.

MAP 9.3 | China after the Han dynasty, 200 C.E. Compare this map with Map 6.2 showing the Han empire at its height. ***What geographical considerations might help explain why the Han empire broke up into the three kingdoms shown here?***

maintained a kind of rough order based on force of arms. In 220 C.E. they abolished the Han dynasty altogether and divided the empire into three large kingdoms.

Once the dynasty had disappeared, large numbers of nomadic peoples migrated into China, especially the northern regions, and they helped to keep China disunited for more than 350 years. Between the fourth and sixth centuries C.E., nomadic peoples established large kingdoms that dominated much of northern China as well as the steppe lands.

Cultural Change in Post-Han China

In some ways the centuries following the fall of the Han dynasty present a spectacle of chaos and disorder. One kingdom toppled another, only to fall in its turn to a temporary successor. War and nomadic invasions led to population decline in much of northern China. By the mid-fifth century, contemporaries reported, the Former Han capital of Chang'an had no more than one hundred households and the Later Han capital of Luoyang resembled a trash heap more than a city.

CULTURAL ADAPTATION OF NOMADIC PEOPLES Beneath the disorderly surface of political events, however, several important social and cultural changes were taking place. First, nomadic peoples increasingly adapted to the Chinese environment and culture, and as the generations passed, distinctions between peoples of nomadic and Chinese ancestry became less and less obvious. Partly because of that development, a new imperial dynasty was eventually able to reconstitute a centralized imperial state in north China.

Second, with the disintegration of political order, the Confucian tradition lost much of its credibility. The original goal of Confucius and his early followers was to find some means to move from chaos to stability during the Period of the Warring States. When the Han dynasty collapsed, Confucianism seemed both ineffective and irrelevant.

Individuals who in earlier centuries might have committed themselves to Confucian values turned instead to Daoism and Buddhism. Daoism, from its origins in the Period of the Warring States, had originally appealed mostly to an educated elite. After the fall of the Han, however, Daoist sages widened its appeal by promising salvation to those who observed their doctrines and rituals and by offering the use of elixirs made of spices, herbs, and drugs that supposedly conferred health and immortality. Daoism attracted widespread interest among a population afflicted by war and disease and became much more popular than before, especially because it faced less competition from the Confucian tradition.

TRADITIONS IN CROSS-CULTURAL EXCHANGES ON THE SILK ROADS. Between the third and the fifth centuries C.E., first China's Han dynasty and then the western Roman Empire collapsed. In what ways did imperial collapse lead peoples across large parts of Eurasia to turn away from cultural encounters and focus instead on local and regional needs and traditions?

POPULARITY OF BUDDHISM Even more important than Daoism for Chinese cultural history was Buddhism. After the fall of the Han empire, Buddhism received strong support from nomadic peoples who migrated into northern China and who in many cases had long been familiar with Buddhism in central Asia. Meanwhile, as a result of missionary efforts, the Indian faith began to attract a following among native Chinese as well. Indeed, between the fourth and sixth centuries C.E., Buddhism became well established in China. When a centralized imperial state took shape in the late sixth century C.E., Buddhism provided an important cultural foundation for the restoration of a unified political order.

THE FALL OF THE ROMAN EMPIRE

A combination of internal problems and external pressures weakened the Roman empire and brought an end to its authority in the western portion of the empire, whereas in the eastern Mediterranean imperial rule continued until the fifteenth century C.E. In the Mediterranean basin as in China, imperial weakness and collapse coincided with significant cultural change, notably the increasing popularity of Christianity.

Internal Decay in the Roman Empire

THE BARRACKS EMPERORS As in the case of the Han dynasty, internal political problems go a long way toward explaining the fall of the Roman empire. Like their Han counterparts, the Roman emperors faced internal opposition. During the half century from 235 to 284 C.E., there were no fewer than twenty-six claimants to the imperial throne. Known as the "barracks emperors," most of them were generals who seized power, held it briefly, and then suddenly lost it when they were displaced by rivals or their own mutinous troops. Not surprisingly, most of the barracks emperors died violently. Only one is known for sure to have succumbed to natural causes.

Confucianism (kuhn-FEW-shun-iz'm)
Daoism (dow-ism)

CONSTANTINE. | Only the colossal head of Constantine survives from a statue that originally stood about 14 meters (46 feet) tall.

The Roman empire also faced problems because of its sheer size. Even during the best of times, when the emperors could count on abundant revenues and disciplined armed forces, the sprawling empire posed a challenge for central governors. After the third century, as epidemics spread throughout the empire and its various regions moved toward local, self-sufficient economies, the empire as a whole became increasingly unmanageable.

THE EMPEROR DIOCLETIAN The emperor Diocletian (reigned 284–305 C.E.) attempted to deal with this problem by dividing the empire into two administrative districts: one in the east and one in the west. A coemperor ruled each district with the aid of a powerful lieutenant, and the four officials, known as the tetrarchs, were able to administer the vast empire more effectively than an individual emperor could. Diocletian was a skillful administrator. He managed to bring Rome's many armies, including unpredictable maverick forces, under firm imperial control. He also tried to deal with a crumbling economy by strengthening the imperial currency, forcing the government to adjust its expenditures to its income, and imposing price caps to dampen inflation. His economic measures were less successful than his administrative reforms, but they helped stabilize an economy ravaged by half a century of civil unrest.

Yet Diocletian's reforms encouraged ambition among the tetrarchs and their generals, and his retirement from the imperial office in 305 C.E. set off a round of internal struggles and bitter civil war. Already in 306 C.E. Constantine, son of Diocletian's coruler Constantius, moved to stake his claim as sole emperor. Once he had consolidated his grip on power in 324 C.E., Constantine ordered the construction of a new capital city, Constantinople, at a strategic site overlooking the Bosporus, the strait linking the Black Sea to the Sea of Marmara and beyond to the wealthy eastern Mediterranean. After 340 C.E. Constantinople became the capital of a united Roman empire.

CONSTANTINE Constantine himself was an able emperor. With the reunion of the eastern and western districts of the empire, however, he and his successors faced the same sort of administrative difficulties that Diocletian had attempted to solve by dividing the empire. As population declined and the economy contracted, emperors found it increasingly difficult to marshall the resources needed to govern and protect the vast Roman empire.

Germanic Invasions and the Fall of the Western Roman Empire

Apart from internal problems, the Roman empire faced a formidable military threat from migratory Germanic peoples. Indeed, during the fifth century C.E., Germanic invasions brought an end to Roman authority in the western half of the empire, although imperial rule survived for an additional millennium in the eastern Mediterranean.

GERMANIC MIGRATIONS Germanic peoples had migrated from their homelands in northern Europe and lived on the eastern and northern borders of the Roman empire since the second century C.E. Most notable were the Visigoths, who came originally from Scandinavia and Russia. Like the nomadic peoples who moved into northern China after the fall of the Han dynasty, the Visigoths settled, adopted agriculture, and drew deep inspiration from Roman society. In the interests of social order, however, the

Diocletian (dah-yuh-KLEE-shuhn)
Constantine (KAHN-stuhn-teen)

Romans discouraged settlement of the Visigoths and other Germanic peoples within the empire, preferring that they constitute buffer societies outside imperial borders.

THE HUNS During the late fourth century, the relationship between Visigoths and Romans changed dramatically when the nomadic Huns began an aggressive westward migration from their homeland in central Asia. The Huns were probably cousins of the nomadic Xiongnu who inhabited the central Asian steppe lands west of China. During the mid-fifth century C.E., the warrior-king Attila organized the Huns into a virtually unstoppable military juggernaut. Under Attila, the Huns invaded Hungary, probed Roman frontiers in the Balkan region, menaced Gaul and northern Italy, and attacked Germanic peoples living on the borders of the Roman empire.

COLLAPSE OF THE WESTERN ROMAN EMPIRE Attila did not create a set of political institutions or a state structure, and the Huns disappeared as a political and military force soon after his death in 453 C.E. By that time, however, the Huns had placed such pressure on Visigoths and other Germanic peoples that they streamed en masse into the Roman empire in search of refuge. Once inside imperial boundaries, they encountered little effective resistance and moved around almost at will. They established

Fall of the Roman empire
www.mhhe.com/bentleybrief2e

Routes of Hun invasions

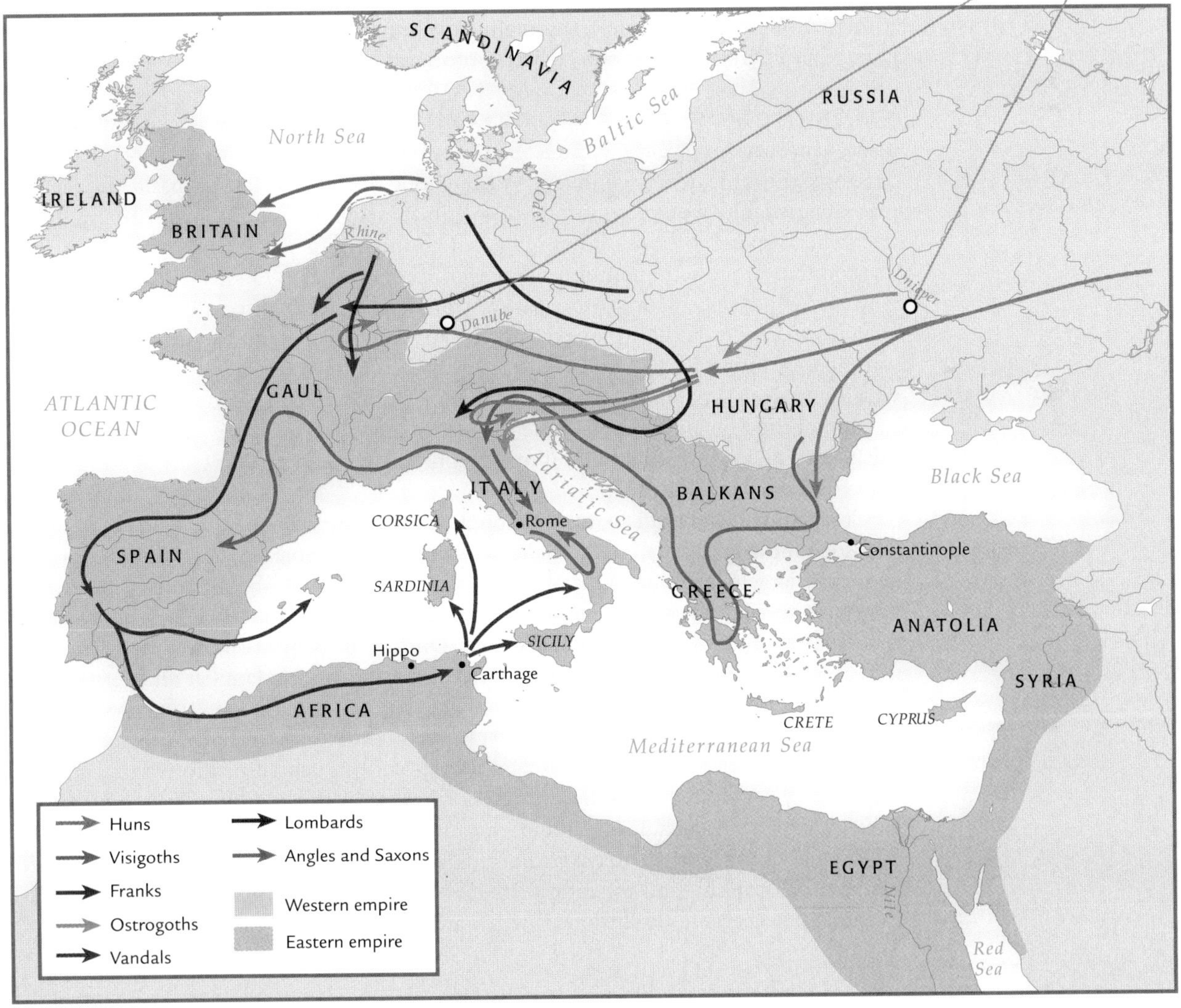

- Huns
- Visigoths
- Franks
- Ostrogoths
- Vandals
- Lombards
- Angles and Saxons
- Western empire
- Eastern empire

MAP 9.4 | Germanic invasions and the fall of the western Roman empire between 450 and 476 C.E. Notice the many different groups that moved into western Roman territory in this period. ***What might have motivated such movement, and why couldn't the western Roman empire prevent it?***

settlements throughout the western half of the empire—Italy, Gaul, Spain, Britain, and north Africa—where populations were less dense than in the eastern Mediterranean. Under the command of Alaric, the Visigoths even stormed and sacked Rome in 410 C.E. By the middle of the fifth century, the western part of the Roman empire was in a shambles. In 476 C.E. imperial authority came to an ignominious end when the Germanic general Odovacer deposed Romulus Augustulus, the last of the Roman emperors in the western half of the empire.

Unlike the Han dynasty, the Roman empire did not entirely disintegrate: imperial authority survived for another millennium in the eastern half of the empire, known after the fifth century C.E. as the Byzantine empire. In the western half, however, Roman authority dissolved, and nomadic peoples built successor states in regions formerly subject to Rome. Vandals and then Visigoths governed Spain, Franks ruled Gaul, Angles and Saxons invaded Britain, and Italy fell under the sway of a variety of peoples, including Visigoths, Vandals, and Lombards.

Cultural Change in the Late Roman Empire

In the Roman empire, as in China, the collapse of the imperial state coincided with important social and cultural changes. The Germanic peoples who toppled the empire looked to their own traditions for purposes of organizing society and government. When they settled in the regions of the former empire, however, they absorbed a good deal of Roman influence. Over time, the mingling of Roman and Germanic traditions led to the emergence of an altogether new society—medieval Europe.

PROMINENCE OF CHRISTIANITY Christianity was perhaps the most prominent survivor of the western Roman empire. During the fourth century C.E., several developments enhanced its influence throughout the Mediterranean basin. In the first place, Christianity won recognition as a legitimate religion in the Roman empire. In 312 C.E., while seeking to establish himself as sole Roman emperor, Constantine experienced a vision that impressed upon him the power of the Christian God. He believed that the Christian God helped him to prevail over his rivals, and he promulgated the Edict of Milan, which allowed Christians to practice their faith openly in the Roman empire. At some point during his reign, perhaps after his edict, Constantine himself converted to Christianity, and in 380 C.E. the emperor Theodosius proclaimed Christianity the official religion of the Roman empire. By the mid-fourth century, Christians held important political and military positions, and imperial sponsorship helped their faith to attract more converts than ever before.

Christianity also began to attract thoughtful and talented converts who articulated a Christian message for the intellectual elites of the Roman empire. The earliest Christians had come largely from the ranks of ordinary working people, and for three centuries the new faith grew as a popular religion of salvation favored by the masses, rather than as a reasoned doctrine of intellectual substance. During the fourth century, however, intellectual elites began to articulate Christianity in terms that were familiar and persuasive to the educated classes.

ST. AUGUSTINE The most important and influential of those figures was St. Augustine (354–430 C.E.), bishop of the north African city of Hippo (modern-day Annaba in Algeria). Augustine had a fine education, and he was conversant with the leading intellectual currents of the day. During his youth he drew great inspiration from Stoicism and Platonism, and for nine years he belonged to a community of Manichaeans. Eventually he became disillusioned with both the Hellenistic philosophical school and

Odovacer (AHD-oh-vah-cer)
Byzantine (BIHZ-uhn-teen)
Theodosius (thee-hu-DOH-see-uhs)

Manichaeism, and in 387 C.E., while studying in Italy, he converted to Christianity. For the remainder of his life, he worked to reconcile Christianity with Greek and Roman philosophical traditions. More than any others, Augustine's writings helped make Christianity an intellectually respectable alternative to Hellenistic philosophy and to popular religions of salvation.

St. Augustine. | This portrait shows St. Augustine holding a copy of his most famous work, *The City of God,* which sought to explain the meaning of history and the world from a Christian point of view. ***In what ways does this portrait seek to represent St. Augustine as a deeply pious man?***

THE INSTITUTIONAL CHURCH Besides winning the right to practice their faith openly and attracting intellectual talent, Christian leaders constructed an institutional apparatus that transformed a popular religion of salvation into a powerful church. In the absence of recognized leadership, the earliest Christians generated a range of conflicting and sometimes contradictory doctrines. To standardize their faith, Christian leaders instituted a hierarchy of church officials. At the top were five religious authorities—the bishop of Rome and the patriarchs of Jerusalem, Antioch, Alexandria, and Constantinople—who resided in the most important spiritual and political centers of the Roman empire. Subordinate to the five principal authorities were bishops, who presided over religious affairs in their districts, known as dioceses, which included all the prominent cities of the Roman empire. When theological disputes arose, the patriarchs and the bishops assembled in church councils to determine which views would prevail as official doctrine. The councils at Nicaea (325 C.E.) and Chalcedon (451 C.E.), for example, took up the difficult and contentious issue of Jesus' nature. Delegates at these councils proclaimed that Jesus was both fully human and fully divine at the same time, in contrast to Nestorians, Arians, and other Christian groups who held that Jesus was either primarily human or primarily divine.

As Roman imperial authority crumbled, the bishop of Rome, known as the pope (from the Latin *papa,* meaning "father"), emerged as spiritual leader of Christian communities in the western regions of the empire. As the only sources of established and recognized authority, the popes and the bishops of other important cities organized local government and defensive measures for their communities. They also mounted missionary campaigns to convert Germanic peoples to Christianity. Although Roman imperial authority disappeared, Roman Christianity survived and served as a foundation for cultural unity in lands that had formerly made up the western half of the Roman empire.

Nicaea (nahy-SEE-uh)
Chalcedon (KAL-suh-dawn)

SUMMARY

Between the last centuries of the first millennium B.C.E. and the first few centuries of the new millennium, the classical societies established a broad zone of exchange throughout much of Eurasia and north Africa. Long-distance trade along what has come to be known as the silk roads profoundly shaped the societies involved. Products like silk, jewels, and spices found new markets in far-distant regions, while ideas and religious beliefs from Buddhism to Christianity found new adherents and converts. Long-distance trade also facilitated the spread of epidemic disease, and by the second and third centuries C.E. disease had wreaked havoc among most of the classical societies. Indeed, coupled with severe internal conflicts as well as external threats, the disorder caused by epidemic disease helped contribute to the collapse of the Chinese Han dynasty as well as the Western Roman empire.

STUDY TERMS

Attila the Hun (179)
Buddhism (170)
Byzantine empire (180)
Christianity (171)
Confucianism (177)
Constantine (178)
Constantinople (178)
Council of Chalcedon (181)
Council of Nicaea (181)
Daoism (177)
Diocletian (178)
Edict of Milan (180)
epidemic disease (173)
Gregory the Wonderworker (171)
Han dynasty (165)
Mani (173)
Manichaeism (173)
Nestorians (172)
Odovacer (180)
pope (181)
silk roads (167)
St. Augustine (180)
tetrarchs (178)
Visigoths (178)
Yellow Turban rebellion (175)

FOR FURTHER READING

Thomas J. Barfield. *The Perilous Frontier: Nomadic Empires and China.* Cambridge, Mass., 1989. Provocative study of the Xiongnu and other central Asian peoples.

Jerry H. Bentley. *Old World Encounters: Cross-Cultural Contacts and Exchanges in Pre-modern Times.* New York, 1993. Studies the spread of cultural and religious traditions before 1500 C.E.

Averil Cameron. *The Later Roman Empire, A.D. 284–430.* Cambridge, Mass., 1993. A lively synthesis.

———. *The Mediterranean World in Late Antiquity, A.D. 395–600.* London, 1993. Like its companion volume just cited, a well-informed synthesis.

Edward Gibbon. *The Decline and Fall of the Roman Empire.* Many editions available. A classic account, still well worth reading, by a masterful historical stylist of the eighteenth century.

C. D. Gordon, ed. *The Age of Attila: Fifth-Century Byzantium and the Barbarians.* Ann Arbor, 1972. Translations of primary sources on the society and history of nomadic and migratory peoples.

Samuel Hugh Moffett. *A History of Christianity in Asia,* vol. 1. San Francisco, 1992. An important volume that surveys the spread of early Christianity east of the Roman empire.

Joseph A. Tainter. *The Collapse of Complex Societies.* Cambridge, 1988. Scholarly review of theories and evidence bearing on the fall of empires and societies.

Susan Whitfield. *Life along the Silk Road.* Berkeley, 1999. Focuses on the experiences of ten individuals who lived or traveled along the silk roads.

Francis Wood. *The Silk Road: Two Thousand Years in the Heart of Asia.* Berkeley, 2002. A brilliantly illustrated volume discussing the history of the silk roads from antiquity to the twentieth century.

Bringing It All Together

Part II The Formation of Classical Societies, 500 B.C.E. to 500 C.E.

In Part II, we have seen that the classical societies that developed in Persia, China, India, and the Mediterranean built on many of the traditions established by the early complex societies discussed in Part I. By the last half-millennium B.C.E., however, the classical societies had surpassed their predecessors in complexity, organization, and sophistication. As a result, they were able to expand further, to control more people and resources, and to trade longer distances than any human societies in the past.

The increased reach of classical societies created an ever-stronger need for rulers to impose their will efficiently across long distances, especially when their territories included diverse and potentially rebellious conquered peoples. Some, like the Achaemenid dynasty of Persia, established carefully designed administrations that divided oversight of their wide realms into manageable portions headed by loyal administrators. Many, including the Achaemenids, the Romans, and the Han dynasty of China, standardized systems of law and taxation as a means of encouraging uniformity throughout their realms. Others, like the rulers of Han China, established a uniform educational system from which all imperial administrators would be drawn.

Classical rulers also sought to impose their will and to promote unity within their realms by sponsoring particular philosophies, cultural practices, or religious beliefs. Thus, Greeks encouraged a sense of commonality between the diverse poleis and colonies by sponsoring the Olympic Games. In India, the Mauryan dynasty advocated Buddhism as a unifying system of belief, the Persian Sasanids sponsored Zoroastrianism as a state religion, and the Romans actively promoted Christianity after 380 C.E. Finally, all the classical societies sought to increase the efficiency of their administrations by establishing long-distance transportation and communication networks. While these networks aided imperial administration, they also allowed for a dramatic increase in long-distance trade. In turn, long-distance trade encouraged both the spread of religions such as Buddhism, Hinduism, and Christianity as well as the diffusion of disease pathogens that ultimately contributed to the disintegration of the classical societies.

By 500 C.E. classical societies in Persia, China, India, and the Mediterranean basin had either collapsed or fallen into decline. Yet all the classical societies left rich legacies that shaped political institutions, social orders, and cultural traditions for centuries to come. Moreover, by sponsoring commercial and cultural relations between different peoples, the classical societies laid a foundation for intensive and systematic cross-cultural interaction in later times.

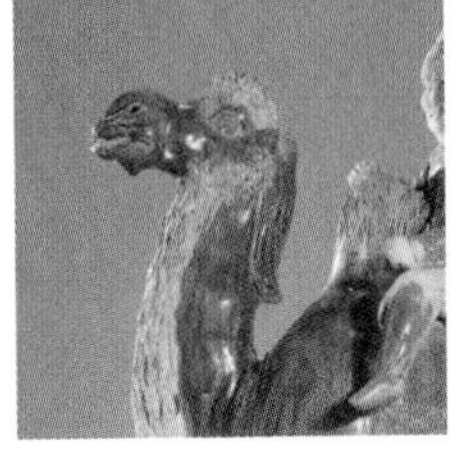

The Postclassical Era, 500 to 1000 C.E.

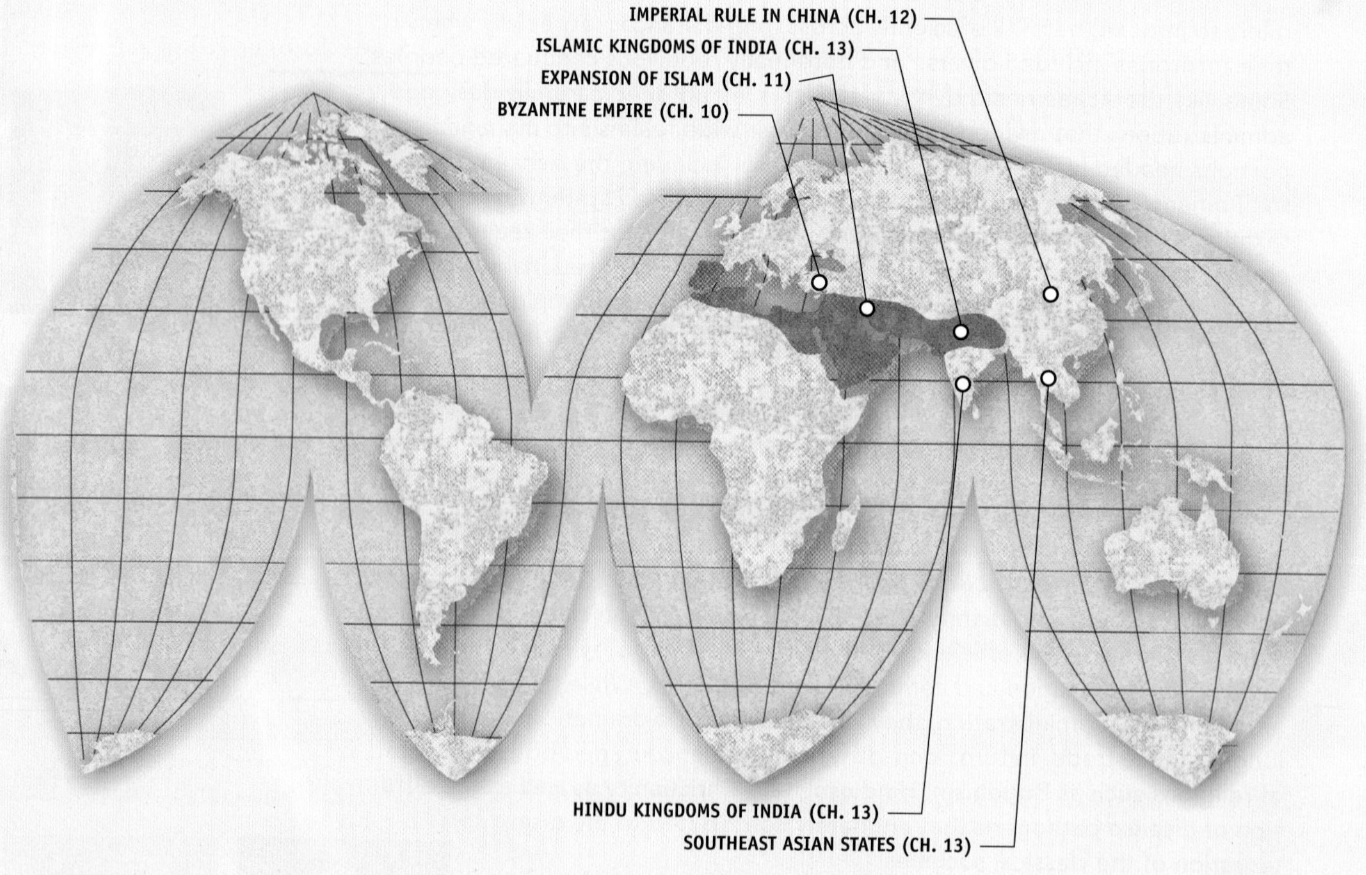

IMPERIAL RULE IN CHINA (CH. 12)
ISLAMIC KINGDOMS OF INDIA (CH. 13)
EXPANSION OF ISLAM (CH. 11)
BYZANTINE EMPIRE (CH. 10)
HINDU KINGDOMS OF INDIA (CH. 13)
SOUTHEAST ASIAN STATES (CH. 13)

The postclassical era was a period of major readjustment for societies throughout the eastern hemisphere. During the early centuries C.E., disease as well as both internal and external pressures brought serious instability to classical societies in China, India, southwest Asia, and the Mediterranean basin. Most of the classical empires collapsed under the strain. During the postclassical era the settled societies of the eastern hemisphere underwent political, social, economic, and cultural change that would shape their experiences over the long term.

The first task that settled societies faced in the postclassical era was the need to restore political and social order. In the eastern Mediterranean the eastern half of the Roman empire survived as the Byzantine empire but underwent political and social reorganization in order to deal with external pressures. In southwest Asia, Arab conquerors inspired by the recently founded Islamic faith asserted their authority over vast areas in southwest Asia and north Africa, and introduced their faith to India as well as Iberia. In China the Sui and Tang dynasties restored centralized imperial authority after almost four centuries of rule by competing regional kingdoms and nomadic conquerors. In India, in contrast, centralized imperial rule did not return: authority devolved instead to a series of regional kingdoms.

The reestablishment of political and social order enabled postclassical societies to revive networks of long-distance trade and participate more actively in processes of cross-cultural communication and exchange. As a result, the postclassical era was a time of rapid economic growth in most of the eastern hemisphere. Meanwhile, increased trade facilitated biological and technological as well as commercial exchanges: agricultural crops migrated far beyond the lands of their origin, and improved techniques of irrigation and cultivation spread through much of Eurasia. As agricultural production increased, so did human population, which allowed growing numbers of people to devote their efforts to trade and manufacturing rather than cultivation.

The postclassical era was also crucially important for the formation and development of cultural and religious traditions. Islam first appeared during the postclassical era, and it soon became the foundation of an expansive empire stretching from north Africa to northern India. Buddhism expanded beyond the Indian subcontinent and central Asia, attracting converts in east and southeast Asia. Christianity was the official faith of the Byzantine empire, where the Eastern Orthodox church emerged and gave shape to a distinctive form of Christianity that eventually spread to much of eastern Europe and Russia.

The empires and regional states of the postclassical era disappeared long ago, but the social, economic, and cultural legacies of the age are noticeable even today. Most notable, perhaps, religious and cultural traditions continue to flourish in lands where they first attracted converts in postclassical times. In some ways, then, the postclassical age survives even in the modern world.

The Christian Commonwealth of Byzantium

10

ccording to the Byzantine historian Procopius, two Christian monks from Persia set out on a momentous journey about the middle of the sixth century C.E. The result of their travels was the introduction of high-quality silk production to the eastern Mediterranean. Although local crafts workers had long produced coarse fabrics from the cocoons of wild silkworms, fine silks had come to the Mediterranean only from China, where manufacturers closely guarded both their carefully bred strains of silkworms and the complex technology that yielded high-quality textiles. Mediterranean consumers obtained silk not directly from Chinese producers but, rather, through intermediaries subject to the Sasanid empire of Persia.

According to Procopius's account, the two Christian monks observed the techniques of silk production during the course of a mission to China. Upon departure they hollowed out their walking staffs and filled them with silkworm eggs, which they smuggled out of China, through their native land of Persia, and into the Byzantine empire.

The monks' motives are unknown. Whatever they may have been, though, it is certain that the monks by themselves could not have introduced a full-blown silk industry to Byzantium. The production of fine, Chinese-style silks required more than a few silkworm eggs. It also required understanding sophisticated technologies and elaborate procedures that must have reached the Byzantine empire by several different routes. Thus it seems that Procopius simplified a much more complex story.

In any case, Byzantine crafts workers did indeed learn how to produce high-quality silk fabrics. By the late sixth century, Byzantine silks matched Chinese silks in quality. Mediterranean consumers no longer relied on Chinese producers and Persian intermediaries, and local production of high-quality silk greatly strengthened the Byzantine economy. Thus Procopius's anonymous monks participated in a momentous transfer of technology between distant lands. Their efforts contributed to the vibrance of Byzantine society, and their story highlights the significance of cross-cultural interactions during the postclassical era.

During the centuries after 200 C.E., most of the classical societies faced a series of problems—epidemic disease, declining population, economic contraction, social and political turmoil, and military threats—that brought about their collapse. Only in the eastern Mediterranean did a classical empire survive. The eastern half of the Roman empire, known as the Byzantine empire, withstood the various problems that brought down other classical societies

‹ A sixth-century icon depicting an enthroned Virgin Mary and infant Jesus attended by angels and saints.

Procopius (proh-KOH-pee-uhs)

CHRONOLOGY

313–337	Reign of Constantine
325	Council of Nicaea
329–379	Life of St. Basil of Caesarea
340	Transfer of Roman government to Constantinople
527–565	Reign of Justinian
717–741	Reign of Leo III
726–843	Iconoclastic controversy
ninth century	Missions of St. Cyril and St. Methodius to the Slavs
976–1025	Reign of Basil II, "the Bulgar-Slayer"
989	Conversion of Prince Vladimir of Kiev to Orthodox Christianity
1054	Beginning of the schism between the eastern and western Christian churches
1071	Battle of Manzikert
1202–1204	Fourth crusade
1453	Fall of Constantinople

and survived for almost a millennium after the collapse of the western Roman empire in the fifth century C.E.

The Byzantine empire did not reconstitute the larger Mediterranean society of classical times. The Roman empire had dominated an integrated Mediterranean basin; the Byzantine empire mostly faced a politically and culturally fragmented Mediterranean region. After the seventh century C.E., Islamic states controlled lands to the east and south of the Mediterranean, Slavic peoples dominated lands to the north, and western Europeans organized increasingly powerful states in lands to the west.

Nevertheless, the Byzantine empire was a political and economic powerhouse of the postclassical era. Until the twelfth century, Byzantine authority dominated the wealthy and productive eastern Mediterranean region. Manufactured goods from the Byzantine empire enjoyed a reputation for high quality in markets from the Mediterranean basin to India. The Byzantine empire also deeply influenced the historical development of the Slavic peoples of eastern Europe and Russia by introducing writing, Christianity, codified law, and sophisticated political organization into their lands. Because Byzantine political, economic, and cultural influence stretched so far, historians often refer to it as the "Byzantine commonwealth." Just as Greek and Roman initiative brought Mediterranean lands into a larger integrated society during classical times, Byzantine policies led to the formation of a large, multicultural zone of trade, communication, interaction, and exchange in eastern Europe and the eastern Mediterranean basin during the postclassical era.

The Early Byzantine Empire

The Byzantine empire takes its name from Byzantion—latinized as Byzantium—a modest village that occupied a site of enormous strategic significance. Situated on a defensible peninsula and blessed with a magnificent natural harbor known as the Golden Horn, Byzantion had the potential to control the Bosporus, the strait of water leading from the Black Sea to the Sea of Marmara and beyond to the Dardanelles, the Aegean Sea, and the Mediterranean. Apart from its maritime significance, Byzantion also offered convenient access to the rich lands of Anatolia, southwestern Asia, and southeastern Europe.

Because of its strategic value, the Roman emperor Constantine designated Byzantion as the site of a new imperial capital, which he named Constantinople ("city of Constantine"). The imperial government moved to Constantinople in 340 C.E., and the new capital rapidly reached metropolitan dimensions. By the late fourth century, it was the most important political and military center of the eastern Roman empire, and it soon became the dominant economic and commercial center in the eastern Mediterranean basin. The city kept the name Constantinople until 1453 C.E., when it fell to the Ottoman Turks, who renamed it Istanbul. By convention, however, historians refer to the realm governed from Constantinople between the fifth and fifteenth centuries C.E. as the Byzantine empire, or simply as Byzantium, in honor of the original settlement.

Byzantine (BIHZ-uhn-teen)
Aegean (ih-JEE-uhn)

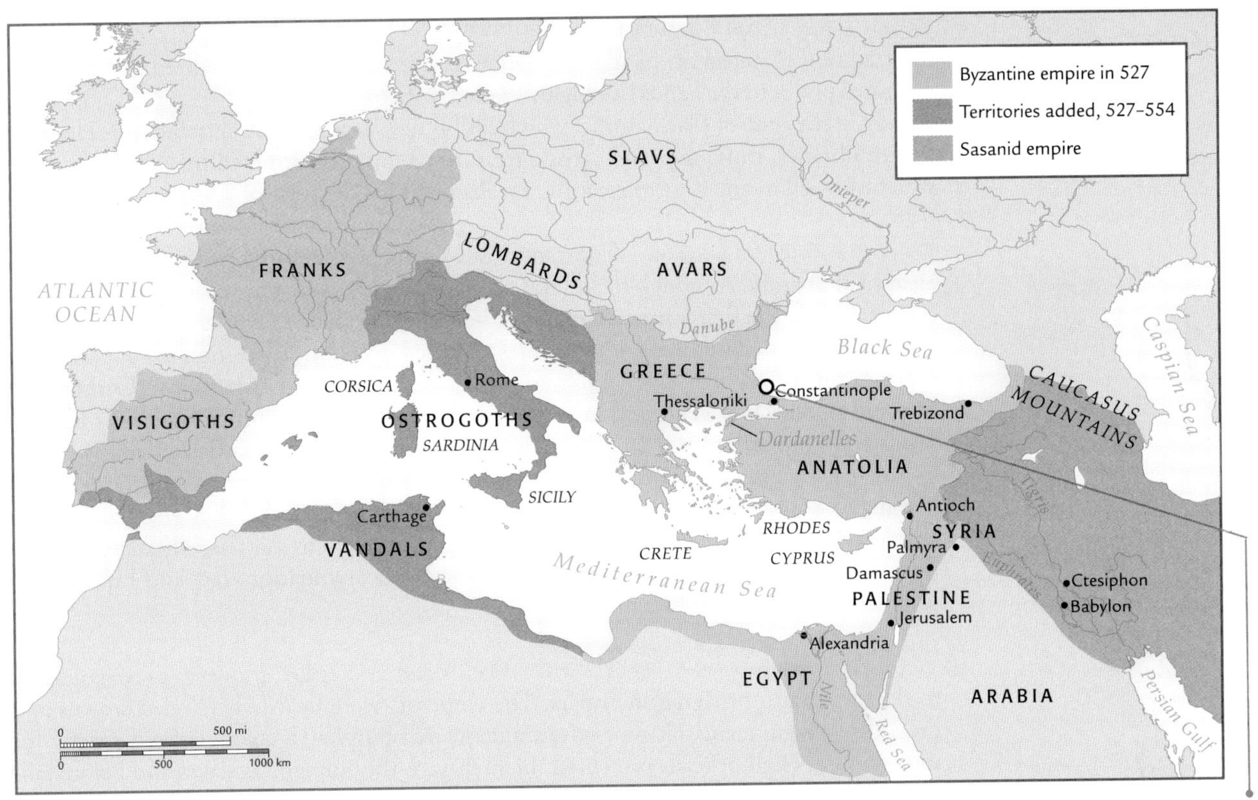

MAP 10.1 | The Byzantine empire and its neighbors, 527–554 C.E. Compare this map with Map 11.2 showing the Roman empire at its height. ***How did the territories of the Byzantine empire differ from those of the classical Roman empire?***

Constantinople became the capital of the Byzantine empire.

The Later Roman Empire and Byzantium

The Byzantine empire originated as the eastern half of the classical Roman empire, which survived the collapse of the western Roman empire in the fifth century C.E. In its early days the Byzantine empire embraced Greece, the Balkan region, Anatolia, Syria, Palestine, Egypt, and northeast Africa. During the seventh and eighth centuries C.E., however, the southern regions of the empire fell into the hands of Arab Muslim conquerors. Nevertheless, Byzantium figured as a major power of the eastern Mediterranean basin until the thirteenth century C.E.

The Byzantine empire
www.mhhe.com/bentleybrief2e

THE LATER ROMAN EMPIRE As the western Roman empire crumbled, the eastern half of the empire remained intact, complete with roads, communications, lines of authority, and a set of functioning imperial institutions, all inherited from Roman predecessors. Yet the early Byzantine emperors faced challenges different from those of their predecessors, and they built a state significantly different from the classical Roman empire.

The principal challenges that confronted the late Roman and early Byzantine empires were the consolidation of the dynamic Sasanid dynasty (226–641 C.E.) in Persia and the invasions of migratory peoples from the north and east. The Sasanid emperors sought to rebuild the Achaemenid empire of classical Persia, a goal that brought them into conflict with Roman forces in Mesopotamia and Syria. Germanic invasions also menaced the late Roman empire. Because they did not have adequate resources to respond strongly to the threat on all fronts, Roman authorities concentrated on maintaining the integrity of the wealthy eastern portion of the empire.

Sasanid (suh-SAH-nid)
Achaemenid (uh-KEE-muh-nihd)

THE EARLY BYZANTINE STATE The Byzantine emperors built a distinctive tradition of statecraft. Its most important feature was tightly centralized rule that concentrated power in the hands of a highly exalted emperor. This characteristic was noticeable already in the time of Constantine, who built his new capital to lavish standards. He filled it with libraries, museums, and artistic treasures, and he constructed magnificent marble structures—all in an effort to create a new Rome fit for the ruler of a mighty empire.

CAESAROPAPISM Constantine also set a precedent by hedging his rule with an aura of divinity. Although he did not claim divine status as some of his imperial predecessors had, as the first Christian emperor he did claim divine favor and sanction for his rule. He intervened in theological disputes and used his political position to support views that he considered orthodox and condemn those he regarded as heretical. Constantine initiated a policy that historians call *caesaropapism,* whereby the emperor not only ruled as secular lord but also played an active and prominent role in ecclesiastical affairs.

Particularly after the sixth century, Byzantine emperors became absolute rulers. According to Roman law, emperors stood above the law: theoretically, they wielded absolute authority in political, military, judicial, financial, and religious matters. They also enjoyed the services of a large and complex bureaucracy. In combination, law and bureaucracy produced an exceptionally centralized state.

THE BYZANTINE COURT Even dress and court etiquette drew attention to the lofty status of Byzantine rulers. The emperors wore heavily bejeweled crowns and dressed in magnificent silk robes dyed a dark, rich purple—a color reserved strictly for imperial use. High officials presented themselves to the emperor as slaves and before taking up matters of business prostrated themselves before him three times and kissed his hands and feet. By the tenth century, engineers had contrived a series of mechanical devices that worked dazzling effects and impressed foreign envoys at the Byzantine court: mechanical lions roared and swished their tails as ambassadors approached the emperor, and sometimes the imperial throne itself moved up and down to emphasize the awesome splendor of the emperor.

Justinian and His Legacy

JUSTINIAN AND THEODORA The most important of the early Byzantine emperors was Justinian (527–565 C.E.), an energetic and tireless worker known to his subjects as "the sleepless emperor," who profoundly influenced the development of the Byzantine empire with the aid of his ambitious wife Theodora. Both were intelligent, strong willed, and disciplined and used those qualities to build a strong empire and a grand imperial court.

PSI img Court of Theodora
www.mhhe.com/
bentleybrief2e

Exterior of Hagia Sophia
www.mhhe.com/
bentleybrief2e

Like Constantine, Justinian lavished resources on the imperial capital. During the early years of his rule, riots against high taxes had destroyed much of Constantinople. After Theodora persuaded him to deploy the imperial army and quash the disturbances, Justinian embarked on an ambitious construction program that thoroughly remade the city. The most notable building erected during that campaign was the church of Hagia Sophia, a magnificent domed structure that ranks as one of the world's most important examples of Christian architecture. Visitors marveled at the church's enormous dome, which they likened to the heavens encircling the earth, and they expressed awe at the gold, silver, and gems that decorated and illuminated Hagia Sophia. Over time, the church even acquired a reputation for working miraculous cures: its columns and doors reportedly healed the illnesses of people who stood beside them or touched them.

JUSTINIAN'S CODE Justinian's most significant political contribution was his codification of Roman law. Almost immediately on taking the throne, Justinian ordered a thorough and systematic review of Roman law. On the basis of that work, he issued the

Hagia Sophia (HAH-yah soh-FEE-uh)

EMPEROR JUSTINIAN. | Justinian wears imperial purple robes in this mosaic from the church of San Vitale in Ravenna. He is pictured in the company of ecclesiastical, military, and court officials. Notice the richness of Justinian's clothing in comparison to those around him.

Corpus iuris civilis (Body of the Civil Law), which immediately won recognition as a definitive work. Later emperors updated Roman law by adding new provisions, but Justinian's code continued to serve as a source of legal inspiration and went on to influence civil law codes throughout much of western Europe.

BELISARIUS AND BYZANTINE CONQUESTS Justinian's most ambitious venture was his effort to reconquer the western Roman empire from Germanic peoples and reestablish Roman authority throughout the Mediterranean basin. Beginning in 533 he sent his brilliant general Belisarius on military campaigns that returned Italy, Sicily, northwestern Africa, and southern Spain to imperial hands. By the end of his reign in 565, Justinian had reconstituted a good portion of the classical Roman empire.

Justinian's accomplishment, however, did not long survive his own rule. Byzantium simply did not possess the resources to sustain Belisarius's conquests. Although Byzantium managed to hold on to a few areas in the Italian peninsula, Justinian's dream of restoring Roman authority throughout the Mediterranean basin soon faded. Indeed, Justinian's efforts clearly showed that the classical Roman empire was beyond recovery. While Justinian devoted his attention to the western Mediterranean, the Sasanids threatened Byzantium from the east and Slavic peoples approached from the north. Justinian's successors had no choice but to withdraw their resources from the western Mediterranean and redeploy them in the east. Even though Belisarius's reconquest of the western Roman empire was a spectacular military accomplishment, it was also something of an anachronism, since the lands of the eastern and western Mediterranean had already begun to follow different historical trajectories.

Islamic Conquests and Byzantine Revival

After the seventh century C.E., the emergence of Islam and the development of a powerful and expansive Islamic state (topics discussed in chapter 11) posed a serious challenge to Byzantium. Inspired by their Islamic faith, Arab peoples conquered the Sasanid empire and overran Byzantine Syria, Palestine, Egypt, and north Africa. During the late seventh and early eighth centuries, Islamic forces even subjected Constantinople to prolonged siege (in 674–678 and again in 717–718). Byzantium resisted this northern thrust of Islam

Corpus iuris civilis (KOR-poos EW-rees sih-VEE-lees)
Belisarius (bel-uh-SAIR-ee-uhs)

The Church of Hagia Sophia ("Holy Wisdom"). | This church was built by Justinian and transformed into a mosque in the fifteenth century. The dome rises almost 60 meters (197 feet) above the floor, and its windows allow abundant light to enter the massive structure.

partly because of military technology. Byzantine forces used a weapon known as Greek fire—a devastating incendiary weapon compounded of sulphur, lime, and petroleum—which they launched at both the fleets and the ground forces of the invaders. Greek fire burned even when floating on water and thus created a serious hazard when deployed around wooden ships. On land it caused panic among enemy forces, since it was very difficult to extinguish and often burned troops to death. As a result of this defensive effort, the Byzantine empire retained its hold on Anatolia, Greece, and the Balkan region.

IMPERIAL ORGANIZATION Though much reduced by the Islamic conquests, the Byzantine empire after the eighth century was also more compact and manageable. Also, Byzantine rulers initiated political and social adjustments that strengthened the empire that remained in their hands. The most important innovation was the reorganization of Byzantine society under the *theme* (imperial province) system. This system placed a *theme* under the jurisdiction of a general, who assumed responsibility for both its military defense and its civil administration. Generals received their appointments from the imperial government, which closely supervised their activities to prevent decentralization of power and authority. Generals recruited armies from the ranks of free peasants, who received allotments of land in exchange for military service. The armies proved to be effective military forces, and the system as a whole strengthened the class of free peasants, which in turn solidified Byzantium's agricultural economy. The *theme* system enabled Byzantine forces to mobilize quickly and resist further Islamic advances and also undergirded the political order and the social organization of the empire from the eighth through the twelfth century.

Indeed, Byzantium vastly expanded its influence between the late ninth and the late eleventh centuries. During the tenth century Byzantine forces shored up defenses in Anatolia and reconquered Syria from Arab Muslims. During the reign of Basil II (976–1025 C.E.), known as "Basil the Bulgar-Slayer," Byzantine armies turned west and crushed the neighboring Bulgars, who had built a large kingdom in the Balkans. After his victory at the battle of Kleidion in 1014 C.E., Basil reportedly commanded his forces to blind fourteen thousand Bulgarian survivors, though he spared one eye in a few, who then guided the others home. By the mid–eleventh century the Byzantine empire embraced lands from Syria and Armenia in the east to southern Italy in the west, from the Danube River in the

Byzantine Manuscript Illustration. | This illustration depicts Byzantine naval forces turning Greek fire on their Arab enemies. © *The Granger Collection, New York.*

north to Cyprus and Crete in the south. Byzantine expansion brought in so much wealth that Basil was able to waive the collection of taxes for two years. Once again, Byzantium dominated the eastern Mediterranean.

Byzantium and Western Europe

TENSIONS BETWEEN BYZANTIUM AND WESTERN EUROPEAN STATES While they went to war with their Arab Muslim and pagan Slavic neighbors, Byzantines also experienced tense relations with their Christian counterparts in the western Mediterranean. The Christian church of Constantinople conducted its affairs in Greek and was heavily influenced by the will of the caesaropapist emperors, whereas the Christian church of Rome conducted its affairs in Latin and rejected imperial interference in ecclesiastical matters. Church authorities in Byzantium regarded Roman Christians as poorly educated and uncouth. In return, church leaders in Rome considered their Byzantine counterparts insincere and insufficiently wary of heresy.

Political grievances also strained relations between Byzantium and western European lands. During the fifth and sixth centuries, imperial authorities could do little more than watch as Germanic peoples established successor states to the western Roman empire—lands that Byzantine emperors regarded as their rightful inheritance. Worse yet, some of the upstart powers claimed imperial authority for themselves. In 800, for example, the Frankish ruler Charlemagne received an imperial crown from the pope in Rome, thereby directly challenging Byzantine claims to imperial authority over western lands. Charlemagne's empire soon dissolved, but in 962 Otto of Saxony lodged his own claim to rule as emperor over the western lands of the former Roman empire. Adding injury to insult, Otto then attacked lands in southern Italy that had been in Byzantine possession since the days of Justinian.

Byzantine Economy and Society

Byzantium dominated the political and military affairs of the eastern Mediterranean largely because of its strong economy. Ever since classical times, the territories embraced by the Byzantine empire had produced abundant agricultural surpluses, supported large numbers of crafts workers, and participated in trade with lands throughout the Mediterranean. Even after the collapse of the Roman empire, those territories continued to provide a solid material foundation for Byzantium, and they helped to make the Byzantine empire an economic powerhouse of the postclassical era.

Charlemagne (SHAHR-leh-mane)

Rural Economy and Society

Until its conquest by Arab forces, Egypt was the major source of grain for Byzantium. Afterward, Anatolia and the lower Danube region served as the imperial breadbasket. All those lands produced reliable and abundant harvests of wheat, which supported large populations in Byzantium's major cities. Indeed, between the fifth and the early thirteenth centuries, Constantinople's population alone approached or exceeded one million people.

THE PEASANTRY Byzantine economy and society were strongest when the empire supported a large class of free peasants who owned small plots of land. Besides serving as the backbone of the Byzantine military system, free peasants cultivated their land intensively in hopes of improving their families' fortunes. As in other societies, however, wealthy families sought to accumulate land and to control the labor of peasants for their own interests. Especially in the early centuries of the Byzantine empire, wealthy cultivators worked to bind peasants to their estates or to force them into sharecropping arrangements from which it was difficult to break free.

However, the invasions of the sixth and seventh centuries broke up many large estates and afforded peasants an opportunity to rebuild small holdings. The *theme* system strengthened the free peasantry by making land available to those who performed military service. The imperial government also made periodic efforts to prevent wealthy landowners from gaining control over peasant lands. Over the long term, however, wealthy landowners built ever-larger estates. From the eleventh century onward, they transformed the peasants into an increasingly dependent class, and by the thirteenth century free peasants accounted for only a small portion of the rural population.

DECLINE OF THE FREE PEASANTRY The accumulation of landholdings in the hands of the wealthy had important implications for financial and military affairs. For one thing, large estates often received tax exemptions and so did not contribute their fair share to imperial coffers. Moreover, the decline of the free peasantry diminished the pool of recruits available for service in military forces organized under the *theme* system. Thus, the concentration of land and rural resources worked against the financial interests of the central government, and it caused political, military, and economic difficulties for the Byzantine state during the last three centuries of its existence.

Industry and Trade

In spite of social and economic problems, Byzantium remained a wealthy land. Byzantine prosperity derived both from the empire's productive capacity and from the importance of Constantinople as a center of trade.

MANUFACTURING ENTERPRISES Indeed, Constantinople was home to many artisans and crafts workers who enjoyed a reputation especially for their glassware, linen and woolen textiles, gems, jewelry, and fine work in gold and silver. In addition, after the arrival of silkworms, crafts workers added high-quality silk textiles to the list of products manufactured in the Byzantine empire. Silk was a most important addition to the economy, and Byzantium became the principal supplier of this fashionable fabric to lands in the Mediterranean basin. The silk industry was so important to the Byzantine economy that the government closely supervised every step in its production and sale. Regulations allowed individuals to participate in only one activity—such as weaving, dyeing, or sales—to prevent the creation of a monopoly in the industry by a few wealthy or powerful entrepreneurs.

TRADE Situated astride routes going east and west as well as north and south, Constantinople also served as the main clearinghouse for trade in the western part of Eurasia. The merchants of Constantinople maintained direct commercial links with manufacturers and merchants in central Asia, Russia, Scandinavia, northern Europe, and the lands of

BYZANTINE WOMEN WORKING. | A manuscript illustration depicts one Byzantine woman weaving cloth (left) while another spins thread (right). Both women veil their hair for modesty. Women workers were prominent in Byzantine textile production.

the Black Sea and the Mediterranean basin. Byzantium dominated trade to such an extent that trading peoples recognized the Byzantine gold coin, the *bezant,* as the standard currency of the Mediterranean basin for more than half a millennium, from the sixth through the twelfth century.

Byzantium drew enormous wealth simply from the control of trade and the levying of customs duties on merchandise that passed through its lands. More important, Byzantium served as the western anchor of a Eurasian trading network that revived the silk roads of classical times. Silk and porcelain came to Constantinople from China, spices from India and southeast Asia. Carpets arrived from Persia, woolen textiles from western Europe, and timber, furs, honey, amber, and slaves from Russia and Scandinavia.

THE ORGANIZATION OF TRADE Banks helped to fuel Byzantine trade by advancing loans to individuals seeking to launch business ventures, and Byzantine merchants often formed partnerships that allowed them to pool their resources and limit their risks. Although neither banking nor partnership was an altogether new technique, Byzantine businessmen made much more extensive use of them than their predecessors had. In doing so, they both supported and stimulated a dynamic commercial economy.

Urban Life

Constantinople had no rival among Byzantine cities. Subjects of the Byzantine empire referred to it simply as "the City." The heart of the City was the imperial palace, which employed twenty thousand workers as palace staff. Peacocks strutted through gardens filled with sculptures and fountains. Most famous was a gold fountain in the shape of a pineapple that spouted wine for imperial guests.

HOUSING IN CONSTANTINOPLE Aristocrats maintained enormous palaces that included courtyards, reception halls, libraries, and chapels. Women lived in separate apartments and did not receive male visitors from outside the household. Indeed, women often did not participate in banquets and parties, especially when wine flowed freely or when the affairs were likely to become so festive that they could compromise a woman's honor.

The less privileged classes of Constantinople occupied less splendid dwellings. Artisans and crafts workers usually lived in rooms above their shops, and clerks and government officials lived in multistory apartment buildings. Workers and the poor occupied dangerous and rickety tenements, sharing kitchens and sanitary facilities with their neighbors.

THINKING ABOUT *Traditions*

TRADITIONS IN THE CHRISTIAN COMMONWEALTH OF BYZANTIUM. From the time of the transfer of Roman government to Constantinople until the city's fall in 1453, the people of the Byzantine empire drew heavily from their historical association with both the western Roman empire as well as classical Greece. In which areas of Byzantine culture and politics were these influences most apparent?

ATTRACTIONS OF CONSTANTINOPLE Even for the poor, though, the City had its attractions. As the heir to Rome, Constantinople was a city of baths, which were sites of relaxation and exercise as well as hygienic bathing. Taverns and restaurants offered settings for social gatherings—checkers, chess, and dice games were especially popular activities at taverns—and theaters provided entertainment in the form of song, dance, and striptease. Mass entertainment took place in the Hippodrome, a large stadium adjacent to the imperial palace. There Byzantine subjects watched chariot races, athletic matches, contests between wild animals, and circuses featuring clowns, jugglers, acrobats, and dwarfs.

CLASSICAL HERITAGE AND ORTHODOX CHRISTIANITY

The first Christian emperor of the Roman empire gave both his name and his faith to Constantinople. Like the Byzantine state, however, Byzantine Christianity developed along distinctive lines, and it became a faith different from the early Christianity of the Roman empire. For one thing, the philosophy and literature of classical Greece had a much deeper influence in Byzantium than in western Europe. Byzantine church leaders also disagreed with their western counterparts on matters of doctrine, ritual, and church authority. By the mid–eleventh century, differences between the eastern and western churches had become so great that their leaders formally divided Mediterranean Christianity into the Eastern Orthodox and Roman Catholic churches.

The Legacy of Classical Greece

Although local inhabitants spoke Greek, the official language of early Constantinople was Latin, the language of Rome. After the sixth century, however, Greek replaced Latin as the language of government in the Byzantine empire. Byzantine scholars often did not learn to read Latin, and they drew intellectual inspiration from the New Testament (originally composed in Greek) and the philosophy and literature of classical Greece rather than classical Rome.

BYZANTINE EDUCATION The legacy of classical Greece was especially noticeable in Byzantine education. The Byzantine state considered education vitally important, since its bureaucracy called for large numbers of literate individuals to administer the empire. As a result, the state organized a school system that offered a primary education in reading, writing, and grammar, followed by studies of classical Greek literature, philosophy, and science. Because of this, basic literacy was widespread in Byzantine society.

BYZANTINE SCHOLARSHIP Like the educational system, Byzantine scholarship reflected the cultural legacy of classical Greece. Byzantine scholars concentrated on the humanities—literature, history, and philosophy—rather than on the natural sciences or medicine. Byzantines with a literary education considered themselves the direct heirs of classical Greece, and they went to great lengths to preserve and transmit the classical legacy. Indeed, almost all literary and philosophical works of classical Greece that survive have come down to the present in copies made between the tenth and twelfth centuries in the Byzantine empire.

The Byzantine Church

PSI img Lid of the Limburg Staurotheca www.mhhe.com/bentleybrief2e

CHURCH AND STATE The most distinctive feature of Byzantine Christianity was its close relationship with the imperial government. From the time of Constantine on, caesaropapist emperors participated actively in religious and theological matters. In 325 C.E., for example, Constantine organized the Council of Nicaea, which brought together bishops, spokesmen, and leaders from all the important Christian churches to consider the views of the Arians, who believed that Jesus had been a mortal human rather than a divine being coeternal with God. Although Constantine originally favored Arian views, he came to accept the view that Jesus was both human and divine and personally attended sessions of the Council of Nicaea to support it. His presence encouraged the council to endorse his preferred view as orthodox and to condemn Arianism as heresy.

The Byzantine emperors, in fact, treated the church as a department of state. They appointed individuals to serve as patriarch of Constantinople—the highest ecclesiastical official in the Byzantine church, counterpart of the pope in Rome—and they instructed patriarchs, bishops, and priests to deliver sermons that supported imperial policy. This caesaropapism was a source of constant conflict between imperial and ecclesiastical authorities, and sometimes even between emperors and their subjects. For example, Emperor Leo III (reigned 717–741 C.E.) sparked riots throughout the empire when he embarked on a policy of iconoclasm (literally, "the breaking of icons") in an attempt to prohibit the use of religious images and icons in churches. Although the policy was ultimately unsuccessful, it generated tremendous bitterness among ordinary people who were deeply attached to the religious imagery in their churches.

GREEK PHILOSOPHY AND BYZANTINE THEOLOGY In its theology, Byzantine Christianity reflected the continuing influence of classical Greek philosophy. Theologians invested a great deal of time and intellectual energy in the examination of religious questions from a philosophical point of view. They looked to classical philosophy, for example, when seeking to understand the nature of Jesus and the extent to which he possessed both human and divine characteristics. Although these debates often became extremely technical, they illustrated an effort to understand Christian doctrine in light of the terms and concepts that classical philosophers had employed in their analysis of the world. A school maintained by the patriarch of Constantinople provided instruction for clergy and church officials in advanced theology of this sort. Thus, although it differed in many ways from Mediterranean society of classical times, Byzantium built its own cultural and religious traditions on a solid classical foundation.

Monasticism and Popular Piety

Caesaropapist emperors, powerful patriarchs, and other high church officials concerned themselves with theological and ritual matters and rarely dealt directly with the lay population of the Byzantine church. Nor did the Byzantine laity have much interest in fine points of theology, and they positively resented policies such as iconoclasm that infringed on cherished patterns of worship. For religious inspiration, then, the laity looked not to the church hierarchy but to the local monasteries.

ASCETICISM Byzantine monasticism grew out of the efforts of devout individuals to lead especially holy lives. Drawing inspiration from early Christian ascetics in Egypt, Mesopotamia, and Persia, these individuals observed regimes of extreme asceticism and self-denial. During the fifth century, for example, a few men and at least two women demonstrated their ascetic commitments by perching for years at a time atop tall pillars. Because of the extreme dedication of ascetics, disciples often gathered around them and established communities of men and women determined to follow their example. These communities became the earliest monasteries of the Byzantine church. They had few rules until St. Basil of Caesarea (329–379 C.E.), the patriarch of Constantinople during the mid–fourth century, urged them to give up their personal possessions and live communally, to observe the rule of elected superiors, and to devote themselves to work and prayer. After the fourth century, Basilian monasticism spread rapidly throughout the Byzantine empire.

Nicaea (nahy-SEE-uh)
patriarch (PAY-tree-ahrk)
iconoclasts (eye-KAHN-oh-klasts)
asceticism (uh-SET-uh-siz-uhm)

BYZANTINE MONASTICISM Unlike their counterparts in western Europe and other lands, Byzantine monasteries for the most part did not become centers of education, study, learning, and scholarship. Yet monasteries under the rule of St. Basil had a reputation for piety and devotion that endeared them to the Byzantine laity. Basilian monks went to great lengths in search of mystical union with God through meditation and prayer. Some retired to remote destinations to lead lives of strict asceticism. The devotion of Basilian monks, in turn, inspired piety among the Byzantine laity because they represented a religious faith more immediate and meaningful than that of the theologians and ecclesiastical bureaucrats of Constantinople.

Monks and nuns also provided social services to their communities. They provided spiritual counsel to local laity, and they organized relief efforts by bringing food and medical attention to communities struck by disasters. They won the support of the Byzantine populace, too, when they vigorously opposed the policy of iconoclasm and fought to restore icons to churches and monasteries. Indeed, by setting examples of devotion and by tending to the needs and interests of the laity, monks helped to maintain support for their faith in the Byzantine empire.

Tensions between Eastern and Western Christianity

Byzantine Christianity developed in tension particularly with the Christian faith of western Europe. During the centuries following Constantine's legalization of Christianity, church leaders in Jerusalem, Alexandria, Antioch, Constantinople, and Rome exercised great influence in the larger Christian community. Yet after Arab peoples conquered most of southwest Asia and introduced Islam there in the seventh century, the influence of the patriarchs in Jerusalem, Alexandria, and Antioch declined, leaving only Constantinople and Rome as the principal centers of Christian authority.

CONSTANTINOPLE AND ROME The specific issues that divided the two Christian communities in Constantinople and Rome were religious and theological. Some ritual and doctrinal differences were relatively minor concerns over forms of worship and the precise wording of theological teachings. Byzantine theologians objected, for example, to the fact that western priests shaved their beards and used unleavened instead of leavened bread when saying Mass. Other differences concerned substantive theological matters, such as the precise relationship between God, Jesus, and the Holy Spirit.

SCHISM Alongside these ritual and doctrinal differences, the Byzantine patriarchs and Roman popes disputed their respective rights and powers. Patriarchs argued for the autonomy of all major Christian jurisdictions, including that of Constantinople, whereas popes asserted the primacy of Rome as the sole seat of authority for all Christendom. Ultimately, relations became so strained that the eastern and western churches went separate ways. In 1054 C.E. the patriarch and the pope excommunicated each other, each refusing to recognize the other's church as properly Christian. Despite efforts at reconciliation, the resulting schism between eastern and western churches persists to the present day. In recognition of the split, historians refer to the eastern Christian church after 1054 as the Eastern Orthodox church and its western counterpart as the Roman Catholic church.

The Influence of Byzantium in Eastern Europe

By the second millennium C.E., a dynamic society founded on the Islamic faith had seized control of the lands on the Mediterranean's southern and eastern rims, and Byzantines and western Europeans contested the northern rim. Hemmed in and increasingly pressured by Islamic and western European societies, Byzantium entered a period of decline beginning about the late eleventh century.

As its Mediterranean influence waned, however, Byzantium turned its attention to eastern Europe and Russia. Through political, commercial, and cultural relations, Byzantium decisively influenced the history of Slavic peoples. The Byzantine state itself came to an end in the fifteenth century C.E. But because of the Byzantine commonwealth—the larger collection of societies in eastern Europe and the eastern Mediterranean basin that developed under Byzantine influence—the legacy of Byzantium survives and continues to shape the lives of millions of people in Russia and eastern Europe.

Domestic Problems and Foreign Pressures

When Basil II, "the Bulgar-Slayer," died in 1025 C.E., the Byzantine empire was a political, military, and economic dynamo. Within fifty years, however, the empire was suffering from serious internal weaknesses and had endured a series of military reverses. Both domestic and foreign problems help to explain this decline.

SOCIAL PROBLEMS Domestic problems arose, ironically, from the success of the *theme* system. Generals who governed the *themes* were natural allies of local aristocrats who held large tracts of land, and together they began to resist the policies of the imperial government. At times, they even mounted rebellions against central authorities. Moreover, by the mid–eleventh century aristocrats had accumulated vast estates that placed the free peasantry under increasing pressure. Since peasants provided the backbone of Byzantium's military system and agricultural economy, this caused both fiscal and military problems for the imperial government.

CHALLENGES FROM THE WEST As domestic problems mounted, Byzantium also faced fresh foreign challenges. From the west came the Normans—a Scandinavian people who had seized and settled in Normandy (in northern France). During the early eleventh century, they established themselves as an independent power in southern Italy, and by midcentury they had taken control of southern Italy and expelled Byzantine authorities there.

During the twelfth and thirteenth centuries, the Normans and other western European peoples mounted a series of crusades—vast military campaigns intended to recapture Jerusalem and other sites holy to Christians from Muslims—and took the opportunity to carve out states in the heart of the Byzantine empire. They even conquered and sacked Constantinople in 1204. Although Byzantine forces recaptured the capital in 1261, the destruction of Constantinople dealt the Byzantine empire a blow from which it never completely recovered.

CHALLENGES FROM THE EAST As Europeans expanded into Byzantine territory from the west, nomadic Turkish peoples invaded from the east. Most important among them were the Muslim Saljuqs, who beginning in the eleventh century sent waves of invaders into Anatolia. Given the military and financial problems of the Byzantine empire, the Saljuqs found Anatolia ripe for plunder. In 1071 they subjected the Byzantine army to a demoralizing defeat at the battle of Manzikert. Byzantine factions then turned on one another in civil war, allowing the Saljuqs almost free rein in Anatolia. By the late twelfth century, the Saljuqs had seized much of Anatolia, and crusaders from western Europe held most of the remainder.

The loss of Anatolia—the principal source of Byzantine grain, wealth, and military forces—sealed the fate of the Byzantine empire. A territorially truncated Byzantium survived until the mid–fifteenth century, but the late Byzantine empire enjoyed little autonomy and continually faced fresh challenges from Italian merchants, western European

Saljuqs (sahl-JYOOKS)

SOURCES FROM THE PAST

Anna Comnena on the Suppression of Bogomil Heretics

Anna Comnena (1083–1148), daughter of the Byzantine emperor Alexius I (reigned 1081–1118), wrote the **Alexiad**, *a laudatory history of her father's reign. In the following selection, she discusses his prosecution in 1110 of Bogomil heretics, who revived the dualist teachings of the Manichaeans. Her account makes it clear that the caesaropapist Byzantine emperors took seriously their commitment to the Orthodox church and their obligation to protect its interests.*

Later . . . there arose an extraordinary "cloud of heretics," a new hostile group, hitherto unknown to the Church. . . . Apparently it was in existence before my father's time, but was unperceived (for the Bogomils' sect is most adept at feigning virtue). No worldly hairstyles are to be seen among Bogomils: their wickedness is hidden beneath cloak and cowl. Your Bogomil wears a somber look; muffled up to the nose, he walks with a stoop, quietly muttering to himself—but inside he's a ravening wolf. This unpleasant race, like a serpent lurking in its hole, was brought to the light and lured out by my father with magical incantations. . . .

The fame of the Bogomils had by now spread to all parts, for the impious sect was controlled with great cunning by a certain monk called Basil. He had twelve followers whom he called "apostles" and also dragged along with him certain female disciples, women of bad character, utterly depraved. In all quarters he made his wicked influence felt and when the evil, like some consuming fire, devoured many souls, the emperor could no longer bear it. He instituted a thorough inquiry into the heresy. . . .

. . . Alexius condemned the heretics out of hand: chorus and chorus-leader alike were to suffer death by burning. When the Bogomils had been hunted down and brought together in one place, some clung to the heresy, but others denied the charges completely, protesting strongly against their accusers and rejecting the Bogomilian heresy with scorn. . . .

The emperor glared at them and said, "Two pyres will have to be lit today. By one a cross will be planted firmly in the ground. Then a choice will be offered to all: those who are prepared to die for their Christian faith will separate themselves from the rest and take up position by the pyre with the cross; the Bogomilian adherents will be thrown on the other. Surely it is better that even Christians should die than live to be hounded down as Bogomils and offend the conscience of the majority. Go away, then, all of you, to whichever pyre you choose." . . .

A huge crowd gathered and stood all about them. Fires were then lit, burning seven times more fiercely than usual. . . . The flames leapt to the heavens. By one pyre stood the cross. Each of the condemned was given his choice, for all were to be burnt. Now that escape was clearly impossible, the orthodox to a man moved over to the pyre with the cross, truly prepared to suffer martyrdom; the godless adherents of the abominable heresy went off to the other. Just as they were about to be thrown on the flames, all the bystanders broke into mourning for the Christians; they were filled with indignation against the emperor (they did not know of his plan). But an order came from him just in time to stop the executioners. Alexius had in this way obtained firm evidence of those who were really Bogomils. The Christians, who were victims of calumny, he released after giving them much advice; the rest [i.e., the Bogomils] were committed once again to prison, but the [Bogomil] "apostles" were kept apart. Later he sent for some of these men every day and personally taught them, with frequent exhortations to abandon their abominable cult. . . . And some did change for the better and were freed from prison, but others died in their heresy, still incarcerated, although they were supplied with plentiful food and clothing.

■ Why did Byzantine rulers go to such lengths to suppress heresy?

SOURCE: Anna Comnena. *The Alexiad of Anna Comnena.* Trans. by E. R. A. Sewter. Harmondsworth: Penguin, 1969, pp. 496–505. (Translation slightly modified.)

adventurers, and Turkish nomads. In 1453, after a long era of decline, the Byzantine empire came to an end when Ottoman Turks captured Constantinople and absorbed its territories into their own expanding realm.

Early Relations between Byzantium and Slavic Peoples

By the time Constantinople fell, Byzantine traditions had deeply influenced the political and cultural development of Slavic peoples in eastern Europe and Russia. Close relations between Byzantium and Slavic peoples date from the sixth century. When Justinian de-

MAP 10.2 | The Byzantine empire and its neighbors, ca. 1100 C.E. After the emergence of Islam, the Byzantine empire shrank dramatically in size. ***To what extent does the expansion of Islam help explain the fact that Byzantine influence was strongest in eastern Europe after the seventh century C.E.?***

Conversions to orthodox Christianity in Bulgaria contributed to the long-term influence of Byzantine culture in eastern Europe.

ployed Byzantium's military resources in the western Mediterranean, Slavic peoples from the north took advantage of the opportunity to move into Byzantine territory. Serbs and Croats moved into the Balkan peninsula, and Bulgars established a powerful kingdom in the lower Danube region.

Relations between Byzantium and Bulgaria were especially tense. By the eighth century, however, Byzantium had begun to influence Bulgarian politics and society. Byzantium and Bulgaria entered into political, commercial, and cultural relations. Members of Bulgarian ruling families often went to Constantinople for a formal education in Greek language and literature and followed Byzantine examples in organizing their court and capital.

CYRIL AND METHODIUS Byzantium also sent missionaries to Balkan lands, and Bulgars and other Slavic peoples began to convert to Orthodox Christianity. The most famous of the missionaries to the Slavs were Saints Cyril and Methodius, two brothers from Thessaloniki in Greece. During the mid–ninth century Cyril and Methodius conducted missions in Bulgaria and Moravia (which included much of the modern Czech, Slovakian, and Hungarian territories). While there, they devised an alphabet, known as the Cyrillic alphabet, for the previously illiterate Slavic peoples. Though adapted from written Greek, the Cyrillic alphabet represented the sounds of Slavic languages more precisely than did the Greek, and it remained in use in much of eastern Europe until supplanted by the Roman alphabet in the twentieth century. In Russia and most other parts of the former Soviet Union, the Cyrillic alphabet survives to the present day.

THINKING ABOUT *Encounters*

ENCOUNTERS IN THE CHRISTIAN COMMONWEALTH OF BYZANTIUM. Although the Mediterranean world inhabited by the Byzantines was more politically fragmented than it had been under the Roman empire, the Byzantine empire nevertheless sustained both hostile and friendly encounters with Islamic peoples to the south and east, Slavic peoples to the north, and Europeans to the west. In what ways did these various encounters shape the Byzantine empire, and in what ways did Byzantine influence shape societies beyond imperial borders?

BULGARIANS IN BYZANTIUM. | This illustration from a twelfth-century manuscript depicts ninth-century incursions of Bulgarians into Byzantine territory, culminating in a lecture by the Bulgarian king to the Byzantine emperor, shown here with bound hands.

Church of the Resurrection
www.mhhe.com/bentleybrief2e

MISSION TO THE SLAVS The Cyrillic alphabet stimulated conversion to Orthodox Christianity. Missionaries translated the Christian scriptures and church rituals into Slavonic, and Cyrillic writing helped them explain Christian values and ideas in Slavic terms. Meanwhile, schools organized by missionaries ensured that Slavs would receive religious instruction alongside their introduction to basic literacy. As a result, Orthodox Christianity deeply influenced the cultural traditions of many Slavic peoples.

Byzantium and Russia

North of Bulgaria another Slavic people began to organize large states: the Russians. About the mid–ninth century Russians created several principalities governed from thriving trading centers, notably Kiev. Strategically situated on the Dnieper River along the main trade route linking Scandinavia and Byzantium, Kiev became a wealthy and powerful center, and it dominated much of the territory between the Volga and the Dnieper from the tenth to the thirteenth century. Russian merchants visited Constantinople in large numbers and became well acquainted with Byzantine society. Russian princes sought alliances with Byzantine rulers and began to express an interest in Orthodox Christianity.

THE CONVERSION OF PRINCE VLADIMIR About 989 Prince Vladimir of Kiev converted to Orthodox Christianity and ordered his subjects to follow his example. After his conversion, Byzantine influences flowed rapidly into Russia. Cyrillic writing, literacy, and Orthodox missions all spread quickly throughout Russia. Byzantine teachers traveled north to establish schools, and Byzantine priests conducted services for Russian converts. For two centuries Kiev served as a conduit for the spread of Byzantine cultural and religious influence in Russia. Indeed, Byzantine art and architecture dominated Kiev and other Russian cities. The onion domes that are a distinctive feature of early Russian churches were the result of architects' efforts to imitate the domed structures of Constantinople using wood as their principal building material.

THE GROWTH OF KIEV The princes of Kiev established firm, caesaropapist control over the Russian Orthodox church—so called to distinguish it from the Eastern Orthodox church of the Byzantine empire. They also drew inspiration from Byzantine legal tradition and compiled a written law code for their lands. By controlling trade with Byzantium and other lands, they gained financial resources to build a flourishing society.

Eventually, Russians even claimed to inherit the imperial mantle of Byzantium. According to a popular theory of the sixteenth century, Moscow was the world's third Rome: the first Rome had fallen to Germanic invaders in the fifth century, whereas the second Rome, Constantinople, had fallen to the Turks a thousand years later. Moscow survived as the third Rome, the cultural and religious beacon that would guide the world to Orthodox Christian righteousness. Inspired by that theory, missionaries took their Russian Orthodox faith to distant lands. Thus, long after the collapse of the eastern Roman empire, the Byzantine legacy continued to work its influence through the outward reach of the Russian Orthodox church.

SUMMARY

The Byzantine empire originated as a survivor of the classical era. Byzantium inherited a hardy economy, a set of governing institutions, an imperial bureaucracy, an official religion, an established church, and a rich cultural tradition from classical Mediterranean society and the Roman empire. Byzantine leaders drew heavily on that legacy as they dealt with new challenges. Throughout Byzantine history, classical inspiration was especially noticeable in the imperial office, the bureaucracy, the church, and the educational system. Yet in many ways Byzantium changed profoundly over the course of its thousand-year history. After the seventh century the Byzantine empire shrank dramatically in size, and after the eleventh century it faced relentless foreign pressure from western Europeans and nomadic Turkish peoples. Changing times also brought transformations in Byzantine social and economic organization. Yet from the fifth to the twelfth century and beyond, Byzantium brought political stability and economic prosperity to the eastern Mediterranean basin, and Byzantine society served as a principal anchor supporting commercial and cultural exchanges in the postclassical world. Through its political, economic, and cultural influence, Byzantium also helped shape the development of the larger Byzantine commonwealth in eastern Europe and the eastern Mediterranean basin.

STUDY TERMS

Arians (197)
asceticism (197)
Basil the Bulgar-Slayer (192)
Basilian monasticism (197)
battle of Manzikert (199)
Belisarius (191)
bezant (195)
Bosporus (188)
Byzantine (188)
caesaropapism (190)
Constantinople (188)
Council of Nicaea (196)
Corpus iuris civilis (191)
Cyrillic alphabet (201)
Eastern Orthodox church (196)
Hagia Sophia (192)
Hippodrome (196)
iconoclasm (197)
Justinian (190)
Normans (199)
patriarch (197)
Prince Vladimir of Kiev (202)
Saljuqs (199)
theme system (194)
Theodora (190)

FOR FURTHER READING

Averil Cameron. *The Mediterranean World in Late Antiquity, A.D. 395–600.* London, 1993. A thoughtful synthesis that places Byzantium in the context of the late Roman empire.

Helen C. Evans, ed. *Byzantium: Faith and Power (1261–1557).* New York, 2004. A lavishly illustrated volume exploring religious life in the late Byzantine empire.

John V. A. Fine Jr. *The Early Medieval Balkans: A Critical Survey from the Sixth to the Late Twelfth Century.* Ann Arbor, 1983. An excellent introduction to Balkan history in the postclassical era.

Garth Fowden. *Empire to Commonwealth: Consequences of Monotheism in Late Antiquity.* Princeton, 1993. A provocative volume that interprets Byzantine political and cultural development as a monotheist Christian society.

Deno John Geanakoplos. *Byzantium: Church, Society, and Civilization Seen through Contemporary Eyes.* Chicago, 1984. Rich collection of translated documents that throw light on all aspects of Byzantine society.

J. M. Hussey. *The Byzantine World.* London, 1982. A brief and reliable survey.

Dimitri Obolensky. *The Byzantine Commonwealth: Eastern Europe, 500–1453.* New York, 1971. A well-informed overview of early Slavic history and relations between Byzantine and Slavic peoples.

Procopius. *History of the Wars, Secret History, and Buildings.* Trans. by A. Cameron. New York, 1967. Translations of writings by the most important historian in the time of Justinian.

Michael Psellus. *Fourteen Byzantine Rulers.* Trans. by E. R. A. Sewter. Harmondsworth, 1966. Memoirs of eleventh-century Byzantium by a highly placed advisor to several emperors.

Mark Whittow. *The Making of Byzantium, 600–1025.* Berkeley, 1996. Concentrates on Byzantine military and political relations with neighboring societies.

عبدالله دوشدی شیبه آه ایدوب دوشدی

The Expansive Realm of Islam

11

In 632 C.E. the prophet Muhammad visited his native city of Mecca from his home in exile at Medina, and in doing so he set an example that devout Muslims have sought to emulate ever since. The *hajj*—the holy pilgrimage to Mecca—draws Muslims by the hundreds of thousands from all parts of the world to Saudi Arabia. Each year Muslims travel to Mecca by land, sea, and air to make the pilgrimage and visit the holy sites of Islam.

In centuries past the numbers of pilgrims were smaller, but their observance of the hajj was no less conscientious. By the ninth century, pilgrimage had become so popular that Muslim rulers went to some lengths to meet the needs of travelers passing through their lands. With the approach of the pilgrimage season, crowds gathered at major trading centers such as Baghdad, Damascus, and Cairo. There they lived in tent cities, surviving on food and water provided by government officials, until they could join caravans bound for Mecca. Muslim rulers invested considerable sums in the maintenance of roads, wells, cisterns, and lodgings that accommodated pilgrims—as well as police forces that protected travelers—on their journeys to Mecca and back.

The hajj was not only solemn observance but also an occasion for joy and celebration. Muslim rulers and wealthy pilgrims often made lavish gifts to caravan companions and others they met en route to Mecca. During her famous hajj of 976–977, for example, the Mesopotamian princess Jamila bint Nasir al-Dawla provided food and fresh green vegetables for her fellow pilgrims and furnished five hundred camels for handicapped travelers. She also purchased freedom for five hundred slaves and distributed fifty thousand fine robes among the common people of Mecca.

Most pilgrims did not have the resources to match Jamila's generosity, but for common travelers, too, the hajj became a special occasion. Merchants and craftsmen arranged business deals with pilgrims from other lands. Students and scholars exchanged ideas during their weeks of traveling together. For all pilgrims, participation in ritual activities lent new meaning and significance to their faith.

The word *Islam* means "submission," signifying obedience to the rule and will of Allah, the only deity recognized in the strictly monotheistic Islamic religion. An individual who accepts the Islamic faith is a *Muslim,* meaning "one who has submitted." Though it began as one man's expression of unqualified faith in Allah, Islam quickly attracted followers. During the

❮ A fifteenth-century Persian manuscript depicts pilgrims praying at Mecca in the mosque surrounding the Ka'ba.

hajj (HAHJ)

CHRONOLOGY

570–632	Life of Muhammad
622	The *hijra*
632	Muhammad's hajj
650s	Compilation of the Quran
661–750	Umayyad dynasty
750–1258	Abbasid dynasty
1050s	Establishment of Saljuq control over the Abbasid dynasty
1126–1198	Life of Ibn Rushd

first century of the new faith's existence, Islam reached far beyond its Arabian homeland, bringing Sasanid Persia and parts of the Byzantine empire into its orbit. By the eighth century the realm of Islam stood alongside the Byzantine empire as a political and economic anchor of the postclassical world.

Islamic society originally reflected the nomadic and mercantile Arabian society from which Islam arose. Yet over time, Muslims drew deep inspiration from other societies as well. After toppling the Sasanid dynasty, Muslim conquerors adopted Persian techniques of government and finance to administer their lands. Persian literature, science, and religious values also found a place in Islamic society. During later centuries Muslims drew inspiration from Greek and Indian traditions as well.

While drawing influence from other societies, however, the Islamic faith thoroughly transformed the cultural traditions that it absorbed. The expansive realm of Islam eventually provided a political framework for trade and diplomacy over a vast portion of the eastern hemisphere, from west Africa to the islands of Southeast Asia. Many lands of varied cultural background thus became part of a larger society often called the *dar al-Islam*—an Arabic term that means the "house of Islam" and that refers to lands under Islamic rule.

A Prophet and His World

Islam arose in the Arabian peninsula, and the new religion faithfully reflected the social and cultural conditions of its homeland. Desert covers most of the peninsula, and agriculture is possible only in the well-watered area of Yemen in the south and in a few other places, such as the city of Medina, where oases provide water. Yet human communities have occupied Arabia for millennia. Nomadic peoples known as bedouin migrated through the deserts to find grass and water for their herds of sheep, goats, and camels. The bedouin organized themselves in family and clan groups. Individuals and their immediate families depended heavily on those kinship networks for support in times of need. In an environment as harsh and unforgiving as the Arabian desert, cooperation with kin often made the difference between life and death. As a result, bedouin peoples developed a strong sense of loyalty to their clans. Indeed, clan loyalties survived for centuries after the appearance of Islam.

Arabia also figured prominently in the long-distance trade networks of the postclassical era. Commodities arrived at ports on the Persian Gulf (near modern Bahrain), the Arabian Sea (near modern Aden), and the Red Sea (near Mecca), and then traveled overland by camel caravan to Palmyra or Damascus, which offered access to the Mediterranean basin. After the third century C.E., Arabia became an increasingly important link in long-distance trade networks. With the weakening of classical empires, trade routes across central Asia became increasingly insecure. In response, merchants abandoned the overland routes in favor of sea-lanes connecting with land routes in the Arabian peninsula. In the process, their trade allowed Arabian cities to thrive.

Muhammad and His Message

MUHAMMAD'S EARLY LIFE The prophet Muhammad came into this world of nomadic bedouin herders and merchants. Born about 570 C.E. into a reputable family of merchants in Mecca, Muhammad ibn Abdullah lost both of his parents as a young child. His grandfather and his uncle raised

bedouin (BEHD-oh-ihn)

Muhammad (muh-HAHM-mahd)

him and provided him with an education, but Muhammad's early life was difficult. As a young man, he worked for a woman named Khadija, a wealthy widow whom he married about the year 595. Through this marriage he gained wealth and a position of some prominence in Meccan society.

By age 30 Muhammad had established himself as a merchant. He made a comfortable life for himself in Arabian society, where peoples of different religious and cultural traditions regularly dealt with one another. Most Arabs recognized many gods, goddesses, demons, and nature spirits, whose favor they sought through prayers and sacrifices. Large communities of Jewish merchants also worked throughout Arabia, and many Arabs had converted to Christianity by Muhammad's time. Although he was not deeply knowledgeable about Judaism or Christianity, Muhammad had a basic understanding of both faiths.

MUHAMMAD'S SPIRITUAL TRANSFORMATION About 610 C.E., as he approached age 40, Muhammad underwent a profound spiritual experience that transformed his life and left a deep mark on world history. His experience left him with the convictions that in all the world there was only one true deity, Allah ("God"), that he ruled the universe, that idolatry and the recognition of other gods amounted to wickedness, and that Allah would soon bring his judgment on the world. Muhammad experienced visions, which he understood as messages or revelations from Allah, delivered through the archangel Gabriel (also recognized by Jews and Christians as a special messenger of God), instructing him to explain his faith to others. In accordance with instructions transmitted to him by Gabriel, Muhammad began to expound his faith to his family and close friends. Gradually, others showed interest in his message, and by about 620 C.E. a zealous and expanding minority of Mecca's citizenry had joined his circle.

THE QURAN Muhammad originally presented oral recitations of the revelations he received during his visions. As the Islamic community grew, his followers prepared written texts of his teachings. During the early 650s devout Muslims compiled these written versions of Muhammad's revelations and issued them as the Quran ("recitation"), the holy book of Islam. A work of magnificent poetry, the Quran communicates in powerful and moving terms Muhammad's understanding of Allah and his relation to the world, and it serves as the definitive authority for Islamic religious doctrine and social organization.

Apart from the Quran, several other sources have provided moral and religious guidance for the Islamic community. Most important after the Quran itself are traditions known as *hadith,* which include sayings attributed to Muhammad and accounts of his deeds. Regarded as less authoritative than the Quran and the *hadith,* but still important as inspirations for Islamic thought, were early works describing social and legal customs, biographies of Muhammad, and pious commentaries on the Quran.

Muhammad's Migration to Medina

CONFLICT AT MECCA The growing popularity of Muhammad's preaching brought him into conflict with the ruling elites at Mecca. Muhammad's insistence that Allah was the only divine power in the universe struck many polytheistic Arabs as offensive and dangerous, since it disparaged long-recognized deities and spirits thought to wield influence over human affairs. The tensions also had a personal dimension. Mecca's ruling elites, who were also the city's wealthiest merchants, took it as a personal affront when Muhammad denounced greed as moral wickedness that Allah would punish.

Muhammad's attack on idolatry also represented an economic threat to those who owned and profited from the many shrines to deities that attracted merchants and pilgrims to Mecca. The best known of these shrines was a large black rock long considered to be the dwelling of a powerful deity. Housed in a cube-shaped building known as the Ka'ba, it drew worshipers from all over Arabia and brought considerable wealth to Mecca. As

Ka'ba at Mecca
www.mhhe.com/bentleybrief2e

Quran (koorr-AHN)
Ka'ba (KAH-bah)

THE QURAN. | Current Islamic doctrine forbids artistic representations of Muhammad and Allah to prevent the worship of their images as idols. Although artists of previous centuries occasionally produced paintings of Muhammad, Islamic art has emphasized geometric design and calligraphy. This handsome page from a Quran written on vellum dates from the ninth or early tenth century.

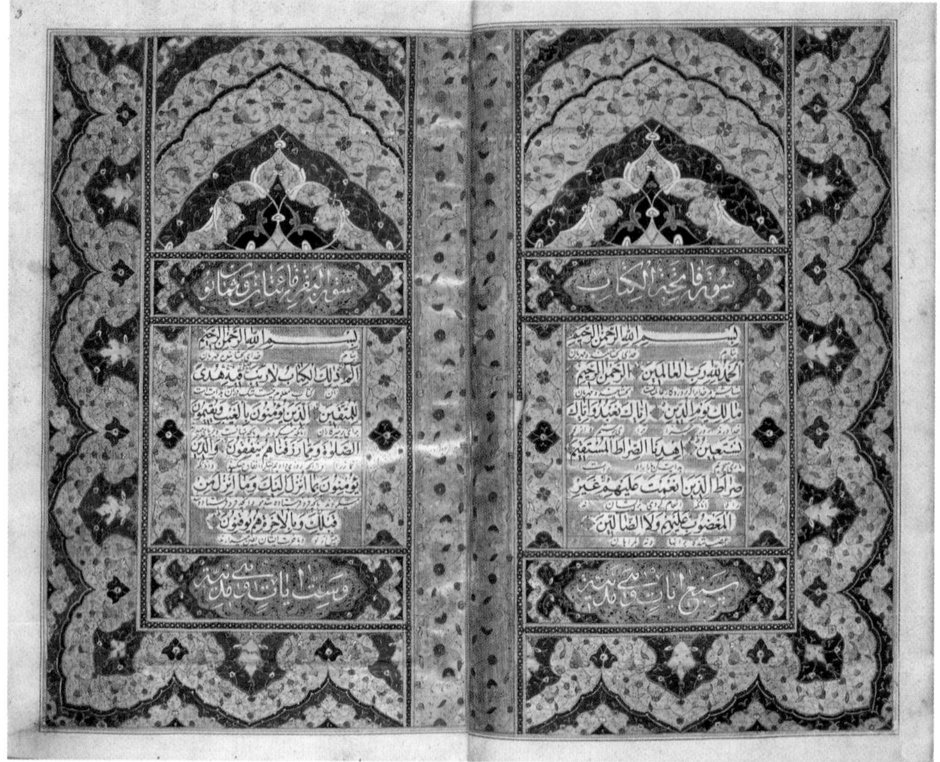

Muhammad relentlessly condemned the idolatry officially promoted at the Ka'ba and other shrines, the ruling elites of Mecca began to persecute the prophet and his followers.

THE HIJRA The pressure became so great that Muhammad and his followers were forced to migrate from Mecca in 622 C.E. They established themselves in Yathrib, a rival trading city north of Mecca, which they renamed Medina ("the city," meaning "the city of the prophet"). Known as the *hijra* ("migration"), Muhammad's move to Medina serves as the starting point of the official Islamic calendar.

THE UMMA Once in Medina, Muhammad found himself at the head of a small but growing society in exile that needed guidance in practical as well as spiritual affairs. He organized his followers into a cohesive community called the *umma* ("community of the faithful") and provided it with a comprehensive legal and social code. He led this community both in daily prayers to Allah and in battle with enemies at Medina, Mecca, and other places. Remembering the difficult days of his own youth, he provided relief for widows, orphans, and the poor, and he made almsgiving a prime moral virtue.

THE "SEAL OF THE PROPHETS" Muhammad's understanding of his religious mission expanded during his years at Medina. He began to refer to himself as a prophet, indeed as the "seal of the prophets"—the final prophet through whom Allah would reveal his message to humankind. Muhammad accepted the authority of earlier Jewish and Christian prophets, including Abraham, Moses, and Jesus, and he held the Hebrew scriptures and the Christian New Testament in high esteem. He also believed that Allah was one and the same as the Jews' Yahweh and the Christians' God. Muhammad taught, however, that the message entrusted to him was a more complete revelation of Allah and his will than Jewish and Christian faiths had made available. Thus, while at Medina, Muhammad came to see himself consciously as the messenger who communicated Allah's wishes and his plan for the world to all humankind.

hijra (HIHJ-ruh)
umma (UM-mah)

The Establishment of Islam in Arabia

MUHAMMAD'S RETURN TO MECCA Throughout their sojourn at Medina, Muhammad and his followers planned ultimately to return to their home in Mecca. In 629 C.E. they arranged with the authorities to participate in the annual pilgrimage to the Ka'ba, but they were not content with a short visit. In 630 they attacked Mecca and conquered the city. They forced the elites to adopt Muhammad's faith, and they imposed a government dedicated to Allah. They also destroyed the pagan shrines and replaced them with mosques, buildings that sought to instill a sense of sacredness and community where Muslims gathered for prayers. Only the Ka'ba escaped their efforts to cleanse Mecca of pagan monuments.

Muhammad and his followers denied that the Ka'ba was the home of a deity, but they preserved the black rock and its housing as a symbol of Mecca's greatness. In 632 Muhammad himself led the first Islamic pilgrimage to the Ka'ba, thus establishing the hajj as an example for all devout Muslims. Building on the conquest of Mecca, Muhammad and his followers launched campaigns against other towns and bedouin clans, and by the time of the prophet's death in 632, shortly after his hajj, they had brought most of Arabia under their control.

THE FIVE PILLARS OF ISLAM Muhammad's faith and his personal leadership decisively shaped the values and the development of the Islamic community. The foundation of the Islamic faith as elaborated by Muhammad consists of obligations known as the Five Pillars of Islam: (1) Muslims must acknowledge Allah as the only god and Muhammad as his prophet. (2) They must pray to Allah daily while facing Mecca. (3) They must observe a fast during the daylight hours of the month of Ramadan. (4) They must contribute alms for the relief of the weak and the poor. (5) Finally, those who are physically and financially able must undertake the hajj and make at least one pilgrimage to Mecca. Although Islam has generated many schools and sects in the centuries since its appearance, the Five Pillars of Islam constitute a powerful framework that has bound the *umma* as a whole into a cohesive community of faith.

JIHAD Some Muslims, though by no means all, have taken *jihad* as an additional obligation for the faithful. The term *jihad* literally means "struggle," and Muslims have understood its imperatives in various ways. In one sense, jihad imposes obligations on Muslims by requiring them to combat vice and evil. In another sense, jihad calls on Muslims to struggle against unbelief by spreading the word of Islam and seeking converts to the faith. In some circumstances, jihad also obliges Muslims to take up the sword and wage war against unbelievers who threaten Islam.

ISLAMIC LAW: THE SHARIA Beyond the general obligations prescribed by the Five Pillars, Islamic holy law, known as the *sharia,* emerged during the centuries after Muhammad and offered detailed guidance on proper behavior in almost every aspect of life. Inspired by the Quran and elaborated by jurists and legal scholars, the sharia offered precise guidance on matters as diverse as marriage and family life, inheritance, slavery, business relationships, political authority, and crime. Through the sharia, Islam became more than a religious doctrine: it developed into a way of life.

THE EXPANSION OF ISLAM

After Muhammad's death the Islamic community might well have unraveled and disappeared. Muhammad had made no provision for a successor, and there was serious division within the *umma* concerning the selection of a new leader. Many of the towns and bedouin clans that had recently accepted Islam took the opportunity of Muhammad's death

The growth of Islam
www.mhhe.com/bentleybrief2e

jihad (jih-HAHD)
sharia (shah-REE-ah)

SOURCES FROM THE PAST

The Quran on Allah and His Expectations of Humankind

The foundation of the Islamic faith is the understanding of Allah, his nature, and his plan for the world as outlined in the Quran. Through his visions Muhammad came to understand Allah as the one and only god, the creator and sustainer of the world in the manner of the Jews' Yahweh and the Christians' God. Those who rejected Allah and his message would suffer eternal punishment, whereas those who recognized and obeyed him would receive his mercy and secure his blessings.

In the name of Allah, most benevolent, ever-merciful.
All praise be to Allah,
Lord of all the worlds,
Most beneficent, ever-merciful,
King of the Day of Judgement.
You alone we worship, and to You
alone turn for help.
Guide us (O Lord) to the path that is straight,
The path of those You have blessed,
Not of those who have earned Your anger,
nor those who have gone astray. . . .
Verily men and women who have come to submission,
men and women who are believers,
men and women who are devout,
truthful men and women,
men and women with endurance,
men and women who are modest,
men and women who give alms,
men and women who observe fasting,
men and women who guard their private parts,
and those men and women who remember God
a great deal,
for them God has forgiveness and a great reward.
No believing men and women have any choice in a matter
after God and His Apostle [i.e., Muhammad] have
decided it.
Whoever disobeys God and His Apostle
has clearly lost the way and gone astray. . . .
O you who believe, remember God a great deal,
And sing His praises morning and evening.
It is He who sends His blessings on you,
as (do) His angels, that He may lead you out of darkness
into light,
for He is benevolent to the believers. . . .
I call to witness
the early hours of the morning,
And the night when dark and still,
Your Lord has neither left you,
nor despises you.
What is to come is better for you
than what has gone before;
For your Lord will certainly give you,
and you will be content.
Did He not find you an orphan
and take care of you?
Did He not find you poor
and enrich you?
So do not oppress the orphan,
And do not drive
the beggar away,
And keep recounting the favours of your Lord. . . .
Say: "He is God
the one the most unique,
God the immanently indispensable.
He has begotten no one,
and is begotten of none.
There is no one comparable to Him."

Compare the Quran's teachings on the relationship between Allah and human beings with the views of Zoroastrians, Jews, and Christians discussed in earlier chapters.

SOURCE: *Al-Qur'an: A Contemporary Translation.* Trans. by Ahmed Ali. Princeton: Princeton University Press, 1984, pp. 11, 358, 359, 540, 559.

to renounce the faith, reassert their independence, and break free from Mecca's control. Within a short time, however, the Islamic community had embarked on a stunningly successful round of military expansion that extended its political and cultural influence far beyond the boundaries of Arabia. Those conquests laid the foundation for the rapid growth of Islamic society.

The Early Caliphs and the Umayyad Dynasty

THE CALIPH Because Muhammad was the "seal of the prophets," it was inconceivable that another prophet should succeed him. Shortly after Muhammad's death his advisors selected Abu Bakr, a genial man who was one of the prophet's closest friends and most devoted disciples, to serve as *caliph* ("deputy"). Thus Abu Bakr and later caliphs led the *umma* not as prophets but as substitutes for Muhammad. Abu Bakr became head of state for the Islamic community as well as chief judge, religious leader, and military commander. Under the new caliph's leadership, the *umma* went on the offensive against people who had renounced Islam after Muhammad's death, and within a year it had compelled them to recognize the faith of Islam and the rule of the caliph.

THE EXPANSION OF ISLAM Indeed, during the century after Muhammad's death, Islamic armies carried their religion and authority throughout Arabia into Byzantine and Sasanid territories and beyond. Although much less powerful than either the Byzantine empire or the Sasanid empire, Muslim armies fought with particular effectiveness because their leaders had unified tribal groups into a powerful state under the banner of Islam. Moreover, they attacked at a moment when the larger empires were preoccupied with internal difficulties. Between 633 and 637 C.E., Muslim forces seized Byzantine Syria

THINKING ABOUT *Traditions*

TRADITIONS IN THE EXPANSIVE REALM OF ISLAM. In the two hundred years after the death of Muhammad in 632, Islam expanded rapidly throughout Arabia and included large portions of west Asia and north Africa as well as part of western Europe. Given the large geographic scope of the Islamic realm, in what ways did the legal, social, and cultural traditions of Islam provide a measure of cultural unity among diverse peoples?

PSI img The Great Mosque at Córdoba www.mhhe.com/bentleybrief2e

Abu-Bakr (a-BOO BAK-uhr)
caliph (KHA-leef)

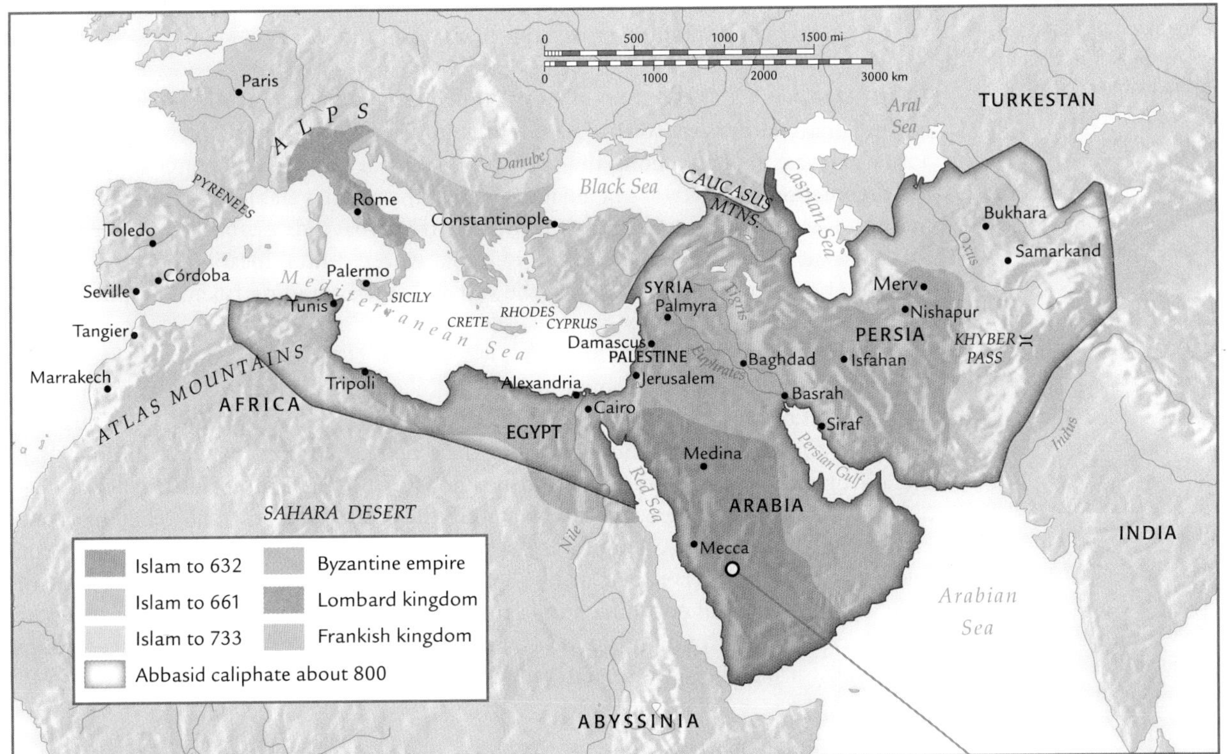

MAP 11.1 | The expansion of Islam, 632–733 C.E. During the seventh and eighth centuries, the new faith of Islam expanded rapidly and dramatically beyond its Arabian homeland. ***How might you explain the spread of a new faith? What political and cultural effects followed from the expansion of Islam?***

Mecca is the holy city of Islam and the destination for pilgrims who make the hajj.

ISLAMIC EXPANSION. The early expansion of Islam was a bloody affair. This illustration from an Arabic manuscript of the thirteenth century depicts a battle between Muhammad's cousin Ali and his adversaries.

Shia pilgrims
www.mhhe.com/bentleybrief2e

and Palestine and took most of Mesopotamia from the Sasanids. During the 640s they conquered Byzantine Egypt and north Africa. In 651 they toppled the Sasanid dynasty and incorporated Persia into their expanding empire. In 711 they conquered the Hindu kingdom of Sind in northwestern India. Between 711 and 718 they extended their authority to northwest Africa and crossed the Strait of Gibraltar, conquering most of the Iberian peninsula and threatening the Frankish kingdom in Gaul. By the mid–eighth century an immense Islamic empire ruled lands from India and the central Asian steppe lands in the east to northwest Africa and Iberia in the west.

During this rapid expansion the empire's rulers encountered problems of governance and administration. One problem had to do with the selection of caliphs. During the early decades after Muhammad's death, leaders of the most powerful Arab clans appointed the first four caliphs. Political ambitions, personal differences, and clan loyalties, however, soon led to the rise of factions and parties within the Islamic community.

THE SHIA Disagreements over succession led to the emergence of the Shia sect, the most important and enduring of all the alternatives to the faith observed by the majority of Muslims, known as Sunni Islam. The Shia sect originated as a party supporting the appointment of Ali—a cousin and son-in-law of Muhammad—and his descendants as caliphs. Ali did serve briefly as the fourth caliph (656–661 C.E.), but his enemies assassinated him, killed many of his relatives, and imposed their own candidate as caliph. Partisans of Ali then organized the Shia ("party") and furiously struggled to return the caliphate to the line of Ali. Although persecuted, the Shia survived and strengthened its identity by adopting doctrines and rituals distinct from those of the Sunnis ("traditionalists"), who accepted the legitimacy of the early caliphs. Shia partisans, for example, observed holy days in honor of their leaders and martyrs to their cause, and they taught that descendants of Ali were infallible, sinless, and divinely appointed to rule the Islamic community.

THE UMAYYAD DYNASTY After the assassination of Ali, the establishment of the Umayyad dynasty (661–750 C.E.) temporarily solved the problem of succession. The Umayyads ranked among the most prominent of the Meccan merchant clans, and their reputation and network of alliances helped them bring stability to the Islamic community. Despite their association with Mecca, the Umayyads established their capital at Damascus, a thriving commercial city in Syria, whose central location enabled them to maintain better communication with the vast and still-expanding Islamic empire.

POLICY TOWARD CONQUERED PEOPLES Although the Umayyads' dynasty solved the problem of succession, their tightly centralized rule and the favor they showed to their fellow Arabs generated an administrative problem. The Umayyads ruled the *dar al-Islam* as conquerors, and their policies favored the Arab military aristocracy by distributing both lands and positions of power among this privileged class. Such policies caused severe discontent among the scores of ethnic and religious groups embraced by the Umayyad empire. In addition, although the Arabs mostly allowed conquered peoples to observe their own religions, they levied a special head tax, called the *jizya,* on those who did not convert to Islam. Moreover, even those who converted did not enjoy access to wealth and positions of authority, which the Umayyads reserved almost exclusively for members of the Arab military aristocracy.

Shia (SHEE-'ah)
Sunni (SOON-nee)
Umayyad (oo-MEYE-ah)
jizya (JIHZ-yah)

UMAYYAD DECLINE Beginning in the early eighth century, the Umayyad caliphs became alienated even from other Arabs as they devoted themselves increasingly to luxurious living rather than to moral leadership of the *umma.* By midcentury the Umayyad caliphs faced not only the continued resistance of the Shia faction but also the discontent of conquered peoples throughout their empire and even the disillusionment of Muslim Arab military leaders.

The Abbasid Dynasty

ABU AL-ABBAS Rebellion in Persia brought the Umayyad dynasty to an end. The chief leader of the rebellion was Abu al-Abbas, a descendant of Muhammad's uncle. Although he was a Sunni Arab, Abu al-Abbas allied readily with Shias and with non-Arab Muslims. During the 740s Abu al-Abbas's party seized control of Persia and Mesopotamia. In 750 his army shattered Umayyad forces in a great battle. Afterward Abu al-Abbas invited the remaining members of the Umayyad clan to a banquet under the pretext of reconciling their differences. Instead, during the festivities his troops slaughtered the Umayyads and annihilated the clan. Abu al-Abbas then founded the Abbasid dynasty, which was the principal source of authority in the *dar al-Islam* until the Mongols toppled it in 1258 C.E.

THE ABBASID DYNASTY The Abbasid dynasty differed considerably from the Umayyad. For one thing, the Abbasid rulers did not show special favor to the Arab military aristocracy. Arabs continued to play a large role in government, but Persians, Egyptians, Mesopotamians, and others also rose to positions of wealth and power.

The Abbasid dynasty differed from the Umayyad also in that it was not a conquering dynasty. The Abbasids did clash intermittently with the Byzantine empire and nomadic peoples from central Asia, and in 751 they defeated a Chinese army at Talas River near Samarkand. The battle of Talas River was exceptionally important: it ended the expansion of China's Tang dynasty into central Asia (discussed in chapter 12), and it opened the door for the spread of Islam among Turkish peoples. Overall, however, the Abbasids did not expand their empire by conquest. The *dar al-Islam* as a whole continued to grow during the Abbasid era, but that was a result of largely autonomous Islamic forces rather than the policies of the caliphs.

ABBASID ADMINISTRATION Instead of conquering new lands, the Abbasids largely contented themselves with administration—a considerable challenge given the empire's diversity of linguistic, ethnic, and cultural groups. In designing their administration, the Abbasids relied heavily on Persian techniques of statecraft. Central authority came from the court at the magnificent new city of Baghdad (capital of modern Iraq). From Baghdad, instructions flowed to the distant reaches of the Abbasid realm. In the provinces, governors represented the caliph and implemented his political and financial policies.

Learned officials known as *ulama* ("people with religious knowledge") and *qadis* ("judges") set moral standards in local communities and resolved disputes. *Ulama* and *qadis* were not priests—Islam does not recognize priests—but they had a formal education that emphasized study of the Quran and the sharia. *Ulama* were pious scholars who sought to develop public policy in accordance with the Quran and the sharia. *Qadis* heard cases at law and rendered decisions based on the Quran and the sharia. Because of their moral authority, *ulama* and *qadis* became extremely influential officials who helped to ensure widespread observance of Islamic values. The Abbasid caliphs also kept a standing army, maintained the network of roads they inherited from the Sasanids, and established bureaucratic ministries in charge of taxation, finance, coinage, and postal services.

ABBASID DECLINE In the early ninth century, however, the Abbasid empire entered a period of decline, and disputes over succession seriously damaged its authority.

Abbasid (ah-BAH-sih)

THINKING ABOUT *Encounters*

ENCOUNTERS IN THE EXPANSIVE REALM OF ISLAM. The expansion of Islam in the seventh and eighth centuries brought societies from Europe, north Africa, and west Asia under the rule of Islamic dynasties. How did encounters with and incorporation of these societies shape the development of Islam itself, in terms of both cultural practices as well as political ideas?

Provincial governors took advantage of disorder in the ruling house by acting independently of the caliphs and building up local bases of power. Meanwhile, popular uprisings and peasant rebellions further weakened the empire.

As a result of these difficulties, the Abbasid caliphs became mere figureheads long before the Mongols extinguished the dynasty in 1258. In 945 members of a Persian noble family seized control of Baghdad and established their clan as the power behind the Abbasid throne. Later, imperial authorities in Baghdad fell under the control of the Saljuq Turks, a nomadic people from central Asia who also invaded the Byzantine empire. By the mid–eleventh century the Saljuqs took possession of Baghdad, and during the following decades they extended their authority to Syria, Palestine, and Anatolia. They retained Abbasid caliphs as nominal sovereigns, but for two centuries, until the arrival of the Mongols, the Saljuq *sultan* ("ruler") was the true source of power in the Abbasid empire.

Economy and Society of the Early Islamic World

In the *dar al-Islam,* as in other agricultural societies, peasants tilled the land while manufacturers and merchants supported a thriving urban economy. Here, as in other lands, the creation of large empires had dramatic economic implications. The Umayyad and Abbasid empires created a zone of trade, exchange, and communication stretching from India to Iberia. Commerce throughout this zone served as a vigorous economic stimulus for both the countryside and the cities of the early Islamic world.

New Crops, Agricultural Experimentation, and Urban Growth

ISLAMIC MAP. | A map produced in the eleventh century by the Arab geographer al-Idrisi shows the lands known and reported by Muslim merchants and travelers. Note that, in accordance with Muslim cartographic convention, this map places south at the top and north at the bottom.

THE SPREAD OF FOOD AND INDUSTRIAL CROPS As soldiers, administrators, diplomats, and merchants traveled throughout the *dar al-Islam,* they encountered plants, animals, and agricultural techniques peculiar to the empire's various regions. They often introduced particularly useful crops to new regions. The most important of the transplants traveled west from India and included staple crops such as sugarcane, rice, and new varieties of sorghum and wheat; vegetables such as spinach and artichokes; fruits such as oranges, bananas, coconuts, and mangoes; and industrial crops such as cotton, indigo, and henna.

EFFECTS OF NEW CROPS The introduction of these crops into the western regions of the Islamic world had wide-ranging effects. New food crops led to a richer and more varied diet. They also increased quantities of food available because they enabled cultivators to extend the growing season: since most of the transplanted crops grew well in high heat, cultivators in southwest Asia and other hot zones could plant an additional crop in the summer months instead of leaving their fields fallow. The result was a dramatic increase in food supplies.

AGRICULTURAL EXPERIMENTATION Travel and communication in the *dar al-Islam* also encouraged experimentation with agricultural methods. Cultivators paid close attention to methods of irrigation, fertilization, crop rotation, and the like, and they outlined their findings in hundreds of agricultural manuals. The combined effect of new crops and improved techniques was a far more productive agricultural economy, which in turn supported vigorous economic growth throughout the *dar al-Islam.*

URBAN GROWTH Increased agricultural production contributed to the rapid growth of cities in all parts of the Islamic world from India to Spain. All these cities—including, for example, Delhi, Merv, Isfahan, Damascus, Cairo, Córdoba, and Tangier—had flourishing markets supporting thousands of artisans, craftsmen, and merchants. Most of them were also important centers of industrial production, particularly of textiles, pottery, glassware, leather, iron, and steel.

One new industry appeared in Islamic cities during the Abbasid era: paper manufacture. When Arab forces defeated a Chinese army at the battle of Talas River in 751, they took prisoners skilled in paper production and learned the technique from them. Paper soon became popular throughout the Islamic world. Paper facilitated the keeping of administrative and commercial records, and it made possible the dissemination of books and treatises in larger quantities than ever before. By the tenth century, mills produced paper in Persia, Mesopotamia, Arabia, Egypt, and Spain, and the industry soon spread to western Europe.

SLAVERY IN THE ISLAMIC WORLD. | In this thirteenth-century manuscript illustration, merchants at a slave market in southern Arabia deal in black slaves captured in sub-Saharan Africa. Slaves traded in Islamic markets also came from Russia and eastern Europe.

The Formation of a Hemispheric Trading Zone

From its earliest days Islamic society drew much of its prosperity from commerce. Muhammad himself was a merchant, and he held merchants in high esteem. By the time of the Abbasid caliphate, elaborate trade networks linked all the regions of the Islamic world and joined it to a larger, hemispheric economy.

OVERLAND TRADE When they overran the Sasanid empire, Muslim conquerors brought the prosperous trading cities of central Asia under control of the expanding *dar al-Islam.* Muslim merchants were then able to take advantage of the extensive road networks originally built during the classical era by imperial authorities in India, Persia, and the Mediterranean basin. To be sure, Umayyad and Abbasid rulers maintained the roads for military and administrative purposes, but those same roads also made excellent highways for merchants as well as missionaries and pilgrims.

A mosque lamp
www.mhhe.com/bentleybrief2e

CAMELS AND CARAVANS Overland trade traveled mostly by camel caravan. Although they are uncooperative beasts, camels endure the rigors of desert travel much better than horses or donkeys. Moreover, camels can carry heavy loads. During the early centuries C.E., camels became the favored beasts of burden in deserts and other dry regions. As camel transport became more common, the major cities of the Islamic world and central Asia built and maintained caravanserais—inns offering lodging for caravan merchants as well as food, water, and care for their animals.

MARITIME TRADE Meanwhile, innovations in nautical technology contributed to a steadily increasing volume of maritime trade in the Red Sea, Persian Gulf, Arabian Sea, and Indian Ocean. Arab and Persian mariners borrowed the compass from its Chinese inventors and used it to guide them on the high seas. From southeast Asian and Indian mariners they borrowed the lateen sail, a triangular sail that increased a ship's maneuverability. From the Hellenistic Mediterranean they borrowed the astrolabe, an instrument that enabled them to calculate latitude. Thus equipped, Arab and Persian mariners ventured throughout the Indian Ocean basin.

BANKS Banking also stimulated the commercial economy of the Islamic world. Banks had operated since classical antiquity, but Islamic banks of the Abbasid period conducted business on a much larger scale than their predecessors. They not only lent money

The Mosque at Córdoba. | This mosque was originally built in the late eighth century and enlarged during the ninth and tenth centuries. One of the largest structures in the *dar al-Islam,* the mosque rests on 850 columns and features nineteen aisles. ***Why are there no representations of Allah in the mosque?***

to entrepreneurs but also served as brokers for investments and exchanged different currencies. They established multiple branches that honored letters of credit known as *sakk* drawn on the parent bank. Thus merchants could settle accounts with distant business partners without having to deal in cash.

THE ORGANIZATION OF TRADE Trade benefited also from refined techniques of business organization. Usually Islamic businessmen preferred not to embark on solo ventures, since an individual could face financial ruin if an entire cargo of commodities fell prey to pirates or went down with a ship that sank in a storm. Instead, like their counterparts in other postclassical societies, Abbasid entrepreneurs often pooled their resources in a variety of group investments designed to distribute individual risks.

As a result of improved transportation, expanded banking services, and refined techniques of business organization, long-distance trade surged in the early Islamic world. Muslim merchants dealt in silk and ceramics from China, spices and aromatics from India and southeast Asia, and jewelry and fine textiles from the Byzantine empire. Merchants also ventured beyond settled societies in China, India, and the Mediterranean basin to distant lands that previously had not engaged systematically in long-distance trade. They crossed the Sahara desert by camel caravan to trade salt, steel, copper, and glass for gold and slaves from the kingdoms of west Africa. They visited the coastal regions of east Africa, where they obtained slaves and exotic local commodities such as animal skins. They engaged in trade with Russia and Scandinavia by way of the Dnieper and Volga rivers and obtained commodities such as animal skins, furs, honey, amber, and slaves as well as bulk goods such as timber and livestock. The vigorous economy of the Abbasid empire thus helped to establish networks of communication and exchange throughout much of the eastern hemisphere.

AL-ANDALUS The prosperity of Islamic Spain, known as al-Andalus, illustrates the far-reaching effects of long-distance trade during the Abbasid era. Most of the Iberian peninsula had fallen into the hands of Muslim Berber conquerors from north Africa during the early eighth century. As allies of the Umayyads, the governors of al-Andalus refused to recognize the Abbasid dynasty, and beginning in the tenth century they styled themselves caliphs in their own right rather than governors subject to Abbasid authority. Despite political and diplomatic tensions, al-Andalus participated actively in the commercial life of the larger Islamic world, which enabled merchants and manufacturers in al-Andalus to conduct thriving businesses in cities such as Córdoba, Toledo, and Seville.

The Changing Status of Women

A patriarchal society had emerged in Arabia long before Muhammad's time, but Arab women enjoyed rights not accorded to women in many other lands. They could legally inherit property, divorce husbands on their own initiative, and engage in business ventures. Khadija, the first of Muhammad's four wives, managed a successful commercial business.

THE QURAN AND WOMEN In some respects the Quran enhanced the security of women in Arabian society. It outlawed female infanticide, and it provided that dowries go directly to brides rather than to their husbands and male guardians. It portrayed women not as the property of their menfolk but as honorable individuals, equal to men before Allah, with their own rights and needs. Muhammad's own kindness and

sakk (sahk)
al-Andalus (al-ahn-duh-LUHS)

generosity toward his wives also served as an example that may have improved the lives of Muslim women.

For the most part, however, the Quran—and later the sharia as well—reinforced male dominance. The Quran and Islamic holy law recognized descent through the male line, and to guarantee proper inheritance, they placed a high premium on genealogical purity. To ensure the legitimacy of heirs, they subjected the social and sexual lives of women to the strict control of male guardians. The Quran and the sharia also permitted men to take up to four wives, whereas women could have only one husband. The Quran and the sharia thus provided a religious and legal foundation for a decisively patriarchal society.

VEILING OF WOMEN When Islam expanded into the Byzantine and Sasanid empires, it encountered strong patriarchal traditions, and Muslims readily adopted long-standing customs such as the veiling of women. Social and family pressures had induced upper-class urban women to veil themselves in Mesopotamia as early as the thirteenth century B.C.E., and long before Muhammad the practice of veiling had spread to Persia and the eastern Mediterranean. When Muslim Arabs conquered these lands, they adopted the practice. A conspicuous symbol of male authority thus found a prominent place in the early Islamic community.

Although the Quran served as the preeminent source of authority in the Islamic world, over the centuries jurists and legal scholars interpreted the Quran in ways that progressively limited the rights of women. To a large extent the increased emphasis on male authority in Islamic law reflected the influence of the strongly hierarchical and patriarchal societies of Mesopotamia, Persia, and eastern Mediterranean lands as Islam developed from a local faith to a large-scale complex society.

ISLAMIC VALUES AND CULTURAL EXCHANGES

Since the seventh century C.E., the Quran has served as the cornerstone of Islamic society. Arising from a rich tradition of bedouin poetry and song, the Quran established Arabic as a flexible and powerful medium of communication. When carrying their faith to new lands during the era of Islamic expansion, Muslim missionaries spread the message of Allah and provided instruction in the Quran's teachings, although they also permitted continued observance of pre-Islamic traditions. Muslim intellectuals drew freely from the long-established cultural traditions of Persia, India, and Greece, which they became acquainted with during the Umayyad and Abbasid eras.

The Formation of an Islamic Cultural Tradition

Muslim theologians and jurists looked to the Quran and other sources of Islamic doctrine in their efforts to formulate moral guidelines appropriate for their society. The body of civil and criminal law embodied in the *sharia* provided a measure of cultural unity for the vastly different lands of the Islamic world. Islamic law did not by any means erase differences, but it established a common cultural foundation that facilitated dealings between peoples of various Islamic lands and that lent substance to the concept of the *dar al-Islam.*

PROMOTION OF ISLAMIC VALUES On a more popular level, *ulama, qadis,* and missionaries helped to spread Islamic values throughout the *dar al-Islam. Ulama* and *qadis* held positions at all Islamic courts. By resolving disputes according to Islamic law and ordering public observance of Islamic social and moral standards, they helped to bring the values of the Quran and the sharia into the lives of peoples living far from the birthplace of Islam.

SUFIS. | Through song, dance, and ecstatic experiences, sometimes enhanced by wine, Persian Sufis expressed their devotion to Allah, as in this sixteenth-century painting.

Formal educational institutions also helped promote Islamic values. For example, many mosques maintained schools that provided an elementary education and religious instruction. By the tenth century, institutions of higher education known as *madrasas* had begun to appear, and by the twelfth century they had become established in the major cities of the Islamic world. Muslim rulers often supported the madrasas in the interests of recruiting literate and learned students for administrative positions.

SUFIS Among the most effective Islamic missionaries were mystics known as Sufis. The term *Sufi* probably came from the patched woolen garments favored by the mystics. Sufis did not deny Islamic doctrine, but they also did not find formal religious teachings to be especially meaningful. Thus, instead of concerning themselves with fine points of doctrine, Sufis worked to deepen their spiritual awareness. Most Sufis led pious and ascetic lives. Some devoted themselves to helping the poor. Many sought a mystical, ecstatic union with Allah, relying on rousing sermons, passionate singing, or spirited dancing to bring them to a state of high emotion. Muslim theologians sometimes mistrusted Sufis, fearing that in their lack of concern for doctrine they would adopt erroneous beliefs. Nevertheless, after the ninth century Sufis became increasingly popular in Muslim societies because of their piety, devotion, and eagerness to minister to the needs of their fellow human beings.

SUFI MISSIONARIES Sufis were especially effective as missionaries because they emphasized devotion to Allah above mastery of doctrine. They sometimes encouraged individuals to revere Allah in their own ways, even if their methods did not have a basis in the Quran. They tolerated the continued observance of pre-Islamic customs, for example, as well as the association of Allah with deities recognized and revered in other faiths. Because of their kindness, holiness, tolerance, and charismatic appeal, Sufis attracted numerous converts, particularly in lands such as Persia and India, where long-established religious faiths such as Zoroastrianism, Christianity, Buddhism, and Hinduism had enjoyed a mass following for centuries.

HAJJ The symbol of Islamic cultural unity was the Ka'ba at Mecca, which from an early date attracted pilgrims from all parts of the Islamic world. Indeed, individuals from far-flung regions made their way to Mecca, visited the holy sites, and learned firsthand the traditions of Islam. Over the centuries these pilgrims helped to spread Islamic beliefs and values to all parts of the Islamic world, and alongside the work of *ulama, qadis,* and Sufi missionaries, their efforts helped to make the *dar al-Islam* not just a name but also a reality.

Islam and the Cultural Traditions of Persia, India, and Greece

As the Islamic community expanded, Muslims of Arab ancestry interacted regularly with peoples from other cultural traditions, especially those of Persia, India, and Greece. In some cases, particularly in lands ruled by the Umayyad and Abbasid dynasties, large numbers of conquered peoples converted to Islam, and they brought elements of their inherited cultural traditions into Islamic society. In other cases, particularly in lands beyond

madrasas (MAH-drahs-ahs)
Sufis (SOO-fees)

the authority of Islamic rulers, Muslims became acquainted with the literary, artistic, philosophical, and scientific traditions of peoples who chose not to convert.

PERSIAN INFLUENCES ON ISLAM Persian traditions quickly found a place in Islamic society, since the culturally rich land fell under Islamic rule at an early date. After the establishment of the Abbasid dynasty and the founding of its capital at Baghdad, Persian administrative techniques were crucial for the organization of the imperial structure through which rulers governed their vast empire. Meanwhile, Persian ideas of kingship—in which kings were wise, benevolent, but nonetheless absolute rulers—profoundly influenced Islamic political thought.

Persian influence was also noticeable in literary works from the Abbasid dynasty. Whereas Arabic served as the language of religion, theology, philosophy, and law, Persian was the principal language of literature, poetry, history, and political reflection. The marvelous collection of stories known as *The Arabian Nights* or *The Thousand and One Nights,* for example, presented popular tales of adventure and romance set in the Abbasid empire and the court of Harun al-Rashid.

INDIAN INFLUENCES ON ISLAM Indian mathematics, science, and medicine also captured the attention of Arab and Persian Muslims who established Islamic states in northern India. Muslims readily adopted what they called "Hindi" numerals, which European peoples later called "Arabic" numerals, since they learned about them through Arab Muslims. Hindi numerals enabled Muslim scholars to develop an impressive tradition of advanced mathematics, concentrating on algebra (an Arabic word) as well as trigonometry and geometry. From a more practical point of view, Indian numerals vastly simplified bookkeeping for Muslim merchants.

Muslims also found much to appreciate in the scientific and medical thought they encountered in India. With the aid of their powerful and flexible mathematics, Indian scholars were able to carry out precise astronomical calculations, which helped inspire the development of Muslim astronomy. Similarly, Indian medicine appealed to Muslims because of its treatments for specific ailments and its use of antidotes for poisons.

GREEK INFLUENCES ON ISLAM Muslims also admired the philosophical, scientific, and medical writings of classical Greece. They became especially interested in Plato and Aristotle, whose works they translated and interpreted in commentaries. For example, Ibn Rushd (1126–1198), *qadi* of Seville in the caliphate of Córdoba, followed Aristotle in seeking to articulate a purely rational understanding of the world. Ibn Rushd's work not only helped to shape Islamic philosophy but also found its way to the schools and universities of western Europe, where Christian scholars knew Ibn Rushd as Averroës. During the thirteenth century, his work profoundly influenced the development of scholasticism, the effort of medieval European philosophers to harmonize Christianity with Aristotelian thought. However, after the thirteenth century, Greek philosophy fell out of favor with Muslim philosophers and theologians, who turned instead to teachings from the Quran and Sufi mystics.

Quite apart from philosophy, Greek mathematics, science, and medicine also appealed strongly to Muslims. Greek mathematics did not make use of Indian numerals, but it offered a solid body of powerful reasoning, particularly when dealing with calculations in algebra and geometry. Greek mathematics supported the development of astronomical and geographical scholarship, and studies of anatomy and physiology served as foundations for medical thought. Muslim scholars quickly absorbed these Greek traditions, combined them with influences from India, and used them as points of departure for their own studies. The result was a brilliant flowering of mathematical, scientific, and medical scholarship that provided Muslim societies with powerful tools for understanding the natural world.

Ibn Rushd (IB-uhn RUSHED)

SUMMARY

The prophet Muhammad did not intend to found a new religion. Instead, his intention was to express his faith in Allah and perfect the teachings of earlier Jewish and Christian prophets by announcing a revelation more comprehensive than those Allah had entrusted to his predecessors. His message soon attracted a circle of devout and committed disciples, and by the time of his death most of Arabia had accepted Islam. During the two centuries following the prophet's death, Arab conquerors spread Islam throughout southwest Asia and north Africa and introduced their faith to central Asia, India, the Mediterranean islands, and Iberia. This rapid expansion of Islam encouraged the development of an extensive trade and communications network: merchants, diplomats, and other travelers moved easily throughout the Islamic world exchanging goods and introducing agricultural crops to new lands. Rapid expansion also led to encounters between Islam and long-established religious and cultural traditions, Persian literature and political thought, and classical Greek philosophy and science. Muslim rulers built a society that made a place for those of different faiths, and Muslim thinkers readily adapted earlier traditions to their own needs. As a result of its expansion, its extensive trade and communications networks, and its engagement with other religious and cultural traditions, the *dar al-Islam* became one of the most prosperous and cosmopolitan societies of the postclassical world.

STUDY TERMS

FOR FURTHER READING

Richard C. Foltz. *Spirituality in the Land of the Noble: How Iran Shaped the World's Religions.* Oxford, 2004. Includes an accessible discussion of Persian influences on the Islamic faith.

Abu Hamid Muhammad al-Ghazzali. *The Alchemy of Happiness.* Trans. by Claude Field. Rev. by Elton L. Daniel. New York, 1991. Translation of one of the classic works of early Islamic religious and moral thought.

Mahmood Ibrahim. *Merchant Capital and Islam.* Austin, 1990. Examines the role of trade in Arabia during Muhammad's time and in early Islamic society.

Ira M. Lapidus. *A History of Islamic Societies.* Cambridge, 1988. Authoritative survey of Islamic history, concentrating on social and cultural issues.

M. Lombard. *The Golden Age of Islam.* Princeton, 2004. Concentrates on the social and economic history of the Abbasid period.

William H. McNeill and Marilyn R. Waldman, eds. *The Islamic World.* New York, 1973. An excellent collection of primary sources in translation.

F. E. Peters. *The Hajj: The Muslim Pilgrimage to Mecca and the Holy Places.* Princeton, 1994. Draws on scores of travelers' reports in studying the Muslim practice through the ages of making a pilgrimage to Mecca.

Al Qur'an: A Contemporary Translation. Trans. by Ahmed Ali. Princeton, 1984. A sensitive translation of the holy book of Islam.

Francis Robinson, ed. *The Cambridge Illustrated History of the Islamic World.* Cambridge, 1996. An excellent and lavishly illustrated introduction to Islam and the Muslim world.

Frances Wood. *The Silk Road: Two Thousand Years in the Heart of Asia.* Berkeley, 2002. A brilliantly illustrated volume discussing the history of the silk roads from antiquity to the twentieth century.

The Resurgence of Empire in East Asia

12

arly in the seventh century C.E., the emperor of China issued an order forbidding his subjects to travel beyond Chinese borders into central Asia. In 629, however, a young Buddhist monk slipped past imperial watchtowers under cover of darkness and made his way west. His name was Xuanzang, and his destination was India, homeland of Buddhism. As a young man, Xuanzang had followed his older brother into a monastery, where he became devoted to Buddhism. While studying the Sanskrit language, Xuanzang noticed that Chinese writings on Buddhism contained many teachings that were confusing or even contradictory to those of Indian Buddhist texts. He decided to travel to India, visit the holy sites of Buddhism, and study with the most knowledgeable Buddhist teachers and sages to learn about his faith from the purest sources.

Xuanzang could not have imagined the difficulties he would face. Immediately after his departure from China, his guide abandoned him in the Gobi desert. After losing his water bag and collapsing in the heat, Xuanzang made his way to the oasis town of Turpan on the silk roads. The Buddhist ruler of Turpan provided the devout pilgrim with travel supplies and rich gifts to support his mission. Among the presents were twenty-four letters of introduction to rulers of lands on the way to India (each one attached to a bolt of silk), thirty horses, twenty-five laborers, and five hundred bolts of silk, along with gold, silver, and silk clothes for Xuanzang to use as travel funds. After departing from Turpan, Xuanzang crossed three of the world's highest mountain ranges—the Tian Shan, Hindu Kush, and Pamir ranges—and lost one-third of his party to exposure and starvation in the Tian Shan.

Yet Xuanzang persisted and arrived in India in 630. He lived there for more than twelve years, devoting himself to the study of languages and Buddhist doctrine, especially at Nalanda, the center of advanced Buddhist education in India. He also amassed a huge collection of relics and images as well as some 657 books, all of which he transported back to China to advance the understanding of Buddhism in his native land.

By the time of his return in 645, Xuanzang had logged more than 16,000 kilometers (10,000 miles) on the road. News of the holy monk's efforts had reached the imperial court, and even

❮ *Buddhist temple in mountain detail.* The Nelson-Atkins Museum of Art, Kansas City, Missouri. Purchase: William Rockhill Nelson Trust, 47-71. Photograph by John Lamberton.

Xuanzang (SHWEN-ZAHNG)
Buddhism (BOO-diz'm)
Sanskrit (SAHN-skriht)
Tian Shan (tyahn shahn)

CHRONOLOGY

589–618	Sui dynasty (China)
602–664	Life of Xuanzang
604–618	Reign of Sui Yangdi
618–907	Tang dynasty (China)
627–649	Reign of Tang Taizong
669–935	Silla dynasty (Korea)
710–794	Nara period (Japan)
755–757	An Lushan's rebellion
794–1185	Heian period (Japan)
960–1279	Song dynasty (China)
960–976	Reign of Song Taizu
1024	First issuance of government-sponsored paper money

though Xuanzang had violated the ban on travel, he received a hero's welcome and an audience with the emperor. Until his death in 664, Xuanzang translated Buddhist treatises into Chinese and promoted his faith. His efforts helped to popularize Buddhism and bring about nearly universal adoption of the faith throughout China.

Xuanzang undertook his journey at a propitious time. For more than 350 years after the fall of the Han dynasty, war, invasion, conquest, and foreign rule disrupted Chinese society. Toward the end of the sixth century, however, centralized imperial rule returned to China. The Sui and Tang dynasties restored order and presided over an era of rapid economic growth in China, especially in the areas of agricultural yields and technological innovations. As a result, China stood alongside the Byzantine and Abbasid empires as a political and economic anchor of the postclassical world.

For China the postclassical era was an age of intense interaction with other peoples. Chinese merchants participated in trade networks that linked most regions of the eastern hemisphere. Buddhism spread beyond its homeland of India and attracted a large popular following in China. A resurgent China also made its influence felt throughout east Asia, especially in Korea, Vietnam, and Japan. Although these lands retained their distinctiveness, each drew deep inspiration from China and participated in a larger east Asian society centered on China.

The Restoration of Centralized Imperial Rule in China

For several centuries following the Han dynasty, none of the remaining regional kingdoms was able to assert lasting authority over all of China. In the late sixth century, however, Yang Jian, an ambitious ruler in northern China, embarked on a series of military campaigns that brought all of China once again under centralized imperial rule. Yang Jian's Sui dynasty survived less than thirty years, but the tradition of centralized rule outlived his house. The Tang dynasty replaced the Sui, and the Song succeeded the Tang. The Tang and Song dynasties organized Chinese society so efficiently that China became a center of exceptional agricultural and industrial production, creating an economy so powerful that it affected much of the eastern hemisphere.

The Sui Dynasty

ESTABLISHMENT OF THE SUI DYNASTY Like Qin Shihuangdi some eight centuries earlier, Yang Jian imposed tight political discipline on his own state and then extended his rule to the rest of China. Yang Jian began his rise to power when a Turkish ruler appointed him duke of Sui in northern China. In 580 Yang Jian's patron died, and one year later he claimed both the throne and the Mandate of Heaven for himself. During the next decade Yang Jian sent military expeditions into central Asia and southern China. By 589 the house of Sui ruled all of China.

Yang Jian (yahng jyahn)

Like the rulers of the Qin dynasty, the emperors of the Sui dynasty (589–618 C.E.) built a strong, centralized government, but only at great human and financial cost. Indeed, the Sui emperors ordered construction projects, repaired defensive walls, and conducted military campaigns, but did so by levying high taxes and demanding compulsory labor services from their subjects.

THE GRAND CANAL The most elaborate project undertaken during the Sui dynasty was the construction of the Grand Canal, which was one of the world's largest waterworks projects before modern times. The second emperor, Sui Yangdi (reigned 604–618 C.E.), wanted the canal to facilitate trade between northern and southern China, particularly to make the abundant supplies of rice and other food crops from the Yangzi River valley available to residents of northern regions. Since Chinese rivers generally flow from west to east, only an artificial waterway could support such a large volume of bulky trade goods trade between north and south.

The Grand Canal was a series of artificial waterways that ultimately reached from Hangzhou in the south to the imperial capital of Chang'an in the west to a terminus near modern Beijing in the north. Sui Yangdi used canals dug as early as the Zhou dynasty, but he linked them into a network that served much of China. When completed, the Grand Canal extended almost 2,000 kilometers (1,240 miles) and reportedly was forty paces wide, with roads running parallel to it on either side.

Though expensive to construct, Sui Yangdi's investment in the Grand Canal paid dividends for more than a thousand years. It integrated the economies of northern and southern China, thereby establishing an economic foundation for political and cultural unity. Until the arrival of railroads in the twentieth century, the Grand Canal served as the principal conduit for internal trade. Indeed, the canal continues to function even today.

Sui Yangdi's construction projects served China well for a long time, but their dependence on high taxes and forced labor generated hostility toward his rule. The Grand Canal alone required the services of conscripted laborers by the millions. In the late 610s, discontented subjects began to revolt against Sui rule. In 618 a disgruntled minister assassinated the emperor and brought the dynasty to an end.

The Tang Dynasty

Soon after Sui Yangdi's death, a rebel leader seized Chang'an and proclaimed himself emperor of a new dynasty that he named Tang after his hereditary title. The dynasty survived for almost three hundred years (618–907 C.E.), and Tang rulers organized China into a powerful, productive, and prosperous society.

TANG TAIZONG Much of the Tang success was due to the energy, ability, and policies of the dynasty's second emperor, Tang Taizong (reigned 627–649 C.E.). Taizong was both ambitious and ruthless: in making his way to the imperial throne, he murdered two of his brothers and pushed his father aside. Once on the throne, however, he displayed a high sense of duty and strove conscientiously to provide an effective, stable government. He built a splendid capital at Chang'an, and he saw himself as a Confucian ruler who heeded the interests of his subjects. Contemporaries reported that banditry ended during his reign, that the price of rice remained low, and that taxes levied on peasants amounted to only one-fortieth of the annual harvest—a 2.5 percent tax rate. These reports suggest that China enjoyed an era of unusual stability and prosperity during the reign of Tang Taizong.

Three policies in particular help to explain the success of the early Tang dynasty: maintenance of a well-articulated transportation and communications network, distribution of land according to the principles of the equal-field system, and reliance on a bureaucracy

Sui Yangdi (sway yahng-dee)

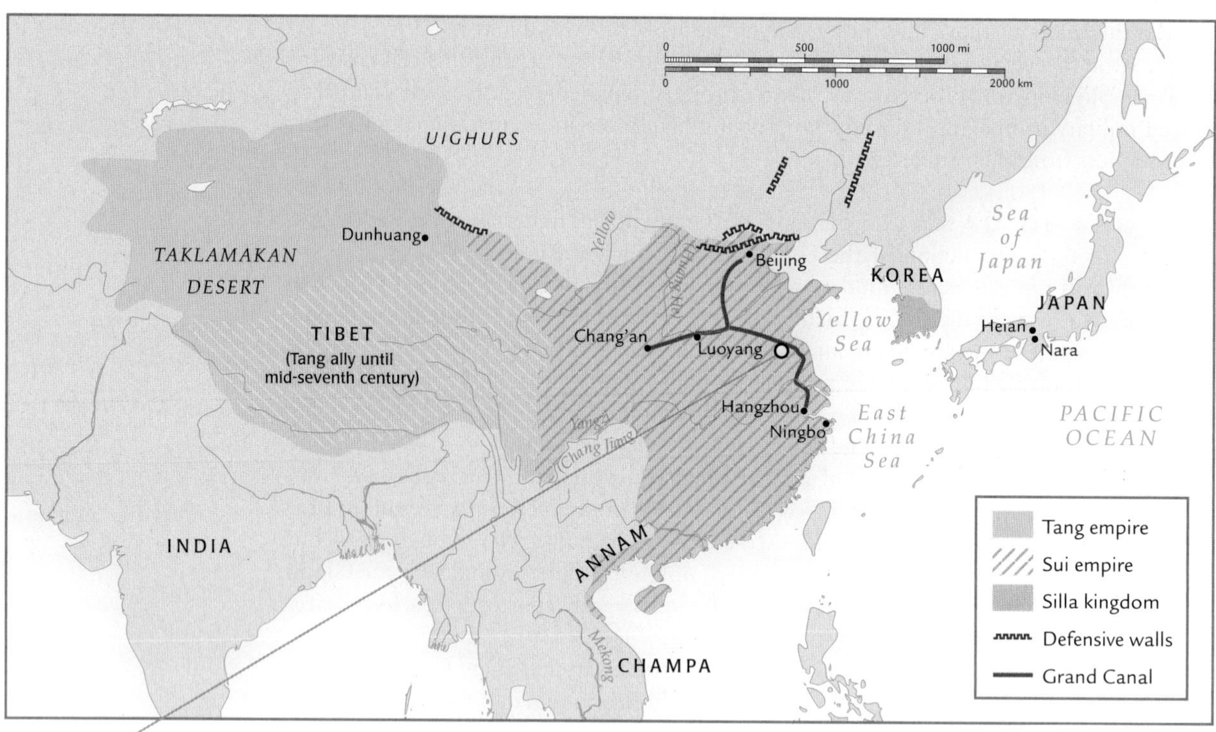

MAP 12.1 | The Sui and Tang dynasties, 589–907 C.E. Compare the size of the Sui and Tang empires. ***Why was the Tang dynasty able to extend its authority over such vast distances?***

based on merit. All three policies originated in the Sui dynasty, but Tang rulers applied them more systematically and effectively than their predecessors.

TRANSPORTATION AND COMMUNICATIONS Apart from the Grand Canal, which served as the principal route for long-distance transportation within China, Tang rulers maintained an extensive network of roads. Along the main routes, Tang officials maintained inns, postal stations, and stables. Using couriers traveling by horse, the Tang court could communicate with the most distant cities in the empire in about eight days. Even human runners provided speedy services: relay teams of some 9,600 runners supplied the Tang court at Chang'an with fresh seafood from Ningbo, more than 1,000 kilometers (620 miles) away!

THE EQUAL-FIELD SYSTEM The equal-field system governed the allocation of agricultural land. Its purpose was to ensure an equitable distribution of land and to avoid the concentration of landed property that had caused social problems during the Han dynasty. The system allotted land to individuals and their families according to the land's fertility and the recipients' needs. About one-fifth of the land became the hereditary possession of the recipients, and the rest remained available for redistribution when the original recipients' needs and circumstances changed.

For about a century, administrators were able to apply the principles of the equal-field system relatively consistently. By the early eighth century, however, a rapidly rising population brought pressure on the land available for distribution. Meanwhile, influential families found ways to retain land scheduled for redistribution. Furthermore, large parcels of land fell out of the system altogether when Buddhist monasteries acquired them. Nevertheless, during the first half of the Tang dynasty, the system provided a foundation for stability and prosperity in the Chinese countryside.

BUREAUCRACY OF MERIT The Tang dynasty also relied heavily on a bureaucracy based on merit. Following the example of the Han dynasty, Sui and Tang rulers recruited government officials from the ranks of candidates who had progressed through

GRAND CANAL. | Barges make their way through a portion of the Grand Canal near the city of Wuxi in southern China.

the Confucian educational system based on the classic works of Chinese literature and philosophy. As a result, most officeholders won their posts because of intellectual ability. Members of this talented class were generally loyal to the dynasty, and they worked to preserve and strengthen the state. In fact, the Confucian educational system and the related civil service served Chinese governments so well that with modifications and an occasional interruption, they survived until the collapse of the Qing dynasty in the early twentieth century.

MILITARY EXPANSION Soon after its foundation, the powerful and dynamic Tang state began to flex its military muscles. In the north, Tang forces brought Manchuria under imperial authority and forced the Silla kingdom in Korea to acknowledge the Tang emperor as overlord. To the south, Tang armies conquered the northern part of Vietnam. To the west, they extended Tang authority as far as the Aral Sea and brought a portion of the high plateau of Tibet under Tang control. Territorially, the Tang empire ranks among the largest in Chinese history.

TANG FOREIGN RELATIONS In an effort to fashion a stable diplomatic order, the Tang emperors revived the Han dynasty's practice of the tribute system. According to Chinese political theory, China was the Middle Kingdom and had the responsibility of bringing order to subordinate lands through a system of tributary relationships. Neighboring lands and peoples would recognize Chinese emperors as their overlords, and envoys from those states would regularly deliver gifts to the court of the Middle Kingdom and perform the kowtow—a ritual prostration during which subordinates knelt before the emperor and touched their foreheads to the ground. In return, tributary states received confirmation of their authority as well as lavish gifts. Because Chinese authorities often had little real influence in these supposedly subordinate lands, there was always something of a fictional quality to the system. Nevertheless, it was extremely important because it institutionalized relations between China and neighboring lands, fostering trade and cultural exchanges as well as diplomatic contacts.

TANG DECLINE Under able rulers such as Taizong, the Tang dynasty flourished. During the mid–eighth century, however, the careless leadership of an emperor more interested in music and his favorite concubine brought the dynasty to a crisis. In 755 one of the dynasty's foremost military commanders, An Lushan, mounted a rebellion and captured the capital at Chang'an and the secondary capital at Luoyang. His revolt was short-lived: by 763 Tang forces had suppressed An Lushan's army and recovered their capitals. But the rebellion left the dynasty gravely weakened, because Tang commanders had to ask a nomadic Turkish people, the Uighurs, to help them win back their capitals. In return, the Uighurs demanded the right to sack Chang'an and Luoyang after the expulsion of the rebels.

The Tang imperial house never again regained control of affairs. The equal-field system deteriorated, and tax receipts dwindled. Imperial armies were unable to resist invasions of Turkish peoples in the late eighth century. During the ninth century a series of rebellions devastated the Chinese countryside. In an effort to control the rebellions, the Tang emperors granted progressively greater power and authority to regional military commanders, who gradually became the effective rulers of China. In 907 the last Tang emperor abdicated his throne, and the dynasty came to an end.

The Song Dynasty

PSI map The Song dynasty www.mhhe.com/bentleybrief2e

Following the Tang collapse, warlords ruled China until the Song dynasty reimposed centralized imperial rule in the late tenth century. Though it survived for more than three centuries, the Song dynasty (960–1279 C.E.) never built a very powerful state. Song rulers mistrusted military leaders, and they placed much more emphasis on civil administration, industry, education, and the arts than on military affairs.

SONG TAIZU The first Song emperor, Song Taizu (reigned 960–976 C.E.), inaugurated this policy. Song Taizu began his career as a junior military officer for a powerful warlord in northern China. He had a reputation for honesty and effectiveness, and in 960 his troops proclaimed him emperor. During the next several years, he and his army subjected the warlords to their authority and consolidated Song control throughout China. He then set about organizing a centralized administration that placed military forces under tight supervision.

Song rulers vastly expanded the bureaucracy by creating more opportunities for individuals to seek a Confucian education and take civil service examinations. They accepted many more candidates into the bureaucracy than their Sui and Tang predecessors, and they provided generous salaries for those who qualified for government appointments. They even placed civil bureaucrats in charge of military forces.

SONG WEAKNESSES The Song approach to administration resulted in a more centralized imperial government than earlier Chinese dynasties had enjoyed, but it caused two big problems that eventually caused the dynasty to fall. The first problem was financial: as the number of bureaucrats and the size of their rewards grew, the imperial treasury came under tremendous pressure. That pressure, in turn, aggravated the peasantry, who were expected to shoulder increased taxes.

The second problem was military. Scholar bureaucrats generally had little talent for military affairs, yet they led Song armies in the field and made military decisions. It was no coincidence that nomadic peoples flourished along China's northern border throughout the Song dynasty. In the early twelfth century, the nomadic Jurchen overran northern China, captured the Song capital at Kaifeng, and proclaimed establishment of the Jin empire. Thereafter the Song dynasty moved its capital to the prosperous port city of Hangzhou and survived only in southern China, so that the latter part of the dynasty is commonly known as the

THINKING ABOUT *Traditions*

TRADITIONS IN THE RESURGENT EAST ASIAN EMPIRES. During the postclassical period, traders and travelers from a wide variety of Eurasian locations came to China, bringing foreign beliefs and values with them. Discuss some of the ways the Chinese transformed these foreign influences into ideas and practices that fit into long-established traditions.

Uighurs (WEE-goors)
Song Taizu (sawng tahy-zoo)

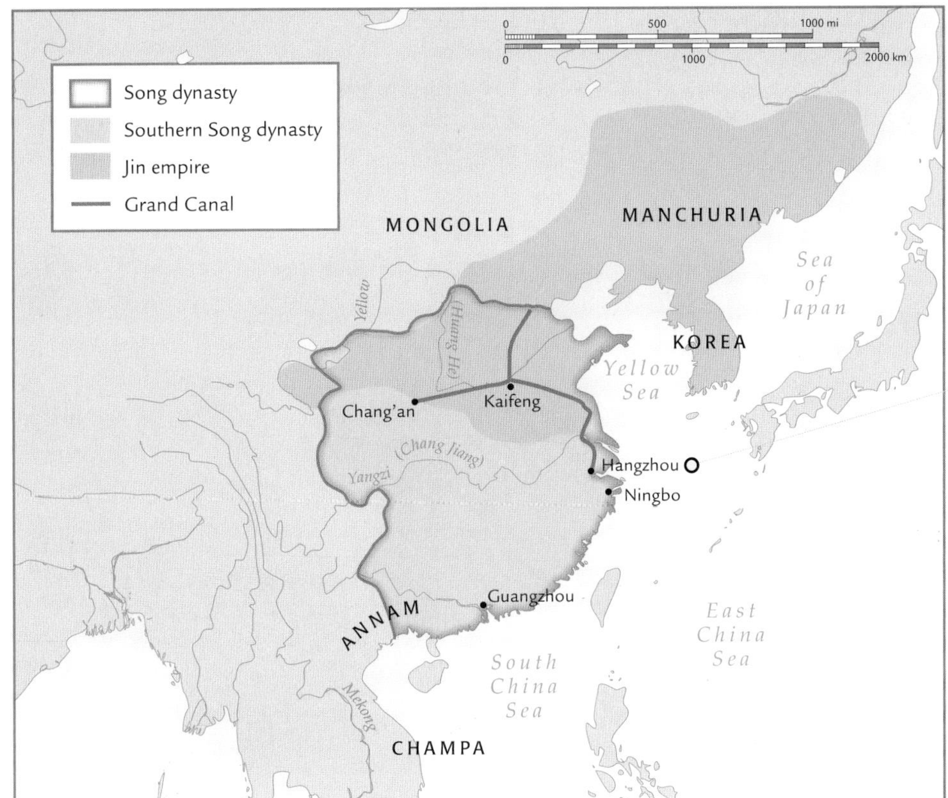

MAP 12.2 | The Song dynasty, 960–1279 C.E. After the establishment of the Jin empire, the Song dynasty moved its capital from Kaifeng to Hangzhou. ***What advantages did Hangzhou offer to the Song rulers?***

The new capital of the Song dynasty.

Southern Song. This truncated Southern Song shared a border with the Jin empire about midway between the Yellow River and the Yangzi River until 1279, when Mongol forces ended the dynasty altogether.

THE ECONOMIC DEVELOPMENT OF TANG AND SONG CHINA

Although the Song dynasty did not develop a strong military capacity, it benefited from a remarkable series of agricultural, technological, industrial, and commercial developments. This economic development originated in the Tang dynasty, but its results became most clear during the Song, which presided over a land of enormous prosperity. The economic surge of Tang and Song times had implications that went well beyond China, since it stimulated trade and production throughout much of the eastern hemisphere for more than half a millennium, from about 600 to 1300 C.E.

Agricultural Development

FAST-RIPENING RICE The foundation of economic development in Tang and Song China was a surge in agricultural production. When Sui and Tang armies ventured into Vietnam, they encountered new strains of fast-ripening rice that enabled cultivators to harvest two crops per year. Transferred to the fertile fields of southern China, fast-ripening rice quickly resulted in an expanded supply of food.

Jurchen (JUHR-chehn)

Chinese Peasant Life. | A wall painting in a Buddhist cave depicts a peasant plowing his field in the rain with the aid of an ox and a heavy plow. Other peasants have found shelter from the rain and consume a midday meal brought to them by their wives. ***How would peasant life have differed from the lives of scholar-bureaucrats?***

NEW AGRICULTURAL TECHNIQUES Chinese cultivators also increased their productivity by adopting improved agricultural techniques. They made increased use of heavy iron plows, and they harnessed oxen (in the north) and water buffaloes (in the south) to help prepare land for cultivation. They enriched the soil with manure and composted organic matter. They also organized extensive irrigation systems. Artificial irrigation made it possible to extend cultivation to new lands, including terraced mountainsides—a development that vastly expanded China's agricultural potential.

POPULATION GROWTH Increased agricultural production resulted in rapid population growth. After the fall of the Han dynasty, the population of China reached a low point of about 45 million in 600 C.E. By 1000 C.E. it had increased to 60 million. By 1127, when the Jurchen conquered the northern half of the Song state, the Chinese population had passed the 100 million mark, and by 1200 it stood at about 115 million.

URBANIZATION Increased food supplies encouraged the growth of cities. During the Tang dynasty the imperial capital of Chang'an was the world's most populous city with as many as two million residents. During the Song dynasty, China was the most urbanized land in the world. In the late thirteenth century, Hangzhou, capital of the Southern Song dynasty, had more than one million residents. They supported hundreds of restaurants, taverns, teahouses, brothels, music halls, theaters, clubhouses, gardens, markets, craft shops, and specialty stores dealing in silk, gems, porcelain, lacquerware, and other goods.

Another result of increased food production was the emergence of a commercialized agricultural economy. Because fast-ripening rice yielded bountiful harvests, many cultivators could purchase inexpensive rice and raise vegetables and fruits for sale on the commercial market. Cultivators specialized in crops that grew well in their own regions, and they often exported their harvests to distant regions. By the twelfth century, for example, the wealthy southern province of Fujian imported rice and devoted its land to the production of lychees, oranges, and sugarcane, which fetched high prices in northern markets.

PATRIARCHAL SOCIAL STRUCTURES Alongside increasing wealth and agricultural productivity, Tang and especially Song China experienced a tightening of patriarchal social structures. During the Song dynasty, for example, the veneration of family ancestors became much more elaborate than before. Indeed, descendants diligently sought the graves of their earliest traceable forefathers and then arranged elaborate graveside rituals in their honor. Whole extended families often traveled great distances to attend annual rituals venerating deceased ancestors—a practice that strengthened the sense of family identity and cohesiveness.

FOOT BINDING Strengthened patriarchal authority also helps to explain the popularity of foot binding, which spread among privileged classes during the Song era. Foot binding involved the tight wrapping of young girls' feet with strips of cloth, which prevented natural growth and resulted in tiny, malformed, curved feet. Women with bound feet could not walk easily or naturally. Usually they needed canes to walk by themselves, and sometimes they depended on servants to carry them around in litters. Foot binding never became universal in China—it was impractical for peasants or lower-class working women in the cities—but wealthy families often bound the feet of their daughters to enhance their attractiveness, display their high social standing, and gain increased control over the girls' behavior. Like the practice of veiling women in the Islamic world, foot binding placed women of privileged classes under tight supervision of their male guardians, who then managed the women's affairs in the interests of the larger family.

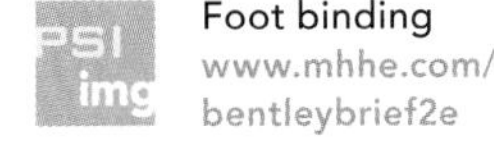

Foot binding
www.mhhe.com/
bentleybrief2e

Technological and Industrial Development

PORCELAIN Abundant supplies of food enabled many people to pursue technological and industrial interests. During the Tang and Song dynasties, Chinese crafts workers generated a remarkable range of technological innovations. During Tang times they discovered techniques for producing high-quality porcelain, which was lighter, thinner, and adaptable to more uses than earlier pottery. Porcelain technology gradually diffused to other societies, yet demand for Chinese porcelain remained high, and the Chinese exported vast quantities of porcelain during the Tang and Song dynasties. Indeed, Chinese porcelain graced the tables of wealthy and refined households in southeast Asia, India, Persia, and the port cities of east Africa. Tang and Song products gained such a reputation that fine porcelain has come to be known generally as *chinaware.*

METALLURGY Tang and Song craftsmen also improved metallurgical technologies, which resulted in a surge of iron and steel production. Chinese craftsmen discovered that they could use coke instead of coal in their furnaces and produce stronger and more useful grades of metal. Between the early ninth and the early twelfth centuries, iron production increased almost tenfold, according to official records. Most of the increased supply of iron and steel went into weaponry and agricultural tools: during the early Song dynasty, imperial armaments manufacturers produced 16.5 million iron arrowheads per year. As in the case of porcelain technology, metallurgical techniques soon diffused to lands beyond China. Indeed, Song military difficulties stemmed partly from the fact that nomadic peoples quickly learned Chinese techniques and fashioned their own iron weapons for use in campaigns against them.

GUNPOWDER Tang and Song craftsmen also invented entirely new products, tools, and techniques, most notably gunpowder, printing, and naval technologies. During the Tang dynasty, Daoist alchemists seeking elixirs to prolong life soon learned that it was unwise to mix charcoal, saltpeter, sulphur, and arsenic because of the volatility of the resulting compound. Military officials, however, recognized opportunity in the explosive mixture. By the mid–tenth century they were using gunpowder in bamboo "fire lances," a kind of flamethrower, and by the eleventh century they had fashioned primitive bombs.

The earliest gunpowder weapons had limited military effectiveness. Over time, however, refinements enhanced their capabilities. Knowledge of gunpowder chemistry quickly

GUNPOWDER. | During the Han Dynasty, Chinese alchemists discovered that a combination of saltpeter, charcoal, and sulfur exploded when lit with a flame. By the 8th century C.E., Chinese strategists began to use gunpowder for military uses.

diffused through Eurasia, and by the late thirteenth century peoples of southwest Asia and Europe were experimenting with metal-barreled cannons.

PRINTING The precise origins of printing are obscure. It is clear, however, that it became common during the Tang era. The earliest printers employed block-printing techniques: they carved a reverse image of an entire page into a wooden block, inked the block, and then pressed a sheet of paper on top. By the mid–eleventh century, printers had also begun to experiment with reusable, movable type: instead of carving images into blocks, they fashioned dies in the shape of ideographs, arranged them in a frame, inked them, and pressed the frame over paper sheets. Printing made it possible to produce texts quickly, cheaply, and in huge quantities. By the late ninth century, printed copies of Buddhist texts, Confucian works, calendars, agricultural treatises, and popular works were abundant, particularly in southwestern China (modern Sichuan province).

NAVAL TECHNOLOGY Chinese inventiveness extended also to naval technology. Before Tang times, Chinese mariners did not venture very far from land, relying instead on foreign ships for long-distance maritime trade. During the Tang dynasty, however, Chinese consumers developed a taste for the spices and exotic products of southeast Asian islands, and Chinese mariners increasingly visited those lands in their own ships. By the time of the Song dynasty, Chinese seafarers sailed ships fastened with iron nails, waterproofed with oils, furnished with watertight bulkheads, driven by canvas and bamboo sails, steered by rudders, and navigated with the aid of the "south-pointing needle"—the magnetic compass. Chinese ships mostly plied the waters between Japan and the Malay peninsula, but some of them called at ports in India, Ceylon, Persia, and east Africa. These long-distance travels helped to diffuse elements of Chinese naval technology, particularly the compass, which soon became the common property of mariners throughout the Indian Ocean basin.

The Emergence of a Market Economy

Increased agricultural production, improved transportation systems, population growth, urbanization, and industrial production combined to stimulate the Chinese economy. China's various regions increasingly specialized in the cultivation of particular food crops or the production of particular manufactured goods. To be sure, the government played an important role in the Chinese economy by regulating the distribution of staple foods and the production of militarily sensitive enterprises such as the iron industry. Nevertheless, millions of cultivators produced fruits and vegetables for sale on the open market, and manufacturers of silk, porcelain, and other goods supplied both domestic and foreign markets. The Chinese economy became more tightly integrated than ever before, and foreign demand for Chinese products fueled rapid economic expansion.

FINANCIAL INSTRUMENTS In fact, trade grew so rapidly during Tang and Song times that China experienced a shortage of the copper coins that served as money for most transactions. To alleviate the shortage, letters of credit came into common use during the early Tang dynasty. Later developments included the use of promissory notes, checks, and even paper money. Indeed, wealthy merchants pioneered the use of printed paper money in the late ninth century. In return for cash deposits from their clients, they issued printed notes that the clients could redeem for merchandise. In a society short of cash, these notes greatly facilitated commercial transactions. Yet they also caused disorder, and sometimes even riots, in the event that merchants were not able to honor their notes.

In the eleventh century, in an effort to forestall such disorder, the Chinese government stepped in and assumed the sole right to issue paper money. The first government-issued paper money appeared in 1024 in Sichuan province, and by the end of the eleventh century it existed throughout imperial China. In spite of continuing problems with paper currency—including counterfeit notes and lapses of public confidence in the government's ability to honor its own notes—printed paper money provided a powerful stimulus to the Chinese economy under the Song.

A COSMOPOLITAN SOCIETY Trade and urbanization transformed Tang and Song China into a prosperous, cosmopolitan society. Trade came to China both by land and by sea. Muslim merchants from the Abbasid empire and central Asia—and even subjects of the Byzantine empire—helped to revive the silk roads network and flocked to large Chinese trading centers. Residents of large Chinese cities such as Chang'an and Luoyang became quite accustomed to merchants from foreign lands. Indeed, musicians and dancers from Persia became popular entertainers in the cities of the Tang dynasty. Meanwhile, Arab, Persian, Indian, and Malay mariners arriving by way of the Indian Ocean and South China Sea established sizable merchant communities in the bustling southern Chinese port cities of Guangzhou and Quanzhou.

CHINA AND THE HEMISPHERIC ECONOMY Indeed, high productivity and trade brought the Tang and Song economy a dynamism that China's borders could not restrain. Chinese consumers developed a taste for exotic goods, which stimulated trade throughout much of the eastern hemisphere. Spices from the islands of southeast Asia made their way to China, along with products as diverse as kingfisher feathers and tortoise shell from Vietnam, pearls and incense from India, and horses and melons from central Asia. In exchange for such exotic items, Chinese sent abroad vast quantities of silk, porcelain, and lacquerware. In central Asia, southeast Asia, India, Persia, and the port cities of east Africa, wealthy merchants and rulers wore Chinese silk and set their tables with Chinese porcelain. China's economic surge during the Tang and Song dynasties thus promoted trade and economic growth throughout much of the eastern hemisphere.

Cultural Change in Tang and Song China

Interactions with peoples of other societies encouraged cultural change in postclassical China. The Confucian and Daoist traditions did not disappear, but they made way for a foreign religion—Mahayana Buddhism—and they developed along new lines that reflected the conditions of Tang and Song society.

Guangzhou (gwahng-joh)
Quanzhou (chwahn-joh)

SOURCES FROM THE PAST

The Arab Merchant Suleiman on Business Practices in Tang China

The Arab merchant Suleiman made several commercial ventures by ship to India and China during the early ninth century C.E. In 851 an Arab geographer wrote an account of Suleiman's travels, describing India and China for Muslim readers in southwest Asia. His report throws particularly interesting light on the economic conditions and business practices of Tang China.

Young and old Chinese all wear silk clothes in both winter and summer, but silk of the best quality is reserved for the kings. . . . During the winter, the men wear two, three, four, five pairs of pants, and even more, according to their means. This practice has the goal of protecting the lower body from the high humidity of the land, which they fear. During the summer, they wear a single shirt of silk or some similar material. They do not wear turbans. . . .

In China, commercial transactions are carried out with the aid of copper coins. The Chinese royal treasury is identical to that of other kings, but only the king of China has a treasury that uses copper coins as a standard. These copper coins serve as the money of the land. The Chinese have gold, silver, fine pearls, fancy silk textiles, raw silk, and all this in large quantities, but they are considered commodities, and only copper coins serve as money.

Imports into China include ivory, incense, copper ingots, shells of sea turtles, and rhinoceros horn, with which the Chinese make ornaments. . . .

The Chinese conduct commercial transactions and business affairs with equity. When someone lends money to another person, he writes up a note documenting the loan. The borrower writes up another note on which he affixes an imprint of his index finger and middle finger together. Then they put the two notes together, roll them up, and write a formula at the point where one touches the other [so that part of the written formula appears on each note]. Next, they separate the notes and entrust to the lender the one on which the borrower recognizes his debt. If the borrower denies his debt later on, they say to him, "Present the note that the lender gave to you." If the borrower maintains that he has no such note from the lender, and denies that he ever agreed to the note with his fingerprints on it, and if the lender's note has disappeared, they say to him, "Declare in writing that you have not contracted this debt, but if later the lender brings forth proof that you have contracted this debt that you deny, you will receive twenty blows of the cane on the back and you will be ordered to pay a penalty of twenty million copper coins." This sum is equal to about 2,000 dinars [gold coins used in the Abbasid empire]. Twenty blows of the cane brings on death. Thus no one in China dares to make such a declaration for fear of losing at the same time both life and fortune. We have seen no one who has agreed when invited to make such a declaration. The Chinese are thus equitable to each other. No one in China is treated unjustly.

■ **In what ways might Chinese policies have encouraged business and trade during the Tang dynasty?**

SOURCE: Gabriel Ferrand, trans. *Voyage du marchand arabe Sulayman en Inde et en Chine.* Paris, 1922, pp. 45, 53–54, 60–61. (Translated into English by Jerry H. Bentley.)

The Establishment of Buddhism

FOREIGN RELIGIONS IN CHINA Buddhist merchants traveling the ancient silk roads visited China as early as the second century B.C.E. During the Han dynasty their faith attracted little interest: Confucianism, Daoism, and cults that honored family ancestors were the most popular cultural alternatives. During the unsettled centuries following the fall of the Han, however, several foreign religions—including Nestorian Christianity, Manichaeism, Zoroastrianism, and Islam—established communities in China. Yet these religions of salvation mostly served the needs of foreign merchants trading in China and converts from nomadic societies and did not win a large popular following.

Confucianism (kuhn-FYEW-shuhn-iz'm)
Daoism (dow-iz'm)
Manichaeism (mahn-ih-kee-iz'm)

DUNHUANG Mahayana Buddhism was different in that it gradually found a popular following in Tang and Song China. Buddhism came to China over the silk roads via the oasis cities of central Asia, and by the fourth century C.E., a sizable Buddhist community had emerged at Dunhuang in western China (modern Gansu province). Between about 600 and 1000 C.E., Buddhists built hundreds of cave temples in the vicinity of Dunhuang and decorated them with murals depicting events in the lives of the Buddha and the boddhisattvas. They also assembled libraries of religious literature and operated scriptoria to produce Buddhist texts. Missions supported by establishments such as those at Dunhuang helped Buddhism to establish a foothold in China.

COSMOPOLITAN SOCIETY. | Foreign music and dance were very popular in the large cities of Tang China. This ceramic model depicts a troupe of musicians from southwest Asia performing on a platform mounted on a camel. Many such models survive from Tang times.

BUDDHISM IN CHINA Buddhism attracted Chinese interest partly because of its high standards of morality, its intellectual sophistication, and its promise of salvation. Yet practical concerns also help to account for its appeal. Buddhist monastic communities in China accumulated sizable estates donated by wealthy converts, and they commonly stored a portion of their harvests for distribution among local residents during hard times. As a result, Buddhist monasteries became important elements in the local economies of Chinese communities.

BUDDHISM AND DAOISM In some ways Buddhism posed a challenge to Chinese cultural and social traditions. Buddhist theologians typically placed great emphasis on written texts and used them to explore elaborate investigations into metaphysical themes such as the nature of the soul. Among Chinese intellectuals, however, only the Confucians placed equal emphasis on written texts, and they devoted their energies mostly to practical rather than metaphysical issues. Meanwhile, Daoists had limited interest in written texts of any kind. Buddhist morality also called for individuals to observe an ascetic ideal by following a celibate, monastic lifestyle. In contrast, Chinese morality centered on the family unit and strongly encouraged procreation so that generations of offspring would be available to venerate family ancestors. Some Chinese held that Buddhist monasteries were economically harmful, because they paid no taxes, whereas others scorned Buddhism because of its foreign origins.

Because of these differences and concerns, Buddhist missionaries sought to tailor their message to Chinese audiences. They explained Buddhist concepts in vocabulary borrowed from Chinese cultural traditions, particularly Daoism. They translated the Indian term *dharma* (the basic Buddhist doctrine) as *dao* ("the way" in the Daoist sense of the term), and they translated the Indian term *nirvana* (personal salvation that comes after an individual soul escapes from the cycle of incarnation) as *wuwei* (the Daoist ethic of noncompetition). While encouraging the establishment of monasteries and the observance of celibacy, they also recognized the validity of family life and offered Buddhism as a religion that would benefit the extended Chinese family: one son in the monastery, they taught, would bring salvation for ten generations of his kin.

Boddhisattva Guide of Souls
www.mhhe.com/bentleybrief2e

Mount Wudang
www.mhhe.com/bentleybrief2e

CHAN BUDDHISM The result was a syncretic faith, a Buddhism with Chinese characteristics. One of the more popular schools of Buddhism in China, for example, was the Chan (also known by its Japanese name, Zen). Chan Buddhists had little interest in written texts but, instead, emphasized sudden flashes of insight in their search for spiritual enlightenment. In that respect they resembled Daoists as much as they did Buddhists.

During the Tang and Song dynasties, this syncretic Buddhism became an immensely popular and influential faith in China. Monasteries appeared in all the major cities, and stupas dotted the Chinese landscape. The monk Xuanzang (602–664) was only one of many devout pilgrims who traveled to India to visit holy sites and learn about Buddhism

nirvana (nuhr-VAH-nuh)
wuwei (woo-WAY)
Chan Buddhism (CHAHN BOO-diz'm)

Xuanzang's Return. This scroll painting depicts the return of the monk Xuanzang to China. His baggage included 657 books, mostly Buddhist treatises but also a few works on grammar and logic, as well as hundreds of relics and images.

in its homeland. Like Xuanzang, many of those pilgrims returned with copies of treatises that deepened the understanding of Buddhism in China. In the process, they played significant roles in establishing Buddhism as a popular faith in China.

HOSTILITY TO BUDDHISM In spite of its popularity, Buddhism met determined resistance from Daoists and Confucians. Daoists resented the popular following of Buddhism, which resulted in diminished resources available for their own tradition. Confucians despised Buddhists' exaltation of celibacy, and they denounced the faith as an alien superstition.

PERSECUTION During the late Tang dynasty, Daoist and Confucian critics of Buddhism found allies in the imperial court. Beginning in the 840s the Tang emperors ordered the closure of monasteries and the expulsion of Buddhists as well as Zoroastrians, Nestorian Christians, and Manichaeans. Yet Tang rulers did not implement the policy in a thorough way, and foreign faiths were not eradicated. Buddhism in particular enjoyed continued support that enabled it not only to survive but also to influence the development of Confucianism during the Song dynasty.

Neo-Confucianism

The Song emperors did not persecute Buddhists, but they actively supported native Chinese cultural traditions in hopes of limiting the influence of foreign religions. They contributed particularly generously to the Confucian tradition by sponsoring the studies of Confucian scholars and subsidizing the printing and dissemination of Confucian writings.

CONFUCIANS AND BUDDHISM Yet the Confucian tradition of the Song dynasty differed from that of earlier times. The earliest Confucians had concentrated resolutely on practical issues of politics and morality, since they were mainly concerned with establishing social order. Confucians of the Song dynasty studied the classic works of their tradition, but they also were inspired by many aspects of Buddhist thought. Indeed, Buddhism both offered a tradition of logical thought and argumentation and dealt with issues not systematically explored by Confucian thinkers, such as the nature of the soul. Because Confucian thought during the Song dynasty reflected the influence of Buddhism as well as original Confucian values, it has come to be known as neo-Confucianism.

neo-Confucianism (nee-oh-kuhn-FYEW-shuhn-iz'm)

NEO-CONFUCIAN INFLUENCE Neo-Confucianism ranks as an important cultural development for two reasons. First, it illustrates the deep influence of Buddhism in Chinese society. Even though the neo-Confucians rejected Buddhism as a faith, their writings adapted Buddhist themes and reasoning to Confucian interests and values. Second, neo-Confucianism influenced east Asian thought over a very long term. In China, neo-Confucianism enjoyed the status of an officially recognized creed from the Song dynasty until the early twentieth century, and in lands that fell within China's cultural orbit—particularly Korea, Vietnam, and Japan—neo-Confucianism shaped philosophical, political, and moral thought for half a millennium and more.

ENCOUNTERS IN THE RESURGENT EAST ASIAN EMPIRES. The postclassical period in China was a time of intense cultural interaction with societies throughout Asia and beyond. In what ways did this interaction influence the long-term development of other east Asian societies in Korea, Vietnam, and Japan?

CHINESE INFLUENCE IN EAST ASIA

Like societies in Byzantium and the *dar al-Islam,* Chinese society influenced the development of neighboring lands during postclassical times. Chinese armies periodically invaded Korea and Vietnam, and Chinese merchants established commercial relations with Japan as well as with Korea and Vietnam. Chinese techniques of government and administration helped shape public life in all three lands, as did Chinese values and cultural traditions. By no means did these lands become absorbed into China: all maintained distinctive identities. Yet they also drew deep inspiration from Chinese examples and built societies that reflected their participation in a larger east Asian society revolving around China.

Korea and Vietnam

During the Tang dynasty, Chinese imperial armies followed in the footsteps of the Qin and Han dynasties by mounting large-scale campaigns of expansion in both Korea and Vietnam. Although the two lands responded differently to Chinese imperial expansion, both borrowed Chinese political and cultural traditions and used them in their own societies.

THE SILLA DYNASTY In the seventh century, Tang armies conquered much of Korea before the native Silla dynasty rallied. Both Tang and Silla authorities preferred to avoid a long and costly conflict, so they agreed to a political compromise: Chinese forces withdrew from Korea, and the Silla king recognized the Tang emperor as his overlord.

Thus Korea entered into a tributary relationship with China. Envoys of the Silla kings regularly delivered gifts to Chinese emperors and performed the kowtow, but those concessions brought considerable benefits to the Koreans. In return for their recognition of Chinese supremacy, they received gifts more valuable than the tribute they delivered to China. Moreover, the tributary relationship opened the doors for Korean merchants to trade in China.

CHINESE INFLUENCE IN KOREA Meanwhile, the tributary relationship facilitated the spread of Chinese political and cultural influences to Korea. Korean rulers began to model their court along Chinese lines, and the Silla kings even built a new capital at Kumsong modeled on the Tang capital at Chang'an. Korean scholars went to China to study Chinese thought and literature and took copies of Chinese writings back to Korea. Their efforts helped to build elite Korean interest in the Confucian tradition, and Chinese schools of Buddhism attracted widespread popular interest.

Sokkuram Grotto
www.mhhe.com/bentleybrief2e

China and Korea differed in many respects. Most notably, perhaps, aristocrats and royal houses dominated Korean society much more than in China. Although the Korean monarchy sponsored Chinese schools and a Confucian examination system, Korea never established a bureaucracy based on merit, and political initiative remained firmly in the hands of the ruling classes. Nevertheless, extensive dealings with its powerful neighbor ensured that Korea reflected the influence of Chinese political and cultural traditions.

Vietnamese Dancer. This Tang dynasty pottery figure is testament to the fact that commercial and tributary relationships introduced southeast Asian performers to China. ***Why might sophisticated urban communities in China have appreciated this kind of entertainment?***

China and Vietnam Chinese relations with Vietnam were far more tense than their relations with Korea. When Tang armies ventured into the land that Chinese called Nam Viet, they encountered spirited resistance on the part of the Viet people, who had settled in the region around the Red River. Tang forces soon won control of Viet towns and cities, and they launched efforts to absorb the Viets into Chinese society. The Viets readily adopted Chinese agricultural methods and irrigation systems as well as Chinese schools and administrative techniques. Like their Korean counterparts, Viet elites studied Confucian texts and took examinations based on a Chinese-style education, and Viet traders marketed their wares in China. Vietnamese authorities even entered into tributary relationships with the Chinese court. Yet the Viets resented Chinese efforts to dominate them, and they mounted a series of revolts against Tang authorities. As the Tang dynasty fell during the early tenth century, the Viets won their independence and successfully resisted later Chinese efforts at imperial expansion to the south.

Like Korea, Vietnam differed from China in many ways. Although Buddhism won a large popular following, many Vietnamese retained their indigenous religions in preference to Chinese cultural traditions. Women played a much more prominent role in Vietnamese society and economy than did their Chinese counterparts. Southeast Asian women had dominated local and regional markets for centuries, and they participated actively in business ventures closed to women in the more rigidly patriarchal society of China. Nevertheless, Chinese traditions found a place in the southern land. Indeed, like Korea, Vietnam absorbed political and cultural influence from China and reflected the development of a larger east Asian society centered on China.

Early Japan

Todaiji
www.mhhe.com/bentleybrief2e

Chinese armies never invaded Japan, but Chinese traditions deeply influenced Japanese political and cultural development. The earliest inhabitants of Japan were nomadic peoples from northeast Asia. They migrated to Japan, perhaps across land bridges that formed during an ice age, about two hundred thousand years ago. Their language, material culture, and religion derived from their parent society in northeast Asia. Later migrants, who arrived in several waves from the Korean peninsula, introduced cultivation of rice, bronze and iron metallurgy, and horses into Japan. As the population of the Japanese islands grew and built a settled agricultural society, small states dominated by aristocratic clans emerged. By the middle of the first millennium C.E., several dozen states ruled small regions.

Nara Japan The establishment of the powerful Sui and Tang dynasties in China had repercussions in Japan, where they suggested the value of centralized imperial government. One of the aristocratic clans in Japan insisted on its precedence over the others, although in fact it had never wielded effective authority outside its own territory in central Japan. Nevertheless, inspired by the Tang example, this clan claimed imperial authority and introduced a series of reforms designed to centralize Japanese politics. The imperial house established a court modeled on that of the Tang, instituted a Chinese-style bureaucracy, implemented an equal-field system, provided official support for Confucianism and Buddhism, and in the year 710 moved to a new capital city at Nara (near modern Kyoto) that was a replica of the Tang capital at Chang'an. Never was Chinese influence more prominent in Japan than during the Nara period (710–794 C.E.).

Shinto temple
www.mhhe.com/bentleybrief2e

Yet Japan did not lose its distinctive characteristics. While adopting Confucian and Buddhist traditions from China, for example, the Japanese continued to observe the rites of Shinto, their indigenous religion, which revolved around the veneration of ancestors and a host of nature spirits and deities.

HEIAN JAPAN The experiences of the Heian, Kamakura, and Muromachi periods clearly illustrate the distinctiveness of Japanese society. Under the Heian (794–1185 C.E.), local rulers on the island of Honshu mostly recognized the emperor as Japan's supreme political authority. Unlike their Chinese counterparts, however, Japanese emperors rarely ruled but, rather, served as ceremonial figureheads and symbols of authority. Effective power lay in the hands of the Fujiwara family, an aristocratic clan that controlled affairs from behind the throne through its influence over the imperial house and manipulation of its members. Indeed, since the Heian period the Japanese political order has almost continuously featured a split between a publicly recognized imperial authority and a separate agent of effective rule. This pattern helps to account for the remarkable longevity of the Japanese imperial house: because emperors have not ruled, they have not been subject to deposition during times of turmoil.

The cultural development of Heian Japan also reflected both the influence of Chinese traditions and the elaboration of peculiarly Japanese ways. Most literature imitated Chinese models and indeed was written in the Chinese language. Boys and young men who received a formal education in Heian Japan learned Chinese, read the classic works of China, and wrote in the foreign tongue. Officials at court conducted business and kept records in Chinese, and literary figures wrote histories and treatises in the style popular in China. Even Japanese writing reflected Chinese influence, since scholars borrowed many Chinese characters and used them to represent Japanese words. They also adapted some Chinese characters into a Japanese syllabic script, in which symbols represent whole syllables rather than a single sound, as in an alphabetic script.

DECLINE OF HEIAN JAPAN In the late eleventh century, changes in the countryside brought an end to the Heian court. The equal-field system gradually fell into disuse, and aristocratic clans accumulated most of the islands' lands into vast estates. Two clans in particular—the Taira and the Minamoto—overshadowed the others. During the mid–twelfth century the two engaged in outright war, and in 1185 the Minamoto emerged victorious. Like the Fujiwara family, the Minamoto did not seek to abolish imperial authority in Japan but, rather, claimed to rule the land in the name of the emperor. They installed the clan leader as *shogun*—a military governor who ruled in place of the emperor—and established the seat of their government at Kamakura, near modern Tokyo, while the imperial court remained at Kyoto. For most of the next four centuries, one branch or another of the Minamoto clan dominated political life in Japan.

POLITICAL DECENTRALIZATION In the Kamakura (1185–1333 C.E.) and Muromachi (1336–1573 C.E.) periods, Japanese society grew ever more distinctive. Indeed, Japan developed a decentralized political order in which provincial lords wielded effective power and authority in local regions where they controlled land and economic affairs. As these lords and their clans vied for power and authority in the countryside, they found little use for the Chinese-style bureaucracy that Nara and Heian rulers had instituted in Japan and still less use for the elaborate protocol and refined conduct that prevailed at the courts. In place of etiquette and courtesy, they valued military talent and discipline. The mounted warrior, the *samurai,* thus came to play the most distinctive role in Japanese political and military affairs.

Shinto (SHIHN-toh)
Heian (HAY-ahn)
shogun (SHOH-gun)
samurai (SAM-uhr-eye)

Thus, although it had taken its original inspiration from the Tang empire in China, the Japanese political order developed along lines different from those of the Middle Kingdom. Yet Japan clearly had a place in the larger east Asian society centered on China. Japan borrowed from China, among other things, Confucian values, Buddhist religion, a system of writing, and the ideal of centralized imperial rule. Though somewhat suppressed during later periods, these elements of Chinese society not only survived in Japan but also decisively influenced Japanese development over the long term.

SUMMARY

The revival of centralized imperial rule in China had profound implications for all of east Asia and indeed for most of the eastern hemisphere. When the Sui and Tang dynasties imposed their authority throughout China, they established a powerful state that guided political affairs throughout east Asia. Tang armies extended Chinese influence to Korea, Vietnam, and central Asia. They did not invade Japan, but the impressive political organization of China prompted the islands' rulers to imitate Tang examples. Moreover, the Sui and Tang dynasties laid a strong political foundation for rapid economic development. Chinese society prospered throughout the postclassical era, partly because of technological and industrial innovation. Tang and Song prosperity touched all of China's neighbors, since it encouraged surging commerce in east Asia. Chinese silk, porcelain, and lacquerware were prized commodities among trading peoples from southeast Asia to east Africa. Chinese inventions such as paper, printing, gunpowder, and the magnetic compass found a place in societies throughout the eastern hemisphere as they diffused across the silk roads and sea-lanes. The postclassical era was an age of religious as well as commercial and technological exchanges: Nestorian Christians, Zoroastrians, Manichaeans, and Muslims all maintained communities in Tang China, and Buddhism became the most popular religious faith in all of east Asia. During the postclassical era, Chinese social organization and economic dynamism helped to sustain interactions between the peoples of the eastern hemisphere on an unprecedented scale.

STUDY TERMS

Chan Buddhism (235)
equal-field system (226)
foot binding (231)
Grand Canal (225)
gunpowder (231)
Heian Japan (239)
Kamakura Japan (239)
Mahayana Buddhism (233)
Muromachi Japan (239)
Nam Viet (238)
Nara period (238)
neo-Confucianism (236)
nirvana (235)
paper money (233)
porcelain (231)
Shinto (239)
Silla dynasty (237)
Song dynasty (228)
Song Taizu (228)
Sui dynasty (224)
Sui Yangdi (225)
Tang dynasty (225)
tribute system (227)
wuwei (235)
Yang Jian (224)

FOR FURTHER READING

Kenneth Ch'en. *Buddhism in China: A Historical Survey.* Princeton, 1964. A clear and detailed account by an eminent scholar.

Hugh R. Clark. *Community, Trade, and Networks: Southern Fujian Province from the Third to the Thirteenth Century.* Cambridge, 1991. Excellent scholarly study exploring the transformation of a region by trade and market forces.

Patricia Buckley Ebrey. *Chinese Civilization: A Sourcebook.* 2nd ed. New York, 1993. A splendid collection of documents in translation.

Mark Elvin. *The Pattern of the Chinese Past.* Stanford, 1973. A brilliant analysis of Chinese history, concentrating particularly on economic, social, and technological themes.

Jacques Gernet. *Daily Life in China on the Eve of the Mongol Invasion, 1250–1276.* Trans. by H. M. Wright. New York, 1962. Rich portrait of Southern Song China, emphasizing social history.

Peter D. Hershock. *Chan Buddhism.* Honolulu, 2005. An accessible introduction to Chan Buddhism focusing on far renowned masters.

Edward H. Schafer. *The Golden Peaches of Samarkand: A Study of T'ang Exotics.* Berkeley, 1963. Deals with relations between China and central Asian lands during the Tang dynasty.

H. Paul Varley. *Japanese Culture.* 4th ed. Honolulu, 2000. An authoritative analysis of Japanese cultural development from early times to the present.

Sally Hovey Wriggins. *Xuanzang: A Buddhist Pilgrim on the Silk Road.* Boulder, 1996. A fascinating and well-illustrated account of Xuanzang's journey to India and his influence on the development of Buddhism in China.

India and the Indian Ocean Basin

13

uzurg ibn Shahriyar was a tenth-century shipmaster from Siraf, a prosperous and bustling port city on the Persian Gulf coast. He probably sailed frequently to Arabia and India, and he may have ventured also to Malaya, the islands of southeast Asia, China, and east Africa. Like all sailors, he heard stories about the distant lands that mariners had visited, the different customs they observed, and the adventures that befell them during their travels. About 953 C.E. he compiled 136 such stories in his *Book of the Wonders of India.*

Buzurg's collection included a generous proportion of tall tales. He told of mermaids and sea dragons, of creatures born from human fathers and fish mothers, of serpents that ate cattle and elephants, of birds so large that they crushed houses, and of a talking lizard. Yet alongside the tall tales, many of Buzurg's stories accurately reflected the conditions of his time. One recounted the story of a king from northern India who converted to Islam and requested translations of Islamic law. Others reported on Hindu customs, shipwrecks, encounters with pirates, and slave trading.

Several of Buzurg's stories tempted readers with visions of vast wealth attainable through maritime trade. For example, Buzurg mentioned a Jewish merchant who left Persia penniless and returned from India and China with a shipload of priceless merchandise. Despite their embellishments, his stories faithfully reflected the trade networks that linked the lands surrounding the Indian Ocean in the tenth century. Although Buzurg clearly thought of India as a distinct land with its own customs, he also recognized a larger world of trade and communication that extended from east Africa to southeast Asia and beyond to China.

Just as China served as the principal inspiration of a larger east Asian society in the postclassical era, India influenced the development of a larger cultural zone in south and southeast Asia. Yet China and India played different roles in their respective spheres of influence. In east Asia, China was clearly the dominant power. In south and southeast Asia, however, there emerged no centralized imperial authority like the Tang dynasty in China. Indeed, although several states organized large regional kingdoms, no single state was able to extend its authority to all parts of the Indian subcontinent, much less to the mainland and islands of southeast Asia.

❮ *Kabir, the blind guru, weaves cloth while discussing religious matters with disciples.*

Though politically disunited, during the postclassical era India remained a coherent and distinct society as a result of powerful social and cultural traditions—especially the caste system and the Hindu religion. Beginning in the seventh century, Islam also began to attract a popular following in India, and after the eleventh century, Islam deeply influenced Indian society alongside the caste system and Hinduism.

CHRONOLOGY

1st to 6th century	Kingdom of Funan
606–648	Reign of Harsha
670–1025	Kingdom of Srivijaya
711	Conquest of Sind by Umayyad forces
850–1267	Chola kingdom
889–1431	Kingdom of Angkor
1001–1027	Raids on India by Mahmud of Ghazni
11th to 12th century	Life of Ramanuja
12th century	Beginning of the bhakti movement
1206–1526	Sultanate of Delhi
1336–1565	Kingdom of Vijayanagar

Beyond the subcontinent Indian traditions helped to shape a larger cultural zone extending to the mainland and islands of southeast Asia. Throughout most of the region, ruling classes adopted Indian forms of political organization and Indian techniques of statecraft. Indian merchants took their Hindu and Buddhist faiths to southeast Asia, where they attracted sustained interest. Somewhat later, Indian merchants also helped introduce Islam to southeast Asia.

While Indian traditions influenced the political and cultural development of southeast Asia, the entire Indian Ocean basin began to move toward economic integration during the postclassical era, as Buzurg ibn Shahriyar's stories suggest. Indeed, innovations in maritime technology, the development of a well-articulated network of sea-lanes, and the building of port cities enabled peoples living around the Indian Ocean to trade and communicate more actively than ever before. As a result, peoples from east Africa to southeast Asia and China increasingly participated in the larger economic, commercial, and cultural life of the Indian Ocean basin.

Islamic and Hindu Kingdoms

Like the Han and Roman empires, the Gupta dynasty came under severe pressure from nomadic invaders. From the mid–fourth to the mid–fifth century C.E., Gupta rulers resisted the pressures and preserved order throughout much of the Indian subcontinent. Beginning in 451 C.E., however, White Huns from central Asia invaded India, and by the mid–sixth century the Gupta state had collapsed. Effective political authority quickly devolved to invaders and independent regional power brokers. From the end of the Gupta dynasty until the sixteenth century, when a Turkish people known as the Mughals extended their authority to most of the subcontinent, India remained a politically divided land.

The Quest for Centralized Imperial Rule

PSI map — States of postclassical India www.mhhe.com/bentleybrief2e

Northern and southern India followed different political trajectories after the fall of the Gupta empire. In the north, local states contested for power and territory, and politics were turbulent and frequently violent. Nomadic Turkish-speaking peoples from central Asia contributed to this unsettled state of affairs by forcing their way into India. They eventually found niches for themselves in the caste system and became completely absorbed into Indian society. However, until processes of social absorption worked themselves out, the arrival of nomadic peoples caused additional disruption in northern India.

HARSHA Even after the collapse of the Gupta dynasty, the ideal of centralized imperial rule did not entirely disappear. During the first half of the seventh century, King Harsha (reigned 606–648 C.E.) temporarily restored unified rule in most of northern India and sought to revive imperial authority. Using a massive military force from his kingdom in the lower Ganges valley, by about 612 Harsha had subdued those who refused to recognize his authority.

COLLAPSE OF HARSHA'S KINGDOM Yet even though Harsha was young, energetic, and an able ruler, he was unable to restore permanent centralized rule. Local rulers had established their authority too securely in India's regions for Harsha to overcome them. Ultimately, he fell victim to an assassin and left no heir to maintain his realm. His empire immediately disintegrated, and local rulers once again turned northern India into a battleground as they sought to enlarge their realms at the expense of their neighbors.

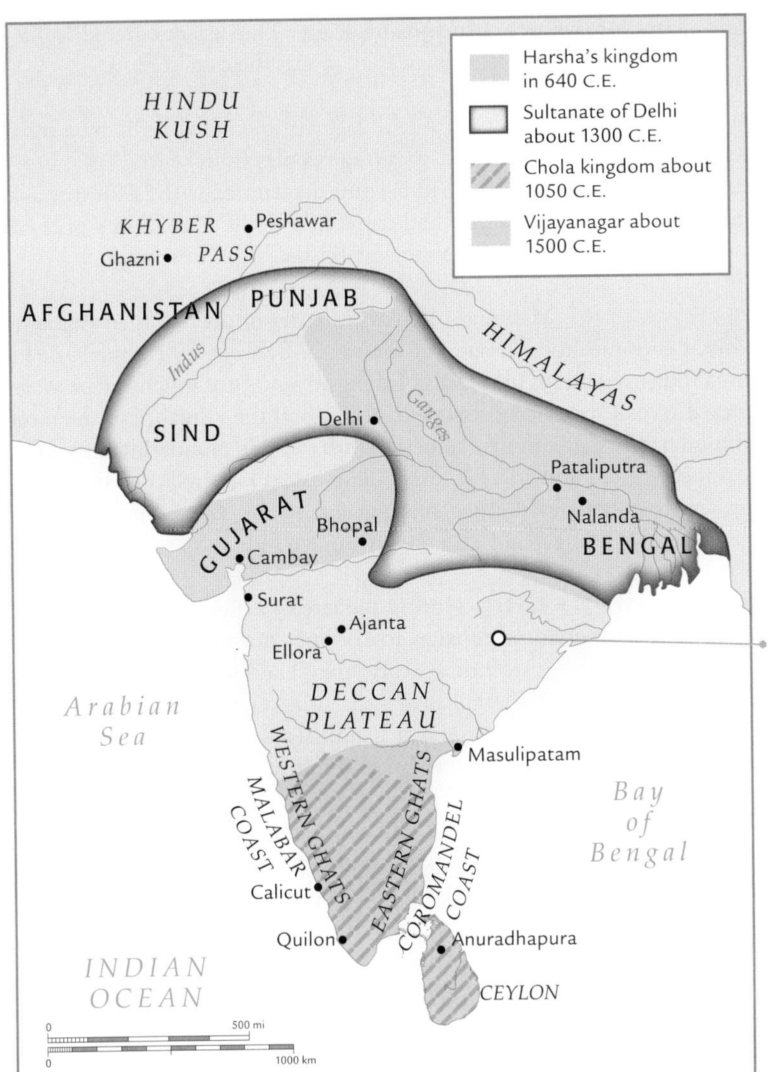

MAP 13.1 | Major states of postclassical India, 600–1600 C.E. Several large rivers and river valleys offered opportunities for inhabitants of northern India. ***How did peoples of southern India organize flourishing states and societies in the absence of major rivers?***

In the postclassical period, India was not dominated by one powerful state.

The Introduction of Islam to Northern India

THE CONQUEST OF SIND Amid nomadic incursions and contests for power, northern India also experienced the arrival of Islam and the establishment of Islamic states. Islam reached India by several routes. One was military: Arab forces entered India as early as the mid–seventh century, although their first expeditions were exploratory ventures rather than campaigns of conquest. In 711, however, a well-organized expedition conquered Sind, the Indus River valley in northwestern India, and incorporated it as a province of the expanding Umayyad empire. At midcentury, along with most of the rest of the *dar al-Islam,* Sind passed into the hands of the Abbasid caliphs. Although political elites eventually took advantage of their distance from the centers of Islamic power to reassert their control over most of Sind, the region remained nominally under the jurisdiction of the caliphs until the collapse of the Abbasid dynasty in 1258.

MERCHANTS AND ISLAM While conquerors brought Islam to Sind, Muslim merchants took their faith to coastal regions in both northern and southern India. Indeed, Muslims dominated trade and transportation networks between India and western lands from the seventh through the fifteenth century. Muslim merchants formed small communities in all the major cities of coastal India, where they played a prominent role in Indian business and commercial life. They frequently married local women, and in many cases they also found places for themselves in Indian society. Thus Islam entered India's port cities in a more gradual but no less effective way than was the case in Sind.

TURKISH MIGRANTS AND ISLAM Islam also entered India by a third route: the migrations and invasions of Turkish-speaking peoples from central Asia. During the tenth century, several Turkish groups had become acquainted with Islam through their dealings with the Abbasid caliphate and had converted to the faith. Some of these Muslim Turks moved into Afghanistan, where they established an Islamic state.

MAHMUD OF GHAZNI Mahmud of Ghazni, leader of the Turks in Afghanistan, soon turned his attention to the rich land to the south. Between 1001 and 1027 he mounted seventeen raiding expeditions into India. Taking advantage of infighting between local rulers, he annexed several states in northwestern India and the Punjab. For the most part, however, Mahmud had less interest in conquering India than in plundering the wealth stored in its many temples. Mahmud and his forces demolished hundreds of Hindu and Buddhist structures and frequently established mosques or Islamic shrines in their place. Not surprisingly, however, Mahmud's raids did not encourage Indians to turn to Islam.

THE SULTANATE OF DELHI During the late twelfth century, Mahmud's successors mounted a more systematic campaign to conquer northern India and place it under Islamic rule. By the early thirteenth century, they had conquered most of the Hindu kingdoms in northern India and established an Islamic state known as the sultanate of Delhi. The sultans established their capital at Delhi, a strategic site controlling access from the Punjab to the Ganges valley, and they ruled northern India at least in name for more than three centuries, from 1206 to 1526.

Medieval fortress from the sultanate of Delhi, 14th C.
www.mhhe.com/bentleybrief2e

During the fourteenth century the sultans of Delhi commanded an army of three hundred thousand, and their state ranked among the most powerful in the Islamic world. Yet for the most part, the authority of the sultans did not extend far beyond Delhi. They had no permanent bureaucracy or administrative apparatus. Even in their immediate domain, they imposed a thin veneer of Islamic political and military authority on a land populated mostly by Hindus, and they depended on the goodwill of Hindu kings to carry out their policies and advance their interests in local regions. They did not even enjoy comfortable control of their own court: of the thirty-five sultans of Delhi, nineteen were killed by assassins. Nevertheless, the sultans prominently sponsored Islam and helped to establish a secure place for their faith in the cultural landscape of India.

The Hindu Kingdoms of Southern India

Bronze statues from the Chola Dynasty
www.mhhe.com/bentleybrief2e

THE CHOLA KINGDOM Although it too remained politically divided, the southern part of the Indian subcontinent largely escaped the invasions, chronic war, and turmoil that troubled the north. Most Hindu rulers in the south presided over small, loosely administered states and did not engage in prolonged or frequent conflicts. Two kingdoms, however, were able to expand enough to exercise at least nominal rule over much of southern India. The first was the Chola kingdom, situated in the deep south, which ruled the Coromandel coast for more than four centuries, from 850 to 1267 C.E. At its high point, during the eleventh century, Chola forces conquered Ceylon and parts of southeast Asia, and its navy dominated the waters from the South China Sea to the Arabian Sea.

Chola rulers did not build a tightly centralized state: they allowed considerable autonomy for local and village institutions as long as they maintained order and delivered tax revenues on time. By the twelfth century, however, revolts reduced the size and power of the Chola state, and it reverted to the status of one regional kingdom among many others in southern India.

Mahmud of Ghazni (mah-muhd of gahz-nee)
Coromandel (kawr-uh-MAN-dul)

THE KINGDOM OF VIJAYANAGAR The second state that dominated much of southern India was the kingdom of Vijayanagar, based in the northern Deccan. The kingdom owed its origin to efforts by the sultans of Delhi to extend their authority to southern India. Officials in Delhi dispatched two brothers, Harihara and Bukka, to represent the sultan and implement court policies in the south. Although they had converted from their native Hinduism to Islam, Harihara and Bukka recognized an opportunity to establish themselves as independent rulers. In 1336 they renounced Islam and proclaimed the establishment of an independent empire of Vijayanagar (meaning "city of victory"). Indeed, the Hindu kingdom of Vijayanagar was the dominant state in southern India from the mid–fourteenth century until 1565, when it fell to Mughal conquerors from the north.

As in northern India, then, political division and conflict between states in southern India characterized its political history in postclassical times. India did not generate the sort of large-scale, centralized, imperial state that guided the fortunes of postclassical societies in the eastern Mediterranean, southwest Asia, or China. Nevertheless, on the basis of trade, common social structures, and inherited cultural traditions, a coherent and distinctive society flourished in postclassical India.

THINKING ABOUT *Traditions*

TRADITIONS IN INDIA AND THE INDIAN OCEAN BASIN. Although Indian societies experienced much economic, social, and religious change during the postclassical period, they nevertheless remained culturally unified by particular social traditions. What were the most important of these traditions, and in what ways did they promote cultural unity?

Production and Trade in the Indian Ocean Basin

As in the Mediterranean, southwest Asia, and China, agricultural yields increased significantly in postclassical India, enabling large numbers of people to devote themselves to trade and manufacturing rather than the production of food. Trade forged links between the various regions of the subcontinent and fostered economic development in southern India. Trade also created links between India and distant lands, as merchants and manufacturers transformed the Indian Ocean basin into a vast zone of communication and exchange. Yet even though the increasing prominence of trade and industry brought change to Indian society, caste identities and loyalties also remained strong, and the caste system continued to serve as the most powerful organizing feature of Indian society.

Vijayanagar (vih-juh-yuh-NUH-guhr)

ELEPHANT STABLES IN VIJAYANAGAR. | The kings of Vijayanagar endowed their capital with splendid buildings and even provided these handsome domed stables for their elephants. ***Why would the kings have invested so much in the construction of these stables?***

Agriculture in the Monsoon World

MONSOONS Because of the rhythms of the monsoons, irrigation was essential for the maintenance of a large, densely populated, agricultural society. During the spring and summer, warm, moisture-laden winds from the southwest bring most of India's rainfall. During the autumn and winter, cool and very dry winds blow from the northeast. To achieve their agricultural potential, Indian lands required a good watering by the southern monsoon, supplemented by irrigation during the dry months. Light rain during the spring and summer months or short supplies of water for irrigation commonly led to drought, reduced harvests, and widespread famine.

IRRIGATION SYSTEMS In northern India, large rivers and plentiful surface water provided abundant opportunities to build irrigation systems. Indeed, irrigation had been a fixture of the countryside in northern India since Harappan times. For the most part, however, southern India is an arid land without rivers that can serve as sources for large-scale irrigation. Thus, as southern India became more densely populated, irrigation systems became crucial. Dams, reservoirs, canals, wells, and tunnels appeared in large numbers. Particularly impressive were monumental reservoirs lined with brick or stone that captured the rains of the spring and summer months and held them until the dry season, when canals carried them to thirsty fields. Projects of this size required enormous investments of human energy, both for their original construction and for continuing maintenance, but they led to significant increases in agricultural productivity.

POPULATION GROWTH As a result of this increased productivity, India's population grew steadily throughout the postclassical era. In 600 C.E., shortly after the fall of the Gupta dynasty, the subcontinent's population stood at about 53 million. By 1000 it had grown 45 percent, to 79 million. During the following centuries the rate of growth slowed, but it took off again about 1500. By 1500, the population of the subcontinent had reached 105 million.

URBANIZATION This demographic surge encouraged the concentration of people in cities. During the fourteenth century, the high point of the sultanate of Delhi, the capital city had a population of about four hundred thousand, which made it second only to Cairo among Muslim cities. Many other cities—particularly ports and trading centers such as Cambay, Surat, Calicut, Quilon, and Masulipatam—had populations well over one hundred thousand.

Trade and the Economic Development of Southern India

Political fragmentation of the subcontinent did not prevent robust trade between the different states and regions of India. As the population grew, opportunities for specialized work became more numerous. Increased trade was a natural result of this process.

INTERNAL TRADE Most regions of the Indian subcontinent were self-sufficient in staple foods such as rice, wheat, barley, and millet. The case was different, however, with metals, salt, and specialized crops that grew well only in certain regions. Iron came mostly from the Ganges River valley near Bengal, copper mostly from the Deccan Plateau, salt

Surat (soo-RAHT)
Quilan (kee-yawn)
Masulipatam (mahsu-lih-pah-tahm)

TEMPLE AT ELLORA. During the eighth century C.E., workers carved a massive temple out of sheer rock at Ellora in central India. Temple communities like the one that grew up at Ellora controlled enormous resources in postclassical India. ***Why did these temple communities control so many resources?***

mostly from coastal regions, and pepper from southern India. These and other commodities sometimes traveled long distances to consumers in remote parts of the subcontinent.

Southern India and Ceylon benefited especially handsomely from this trade. As invasions and conflicts disrupted northern India, southern regions experienced rapid economic development. The Chola kingdom provided relative stability in the south, and Chola expansion in southeast Asia opened markets for Indian merchants and producers.

TEMPLES AND SOCIETY The Chola rulers allowed considerable autonomy to their subjects, and the towns and villages of southern India largely organized their own affairs. Public life revolved around Hindu temples, which organized agricultural activities, coordinated work on irrigation systems, and maintained reserves of surplus production for use in times of need. Temples often possessed large tracts of agricultural land, and they sometimes employed hundreds of people. To meet their financial obligations to employees, temple administrators collected a portion of the agricultural yield from lands subject to temple authority.

Temple at Mamallapuram
www.mhhe.com/bentleybrief2e

Administrators were also responsible for keeping order in their communities and delivering tax receipts to the Cholas and other political authorities. In addition, temple authorities served as bankers, made loans, and invested in commercial and business ventures. They also frequently cooperated with the leaders of merchant guilds in seeking commercial opportunities to exploit. Temples thus grew prosperous and became crucial to the economic health of southern India.

SOURCES FROM THE PAST

Cosmas Indicopleustes on Trade in Southern India

Cosmas Indicopleustes was a Christian monk from Egypt who lived during the sixth century C.E. and traveled widely throughout north Africa and southwest Asia. On one of his trips, he ventured as far as India and Ceylon, which he described at some length in a work titled The Christian Topography. *Cosmas's account clearly shows that sixth-century India and Ceylon played prominent roles in the larger economy of the Indian Ocean basin.*

Ceylon lies on the other side of the pepper country [southern India]. Around it are numerous small islands all having fresh water and coconut trees. They nearly all have deep water close up to their shores. . . . Ceylon is a great market for the people in those parts. The island also has a church of Persian Christians who have settled there, and a priest who is appointed from Persia, and a deacon and a complete ecclesiastical ritual. But the natives and their kings are heathens. . . .

Since the island of Ceylon is in a central position, it is much frequented by ships from all parts of India and from Persia and Ethiopia, and it likewise sends out many of its own. And from the remotest countries—I mean China and other trading places—it receives silk, aloes, cloves, sandalwood, and other products, and these again are passed on to markets on this side, such as Male [the western coast of southern India], where pepper grows, and to Calliana [a port city near modern Bombay], which exports copper and sesame logs and cloth for making dresses, for it also is a great place of business. And also to Sind [Gujarat], where musk and castor and spice are procured, and to Persia and the Homerite country [Anatolia], and to Adule [in Ethiopia]. And this island [Ceylon] receives imports from all these markets that we have mentioned and passes them on to the remoter ports, while at the same time exporting its own produce in both directions. . . .

The kings of various places in India keep elephants. . . . They may have six hundred each, or five hundred, some more, some fewer. Now the king of Ceylon gives a good price both for the elephants and for the horses that he has. The elephants he pays for by the cubit [a unit of measurement equivalent to about half a meter or twenty inches]. For the height is measured from the ground, and the price is reckoned at so many gold coins for each cubit—fifty [coins] it may be, or a hundred, or even more. Horses they bring to him from Persia, and he buys them, exempting the importers of them from paying custom duties. The kings of the Indian subcontinent tame their elephants, which are caught wild, and employ them in war.

■ Why did Ceylon become such an important location for Indian Ocean trade?

SOURCE: Cosmas Indicopleustes. *The Christian Topography of Cosmas, an Egyptian Monk.* Trans. by J. W. McCrindle. London: Hakluyt Society, 1897, pp. 364–72. (Translation slightly modified.)

Cross-Cultural Trade in the Indian Ocean Basin

Indian prosperity sprang partly from the productivity of Indian society, but it depended also on the vast wealth that circulated in the commercial world of the Indian Ocean basin. Trade in the Indian Ocean was not new in postclassical times: Indian merchants had already ventured to southeast Asia during the classical era, and they dealt regularly with mariners from the Roman empire who traveled to India in search of pepper. During the postclassical era, however, larger ships and improved commercial organization supported a dramatic surge in the volume and value of trade in the Indian Ocean basin.

As larger, more stable ships came into use, mariners increasingly entrusted their crafts and cargoes to the reasonably predictable monsoons and sailed directly across the Arabian Sea and the Bay of Bengal. In the age of sail, however, it was impossible to make a round trip across the entire Indian Ocean without spending months at distant ports waiting for the winds to change, so merchants usually conducted their trade in stages.

EMPORIA Because India stood in the middle of the Indian Ocean basin, it was a natural site for emporia and warehouses. Merchants coming from east Africa or Persia exchanged their cargoes at Cambay, Calicut, or Quilon for goods to take back west with the winter monsoon. Mariners from China or southeast Asia called at Indian ports and traded their cargoes for goods to ship east with the summer monsoon. Indeed, because of their central location, Indian ports became the principal clearinghouses of trade in the Indian Ocean basin, and they became remarkably cosmopolitan centers. Hindus, Buddhists, Muslims, Jews, and others who inhabited the Indian port cities did business with counterparts from all over the eastern hemisphere.

Particularly after the establishment of the Umayyad and Abbasid dynasties in southwest Asia and the Tang and Song dynasties in China, trade in the Indian Ocean surged. Generally, Arabs and Persians dominated the carrying trade between India and points west. During the Song dynasty, Chinese junks also ventured into the western Indian Ocean and called at ports as far away as east Africa. To the east, in the Bay of Bengal and the China seas, Malay and Chinese vessels were most prominent.

SPECIALIZED PRODUCTION As the volume of trade in the Indian Ocean basin increased, lands around the ocean began to engage in specialized production of commodities for the commercial market. Indian artisans, for example, built thriving local industries around the production of high-quality cotton textiles. These industries influenced the structure of the Indian economy: they created a demand for specific agricultural products, provided a livelihood for thousands of artisans, and enabled consumers to import goods from elsewhere in the Indian Ocean basin.

Other lands concentrated on the production of different manufactured goods and agricultural commodities: China produced silk, porcelain, and lacquerware; southeast Asian lands provided fine spices; incense, horses, and dates came from southwest Asia; and east Africa contributed gold, ivory, and slaves. Thus trade encouraged specialized production

Note India's central position in the Indian Ocean basin.

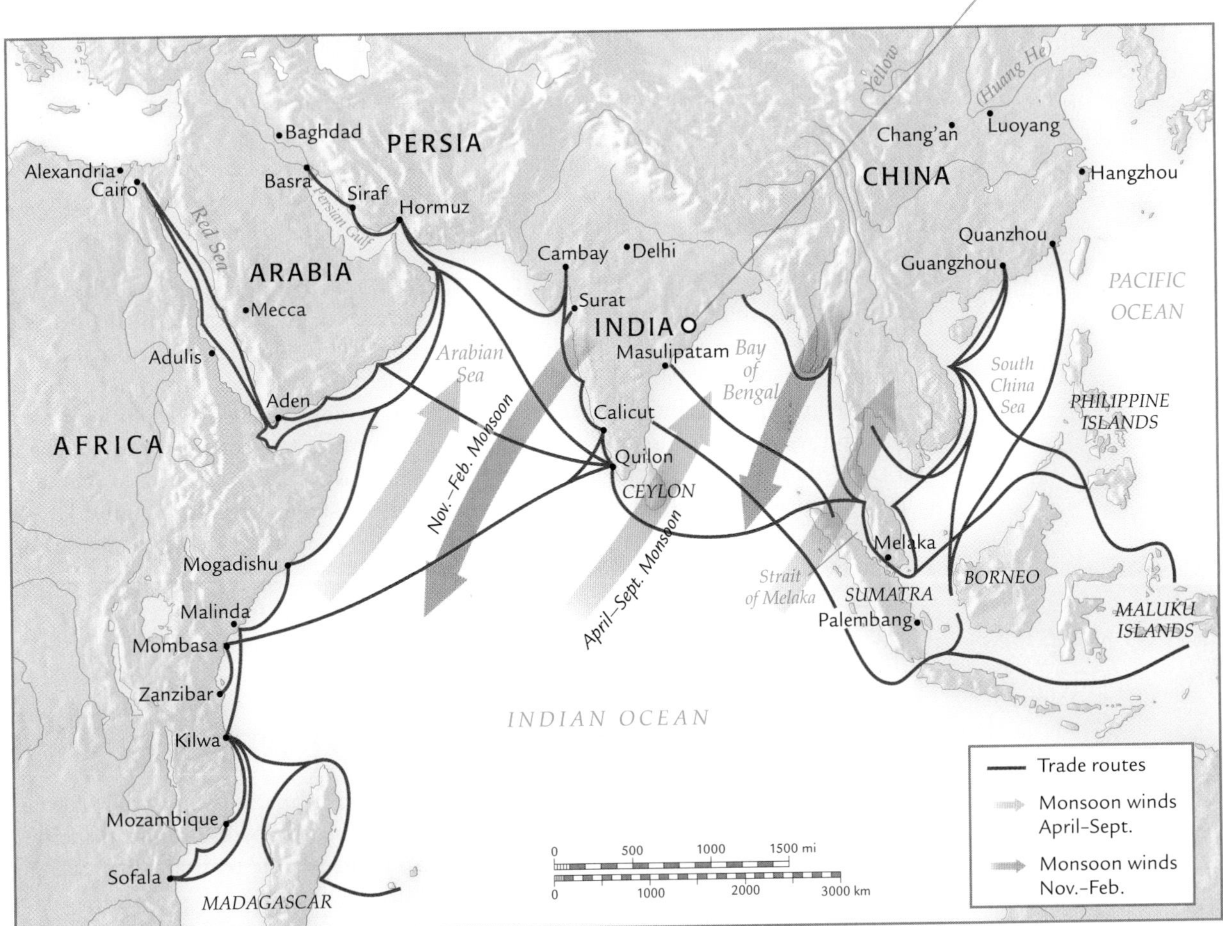

MAP 13.2 | The trading world of the Indian Ocean basin, 600–1600 C.E. Note the directions of seasonal winds in the Indian Ocean basin. ***How would mariners take advantage of these winds to reach their destinations?***

and economic development in all lands participating in the trade networks of the Indian Ocean: cross-cultural trade in postclassical times influenced the structure of economies and societies throughout much of the eastern hemisphere.

Caste and Society

The political, economic, and social changes of the postclassical era brought a series of challenges for India's caste system. Migrations, the growing prominence of Islam, economic development, and urbanization all placed pressures on the caste system as it had developed during the Vedic and classical eras. But the caste system has never been a rigid, unchanging structure. Rather, individuals and groups have continuously adjusted it and adapted it to new circumstances. Adjustments and adaptations of the postclassical era resulted in a caste system that was more complex than in earlier ages and that also extended its geographic reach deeper into southern India than ever before. In the absence of strong central governments, the caste system helped maintain order in local communities by providing guidance on individuals' roles in society and their relationships with others.

CASTE AND MIGRATION The caste system closely reflected changes in Indian society. It adapted to the arrival of migrants, for example, and helped to integrate them into Indian society. As Turkish peoples or Muslim merchants pursued opportunities in India, they gained recognition as distinct groups under the umbrella of the caste system. They established codes of conduct both for the regulation of behavior within their own groups and for guidance in dealing with members of other castes. Within a few generations their descendants had become absorbed into Indian society.

CASTE AND SOCIAL CHANGE The caste system also accommodated the social changes brought about by trade and economic development. Even before the postclassical era, individuals tended to identify most closely with their *jati* (subcastes), which were usually organized by occupation. In postclassical times, as merchants and manufacturers became increasingly important in the larger economy, they organized powerful workers' guilds to represent their interests. These guilds, however, were largely incorporated into the caste system as distinct *jati.* Thus merchants specializing in particular types of commerce, such as the silk, cotton, or spice trade, established themselves as subcastes, as did artisans working in particular industries, such as the iron, steel, or leather business.

EXPANSION OF THE CASTE SYSTEM Besides becoming more complex, the caste system also extended its geographic reach. Caste distinctions first became prominent in northern India following the Aryan migrations. During the postclassical era, the caste system became securely established in southern India as well. Economic development aided this process by encouraging commercial relationships between southern merchants and their caste-conscious counterparts in the north. The emergence of merchant and craft guilds in southern regions strengthened the caste system, since guild members usually organized as a subcaste. Powerful temples also fostered caste distinctions, largely because of the influence of caste-conscious brahmins who supervised temple activities. As a result, by about the eleventh century C.E., caste had become the principal basis of social organization in southern India.

THE MEETING OF HINDU AND ISLAMIC TRADITIONS

The Indian cultural landscape underwent a thorough transformation during the postclassical era. Jainism and Buddhism lost much of their popular following, although neither belief completely disappeared. In their place, Hindu and Islamic traditions increasingly dominated the cultural and religious life of India after 1000 C.E.

Hinduism and Islam differed profoundly. The Hindu pantheon made places for numerous gods and spirits, for example, whereas Islamic theology stood on the foundation of a firm and uncompromising monotheism. Yet both religions attracted large popular followings throughout the subcontinent, with Hinduism predominating in southern India and Islam in the north.

The Development of Hinduism

Toward the end of the first millennium C.E., Buddhism flourished in east Asia, central Asia, and parts of southeast Asia but came under great pressure in India. Like Mahayana Buddhism, both Hinduism and Islam promised salvation to devout individuals, and they gradually attracted Buddhists to their own communities. Invasions of India by Turkish peoples also hastened the decline of Buddhism because the invaders looted and destroyed Buddhist stupas and shrines. In 1196 Muslim forces overran the Buddhist schools in the city of Nalanda, torched the libraries, and killed or exiled thousands of monks. Buddhism soon became a minor faith in the land of its birth.

SHIVA. | Southern Indian artists often portrayed Shiva in bronze sculptures as a four-armed lord of dancers. In this figure from the Chola dynasty, Shiva crushes with his foot a dwarf demon symbolizing ignorance. One hand holds a bell to awaken his devotees, another bears the fire used by Shiva as creator and destroyer of the world, and a third gestures Shiva's benevolence toward his followers.

VISHNU AND SHIVA Hinduism benefited from the decline of Buddhism. One reason for the increasing popularity of Hinduism was the remarkable growth of devotional cults, particularly those dedicated to Vishnu and Shiva, two of the most important deities in the Hindu pantheon. Vishnu was the preserver of the world, a god who observed the universe from the heavens and who occasionally entered the world in human form to resist evil or communicate his teachings. In contrast, Shiva was both a god of fertility and a destructive deity: he brought life but also took it away when its season had passed.

DEVOTIONAL CULTS Hindus embraced the new cults warmly because they promised salvation. Devotional cults became especially popular in southern India, where individuals or family groups went to great lengths to honor their chosen deities. Often cults originated when individuals identified Vishnu or Shiva with a local spirit or deity associated with a particular region or a prominent geographic feature. By venerating images of Vishnu or Shiva, offering them food and drink, and meditating on the deities and their qualities, Hindus hoped to achieve a mystic union with the gods that would bring grace and salvation.

SHANKARA The significance of Hinduism extended well beyond popular religion: it also influenced philosophy. Just as Buddhism, Christianity, and Islam influenced moral thought and philosophy in other lands, devotional Hinduism guided the efforts of the most prominent philosophers in postclassical India. Brahmin philosophers such as Ramanuja took the Upanishads as a point of departure for subtle reasoning and sophisticated metaphysics. Ramanuja, a devotee of Vishnu who was active during the eleventh and early twelfth centuries C.E., believed that genuine bliss came from salvation and identification of individuals with their gods. He followed the *Bhagavad Gita* in recommending intense devotion to Vishnu, and he taught that by placing themselves in the hands of Vishnu, devotees would win the god's grace and live forever in his presence. Thus, Ramanuja's

Vishnu dreaming the universe
www.mhhe.com/bentleybrief2e

Buddhism (BOO-diz'm)
Vishnu (VIHSH-noo)
Shiva (SHIH-vuh)
Bhagavad Gita (BUHG-uh-vuhd gee-tah)

philosophy pointed toward a Hindu theology of salvation. Indeed, his thought inspired the development of devotional cults throughout India, and it serves even today as a philosophical foundation for Hindu popular religion.

Islam and Its Appeal

The Islamic faith did not attract much immediate interest among Indians when it arrived in the subcontinent. It won gradual acceptance in merchant communities where foreign Muslim traders took local spouses and found a place in Indian society. Elsewhere, however, circumstances did not favor its adoption, since it often arrived with conquering peoples. Muslim conquerors generally reserved important political and military positions for their Arab, Persian, and Turkish companions. Only rarely did they allow Indians—even those who had converted to Islam—to hold sensitive posts. Because of that policy, conquerors offered little incentive for Indians to convert to Islam.

CONVERSION TO ISLAM Gradually, however, many Indians converted to Islam. By 1500 C.E. Indian Muslims numbered perhaps twenty-five million—about one-quarter of the subcontinent's population. Some Indians adopted Islam in hopes of improving their positions in society: Hindus of lower castes, for example, hoped to escape discrimination by converting to a faith that recognized the equality of all believers. In fact, Hindus rarely improved their social standing by conversion. Often members of an entire caste or subcaste adopted Islam en masse, and after conversion they continued to play the same social and economic roles that they had before.

SUFIS In India as elsewhere, the most effective agents of conversion to Islam were Sufi mystics. Sufis encouraged a personal, emotional, devotional approach to Islam. They did not insist on fine points of doctrine, and they sometimes even permitted their followers to observe rituals or venerate spirits not recognized by the Islamic faith. Because of their piety and sincerity, however, Sufi missionaries attracted individuals searching for a faith that could provide comfort and meaning for their personal lives. Thus, like Hinduism, Indian Islam emphasized piety and devotion. Even though Hinduism and Islam were profoundly different religions, they encouraged the cultivation of similar spiritual values that transcended the social and cultural boundary lines of postclassical India.

THE BHAKTI MOVEMENT In some ways the gap between Hinduism and Islam narrowed in postclassical India because both religions drew on long-established and long-observed cultural traditions. Sufis, for example, often attracted schools of followers in the manner of Indian gurus, spiritual leaders who taught Hindu values to disciples who congregated around them. Even more important was the development of the *bhakti* movement, a cult of love and devotion that ultimately sought to erase the distinction between Hinduism and Islam. The bhakti movement emerged in southern India during the twelfth century, and it originally encouraged a traditional piety and devotion to Hindu values. As the movement spread to the north, bhakti leaders increasingly encountered Muslims and became deeply attracted to certain Islamic values, especially monotheism and the notion of spiritual equality of all believers. Eventually, the bhakti movement rejected the exclusive features of both Hinduism and Islam, and some believers taught that Shiva, Vishnu, and Allah were all manifestations of a single, universal deity. The bhakti movement did not succeed in harmonizing Hinduism and Islam. Nevertheless, like the Sufis, bhakti teachers promoted values that helped build bridges between India's social and cultural communities.

Sufis (SOO-fees)

bhakti (BHUK-tee)

The Influence of Indian Society in Southeast Asia

Just as China stood at the center of a larger east Asian society, India served as the principal source of political and cultural traditions widely observed throughout south and southeast Asia. For a millennium and more, southeast Asian peoples adapted Indian political structures and religions to local needs and interests. Although Indian armed forces rarely ventured into the region, southeast Asian lands reflected the influence of Indian society, as merchants introduced Hinduism, Buddhism, Sanskrit writings, and Indian forms of political organization. Beginning about the twelfth century, Islam also found solid footing in southeast Asia, as Muslim merchants, many of them Indians, established trading communities in the important port cities of the region. Over the next five hundred years, Islam attracted a sizable following and became a permanent feature in much of southeast Asia.

The States of Southeast Asia

INDIAN INFLUENCE IN SOUTHEAST ASIA Indian merchants visited the islands and mainland of southeast Asia from an early date, perhaps as early as 500 B.C.E. By the early centuries C.E., they had become familiar figures throughout southeast Asia, and their presence brought opportunities for the native ruling elites of the region. In exchange for spices and exotic products, Indian merchants brought textiles, beads, gold, silver, and manufactured metal goods. Southeast Asian rulers used the profits from this trade to consolidate their political control.

Meanwhile, southeast Asian ruling elites became acquainted with Indian political and cultural traditions. Without necessarily giving up their own traditions, they borrowed Indian forms of political organization and accepted Indian religious faiths. On the model of Indian states, for example, they adopted kingship as the principal form of political authority, and they surrounded themselves with courts featuring administrators and rituals similar to those found in India.

Ruling elites also sponsored the introduction of Hinduism or Buddhism—sometimes both—into their courts. They embraced Indian literature such as the *Ramayana* and the *Mahabharata,* which promoted Hindu values, as well as treatises that explained Buddhist views of the world. At the same time, however, they did not show much enthusiasm for the Indian caste system and continued to acknowledge the deities and nature spirits that southeast Asian peoples had venerated for centuries.

FUNAN The first state known to have incorporated Indian influence into its own traditions was Funan, which dominated the lower reaches of the Mekong River (including parts of modern Cambodia and Vietnam) between the first and the sixth centuries C.E. Funan grew enormously wealthy because it dominated the Isthmus of Kra, the narrow portion of the Malay peninsula where merchants transported trade goods between China and India. (The short portage enabled them to avoid a long voyage around the Malay peninsula.) The rulers of Funan used the profits from this trade to construct an elaborate irrigation system that supported a highly productive agricultural economy in the Mekong delta.

As trade with India became an increasingly important part of Funan's economy, the ruling classes adopted Indian political, cultural, and religious traditions. They took the Sanskrit term *raja* ("king") for themselves and claimed divine sanction for their rule in the manner of Hindu rulers in India. They established positions for administrators and bureaucrats such as those found at Indian courts and conducted official business in

Isthmus of Kra (ihs-muhs of krah)

THINKING ABOUT *Encounters*

ENCOUNTERS IN INDIA AND THE INDIAN OCEAN BASIN. During the postclassical period, Indian societies became critical players in the vast trading networks that crisscrossed the Indian Ocean basin. Why did these trading relationships encourage other societies, particularly in southeast Asia, to adopt Indian social, religious, and political structures? How did these adoptions shape the development of southeast Asian societies?

Khwaja Khidr. | In India as in other lands, Sufi mystics were the most effective Muslim missionaries. This eighteenth-century painting depicts the Sufi Khwaja Khidr, beloved in Muslim communities throughout northern India as one associated with springtime, fertility, and happiness.

Sanskrit. They introduced Indian ceremonies and rituals and worshiped Vishnu, Shiva, and other Hindu deities. They continued to honor local deities, but they eagerly welcomed Hinduism, which offered additional recognition and divine legitimacy for their rule. At first, Indian cultural and religious traditions were most prominent and most often observed at ruling courts. Over the longer term, however, those traditions extended well beyond ruling elites and won a secure place in southeast Asian society.

SRIVIJAYA During the sixth century C.E., a bitter power struggle weakened Funan internally, and by late century it had passed into oblivion. After the fall of Funan, political leadership in southeast Asia passed to the kingdom of Srivijaya (670–1025 C.E.) based on the island of Sumatra. The kings of Srivijaya built a powerful navy and controlled commerce in southeast Asian waters. They compelled port cities in southeast Asia to recognize their authority, and they financed their navy and bureaucracy from taxes levied on ships passing through the region. They maintained an all-sea trade route between China and India, eliminating the need for the portage of trade goods across the Isthmus of Kra. As the volume of trade with India increased in the postclassical era, the rulers of Srivijaya—like the rulers of Funan—borrowed heavily from Indian cultural traditions. Unlike their

raja (RAH-juh)
Srivijaya (sree-vih-JUH-yuh)

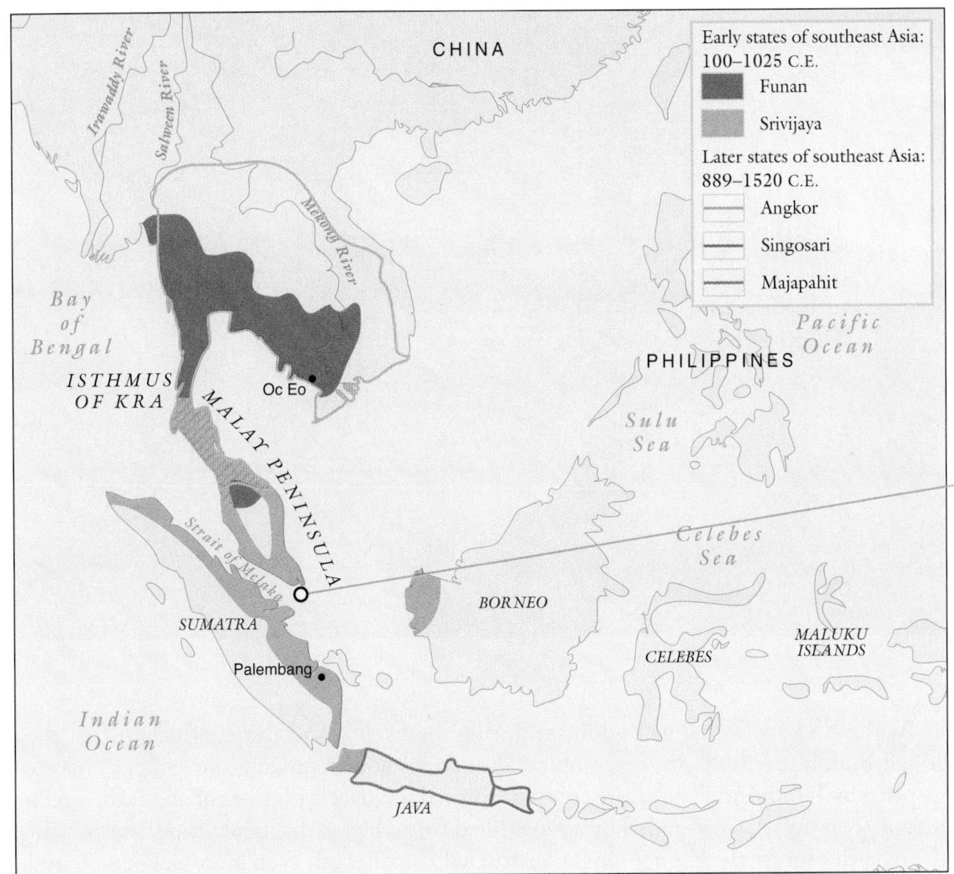

MAP 13.3 | Major states of southeast Asia between about 100 and 1520 C.E. Notice the strategic location of these southeast Asian states on the trade routes between China to the east and India to the west. ***How might this have affected the development of states in southeast Asia?***

Most postclassical southeast Asian states grew powerful as a result of their position between China and India.

counterparts in Funan, however, the rulers of Srivijaya were most attracted to the teachings and practices associated with Buddhism. The Srivijaya kingdom prospered on the fruits of the Indian Ocean trade until the expansive Chola kingdom of southern India eclipsed it in the eleventh century. In the process, Srivijaya played an important role in facilitating cultural exchange in the Indian Ocean world.

With the decline of Srivijaya, the kingdoms of Angkor (889–1431 C.E.), Singosari (1222–1292 C.E.), and Majapahit (1293–1520 C.E.) dominated affairs in southeast Asia. Whereas Angkor had its base in Cambodia, Singosari and Majapahit were island states based on Java. Angkor made deep commitments to Buddhism; Majapahit was largely a Hindu state. Singosari represented a unique blend of Indian and indigenous traditions. Indeed, at the court of Singosari, religious authorities fashioned a cultural blend of Hindu, Buddhist, and indigenous values. Sculptures at the Singosari court depicted Hindu and Buddhist personalities, for example, but used them to honor local deities and natural spirits rather than Indian deities.

ANGKOR The magnificent monuments of Angkor testify eloquently to the influence of Indian traditions in southeast Asia. Beginning in the ninth century, the kings of the Khmers began to build a capital city at Angkor Thom. With the aid of brahmin advisors from India, the kings designed the city as a microcosmic reflection of the Hindu world order. At the center, they built a temple representing the Himalayan Mount Meru, the sacred abode of Shiva, and surrounded it with numerous smaller temples representing other parts of the Hindu universe.

Angkor Wat
www.mhhe.com/bentleybrief2e

Angkor (AHN-kohr)
Singosari (sihng-oh-sah-ree)
Majapahit (mah-jah-PAH-hit)

Buddhist Temple Carving. | Maritime trade flourished in southeast Asia during postclassical times. This ninth-century relief carving from the Buddhist temple at Borobodur in Java depicts a typical southeast Asian ship.

As the Khmers turned to Buddhism during the twelfth and thirteenth centuries, they added Buddhist temples to the complex, though without removing the earlier structures inspired by Hinduism. The entire complex formed a square with sides of about three kilometers (two miles), surrounded by a moat filled from the nearby Tonle Sap River. During the twelfth century the Khmer kings constructed a smaller but even more elaborate temple center at Angkor Wat, about one kilometer (just over half a mile) from Angkor Thom.

The Khmers abandoned Angkor in 1431 after Thai peoples invaded the capital and left much of it in ruins. Soon the jungle reclaimed both Angkor Thom and Angkor Wat, which remained largely forgotten until French missionaries and explorers rediscovered the sites in the mid–nineteenth century. Today the temple complexes of Angkor stand as vivid reminders of the influence of Indian political, cultural, and religious traditions in southeast Asia.

The Arrival of Islam

Muslim merchants had ventured into southeast Asia by the eighth century, but only during the tenth century did they become prominent in the region. Some came from southern Arabia or Persia, but most were Indians from Gujarat or the port cities of southern India. Thus Indian influence helped to establish Islam as well as Hinduism and Buddhism in southeast Asia.

CONVERSION TO ISLAM For several centuries Islam maintained a quiet presence in southeast Asia. Small communities of foreign merchants observed their faith in the port cities of the region but attracted little interest on the part of the native inhabitants. Gradually, however, ruling elites, traders, and others who had regular dealings with foreign Muslims became interested in the faith.

Like Hinduism and Buddhism, Islam did not enter southeast Asia as an exclusive faith. Ruling elites who converted to Islam often continued to honor Hindu, Buddhist, or native southeast Asian traditions. They adopted Islam less as an absolute creed than as a faith that facilitated their dealings with foreign Muslims and provided additional divine sanction for their rule. Rarely did they push their subjects to convert to Islam, although they allowed Sufi mystics to preach their faith before popular audiences. As in India, Sufis in southeast Asia appealed to a large public because of their reputation for sincerity and holiness. They allowed converts to retain inherited customs while adapting the message of Islam to local needs and interests.

ANGKOR WAT. | General view of the temple complex dedicated to Vishnu at Angkor Wat in modern Cambodia.

MELAKA During the fifteenth century the spread of Islam gained momentum in southeast Asia, largely because the powerful state of Melaka sponsored the faith throughout the region. Founded during the late fourteenth century by Paramesvara, a rebellious prince from Sumatra, Melaka took advantage of its strategic location in the Strait of Melaka, near modern Singapore, and soon became prominent in the trading world of southeast Asia. By the mid–fifteenth century, Melaka had built a substantial navy that patrolled the waters of southeast Asia and protected the region's sea-lanes. Melakan fleets compelled ships to call at the port, where ruling authorities levied taxes on the value of their cargoes. Thus, like southeast Asian states of earlier centuries, Melaka became a powerful state through the control of maritime trade.

In one respect, though, Melaka differed significantly from the earlier states. Although it began as a Hindu state, Melaka soon became predominantly Islamic. About the mid–fifteenth century the Melakan ruling class converted to Islam. It welcomed theologians, Sufis, and other Islamic authorities to Melaka and sponsored missionary campaigns to spread Islam throughout southeast Asia. By the end of the fifteenth century, mosques had begun to define the urban landscapes of Java, Sumatra, and the Malay peninsula, and Islam had made its first appearance in the spice-bearing islands of Maluku and in the southern islands of the Philippine archipelago.

Thus, within several centuries of its arrival, Islam was a prominent feature in the cultural landscape of southeast Asia. Along with Hinduism and Buddhism, Islam helped link southeast Asian lands to the larger cultural world of India and to the larger commercial world of the Indian Ocean basin.

Melaka (may-LAHK-kah)

SUMMARY

With respect to political organization, India differed from postclassical societies in China, southwest Asia, and the eastern Mediterranean basin: it did not experience a return of centralized imperial rule such as that provided by the Tang and Song dynasties, the Umayyad and Abbasid dynasties, and the Byzantine empire. In other respects, however, India's development was similar to that of other postclassical societies. Increased agricultural production fueled population growth and urbanization, while trade encouraged specialized industrial production and rapid economic growth. The vigorous and voluminous commerce of the Indian Ocean basin influenced the structure of economies and societies from east Asia to east Africa. It brought prosperity especially to India, which not only contributed cotton, pepper, sugar, iron, steel, and other products to the larger hemispheric economy but also served as a major clearinghouse of trade. Like contemporary societies, postclassical India experienced cultural change, and Indian traditions deeply influenced the cultural development of other lands. Hinduism and Islam emerged as the two most popular religious faiths within the subcontinent, and Indian merchants helped to establish Hinduism, Buddhism, and Islam in southeast Asian lands. Throughout the postclassical era, India participated fully in the larger hemispheric zone of cross-cultural communication and exchange.

STUDY TERMS

Angkor (257)
Angkor Thom (257)
Angkor Wat (258)
bhakti movement (254)
Buddhism (253)
caste system (252)
Chola kingdom (246)
Funan (255)
Gupta dynasty (244)
irrigation systems (248)
jati (252)
King Harsha (244)
Mahmud of Ghazni (246)
Majapahit (257)
Melaka (259)
Ramanuja (253)
Shiva (253)
Singosari (257)
Srivijaya (256)
Sufis (254)
Sultanate of Delhi (246)
Vijayanagar Kingdom (247)
Vishnu (253)

FOR FURTHER READING

Aziz Ahmad. *Studies in Islamic Culture in the Indian Environment.* Oxford, 1964. A scholarly analysis of the arrival of Islam and its effects in India.

Buzurg ibn Shahriyar. *The Book of the Wonders of India: Mainland, Sea and Islands.* Trans. by G. S. P. Freeman-Grenville. London, 1981. Stories and tall tales of a tenth-century mariner who sailed frequently between Persia and India.

K. N. Chaudhuri. *Asia before Europe: Economy and Civilisation of the Indian Ocean from the Rise of Islam to 1750.* Cambridge, 1990. Controversial and penetrating analysis of economic, social, and cultural structures shaping societies of the Indian Ocean basin.

Ainslie T. Embree and Stephen Hay, eds. *Sources of Indian Tradition.* 2 vols. 2nd ed. New York, 1988. An important collection of primary sources in English translation.

Kenneth R. Hall. *Maritime Trade and State Development in Early Southeast Asia.* Honolulu, 1985. Examines the link between long-distance trade and state building in southeast Asia.

Charles Higham. *The Civilization of Angkor.* London, 2001. Draws usefully on recent archaeological research in placing Angkor in historical context.

S. M. Ikram. *Muslim Civilization in India.* Ed. by A. T. Embree. New York, 1964. Important survey of Islam and its impact in India.

Patricia Risso. *Merchants and Faith: Muslim Commerce and Culture in the Indian Ocean.* Boulder, 1995. Surveys the activities of Muslim merchants in the Indian Ocean basin from the seventh to the nineteenth century.

Burton Stein. *Vijayanagara.* Cambridge, 1989. A study of the southern Hindu kingdom concentrating on political and economic history.

Ramila Thapar. *Early India: From the Origins to A.D. 1300.* Berkeley, 2003. A fresh view by one of the leading scholars of early Indian history.

Bringing It All Together

Part III | The Postclassical Era, 500 to 1000 C.E.

After the collapse of classical societies in Persia, China, India, and the Mediterranean, societies in much of the eastern hemisphere were faced with the monumental tasks of restoring internal order as well as rebuilding networks of contact and exchange that had fallen into disuse. Although the ways societies accomplished these tasks varied, it is nevertheless clear that large portions of Eurasia and North Africa once again came under stable rule between 500 and 1000 C.E. As a consequence, during the postclassical era much of the eastern hemisphere both reintegrated and enhanced the trade networks that had once linked so many of the classical societies.

Religion played an important role in the maintenance of internal order in most postclassical societies, including the Byzantine Empire, the Islamic world, and India. Byzantine emperors claimed divine status within the Christian Orthodox church, dramatically enhancing their authority among their subjects. In the Islamic world, the new Muslim faith provided a common language, doctrine, culture, and legal system that served to unite diverse conquered peoples in a common community of believers. In India, the caste system central to Hinduism lent cultural unity to the subcontinent even though it was not ruled by a single power. Because the caste system determined the social role of both groups and individuals, it was a critical factor in maintaining a stable society.

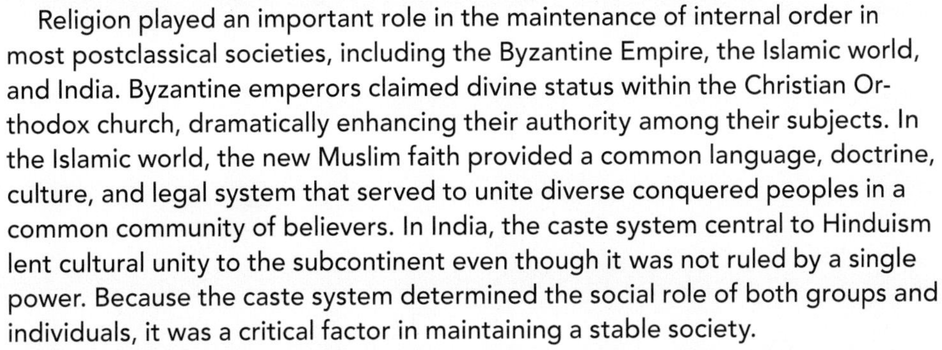

Once they had restored internal order, the postclassical societies reestablished and expanded the trade networks that had once linked the classical societies. This encouraged the exchange of goods, of course, but also encouraged the transfer of technologies and food items that allowed for improved agricultural practices and greater crop productivity—both of which led to population growth. As in the classical era, interaction triggered by trade was also accompanied by cultural interaction. The vast networks of roads and sealanes that linked postclassical societies became highways for the exchange of ideas and beliefs as well.

Of these myriad cultural interactions, the spread of religion—including Islam, Buddhism, Hinduism, and Christianity—was perhaps the most obvious and important. In fact, each of these religions spread far beyond their origins in the postclassical era. As a result of Indian Ocean trading networks, Indian merchants brought Hinduism to much of southeast Asia; Islamic traders from both India and Arabia later did the same with their faith. Meanwhile, Buddhists from India and central Asia brought their faith to China, where for a time it enjoyed immense popularity. Finally, Orthodox Christians in Byzantium introduced their faith to the peoples of eastern Europe, who adopted it as their own. As a result of these and other exchanges, the legacies of postclassical societies remain very much with us in the present day.

IV

An Age of Cross-Cultural Interaction, 1000 to 1500 C.E.

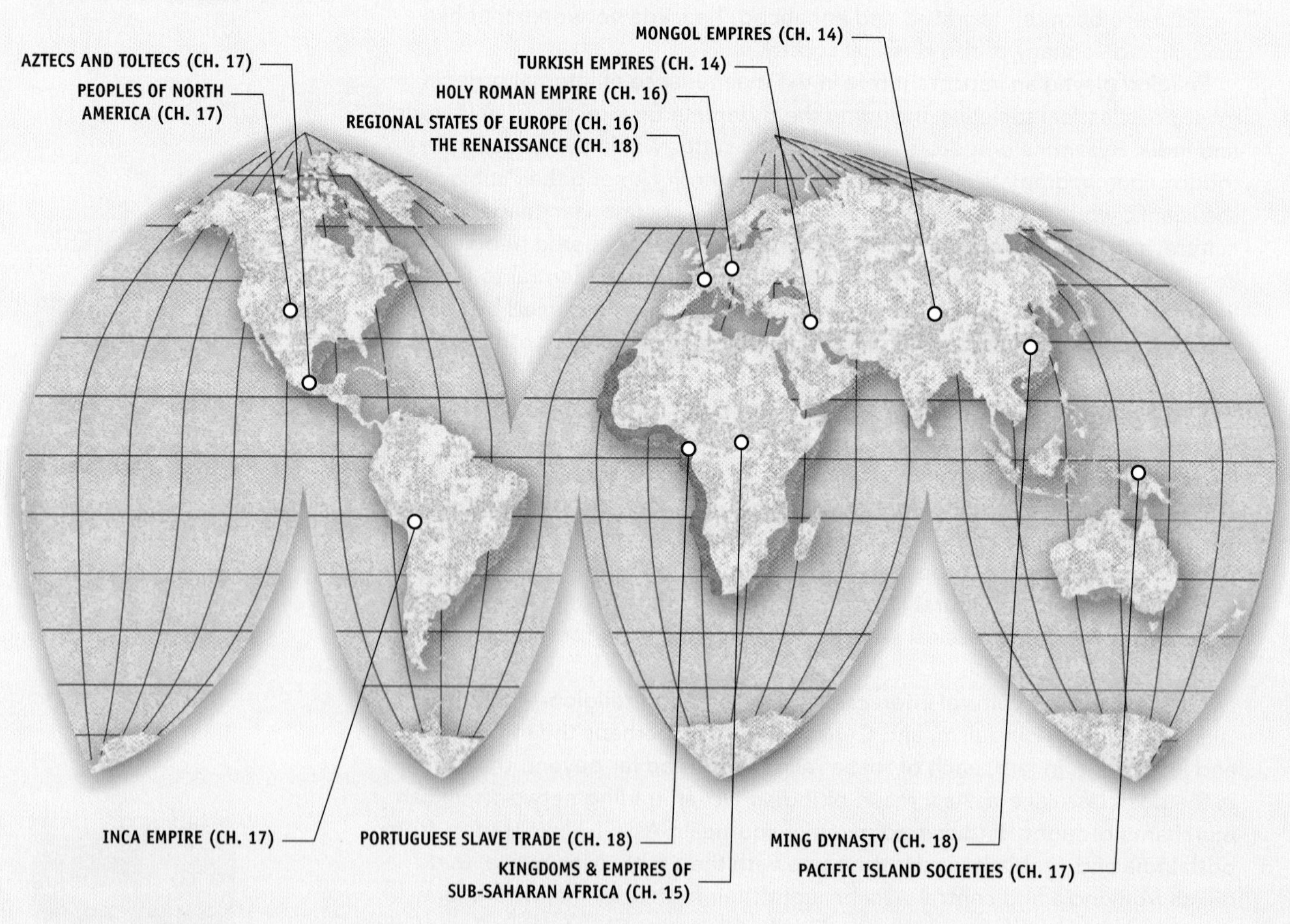

The half millennium from 1000 to 1500 C.E. differed markedly from earlier eras. During classical and postclassical times, large, regional societies situated in China, India, southwest Asia, and the Mediterranean basin dominated the eastern hemisphere. From 1000 to 1500 C.E., however, nomadic Turkish and Mongol peoples overran settled societies and established vast transregional empires from China to eastern Europe.

Nomadic peoples toppled several postclassical states, most notably the Song empire in China and the Abbasid realm in southwest Asia. By building empires that transcended the boundaries of postclassical states, however, nomadic Turks and Mongols laid a political foundation for sharply increased trade and communication between peoples of different societies and cultural regions.

Increased trade in the Indian Ocean basin also promoted more intense cross-cultural communications. Maritime trade built on the political stability, economic expansion, and demographic growth of the postclassical era. This trade indicated a movement toward economic integration as societies of the Indian Ocean basin concentrated increasingly on cultivating crops or producing goods for export while importing foods or goods that they could not produce very well themselves.

Demographic growth, economic expansion, and increased trade were not limited to the Indian Ocean basin, China, and southwest Asia in this period. Indeed, the intensification of trade across much of Eurasia also brought relatively isolated areas like sub-Saharan Africa and western Europe into sustained cross-cultural relationships with far distant places. These relationships brought increased prosperity to both regions, which in turn encouraged political centralization and the consolidation of state power.

The indigenous peoples of the Americas and Oceania also built larger and more centralized societies from 1000 to 1500 C.E., with centralized empires appearing in Mesoamerica and Andean South America and agricultural societies emerging in several regions of North America. Although Pacific islanders had limited resources with which to build empires, within their own agricultural and fishing societies they established tightly centralized kingdoms.

During the fourteenth and fifteenth centuries C.E., much of the eastern hemisphere experienced difficulties not only because of warfare arising from the conquests of nomadic peoples but also because of epidemic bubonic plague and global climatic changes that brought cooler temperatures. Together, these problems led to political, social, and economic turmoil throughout much of the eastern hemisphere.

Nevertheless, by the mid–fifteenth century, peoples from China to western Europe were recovering from those difficulties and rebuilding prosperous societies. In their own quest for prosperity, western European peoples unwittingly laid the foundations of a new era in world history. While searching for sea routes to Asian markets, European mariners happened on the continents of North and South America. Their voyages brought the world's various peoples for the first time into permanent and sustained communication, and their interactions triggered a series of consequences that profoundly influenced modern world history. Yet it is important to remember that the European voyages that gave rise to this interdependent and interconnected world occurred precisely because Europeans were seeking to become more involved in the vibrant trade networks that characterized much of the eastern hemisphere in the half-millennium after 1000 C.E.

Nomadic Empires and Eurasian Integration

14

Guillaume Boucher was a goldsmith who lived during the early and middle decades of the thirteenth century. During the 1230s, he left his native Paris and went to Budapest, which was then a part of the kingdom of Hungary. There he was captured by Mongol warriors campaigning in Hungary. The Mongols noticed and appreciated Boucher's talents, and when they left Hungary in 1242, they took him and other skilled captives to their central Asian homeland.

For at least the next fifteen years, Boucher lived at the Mongol capital at Karakorum. Though technically a slave, he enjoyed some prestige. He supervised fifty assistants in a workshop that produced decorative objects of gold and silver for the Mongol court. His most ingenious creation was a spectacular silver fountain in the form of a tree. Four pipes, concealed by the tree's trunk, carried wines and other intoxicating drinks to the top of the tree and then dispensed them into silver bowls from which guests filled their cups. Apart from his famous fountain, Boucher also produced statues in gold and silver, built carriages, designed buildings, and even sewed ritual garments for Roman Catholic priests who conducted services for Christians living at Karakorum.

Boucher was by no means the only European living at the Mongol court. His wife was a woman of French ancestry whom Boucher had met and married in Hungary. The Flemish missionary William of Rubruck visited Karakorum in 1254, and during his sojourn there he encountered men and women from France, Russia, Greece, and England. Other European visitors to the Mongol court found Germans, Slavs, and Hungarians as well as Chinese, Koreans, Turks, Persians, and Armenians, among others. Many thirteenth-century roads led to Karakorum.

Nomadic peoples had made their influence felt throughout much of Eurasia as early as classical times. The Xiongnu confederation dominated central Asia and threatened the Han dynasty in China from the third to the first century B.C.E. During the second and third centuries C.E., the Huns and other nomadic peoples from central Asia launched migrations that helped bring down the western Roman empire, and later migrations of the White Huns destroyed the Gupta state in India. Turkish peoples ruled a large central Asian empire from the sixth through the ninth century, and the Uighur Turks even seized the capital cities of the Tang dynasty in the mid–seventh century.

Between the eleventh and fifteenth centuries, nomadic peoples became more prominent than ever before in Eurasian

❮ Chabi, a Nestorian Christian and the favorite wife of Khubilai Khan, wearing the distinctive headgear reserved for Mongol women of the ruling class.

Karakorum (kahr-uh-KOR-uhm)

CHRONOLOGY

1055	Tughril Beg named sultan
1071	Battle of Manzikert
1206–1227	Reign of Chinggis Khan
1211–1234	Mongol conquest of northern China
1219–1221	Mongol conquest of Persia
1237–1241	Mongol conquest of Russia
1258	Mongol capture of Baghdad
1264–1279	Mongol conquest of southern China
1264–1294	Reign of Khubilai Khan
1279–1368	Yuan dynasty
1295	Conversion of Ilkhan Ghazan to Islam
1336–1405	Life of Tamerlane
1453	Ottoman capture of Constantinople

affairs. Turkish peoples migrated to Persia, Anatolia, and India, where they established new states. During the thirteenth and fourteenth centuries, the Mongols established themselves as the most powerful people of the central Asian steppes and then turned on settled societies in China, Persia, Russia, and eastern Europe. By the early fourteenth century, the Mongols had built the largest empire the world has ever seen, stretching from Korea and China in the east to Russia and Hungary in the west.

Most of the Mongol states collapsed during the late fourteenth and fifteenth centuries, but the decline of the Mongols did not signal the end of nomadic peoples' influence on Eurasian affairs. Although a native Chinese dynasty replaced the Mongol state in China, the Mongols continued to threaten its central Asian frontier. Moreover, from the fourteenth through the seventeenth century, Turkish peoples embarked on new campaigns of expansion that eventually brought most of India, much of central Asia, all of Anatolia, and a good portion of eastern Europe under their domination.

The military campaigns of nomadic peoples were sometimes exceedingly destructive. Nomadic warriors demolished cities, slaughtered urban populations, and ravaged surrounding agricultural lands. Yet those same forces also encouraged systematic peaceful interaction between peoples of different societies. Between the eleventh and fifteenth centuries, the imperial campaigns of Turkish and Mongol peoples forged closer links than ever before between Eurasian lands. By fostering cross-cultural communication and exchange on an unprecedented scale, the nomadic empires integrated the lives of peoples throughout much of the eastern hemisphere.

TURKISH MIGRATIONS AND IMPERIAL EXPANSION

Turkish peoples never formed a single, homogeneous group but, rather, organized themselves into clans and tribes that often fought bitterly with one another. All Turkish peoples spoke related languages, and all were nomads or descendants of nomads. From modest beginnings they expanded their influence until they dominated not only the steppes of central Asia but also settled societies in Persia, Anatolia, and India.

Nomadic Economy and Society

Nomadic societies in central Asia developed by adapting to the ecological conditions of arid lands. Central Asia does not receive enough rain to support large-scale agriculture. Oases permit cultivation of limited regions, but for the most part only grasses and shrubs grow on the central Asian steppe lands, and there are no large rivers or other sources of water to support large-scale irrigation systems. Yet grazing animals thrive on grasses and shrubs, and the peoples of central Asia took advantage of this by herding sheep, horses, cattle, goats, and camels.

NOMADIC PEOPLES AND THEIR ANIMALS Nomadic peoples drove their herds and flocks to lands with abundant grass and then moved them along as the animals thinned the vegetation. They carefully followed migratory cycles that took account of the seasons and local climatic

NOMADIC LIFE. | A painting from the late fourteenth century by the central Asian artist Mehmed Siyah Qalem suggests the physical hardships of nomadic life. In this scene from a nomadic camp, two men wash clothes (upper left), while another blows on a fire, and a companion tends to a saddle. Bows, arrows, and other weapons are readily available (top right).

conditions and lived mostly off the meat, milk, and hides of their animals. They used animal bones for tools and animal dung as fuel. They made shoes and clothes out of wool from their sheep and skins from their other animals. Their dwellings—large tents called *yurts*—were fashioned with felt made from the wool of their sheep. They even prepared an alcoholic drink from their animals by fermenting mare's milk into a potent concoction known as *kumiss.*

NOMADIC AND SETTLED PEOPLES The aridity of the climate and the nomadic lifestyle limited the development of human societies in central Asia. Intensive agriculture was impossible except in oases, and the need to regularly follow the herds made large-scale craft production impractical. As a result, nomads avidly sought opportunities to trade with settled peoples. Much of that commerce took place on a small scale as nomads sought agricultural products and manufactured goods to satisfy their immediate needs. Often, however, nomads also participated in long-distance trade networks. Because of their mobility and their familiarity with large regions of central Asia, nomadic peoples were ideally suited to organize and lead the caravans that crossed central Asia and linked settled societies from China to the Mediterranean basin. During the postclassical era and later, Turkish peoples were especially prominent on the caravan routes of central Asia.

NOMADIC SOCIETY Nomadic society generated two social classes: nobles and commoners. Charismatic leaders won recognition as nobles and thereby acquired the prestige needed to organize clans and tribes into alliances. Normally, nobles did little governing, since clans and tribes looked after their own affairs and resented interference. During times of war, however, nobles wielded absolute authority over the forces within their alliances.

yurts (yuhrts)

The nobility was a fluid class. Leaders passed noble status along to their heirs, but the heirs could lose their status if they did not continue to provide appropriate leadership for their clans and tribes. Over the course of a few generations, nobles could return to the status of commoners. Meanwhile, commoners could win recognition as nobles by outstanding conduct, particularly by courageous behavior during war. Then, if they were clever diplomats, they could arrange alliances between clans and tribes and gain enough support to displace established leaders.

NOMADIC RELIGION The earliest religion of the Turkish peoples revolved around shamans—religious specialists who possessed supernatural powers, communicated with the gods and nature spirits, and invoked divine aid on behalf of their communities. Yet many Turkish peoples became attracted to the religious and cultural traditions they encountered when trading with peoples of settled societies, and by the sixth century C.E. many Turks had converted to Buddhism, Nestorian Christianity, or Manichaeism. Partly because of their newly adopted religious traditions and partly because of their prominence in Eurasian trade networks, Turkish peoples also developed a written script.

TURKISH CONVERSION TO ISLAM Between the tenth and the fourteenth centuries, most Turkish clans on the steppes of central Asia converted to Islam. Their conversion had great significance. When Turkish peoples began to migrate into settled societies in large numbers, they helped spread Islam to new lands, particularly Anatolia and northern India. The boundaries of the Islamic world thus expanded along with the political and military influence of Turkish peoples.

MILITARY ORGANIZATION This expansion took place when nomadic leaders organized vast confederations of peoples under the leadership of a *khan* ("ruler"). In fact, khans rarely ruled directly, instead ruling through the leaders of allied tribes. Yet when organized on a large scale, nomadic peoples wielded enormous military power due mostly to their outstanding cavalry forces. Nomadic warriors had superior equestrian skills. Their arrows flew with deadly accuracy even when launched from the backs of galloping horses. Moreover, units of warriors coordinated their movements to outmaneuver and overwhelm their opponents. Indeed, few armies were able to resist the mobility and discipline of well-organized nomadic warriors. With such military capabilities, several groups of Turkish nomads began in the tenth century C.E. to seize the wealth of settled societies and build imperial states in the regions surrounding central Asia.

Turkish Empires in Persia, Anatolia, and India

SALJUQ TURKS AND THE ABBASID EMPIRE Turkish peoples entered Persia, Anatolia, and India at different times and for different purposes. They approached Abbasid Persia much as Germanic peoples had earlier approached the Roman empire. From about the mid–eighth to the mid–tenth century, Turkish peoples lived mostly on the borders of the Abbasid realm. By the mid– to late tenth century, large numbers of Saljuq Turks served in Abbasid armies and lived in the Abbasid realm itself. By the mid–eleventh century the Saljuqs overshadowed the Abbasid caliphs so much that in 1055 the caliph recognized the Saljuq leader Tughril Beg as *sultan* ("chieftain"). Tughril first consolidated his hold on the Abbasid capital at Baghdad, then he and his successors extended Turkish rule to Syria, Palestine, and other parts of the realm. For the last two

Nestorian (neh-STOHR-eeuhn)
Manichaeism (MAN-ih-kee-ism)
Abbasid (ah-BAH-sih)
Saljuqs (sahl-JYOOKS)

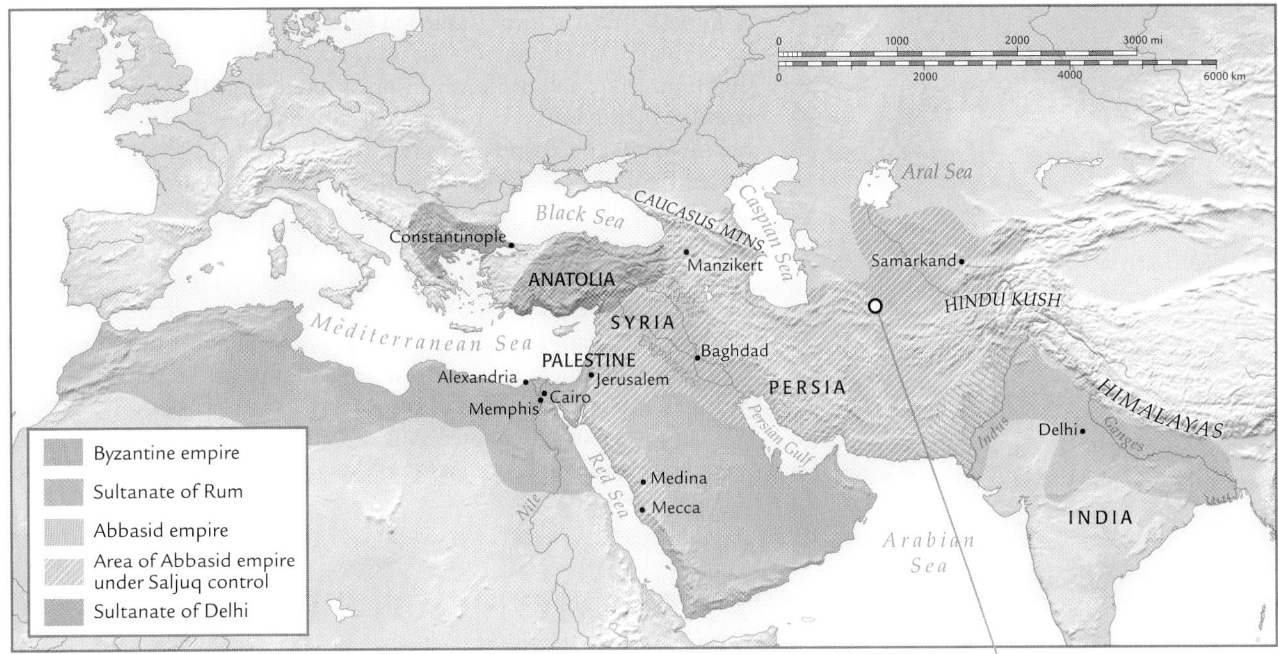

MAP 14.1 | Turkish empires and their neighbors, ca. 1210 C.E. After about 1000 C.E., nomadic Turkish peoples conquered and ruled settled agricultural societies in several regions of Eurasia and north Africa. ***How were Turkish peoples able to venture so far from their central Asian homeland?***

centuries of the Abbasid state, the caliphs served only as figureheads: actual governance lay in the hands of the Turkish sultans.

SALJUQ TURKS AND THE BYZANTINE EMPIRE Some Saljuq Turks began to turn their attention to the rich land of Anatolia, and in the early eleventh century they began migrating there in large numbers. In 1071 Saljuq forces inflicted a devastating defeat on the Byzantine army at Manzikert in eastern Anatolia and took the Byzantine emperor captive. Following that victory Saljuqs and other Turkish groups entered Anatolia almost at will. The peasants of Anatolia, who mostly resented their Byzantine overlords, tended to look on the Saljuqs as liberators rather than as conquerors.

The migrants thoroughly transformed Anatolia. Turkish groups displaced Byzantine authorities and set up their own political and social institutions. They levied taxes on the Byzantine church, restricted its activities, and sometimes confiscated church property. Meanwhile, they welcomed converts to Islam and made political, social, and economic opportunities available to them. By 1453, when Ottoman Turks captured the Byzantine capital at Constantinople, Byzantine and Christian Anatolia had become largely a Turkish and Islamic land.

GHAZNAVID TURKS AND THE SULTANATE OF DELHI While the Saljuqs spearheaded Turkish migrations in Abbasid Persia and Byzantine Anatolia, in the early eleventh century Mahmud of Ghazni led the Turkish Ghaznavids of Afghanistan in raids on lucrative sites in northern India. Although their original goal was plunder, they gradually became more interested in permanent rule. They asserted their authority first over the Punjab and then over Gujarat and Bengal. By the thirteenth century the Turkish sultanate of Delhi claimed authority over all of northern India. Several of the Delhi sultans conceived plans to conquer southern India, but none was able to realize those ambitions. Indeed, the sultans faced constant challenges from Hindu princes in neighboring lands, and they periodically had to defend their northern frontiers from new Turkish or Mongol invaders. They maintained an enormous army with a large elephant corps, but those forces only enabled them to hold on to territories they already had.

THINKING ABOUT *Traditions*

TRADITIONS IN NOMADIC EMPIRES AND EURASIAN INTEGRATION. The nomadic peoples of central Asia developed particular social and cultural traditions—such as superior equestrian skills and merit-based leadership—in accordance with the ecological conditions of their arid homelands. In what ways did these traditions aid nomadic peoples in their various quests for expansion between 1000 and 1500 C.E.?

Turkish rule had great social and cultural implications in India, as it did in Anatolia. Mahmud of Ghazni was a zealous foe of Buddhism and Hinduism alike, and his forces stripped Buddhist and Hindu establishments of their wealth, destroyed their buildings, and often slaughtered their residents and attendants as well. As Mahmud of Ghazni's forces repressed Buddhism and Hinduism, they encouraged conversion to Islam and enabled their faith to establish a secure presence in northern India.

Though undertaken by different groups and for different reasons, the Turkish conquests of Persia, Anatolia, and India represented part of a larger expansive movement by nomadic peoples. In all three cases the formidable military prowess of Turkish peoples enabled them to dominate settled societies. By the thirteenth century, the influence of nomadic peoples was greater than ever before in Eurasian history. Yet the Turkish conquests represented only a prelude to an astonishing round of empire building launched by the Mongols during the thirteenth and fourteenth centuries.

THE MONGOL EMPIRES

For most of history the nomadic Mongols lived on the high steppe lands of eastern central Asia. Like other nomadic peoples, they displayed deep loyalty to kin groups organized into families, clans, and tribes. They frequently allied with Turkish peoples who built empires on the steppes, but they rarely played a leading role in the organization of states before the thirteenth century. Strong loyalties to kinship groups made it difficult for the Mongols to organize a stable society on a large scale. During the early thirteenth century, however, Chinggis Khan (sometimes spelled "Genghis Khan") forged the various Mongol tribes into a powerful alliance that built the largest empire the world has ever seen. Although the vast Mongol realm soon dissolved into a series of smaller empires—most of which disappeared within a century—the Mongols' imperial venture brought the societies of Eurasia into closer contact than ever before.

Chinggis Khan and the Making of the Mongol Empire

The unifier of the Mongols was Temüjin, born about 1167 into a noble family. His father was a prominent warrior who forged an alliance between several Mongol clans and seemed likely to become a powerful leader. When Temüjin was about ten years old, however, rivals poisoned his father and destroyed the alliance. Abandoned by his father's allies, Temüjin led a precarious existence for some years. He lived in poverty, since rivals seized the family's animals, and several times eluded enemies seeking to eliminate him. A rival once captured him and imprisoned him in a wooden cage, but Temüjin made a daring midnight escape and regained his freedom.

CHINGGIS KHAN'S RISE TO POWER During the late twelfth century, Temüjin made an alliance with a prominent Mongol clan leader. He also mastered the art of steppe diplomacy, which called for displays of personal courage in battle, combined with intense loyalty to allies, a willingness to betray others to improve one's position, and the ability to entice other tribes into cooperative relationships. Temüjin gradually strengthened his position, sometimes by forging useful alliances, often by conquering rival contenders for power, and occasionally by turning suddenly against a troublesome

Chinggis Khan (CHIHN-gihs Kahn)
Temüjin (TEM-oo-chin)

ally. He eventually brought all the Mongol tribes into a single confederation, and in 1206 an assembly of Mongol leaders recognized Temüjin's supremacy by proclaiming him Chinggis Khan ("universal ruler").

CHINGGIS KHAN. | This painting by a Chinese artist depicts Chinggis Khan at about age sixty. Though most of his conquests were behind him, Chinggis Khan's focus and determination are readily apparent in this portrait.

MONGOL POLITICAL ORGANIZATION Chinggis Khan's policies greatly strengthened the Mongol people. Earlier nomadic state builders had ruled largely through the leaders of allied tribes. But Chinggis Khan mistrusted the Mongols' tribal organization, so he broke up the tribes and forced men of fighting age to join new military units with no tribal affiliations. He chose high military and political officials not on the basis of kinship or tribal status but because of their talents or their loyalty to him. Although he spent most of his life on horseback, Chinggis Khan also established a capital at Karakorum—present-day Har Horin, located about 300 kilometers (186 miles) west of the modern Mongolian capital of Ulaanbaatar—where he built a luxurious palace. As command center of Chinggis Khan's empire, Karakorum symbolized a source of Mongol authority superior to the clan or tribe. Chinggis Khan's policies created a Mongol state that was not only much stronger than any earlier nomadic confederation but also less troubled by conflicts between clans and tribes.

The most important institution of the Mongol state was the army, which magnified the power of the small population. In the thirteenth century the Mongol population stood at about one million people—less than 1 percent of China's numbers. During Chinggis Khan's life, his army numbered only 100,000 to 125,000 Mongols, although allied peoples also contributed forces. How was it possible for so few people to conquer the better part of Eurasia?

MONGOL ARMS Like earlier nomadic armies, Mongol forces relied on outstanding equestrian skills. In addition, their bows were short enough for archers to use while riding, and their arrows could fell enemies at 200 meters (656 feet). Mongol horsemen were among the most mobile forces of the premodern world, sometimes traveling more than 100 kilometers (62 miles) per day to surprise an enemy. Furthermore, the Mongols understood the psychological dimensions of warfare and used them to their advantage. If enemies surrendered without resistance, the Mongols usually spared their lives, and they provided generous treatment for artisans, crafts workers, and those with military skills. In the event of resistance, however, the Mongols ruthlessly slaughtered whole populations, sparing only a few, whom they sometimes drove before their armies as human shields during future conflicts.

The Palace of Great Khan
www.mhhe.com/
bentleybrief2e

Once he had united the Mongols, Chinggis Khan turned his army and his attention to other parts of central Asia, particularly to nearby settled societies. He attacked the various Turkish peoples ruling in Tibet, northern China, Persia, and the central Asian steppes. Those conquests were important because they protected him against the possibility that other nomadic leaders might challenge his rule. But the Mongol campaigns in China and Persia had especially far-reaching consequences.

MONGOL CONQUEST OF NORTHERN CHINA Chinggis Khan himself extended Mongol rule to northern China, dominated since 1127 C.E. by the nomadic Jurchen people, while the Song dynasty continued to rule in southern China. In 1211 C.E. Mongol raiding parties invaded the Jurchen realm, and by 1215 the Mongols

The Mongol empires
www.mhhe.com/
bentleybrief2e

Ulaanbaatar (OOLAHN-bah-tahr)
Jurchen (JUHR-chehn)
Song (SOHNG)

CHINGGIS KHAN AT WAR. | A Persian manuscript illustration depicts Chinggis Khan and his cavalry in hot pursuit of retreating forces.

History of the Mongols
www.mhhe.com/bentleybrief2e

had captured the capital near modern Beijing. This city, under the new name of Khanbaliq ("city of the khan"), also served as the Mongol capital in China. By 1220 the Mongols had largely established control over northern China.

MONGOL CONQUEST OF PERSIA Next, Chinggis Khan led another force to Afghanistan and Persia, ruled at that time by a successor to the Saljuqs known as the Khwarazm shah. The mission was one of revenge, for in 1218 the Khwarazm shah had spurned a diplomatic envoy sent by Chinggis Khan by murdering the whole group. In response, the following year Chinggis Khan took his army west, pursued the Khwarazm shah to an island in the Caspian Sea (where he died), shattered his army, and seized control of his realm.

To ensure that the shah's state would never constitute a challenge to his own empire, Chinggis Khan wreaked destruction on the conquered land. The Mongols ravaged one city after another, demolishing buildings and massacring hundreds of thousands of people. Some cities never recovered. The Mongols also destroyed the delicate *qanat* irrigation systems that sustained agriculture in the arid region, resulting in severely reduced agricultural production. For centuries after the Mongol conquest, Persian chroniclers cursed the invaders and the devastation they visited on the land.

By the time of his death in 1227, Chinggis Khan had laid the foundation of a vast and mighty empire. He had united the Mongols, established Mongol supremacy in central Asia, and extended Mongol control to northern China in the east and Persia in the west. But Chinggis Khan was a conqueror, not an administrator. He ruled the Mongols themselves through his control over the army, but he did not establish a central government for the lands that he conquered. Instead, he assigned Mongol overlords to supervise local administrators and to extract a generous tribute for the Mongols' own uses. Chinggis Khan's heirs continued his conquests, but they also undertook the task of designing a more permanent administration to guide the fortunes of the Mongol empire.

The Mongol Empires after Chinggis Khan

Chinggis Khan and his sons
www.mhhe.com/bentleybrief2e

Chinggis Khan's death touched off a struggle for power among his sons and grandsons. Eventually, his heirs divided Chinggis Khan's vast realm into four regional empires. The great khans ruled China, the wealthiest of Mongol lands. Descendants of Chaghatai, one of Chinggis Khan's sons, ruled the khanate of Chaghatai in central Asia. Persia fell under the authority of rulers known as the ilkhans, and the khans of the Golden Horde dominated Russia. The great khans were nominally superior to the others, but they were rarely able to enforce their claims to authority. In fact, for as long as the Mongol empires survived, ambition fueled constant tension and occasional conflict among the four khans.

KHUBILAI KHAN The consolidation of Mongol rule in China came during the reign of Khubilai (sometimes spelled Qubilai), one of Chinggis Khan's grandsons. Khubilai was perhaps the most talented of the great conqueror's descendants. He unleashed ruthless attacks against his enemies, but he also took an interest in cultural matters and worked to improve the welfare of his subjects. He actively promoted Buddhism, and he provided support also for Daoists, Muslims, and Christians in his realm. The famous Venetian traveler Marco Polo, who lived almost two decades at Khubilai's court, praised him for his generosity toward the poor and his efforts to build roads. From 1264 until his death in 1294, Khubilai Khan presided over the Mongol empire at its height.

Khubilai (KOO-bih-lie)
Buddhism (BOO-diz'm)

SOURCES FROM THE PAST

Marco Polo on Mongol Military Tactics

The Venetian Marco Polo traveled extensively through central Asia and China in the late thirteenth century, when Mongol empires dominated Asia. His book of travel writings is an especially valuable source of information about the Mongol age. Among other things, he described the Mongol way of making war.

Their arms are bows and arrows, sword and mace; but above all the bow, for they are capital archers, indeed the best that are known. . . .

When a Mongol prince goes forth to war, he takes with him, say, 100,000 men. Well, he appoints an officer to every ten men, one to every hundred, one to every thousand, and one to every ten thousand, so that his own orders have to be given to ten persons only, and each of these ten persons has to pass the orders only to another ten, and so on, no one having to give orders to more than ten. And every one in turn is responsible only to the officer immediately over him; and the discipline and order that comes of this method is marvellous, for they are a people very obedient to their chiefs. . . .

When they are going on a distant expedition they take no gear with them except two leather bottles for milk, a little earthenware pot to cook their meat in, and a little tent to shelter them from rain. And in case of great urgency they will ride ten days on end without lighting a fire or taking a meal. On such an occasion they will sustain themselves on the blood of their horses, opening a vein and letting the blood jet into their mouths, drinking till they have had enough, and then staunching it. . . .

When they come to an engagement with the enemy, they will gain the victory in this fashion. They never let themselves get into a regular medley, but keep perpetually riding round and shooting into the enemy. And as they do not count it any shame to run away in battle, they will sometimes pretend to do so, and in running away they turn in the saddle and shoot hard and strong at the foe, and in this way make great havoc. Their horses are trained so perfectly that they will double hither and thither, just like a dog, in a way that is quite astonishing. Thus they fight to as good purpose in running away as if they stood and faced the enemy because of the vast volleys of arrows that they shoot in this way, turning round upon their pursuers, who are fancying that they have won the battle. But when the Mongols see that they have killed and wounded a good many horses and men, they wheel round bodily and return to the charge in perfect order and with loud cries, and in a very short time the enemy are routed. In truth they are stout and valiant soldiers, and inured to war. And you perceive that it is just when the enemy sees them run, and imagines that he has gained the battle, that he has in reality lost it, for the Mongols wheel round in a moment when they judge the right time has come. And after this fashion they have won many a fight.

■ **In what ways do the military practices described by Marco Polo reflect the influence of the steppe environment on the Mongols?**

SOURCE: Marco Polo. *The Book of Ser Marco Polo,* 3rd ed. Trans. and ed. by Henry Yule and Henri Cordier. London: John Murray, 1921, pp. 260–63. (Translation slightly modified.)

MONGOL CONQUEST OF SOUTHERN CHINA Khubilai extended Mongol rule to all of China. From his base at Khanbaliq, he relentlessly attacked the Song dynasty in southern China. The Song capital at Hangzhou fell to Mongol forces in 1276, and within three years Khubilai had eliminated resistance throughout China. In 1279 he proclaimed himself emperor and established the Yuan dynasty, which ruled China until its collapse in 1368.

Beyond China, Khubilai had little success as a conqueror. During the 1270s and 1280s, he launched several unsuccessful invasions of Vietnam, Cambodia, and Burma as well as a failed naval expedition against Java involving 500 to 1,000 ships and twenty thousand troops. In 1274 and again in 1281, Khubilai also attempted seaborne invasions of Japan, but on both occasions typhoons thwarted his plans. The storm of 1281 was especially vicious:

Khanbaliq (Kahn-bah-LEEK)
Yuan (yoo-AHN)

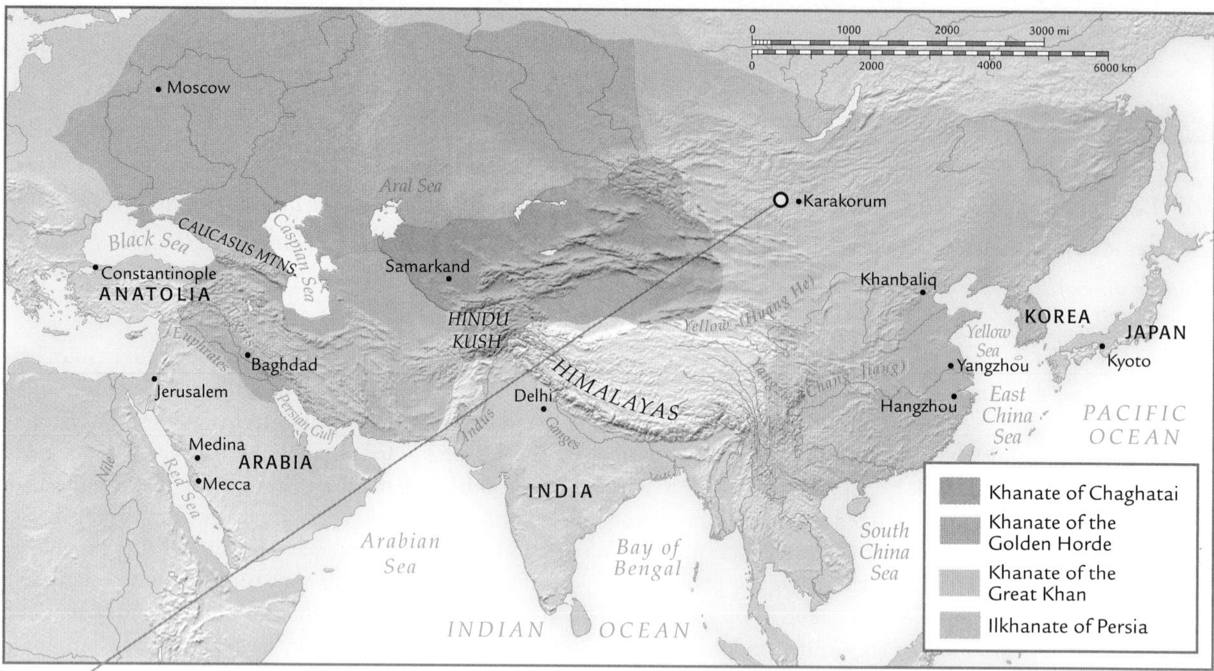

The Mongol capital under Chinggis Khan

MAP 14.2 | The Mongol empires, ca. 1300 C.E. The Mongol empires stretched from Manchuria and China to Russia and eastern Europe. ***In what ways did Mongol empires and Mongol policies facilitate trade, travel, and communication throughout Eurasia?***

it destroyed about 4,500 Mongol vessels carrying more than one hundred thousand armed troops—the largest seaborne expedition before World War II.

THE GOLDEN HORDE As Khubilai consolidated his hold on east Asia, his cousins and brothers tightened Mongol control on lands to the west. Mongols of the group known as the Golden Horde overran Russia between 1237 and 1241 and then mounted exploratory expeditions into Poland, Hungary, and eastern Germany in 1241 and 1242. Mongols of the Golden Horde prized the steppes north of the Black Sea as prime pastureland for their horses, and they used them to maintain a large army. They did not occupy Russia, which they regarded as an unattractive land of forests, but they extracted tribute from the Russian cities and agricultural provinces. The Golden Horde maintained its hegemony in Russia until the mid–fifteenth century, when the princes of Moscow built a powerful Russian state. By the mid–sixteenth century Russian conquerors had extended their control to the steppes, but Mongol khans descended from the Golden Horde continued to rule the Crimea until the late eighteenth century.

THE ILKHANATE OF PERSIA While the Golden Horde established its authority in Russia, Khubilai's brother Hülegü toppled the Abbasid empire and established the Mongol ilkhanate in Persia. In 1258 he captured the Abbasid capital of Baghdad after a brief siege. His troops looted the city, executed the caliph, and massacred more than two hundred thousand residents. From Persia, Hülegü's army ventured into Syria, but Muslim forces from Egypt soon expelled them and placed a limit on Mongol expansion to the southwest.

When the Mongols crushed ruling regimes in large settled societies, they discovered that they needed to become governors as well as conquerors. The Mongols had no experience administering complex societies, where successful governance required talents

Hülegü (Hoo-LAY-goo)
ilkhanate (EEL-kahn-ate)

The siege of Baghdad. A Persian manuscript illustration depicts Mongol forces camped outside the city walls while residents huddle within. Note that the Mongols killed about 200,000 residents once the city fell.

beyond the equestrian and military skills esteemed on the steppes. They had a difficult time adjusting to their role as administrators, and in fact most of their conquests fell out of their hands within a century.

MONGOL RULE IN PERSIA The Mongols adopted different tactics in the different lands they ruled. In Persia they made important concessions to local interests. Although Mongols and their allies occupied the highest administrative positions, they basically allowed the Persians to run the ilkhanate as long as they delivered tax receipts and maintained order.

Over time, the Mongols even assimilated to Persian cultural traditions. The early Mongol rulers of Persia mostly observed their native shamanism, but they tolerated all religions—including Islam, Nestorian Christianity, Buddhism, and Judaism. Gradually, however, the Mongols gravitated toward Islam. In 1295 Ilkhan Ghazan publicly converted to Islam, and most of the Mongols in Persia followed his example. Ghazan's conversion sparked large-scale massacres of Christians and Jews, and it signaled the absorption of the Mongols into Muslim Persian society.

MONGOL RULE IN CHINA In China, in contrast, the Mongol overlords stood aloof from their subjects, whom they scorned as mere cultivators. They outlawed intermarriage between Mongols and Chinese and forbade the Chinese to learn the Mongol language. Some of the victors went so far as to suggest that the Mongols exterminate the Chinese people and convert China itself into pastureland for their horses. In the end, the Mongols decided simply to extract as much revenue as possible from their Chinese subjects. Unlike their counterparts in Persia, the Mongols in China did not make much use of native administrative talent. Instead, they brought foreign administrators—including Arabs, Persians, and even Europeans—into China and placed them in charge.

The Mongols also resisted assimilation to Chinese cultural traditions. They ended the privileges enjoyed by the Confucian scholars, and they dismantled the Confucian educational and examination system, which had produced generations of civil servants for the Chinese bureaucracy. They did not persecute Confucians, but they allowed the Confucian

shamanism (SHAH-mah-niz'm)

tradition to wither in the absence of official support. Meanwhile, although the Mongols mostly continued to follow their native shamanist cults, they tolerated all cultural and religious traditions in China, including Confucianism, Daoism, Buddhism, and Christianity. Of Khubilai Khan's four wives, his favorite was Chabi, a Nestorian Christian.

The Mongols and Eurasian Integration

In building their vast empire, the Mongols brought tremendous destruction to lands throughout much of the Eurasian landmass. Yet they also sponsored interaction among peoples of different societies and linked Eurasian lands more directly than ever before. Indeed, Mongol rulers positively encouraged travel and communication over long distances. Recognizing the value of regular communications for their vast empire, Chinggis Khan and his successors maintained a courier network that rapidly relayed news, information, and government orders. The network included relay stations with fresh horses and riders so that messages could travel almost nonstop throughout Mongol territories. The Mongols' encouragement of travel and communication facilitated trade, diplomatic travel, missionary efforts, and movements of peoples to new lands.

THE MONGOLS AND TRADE As a nomadic people dependent on commerce with settled agricultural societies, the Mongols worked to secure trade routes and ensure the safety of merchants passing through their territories. The Mongol khans frequently fought among themselves, but they maintained reasonably good order within their realms and allowed merchants to travel unmolested through their empires. As a result, long-distance travel and trade became much less risky than in earlier times. Merchants increased their commercial investments, and the volume of long-distance trade across central Asia dwarfed that of earlier eras. Lands as distant as China and western Europe became directly linked for the first time because of the ability of individuals to travel across the entire Eurasian landmass.

PSI doc Letter from John Montecorvino www.mhhe.com/bentleybrief2e

DIPLOMATIC MISSIONS Like trade, diplomatic communication was essential to the Mongols, and their protection of roads and travelers benefited ambassadors as well as merchants. Throughout the Mongol era the great khans in China, the ilkhans in Persia, and the other khans maintained close communications by means of diplomatic embassies. They also had diplomatic dealings with rulers in Korea, Vietnam, India, and western Europe, and in other lands as well. Some diplomatic travelers crossed the entire Eurasian landmass. Several European ambassadors traveled to Mongolia and China to deliver messages from authorities seeking to ally with the Mongols against Muslim states in southwest Asia. Diplomats also traveled west: Rabban Sauma, a Nestorian Christian monk born in Khanbaliq, visited Italy and France as a representative of the Persian ilkhan.

MISSIONARY EFFORTS Like the silk roads in earlier times, Eurasian routes during the era of the Mongol empires served as highways for missionaries as well as merchants and diplomats. Sufi missionaries helped popularize Islam among Turkish peoples in central Asia, and Nestorian Christians found new opportunities to win converts when they went to China to serve as administrators for Mongol rulers. Roman Catholic Christians also mounted missionary campaigns in China. (See chapter 18 for further discussion of travel during the Mongol era.)

RESETTLEMENT Another Mongol policy that encouraged Eurasian integration was the practice of resettling peoples in new lands. As a nomadic people, the Mongols had limited numbers of skilled artisans and educated individuals, but the more their empire expanded, the more they needed the services of specialized crafts workers and literate administrators. Mongol overlords recruited the talent they needed largely from the ranks

---

Daoism (DOW-iz'm)

of their allies and the peoples they conquered, and they often moved people far from their homelands to sites where they could best make use of their services. Among the most important of the Mongols' allies were the Uighur Turks, who lived mostly in oasis cities along the silk roads. The Uighurs were literate and often highly educated, and they provided not only many of the clerks, secretaries, and administrators who ran the Mongol empires but also units of soldiers who bolstered Mongol garrisons. Arab and Persian Muslims were also prominent among those who administered the Mongols' affairs far from their homelands.

Conquered peoples also supplied the Mongols with talent. When they overcame a city, Mongol forces surveyed the captured population, separated out those with specialized skills, and sent them where there was demand for their services. After the 1230s the Mongols often took censuses of lands they conquered, partly to levy taxes and conscript military forces and partly to locate talented individuals. The Parisian goldsmith Guillaume Boucher was only one among thousands of foreign-born individuals who became permanent residents of the Mongol capital at Karakorum because of their special talents. Like their protection of trade and diplomacy, the Mongols' policy of resettling allies and conquered peoples promoted Eurasian integration by increasing communication and exchange between peoples of different societies.

ENCOUNTERS IN NOMADIC EMPIRES AND EURASIAN INTEGRATION. In the thirteenth and fourteenth centuries, the Mongols conquered vast portions of the Eurasian landmass, creating the largest empire in history. Why, despite the extreme violence of Mongol conquest in many areas, did Mongol rule lead to greater cultural interaction among the peoples of Eurasia than ever before?

Decline of the Mongols in Persia and China

COLLAPSE OF THE ILKHANATE Soon after the long and prosperous reign of Khubilai Khan, the Mongols encountered serious difficulties governing Persia and China. In Persia excessive spending strained the treasury, and overexploitation of the peasantry led to reduced revenues. When the ilkhan tried to resolve his financial difficulties by ordering the use of paper money in the 1290s, merchants refused to accept paper they regarded as worthless. Commerce ground to a halt until the ilkhan rescinded his order. Meanwhile, factional struggles plagued the Mongol leadership. When the last of the Mongol rulers died without an heir in 1335, the ilkhanate itself simply collapsed. Government in Persia devolved to local levels until late in the fourteenth century, when Turkish peoples reintroduced effective central government.

DECLINE OF THE YUAN DYNASTY Mongol decline in China was a more complicated affair. As in Persia, it had an economic dimension. The Mongols continued to use the paper money that the Chinese had introduced during the Tang and Song dynasties, but they did not maintain adequate reserves of the bullion that backed up paper notes. The general population soon lost confidence in paper money, and its value plummeted. As in Persia, too, factions and infighting hastened Mongol decline in China. Beginning in the 1320s power struggles, imperial assassinations, and civil war convulsed the Mongol regime in China.

BUBONIC PLAGUE Apart from financial difficulties and factional divisions, the Mongol rulers of China also faced an onslaught of epidemic disease. By facilitating trade and communications throughout Eurasia, the Mongols unwittingly expedited the spread of bubonic plague (discussed in chapter 18). During the 1330s plague erupted in southwestern China. From there it spread throughout China and central Asia, and by the late 1340s it had reached southwest Asia and Europe, where it became known as the Black Death. Bubonic plague sometimes killed half or more of an exposed population, particularly during the furious initial years of the epidemic, and it seriously disrupted economies

Uighurs (WEE-goors)

and societies throughout much of Eurasia. In China depopulation and labor shortages that followed on the heels of epidemic plague weakened the Mongol regime.

Because they treated their Chinese subjects as inferiors, the Mongols also faced a rebellious subject population in China. Beginning in the 1340s southern China became a hotbed of peasant rebellion and banditry, which the Mongols could not control. In 1368 rebel forces captured Khanbaliq, and the Mongols departed China en masse and returned to the steppes.

SURVIVING MONGOL KHANATES Despite the collapse of the Mongol regimes in Persia and China, Mongol states did not completely disappear. The khanate of Chaghatai continued to prevail in central Asia, and Mongols posed a threat to the northwestern borders of China until the eighteenth century. Meanwhile, the khanate of the Golden Horde continued to dominate the Caucasus and the steppe lands north of the Black Sea and Caspian Sea until the mid–sixteenth century, when a resurgent Russian state brought the Golden Horde down. Like Mongols in China, however, Mongols in Russia continued to threaten until the eighteenth century, and Mongols who had settled in the Crimean peninsula retained their identity until Josef Stalin forcibly moved them to other parts of the Soviet Union in the mid–twentieth century.

After the Mongols

By no means did the decline of the Mongols signal the end of nomadic peoples' influence in Eurasia. As Mongol strength waned, Turkish peoples resumed the expansive campaigns that the Mongols had interrupted. During the late fourteenth and early fifteenth centuries, the Turkish conqueror Tamerlane built a central Asian empire rivaling that of Chinggis Khan himself. Although Tamerlane's empire foundered soon after his death, it deeply influenced three surviving Turkish Muslim states—the Mughal empire in India, the Safavid empire in Persia, and the Ottoman empire based in Anatolia—and embraced much of southwest Asia, southeastern Europe, and north Africa.

TAMERLANE'S TOMB. Spoils from Tamerlane's campaigns and raids enriched the conqueror's capital at Samarkand. They financed, among other buildings, the magnificent tomb where Tamerlane's remains still rest.

Tamerlane the Whirlwind

THE LAME CONQUEROR The rapid collapse of the Mongol states left gaping power vacuums in China and Persia. While the native Ming dynasty filled the vacuum in China, a self-made Turkish conqueror named Timur moved on Persia. Because he walked with a limp, contemporaries referred to him as Timur-i lang—"Timur the Lame," an appellation that made its way into English as Tamerlane.

Born about 1336 near Samarkand, Tamerlane took Chinggis Khan as his model. Like Chinggis Khan, Tamerlane came from a family of the minor nobility and had to make his own way to power. Also like Chinggis Khan, he was a charismatic leader and a courageous warrior, and he attracted a band of loyal followers. During the 1360s he eliminated rivals to power, either by persuading them to join him as allies or by defeating their armies on the battlefield, and he won recognition as leader of his own tribe. By 1370

Timur-i lang (tee-MOOR-yee LAHNG)

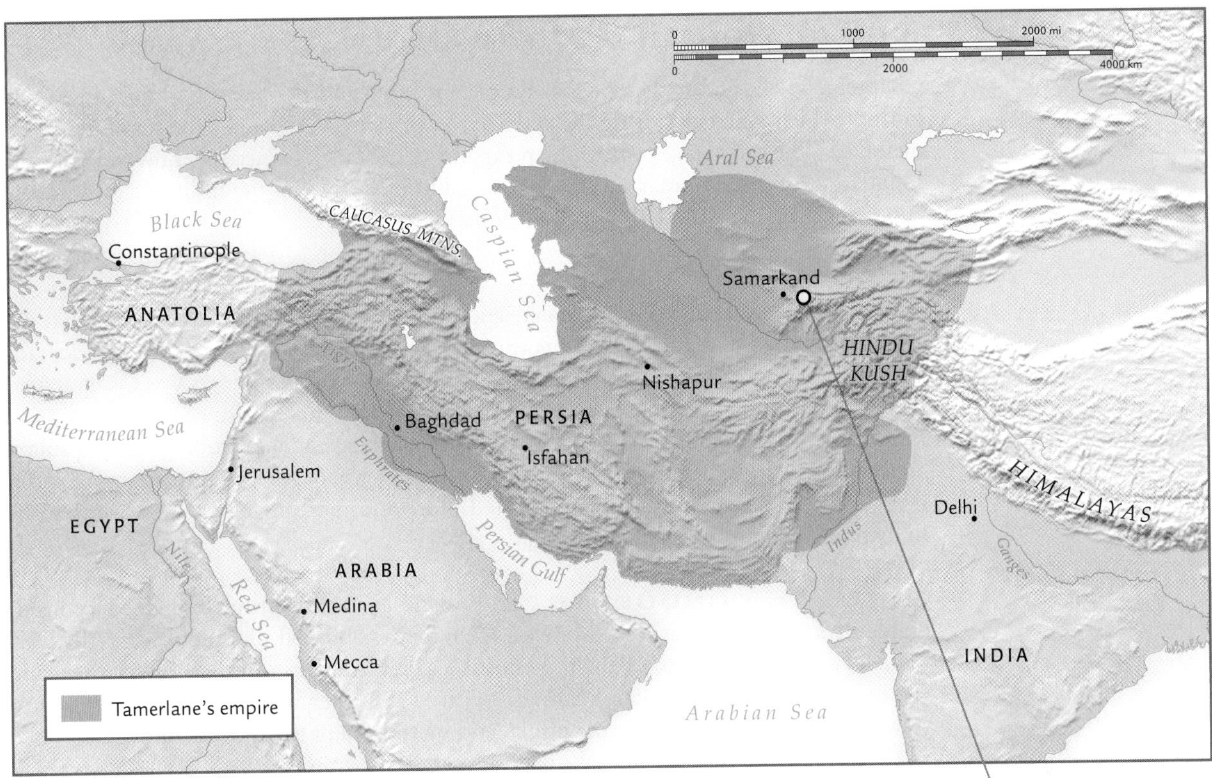

MAP 14.3 | Tamerlane's empire, ca. 1405 C.E. Notice the similarity between Tamerlane's empire and the ilkhanate of Persia shown on Map 14.2. ***To what extent do you think the cities and the administrative infrastructure of the region facilitated Tamerlane's efforts to control his empire?***

Samarkand was the capital of Tamerlane's empire.

Tamerlane the Conqueror
www.mhhe.com/bentleybrief2e

he had extended his authority throughout the khanate of Chaghatai and had begun to build a magnificent imperial capital in Samarkand.

For the rest of his life, Tamerlane led his armies on campaigns of conquest. He turned first to the region between Persia and Afghanistan, and he took special care to establish his authority in the rich cities so that he could levy taxes on trade and agricultural production. Next he attacked the Golden Horde in the Caucasus region and Russia, and by the mid-1390s he had severely weakened it. During the last years of the century, he invaded India and subjected Delhi to a ferocious sack. Later Tamerlane campaigned along the Ganges, although he never attempted to incorporate India into his empire. He opened the new century with campaigns in southwest Asia and Anatolia. In 1404 he began preparations for an invasion of China, and he was leading his army east when he fell ill and died in 1405.

Like his model Chinggis Khan, Tamerlane was a conqueror, not a governor. He spent most of his adult life planning and fighting military campaigns. He did not create an imperial administration but, rather, ruled through tribal leaders who were his allies. He appointed overlords in the territories he conquered, but they relied on existing bureaucratic structures and simply received taxes and tributes on his behalf.

TAMERLANE'S HEIRS Given its loose organization, it is not surprising that Tamerlane's empire experienced stresses and strains after the conqueror's death. Tamerlane's sons and grandsons engaged in a long series of bitter conflicts that resulted in the contraction of his empire and its division into four main regions. For a century after Tamerlane's death, however, they maintained control over the region from Persia to Afghanistan. When the last vestiges of Tamerlane's imperial creation disappeared, in the early sixteenth century, the Mughal, Safavid, and Ottoman empires that replaced it all clearly reflected the Turkish Muslim legacy of the lame conqueror.

The Foundation of the Ottoman Empire

Chapter 25 will discuss the Mughal Empire in India and the Safavid Empire in Persia, both of which emerged during the early sixteenth century as Tamerlane's empire finally dissolved. The early stages of Ottoman expansion predated Tamerlane, however, and the foundation of the Ottoman empire throws additional light on the influence of nomadic peoples during the period 1000 to 1500 C.E.

OSMAN After the Mongol conquest of Persia, large numbers of nomadic Turks migrated from central Asia to the ilkhanate and beyond to the territories in Anatolia that the Saljuq Turks had seized from the Byzantine empire. There they followed charismatic leaders who organized further campaigns of conquest. Among those leaders was Osman, who during the late thirteenth and early fourteenth centuries carved a small state for himself in northwestern Anatolia. In 1299 Osman declared independence from the Saljuq sultan and launched a campaign to build a state at the expense of the Byzantine empire. After every successful operation Osman attracted more and more followers, who came to be known as Osmanlis or Ottomans.

OTTOMAN CONQUESTS During the 1350s the Ottomans gained a considerable advantage over their Turkish rivals when they established a foothold across the Dardanelles at Gallipoli on the Balkan peninsula. The Ottomans quickly moved to expand the boundaries of their Balkan holdings. By the 1380s they had become by far the most powerful people in the Balkan peninsula, and by the end of the century they were poised to capture Constantinople and take over the Byzantine empire.

Tamerlane temporarily delayed Ottoman expansion in the Byzantine realm. In 1402 his forces crushed the Ottoman army, captured the sultan, and subjected the Ottoman state to the conqueror's authority. After Tamerlane's death, Ottoman leaders had to re-establish their rule in their own realm. Yet by the 1440s the Ottomans had recovered their balance and had begun again to expand in the Byzantine empire.

PSI img The siege of Constantinople www.mhhe.com/bentleybrief2e

THE CAPTURE OF CONSTANTINOPLE The campaign culminated in 1453 when Sultan Mehmed II, known as Mehmed the Conqueror, captured the Byzantine capital of Constantinople. After subjecting it to a sack, he made the city his own capital under the Turkish name of Istanbul. With Istanbul as a base, the Ottomans quickly absorbed the remainder of the Byzantine empire. By 1480 they controlled all of Greece and the Balkan region. They continued to expand throughout most of the sixteenth century as well, extending their rule to southwest Asia, southeastern Europe, Egypt, and north Africa. Once again, then, a nomadic people asserted control over a long-settled society and quickly built a vast empire.

Osman (os-MAHN)

SUMMARY

During the half millennium from 1000 to 1500 C.E., nomadic peoples of central Asia played a larger role than ever before in world history. As early as the second millennium B.C.E., they had periodically threatened states from China to the eastern Mediterranean region, and from classical times on they had traded regularly and actively with peoples of settled societies. From 1000 to 1500 their relations with neighboring peoples changed, as they dominated affairs in most of Eurasia through their conquests and their construction of vast transregional empires. Turkish peoples built the most durable of the nomadic empires, but the spectacular conquests of the Mongols most clearly demonstrated the potential of nomadic peoples to project their formidable military power to settled agricultural societies. By establishing connections that spanned the Eurasian landmass, the nomadic empires laid the foundation for increasing communication, exchange, and interaction among peoples of different societies and thereby fostered the integration of the eastern hemisphere. The age of nomadic empires, from 1000 to 1500 C.E., foreshadowed the integrated world of modern times.

STUDY TERMS

Abbasids (268)
Chinggis Khan (270)
Ghaznavids (269)
Hülegü (274)
Ilkhan Ghazan (275)
ilkhans (272)
Karakorum (271)
khan (268)
khanate of Chagatai (272)
Khanbaliq (272)
khans of the Golden Horde (272)
Khubilai Khan (272)
Khwarazm shah (272)
Mehmed the Conqueror (280)
Mongols (270)
Osman (280)
Rabban Sauma (276)
Saljuqs (268)
shamanism (268)
sultan (268)
sultanate of Delhi (269)
Tamerlane (278)
Turkish peoples (266)
Uighur Turks (277)
Yuan dynasty (273)

FOR FURTHER READING

S. A. M. Adshead. *Central Asia in World History.* New York, 1993. A provocative essay on central Asia and its place in the larger world.

Thomas J. Barfield. *The Nomadic Alternative.* Englewood Cliffs, N.J., 1993. A sensitive study of nomadic societies in Africa and Eurasia by a leading anthropologist.

Charles J. Halperin. *Russia and the Golden Horde: The Mongol Impact on Medieval Russian History.* Bloomington, 1985. An insightful study of the Golden Horde and its influence on Russian society.

Halil Inalcik. *The Ottoman Empire: The Classical Age, 1300–1600.* Trans. by N. Itzkowitz and C. Imber. New York, 1973. The best short introduction to early Ottoman history.

Paul Kahn, ed. *The Secret History of the Mongols: The Origin of Chingis Khan.* Adapted from the translation of F. W. Cleaves. San Francisco, 1984. A translation of the Mongols' history of their own society, adapted for modern readers.

Adam T. Kessler. *Empires beyond the Great Wall: The Heritage of Genghis Khan.* Los Angeles, 1993. Well-illustrated survey of nomadic states in central Asia from the Xiongnu to the Mongols.

Beatrice Forbes Manz. *The Rise and Rule of Tamerlane.* Cambridge, 1989. Scholarly analysis of Tamerlane's career and his empire.

David Morgan. *Medieval Persia, 1040–1797.* London, 1988. A brief and insightful survey concentrating on the eras of Turkish and Mongol dominance in Persia.

———. *The Mongols.* Oxford, 1986. Lucid and witty study: the best short work on the Mongols.

Morris Rossabi. *Khubilai Khan: His Life and Times.* Berkeley, 1988. Excellent scholarly study of the greatest of the great khans.

States and Societies of Sub-Saharan Africa

15

A remarkable oral tradition preserves the story of the lion prince Sundiata, thirteenth-century founder of the Mali empire in west Africa. Oral traditions include stories, histories, epics, and other accounts transmitted by professional singers and storytellers known in Africa as griots. Until scholars began to collect and publish African oral traditions in the middle of the twentieth century, the story of Sundiata was available only when a griot recited it.

According to the oral tradition, Sundiata's father ruled a small west African kingdom in the northeastern part of what is now Guinea. Despite his royal parentage, Sundiata had a difficult childhood, because a congenitally defective leg left him partially crippled. When the old king died, his enemies invaded the kingdom and killed the royal offspring, sparing Sundiata because they thought his physical condition would prevent him from posing a threat to their ambitions. But Sundiata overcame his injury, learned to use the bow and arrow, and strengthened himself by hunting in the forest. As Sundiata grew stronger, his enemies began to fear him, and they forced him to seek refuge in a neighboring kingdom. While in exile, Sundiata distinguished himself as a warrior and assembled a powerful cavalry force staffed by loyal followers and allies.

About 1235 Sundiata returned to his homeland and claimed the throne. His cavalry slashed through the countryside and defeated his enemies. Within a few years he had overcome resistance, established the Mali empire, and consolidated his rule throughout the valley of the Niger River. Although he respected traditional religious beliefs and magical powers, Sundiata was a Muslim, and he welcomed Muslim merchants from north Africa into his realm. He built a capital city at Niani, which soon became a thriving commercial center. For two centuries after Sundiata's death about 1260, the lion prince's legacy shaped the lives of west African peoples and linked west Africa with north Africa and the Mediterranean basin.

From the classical era forward, peoples from east Asia to the Mediterranean basin established extensive networks of trade and communication. African peoples living south of the Sahara desert participated in the larger economy of the eastern hemisphere, though not as fully as their counterparts in north Africa. Geographic conditions help to explain why trade and communication networks

❮ The magnificent mosque at Jenne, constructed in the fourteenth century, served as a principal center of Islamic education and scholarship in the Mali empire.

Sundiata (soon-JAH-tuh)
Mali (MAH-lee)
griot (GREE-oh)

CHRONOLOGY

4th century C.E.	Introduction of bananas to Africa
11th to 13th century	Kingdom of Ghana
11th to 15th century	Swahili cities
12th to 15th century	Kingdom of Great Zimbabwe
12th to 16th century	Christian kingdom of Axum
13th to 15th century	Mali empire
1230–1255	Reign of Sundiata
14th to 17th century	Kingdom of Kongo
1312–1337	Reign of Mansa Musa
1324–1325	Mansa Musa's pilgrimage to Mecca

did not embrace sub-Saharan Africa as readily as they did other regions: the Sahara desert poses a formidable challenge to overland travelers, the African coastlines offer few good natural harbors, and cataracts complicate travel up the continent's major rivers.

Nevertheless, like their Eurasian and north African counterparts, peoples of sub-Saharan Africa organized productive societies, built powerful states, and participated in large-scale networks of communication and exchange. Internal African processes drove much of this development. Between 1000 and 1500 C.E., in the wake of the Bantu and other migrations (discussed in chapter 2), population increases in sub-Saharan Africa led societies there to organize states, develop centers of economic specialization, and conduct interregional trade. Alongside these internal processes, relations with other peoples of the eastern hemisphere also profoundly influenced the development of African societies. From the early centuries C.E. to 1500 and later as well, trade with lands of the Mediterranean and the Indian Ocean basins encouraged African peoples to produce commodities desired by consumers throughout much of the eastern hemisphere. This trade promoted urban development, the organization of large states and empires, and the introduction of new food crops and new religious beliefs into sub-Saharan Africa.

Effects of Early African Migrations

By 1000 C.E. Bantu-speaking peoples had settled in most parts of Africa south of the equator, and Kushite, Sudanese, Mande, and other peoples had also established communities in lands far from their original homes. For the next several centuries, African peoples built societies on the foundation of small communities that the Bantu and other migrations had generated.

Agriculture and Population Growth

The principal early result of the Bantu and other migrations was to spread agriculture and herding to almost all parts of Africa. As they established agricultural societies, cultivators and herders displaced or absorbed many of the hunting, gathering, and fishing peoples who previously inhabited sub-Saharan Africa. After about 500 B.C.E., most Bantu peoples possessed iron metallurgy, which enabled them to fashion iron tools that facilitated further clearing of lands and extension of agriculture. By the early centuries C.E., cultivation and herding had reached the southernmost parts of Africa. The expansion of agriculture, in turn, resulted in increased agricultural production, rising population, and pressure for continuing migration to new territories.

BANANAS The introduction of bananas to Africa encouraged a fresh migratory surge. First domesticated in southeast Asia, bananas entered Africa by way of the Indian Ocean. Between about 300 and 500 C.E., Malay seafarers from the islands that make up modern Indonesia colonized the island of Madagascar and established banana cultivation there. From Madagascar, bananas easily made the jump to the east African mainland. By 500 C.E. several varieties of bananas had become well established in Africa.

Cultivation of bananas allowed the Bantu to expand into heavily forested regions where yams and millet did not grow well. Indeed, bananas increased the supply of available food, enriched the Bantu diet, and allowed sub-Saharan populations to expand more rapidly than before.

POPULATION GROWTH The population history of sub-Saharan Africa clearly reflects the significance of iron metallurgy and bananas. In 400 B.C.E., before iron working had deeply influenced the continent's societies, the population of sub-Saharan Africa stood at about 3.5 million. By 800 C.E., after banana cultivation had spread throughout the continent, the sub-Saharan population had climbed to 17 million. And by 1000, when the Bantu migrations had introduced agriculture and iron metallurgy to most regions of sub-Saharan Africa, the population had passed 22 million.

The continuing Bantu migrations, the expansion of Bantu population, and the establishment of new Bantu communities contributed to changes in relationships between Bantu and foraging peoples such as the forest dwellers of central Africa (the people once referred to as pygmies). In the past, the Bantu had often relied on the foragers as guides as they expanded into unfamiliar forest environments. However, as Bantu populations surged, many foragers were displaced by growing numbers of agricultural settlements. As a result, some forest peoples joined the cultivators and effectively integrated into Bantu society, while others retreated deeper into the forest to sustain their small-scale societies.

African Political Organization

By 1000 C.E., the Bantu had approached the limits of their expansion. Because agricultural peoples already occupied most of the continent, migrating into new territories and forming new settlements was much more difficult than before. Instead of migrating in search of new lands to cultivate, then, African peoples developed increasingly complex forms of government that enabled them to organize their existing societies more efficiently.

KIN-BASED SOCIETIES Most early Bantu societies did not depend on an elaborate hierarchy of officials or a bureaucratic apparatus to administer their affairs. Instead, Bantu peoples governed themselves mostly through family and kinship groups. Usually, Bantu peoples settled in villages with populations averaging about one hundred people. Male heads of families constituted a village's ruling council, which decided public affairs for the entire group. The most prominent of the family heads presided over the village as a chief and represented the settlement when it dealt with neighboring peoples. A group of villages constituted a district, which became the principal focus of loyalties. Usually, there was no chief or larger government for the district. Instead, village chiefs negotiated on matters concerning two or more villages. Meanwhile, within individual villages, family and kinship groups disciplined their own members as necessary.

CHIEFDOMS This type of organization lends itself particularly well to small-scale communities, but kin-based societies often grew to large proportions. After about 1000 C.E., kin-based societies faced difficult challenges as population growth strained resources. Conflicts between villages and districts became more frequent and more intense. Increased conflict encouraged Bantu communities to organize military forces for both offensive and defensive purposes, and military organization in turn encouraged the development of more formal structures of government.

Many districts fell under the leadership of powerful chiefs, who overrode kinship networks and imposed authority on their territories. Some of these chiefs conquered their neighbors and consolidated their lands into small kingdoms. These local kingdoms emerged in several regions of sub-Saharan Africa after about 1000 C.E. The kingdoms of Ife and Benin, for example, arose in the forested regions of west Africa. Both realms were city-states in which the court and urban residents controlled the surrounding countryside through family relationships and political alliances. Both Ife and Benin also produced magnificent sculptures that put human faces and figures to the early history of sub-Saharan Africa. Local kingdoms appeared also in southern Africa and central Africa.

Ife (EE-fehy)
Benin (beh-NEEN)

Ife Sculpture. | According to legend, this handsome terra-cotta head represents an ambitious warrior who usurped power in the small state of Ife (in modern Nigeria). Produced shortly after 1000 C.E., it testifies to the increasing tensions in sub-Saharan politics after the turn of the millennium.

KINGDOM OF KONGO One of the most active areas of political development was the basin of the Congo River (also known as the Zaire River). After about 1000 C.E. population pressures and military challenges encouraged kin-based societies in the Congo region to form small states embracing a few villages each. By 1200 conflict between these small states had resulted in the organization of larger, regional principalities that could better resist political and military pressures. One of the more prosperous of the Congolese states was the kingdom of Kongo, which participated actively in trade networks involving copper, raffia cloth, and nzimbu shells from the Atlantic Ocean. During the fourteenth century the kingdom of Kongo came to embrace much of the modern-day Republic of the Congo and Angola.

The central government of Kongo included the king and officials who oversaw military, judicial, and financial affairs (including a royal currency system based on cowry shells). Beneath the central government were six provinces administered by governors, each of whom supervised several districts administered by subordinate officials. Within the districts, villages ruled by chiefs provided local government. Though not the only kingdom in sub-Saharan Africa, Kongo was perhaps the most tightly centralized of the early Bantu kingdoms. The kingdom of Kongo provided effective organization from the fourteenth until the mid–seventeenth century, when Portuguese slave traders undermined the authority of the kings and the central government.

Kin-based societies did not disappear with the emergence of formal states. In fact, many survived well into the nineteenth century. Yet regional states and large kingdoms became increasingly prominent during the centuries after 1000 C.E. as Bantu and other African peoples responded to population pressures and military challenges facing their societies.

African Society and Cultural Development

By the eleventh century C.E., Africa was a land of enormous diversity. The peoples of sub-Saharan Africa spoke some eight hundred languages, and the continent supported a wide variety of societies and economies: mobile bands of hunting and gathering peoples, fishing peoples who lived alongside the continent's lakes and coasts, nomadic herders, subsistence farmers who migrated periodically to fresh lands, settled cultivators, and city-based societies that drew their livelihoods from mining, manufacturing, and trade. Although that diversity makes it difficult to speak of African society and cultural development in general terms, certain social forms and cultural patterns appeared widely throughout sub-Saharan Africa.

THINKING ABOUT *Traditions*

TRADITIONS IN STATES AND SOCIETIES IN SUB-SAHARAN AFRICA. Geographic barriers posed many difficulties for cross-cultural interaction between sub-Saharan African societies and other societies in north Africa and Eurasia. In what ways did the relative isolation imposed by these barriers contribute to the persistence of distinctly sub-Saharan traditions regarding religion, culture, and community organization in this period?

Social Classes

In kingdoms, empires, and city-states, such as Kongo, Mali, and Kilwa, respectively, African peoples developed complex societies with clearly defined classes: ruling elites, military nobles, administrative officials, religious authorities, merchants, artisans, peasants, and slaves. These societies more or less resembled those found in other settled, agricultural lands of Eurasia organized by powerful states.

In the small states and kin-based societies of sub-Saharan Africa, however, social structures were different. Small states often generated an aristocratic or ruling elite, and they always recognized a class of religious authorities. Yet in general, kinship, sex and gender expectations, and age groupings were the principal considerations that determined social position in such societies.

KINSHIP GROUPS Extended families and clans served as the main foundation of social and economic organization in small-scale agricultural societies. The institution of privately owned property, found in most societies in north Africa and Eurasia, did not exist in sub-Saharan

Africa. Instead, communities claimed rights to land and used it in common. The villages of sub-Saharan Africa, where most of the population lived, generally consisted of several extended family groups. Male heads of families jointly governed the village and organized the work of their own groups. They allocated portions of the communal lands for their relatives to cultivate and were responsible for distributing harvests equitably among all members of their groups.

SEX AND GENDER RELATIONS Sex and gender relations also influenced the roles and occupations of individuals in society. Workers with special skills were mostly men. Leather tanning, for example, was the work of men who carefully guarded knowledge of their techniques and passed them down to their heirs. Iron working, which was highly prestigious, was also the work of men. Blacksmiths often served as community leaders, and like leather tanners, they passed knowledge of their craft down to their heirs. Men usually undertook the heavy labor of clearing land and preparing it for cultivation, although both men and women participated in the planting and harvesting of crops. Women's roles also included tending to domestic chores and taking primary responsibility for child rearing.

WOMEN'S ROLES As in other societies, men largely monopolized public authority. Yet women in sub-Saharan Africa generally had more opportunities open to them than did their counterparts in other lands. Women enjoyed high honor as the sources of life. On at least a few occasions, women made their ways to positions of power, and aristocratic women often influenced public affairs. Women merchants commonly traded at markets, and they participated actively in both local and long-distance trade in Africa. Sometimes women even engaged in combat and organized all-female military units.

The arrival of Islam did not change the status of women in sub-Saharan Africa as dramatically as it did in Arabia and southwest Asia. South of the Sahara, early converts to Islam came mostly from the ranks of the ruling elites and the merchant classes. Because it did not become a popular faith for several centuries after its introduction, Islam did not deeply influence the customs of most Africans. Even at royal courts where Islam attracted eager converts, Muslims of sub-Saharan Africa simply did not honor the same social codes as their counterparts elsewhere. For the most part, Muslim women in sub-Saharan Africa socialized freely with men outside their immediate families, and they continued to appear and work openly in society. Thus Islam did relatively little to curtail the opportunities available to women or to compromise their status in sub-Saharan Africa.

AGE GRADES Apart from kinship and expectations based on sex and gender roles, African society also made a place for age groups that included all individuals within a given community born within a few years of one another. Members of age grades performed tasks appropriate for their levels of development, and they often bonded with one another to form tight circles of friends and political allies. Members of an age grade might provide labor for community projects, for example, or take joint responsibility for looking after village elders. They aided members who experienced adversities and helped one another at crucial junctures, such as marriage and the building of a new household. Thus age grades had the effect of establishing social ties that crossed the lines of family and kinship.

SLAVERY One class of individuals stood apart from the other social groups: slaves. As in other lands, the institution of slavery had had a place in Africa since antiquity. Most slaves were captives of war. Others came from the ranks of debtors, suspected witches, and criminals. Within Africa most slaves probably worked as agricultural laborers, although many also worked as construction laborers, miners, or porters. Slaves were an important form of personal wealth in sub-Saharan Africa. In the absence of private property, sub-Saharans could not become wealthy through the accumulation of landholdings. Instead, the accumulation of slaves enabled individuals or families to display their wealth, to enhance their positions in society, and also to increase their agricultural production. For those reasons, slave trading and slaveholding were prominent features of sub-Saharan African society.

SLAVE TRADING After about the ninth century C.E., the expansion of the trans-Saharan and Indian Ocean trade networks stimulated increased traffic in African slaves. In previous centuries, eastern Europeans had been the main source of slaves in the trading networks of Muslim merchants. Yet the demand for slaves became greater than eastern Europe could supply. As a result, Muslim merchants turned increasingly to sub-Saharan Africa as an alternative source for slaves.

In response to that demand, slave raiding became an increasingly prominent activity within Africa itself. Rulers of large-scale states and empires began to make war on smaller, weaker states and kin-based societies in search of captives. In some years, ten to twenty thousand Africans left their homes as slaves. Indeed, although smaller than the Atlantic slave trade of modern times, the Islamic slave trade was a sizable affair: between 750 and 1500 C.E. the number of African slaves transported to foreign lands may have exceeded ten million. The high demand led to the creation of networks within Africa that supplied slaves and served as a foundation for the Atlantic slave trade in later centuries. Although records of the Islamic slave trade are scarce, a lengthy uprising known as the *Zanj* revolt allows a glimpse of the harsh conditions under which many of these slaves toiled. The term *Zanj* referred to black slaves from the Swahili coast, many of whom worked on sugarcane plantations or cleared land for cultivation in southern Mesopotamia by the seventh century C.E. Slave revolts were not uncommon, and about 869 a rebel slave named Ali bin Muhammad organized about fifteen thousand Zanj slaves into a massive force that captured Basra, the most important city of southern Mesopotamia. The rebels then proceeded to establish a state in the region, which was only defeated by the Abbasid rulers fourteen years later.

African Religion

Peoples of sub-Saharan Africa developed a wide range of languages, societies, and cultural traditions. Religious beliefs and practices in particular took many forms. The continent's peoples referred to their deities by different names, told different stories about them, and honored them with different rituals. Yet certain features were common to many religions of sub-Saharan Africa. In combination, these features offer considerable insight into the cultural and religious climate of sub-Saharan Africa in premodern times.

CREATOR GOD Many African peoples had held monotheistic beliefs from the early days of Sudanic agriculture. Although those beliefs were not static over time, many peoples recognized a single divine force as the agent responsible for setting the world in motion and providing it with order. Some peoples believed that this god also sustained the world, intervening indirectly, through spirits, to influence the course of human affairs. Some considered this deity to be all-powerful, others regarded it as all-knowing, and many considered it both omnipotent and omniscient.

LESSER GODS AND SPIRITS Apart from the superior creator god, Africans recognized many lesser gods and spirits often associated with the elements and with natural features. Unlike the creator god, these lesser deities participated actively in the workings of the world. They could confer or withhold benefits and bring favor or injury to humans. Similarly, most Africans believed that the souls of departed ancestors had the power to intervene in the lives of their descendants: the departed could bring good fortune to descendants who behaved properly and honored their ancestors, and they could also bring misfortune as punishment for evil behavior and neglect of their ancestors' memory. Much of the ritual of African religions focused on honoring deities, spirits, or ancestors' souls to win their favor or regain their goodwill. The rituals included prayers, animal sacrifices, and ceremonies marking important stages of life—such as birth, circumcision, marriage, and death.

DIVINERS Like other peoples of the world, Africans recognized classes of religious specialists—individuals who had the power to mediate between humanity and supernatural beings. Often referred to as diviners, they were intelligent people, usually men though

Zanj (zahn-jee)

sometimes women, who understood clearly the networks of political, social, economic, and psychological relationships within their communities. When afflicted by illness, sterility, crop failure, or some other disaster, individuals or groups consulted diviners to learn the cause of their misfortune. Diviners then consulted oracles, identified the causes of the trouble, and prescribed medicine, rituals, or sacrifices designed to eliminate the problem and bring about a return to normality.

For the most part, African religion concerned itself not with matters of theology but, rather, with the more practical business of explaining, predicting, and controlling the experiences of individuals and groups in the world. Thus African religion strongly emphasized morality and proper behavior as essential to the maintenance of an orderly world. Failure to observe high moral standards would displease deities, spirits, and departed ancestors and ensure that misfortune befell the negligent parties. Because proper moral behavior was so important to their fortunes, family and kinship groups took responsibility for policing their members and disciplining those who fell short of expected standards.

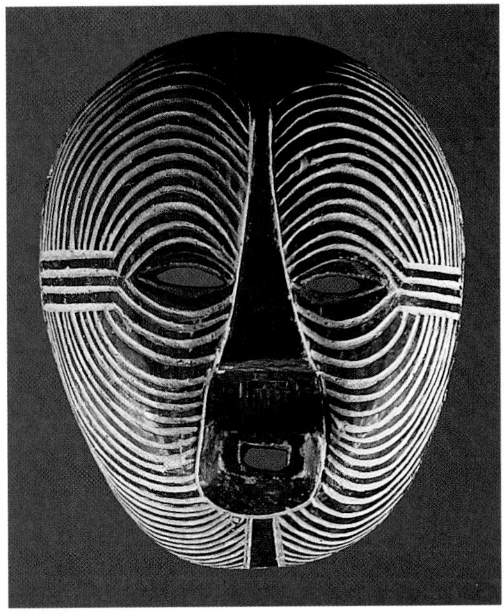

CONGOLESE MASK. | Entrancing and enthralling masks like this one from Congo were essential to the proper observance of religious rituals, which often involved communicating with natural or animal spirits. Masks transformed diviners and provided them with powers not accessible to normal humans. ***What kinds of feelings might a mask like this have elicited from observers?***

The Arrival of Christianity

EARLY CHRISTIANITY IN NORTH AFRICA Alongside religions that concentrated on the practical matter of maintaining an orderly world, Christianity reached Egypt and north Africa during the first century C.E., soon after the faith's appearance. Alexandria in Egypt became one of the most prominent centers of early Christian thought, and north Africa was the home of St. Augustine, an important leader of the fledgling church.

THE CHRISTIAN KINGDOM OF AXUM About the middle of the fourth century C.E., Christianity established a foothold in the kingdom of Axum, located in the highlands of modern Ethiopia. The first Axumite converts were probably local merchants who traded with Mediterranean Christians calling at the port of Adulis on the Red Sea. As missionaries visited Ethiopia, the kings of Axum also converted to Christianity. Indeed, the kings of Axum were some of the first royal converts to Christianity, adopting the faith shortly after the Roman emperor Constantine himself. Missionaries later established monasteries, translated the Bible into the Ethiopian language, and worked to popularize Christianity throughout the kingdom.

The fortunes of Christianity in Ethiopia reflected the larger political experience of the region. In the late seventh century C.E., the ruling house of Axum fell into decline, and during the next several centuries the expansion of Islam left an isolated island of Christianity in the Ethiopian highlands. During the twelfth century, however, a new ruling dynasty undertook a centralizing campaign and enthusiastically promoted Christianity as a faith that could provide cultural unity for the land. From the twelfth through the sixteenth century, Christianity enjoyed particular favor in Ethiopia. During the twelfth century, the Ethiopian kings ordered the carving of eleven massive churches out of solid rock—a monumental work of construction that required enormous resources. During the thirteenth century, rulers of Ethiopia's Solomonic dynasty claimed descent from the Israelite kings David and Solomon in an effort to lend additional biblical luster to their authority. The fictional work *Kebra Negast (The Glory of Kings),* which undertook to trace that lineage, has recently become popular among Rastafarians and devotees of reggae music in Ethiopia, Jamaica, and other lands. Meanwhile, Christianity retained its privileged status in Ethiopia until it fell out of favor following the socialist revolution of 1974.

Axum (AHK-soom)
Kebra Nagast (kee-brah NAH-gahst)

Church of St. George. Worshipers gather at the church of St. George at Lalibela, Ethiopia, a massive structure in the form of a cross. Workers excavated the surrounding earth and then carved the church itself out of a rock.

ETHIOPIAN CHRISTIANITY During the centuries after the Islamic conquests of Egypt, the Sudan, and northern Africa, Ethiopian Christians had little contact with Christians in other lands. As a result, although Ethiopian Christianity retained basic Christian theology and rituals, it increasingly reflected the interests of its African devotees. Ethiopian Christians believed that a large host of evil spirits populated the world, for example, and carried amulets or charms for protection against these menacing spirits. The twelfth-century carved-rock churches themselves harked back to pre-Christian values, since rock shrines had long been a prominent feature in Ethiopian religion. Not until the sixteenth century, when Portuguese mariners began to visit Ethiopia en route to India, did Ethiopians reestablish relations with Christians from other lands. By that time the Portuguese had introduced their Roman Catholic faith to the kingdom of Kongo, and Christianity began to win a place for itself elsewhere in sub-Saharan Africa.

Islamic Kingdoms and Empires

After the eighth century C.E., Islam was also introduced to Africa. Islam arrived by two routes: it went to west Africa overland by trans-Saharan camel caravans, and it traveled to coastal east Africa over the sea-lanes of the Indian Ocean in the vessels of merchant mariners. After its introduction, Islam profoundly influenced the political, social, and economic development of sub-Saharan Africa as well as its cultural and religious development. At the same time, Africans in both west and east Africa adapted Islam to their own cultures, giving African Islam distinctly African characteristics.

Trans-Saharan Trade and Islamic States in West Africa

The Sahara desert has never served as an absolute barrier to communication between human societies. Small numbers of nomadic peoples have lived in the desert itself since about 5000 B.C.E. These nomads migrated around the desert and had dealings with other peoples settled on its fringes. In addition, merchants occasionally organized commercial expeditions across the desert even in ancient and classical times.

CAMELS Yet travel across the Sahara quickened substantially with the arrival of the camel. Camels came to north Africa from Arabia about the seventh century B.C.E. During the late centuries B.C.E., a special camel saddle, which took advantage of the animals' distinctive physical structure, also made its way to north Africa. Because a caravan took seventy to ninety days to cross the Sahara and because camels could travel long distances before needing water, they proved to be extremely useful beasts of burden in such an arid region. After about 300 C.E. camels became the preferred transport animals throughout the Sahara.

When Arab conquerors established their Islamic faith in north Africa during the seventh and eighth centuries, they also integrated the region into a rapidly expanding zone of commerce and communication. Soon afterward, Muslims in north Africa began to explore the potential of trade across the Sahara. By the late eighth century, Islamic merchants had trekked across the desert and established commercial relations with societies in sub-Saharan west Africa. There they found a series of long-established trading centers such as Gao, a terminus of caravan routes across the Sahara that offered access to the Niger River valley, which was a flourishing market for copper, ironware, cotton textiles, salt, grains, and carnelian beads.

Kingdoms & empires of Africa
www.mhhe.com/bentleybrief2e

THE KINGDOM OF GHANA The principal state of west Africa at the time of the Muslims' arrival was the kingdom of Ghana (not related to the modern state of Ghana), situated between the Senegal and Niger rivers in a region straddling the border between the modern states of Mali and Mauritania. Ghana emerged as a kingdom at an uncertain but early date: according to legends preserved by Arab travelers, as many as twenty-two kings ruled in Ghana before Muhammad and his companions embarked on the *hijra.* Ghana probably developed as a state during the fourth or fifth century C.E. when agricultural peoples sought to protect their societies from the raids of camel-riding nomads who increasingly came out of the Sahara. When Muslims arrived in west Africa, the kingdom of Ghana was a regional state much like others that were emerging elsewhere in sub-Saharan Africa.

GOLD TRADE As trade and traffic across the desert increased, Ghana underwent a dramatic transformation. It became the most important commercial site in west Africa because it was the center for trade in gold, which was in high demand throughout the eastern hemisphere. Muslim merchants flocked to camel caravans traveling across the Sahara to Ghana in search of gold for consumers in the Mediterranean basin and elsewhere in the Islamic world. Ghana itself did not produce gold, but the kings procured nuggets from lands to the south—probably from the region around the headwaters of the Niger, Gambia, and Senegal rivers, which enjoyed the world's largest supply of gold available at the time. By controlling and taxing trade in the precious metal, the kings both enriched and strengthened their realm. Apart from gold, merchants from Ghana provided ivory and slaves for traders from north Africa. In exchange, they received horses, cloth, small manufactured wares, and salt.

KOUMBI-SALEH Integration into trans-Saharan trade networks brought enormous wealth and considerable power to Ghana. The kingdom's capital and principal trading site stood at Koumbi-Saleh, a small town today but a thriving commercial center with a population of some fifteen to twenty thousand people at its peak between the ninth and twelfth centuries. Al-Bakri, a Spanish Muslim traveler of the mid–eleventh century,

---

Ghana (GAH-nuh)

MAP 15.1 | Kingdoms, empires, and city-states of sub-Saharan Africa, 800–1500 C.E. After the emergence of Islam, trans-Saharan overland routes linked sub-Saharan west Africa with the Mediterranean region, and maritime trade routes linked sub-Saharan east Africa to the Indian Ocean basin. ***What role did trade play in the emergence of cities and states in sub-Saharan Africa?***

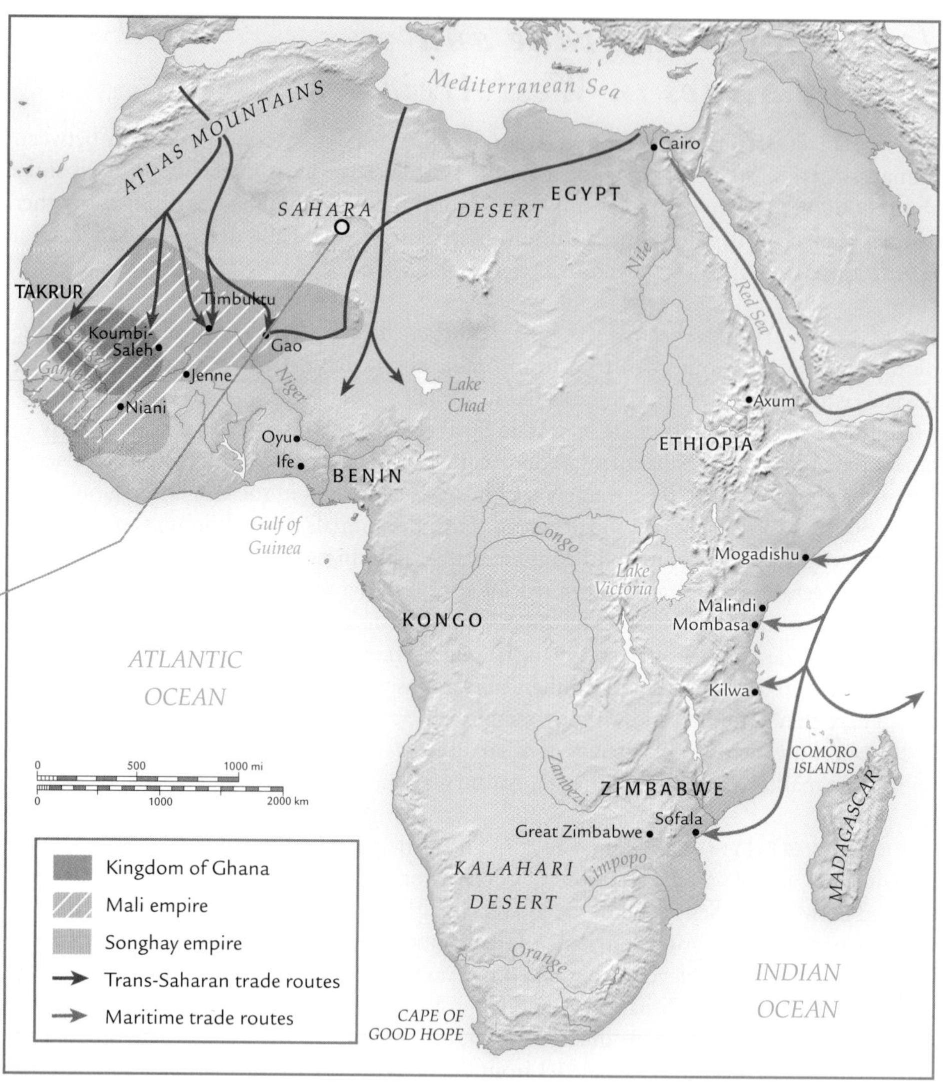

It took 70–90 days for a camel caravan to cross the Sahara Desert.

described Koumbi-Saleh as a flourishing site with buildings of stone and more than a dozen mosques. From taxes levied on trade passing through Ghana, the kings financed a large army—al-Bakri reported that they could field two hundred thousand warriors—that protected the sources of gold, maintained order in the kingdom, kept allied and tributary states in line, and defended Ghana against nomadic incursions from the Sahara.

ISLAM IN WEST AFRICA By about the tenth century, the kings of Ghana had converted to Islam. Their conversion led to improved relations with Muslim merchants from north Africa as well as Muslim nomads from the desert who transported trade goods across the Sahara. It also brought them recognition and support from Muslim states in north Africa. The kings of Ghana made no attempt to impose Islam forcibly on their society, nor did they accept Islam exclusively even for their own purposes. Instead, they continued to observe traditional religious customs: al-Bakri mentioned, for example, that native religious specialists practiced magic and kept idols in the woods surrounding the royal palace at Koumbi-Saleh. Even in the absence of efforts to impose Islam on Ghana, however, the faith attracted converts, particularly among those engaged in trade with Muslim merchants from the north.

As the kingdom expanded to the north, it became vulnerable to attacks by nomadic peoples from the Sahara who sought to seize some of the kingdom's wealth. During the early thirteenth century, raids from the desert weakened the kingdom, and it soon collapsed. Political leadership in west Africa then fell to the powerful Mali empire, which emerged just as the kingdom of Ghana dissolved.

SUNDIATA The lion prince Sundiata (reigned 1230–1255) built the Mali empire during the first half of the thirteenth century. Through alliances with local rulers, a reputation for courage in battle, and a large army dominated by cavalry, Sundiata had consolidated his hold on the Mali empire by about 1235. The empire embraced Ghana as well as other, neighboring kingdoms in the regions surrounding the Senegal and Niger rivers.

THE MALI EMPIRE AND TRADE Mali benefited from trans-Saharan trade on an even larger scale than Ghana had. From the thirteenth until the late fifteenth century, Mali controlled and taxed almost all trade passing through west Africa. Enormous caravans with as many as twenty-five thousand camels linked Mali to north Africa. The capital city of Niani attracted merchants seeking gold, and market cities on the caravan routes such as Timbuktu, Gao, and Jenne grew crowded and wealthy. Like the earlier kings of Ghana, the rulers of Mali honored Islam and provided protection, lodging, and comforts for Muslim merchants from the north. Also like the Ghanaian kings, they did not force Islam on their realm. Rather, they encouraged its spread on a voluntary basis.

WEST AFRICAN SCULPTURE. | This terra-cotta sculpture from the thirteenth or fourteenth century depicts a helmeted and armored warrior astride a horse with elaborate harness and head protection. ***What can this sculpture tell us about the values of the society that produced it?***

MANSA MUSA The significance of trade and Islam for west Africa became clearest during the reign of Sundiata's grand-nephew Mansa Musa, who ruled Mali from 1312 to 1337, during the high point of the empire. Mansa Musa observed Islamic tradition by making his pilgrimage to Mecca in 1324–1325. His party formed a huge caravan that included thousands of soldiers, attendants, subjects, and slaves as well as a hundred camels carrying satchels of gold. In fact, during his three-month visit to Cairo along the way, Mansa Musa distributed so much gold that the metal's value declined by as much as 25 percent on local markets.

MANSA MUSA AND ISLAM Mansa Musa drew great inspiration from his pilgrimage to Mecca, and on returning to Mali he took his religion even more seriously than before. He built mosques, and he sent promising students to study with distinguished Islamic scholars in north Africa. He also established religious schools and brought in Arabian and north African teachers, including four descendants of Muhammad, to make Islam better known in Mali.

Within a century of Mansa Musa's reign, Mali was in serious decline: factions crippled the central government, provinces seceded from the empire, and military pressures came both from neighboring kingdoms and from desert nomads. By the late fifteenth century, the Songhay empire had completely overcome Mali. Yet Mansa Musa and other Mali rulers had established a tradition of centralized government that the Songhay realm would continue, and they had ensured that Islam would have a prominent place in west African society over the long term.

Mansa Musa, king of Mali
www.mhhe.com/bentleybrief2e

Great Mosque at Timbuktu
www.mhhe.com/bentleybrief2e

The Indian Ocean Trade and Islamic States in East Africa

While trans-Saharan caravan traffic linked west Africa to the larger trading world of the eastern hemisphere, merchant mariners sailing the sea-lanes of the Indian Ocean performed a similar service for Swahili societies in coastal east Africa. *Swahili* is an Arabic term meaning "coasters," referring to those who engaged in trade along the east African coast. Swahili society developed as a result of Bantu migrations to east Africa in the early centuries C.E. These migrants introduced agriculture, cattle herding, and iron metallurgy to the region, and here, as elsewhere in sub-Saharan Africa, they founded complex societies governed by small, local states. As their population increased, Bantu peoples founded settlements on the coasts and

Timbuktu (tim-buhk-TOO)
Gao (gou)
Jenne (jehn-neh)
Mansa Musa (MAHN-suh MOO-suh)

MANSA MUSA. | Mansa Musa enjoyed a widespread reputation as the wealthiest king in the world. On this map, prepared in 1375 by a cartographer from the Mediterranean island of Majorca, Mansa Musa holds a gold nugget about the size of a grapefruit. ***What kinds of objects surround Mansa Musa?***

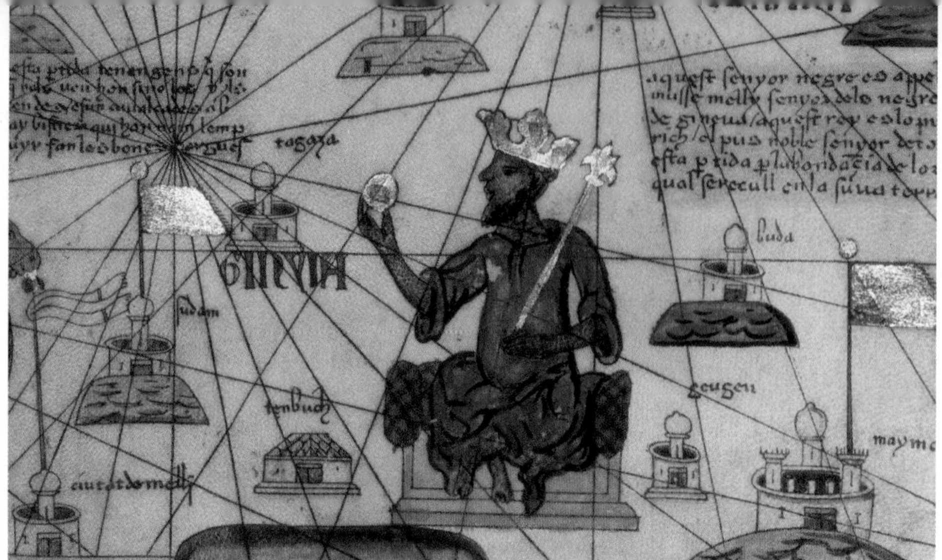

offshore islands as well as the interior regions of east Africa. These coast dwellers supplemented their agricultural production with ocean fishing and maritime trade.

THE SWAHILI The Swahili dominated the east African coast from Mogadishu in the north to Kilwa, the Comoro Islands, and Sofala in the south. They spoke a Bantu language, also known as Swahili, supplemented with words and ideas borrowed from Arabic. Swahili peoples developed different dialects, but they communicated readily among themselves because individuals frequently visited other Swahili communities in their ocean-going craft. Indeed, all along the east African coast, Swahili society underwent similar patterns of development with respect to language, religion, architecture, and technology.

In the tenth century, Swahili society attracted increasing attention from Islamic merchants. From the interior regions of east Africa, the Swahili obtained gold, slaves, ivory, and exotic local products, which they traded for pottery, glass, and textiles that Muslim merchants brought from Persia, India, and China.

THE SWAHILI CITY-STATES By the eleventh and twelfth centuries, trade had brought important changes to coastal east Africa, just as it had done in west Africa. By controlling and taxing trade within their jurisdictions, local chiefs grew wealthy, strengthened their own authority, and increased the influence of their communities. Gradually, trade concentrated at several coastal and island port cities that enjoyed especially convenient locations: Mogadishu, Lamu, Malindi, Mombasa, Zanzibar, Kilwa, Mozambique, and Sofala. Each of these sites developed into a powerful city-state governed by a king who supervised trade and organized public life in the region.

The cities themselves underwent an impressive transformation. Whereas most buildings were traditionally made of wood and dried mud, by about the twelfth century Swahili peoples began to construct large coral buildings, and by the fifteenth century the main Swahili towns boasted handsome stone mosques and public buildings. Meanwhile, urban Swahili elites dressed in silk and fine cotton clothes, and they set their tables with porcelain imported from China.

PSI img — Ruins of a great mosque at Kilwa
www.mhhe.com/bentleybrief2e

KILWA Travelers' reports and recent archaeological discoveries have thrown especially clear light on the development of Kilwa, one of the busiest city-states on the east African coast. With a population of about twelve thousand, Kilwa was a thriving city with many stone buildings and mosques. Residents imported cotton and silk textiles as well as perfumes and pearls from India, and archaeologists have unearthed a staggering amount of Chinese porcelain. Merchants of Kilwa imported these products in exchange for gold, slaves, and ivory obtained from interior regions. By the late fifteenth century, Kilwa exported about a ton of gold per year.

Swahili (swah-HEE-lee)

ZIMBABWE The influence of long-distance trade also had important effects on the interior regions of east Africa. Indeed, trade and the wealth that it brought underwrote the establishment of large and powerful kingdoms in east and central Africa. The best known of these kingdoms was Zimbabwe. The term *zimbabwe* simply refers to the dwelling of a chief. About the early thirteenth century, interior peoples built a magnificent stone complex known as Great Zimbabwe near Nyanda in the modern state of Zimbabwe. Within stone walls 5 meters (16 feet) thick and 10 meters (32 feet) tall, Great Zimbabwe was a city of stone towers, palaces, and public buildings that served as the capital of a large kingdom. At the time of its greatest extent in the late fifteenth century, up to eighteen thousand people may have lived in the vicinity of Great Zimbabwe, and the kingdom stretched from the outskirts of the Swahili city of Sofala deep into the interior of south-central Africa.

Kings residing at Great Zimbabwe controlled and taxed the trade between the interior and coastal regions. They organized the flow of gold, ivory, slaves, and local products from sources of supply to the coast. Their control over these products enabled them to forge alliances with local leaders and to profit handsomely from commercial transactions. Just as the trans-Saharan trade encouraged the building of states and empires in west Africa, the Indian Ocean trade generated wealth that financed the organization of city-states on the coast and large kingdoms in the interior regions of east and central Africa.

THINKING ABOUT *Encounters*

ENCOUNTERS IN STATES AND SOCIETIES IN SUB-SAHARAN AFRICA. Despite geographical barriers, the period after the eighth century C.E. witnessed increasing cross-cultural interaction between sub-Saharan Africans in west and east Africa with Islamic traders from the north. How did the introduction of Islam shape sub-Saharan societies and, conversely, how did sub-Saharan societies shape Islam?

Distant view of Great Zimbabwe
www.mhhe.com/bentleybrief2e

ISLAM IN EAST AFRICA In east Africa, as in west Africa, trade brought cultural as well as political changes. Like their counterparts in west Africa, the ruling elites and the wealthy merchants of east Africa converted to the Islamic faith. They did not necessarily give up their religious and cultural traditions but, rather, continued to observe them for purposes of providing cultural leadership in their societies. By adopting Islam, however, they laid a cultural foundation for close cooperation with Muslim merchants. Moreover, Islam served as a fresh source of legitimacy for their rule, since they gained recognition from Islamic states in southwest Asia, and their conversion opened the door to political alliances with Muslim rulers in other lands. Even though the conversion of elite classes did not bring about the immediate spread of Islam throughout their societies, it enabled Islam to establish a presence in east Africa under the sponsorship of influential patrons. The faith eventually attracted interest in larger circles and became one of the principal cultural and religious traditions of east Africa.

Kilwa (KILH-wah)
Zimbabwe (zihm-BAHB-way)

GREAT ZIMBABWE. | Built between the 11th and 15th centuries C.E. in what is now modern Zimbabwe, this stone city complex covered 1,800 acres.

SOURCES FROM THE PAST

Ibn Battuta on Muslim Society at Mogadishu

During the fourteenth century the Moroccan jurist Ibn Battuta traveled throughout much of the eastern hemisphere. Twice he visited sub-Saharan Africa: in 1331, when he traveled along the Swahili coast, and in 1351–1352, when he visited the Mali empire. His account of his visit to the Swahili city of Mogadishu offers insight into the mercantile and social customs of the city as well as the hospitality accorded to distinguished visitors.

[Mogadishu] is a town of enormous size. Its inhabitants are merchants possessed of vast resources: they own large numbers of camels, of which they slaughter hundreds every day [for food], and also have quantities of sheep. In this place are manufactured the woven fabrics called after it, which are unequalled and exported from it to Egypt and elsewhere. It is the custom of the people of this town that, when a vessel reaches the anchorage, the sumbuqs, which are small boats, come out to it. In each sumbuq there are a number of young men of the town, each one of whom brings a covered platter containing food and presents it to one of the merchants on the ship saying "This is my guest," and each of the others does the same. The merchant, on disembarking, goes only to the house of his host among the young men, except those of them who have made frequent journeys to the town and have gained some acquaintance with its inhabitants; these lodge where they please. When he takes up residence with his host, the latter sells his goods for him and buys for him; and if anyone buys anything from him at too low a price or sells to him in the absence of his host, that sale is held invalid by them. This practice is a profitable one for them.

When the young men came on board the vessel in which I was, one of them came up to me. My companions said to him "This man is not a merchant, but a doctor of the law," whereupon he called out to his friends and said to them "This is the guest of the qadi." There was among them one of the qadi's men, who informed him of this, and he came down to the beach with a number of students and sent one of them to me. I then disembarked with my companions and saluted him and his party. He said to me "In the name of God, let us go to salute the Shaikh." "And who is the Shaikh?" I said, and he answered, "The Sultan," for it is their custom to call the sultan "the Shaikh." . . .

When I arrived with the qadi . . . at the sultan's residence, one of the serving-boys came out and saluted the qadi, who said to him "Take word to the intendant's office and inform the Shaikh that this man has come from the land of al-Hijaz [Arabia]." So he took the message, then returned bringing a plate on which were some leaves of betel and areca nuts, the same to the qadi, and what was left on the plate to my companions and the qadi's students. He brought also a jug of rose-water of Damascus, which he poured over me and over the qadi [i.e., over our hands], and said "Our master commands that he be lodged in the students' house," this being a building equipped for the entertainment of students of religion. . . .

We stayed there three days, food being brought to us three times a day, following their custom. On the fourth day, which was a Friday, the qadi and students and one of the Shaikh's viziers came to me, bringing a set of robes; these [official] robes of theirs consist of a silk wrapper which one ties round his waist in place of drawers (for they have no acquaintance with these), a tunic of Egyptian linen with an embroidered border, a furred mantle of Jerusalem stuff, and an Egyptian turban with an embroidered edge. They also brought robes for my companions suitable to their position. We went to the congregational mosque and made our prayers behind the maqsura [private box for the sultan]. When the Shaikh came out of the door of the maqsura I saluted him along with the qadi; he said a word of greeting, spoke in their tongue with the qadi, and then said in Arabic "You are heartily welcome, and you have honored our land and given us pleasure."

■ **From Ibn Battuta's report, how could you characterize the role of hospitality on the Swahili coast?**

SOURCE: H. A. R. Gibb, trans. *The Travels of Ibn Battuta, A.D. 1325–1354,* 4 vols. Cambridge: Hakluyt Society, 1958–94, 2:374–77.

SUMMARY

States and societies of sub-Saharan Africa differed considerably from those in other parts of the eastern hemisphere. The foundations of most sub-Saharan societies were the agricultural economy and iron-working skills that Bantu and other peoples spread throughout most of the African continent. As these peoples migrated to new regions and established new communities, they usually based their societies on kin groups rather than the state structures that predominated elsewhere in the eastern hemisphere. When different societies came into conflict with one another, however, they increasingly established formal political authorities to guide their affairs. African peoples organized states of various sizes, some very small and others quite large. When they entered into commercial relationships with Muslim peoples in southwest Asia and north Africa, they also built formidable imperial states in west Africa and bustling city-states in coastal east Africa. These states had far-reaching implications for sub-Saharan societies because they depended on a regular and reliable flow of trade goods—particularly gold, ivory, and slaves—and they encouraged African peoples to organize themselves politically and economically to satisfy the demands of foreign Muslim merchants. Trade also had cultural implications because it facilitated the introduction of Islam, which together with native African traditions profoundly influenced the development of sub-Saharan societies. After the eighth century, ruling elites in both west Africa and coastal east Africa mostly accepted Islam and strengthened its position in their societies by building mosques, consulting Muslim advisors, and supporting Islamic schools. By 1500 C.E. African traditions and Islamic influences had combined to fashion a series of powerful, productive, and distinctive societies in sub-Saharan Africa.

STUDY TERMS

age grades (287)
Axum (289)
bananas (284)
Bantu peoples (284)
Benin (285)
camels (291)
Ghana (291)
Great Zimbabwe (295)
Ife (285)
Islamic slave trade (288)
Kebra Negast (289)
Kilwa (294)
kin-based societies (285)
kingdom of Kongo (286)
Koumbi-Saleh (291)
Mansa Musa (293)
Sundiata (283)
Swahili (293)
trans-Saharan trade (291)
Zanj revolt (288)

FOR FURTHER READING

Ibn Battuta. *Ibn Battuta in Black Africa.* Ed. and trans. by Said Hamdun and Noel King. Princeton, 1998. Translations of travel accounts of visits to coastal east Africa and the empire of Mali by a famous fourteenth-century Moroccan traveler.

Paul Bohannan and Philip D. Curtin. *Africa and Africans.* 3rd ed. Prospect Heights, Ill., 1988. Exploration of themes in African history, society, and culture by an anthropologist and a historian.

Christopher Ehret. *The Civilizations of Africa: A History to 1800.* Charlottesville, Va., 2002. An important contribution that views Africa in the context of world history.

J. F. P. Hopkins and N. Levtzion, eds. *Corpus of Early Arabic Sources for West African History.* Princeton, 2000. Translations of numerous important accounts by Muslim merchants and geographers who reported on conditions in west Africa before modern times.

Ali A. Mazrui. *The Africans: A Triple Heritage.* Boston, 1986. Emphasizes the legacies of indigenous, Islamic, and western influences on African history.

John S. Mbiti. *African Religions and Philosophy.* 2nd ed. London, 1990. A thorough and systematic study of traditional African religions in their cultural context.

Roderick James McIntosh. *The Peoples of the Middle Niger: The Island of Gold.* Oxford, 1998. Fascinating volume emphasizing the environmental context of west African history.

John Middleton. *The World of the Swahili: An African Mercantile Civilization.* New Haven, 1992. Rich scholarly analysis that places modern Swahili society and culture in its historical context.

D. T. Niane, ed. *Sundiata: An Epic of Old Mali.* Trans. by G. D. Pickett. London, 2006. Translation of the story of Sundiata, founder of the Mali empire, as preserved in African oral tradition.

Jan Vansina. *Paths in the Rainforests: Toward a History of Political Tradition in Equatorial Africa.* Madison, 1990. A brilliant synthesis of early African history by one of the world's foremost historians of Africa.

Christian Western Europe during the Middle Ages

16

In 1260 C.E. two brothers, Niccolò and Maffeo Polo, traveled from their native Venice to Constantinople. The Polo brothers were jewel merchants, and while in Constantinople, they decided to pursue opportunities farther east. They went first to trading cities on the Black Sea and the Volga River and then spent three years in the great central Asian trading city of Bokhara. While in Bokhara, they received an invitation to join a diplomatic embassy going to the court of Khubilai Khan. They readily agreed and traveled by caravan to the Mongol court, where the great khan received them and inquired about their land, rulers, and religion.

Khubilai was especially interested in learning more about Roman Catholic Christianity. Thus he asked the Polo brothers to return to Europe and request the pope to send learned theologians who could serve as authoritative sources of information on Christian doctrine. They accepted the mission and returned to Italy in 1269 as envoys of the great khan.

The Polo brothers were not able to satisfy the great khan's desire for expertise in Christian doctrine. The pope designated two missionaries to accompany the Polos, and the party set out in 1271, together with Niccolò's seventeen-year-old son, Marco Polo. Soon, however, the missionaries became alarmed at fighting along the route, and they decided to abandon the embassy and return to Europe. Only the Polos completed the journey, arriving at the Mongol court of Shangdu in 1274. Although they presented Khubilai with presents and letters from the pope rather than the requested missionaries, the great khan received them warmly. In fact, they remained in China in the service of the great khan for the next seventeen years. Their mission gave rise to Marco Polo's celebrated account of his travels, and it signaled the reintegration of Europe into the political and economic affairs of the larger eastern hemisphere.

Khubilai Khan with the Polo brothers
www.mhhe.com/bentleybrief2e

During the early middle ages—from about 500 to 1000 C.E.—western Europe was a violent and disorderly land. The collapse of the western Roman empire and invasions by migratory peoples wrecked European society and the economy. The Germanic Carolingian empire—ruled most famously by Charlemagne—provided order in much of Europe only for a short time before a new series of invasions brought it down in 843 C.E. As a result of the turmoil and disarray that plagued Europe during the half millennium from 500 to 1000 C.E., western Europeans played little role in the development of a hemispheric economy during the era dominated by the Tang, Song, Abbasid, and Byzantine empires.

❮ *A street scene of fabric and furniture merchants.*

Khubilai Khan (KOO-bih-lie Kahn)

CHRONOLOGY

476	Fall of the western Roman empire
480–547	Life of St. Benedict of Nursia
481–511	Reign of Clovis
482–543	Life of St. Scholastica
590–604	Reign of Pope Gregory I
751–843	Carolingian kingdom
768–814	Reign of Charlemagne
800	Coronation of Charlemagne as emperor
843	Dissolution of the Carolingian empire
936–973	Reign of King Otto I of Saxony
962	Coronation of Otto I as Holy Roman Emperor
1066	Norman invasion of England
1096–1099	First crusade
1170–1221	Life of St. Dominic
1182–1226	Life of St. Francis
1187	Recapture of Jerusalem by Saladin
1202–1204	Fourth Crusade
1225–1274	Life of St. Thomas Aquinas
1271–1295	Marco Polo's trip to China

However, Europeans did begin to lay the foundations of a more dynamic society in the early middle ages. For example, regional states began to provide a stable political order. New tools and technologies led to increased agricultural production and economic growth. In addition, the western Christian church brought cultural and religious unity to most of Europe. Based on such political, economic, and cultural foundations, Europeans were able to build a vibrant and powerful society from about 1000 to 1300 C.E.—the period known in Europe as the "high middle ages."

Although the idea of empire continued to fascinate European leaders, no one managed to bring all of Europe under their control during the high middle ages. Instead, local rulers organized powerful regional states. Increased agricultural production fueled rapid population growth. Economic expansion led to increased long-distance trade, enriched cities, and helped to create new towns.

Political organization, demographic increase, and economic growth pushed Europeans once again into the larger world. European merchants began to participate directly in the commercial economy of the eastern hemisphere, sometimes traveling as far as China in search of luxury goods. Ambitious military and political leaders expanded the boundaries of Christendom by seizing Muslim-held territories in Spain and the Mediterranean islands. European forces even mounted a series of military crusades that sought to recapture Palestine and the city of Jerusalem from Muslim control. Those efforts clearly demonstrated that Europeans were beginning to play a much larger role in the world than they had for the previous half millennium.

The Quest for Order and the Establishment of Regional States

Long after its disappearance in the late fifth century C.E. the Roman empire inspired European leaders, who dreamed of a centralized political structure embracing all of Christian Europe. Yet it was not until the late eighth and ninth centuries that a Germanic group, the Franks, temporarily reestablished imperial authority in western Europe. Even then, imperial authority was short-lived and collapsed by the late ninth century. In the late tenth century, a new attempt was made by German princes who formed the Holy Roman Empire, which they viewed as a Christian revival of the earlier Roman empire. In fact, however, the Roman empire returned only in name. All attempts to extend its influence beyond Germany met stiff resistance from the popes and from the princes of other European lands. Medieval Europe became a political mosaic of independent and competing regional states. Independent monarchies emerged in France and England, and other authorities ruled the various regions of Italy and Spain. These states frequently clashed with one another, and they all faced perennial challenges from within. Yet they organized their own territories efficiently, and they laid the foundations for the emergence of powerful national states in a later era.

The Franks and the Temporary Revival of Empire

CHARLEMAGNE. | A bronze statue depicts Charlemagne riding a horse and carrying an orb symbolizing his imperial authority.

Just a few decades after the Germanic general Odovacer deposed the last of the western Roman emperors in 476 C.E., the invaders organized a series of Germanic kingdoms as successor states in place of the Roman Empire. However, from the fifth through the eighth centuries, continuing invasions and conflicts among the invaders themselves left western Europe in a shambles. A major problem was that none of the Germanic peoples possessed the resources—much less the political and social organization—to dominate all the others and establish their hegemony throughout western Europe. Yet by the ninth century, one of these groups—the Franks—not only became the most powerful of the Germanic peoples, but also built an impressive imperial state that temporarily organized about half of the territories formerly embraced by the western Roman empire.

CHARLEMAGNE The Franks had won their dominance over other Germanic peoples as a result of strong military leadership as well as the support of the popes in Rome, who appreciated the Franks' conversion to Roman Christianity in the late fifth century. The Frankish realm reached its high point under the rule of the Carolingian family line during the reign of Charlemagne ("Charles the Great"), who ruled from 768 to 814. Charlemagne possessed enormous energy, and the building of the Carolingian empire was in large measure his personal accomplishment. Although barely literate, Charlemagne was extremely intelligent. He spoke Latin, understood some Greek, and regularly conversed with theologians and other learned men. He also maintained diplomatic relations with the Byzantine empire and the Abbasid caliphate. When Charlemagne inherited the Frankish throne, his realm included most of modern France as well as the lands that now form Belgium, the Netherlands, and southwestern Germany. By the time of his death in 814, Charlemagne had extended his authority to northeast Spain, Bavaria, northern Germany, and Italy as far south as Rome.

CHARLEMAGNE'S ADMINISTRATION Charlemagne established a court and capital at Aachen (in modern Germany), but he spent most of his reign traveling throughout his realm to maintain his authority. In his absence, Charlemagne relied on aristocratic deputies, known as counts, who held political, military, and judicial authority in local jurisdictions. However, because the counts often had their own political ambitions that were not the same as those of the central government, Charlemagne instituted a new group of imperial officials known as *missi dominici* ("envoys of the lord ruler"), who traveled annually to review the accounts of all local authorities.

CHARLEMAGNE AS EMPEROR Charlemagne worked extremely hard to keep his territories together. Although he had built the Frankish kingdom into an empire, he hesitated to call himself emperor because he knew the title would constitute a direct challenge to the Byzantine emperors who had inherited the eastern Roman empire. In 800, however, Charlemagne did accept the title when Pope Leo III publicly recognized his accomplishments by proclaiming him emperor during religious services on Christmas Day.

DISSOLUTION OF THE CAROLINGIAN EMPIRE Yet Charlemagne's empire did not last long after his death. Indeed, both internal disunity and external invasions brought the Carolingian empire to an early end. By 843 Charlemagne's

Odoacer (AHD-oh-ah-cer)
Charlemagne (SHAHR-leh-mane)
Carolingian (kah-roe-LIN-gee-uhn)
Aachen (AH-kehn)

MAP 16.1 | The Carolingian empire, 814 C.E. Notice the location of Charlemagne's capital at Aachen and also the extent of his empire. ***What geographical challenges did he face in his efforts to hold his empire together?***

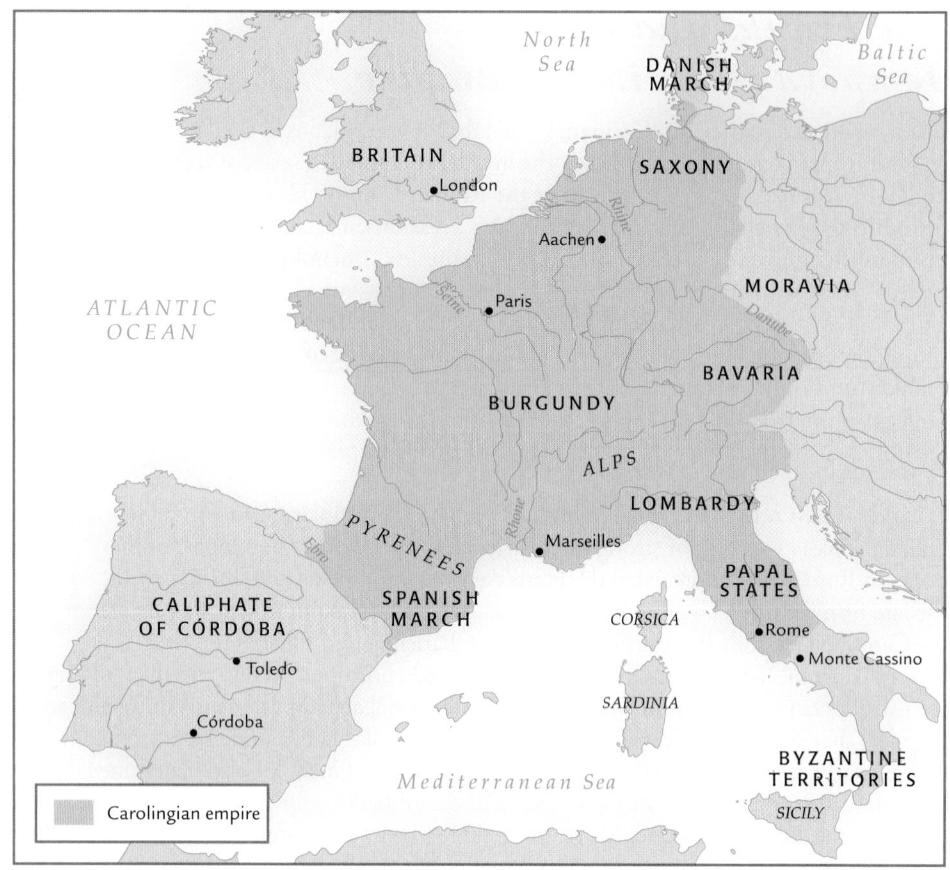

three grandsons—who fought bitterly between themselves for the title of emperor—decided that they would solve the problem by dividing the empire into three kingdoms. Even had the empire remained unified, however, it was already apparent that local counts in the empire's vast realms were increasingly ignoring the central imperial government in favor of their own interests. Moreover, Muslim invaders from the south, Hungarian Magyar invaders from the east, and Viking invaders from the north all contributed to massive instability in the region and helped to ensure the ultimate dissolution of the empire.

The Holy Roman Empire

OTTO I As the Carolingian empire faded during the ninth century, local authorities took responsibility for providing order in their own regions. Gradually, some of them extended their influence beyond their own jurisdictions and built larger states. Otto of Saxony was particularly aggressive. By the mid–tenth century, he had established himself as king in northern Germany, and twice he ventured into Italy to quell political disturbances, protect the church, and seek opportunities in the south. In appreciation for his aid to the church, Pope John XII proclaimed Otto emperor in 962 C.E. Thus was born the Holy Roman Empire.

The imperial title had considerable cachet, and on several occasions energetic emperors almost transformed the Holy Roman Empire into a hegemonic state that might have reintroduced imperial unity to Europe. Conflict with the papacy, however, prevented the emperors from building a strong and dynamic state. Although the popes crowned the medieval emperors, their relations were usually tense, since both popes and emperors made large claims to authority in Christian Europe. Relations became especially strained when emperors sought to influence the selection of church officials, which the popes regarded as their own prerogative, or when emperors sought to extend their authority into

MAP 16.2 | The regional states of medieval Europe, 1000–1300 C.E. Note the large number of states and the different kinds of states that claimed sovereignty in medieval Europe. ***How would this variety of states have contributed to instability in Europe?***

Italy, where the popes had long provided political leadership. Thus when the popes felt threatened by the pretensions of the Holy Roman Empire, they entered into alliances with other European authorities to check the power of the emperors. Because of that, the Holy Roman Empire remained an empire principally in name. Voltaire, the eighteenth-century French writer, once quipped that the Holy Roman Empire was "neither holy, nor Roman, nor an empire." Instead, it was a regional state that ruled Germany and occasionally sought to wield influence in eastern Europe and Italy.

Regional Monarchies in France and England

In the absence of an effective imperial power, regional states emerged throughout medieval Europe. In France and England, princes established regional monarchies on the basis of relationships between lords and their retainers.

CAPETIAN FRANCE The French monarchy grew slowly from humble beginnings. When the last of the Carolingians died, in 987 C.E., the lords of France elected a minor noble named Hugh Capet to serve as king. Capet held only a small territory around

Capet (KAHP-it)

Paris, and some of his retainers were far more powerful than he. Over the next three centuries, however, his descendants, known as the Capetian kings, gradually added to their resources, expanded their political influence, and established the right to administer justice throughout the realm. By the early fourteenth century, the Capetian kings had gradually centralized power and authority in France.

PSI doc Statutes of William the Conqueror www.mhhe.com/bentleybrief2e

THE NORMANS The English monarchy developed quite differently. Its founders were Normans—descendants of Vikings who carved out a state on the peninsula of Normandy in France during the ninth century. Though nominally subject to Carolingian and later to Capetian rulers, the dukes of Normandy in fact pursued their own interests with little regard for their lords. Within Normandy the dukes built a tightly centralized state in which all authority stemmed from the dukes themselves. The dukes also retained title to all land in Normandy and strictly limited the right of their retainers to grant land to others. In 1066 Duke William of Normandy invaded England, then ruled by descendants of the Angles, the Saxons, and other Germanic peoples. Following a speedy military victory, the duke, now known as William the Conqueror, introduced Norman principles of government and land tenure to England and quickly established a tightly centralized realm.

Both the Capetians and the Normans faced internal challenges from retainers seeking to pursue independent policies or enlarge their powers. Both dynasties also faced external challenges: indeed, they often battled each other, since the Normans periodically sought to expand their possessions in France. On the basis of relationships between lords and retainers, however, both the Capetians and the Normans managed to organize regional monarchies that maintained order and provided reasonably good government.

Regional States in Italy and Iberia

ITALIAN STATES Regional states emerged also in other lands of medieval Europe, though not on such a large scale as the monarchies of France and England. In Italy, for example, a series of ecclesiastical states, city-states, and principalities competed for power and position. By about the twelfth century, a series of prosperous city-states—including Florence, Bologna, Genoa, Milan, and Venice—dominated not only their own urban districts but also the surrounding hinterlands. Meanwhile, in southern Italy, Norman adventurers invaded territories still claimed by the Byzantine empire and various Muslim states. With papal approval and support, they overcame Byzantine and Muslim authorities, brought southern Italy into the orbit of Roman Catholic Christianity, and laid the foundations for the emergence of the powerful kingdom of Naples.

PSI img The Alhambra in Granada www.mhhe.com/bentleybrief2e

CHRISTIAN AND MUSLIM STATES IN IBERIA As in Italy, a series of regional states competed for power on the Iberian peninsula. From the eighth to the eleventh century, Muslim conquerors ruled most of the peninsula except for a few small states in northern Spain. Beginning in the mid–eleventh century, though, Christian adventurers from these states began to attack Muslim territories and enlarge their own domains. By the late thirteenth century, the Christian kingdoms of Castile, Aragon, and Portugal controlled most of the Iberian peninsula, leaving only the small kingdom of Granada in Muslim hands.

With its Holy Roman Empire, regional monarchies, ecclesiastical principalities, city-states, and new states founded on conquest, medieval Europe might seem to present a stark contrast to a centralized, reunified land such as China. Moreover, European rulers constantly campaigned to enlarge their holdings at the expense of their neighbors and thus endlessly complicated medieval European politics. Yet the regional states of the middle ages effectively tended to public affairs in limited regions. In doing so, they fashioned alternatives to a centralized empire as a form of political organization.

Economic Growth and Social Development

As regional states provided increasingly effective political organization, regional lords and their vassals took charge of political and military affairs in a system historians have commonly referred to as feudalism. The relative order and stability provided by feudalism eventually encouraged dramatic economic growth and social development in medieval Europe. This economic revival closely resembled the processes that in an earlier era had strengthened China, India, and the Islamic world. Thus, even in the absence of centralized imperial authority, the increased agricultural production, urbanization, manufacturing, and trade spurred by feudalism transformed Europe and drew it once again into commercial relationships with distant lands.

Organizing a Decentralized Society

When the short-lived Carolingian empire dissolved, European nobles had little choice but to take responsibility for maintaining order in their own territories. Although most nobles owed nominal allegiance to a higher authority, in reality they acted with growing independence: they collected rents and fees, administered local affairs, mobilized armed forces, and decided legal disputes.

LORDS AND RETAINERS To organize their territories the local nobles built military and political relationships with other prominent individuals in their territories. In doing so, they mobilized small private armies by attracting armed retainers into their service with grants of land or money. These grants enabled retainers to devote their energies to the service of their lords rather than the tasks of cultivating food for their families. Retainers became responsible for the organization of local public works projects, the resolution of disputes, and the administration of justice. In exchange, retainers owed loyalty, obedience, and military service to their lords. As a result of these mutual obligations, lords and retainers merged into a hereditary noble class that lived off the surplus agricultural production it extracted from cultivators.

This decentralized political order developed into a complicated network of relationships between lords and retainers. Indeed, a lord with several retainers might himself be a retainer to a higher lord, who in turn might be one of several retainers to an even greater lord in a web of relationships extending from local communities to a king. Although this decentralized political order had the potential to lead to chaos if retainers decided to pursue their own interests, in several places—including England, Germany, and France—high-ranking lords built powerful states on such foundations.

Serfs, Manors, and the Growth of the Agricultural Economy

SERFS The development of a decentralized political order accompanied fundamental changes in European society. Among the most important of these changes was the creation, during the mid-seventh century, of a new category of peasants called serfs. Serfs were not slaves subject to sale, but neither were they fully free. Instead, landlords allocated serfs a certain portion of land to farm, and in exchange required both labor services as well as a portion of the serfs' harvest. Male serfs typically worked three days a week in the fields of their lords and provided additional labor services during planting and harvesting seasons, while women churned butter, made cheese, brewed beer, spun thread, wove cloth, or sewed clothes for the lords and their families. Because landlords provided them with land to cultivate and sometimes with tools and animals as well, serfs had little opportunity to move to different lands. Indeed, they were able to do so only with the permission of

MANOR HOUSE. | In this landscape painting from the late fifteenth century, the lord of the manor (in robes) watches his laborers plant grapevines and pick grapes.

their lord. They even had to pay a fee for the right to marry a serf who worked for a different lord.

MANORS During the early middle ages, the institution of serfdom encouraged the development of the manor as the principal form of agricultural organization in western Europe. A manor was a large estate consisting of fields, meadows, forests, domestic animals, and serfs bound to the land. The lord of the manor was a prominent political or military figure who provided government, administration, and justice for the manor. In the absence of thriving cities, manors became largely self-sufficient communities. Lords of the manors maintained mills, bakeries, breweries, and wineries, and serfs produced most of the iron tools, leather goods, domestic utensils, and textiles that the manorial community needed. During the high middle ages, craft skills developed on manors would help fuel an impressive round of economic development in western Europe.

NEW CROPS AND TOOLS Peasant cultivators on manors also cleared forests, drained swamps, and increased the amount of land devoted to agriculture during the middle ages. As they did so, they also experimented with new agricultural techniques and implements. By the high middle ages European cultivators were experimenting with new crops and with different cycles of crop rotation to ensure the most abundant harvests without compromising the fertility of the soil. They increased cultivation especially of beans, which not only provided dietary protein but also enriched the land because of their property of fixing nitrogen in the soils where they grow. In addition, European peoples expanded their use of watermills and heavy plows, and introduced new tools like the horseshoe and horse collar—both of which increased the efficiency of agricultural labor. By the thirteenth century, observation and experimentation with new crops and new techniques had vastly increased understanding of agricultural affairs. News of these discoveries circulated widely throughout Europe in books and treatises on household economics and agricultural methods, which in turn led to increased agricultural productivity.

POPULATION GROWTH Expansion of land under cultivation, improved methods of cultivation, and the use of new tools combined to increase both the quantity and the quality of food supplies. During the centuries from 1000 to 1300, European diets expanded from an almost complete reliance on grains to include meat, dairy products, fish, vegetables, and legumes such as beans and peas. This increase in agricultural productivity supported rapid population growth. In 600 C.E., as the Franks were beginning to

SOURCES FROM THE PAST

Life on an Early Medieval Manor

Some useful insights into the lives and experiences of common people come from a decree known as the "Capitulary de Villis" issued by the emperor Charlemagne in 807 C.E. as a guide for stewards of Carolingian estates. The decree envisions a community with sophisticated agricultural and craft skills. Probably few estates observed all provisions of Charlemagne's decree, but the capitulary nonetheless communicates clearly how lords hoped to control their manors and profit from their production.

Each steward shall make an annual statement of all our income: an account of our lands cultivated by the oxen which our ploughmen drive and of our lands which the tenants of farms ought to plough; an account of the pigs, of the rents, of the obligations and fines; of the game taken in our forests without our permission; . . . of the mills, of the forest, of the fields, of the bridges, and ships; of the free men and the hundreds who are under obligations to our treasury; of markets, vineyards, and those who owe wine to us; of the hay, firewood, torches, planks, and other kinds of lumber; of the waste lands; of the fruits of the trees, of the nut trees, larger and smaller; of the grafted trees of all kinds; of the gardens; of the turnips; of the fish ponds; of the hides, skins, and horns; of the honey, wax; of the fat, tallow and soap; of the mulberry wine, cooked wine, mead, vinegar, beer, wine new and old; of the new grain and the old; of the hens and eggs; of the geese; the number of fishermen, [metal] smiths, sword-makers, and shoemakers; . . . of the forges and mines, that is iron and other mines; of the lead mines; . . . of the colts and fillies; they shall make all these known to us, set forth separately and in order, at Christmas, in order that we may know what and how much of each thing we have. . . .

[Stewards] must provide the greatest care, that whatever is prepared or made with the hands, that is, lard, smoked meat, salt meat, partially salted meat, wine, vinegar, mulberry wine, cooked wine . . . mustard, cheese, butter, malt, beer, mead, honey, wax, flour, all should be prepared and made with the greatest cleanliness. . . .

[Stewards should ensure] that in each of our estates, the chambers [living quarters] shall be provided with counterpanes, cushions, pillows, bed clothes, coverings for the tables and benches; vessels of brass, lead, iron and wood; andirons, chains, pot-hooks, adzes, axes, augers, cutlasses and all other kinds of tools, so that it shall never be necessary to go elsewhere for them, or to borrow them. And the weapons, which are carried against the enemy, shall be well cared for, so as to keep them in good condition; and when they are brought back they shall be placed in the chamber.

For our women's work they are to give at the proper time, as has been ordered, the materials, that is the linen, wool, woad, vermillion, madder, wool-combs, teasels, soap, grease, vessels and the other objects which are necessary.

Of the food products other than meat, two-thirds shall be sent each year for our own use, that is of the vegetables, fish, cheese, honey, mustard, vinegar, millet, panic [a grain similar to millet], dried and green herbs, radishes, and in addition of the wax, soap and other small products; and they shall tell us how much is left by a statement, as we have said above; and they shall not neglect this as in the past; because from those two-thirds, we wish to know how much remains.

Each steward shall have in his district good workmen, namely, blacksmiths, goldsmiths, silversmiths, shoemakers, [wood] turners, carpenters, sword-makers, fishermen, foilers [fine metalworkers], soap-makers, men who know how to make beer, cider, berry, and all other kinds of beverages, bakers to make pastry for our table, net-makers who know how to make nets for hunting, fishing and fowling, and the others who are too numerous to be designated.

■ **On the basis of the "Capitulary de Villis," how would you characterize the conditions of material life in the Carolingian countryside?**

SOURCE: *Translations and Reprints from the Original Sources of European History*, vol. 2. Philadelphia: University of Pennsylvania Press, 1900. (Translation slightly modified.)

gain dominance in western Europe, the European population stood at about twenty-six million. By 1000, when regional states had ended invasions and restored order, it had edged up to thirty-six million. By 1300, only three hundred years later, the population had reached seventy-nine million. Such rapid demographic growth in turn helped stimulate a vigorous revival of towns and trade in medieval Europe.

VENICE. | This city, the home of Marco Polo and a legion of merchants, drew enormous prosperity from trade. Street vendors, shopkeepers, and merchant ships figure prominently in this illustration from a fourteenth-century manuscript. ***What advantages did proximity to the water lend to Venetian merchants?***

The Revival of Towns and Trade

URBANIZATION With the abundant supplies of food produced on manors during the middle ages, by 1000 C.E. European society was able to support large numbers of urban residents. Attracted by urban opportunities, people from the countryside flocked to established cities and founded new towns at strategically located sites. Cities founded during Roman times, such as Paris, London, and Toledo, became thriving centers of government and business, and new urban centers—such as Venice in northern Italy—also emerged. Northern Italy and Flanders (the northwestern part of modern Belgium) experienced especially strong urbanization. Thus, for the first time since the fall of the western Roman empire, cities began to play a major role in European economic and social development.

TEXTILE PRODUCTION The growth of towns and cities brought about increasing specialization of labor, which in turn resulted in the dramatic expansion of manufacturing and trade. Manufacturing concentrated especially on the production of wool textiles. In fact, trade in wool products helped to fuel economic development, commercial exchange, and urbanization throughout Europe.

MEDITERRANEAN TRADE The revival of urban society was most pronounced in Italy, which was geographically well situated to participate in the trade networks of the Mediterranean basin. During the tenth century, for example, the cities of Amalfi and Venice served as ports for merchants engaged in trade with Byzantine and Muslim partners in the eastern Mediterranean. Italian merchants exchanged salt, olive oil, wine, wool fabrics, leather products, and glass for luxury goods such as gems, spices, silk, and other goods from India, southeast Asia, and China that Muslim merchants brought to eastern Mediterranean markets.

As trade expanded, Italian merchants established sizable communities in the major ports and commercial centers of the Mediterranean and the Black Sea, and by the mid–

In addition, most guilds admitted women into their ranks, and some guilds had exclusively female memberships. Indeed, the increasing prominence of women in European society illustrates the significance of towns and cities as agents of social change in medieval Europe.

European Christianity during the Middle Ages

One of the most important developments of the early middle ages was the conversion of western Europe to Roman Christianity. The Franks, the popes, and the monasteries played important roles in bringing about this conversion. The adoption of Roman Christianity ensured that medieval Europe would inherit crucial cultural elements from classical Roman society, including the Latin language and the institutional Roman church. In addition, Roman Catholic Christianity guided European thought on religious, moral, and ethical matters. Representatives of the Roman church administered the rituals associated with birth, marriage, and death. Most of the art, literature, and music of the middle ages drew inspiration from Christian doctrines and stories. Just as mosques and minarets defined the skylines of Muslim cities, the spires of churches and cathedrals dominated the landscape of medieval Europe, testifying visually to the importance of religion and the pervasive presence of the Roman Catholic church.

Western Christianity also changed in several ways during the late middle ages. As the Roman Catholic church developed an identity distinct from the Eastern Orthodox church, western theologians became reacquainted with the works of Aristotle—mostly unknown to European scholars of the early middle ages—and they produced an impressive synthesis of Aristotelian philosophy and Christian values. Meanwhile, lay classes elaborated a rich tradition of popular religion that represented an effort to express Christianity in meaningful terms.

The Politics of Conversion

THE FRANKS AND THE CHURCH Although Christianity was the principal source of religious, moral, and cultural authority in the Mediterranean basin by the time the Roman empire collapsed, western Europeans did not demonstrate a deep commitment to Christianity until the Franks converted to the religion in the late fifth century. By the time of Charlemagne, the Carolingian Franks viewed themselves as protectors of the papacy, and offered the popes both political and military support. Charlemagne also worked to spread Christianity in northern lands through both peaceful and military means. Between 772 and 804, for example, he waged a bitter campaign against the Saxons, a pagan people inhabiting northern Germany. When he finally claimed victory, Charlemagne insisted, not only that the Saxons acknowledge him as their political lord, but that they replace their pagan traditions with Christianity. Through campaigns such as this, as well as through diplomacy and the work of missionaries, by the year 1000 C.E. Christianity had won the allegiance of most people throughout western Europe and the Nordic lands.

The Papacy

In addition to the support it received from the Franks, the Roman church increased its authority in Europe through strong papal leadership. When the western Roman empire collapsed, the papacy survived and claimed spiritual authority over all the lands formerly embraced by the empire. Initially, the popes cooperated closely with the Byzantine emperors, who as leaders of the eastern Roman empire seemed to be the natural heirs to Roman authority. Beginning in the late sixth century, however, the popes began increasingly to distinguish the western Christian church based in Rome from the eastern Christian church based in Constantinople. By 1054 C.E., the two churches differed so violently on so many issues that the pope and the patriarch of the eastern church excommunicated each other. After the eleventh century the two branches of Christianity formed distinct identities as the Roman Catholic and Eastern Orthodox churches.

POPE GREGORY I The individual most important in providing the Roman church with its sense of identity and direction was Pope Gregory I (590–604 C.E.), also known as Gregory the Great. Most important, Gregory strengthened the pope's control over church doctrine by reasserting papal primacy—the claim that the bishop of Rome was the ultimate authority in the Christian church. Gregory also enhanced the influence of the Roman church in the lives of individuals by emphasizing the sacrament of penance, which required individuals to confess their sins to their priests and then to atone for their sins by penitential acts prescribed by the priests. In addition, Gregory further strengthened the Roman church by extending its appeal and winning new converts in western Europe through the efforts of missionaries, most of whom were monks. Indeed, Pope Gregory himself was a monk, and he relied heavily on the energies of his fellow monks in seeking converts throughout Europe.

Monasticism

Christian monasticism had its origin in the second century C.E. in Egypt, where devout Christians had formed communes to devote themselves to the pursuit of holiness. When Christianity became legal during the fourth century, the monastic lifestyle became an increasingly popular alternative throughout the Roman empire.

ST. BENEDICT AND THE *RULE* During the early days of monasticism, each community developed its own rules, procedures, and priorities. Some communities demanded that their inhabitants follow extremely austere lifestyles that sapped the energy of the monks, whereas others did not establish any clear expectations of their recruits. In response to those haphazard conditions, St. Benedict of Nursia (480–547 C.E.) strengthened the early monastic movement by providing it with discipline and a sense of purpose. In 529 St. Benedict prepared a set of regulations known as Benedict's *Rule* for the monastic community that he had founded at Monte Cassino, near Rome. The *Rule* required monks to take vows to lead communal, celibate lives under the absolute direction of the abbot who supervised the monastery: poverty, chastity, and obedience became the prime virtues for Benedictine monks.

ST. SCHOLASTICA Through the influence of St. Benedict's sister, the nun St. Scholastica (482–543), an adaptation of the *Rule* soon provided guidance for the religious life of women living in convents. Within a century most European monasteries and convents observed the Benedictine *Rule.* Even today most Roman Catholic monasteries observe rules that reflect the influence of the Benedictine tradition.

Strengthened by the discipline that the Benedictine *Rule* introduced, monasteries became a dominant feature in the social and cultural life of western Europe throughout the middle ages. Monasteries helped to provide order in the countryside, for example, and to expand agricultural production. Monasteries accumulated large landholdings—as well as authority over serfs working their lands—from the bequests of wealthy individuals, and on those lands they mobilized both monks and serfs to clear forests, drain swamps, and prepare lands for cultivation. Indeed, monasteries organized much of the labor that brought about the expansion of agricultural production in early medieval Europe.

MONASTICISM AND SOCIETY Like Buddhist monasteries in Asian lands and charitable religious foundations in Muslim lands, European monasteries provided a variety of social services. They served as inns, places of refuge, orphanages, hospitals,

St. Scholastica (skuh-LAS-tih-kah)

and schools. Some monasteries maintained libraries and scriptoria, where monks copied works of classical literature and philosophy as well as the scriptures and other Christian writings. Almost all works of Latin literature that have come down to the present survive because of copies made by medieval monks. Finally, monasteries served as a source of literate, educated, and talented individuals whose secretarial and administrative services were crucial for the organization of effective government in early medieval Europe.

Because of the various roles they played in the larger society, monasteries were particularly effective agents in the spread of Christianity. While they organized life in the countryside and provided social services, monks also zealously preached Christianity and tended to the spiritual needs of rural populations. Monks patiently and persistently served the needs of rural populations, and over the decades and centuries they helped to instill Christian values in countless generations of European peasants.

Monastery Life. Monasteries were the principal centers of literacy in western Europe during the early middle ages. In this manuscript illustration, one monk copies a manuscript, another makes geometric calculations, and a third cuts parchment, while two work on the building and one more rings the bells that call monks and members of the surrounding community to religious services.

Schools, Universities, and Scholastic Theology

CATHEDRAL SCHOOLS By the high middle ages, Europe's increasing wealth and social complexity created a strong demand for educated individuals who could deal with complicated political, legal, and theological issues. In response to such demand, by the eleventh century bishops and archbishops in France and northern Italy organized schools in their cathedrals and invited well-known scholars to serve as master teachers.

By the twelfth century the cathedral schools had established formal curricula. Instruction concentrated on the liberal arts, especially literature and philosophy. Students read the Bible and the writings of the church fathers, as well as classical Latin literature and the few works of Plato and Aristotle that were available in Latin translation. Some cathedral schools also offered advanced instruction in law, medicine, and theology.

UNIVERSITIES About the mid–twelfth century, students and teachers organized academic guilds and persuaded political authorities to grant charters guaranteeing their rights. Student guilds demanded rigorous, high-quality instruction from their teachers, while faculty sought to vest teachers with the right to bestow academic degrees and to control the curriculum in their own institutions. These guilds had the effect of transforming cathedral schools into universities. By the late thirteenth century, universities had appeared in cities throughout Europe.

PSI doc Founding of the University of Heidelberg www.mhhe.com/bentleybrief2e

SCHOLASTICISM: ST. THOMAS AQUINAS The evolution of the university coincided with the rediscovery of the works of Aristotle, which European scholars learned about through increased contacts with Byzantine as well as Muslim philosophers. During the thirteenth century, Latin translations of Aristotle's works spread throughout Europe, and they profoundly influenced almost all branches of thought. The most notable result was the emergence of scholastic theology, which sought to synthesize the beliefs and values of Christianity with the logical rigor of Greek philosophy. The most famous of the scholastic theologians was St. Thomas Aquinas (1225–1274), who spent most of his career teaching at the University of Paris. While holding fervently to his Christian convictions, St. Thomas believed that Aristotle had understood and explained the workings of the world better than any other thinker. St. Thomas saw no contradiction between Aristotle and Christian revelation. In his view, Aristotle explained the world according to human reason, while Christianity explained it as part of a divine plan. Thus, scholastic theology represented the synthesis of reason and faith. Like the neo-Confucianism of Zhu Xi or

St. Thomas Aquinas (uh-KWAHY-nuhs)

NÔTRE DAME CATHEDRAL. | Architects and laborers sometimes worked more than a century to construct the massive gothic cathedrals of medieval Europe. Built during the twelfth and thirteenth centuries, the magnificent cathedral of Notre Dame in Paris honors the Virgin Mary. ***What kinds of feelings might such massive structures have evoked in worshipers?***

the Islamic philosophy of Ibn Rushd, scholastic theology reinterpreted inherited beliefs in light of the most advanced knowledge of the time.

Popular Religion

St. Thomas and the other scholastic theologians addressed a sophisticated, intellectual elite rather than the common people of medieval Europe. The popular masses neither knew nor cared much about Aristotle. For their purposes, Christianity was important primarily as a set of beliefs, ceremonies, and rituals that gave meaning to individual lives and that bound them together into coherent communities.

SACRAMENTS Popular piety generally entailed observance of the sacraments and devotion to the saints recognized by the Roman Catholic church. Sacraments are holy rituals that bring spiritual blessings on the observants. The church recognized seven sacraments, including baptism, matrimony, penance, and the Eucharist. By far the most popular was the Eucharist, during which priests offered a ritual meal commemorating Jesus' last meal with his disciples before his trial and execution by Roman authorities. Because the sacrament kept individuals in good standing with the church, conscientious believers observed it weekly, and the especially devout on a daily basis. Popular beliefs held that the sacrament would protect individuals from sudden death and advance their worldly interests.

DEVOTION TO SAINTS Popular religion also took the form of devotion to the saints. According to church teachings, saints were human beings who had led such exemplary lives that God held them in special esteem. As a result, they enjoyed special influence with heavenly authorities and were able to intervene on behalf of individuals living in the world. Medieval Europeans frequently invoked the aid of saints, who had reputations for helping living people as well as souls of the dead. Tradition held that certain saints could cure diseases, relieve toothaches, and guide sailors through storms to a port.

THE VIRGIN MARY During the high middle ages, the most popular saint was always the Virgin Mary, mother of Jesus, who personified the Christian ideal of womanhood, love, and sympathy, and who reportedly lavished aid on her devotees. During the twelfth and thirteenth centuries, Europeans dedicated hundreds of churches and cathedrals to the Virgin, among them the splendid cathedral of Notre Dame ("Our Lady") of Paris.

SAINTS' RELICS Medieval Europeans went to great lengths to express their adoration of the Virgin and other saints through veneration of their relics and physical remains, widely believed to retain the powers associated with the holy individuals themselves. Churches assembled vast collections of relics, such as clothes, locks of hair, teeth, and bones of famous saints. Especially esteemed were relics associated with Jesus or the Virgin, such as the crown of thorns that Jesus reportedly wore during his crucifixion or drops of the Virgin's milk miraculously preserved in a vial.

PILGRIMAGE Some collections of relics became famous well beyond their own regions. Like Muslims making the hajj, pilgrims trekked long distances to honor the saints the relics represented. The making of pilgrimages became so common during the high middle ages that a travel industry emerged to serve the needs of pilgrims. Inns dotted the routes leading to popular churches and shrines, and guides shepherded groups of pilgrims to religious sites and explained their significance. There were even guidebooks that pointed out the major attractions along pilgrims' routes and warned them of difficult terrain and unscrupulous scoundrels who took advantage of visitors.

THINKING ABOUT *Traditions*

TRADITIONS IN WESTERN EUROPE DURING THE MIDDLE AGES. When a strong and sustained imperial authority failed to emerge in Europe in the centuries after the fall of the Roman empire, a wide variety of regional, self-sufficient states emerged to organize local affairs. In the early middle ages, most of these states did not have the wealth or capability to engage in long-distance trade or communication with the rest of the eastern hemisphere. In what ways did the relative isolation of European states in this period affect the development of cultural, political, and social traditions?

The Medieval Expansion of Europe

During the high middle ages, the relationship between western European peoples and their neighbors underwent dramatic change. Powerful states, economic expansion, and demographic growth all strengthened European society, while church officials encouraged the colonization of pagan and Muslim lands as a way to extend the influence of Roman Catholic Christianity. Beginning about the mid–eleventh century, Europeans embarked on expansive ventures on several fronts: Atlantic, Baltic, and Mediterranean. All those ventures signaled clearly that Europeans were beginning to play a much larger role in the affairs of the eastern hemisphere than they had during the early middle ages.

Relic of John the Baptist
www.mhhe.com/bentleybrief2e

Atlantic and Baltic Colonization

VINLAND During the ninth and tenth centuries, seafaring peoples from the Nordic Scandinavian lands began to venture far from Europe to the islands of the North Atlantic Ocean. They occupied Iceland beginning in the late ninth century, and by the end of the tenth century they had discovered Greenland and established a small colony there. About 1000 C.E. Leif Ericsson left the colony at Greenland and took an exploratory party south and west, arriving eventually at modern Newfoundland in Canada. Because of the wild grapes growing in the region, Leif called it Vinland. During the years following Leif's voyage, Greenlanders made several efforts to establish permanent colonies in Vinland. Ultimately, however, their efforts failed because they did not have the resources to sustain a settlement over the stormy seas of the North Atlantic Ocean. Nonetheless, the establishment of even a short-lived colony indicated a growing capacity of Europeans to venture into the larger world.

CHRISTIANITY IN SCANDINAVIA While Scandinavians explored the North Atlantic, the Roman Catholic church drew Scandinavia itself into the community of Christian Europe. The kings of Denmark and Norway converted to Christianity in the

Leif Ericsson (leef ER-ik-suhn)

tenth century. Conversion of their subjects came gradually and with considerable resistance, but royal support for the Roman Catholic church ensured that Christianity would have a place in Danish and Norwegian societies. Between the twelfth and fourteenth centuries, Sweden and Finland followed their neighbors into the Christian faith.

CRUSADING ORDERS AND BALTIC EXPANSION In the Baltic lands of Prussia, Livonia, and Lithuania, Christian authority arrived in the wake of military conquest. During the era of crusades, zealous Christians formed a series of military-religious orders. The most prominent were the Templars, Hospitallers, and Teutonic Knights, who pledged to devote their lives to the struggle against Muslims and pagans. The Teutonic Knights were most active in the Baltic region, where they waged military campaigns against the pagan Slavic peoples during the twelfth and thirteenth centuries. Aided by German missionaries, the Knights founded churches and monasteries in the territories they subdued. By the late thirteenth century, the Roman Catholic church had established its presence throughout the Baltic region, which progressively became absorbed into the larger society of Christian Europe.

The Reconquest of Sicily and Spain

The boundaries of Christian Europe also expanded in the Mediterranean basin. There Europeans came into conflict with Muslims, whose ancestors had conquered the major Mediterranean islands and most of the Iberian peninsula between the eighth and tenth centuries. As their society became stronger, Europeans undertook to reconquer those territories and reintegrate them into Christian society.

THE RECONQUEST OF SICILY Most important of the islands was Sicily, which Muslims had conquered in the ninth century. During the eleventh century, Norman warriors returned Sicily to Christian hands after almost twenty years of conflict. Islam did not disappear immediately, but as Muslims either left Sicily or converted to Christianity, Islam gradually disappeared from the island.

THE RECONQUISTA OF SPAIN The reconquest of Spain—known as the *reconquista*—took a much longer time than the recapture of Sicily. Following the Muslim invasion and conquest of the early eighth century, the caliphate of Córdoba ruled almost all of the Iberian peninsula. A small Christian state survived in Catalonia in the far northeast, and the kingdom of León resisted Muslim advances in the far northwest. The process of *reconquista* began in the 1060s from these Christian toeholds. By 1150 Christian forces had recaptured Lisbon and established their authority over half of the peninsula. Their successes lured reinforcements from France and England, and in the first half of the thirteenth century a new round of campaigns brought most of Iberia into Christian hands. Only the kingdom of Granada in the far south of the peninsula remained Muslim. It survived as an outpost of Islam until 1492, when Christian forces mounted a campaign that conquered Granada and completed the *reconquista.*

The political, economic, and demographic strength of Christian Europe helps to explain the reconquests of Sicily and Spain as military ventures. Especially in the case of Spain, however, it is clear that religious concerns also helped to drive the *reconquista.* The popes and other leading clergy of the Roman Catholic church regarded Islam as an affront to Christianity, and they enthusiastically encouraged campaigns against the Muslims. When reconquered territories fell into Christian hands, church officials immediately established bishoprics and asserted Christian authority. They also organized campaigns to convert local populations. As a result of those efforts, the Roman Catholic church began to displace Islam in conquered Spain.

reconquista (ray-kohn-KEES-tah)

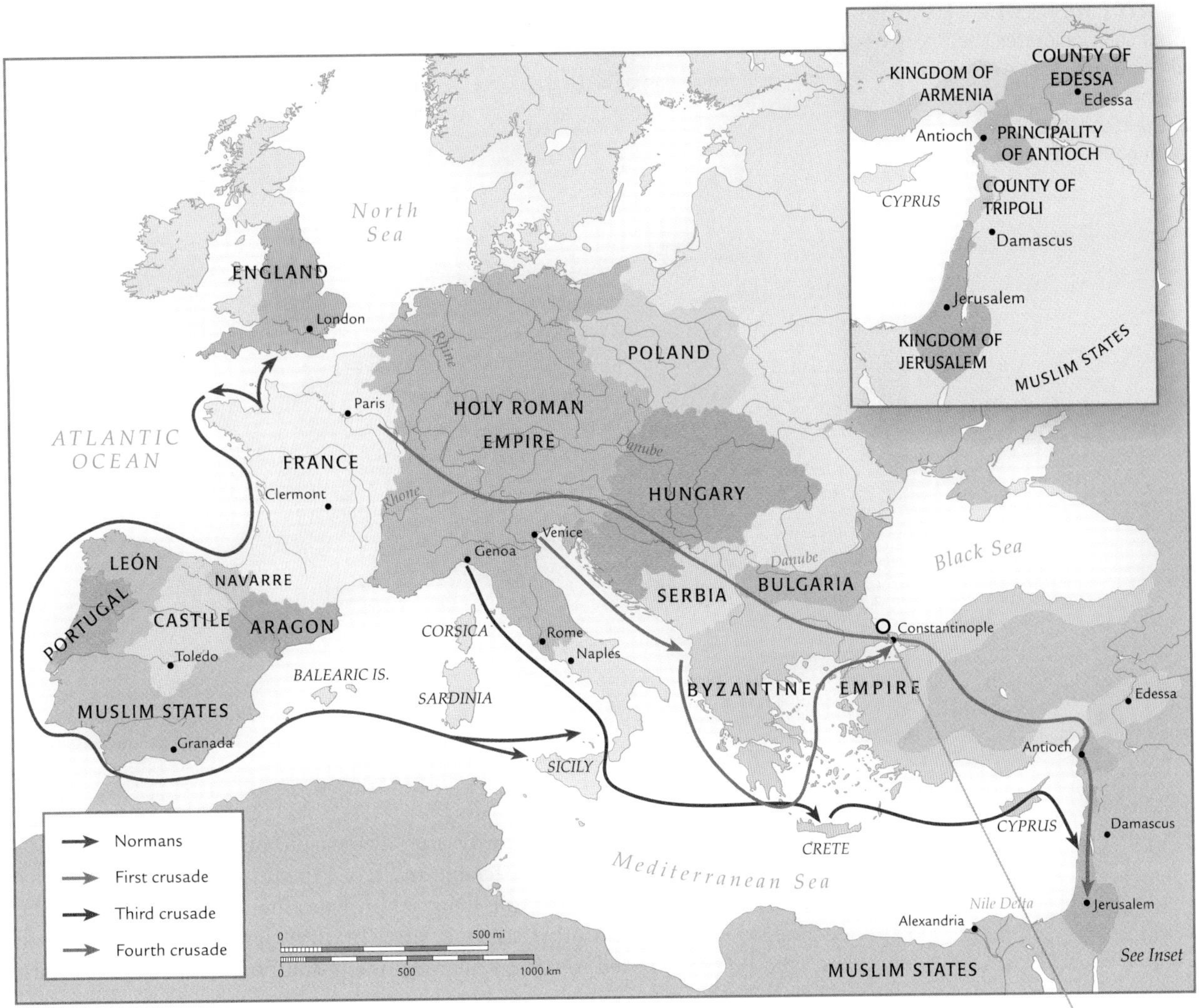

MAP 16.3 | Medieval expansion of Europe, 1000–1250 C.E. Observe the paths taken by the European crusaders and invaders. ***What does the distance of these paths tell you about the military and organizational capabilities of Europeans in the high middle ages?***

The fourth crusade was diverted to Constantinople, where crusaders sacked the city.

The Crusades

The term *crusade* refers to a holy war. It derives from the Latin word *crux,* meaning "cross," the device on which Roman authorities had executed Jesus. When a pope declared a crusade, warriors would "take up the cross" as a symbol of their faith, sew strips of cloth in the form of a cross on the backs of their garments, and venture forth to fight on behalf of Christianity. The most famous of these crusades were the enormous expeditions that Roman Catholic Christians mounted in an effort to recapture Palestine and the holy city of Jerusalem from Muslim authorities.

Summons to the crusade www.mhhe.com/bentleybrief2e

URBAN II Pope Urban II launched these crusades in 1095. The response to Urban's appeal was immediate and enthusiastic. A zealous preacher named Peter the Hermit traveled throughout France, Germany, and the Low Countries whipping up support among popular audiences. Within a year of Pope Urban's call, the Hermit had organized a ragtag army of poor knights and enthusiastic peasants—including women—and set out for Palestine without training, discipline, weapons, supplies, or plans. Not surprisingly, the campaign was a disaster: many members of Peter's band died, and few made it back to Europe. Yet the campaign indicated the high level of interest that the crusading idea generated among the European public.

THE THIRD CRUSADE. This painting commemorates the fall of Ptolemais (St. Jean d'Acre) to the Christian forces of King Richard I (the Lionheart) of England and King Philip II of France in 1191.

PSI map The crusades www.mhhe.com/bentleybrief2e

THE FIRST CRUSADE Shortly after Peter's ill-fated venture, French and Norman nobles organized a more respectable military expedition to the holy land. In late 1096 the crusading armies began the long trek to Palestine. In 1097 and 1098 they captured Edessa, Antioch, and other strategic sites. In 1099 Jerusalem itself fell to the crusaders, who then proceeded to extend their conquests and carve conquered territories into Christian states.

Although the crusaders did not realize it, hindsight shows that their quick victories came largely because of division and disarray in the ranks of their Muslim foes. The crusaders' successes, however, encouraged Turks, Egyptians, and other Muslims to settle their differences, at least temporarily, in the interests of expelling European Christians from the eastern Mediterranean. By the mid–twelfth century the crusader communities had come under tremendous pressure. The crusader state of Edessa fell to Turks in 1144, and the Muslim leader Salah al-Din, known to Europeans as Saladin, recaptured Jerusalem in 1187. Crusaders maintained several of their enclaves for another century and even embarked on several more military expeditions, but Saladin's victories sealed the fate of Christian forces in the eastern Mediterranean.

Europeans did not immediately concede Palestine to the Muslims. By the mid–thirteenth century they had launched five major crusades, but none of the later ventures succeeded in reestablishing a Christian presence in Palestine. The fourth crusade (1202–1204) went badly astray. Venetian authorities contracted with military leaders to supply enough ships to transport some thirty thousand crusaders to Palestine. When crusaders could not come up with sufficient funds, Venetians directed them instead to conquer the Italian port city of Zara—a commercial rival of Venice—and then to attack Constantinople, the most important commercial center in the eastern Mediterranean. In fact, the fourth crusade never made it to Palestine. The ignoble venture ended after the crusaders conquered Constantinople, subjected the city to a ruthless sack, and installed a Roman Catholic regime that survived until 1261. The

THINKING ABOUT *Encounters*

ENCOUNTERS IN WESTERN EUROPE DURING THE MIDDLE AGES. By the high middle ages, increasing wealth and productivity in Europe encouraged many Europeans to rebuild lines of communication with the rest of the eastern hemisphere through trade, diplomacy, religious crusades, and exploration. In what specific ways did these encounters with a wider world change European trading patterns, tastes, technologies, and ideas?

Byzantine empire never fully recovered from this blow, and lumbered along in serious decline until Ottoman Turks toppled it in 1453. Yet even though the later crusades failed in their principal objective, they inspired European dreams of conquest in the eastern Mediterranean until the late sixteenth century.

CONSEQUENCES OF THE CRUSADES As holy wars intended to reestablish Roman Catholic Christianity in the eastern Mediterranean basin, the crusades were wars of military and political expansion. Yet in the long run, the crusades were much more important for their social, economic, commercial, and cultural consequences. Even as European armies built crusader states in Palestine and Syria, European scholars and missionaries dealt with Muslim philosophers and theologians, and European merchants traded eagerly with their Muslim counterparts. The result was a large-scale exchange of ideas, technologies, and trade goods that profoundly influenced European development. Through their sojourns in Palestine and their regular dealings with Muslims throughout the Mediterranean basin, European Christians became acquainted with the works of Aristotle, Islamic science and astronomy, "Arabic" numerals (which Muslims had borrowed from India), and techniques of paper production (which Muslims had learned from China). They also learned to appreciate new food and agricultural products such as spices, granulated sugar, coffee, and dates as well as trade goods such as silk products, cotton textiles, carpets, and tapestries.

In the early days of the crusades, Europeans had little to exchange for those products other than rough wool textiles, furs, and timber. During the crusading era, however, Italian merchants seeking to meet the rising demand for luxury goods developed new products and marketed them in commercial centers and port cities. Thus Niccolò, Maffeo, and Marco Polo traded in gems and jewelry, and other merchants marketed fine woolen textiles or glassware. By the thirteenth century, large numbers of Italian merchants had begun to travel well beyond Egypt, Palestine, and Syria to avoid Muslim intermediaries and to deal directly with the producers of silks and spices in India, China, and southeast Asia. Thus, although the crusades largely failed as military ventures, they helped encourage the reintegration of western Europe into the larger economy of the eastern hemisphere.

SUMMARY

Like societies in China, India, southwest Asia, and the eastern Mediterranean, western European society experienced massive change from 500 to 1300 C.E. Unlike those societies, however, rulers of medieval Europe were unable to reinstate an imperial form of government for long, and for centuries they did not participate actively in the larger trading world of the eastern hemisphere. Yet western Europeans found ways to maintain relative order and stability by decentralizing political responsibilities and relying on local authorities and regional states for political organization. The development of self-sufficient manors allowed western Europeans to expand agricultural production, which in turn spurred population growth as well as trade. In addition, western Christianity preserved elements of classical Roman society and established a foundation for cultural unity in western Europe. It was on these solid foundations that western Europe underwent thorough political and economic reorganization in the later middle ages. Regional states maintained good order and fostered rapid economic growth. Agricultural improvements brought increased food supplies, which encouraged urbanization, manufacturing, and trade. By the thirteenth century, European peoples traded actively throughout the Mediterranean, Baltic, and North Sea regions, and a few merchants even ventured as far away as China in search of commercial opportunities. The Roman Catholic church prospered, and advanced educational institutions reinforced the influence of Christianity throughout Europe. Christianity even played a role in European political and military expansion, since church officials encouraged crusaders to conquer pagan and Muslim peoples in Baltic and Mediterranean lands. Thus even in the absence of a strong imperial power, by 1300 western European peoples had strengthened their own society and began in various ways to interact regularly with their counterparts in other regions of the eastern hemisphere.

STUDY TERMS

Capetian kings (303)
Carolingian empire (301)
cathedral schools (313)
Charlemagne (301)
chivalry (309)
crusades (317)
Eastern Orthodox Church (311)
Eucharist (314)
feudalism (305)
Franks (301)
guilds (310)
Hanseatic League (309)
Holy Roman Empire (302)
manors (306)
Normans (304)
Otto of Saxony (302)
Pope Gregory I (312)
Pope Urban II (317)
relics (315)
reconquista (316)
Roman Catholic Church (311)
sacraments (314)
scholasticism (313)
serfs (305)
St. Benedict of Nursia (312)
St. Scholastica (312)
St. Thomas Aquinas (313)
William the Conqueror (304)

FOR FURTHER READING

Robert Bartlett. *The Making of Europe: Conquest, Colonization, and Cultural Change, 950–1350.* Princeton, 1993. A well-documented examination of European expansion from a cultural point of view.

Rosalind Brooke and Christopher Brooke. *Popular Religion in the Middle Ages: Western Europe, 1000–1300.* London, 1984. Well-illustrated essays on the faith of the masses.

Peter Brown. *The Rise of Western Christendom: Triumph and Diversity, A.D. 200–1000.* 2nd ed. Oxford, 2003. A landmark analysis of early Christian history that incorporates the findings of recent scholarship.

Georges Duby. *Rural Economy and Country Life in the Medieval West.* Trans. by C. Postan. Columbia, S.C., 1968. Authoritative and well-documented study of the medieval agrarian world by a distinguished scholar.

Patrick J. Geary, ed. *Readings in Medieval History.* Lewiston, N.Y., 1989. Offers substantial English translations of primary sources.

David Herlihy. *Opera Muliebra: Women and Work in Medieval Europe.* New York, 1990. Examines women's roles both in their own households and in the larger society of medieval Europe.

Richard Hodges and David Whitehouse. *Mohammed, Charlemagne, and the Origins of Europe: Archaeology and the Pirenne Thesis.* Ithaca, 1983. Draws on archaeological discoveries in placing the early medieval European economy in hemispheric context.

Hans Eberhard Mayer. *The Crusades,* 2nd ed. Oxford, 1988. Perhaps the best short history of the crusades.

Michael McCormick. *Origins of the European Economy: Communications and Commerce, A.D. 300–900.* Cambridge, Mass., 2001. A thorough and comprehensive analysis that emphasizes the participation of early medieval Europe in a larger Mediterranean economy.

J. R. S. Phillips. *The Medieval Expansion of Europe.* Oxford, 1988. Excellent survey of European ventures in the larger world during the high and late middle ages.

Susan Reynolds. *Kingdoms and Communities in Western Europe, 900–1300.* Oxford, 1984. An imaginative study focusing on the political and social values that undergirded western European society.

———. *Fiefs and Vassals: The Medieval Evidence Reinterpreted.* Oxford, 1994. A powerful scholarly critique of the concept of feudalism.

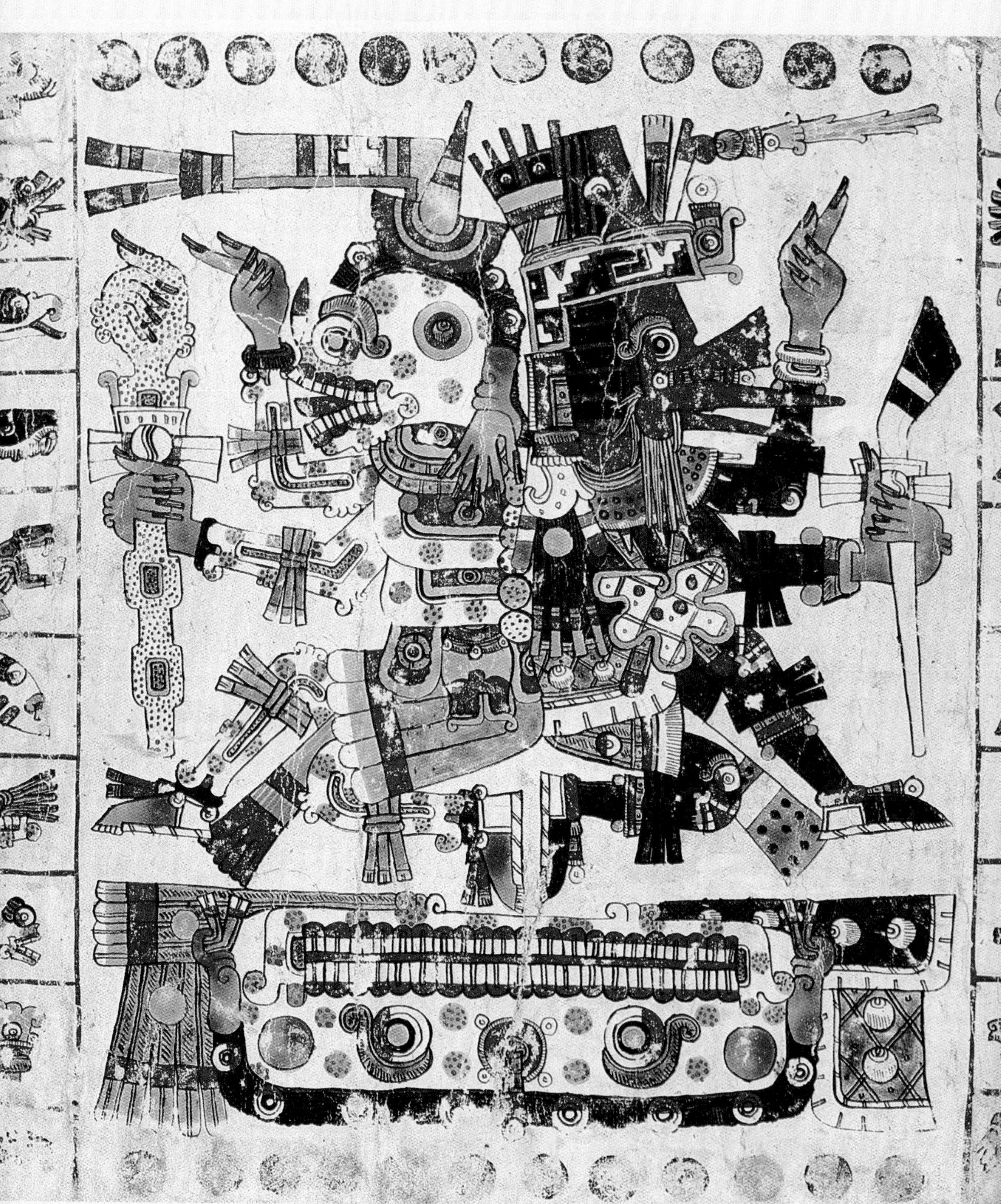

Worlds Apart: The Americas and Oceania

17

n November 1519 a small Spanish army entered Tenochtitlan, capital city of the Aztec empire. Although they had heard many reports about the wealth of the Aztec empire, nothing prepared them for what they saw. Years after the conquest of the Aztec empire, Bernal Díaz del Castillo, a soldier in the Spanish army, described Tenochtitlan at its high point. The city itself sat in the water of Lake Texcoco, connected to the surrounding land by three broad causeways, and, as in Venice, canals allowed canoes to navigate to all parts of the city. The imperial palace included many large rooms and apartments, and its armory was well stocked with swords, lances, knives, bows, arrows, slings, armor, and shields.

To Bernal Díaz the two most impressive sights were the markets and the temples of Tenochtitlan. The markets astonished him because of their size, the variety of goods they offered, and the order that prevailed there. In the principal market at Tlatelolco, a district of Tenochtitlan, Bernal Díaz found gold and silver jewelry, gems, feathers, embroidery, slaves, cotton, cacao, animal skins, maize, beans, vegetables, fruits, poultry, meat, fish, salt, paper, and tools. It would take more than two days, he said, to walk around the market and investigate all the goods offered for sale. His well-traveled companions-in-arms compared the markets favorably to those of Rome and Constantinople.

PSI img The city of Tenochtitlan www.mhhe.com/bentleybrief2e

The temples also struck Bernal Díaz, though in a different way. Aztec temples were the principal sites of rituals involving human sacrifice. Bernal Díaz described interior rooms of the temple so encrusted with blood that their walls and floors had turned black. Some of the interior rooms held the dismembered limbs of sacrificial victims, and others were resting places for thousands of human skulls and bones.

The contrast between Tenochtitlan's markets and temples challenged Bernal Díaz and his fellow soldiers. In the markets they witnessed peaceful exchange of the kind that took place all over the world. In the temples, however, they saw signs of human sacrifice on a scale rarely matched, if ever, anywhere else in the world. Yet, by the cultural standards of the Aztec empire, both the commercial activity of the marketplaces and the human sacrifice of the temples had a place in the maintenance of the world: trade enabled a complex society to function, and

PSI img Aztec human sacrifice www.mhhe.com/bentleybrief2e

❮ A Mexica manuscript known as the Codex Borgia depicts Quetzalcóatl (left) as the lord of life and Tezcatlipoca (right) as the god of death.

Tenochtitlan (teh-noch-tee-TLAHN)
Texcoco (TEHS-co-co)
Tlatelolco (tl-tay-LOL-ko)

CHRONOLOGY

AMERICAS	
950–1150	High point of the Toltec empire
1175	Collapse of the Toltec empire
1250	Inca settlement near Cuzco
1345	Foundation of Tenochtitlan by the Mexica
1400	Emergence of the five Iroquois nations
1428–1440	Reign of the Aztec ruler Itzcóatl
1438–1471	Reign of the Inca ruler Pachacuti
1440–1469	Reign of the Aztec ruler Motecuzoma I
1502–1520	Reign of the Aztec ruler Motecuzoma II
1519	Arrival of Spanish conquerors in Mexico
OCEANIA	
Eleventh century	Beginning of population growth in Pacific islands
Thirteenth century	Emergence of distinct social classes and chiefly states
Fourteenth century	Construction of fishponds in Hawai`i

sacrificial rituals pleased the gods and persuaded them to keep the world going.

Although the peoples of Africa, Asia, and Europe interacted regularly before modern times, before 1492 the indigenous peoples of the Americas had only fleeting and random dealings with their contemporaries across the oceans. Yet between 1000 and 1500 C.E. the peoples of North and South America, like their counterparts in the eastern hemisphere, organized large empires with distinctive cultural and religious traditions, and they created elaborate trade networks touching most regions of the Americas.

The indigenous peoples of Australia and the Pacific islands had irregular and sporadic dealings with peoples outside Oceania. Within Oceania itself, Pacific islanders did maintain links between various island groups by sailing over the open ocean. Yet to a greater extent than their counterparts in the eastern hemisphere, the indigenous peoples of Australia and the Pacific islands built self-sufficient societies that tended to their own needs. Even though they had extremely limited amounts of land and other natural resources to work with, by the thirteenth century C.E. they had established well-organized agricultural societies and chiefly states throughout the Pacific islands.

States and Empires in Mesoamerica and North America

Mesoamerica entered an era of war and conquest in the eighth century C.E. Great stores of wealth had accumulated in Teotihuacan, the largest early city in Mesoamerica. When Teotihuacan declined, it became a target for less-prosperous but well-organized forces from the countryside and northern Mexico. Attacks on Teotihuacan opened a long era of militarization and empire building in Mesoamerica that lasted until Spanish forces conquered the region in the sixteenth century. Most prominent of the peoples contesting for power in Mesoamerica were the Mexica, the architects of the Aztec empire.

The Toltecs and the Mexica

During the ninth and early tenth centuries, after the collapse of Teotihuacan, several regional states dominated portions of the high central valley of Mexico, the area surrounding Mexico City. Although these successor states and their societies shared the religious and cultural traditions of Teotihuacan, they fought relentlessly among themselves. Their capital cities all stood on well-defended hill sites, and warriors figured prominently in their works of art.

Teotihuacan (teh-o-tee-WAH-kahn)
Mexica (MEHK-si-kah))

TOLTECS With the emergence of the Toltecs and later the Mexica, much of central Mexico again came under unified rule. The Toltecs began to migrate into the area from the arid land of northwestern Mexico about the eighth century. They settled mostly at Tula, about 50 kilometers (31 miles) northwest of modern Mexico City. There, the Toltecs tapped the waters of the nearby River Tula to irrigate crops of maize, beans, peppers, tomatoes, chiles, and cotton. At its high point, from about 950 to 1150 C.E., Tula supported a population that might have reached sixty thousand people, and another sixty thousand lived in the surrounding region.

The Toltecs also built a compact regional empire with their large and powerful army, and they transformed their capital into a wealthy city with the tribute they exacted from subject peoples. Indeed, the city of Tula became an important center of weaving, pottery, and obsidian work, and residents imported large quantities of jade, turquoise, animal skins, exotic bird feathers, and other luxury goods from elsewhere in Mesoamerica. The Toltecs maintained close relations with societies on the Gulf coast as well as with the Maya of Yucatan. Indeed, Tula shared numerous architectural designs and art motifs with the Maya city of Chichén Itzá some 1,500 kilometers (932 miles) to the east.

Beginning about 1125 C.E. the Toltec empire faced serious difficulties as conflicts between the different ethnic groups living at Tula led to civil strife. By the mid–twelfth century large numbers of migrants—mostly nomadic peoples from northwestern Mexico—had entered Tula and settled in the surrounding area. By 1175 the combination of civil conflict and nomadic incursion had destroyed the Toltec state.

THE MEXICA Among the migrants drawn to central Mexico from northwestern regions was a people who called themselves the Mexica, often referred to as Aztecs because they dominated the alliance that built the Aztec empire in the fifteenth century. (The term *Aztec* derives from *Aztlán,* "the place of the seven legendary caves," which the Mexica remembered as the home of their ancestors.) The Mexica arrived in central Mexico about the middle of the thirteenth century. They had a reputation for making trouble by kidnapping women from nearby communities and seizing land already cultivated by others. On several occasions their neighbors became tired of their disorderly behavior and forced them to move. For a century they migrated around central Mexico, fighting with other peoples and sometimes surviving only by eating fly eggs and snakes.

TENOCHTITLAN About 1345 the Mexica settled on an island in a marshy region of Lake Texcoco and founded the city that would become their capital—Tenochtitlan, on top of which Spanish conquerors later built Mexico City. The site offered several advantages. The lake harbored plentiful supplies of fish, frogs, and waterfowl, and it also enabled the Mexica to develop the *chinampa* system of agriculture. The Mexica dredged the fertile muck from the lake's bottom and built it up into small plots of land known as *chinampas.* During the dry season, cultivators tapped water from canals leading from the lake to their plots, and in the temperate climate they grew crops year-round. *Chinampas* were so productive that cultivators were sometimes able to harvest seven crops per year. The lake also served as a natural defense: waters protected Tenochtitlan on all sides, and Mexica warriors patrolled the three causeways that eventually linked their capital to the surrounding mainland.

THE AZTEC EMPIRE By the early fifteenth century, the Mexica were powerful enough to overcome their immediate neighbors and demand tribute from their new subjects. During the middle decades of the century, the Mexica launched ambitious campaigns of imperial expansion. Under the rule of "the Obsidian Serpent" Itzcóatl (1428–1440) and Motecuzoma I (1440–1469), also known as Moctezuma or Montezuma, they

Toltec and Aztec empires
www.mhhe.com/
bentleybrief2e

Yucatan (yoo-kuh-TAN)

Itzcóatl (tsee-ko-atl)

Motecuzoma (mo-tec-oo-ZO-ma)

The Aztec built their capital in the middle of Lake Texcoco, which made for easier defense.

MAP 17.1 | The Toltec and Aztec empires, 950–1520 C.E. The Aztec empire stretched from the Gulf of Mexico to the Pacific Ocean. ***How were Aztec rulers able to control these diverse territories?***

first advanced against Oaxaca in southwestern Mexico. After conquering the city and slaying many of its inhabitants, they populated Oaxaca with colonists, and the city became a bulwark for the emerging Mexica empire.

The Mexica next turned their attention to the Gulf coast. Finally, they conquered the cities of the high plateaus between Tenochtitlan and the Gulf coast. About the mid–fifteenth century the Mexica joined forces with two neighboring cities, Texcoco and Tlacopan (modern Tacuba), to create a triple alliance that guided the Aztec empire. Dominated by the Mexica and Tenochtitlan, the allies imposed their rule on about twelve million people and most of Mesoamerica, excluding only the arid northern and western regions and a few small, independent states.

TRIBUTE AND TRADE The main objective of the triple alliance was to exact tribute from subject peoples. From nearby peoples the Mexica and their allies received food crops and manufactured items. Tribute obligations were sometimes very oppressive for subject peoples. The annual tribute owed by the state of Tochtepec on the Gulf coast, for example, included 9,600 cloaks, 1,600 women's garments, 200 loads of cacao (the source of cocoa and chocolate), and 16,000 rubber balls. Ruling elites entrusted some of these tribute items to officially recognized merchants, who took them to distant lands and exchanged them for local products including luxury items such as translucent jade, tortoise shells, jaguar skins, parrot feathers, and seashells. The tropical lowlands also supplied vanilla beans and cacao, from which Mexica elites prepared tasty beverages.

Unlike imperial states in the eastern hemisphere, the Aztec empire had no elaborate bureaucracy or administration. The Mexica and their allies simply conquered their subjects and assessed tribute, leaving local governance and the collection of tribute in the hands of the conquered peoples themselves. The allies did not even maintain military garrisons throughout their empire. Nor did they keep a permanent, standing army. Nevertheless, the Mexica in particular had a reputation for military prowess, and fear of reprisal kept most subject peoples in line.

At the high point of the Aztec empire in the early sixteenth century, tribute from some 489 subject territories flowed into Tenochtitlan, which was an enormously wealthy city.

Oaxaca (wah-hah-kah)

Tlacopan (Tee-laaa-co-pawn)

The Mexica capital had a population of about two hundred thousand people, and three hundred thousand more lived in nearby towns and suburban areas. The principal market had separate sections for merchants dealing in gold, silver, slaves, cloth, shoes, animal skins, turkeys, dogs, wild game, maize, beans, peppers, cacao, and fruits.

MEXICA TRIBUTE LIST. A Spanish copy of a Mexica list records tribute owed by six northwestern towns to the ruler Motecuzoma II. Every two years the towns delivered, among other items, women's skirts and blouses, men's shirts, warriors' armor and shields, an eagle, and various quantities of maize, beans, and other foods.

Mexica Society

More information survives about the Mexica and their subjects than about any other people of the pre-Columbian Americas. A few Mexica books survived the Spanish conquest of the Aztec empire, and they offer direct testimony about the Mexica way of life. Moreover, a great deal of information survives from interviews conducted by Spanish missionaries with priests, elders, and other leaders of the Mexica during the mid–sixteenth century. In combination, these sources shed considerable light on Mexica society.

SOCIAL STRUCTURE Mexica society was rigidly hierarchical, with public honors and rewards going mostly to the military elite. The Mexica looked on all males as potential warriors, but for the most part the military elite came from the Mexica aristocracy. Men of noble birth received the most intense training in military affairs, and they enjoyed the best opportunities to display their talents on the battlefield.

WARRIORS The Mexica showered wealth and honors on the military elite. Accomplished warriors received extensive land grants as well as tribute from commoners for their support. The most successful warriors formed a council whose members selected the ruler, discussed public issues, and filled government positions. They ate the best foods, and they consumed most of the luxury items that came into Mexica society by way of trade or tribute. Even dress reflected social status in Mexica society. Sumptuary laws required commoners to wear coarse, burlaplike garments made of henequen but permitted aristocrats to drape themselves in cotton. Successful warriors also enjoyed the right to don brightly colored capes and adorn themselves with lip plugs and eagle feathers.

MEXICA WOMEN Women played almost no public role in a society so dominated by military values, but they wielded influence within their families and enjoyed honor as mothers of warriors. Mexica women did not inherit property or hold official positions, and the law subjected them to the strict authority of their fathers and husbands. However, women were prominent in the marketplaces, as well as in crafts involving embroidery and needlework.

With the exception of a few who dedicated themselves to the service of a temple, all Mexica women married. Mexica values taught that their principal function was to bear children, and society recognized the bearing of children as equal to a warrior's capture of enemies in battle. Indeed, women who died in childbirth won the same fame as warriors who died valiantly on the battlefield.

PRIESTS Alongside the military aristocracy, a priestly class also ranked among the Mexica elite. Priests received a special education in calendrical and ritual lore, and they presided over religious ceremonies that the Mexica viewed as crucial to the continuation of the world. Priests read omens and explained the forces that drove the world, thereby wielding considerable influence as advisors to Mexica rulers. On a few occasions, priests even became supreme rulers of the Aztec empire: the ill-fated Motecuzoma II (reigned 1502–1520), ruler of the Aztec empire when Spanish invaders appeared in 1519, was a priest of the most popular Mexica cult.

CULTIVATORS AND SLAVES The bulk of the Mexica population consisted of commoners who lived in hamlets cultivating lands allocated to their families by community groups known as *calpulli.* Originally, *calpulli* members claimed descent from common ancestors, but over time ancestry became less important than the fact that groups of families lived together in communities, organized their own affairs, and allocated community property to individual families. In addition to cultivating plots assigned by their *calpulli,* Mexica commoners also worked on the lands of aristocrats or warriors and contributed labor services to public works projects. Cultivators delivered periodic tribute payments to state agents, who distributed a portion of what they collected to the elite classes and stored the remainder in state granaries and warehouses. In addition to these cultivators of common birth, Mexica society included a large number of slaves, who usually worked as domestic servants. Most slaves were not foreigners, but Mexica who entered slavery because of financial distress or criminal behavior.

ARTISANS AND MERCHANTS Skilled artisans, particularly those who worked with gold, silver, and other items destined for consumption by the elite, enjoyed considerable prestige in Mexica society. Merchants specializing in long-distance trade occupied an important but somewhat more tenuous position in Mexica society. Indeed, although these merchants supplied important luxuries to the elite as well as political and military intelligence about the lands they visited, they often fell under suspicion as greedy profiteers.

Mexica Religion

When they migrated to central Mexico, the Mexica already spoke the Nahuatl language, which had been the prevalent tongue in the region since the time of the Toltecs. The Mexica soon adopted other cultural and religious traditions, some of which dated from the time of the Olmecs, shared by all the peoples of Mesoamerica. Most Mesoamerican peoples played a ball game in formal courts, for example, and maintained a complicated calendar based on a solar year of 365 days and a ritual year of 260 days. The Mexica enthusiastically adopted the ball game, and they also kept a sophisticated calendar.

MEXICA GODS The Mexica also absorbed the religious beliefs common to Mesoamerica. Two of their principal gods—Tezcatlipoca, "the Smoking Mirror," and Quetzalcoatl, "the Feathered Serpent"—had figured in Mesoamerican pantheons at least since the time of Teotihuacan. Tezcatlipoca was a powerful figure, the giver and taker of life and the patron deity of warriors, whereas Quetzalcoatl supported arts, crafts, and agriculture. Like their predecessors, the Mexica believed that their gods had set the world in motion through acts of individual sacrifice. By letting their blood flow, the gods had given the earth the moisture it needed to bear maize and other crops. To win the favor of the gods and ensure the continuation of the world, the Mexica also engaged in sacrificial bloodletting. Mexica priests regularly performed acts of self-sacrifice, piercing their earlobes or penises with cactus spines in honor of the primeval acts of their gods.

RITUAL BLOODLETTING Mexica priests also presided over the sacrificial killing of human victims. From at least the time of the Olmecs, Mesoamerican peoples had regarded the ritual sacrifice of human beings as essential to the world's survival. The Mexica, however, placed much more emphasis on human sacrifice than their predecessors had. To a large extent the Mexica enthusiasm for human sacrifice followed from their devotion to the god Huitzilopochtli as the patron deity of Mexica warriors. Military successes in the fourteenth century, when the Mexica subjected neighboring peoples to their

calpulli (kal-po-lee)
Nahuatl (na-watl)
Tezcatlipoca (tehs-cah-tlee-poh-cah)
Quetzalcoatl (keh-tzahl-koh-AHTL)

Mexica Sacrificial Bloodletting. | In this manuscript illustration an aide stretches a victim over a sacrificial altar while a priest opens his chest, removes the still-beating heart, and offers it to Huitzilopochtli. At the bottom of the structure, attendants remove the body of an earlier victim.

rule, increasingly persuaded them of Huitzilopochtli's favor. As Mexica military successes mounted, the priests of Huitzilopochtli's cult demanded sacrificial victims to keep the war god appeased.

Some of the victims were Mexica criminals, and others came as tribute from neighboring peoples or from the ranks of warriors captured on the battlefield. In all cases the Mexica viewed human sacrifice not as a gruesome form of entertainment but, rather, as a ritual essential to the world's survival. They believed that the blood of sacrificial victims sustained the sun and secured a continuing supply of moisture for the earth, thus ensuring that human communities would be able to cultivate their crops and perpetuate their societies.

Peoples and Societies of the North

Beyond Mexico the peoples of North America developed a rich variety of political, social, and cultural traditions. Many North American peoples depended on hunting, fishing, and foraging. In the arctic and subarctic regions, for example, diets included whale, seal, and walrus supplemented by land mammals such as moose and caribou. Peoples in coastal regions consumed fish, and in interior regions they hunted large animals such as bison and deer. Throughout the continent nuts, berries, roots, and grasses supplemented the meat provided by hunters and fishers. Like their counterparts elsewhere, hunting, fishing, and foraging peoples of North America built societies on a relatively small scale, since food resources in the wild would not support dense populations.

PUEBLO AND NAVAJO SOCIETIES In several regions of North America, agricultural economies enabled peoples to maintain settled societies with large populations. In what is now the American southwest, for example, Pueblo and Navajo peoples tapped river waters to irrigate crops of maize, which constituted as much as 80 percent of

Huitzilopochtli (we-tsee-loh-POCK-tlee)
Pueblo (PWEB-loh)
Navajo (NAH-vah-ho)

THINKING ABOUT *Traditions*

TRADITIONS IN THE AMERICAS AND OCEANIA. In contrast to societies in Eurasia, which were linked across vast areas through complex networks of seaborne and overland trade, societies in the Americas and in Oceania were unable to maintain similar connections across areas of comparable size. In what ways can geographical obstacles in both the Americas and Oceania help to explain the difficulties of maintaining comparable long-distance connections? How might the presence of these obstacles have shaped the development of cultural, social, and political traditions?

their diets. Although the hot and dry environment periodically brought drought and famine, by about 700 C.E. the Pueblo and the Navajo had begun to construct permanent stone and adobe buildings. Archaeologists have discovered about 125 sites where agricultural peoples built such communities.

IROQUOIS PEOPLES Large-scale agricultural societies also emerged in the woodlands east of the Mississippi River. Woodlands peoples began to cultivate maize and beans during the early centuries C.E., and after about 800 these cultivated foods made up the bulk of their diets. By 1000 the Owasco people had established a distinct society in what is now upstate New York, and by about 1400 the five Iroquois nations (Mohawk, Oneida, Onondaga, Cayuga, and Seneca) had emerged from Owasco society. Women were in charge of Iroquois villages and longhouses, in which several related families lived together, and supervised cultivation of fields surrounding their settlements. Men took responsibility for affairs beyond the village—hunting, fishing, and war.

MOUND-BUILDING PEOPLES The most impressive structures of the woodlands were the enormous earthen mounds that dotted the countryside throughout the eastern half of North America. Woodlands peoples used these mounds as stages for ceremonies and rituals, as platforms for dwellings, and occasionally as burial sites. Although modern development has destroyed most of these mounds, several surviving examples demonstrate that they sometimes reached gigantic proportions.

PSI img Cahokia
www.mhhe.com/bentleybrief2e

CAHOKIA The largest surviving structure is a mound at Cahokia near East St. Louis, Illinois. More than 30 meters (100 feet) high, 300 meters (1,000 feet) long, and 200 meters (650 feet) wide, it was the third-largest structure in the western hemisphere before the arrival of Europeans. Only the temple of the sun in Teotihuacan and the tem-

Iroquois (EER-uh-kwah)
Cahokia (kuh-HOH-kee-uh)

THE GREAT SERPENT MOUND. | Originally constructed about 1000 C.E., this mound sits atop a ridge in modern Ohio. The serpent's coiled tail is visible at the left, while its open mouth holds an egg on the right. ***Why would the builders of this mound have adopted an aerial perspective?***

ple of Quetzalcóatl in Cholula were larger. When the Cahokia society was at its height, from approximately 900 to 1250 C.E., more than one hundred smaller mounds stood within a few kilometers of the highest and most massive mound. Scholars have estimated that during the twelfth century, fifteen thousand to thirty-eight thousand people lived in the vicinity of the Cahokia mounds.

TRADE Because peoples north of Mexico had no writing, information about their societies comes almost exclusively from archaeological discoveries. Burial sites reveal that mound-building peoples recognized social classes, since they bestowed grave goods of differing quality and quantities on their departed kin. Archaeologists have shown, too, that trade linked widely separated regions and peoples of North America. An elaborate network of rivers—notably the Mississippi, Missouri, Ohio, and Tennessee rivers—facilitated travel and trade by canoe in the eastern half of North America. Throughout the eastern woodlands, archaeologists have turned up stones with sharp cutting edges from the Rocky Mountains, copper from the Great Lakes region, seashells from Florida, minerals from the upper reaches of the Mississippi River, and mica from the southern Appalachian mountains. Indeed, the community at Cahokia probably owed its size and prominence to its location at the hub of North American trade networks. Situated near the confluence of the Mississippi, Missouri, and Ohio rivers, Cahokia was most likely the center of trade and communication networks linking the eastern woodlands of North America with the lower Mississippi valley and lands bordering the Gulf of Mexico.

States and Empires in South America

Like the peoples north of Mexico, South American peoples had no tradition of writing before the arrival of Spanish invaders in the early sixteenth century. As a result, the experiences of early South American societies have been reconstructed largely on the basis of archaeological evidence and information recorded by Spanish conquerors. As in Mesoamerica, cities and secular government in South America began to overshadow ceremonial centers and priestly regimes during the centuries from 1000 to 1500 C.E. Toward the end of the period, like the Mexica in Mesoamerica, the Incas built a powerful state, extended their authority over a vast region, and established the largest empire South America had ever seen.

The Coming of the Incas

After the disappearance of the Chavín and Moche societies, a series of autonomous regional states organized public affairs in Andean South America. The states frequently clashed, but rarely did one of them gain a long-term advantage over the others. For the most part they controlled areas either in the mountainous highlands or in the valleys and coastal plains.

CHUCUITO In the highlands, people depended on the cultivation of potatoes and the herding of llamas and alpacas—camel-like beasts that were the only large domesticated animals anywhere in the Americas before the sixteenth century. After the twelfth century the kingdom of Chucuito dominated the highland region on the border between modern Peru and Bolivia. There, inhabitants built elaborately terraced fields where cultivators harvested potatoes of many different colors, sizes, and tastes.

CHIMU Inhabitants of the coastal lowlands depended not on potatoes but on maize and sweet potatoes, which were grown with the aid of irrigation networks that tapped the rivers and streams flowing from the Andes mountains. Some lowland societies, such as

Chucuito (CHEW-keeto)

MAP 17.2 | The Inca empire, 1471–1532 C.E. The Incas built the largest empire in the pre-Columbian Americas. ***How were they able to maintain control over their extensive realm?***

The Inca capital of Cuzco was situated high in the Andes mountains.

the kingdom of Chimu, grew large and powerful in the half millennium before the emergence of the Incas in the mid–fifteenth century. Indeed, Chimu's capital city, Chanchan, had a population that exceeded fifty thousand and may have approached one hundred thousand.

For several centuries, regional states such as Chucuito and Chimu maintained order in Andean South America. Yet within a period of about thirty years, they and other regional states fell under the domination of the dynamic and expansive society of the Incas. The word *Inca* originally was the title of the rulers of a small kingdom in the valley of Cuzco, but in modern usage the term refers more broadly to those who spoke the Incas' Quechua language, or even to all subjects of the Inca empire.

THE INCA EMPIRE After a long period of migration in the highlands, the Incas settled in the highland region around Lake Titicaca about the mid–thirteenth century. At first they lived as one among many peoples inhabiting the region. About 1438, however, the Inca ruler Pachacuti (reigned 1438–1471) launched a series of military campaigns that vastly expanded the Incas' authority. Pachacuti first extended Inca control over the southern and northern highlands and then turned his forces on the coastal kingdom of Chimu. Though well defended, Chimu had to submit to the Incas when Pachacuti gained control of the waters that supplied Chimu's irrigation system.

By the late fifteenth century, the Incas had built a huge empire stretching more than 4,000 kilometers (2,500 miles) from modern Quito to Santiago. It embraced almost all of modern Peru, most of Ecuador, much of Bolivia, and parts of Chile and Argentina. Only the tropical rain forests of the Amazon and other river valleys set a limit to Inca expansion to the east, and the Pacific Ocean defined its western boundary. With a population of about 11.5 million, the Inca empire easily ranked as the largest state ever built in South America.

Andean South America
www.mhhe.com/bentleybrief2e

The Incas ruled as a military and administrative elite. They led armies composed mostly of conquered peoples, and they staffed the bureaucracy that managed the empire's political affairs. But the Incas themselves were not numerous enough to overwhelm their subjects. Thus, they sought to encourage obedience among subject peoples by taking hostages from their ruling classes and forcing them to live at the Inca capital. Also, when conquered peoples became restive or uncooperative, the Incas sent loyal subjects to colonize the area and to establish military garrisons. When conquered peoples rebelled, Inca armies resettled them in distant parts of the empire.

QUIPU AND INCA ADMINISTRATION Administration of the Inca empire rested with a large class of bureaucrats. In the absence of writing, bureaucrats relied on a mnemonic aid known as *quipu* to keep track of their responsibilities. Quipu consisted of an array of small cords of various colors and lengths, all suspended from one large, thick

Chanchan (CHAHN-chahn)
Quechua (keh-CHUA)
Pachacuti (pah-cha-KOO-tee)
quipu (KEE-poo)

Inca City. | Machu Picchu, an Inca settlement built beginning in 1430, was 8,000 feet above sea level. ***What kinds of technology would the Inca have needed to construct a stone city at such a high altitude?***

cord. Experts tied a series of knots in the small cords, which sometimes numbered a hundred or more, to help them remember certain kinds of information. Most quipu recorded statistical information having to do with population, state property, taxes, and labor services that communities owed to the central government. Occasionally, though, quipu also helped experts to remember historical information having to do with the establishment of the Inca empire, the Inca rulers, and their deeds. Although much more unwieldy and less flexible than writing, quipu enabled Inca bureaucrats to keep track of information well enough to run an orderly empire.

CUZCO The Inca capital at Cuzco served as the administrative, religious, and ceremonial center of the empire. At its high point in the late fifteenth century, Cuzco's population may have reached three hundred thousand. Most prominent of the residents were the Inca rulers and high nobility, the high priests of the various religious cults, and the hostages of conquered peoples who lived with their families under the watchful eyes of Inca guardians. Cuzco had many handsome buildings of red stone, and the most important temples and palaces sported gold facings.

INCA ROADS A magnificent and extensive road system enabled the central government at Cuzco to communicate with all parts of the far-flung Inca empire and to dispatch large military forces rapidly to distant trouble spots. Two roads linked the Inca realm from north to south—one through the mountains, the other along the coast. Scholars have estimated the combined length of these roads at 16,000 kilometers (9,944 miles). A corps of official runners carried messages along the roads so that news and information could travel between Cuzco and the most distant parts of the empire within a few days. When the Inca rulers desired a meal of fresh fish, they dispatched runners from Cuzco to the coast more than 320 kilometers (200 miles) away and had their catch within two days. Like roads in empires in other parts of the world, the Incas' roads favored their efforts at centralization.

Inca Society and Religion

TRADE Despite these splendid roads, Inca society did not generate large classes of merchants and skilled artisans. On the local level the Incas and their subjects bartered agricultural produce and handcrafted goods among themselves. Long-distance trade, however, fell under the supervision of the central government. Administrators organized exchanges of agricultural products, textiles, pottery, jewelry, and craft goods, but the Inca state did not permit individuals to become independent merchants. In the absence of a market economy, then, there was no opportunity for a large class of professional, skilled artisans to emerge.

INCA GOD-KING. This painting depicts Pachacuti (r. 1438–1471), the ruler responsible for expanding Inca territory into an empire.

RULING ELITES The main classes in Inca society were the rulers, aristocrats, priests, and peasant cultivators of common birth. The Incas considered their chief ruler a deity descended from the sun. In theory, this god-king owned everything in the Inca realm, which he governed as an absolute and infallible ruler. Inca rulers retained their prestige even after death. Their descendants mummified the royal remains and regarded departed kings as intermediaries with the gods. Succeeding rulers often deliberated state policy in the presence of royal mummies so as to benefit from their counsel. Indeed, on the occasion of certain festivals, rulers brought out the mummified remains of their ancestors, dressed them in fine clothes, and presented them with offerings of food and drink to maintain cordial relations with former rulers.

ARISTOCRATS AND PRIESTS Like the ruling elites, Inca aristocrats and priests led privileged lives. Aristocrats consumed fine foods and dressed in embroidered clothes provided by common subjects. Aristocrats also had the right to wear large ear spools that distended their lobes so much that Spanish conquerors referred to them as "big ears." Priests often came from royal and aristocratic families. They led celibate and ascetic lives, but they deeply influenced Inca society because of their education and their responsibility for overseeing religious rituals. The major temples supported hundreds of priests, along with attendants and virgin women devoted to divine service who prepared ceremonial meals and wove fine ritual garments for the priestly staff.

PEASANTS The cultivators were mostly peasants of common birth who lived in communities known as *ayllu,* similar to the Mexica's *calpulli,* which were the basic units of rural society. Ranging in size from small villages to larger towns, each *ayllu* consisted of several families who lived together, sharing land, tools, animals, crops, and work. Instead of paying taxes or tribute, peasants also worked on state lands administered by aristocrats. Much of the production from these state lands went to support the ruling, aristocratic, and priestly classes. The rest went into state storehouses for public relief in times of famine and for the support of widows, orphans, and others unable to cultivate land for themselves. Apart from agricultural work, peasants also owed compulsory labor services to the Inca state. Men provided the heavy labor required for the construction, maintenance, and repair of roads, buildings, and irrigation systems. Women delivered tribute in the form of textiles, pottery, and jewelry. With the aid of quipu, Inca bureaucrats kept track of the labor service and tribute owed by local communities.

INCA GODS: INTI AND VIRACOCHA Members of the Inca ruling class venerated the sun as a god and as their major deity, whom they called Inti. They also recognized the moon, the stars, the planets, the rain, and other natural forces as divine. Some Incas, including the energetic ruler Pachacuti, also showed special favor to the god Viracocha, creator of the world, humankind, and all else in the universe. The cult of the

Inti (ihn-tee)
Viracocha (veer-rah-coh-chah)

sun, however, outshone all the others. In Cuzco alone some four thousand priests, attendants, and virgin devotees served Inti, whose temple attracted pilgrims from all parts of the Inca empire. Priests of all cults honored their deities with sacrifices, which in Inca society usually took the form of agricultural produce or animals such as llamas and guinea pigs rather than humans.

MORAL THOUGHT Alongside sacrifices and ritual ceremonies, Inca religion had a strong moral dimension. The Incas taught a concept of sin as a violation of the established social or natural order, and they believed in a life beyond death during which individuals would receive rewards or punishments based on the quality of their earthly lives. Sin, they believed, would bring divine disaster both for individuals and for their larger communities. The Incas also observed rituals of confession and penance by which priests absolved individuals of their sins and returned them to the good graces of the gods.

The Societies of Oceania

Inhabitants of Oceania did not interact with peoples of different societies as frequently or systematically as did their counterparts in the eastern hemisphere, but they built and maintained flourishing societies. The aboriginal peoples of Australia ventured over vast stretches of their continent and created networks of trade and exchange between hunting and gathering societies. Meanwhile, throughout the Pacific Ocean, islanders built complex agricultural societies. By the time European mariners sailed into the Pacific Ocean in the sixteenth century, the larger island groups had sizable populations, hierarchical social orders, and hereditary chiefly rulers. In the central and western Pacific, mariners sailed regularly between island groups and established elaborate trade networks. Islanders living toward the eastern and western edges of the Pacific Ocean also had occasional dealings with American and Asian peoples, sometimes with significant consequences for the Pacific island societies.

The Nomadic Foragers of Australia

Aborigine of the Naomi tribe
www.mhhe.com/bentleybrief2e

Although the aboriginal peoples of Australia learned how to expertly exploit the resources of the continent, they did not turn to agriculture as did their neighbors to the north in New Guinea. The inhabitants of New Guinea began to herd swine and cultivate root crops about 5000 B.C.E., and the inhabitants of islands in the Torres Strait (which separates Australia from New Guinea) took up gardening soon thereafter. In contrast, the aboriginal peoples of northern Australia maintained nomadic, foraging societies until European peoples migrated to Australia in large numbers during the nineteenth and twentieth centuries.

TRADE As a result of their mobile and nomadic way of life, aboriginal Australians frequently interacted with peoples of neighboring societies. Even though as nomads they did not accumulate large quantities of material goods, groups regularly exchanged surplus food and small items when they met. Eventually, this sort of small-scale exchange enabled trade goods to spread throughout most of Australia. Pearly oyster shells were among the most popular trade items. Archaeologists have turned up many of these shells fashioned into jewelry more than 1,600 kilometers (1,000 miles) from the waters where the oysters bred. Peoples on the north coast also engaged in a limited amount of trade with mariners from New Guinea and the islands of southeast Asia. Australian spears and pearly shells went north in exchange for items such as iron axes, which were much coveted by aboriginal peoples who had no tradition of metallurgy.

CULTURAL AND RELIGIOUS TRADITIONS In spite of seasonal migrations, frequent encounters with peoples from other aboriginal societies, and trade, the cultural traditions of Australian peoples did not diffuse much beyond the regions inhabited by individual societies. Aboriginal peoples paid close attention to the prominent geographic features of the lands around them. Often they conducted religious observances designed to ensure continuing supplies of animals, plant life, and water. Given the intense concern of aboriginal peoples with their immediate environments, their cultural and religious traditions focused on local matters and did not appeal to peoples from other regions.

The Development of Pacific Island Societies

By the early centuries C.E., human migrants had established agricultural societies in almost all the island groups of the Pacific Ocean. About the middle of the first millennium C.E., they ventured to the large islands of New Zealand—the last large, habitable region of the earth to receive members of the human species. After 1000 C.E. Polynesians inhabiting the larger Pacific islands grew especially numerous, and their surging population prompted remarkable social and political development.

TRADE BETWEEN ISLAND GROUPS In the central and western regions of the Pacific, where several clusters of islands are relatively close to one another, mariners linked island societies. Regional trade networks facilitated exchanges of useful goods such as axes and pottery, exotic items such as shells and decorative ornaments, and sometimes even foodstuffs. Regional trade within individual island groups served social and political as well as economic functions, since it helped ruling elites establish and maintain harmonious relations with one another. In some cases, trade crossed longer distances and linked different island groups. Inhabitants of the Tonga, Samoa, and Fiji islands traded mats and canoes, for example, and also intermarried, thus creating political and social relationships.

New Zealand was the last large habitable area to be settled by humans.

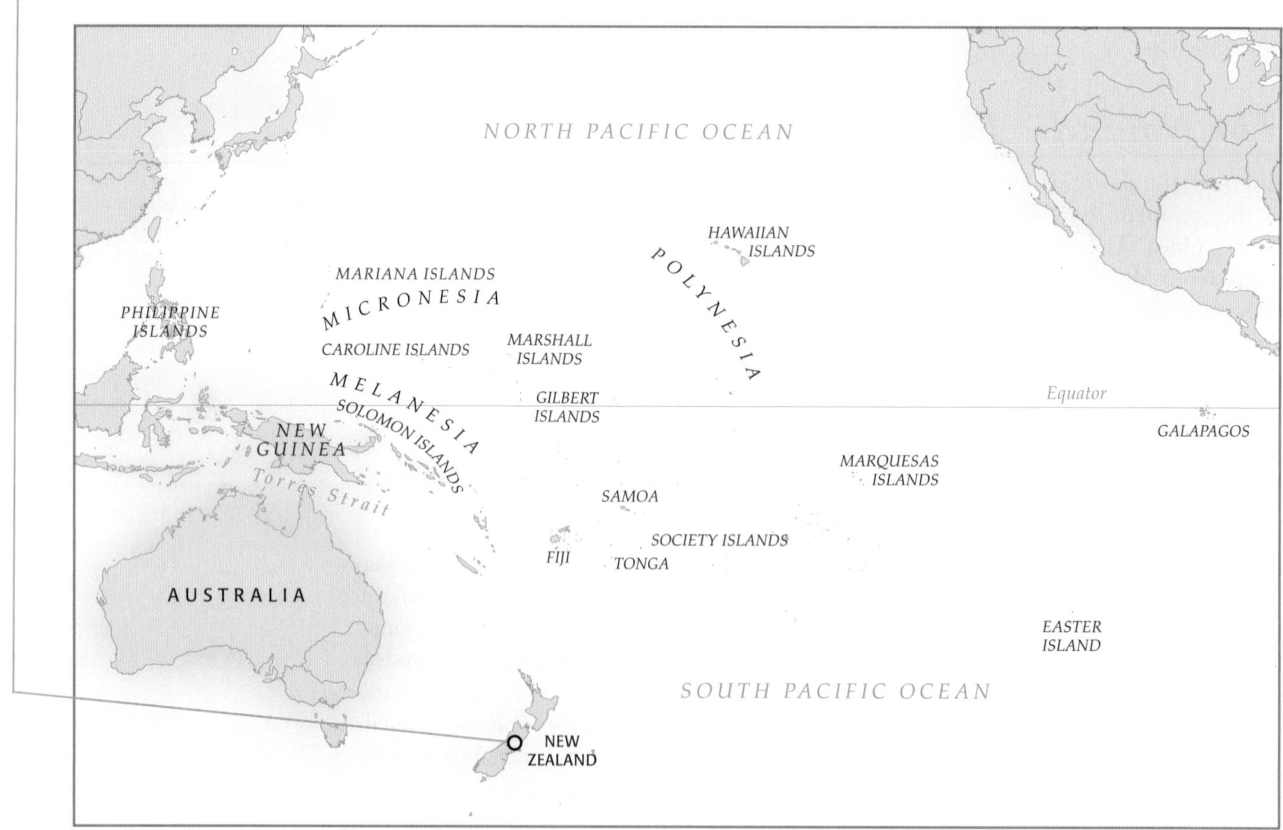

MAP 17.3 | The societies of Oceania. Islands are much more numerous and much closer together in the western Pacific than in the eastern Pacific. ***In what ways did proximity to or distance from other islands influence the development of Pacific island societies?***

HAWAI`I.** | A painting from 1825 shows several fishponds in active use near Honolulu in Hawai`i. ***How might these fishponds be compared to farming livestock?*

LONG-DISTANCE VOYAGING Elsewhere in Polynesia, vast stretches of deep blue water made it much more complicated to travel between different island groups and societies. As a result, regular trade networks did not emerge in the eastern Pacific Ocean. Nevertheless, mariners undertook lengthy voyages on an intermittent basis, sometimes with momentous results. After the original settlement of Easter Island about 300 C.E., for example, Polynesian mariners probably ventured to the western coast of South America, where they learned about the cultivation of sweet potatoes. Between about 400 and 700 C.E., mariners spread sweet potatoes throughout Polynesia and beyond. The new crop quickly became a prominent source of food in all the islands it reached. Thus long-distance voyages were responsible for the dissemination of sweet potatoes to remote islands situated thousands of kilometers from the nearest inhabited lands.

Another case of long-distance voyaging prompted social changes in the Hawaiian Islands. For centuries after the voyages that brought the original settlers to the islands in the early centuries C.E., there was little travel or communication between Hawai`i and other Polynesian societies. During the twelfth and thirteenth centuries, however, a series of two-way voyages linked Hawai`i with Tahiti and the Marquesas Islands. Memories of those voyages survive in oral traditions that relate the introduction into Hawai`i of new chiefly and priestly lines from Tahiti. Evidence for the voyages comes also from Hawaiian adoption of fishhook styles from Tahiti and words from the Tahitian language.

POPULATION GROWTH While undertaking regular or intermittent voyages over long distances, islanders throughout the Pacific Ocean also built productive agricultural and fishing societies. They cultivated taro, yams, sweet potatoes, bananas, breadfruit, and coconuts, and they kept domesticated pigs and dogs. They also fed on abundant supplies of fish. After about the fourteenth century, as their population increased, the inhabitants of Hawai`i built ingenious fishponds that allowed small fry to swim from the ocean through narrow gates into rock-enclosed spaces but prevented larger fish from escaping. Fishponds thus enabled Hawaiians to harvest large quantities of mature fish with relative ease. The establishment of agricultural and fishing societies led to rapid population growth in all the larger Pacific island groups. In Hawai`i, the most heavily populated of the Polynesian island groups, the human population may have exceeded five hundred thousand when European mariners arrived in the late eighteenth century.

NAN MADOL. | A massive wall constructed of basalt rock protects a burial site at Nan Madol in Pohnpei.

Dense populations sometimes led to environmental degradation and social strife on small islands with limited resources. Easter Island in particular was the site of dramatic problems arising from overpopulation. Polynesian migrants originally settled Easter Island in the early centuries C.E., and during the era from about 1100 to 1500, their descendants numbered about ten thousand. This population placed tremendous pressure on the island's resources. By 1500, islanders fought one another ferociously for those resources, engaging in brutal massacres of their enemies and the desecration of their bodies. As their society disintegrated, they sometimes resorted to cannibalism for lack of sufficient food.

NAN MADOL In other lands, dense populations promoted social organization on a scale never before seen in Oceania. On Pohnpei in the Caroline Islands, for example, the Sandeleur dynasty built a powerful state and organized construction of a massive stone palace and administrative center at Nan Madol. Built mostly during the period from 1200 to 1600, the complex included ninety-three artificial islets protected by seawalls and breakwaters on three sides.

DEVELOPMENT OF SOCIAL CLASSES Indeed, beginning about the thirteenth century, expanding populations prompted residents of many Pacific islands to develop increasingly complex social and political structures. Especially on the larger islands, workers became more specialized: some concentrated on cultivating certain crops while others devoted their efforts to fishing or crafts production. Distinct classes emerged as well. The islands of Tonga, Tahiti, and Hawai`i had especially stratified societies with sharp distinctions between various classes of high chiefs, lesser chiefs, and commoners. Hawaiian society also recognized distinct classes of priests and skilled artisans as well as common classes.

THE FORMATION OF CHIEFLY STATES In addition to distinct social classes, island societies generated strong political leadership. Ruling chiefs generally oversaw public affairs in portions of an island, in an entire island, or occasionally in several islands situated

THINKING ABOUT *Encounters*

ENCOUNTERS IN THE AMERICAS AND OCEANIA. Within limited regions, societies in the Americas and Oceania established trade networks, tributary relations, or imperial authority over neighboring peoples. In addition, some societies supported networks of long-distance trade. What are some examples in which long-distance trade altered or shaped societies in either the Americas or Oceania?

SOURCES FROM THE PAST

Mo`ikeha's Migration from Tahiti to Hawai`i

A group of Polynesian oral traditions preserves memories of numerous two-way voyages between Tahiti and Hawai`i in the twelfth and thirteenth centuries. One of them has to do with Mo`ikeha, a high chief who left Tahiti because of domestic difficulties and migrated to Hawai`i, where he founded a new chiefly line. The legend recounts several voyages between Tahiti and Hawai`i. The following excerpts deal with Mo`ikeha's establishment as a chief in Hawai`i and the later arrival of his Tahitian son La`amaikahiki, who is credited with the introduction of Tahitian religious and cultural traditions to Hawai`i.

It was dark by the time they arrived [at the Hawaiian island of Kaua`i], so they did not land, instead, mooring their canoe offshore. Early the next morning the people saw this double-hulled canoe floating offshore with the kapu sticks of a chief aboard. The canoe was brought ashore and the travelers got off. Meanwhile the locals were gathering in a crowd to go surf-riding. . . . Among them were the two daughters of the ali`i nui [chief] of Kaua`i, Ho`oipoikamalanai and Hinauu.

Mo`ikeha and his companions saw the crowd and followed along to take part in the morning exercise. Mo`ikeha was a handsome man with dark reddish hair and a tall, commanding figure.

When Ho`oipoikamalanai and her sister saw Mo`ikeha, they immediately fell in love with him, and they decided to take him for their husband. Mo`ikeha in the meantime was also struck with the beauty and grace of the two sisters, and he, too, fell in love with them and decided to take one of them to be his wife. After enjoying the surf for a time, Ho`oipoikamalanai and her sister returned home and told their father about the new arrival and said: "We wish to take that young chief as a husband for one of us." The father approved.

Orders were issued that Mo`ikeha be brought to the house of the two ali`i women. Mo`ikeha and his company were sent for and brought in the presence of the king [the ali`i nui of Kaua`i]. The love of these young people being mutual, Ho`oipoikamalanai and Hinauu took Mo`ikeha to be their husband. Mo`ikeha became ali`i nui of Kaua`i after the death of his father-in-law. . . .

Mo`ikeha worked to make his two wives and five children happy, giving his undivided attention to the bringing up of his boys. He thought no more of Lu`ukia [his lover in Tahiti], but after a while, he began to feel a yearning desire to see his son La`amaikahiki, his child by his first wife Kapo. So he called his five sons together and said to them: "I'm thinking of sending one of you boys to bring your elder brother to Hawai`i.". . .

[After Mo`ikeha's son Kila sailed to Tahiti and found his elder half-brother] La`amaikahiki immediately prepared to accompany his brother to Hawai`i, as Mo`ikeha wished. La`amaikahiki took his priests and his god Lonoika`ouali`i, and set sail for Hawai`i with the men who had come with Kila. When they were approaching Kaua`i, La`amaikahiki began beating his drum. Mo`ikeha heard his drum and ordered everything, the land as well as the house, to be made ready for the reception of the chief La`amaikahiki. Upon the arrival of La`amaikahiki and Kila, the high priest of Kaua`i, Poloahilani, took La`amaikahiki and his god Lonoika`ouali`i ("Lono at the Chiefly Supremacy") to the heiau [temple]. It is said that La`amaikahiki was the first person to bring a god (akua) to Hawai`i. . . .

[After returning to Tahiti, then sailing again to Hawai`i, La`amaikahiki] set sail again, going up the Kona coast [of Hawai`i Island]. . . . It was on this visit that La`amaikahiki introduced hula dancing, accompanied by the drum, to Hawai`i. . . .

La`amaikahiki stayed a long time on Kaua`i teaching the people the art of dancing. From Kaua`i La`amaikahiki visited all the other islands of this group and thus the drum dance (hula ka`eke) spread to the other islands.

■ **How would you characterize the political, social, and cultural significance of two-way voyaging between Tahiti and Hawai`i?**

SOURCE: Teuira Henry and others. *Voyaging Chiefs of Havai`i.* Ed. by Dennis Kawaharada. Honolulu: Kalamaku Press, 1995, pp. 138–39, 144–46.

close to one another. In Tonga and Hawai`i, high chiefs frequently launched campaigns to bring additional islands under their control and create large centralized states. Rarely, however, were these militant chiefs able to overcome geographic and logistic difficulties and realize their expansionist ambitions before the nineteenth century.

Nevertheless, high chiefs guided the affairs of complex societies throughout Polynesia. They allocated lands to families, mobilized labor for construction projects, and organized men into military forces. They commanded enormous respect within their societies. In Hawai`i, for example, the classes of high chiefs known as *ali`i nui* intermarried, ate the best fish and other foods that were *kapu* ("taboo") to commoners, and had the right to wear magnificent cloaks adorned with thousands of bright red and yellow bird feathers. Indeed, a *kapu* forbade commoners to approach or even cast a shadow on the *ali`i nui.*

POLYNESIAN RELIGION High chiefs worked closely with priests, who served as intermediaries between human communities and the gods. Gods of war and agriculture were common throughout the Pacific islands, but individual islands and island groups recognized deities particular to their own regions and interests. The most distinctive architecture of early Pacific societies was the ceremonial precinct and temple structure known as *marae* (or *heiau* in Hawaiian). *Marae* often had several terraced floors, with a rock or coral wall designating the boundaries of the sacred space. In Tonga and Samoa, temples made of timber and thatched roofs served as places of worship, sacrifice, and communication between priests and the gods, whereas in eastern Polynesia religious ceremonies took place on platforms in open-air courtyards.

Pacific island societies did not enjoy access to the range of technologies developed by continental peoples until after the sixteenth century. Yet Pacific islanders cleverly exploited their environments, established productive agricultural economies, built elaborate, well-organized societies, and reached out when possible to engage in trade with their neighbors. Their achievements testify anew to the human impulses toward densely populated communities and interaction with other societies.

SUMMARY

The original inhabitants of the Americas and Oceania lived in societies that were considerably smaller than those of the eastern hemisphere. Unlike their counterparts in the eastern hemisphere, they did not possess metallurgical technologies or transportation technologies based on wheeled vehicles and domesticated animals. Nevertheless, long before they entered into sustained interaction with European and other peoples, they built complex societies and developed sophisticated cultural and religious traditions. Indigenous peoples established foraging, fishing, and agricultural societies throughout the Americas, and they fashioned tools from wood, stone, and bone that enabled them to produce enough food to support sizable communities. In Mesoamerica and Andean South America, they also built imperial states that organized public affairs on a large scale.

The original inhabitants of Australia and the Pacific islands built societies on a smaller scale than did the peoples of the Americas, but they too devised effective means of exploiting the natural environment and organizing flourishing communities. Australia was a continent of foraging nomadic peoples, whereas the Pacific islands supported densely populated agricultural societies. Although they had limited communication with peoples of the Americas or the eastern hemisphere, the peoples of Oceania traded and interacted regularly with their neighbors, and inhabitants of the Pacific islands sometimes undertook lengthy voyages to trade with distant island groups.

STUDY TERMS

aboriginal peoples (335)
ali'i nui (340)
ayllu (334)
Aztec (325)
Cahokia (330)
calpulli (328)
Chimu (331)
chinampa system (325)
Cuzco (333)
Huitzilopochtli (328)
Inca (332)
Inti (334)
Iroquois (330)
kapu (340)
marae (340)
Mexica (324)
Nahuatl (328)
Nan Madol (338)
Navajo (329)
Pachacuti (332)
Polynesians (336)
Pueblo (329)
Quechua (332)
Quetzalcoatl (328)
quipu (332)
Tenochtitlan (323)
Teotihuacan (324)
Tezcatlipoca (328)
Toltecs (324)
Viracocha (334)

FOR FURTHER READING

Peter Bellwood. *The Polynesians: Prehistory of an Island People.* Rev. ed. London, 1987. Well-illustrated popular account emphasizing the origins and early development of Polynesian societies.

Geoffrey Blainey. *Triumph of the Nomads: A History of Aboriginal Australia.* Melbourne, 1975. A sympathetic account of Australia before European arrival, well informed by archaeological discoveries.

Inga Clendinnen. *Aztecs: An Interpretation.* Cambridge, 1991. A brilliant re-creation of the Mexica world, concentrating on cultural and social themes.

George A. Collier, Renato I. Rosaldo, and John D. Wirth, eds. *The Inca and Aztec States, 1400–1800: Anthropology and History.* New York, 1982. Seventeen well-focused essays represent approaches that scholars have taken to the Inca and Aztec empires.

Ben Finney. *Voyage of Rediscovery: A Cultural Odyssey through Polynesia.* Berkeley, 1994. Fascinating account of efforts to understand ancient Polynesian techniques of seafaring and to chart the courses of Polynesian migrations.

Patrick V. Kirch. *On the Road of the Winds: An Archaeological History of the Pacific Islands before European Contact.* Berkeley, 2000. A valuable synthesis of recent scholarship by the foremost contemporary archaeologist of the Pacific islands.

Miguel León-Portilla. *The Aztec Image of Self and Society: An Introduction to Nahua Culture.* Salt Lake City, 1992. An excellent guide to Mexica social and cultural history by the foremost student of the Mexica.

Charles C. Mann. *1491: New Revelations of the Americas before Columbus.* New York, 2006. Summarizes a great deal of archaeological research on the pre-Columbian Americas.

Lynda Norene Shaffer. *Native Americans before 1492: The Mound-building Centers of the Eastern Woodlands.* Armonk, N.Y., 1992. Places the societies of mound-building peoples in larger historical context.

Muriel Porter Weaver. *The Aztecs, Maya, and Their Predecessors: Archaeology of Mesoamerica.* 3rd ed. New York, 1993. An up-to-date survey based on historical and archaeological research.

Reaching Out: Cross-Cultural Interactions

18

One of the great world travelers of all time was the Moroccan legal scholar Ibn Battuta. Born in 1304 at Tangier, Ibn Battuta followed family tradition and studied Islamic law. In 1325 he left Morocco to make a pilgrimage to Mecca. He traveled by caravan across north Africa and through Egypt, Palestine, and Syria, arriving at Mecca in 1326. After completing his hajj, Ibn Battuta spent a year visiting Mesopotamia and Persia, then traveled by ship through the Red Sea and down the east African coast as far south as Kilwa. By 1330 he had returned to Mecca, but then soon set off for India when he learned that the sultan of Delhi offered handsome rewards to foreign legal scholars. In 1333 he arrived in Delhi after following a long and circuitous land route that took him through Egypt, Syria, Anatolia, Constantinople, the Black Sea, and the great trading cities of central Asia, Bokhara and Samarkand.

Ibn Battuta in China
www.mhhe.com/bentleybrief2e

For the next eight years, Ibn Battuta remained in India, serving mostly as a *qadi* (judge) in the government of the sultan of Delhi. In 1341 Ibn Battuta began his travels again, this time making his way around southern India, Ceylon, and the Maldive Islands before continuing to China about 1345. He visited the bustling southern Chinese port cities of Quanzhou and Guangzhou, where he found large communities of Muslim merchants, before returning to Morocco in 1349 by way of southern India, the Persian Gulf, Syria, Egypt, and Mecca.

Still, Ibn Battuta's travels were not complete. In 1350 he made a short trip to the kingdom of Granada in southern Spain, and in 1353 he joined a camel caravan across the Sahara desert to visit the Mali empire, returning to Morocco in 1355. During his travels Ibn Battuta visited the equivalent of forty-four modern countries and logged more than 117,000 kilometers (73,000 miles). His account of his adventures stands with Marco Polo's book among the classic works of travel literature.

Between 1000 and 1500 C.E., the peoples of the eastern hemisphere traveled, traded, communicated, and interacted more regularly and intensively than ever before. The large empires of the Mongols and other nomadic peoples provided a political foundation for that cross-cultural interaction. When they conquered and pacified vast regions, nomadic peoples provided safe roads for merchants, diplomats, missionaries, and other travelers. Quite apart from the nomadic empires, improvements in maritime technology led to increased traffic in the sea-lanes of the Indian Ocean and the South China Sea. As a result, long-distance travel became much more common than in earlier eras.

❮ A giraffe from east Africa sent as a present to China in 1414 and painted by a Chinese artist at the Ming zoo.

Ibn Battuta (ih-bun BAH-too-tah)

CHRONOLOGY

1253–1324	Life of Marco Polo
1287–1288	Rabban Sauma's embassy to Europe
1304–1369	Life of Ibn Battuta
1304–1374	Life of Francesco Petrarca
1330s	First outbreaks of bubonic plague in China
1347	Arrival of bubonic plague in the Mediterranean basin
1368–1644	Ming Dynasty
1405–1433	Zheng He's expeditions in the Indian Ocean
1466–1536	Life of Desiderius Erasmus of Rotterdam
1488	Bartolomeu Dias's voyage around Africa
1492	Christopher Columbus's first voyage to the western hemisphere
1497–1498	Vasco da Gama's voyage to India

Merchants and travelers exchanged more than trade goods. They diffused technologies and spread religious faiths. They also exchanged diseases that caused deadly epidemics. During the middle decades of the fourteenth century, bubonic plague traveled the trade routes and spread through most of Eurasia. During its initial, furious onslaught, bubonic plague caused death and destruction on a huge scale and interrupted long-distance trade networks.

By the early fifteenth century, however, societies had begun to recover from the plague. Chinese and western European peoples in particular had restabilized their societies and begun to renew cross-cultural contacts. In Europe, this effort had profound consequences for modern world history. As they sought entry to the markets of Asia, European mariners sailed to the western hemisphere and the Pacific Ocean. Their voyages brought the peoples of the eastern hemisphere, the western hemisphere, and Oceania into permanent and sustained interaction with one another. Thus between 1000 and 1500, cross-cultural interactions pointed toward global interdependence, a principal characteristic of modern world history.

Long-Distance Trade and Travel

Travelers embarked on long-distance journeys for a variety of reasons. Three of the more important motives for long-distance travel between 1000 and 1500 C.E. were trade, diplomacy, and missionary activity. The cross-cultural interactions that resulted helped spread technological innovations throughout the eastern hemisphere.

Patterns of Long-Distance Trade

Merchants engaged in long-distance trade relied on two principal networks of trade routes. Luxury goods of high value relative to their weight, such as silk textiles and precious stones, often traveled overland on the silk roads. Bulkier commodities, such as steel, stone, and building materials, traveled the sea-lanes of the Indian Ocean, because it would have been unprofitable to transport them overland. The silk roads linked all of the Eurasian landmass, and trans-Saharan caravan routes drew west Africa into the larger economy of the eastern hemisphere. The sea-lanes of the Indian Ocean served ports in southeast Asia, India, Arabia, and east Africa while also offering access via the South China Sea to ports in China, Japan, Korea, and the islands of southeast Asia. Thus, in combination, land and sea routes touched almost every corner of the eastern hemisphere.

TRADING CITIES As the volume of trade increased, the major trading cities and ports grew rapidly, attracting buyers, sellers, brokers, and bankers from parts near and far. When a trading or port city enjoyed a strategic location, maintained good order, and resisted the temptation to levy excessive customs fees, it had the potential to become a major emporium. A case in point is Melaka (in modern Malaysia). Founded in the 1390s, within a few decades Melaka became the principal clearinghouse of trade in the eastern Indian Ocean. The city's authorities policed the strategic Strait of Melaka and maintained

Melaka (may-LAH-kah)

a safe market that welcomed all merchants and levied reasonable fees on goods exchanged there. By the end of the fifteenth century, Melaka had a population of some fifty thousand people, and, according to one report, more than eighty languages could be heard in the city's streets.

Although the early period of Mongol conquest in the first half of the thirteenth century caused economic decline, especially in China and southwest Asia, eventually Mongol rule proved to be a boon for overland trade. Under Mongol rule, merchants traveling the silk roads faced less risk of banditry or political turbulence than in previous times. Meanwhile, strong economies in China, India, and western Europe fueled demand for foreign commodities.

MARCO POLO The best-known long-distance traveler of Mongol times was the Venetian Marco Polo (1253–1324), who, with his father and his uncle, traveled and traded throughout Mongol lands in the late thirteenth century. When Marco Polo returned to Europe in 1295, stories of his adventures were compiled by a third party and circulated widely throughout Europe. In spite of occasional exaggerations and tall tales, Marco's stories about the textiles, spices, gems, and other goods he observed during his travels deeply influenced European readers eager to participate in the lucrative trade networks of Eurasia. Indeed, in the wake of the Polos came hundreds of others, whose travels helped to increase European participation in the larger economy of the eastern hemisphere.

Political and Diplomatic Travel

Marco Polo came from a family of merchants, and merchants were among the most avid readers of his stories. Yet his experiences also throw light on long-distance travel undertaken for political and diplomatic purposes. Khubilai Khan and the other Mongol rulers of China did not entirely trust their Chinese subjects and regularly appointed foreigners to administrative posts. Indeed, while in China Marco reported that Khubilai appointed him governor of the large trading city of Yangzhou, and that he represented Khubilai Khan's interests on diplomatic missions.

Khubilai Khan with the Polos
www.mhhe.com/bentleybrief2e

MONGOL-CHRISTIAN DIPLOMACY The emergence of elaborate trading networks and the establishment of vast imperial states created great demand for political and diplomatic representation during the centuries after 1000 C.E. The thirteenth century was a time of especially active diplomacy involving distant parties. During the 1240s and 1250s, for example, Pope Innocent IV dispatched a series of envoys who invited the Mongol khans to convert to Christianity and join Europeans in an alliance against the Muslims in control of Jerusalem. The khans declined the invitation, proposing in reply that the pope and European Christians submit to Mongol rule or face destruction.

RABBAN SAUMA Although the early round of Mongol-European diplomacy offered little promise of cooperation, the Mongols later initiated another effort. In 1287 the Mongol ilkhan of Persia planned to invade the Muslim-held lands of southwest Asia and capture Jerusalem. In hopes of attracting support for the project, he dispatched Rabban Sauma, a Nestorian Christian priest of Turkish ancestry, as an envoy to the pope and European political leaders. Although his efforts did not succeed in garnering European support for Mongol plans, such diplomatic activity illustrates the complexity of political affairs in the eastern hemisphere and the need for diplomatic consultation over long distances.

The expansion of Islamic influence in the eastern hemisphere encouraged a different kind of politically motivated travel. Legal scholars and judges played a crucial role in Islamic societies, since the *sharia* prescribed religious observances and social relationships based on the Quran. Conversions to Islam and the establishment of Islamic states in India, southeast Asia, and sub-Saharan Africa created a demand for Muslims educated in Islamic law. After about the eleventh century, educated Muslims from southwest Asia and north Africa regularly traveled to recently converted lands to help instill Islamic values.

MAP 18.1 | Travels of Marco Polo and Ibn Battuta. Compare the routes taken by Marco Polo and Ibn Battuta during their travels. ***How did the two men choose where to travel? What conditions made it possible for them to travel so far from their homes?***

Between them, Ibn Battuta and Marco Polo traveled across much of the Eurasian landmass as well as parts of Africa and southeast Asia.

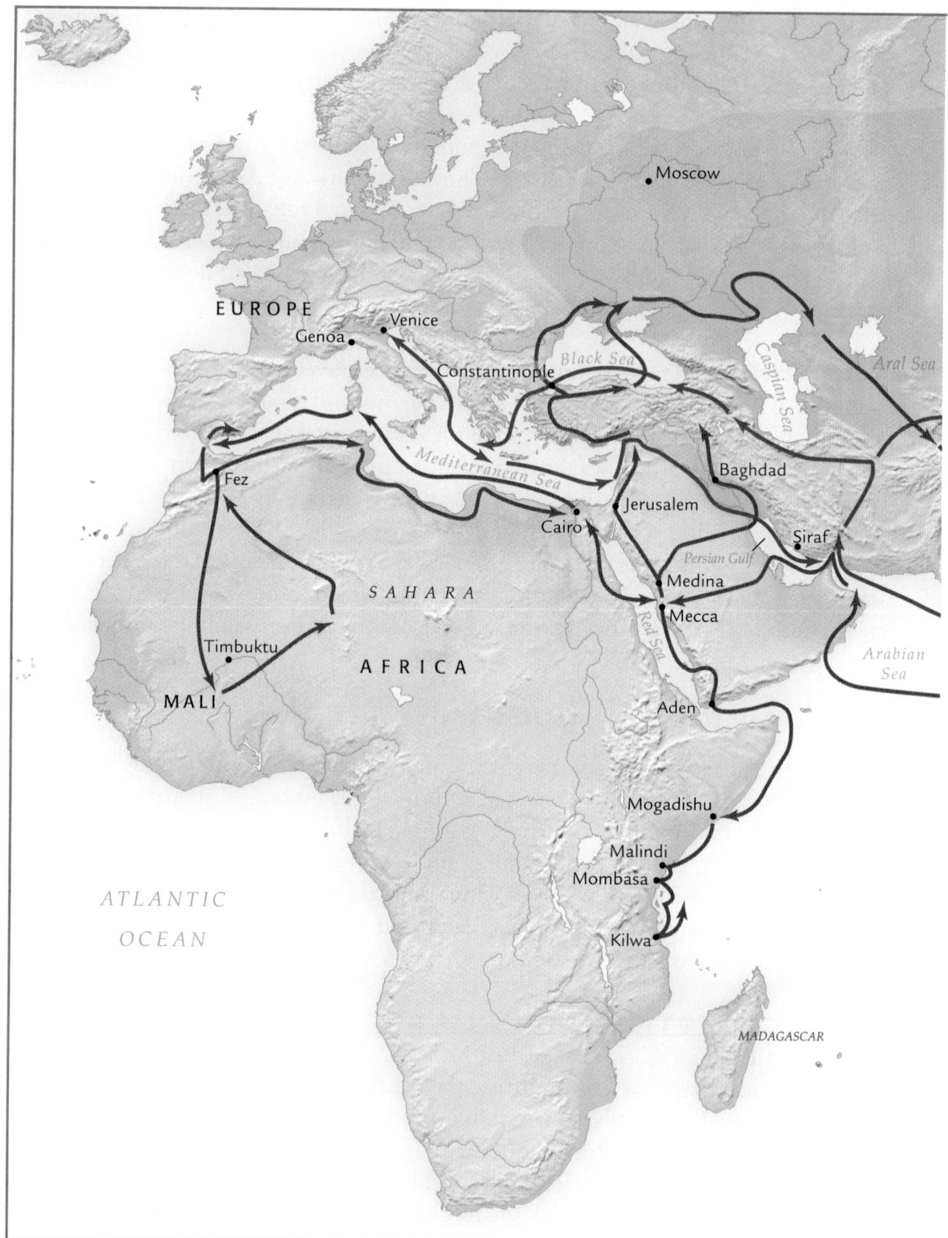

IBN BATTUTA Best known of the Muslim travelers was Ibn Battuta (1304–1369). Islamic rulers governed most of the lands Ibn Battuta visited, but very few Muslims educated in the law were available in those lands. With his legal credentials Ibn Battuta had little difficulty finding government positions. As *qadi* and advisor to the sultan of Delhi, he supervised the affairs of a wealthy mosque and heard cases at law, which he strictly enforced according to Islamic standards of justice. On one occasion Ibn Battuta sentenced a man to receive eighty lashes because he had drunk wine eight years earlier. Ibn Battuta also served as *qadi* in both east and west Africa, where he consulted with Muslim rulers and offered advice about government, women's dress, and proper relationships between the sexes. Like many other legal scholars whose stories went unrecorded, Ibn Battuta provided guidance in the ways of Islam in societies recently converted to the faith.

qadi (KAH-dee)

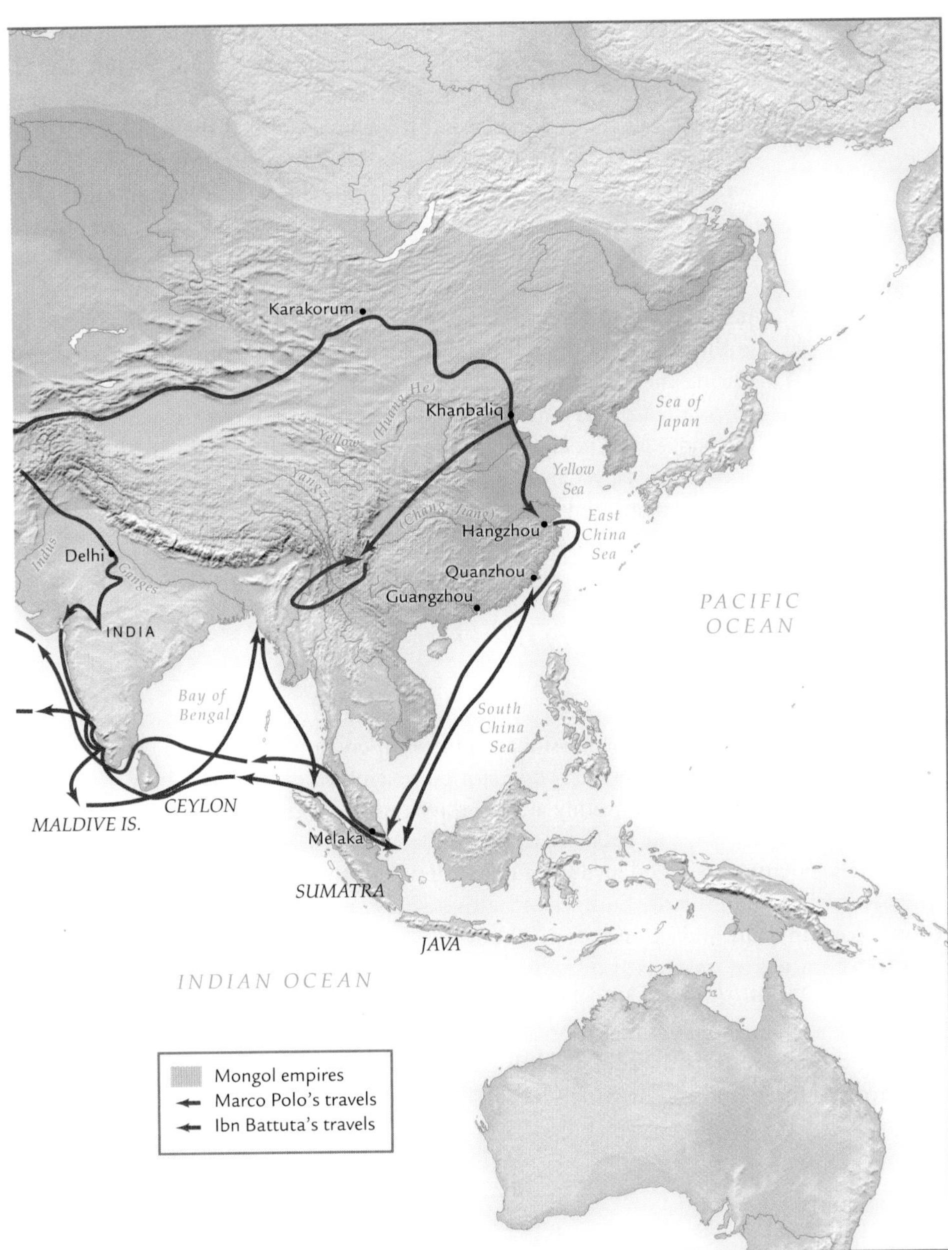

Missionary Campaigns

SUFI MISSIONARIES Islamic values spread not only through the efforts of legal scholars but also through the missionary activities of Sufi mystics. As in the early days of Islam, Sufis in the period from 1000 to 1500 ventured to recently conquered or converted lands and sought to win a popular following for the faith in India, southeast Asia, and sub-Saharan Africa. Sufis did not insist on a strict, doctrinally correct understanding of Islam but, rather, emphasized piety and devotion to Allah. They even tolerated continuing reverence of traditional deities. By taking a flexible approach to their missions, the Sufis spread Islamic values without facing the resistance that unyielding and doctrinaire campaigns might have provoked.

Sufis (SOO-fees)

THINKING ABOUT *Traditions*

TRADITIONS IN CROSS-CULTURAL INTERACTIONS. In spite of unprecedented cross-cultural trade and interaction between 1000 and 1500 C.E., societies in Eurasia maintained distinctive characteristics based on historical traditions, religion, cultural practices, and state structures. Using the experiences of travelers like Ibn Battuta, Marco Polo, and Zheng He, discuss how the cultural traditions embraced by individuals could shape responses to cultures very different from theirs.

CHRISTIAN MISSIONARIES Meanwhile, Roman Catholic missionaries also traveled long distances in the interests of spreading Christianity. Missionaries accompanied the crusaders and other forces to all the lands where Europeans extended their influence after the year 1000. In lands where European conquerors maintained a long-term presence—such as the Baltic lands, the Balkan region, Sicily, and Spain—missionaries attracted converts in large numbers, and Roman Catholic Christianity became securely established.

The most ambitious missions sought to convert Mongols and Chinese to Roman Catholic Christianity. Yet even though Roman Catholic authorities in Europe dispatched many priests and missionaries to China during the early fourteenth century, they ultimately won few converts. In part, east Asia was just too distant for the resources available to the Roman Catholic church. Moreover, Christianity seemed to have little appeal to east Asian peoples, who already possessed sophisticated religious and cultural traditions.

Long-Distance Travel and Cross-Cultural Exchanges

CULTURAL EXCHANGES Long-distance travel of all kinds, whether for commercial, political, diplomatic, or missionary purposes, encouraged cultural exchanges between peoples of different societies. Songs, stories, religious ideas, philosophical views, and scientific knowledge all passed readily among travelers who ventured into the larger world during the era from 1000 to 1500 C.E. The troubadours of western Europe, for example, drew on the poetry, music, and love songs of Muslim performers when developing the literature of courtly love. Similarly, European scientists avidly consulted their Muslim and Jewish counterparts in Sicily and Spain to learn about their understanding of the natural world.

Large numbers of travelers also facilitated agricultural and technological diffusion during the period from 1000 to 1500. The magnetic compass, for example, invented in China during the Tang or Song dynasty, spread throughout the Indian Ocean basin during the eleventh century, and by the mid–twelfth century European mariners used compasses in the Mediterranean and the Atlantic Ocean. The compass was a boon to maritime trade,

THE SIEGE OF BAGHDAD. | Mongol troops under the leadership of Hulagu Khan storm and capture Baghdad in 1258 after besieging the city. ***How did the Mongols make use of catapults during the siege?***

SOURCES FROM THE PAST

Ibn Battuta on Customs in the Mali Empire

Long-distance travelers often encountered unfamiliar customs in foreign societies. The Moroccan traveler Ibn Battuta approved heartily when staying with hosts who honored the values of his own Muslim society, but he had little tolerance for those who did not. Here he describes what he witnessed at the sultan's court in the Mali empire.

The blacks are the most humble of men before their king and the most extreme in their self-abasement before him. They swear by his name, saying "Mansa Sulaimanki" [the law of Mansa Sulaiman, the Mali sultan]. When he calls one of them while he is in session . . . the man invited takes off his clothes and wears patched clothes, takes off his turban, puts on a dirty cap, and goes in raising his clothes and trousers up his legs halfway to his knees. He advances with humility looking like a beggar. He hits the ground with his elbows, he hits it hard. He stands bowed, like one . . . in prayer, listening to what the king says. When one of them speaks to the sultan and he gives him an answer, he removes his clothes from his back and throws dust on his head and back, as a person does when bathing with water. I used to wonder how they do not blind their eyes. . . .

Sometimes one of them would stand before him and recall what he had done in his [the sultan's] service, saying, "I did such and such on such a day," and, "I killed so and so on such a day." Those who know this confirm that he is telling the truth. Their confirmation is by pulling the strings of their bows and letting them go, as one does when one is shooting. If the sultan says to him that he has spoken the truth or thanks him, he takes off his clothes and dusts. This is good manners among them. . . .

Amongst their good qualities is the small amount of injustice amongst them, for of all people they are the furthest from it. . . .

Another of the good habits amongst them is the way they meticulously observe the times of the prayers and attendance at them, so also it is with regard to their congregational services and their beating of their children to instill these things in them.

When it is Friday, if a man does not come early to the mosque he will not find a place to pray because of the numbers of the crowd. It is their custom for every man to send his boy [i.e., servant] with his prayer mat. He spreads it for him in a place commensurate with his position and keeps the place until he comes to the mosque. . . .

Among their good qualities is their putting on of good white clothes on Friday. If a man among them has nothing except a tattered shirt, he washes and cleans it and attends the Friday prayer in it. Another of their good qualities is their concern for learning the sublime Quran by heart. . . .

Among the bad things which they do—their serving women, slave women and little daughters appear before people naked, exposing their private parts. I used to see many of them in this state in [the fasting month of] Ramadan, for it was the custom of the *farariyya* [commanders] to break the fast in the sultan's house. Everyone of them has his food carried in to him by twenty or more of his slave girls and they are naked, every one. Also among their bad customs is the way women will go into the presence of the sultan naked, without any covering; and the nakedness of the sultan's daughters—on the night of the twenty-seventh of Ramadan, I saw about a hundred slave girls coming out of his palace with food, with them were two of his daughters, they had full breasts and no clothes on. Another of their bad customs is their putting of dust and ashes on their heads as a sign of respect. . . . And another is that many of them eat animals not ritually slaughtered, and dogs and donkeys.

■ Discuss the various ways in which Islamic influences and established local customs came together in the Mali empire.

SOURCE: Said Hamdun and Noel King, eds. *Ibn Battuta in Black Africa*. Princeton: Markus Wiener, 1998, pp. 49–50, 58–59.

because it allowed mariners to sail over long stretches of deep water with confidence in their ability to find their destinations and return home safely.

SPREAD OF CROPS Long-distance journeys enabled Muslim travelers to introduce new food and commercial crops—such as citrus fruits and Asian rice—to sub-Saharan Africa, which enriched west African diets after the eleventh century. Muslims also introduced cotton to west Africa, and by 1500 it was the principal textile produced in sub-Saharan Africa.

SUGARCANE Muslims were also instrumental in the continuing diffusion of sugarcane. Muslim merchants and other travelers had begun large-scale cultivation of sugarcane in southwest Asia and north Africa during the Abbasid caliphate. After the twelfth century, Muslims facilitated the westward spread of sugarcane by acquainting European crusaders with crystallized sugar refined from cane. Up to that time Europeans had little access to refined sugar, and they relied on honey and fruits as sweeteners. They immediately appreciated the convenience of refined sugar. Italian entrepreneurs began to organize sugarcane plantations on Mediterranean islands such as Sicily, Cyprus, Crete, and Rhodes, and investors began to seek suitable locations throughout the Mediterranean basin. The cultivation of sugarcane had deep social and economic implications. Like their Muslim predecessors, European sugar producers often staffed their plantations with slave laborers, and the growth of plantations fueled an increasing demand for Muslim war captives and black Africans who could supply labor services.

GUNPOWDER TECHNOLOGIES Although Muslim merchants and travelers were especially prominent agents of diffusion, Mongols also contributed to the process, notably by helping to spread gunpowder technologies west from China. Mongol invaders learned about gunpowder from Chinese military engineers in the early thirteenth century and soon incorporated gunpowder-based weapons into their arsenal. During the 1250s, as they campaigned in Persia and southwest Asia, the Mongols used catapults and trebuchets to lob gunpowder bombs into cities under siege. Muslim armies soon developed similar weapons in response.

By the mid–thirteenth century gunpowder had reached Europe. By the early fourteenth century, armies from China to Europe possessed primitive cannons. Although not especially accurate, the weapons were powerful enough to blow holes in the defensive walls of cities under siege. Thus, with the assistance of Mongol warriors, gunpowder technology rapidly spread from its homeland in China across the entire Eurasian landmass and changed forever the nature of war.

Agricultural and technological diffusions of the era 1000 to 1500 were by no means unique processes in world history. For millennia, agricultural crops and technological skills had spread widely whenever peoples of different societies interacted with one another. Because of the particularly intense interactions of the period from 1000 to 1500, however, agricultural and technological diffusion profoundly influenced the lives of peoples throughout the eastern hemisphere on an unprecedented scale.

Crisis and Recovery

As Eurasian peoples traveled over long distances, they exchanged trade goods, agricultural crops, and technological expertise, and they also unwittingly spread disease pathogens. When diseases broke out among previously unexposed populations, they often caused widespread epidemics that severely disrupted whole societies. During the fourteenth century, bubonic plague erupted in epidemics that ravaged societies throughout most of Asia, Europe, and north Africa. Epidemic plague struck intermittently until the seventeenth century, but by the fifteenth century Chinese and western European societies in particular had begun to recover from its effects.

Bubonic Plague

THE LITTLE ICE AGE About 1300 C.E. a process of global climatic change caused temperatures to decline significantly throughout the world. For more than five hundred years, the earth experienced a "little ice age," when temperatures were much cooler than before. Markedly cooler temperatures meant shorter growing seasons, which caused agricultural production to decline in many lands. That, in turn, led to famine and sometimes even starvation. In some northerly lands, such as Greenland, agriculture ceased to be a practical possibility.

ORIGINS OF EPIDEMIC BUBONIC PLAGUE Just after the onset of the little ice age, peoples in much of the eastern hemisphere suddenly encountered a new challenge in the form of devastating epidemic disease. Bubonic plague spread from the Yunnan region of southwestern China, where it probably had been endemic for centuries. The plague bacillus infects rodents such as rats, squirrels, and prairie dogs, and fleas transmit the pathogen from one rodent to another. If rodent populations decline, fleas seek other hosts and sometimes spread the disease to human victims. In the early fourteenth century, Mongol military campaigns helped spread plague from Yunnan to China's interior, and by the 1350s it had spread to widely scattered regions of China. In some afflicted areas contemporaries reported that plague carried away two-thirds of the population.

THE BUBONIC PLAGUE IN EUROPE. | A painting of 1503 graphically communicates the horror felt by medieval Europeans when bubonic plague struck their communities. Here death takes away a victim, while others die beside the road.

SPREAD OF PLAGUE During the 1340s Mongols, merchants, and other travelers helped spread the disease along trade routes west of China. By 1346 it had reached the Black Sea ports of Caffa and Tana. In 1347 Italian merchants fled plague-infected Black Sea ports and unwittingly spread the disease throughout the Mediterranean basin. By 1348, following the trade routes, plague had sparked epidemics in most of western Europe.

Wherever it appeared, bubonic plague—which Europeans referred to as the "Black Death"—struck with frightful effects. Victims developed inflamed lymph nodes, particularly in the neck, armpit, and groin areas, and most died within a few days after the onset of symptoms. Internal hemorrhaging often discolored the inflammations to a black or purple hue. These swellings were called buboes, which gave rise to the term *bubonic plague.* Bubonic plague typically killed 60 to 70 percent of its human victims. In some small villages and towns, disease wiped out the entire population. Plague also returned to claim new victims. In Europe plague erupted intermittently from the 1340s until the late 1600s.

Some parts of the eastern hemisphere did not suffer directly from plague epidemics. The long, cold winters of Scandinavia, for example, discouraged the proliferation of plague-bearing rodents and fleas. For reasons unknown, India also seems to have avoided the worst effects of the plague. In fact, Indian population grew from 91 million in the year 1300 to 97 million a century later. Epidemics also largely bypassed sub-Saharan Africa.

The bubonic plague
www.mhhe.com/
bentleybrief2e

POPULATION DECLINE In lands hard hit by plague, however, it took a century and more to begin recovery from the demographic consequences of the disease. In 1300 China's population, already reduced by conflicts with the Mongols, stood at eighty-five million. In 1400, after about seventy years of epidemic plague, China's population amounted to only seventy-five million. A century later demographic recovery was under way, and China's population rebounded to one hundred million. European society also reeled from the effects of bubonic plague. From seventy-nine million in 1300, European population dropped by almost 25 percent to sixty million in 1400. As in China, demographic recovery in Europe was under way in 1500, when European population climbed to eighty-one million. Islamic societies in southwest Asia, Egypt, and north Africa also suffered devastating population losses, and demographic recovery took much longer there than in China and Europe. In Egypt, human population probably did not reach preplague levels until the nineteenth century.

SOCIAL AND ECONOMIC EFFECTS Because of its heavy demographic toll, bubonic plague disrupted societies and economies throughout Eurasia and north Africa. Such high death rates caused huge labor shortages, which in turn generated social unrest. In western Europe, for example, urban workers demanded higher wages, and many left their homes in search of better conditions. Political authorities responded by freezing wages and forbidding workers to leave their homes. Peasants in the countryside also sought to improve their circumstances by moving to regions where landlords offered better terms. Landlords responded to this challenge by restricting the freedom of peasants to move. As a result of sharply conflicting interests, disgruntled workers and peasants mounted a series of rebellions that rocked both the towns and the countryside of western Europe and were extinguished only after considerable social disruption and loss of life.

By the seventeenth century the plague had lost much of its ferocity. Epidemics occurred more sporadically, and they did not seriously diminish human populations. Since the 1940s antibiotic drugs have brought the disease largely under control among human populations, although it survives in rodent communities throughout much of the world.

Recovery in China: The Ming Dynasty

By the mid–fourteenth century the Mongol's Yuan dynasty was experiencing very difficult times. Financial mismanagement led to serious economic difficulties, and political conflicts led to factional fighting among the Mongols themselves. In 1368, with bubonic plague raging, the Yuan dynasty collapsed, and the Mongols departed China en masse, leaving China in a state of both demographic and political turmoil. However, an increasing birthrate soon helped to replenish human numbers, and political recovery accompanied the demographic rebound.

HONGWU When the Yuan dynasty fell, the governance of China returned to Chinese hands. The new emperor came from a family so poor that he spent much of his youth as a beggar. Because of his size and strength, he came to the notice of military commanders, and he made his way through the ranks to lead the rebellious forces that toppled the Yuan dynasty. In 1368 he became Emperor Hongwu, and he proclaimed the establishment of the Ming ("brilliant") dynasty, which lasted until 1644.

MING CENTRALIZATION Hongwu immediately set about eliminating all traces of Mongol rule and establishing a government on the model of traditional Chinese dynasties. Although Hongwu had little interest in scholarly matters, he reestablished the Confucian educational and civil service systems to ensure a supply of talented officials and bureaucrats. At the same time, he moved to centralize his authority. In 1380, when he suspected his chief minister of involvement in a treasonous plot, Hongwu executed the minister and his allies and then abolished the minister's position altogether. From that time forward the Ming emperors ruled directly, without the aid of chief ministers.

MANDARINS AND EUNUCHS The Ming emperors insisted on absolute obedience to the policies and initiatives of the central government. They relied heavily on the mandarins, a special class of officials sent out as emissaries of the central government to ensure local compliance with imperial policy. The Ming emperors also relied more heavily on eunuchs than had any of their predecessors. Eunuchs had long been considered reliable because they could not generate families and build power bases that might challenge ruling houses. Yet Ming emperors intent on centralization placed even more importance on the service of eunuchs, because they expected that servants whose fortunes depended exclusively on the emperors' favor would work especially diligently to advance the emperors' interests.

The tightly centralized administration instituted by the early Ming emperors lasted more than five hundred years. Although the dynasty fell in 1644 to Manchu invaders, who founded the Qing dynasty, the Manchus retained the administrative framework of

Yuan (yoo-AHN)
Hongwu (hawng-woo)
eunuchs (YOO-nihks)

the Ming state, which largely survived until the collapse of the Qing dynasty in 1911.

MING JAR. | Ming artisans won worldwide fame for their blue-and-white porcelain, which inspired the founders of the Delft porcelain factory in the Netherlands. This covered jar dates from the early fifteenth century.

ECONOMIC RECOVERY While building a centralized administration, the Ming emperors also worked toward economic recovery. The new rulers conscripted laborers to rebuild irrigation systems that had fallen into disrepair, and agricultural production surged as a result. At the same time, they promoted the manufacture of porcelain, lacquerware, and fine silk and cotton textiles. They did not actively promote trade with other lands, but private Chinese merchants conducted a thriving business marketing Chinese products in ports and trading cities from Japan to the islands of southeast Asia. Meanwhile, domestic trade surged within China, reflecting increasing productivity and prosperity.

CULTURAL REVIVAL Alongside political and economic recovery, the Ming dynasty sponsored a kind of cultural revival in China. Emperor Hongwu tried to eradicate all signs of the recent nomadic occupation by discouraging the use of Mongol names and the wearing of Mongol dress. Ming emperors actively promoted Chinese cultural traditions, particularly the Confucian and neo-Confucian schools. Hongwu's successor, Yongle, even organized the preparation of a vast encyclopedia that compiled all significant works of Chinese history, philosophy, and literature. This *Yongle Encyclopedia* ran to almost twenty-three thousand manuscript rolls, each equivalent to a medium-size book, and was a clear signal of Ming interest in supporting native Chinese cultural traditions.

Ming dynasty tea shop
www.mhhe.com/bentleybrief2e

Recovery in Western Europe: State Building

Demographic recovery strengthened states in western Europe as it did in China. In Europe, however, political authority rested with a series of regional states rather than a centralized empire. By the late fifteenth century, states in Italy, Spain, France, and England had devised techniques of government that vastly enhanced their power.

During the later middle ages (1300–1500), internal problems as well as bubonic plague complicated European political affairs. The Holy Roman Empire survived in name, but effective authority lay with the German princes and the Italian city-states rather than the emperor. In Spain descendants of Muslim conquerors held the kingdom of Granada in the southern portion of the Iberian peninsula. Meanwhile, the kings of France and England sparred constantly over lands claimed by both.

TAXES AND ARMIES By the late fifteenth century, however, regional states in western Europe had greatly strengthened their societies. The state-building efforts of the later middle ages involved two especially important elements. The first was the development of fresh sources of finance, usually through new taxes levied directly on citizens and subjects. The second was the maintenance of large standing armies, often composed of mercenary forces and equipped with gunpowder weapons, supported by state funds.

ITALIAN STATES The state-building process began in Italy, where profits from industrial production and trade enriched the major cities. Beginning in the thirteenth century, the principal Italian states—the city-states of Milan, Venice, and Florence, the papal state based in Rome, and the kingdom of Naples—began to finance their needs for military forces and larger bureaucracies by levying direct taxes and issuing long-term bonds that they repaid from treasury receipts. With fresh sources of finance, the principal

Qing (ching)
Yongle (YAWNG-leh)

The Cathedral of Florence. | Brunelleschi's magnificent dome on the cathedral of Florence dominates the city's skyline even today. ***Why was such a dome considered revolutionary during the Renaissance?***

Italian states strengthened their authority within their boundaries as well as in their surrounding areas.

FRANCE AND ENGLAND During the fourteenth and fifteenth centuries, Italian administrative methods made their way beyond the Alps. Partly because of the enormous expenses they incurred during wars against each other, the kings of France and England began to levy direct taxes and assemble powerful armies. Rulers in both lands asserted the authority of the central government over the nobility. In France, King Louis XI (reigned 1461–1483) accomplished this by maintaining a permanent army of about fifteen thousand well-armed troops. Because the expense of maintaining such forces was beyond the means of the nobility, Louis and his successors enjoyed a decisive edge over ambitious subordinates seeking to challenge royal authority.

SPAIN The process of state building was most dramatic in Spain, where the marriage in 1469 of Fernando of Aragon and Isabel of Castile united the two wealthiest Iberian realms. Receipts from the sales tax, the primary source of royal income, supported a powerful standing army. Under Fernando and Isabel, popularly known as the Catholic Kings, Christian forces completed the *reconquista* by conquering the kingdom of Granada and absorbing it into their state. The Catholic Kings also projected their authority beyond Iberia. When a French army threatened the kingdom of Naples in 1494, they seized southern Italy, and by 1559 Spanish forces had established their hegemony throughout most of the Italian peninsula.

Competition between European states intensified as they tightened their authority in their territories. This competition led to frequent small-scale wars between European states, and it encouraged the rapid development of military and naval technology. As states sought technological advantages over their neighbors, they encouraged the refinement and improvement of weapons, ships, and sails. When one state acquired powerful weapons—such as ships equipped with cannons—neighboring states sought to outdo their rivals with more advanced devices. Thus technological innovations vastly strengthened European armies just as they began to venture again into the larger world.

Fernando and Isabel receive Boabdil
www.mhhe.com/bentleybrief2e

Recovery in Western Europe: The Renaissance

Demographic recovery and state-building efforts in western Europe coincided with a remarkable cultural flowering known as the Renaissance. The French word *renaissance* means "rebirth," and it refers here to a period of artistic and intellectual creativity from the fourteenth to the sixteenth century in western Europe. Painters, sculptors, and architects of the Renaissance era drew inspiration from classical Greek and Roman artists rather

Fernando of Aragon (fer-NAWN-doh of ah-ruh-GAWN)
Isabel of Castile (IHZ-uh-bel of ka-steel)
reconquista (ray-kohn-KEES-tah)
Renaissance (ren-uh-SAHNS)

than from their medieval predecessors. In their efforts to revive classical aesthetic standards, they transformed European art. Meanwhile, Renaissance scholars known as humanists looked to classical rather than medieval literary models, and they sought to update medieval moral thought and adapt it to the needs of a bustling urban society.

ITALIAN RENAISSANCE ART Just as they pioneered new techniques of statecraft, the Italian city-states also pioneered Renaissance innovations in art and architecture. In search of realistic depictions, Italian artists studied the human form and represented the emotions of their subjects. Italian painters such as Leonardo da Vinci (1452–1519) relied on the technique of linear perspective to represent the three dimensions of real life on two-dimensional surfaces. Sculptors such as Donatello (1386–1466) and Michelangelo Buonarotti (1475–1564) sought to depict their subjects in natural poses that reflected the actual workings of human muscles rather than the awkward and rigid postures of earlier sculptures.

The Vitruvian Man
www.mhhe.com/bentleybrief2e

RENAISSANCE ARCHITECTURE Renaissance architects designed buildings in the simple, elegant style preferred by their classical Greek and Roman predecessors. Their most impressive achievement was the construction of domed buildings. Roman architects had built domes, but their technology and engineering did not survive the collapse of the Roman empire. In the early fifteenth century, however, the Florentine architect Filippo Brunelleschi (1377–1446) reinvented equipment and designs for a large dome. During the 1420s and 1430s, he oversaw the construction of a magnificent dome on the cathedral of Florence, which residents took as a symbol of the city's wealth and leadership in artistic and cultural affairs.

THE HUMANISTS Like Renaissance artists and architects, scholars and literary figures known as humanists drew inspiration from classical models. The term *humanist* referred to scholars interested in the humanities—literature, history, and moral philosophy. Renaissance humanists were also deeply committed to Christianity. Several humanists worked diligently to prepare accurate texts and translations of the New Testament and other important Christian writings. Most notable of them was Desiderius Erasmus of Rotterdam (1466–1536), who in 1516 published the first edition of the Greek New Testament along with a revised Latin translation and copious annotations.

Humanists scorned the dense and often convoluted writing style of the scholastic theologians. Instead, they preferred the elegant and polished language of classical Greek and Roman authors and the early church fathers, whose works they considered more engaging and more persuasive than those of medieval philosophers and theologians. Thus humanists such as the Florentine Francesco Petrarca, known in English as Petrarch (1304–1374), traveled throughout Europe searching for manuscripts of classical works. In the monastic libraries of Italy, Switzerland, and southern France, they found hundreds of Latin writings that medieval scholars had overlooked. During the fifteenth century, Italian humanists became acquainted with Byzantine scholars and enlarged the body of classical Greek as well as Latin works available to scholars.

HUMANIST MORAL THOUGHT Classical Greek and Latin values encouraged the humanists to reconsider medieval ethical teachings. Medieval moral philosophers had taught that the most honorable calling was that of monks and nuns who withdrew from the world and dedicated their lives to prayer and contemplation, but the humanists drew inspiration from classical authors such as Cicero, who demonstrated that it was possible to lead a morally virtuous life while participating actively in the affairs of the world.

Leonardo da Vinci (lee-uh-NAHR-doh duh VIHN-chee)
Michelangelo Buonarotti (mik-uhl-AN-juh-loh baw-nahr-RAW-tee)
Desiderius Erasmus (des-i-DEER-ee-uhs ih-raz-muhs)
Francesco Petrarca (frahn-CHES-kaw PEE-trahrk-a)

Renaissance humanists argued that it was perfectly honorable for Christians to enter into marriage, business relationships, and public affairs. Humanist moral thought thus represented an effort to reconcile Christian values and ethics with the increasingly urban and commercial society of Renaissance Europe.

RENAISSANCE EUROPE AND THE LARGER WORLD Quite apart from the conscious effort to draw inspiration from classical antiquity, Renaissance art and thought also reflected increasing European participation in the affairs of the eastern hemisphere. As merchants linked Europe to the larger hemispheric economy, European peoples experienced increased prosperity, which enabled them to invest resources in artistic production and support for scholarship. Renaissance painters filled their canvases with images of silk garments, lacquered wood, spice jars, and foreign peoples that had recently come to European attention. Princes and wealthy patrons commissioned hundreds of these paintings, which brought a cosmopolitan look to their palaces, residences, and places of business.

EXPLORATION AND COLONIZATION

As peoples of the eastern hemisphere recovered from demographic collapse and restored order to their societies, they also sought to revive the networks of long-distance trade and communication that epidemic plague had disrupted. Most active in that effort were China and western Europe—the two societies that recovered most rapidly from the disasters of the fourteenth century. During the early Ming dynasty, Chinese ports accommodated foreign traders, and mariners mounted a series of enormous naval expeditions that visited almost all parts of the Indian Ocean basin. Meanwhile, by the end of the fifteenth century, Europeans not only had established sea-lanes to India but also had made several return voyages to the American continents, thus inaugurating a process that brought all the world's peoples into permanent and sustained interaction.

The Chinese Reconnaissance of the Indian Ocean Basin

Having ousted the Mongols, the early Ming emperors were not eager to have large numbers of foreigners residing in China. Yet the emperors permitted foreign merchants to trade in the closely supervised ports of Quanzhou and Guangzhou, where they obtained Chinese silk, porcelain, and manufactured goods in exchange for pearls, gems, spices, and cotton fabrics. The early Ming emperors also refurbished the large Chinese navy built during the Song dynasty, and they allowed Chinese merchants to participate in overseas trading ventures in Japan and southeast Asia.

ZHENG HE'S EXPEDITIONS Moreover, for almost thirty years, the Ming government sponsored a series of seven unprecedented naval expeditions designed to establish a Chinese presence in the Indian Ocean basin. Emperor Yongle organized the expeditions for two main purposes: to impose imperial control over foreign trade with China and to impress foreign peoples with the power and might of the Ming dynasty. Indeed, he might well have hoped to extend the tributary system, by which Chinese dynasties traditionally recognized foreign peoples, to lands in the Indian Ocean basin.

The expeditions took place between 1405 and 1433. Leading them was the eunuch admiral Zheng He, a Muslim from Yunnan in southwestern China who became a trusted advisor of Yongle. Zheng He embarked on each voyage with an awesome fleet of vessels

Zheng He (jung ha)

complemented by armed forces large enough to overcome resistance at any port where the expedition called. On the first voyage, for example, Zheng He's fleet consisted of 317 ships accompanied by almost twenty-eight thousand armed troops. Many of these vessels were mammoth, nine-masted ships with four decks capable of accommodating five hundred or more passengers. Measuring up to 124 meters (408 feet) long and 51 meters (166 feet) wide, these ships were by far the largest marine craft the world had ever seen.

On the first three voyages, Zheng He took his fleet to southeast Asia, India, and Ceylon. The fourth expedition went to the Persian Gulf and Arabia, and later expeditions ventured down the east African coast, calling at ports as far south as Malindi in modern Kenya. Throughout his travels, Zheng He liberally dispensed gifts of Chinese silk, porcelain, and other goods. In return he received rich and unusual presents, including African zebras and giraffes.

CHINESE NAVAL POWER Zheng He generally sought to attain his goals through diplomacy, and for the most part he had little need to engage in hostilities. But a contemporary reported that Zheng He did not shrink from violence when he considered it necessary to impress foreign peoples with China's military might. He ruthlessly suppressed pirates who had long plagued Chinese and southeast Asian waters. He also intervened in a civil disturbance to establish his authority in Ceylon, and he made displays of military force when local officials threatened his fleet in Arabia and east Africa. The seven expeditions established a Chinese presence and reputation in the Indian Ocean basin. Returning from his fourth voyage, Zheng He brought envoys from thirty states who traveled to China and paid their respects at the Ming court.

END OF THE VOYAGES Yet suddenly, in the mid-1430s, the Ming emperors decided to end the expeditions. Confucian ministers, who mistrusted Zheng He and the eunuchs who supported the voyages, argued that resources committed to the expensive expeditions should go to better uses. Moreover, during the 1420s and 1430s the Mongols mounted a new military threat from the northwest, and land forces urgently needed financial support.

Thus in 1433, after Zheng He's seventh voyage, the expeditions ended. Chinese merchants continued to trade in Japan and southeast Asia, but imperial officials destroyed most of the nautical charts that Zheng He had carefully prepared. The decommissioned ships sat in harbors until they rotted away, and Chinese craftsmen forgot the technology of building such large vessels. Yet Zheng He's voyages demonstrated clearly that China could exercise military, political, and economic influence throughout the Indian Ocean basin.

European Exploration in the Atlantic and Indian Oceans

As Chinese fleets reconnoitered the Indian Ocean, European mariners were preparing to enter both the Atlantic and the Indian Ocean basins. Unlike Zheng He and his companions, however, Europeans ventured onto the seas not for diplomatic reasons but to expand the boundaries of Roman Catholic Christianity and to profit from commercial opportunities.

PORTUGUESE EXPLORATION The experience of Portugal illustrates that mixture of motives. During the fifteenth century Prince Henrique of Portugal, often called Prince Henry the Navigator, embarked on an ambitious campaign to spread Christianity and increase Portuguese influence on the seas. In 1415 he watched as Portuguese forces seized the Moroccan city of Ceuta, which guarded the Strait of Gibraltar from the south. He regarded his victory both as a blow against Islam and as a strategic move enabling Christian vessels to move freely between the Mediterranean and the Atlantic.

King Afonso V to his sea captains
www.mhhe.com/bentleybrief2e

Ceuta (SYOO-tuh)

MAP 18.2 | Chinese and European voyages of exploration, 1405–1498. Although they followed different routes, all the voyagers represented on this map were seeking destinations in the Indian Ocean basin. ***Why did Chinese and Iberian mariners want to establish a presence in the Indian Ocean during the fifteenth century?***

Columbus believed he had found a shorter route to the Indian Ocean basin when he landed on San Salvador.

COLONIZATION OF THE ATLANTIC ISLANDS Following the capture of Ceuta, Henrique encouraged Portuguese mariners to venture into the Atlantic. During their voyages they discovered the Madeiras and Azores Islands, all uninhabited, which they soon colonized. Later discoveries included the Cape Verde Islands, Fernando Po, São Tomé, and Principe off the west African coast. Because these Atlantic islands enjoyed fertile soils and a Mediterranean climate, Portuguese entrepreneurs soon began to cultivate sugarcane there, often in collaboration with Italian investors. Italians had financed sugar plantations in the Mediterranean islands since the twelfth century, and their commercial networks provided a ready means to distribute sugar to Europeans, who were rapidly developing a taste for sweets.

SLAVE TRADE During the middle decades of the fifteenth century, a series of Portuguese fleets also explored the west African coast. Originally, the Portuguese traded guns, textiles, and other manufactured items for African gold and slaves. Soon, Portuguese traders changed the nature of the African slave trade by dramatically increasing its volume and by sending slaves to new destinations. In the mid–fifteenth century the Portuguese dispatched thousands of slaves annually to recently founded plantations in the Atlantic islands, where the slaves worked as laborers. The use of African slaves to perform heavy labor on commercial plantations soon became common practice, and it fueled the development of a huge, Atlantic-wide trade that, by the end of the nineteenth century, delivered as many as twelve million enslaved Africans to destinations in North America, South America, and the Caribbean region.

THINKING ABOUT *Encounters*

ENCOUNTERS IN CROSS-CULTURAL INTERACTIONS. The period from 1000 to 1500 C.E. witnessed enormous and unprecedented cross-cultural trade and travel across Eurasia and Africa and, for the first time, between Eurasia and the Americas. Using specific examples, discuss the ways in which these numerous encounters encouraged technological, intellectual, and material changes in far-distant societies.

INDIAN OCEAN TRADE While some Portuguese mariners traded profitably in west Africa, others sought to eliminate the role of Muslim and Italian intermediaries in the Asian silk and spice trades by finding a sea-lane from Europe around Africa and into the Indian Ocean. By 1488 Bartolomeu Dias had sailed around the Cape of Good Hope and entered the Indian Ocean. In 1497 Vasco da Gama departed Portugal with the intention of sailing to India. After rounding the Cape of Good Hope, he cruised up the east African coast and found a Muslim pilot who showed him how to take advantage of the seasonal monsoon winds to sail across the Arabian Sea to India. In 1498 he arrived at Calicut, and by 1499 he had returned to Lisbon with a hugely profitable cargo of pepper and spices.

For most of the following century, Portuguese merchants and mariners dominated trade between Europe and Asia. Indeed, they attempted to control all shipping in the Indian Ocean by overpowering the vessels of Arabs, Persians, Indians, and southeast Asians. They did not have enough ships to oversee all trade in the region, but the entry of Portuguese mariners into the Indian Ocean signaled the beginning of European imperialism in Asia.

CHRISTOPHER COLUMBUS While Portuguese seafarers sought a sea route around Africa to India, the Genoese mariner Cristoforo Colombo, known in English as Christopher Columbus, conceived the idea of sailing west to reach Asian markets. Because geographers in the eastern hemisphere knew nothing of the Americas, Columbus's notion made a certain amount of sense, although many doubted that his plan could lead to profitable trade because of the long distances involved. After the king of Portugal declined to sponsor an expedition to test Columbus's plan, Fernando and Isabel of Spain agreed to underwrite a voyage. In 1492 Columbus set sail. Later that year his fleet of three ships reached land at San Salvador (Watling Island) in the Bahamas.

Bartolomeu Dias (bahr-tol-oh-mew DEE-uhs)
Vasco da Gama (VAS-koh duh GAM-uh)
Cristoforo Colombo (crihs-toh-for-oh kuh-LUHM-boh)

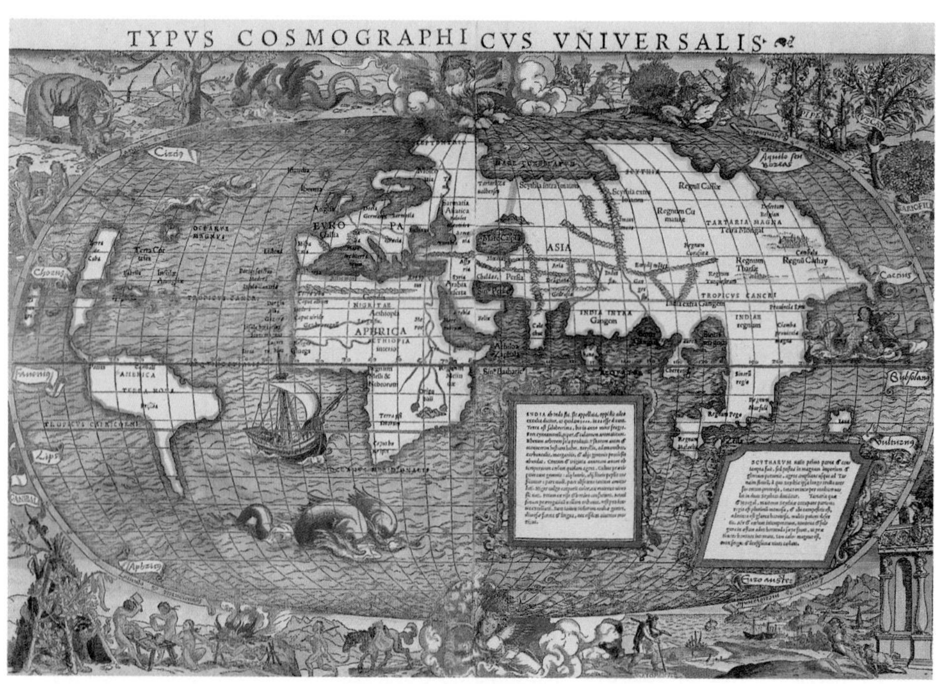

SIXTEENTH-CENTURY EUROPEAN MAP OF THE WORLD. | Although Christopher Columbus believed that he had sailed into Asian waters, later mariners soon realized that the Americas were continents unknown to geographers of the eastern hemisphere. This map, prepared in 1532 by the German cartographer Sebastian Münster, shows that by the early sixteenth century European geographers had acquired a rough but accurate understanding of South America but had reconnoitered only the Atlantic coastline of North America.

Columbus returned to Spain without the gold, silk, and spices that he had expected to find, but he persistently held that he had reached islands near the Asian mainland and the markets of China and Japan. Yet although Columbus himself never acknowledged that his expeditions had not reached Asia, by the end of the fifteenth century other mariners who came to explore the Caribbean and the American continents realized that the western hemisphere constituted a world apart from Europe, Asia, and Africa.

SUMMARY

In the five centuries between 1000 and 1500 C.E., peoples in the eastern hemisphere interacted with more frequency than ever before. In part this was because of the stability created by the large empires of the Mongols and other nomadic peoples. Although conquest by these empires brought initial destruction to many societies, the pacification of large areas that occurred after conquest allowed safe travel for traders, diplomats, and missionaries. The relative safety of long-distance travel encouraged peoples of the eastern hemisphere to exchange technologies, ideas, crops, and religious faiths with one another with ever-increasing frequency. Yet just as we saw at the end of the classical period, one of the unintended consequences of increased cross-cultural interaction was the spread of epidemic disease to distant regions. Indeed, in the fourteenth century bubonic plague tore through much of Eurasia, leaving death and destruction in its wake and severely weakening cross-cultural ties. However, by the early fifteenth century societies had begun to recover from the plague, and China and Europe in particular began to renew cross-cultural contacts. Although both Chinese and European efforts at renewing these contacts had momentous consequences, the ocean voyages of Europeans in this period fundamentally shaped modern world history when they accidentally made contact with peoples from the western hemisphere. For the first time in human history, cross-cultural interactions began to connect peoples from both hemispheres, with enormous significance for the entire globe.

STUDY TERMS

Bartolomeu Dias (360)
bubonic plague (344)
Christopher Columbus (360)
Desiderius Erasmus (355)
eunuchs (352)
Filippo Brunelleschi (355)
gunpowder (350)
Hongwu (352)
Ibn Battuta (343)
Isabel of Castile and Fernando of Aragon (354)
Khubilai Khan (345)
Leonardo da Vinci (355)
mandarins (352)
Marco Polo (345)
Melaka (344)
Michelangelo Buonarotti (355)
Ming dynasty (352)
Petrarch (355)
Prince Henry the Navigator (357)
reconquista (354)
Renaissance (354)
Sufis (347)
sugarcane (350)
Vasco da Gama (360)
Yongle (353)
Zheng He (356)

FOR FURTHER READING

Janet L. Abu-Lughod. *Before European Hegemony: The World System, A.D. 1250–1350.* New York, 1989. An important study of long-distance trade networks during the Mongol era.

Jerry H. Bentley. *Old World Encounters: Cross-Cultural Contacts and Exchanges in Pre-modern Times.* New York, 1993. Studies cultural and religious exchanges in the eastern hemisphere before 1500 C.E.

Jerry Brotton. *The Renaissance Bazaar: From the Silk Road to Michelangelo.* Oxford, 2002. A provocative and well-illustrated study arguing that encounters in the larger world deeply influenced Renaissance cultural development in Europe.

K. N. Chaudhuri. *Asia before Europe: Economy and Civilisation of the Indian Ocean from the Rise of Islam to 1750.* Cambridge, 1990. Controversial and penetrating analysis of economic, social, and cultural structures shaping societies of the Indian Ocean basin.

Ross E. Dunn. *The Adventures of Ibn Battuta: A Muslim Traveler of the 14th Century.* Berkeley, 1986. Fascinating reconstruction of Ibn Battuta's travels and experiences.

Robert S. Gottfried. *The Black Death: Natural and Human Disaster in Medieval Europe.* New York, 1983. The best general study of bubonic plague and its effects in Europe.

John Larner. *Marco Polo and the Discovery of the World.* New Haven, 1999. Excellent study of Marco Polo and his significance, based on a thorough review of both textual evidence and recent scholarship.

Louise L. Levathes. *When China Ruled the Seas: The Treasure Fleet of the Dragon Throne, 1405–1433.* New York, 1994. Excellent popular account of Zheng He's voyages.

William D. Phillips Jr. and Carla Rahn Phillips. *The Worlds of Christopher Columbus.* New York, 1992. The best general work on Christopher Columbus.

Frances Wood. *The Silk Road: Two Thousand Years in the Heart of Asia.* Berkeley, 2002. A brilliantly illustrated volume discussing the history of the silk roads from antiquity to the twentieth century.

Bringing It All Together

Part IV | An Age of Cross-Cultural Interaction, 1000 to 1500 C.E.

Although the postclassical societies of the eastern hemisphere had restored order and stability to the region by 1000 C.E., invasions and conquest by nomadic peoples caused most postclassical societies to collapse between the eleventh and the fourteenth centuries. These nomadic invaders included the Mongols, who conquered so much of Eurasia in the thirteenth and fourteenth centuries that they built the largest empire the world has ever seen.

Mongol conquest initially resulted in monumental human and physical destruction. However, once conquest was complete, Mongol overlords facilitated accelerated communication within their vast imperial domains. Thus, from China to eastern Europe, traders, diplomats, missionaries, travelers, and pilgrims moved overland with greater ease than ever before, and encouraged ever-stronger networks of communication and exchange.

The Indian Ocean basin also grew far more integrated in the centuries between 1000 and 1500 C.E. Indeed, by 1500 the Indian Ocean served as a highway linking peoples from China to east Africa. As with the overland routes of the Mongol empire, this Indian Ocean highway encouraged the diffusion of scientific and intellectual knowledge, technologies like gunpowder and the compass, and food crops such as cotton and sugarcane—all of which profoundly influenced the development of societies throughout the eastern hemisphere.

Yet as at the end of the classical period, increased overland and seaborne interaction in the eastern hemisphere also led to the diffusion of disease pathogens. In the fourteenth century, the bubonic plague spread rapidly from China across most of Eurasia, leaving millions dead in its wake. Such massive fatalities severely disrupted networks of communication and trade. However, by the end of the fifteenth century these networks had recovered once again. Indeed, they recovered so well that western Europeans—who had long been on the margins of Eurasian trade networks—sought eagerly to find alternate routes to the lucrative markets of east and southeast Asia. In one attempt to reach these markets by sailing west rather than east, Europeans instead stumbled on the Americas.

As European mariners ventured across the Atlantic and into the Americas, they unwittingly inaugurated a new era in world history, because they initiated a long-term process that brought all regions and peoples of the earth into permanent and sustained interaction for the first time in human history. Indeed, the formation and reconfiguration of global networks of power, communication, and exchange that followed from the initial contact between the two hemispheres rank among the most prominent themes of modern world history.

V The Origins of Global Interdependence, 1500–1800

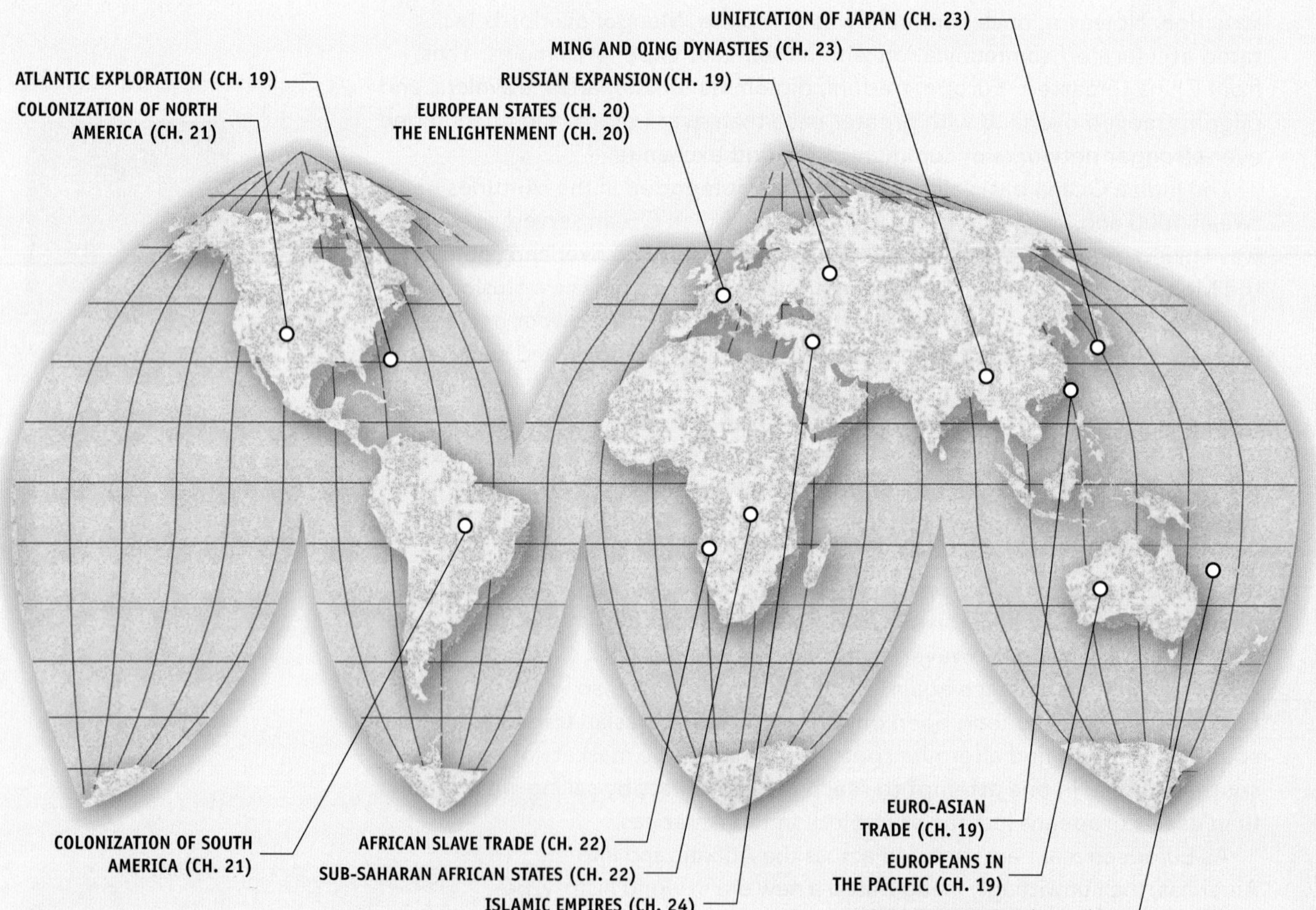

UNIFICATION OF JAPAN (CH. 23)
MING AND QING DYNASTIES (CH. 23)
ATLANTIC EXPLORATION (CH. 19)
RUSSIAN EXPANSION(CH. 19)
COLONIZATION OF NORTH AMERICA (CH. 21)
EUROPEAN STATES (CH. 20)
THE ENLIGHTENMENT (CH. 20)

EURO-ASIAN TRADE (CH. 19)
COLONIZATION OF SOUTH AMERICA (CH. 21)
AFRICAN SLAVE TRADE (CH. 22)
SUB-SAHARAN AFRICAN STATES (CH. 22)
EUROPEANS IN THE PACIFIC (CH. 19)
ISLAMIC EMPIRES (CH. 24)
PACIFIC EXPLORATION (CH. 19)

By 1500 C.E. peoples throughout the world had built well-organized societies with distinctive cultural traditions. Powerful agricultural societies dominated most of Asia, the Mediterranean basin, Europe, much of sub-Saharan Africa, Mexico, and the central Andean region. By 1500 peoples of the world had also established intricate transportation networks that supported travel, communication, and exchange. Although pioneered by merchants in the interests of trade, these routes also enabled the diffusion of religion, food crops, animal stocks, and disease pathogens.

Yet the commercial, cultural, and biological exchanges of premodern times prefigured much more intense cross-cultural interactions after 1500. Beginning in the fifteenth century, European mariners established trade routes linking the lands of the Indian, Atlantic, and Pacific Ocean basins. These routes in turn fostered direct contact between the peoples of the eastern hemisphere, the western hemisphere, and Oceania.

The establishment of links between all the world's regions and peoples gave rise to the early modern era of world history, approximately 1500 to 1800 C.E. The early modern era differed from the period from 1000 to 1500, when there were only sporadic contacts between peoples of the eastern hemisphere, the western hemisphere, and Oceania. It also differed from the modern era, from 1800 to the present, when national states, heavy industry, powerful weapons, and efficient technologies of transportation and communication enabled peoples of European ancestry to achieve political and economic dominance in the world.

During the early modern era, several global processes touched peoples in all parts of the world and influenced the development of their societies. One involved biological exchange: plants, animals, diseases, and human communities crossed the world's oceans and established themselves in new lands, where they dramatically affected both the natural environment and established societies. Another involved commercial exchange: merchants took advantage of newly established sea-lanes to inaugurate a genuinely global economy. Yet another process involved the diffusion of technologies and cultural traditions: printing and gunpowder spread throughout the world, and Christianity and Islam attracted increasing numbers of converts.

These global processes had different effects for different peoples. In the Americas and Oceania, diseases introduced from the eastern hemisphere ravaged indigenous populations and sometimes led to the collapse of whole societies. In contrast, Europeans claimed vast stretches of land in the Americas, where they founded colonies and cultivated crops for sale on the open market. In sub-Saharan Africa, millions of enslaved individuals underwent a forced migration to the western hemisphere, where they suffered both physical and psychological abuse. Meanwhile, east Asian and Islamic peoples prospered from increased trade but restricted the introduction of foreign ideas and technologies into their societies.

Although European peoples benefited from global processes of the period 1500 to 1800, by no means did they dominate world affairs in early modern times. Indeed, most of the western hemisphere and Africa lay beyond their control until the nineteenth century. Nevertheless, European peoples played a more prominent role in world affairs than any of their ancestors, and their efforts helped foster the development of an increasingly interdependent world.

Transoceanic Encounters and Global Connections

19

On 8 July 1497 the Portuguese mariner Vasco da Gama led a small fleet of four armed merchant vessels with 170 crewmen out of the harbor at Lisbon. His destination was India, which he planned to reach by sailing around the continent of Africa and through the Indian Ocean. He carried letters of introduction from the king of Portugal as well as cargoes of gold, wool textiles, and other goods that he hoped to exchange for pepper and spices in India.

Before there would be an opportunity to trade, however, da Gama and his crew had a prolonged voyage through two oceans. They sailed south from Portugal to the Cape Verde Islands off the west coast of Africa, where they took on fresh provisions. On 3 August they headed southeast into the Atlantic Ocean to take advantage of the prevailing winds. For the next ninety-five days, the fleet saw no land. By October, da Gama had found westerly winds in the southern Atlantic, rounded the Cape of Good Hope, and entered the Indian Ocean. The fleet slowly worked its way up the east coast of Africa as far as Malindi, where da Gama secured the services of an Indian Muslim pilot to guide his ships across the Arabian Sea. On 20 May 1498—more than ten months after its departure from Lisbon—the fleet anchored at Calicut in southern India.

In India the Portuguese fleet found a wealthy, cosmopolitan society. The markets of Calicut offered not only pepper, ginger, cinnamon, and other spices but also rubies, emeralds, gold jewelry, and fine cotton textiles. Alas, apart from gold and some striped cloth, the goods that da Gama had brought attracted little interest among merchants at Calicut. Nevertheless, da Gama managed to exchange gold for a cargo of pepper and cinnamon that turned a handsome profit when the fleet returned to Portugal in August 1499. Da Gama's expedition also opened the door to direct maritime trade between European and Asian peoples and helped to establish permanent links between the world's various regions.

Cross-cultural interactions have been a persistent feature of historical development. Even in ancient times mass migration, campaigns of imperial expansion, and long-distance trade deeply influenced societies throughout the world. Yet after 1500 C.E. cross-cultural interactions took place on a much larger geographic scale than ever before, and encounters were often more disruptive than in earlier centuries. Equipped with advanced technologies and a powerful military arsenal, western European peoples began to cross the world's

‹ This 16th century tapestry depicts the arrival of Portuguese mariner Vasco da Gama in the city of Calcutta, India, in May, 1498.

Vasco da Gama (VAS-koh duh GAM-uh)

CHRONOLOGY

1394–1460	Life of Prince Henry the Navigator of Portugal
1488	Bartolomeu Dias's voyage around the Cape of Good Hope into the Indian Ocean
1492	Christopher Columbus's first voyage to the western hemisphere
1497–1499	Vasco da Gama's first voyage to India
1519–1522	Ferdinand Magellan's circumnavigation of the world
1565–1575	Spanish conquest of the Philippines
1768–1780	Captain James Cook's voyages in the Pacific Ocean

oceans in large numbers during the early modern era. At the same time, Russian adventurers built an enormous Eurasian empire and ventured tentatively into the Pacific Ocean.

Europeans were not the only peoples who actively explored the larger world during the early modern era. In the early fifteenth century, the Ming emperors of China sponsored a series of seven enormous maritime expeditions that visited all parts of the Indian Ocean basin. In the sixteenth century Ottoman mariners also ventured into the Indian Ocean. Following the Ottoman conquest of Egypt in 1517, both merchant and military vessels established an Ottoman presence throughout the Indian Ocean basin.

Although other peoples also made their way into the larger world, only Europeans linked the lands and peoples of the eastern hemisphere, the western hemisphere, and Oceania. Because of that, European peoples benefited from unparalleled opportunities to increase their power, wealth, and influence. As a result, after 1500, European peoples became much more prominent in the larger world than before.

The expansion of European influence resulted in the establishment of global networks of transportation, communication, and exchange. Indeed, a worldwide diffusion of plants, animals, diseases, and human communities followed European ventures across the oceans, and intricate trade networks eventually gave birth to a global economy.

The European Reconnaissance of the World's Oceans

Between 1400 and 1800, European mariners launched a remarkable series of exploratory voyages that took them to nearly all the earth's waters. Those voyages were very expensive affairs. Yet private investors and government authorities had strong motives to underwrite the expeditions and outfit them with the latest nautical technology. The voyages of exploration paid large dividends: they enabled European mariners to chart the world's ocean basins and develop an accurate understanding of world geography. On the basis of that knowledge, European merchants and mariners established global networks of communication, transportation, and exchange—and profited handsomely from their efforts.

Mediterranean map—17th century
www.mhhe.com/bentleybrief2e

Motives for Exploration

A complex combination of motives prompted Europeans to explore the world's oceans. Most important of those motives were the search for basic resources and lands suitable for the cultivation of cash crops, the desire to establish new trade routes to Asian markets, and the aspiration to expand the influence of Christianity.

PORTUGUESE EXPLORATION Mariners from the relatively poor kingdom of Portugal were most prominent in the search for fresh resources and lands. Beginning in the thirteenth century, Portuguese seamen ventured away from the coasts and into the open Atlantic Ocean to supplement their own meager resources. By the early fourteenth century, they had discovered the uninhabited Azores and Madeiras Islands and called frequently at the Canary Islands, inhabited by the indigenous Guanche people. These Atlantic islands proved ideal for the cultivation of sugar, a product that enjoyed a strong European demand. In the fifteenth century, Italian investors—who had organized sugar plantations in the Mediterranean since the twelfth century—helped Portuguese mariners establish plantations in the

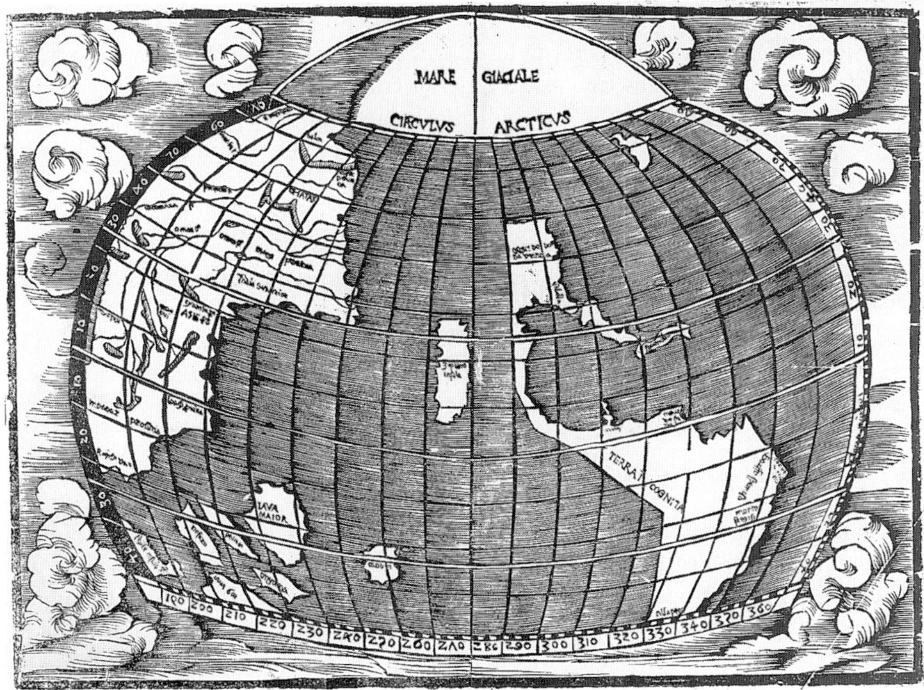

1512 WORLD MAP. | This map, prepared about 1512 by the Polish cartographer Jan Stobnicza, shows eloquently that it took a long time for geographers to realize the extent of the Americas and the Pacific Ocean. Here "Cipangu" (Japan) lies just west of Mexico, with the Asian mainland nearby.

Atlantic islands. Continuing Portuguese voyages also led to the establishment of plantations on the Cape Verde Islands, São Tomé, Principe, and Fernando Po.

THE LURE OF TRADE Even more alluring than the exploitation of fresh lands and resources was the goal of establishing maritime trade routes to the markets of Asia. During the era of the Mongol empires, European merchants often traveled overland as far as China to trade for Asian goods. When the Mongol empires collapsed and bubonic plague spread across Eurasia in the fourteenth century, however, travel on the silk roads became much more dangerous. As a result, Europeans relied on Muslim mariners to bring Asian goods through the Indian Ocean and the Red Sea to Cairo, where Italian merchants purchased them for distribution in western Europe. But prices at Cairo were high, and Europeans sought ever-larger quantities of Asian goods, particularly spices.

By the fourteenth century the wealthy classes of Europe regarded Indian pepper and Chinese ginger as expensive necessities, and they especially prized cloves and nutmeg from the spice islands of Maluku. Merchants and monarchs alike realized that by gaining direct access to Asian markets and eliminating Muslim intermediaries, they could increase the quantities of spices and other Asian goods available in Europe while making enormous profits.

African trade also beckoned to Europeans and called them to the sea. Since the twelfth century, Europeans had purchased west African gold, ivory, and slaves brought to north African ports by Muslim merchants. West African gold was especially important to Europeans because it was their principal form of payment for Asian luxury goods. As in the case of Asian trade, Europeans realized that they could profit from eliminating Muslim middlemen and establishing maritime routes that offered direct access to African markets.

MISSIONARY EFFORTS Alongside material incentives, the goal of expanding the boundaries of Christianity drove Europeans into the larger world. Like Buddhism and Islam, Christianity is a missionary religion that directs believers to spread the faith.

Sometimes such efforts were attempted through peaceful persuasion. At other times the expansion of Christianity could be quite violent. Beginning in the eleventh century, for example, western Europeans launched a series of crusades against Muslims in Palestine, the Mediterranean islands, and Iberia. In Iberia, in fact, the Muslim kingdom of Granada fell to Spanish Christian forces just weeks before Christopher Columbus set sail on his famous first voyage to the western hemisphere in 1492. Whether through persuasion or violence, overseas voyages offered fresh opportunities for western Europeans to spread their faith.

PSI img Vasco da Gama in Calcutta in 1489 www.mhhe.com/bentleybrief2e

In practice, the various motives for exploration combined and reinforced one another. When the Portuguese mariner Vasco da Gama reached the Indian port of Calicut in 1498, local authorities asked him what he wanted there. His reply: "Christians and spices." The goal of spreading Christianity thus became a powerful justification and reinforcement for the more material motives for the voyages of exploration.

The Technology of Exploration

Without advanced nautical technology and navigational skills, even the strongest motives would not have enabled European mariners to reconnoiter the world's oceans. They also needed sturdy ships, good navigational equipment, and knowledge of sailing techniques. These they devised by combining Chinese and Arabic technologies with their own inherited nautical technologies from the Mediterranean and northern Europe.

SHIPS AND SAILS From their experiences in the rough coastal waters of the Atlantic, European sailors learned to construct ships strong enough to brave most adverse conditions. Beginning about the twelfth century, they increased the maneuverability of their craft by building a rudder onto the stern. (The sternpost rudder was a Chinese invention that had diffused across the Indian Ocean.) They outfitted their vessels with two types of sails: square sails (which enabled them to take full advantage of a wind blowing from behind) and triangular lateen sails (which could catch winds from the side as well as from behind). With a combination of square and lateen sails, European ships were able to use whatever winds arose. Their ability to tack—to advance against the wind by sailing across it—was crucial for the exploration of regions with uncooperative winds.

PSI img 18th-century magnetic compass www.mhhe.com/bentleybrief2e

NAVIGATIONAL INSTRUMENTS The most important navigational equipment on board these vessels were magnetic compasses (which determined heading) and astrolabes (which determined latitude). The compass was a Chinese invention that had diffused throughout the Indian Ocean basin in the eleventh century and had reached European mariners by the mid–twelfth century. The astrolabe was a simplified version of an instrument used by Greek and Persian astronomers to measure the angle of the sun or the pole star above the horizon. In the late fifteenth century, however, Portuguese mariners encountered Arab sailors in the Indian Ocean using simpler and more serviceable instruments for determining latitude, which the Portuguese then used as models for the construction of cross-staffs and back-staffs.

THE CROSS-STAFF. | By using cross-staffs to measure the angle of the sun or the pole star above the horizon, mariners could determine latitude.

KNOWLEDGE OF WINDS AND CURRENTS European mariners' ability to determine direction and latitude enabled them to assemble a vast body of data about the earth's geography and to find their way around the world's oceans with tolerable accuracy and efficiency. Equipped with advanced technological hardware, European mariners ventured into the oceans and gradually compiled a body of practical knowledge about winds and currents. Indeed, as they became familiar with the wind systems of the world's oceans, European mariners developed the ability to travel reliably to coastlines throughout the world.

astrolabe (AS-truh-leyb)

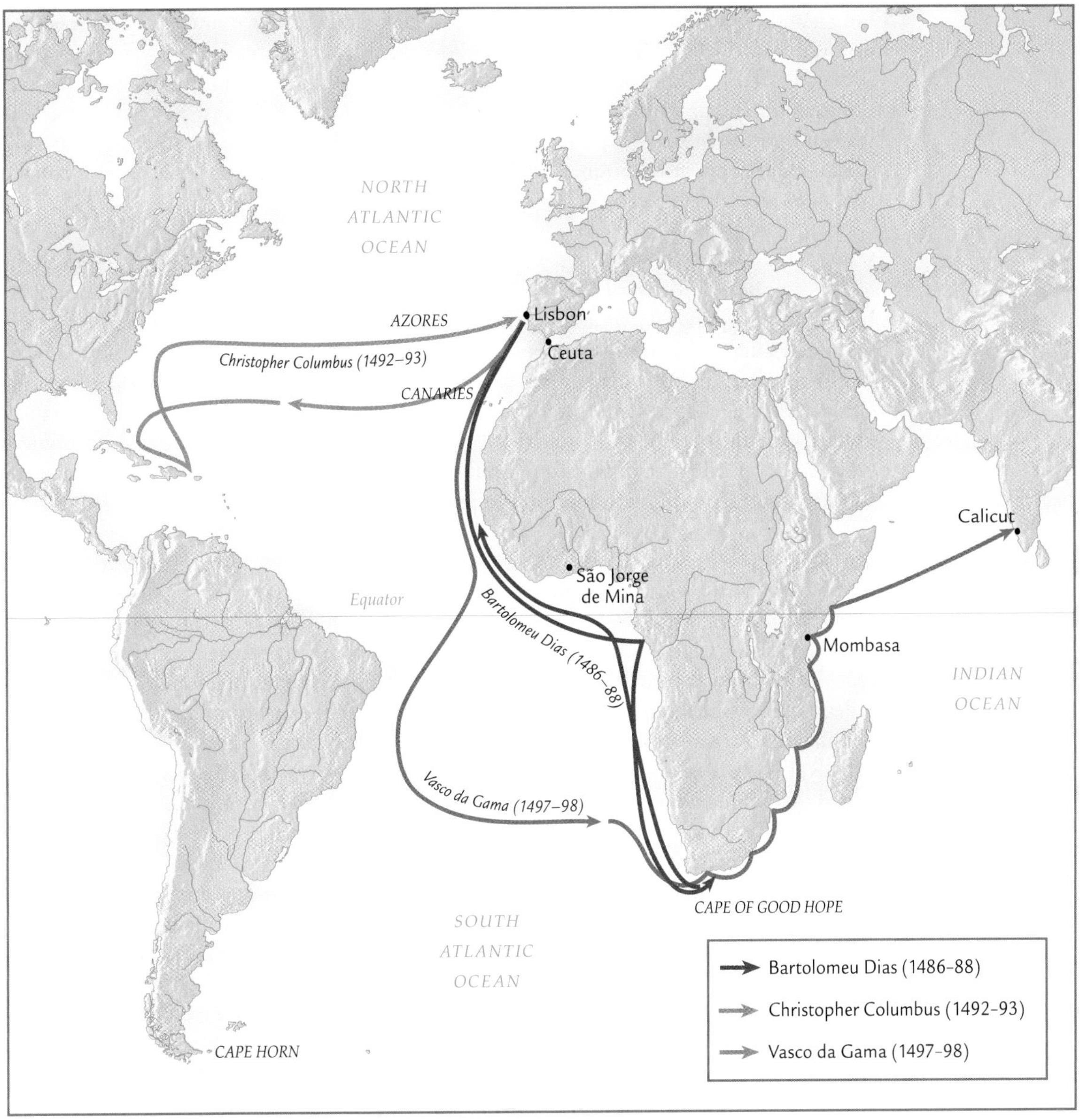

MAP 19.1 | European exploration in the Atlantic Ocean, 1486–1498. Observe the difference between Bartolomeu Dias's journey and Vasco da Gama's journey around the Cape of Good Hope. ***Why did da Gama go so far out into the Atlantic before rounding the Cape?***

European voyagers traveled around the Horn of Africa as well as westward in the hopes of gaining direct access to Asian markets.

Voyages of Exploration: From the Mediterranean to the Atlantic

Afonso V to his captains
www.mhhe.com/bentleybrief2e

PRINCE HENRY OF PORTUGAL Although European exploratory voyaging began as early as the thirteenth century, the pace quickened decisively after 1415. In that year, Prince Henry of Portugal (1394–1460), often called Prince Henry the Navigator, conquered the Moroccan port of Ceuta and sponsored a series of voyages down the west African coast. Portuguese merchants soon established fortified trading posts at São Jorge da Mina (in modern Ghana) and other strategic locations. There they exchanged European

Ceuta (SYOO-tuh)
São Jorge de Mina (sou hor-hay day meena)

horses and goods for gold and slaves. Portuguese explorations continued after Henry's death, and in 1488 Bartolomeu Dias rounded the Cape of Good Hope and entered the Indian Ocean. He did not proceed farther because of storms and a restless crew, but the route to India, China, and the spice-bearing islands of southeast Asia lay open. The sea route to the Indian Ocean offered European merchants the opportunity to buy silk, spices, and pepper at the source, rather than through Muslim intermediaries, and to take part in the flourishing trade of Asia.

VASCO DA GAMA As we have already seen, in 1497 Vasco da Gama sought to do just that, departing Lisbon with a fleet of four armed merchant ships bound for India. His experience was not altogether pleasant. His fleet went more than three months without seeing land, and his cargoes excited little interest in Indian markets. Moreover, less than half of his crew made it safely back to Portugal. Yet his cargo of pepper and cinnamon was hugely profitable, and Portuguese merchants began immediately to organize further expeditions. By 1500 they had built a trading post at Calicut, and Portuguese mariners soon called at ports throughout the Indian Ocean basin. By the late sixteenth century, English and Dutch mariners followed suit.

CHRISTOPHER COLUMBUS While Portuguese navigators plied the sea route to India, the Genoese mariner Cristoforo Colombo, known in English as Christopher Columbus (1451–1506), proposed sailing to the markets of Asia by a western route. On the basis of wide reading in the existing geographical literature, Columbus believed that the earth was a relatively small sphere with a circumference of about 17,000 nautical miles. (In fact, the earth's circumference is almost 25,000 nautical miles.) By Columbus's calculations, Japan should have been less than 2,500 nautical miles west of the Canary Islands. (The actual distance is more than 10,000 nautical miles.) This geography suggested that sailing west from Europe to Asian markets would be profitable, and Columbus sought royal sponsorship for a voyage to prove his ideas.

Eventually Fernando and Isabel of Spain agreed to underwrite Columbus's expedition, and in August 1492 his fleet of three ships departed southern Spain. He sailed south to the Canaries, picked up supplies, and then turned west with the trade winds. On the morning of 12 October 1492, he made landfall at an island in the Bahamas that the native Taino inhabitants called Guanahaní and that Columbus rechristened San Salvador (also known as Watling Island). Thinking that he had arrived in the spice islands known familiarly as the Indies, Columbus called the Tainos "Indians." He sailed around the Caribbean for almost three months in search of gold, and at the large island of Cuba he sent a delegation to seek the court of the emperor of China. When Columbus returned to Spain, he reported to his royal sponsors that he had reached islands just off the coast of Asia.

PSI img Waldseemuller's world map—first to name America www.mhhe.com/bentleybrief2e

HEMISPHERIC LINKS Columbus never reached the riches of Asia, and he obtained very little gold in the Caribbean. Yet news of his voyage spread rapidly throughout Europe, and hundreds of Spanish, English, French, and Dutch mariners soon followed in his wake. Initially, many of them continued to seek the passage to Asian waters that Columbus himself had pursued. Over a longer term, however, it became clear that the American continents and the Caribbean islands themselves held abundant opportunities for entrepreneurs. Thus Columbus's voyages to the western hemisphere had unintended but momentous consequences, since they established links between the eastern and western hemispheres and paved the way for the conquest, settlement, and exploitation of the Americas by European peoples.

Bartolomeu Dias (bahr-tol-uh-MEY-oh dee-as)
Taino (tah-EE-no)
Guanahaní (Gwah-nah-nee)

SOURCES FROM THE PAST

Christopher Columbus's First Impressions of American Peoples

Christopher Columbus kept journals of his experiences during his voyages to the western hemisphere. The journal of his first voyage survives mostly in summary, but it clearly communicates Columbus's first impressions of the peoples he met in the Caribbean islands. The following excerpts show that Columbus, like other European mariners, had both Christianity and commerce in mind when exploring distant lands.

Thursday, 11 October [1492]. . . .
I . . . in order that they would be friendly to us—because I recognized that they were people who would be better freed [from error] and converted to our Holy Faith by love than by force—to some of them I gave red caps, and glass beads which they put on their chests, and many other things of small value, in which they took so much pleasure and became so much our friends that it was a marvel. Later they came swimming to the ships' launches where we were and brought us parrots and cotton thread in balls and javelins and many other things, and they traded them to us for other things which we gave them, such as small glass beads and bells. In sum, they took everything and gave of what they had willingly.

But it seemed to me that they were a people very poor in everything. All of them go as naked as their mothers bore them; and the women also, although I did not see more than one quite young girl. And all those that I saw were young people, for none did I see of more than 30 years of age. They are very well formed, with handsome bodies and good faces. Their hair [is] coarse—almost like the tail of a horse—and short. They wear their hair down over their eyebrows except for a little in the back which they wear long and never cut. . . .

They do not carry arms nor are they acquainted with them, because I showed them swords and they took them by the edge and through ignorance cut themselves. They have no iron. Their javelins are shafts without iron and some of them have at the end a fish tooth and others of other things. All of them alike are of good-sized stature and carry themselves well. I saw some who had marks of wounds on their bodies and I made signs to them asking what they were; and they showed me how people from other islands nearby came there and tried to take them, and how they defended themselves and I believed and believe that they come here from *tierra firme* [the continent] to take them captive. They should be good and intelligent servants, for I see that they say very quickly everything that is said to them; and I believe that they would become Christians very easily, for it seemed to me that they had no religion. . . .

Monday, 12 November. . . .
They are very gentle and do not know what evil is; nor do they kill others, nor steal; and they are without weapons and so timid that a hundred of them flee from one of our men even if our men are teasing them. And they are credulous and aware that there is a God in heaven and convinced that we come from the heavens; and they say very quickly any prayer that we tell them to say, and they make the sign of the cross. So that Your Highnesses ought to resolve to make them Christians: for I believe that if you begin, in a short time you will end up having converted to our Holy Faith a multitude of peoples and acquiring large dominions and great riches and all of their peoples for Spain. Because without doubt there is in these lands a very great quantity of gold; for not without cause do these Indians that I bring with me say that there are in these islands places where they dig gold and wear it on their chests, on their ears, and on their arms, and on their legs; and they are very thick bracelets. And also there are stones, and there are precious pearls and infinite spicery. . . . And also here there is probably a great quantity of cotton; and I think that it would sell very well here without taking it to Spain but to the big cities belonging to the Grand [Mongol] Khan.

■ On the basis of Columbus's account, what inferences can you draw about his plans for American lands and peoples?

SOURCE: Christopher Columbus. *The* Diario *of Christopher Columbus's First Voyage to America.* Trans. by Oliver Dunn and James E. Kelley Jr. Norman: University of Oklahoma Press, 1989, pp. 65–69, 143–45.

Voyages of Exploration: From the Atlantic to the Pacific

While some Europeans sought opportunities in the Americas, others continued to seek a western route to Asian markets. However, in the early sixteenth century no one suspected the vast size of the Pacific Ocean, which covers one-third of the earth's surface.

MAP 19.2 | Voyages of European exploration in the Pacific Ocean, 1519–1780. Note the vast expanses of blue water mariners had to cross in these voyages. ***What technologies made such extensive voyages possible?***

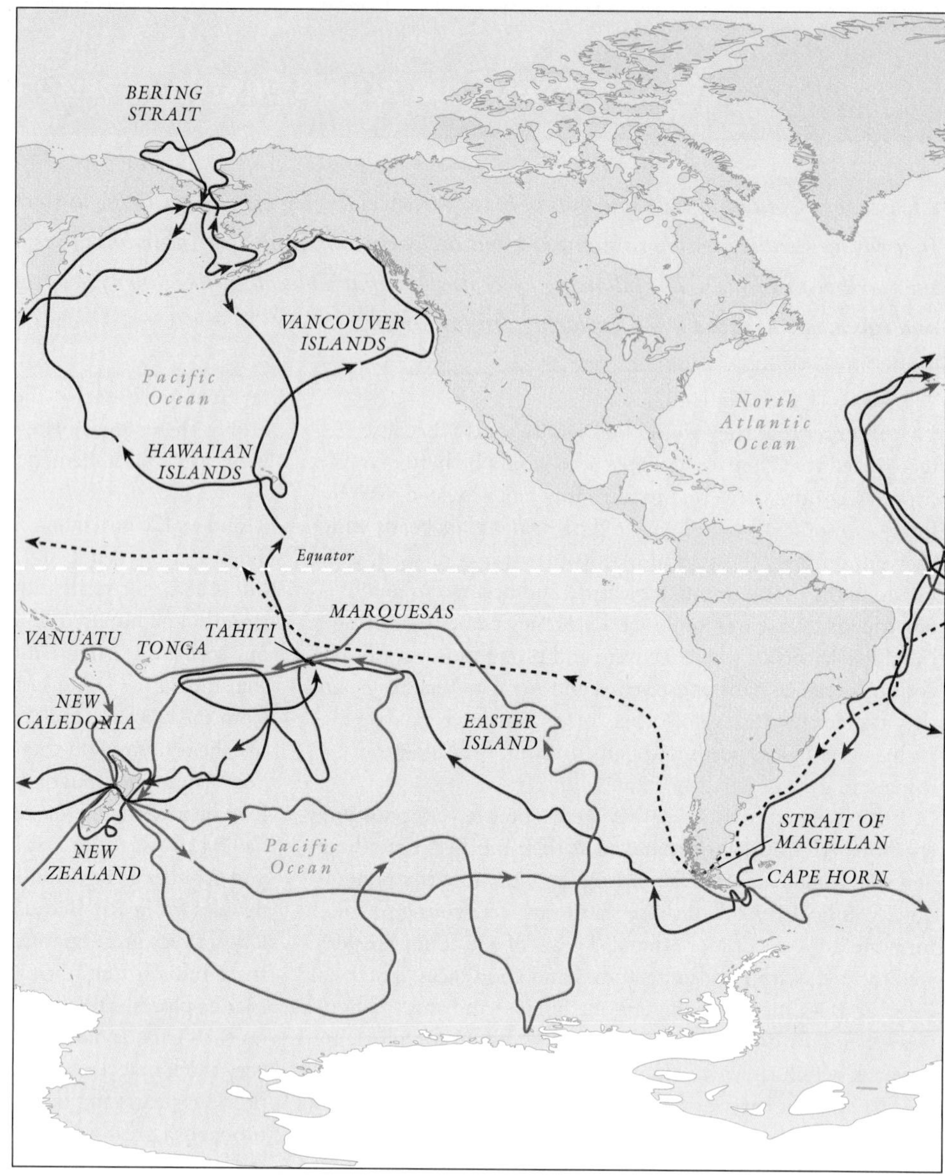

FERDINAND MAGELLAN The reconnaissance of the Pacific Ocean basin began with the Portuguese navigator Fernão de Magalhães (1480–1521), better known as Ferdinand Magellan. While sailing in the service of Portugal, Magellan had visited ports throughout the Indian Ocean basin and had traveled east as far as the spice islands of Maluku. He believed that the spice islands and Asian markets lay fairly close to the western coast of the Americas, and he decided to pursue Christopher Columbus's goal of establishing a western route to Asian waters. Because Portuguese mariners had already reached Asian markets through the Indian Ocean, they had little interest in Magellan's proposed western route. Thus, on his Pacific expedition and circumnavigation of the world (1519–1522), Magellan sailed in the service of Spain.

THE CIRCUMNAVIGATION Magellan's voyage was an exercise in endurance. He began by probing the eastern coast of South America in search of a strait leading to the Pacific. Eventually he found and sailed through the treacherous Strait of Magellan near the southern tip of South America. His fleet then sailed almost four months before tak-

Ferdinand Magellan (FUR-dih-nand muh-JEHL-uhn)

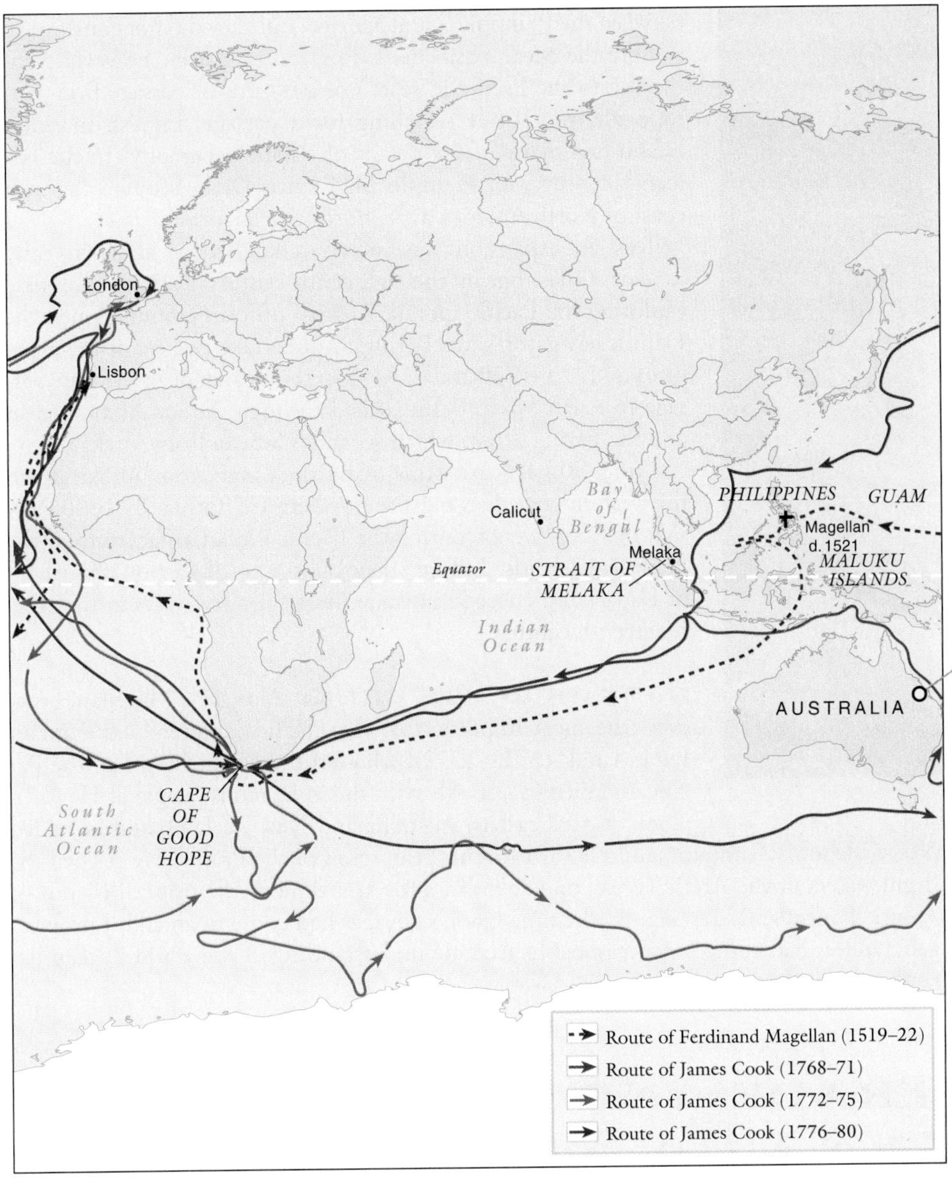

Note that these voyages only explored the eastern coast of the Australian continent.

Route of Ferdinand Magellan (1519–22)
Route of James Cook (1768–71)
Route of James Cook (1772–75)
Route of James Cook (1776–80)

ing on fresh provisions at Guam. During that period crewmen survived on worm-ridden biscuits, ship's rats, leather they had softened in the ocean, and water gone foul. Lacking fresh fruits and vegetables in their diet, many of the crew fell victim to the dreaded disease of scurvy, which caused painful rotting of the gums, loss of teeth, abscesses, hemorrhaging, and in most cases death. Scurvy killed 29 members of Magellan's crew during the Pacific crossing.

James Cook, English explorer
www.mhhe.com/bentleybrief2e

Conditions improved after the fleet called at Guam, but its ordeal had not come to an end. From Guam, Magellan proceeded to the Philippine Islands, where he and 40 of his crew were killed in a local political dispute. The survivors continued on to the spice islands of Maluku, where they took on a cargo of cloves. They then sailed home through the familiar waters of the Indian Ocean—and thus completed the first circumnavigation of the world—returning to Spain after a voyage of almost exactly three years. Of Magellan's five ships and 280 men, only one ship with 18 of the original crew returned. (An additional 17 crewmen returned later by other routes.)

EXPLORATION OF THE PACIFIC The Pacific Ocean is so vast that it took European explorers almost three centuries to chart its features. Spanish merchants built on information gleaned from Magellan's expedition and established a trade route

Captain James Cook. A portrait of Captain James Cook painted by William Hodges about 1775 depicts a serious and determined man. ***What physical prop is included in the portrait, and why?***

between the Philippines and Mexico, but they did not continue to explore the ocean basin itself. English navigators, however, ventured into the Pacific in search of a northwest passage from Europe to Asia. While searching for a passage, English mariners established many of the details of Pacific geography. In the sixteenth century, for example, Sir Francis Drake scouted the west coast of North America as far north as Vancouver Island.

Russian expansion was mostly a land-based affair in early modern times, but by the eighteenth century Russians also were exploring the Pacific Ocean. Russian officials commissioned the Danish navigator Vitus Bering to undertake two maritime expeditions (1725–1730 and 1733–1742) in search of a northeast passage to Asian ports. Bering sailed through the icy Arctic Ocean and the Bering Strait, which separates Siberia from Alaska.

Other Russian explorers made their way from Alaska down the western Canadian coast to northern California. By 1800 Russian mariners were scouting the Pacific Ocean as far south as the Hawaiian Islands. Indeed, they built a small fort on the island of Kaua`i and engaged in trade there for a few years in the early nineteenth century.

CAPTAIN JAMES COOK Alongside Magellan, however, the most important of the Pacific explorers was Captain James Cook (1728–1779), who led three expeditions to the Pacific and died in a scuffle with the indigenous people of Hawai`i. Cook charted eastern Australia and New Zealand, and he added New Caledonia, Vanuatu, and Hawai`i to European maps of the Pacific. He probed the frigid waters of the Arctic Ocean and spent months at a time in the tropical islands of Tahiti, Tonga, and Hawai`i. By the time Cook's voyages had come to an end, European geographers had compiled a reasonably accurate understanding of the world's ocean basins, their lands, and their peoples.

Trade and Conflict in Early Modern Asia

The voyages of exploration taught European mariners how to sail to almost any coastline in the world and return safely. Once they arrived at their destinations, they sought commercial opportunities. In the eastern hemisphere they built a series of fortified trading posts that offered footholds in regions where established commercial networks had held sway for centuries. They even attempted to control the spice trade in the Indian Ocean, but with limited success. For the most part, they did not have the human numbers or the military power to impose their rule in the eastern hemisphere. In a parallel effort involving expansion across land rather than the sea, Russian explorers and adventurers established a presence in central Asia and Siberia, thus laying the foundations for a vast Eurasian empire. Commercial and political rivalries in both the eastern and the western hemispheres also led to conflict between European peoples, which resulted in numerous wars between competing powers for both territory and resources.

Trading-Post Empires

PORTUGUESE TRADING POSTS Portuguese mariners built the earliest trading-post empire. Their goal was not to conquer territories but to control trade routes by forcing merchant vessels to call at fortified trading sites and pay duties there. Vasco da Gama obtained permission from local authorities to establish a trading post at Calicut

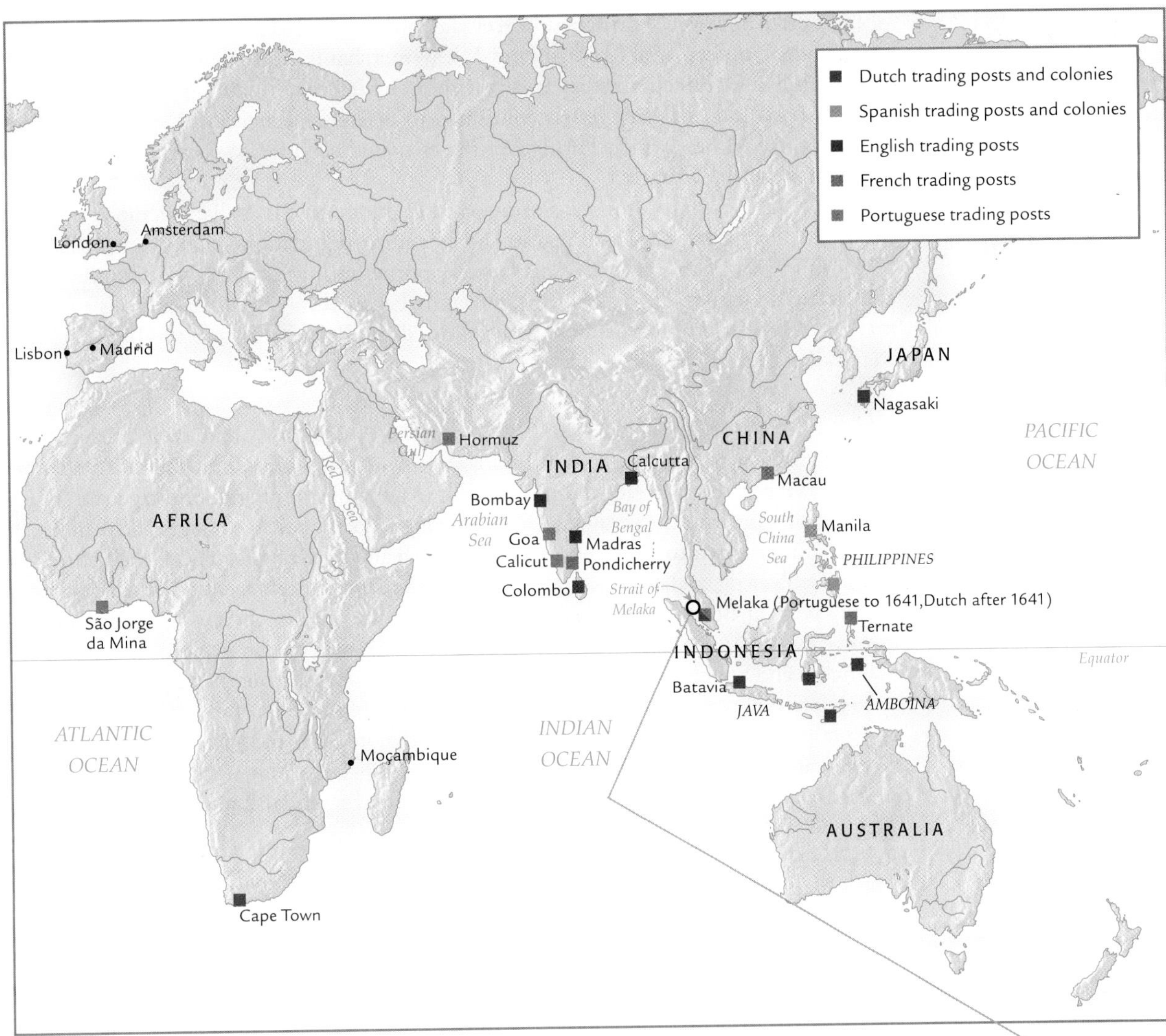

MAP 19.3 | European trading posts in Africa and Asia, ca. 1700. Note how many more trading posts there were in Asia than in Africa. ***What accounts for the difference?***

The Strait of Melaka was a crucial strategic point, because it controlled the entry and exit of ships passing between the Indian Ocean and the South China Sea.

when he arrived there in 1498. By the mid–sixteenth century, Portuguese merchants had built more than fifty trading posts between west Africa and east Asia.

AFONSO D'ALBOQUERQUE Equipped with heavy artillery, Portuguese vessels were able to overpower most other craft they encountered, and they sometimes trained their cannon effectively onshore. The architect of their aggressive policy was Afonso d'Alboquerque, commander of Portuguese forces in the Indian Ocean during the early sixteenth century. Alboquerque's fleets seized Hormuz in 1508, Goa in 1510, and Melaka in 1511. From these strategic sites, Alboquerque sought to control Indian Ocean trade by forcing all merchant ships to purchase safe-conduct passes and present them at Portuguese trading posts. Ships without passes were subject to confiscation, along with their cargoes. Alboquerque's forces punished violators of his policy by executing them or cutting off their hands. Alboquerque was confident of Portuguese naval superiority and its ability to control trade in the Indian Ocean.

Afonso d'Alboquerque (al-FAWN-soo d'AL-buh-kur-kee)

In reality, however, Portuguese forces did not have enough vessels to enforce their commander's orders. Arab, Indian, and Malay merchants continued to play prominent roles in Indian Ocean commerce, usually without taking the precaution of securing a safe-conduct pass. Indeed, Arab vessels continued to deliver shipments of pepper and spices through the Red Sea, which Portuguese forces never managed to control, to Cairo and Mediterranean trade routes.

By the late sixteenth century, Portuguese hegemony in the Indian Ocean was growing weak. Portugal was a small country with a small population—about one million in 1500—and was unable to sustain its large seaborne trading empire. In addition, by the late sixteenth century, investors in other lands began to organize expeditions to Asian markets. Most prominent of those who followed the Portuguese into the Indian Ocean were English and Dutch mariners.

ENGLISH AND DUTCH TRADING POSTS Like their predecessors, English and Dutch merchants built trading posts on Asian coasts and sought to channel trade through them, but they did not attempt to control shipping on the high seas. They also occasionally seized Portuguese sites, although Portuguese authorities held many of their trading posts into the twentieth century. Meanwhile, English and Dutch entrepreneurs established parallel networks. English merchants concentrated on India and built trading posts at Bombay, Madras, and Calcutta, while the Dutch operated more broadly from Cape Town, Colombo, and Batavia (modern Jakarta on the island of Java).

English and Dutch merchants enjoyed two main advantages over their Portuguese predecessors. They sailed faster, cheaper, and more powerful ships, which offered both an economic and a military edge over their competitors. Furthermore, they conducted trade through an exceptionally efficient form of commercial organization—the joint-stock company—which enabled investors to realize handsome profits while limiting the risk to their investments.

THE TRADING COMPANIES English and Dutch merchants formed two especially powerful joint-stock companies: the English East India Company, founded in 1600, and its Dutch counterpart, the United East India Company, known from its initials as the VOC (Vereenigde Oost-Indische Compagnie), established in 1602. Private merchants advanced funds to launch these companies, outfit them with ships and crews, and provide them with commodities and money to trade. Although they enjoyed government support, the companies were privately owned enterprises. Unhampered by political oversight, company agents concentrated strictly on profitable trade. Their charters granted them the right to buy, sell, build trading posts, and even make war.

The English and Dutch companies experienced immediate financial success. In 1601, for example, five English ships set sail from London with cargoes mostly of gold and silver coins valued at thirty thousand pounds sterling. When they returned in 1603, the spices that they carried were worth more than one million pounds sterling. Because of their advanced nautical technology, powerful military arsenal, efficient organization, and relentless pursuit of profit, the English East India Company and the VOC contributed to the early formation of a global network of trade.

THINKING ABOUT *Traditions*

TRADITIONS IN TRANSOCEANIC ENCOUNTERS AND GLOBAL CONNECTIONS. From the fifteenth to the eighteenth century, European mariners explored vast areas in the Atlantic, Indian, and Pacific oceans. In what ways were their motivations for this exploration—as well as their behaviors when making contact with people in other lands—shaped by the Christian traditions of their cultures?

European Conquests in Southeast Asia

Following voyages of exploration to the western hemisphere, Europeans conquered indigenous peoples, built territorial empires, and established colonies settled by European migrants. In the eastern hemisphere, however, they were mostly unable to force their will on large Asian populations and powerful centralized states. With the decline of the Portuguese effort to control shipping in the Indian Ocean, Europeans mostly traded peacefully in Asian waters alongside Arab, Indian, Malay, and Chinese merchants.

Yet in two island regions of southeast Asia—the Philippines and Indonesia—Europeans conquered existing authorities and imposed their rule. Though densely populated, neither the Philippines nor Indonesia had a powerful state when Europeans arrived there in the sixteenth century. Nor did imperial authorities in China or India lay claim to the island regions. Heavily armed ships enabled Europeans to bring overwhelming force to bear and to establish imperial regimes that favored the interests of European merchants.

THE SPICE TRADE. | Harvesting mace on the island of Lontor in the Banda Islands.

CONQUEST OF THE PHILIPPINES Spanish forces approached the Philippines in 1565 under the command of Miguel López de Legazpi, who named the islands after King Philip II of Spain. Because the Philippines had no central government, there was no organized resistance to the intrusion. By 1575 Spanish forces controlled the coastal regions of the central and northern islands, and during the seventeenth century they extended their authority to most parts of the archipelago except the southern island of Mindanao, where a large Muslim community stoutly resisted Spanish expansion.

MANILA Spanish policy in the Philippines revolved around trade and Christianity. Manila soon emerged as a bustling, multicultural port city—an entrepôt for trade, particularly in silk—and it quickly became the hub of Spanish commercial activity in Asia. Chinese merchants were especially prominent in Manila. They occupied a specially designated commercial district of the city and supplied silk goods that Spanish traders shipped to Mexico in the Manila galleons. Their commercial success brought suspicion on the Chinese community, however, and resentful Spanish and Filipino residents massacred Chinese merchants in several eruptions of violence over the next few hundred years. Meanwhile, the Spanish also sought to Christianize the Philippines. Spanish rulers and missionaries pressured prominent Filipinos to convert to Christianity in hopes of persuading others to follow their example. They opened schools to teach the fundamentals of Christian doctrine, along with basic literacy, in densely populated regions throughout the islands. Although Spanish missionaries initially faced resistance, over the long term Filipinos turned increasingly to Christianity, and by the nineteenth century the Philippines had become one of the most fervent Roman Catholic lands in the world.

CONQUEST OF JAVA Dutch mariners who imposed their rule on the islands of Indonesia did not worry about seeking converts to Christianity but concentrated instead on the trade in spices, particularly cloves, nutmeg, and mace. The architect of Dutch policy was Jan Pieterszoon Coen, who in 1619 founded Batavia on the island of Java to serve as an entrepôt for the VOC. Coen's plan was to establish a VOC monopoly over spice production and trade, thus enabling Dutch merchants to reap enormous profits in European markets. Coen brought his naval power to bear on the small Indonesian islands and forced them to deliver spices only to VOC merchants. By the late seventeenth century, the VOC controlled all the ports of Java as well as most of the important spice-bearing islands throughout the Indonesian archipelago.

Dutch numbers were too few for them to rule directly over their whole southeast Asian empire. They made alliances with local authorities to maintain order in most regions, reserving only Batavia and the most important spice-bearing islands for direct Dutch rule. The Dutch did not embark on campaigns of conquest for purposes of adding to their holdings, but they uprooted spice-bearing plants on islands they did not control and mercilessly

Miguel López de Legazpi (mee-GEHL LOH-pess de le-GAHS-pee)
Mindanao (min-duh-NAH-oh)
Jan Pieterszoon Coen (yahn PEE-tuhr-sohn KOH-uhn)

attacked peoples who sold their spices to merchants not associated with the VOC. Monopoly profits from the spice trade not only enriched the VOC but also made the Netherlands the most prosperous land in Europe throughout most of the seventeenth century.

Foundations of the Russian Empire in Asia

While western European peoples were building maritime empires, Russians were laying the foundations for a vast land empire that embraced most of northern Eurasia. This round of expansion began in the mid–sixteenth century, as Russian forces took over several Mongol khanates in central Asia. Those acquisitions resulted in Russian control over the Volga River and offered opportunities for trade with the Ottoman empire, Iran, and even India through the Caspian Sea. In the eighteenth century, Russian forces extended their presence in the Caspian Sea region by absorbing much of the Caucasus, a vibrant multiethnic region embracing the modern-day states of Georgia, Armenia, and Azerbaijan.

SIBERIA Far more extensive were Russian acquisitions in northeastern Eurasia. The frozen tundras and dense forests of Siberia posed formidable challenges, but explorers and merchants made their way into the region in a quest for fur. In the late sixteenth century, Russian explorers pushed into the interior regions of Siberia by way of the region's great rivers. By 1639 they had made their way across the Eurasian landmass and reached the Pacific Ocean.

NATIVE PEOPLES OF SIBERIA Siberia was home to about twenty-six major ethnic groups that lived by hunting, trapping, fishing, or herding reindeer. These indigenous peoples varied widely in language and religion, and they responded in different ways to the arrival of Russian adventurers who sought to exact tribute from them by coercing them to supply animal pelts on a regular basis. Some groups readily accepted iron tools, woven cloth, flour, tea, and liquor for the skins of fur-bearing animals such as otter, lynx, and especially sable. Others resented the ever-increasing demands for tribute and resisted Russian encroachment on their lands. For example, the Yakut people of the Lena and Aldan river valleys in central Siberia mounted a revolt against Russian oppression in 1642. The Russian response was brutal: over a period of forty years, Russian forces drove many Yakut out of their settlements and reduced their population by an estimated 70 percent. Quite apart from military violence, the peoples of Siberia reeled from epidemic diseases that reduced many populations by more than half.

THE RUSSIAN OCCUPATION OF SIBERIA Despite the region's harsh climate, Russian migrants—some of whom were social misfits or convicted criminals—gradually filtered into Siberia and thoroughly altered its demographic complexion. Small agricultural settlements grew up near many trading posts, particularly in the fertile Amur River valley. Over time, Siberian trading posts developed into Russian towns with Russian-speaking populations attending Russian Orthodox churches. By 1763 some 420,000 Russians lived in Siberia, nearly double the number of indigenous inhabitants. In the nineteenth century, large numbers of additional migrants moved east to mine Siberian gold, silver, copper, and iron, and the Russian state was well on the way toward consolidating its control over the region.

European Commercial Rivalries

Exploration and imperial expansion led to conflicts not only between Europeans and Asians but also among the Europeans. Mariners competed vigorously for trade in Asia and the Americas, and their efforts to establish markets—and sometimes monopolies—led frequently to clashes with their counterparts from different lands.

COMPETITION AND CONFLICT Indeed, throughout the seventeenth and early eighteenth centuries, commercial and political rivalries led to running wars between ships flying different flags. Dutch vessels were most numerous in the Indian Ocean, and

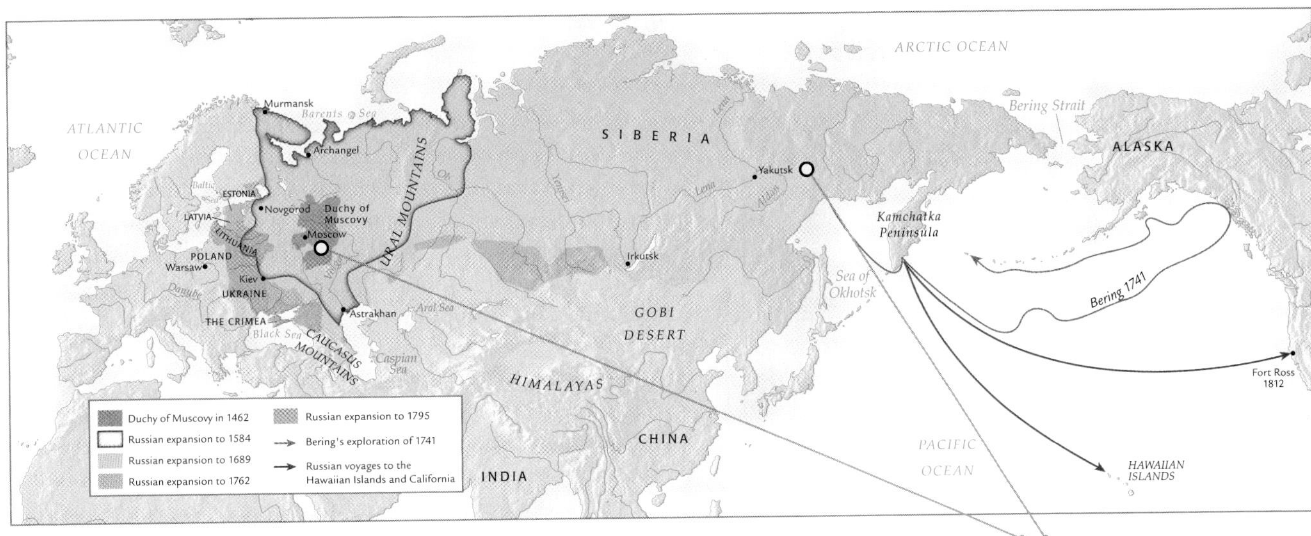

MAP 19.4 | Russian expansion, 1462–1795. Observe how vast the empire became after it added the territory of Siberia. ***How did Russians exert their control over such a huge and unforgiving territory?***

they enabled the VOC to dominate the spice trade. Dutch forces expelled most Portuguese merchants from southeast Asia and prevented English mariners from establishing secure footholds there. By the early eighteenth century, trade in Indian cotton and tea from Ceylon had begun to overshadow the spice trade, and English and French merchants working from trading posts in India became the dominant carriers in the Indian Ocean. Fierce competition again generated violence: in 1746 French forces seized the English trading post at Madras, one of the three principal centers of British operations in India.

Commercial competition led to conflict also in the Caribbean and the Americas. English pirates and privateers preyed on Spanish shipping from Mexico, often seizing vessels carrying cargoes of silver. English and French forces constantly skirmished and fought over sugar islands in the Caribbean while also contesting territorial claims in North America. In addition, almost all conflicts between European states in the eighteenth century spilled over into the Caribbean and the Americas.

Global Exchanges

European explorers and those who followed them established links between all lands and peoples of the world. Interaction between peoples in turn resulted in an unprecedented volume of exchange across the boundary lines of societies and cultural regions. Some of that exchange involved biological species: plants, food crops, animals, human populations, and disease pathogens all spread to regions they had not previously visited. These biological exchanges had differing and dramatic effects on human populations, destroying some of them through epidemic diseases while enlarging others through increased food supplies and richer diets. Commercial exchange also flourished in the wake of the voyages of exploration as European merchants traveled to ports throughout the world in search of trade. Indeed, by the mid–eighteenth century they had established globe-girdling networks of trade and communication.

The Columbian Exchange

BIOLOGICAL EXCHANGES Processes of biological exchange were prominent features of world history well before modern times. The early expansion of Islam, for example, had facilitated the diffusion of plants and food crops throughout much of the eastern hemisphere during the period from about 700 to 1100 C.E., some of which helped spark demographic and economic growth in the lands where they took root. Yet the *Columbian*

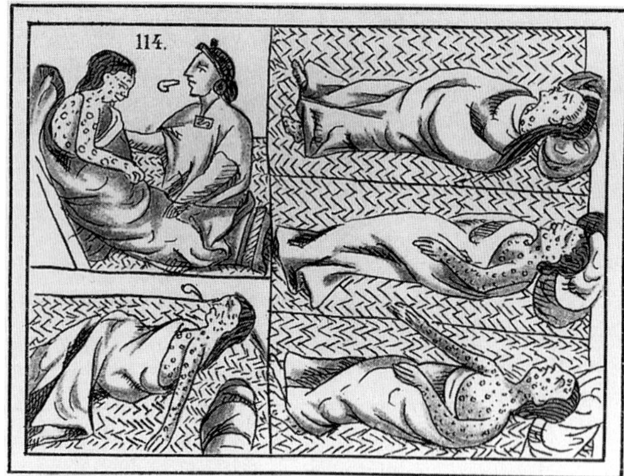

Epidemic Disease in the Americas. | Smallpox victims in the Aztec empire. The disease killed most of those it infected and left disfiguring scars on survivors. ***According to this depiction, what were the symptoms of smallpox?***

exchange—the global diffusion of plants, food crops, animals, human populations, and disease pathogens that took place after voyages of exploration by Christopher Columbus and other European mariners—had consequences much more profound than earlier rounds of biological exchange. Unlike earlier processes, the Columbian exchange involved lands with radically different flora, fauna, and diseases. For thousands of years the various species of the eastern hemisphere, the western hemisphere, and Oceania had evolved along separate lines. By creating links between these biological zones, the European voyages of exploration set off a round of biological exchange that permanently altered the world's human geography and natural environment.

Beginning in the early sixteenth century, infectious and contagious diseases brought sharp demographic losses to indigenous peoples of the Americas and the Pacific islands. The worst scourge was smallpox, but measles, diphtheria, whooping cough, and influenza also took heavy tolls. Before the voyages of exploration, none of the peoples of the western hemisphere or Oceania possessed inherited or acquired immunities to those pathogens. In the eastern hemisphere, these diseases were endemic: they claimed a certain number of victims from the ranks of infants and small children, but survivors gained immunity to the diseases through exposure at an early age. In some areas of Europe, for example, smallpox was responsible for 10 to 15 percent of deaths, but most victims were age ten or younger. Although its individual effects were tragic, smallpox did not pose a threat to European society as a whole because it did not carry away economically and socially productive adults.

EPIDEMIC DISEASES AND POPULATION DECLINE When infectious and contagious diseases traveled to previously unexposed populations, however, they touched off ferocious epidemics that sometimes destroyed entire societies. Beginning in 1519, epidemic smallpox ravaged the Aztec empire in combination with other diseases, and within a century the indigenous population of Mexico had declined by as much as 90 percent, from about 17 million to 1.3 million. By that time Spanish conquerors had imposed their rule on Mexico, and the political, social, and cultural traditions of the indigenous peoples had either disappeared or fallen under Spanish domination.

Imported diseases took their worst tolls in densely populated areas such as the Aztec and Inca empires, but they did not spare other regions. Smallpox and other diseases were so easily transmissible that they raced to remote areas of North and South America and sparked epidemics well before the first European explorers arrived in those regions. By the 1530s smallpox may have spread as far from Mexico as the Great Lakes in the north and the pampas of Argentina in the south.

When introduced to the Pacific islands, infectious and contagious diseases struck vulnerable populations with the same horrifying effects as in the Americas. All told, disease epidemics sparked by the Columbian exchange probably caused the worst demographic calamity in all of world history. Between 1500 and 1800, upward of 100 million people may have died of diseases imported into the Americas and Pacific islands.

FOOD CROPS AND ANIMALS Over a longer term, however, the Columbian exchange increased rather than diminished human population because of the global spread of food crops and animals that it sponsored. For example, wheat, vines, horses, cattle, pigs, sheep, goats, and chickens went from Europe to the Americas, where they sharply increased supplies of food and animal energy. Food crops native to the Americas also played prominent roles in the Columbian exchange. American crops that took root in Africa, Asia, and Europe include maize, potatoes, beans, tomatoes, peppers, peanuts, manioc, papayas, guavas, avocados, tobacco, pineapples, and cacao, to name only a few. Residents of the eastern hemisphere only gradually developed a taste for American crops, but by the eighteenth century maize and potatoes had contributed to a sharply increased number of calories in Eurasian diets. In tropical regions, peanuts and manioc flourished in soils that otherwise would not produce large yields or support large populations.

POPULATION GROWTH The Columbian exchange of plants and animals fueled a surge in world population. In 1500, as Eurasian peoples were recovering from epidemic bubonic plague, world population stood at about 425 million. By 1600 it had increased more than 25 percent, to 545 million. By 1750 human population stood at 720 million, and by 1800 it had surged to 900 million, having grown by almost 50 percent during the previous century. Much of the rise was due to the increased nutritional value of diets enriched by the global exchange of food crops and animals.

THINKING ABOUT *Encounters*

ENCOUNTERS IN TRANSOCEANIC ENCOUNTERS AND GLOBAL CONNECTIONS. When European mariners made contact with the Americas at the end of the fifteenth century, they set in motion a process of interaction and exchange that had profound consequences for the entire world. What are some of the specific ways this Columbian exchange transformed human populations, both in the Americas and in Eurasia?

MIGRATION Alongside disease pathogens and plant and animal species, the Columbian exchange involved the spread of human populations through transoceanic migration, whether voluntary or forced. During the period from 1500 to 1800, the largest contingent of migrants consisted of enslaved Africans transported involuntarily to the Americas. A smaller migration involved Europeans who traveled to the Americas and settled in lands depopulated by infectious and contagious diseases. During the nineteenth century, European peoples traveled in huge numbers to the western hemisphere and also to south Africa, Australia, and Pacific islands, and Asian peoples migrated to tropical and subtropical destinations throughout much of the world. In combination, those migrations have profoundly influenced modern world history.

The Origins of Global Trade

The trading-post empires established by Portuguese, Dutch, and English merchants linked Asian markets with European consumers and offered opportunities for European mariners to participate in the carrying trade within Asia. Indeed, by the late sixteenth century, European merchants carrying carpets, spices, silks, and silver were as prominent as Arabs in the trading world of the Indian Ocean basin.

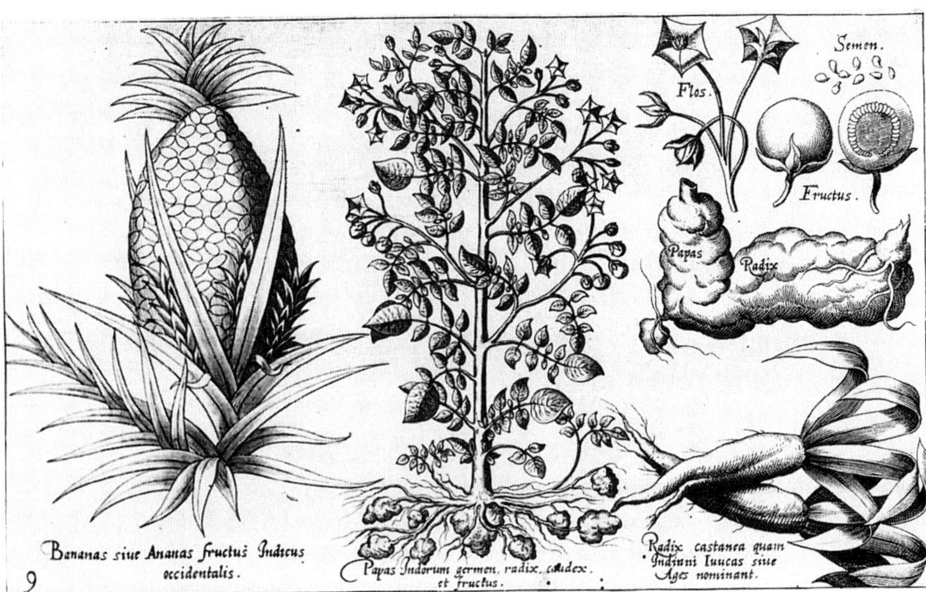

THE COLUMBIAN EXCHANGE OF FOODS. | Illustrations in an early-seventeenth-century book depict pineapple, potatoes, and cassava—all plants native to the Americas and unknown to Europeans before the sixteenth century.

TRANSOCEANIC TRADE Besides stimulating commerce in the eastern hemisphere, the voyages of European merchant mariners encouraged the emergence of a genuinely global trading system. As Europeans established colonies in the Caribbean and the Americas, for example, trade networks extended to all corners of the Atlantic Ocean basin. European manufactured goods traveled west across the Atlantic in exchange for silver from Mexican and Peruvian mines and agricultural products such as sugar and tobacco, both of which were in high demand among European consumers. Trade in human beings also figured in Atlantic commerce. European manufactured goods went south to west Africa, where merchants exchanged them for African slaves, who then went to the tropical and subtropical regions of the western hemisphere to work on plantations.

PSI img A Spanish galleon—1643 www.mhhe.com/bentleybrief2e

THE MANILA GALLEONS The experience of the Manila galleons illustrates the early workings of the global economy in the Pacific Ocean basin. For 250 years, from 1565 to 1815, Spanish galleons—sleek, fast, heavily armed ships capable of carrying large cargoes—regularly plied the waters of the Pacific Ocean between Manila in the Philippines and Acapulco on the west coast of Mexico. From Manila they took Asian luxury goods to Mexico and exchanged them for silver. Most of the precious metal made its way to China, where a thriving domestic economy demanded increasing quantities of silver. Meanwhile, some of the Asian luxury goods from Manila remained in Mexico or went to Peru, where they contributed to a comfortable way of life for Spanish ruling elites. Most, however, went overland across Mexico and then traveled by ship across the Atlantic to Spain and European markets.

ENVIRONMENTAL EFFECTS OF GLOBAL TRADE As silver lubricated growing volumes of global trade, pressures increased on several animal species that had the misfortune to become commodities on the world market. Fur-bearing animals came under particularly intense pressure, as hunters sought their pelts for sale to consumers in China, Europe, and North America. During the seventeenth century, an estimated two hundred to three hundred thousand sable pelts flowed annually from Siberia to the global market, and during the eighteenth century, more than sixteen million North American beaver pelts fed consumers' demands for fur hats and cloaks. Wanton hunting of fur-bearing animals soon drove many species into extinction or near extinction, permanently altering the environments they had formerly inhabited. Early modern hunters also harvested enormous numbers of deer, codfish, whales, walruses, and seals as merchants sought to supply animal products for global consumers.

In the seventeenth and eighteenth centuries, the volume of global trade expanded rapidly. During the seventeenth century, for example, Dutch merchants imported, among other commodities, wheat from south Africa, cowry shells from India, and sugar from Brazil. The wheat fed domestic consumers, who increasingly worked as merchants, bankers, or manufacturers rather than as cultivators. English, Dutch, and other merchants eagerly purchased the cowry shells—which served as currency in much of sub-Saharan Africa—and exchanged them for slaves destined for plantations in the western hemisphere. The sugar went on the market at Amsterdam and found its way to consumers throughout Europe. And that was just the beginning. By 1750 all parts of the world except Australia participated in global networks of commercial relations in which European merchant mariners played prominent roles.

SUMMARY

Global commercial and biological exchanges arose from the efforts of European mariners to explore the world's waters and establish sea-lanes that would support long-distance trade. Their search for sea routes to Asia led them to the western hemisphere and the vast expanse of the Pacific Ocean. The geographic knowledge that they accumulated enabled them to link the world's regions into a finely articulated network of trade. But commercial exchange was not the only result of this global network. Food crops, animal stocks, disease pathogens, and human migrants also traveled the sea-lanes and dramatically influenced societies throughout the world. Transplanted crops and animal species led to improved nutrition and increasing populations throughout the eastern hemisphere. Epidemics sparked by unfamiliar disease pathogens ravaged indigenous populations in the Americas and the Pacific islands. Mass migrations of human communities transformed the social and cultural landscape of the Americas and encouraged increased mingling of the world's peoples. The European voyages of exploration, transoceanic trade networks, and the Columbian exchange pushed the world's regions toward interdependence and global integration.

STUDY TERMS

Afonso d'Alboquerque (377)
astrolabe (370)
Bartolomeu Dias (371)
Captain James Cook (376)
Christopher Columbus (372)
Columbian exchange (381)
cross-staff (370)
East India Company (378)
epidemic disease (382)
Fernando Magellan (374)
joint-stock company (378)
magnetic compass (370)
Manila galleons (379)
Prince Henry the Navigator (371)
Taino (372)
Vasco da Gama (367)
Vitus Bering (376)
VOC (378)

FOR FURTHER READING

K. N. Chaudhuri. *Trade and Civilisation in the Indian Ocean: An Economic History from the Rise of Islam to 1750.* Cambridge, 1985. A brilliant analysis that places the European presence in the Indian Ocean in its larger historical context.

Christopher Columbus. *The* Diario *of Christopher Columbus's First Voyage to America.* Trans. by Oliver Dunn and James E. Kelley Jr. Norman, Okla., 1989. A careful translation.

Alfred W. Crosby. *The Columbian Exchange: Biological and Cultural Consequences of 1492.* Westport, Conn., 1972. Focuses on early exchanges of plants, animals, and diseases between Europe and America.

Philip D. Curtin. *Cross-Cultural Trade in World History.* New York, 1984. Focuses on the roles of cross-cultural brokers in facilitating trade between different societies.

Andre Gunder Frank. *ReORIENT: Global Economy in the Asian Age.* Berkeley, 1998. Important and challenging analysis of global economic integration in the early modern world.

Antonio Pigafetta. *Magellan's Voyage: A Narrative Account of the First Circumnavigation.* 2 vols. Trans. by R. A. Skelton. New Haven, 1969. Valuable account by a crewman on Magellan's circumnavigation of the world.

Kenneth Pomeranz. *The Great Divergence: China, Europe, and the Making of the Modern World Economy.* Princeton, 2000. Path-breaking scholarly study that illuminates the economic history of the early modern world through comparison of economic development in Asian and European lands.

John F. Richards. *The Unending Frontier: An Environmental History of the Early Modern World.* Berkeley, 2003. Thoroughly explores the environmental effects of the global historical processes that shaped the early modern world.

Stuart B. Schwartz, ed. *Implicit Understandings: Observing, Reporting, and Reflecting on the Encounters between Europeans and Other Peoples in the Early Modern Era.* Cambridge, 1994. Fascinating collection of essays by specialists on cross-cultural perceptions in early modern times.

Yuri Slezkine. *Arctic Mirrors: Russia and the Small Peoples of the North.* Ithaca, N.Y., 1994. Thoughtful analysis of Russian relations with the hunting, fishing, and herding peoples of Siberia.

The Transformation of Europe

20

In 1517 an obscure German monk posed a challenge to the Roman Catholic church. Martin Luther of Wittenberg denounced the church's sale of indulgences, a type of pardon that excused individuals from doing penance for their sins. Indulgences had been available since the eleventh century, but to raise funds for the reconstruction of St. Peter's basilica in Rome, church authorities began to market indulgences aggressively in the early sixteenth century. From their point of view, indulgences were splendid devices: they encouraged individuals to reflect piously on their behavior while also bringing large sums of money into the church's treasury.

To Martin Luther, however, indulgences were signs of greed, hypocrisy, and moral rot in the Roman Catholic church. Luther believed that no human being had the power to absolve individuals of their sins and grant them admission to heaven, so for him the sale of indulgences constituted a vast fraud. In October 1517, following academic custom, he offered to debate publicly with anyone who wished to dispute his views, and he denounced the sale of indulgences in a document called the *Ninety-five Theses.*

Luther did not nail his work to the church door in Wittenberg, although a popular legend credits him with that gesture, but news of the *Ninety-five Theses* spread instantly: within a few weeks, printed copies were available throughout Europe. Luther's challenge galvanized both strong support and severe criticism. Religious and political authorities seeking to maintain the established order were especially critical. Church officials judged Luther's views erroneous, and in 1520 Pope Leo X excommunicated him. In 1521 the Holy Roman emperor Charles V, a devout Roman Catholic, summoned Luther and demanded that he recant his views. Luther's response: "I cannot and will not recant anything, for it is neither safe nor right to act against one's conscience. Here I stand. I can do no other. God help me. Amen."

Martin Luther's challenge held enormous religious and political implications. Though expelled from the church, Luther still considered himself Christian, and he held religious services for a community of devoted followers. By the 1520s, religious dissent had spread through much of Germany and Switzerland. During the 1530s dissidents known as Protestants—because of their protest against the established order—organized movements also in France, England, the Low Countries, Italy, and Spain. By mid-century Luther's act of individual rebellion had mushroomed into the Protestant Reformation, which shattered the religious unity of western Christendom.

❮ This detail from a sixteenth-century painting by François Dubois depicts the brutal murder of French Protestants in Paris during the St. Bartholomew's Day Massacre on August 23rd, 1572.

For all its unsettling effects, the Protestant Reformation was only one of several powerful movements that transformed European society during the early modern era. Another was the

CHRONOLOGY

1473–1543	Life of Nicolaus Copernicus
1478	Foundation of the Spanish Inquisition
1483–1546	Life of Martin Luther
1517	Publication of the *Ninety-five Theses*
1540	Foundation of the Society of Jesus
1545–1563	Council of Trent
1564–1642	Life of Galileo Galilei
1571–1630	Life of Johannes Kepler
1618–1648	Thirty Years' War
1642–1727	Life of Isaac Newton
1643–1715	Reign of King Louis XIV
1648	Peace of Westphalia
1694–1778	Life of Voltaire
1723–1790	Life of Adam Smith

consolidation of strong centralized states, which took shape partly because of the Reformation. Between the sixteenth and eighteenth centuries, monarchs in western Europe took advantage of religious quarrels to tighten control over their societies. By the mid–eighteenth century, some rulers had concentrated so much power in their own hands that historians refer to them as absolute monarchs.

Alongside religious conflict and the building of powerful states, capitalism and early modern science profoundly influenced western European society in early modern times. Early capitalism encouraged European merchants and manufacturers to reorganize their businesses in search of maximum efficiency. Early modern science challenged traditional ways of understanding the world and the universe and prompted European intellectuals to seek an entirely rational understanding of human society as well as the natural world.

Thus between 1500 and 1800, western Europe underwent a thorough transformation. Although the changes were unsettling and often disruptive, they also strengthened European society. Indeed, by 1800 several European states had become especially powerful, wealthy, and dynamic. They stood poised to play major roles in world affairs during the nineteenth and twentieth centuries.

The Fragmentation of Western Christendom

Although the peoples of western Europe spoke different languages and observed different customs, the church of Rome provided them with a common religious and cultural heritage. During the sixteenth and seventeenth centuries, however, revolts against the Roman Catholic church shattered the religious unity of western Europe. Followers of Martin Luther and other Protestant reformers established a series of churches independent of Rome, and Roman Catholic leaders strengthened their own church against the challengers. Throughout early modern times, religious controversies fueled social tensions.

The Protestant Reformation

MARTIN LUTHER Martin Luther (1483–1546) quickly attracted enthusiastic support from others who resented the policies of the Roman church. Luther was a talented writer, and he published scores of works condemning the Roman church. His cause benefited enormously from the printing press, which had first appeared in Europe in the mid–fifteenth century. A sizable literate public inhabited European cities and towns, and readers eagerly consumed printed works on religious as well as secular themes. Printed editions of Luther's writings appeared throughout Europe and sparked spirited debates on theological issues. His supporters and his critics took their own works to the printers, and religious controversies kept the presses busy churning out pamphlets and treatises for a century and more.

PSI img Martin Luther posting *Ninety-five Theses* www.mhhe.com/bentleybrief2e

Luther attacked the Roman church for a wide range of abuses and called for thorough reform of Christendom. He advocated the closure of monasteries, translation of the Bible from Latin into vernacular lan-

vernacular (ver-NA-kyoo-lar)

guages, and an end to priestly authority, including the authority of the pope himself. Most important, Luther believed that salvation could never be earned through good works or through the prayers of others. Instead, he argued, humans could be saved only through faith in the promises of God as revealed in the Bible. This idea of "justification by faith alone" became the core of Protestant belief. When opponents pointed out that Luther's reform program ran counter to church policy, he rejected the authority of the church hierarchy and proclaimed that the Bible was the only source of Christian religious authority.

REFORM OUTSIDE GERMANY Luther's works drew an enthusiastic popular response, and in Germany they fueled a movement to reform the church along the lines of Luther's teachings. Lay Christians flocked to hear Luther preach in Wittenberg, and several princes of the Holy Roman Empire warmed to Luther's views—partly because of personal conviction but partly also because religious controversy offered opportunities for them to build their own power bases, During the 1520s and 1530s, many of the most important German cities—Strasbourg, Nuremberg, and Augsburg, among others—passed laws requiring all religious services to follow Protestant doctrine and procedures. By the mid–sixteenth century about half the German population had adopted Lutheran Christianity, and reformers had launched Protestant movements and established alternative churches in other lands as well. By the late 1520s the prosperous cities of Switzerland—Zurich, Basel, and Geneva—had fledgling Protestant churches. The heavily urbanized Low Countries also responded enthusiastically to Protestant appeals. Protestants appeared even in Italy and Spain, although authorities in those lands handily suppressed their challenge to the Roman church.

JOHN CALVIN Meanwhile, an even more influential reformation was taking shape in France and French-speaking Switzerland. The initiator was a French lawyer, John Calvin (1509–1564), who in the 1530s converted to Protestant Christianity. Because the French monarchy sought to suppress Protestants, Calvin moved to French-speaking Geneva in Switzerland, where he organized a tight-knit Protestant community. Calvin also composed an influential treatise, *Institutes of the Christian Religion* (first published in 1536), that presented Protestant teachings as a coherent and organized package. Although Calvin believed in the basic elements of Luther's Protestant teachings, his ideas differed from those of Luther in important ways. Most fundamentally, Calvin emphasized the awesome power of God more than Luther did. Indeed, he believed not only that humans could never earn salvation but also that God had in fact already determined which individuals would be saved from damnation before they were even born. These individuals, known as "the elect," were predestined to salvation regardless of their deeds on earth. This doctrine of "predestination," as it became known, grew increasingly important to the Calvinist church in the generations after Calvin's death.

Calvin's Geneva was based on a strict code of morality and discipline. Calvinists were supposed to dress simply, to study the Bible regularly, and to refrain from activities such as playing cards and dancing. It was, in effect, a model Protestant community. Geneva also became an important missionary center from which Calvinist doctrine spread to other parts of Europe. Calvinist missionaries were most active in France, where they attracted strong interest in the cities, but they ventured also to Germany, the Low Countries, England, Hungary, and—most successfully—the Netherlands and Scotland.

THE ENGLISH REFORMATION In England a reformation took place for political as well as religious reasons. Lutherans and other Protestants worked to build a following in England from the 1520s on, but they faced stout government resistance until King Henry VIII (reigned 1509–1547) came into conflict with the pope. Henry wanted to divorce his wife, who had not borne a male heir, but the pope refused to allow him to do so. Henry's response was to sever relations with the Roman church and make himself supreme head of the Anglican church—an English pope, as it were. While Henry reigned, the theology of the English church changed little, but his successors replaced Roman Catholic with Protestant doctrines and rituals. By 1560 England had permanently left the

Roman Catholic community. Indeed, by the late sixteenth century, Lutherans, Calvinists, and Anglicans in Europe had built communities large enough that a return to religious unity in western Christendom was inconceivable.

The Catholic Reformation

In response to the Protestant Reformation, Roman Catholic authorities undertook a wide-ranging reform effort of their own. Their purpose was to clarify differences between Roman and Protestant churches, to persuade Protestants to return to the Roman church, and to deepen the sense of spirituality and religious commitment in their own community. Taken together, their efforts constituted the Catholic Reformation.

THE COUNCIL OF TRENT Two institutions were especially important for defining the Catholic Reformation and advancing its goals—the Council of Trent and the Society of Jesus. The Council of Trent was an assembly of high church officials who met intermittently between 1545 and 1563 to address matters of doctrine and reform. During the meetings, the council defined the elements of Roman Catholic theology in detail. The council also took steps to reform the church by demanding that church authorities observe strict standards of morality and requiring them to establish schools and seminaries to prepare priests properly for their roles.

ST. IGNATIUS OF LOYOLA While the Council of Trent dealt with doctrine and reform, the Society of Jesus sought to extend the boundaries of the reformed Roman church. The society's founder was St. Ignatius Loyola (1491–1556), a Basque nobleman and soldier who in 1521 suffered a leg wound that ended his military career. While recuperating he read spiritual works and popular accounts of saints' lives, and he resolved to put his energy into religious work. In 1540, together with a small band of disciples, he founded the Society of Jesus.

THE SOCIETY OF JESUS Ignatius required that members of the society, known as Jesuits, complete a rigorous and advanced education in theology, philosophy, languages, history, literature, and science. As a result of that preparation, the Jesuits made extraordinarily effective missionaries. They also acquired a reputation for discipline and determination, and often served as counselors to kings and other rulers. They also were the most prominent of the early Christian missionaries outside Europe: in the wake of the European reconnaissance of the world's oceans, Jesuits attracted converts in India, China, Japan, the Philippines, and the Americas, thus making Christianity a genuinely global religion.

THINKING ABOUT *Traditions*

TRADITIONS IN THE TRANSFORMATION OF EUROPE. Until the early sixteenth century, most of Europe was culturally united by the common practice of Roman Christianity. As a result of the Reformation, however, European peoples formed new identities and traditions based on their practice of either reformed Roman Catholicism or the various Protestant faiths. What makes it possible for well-established traditions to change over time, and how are new traditions created?

Witch Hunts and Religious Wars

Europeans took religion seriously in the sixteenth century, and religious divisions helped to fuel social and political conflict. Apart from wars, the most destructive violence that afflicted early modern Europe was the hunt for witches, which was especially prominent in regions, such as the Rhineland, where tensions between Protestants and Roman Catholics ran high.

Like many other peoples, Europeans had long believed that certain individuals possessed unusual or supernatural powers. During the late fifteenth century, theologians developed a theory that some of these people were witches who derived their powers—such as the ability to fly through the night on brooms or pitchforks—from the devil. Theorists believed that witches regularly flew off to distant places to attend the witches' sabbath, a gathering that featured devil worship and the concoction of secret potions and culminated in sexual relations with the devil himself. Indeed, witchcraft became a convenient explanation

Witch's Sabbath. In this etching from 1620 c.e., the artist portrays women cavorting with the devil and concocting potions in a nocturnal gathering of witches.

for any unpleasant turn of events—failure of a crop, an unexpected death, or inability to conceive a child.

WITCH-HUNTING In the sixteenth and seventeenth centuries, fears that individuals were making alliances with the devil sparked a widespread hunt for witches. About 110,000 individuals underwent trial as suspected witches, and about 60,000 of them died either by hanging or by burning at the stake. Most of the victims—perhaps 95 percent—were poor, old, single, or widowed women who lived on the margins of their societies and thus were easy targets for accusers. Although the fear of witches had largely diminished by 1700, the intermittent pursuit of witches for the better part of two centuries revealed clearly the stresses and strains—both secular and religious—that afflicted European society during early modern times.

RELIGIOUS WARS Religious tensions also led to outright war between Protestant and Roman Catholic communities. Religious wars wracked France for thirty-six years (1562–1598), for example, and they also complicated relations between Protestant and Roman Catholic states. In 1588 King Philip II of Spain (reigned 1556–1598) attempted to force England to return to the Roman Catholic church by sending the Spanish Armada—a huge flotilla consisting of 130 ships and 30,000 men—to dethrone the Protestant Queen Elizabeth. The effort collapsed, however, when English forces disrupted the Spanish fleet by sending blazing, unmanned ships into its midst. Then a ferocious gale scattered Spanish vessels throughout the North Sea.

Religious convictions also aggravated relations between the Netherlands and Spain by fueling the revolt of the Dutch provinces from their overlord, the king of Spain. In 1567 resistance escalated into a full-scale rebellion. By 1610 the seven northern provinces (the modern Netherlands) had won their independence and formed a republic known as the United Provinces, leaving ten southern provinces (modern Belgium) under Spanish and later Austrian rule until the late eighteenth century.

THE THIRTY YEARS' WAR The religious wars culminated in a great continental conflict known as the Thirty Years' War (1618–1648). The war opened after the Holy Roman emperor attempted to force his Bohemian subjects to return to the Roman Catholic church, and the main battleground was the emperor's territory in Germany. By the time the war ended, however, Spanish, French, Dutch, German, Swedish, Danish, Polish, Bohemian, and Russian forces had taken part in the conflict. The war itself was the most destructive European conflict before the twentieth century. Quite apart from violence and brutalities committed by undisciplined soldiers, the war damaged economies and societies throughout Europe and led to the deaths of about one-third of the German population. And though religious differences were not the only issues of the war, they complicated other issues and made them more difficult to resolve.

The Consolidation of Sovereign States

Although fundamentally a religious movement, the Reformation had strong political implications, and centralizing monarchs readily made use of religious issues in their efforts to strengthen their states and enhance their authority. Indeed, after the devastation of the Thirty Years' War, rulers of these states devised a diplomatic system that sought to maintain order among the many independent and competitive European states.

Note how much more dispersed the Spanish Habsburg territories were in comparison to the Austrian Habsburgs.

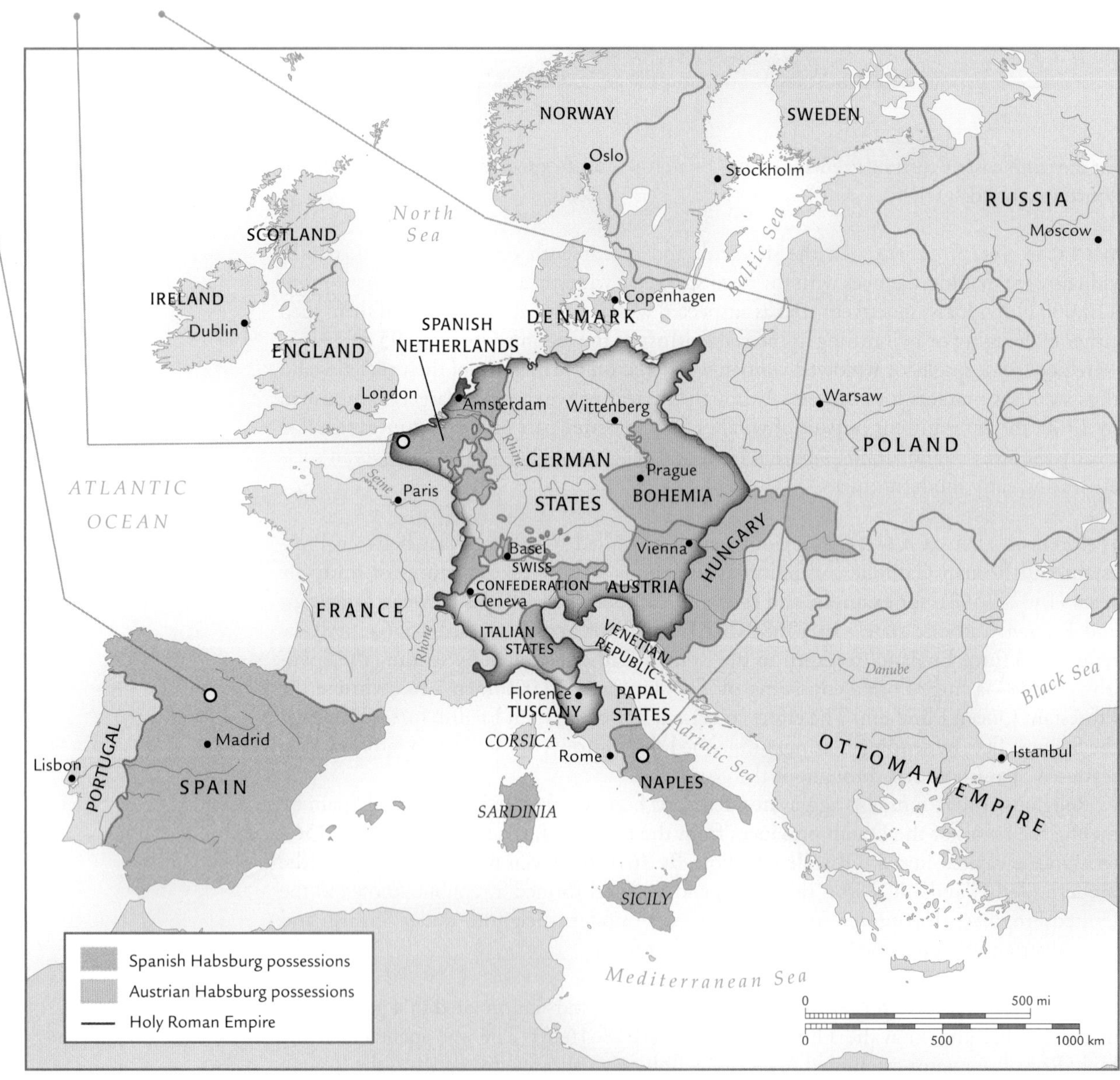

MAP 20.1 | Sixteenth-century Europe. Note the extent of Habsburg territories and the wide boundaries of the Holy Roman Empire. ***With such powerful territories, what prevented the Habsburgs from imposing imperial rule on most of Europe?***

The Attempted Revival of Empire

After the dissolution of the Carolingian empire in the ninth century C.E., there was no effective imperial government in western Europe. The Holy Roman Empire emerged in the tenth century, but its authority extended only to Germany and northern Italy, and even there its power was contested. During the early sixteenth century, it seemed that Emperor Charles V (reigned 1519–1556) might establish the Holy Roman Empire as the preeminent political authority in Europe, but by midcentury it was clear that there would be no revival of empire. Thus, unlike China, India, and the Ottoman empire, early modern Europe developed as a region of independent states.

CHARLES V After 1438 the Habsburg family, with extensive dynastic holdings in Austria, dominated the Holy Roman Empire. Through marriage alliances, the Habsburgs accumulated rights and titles to lands throughout Europe and beyond. Indeed, when Charles V became emperor in 1519, his empire stretched from Vienna in Austria to Cuzco in Peru. In spite of his far-flung holdings, Charles did not extend his authority throughout Europe. Part of the reason was that throughout his reign Charles had to devote much of his attention and energy to the Lutheran movement and to putting down imperial princes who took advantage of religious controversy to assert their independence. Foreign difficulties also played a role, because Charles's neighbors to the west and east—in France and the Ottoman empire, respectively—actively opposed the creation of a powerful Holy Roman Empire.

To ensure that Charles's territories remained in disarray, for example, the Roman Catholic French kings aided German Lutherans in their rebellion against the Holy Roman Empire. The French kings even allied with the Muslim Ottoman Turks against the emperor, who did not want a powerful Christian empire to threaten their holdings in eastern Europe and the Mediterranean basin.

Thus domestic and foreign problems prevented Charles V from establishing his vast empire as the supreme political authority in Europe. In 1556, disappointed especially in his inability to suppress the Lutherans in his territories, the emperor abdicated his throne and retired to a monastery in Spain. His empire did not survive. Charles bestowed his holdings in Spain, Italy, the Low Countries, and the Americas on his son, King Philip II of Spain, and his brother Ferdinand inherited the Habsburg family lands in Austria and the imperial throne.

The New Monarchs

In the absence of effective imperial power, public affairs fell to the various regional states that had emerged during the middle ages. In this period, however, the most powerful European states were the kingdoms of England, France, and Spain. During the late fifteenth and sixteenth centuries, rulers of these lands, known as the "new monarchs," marshaled their resources, curbed the nobility, and built strong centralized regimes.

FINANCE The new monarchs included Henry VIII of England, Louis XI and Francis I of France, and Fernando and Isabel of Spain. All the new monarchs sought to enhance their treasuries by developing new sources of finance. The French kings levied direct taxes on sales, households, and the salt trade. A new sales tax dramatically boosted Spanish royal income in the sixteenth century, and English kings increased revenues by raising fines and fees for royal services. Moreover, after Henry VIII severed ties between the English and Roman churches, he confiscated all church properties in England, which dramatically increased the size and wealth of the state.

STATE POWER With their increased income the new monarchs enlarged their administrative staffs, which enabled them to collect taxes and implement royal policies more reliably than before. Increased wealth also allowed the new monarchs to raise powerful

Carolingian (kar-uh-LIHN-jee-uhn)

The Spanish Inquisition. | When the Spanish Inquisition detected traces of Protestant heresy, the punishment could be swift and brutal. In this engraving of about 1560, a large crowd observes the execution of heretics (top right) by burning at the stake. ***Why were heretics burned rather than hung?***

armies when the need arose. That, in turn, resulted in increased control over the nobility, who could no longer compete with the power and wealth of the state.

THE SPANISH INQUISITION The debates and disputes launched by the Protestant Reformation also helped monarchs increase their power. Whereas monarchs in Protestant lands—including England, much of Germany, Denmark, and Sweden—expropriated church wealth to expand their powers, others relied on religious justifications to advance state ends. The Spanish Inquisition was the most distinctive institution of that kind. Fernando and Isabel founded the Spanish Inquisition in 1478, and they obtained papal license to operate the institution as a royal agency. Its original task was to ferret out those who secretly practiced Judaism or Islam, but Charles V charged it with responsibility also for detecting Protestant heresy in Spain.

Inquisitors had broad powers to investigate suspected cases of heresy. Popular legends have created an erroneous impression of the Spanish Inquisition as an institution running amok, framing innocent victims and routinely subjecting them to torture. In fact, inquisitors usually observed rules of evidence, and they released many suspects after investigation. Yet when they detected heresy, inquisitors could be ruthless. They sentenced hundreds of victims to hang from the gallows or burn at the stake and imprisoned many others for extended periods of time. Fear of the Inquisition deterred nobles from adopting Protestant views out of political ambition, and inquisitors also used their influence to silence those who threatened the Spanish monarchy. From 1559 to 1576, for example, inquisitors imprisoned the archbishop of Toledo—the highest Roman Catholic church official in all of Spain—because of his political independence.

Constitutional States

During the seventeenth and eighteenth centuries, as they sought to restore order after the Thirty Years' War, European states developed along two lines. Rulers in England and the Netherlands shared authority with representative institutions and created constitutional

The Execution of King Charles I. | In this contemporary painting, the executioner holds up the just-severed head of King Charles I of England. The sight of a royal execution overcomes one woman, who faints (at bottom). *The Granger Collection, New York.*

states, whereas monarchs in France, Spain, Austria, Prussia, and Russia concentrated power in their own hands and created a form of state known as absolute monarchy.

CONSTITUTIONAL STATES During the seventeenth century the island kingdom of England and the maritime Dutch republic evolved governments that recognized rights pertaining to individuals and representative institutions. Their constitutional states took different forms: in England a constitutional monarchy emerged, whereas in the Netherlands a republic based on representative government emerged. In neither land did constitutional government come easily into being: in England it followed a civil war (1642–1649), and in the Netherlands it followed a long struggle for independence in the late sixteenth century. In both lands, however, constitutional government strengthened the state and provided a political framework that enabled merchants to flourish as never before in European experience.

THE ENGLISH CIVIL WAR Constitutional government came to England after political and religious disputes led to the English civil war. Politically, disputes arose between the king and the parliament over the king's ability to institute new taxes without parliamentary approval, while religious tensions between the Anglican king and a vocal group of zealous, reform-minded Calvinists in Parliament created a deep rift between the two branches of government. By 1641 King Charles I and Parliament were at loggerheads. Both sides raised armies. In the conflicts that followed, Parliamentary forces captured Charles and in 1649 executed him for tyranny. Yet English problems of government continued through a dictatorial Puritan regime as well as the restoration of the monarchy in 1660, until in 1688 Parliament deposed King James II and invited his daughter Mary and her Dutch husband, William of Orange, to assume the throne. The resulting arrangement provided that kings would rule in cooperation with Parliament, thus guaranteeing that nobles, merchants, and other constituencies would enjoy representation in government affairs.

Charles I of England
www.mhhe.com/bentleybrief2e

THE DUTCH REPUBLIC As in England, a combination of political and religious tensions led to conflict from which constitutional government emerged in the Netherlands. In the mid–sixteenth century, authority over the Low Countries, including modern-day Belgium as well as the Netherlands, rested with King Philip II of Spain.

In 1566 Philip, a devout Roman Catholic, moved to suppress an increasingly popular Calvinist movement in the Netherlands—a measure that provoked large-scale rebellion against Spanish rule. In 1581 a group of Dutch provinces proclaimed themselves the independent United Provinces. Representative assemblies organized local affairs in each of the provinces, and on that foundation political leaders built a Dutch republic. Although Spain did not officially recognize the independence of the United Provinces until 1648, the Dutch republic was effectively organizing affairs in the northern Low Countries by the early seventeenth century.

In both England and the Dutch republic, merchants were especially prominent in political affairs, and state policy in both lands favored maritime trade and the building of commercial empires overseas. The constitutional states allowed entrepreneurs to pursue their economic interests with minimal interference from public authorities, and during the late seventeenth and eighteenth centuries both states experienced extraordinary prosperity as a result of those policies. Indeed, in many ways the English and Dutch states represented an alliance between merchants and rulers that worked to the benefit of both. Merchants supported the state with the wealth that they generated through trade—especially overseas trade—and rulers followed policies that looked after the interests of their merchants.

Absolute Monarchies

Whereas constitutional states devised ways to share power and authority, absolute monarchies stood on a theoretical foundation known as the divine right of kings. This theory held that kings derived their authority from God and served as "God's lieutenants upon earth." There was no role in divine-right theory for common subjects or even nobles in public affairs: the king made law and determined policy. In fact, absolute monarchs always relied on support from nobles and other social groups, but the claims of divine-right theory clearly reflected efforts at royal centralization.

The most conspicuous absolutist state was the French monarchy. The architect of French absolutism was a prominent church official, Cardinal Richelieu, who served as chief minister to King Louis XIII from 1624 to 1642. Richelieu worked systematically to undermine the power of the nobility and enhance the authority of the king. He destroyed nobles' castles and ruthlessly crushed aristocratic conspiracies. As a counterweight to the nobility, Richelieu built a large bureaucracy staffed by commoners loyal to the king. He also appointed officials to supervise the implementation of royal policy in the provinces.

Louis XIV and Molière
www.mhhe.com/bentleybrief2e

THE SUN KING The ruler who best epitomized royal absolutism was King Louis XIV (reigned 1643–1715). In fact, Louis XIV once reportedly declared that he was himself the state: "*l'état c'est moi.*" Known as *le roi soleil*—"the sun king"—Louis surrounded himself with splendor befitting one who ruled by divine right. During the 1670s he built a magnificent residence at Versailles, and in the 1680s he moved his court there. Louis's palace at Versailles was the largest building in Europe, with 230 acres of formal gardens and 1,400 fountains. All prominent nobles established residences at Versailles for their families and entourages. Louis strongly encouraged them to live at court, where he and his staff could keep an eye on them, and ambitious nobles gravitated there anyway in hopes of winning influence with the king. While nobles living at Versailles mastered the intricacies of court ritual and attended banquets, concerts, operas, balls, and theatrical performances, Louis and his ministers ran the state, maintained a huge army, waged war, and promoted economic development. In effect, Louis provided the nobility with luxurious accommodations and endless entertainment in exchange for absolute rule.

Richelieu (RISH-uh-loo)
Louis (LOO-ee)
Versailles (vehr-SEYE)

VERSAILLES. | King Louis XIV and his entourage approach the main gate of Versailles (bottom right). Though only partially constructed at the time of this painting (1668), Versailles was already a spacious and luxurious retreat for Louis and his court.

ABSOLUTISM IN RUSSIA UNDER PETER I Louis XIV was not the only absolute monarch of early modern Europe: Spanish, Austrian, and Prussian rulers embraced similar policies. Yet the potential of absolutism to increase state power was particularly conspicuous in the case of Russia, where tsars of the Romanov dynasty (1613–1917) tightly centralized government functions. Most important of the Romanov tsars was Peter I (reigned 1682–1725), widely known as Peter the Great, who inaugurated a thoroughgoing process of state transformation. Peter had a burning desire to transform Russia, a huge but underpopulated land, into a great military power like those that had recently emerged in western Europe. In 1697–1698 he led a large party of Russian observers on a tour of Germany, the Netherlands, and England to learn about western European administrative methods and military technology. His traveling companions often behaved crudely by western European standards: they consumed beer, wine, and brandy in quantities that astonished their hosts, and King William III sent Peter a bill for damages done by his entourage at the country house where they lodged in England.

On his return to Moscow, Peter set Russia spinning. He reformed the army by providing his forces with extensive training and equipping them with modern weapons. He ordered aristocrats to study mathematics and geometry so that they could calculate how to aim cannons accurately, and he began the construction of a navy. He also overhauled the government bureaucracy to facilitate tax collection and improve administrative efficiency. He even commanded his aristocratic subjects to wear western European fashions and ordered men to shave their traditional beards. These measures provoked spirited protest among those who resented the influence of western European ways. Yet Peter was so insistent on

Romanov (ruh-MAH-nuhf)

the observance of his policies that he reportedly went into the streets and personally hacked the beards off recalcitrants' faces. Perhaps the best symbol of his policies was St. Petersburg, a newly built seaport that Peter opened in 1703 to serve as a magnificent capital city and a haven for Russia's fledgling navy.

CATHERINE II AND THE LIMITS OF REFORM The most able of Peter's successors was Catherine II (reigned 1762–1796), also known as Catherine the Great. Like Peter, Catherine sought to make Russia a great power. She worked to improve governmental efficiency, and she promoted economic development in Russia's towns. For a while, she even worked to improve the conditions of Russia's oppressed peasantry by restricting the punishments—such as torture, beating, and mutilation—that noble landowners could inflict on the serfs who worked their lands.

However, Catherine's interest in social reform cooled rapidly when it seemed to inspire challenges to her rule. She faced a particularly unsettling trial in 1773 and 1774, when a disgruntled former soldier named Yemelian Pugachev mounted a rebellion in the steppe lands north of the Caspian Sea. Pugachev raised a motley army of adventurers, exiles, peasants, and serfs who killed thousands of noble landowners and government officials before imperial forces crushed the uprising. Government authorities took the captured Pugachev to Moscow in chains, beheaded him, quartered his body, and displayed his parts throughout the city as a warning against rebellion. Thereafter, Catherine's first concern was the preservation of autocratic rule rather than the transformation of Russia according to western European models.

Thus, in Russia as in other European lands, absolutist policies resulted in tight centralization and considerable strengthening of the state. The enhanced power that flowed from absolutism became dramatically clear in the period 1772 to 1797, when Austria, Prussia, and Catherine II's Russia picked the weak kingdom of Poland apart. In a series of three "partitions," the predatory absolutist states seized Polish territory and absorbed it into their own realms, ultimately wiping Poland entirely off the map. The lesson of the partitions was clear: any European state that hoped to survive needed to construct an effective government that could respond promptly to challenges and opportunities.

The European States System

Whether they relied on absolutist or constitutional principles, European governments of early modern times built states much more powerful than those of their medieval predecessors. This round of state development led to difficulties within Europe, since conflicting interests fueled interstate competition and war. In the absence of an imperial authority capable of imposing and maintaining order in Europe, sovereign states had to find ways to resolve conflicts by themselves.

PSI map The Peace of Westphalia www.mhhe.com/bentleybrief2e

THE PEACE OF WESTPHALIA The Thirty Years' War demonstrated the chaos and devastation that conflict could bring. In an effort to avoid tearing their society apart, European states ended the Thirty Years' War with the Peace of Westphalia (1648), which laid the foundations for a system of independent, competing states. By the treaty's terms, the European states regarded one another as sovereign and equal. They also mutually recognized their rights to organize their own domestic and religious affairs and agreed that political and diplomatic affairs were to be conducted by states acting in their own interests. European religious unity had disappeared, and the era of the sovereign state had arrived.

The Peace of Westphalia did not bring an end to war. Indeed, war was almost constant in early modern Europe. Most conflicts were minor affairs, but some grew to sizable proportions. Most notable among them were the wars of Louis XIV and the Seven Years' War. Between 1668 and 1713, the sun king sought to expand his borders east into

Yemelian Pugachev (yehm-eel-ian puh-gah-chehf)
Westphalia (west-FEY-lee-uh)

MAP 20.2 | Europe after the Peace of Westphalia, 1648. Both England and the Netherlands became constitutional states with strong commercial interests. Compare this map with map 20.1 ***How have the boundaries of the Holy Roman Empire changed, and why?***

Germany and to absorb Spain and the Spanish Netherlands into his kingdom. That prospect prompted England, the United Provinces, and Austria to mount a coalition against Louis. Later the Seven Years' War (1756–1763) pitted France, Austria, and Russia against Britain and Prussia, and it merged with conflicts between France and Britain in India and North America to become a global war for imperial supremacy.

THE BALANCE OF POWER These shifting alliances illustrate the principal foundation of European diplomacy in early modern times—the balance of power. No ruler wanted to see another state dominate all the others. Thus, when any particular state began to wax strong, others formed coalitions against it. By playing balance-of-power politics, statesmen prevented the building of empires and ensured that Europe would be a land of independent, sovereign, competing states.

MILITARY DEVELOPMENT Frequent wars and balance-of-power diplomacy drained the resources of individual states but strengthened European society as a whole. European states competed vigorously and sought to develop the most expert military leadership and the most effective weapons for their arsenals. States organized military academies where officers received advanced education in strategy and tactics. Demand for powerful weapons stimulated the development of a sophisticated armaments industry. Gun foundries manufactured cannons of increasing size, range, power, and accuracy as well as small arms that allowed infantry to unleash withering volleys against their enemies.

In China, India, and Islamic lands, imperial states had little incentive to encourage similar technological innovation in the armaments industry. These states possessed the forces and weapons they needed to maintain order within their boundaries, and they rarely encountered foreign threats backed up with superior armaments. In Europe, however, failure to keep up with the latest improvements in arms technology could lead to defeat on the battlefield and decline in state power. Thus Europeans continuously sought to improve their military arsenals, and as a result, by the eighteenth century European armaments outperformed all others.

Early Capitalist Society

While the Protestant Reformation and the emergence of sovereign states brought religious and political change, a rapidly expanding population and economy encouraged the development of capitalism, which in turn led to a restructuring of European economy and society. Technologies of communication and transportation enabled businessmen to profit from distant markets, and merchants and manufacturers increasingly organized their affairs with the market rather than local communities in mind. Although capitalism generated considerable wealth, its effects were uneven and sometimes unsettling. Even in western Europe, where development and prosperity were most noticeable, early capitalism sometimes required painful adjustments to new conditions.

Population Growth and Urbanization

AMERICAN FOOD CROPS The foundation of European economic expansion in early modern times was a rapidly growing population, which reflected improved nutrition and decreasing mortality. The Columbian exchange enriched European diets by introducing new food crops to European fields and tables. Most notable of the introductions was the potato, which provided a welcome and inexpensive source of carbohydrates for peasants and laborers all over Europe. Other American crops, such as tomatoes and peppers, added vitamins and tangy flavor to European diets.

PSI map — Black Death www.mhhe.com/bentleybrief2e

Since better-nourished populations are less susceptible to illness, new food crops also improved the overall resistance of Europeans to old diseases such as smallpox, dysentery, influenza, and typhus. Bubonic plague, a devastating epidemic killer during the fourteenth and fifteenth centuries, also receded from European society. Although plague made periodic appearances throughout the early modern era, epidemics were rare and isolated events after the mid–seventeenth century.

ENCOUNTERS IN THE TRANSFORMATION OF EUROPE. During the sixteenth and seventeenth centuries, the peoples of different European states frequently encountered one another through long and bloody wars. Although such wars caused widespread destruction, in what ways did the constant competition between states also strengthen European society?

POPULATION GROWTH AND URBANIZATION Although European birthrates did not rise dramatically in early modern times, decreasing mortality resulted in rapid population growth. In 1500 the population of Europe, including Russia, was about 81 million. By 1700 the population had risen to 120 million, and in the next century it reached 180 million. Such rapid population growth drove a process of equally rapid urbanization. In the mid–sixteenth century, for example, the population of Paris was about 130,000, and that of London was about 60,000. A century later the populations of both cities had risen to 500,000. Other European cities also experienced rapid growth, including Madrid, Amsterdam, Berlin, Copenhagen, Dublin, Stockholm, and Vienna, to name only a few.

Early Capitalism and Protoindustrialization

THE NATURE OF CAPITALISM Population growth and rapid urbanization helped spur a round of remarkable economic development. That economic growth coincided with the emergence of capitalism—an economic system in which private parties make their goods and services available on a free market and seek to take advantage of market conditions to profit from their activities. Private parties own the land, machinery, tools, equipment, buildings, workshops, and raw materials needed for production. Private parties also hire workers and decide for themselves what to produce: economic decisions are the prerogative of capitalist businessmen, not governments or social superiors. The center of a capitalist system is the market in which businessmen compete with one another, and the forces of supply and demand determine the prices received for goods and services. The goal is to realize handsome profits from these activities.

SUPPLY AND DEMAND The desire to accumulate wealth and realize profits was by no means new. Indeed, for several thousand years before the early modern era, merchants in China, southeast Asia, India, southwest Asia, the Mediterranean basin, and sub-Saharan Africa had pursued commercial ventures in hopes of realizing profits. During early modern times, however, European merchants and entrepreneurs transformed their society in a way that none of their predecessors had done. The capitalist economic order developed as businessmen learned to take advantage of market conditions in distant places via efficient networks of transportation and communication. For example, Dutch merchants might purchase cheap grain from Poland, store it in Amsterdam until they learned about a famine in the Mediterranean, and then transport it and sell it in southern France or Spain at an enormous profit.

Private parties organized an array of institutions and services to support early capitalism. Banks, for example, appeared in all the major commercial cities of Europe: they held funds on account for safekeeping and granted loans to merchants or entrepreneurs launching new business ventures. Insurance companies mitigated financial losses from risky undertakings such as transoceanic voyages, and stock exchanges provided markets where investors could buy and sell shares in joint-stock companies and trade in other commodities as well.

JOINT-STOCK COMPANIES Joint-stock companies were especially important institutions in early capitalist society. Large trading companies such as the English East India Company and its Dutch counterpart, the Vereenigde Oost-Indische Compagnie (VOC), spread the risks attached to expensive business enterprises and also took advantage of extensive communications and transportation networks. The trading companies organized commercial ventures on a larger scale than ever before in world history. They were the principal foundations of the global economy that emerged in early modern times, and they were the direct ancestors of contemporary multinational corporations.

POLITICS AND EMPIRE Capitalism did not develop in a political vacuum. On the contrary, it emerged with the active support of government authorities who saw a capitalist order as the one best suited to their individual and collective interests. Merchants were especially influential in the affairs of the English and Dutch states, so it is not surprising that these lands adopted policies that were most favorable to capitalist enterprises throughout the early modern era. The English and Dutch states recognized individuals' rights to possess private property and protected their financial interests. They also authorized joint-stock companies to explore and colonize distant lands in search of commercial opportunities. Indeed, imperial expansion and colonial rule were crucial for the development of capitalism, since they enabled European merchants to gain access to the natural resources and commodities that they distributed so effectively through their transportation networks.

Quite apart from its influence on trade and the distribution of goods, capitalism also encouraged European entrepreneurs to organize new ways to manufacture goods. For centuries,

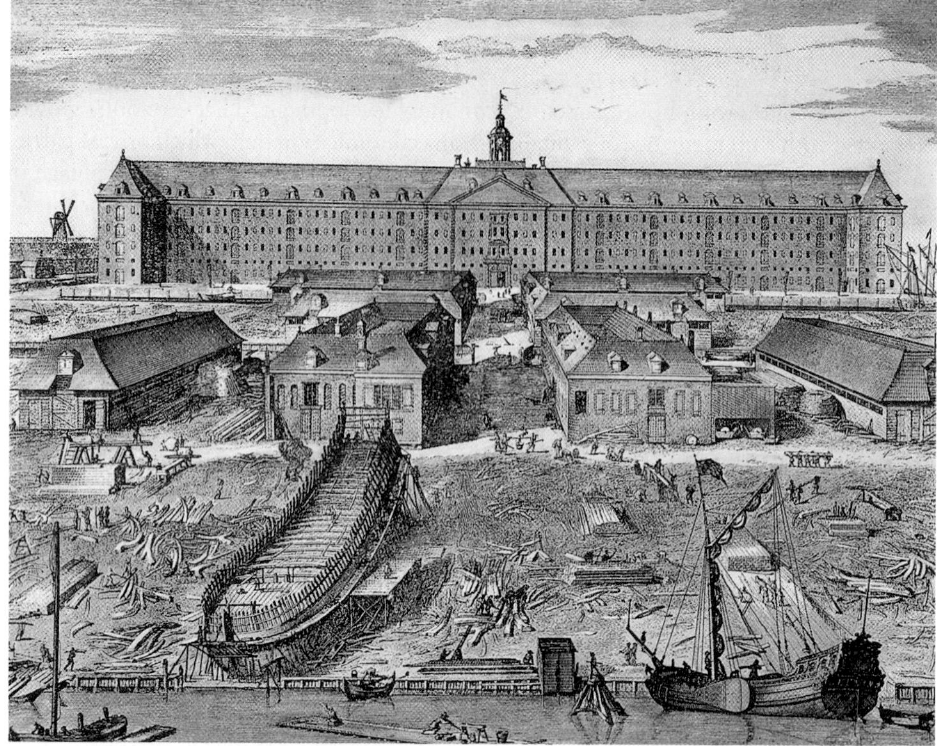

DUTCH SHIPYARD. An anonymous engraving depicts workers building a massive, ocean-going sailing ship. In the seventeenth century, Dutch ships were inexpensive to operate, yet they accommodated abundant cargoes. ***What kinds of cargoes were Dutch ships likely to carry in this period?*** *© The Granger Collection, New York.*

craft guilds had monopolized the production of goods such as textiles and metalwares in European towns and cities. Guilds fixed prices and wages, and they regulated standards of quality. They sought not to realize profits so much as to protect markets and preserve their members' places in society. As a result, they actively discouraged competition.

THE PUTTING-OUT SYSTEM Capitalist entrepreneurs seeking profits found the guilds inflexible, so they sidestepped them and moved production into the countryside. There, they organized a "putting-out system" by which they delivered unfinished materials such as raw wool to rural households. Men and women in the countryside would spin and weave the wool into cloth and then cut and assemble the cloth into garments. The entrepreneur picked up the finished goods, paid the workers, and sold the items on the market for a handsome profit. The putting-out system represented an early effort to organize efficient industrial production and remained a prominent feature of European society until the nineteenth century. In fact, some historians refer to the seventeenth and eighteenth centuries as an age of "protoindustrialization."

Social Change in Early Modern Europe

Capitalist economic development brought unsettling change to European lands. In western Europe, the putting-out system introduced considerable sums of money into the countryside, which tended to undermine long-established patterns of rural life even as it brought material benefits such as improved food, clothing, and furnishings to rural households. Increased wealth meant that individuals suddenly acquired incomes that enabled them to become financially independent of their families and neighbors, and many feared that these individuals—especially young adults and women—might abandon their kin and way of life altogether as a result.

In eastern Europe, the putting-out system did not become a prominent feature of production, but early capitalism prompted deep social change there as well. Eastern Europe had very few cities in early modern times, so in agrarian states such as Poland, Bohemia, and Russia, most people had no alternative to working in the countryside. Landlords took advantage of this situation by forcing peasants to work under extremely harsh conditions.

SERFDOM IN RUSSIA Russia in particular was a vast but sparsely populated empire with little trade or manufacturing. Out of a concern to retain the allegiance of the powerful nobles who owned most of Russia's land, the Romanov tsars restricted the freedoms of most Russian peasants and tied them to the land as serfs. The institution of serfdom had emerged in the early middle ages as a labor system that required peasants to provide labor services for landowners and prevented them from marrying or moving away without their landlords' permission. Although serfdom came to an end in western Europe after the fifteenth century, in eastern Europe landowners and rulers tightened restrictions on peasants during the sixteenth century. In Russia, for example, landlords commonly sold serfs to one another as if they were private property. In effect, the Romanovs won the support of the Russian nobles by ensuring them that laborers would be available to work their estates, which otherwise would have been worthless. Under these conditions, landlords operated estates with inexpensive labor and derived enormous incomes from the sale of agricultural products on the market.

These arrangements played crucial roles in the emergence of capitalism. In the larger economy of early modern Europe, eastern European lands produced agricultural products and raw materials based on semi-free labor, which were then exported to western Europe to sustain its large and growing free wage labor force. Already by the early sixteenth century, consumers in the Netherlands depended for their survival on grains imported from Poland and Russia through the Baltic Sea. Thus it was possible for capitalism to flourish in western Europe only because the peasants and semi-free serfs of eastern Europe provided inexpensive foods and raw materials that fueled economic development. From its earliest days, capitalist economic organization had implications for peoples and lands far removed from the centers of capitalism itself.

PROFITS AND ETHICS Capitalism also posed moral challenges. Medieval theologians had regarded profit making as morally dangerous, since profiteers looked to their own advantage rather than to the welfare of the larger community. But capitalism found advocates who sought to explain its principles and portray it as a socially beneficial form of economic organization. Most important of the early apostles of capitalism was the Scottish philosopher Adam Smith (1723–1790), who held that society would prosper when individuals pursued their own economic interests.

Nevertheless, prosperity was unattainable for all or even most early modern Europeans, which meant that the transition to capitalist economic practices was a long and painful process that generated deep social strains throughout Europe. Those strains often manifested themselves in violence: bandits plagued the countryside of early modern Europe, and muggers turned whole sections of large cities into danger zones. Some historians believe that witch-hunting activities reflected social tensions generated by early capitalism and that accusations of witchcraft represented hostility toward women who were becoming economically independent of their husbands and families.

THE NUCLEAR FAMILY In some ways capitalism favored the nuclear family as the principal unit of society. Although for centuries European couples had set up independent households, early capitalism offered further opportunities for independent families to increase their wealth by producing goods for sale on the market. As nuclear families became more important economically, they also became more socially and emotionally independent. Love between a man and a woman became a more important consideration in the making of marriages than the interests of the larger extended families, and affection between parents and their children became a more important ingredient of family life. Capitalism did not necessarily cause these changes in family life, but it may have encouraged developments that helped to define the nature and the role of the family in modern European society.

PTOLEMAIC UNIVERSE. | A woodcut illustration depicts the Ptolemaic universe with the earth at the center surrounded by spheres holding the planets and the stars.

SCIENCE AND ENLIGHTENMENT

While experiencing religious, political, economic, and social change, western Europe also underwent intellectual and cultural transformation. Astronomers and physicists rejected classical Greek and Roman authorities, whose theories had dominated scientific thought during the middle ages, and based their understanding of the natural world on direct observation and mathematical reasoning. During the seventeenth and eighteenth centuries, they elaborated a new vision of the earth and the larger universe in a process known as the scientific revolution. Some European intellectuals then sought to use scientific methods and reason to overhaul moral, social, and political thought. In the process, they weakened the influence of churches in western Europe and encouraged the development of secular values.

The Reconception of the Universe

THE PTOLEMAIC UNIVERSE Until the seventeenth century, European astronomers based their understanding of the universe on the work of the Greek scholar Claudius Ptolemy of Alexandria. In the middle of the second century C.E., Ptolemy produced a work known as the *Almagest,* which envisioned a motionless earth surrounded by a series of nine hollow, concentric spheres that revolved around it. Each of the first seven spheres had one of the observable heavenly bodies embedded in its shell. The eighth sphere held the stars, and an empty ninth sphere surrounded the whole cosmos and provided the spin that kept all the others moving. Beyond the spheres Christian astronomers located heaven, the realm of God.

Ptolemaic system
www.mhhe.com/
bentleybrief2e

Following Ptolemy, astronomers believed that the heavens consisted of a pure substance that did not experience change or corruption and was not subject to the physical laws that governed the world below the moon. They also held that heavenly bodies followed perfect circular paths in making their revolutions around the earth.

PLANETARY MOVEMENT This cosmology, however, did not mesh readily with the erratic movements of the planets, which sometimes slowed down, stopped, or even turned back on their courses. Astronomers went to great lengths to explain planetary behavior as the result of perfect circular movements. The result was an awkward series of adjustments known as epicycles—small, circular revolutions that planets made around a point in their spheres, even while the spheres themselves revolved around the earth.

THE COPERNICAN UNIVERSE In 1543, however, the Polish astronomer Nicolaus Copernicus published *On the Revolutions of the Heavenly Spheres,* which broke with Ptolemaic theory. Copernicus argued that the sun rather than the earth stood at the center of the universe and that the planets, including the earth, revolved around the sun. Although this new theory harmonized much better with observational data, it did not receive a warm welcome. Copernicus's ideas not only challenged prevailing scientific theories but also threatened cherished religious beliefs, which held that the earth and humanity were unique creations of God.

Ptolemaic (TAWL-oh-may-ihk)

SOURCES FROM THE PAST

Galileo Galilei, Letter to the Grand Duchess Christina

The Italian physicist and astronomer Galileo Galilei (1564–1642) was one of the most important European scientists in the early 1600s. His staunch defense of Nicolaus Copernicus' theory of a sun-centered universe threatened Catholic clergy, who were worried that such a theory threatened the authority of both the Bible and the Church. In 1615 Galileo, himself a devout Catholic, defended his scientific beliefs in a published letter to Christina, the grand duchess of Tuscany. Although the Church forced Galileo to publicly renounce his scientific beliefs in 1632, over the long term his writings contributed greatly to the reconception of the universe using the new scientific methodology.

Some years ago, as Your Serene Highness well knows, I discovered in the heavens many things that had not been seen before our own age. The novelty of these things, as well as some consequences which followed from them in contradiction to the physical notions commonly held among academic philosophers, stirred up against me no small number of professors—as if I had placed these things in the sky with my own hands in order to upset nature and overturn the sciences. They seemed to forget that the increase of known truths stimulates the investigation, establishment, and growth of the arts; not their diminution or destruction. . . .

Persisting in their original resolve to destroy me and everything mine by any means they can think of, these men are aware of my views in astronomy and philosophy. They know that as to the arrangement of the parts of the universe, I hold the sun to be situated motionless in the center of the revolution of the celestial orbs while the earth rotates on its axis and revolves around the sun. They know also that I support this position not only by refuting the arguments of Ptolemy and Aristotle, but by producing many counter-arguments; in particular, some which relate to physical effects whose causes can perhaps be assigned in no other way. In addition there are astronomical arguments derived from many things in my new celestial discoveries that confute the Ptolemaic system while admirably agreeing with and confirming the contrary hypothesis. Possibly because they are disturbed by the known truth of other propositions of mine which differ from those commonly held, and therefore mistrusting their defense so long as they confine themselves to the field of philosophy, these men have resolved to fabricate a shield for their fallacies out of the mantle of pretended religion and the authority of the Bible. These they apply, with little judgment, to the refutation of arguments that they do not understand and have not even listened to. . . .

. . . I think that in discussions of physical problems we ought to begin not from the authority of scriptural passages but from sense-experiences and necessary demonstrations; for the holy Bible and the phenomena of nature proceed alike from the divine Word, the former as the dictate of the Holy Ghost and the latter as the observant executrix of God's commands. It is necessary for the Bible, in order to be accommodated to the understanding of every man, to speak many things which appear to differ from the absolute truth so far as the bare meaning of the words is concerned. But Nature, on the other hand, is inexorable and immutable; she never transgresses the laws imposed upon her, or cares a whit whether her abstruse reasons and methods of operation are understandable to men. For that reason it appears that nothing physical which sense-experience sets before our eyes, or which necessary demonstrations prove to us, ought to be called in question (much less condemned) upon the testimony of biblical passages which may have some different meaning beneath their words. For the Bible is not chained in every expression to conditions as strict as those which govern all physical effects; nor is God any less excellently revealed in Nature's actions than in the sacred statements of the Bible.

■ **Why did Galileo's critics, mentioned in the passage above, find fault with his scientific observations?**

SOURCE: Alfred J. Andrea and James H. Overfield. *The Human Record: Sources of Global History,* 3rd ed., vol. II: *Since 1500.* Boston and New York: Houghton Mifflin, 1998.

The Scientific Revolution

In time, though, Copernicus's theory inspired some astronomers to examine the heavens in fresh ways, using precise observational data and mathematical reasoning. Gradually, they abandoned the Ptolemaic in favor of the Copernican model of the universe. Some also began to apply their analytical methods to mechanics—the branch of science that deals with moving bodies—and by the mid–seventeenth century accurate observation and mathematical reasoning dominated both mechanics and astronomy. Indeed, reliance on observation and mathematics transformed the study of the natural world and brought about the scientific revolution.

GALILEO GALILEI The works of two mathematicians—Johannes Kepler of Germany and Galileo Galilei of Italy—rang the death knell for the Ptolemaic universe. Kepler (1571–1630) demonstrated that planetary orbits are elliptical, not circular as in Ptolemaic theory. Galileo (1564–1642) showed that the heavens were not the perfect, unblemished realm that Ptolemaic astronomers assumed. Using the recently invented telescope, Galileo was able to observe spots on the sun and mountains on the moon. He also caught sight of distant stars previously undetectable to the naked eye, which implied that the universe was much larger than anyone had previously suspected.

ISAAC NEWTON The new approach to science culminated in the work of the English mathematician Isaac Newton (1642–1727), who depended on accurate observation and mathematical reasoning to construct a powerful synthesis of astronomy and mechanics. Newton outlined his views on the natural world in an epoch-making volume of 1687 titled *Mathematical Principles of Natural Philosophy.* Newton's work united the heavens and the earth in a vast, cosmic system. He argued that a law of universal gravitation regulates the motions of bodies throughout the universe, and he offered precise mathematical explanations of the laws that govern movements of bodies on the earth. His laws also allowed him to explain a vast range of seemingly unrelated phenomena, such as the ebb and flow of the tides and the eccentric orbits of planets and comets. Until the twentieth century, Newton's universe served as the unquestioned framework for the physical sciences.

Inspired by the dramatic discoveries of astronomers and physicists, other scientists began to construct fresh approaches to understanding the natural world. During the seventeenth and eighteenth centuries, anatomy, physiology, microbiology, chemistry, and botany underwent a thorough overhaul, as scientists tested their theories against direct observation of natural phenomena and explained them in rigorous mathematical terms.

The Enlightenment

Newton's vision of the universe was so powerful and persuasive that its influence extended well beyond science. His work suggested that rational analysis of human behavior and institutions could lead to fresh insights about the human as well as the natural world. From Scotland to Sicily and from Philadelphia to Moscow, European and Euro-American thinkers launched an ambitious project to discover natural laws that governed human society in the same way that Newton's laws regulated the universe. They went about this project in different ways. Some, such as John Locke (1632–1704), sought the natural laws of politics. Others, such as Adam Smith, sought to comprehend the laws of economics. Like the early modern scientists, however, they all abandoned Aristotelian philosophy and Christian religion as sources of authority in their quest to subject the human world to purely rational analysis. The result of their work was a movement known as the Enlightenment.

The center of Enlightenment thought was France, where prominent intellectuals known collectively as *philosophes* ("philosophers") advanced the cause of reason. The philosophes addressed their works more to the educated public than to scholars: instead of formal philosophical treatises, they mostly composed histories, novels, dramas, satires, and pamphlets on religious, moral, and political issues.

PSI doc Voltaire on nobility
www.mhhe.com/bentleybrief2e

VOLTAIRE More than any other philosophe, François-Marie Arouet (1694–1778) epitomized the spirit of the Enlightenment. Writing under the pen name Voltaire, he championed individual freedom and attacked any institution sponsoring intolerant or op-

Voltaire (vohl-TAIR)

TYCHO BRAHE'S OBSERVATORY. | In this specialized but eccentric observatory called Uraniborg, the scientist Tycho Brahe collected data related to astronomical phenomena. Although the castle was custom built for Brahe in 1584 on a Danish island, the withdrawal of support from the Danish king led Brahe to abandon it in 1597.

pressive policies. Targets of his often caustic wit included the French monarchy and the Roman Catholic church. When the king of France sought to save money by reducing the number of horses kept in royal stables, for example, Voltaire suggested that it would be more effective to get rid of the asses who rode the horses. Voltaire also waged a long literary campaign against the Roman Catholic church, which he held responsible for fanaticism, intolerance, and incalculable human suffering. Indeed, Voltaire himself—like many other philosophes—was a deist and denied the supernatural teachings of Christianity. Instead, deists held that, although a powerful god had created the universe, once created, the universe operated by itself according to rational and natural laws.

THE THEORY OF PROGRESS Most philosophes were optimistic about the future of the world and humanity. In fact, they believed that rational understanding of human and natural affairs would bring about a new era of progress and individual freedom and would lead to the construction of a prosperous, just, and equitable society. Although those fond wishes did not come to pass, the Enlightenment did indeed help to bring about a thorough cultural transformation of European society. For one thing, it weakened the influence of organized religion by encouraging the replacement of Christian values with a new set of secular values based on reason. Furthermore, the Enlightenment encouraged political and cultural leaders to subject society to rational analysis and intervene actively in its affairs in the interests of promoting progress and prosperity. In many ways the Enlightenment legacy continues to influence European and Euro-American societies.

deism (DEE-iz'm)

SUMMARY

During the early modern era, European society experienced a series of profound and sometimes unsettling changes. The Protestant Reformation ended the religious unity of western Christendom and led to more than a century of religious conflict. Centralizing monarchs strengthened their realms and built a society of sovereign, autonomous, and intensely competitive states. Capitalist entrepreneurs reorganized the production and distribution of manufactured goods, and although their methods led to increased wealth, their quest for efficiency and profits clashed with traditional values. Modern science based on direct observation and mathematical explanations emerged as a powerful tool for the investigation of the natural world. Some people used scientific methods to investigate the human world and created a new moral thought based strictly on science and reason. At just the time that European merchants, colonists, and adventurers were seeking opportunities in the larger world, European society was becoming more powerful, more experimental, and more competitive than ever before.

STUDY TERMS

absolutism (396)
Anglicans (390)
Calvinists (389)
capitalism (400)
Catherine the Great (398)
constitutional states (395)
Enlightenment (406)
Galileo Galilei (406)
Habsburgs (393)
Isaac Newton (406)
Johannes Kepler (406)
Louis XIV (396)
Martin Luther (387)
Nicolaus Copernicus (404)
Ninety-five Theses (387)
Peace of Westphalia (398)
Peter the Great (397)
philosophes (406)
Protestant Reformation (387)
protoindustrialization (401)
Ptolemaic system (404)
scientific revolution (404)
Society of Jesus (390)
Spanish Inquisition (394)
Thirty Years' War (391)
Voltaire (406)
witch hunts (391)

FOR FURTHER READING

Fernand Braudel. *Civilization and Capitalism, 15th to 18th Century.* 3 vols. Trans. by S. Reynolds. New York, 1981–84. A rich analysis of early capitalist society by one of the greatest historians of the twentieth century.

Paul Dukes. *The Making of Russian Absolutism, 1613–1801.* 2nd ed. London, 1990. A succinct study of two disparate centuries, the seventeenth and eighteenth, and two influential tsars, Peter and Catherine.

Robert S. Duplessis. *Transitions to Capitalism in Early Modern Europe.* Cambridge, 1997. A valuable synthesis of recent research on early capitalism and protoindustrialization.

Margaret Jacob. *The Cultural Meaning of the Scientific Revolution.* New York, 1989. Explores the larger cultural and social implications of early modern science.

E. L. Jones. *The European Miracle: Environments, Economies, and Geopolitics in the History of Europe and Asia.* 2nd ed. Cambridge, 1987. Examines European politics and economic growth in comparative perspective.

Thomas S. Kuhn. *The Structure of Scientific Revolutions.* 3rd ed. Chicago, 1997. An influential theoretical work that views scientific thought in larger social and cultural context.

William H. McNeill. *The Pursuit of Power: Technology, Armed Force, and Society since A.D. 1000.* Chicago, 1982. Insightful analysis exploring the influence of sovereign states and early capitalism on military technology and organization.

Eugene F. Rice Jr. and Anthony Grafton. *The Foundations of Early Modern Europe, 1460–1559.* 2nd ed. New York, 1994. Excellent introduction to political, social, economic, and cultural developments.

Simon Schama. *The Embarrassment of Riches: An Interpretation of Dutch Culture in the Seventeenth Century.* New York, 1987. A marvelous popular study of the wealthy Dutch republic at its height.

Keith Thomas. *Religion and the Decline of Magic.* New York, 1971. A riveting analysis of popular culture in early modern times, especially strong on the explanation of magic and witchcraft.

New Worlds: The Americas and Oceania

21

A remarkable young woman played a pivotal role in the Spanish conquest of Mexico. Originally called Malintzin, she is better known by her Spanish name, Doña Marina. Born about 1500 to a noble family in central Mexico, Doña Marina's mother tongue was Nahuatl, the principal language of the Aztec empire. When she was a girl, Doña Marina's family sent her to the Mexican coast as a slave. Her new family later passed her on to their neighbors on the Yucatan peninsula, where she also became fluent in the Maya language.

When Hernán Cortés arrived on the Mexican coast in 1519, only one of his soldiers could speak the Maya language spoken by coastal peoples. But he had no way to communicate with the Nahuatl-speaking peoples of central Mexico until a Maya chieftain presented him with twelve young women, including Doña Marina, as a token of alliance. Doña Marina's linguistic talents enabled Cortés to communicate through an improbable chain of languages—from Spanish to Maya to Nahuatl and then back again—while making his way to the Aztec capital of Tenochtitlan. (Doña Marina soon learned Spanish and thus eliminated the Maya link in the linguistic chain.)

Doña Marina provided Cortés with intelligence and diplomatic as well as linguistic services. On several occasions she learned of plans by native peoples to overwhelm and destroy the tiny Spanish army, and she alerted Cortés to the danger in time for him to forestall an attack. She also helped Cortés negotiate with emissaries from the major cities of central Mexico. Indeed, in the absence of Doña Marina's services, it is difficult to see how Cortés's small band could have survived to see the Aztec capital.

Apart from facilitating the Spanish conquest of the Aztec empire, Doña Marina also played a role in the formation of a new society in Mexico. In 1522 she gave birth to a son fathered by Cortés, and in 1526 she bore a daughter to a Spanish captain whom she had married. Her offspring thus symbolize the early emergence of a mestizo population in Mexico. Doña Marina died soon after the birth of her daughter, probably in 1527, but during her short life she contributed to the thorough transformation of Mexican society. Doña Marina's role in the Spanish conquest of Mexico underscored the existing divisions within sixteenth-century Mesoamerican society. Among some groups, she was remembered as the mother of the Mexican people, while recollection

❮ Doña Marina is depicted between a Tlaxcalan chief and Hernánd Cortés.

Malintzin (mal-een-tzeen)
Nahuatl (na-watl)
Hernán Cortés (er-NAHN kawr-TEZ)
Tenochtitlan (teh-noch-tee-TLAHN)

CHRONOLOGY

1492	First voyage of Christopher Columbus to the western hemisphere
1494	Treaty of Tordesillas
1500	Brazil claimed for Portugal by Pedro Alvarez de Cabral
1518	Smallpox epidemic in the Caribbean
1519–1521	Spanish conquest of Mexico
1532–1540	Spanish conquest of Peru
1545	Spanish discovery of silver near Potosí
1604	Foundation of Port Royal (Nova Scotia)
1607	Foundation of Jamestown
1608	Foundation of Quebec
1623	Foundation of New Amsterdam
1630	Foundation of the Massachusetts Bay Colony
1688	Smallpox epidemic on Guam
1768–1779	Captain James Cook's exploration of the Pacific Ocean
1788	Establishment of the first European colony in Australia

of her collaboration with Spaniards led other groups to call her La Malinche: the traitor.

Until 1492 the peoples of the eastern and western hemispheres had few dealings with one another. Sporadic encounters between Europeans and North Americans did occur, and it is likely that an occasional Asian or Austronesian mariner reached the Pacific coast of the Americas before 1492. Yet travel between the eastern hemisphere, the western hemisphere, and Oceania was too irregular and infrequent to generate sustained interaction until the fifteenth century.

After 1492, however, the voyages of European mariners led to permanent and continuous contact between the peoples of all these areas. The resulting encounters brought profound and often violent change to both American and Pacific lands. European peoples possessed powerful weapons, horses, and ships that provided them with technological advantages over the peoples they encountered in the Americas and the Pacific islands. Moreover, most Europeans also enjoyed complete or partial immunity to diseases that caused devastating epidemics when introduced to the western hemisphere and Oceania. Because of their technological advantages and the depopulation that followed from epidemic diseases, European peoples were able to establish a presence throughout the Americas and much of the Pacific Ocean basin.

COLLIDING WORLDS

When European peoples first sought to establish their presence in the Americas, they brought technologies unavailable to the peoples they encountered in the western hemisphere. More important than technology, however, were the divisions between indigenous peoples that Europeans were able to exploit and the effects of epidemic diseases that devastated native societies. Soon after their arrival in the western hemisphere, Spanish conquerors toppled the Aztec and Inca empires and imposed their own rule in Mexico and Peru. In later decades Portuguese planters built sugar plantations on the Brazilian coastline. French, English, and Dutch migrants displaced indigenous peoples in North America and established settler colonies under the rule of European peoples.

The Spanish Caribbean

TAINOS The first site of interaction between European and American peoples was the Caribbean. When Spanish mariners arrived there, the Tainos (also known as Arawaks) were the most prominent people in the region. The Tainos cultivated manioc and other crops, and they lived in small villages under the authority of chiefs who allocated land to families and supervised community affairs.

SPANISH ARRIVAL Christopher Columbus and his immediate followers made the island of Hispaniola (modern Haiti and the Dominican Republic) the base of Spanish operations in the Caribbean. Columbus's original plan was to build forts and trading posts where merchants could trade with local peoples for products desired by European consumers. However, it soon became clear that the Caribbean

Taino (tah-EE-noh)

European Representations of Native Americans. | One of the earliest European depictions of native Americans was this engraving of 1505. The caption informed readers that American peoples lived in communal society, where men took several wives but none had private possessions, and that they routinely smoked and consumed the bodies of slain enemies. ***How might such representations have shaped European ideas about native Americans?***

region offered no silks or spices for the European market. If Spanish settlers wanted to maintain their presence in the Caribbean, they would need to find some way to make a living.

The settlers first attempted to support their society by mining gold. Spanish settlers were few in number and were not inclined to perform heavy labor, so they recruited the labor they needed from the ranks of the Tainos. This was done through an institution known as the *encomienda,* which gave *encomenderos* (Spanish settlers) the right to compel Tainos to work in their mines or fields. In return for labor, *encomenderos* were supposed to look after their workers' welfare and encourage their conversion to Christianity.

Conscription of Taino labor was a brutal business. *Encomenderos* worked their charges hard and punished them severely. Tainos occasionally organized rebellions, but their bows, arrows, and slings had little effect against Spanish steel. By about 1515, social disruption and physical abuse caused Taino populations to decline on the large Caribbean islands—Hispaniola, Jamaica, Puerto Rico, and Cuba—favored by Spanish settlers.

Latin American slavery
www.mhhe.com/bentleybrief2e

SMALLPOX After 1518 serious demographic decline set in when smallpox reached the Caribbean and touched off devastating epidemics. To replace laborers lost to disease, *encomenderos* resorted to kidnapping and enslaving Tainos and other peoples. That tactic, however, only exposed additional victims to disease. As a result of epidemic disease, the native population of the Caribbean plummeted from about four million in 1492 to a few thousand in the 1540s. Entire native societies passed out of existence. By the middle of the sixteenth century, a few surviving words—*canoe, hammock, hurricane, barbecue, maize,* and *tobacco*—were all that was left of Taino society.

encomienda (ehn-koh-MYEN-dah)

HERNÁN CORTÉS. | This portrait depicts Cortés, the Spanish conqueror of Mexico, in military armor.

FROM MINING TO PLANTATION AGRICULTURE After the mid–sixteenth century, when it was clear that gold supplies in the region were thin, the Caribbean became a sleepy backwater of the Spanish empire. In the 1640s, French, English, and Dutch settlers began to take the place of the Spanish and flocked to the Caribbean with the intention of establishing plantations. Indeed, they found that the Caribbean offered ideal conditions for the cultivation of cash crops, particularly sugar and tobacco. Meanwhile, because indigenous populations were extinct, planters imported several million slaves to provide labor. By 1700 Caribbean society consisted of a small class of European administrators and large numbers of African slaves.

The Conquest of Mexico and Peru

Spanish interest shifted quickly from the Caribbean to the American mainland in the quest for resources. During the early sixteenth century, Spanish *conquistadores* ("conquerors") pressed west into Mexico and south into Panama and Peru. Between 1519 and 1521 Hernán Cortés and a small band of men brought down the Aztec empire in Mexico, and between 1532 and 1533 Francisco Pizarro and his followers toppled the Inca empire in Peru. Those conquests laid the foundations for colonial regimes that would transform the Americas.

In Mexico and Peru, Spanish explorers found societies quite different from those of the Caribbean islands. Both Mexico and Peru had been sites of agricultural societies, cities, and large states for more than a millennium. In the early fifteenth century, both lands fell under the sway of powerful imperial states: the Mexica people and their allies founded the Aztec empire, which expanded to embrace most of Mesoamerica, and the Incas imposed their rule on a vast realm extending from modern Ecuador in the north to modern Chile in the south. (See chapter 17.)

Toltec and Aztec empires
www.mhhe.com/bentleybrief2e

HERNÁN CORTÉS The conquest of Mexico began in 1519 when Cortés led about 450 soldiers from Veracruz on the Gulf coast to the island city of Tenochtitlan, the stunningly beautiful Aztec capital situated in Lake Texcoco. They seized the emperor Motecuzoma II, who died in 1520 during a skirmish between Spanish forces and residents of Tenochtitlan. Aztec forces soon drove the conquistadores from the capital, but Cortés built a small fleet of ships, placed Tenochtitlan under siege, and in 1521 starved the city into surrender.

Spanish weapons and horses offered Cortés and his soldiers some advantage over the forces they met and help to account for the Spanish conquest of the Aztec empire. Yet weaponry alone clearly was not enough to overcome such a large, densely populated society. Indeed, Cortés's expedition also benefited from divisions among the indigenous peoples of Mexico and made important alliances with peoples who resented Aztec domination. Native allies reinforced the small Spanish army with thousands of veteran warriors and provided Spanish forces with logistical support and secure bases in friendly territory.

Andean South America
www.mhhe.com/bentleybrief2e

EPIDEMIC DISEASE Epidemic disease also aided Spanish efforts. During the siege of Tenochtitlan, smallpox raged through the city, killing inhabitants by the tens of thousands. It then spread beyond the capital and raced through Mexico, carrying off so

---

conquistadores (kon-kees-tah-DOH-rayz)
Motecuzoma (mo-tec-oo-ZO-ma)

many people that Aztec society was unable to function. Only in the context of this enormous depopulation is it possible to understand the Spanish conquest of Mexico.

FRANCISCO PIZARRO Francisco Pizarro experienced similar results when he led a Spanish expedition from Central America to Peru. Pizarro set out in 1530 with 180 soldiers, later joined by reinforcements to make a force of about 600. The conquistadores arrived in Peru just after a bitter dispute within the Inca ruling house, and it was easy for them to exploit differences between the factions. By 1533 they had taken the Inca capital at Cuzco. Under pretext of holding a conference, they called the Inca ruling elites together, seized them, and killed most of them. They spared the Inca ruler Atahualpa until he had delivered a large quantity of gold to Pizarro. Then they strangled him and decapitated his body. Pizarro and his conquistadores proceeded to loot gold and silver from Cuzco's temples and public buildings, and even to loot jewelry and ornaments from the embalmed bodies of deceased Inca rulers.

As Cortés's expedition had done to the Aztecs in Mexico, Pizarro's tiny force toppled the Inca empire by exploiting divisions among native peoples. Many Inca subjects despised their overlords and thus either allied with or did not resist Pizarro's forces. In addition, smallpox had spread to the Inca empire in the 1520s, long before Pizarro's arrival, and had already taken a heavy toll among Andean populations. As a result, by 1540 Spanish forces had established themselves securely as lords of the land.

Iberian Empires in the Americas

SPANISH COLONIAL ADMINISTRATION The conquests of Mexico and Peru were the results not of Spanish royal policy but, rather, of individual efforts by freelance adventurers. Gradually, however, the Spanish monarchy extended its control over the growing American empire, and by about 1570 it had established formal rule under the Spanish crown. Spanish administrators established two main centers of authority in the Americas—Mexico (which they called New Spain) and Peru (known as New Castile)—each governed by a viceroy who was responsible to the king of Spain. In Mexico they built a new capital, Mexico City, on top of Tenochtitlan. In Peru they moved the seat of government from the high-altitude Inca capital of Cuzco to the Peruvian coast and in 1535 founded the new capital of Lima.

The viceroys were the king's representatives in the Americas, and they wielded considerable power. The kings of Spain attempted to hold them in check by subjecting them to the review of courts known as *audiencias* staffed by university-educated lawyers. The *audiencias* heard appeals against the viceroys' decisions and policies and had the right to address their concerns directly to the Spanish king. Furthermore, the *audiencias* conducted reviews of viceroys' performance at the end of their terms, and negative reviews could lead to severe punishment.

Gutiérrez map of Spanish claims
www.mhhe.com/bentleybrief2e

In many ways, Spanish administration in the Americas was a ragged affair. Transportation and communication difficulties limited the ability of viceroys to supervise their own extensive territories. The jurisdiction of the viceroyalty of New Spain, for example, reached from Mexico City as far as St. Augustine in Florida (founded in 1565). Distance also prevented Spanish monarchs from exercising much influence on American affairs. It often took two years for the central government in Spain to respond to a query from Mexico or Peru, and when viceroys received clear orders that they did not like, it was easy to procrastinate.

PORTUGUESE BRAZIL While the Spanish built a territorial empire in Mexico and Peru, Portuguese forces established an imperial presence in Brazil. The Portuguese presence came about by an odd twist of diplomatic convention. In 1494 Spain and

Cuzco (KOOS-koh)
Atahualpa (ah-tah-WAHL-pah)
audiencias (AW-dee-uhns-cee-ahs)

SOURCES FROM THE PAST

First Impressions of Spanish Forces

The following document, based on indigenous accounts but filtered through imperial Spanish sensibilities, suggested that Motecuzoma reacted with fright when presented with reports that were less than reassuring since they focused on fearsome weapons and animals of the Spanish. Given the martial response of the Aztecs to the Spanish invasion, it seems highly unlikely that Motecuzoma or the Aztecs would have expressed terror in such a humiliating fashion.

And when [Motecuzoma] had heard what the messengers reported, he was terrified, he was astounded. . . .

Especially did it cause him to faint away when he heard how the gun, at [the Spaniards'] command, discharged [the shot]; how it resounded as if it thundered when it went off. It indeed bereft one of strength; it shut off one's ears. And when it discharged, something like a round pebble came forth from within. Fire went showering forth; sparks went blazing forth. And its smoke smelled very foul; it had a fetid odor which verily wounded the head. And when [the shot] struck a mountain, it was as if it were destroyed, dissolved. And a tree was pulverized; it was as if it vanished; it was as if someone blew it away.

All iron was their war array. In iron they clothed themselves. With iron they covered their heads. Iron were their swords. Iron were their crossbows. Iron were their shields. Iron were their lances.

And those which bore them upon their backs, their deer [that is, horses], were as tall as roof terraces.

And their bodies were everywhere covered; only their faces appeared. They were very white; they had chalky faces; they had yellow hair, though the hair of some was black. Long were their beards; they also were yellow. They were yellow-headed. [The black men's hair] was kinky, it was curly.

And their food was like fasting food—very large, white, not heavy like [tortillas]; like maize stalks, good-tasting as if of maize stalk flour; a little sweet, a little honeyed. It was honeyed to eat; it was sweet to eat.

And their dogs were very large. They had ears folded over; great dragging jowls. They had fiery eyes—blazing eyes; they had yellow eyes—fiery yellow eyes. They had thin flanks—flanks with ribs showing. They had gaunt stomachs. They were very tall. They were nervous; they went about panting, with tongues hanging out. They were spotted like ocelots; they were varicolored.

And when Motecuzoma heard all this, he was much terrified. It was as if he fainted away. His heart saddened; his heart failed him.

■ What did the Spanish and their indigenous allies hope to gain by presenting this image of Motecuzoma?

SOURCE: Bernardino de Sahagún. *Florentine Codex: General History of the Things of New Spain,* 13 vols. Trans. by Arthur J. O. Anderson and Charles E. Dibble. Salt Lake City: University of Utah Press, 1950–82, 13:19–20. (Translation slightly modified.)

Portugal signed the Treaty of Tordesillas, which divided the world along an imaginary north-south line 370 leagues west of the Azores and Cape Verde Islands. According to this agreement, Spain could claim any non-Christian lands west of that line, and Portugal gained the same rights for lands east of the line. Thus Portugal gained territory along the northeastern part of the South American continent, a region known as Brazil from the many brazilwood trees that grew along the coast, and the remainder of the western hemisphere fell under Spanish control. Brazil did not attract significant Portuguese interest, however, until entrepreneurs began establishing sugar plantations on the coast after the mid–sixteenth century. Once it was clear the plantations would be profitable, Portuguese interest—and settlement—surged.

COLONIAL AMERICAN SOCIETY Both the Spanish and the Portuguese rapidly established cities throughout their territories. Like their compatriots in Europe, colonists preferred to live in cities even when they derived their income from the agricultural production of their landed estates, and they made every attempt to model their new cities along European lines. Away from urban areas, however, indigenous ways of life largely persisted. In places such as the Amazon basin and Paraguay, for example, where there were no mineral deposits to attract European migrants, European visitors learned to adapt to indigenous societies and customs: they ate bread made of manioc flour, made use of native hammocks and canoes, and communicated in the Guaraní and Tupí languages. Indeed, indigenous languages flourish even today throughout much of Latin America: among the more prominent are Nahuatl in Mexico, Quiché in Mexico and Guatemala, Guaraní in Paraguay, and Quechua in the Andean highlands of Peru, Ecuador, and Bolivia.

Spanish and Portuguese peoples always saw the western hemisphere more as a land to exploit and administer than as a place to settle and colonize. Nevertheless, upward of five hundred thousand Spaniards and one hundred thousand Portuguese settled permanently in the Americas between 1500 and 1800. Their presence contributed to the making of a new world—a world characterized by intense interaction between the peoples of Europe, Africa, and the Americas—in the western hemisphere.

Settler Colonies in North America

Throughout the sixteenth century, Spanish explorers sought opportunities north of Mexico and the Caribbean. They established towns, forts, and missions from modern Florida as far north as Virginia, and they scouted shorelines off Maine and Newfoundland. On the west coast they established a fort on Vancouver Island in modern Canada. By mid-century, however, French, English, and Dutch mariners were dislodging Spanish colonists north of Florida. Originally, they came in a fruitless search for a northwest passage to Asia. Instead, they found immense quantities of codfish, which they exploited from the banks off Labrador, Newfoundland, Nova Scotia, and New England.

FOUNDATION OF COLONIES More important, in the early seventeenth century they began to plant permanent colonies on the North American mainland. French settlers established colonies at Port Royal (Nova Scotia) in 1604 and Quebec in 1608, and English migrants founded Jamestown in 1607 and the Massachusetts Bay Colony in 1630. Dutch entrepreneurs built a settlement at New Amsterdam in 1623, but in 1664 an English fleet seized and rechristened it New York and absorbed it into English colonial holdings. During the seventeenth and eighteenth centuries, French migrants settled in eastern Canada, and French explorers and traders scouted the St. Lawrence, Ohio, and Mississippi rivers, building forts all the way to the Gulf of Mexico. Meanwhile, English settlers established colonies along the east coast of the present-day United States of America.

Life in those early settlements was extremely difficult. Most of the settlers hoped to sustain their communities not through farming but by producing valuable commodities such as fur, pitch, tar, or lumber, if not silver and gold. They relied heavily on provisions sent from Europe, and when supply ships did not arrive as expected, they sometimes avoided starvation only because indigenous peoples provided them with food. In Jamestown, food shortages and disease became so severe that only sixty of the colony's five hundred inhabitants survived the winter of 1609–1610. Some settlers went so far as to disinter corpses and consume the flesh of their departed neighbors.

COLONIAL GOVERNMENT The French and English colonies in North America differed in several ways from Iberian territories to the south. Whereas Iberian explorations had royal backing, private investors played larger roles in French and English colonial efforts. Because of that, individuals retained much more control over their colonies' affairs than did their Iberian counterparts. Thus settlers in the English colonies—though ultimately subject to royal authority—maintained their own assemblies and influenced the choice of royal governors: there were no viceroys or *audiencias* in the North American colonies.

Quiché (keesh-AY)
Guaraní (gwahr-uh-NEE)
Quechua (keh-CHUA)

MAP 21.1 | European empires and colonies in the Americas, ca. 1700. Locate the major cities and settlements of each imperial power. ***What factors decided where settlements would be placed, and why are there so few settlements in the interior of either North or South America?***

Potosí and Zacatecas were the two most important silver mining sites in the Americas.

RELATIONS WITH INDIGENOUS PEOPLES French and English colonies differed from Iberian territories also in their relationships with indigenous peoples. French and English migrants did not find large, densely settled, centralized states like the Aztec and Inca empires. Although many of the native societies in eastern North America practiced agriculture, most also relied on hunting and consequently moved their villages frequently in pursuit of game. They did not claim ownership of precisely bounded territories, but they regularly migrated between well-defined regions.

When European settlers saw forested lands not bearing crops, they staked out farms for themselves. The availability of fertile farmland soon attracted large numbers of European migrants. Upward of 150,000 English migrants moved to North America during the seventeenth century alone, and sizable French, German, Dutch, and Irish contingents soon joined them.

European migrants took pains to justify their claims to American lands. Some, such as the English, sought to provide legal cover for their settlements by negotiating treaties with the peoples whose lands they colonized. Other migrants claimed that they were making productive use of lands that native peoples only used as hunting parks. Such justifications

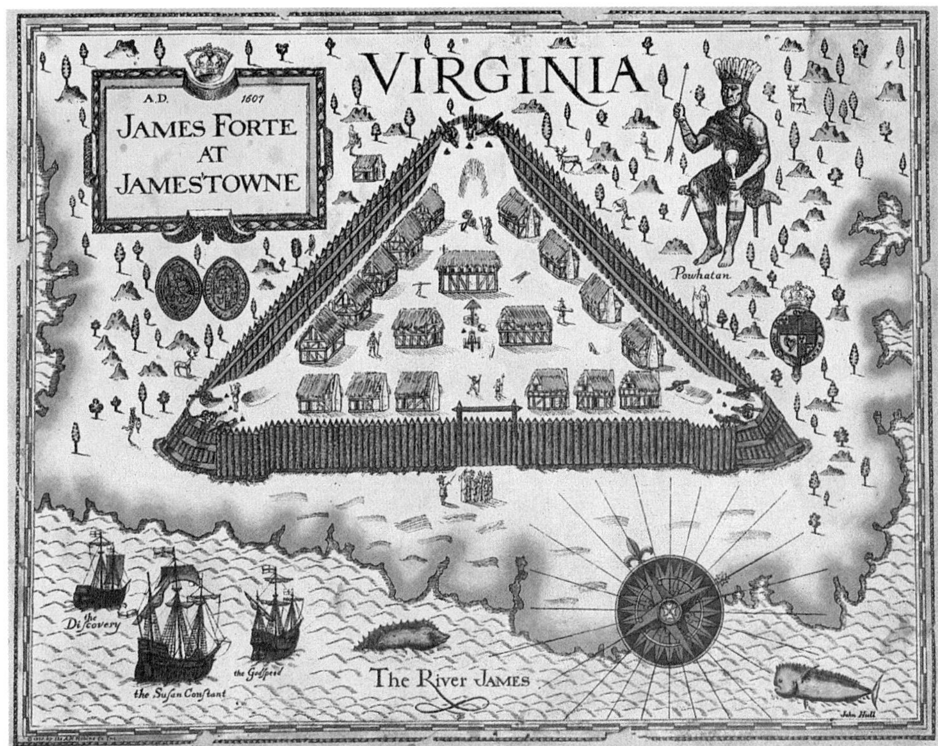

JAMESTOWN. | A painting of the English settlement at Jamestown in the early seventeenth century illustrates the precarious relations between European settlers and indigenous peoples. Note the heavy palisades and numerous cannons deployed within the fort, as well as the imposing figure of the native chief Powhatan depicted outside the settlement's walls.

did not convince native peoples, who frequently clashed with colonists over the right to use their hunting grounds, whether treaties existed or not. In 1622, for example, native peoples angry over European intrusions massacred almost one-third of the English settlers in the Chesapeake region.

Such attacks did not stem the tide of European migrants, however. Between 1600 and 1800, about one million European migrants arrived in North America, many of whom actively sought to displace native peoples from their lands. Violent conflict, indeed, took a heavy toll on native populations. Yet as in the Iberian territories, epidemic disease also dramatically reduced the indigenous population of North America in early modern times. In 1492 the native population of the territory now embraced by the United States was greater than five million, perhaps as high as ten million. By the mid–sixteenth century, however, smallpox and other diseases spread north from Mexico and ravaged native societies in the plains and eastern woodlands of North America. By 1800 only six hundred thousand indigenous peoples remained, as against almost five million settlers of European ancestry and about one million slaves of African ancestry. Although the settler colonies of North America differed markedly from the Iberian territorial empires, they too contributed greatly to the transformation of the western hemisphere.

COLONIAL SOCIETY IN THE AMERICAS

The European migrants who flooded into the western hemisphere interacted both with the native inhabitants and with African peoples whom they imported as enslaved laborers. Throughout the Americas, relations between individuals of American, European, and African ancestry soon led to the emergence of mestizo populations. Yet European peoples and their Euro-American offspring increasingly dominated political and economic affairs in the Americas. They mined precious metals, cultivated cash crops such as sugar and tobacco, and trapped fur-bearing animals to supply capitalist markets that met the voracious demands of European

THINKING ABOUT *Traditions*

TRADITIONS IN THE AMERICAS AND OCEANIA. In spite of conquest and massive depopulation from epidemic disease, the peoples of the Americas managed to preserve aspects of their social, religious, and cultural identities. In what specific ways did native American traditions persist, especially in terms of culture and religion?

Mestizo Family. A Spaniard rests his hand on the shoulder of his Indian wife in this eighteenth century painting from Mexico. Between them, their mestizo son reaches into his mother's basket.

PSI map The Atlantic world www.mhhe.com/bentleybrief2e

and Asian consumers. Over time they also established their Christian religion as the dominant faith of the western hemisphere.

The Formation of Multicultural Societies

Many parts of the Americas remained outside European control until the nineteenth century. Only rarely did Europeans venture into the interior regions of the American continents in the sixteenth century, and those who did often found themselves at the mercy of the native inhabitants. But even though their influence reached the American interior only gradually, European migrants radically transformed the social order in the regions where they established colonies.

MESTIZO SOCIETIES In Spanish and Portuguese territories, society quickly became both multicultural and ethnically mixed, largely because of migration patterns. Indeed, more than 85 percent of Spanish migrants were men, and the percentage of men was even higher for the Portuguese. Because there were so few European women, Spanish and Portuguese migrants entered into relationships with native women, which soon gave rise to an increasingly mestizo society.

This pattern was especially pronounced in the Portuguese colony of Brazil, where there were very few European women. There, Portuguese men entered into relationships with both native and African slave women. Brazil soon had large populations not only of mestizos but also of mulattoes, born of Portuguese and African parents; *zambos,* born of indigenous and African parents; and other combinations arising from these groups themselves. Indeed, marriages between members of different racial and ethnic communities became very common in colonial Brazil.

zambos (SAHM-bohs)
mestizo (mehs-TEE-soh)

THE SOCIAL HIERARCHY In both the Spanish and the Portuguese colonies, migrants born in Europe known as *peninsulares* (people from the Iberian peninsula) stood at the top of the social hierarchy, followed by *criollos,* or creoles, individuals born in the Americas of Iberian parents. As the numbers of mestizos grew, they also became essential contributors to their societies, especially in Mexico and Brazil. Meanwhile, mulattoes, zambos, and other individuals of mixed parentage became prominent groups in Brazilian society, although they were usually subordinate to *peninsulares,* creoles, and even mestizos. In all the Iberian colonies, imported slaves and native peoples stood at the bottom of the social hierarchy.

NORTH AMERICAN SOCIETIES The social structure of the French and English colonies in North America differed markedly from that of the Iberian colonies. Women were more numerous, especially among the English migrants, and settlers mostly married within their own groups. Although French fur traders often associated with native women and generated *métis* (the French equivalent of mestizos) in regions around trading posts, such arrangements were less common in French colonial cities such as Port Royal and Quebec.

Mingling between peoples of different ancestry was least common in the English colonies of North America. Colonists regarded the native peoples they encountered as lazy heathens who did not exert themselves to cultivate the land. Later they also scorned African slaves as inferior beings. Those attitudes fueled a virulent racism, and English settlers worked to maintain sharp boundaries between themselves and peoples of American and African ancestry.

Yet English settlers readily borrowed useful cultural elements from other communities. From native communities, for example, they learned about American plants and animals, and they adapted moccasins and deerskin clothes. From their slaves they borrowed African food crops and techniques for the cultivation of rice. Yet, unlike their Iberian neighbors, English settlers strongly discouraged relationships between individuals of different ancestry and mostly refused to accept offspring of mixed parentage.

Mining and Agriculture in the Spanish Empire

From the Spanish perspective, the greatest attractions of the Americas were precious metals. Once the conquistadores had thoroughly looted the treasures of the Aztec and Inca empires, their followers opened mines to extract the mineral wealth of the Americas in a more systematic fashion.

SILVER MINING Silver was the most abundant American treasure, and much of Spain's American enterprise focused on its extraction. Silver production concentrated on two areas: the thinly populated Mexican north, particularly the region around Zacatecas, and the high central Andes, particularly the stunningly rich mines of Potosí. Both sites employed large numbers of indigenous laborers. Many laborers went to Zacatecas voluntarily to escape the pressures of conquest and disease. Over time they became professional miners, spoke Spanish, and lost touch with the communities of their birth.

Meanwhile, Spanish prospectors discovered a large vein of silver near Potosí in 1545 and began large-scale mining there in the 1580s. By 1600 Potosí had a booming population

peninsulares (pehn-IHN-soo-LAH-rayz)
criollos (KRYO-yohs)
métis (may-TEE)
Zacatecas (sah-kah-TEH-kahs)
Potosí (paw-taw-SEE)

of 150,000. Such rapid growth created an explosive demand for labor. As in the Mexican mines, Spanish administrators relied mostly on voluntary labor, but they also adapted the Inca practice of requisitioning draft labor, known as the *mita* system, to recruit workers for particularly difficult and dangerous chores. Under the *mita* system, each native village was required to send one-seventh of its male population to work for four months in the mines at Potosí. Draft laborers received very little payment for their work, and conditions were extremely harsh. Death rates of draft laborers were high, and many native men sought to evade *mita* obligations by fleeing to cities or hiding in distant villages.

THE GLOBAL SIGNIFICANCE OF SILVER The mining industries of Mexico and Peru powered the Spanish economy in the Americas and even stimulated the world economy of early modern times. Indeed, the Spanish government's share—one-fifth of all silver production, called the *quinto*—represented the principal revenue the crown derived from its American possessions. Most American silver made its way across the Atlantic to Spain, where it financed Spain's army and bureaucracy and lubricated markets throughout Europe. From Europe, merchants used it to trade for silk, spices, and porcelain in the markets of Asia. Silver also traveled from Acapulco on the west coast of Mexico across the Pacific in the Manila galleons, and from Manila it also made its way to Asian markets. No matter which direction it went, American silver powerfully stimulated global trade.

THE HACIENDA Apart from mining, the principal occupations in Spanish America were farming, stock raising, and craft production. By the seventeenth century the most prominent site of agricultural and craft production in Spanish America was the hacienda, or estate, which produced goods for sale to local markets in nearby mining districts, towns, and cities. Bordering the large estates were smaller properties owned by Spanish migrants or creoles as well as sizable tracts of land held by indigenous peoples who practiced subsistence agriculture.

LABOR SYSTEMS The major source of labor for the haciendas was the indigenous population. As in the Caribbean, Spanish conquerors first organized native workforces under the *encomienda* system. Yet from the 1520s to the 1540s, this system led to rampant abuse, as Spanish landowners overworked their laborers and skimped on their maintenance. After midcentury, *encomenderos* in agriculturally productive regions increasingly required their subject populations to provide tribute but not labor. That didn't solve the problem of labor, however, so Spanish landowners resorted to a system of debt peonage to recruit workers for their haciendas. Under this system, landowners advanced loans to native peoples so that they could buy seeds, tools, and supplies for their farms. The debtors then repaid the loans with labor, but wages were so low that they were never able to pay off their debts. Thus, landowners helped create a cycle of debt that ensured them a dependent labor force to work their estates.

RESISTANCE TO SPANISH RULE The Spanish regimes in the Americas met considerable resistance from indigenous peoples. Resistance took various forms: armed rebellion, halfhearted work, and retreat into the mountains and forests. On some occasions, indigenous peoples turned to Spanish law in search of aid against oppressive colonists. In 1615, for example, Felipe Guaman Poma de Ayala, a native of Peru, fired off a 1,200-page letter to King Philip III of Spain asking for protection for native peoples against rapacious colonists. He wrote passionately of men ruined by overtaxation and women driven to prostitution, of Spanish colonists who grabbed the lands of native peoples and Spanish priests who seduced the wives of native men. Guaman Poma warned the king that if Philip wanted anything to remain of his Andean empire, he should intervene and protect the indigenous

quinto (KEEN-toh)
hacienda (ah-SYEN-dah)

peoples of the land. Unfortunately for Guaman Poma, the king never saw the letter. Instead, it ended up in Denmark, where it remained unknown in a library until 1908.

Sugar and Slavery in Portuguese Brazil

Whereas the Spanish American empire concentrated on the extraction of silver, the Portuguese empire in Brazil depended on the production and export of sugar. The different economic and social foundations of the Spanish and Portuguese empires led to different patterns of labor recruitment. The Spanish forced native peoples to provide labor; the Portuguese relied instead on imported African slaves. Because of that, Africans and their descendants became the majority of the population in Brazil.

THE ENGENHO Colonial Brazilian life revolved around the *engenho,* or sugar mill, which came to represent a complex of land, labor, buildings, animals, capital, and technical skills related to the production of sugar. Unlike other crops, sugarcane required extensive processing to yield molasses or refined sugar. Thus *engenhos* needed both heavy labor for the planting and harvesting of cane and specialized skills for the intricacies of processing.

THE SEARCH FOR LABOR Like their Spanish counterparts, Portuguese colonists first tried to enlist local populations as laborers. Unlike the inhabitants of Mexico and Peru, however, the peoples of Brazil were not sedentary cultivators. They resisted efforts to commandeer their labor and evaded the Portuguese simply by retreating to interior lands. In addition, in Brazil as elsewhere in the Americas, epidemic diseases devastated indigenous populations. After smallpox and measles ravaged the Brazilian coast in the 1560s, Portuguese settlers had a hard time even finding potential laborers, let alone forcing them to work.

SLAVERY Faced with those difficulties, the colonists turned to another labor source: African slaves. Portuguese plantation managers imported slaves as early as the 1530s, but they began to rely on African labor on a large scale only in the 1580s. The toll on slave communities was extremely heavy: arduous working conditions, mistreatment, poor nutrition, and inadequate housing combined to produce high rates of disease and mortality. Indeed, *engenhos* typically lost 5 to 10 percent of their slaves annually, so there was a constant demand for more slaves.

Owners had little economic incentive to improve conditions for slaves or to encourage them to reproduce naturally. If a slave lived five to six years, the investment of the average owner doubled and permitted him to purchase a new and healthy slave without taking a monetary loss. Children required financial outlays for at least twelve years, which from the perspective of the owner represented a financial loss. To them the balance sheet of sugar production was about profit, not about slaves' lives. All told, the business of producing Brazilian sugar was so brutal that every ton of the sweet substance cost one human life.

Fur Traders and Settlers in North America

THE FUR TRADE European mariners first frequented North American shores in search of fish. Over time, though, trade in furs became far more lucrative. After explorers found a convenient entrance to rich fur-producing regions through the Hudson Strait and Hudson Bay, they began to connect large parts of the North American interior by a chain of forts and trading posts. Indigenous peoples trapped animals for Europeans and exchanged the pelts for manufactured goods. The hides went mostly to Europe, where there was strong demand for beaver skin hats and fur clothing.

Champlain's explorations
www.mhhe.com/bentleybrief2e

engenho (en-GEHN-ho)

Tobacco Use in Europe. | European moralists often denounced tobacco as a noxious weed, and they associated its use with vices such as drunkenness, gambling, and prostitution. Nevertheless, its popularity surged in Europe, and later in Africa and Asia as well, after its introduction from the Americas. ***Does this engraving seem to promote or discourage the use of tobacco?***

Conditions in the Virginia colony
www.mhhe.com/bentleybrief2e

EFFECTS OF THE FUR TRADE The fur trade generated tremendous conflict between native groups. As overhunting caused American beaver populations to plummet, native trappers constantly had to push farther inland in search of hides. This frequently led native peoples to invade others' territories, which in turn often led to war. The fur trade also took place in the context of competition between European states. This competitive atmosphere contributed to further conflict, as indigenous peoples became embroiled in their patrons' rivalries.

SETTLER SOCIETY European settler-cultivators posed an even more serious challenge to native ways of life than the fur traders, since they displaced indigenous peoples from the land and turned hunting grounds into plantations. And, as colonists' numbers increased, they sought to integrate their American holdings into the larger economy of the Atlantic Ocean basin by producing cash crops—such as tobacco, rice, and indigo—that they could market in Europe.

TOBACCO Tobacco farming quickly became critical to settler societies in eastern North America. Although originally hailed for its medicinal uses, this native American plant quickly became wildly popular with Europeans as a recreational drug. Indeed, just a few decades after English settlers cultivated the first commercial crop of tobacco in Virginia in 1612, Europeans were smoking tobacco socially in huge numbers. This widespread popularity was due to the addictive nature of nicotine, an oily, toxic substance present in tobacco leaves. As a result, it was easy for tobacco users to become dependent on nicotine, which in turn kept demand for tobacco high. Moreover, merchants and mariners soon spread the use of tobacco throughout Europe and to all parts of the world that European ships visited—a process that helped, at least in the short term, to expand the markets for American tobacco.

INDENTURED LABOR Cash-crop plantations created high demand for cheap labor. Unlike their counterparts in the Spanish territories, indigenous peoples in North America could not be induced to labor in the colonists' fields. Instead, planters turned to indentured servants from Europe for their labor needs. Under this system, people who had little future in Europe—the chronically unemployed, orphans, criminals—received free passage across the Atlantic in exchange for providing four to seven years of labor. Although thousands of indentured servants came to the American colonies with high hopes for making a new start, the system was far from ideal—many died of disease or overwork before completing their terms of labor, and others found only marginal employment.

SLAVERY IN NORTH AMERICA English settlers in North America also found uses for African slaves. In 1619 a group of about twenty Africans reached Virginia, where they worked alongside European laborers as indentured servants. After about 1680, however, planters increasingly replaced indentured servants with African slaves. By 1750 some 120,000 black slaves tilled Chesapeake tobacco, and 180,000 others cultivated Carolina rice.

Slave labor was not prominent in the northern colonies, mostly because the land and the climate were not suitable for the cultivation of labor-intensive cash crops. Nevertheless, the economies of these colonies also profited handsomely from slavery. Many New England merchants traded in slaves destined for the West Indies: by the mid–eighteenth century, half the merchant fleet of Newport carried human cargo. The economies of New York and Philadelphia also benefited from the building and outfitting of slave vessels, and the seaports of New England became profitable centers for the distillation of rum. The chief ingredient of that rum was slave-produced sugar from the West Indies,

PLANTATION SOCIETY. The Goober-gatherers, 1890 (engraving), by Horace Bradley (fl. 1890).

and merchants traded much of the distilled spirits for slaves on the African coast. Thus, although the southern plantation societies became most directly identified with slavery, all the North American colonies participated in and profited from the slave trade.

Christianity and Native Religions in the Americas

Like Buddhists and Muslims in earlier centuries, European explorers, conquerors, merchants, and settlers took their religious traditions with them when they traveled overseas. The desire to spread Christianity was a prominent motive behind European ventures overseas, and missionaries soon made their way to the Americas.

SPANISH MISSIONARIES From the beginning of Spanish colonization in Mexico and Peru, Franciscan, Dominican, and Jesuit missionaries campaigned to Christianize indigenous peoples. Over time, and despite considerable initial resistance, Christianity did win adherents in Spanish America. In the wake of conquest and epidemic disease, many native leaders in Mexico concluded that their gods had abandoned them and looked to the missionaries for spiritual guidance. When native peoples adopted Christianity, however, they blended their own interests and traditions with the faith taught by Spanish missionaries. When they learned about Roman Catholic saints, for example, they revered saints with qualities like those of their inherited gods or those whose feast days coincided with traditional celebrations.

THE VIRGIN OF GUADALUPE In Mexico, Christianity became especially popular after the mid–seventeenth century, as an increasingly mestizo society took the Virgin of Guadalupe almost as a national symbol. According to legends, the Virgin Mary appeared before a peasant near Mexico City in 1531. The site of the apparition soon became a popular local shrine visited mostly by Spanish settlers. By the 1640s the shrine attracted pilgrims from all parts of Mexico, and the Virgin of Guadalupe gained a reputation for

Virgin of Guadalupe (gwah-dah-LOO-pay)

working miracles on behalf of individuals who visited her shrine. The popularity of the Virgin of Guadalupe helped to ensure not only that Roman Catholic Christianity would dominate cultural and religious matters in Mexico but also that Mexican religious faith would retain strong indigenous influences.

FRENCH AND ENGLISH MISSIONS French and English missionaries did not attract nearly as many converts to Christianity in North America as their Spanish counterparts did in Mexico and Peru, partly because French and English colonists did not rule over sedentary cultivators: it was much more difficult to conduct missions among peoples who frequently moved about the countryside than among those who lived permanently in villages, towns, or cities. Even so, French missionaries did work actively among native communities in the St. Lawrence, Mississippi, and Ohio river valleys and experienced modest success for their efforts. English colonists, in contrast, displayed little interest in converting indigenous peoples to Christianity, nor did they welcome native converts into their agricultural and commercial society. Yet even without native conversion to Christianity, the growing settlements of French and especially English colonists guaranteed that European religious traditions would figure prominently in North American society.

Europeans in the Pacific

Though geographically distant from the Americas, Australia and the Pacific islands underwent experiences similar to those that transformed the western hemisphere in early modern times. Like their American counterparts, the peoples of Oceania had no inherited or acquired immunities to diseases that were common to peoples throughout the eastern hemisphere, and their numbers plunged when epidemic disease struck their populations. For the most part, however, Australia and the Pacific islands experienced epidemic disease and the arrival of European migrants later than did the Americas. European mariners thoroughly explored the Pacific basin between the sixteenth and eighteenth centuries, but only in Guam and the Mariana Islands did they establish permanent settlements before the late eighteenth century. Nevertheless, their scouting of the region laid a foundation for much more intense interactions between European, Euro-American, Asian, and Oceanic peoples during the nineteenth and twentieth centuries.

Australia and the Larger World

DUTCH EXPLORATION At least from the second century C.E., European geographers had speculated about *terra australis incognita*—"unknown southern land"—that they thought must exist in the world's southern hemisphere to balance the huge landmasses north of the equator. Although Portuguese mariners most likely charted much of the western and northern coasts of Australia as early as the 1520s, Dutch sailors based in the Indonesian islands made the first recorded European sighting of the southern continent in 1606. The Dutch VOC authorized exploratory voyages, but mariners found little to encourage further efforts. In 1623, after surveying the landscape of western Australia, the Dutch mariner Jan Carstenzs described the land as "the most arid and barren region that could be found anywhere on earth."

Nevertheless, Dutch mariners continued to visit Australia. By the mid–seventeenth century they had scouted the continent's northern, western, and southern coasts and had fleeting encounters with indigenous populations. Yet because those peoples were nomadic foragers rather than sedentary cultivators, Europeans mostly considered them wretched savages. In the absence of tempting opportunities to trade, European mariners made no effort to establish permanent settlements in Australia.

BRITISH COLONISTS Only after James Cook charted the eastern coast in 1770 did European peoples become seriously interested in Australia. Cook dropped anchor for a week at Botany Bay (near modern Sydney) and reported that the region was suitable for settlement. In 1788 a British fleet arrived at Sydney carrying about one thousand passengers, eight hundred of them convicts, who established the first European settlement in Australia as a penal colony. For half a century Europeans in Australia numbered only a few thousand, most of them convicts. In fact, free settlers did not outnumber convicted criminal migrants until the 1830s. Thus, despite early fleeting encounters between European and aboriginal Australian peoples, it was only in the nineteenth and twentieth centuries that a continuing stream of European migrants and settlers linked Australia more directly to the larger world.

> THINKING ABOUT *Encounters*
>
> **ENCOUNTERS IN THE AMERICAS AND OCEANIA.** As in many other places and times, encounters between Europeans and the peoples of the Americas and Oceania spurred huge cultural, social, and economic changes for everyone involved. Yet the transformations that occurred among the peoples of the Americas and Oceania as a result of these encounters were disproportionately drastic and difficult. Why did these encounters cause such hardship for both native Americans and Oceanians?

The Pacific Islands and the Larger World

The entry of European mariners into the Pacific Ocean basin did not bring immediate change to most of the Pacific islands. In these islands, as in Australia, European merchants and settlers did not arrive in large numbers until the late eighteenth century. However, in Guam and the Mariana Islands, dramatic change was already under way by the sixteenth century.

SPANISH VOYAGES IN THE PACIFIC Ferdinand Magellan and his crew became the first Europeans to cross the Pacific Ocean, in 1521. Before reaching the Philippines, they encountered only one inhabited island group—the Marianas, dominated by Guam. In 1565 Spanish mariners inaugurated the Manila galleon trade between Manila and Acapulco. Because their primary goal was to link New Spain to Asian markets, they rarely went out of their way to explore the Pacific Ocean or to search for other islands. Although a few Spanish vessels visited some of the other Pacific islands in the sixteenth century, Spanish mariners found little to interest them and did not establish regular communications with island peoples.

GUAM The only Pacific islands that attracted substantial Spanish interest in the sixteenth century were Guam and the Marianas. Manila galleons called regularly at Guam, which lay directly on the route from Acapulco to Manila. For more than a century, they took on fresh provisions and engaged in mostly peaceful trade with the indigenous Chamorro people. Then, in the 1670s and 1680s, Spanish authorities decided to bring the Mariana Islands under the control of the viceroy of New Spain in Mexico. They dispatched military forces to the islands to impose Spanish rule and subject the Chamorro to the spiritual authority of the Roman Catholic church. The Chamorro stoutly opposed those efforts, but a smallpox epidemic in 1688 severely reduced their numbers and crippled their resistance. By 1695 the Chamorro population had declined from about fifty thousand at midcentury to five thousand, mostly because of smallpox. By the end of the seventeenth century, Spanish forces had established garrisons throughout the Mariana Islands and relocated surviving Chamorro into communities supervised by Spanish authorities.

VISITORS AND TRADE By the late eighteenth century, growing European and Euro-American interest in the Pacific Ocean basin led to sharply increased interactions between islanders and mariners. English and French mariners explored the Pacific basin in search of commercial opportunities and the elusive northwest passage from Europe to Asia. They frequently visited Tahiti after 1767, and they soon began to trade with the islanders: European mariners received provisions and engaged in sexual relations with Tahitian women in exchange for nails, knives, iron tools, and textiles.

Chamorro (chuh-MAWR-oh)

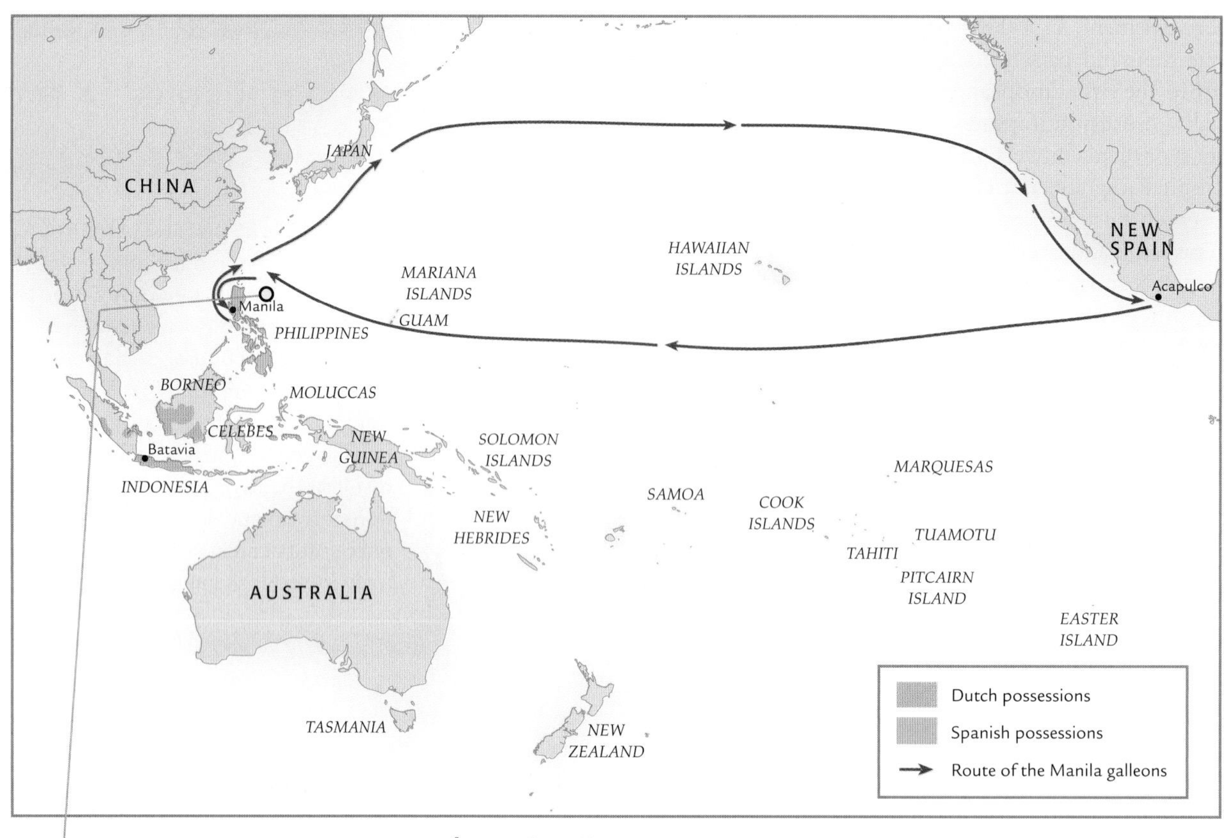

The Manila galleons meant that Spanish silver mined in the Americas could now be shipped directly to Asia.

MAP 21.2 | Manila galleon route and the lands of Oceania, 1500–1800. Note the route taken by the Manila galleons in relation to the majority of the Pacific islands. ***Why weren't Spanish mariners more interested in exploring the rest of the Pacific as they made their way to the Philippines?***

CAPTAIN COOK AND HAWAI'I After 1778 the published writings of Captain James Cook, who happened across the Hawaiian Islands in that year, galvanized even greater interest in the Pacific. European whalers, missionaries, and planters came in large numbers in search of opportunities. As a result, by the early nineteenth century, European and Euro-American peoples had become prominent figures in all the major Pacific island groups. In the next two centuries, interactions between islanders, visitors, and migrants brought rapid and often unsettling change to Pacific island societies.

SUMMARY

The Americas underwent thorough transformation in early modern times. Smallpox and other diseases sparked ferocious epidemics that devastated indigenous populations and undermined their societies. In the wake of severe depopulation, European peoples toppled imperial states, established mining and agricultural enterprises, imported enslaved African laborers, and founded colonies throughout much of the western hemisphere. Some indigenous peoples disappeared entirely as distinct groups. Others maintained their communities, identities, and cultural traditions but fell increasingly under the influence of European migrants and their Euro-American offspring. In Oceania only Guam and the Mariana Islands felt the full effects of epidemic disease and migration in the early modern era. By the late eighteenth century, however, European and Euro-American peoples with advanced technologies had thoroughly explored the Pacific Ocean basin, and epidemic diseases traveled with them to Australia and the Pacific islands. As a result, during the nineteenth and twentieth centuries, Oceania underwent a social transformation similar to the one experienced earlier by the Americas.

STUDY TERMS

audiencias (415)
Brazil (415)
conquistadores (414)
criollos (421)
Doña Marina (411)
encomienda (413)
engenho (423)
epidemic disease (413)
Francisco Pizarro (414)
fur trade (423)
hacienda (422)
Hernán Cortés (414)
indentured labor (424)
James Cook (426)
Manila galleons (427)
mestizo/métis (420)
mita system (422)
Motecuzoma II (414)
mulattoes (421)
New Spain (415)
peninsulares (421)
Peru (414)
Potosí (421)
quinto (422)
sugarcane (414)
tobacco (424)
viceroy (415)
Virgin of Guadalupe (425)
Zacatecas (421)

FOR FURTHER READING

Colin G. Callaway. *New Worlds for All: Indians, Europeans, and the Remaking of Early America.* Baltimore, 1997. Scholarly synthesis examining interactions and cultural exchanges between European and indigenous American peoples.

William Cronon. *Changes in the Land: Indians, Colonists, and the Ecology of New England.* New York, 1983. Brilliant study concentrating on the different ways English colonists and native peoples in colonial New England used the environment.

Philip D. Curtin. *The Rise and Fall of the Plantation Complex: Essays in Atlantic History.* 2nd ed. Cambridge, 1998. Examines plantation societies and slavery as institutions linking lands throughout the Atlantic Ocean basin.

K. R. Howe. *Where the Waves Fall: A New South Sea Island History from First Settlement to Colonial Rule.* Honolulu, 1984. A thoughtful survey of Pacific island history emphasizing interactions between islanders and visitors.

John E. Kicza. *Resilient Cultures: America's Native Peoples Confront European Colonization, 1500–1800.* Upper Saddle River, N.J., 2002. A comprehensive comparative study assessing the impact of colonization on indigenous American peoples as well as native influences on American colonial history.

Karen Ordahl Kupperman. *Indians and English: Facing Off in Early America.* Ithaca, N.Y., 2000. Fascinating reconstruction of the early encounters between English and indigenous American peoples, drawing on sources from all parties to the encounters.

Miguel León-Portilla. *The Broken Spears: The Aztec Account of the Conquest of Mexico.* Rev. ed. Boston, 1992. Offers translations of indigenous accounts of the Spanish conquest of the Aztec empire.

James Lockhart and Stuart B. Schwartz. *Early Latin America: A History of Colonial Spanish America and Brazil.* New York, 1982. The best survey of colonial Latin American history.

Gary B. Nash. *Red, White, and Black: The Peoples of Early America.* 3rd ed. Englewood Cliffs, N.J., 1992. Outstanding survey of early American history focusing on the interactions between peoples of European, African, and American ancestry.

Steve J. Stern. *Peru's Indian Peoples and the Challenge of Spanish Conquest.* 2nd ed. Madison, 1993. Scholarly analysis concentrating on the social history of indigenous peoples following the Spanish conquest of Peru.

Africa and the Atlantic World

22

etween 1760 and 1792, a west African man known as Thomas Peters crossed the Atlantic Ocean four times. In 1760 slave raiders captured Peters, whose original African name is unknown, marched him to the coast, and sold him to French slave merchants. He traveled in a slave ship to the French colony of Louisiana, where he probably worked on a sugar plantation. But Peters was not a docile servant. He attempted to escape at least three times, and his master punished him by beating him and branding him with a hot iron. During the 1760s his French master sold Peters to an English planter, and about 1770 a Scottish landowner in North Carolina bought him.

During the 1770s, as English colonists in North America prepared to rebel against the British government, slaves of African ancestry considered their own prospects and looked for ways to obtain personal freedom. Peters was among them. When war broke out, he made his way with his wife and daughter to British lines and joined the Black Pioneers, a company of escaped slaves who fought to maintain British rule in the colonies. When the colonists won the war, Peters escaped to Nova Scotia with his family and many other former slaves.

Blacks were legally free in Nova Scotia, but the white ruling elites forced them to till marginal lands and live in segregated villages. In hopes of improving their lot, some two hundred black families sent Peters to London in 1790, where he promoted the establishment of a colony for former slaves in Sierra Leone. His efforts succeeded, and the next year he returned to Nova Scotia to seek recruits for the colony. In 1792 he led 1,196 blacks aboard a convoy of fifteen ships and began his fourth crossing of the Atlantic Ocean. The colonists arrived safely at Freetown, and Peters served as a leader of the black community there. Although he lived less than four months after arriving in Sierra Leone, his life and experiences personified the links connecting the lands of the Atlantic Ocean basin.

For the most part, the peoples of sub-Saharan Africa continued to follow established patterns of life in early modern times. They built states and organized societies based on kinship groups, and in west Africa and coastal east Africa they continued to trade regularly with Muslim merchants from north Africa and southwest Asia.

❮ Armed escorts march a group of freshly captured Africans to the coast for sale in slave markets.

Yet the establishment of global trade networks brought deep change to sub-Saharan Africa. Commercial opportunities drew Europeans to the coasts of west Africa, and maritime trade soon turned west African attention to the Atlantic. Maritime commerce also helped promote the emergence of prosperous port cities and the establishment of powerful coastal kingdoms that traded through the ocean rather than the desert. In central

CHRONOLOGY

1441	Beginning of the Portuguese slave trade
1464–1493	Reign of Sunni Ali
1464–1591	Songhay empire
1506–1542	Reign of King Afonso I of Kongo
1623–1663	Reign of Queen Nzinga of Ndongo
1706	Execution of Doña Beatriz
1745–1797	Life of Olaudah Equiano
1793–1804	Haitian revolution
1807	End of the British slave trade
1865	Abolition of slavery in the United States

Africa and south Africa, European merchants brought the first substantial opportunities for long-distance trade, since Muslim merchants had not ventured to those regions in large numbers.

Trade through the Atlantic profoundly affected African society because it involved human beings. Slavery had been a part of African societies for centuries, and Africans had long supplied slaves to Muslim merchants involved in trans-Saharan trade networks. The Atlantic slave trade, however, was vastly larger than the African and Islamic slave trades, and it had more serious consequences for African society. Between the fifteenth and the nineteenth centuries, it not only siphoned millions of people from their own societies but also provoked turmoil in much of sub-Saharan Africa.

The vast majority of Africans sold into the Atlantic slave trade went to the Caribbean or the Americas. Most worked on plantations cultivating cash crops for export, although some worked as domestic servants, miners, or laborers. Together they made up the largest migration in history before the nineteenth century and gave rise to an African diaspora in the western hemisphere. Under the restrictive conditions of slavery, they could not reconstitute African societies, but they preserved some African traditions and blended them with European and American traditions to create hybrid African-American societies.

African Politics and Society in Early Modern Times

At the start of the early modern era, African peoples lived under a variety of political organizations, including clans governed by kinship groups, regional kingdoms, city-states, and large imperial states that drew their power from the trans-Saharan trade. Under the influence of maritime trade, however, African patterns of state development changed. In west Africa, regional kingdoms replaced imperial states as peoples organized their societies to take advantage of Atlantic as well as trans-Saharan commerce. In east Africa, Swahili city-states fell under the domination of Portuguese merchant-mariners seeking commercial opportunities in the Indian Ocean basin. The extension of trade networks also led to the formation of regional kingdoms in central Africa and south Africa. As the volume of long-distance trade grew, both Islam and Christianity became more prominent in sub-Saharan African societies.

The States of West Africa and East Africa

Between the eighth and the sixteenth centuries, powerful kingdoms and imperial states ruled the savannas of west Africa. The earliest was the kingdom of Ghana, which originated as early as the fourth or fifth century and established its dominance in the region in the eighth century. By controlling and taxing the trans-Saharan trade in gold, the kings of Ghana gained the resources they needed to field a large army and influence affairs in much of west Africa. In the thirteenth century the Mali empire replaced Ghana as the preeminent power in west Africa and continued the Ghana policy of controlling trans-Saharan trade.

THE SONGHAY EMPIRE In the fifteenth century the expansive state of Songhay emerged to take Mali's place as the dominant power of the western grasslands. Based in the trading city of Gao, Songhay rulers built a flourishing city-state as early as the eighth century. In the early fifteenth century,

Ghana (GAH-nuh)
Songhay (song-AHY)

TIMBUKTU. | The city of Timbuktu, as sketched by a French traveler in 1828, was the commercial and cultural center of the Mali and Songhay empires. Though long in decline, the city's mosques, mud-brick dwellings, and crowds of people bespeak a prosperous community.

they rejected Mali authority, and in 1464 the Songhay ruler Sunni Ali (reigned 1464–1493) conquered his neighbors and consolidated the Songhay empire (1464–1591). He brought the important trading cities of Timbuktu and Jenne under his control and used their wealth to dominate the central Niger valley.

SONGHAY ADMINISTRATION Sunni Ali built an elaborate administrative and military apparatus to oversee affairs in his realm. He instituted a hierarchy of command that turned his army into an effective military force. He also created an imperial navy to patrol the Niger River, which was an extremely important commercial highway. Songhay military might enabled Sunni Ali's successors to extend their authority north into the Sahara, east toward Lake Chad, and west toward the upper reaches of the Niger River.

The Songhay emperors presided over a prosperous land. The capital city of Gao had about seventy-five thousand residents, many of whom participated in the lucrative trans-Saharan trade that brought salt, textiles, and metal goods south in exchange for gold and slaves. The emperors were all Muslims: they supported mosques, built schools to teach the Quran, and maintained an Islamic university at Timbuktu. Like the rulers of Ghana and Mali, the Songhay emperors valued Islam as a cultural foundation for cooperation with Muslim merchants and Islamic states in north Africa.

FALL OF SONGHAY The Songhay empire dominated west Africa for most of the sixteenth century, but it was the last of the great imperial states of the grasslands. In 1591 a musket-bearing Moroccan army trekked across the Sahara and opened fire on the previously invincible Songhay military machine. Songhay forces withered under the attack, and subject peoples took the opportunity to revolt against Songhay domination.

As the Songhay empire crumbled, a series of small, regional kingdoms and city-states emerged in west Africa. On the coasts Diula, Mande, and other trading peoples established

Sunni Ali (soon-ee ah-lee)
Timbuktu (tim-buhk-TOO)
Jenne (jehn-neh)
Diula (dih-uh-lah)
Mande (MAHN-dey)

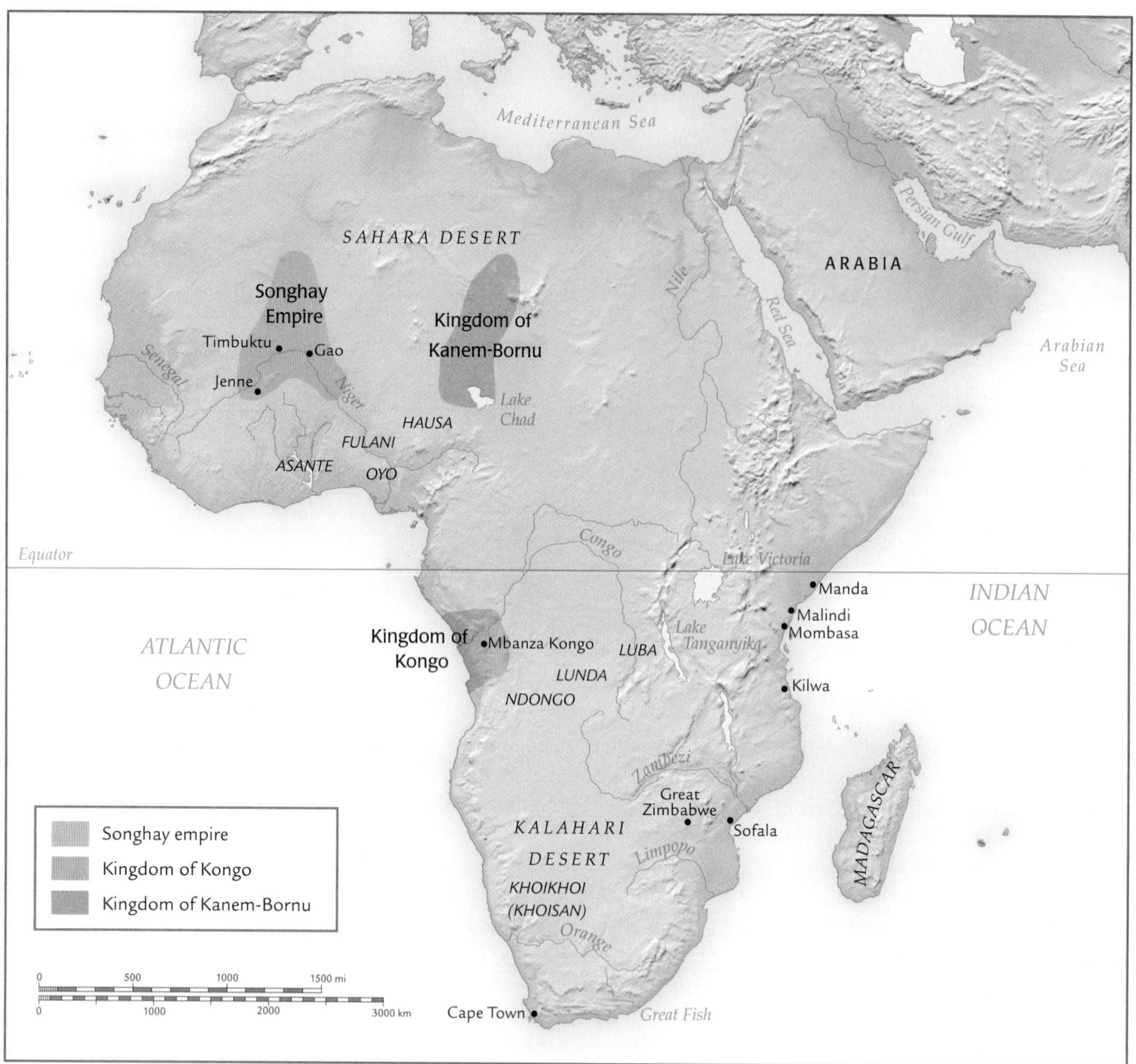

MAP 22.1 | African states, 1500–1650. Locate the three largest states of Songhay, Kongo, and Kanem-Bornu. ***What was it about their respective locations that favored the development of such large polities?***

a series of states that entered into commercial relations with European merchant-mariners who called at west African ports after the fifteenth century. The increasing prominence of Atlantic trade in west African society worked against the interests of imperial states such as Mali and Songhay, which had relied on control of trans-Saharan trade to finance their empires.

SWAHILI DECLINE While regional states displaced the Songhay empire in west Africa, the Swahili city-states of east Africa fell on hard times. In 1505 a huge Portuguese naval expedition subdued all the Swahili cities from Sofala to Mombasa. Portuguese forces built administrative centers at Mozambique and Malindi and constructed forts throughout the region in hopes of controlling trade in east Africa. They did not succeed in that effort, but they disrupted trade patterns enough to send the Swahili cities into a decline from which they never fully recovered.

Swahili (swah-HEE-lee)
Mozambique (moh-zam-BEEK)
Malindi (mah-LIN-dee)

The Kingdoms of Central Africa and South Africa

THE KINGDOM OF KONGO As trade networks multiplied and linked all regions of sub-Saharan Africa, an increasing volume of commerce encouraged state building in central and south Africa. In central Africa the principal states were the kingdoms of Kongo, Ndongo, Luba, and Lunda in the Congo River basin. Best known of them was the kingdom of Kongo, which emerged in the fourteenth century. Its rulers built a centralized state with officials overseeing military, judicial, and financial affairs, and by the late fifteenth century Kongo embraced much of the modern-day Republic of the Congo and Angola.

In 1483 a small Portuguese fleet initiated commercial relations with the kingdom of Kongo. Within a few years, Portuguese merchants had established a close political and diplomatic relationship with the kings of Kongo. They supplied the kings with advisors, provided a military garrison to support the kings and protect Portuguese interests, and brought artisans and priests to Kongo.

The kings of Kongo converted to Christianity as a way to establish closer commercial and diplomatic relations with the Portuguese. The kings appreciated the fact that Christianity offered a strong endorsement of their monarchical rule and found similarities between Roman Catholic saints and the spirits recognized in Kongolese religion. King Nzinga Mbemba of Kongo, also known as King Afonso I (reigned 1506–1542), became a devout Roman Catholic and sought to convert all his subjects to Christianity. Portuguese priests in Kongo reported that he attended religious services daily and studied the Bible so zealously that he sometimes neglected to eat.

PSI img King of the Kongo www.mhhe.com/bentleybrief2e

SLAVE RAIDING IN KONGO Relations with Portugal brought wealth and foreign recognition to Kongo but also led eventually to the destruction of the kingdom. In exchange for their goods and services, Portuguese merchants sought high-value merchandise such as copper, ivory, and, most of all, slaves. They sometimes embarked on slaving expeditions themselves, but more often they made alliances with local authorities in interior regions and provided them with weapons in exchange for slaves. Such tactics undermined the authority of the kings, who appealed repeatedly for the Portuguese to cease or at least to limit their trade in slaves.

Over time, relations between Kongo and Portugal deteriorated, particularly after Portuguese agents began to pursue opportunities south of Kongo. In 1665 Portuguese colonists to the south even went to war with Kongo. Portuguese forces quickly defeated the Kongolese army and decapitated the king. Soon thereafter, Portuguese merchants began to withdraw from Kongo in search of more profitable business in the kingdom of Ndongo to the south. By the eighteenth century the kingdom of Kongo had largely disintegrated.

THE KINGDOM OF NDONGO Meanwhile, Portuguese explorers were developing a brisk slave trade to the south in the kingdom of Ndongo, which the Portuguese referred to as Angola from the title of the king, *ngola.* During the sixteenth century, Ndongo had grown from a small chiefdom subject to the kings of Kongo to a powerful regional kingdom, largely on the basis of the wealth it was able to attract by trading directly with Portuguese merchants rather than through Kongolese intermediaries. After 1611 the Portuguese steadily increased their influence inland by allying with neighboring peoples who delivered increasing numbers of war captives to feed the growing slave trade. Over the next several decades, Portuguese forces campaigned in Ndongo in an effort to establish a colony that would support large-scale trading in slaves.

Ndongo (n'DAWN-goh)
Nzinga Mbemba (IN-zinga MEHM-bah)

QUEEN NZINGA OF NDONGO. | In this engraving, the queen speaks with the Portuguese governor of Angola at his headquarters. The diplomat refused to provide Nzinga with a chair, so she seated herself on the back of a servant while her "concubines" looked on at the right.

QUEEN NZINGA The conquest of Angola did not come easily. For forty years Queen Nzinga (reigned 1623–1663) led spirited resistance against Portuguese forces. Nzinga came from a long line of warrior-kings. She dressed as a male warrior when leading troops in battle and insisted that her subjects refer to her as king rather than queen. She mobilized central African peoples against her Portuguese adversaries, and she allied with Dutch mariners who also traded on the African coast. Her aim was to drive the Portuguese from her land, then expel the Dutch, and finally create a central African empire embracing the entire lower Congo basin.

THE PORTUGUESE COLONY OF ANGOLA Although she was an effective military leader, Nzinga was unable to oust Portuguese forces from Ndongo. When Nzinga died, Portuguese forces faced less capable resistance, and they both extended and tightened their control over Angola, the first European colony in sub-Saharan Africa.

Great Zimbabwe
www.mhhe.com/bentleybrief2e

REGIONAL KINGDOMS IN SOUTH AFRICA In south Africa, as in central Africa, regional kingdoms dominated political affairs. Kingdoms had begun to emerge as early as the eleventh century, largely under the influence of trade. Merchants from the Swahili city-states of coastal east Africa sought gold, ivory, and slaves from the interior regions of south Africa. By controlling local commerce, chieftains increased their wealth, enhanced their power, and extended their authority. By 1300 rulers of one such kingdom had built a massive, stone-fortified city known as Great Zimbabwe, near the city of Nyanda in modern Zimbabwe, and they dominated the gold-bearing plain between the Zambesi and Limpopo rivers until the late fifteenth century.

EUROPEAN ARRIVAL IN SOUTH AFRICA After the fifteenth century a series of smaller kingdoms displaced the rulers of Great Zimbabwe, and Portuguese and Dutch mariners began to play a role in south African affairs. They became especially active after Dutch mariners built a trading post at Cape Town in 1652. With the

Zimbabwe (zihm-BAHB-way)

aid of firearms, they claimed lands for themselves and commandeered the labor of indigenous Khoikhoi peoples. By 1700 large numbers of Dutch colonists had begun to arrive in south Africa, and by midcentury they had established settlements in the region. Their conquests laid the foundation for a series of prosperous Dutch and British colonies in sub-Saharan Africa.

> THINKING ABOUT *Traditions*
>
> **TRADITIONS IN AFRICA AND THE ATLANTIC WORLD.** As a result of the Atlantic slave trade, millions of Africans from a wide variety of states and regions were forced to migrate to the Americas without the benefit of material possessions, family, or the freedom to live where and how they liked. In spite of these hardships, many African traditions survived and grew to shape many aspects of cultural life for all peoples of the Americas. What kinds of African traditions persisted in the Americas, and what made their survival possible?

Islam and Christianity in Early Modern Africa

Indigenous religions remained influential throughout sub-Saharan Africa in early modern times. Although many African peoples recognized a supreme, remote creator god, they devoted most of their attention to powerful spirits who were thought to intervene directly in human affairs. Some of those spirits were associated with geographic features such as mountains, waters, or forests, and others were believed to be the spirits of ancestors who roamed the world.

ISLAM IN SUB-SAHARAN AFRICA Although most Africans continued to observe their inherited religions, both Islam and Christianity attracted increasing interest in sub-Saharan Africa. Islam was most popular in the commercial centers of west Africa and the Swahili city-states of east Africa. In the sixteenth century the trading city of Timbuktu had a prominent Islamic university and 180 schools that taught the Quran. Students flocked to Timbuktu by the thousands from all parts of west Africa.

Most African Muslims blended Islam with indigenous beliefs and customs. The result was a syncretic brand of Islam that not only made a place for African beliefs but also permitted men and women to associate with one another on much more familiar terms than was common in north Africa and Arabia. This syncretic Islam frequently struck many devout Muslims as impure and offensive. Muslim merchants and travelers from north Africa and Arabia often commented on their shock at seeing women in tropical Africa who went out in public with bare breasts and socialized freely with men outside their own families.

THE FULANI AND ISLAM Some Muslims in sub-Saharan Africa also shared these concerns about the purity of Islam. Most important of them were the Fulani of the west African savannas, who observed a strict form of Islam like that practiced in north Africa and Arabia. Beginning about 1680 and continuing through the nineteenth century, the Fulani led a series of military campaigns to establish Islamic states and impose their own brand of Islam in west Africa. They founded powerful states in what is now Guinea, Senegal, Mali, and northern Nigeria, and they promoted the spread of Islam beyond the cities to the countryside by establishing Islamic schools in remote towns and villages. Their campaigns did not stamp out African religions, but they strengthened Islam in sub-Saharan Africa and laid a foundation for new rounds of Islamic state-building and conversion efforts in the nineteenth and twentieth centuries.

CHRISTIANITY IN SUB-SAHARAN AFRICA Like Islam, Christianity blended with traditional beliefs and customs when it spread in sub-Saharan Africa and sometimes formed syncretic cults. A particularly influential syncretic cult was the Antonian movement in Kongo, which flourished in the early eighteenth century. The Antonian movement began in 1704 when an aristocratic woman named Doña Beatriz proclaimed that St. Anthony of Padua had possessed her and chosen her to communicate his messages. St. Anthony was a thirteenth-century Franciscan missionary and popular

Khoikhoi (KOY-koy)
Fulani (foo-LAH-nee)

SOURCES FROM THE PAST

King Afonso I Protests Slave Trading in the Kingdom of Kongo

King Afonso I of Kongo wrote some twenty-four official letters to his fellow monarchs, the kings of Portugal. The letters touch on many themes—relations between Portugal and Kongo, Afonso's devotion to Christianity, and the slave trade. The following excerpts come from two letters of 1526, when Portuguese slave trading was causing serious disruption in Kongo, prompting Afonso to request help in controlling the activities of Portuguese merchants.

And we cannot reckon how great the damage [caused by Portuguese merchants] is, since the mentioned merchants are taking every day our natives, sons of the land and the sons of our noblemen and vassals and our relatives, because the thieves and men of bad conscience grab them wishing to have the things and wares of this Kingdom which they are ambitious of; they grab them and get them to be sold; and so great, Sir, is the corruption and licentiousness that our country is being completely depopulated, and Your Highness should not agree with this nor accept it as in your service. And to avoid it we need from [your] Kingdoms no more than some priests and a few people to teach in schools, and no other goods except wine and flour for the holy sacrament. That is why we beg of Your Highness to help and assist us in this matter, commanding your factors that they should not send here either merchants or wares, because it is *our will that in these Kingdoms there should not be any trade of slaves nor outlet for them.* Concerning what is referred [to] above, again we beg of Your Highness to agree with it, since otherwise we cannot remedy such an obvious damage. . . .

Moreover, Sir, in our Kingdoms there is another great inconvenience which is of little service to God, and this is that many of our people, keenly desirous as they are of the wares and things of your Kingdoms, which are brought here by your people, and in order to satisfy their voracious appetite, seize many of our people, freed and exempt men, and very often it happens that they kidnap even noblemen and the sons of noblemen, and our relatives, and take them to be sold to the white men who are in our Kingdoms. . . .

And as soon as they are taken by the white men they are immediately ironed and branded with fire, and when they are carried to be embarked, if they are caught by our guards' men the whites allege that they have bought them but they cannot say from whom, so that it is our duty to do justice and to restore to the freemen their freedom, but it cannot be done if your subjects feel offended, as they claim to be.

And to avoid such a great evil we passed a law so that any white man living in our Kingdoms and wanting to purchase goods [i.e., slaves] in any way should first inform three of our noblemen and officials of our court whom we rely upon in this matter, . . . who should investigate if the mentioned goods are captives or free men, and if cleared by them there will be no further doubt nor embargo for them to be taken and embarked. But if the white men do not comply with it they will lose the aforementioned goods. And if we do them this favor and concession it is for the part Your Highness has in it, since we know that it is in your service too that these goods are taken from our Kingdom, otherwise we should not consent to this.

■ **On the basis of these letters, does it appear that King Afonso opposed all slave trading or only certain kinds of slave trading?**

SOURCE: Basil Davidson. *The African Past.* Boston: Little, Brown, 1964, pp. 191–93.

preacher, and he became the patron saint of Portugal. Doña Beatriz gained a reputation for working miracles and curing diseases, and she used her prominence to promote an African form of Christianity. She taught that Jesus Christ had been a black African man, that Kongo was the true holy land of Christianity, and that heaven was for Africans. She urged Kongolese to ignore European missionaries and heed her disciples instead, and she sought to harness the widespread popular interest in her teachings and use it to end the wars plaguing Kongo.

Doña Beatriz's movement was a serious challenge to Christian missionaries in Kongo. In 1706 they persuaded King Pedro IV of Kongo to arrest the charismatic prophetess on suspicion of heresy. After examining her, the missionaries determined that Doña Beatriz knowingly taught false doctrine. On their recommendation the royal government sentenced her to death and burned her at the stake. Yet the Antonian movement did not disappear: in 1708 an army of almost twenty thousand Antonians challenged King Pedro, whom they considered an unworthy ruler. Their efforts illustrate clearly the tendency of Kongolese Christians to fashion a faith that reflected their own needs and concerns as well as the interests of European missionaries.

Social Change in Early Modern Africa

Despite increased state-building activity and political turmoil, African society followed long-established patterns during the early modern era. Kinship groups, for example, continued to serve as the basis of social organization and sometimes political organization as well. Within agricultural villages throughout sub-Saharan Africa, clans under the leadership of prominent individuals organized the affairs of their kinship groups and disciplined those who violated community standards. Even in lands ruled by formal states, clan leaders usually implemented state policy at the village level.

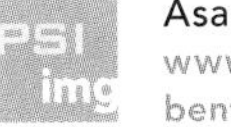

Asante Yam Festival
www.mhhe.com/bentleybrief2e

AMERICAN FOOD CROPS IN SUB-SAHARAN AFRICA Yet interaction with European peoples brought change to African society in early modern times. Trade brought access to European textiles and metal goods, which became popular as complements to native African wares. Trade also brought new food crops to sub-Saharan Africa. In the mid–sixteenth century, American crops such as manioc, maize, and peanuts arrived in Africa aboard Portuguese ships. These crops supplemented bananas, yams, rice, and millet, the principal staple foods of sub-Saharan Africa. The most important American crop was manioc because of its high yield and because it thrived in tropical soils not well suited to cultivation of the other crops.

POPULATION GROWTH By the eighteenth century, bread made from manioc flour had become a staple food in much of west Africa and central Africa, where it helped to underwrite steady population growth. In 1500 C.E. the population of sub-Saharan Africa was about thirty-four million. By 1600 it had increased to forty-four million, and it continued climbing to sixty million in 1800. This strong demographic expansion is all the more remarkable because it took place precisely when millions of Africans underwent an involuntary, forced migration to destinations in the Caribbean and the Americas.

THE ATLANTIC SLAVE TRADE

Of all the processes that linked Africa to the larger Atlantic world in early modern times, the most momentous was the Atlantic slave trade. From the fifteenth to the nineteenth century, European peoples looked to Africa as a source of labor for large plantations that they established in the western hemisphere. In exchange for slaves, African peoples received European manufactured products—most notably firearms. Only in the nineteenth century did the Atlantic slave trade and, in most places, slavery itself come to an end.

Foundations of the Slave Trade

SLAVERY IN AFRICA Until the nineteenth century many settled peoples of the world utilized slave labor in some form. Slavery was common throughout Africa after the Bantu migrations spread agriculture to all parts of the continent. As in other societies, most slaves in Africa were war captives, although criminals and individuals expelled from their clans also fell into slavery. Once enslaved, an individual had no personal or civil rights. Owners could punish slaves at will and sell them as chattel. African slaves usually worked as cultivators in societies far from their homes, although some worked as administrators, soldiers, or even highly placed advisors. The Songhay emperors, for example, often employed slaves as administrators and soldiers, since the rulers distrusted free nobles, whom they considered excessively ambitious and undependable.

Law and society made African slavery different from bondage in Europe, Asia, and other lands. African law did not recognize private property but, rather, vested ownership of land in communities. Thus wealth and power in Africa came not from the possession of land but from control over the human labor that made land productive. Slaves were thus an important means of measuring wealth. Those who controlled large numbers of individuals were able to harvest more crops and accumulate more wealth than others. Africans routinely purchased slaves to enlarge their families, and they often assimilated slaves into their kinship groups so that within a generation a slave might obtain both freedom and an honorable position in a new family or clan.

THE ISLAMIC SLAVE TRADE After the eighth century, Muslim merchants from north Africa, Arabia, and Persia sought African slaves for sale and distribution to destinations in the Mediterranean basin, southwest Asia, India, and even southeast Asia and China. When traditional sources proved insufficient to satisfy the demand for slaves, merchants created new supplies by raiding villages and capturing innocent individuals. Merchants then transported the freshly recruited slaves across the Sahara desert or boarded them on ships at the Swahili port cities of east Africa. Between the eighth and the twentieth centuries, as many as ten million Africans may have left their homeland to feed the Islamic slave trade.

By the time Europeans ventured to sub-Saharan Africa in the fifteenth and sixteenth centuries, traffic in slaves was a well-established feature of African society, and a system for capturing, selling, and distributing slaves had functioned effectively for more than five hundred years. After 1450 European peoples tapped existing networks and dramatically expanded commerce in African slaves even as they shifted its focus to the Atlantic Ocean basin. This Atlantic slave trade profoundly influenced the development of societies throughout the Atlantic Ocean basin.

Human Cargoes

Slave-trading post on the African coast
www.mhhe.com/bentleybrief2e

The Atlantic slave trade began small, but it grew steadily and eventually reached enormous proportions. The earliest European slave traders were Portuguese explorers who, in 1441, seized twelve African men and took them to Portugal as slaves. Portuguese mariners encountered stiff resistance when they attempted to capture slaves, as African warriors fired thousands of poison-tipped arrows at gangs of would-be slave raiders. Soon, however, the mariners learned that they could purchase slaves rather than capture them. By 1460 they were delivering five hundred slaves per year to Portugal and Spain, where they usually worked as miners, porters, or domestic servants.

THE EARLY SLAVE TRADE Slave traders also delivered their human cargoes to Portuguese island colonies in the Atlantic. There was no supply of labor to work plantations in the Azores, the Madeiras, the Cape Verde Islands, and São Tomé, all of which were uninhabited when explorers discovered them in the fifteenth century. Sugar planters on the island of São Tomé in particular called for slaves in increasing quantities. By the 1520s some two thousand slaves per year went to São Tomé. By the 1530s Portuguese entrepreneurs had extended the use of slave labor to Brazil, which eventually became the wealthiest of the sugar-producing lands of the western hemisphere.

Spanish explorers and conquerors also sought laborers to work lands in the Caribbean and the Americas. As imported diseases ravaged indigenous populations, the conquerors found themselves with few laborers to work the land. Gradually Spanish settlers began to rely on imported African slaves as laborers. In 1518 the first shipment of slaves went directly from west Africa to the Caribbean, where they worked on recently established

Azores (uh-ZAWRZ)
Madeiras (muh-DEER-uhs)
São Tomé (SOU tuh-MEY)

sugar plantations. By the early seventeenth century, English colonists had introduced slaves also to the North American mainland.

Middle Passage. Below decks on an illegal slave ship seized by a British anti-slavery patrol in 1846. ***What kinds of conditions are depicted in this drawing?***

TRIANGULAR TRADE The demand for labor in the western hemisphere stimulated a profitable commerce known as the triangular trade, since European ships often undertook voyages of three legs. On the first leg they carried horses and European manufactured goods—especially firearms—which they exchanged in Africa for slaves. The second leg took Africans to Caribbean and American destinations.

On arrival merchants sold their human cargoes to plantation owners for two to three times what they had cost in Africa. In sugar-producing regions they often bartered slaves for sugar or molasses. Then they filled their vessels' hulls with American products before embarking on their voyage back to Europe.

At every stage of the process, the slave trade was a brutal and inhumane business. The original capture of slaves in Africa was almost always a violent affair. As European demand for slaves grew, some African chieftains organized raiding parties to seize individuals from neighboring societies. Others launched wars for the purpose of capturing victims for the slave trade. They often snatched individuals right out of their homes, fields, or villages: millions of lives changed instantly, as slave raiders grabbed their quarries and then immediately spirited them away in captivity. Bewilderment and anger was the lot not only of the captives but also of their family members, who would never again see their kin.

A slave ship
www.mhhe.com/
bentleybrief2e

THE MIDDLE PASSAGE Following capture, enslaved individuals underwent a forced march to the coast, where they lived in holding pens until a ship arrived to transport them to the western hemisphere. Then they embarked on the dreadful middle passage, the trans-Atlantic journey aboard filthy and crowded slave ships. Enslaved passengers traveled belowdecks in hideously cramped quarters. Conditions were so bad that many slaves attempted to starve themselves to death or mounted revolts. Ship crews often treated the unwilling passengers with cruelty and contempt. Crew members used tools to pry open the mouths of those who refused to eat and pitched sick individuals into the ocean rather than have them waste limited supplies of food.

Barring difficulties, the journey to Caribbean and American destinations took four to six weeks, during which heat, cold, and disease levied a heavy toll on the human cargo. During the early days of the slave trade, mortality could exceed 50 percent. As the volume of the trade grew, slavers provided better nourishment and facilities for their cargoes, and mortality eventually declined to about 5 percent per voyage. Over the course of the Atlantic slave trade, however, approximately 25 percent of individuals enslaved in Africa did not survive the middle passage.

The Impact of the Slave Trade in Africa

VOLUME OF THE SLAVE TRADE Before 1600 the Atlantic slave trade operated on a modest scale: on average about two thousand slaves left Africa annually during the late fifteenth and sixteenth centuries. During the seventeenth century, slave exports rose dramatically to twenty thousand per year. The high point of the slave trade came in the eighteenth century, when the number of slaves exported to the Americas averaged fifty-five

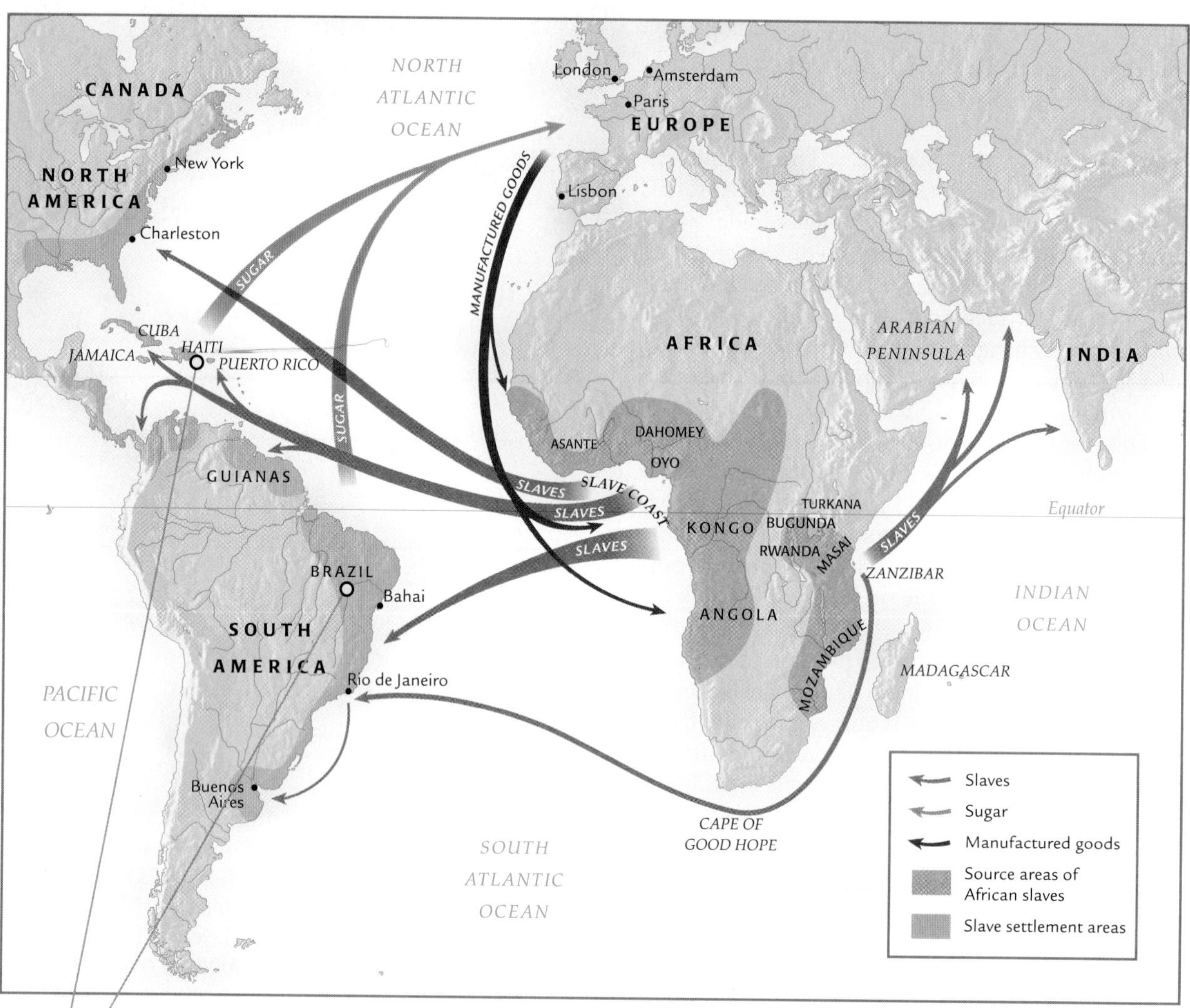

Over 80% of all slaves shipped across the Atlantic were sent to the Caribbean islands and Brazil.

MAP 22.2 | The Atlantic slave trade, 1500–1800. Note the triangular pattern of the Atlantic trade routes between Europe, Africa, and the Americas. ***Why were most slaves in the Atlantic system taken from west/central Africa, and where were they taken?***

thousand per year. During the 1780s slave arrivals averaged eighty-eight thousand per year, and in some individual years they exceeded one hundred thousand. From beginning to end the Atlantic slave trade brought about twelve million Africans to the western hemisphere. An additional four million or more died before arriving.

The impact of the slave trade varied over time and from one African society to another. Some societies largely escaped the slave trade because their lands were distant from the major slave ports on the west African coast. Those societies that raided, took captives, and sold slaves to Europeans profited handsomely from the trade, as did the port cities and the states that coordinated trade with European merchants. Asante, Dahomey, and Oyo peoples, for example, took advantage of the slave trade to obtain firearms from European merchants and build powerful states in west Africa.

SOCIAL EFFECTS OF THE SLAVE TRADE On the whole, however, Africa suffered serious losses from the slave trade. The Atlantic slave trade alone deprived African societies of about sixteen million individuals, in addition to several million others consumed by the continuing Islamic slave trade during the early modern era. Although

Asante (uh-SAN-tee)

Dahomey (dah-HO-meh)

Oyo (OH-yoh)

Plantation Life. | In an engraving of 1667, a European supervisor (lower right) directs slaves on a sugar plantation in Barbados as they haul cane, crush it to extract its juice, boil it to produce molasses, and distill the product into rum.

total African population rose during the early modern era, partly because American food crops enriched diets, several individual societies experienced severe losses because of the slave trade. West African societies between Senegal and Angola were especially vulnerable to slave raiding because of their proximity to the most active slave ports.

While diverting labor from Africa to other lands, the slave trade also distorted African sex ratios, since approximately two-thirds of all exported slaves were males. Slavers preferred young men between ages fourteen and thirty-five, since they had the best potential to provide heavy labor over an extended period of time. This preference for male slaves had social implications for lands that provided slaves. By the late eighteenth century, for example, women made up more than two-thirds of the adult population of Angola. This sexual imbalance encouraged Angolans to practice polygamy and forced women to take on duties that in earlier times had been the responsibility of men.

POLITICAL EFFECTS OF THE SLAVE TRADE Apart from its demographic and social effects, the slave trade brought turmoil to African societies. Violence escalated especially after the late seventeenth century, when African peoples increasingly exchanged slaves for European firearms. When the kingdom of Dahomey obtained effective firearms, for example, its armies were able to capture slaves from unarmed neighboring societies and exchange them for more weapons. During the eighteenth century, Dahomey expanded rapidly and absorbed neighboring societies by increasing its arsenal of firearms and maintaining a constant flow of slaves to the coast. By no means did all African states take such advantage of the slave trade, but Dahomey's experience illustrates the potential of the slave trade to alter the patterns of African politics and society.

The African Diaspora

Some slaves worked as urban laborers or domestic servants, and in Mexico and Peru many worked also as miners. The vast majority, however, provided agricultural labor on plantations in the Caribbean or the Americas. There they cultivated cash crops that made their way into commercial arteries linking lands throughout the Atlantic Ocean basin. Although deprived of their freedom, slaves often resisted their bondage, and they built hybrid cultural traditions compounded of African, European, and American elements. Most European and American states ended the slave trade and abolished slavery during the nineteenth century. By that time the African diaspora—the dispersal of African peoples and their descendants—had left a permanent mark throughout the western hemisphere.

diaspora (dahy-AS-per-uh)

Plantation Societies

Most African slaves went to plantations in the tropical and subtropical regions of the western hemisphere. Spanish colonists established the first of these plantations in 1516 on the island of Hispaniola (modern Haiti and the Dominican Republic) and soon extended them to Mexico as well. Beginning in the 1530s Portuguese entrepreneurs organized plantations in Brazil, and by the early seventeenth century English, Dutch, and French plantations had also appeared in the Caribbean and the Americas.

Gathering cane www.mhhe.com/bentleybrief2e

CASH CROPS Many of these plantations produced sugar, which was one of the most lucrative cash crops of early modern times. But plantations produced other crops as well, including tobacco, rice, and indigo. By the eighteenth century many plantations concentrated on the cultivation of cotton, and coffee had begun to emerge as a plantation specialty.

Regardless of the crops they produced, Caribbean and American plantations had certain elements in common. All of them specialized in the production and export of commercial crops. They all also relied almost exclusively on slave labor. Plantations also featured a sharp, racial division of labor: small numbers of European or Euro-American supervisors governed plantation affairs, and large numbers of African or African-American slaves performed most of the community's physical labor.

REGIONAL DIFFERENCES In spite of their structural similarities, plantation societies differed considerably from one region to another. In the Caribbean and South America, slave populations usually were unable to sustain their numbers by natural means. This was due partly to the impact of tropical diseases such as malaria and yellow fever and partly to the brutal working conditions the slaves faced on the plantations. Moreover, since most slaves were male, slave communities did not reproduce quickly.

Thus, in the Caribbean and South America, plantation owners demanded a continuous supply of slaves to maintain their workforces. Of all the slaves delivered from Africa to the western hemisphere, about half went to Caribbean destinations, and a third more went to Brazil.

Slave codes www.mhhe.com/bentleybrief2e

Only about 5 percent of enslaved Africans went to North American destinations. Diseases there were less threatening than in the Caribbean and Brazil. Moreover, North American planters imported larger numbers of female slaves and encouraged their slaves to form families and bear children. Their support for slave families was especially strong in the eighteenth century, when the prices of slaves direct from Africa rose dramatically.

RESISTANCE TO SLAVERY No matter where they lived, slaves did not meekly accept their status but, like Thomas Peters, resisted it in numerous ways. Some forms of resistance were mild but costly to slave owners: slaves often worked slowly for their masters but diligently in their own gardens, for example. Sometimes they sabotaged plantation equipment or work routines. More seriously, slaves resisted by running away. Runaways known as maroons gathered in remote regions and built their own self-governing communities. Many maroons had gained military experience in Africa, and they organized escaped slaves into effective military forces. Maroon communities flourished throughout slaveholding regions of the western hemisphere, and some of them survived for centuries. In present-day Suriname, for example, the Saramaka people maintain an elaborate oral tradition that traces their descent from eighteenth-century maroons.

SLAVE REVOLTS The most dramatic form of resistance to slavery was the slave revolt. Slaves far outnumbered others in most plantation societies, and thus slave revolts brought stark fear to plantation owners and supervisors. Yet slave revolts almost never

---

Suriname (SOOR-uh-nahm)
Saramaka (sar-ah-MAH-kah)

TREATMENT OF SLAVES. | Slaves were vulnerable to cruel treatment that often provoked them to run away from their plantations or even mount revolts. A French visitor to Brazil in the early nineteenth century depicted a Portuguese overseer administering a brutal whipping to a bound slave on a plantation near Rio de Janeiro. ***What function might the branch behind this slave's knees have had?***

brought slavery itself to an end, because the European and Euro-American ruling elites had access to military forces that extinguished most rebellions. Only in the French sugar colony of Saint-Domingue did a slave revolt abolish slavery as an institution (1793). Indeed, the slaves of Saint-Domingue declared independence from France, renamed the land Haiti, and established a self-governing republic (1804). The Haitian revolution terrified slave owners and inspired slaves throughout the western hemisphere, but no other slave rebellion matched its accomplishments.

SLAVERY AND ECONOMIC DEVELOPMENT The physical labor of African and African-American slaves made crucial contributions to the building of new societies in the Americas and also to the making of the early modern world as a whole. Slave labor cultivated many of the crops and extracted many of the minerals that made their way around the world in the global trade networks of the early modern era. Although slaves themselves did not enjoy the fruits of their labors, without them it would have been impossible for prosperous new societies to emerge in the Americas during the early modern era.

The Making of African-American Cultural Traditions

Enslaved Africans did not enjoy the luxury of maintaining their inherited cultural traditions in the western hemisphere. When packed in slave ships for the middle passage, they found themselves in the company of Africans from societies other than their own. When sold to masters in the Caribbean and the Americas, they joined societies shaped by European and American traditions. In those new circumstances, then, slaves constructed distinctive African-American cultural traditions.

Saint-Domingue (san doe-MANG)

THINKING ABOUT *Encounters*

ENCOUNTERS IN AFRICA AND THE ATLANTIC WORLD. Although many of the peoples of sub-Saharan Africa continued to follow established patterns of life in the early modern period, the opening of the Atlantic slave trade ushered in a new era of intense and destructive encounters between Africans and Europeans. In what ways did these encounters shape African societies in Africa itself, and in what ways did they shape the emerging societies of the Americas?

AFRICAN AND CREOLE LANGUAGES European languages were the dominant tongues in the slave societies of the western hemisphere, but slave communities frequently spoke a creole tongue that drew on several African and European languages. In the low country of South Carolina and Georgia, for example, slaves made up about three-quarters of the population in the eighteenth century and regularly communicated in the creole languages Gullah and Geechee, respectively.

AFRICAN-AMERICAN RELIGIONS Like their languages, slaves' religions combined elements from different societies. Some slaves from Africa were Christians, and many others converted to Christianity after their arrival in the western hemisphere. Most Africans and African-Americans, however, practiced a syncretic faith that made considerable room for African interests and traditions. Because they developed mostly in plantation societies under conditions of slavery, these syncretic religions usually did not create an institutional structure or establish a hierarchy of priests and officials. Yet in several cases—most notably Voudou in Haiti, Santeria in Cuba, and Candomblé in Brazil—they became exceedingly popular.

All the syncretic African-American religions drew inspiration from Christianity: they met in parish churches, sought personal salvation, and made use of Christian paraphernalia such as holy water, candles, and statues. Yet they also preserved African traditions. They associated African deities with Christian saints and relied heavily on African rituals such as drumming, dancing, and sacrificing animals. They also preserved beliefs in spirits and supernatural powers: magic, sorcery, witchcraft, and spirit possession all played prominent roles in African-American religions.

AFRICAN-AMERICAN MUSIC As in their languages and religions, slaves relied on their African traditions in creating musical forms attuned to the plantation landscape. African slaves in the Americas adapted African musical traditions, including both their rhythmic and oratorical elements, to their new environments as a means of buffering the shock of transition, as a way to survive and to resist the horrid conditions of their new lives. In the process, they managed to create musical forms that made their influence felt not just in the slave quarters but also in the multicultural societies of the Caribbean and the Americas.

Slaves fashioned a new sense of identity and strength by adapting west African instruments and musical traditions to suit European languages, Christian religion, and the work routines of American plantations. Slave musicians played drums and stringed instruments like banjos that closely resembled traditional African instruments. They also adapted west African call-and-response patterns of singing to the rhythms of field work on plantations. Indeed, from work songs and spirituals to the blues, jazz, and soul, African-American music evolved to mirror the difficult and often chaotic circumstances of black life in the Americas.

AFRICAN-AMERICAN CULTURAL TRADITIONS African traditions also made their effects felt throughout much of the western hemisphere. Slaves introduced African foods to Caribbean and American societies and helped give rise to distinctive hybrid cuisines. They combined African okra, for example, with European-style sautéed vegetables and American shellfish to produce magnificent gumbos, which found their way to Euro-American as well as African-American tables. Slaves introduced rice cultivation to tropical and subtropical regions. They also built houses, fashioned clay pots,

Gullah (GUHL-uh)
Geechee (GEE-chee)
Voudou (voo-doo)
Santeria (sahn-tuh-REE-uh)
Candomblé (kan-duhm-BLEH)

and wove grass baskets in west African styles. In many ways the African diaspora influenced the ways all peoples lived in plantation societies.

The End of the Slave Trade and the Abolition of Slavery

OLAUDAH EQUIANO. The abolitionist former slave as depicted in the first edition of his autobiography (1789).

OLAUDAH EQUIANO Almost as old as the Atlantic slave trade itself were voices calling for its abolition. The American and French revolutions, with their calls for liberty and universal human rights, stimulated the abolitionist cause. Africans also took up the struggle to abolish commerce in human beings. Frequent slave revolts in the eighteenth and nineteenth centuries made the institution of slavery an expensive and dangerous business. Some freed slaves contributed to the abolitionist cause by writing books that exposed the brutality of institutional slavery. Most notable of them was the west African Olaudah Equiano (1745–1797), who in 1789 published an autobiography detailing his experiences as a slave and a free man. Captured at age ten in his native Benin (in modern Nigeria), Equiano worked as a slave in the West Indies, Virginia, and Pennsylvania. He accompanied one of his masters on several campaigns of the Seven Years' War before purchasing his freedom in 1766. The book became a best seller, and Equiano traveled throughout the British Isles giving speeches and denouncing slavery as an evil institution. He lobbied government officials and members of Parliament, and his efforts strengthened the antislavery movement in England.

THE ECONOMIC COSTS OF SLAVERY Quite apart from moral and political arguments, economic forces contributed to the end of slavery and the slave trade. Indeed, it gradually became clear that slave labor did not come cheap. The possibility of rebellion forced slave societies to maintain expensive military forces. Even in peaceful times slaves were often unwilling and unproductive workers. Furthermore, in the late eighteenth century a rapid expansion of Caribbean sugar production led to declining prices. About the same time, African slave traders and European merchants sharply increased the prices they charged for fresh slaves.

As the profitability of slavery declined, Europeans began to shift their investments from sugarcane and slaves to newly emerging manufacturing industries. Investors soon found that wage labor in factories was cheaper than slave labor on plantations. As an additional benefit, free workers spent much of their income on manufactured goods. Meanwhile, European investors realized that leaving Africans in Africa, where they could secure raw materials and buy manufactured goods in exchange, was good business.

END OF THE SLAVE TRADE Denmark abolished trade in slaves in 1803, and other lands followed suit: Great Britain in 1807, the United States in 1808, France in 1814, the Netherlands in 1817, and Spain in 1845. The end of the slave trade did not abolish the institution of slavery itself, however, and as long as plantation slavery continued, a clandestine trade shipped slaves across the Atlantic. British naval squadrons sought to prevent this trade by conducting search-and-seizure operations, and gradually the illegal slave trade ground to a halt. The last documented ship that carried slaves across the Atlantic arrived in Cuba in 1867.

The abolition of the institution of slavery itself was a long-drawn-out process: emancipation of all slaves came in 1833 in British colonies, 1848 in French colonies, 1865 in the United States, 1886 in Cuba, and 1888 in Brazil. Saudi Arabia and Angola abolished

Olaudah Equiano (oh-LAU-duh ay-kwee-AHN-oh)

slavery in the 1960s. Officially, slavery no longer exists, but millions of people live in various forms of involuntary servitude even today. According to the Anti-slavery Society for the Protection of Human Rights, debt bondage, contract labor, sham adoptions, servile marriages, and other forms of servitude still oppress more than two hundred million people, mostly in Africa, south Asia, and Latin America. Meanwhile, the legacy of the Atlantic slave trade remains visible throughout much of the western hemisphere, where the African diaspora has given rise to distinctive African-American communities.

SUMMARY

During the early modern era, the peoples of sub-Saharan Africa built states and traded with Islamic societies as they had since the eighth century C.E. Yet African peoples also experienced dramatic changes as they participated in the formation of an integrated Atlantic Ocean basin. The principal agents of change were European merchant-mariners who sought commercial opportunities in sub-Saharan Africa. They brought European manufactured goods and introduced American food crops that fueled population growth throughout Africa. But they also encouraged vast expansion of existing slave-trading networks as they sought laborers for plantations in the western hemisphere. The Atlantic slave trade violently removed at least sixteen million individuals from their home societies and caused political turmoil and social disruption throughout much of sub-Saharan Africa. Enslaved Africans and their descendants were mostly unable to build states or organize societies in the western hemisphere. But they formed an African diaspora that maintained some African traditions and profoundly influenced the development of societies in all slave-holding regions of the Caribbean and the Americas. They also collaborated with others to bring about an end to the slave trade and the abolition of slavery itself.

STUDY TERMS

African diaspora (443)
Angola (436)
Antonian movement (437)
Atlantic slave trade (439)
Cape Town (436)
creole language (446)
Dahomey (443)
Doña Beatriz (437)
Fulani (437)
Great Zimbabwe (436)
Haiti (445)
Islamic slave trade (440)
King Afonso I (438)
kingdom of Kongo (435)
Mali empire (432)
manioc (439)
middle passage (441)
Olaudah Equiano (447)
plantation (444)
Queen Nzinga (436)
Songhay empire (432)
triangular trade (441)

FOR FURTHER READING

Michael L. Conniff and Thomas J. Davis. *Africans in the Americas: A History of the Black Diaspora.* New York, 1994. A comprehensive survey of African-European relations, the slave trade, and the African diaspora.

Philip D. Curtin. *The Rise and Fall of the Plantation Complex: Essays in Atlantic History.* 2nd ed. Cambridge, 1998. Examines plantation societies and slavery as institutions linking lands throughout the Atlantic Ocean basin.

———, ed. *Africa Remembered: Narratives by West Africans from the Era of the Slave Trade.* Madison, 1967. Translations of works in which ten enslaved Africans recounted their memories of early modern Africa.

Christopher Ehret. *The Civilizations of Africa: A History to 1800.* Charlottesville, Va., 2002. An important contribution that views Africa in the context of world history.

David Eltis. *The Rise of African Slavery in the Americas.* Cambridge, 1999. Emphasizes both the economic and the cultural foundations of Atlantic slavery.

Joseph E. Harris, ed. *Global Dimensions of the African Diaspora.* 2nd ed. Washington, 1993. A collection of scholarly essays on Africans in the Americas and the larger world.

Patrick Manning. *Slavery and African Life: Occidental, Oriental, and African Slave Trades.* Cambridge, 1990. Concentrates on the impact of the slave trade on Africa.

Sidney Mintz. *Sweetness and Power: The Place of Sugar in Modern History.* New York, 1985. Important study of sugar, slavery, politics, and society by a prominent anthropologist.

John Thornton. *Africa and Africans in the Making of the Atlantic World, 1400–1800.* 2nd ed. New York, 1997. A rich analysis of African peoples and their roles in the Atlantic Ocean basin.

Jan Vansina. *Paths in the Rainforest: Toward a History of Political Tradition in Equatorial Africa.* Madison, 1990. A thoughtful analysis that considers both native traditions and external influences on African history.

Tradition and Change in East Asia

23

n January 1601 a mechanical clock chimed the hours for the first time in the city of Beijing. In the early 1580s, devices that Chinese called "self-ringing bells" had arrived at the port of Macau with Portuguese merchants. Reports of them soon spread to the emperor in Beijing. The Roman Catholic missionary Matteo Ricci conceived the idea of awing the emperor with mechanical clocks and then persuading him and his subjects to convert to Christianity. From his post at Macau, Ricci let imperial authorities know that he could supply the emperor with a chiming clock. When the emperor Wanli granted him permission to travel to Beijing and establish a mission, Ricci took with him a large mechanical clock intended for public display and a smaller clock for the emperor's personal use.

Chiming mechanical clocks enchanted Wanli and his court and soon became the rage in elite society throughout China. Wealthy Chinese merchants paid handsome sums for them, and Europeans often found that business went better if they presented clocks to the government officials they dealt with. By the eighteenth century the imperial court maintained a workshop to manufacture and repair mechanical clocks and watches. Although most Chinese could not afford to purchase mechanical clocks, commoners could admire the large, chiming clock Matteo Ricci installed outside his residence in Beijing.

Chiming clocks did not have the effect that Ricci desired. The emperor showed no interest in Christianity, and the missionaries attracted only small numbers of Chinese converts. Yet, by opening the doors of the imperial court to the missionaries, the self-ringing bells symbolized the increasing engagement between Asian and European peoples.

By linking all the world's regions and peoples, the European voyages of exploration inaugurated a new era in world history. Yet transoceanic connections influenced different societies in very different ways. In contrast to sub-Saharan Africa, where the Atlantic slave trade provoked turmoil, east Asian lands benefited greatly from long-distance trade, since it brought silver, which stimulated their economies. East Asian societies benefited also from American plant crops that made their way across the seas as part of the Columbian exchange.

Unlike societies in the Americas, where Europeans profoundly influenced historical development from the time of their arrival,

❮ Although the Great Wall of China had precedents as early as the 4th century B.C.E., this 2500 kilometer (1550 mile) stone and brick wall was built by the Ming emperors in the 15th and 16th centuries to protect China from invaders.

Matteo Ricci (maht-TAY-oh REET-chee)
Wanli (wahn-LEE)

CHRONOLOGY

1368–1644	Ming dynasty (China)
1368–1398	Reign of Hongwu
1403–1424	Reign of Yongle
1552–1610	Life of Matteo Ricci
1572–1620	Reign of Emperor Wanli
1600–1867	Tokugawa shogunate (Japan)
1616–1626	Reign of Nurhaci
1642–1693	Life of Ihara Saikaku
1644–1911	Qing dynasty (China)
1661–1722	Reign of Kangxi
1736–1795	Reign of Qianlong
1793	British trade mission to China

east Asian societies largely controlled their own affairs until the nineteenth century. Because of its political and cultural preeminence, China remained the dominant power in east Asia. China was also a remarkably prosperous land. Indeed, with its huge population, enormous productive capacity, and strong demand for silver, China was a leading economic powerhouse driving world trade in early modern times. By the late eighteenth century, however, China was experiencing social and economic change that eventually caused instability.

During the seventeenth and eighteenth centuries, Japan also underwent major transformations. The Tokugawa shoguns unified the Japanese islands for the first time and laid a foundation for long-term economic growth. While tightly restricting contacts and relations with the larger world, Tokugawa Japan generated a distinctive set of social and cultural traditions. Those developments helped fashion a Japan that would play a decisive role in global affairs by the twentieth century.

THE QUEST FOR POLITICAL STABILITY

During the thirteenth and fourteenth centuries, China was ruled by the Yuan dynasty (1279–1368) of nomadic Mongol warriors. Mongol overlords ignored Chinese political and cultural traditions, and they displaced Chinese bureaucrats in favor of foreign administrators. When the Yuan dynasty came to an end, the Ming emperors who succeeded it sought to erase all signs of Mongol influence and restore traditional ways to China. Looking to the Tang and Song dynasties for inspiration, they built a powerful imperial state, revived the civil service staffed by Confucian scholars, and promoted Confucian thought. Rulers of the succeeding Qing dynasty were themselves Manchus of nomadic origin, but they too worked zealously to promote Chinese ways. Ming and Qing emperors alike were deeply conservative: their principal concern was to maintain stability in a large agrarian society, so they adopted policies that favored Chinese political and cultural traditions. The state they fashioned governed China for more than half a millennium.

The Ming Dynasty

MING GOVERNMENT When the Yuan dynasty collapsed, the Ming dynasty (1368–1644) restored native rule to China. Hongwu (reigned 1368–1398), founder of the Ming ("brilliant") dynasty, built a tightly centralized state. As emperor, Hongwu made extensive use of mandarins, imperial officials who oversaw implementation of government policies throughout China. He also placed great trust in eunuchs on the assumption that they could not generate families who might one day challenge imperial

Tokugawa (TOH-koo-GAH-wah)
shogun (SHOH-gun)
Qing (chihng)
Hongwu (hawng-woo)
eunuch (YOO-nuhk)

MAP 23.1 | Ming China, 1368–1644. Locate the old Ming capital at Nanjing and the new Ming capital at Beijing. ***Why would the Ming emperors have wanted to move so far north?***

The Ming-era Great Wall was about 2500 km long, and was designed to keep nomadic invaders from the north at bay.

authority. The emperor Yongle (reigned 1403–1424) launched a series of naval expeditions that went as far as Malindi in east Africa. Yongle's successors discontinued the expeditions but maintained the centralized state that Hongwu had established.

The Ming dynasty www.mhhe.com/ bentleybrief2e

The Great Wall of China www.mhhe.com/ bentleybrief2e

THE GREAT WALL The Ming emperors were determined to prevent new invasions. In 1421 Yongle moved the capital from Nanjing in the south to Beijing to keep closer watch on the Mongols and other nomadic peoples in the north. The later Ming emperors sought to protect their realm by building new fortifications, including the Great Wall of China, along the northern border. The Great Wall had precedents dating back to the fourth century B.C.E., but its construction was a Ming-dynasty project. Workers by the hundreds of thousands labored throughout the late fifteenth and sixteenth centuries to build a stone and brick barrier that ran some 2,500 kilometers (1,550 miles). The Great Wall was 10 to 15 meters (33 to 49 feet) high, and it featured watch towers, signal towers, and accommodations for troops deployed on the border.

The Ming emperors also set out to eradicate Mongol and other foreign influences and to create a stable society in the image of the Chinese past. Respect for Chinese traditions facilitated the restoration of institutions that the Mongols had ignored or suppressed. The government sponsored study of Chinese cultural traditions, especially Confucianism and the reestablishment of imperial academies and regional colleges. Most important, the Ming state restored the system of civil service examinations that Mongol rulers had neglected.

MING DECLINE The vigor of early Ming rule did not survive beyond the mid–sixteenth century, when a series of problems weakened the dynasty. From the 1520s to the 1560s, pirates and smugglers operated almost at will along the east coast of China.

Yongle (yong-lay)

THE FORBIDDEN CITY. | The emperor Yongle designed the Forbidden City as a vast, walled imperial retreat in central Beijing. Here a sculptured lion guards the Forbidden City's Gate of Supreme Harmony.

Suppression of pirates took more than forty years, partly because of an increasingly inept imperial government. The later Ming emperors lived extravagantly in the Forbidden City, a vast imperial enclave in Beijing, and received news about the outside world only from eunuch servants and administrators. The emperors sometimes ignored government affairs for decades on end, while powerful eunuchs won favor by providing for their amusement. As the eunuchs' influence increased, corruption and inefficiency spread throughout the government and weakened the Ming state.

MING COLLAPSE When a series of famines struck China during the early seventeenth century, the government was unable to organize effective relief efforts. During the 1630s peasants organized revolts throughout China. To complicate matters further, Manchu forces invaded from the north. In 1644 Chinese rebel forces captured the Ming capital at Beijing. Manchu invaders allied with an army loyal to the Ming, crushed the rebels, and recovered Beijing. The Manchus portrayed themselves as avengers who saved the capital from dangerous rebels, but they neglected to restore Ming rule. Instead, they moved their own capital to Beijing and displaced the Ming dynasty.

The Qing Dynasty

THE MANCHUS When the Ming dynasty fell, Manchus poured south into China from their homeland of Manchuria. The victors proclaimed a new dynasty, the Qing ("pure"), which ruled China until the early twentieth century (1644–1911). The Manchus mostly were pastoral nomads whose remote ancestors had traded with China since the Qin dynasty. During the late sixteenth and early seventeenth centuries, an ambitious chieftain named Nurhaci (reigned 1616–1626) unified Manchu tribes into a centralized state and organized a powerful military force. During the 1620s and 1630s, the Manchu army captured Korea and Mongolia and launched small-scale invasions into China. After their seizure of Beijing in 1644, the Manchus moved to extend their authority throughout China. By the early 1680s they had consolidated the Qing dynasty's hold throughout the land.

The establishment of the Qing dynasty was due partly to Manchu military prowess and partly to Chinese support for the Manchus. During the 1630s and 1640s, many Chinese generals and Confucian scholar-bureaucrats deserted the Ming dynasty because of its corruption and inefficiency. The Manchu ruling elites were schooled in Chinese language and Confucian thought, and they often enjoyed more respect from the scholar-bureaucrats than the high administrators of the Ming dynasty itself.

The Manchus were careful to preserve their own ethnic and cultural identity. They outlawed intermarriage between Manchus and Chinese and forbade Chinese to travel to Manchuria or to learn the Manchurian language. Qing authorities also forced Chinese men to shave the front of their heads and grow a Manchu-style queue as a sign of submission to the dynasty.

Nurhaci (NOOR-hacheh)

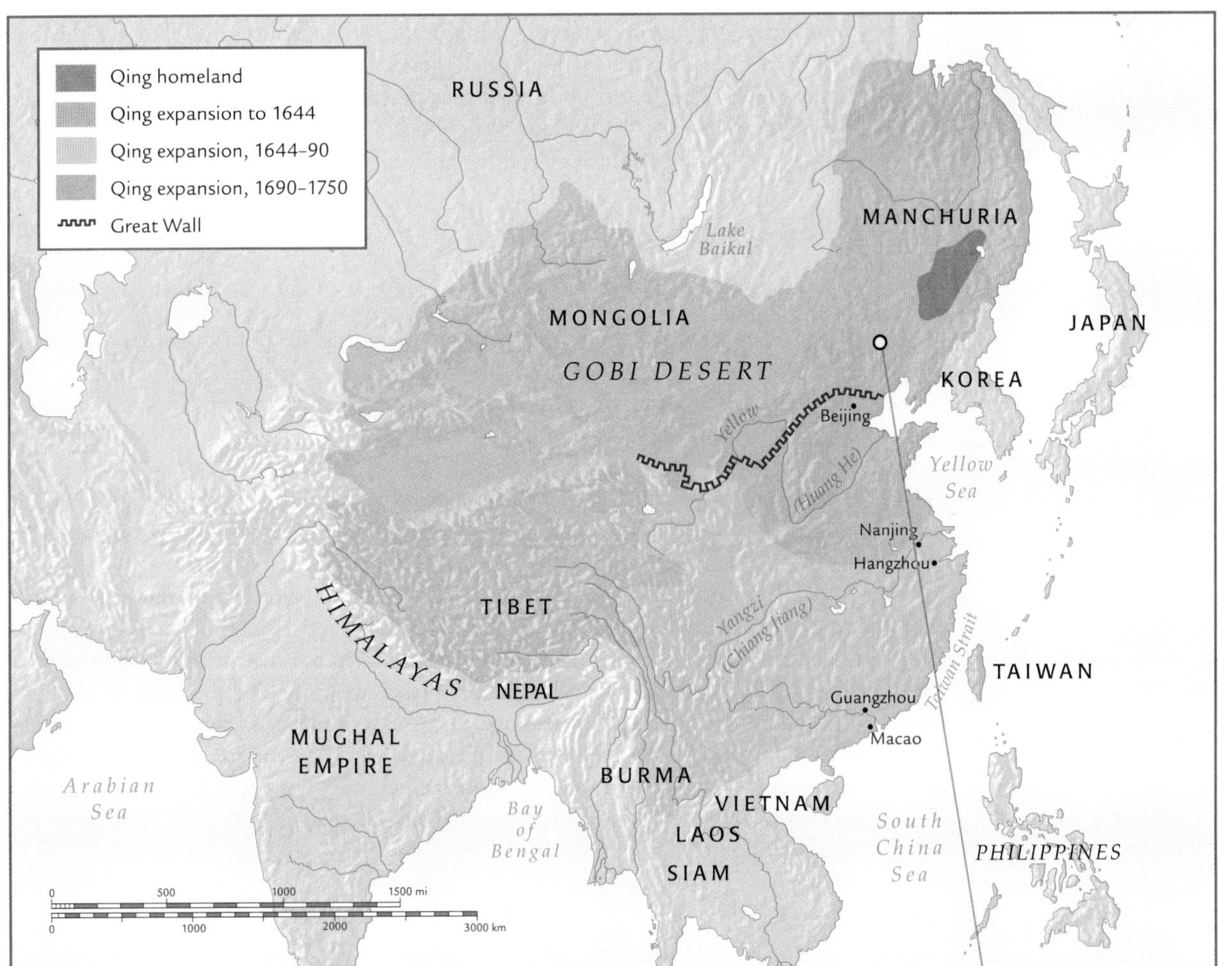

MAP 23.2 | The Qing empire, 1644–1911. Compare this map with Map 23.1. ***Why would the Qing emperors have wanted to incorporate such extensive territories in Mongolia and Tibet into their empire?***

The Qing, who were originally from Manchuria, did not allow ethnic Chinese to travel to their homeland.

KANGXI. | Though painted in the nineteenth century, this portrait depicts Kangxi in his imperial regalia as he looked at about age fifty.

KANGXI AND HIS REIGN The long reigns of two particularly effective emperors, Kangxi (1661–1722) and Qianlong (1736–1795), helped mute the tensions between Manchus and Chinese and allowed the Manchus to consolidate their hold on China. Kangxi was a Confucian scholar as well as an enlightened ruler. He studied the Confucian classics and sought to apply their teachings through his policies. Thus, for example, he organized flood-control and irrigation projects on the Confucian precept that rulers should look after the welfare of their subjects and promote agriculture. He also generously patronized Confucian schools and academies.

Kangxi was also a conqueror, and he oversaw the construction of a vast Qing empire. He conquered the island of Taiwan, where Ming loyalists had retreated after their expulsion from southern China, and absorbed it into his empire. Like his predecessors of the Han and Tang dynasties, Kangxi sought to forestall problems with nomadic peoples by projecting Chinese influence into central Asia. His conquests in Mongolia and central Asia extended almost to the Caspian Sea, and he imposed a Chinese protectorate over Tibet. Kangxi's grandson Qianlong continued this expansion of Chinese influence by consolidating Kangxi's conquests in central Asia and by making Vietnam, Burma, and Nepal vassal states of the Qing dynasty.

QIANLONG AND HIS REIGN Qianlong's reign marked the height of the Qing dynasty. Like Kangxi, Qianlong was a sophisticated and learned man. During his long, stable, and prosperous reign, the imperial treasury bulged so much that on four occasions Qianlong canceled tax collections. Toward the end of his reign, however, Qianlong delegated many responsibilities to his favorite eunuchs. His successors continued that practice, and by the nineteenth century the Qing dynasty faced serious difficulties. Throughout the reign of Qianlong, however, China remained a wealthy and well-organized land.

The Son of Heaven and the Scholar-Bureaucrats

Although Qing rulers usually appointed Manchus to the highest political posts, they relied on the same governmental apparatus that the Ming emperors had established. Indeed, for more than five hundred years, the autocratic state created by the Ming emperor Hongwu governed China's fortunes.

THE SON OF HEAVEN If the emperor of China during the Ming and Qing dynasties was not quite a god, he certainly was more than a mere mortal. Chinese tradition held that he was the "Son of Heaven," the human being designated by heavenly powers to maintain order on the earth. He led a privileged life within the walls of the Forbidden City. Hundreds of concubines resided in his harem, and thousands of eunuchs looked after his desires. Everything about his person and the institution he represented conveyed a sense of awesome authority. The imperial wardrobe and personal effects bore designs forbidden to all others, for instance, and the written characters of the emperor's name were taboo throughout the realm. Individuals who had the rare privilege of a personal audience with the emperor had to perform the kowtow—three kneelings and nine head knockings. Those who gave even minor offense faced having their bare buttocks flogged with bamboo canes.

Kangxi (kahng-shee)
Qianlong (chyahn-lawng)
kowtow (kou-tou)

THE SCHOLAR-BUREAUCRATS Day-to-day governance of the empire fell to scholar-bureaucrats appointed by the emperor. With few exceptions these officials came from the class of well-educated and highly literate men known as the scholar-gentry. These men had earned academic degrees by passing rigorous civil service examinations, and they dominated China's political and social life.

Preparations for the examinations began at an early age, either in local schools or with private tutors. By the time students were eleven or twelve years old, they had memorized several thousand characters that were necessary to deal with the Confucian curriculum, including the *Analects* of Confucius and other standard works. They followed those studies with instruction in calligraphy, poetry, and essay composition.

CIVIL SERVICE EXAMINATIONS The examinations consisted of a battery of tests administered at the district, provincial, and metropolitan levels. Stiff official quotas restricted the number of successful candidates in each examination—only three hundred students could pass metropolitan examinations—and students frequently took the examinations several times before earning a degree.

THE EXAMINATION SYSTEM AND CHINESE SOCIETY The possibility of bureaucratic service—with prospects for rich social and financial rewards—ensured that competition for degrees was ferocious at all levels. Yet a degree did not ensure government service. During the Qing dynasty the empire's one million degree holders competed for twenty thousand official civil service positions, and only those who passed the metropolitan examinations could look forward to powerful positions in the imperial bureaucracy.

Yet the examination system was a pivotal institution. By opening the door to honor, power, and rewards, the examinations encouraged serious pursuit of a formal education. Furthermore, since the system did not erect social barriers before its recruits, it provided an avenue for upward social mobility. Finally, in addition to selecting officials for government service, the education and examination system molded the personal values of those who managed day-to-day affairs in imperial China. By concentrating on Confucian classics and neo-Confucian commentaries, the examinations guaranteed that Confucianism would be at the heart of Chinese education and that Confucians would govern the state.

ECONOMIC AND SOCIAL CHANGES

By modeling their governmental structure on the centralized imperial states of earlier Chinese dynasties, the Ming and Qing emperors succeeded in their goal of restoring and maintaining traditional ways in China. They also sought to preserve the traditional hierarchical and patriarchal social order. Yet, while the emperors promoted conservative political and social policies, China experienced economic and social changes, partly as a result of influences from abroad. Agricultural production increased dramatically and fueled rapid population growth, and global trade brought China enormous wealth. These developments deeply influenced Chinese society and partly undermined the stability that the Ming and Qing emperors sought to preserve.

The Patriarchal Family

FILIAL PIETY Moralists portrayed the Chinese people as one large family, and they extended family values to the larger society. Filial piety, for example, implied not only duties of children toward their fathers but also loyalty of subjects toward the emperor. Like the imperial government, the Chinese family was hierarchical, patriarchal, and authoritarian. The father was head of the household, and he passed leadership of the family to his eldest son. The veneration of ancestors, which the state promoted as a matter of Confucian propriety, strengthened the authority of the patriarchs by honoring the male line of descent. Filial piety was the cornerstone of family values. Children had the duty to look after their parents' happiness and well-being, especially in their old age. Young children heard stories of sons who went so far as to cut off parts of their bodies to ensure that their parents had enough to eat.

The social assumptions of the Chinese family extended into patrilineal descent groups such as the clan. Clans—whose members sometimes numbered in the thousands—assumed responsibilities such as the maintenance of local order, organization of local economies, and provision for welfare. Clan-supported education gave poor but promising relatives the opportunity to succeed in the civil service examinations. Finally, clans served as a means for the transmission of Confucian values from the gender leaders to all social classes within the clan.

GENDER RELATIONS Within the family, Confucian principles subjected women to the authority of men. The subordination of females began at an early age. Chinese parents preferred boys over girls. Whereas a boy might have the opportunity to take the official examinations and become a government official, parents regarded a girl as a social and financial liability. Under those circumstances it was not surprising that girls were the primary victims of infanticide.

During the Ming and Qing dynasties, patriarchal authority over females probably became tighter than ever before in China. Since ancient times, relatives had discouraged widows from remarriage, but social pressures increased during the Ming dynasty. Friends and relatives not only encouraged widows to honor the memory of their departed husbands but also heaped posthumous honors on those who committed suicide and followed their spouses to the grave.

PSI img Chinese foot binding www.mhhe.com/bentleybrief2e

FOOT BINDING Moreover, foot binding, a custom that probably originated in the Song dynasty, became exceptionally popular during the late Ming and Qing dynasties. Tightly constrained and deformed by strips of linen, bound feet could not grow naturally and so would not support the weight of an adult woman. Bound feet were small and dainty, and they sometimes inspired erotic arousal among men. The practice of foot binding became most widespread among the wealthy classes, since it demonstrated an ability to support women who could not perform physical labor, but commoners sometimes bound the feet of especially pretty girls in hopes of arranging favorable marriages.

Marriage itself was a contractual affair whose principal purpose was to continue the male line of descent. A bride became a member of the husband's family, and her position there was one of unambiguous subservience. Women could not divorce their husbands, but men could put aside their wives in cases where there were no offspring or where the wife was guilty of adultery, theft, or disobedience.

Thus custom and law combined to strengthen patriarchal authority in Chinese families during the Ming and Qing dynasties. Yet, while family life continued to develop along traditional lines, the larger Chinese society underwent considerable change between the sixteenth and the eighteenth centuries.

TRADITIONS IN EAST ASIA. Between 1500 and 1800, the Ming and Qing dynasties in China sought to promote stability within their realms by encouraging Chinese people to restore and then maintain the cultural traditions of past eras. What traditions were both dynasties particularly keen to encourage, and how did they promote their restoration?

Population Growth and Economic Development

China was a predominantly agricultural society, a fact that meshed agreeably with the Confucian view that land was the source of everything praiseworthy. Yet only a small fraction of China's land is suitable for planting: even today only about 11 percent is in cultivation. To feed the country's large population, China's farmers relied on intensive, garden-style agriculture that was highly productive. On its strong agrarian foundation, China supported a large population and built the most highly commercialized economy of the preindustrial world.

AMERICAN FOOD CROPS By intensively cultivating every available parcel of land, Chinese peasants increased their yields of traditional food crops—especially rice, wheat, and millet—until the seventeenth century. As peasants approached the upper limits of agricultural productivity, Spanish merchants coming by way of the Philippines introduced American food crops to China. American maize, sweet potatoes, and peanuts permitted Chinese farmers to take advantage of soils that previously had gone uncultivated. The introduction of new crops increased the food supply and supported further population growth.

POPULATION GROWTH In spite of recurring epidemic diseases such as plague, China's population rose rapidly from 100 million in 1500 to 160 million in 1600. By 1750 it had surged to 225 million. However, this rapid demographic growth set the stage for future economic and social problems, since agricultural production could not keep pace with population over a long term.

Although an increasing population placed pressure on Chinese resources, it offered opportunities for entrepreneurs. Indeed, entrepreneurs had access to a large labor force, which meant they were able to recruit workers readily at low cost. After the mid–sixteenth century the Chinese economy benefited also from the influx of Japanese and American silver, which stimulated trade and financed further commercial expansion.

Silk Production. A Ming-era vase painting depicts a woman weaving silk as an attendant pours tea.

FOREIGN TRADE Global trade brought tremendous prosperity to China, especially during the early Qing dynasty. Chinese workers produced vast quantities of silk, porcelain, lacquerware, and tea for consumers in the Indian Ocean basin, central Asia, and Europe. Chinese imports were relatively few, and thus the most important form of compensation for exports was silver bullion, which supported the silver-based Chinese economy and fueled manufacturing.

Economic growth and commercial expansion took place mostly in an atmosphere of tight government regulation. Although the Ming emperor Yongle had sponsored a series of maritime expeditions (1405–1433) in the Indian Ocean basin, his successors withdrew their support for such activities and even tried to prevent Chinese subjects from dealing with foreign peoples. In its effort to pacify southern China during the later seventeenth century, the Qing government tried to end maritime activity altogether. An imperial edict of 1656 forbade "even a plank from drifting to the sea," and in 1661 the emperor Kangxi ordered evacuation of the southern coastal regions. Those policies had only a limited effect, and when Qing forces pacified southern China in the 1680s, government authorities rescinded the strictest measures. Thereafter, however, Qing authorities closely supervised the activities of foreign merchants in China. Portuguese merchants were allowed to operate only at the port of Macau, and British agents had to deal exclusively with the official merchant guild in Guangzhou.

Government policies also discouraged the organization of large-scale commercial ventures by Chinese merchants. As a result, it was impossible to maintain shipyards that could construct large sailing ships capable of traveling long distances. Similarly, it was impossible to organize large trading firms like the English East India Company or the Dutch VOC.

TRADE AND MIGRATION TO SOUTHEAST ASIA Nevertheless, thousands of Chinese merchants worked either individually or in partnerships, plying the waters of the China seas to link China with global trade networks. Chinese merchants were especially prominent in Manila, where they exchanged silk and porcelain for American silver that came across the Pacific Ocean from Mexico. They were also frequent visitors at the Dutch colonial capital of Batavia, where they supplied the VOC with silk and porcelain in exchange for silver and Indonesian spices. Entrepreneurial Chinese merchants ventured also to lands throughout southeast Asia in search of exotic tropical products for Chinese consumers. Indeed, the early modern era was an age when merchants established a prominent Chinese presence throughout southeast Asia.

PSI img Beijing Observatory www.mhhe.com/bentleybrief2e

GOVERNMENT AND TECHNOLOGY China's economic expansion took place largely in the absence of technological innovation. During the Tang and Song dynasties, Chinese engineers had produced a veritable flood of inventions, and China was the world's leader in technology. Yet by early Ming times, technological innovation had slowed. Part of the explanation for the slowdown has to do with role of the government. During the Tang and Song dynasties, the imperial government had encouraged technological innovation as a foundation of military and economic strength. In contrast, the Ming and Qing regimes favored political and social stability over technological innovation.

Alongside government policy, the abundance of skilled workers discouraged technological innovation. When employers wanted to increase production, they found that hiring additional workers was less costly than making investments in new technologies. In the short run this tactic kept most of China's population gainfully employed. Over the longer term, however, it meant that China lost technological ground to European peoples, who embarked on a round of stunning technological innovation beginning about the mid–eighteenth century.

Gentry, Commoners, Soldiers, and Mean People

PRIVILEGED CLASSES Besides the emperor and his family, scholar-bureaucrats and gentry occupied the most exalted positions in Chinese society. Scholar-bureaucrats had much in common with the gentry: they came largely from gentry ranks, and after leaving government service they usually rejoined gentry society. The scholar-bureaucrats and the gentry functioned as intermediaries between the imperial government and local society. By organizing water-control projects and public security measures, they played a crucial role in the management of local society.

Scholar-bureaucrats and gentry were easy to identify. They wore distinctive clothing—black gowns with blue borders adorned with various rank insignia—and commoners addressed them with honorific terms. They also received favorable legal treatment and enjoyed immunity from corporal punishment as well as exemption from labor service and taxes.

Most of the gentry owned land, which was their major source of income. Some were also silent business partners of merchants and entrepreneurs. Their principal source of income, however, was the government service to which their academic degrees gave them access. In contrast to landed elites elsewhere, who often lived on rural estates, China's gentry resided largely in cities and towns, where they tended to political, social, and financial affairs.

CHINESE PEASANTS. | This engraving depicts a peasant couple in harness pulling a plow. Note that the man wears the braided queue that Manchus required their male Chinese subjects to wear. ***Why would the peasants have been pulling the plow themselves?***

WORKING CLASSES Confucian tradition ranked three broad classes of commoners below the gentry: peasants, artisans or workers, and merchants. By far the biggest class consisted of peasants: a designation that covered everyone from day laborers to petty landlords. Confucian principles regarded peasants as the most honorable of the three classes, since they performed honest labor and supplied the entire population with food.

The category of artisans and workers encompassed a wide spectrum of occupations. Despite their lower status, crafts workers, tailors, barbers, and physicians generally enjoyed higher income than peasants did. Artisans and workers were usually employees of the state or of gentry and merchant families, but they also pursued their occupations as self-employed persons.

MERCHANTS Merchants, from street peddlers to individuals of enormous wealth and influence, ranked at the bottom of the Confucian social hierarchy. Because moralists looked on them as unscrupulous social parasites, merchants enjoyed little legal protection. Yet Chinese merchants often garnered official support for their enterprises through bribery of government bureaucrats or through profit-sharing arrangements with gentry families. Indeed, the participation of gentry families in commercial ventures such as warehousing, moneylending, and pawnbroking blurred the distinction between gentry and merchants. In addition, merchants blurred the distinction further by preparing their sons for government examinations, which could result in appointment to civil service positions and promotion to gentry status.

Although China was still a basically agricultural land under the Ming and the Qing, the increasing prominence of artisans and merchants demonstrated that manufacturing and commerce had become much more economically important than in ancient times. As a result, those who could exploit opportunities had the potential to lead comfortable lives and even to climb into the ranks of the privileged gentry class. Yet Chinese merchants and artisans did not forge cooperative relationships with government authorities as their counterparts in England and the Netherlands did.

The principal concern of late Ming and Qing authorities was to preserve the stability of a large agrarian society, not to promote rapid economic development through trade. Thus Chinese authorities did not adopt policies designed to strengthen both merchants and the state by authorizing merchants to pursue their efforts aggressively in the larger world.

LOWER CLASSES Beyond the Confucian social hierarchy were members of the military forces and the so-called mean people, such as slaves, indentured servants, entertainers, and prostitutes. Confucian moralists regarded armed forces as a wretched but necessary evil and attempted to avoid military dominance of society by placing civilian bureaucrats in the highest command positions, even at the expense of military effectiveness.

The Confucian Tradition and New Cultural Influences

The Ming and Qing emperors looked to Chinese traditions for guidance in framing their cultural as well as their political and social policies. They provided generous support for Confucianism, and they ensured that formal education in China revolved around Confucian thought and values. Yet demographic and urban growth also encouraged the emergence of a vibrant popular culture in Chinese cities, and European missionaries acquainted the Chinese with Roman Catholic Christianity and European science and technology as well.

Neo-Confucianism and Pulp Fiction

Imperial sponsorship of Chinese cultural traditions meant primarily support for the Confucian tradition, especially as systematized by the Song dynasty scholar Zhu Xi, the most prominent architect of neo-Confucianism. Zhu Xi combined the moral, ethical, and political values of Confucius with the logical rigor and speculative power of Buddhist philosophy. He emphasized the values of self-discipline, filial piety, and obedience to

Zhu Xi (ZHOO SHEE)
neo-Confucianism (NEE-oh kuhn-FYEW-shuhn-iz'm)

established rulers, all of which appealed to Ming and Qing emperors seeking to maintain stability in their vast realm. To promote Confucian values, the Ming and Qing emperors supported educational programs at many levels throughout the land.

POPULAR CULTURE While the imperial courts promoted Confucianism, a lively popular culture took shape in the cities of China. Most urban residents did not have an advanced education and knew little about Confucius. Many were literate, however, and they found that popular novels met their needs for entertainment and diversion. Although Confucian scholars thought popular novels were crude, printing made it possible to produce them cheaply and in large numbers, and urban residents eagerly consumed them. Many of the novels had little literary merit, but their tales of conflict, horror, wonder, excitement, and sometimes unconcealed pornography appealed to readers.

POPULAR NOVELS Some popular novels, however, did offer thoughtful reflections on the world and human affairs. The historical novel *The Romance of the Three Kingdoms,* for example, explored the political intrigue that followed the collapse of the Han dynasty. *The Dream of the Red Chamber* told the story of cousins deeply in love who could not marry because of their families' wishes. Through the prism of a sentimental love story, the novel shed fascinating light on the dynamics of wealthy scholar-gentry families.

The Return of Christianity to China

Nestorian Christians had established churches and monasteries in China as early as the seventh century C.E., and Roman Catholic communities were prominent in Chinese commercial centers during the Yuan dynasty. After the outbreak of epidemic plague and the collapse of the Yuan dynasty in the fourteenth century, however, Christianity disappeared from China. When Roman Catholic missionaries returned in the sixteenth century, they had to start from scratch in their efforts to win converts.

MATTEO RICCI Founder of the mission to China was the Italian Jesuit Matteo Ricci (1552–1610), who had the ambitious goal of converting China to Christianity, beginning with the Ming emperor Wanli. Ricci was a brilliant and learned man as well as a polished diplomat, and he became a popular figure at the Ming court. On arrival at Macau in 1582, Ricci immersed himself in the study of the Chinese language and the Confucian classics. By the time he first traveled to Beijing and visited the imperial court in 1601, Ricci was able to write learned Chinese and converse fluently with Confucian scholars.

Ricci's mastery of Chinese language and literature opened doors for the Jesuits, who then dazzled their hosts with European science, technology, and mechanical gadgetry such as glass prisms, harpsichords, and especially "self-ringing bells"—spring-driven mechanical clocks that chimed the hours.

CONFUCIANISM AND CHRISTIANITY The Jesuits sought to capture Chinese interest with European science and technology, but their ultimate goal was to win converts. Ricci, for example, tried to make Christianity seem familiar by arguing that the doctrines of Confucius and Jesus were very similar, if not identical. The Jesuits also held religious services in the Chinese language and allowed converts to continue the time-honored practice of venerating their ancestors.

In spite of their tolerance, flexibility, and genuine respect for their hosts, the Jesuits attracted few converts in China. By the mid–eighteenth century, Chinese Christians numbered about 200,000—a tiny proportion of the Chinese population of 225 million. Many Chinese hesitated to adopt Christianity partly because of its exclusivity: like Islam, Christianity claimed to be the only true religion, so conversion implied that the time-honored traditions of Confucianism, Daoism, and Buddhism were fallacious creeds—a proposition most Chinese were unwilling to accept.

Buddhism (BOO-diz'm)

END OF THE JESUIT MISSION Ultimately, the Roman Catholic mission in China came to an end because of squabbles between the Jesuits and members of the Franciscan and Dominican orders, who also sought converts in China. Jealous of the Jesuits' presence at the imperial court, they complained to the pope about their rivals' tolerance of Chinese traditions. The pope sided with the critics and in the early eighteenth century issued several proclamations ordering missionaries in China to conduct services according to European standards. In response, the emperor Kangxi ordered an end to the preaching of Christianity in China. By the mid–eighteenth century, the mission had weakened so much that it had effectively come to an end.

The Roman Catholic mission to China did not attract large numbers of converts, but it nonetheless had important cultural effects. In letters, reports, and other writings distributed widely throughout Europe, the Jesuits described China as an orderly and rational society. The rational morality of Confucianism appealed to the Enlightenment philosophes, who sought alternatives to Christianity as the foundation for ethics and morality. Thus for the first time since Marco Polo, strong European interest in east Asian societies was stimulated.

THE UNIFICATION OF JAPAN

During the late sixteenth and early seventeenth centuries, the political unification of Japan ended an extended period of civil disorder. Like the Ming and Qing emperors in China, the Tokugawa shoguns sought to lay a foundation for long-term political and social stability by promoting conservative values and tightly restricting foreign influence in Japan. As in China, however, demographic expansion and economic growth fostered social and cultural change in Japan, and merchants introduced Chinese and European influences into Japan.

The Golden Pavilion
www.mhhe.com/
bentleybrief2e

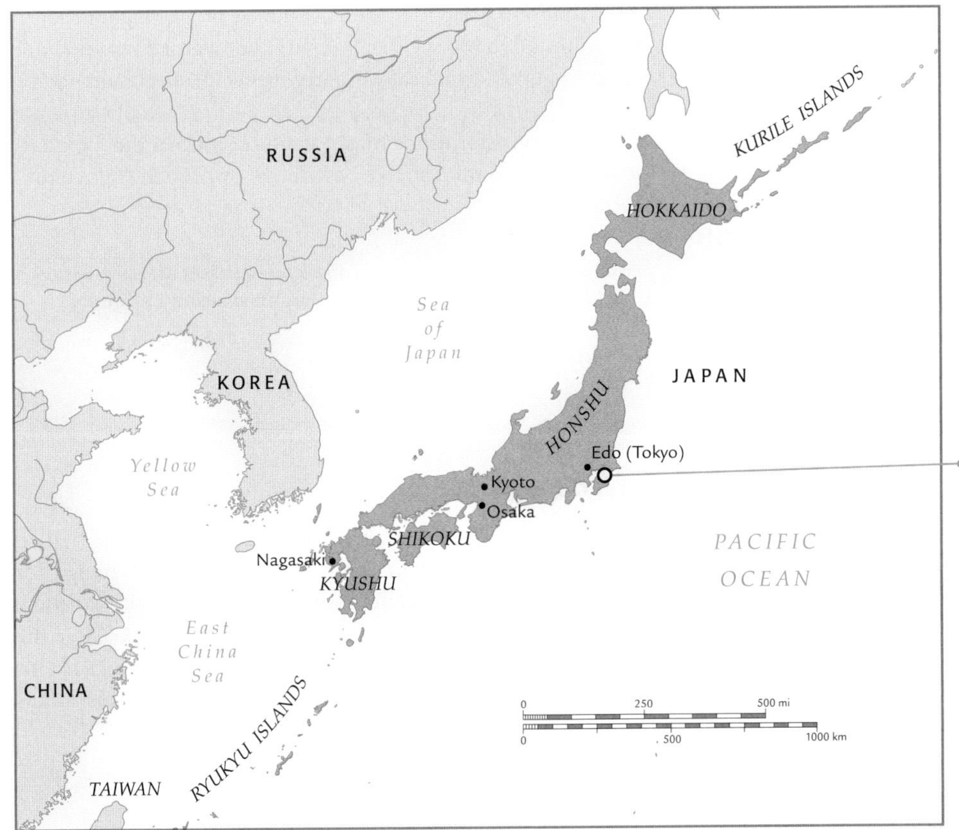

MAP 23.3 | Tokugawa Japan, 1600–1867. Consider Japan's position with regard to China, Korea, and Russia. ***Would it have been easy or difficult to enforce the ban on foreign trade during most of the period?***

The Tokugawa shogunate made their capital at Edo.

SOURCES FROM THE PAST

Qianlong on Chinese Trade with England

Qing administrators tightly restricted foreign trade. Foreign merchants had to deal with government-approved agents outside the city walls of Guangzhou and had to depart as soon as they had completed their business. In 1793 a British diplomat representing King George III of England bestowed gifts on the emperor Qianlong and petitioned for the right to trade at ports other than Guangzhou. In a letter to King George, Qianlong outlined his views on Chinese trade with England. His letter also bespeaks clearly the importance of government policy for commerce and economic affairs in China.

You, O king, from afar have yearned after the blessings of our civilization, and in your eagerness to come into touch with our influence have sent an embassy across the sea bearing a memorandum. I have already taken note of your respectful spirit of submission, have treated your mission with extreme favor and loaded it with gifts, besides issuing a mandate to you, O king, and honoring you with the bestowal of valuable presents. . . .

Yesterday your ambassador petitioned my ministers to memorialize me regarding your trade with China, but his proposal is not consistent with our dynastic usage and cannot be entertained. Hitherto, all European nations, including your own country's barbarian merchants, have carried on their trade with our Celestial Empire at Guangzhou. Such has been the procedure for many years, although our Celestial Empire possesses all things in prolific abundance and lacks no product within its own borders. There was therefore no need to import the manufactures of outside barbarians in exchange for our own produce. But as the tea, silk, and porcelain which the Celestial Empire produces are absolute necessities to European nations and to yourselves, we have permitted, as a signal mark of favor, that trading agents should be established at Guangzhou, so that your wants might be supplied and your country thus participate in our beneficence. But your ambassador has now put forward new requests which completely fail to recognize our throne's principle to "treat strangers from afar with indulgence," and to exercise a pacifying control over barbarian tribes the world over. . . . Your England is not the only nation trading at Guangzhou. If other nations, following your bad example, wrongfully importune my ear with further impossible requests, how will it be possible for me to treat them with easy indulgence? Nevertheless, I do not forget the lonely remoteness of your island, cut off from the world by intervening wastes of sea, nor do I overlook your excusable ignorance of the usages of our Celestial Empire. I have consequently commanded my ministers to enlighten your ambassador on the subject, and have ordered the departure of the mission. . . .

If, after the receipt of this explicit decree, you lightly give ear to the representations of your subordinates and allow your barbarian merchants to proceed to Zhejiang and Tianjin, with the object of landing and trading there, the ordinances of my Celestial Empire are strict in the extreme, and the local officials, both civil and military, are bound reverently to obey the law of the land. Should your vessels touch the shore, your merchants will assuredly never be permitted to land or to reside there, but will be subject to instant expulsion. In that event your barbarian merchants will have had a long journey for nothing. Do not say that you were not warned in due time! Tremblingly obey and show no negligence! A special mandate!

■ What considerations might have prompted the Chinese government to take such a restrictive approach to foreign trade?

SOURCE: J. O. P. Bland. *Annals and Memoirs of the Court of Peking.* Boston: Houghton Mifflin, 1914, pp. 325–31. (Translation slightly modified.)

The Tokugawa Shogunate

From the twelfth through the sixteenth century, a *shogun* ("military governor") ruled Japan through retainers who received political rights and large estates in exchange for military services. Theoretically, the shogun ruled as a temporary stand-in for the Japanese emperor. In fact, however, the emperor was nothing more than a figurehead. After the fourteenth century the conflicting ambitions of shoguns and retainers led to constant turmoil, and by the sixteenth century Japan was in a state of civil war. Japanese historians often refer to the sixteenth century as the era of *sengoku*—"the country at war."

Sengoku (sehn-goh-koo)

Tokugawa Castle, Kyoto
www.mhhe.com/bentleybrief2e

TOKUGAWA IEYASU Toward the end of the sixteenth century, a series of military leaders brought about the unification of the land. In 1600 the last of those leaders, Tokugawa Ieyasu (reigned 1600–1616), established a military government known as the Tokugawa *bakufu* ("tent government," since it theoretically was only a temporary replacement for the emperor's rule). Ieyasu and his descendants ruled the bakufu as shoguns from 1600 until the end of the Tokugawa dynasty in 1867.

The principal aim of the Tokugawa shoguns was to prevent the return of civil war. Consequently, the shoguns needed to control the *daimyo* ("great names"), powerful territorial lords who ruled most of Japan from their vast, hereditary landholdings. Each maintained a government, an independent judiciary, and schools, and each circulated paper money. Moreover, after the mid–sixteenth century, many daimyo established relationships with European mariners, from whom they learned how to manufacture and use gunpowder weapons, which they turned against one another.

CONTROL OF THE DAIMYO From the castle town of Edo (modern Tokyo), the shogun sought to extend his control over the daimyo through the policy of "alternate attendance," which required daimyo to maintain their families at Edo and spend every other year at the Tokugawa court. This policy enabled the shoguns to keep an eye on the daimyo, and it encouraged daimyo to spend their money on comfortable lives in Edo rather than on military forces that could challenge the bakufu. The shoguns also discouraged the daimyo from visiting one another and even required daimyo to obtain permission to meet with the emperor.

CONTROL OF FOREIGN RELATIONS In an effort to prevent European influences from destabilizing the land, the Tokugawa shoguns closely controlled relations between Japan and the outside world. A primary concern was that Europeans might threaten the bakufu by making alliances with daimyo and supplying them with weapons. Thus during the 1630s the shoguns issued a series of edicts sharply restricting Japanese relations with other lands.

The policy forbade Japanese to go abroad on pain of death and prohibited the construction of large ships. It expelled Europeans from Japan and prohibited foreign merchants from trading in Japanese ports. The policy did, however, allow carefully controlled trade with Asian lands, and it also permitted small numbers of Chinese and Dutch merchants to trade under tight restrictions at the southern port city of Nagasaki. As a result, Japan was never completely isolated from the outside world.

Economic and Social Change

By ending civil conflict and maintaining political stability, the Tokugawa shoguns set the stage for economic growth in Japan. Ironically, peace and a booming economy encouraged social change that undermined the order that the bakufu sought to preserve. Economic growth had its roots in increased agricultural production, especially of rice, cotton, silk, and indigo. In many parts of Japan, villages moved away from subsistence farming in favor of production for the market.

POPULATION GROWTH Increased agricultural production brought about rapid demographic growth: during the seventeenth century the Japanese population rose by almost one-third, from twenty-two million to twenty-nine million. Thereafter, however, many families practiced population control to maintain or raise their standard of living. Between 1700 and 1850 the Japanese population grew only moderately, from twenty-nine million to thirty-two million. Contraception, late marriage, and abortion

Tokugawa (TAW-koo-GAH-wah)
bakufu (bah-kuh-fuh)
daimyo (DEYEM-yoh)

Nagasaki Harbor. Dutch sailing ships and smaller Japanese vessels mingle in Nagasaki harbor. Dutch merchants conducted their business on the artificial island of Deshima, at left. ***Why was the island so densely populated?***

© Carousel/Laurie Platt Winfrey, Inc.

all played roles in limiting population growth, but the principal method of control was infanticide, euphemistically referred to as "thinning out the rice shoots." Japanese families resorted to these measures primarily because Japan was land poor, which made it easy for populations to strain available resources.

SOCIAL CHANGE The Tokugawa era was an age of social as well as demographic change in Japan. Because of Chinese cultural influence, the Japanese social hierarchy followed Confucian precepts in ranking the ruling elites—including the daimyo and samurai warriors—as the most privileged class of society, followed by peasants and artisans. As in China, merchants ranked at the bottom. Yet the extended period of peace ushered in by Tokugawa rule undermined the social position of the ruling elites, who found their traditional role as local administrators redundant. Many of the ruling elite also fell into financial difficulty in this period because of rising prices and lavish lifestyles. As a result, many became indebted to rice brokers and gradually declined into genteel poverty.

Meanwhile, as in China, merchants in Japan became increasingly wealthy and prominent. Japanese cities flourished throughout the Tokugawa era—the population of Edo approached one million by 1700—and merchants prospered in the vibrant urban environment. Rice dealers, pawnbrokers, and sake merchants soon controlled more wealth than the ruling elites.

Neo-Confucianism and Floating Worlds

NEO-CONFUCIANISM IN JAPAN Japan had gone to school in China, and the influence of China continued throughout the Tokugawa era. Formal education began with study of Chinese language and literature. As late as the nineteenth century, many Japanese scholars wrote their philosophical, legal, and religious works in Chinese. The common people embraced Buddhism, which had come to Japan from China, and Confucianism was the most influential philosophical system. Indeed, by the early eighteenth century, neo-Confucianism had become the official ideology of the Tokugawa bakufu.

NATIVE LEARNING Yet even with Tokugawa sponsorship, neo-Confucianism did not dominate intellectual life in Japan. Some scholars sought to establish a sense of Japanese identity that did not depend on cultural kinship with China. Particularly during the eighteenth century, scholars of "native learning" scorned neo-Confucianism and even Buddhism as alien cultural imports and emphasized instead the importance of folk traditions and the indigenous Shinto religion for Japanese identity. Many scholars of native learning viewed Japanese people as superior to all others and glorified the supposed purity of Japanese society before its adulteration by Chinese and other foreign influences.

Meanwhile, the emergence of a prosperous merchant class encouraged the development of a vibrant popular culture. During the seventeenth and eighteenth centuries, an exuberant middle-class culture flourished in cities such as Kyoto, Edo, and Osaka. In those and other cities, Japan's finest creative talents catered to middle-class appetites.

FLOATING WORLDS The centers of Tokugawa urban culture were the *ukiyo* ("floating worlds"), entertainment and pleasure quarters where teahouses, theaters, brothels, and public baths offered escape from the rigid rules of conduct that governed public behavior in Tokugawa society. In contrast to the solemn, serious proceedings of the impe-

Shintoism (SHIHN-toh-iz'm)

Kabuki Theater. A colored woodcut by Okumura Masanobu depicts the audience at a seventeenth-century kabuki theater. Enthusiastic actors often ran down wooden ramps and played their roles among the audience.

rial court and the bakufu, the popular culture of urban residents was secular, satirical, and even scatological. The main expressions of this lively culture were prose fiction and new forms of theater.

Ihara Saikaku (1642–1693), one of Japan's most prolific poets, helped create a new genre of prose literature, the "books of the floating world." Much of his fiction revolved around the theme of love. In *The Life of a Man Who Lived for Love,* for example, Ihara chronicled the experiences of a townsman who devoted his life to a quest for sexual pleasure. Ihara's treatment of love stressed the erotic rather than the aesthetic, and the brief, episodic stories that made up his work appealed to literate urban residents who were not inclined to pore over dense neo-Confucian treatises.

Beginning in the early seventeenth century, two new forms of drama became popular in Japanese cities. One was *kabuki* theater, which usually featured several acts consisting of lively and sometimes bawdy skits where stylized acting combined with lyric singing, dancing, and spectacular staging. The other new dramatic form was *bunraku,* the puppet theater. In bunraku, chanters accompanied by music told a story acted out by puppets. Manipulated by a team of three, each puppet could execute the subtlest and most intricate movements, such as brushing a tear from the eye with the sleeve of a kimono. Both kabuki and bunraku attracted enthusiastic audiences in search of entertainment and diversion.

ENCOUNTERS IN EAST ASIA. Although both the Chinese and Japanese states sought to minimize cultural contacts with outsiders from overseas, encounters with the wider world nevertheless affected each state in important ways. Describe the ways encounters with foreign traders and missionaries shaped the internal development of China and Japan in economic, social, and cultural terms.

Christianity and Dutch Learning

CHRISTIAN MISSIONS Christian missionaries and European merchants also contributed their own distinctive threads to the cultural fabric of Tokugawa Japan. The Jesuit Francis Xavier opened the first Roman Catholic mission in 1549 and for a few decades experienced remarkable success. Several powerful daimyo adopted Christianity and ordered their subjects to do likewise. Many Japanese converts

kabuki (kah-BOO-kee)
bunraku (boon-RAH-koo)
Francis Xavier (fran-sis ZEY-vee-er)

became enthusiastic Christians and worked to convert their compatriots to the new faith. By the 1580s about 150,000 Japanese had converted to Christianity, and by 1615 Japanese Christians numbered about 300,000.

Although Christians were only a tiny minority of the Japanese population, the popularity of Christianity generated a backlash among those seeking to preserve Japanese religious and cultural traditions. The Tokugawa shoguns restricted European access to Japan largely because of concerns that Christianity might serve as a cultural bridge for alliances between daimyo and European adventurers, which in turn could threaten the bakufu. Meanwhile, Buddhist and Confucian scholars resented the Christian conviction that their faith was the only true doctrine.

PSI img Persecution of Catholics
www.mhhe.com/bentleybrief2e

ANTI-CHRISTIAN CAMPAIGN Between 1587 and 1639, shoguns promulgated several decrees ordering a halt to Christian missions and commanding Japanese Christians to renounce their faith. In 1612 the shoguns began rigorous enforcement of these decrees. They tortured and executed European missionaries who refused to leave the islands as well as Japanese Christians who refused to abandon their faith. The campaign was so effective that even some European missionaries abandoned Christianity. Most notable was the Portuguese Jesuit Christovão Ferreira, head of the Jesuit mission in Japan, who gave up Christianity under torture, adopted Buddhism, and interrogated many Europeans who fell into Japanese hands in the mid–seventeenth century. By the late seventeenth century, the anti-Christian campaign had claimed tens of thousands of lives, and Christianity survived only as a secret, underground religion.

DUTCH LEARNING Tokugawa policies ensured that Christianity would not soon reappear in Japan, but they did not entirely prevent contacts between Europeans and Japanese. After 1639 Dutch merchants trading at Nagasaki became Japan's principal source of information about the world beyond east Asia. A small number of Japanese scholars learned Dutch to communicate with the foreigners. Their studies, which they called "Dutch learning," brought considerable knowledge of the outside world to Japan. After 1720 Tokugawa authorities lifted the ban on foreign books, and Dutch learning—especially European art and science—began to play a significant role in Japanese intellectual life. Indeed, by the mid–eighteenth century the Tokugawa shoguns themselves had become enthusiastic proponents of Dutch learning, and schools of European medicine and Dutch studies flourished in several Japanese cities.

Christovão Ferreira (chris-STOH-voh feh-RAY-rah)

SUMMARY

Both China and Japan controlled their own affairs throughout the early modern era and avoided the turmoil that afflicted societies in the Americas and much of sub-Saharan Africa. Rulers of the Ming dynasty built a powerful centralized state in China. They worked diligently to restore traditional ways by reviving Chinese political institutions and providing state sponsorship for neo-Confucianism. In the interest of stability, authorities also restricted foreign merchants' access to China and limited the activities of Christian missionaries. The succeeding Qing dynasty pursued similar policies. The Ming and Qing dynasties both brought political stability, but China experienced considerable social and economic change in early modern times. American food crops helped increase agricultural production, which fueled rapid population growth, and global trade stimulated the Chinese economy, which improved the position of merchants and artisans in society. The experience of the Tokugawa era in Japan was much like that of the Ming and Qing eras in China. The Tokugawa bakufu brought political order to the Japanese islands and closely controlled foreign relations, but a vibrant economy promoted social change that enhanced the status of merchants and artisans.

STUDY TERMS

bakufu (465)
bunraku (467)
civil service examinations (457)
daimyo (465)
Dutch learning (468)
filial piety (457)
floating worlds (466)
Forbidden City (454)
Great Wall (453)
Hongwu (452)
Jesuits (462)
kabuki (467)
Kangxi (456)
Manchu (454)
Matteo Ricci (451)
Ming dynasty (452)
neo-Confucianism (466)
Qianlong (456)
Qing dynasty (454)
Shinto (466)
shogun (464)
Son of Heaven (456)
Tokugawa Ieyasu (465)
Tokugawa shogunate (464)
Yongle (453)

FOR FURTHER READING

Timothy Brook. *The Confusions of Pleasure: Commerce and Culture in Ming China.* Berkeley, 1998. Fascinating social and cultural analysis of Ming China focusing on the role of commerce as an agent of social change.

Mark C. Elliott. *The Manchu Way: The Eight Banners and Ethnic Identity in Late Imperial China.* Stanford, 2001. Important scholarly study focusing on relations between Manchus and Chinese during the Qing dynasty.

Mark Elvin. *The Pattern of the Chinese Past: A Social and Economic Interpretation.* Stanford, 1973. A brilliant analysis of Chinese history concentrating on economic, social, and technological themes.

Ray Huang. *1587: A Year of No Significance.* New Haven, 1981. A very good history of the late Ming, with insights into daily life.

Susan Naquin and Evelyn S. Rawski. *Chinese Society in the Eighteenth Century.* New Haven, 1987. A lucid and well-organized discussion of Chinese social history.

Kenneth Pomeranz. *The Great Divergence: China, Europe, and the Making of the Modern World Economy.* Princeton, 2000. Path-breaking scholarly study that illuminates the economic history of the early modern world through comparison of economic development in Asian and European lands.

Jonathan D. Spence. *The Death of Woman Wang.* New York, 1978. Engaging reconstruction of life in rural China during the early Qing dynasty.

Conrad Totman. *Early Modern Japan.* Berkeley, 1993. An outstanding survey of Tokugawa ecological, political, social, economic, and cultural history.

H. Paul Varley. *Japanese Culture.* 4th ed. Honolulu, 2000. Places the cultural history of the Tokugawa era in its larger historical context.

Frederic Wakeman Jr. *The Great Enterprise: The Manchu Reconstruction of the Imperial Order in Seventeenth-Century China.* 2 vols. Berkeley, 1985. Important scholarly analysis of early Qing history.

The Islamic Empires

24

n 1635 Shah Jahan, the emperor of Mughal India, took his seat on the Peacock Throne. Seven years in the making, the Peacock Throne is probably the most spectacular seat on which any mortal human being has rested. Shah Jahan ordered the throne encrusted with ten million rupees' worth of diamonds, rubies, emeralds, and pearls. Atop the throne itself stood a magnificent, golden-bodied peacock with a huge ruby and a fifty-carat, pear-shaped pearl on its breast and a brilliant tail fashioned of sapphires and gems.

Yet, for all its splendor, the Peacock Throne ranks a distant second among Shah Jahan's artistic projects: pride of place goes to the incomparable Taj Mahal. Built over a period of eighteen years as a tomb for Shah Jahan's beloved wife, Mumtaz Mahal, who died during childbirth in 1631, the Taj Mahal is a graceful and elegant monument both to the departed empress and to Shah Jahan's Islamic faith.

The emperor and his architects conceived the Taj Mahal as a vast allegory in stone symbolizing the day when Allah would cause the dead to rise and undergo judgment. Its gardens represented the gardens of paradise, and the four water channels running through them symbolized the four rivers of the heavenly kingdom. The domed marble tomb of Mumtaz Mahal represented the throne of Allah. The main gateway to the structure features the entire text of the chapter promising that on the day of judgment, Allah will punish the wicked and gather the faithful into his celestial paradise.

The Peacock Throne and the Taj Mahal testify to the wealth of the Mughal empire, and the tomb of Mumtaz Mahal bespeaks also the fundamentally Islamic character of the ruling dynasty. But the Mughal realm was not the only well-organized Islamic empire of early modern times. The Ottoman dynasty ruled a powerful empire that expanded from its base in Anatolia to embrace much of eastern Europe, Egypt, and north Africa. The Safavid dynasty challenged the Ottomans for dominance in southwest Asia and prospered from its role in trade networks linking China, India, Russia, southwest Asia, and the Mediterranean basin.

All three Islamic empires of early modern times had dynasties that originated with nomadic, Turkish-speaking peoples from the steppes of central Asia. All three dynasties retained political and cultural traditions that their ancestors had adopted on the steppes, but they also adapted readily to the city-based agricultural societies that they conquered. The Ottoman dynasty made especially effective

❮ The Taj Mahal, a sumptuous mosque and tomb built between 1632 and 1649 by Shah Jahan in memory of his wife, Mumtaz Mahal.

Shah Jahan (shah jah-han)
Mumtaz Mahal (moom-tahz muh-HAHL)

CHRONOLOGY

1289–1923	Ottoman dynasty
1451–1481	Reign of Mehmed the Conqueror
1453	Ottoman conquest of Constantinople
1501–1524	Reign of Shah Ismail
1501–1722	Safavid dynasty
1514	Battle of Chaldiran
1520–1566	Reign of Süleyman the Magnificent
1526–1858	Mughal dynasty
1556–1605	Reign of Akbar
1588–1629	Reign of Shah Abbas the Great
1659–1707	Reign of Aurangzeb

use of gunpowder weapons, and the Safavids and the Mughals also incorporated gunpowder weapons into their arsenals. All three dynasties officially embraced Islam and drew cultural guidance from Islamic values.

During the sixteenth and early seventeenth centuries, the three Islamic empires presided over expansive and prosperous societies. About the mid–seventeenth century, however, they all began to weaken. Each empire waged long, costly wars that drained resources without bringing compensating benefits. The empires also faced domestic difficulties. Each of them was an ethnically and religiously diverse realm, and each experienced tensions when conservative Muslim leaders lobbied for strict observance of Islam while members of other communities sought greater freedom for themselves. Furthermore, the Islamic empires made little investment in economic and technological development. By the mid–eighteenth century the Safavid empire had collapsed, and the Ottoman and Mughal realms were rapidly falling under European influence.

Formation of the Islamic Empires

The Islamic empires began as small warrior principalities in frontier areas. As they grew, they devised elaborate administrative and military institutions. Under the guidance of talented and energetic rulers, each empire organized an effective governmental apparatus and presided over a prosperous society.

The Ottoman Empire

OSMAN The Ottoman empire was an unusually successful frontier state. The term *Ottoman* derived from Osman Bey, founder of the dynasty that continued in unbroken succession from 1289 until the dissolution of the empire in 1923. Osman was *bey* (chief) of a band of seminomadic Turks who migrated to northwestern Anatolia in the thirteenth century. Osman and his followers sought above all to become *ghazi,* Muslim religious warriors who fought on behalf of the faith.

OTTOMAN EXPANSION The Ottomans' location on the borders of the Byzantine empire afforded them ample opportunity to wage holy war. Their first great success came in 1326 with the capture of the Anatolian city of Bursa, which became the capital of the Ottoman principality. About 1352 they established a foothold in Europe when they seized the fortress of Gallipoli. The city of Edirne (Adrianople) became a second Ottoman capital and served as a base for further expansion into the Balkans. As warriors settled in frontier districts and pushed their boundaries forward, they took spoils and gathered revenues that enriched both the *ghazi* and the central government.

Driving Ottoman expansion was a formidable military machine, which included light cavalry, volunteer infantry, and—as the state grew larger—heavy cavalry. After expanding into the Balkans, the Ottomans created an important force composed of slave troops. Through an institution known as the *devshirme,* the Ottomans required the Christian population of the Balkans to contribute young boys to become slaves

Osman Bey (oz-MAHN beh)
ghazi (GAH-zee)
Byzantine (BIHZ-uhn-teen)

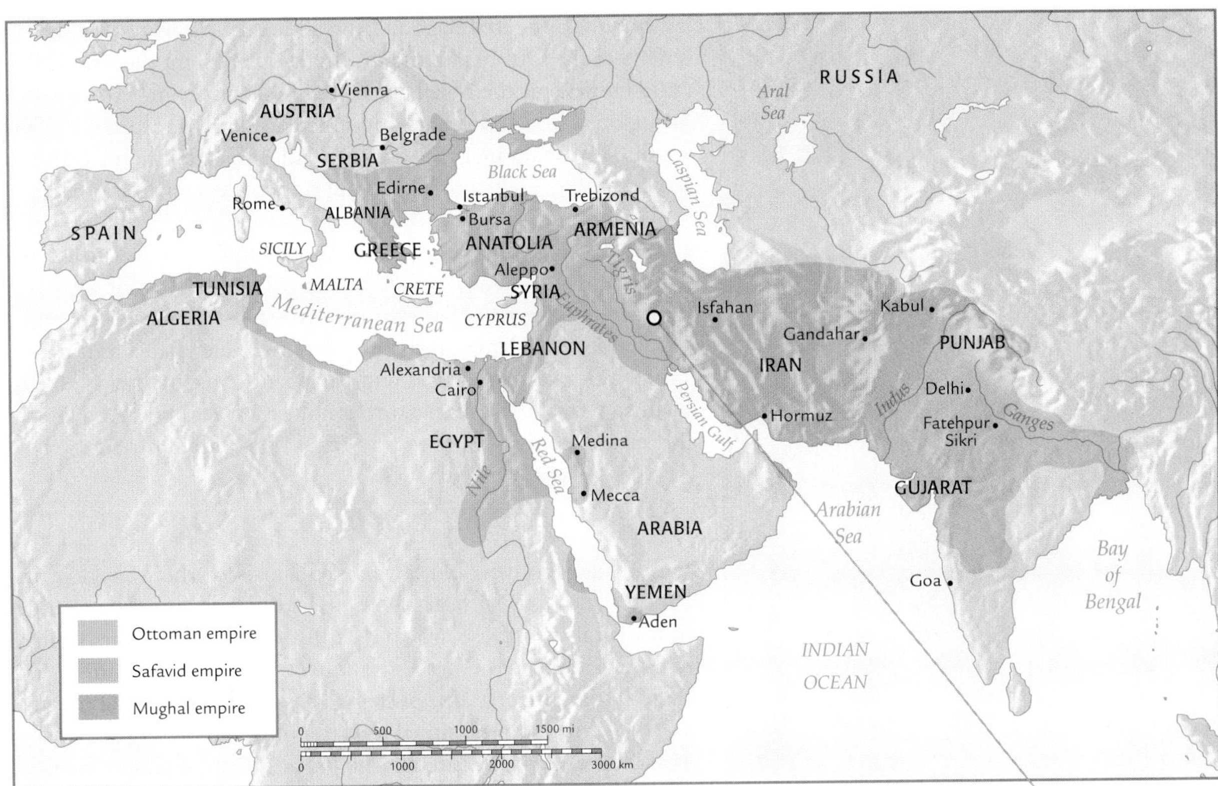

MAP 24.1 | The Islamic empires, 1500–1800. Locate the Ottoman capital of Istanbul, the Safavid capital of Isfahan, and the Mughal capital of Delhi. ***What strategic or commercial purposes did each of these capitals fulfill, and how would their locations have aided or hindered imperial administration?***

The proximity of the Sunni Ottoman empire to the Shiite Safavid empire encouraged frequent conflict between the two.

of the sultan. The boys received special training, learned Turkish, and converted to Islam. According to individual ability, they entered either the Ottoman civilian administration or the military. Those who became soldiers were known as Janissaries, from the Turkish *yeni cheri* ("new troops"). The Janissaries quickly gained a reputation for esprit de corps, loyalty to the sultan, and readiness to employ new military technology. The Ottomans also outfitted their forces with gunpowder weapons and used them effectively in battles and sieges.

PSI map The Ottoman empire www.mhhe.com/bentleybrief2e

MEHMED THE CONQUEROR The capture of Constantinople in 1453 by Mehmed II (reigned 1451–1481)—known as Mehmed the Conqueror—opened a new chapter in Ottoman expansion. With its superb location and illustrious heritage, Constantinople became the new Ottoman capital, subsequently known as Istanbul. With the capture of the great city behind him, Mehmed presented himself not just as a warrior-sultan but as a true emperor. He laid the foundations for a tightly centralized, absolute monarchy, and his army faced no serious rival. He completed the conquest of Serbia, moved into southern Greece and Albania, eliminated the last Byzantine outpost at Trebizond, captured Genoese ports in the Crimea, initiated a naval war with Venice in the Mediterranean, and reportedly hoped to march on Rome and capture the pope. Toward the end of his life, he launched an invasion of Italy and briefly occupied Otranto, but his successors abandoned plans for expansion in western Europe.

SÜLEYMAN THE MAGNIFICENT The Ottomans continued their expansion in the early sixteenth century by occupying Syria and Egypt. Ottoman imperialism climaxed in the reign of Süleyman the Magnificent (reigned 1520–1566). In 1534

Istanbul (iss-TAHN-bull)
Süleyman (SOO-lehy-mahn)

Süleyman conquered Baghdad and added the Tigris and Euphrates valleys to the Ottoman domain. In Europe he kept the rival Habsburg empire on the defensive throughout his reign. He captured Belgrade in 1521, defeated and killed the king of Hungary at the battle of Mohács in 1526, and in 1529 subjected the Habsburgs' prized city of Vienna to a brief but nonetheless terrifying siege.

Under Süleyman the Ottomans also became a major naval power. In addition to their own Aegean and Black Sea fleets, the Ottomans inherited the navy of the Mamluk rulers of Egypt. A Turkish corsair, Khayr al-Din Barbarossa Pasha, placed his pirate fleet under the Ottoman flag and became Süleyman's leading admiral. With such resources and leadership, Süleyman was able to challenge Christian vessels throughout the Mediterranean as well as Portuguese fleets in the Red Sea and the Indian Ocean.

SÜLEYMAN THE MAGNIFICENT. | Sultan Süleyman (center, on horse) leads Ottoman forces as they march on Europe.

The Safavid Empire

In 1499 a twelve-year-old boy named Ismail left the swamps of Gilan near the Caspian Sea, where he had hidden from the enemies of his family for five years, to seek his revenge. Two years later he entered Tabriz at the head of an army and laid claim to the ancient Persian imperial title of shah. The young Shah Ismail (reigned 1501–1524) also proclaimed that the official religion of his realm would be Twelver Shiism, and he proceeded to impose it, by force when necessary, on the formerly Sunni population. Over the next decade he seized control of the Iranian plateau and launched expeditions into the Caucasus, Anatolia, Mesopotamia, and central Asia.

THE SAFAVIDS Shah Ismail and his successors traced their ancestry back to Safi al-Din (1252–1334), leader of a Sufi religious order in northwestern Persia. The famous tomb and shrine of Safi al-Din at Ardabil became the home of Shah Ismail's family (named "Safavids" after the holy man himself), the headquarters of his religious movement, and the center of a determined, deliberate conspiracy to win political power for his descendants. The Safavids changed their religious preferences several times in the hope of gaining popular support before settling on a form of Shiism that appealed to the nomadic Turkish tribes who were moving into the area.

TWELVER SHIISM Twelver Shiism held that there had been twelve infallible imams (or religious leaders) after Muhammad, beginning with the prophet's cousin and son-in-law Ali. The twelfth, or "hidden," imam had gone into hiding about 874 to escape persecution, but the Twelver Shiites believed he was still alive and would one day return to take power and spread the true religion. Ismail's father had instructed his Turkish followers to wear a distinctive red hat with twelve pleats in memory of the twelve Shiite imams, and they subsequently became known as the *qizilbash* ("red heads"). Safavid propaganda also suggested that Ismail was himself the hidden imam, or even an incarnation of Allah. Although most Muslims would have regarded those pretensions as utterly blasphemous, the *qizilbash* enthusiastically accepted them, since they resembled traditional

Shah Ismail (shah IZ-may-el)
Shiism (SHEE-izm)
Sunni (SOON-nee)
Safavid (SAH-fah-vihd)
qizilbash (gih-ZIHL-bahsh)

Turkish conceptions of leadership that associated military leaders with divinity. The *qizilbash* believed that Ismail would make them invincible in battle, and they became fanatically loyal to the Safavid cause.

Shah Ismail's curious blend of Shiism and Turkish militancy created some powerful enemies. Foremost among them were the staunchly Sunni Ottomans, who detested the Shiite Safavids and feared the spread of Safavid propaganda among the nomadic Turks in their own territory. As a result, Ottomans launched a full-scale invasion of Safavid territory in the early sixteenth century.

BATTLE OF CHALDIRAN At a battle on the plain of Chaldiran (1514), the Ottomans deployed heavy artillery and thousands of Janissaries equipped with firearms behind a barrier of carts. Although the Safavids knew about gunpowder technology, they declined to use devices that they saw as unreliable and unmanly. Trusting in the protective charisma of Shah Ismail, the *qizilbash* cavalry fearlessly attacked the Ottoman line and suffered devastating casualties. Ismail had to slip away, and the Ottomans temporarily occupied his capital at Tabriz. The Ottomans badly damaged the Safavid state but lacked the resources to destroy it, and the two empires remained locked in intermittent conflict for the next two centuries.

SHAH ABBAS THE GREAT Later Safavid rulers prudently abandoned the extreme Safavid ideology that associated the emperor with Allah in favor of more conventional Twelver Shiism, from which they still derived legitimacy as descendants and representatives of the imams. In the late sixteenth century, Shah Abbas the Great (reigned 1588–1629) fully revitalized the Safavid empire. He moved the capital to the more central location of Isfahan, encouraged trade with other lands, and reformed the administrative and military institutions of the empire. With newly strengthened military forces, Shah Abbas led the Safavids to numerous victories. He attacked and defeated the nomadic Uzbeks in central Asia, expelled the Portuguese from Hormuz, and harassed the Ottomans mercilessly in a series of wars from 1603 to the end of his reign. His campaigns brought most of northwestern Iran, the Caucasus, and Mesopotamia under Safavid rule.

SHAH ISMAIL AND THE *QIZILBASH*. | This miniature painting from a Safavid manuscript depicts the shah and his *qizilbash* warriors wearing the distinctive red pleated cap that was their emblem of identity.

The Mughal Empire

BABUR In 1523 Zahir al-Din Muhammad, known as Babur ("the Tiger"), a Chagatai Turk who claimed descent from both Chinggis Khan and Tamerlane, appeared in northern India. Unlike the Ottomans or Safavids, who fought on behalf of Islam, Babur made little pretense to be anything more than a soldier of fortune in the manner of his illustrious ancestors. His father had been the prince of Farghana, and Babur's great ambition was to transform his inheritance into a glorious central Asian empire. Yet envious relatives and Uzbek enemies frustrated his ambitions.

Chaldiran (chahld-ih-rahn)
Mughal (MOO-guhl)
Babur (BAH-ber)
Zahir al-Din Muhammad (zah-here ahl-dihn muh-HAHM-mud)
Chagatai (chah-guh-TAHY)

SOURCES FROM THE PAST

Sultan Selim I, Letter to Shah Ismail of Persia

In 1514, the Ottoman Sultan Selim I (reigned 1512–1520) wrote the following letter to the founder of the Safavid Empire, Ismail I (reigned 1501–1524). Ismail had recently invaded Ottoman territory in eastern Anatolia, and war seemed certain. In addition, Ismail was the leader of the emerging Shi'ite interpretation of Islam, while Selim was a Sunni Muslim. This letter reveals the deep bitterness that developed between Shi'ites and Muslims in the early modern period. Although Selim's forces did in fact defeat Ismail's army at the battle of Chaldiran, Ismail retained control of Persia and thus helped to ensure the survival of Shi'ism.

The Supreme Being who is at once the sovereign arbiter of the destinies of men and the source of all light and knowledge, declares in the holy book [the Qur'an] that the true faith is that of the Muslims, and that whoever professes another religion, far from being hearkened to and saved, will on the contrary be cast out among the rejected on the great day of the Last Judgment. . . . Place yourself, O Prince, among the true believers, those who walk in the path of salvation, and who turn aside with care from vice and infidelity. . . .

I, sovereign chief of the Ottomans, master of the heroes of the age . . . address myself graciously to you, Amir Isma'il, chief of troops of Persia. . . . [M]an is the only being who can comprehend the attributes of the divinity and adore its sublime beauties; but he possesses this rare intelligence, he attains this divine knowledge only in our religion and by observing the precepts of the prince of prophets, the Caliph of Caliphs, the right arm of the God of Mercy; it is then only by practicing the true religion that man will prosper in this world and merit eternal life in the other. As to you, Amir Isma'il, such a recompense will not be your lot; because you have denied the sanctity of the divine laws; because you have deserted the path of salvation and the sacred commandments; because you have impaired the purity of the dogmas of Islam; because you have dishonoured, soiled and destroyed the altars of the Lord, usurped the sceptre of the East by unlawful and tyrannical means, because coming forth from the dust, you have raised yourself by odious devices to a place shining with splendor and magnificence. . . . Now as the first duty of a Muslim and above all of a pious prince is to obey the commandment, "O, you faithful who believe, be the executors of the decrees of God!" the *ulama* and our doctors have pronounced sentence of death against you, perjurer and blasphemer, and have imposed on every Muslim the sacred obligation to arm in defense of religion and destroy heresy and impiety in your person and that of all your partisans.

. . . However, anxious to conform to the spirit of the law of the Prophet, we come, before commencing war, to set out before you the words of the Qur'an, in place of the sword, and to exhort you to embrace the true faith; this is why we address this letter to you. . . . We urge you to look into yourself, to renounce your errors, and to march towards the good with a firm and courageous step; we ask further that you give up possession of the territory violently seized from our state and to which you have only illegitimate pretensions. . . .

But if, to your misfortune, you persist in your past conduct . . . you will see in a few days your plains covered with our tents and inundated with our battalions. Then prodigies of valor will be done, and we shall see the decrees of the Almighty, Who is the God of Armies, and sovereign judge of the actions of men, accomplished. For the rest, victory to him who follows the path of salvation!

■ According to Selim I, why did Ismail's Shi'ite faith constitute a blasphemy against Islam? Why might Selim have viewed Shi'ism as such a threat?

SOURCE: Alfred J. Andrea and James H. Overfield. *The Human Record: Sources of Global History,* 3rd ed., vol. II: *Since 1500.* Boston and New York: Houghton Mifflin, 1998.

Mughal dynasty
www.mhhe.com/bentleybrief2e

Unable to accomplish his goals in central Asia, Babur turned his attention to India. With the aid of gunpowder weapons, including artillery and firearms, Babur took Delhi in 1526. Ironically, Babur cared little for the land he had conquered. Many in his entourage wanted to take their spoils of war and leave the hot and humid Indian climate, which ruined their finely crafted compound bows, but Babur elected to stay. By the time of his death in 1530, Babur had built a loosely knit empire that stretched from Kabul through the Punjab to the borders of Bengal. He founded a dynasty called the *Mughal* (a Persian term for "Mongol"), which expanded to embrace almost all the Indian subcontinent.

AKBAR The real architect of the Mughal empire was Babur's grandson Akbar (reigned 1556–1605), a brilliant and charismatic ruler. During his reign, Akbar created a centralized administrative structure with ministries regulating the various provinces of the empire. His military campaigns consolidated Mughal power in Gujarat and Bengal. He destroyed the Hindu kingdom of Vijayanagar, thus laying the foundation for later Mughal expansion in southern India.

In addition to being an able ruler, Akbar was a thoughtful, reflective man deeply interested in religion and philosophy. He pursued a policy of religious toleration that he hoped would reduce tensions between Hindu and Muslim communities in India. Although illiterate (probably due to dyslexia), he was extremely intelligent and had books read to him daily. Instead of imposing Islam on his subjects, he encouraged the elaboration of a syncretic religion called the "divine faith" that focused attention on the emperor as a ruler common to all the religious, ethnic, and social groups of India.

AURANGZEB The Mughal empire reached its greatest extent under Aurangzeb (reigned 1659–1707). During his long reign, Aurangzeb waged a relentless campaign of expansion. By the early eighteenth century, Mughals ruled the entire subcontinent except for a small region at the southern tip. Although he greatly expanded Mughal boundaries, Aurangzeb presided over a troubled empire. Aurangzeb was a devout Muslim, and he broke with Akbar's policy of religious toleration. He demolished several famous Hindu temples and replaced them with mosques. He also imposed a tax on Hindus in an effort to encourage conversion to Islam. His promotion of Islam appealed strongly to Indian Muslims, but it provoked deep hostility among Hindus and enabled local leaders to organize movements to resist or even rebel against Mughal authority.

Aurangzeb at prayer
www.mhhe.com/bentleybrief2e

IMPERIAL ISLAMIC SOCIETY

Despite many differences, there were striking similarities in the development of Ottoman, Safavid, and Mughal societies. All relied on bureaucracies that drew inspiration from the steppe traditions of Turkish and Mongol peoples as well as from the heritage of Islam. They adopted similar economic policies and sought ways to maintain harmony in societies that embraced many different religious and ethnic groups. Rulers of all the empires also sought to enhance the legitimacy of their regimes by providing for public welfare and associating themselves with literary and artistic talent.

The Dynastic State

The Ottoman, Safavid, and Mughal empires were all military creations, regarded by their rulers as personal possessions by right of conquest. The rulers exercised personal command of the armies, appointed and dismissed officials at will, and adopted whatever policies they wished. In theory, the emperors owned all land and granted use of it in return for the payment of fixed taxes. The emperors and their families derived revenues from crown lands, and revenues from other lands supported military and administrative officials.

THE EMPERORS AND ISLAM In the Ottoman, Safavid, and Mughal empires, the prestige and authority of the dynasty derived from the personal piety and the military prowess of the ruler and his ancestors. Devotion to Islam encouraged rulers to extend their faith to new lands. Moreover, the *ghazi* ideal of spreading Islam by fighting infidels or heretics resonated with the traditions of Turkish and Mongolian peoples, who were accustomed both to warfare and to leadership by warriors.

STEPPE TRADITIONS The autocratic authority wielded by the rulers of the Islamic empires also reflected steppe traditions. The early emperors largely did as they pleased, irrespective of religious and social norms. The Ottoman sultans, for example, unilaterally issued numerous legal edicts, and Safavid and Mughal rulers unabashedly asserted their spiritual authority over their subjects. Yet steppe practices also brought problems to

AKBAR. | This manuscript illustration from about 1590 depicts Akbar (at top, shaded by attendants) inspecting construction of a new imperial capital at Fatehpur Sikri. ***What kinds of projects are laborers working on?***

the Islamic empires, especially regarding succession issues. In the steppe empires the ruler's relatives often managed components of the states, and succession to the throne became a hot contest between competing members of the family. This was reflected in the Mughal empire, where conflicts among princes and rebellions of sons against fathers were recurrent features throughout its history. The Safavids also engaged in murderous struggles for the throne. Shah Abbas himself lived in fear that another member of the family would challenge him. He kept his sons confined to the palace and killed or blinded relatives he suspected, almost wiping out his family in the process.

Succession issues also became a problem for the Ottomans. After the fifteenth century, the sultans increasingly moved to protect their position by eliminating family rivals. Mehmed the Conqueror decreed that a ruler could legally kill off his brothers after taking the throne. His successors observed that tradition in Turko-Mongol style—by strangling victims with a silk bow string so as not to shed royal blood—until 1595, when the new sultan executed nineteen brothers, many of them infants, as well as fifteen expectant mothers. After that episode, sultans confined their sons in special quarters of the imperial harem and forbade them to go outside except to take the throne.

WOMEN AND POLITICS Even though Muslim theorists universally agreed that women should have no role in public affairs, women played important roles in managing the Islamic empires. Many Ottoman, Safavid, and Mughal emperors followed the example of Chinggis Khan, who revered his mother and his first wife. In the Islamic empires the ruler's mother and his chief wife or favorite concubine enjoyed special privileges and authority. Ottoman courtiers often complained loudly about the "rule of women," thus offering eloquent testimony to the power that women could wield. Süleyman the Magnificent, for example, became infatuated with Hürrem Sultana (also known as Roxelana), a concubine of Ukrainian origin. Süleyman elevated her to the status of a legal wife, consulted her on state policies, and deferred to her judgment even to the point of executing his eldest son when Hürrem wanted to secure the succession of her child.

Women also played prominent political roles in the Safavid and Mughal empires. In Safavid Persia, Mahd-e Olya, the wife of one shah, was the de facto ruler. Her efforts to limit the power of the *qizilbash* so enraged them that they murdered her. The aunt of another shah scolded the ruler for neglecting his duties and used her own money to raise an army to put down a revolt. The Mughal emperor Jahangir was content to let his wife Nur Jahan run the government, and even the conscientious Muslim Aurangzeb listened to his daughter's political advice.

Agriculture and Trade

FOOD CROPS Productive agricultural economies were the foundations of all the Islamic empires. Each empire extracted surplus agricultural production and used it to finance armies and bureaucracies. Mostly the Islamic empires relied on crops of wheat and rice that had flourished for centuries in the lands they ruled. The Columbian exchange brought American crops to all the Islamic empires but without the same dramatic effects as in Europe, east Asia, and Africa. European merchants did introduce maize, potatoes, tomatoes, and other crops to the Islamic empires, however, and although the new arrivals did not become staples, they enlivened regional cuisines with new tastes and textures.

Two products of the Columbian exchange that caught on extremely well in both the Ottoman and the Safavid empires were coffee and tobacco. Although native to Ethiopia

OTTOMAN COFFEEHOUSE. | This 19th-century depiction of a coffeehouse in Istanbul demonstrates the centrality of tobacco smoking to the experience. In the Ottoman empire, men socialized in coffeehouses while smoking from elaborate water pipes called hookahs. ***In this picture, what seems most central—coffee or tobacco?***

and cultivated in southern Arabia, coffee did not become popular in Islamic lands until the sixteenth century. Like sugar, coffee had traveled to Europe and from there to the Americas, where plantations specialized in the production of both tropical crops for the world market. By the eighteenth century, American producers and European merchants supplied Muslim markets with coffee as well as sugar.

TOBACCO According to the Ottoman historian Ibrahim Pechevi, English merchants introduced tobacco about 1600, claiming it was useful for medicinal purposes. Within a few decades it had spread throughout the Ottoman empire. The increasing popularity of coffee drinking and pipe smoking encouraged entrepreneurs to establish coffeehouses where customers could indulge their appetites for caffeine and nicotine at the same time. The popularity of coffeehouses provoked protest from moralists who worried that these popular attractions were dens of iniquity. Pechevi himself complained about the hideous odor of tobacco and the messy ashes, and religious leaders claimed that it was worse to frequent a coffeehouse than a tavern. Sultan Murad IV went so far as to outlaw coffee and tobacco and to execute those who continued to partake. That effort, however, was a losing battle. Both pastimes eventually won widespread acceptance, and the coffeehouse became a prominent social institution in the Islamic empires.

POPULATION GROWTH American food crops had less demographic effect in the Islamic empires than in other parts of the world. The population of India surged during early modern times, growing from 105 million in 1500 to 190 million in 1800. But population growth in India resulted more from intensive agriculture along traditional lines than from the influence of new crops. The Safavid population grew less rapidly, from 5 million in 1500 to 8 million in 1800. Ottoman numbers grew from 9 million in 1500 to about 24 million about 1800, but those numbers reflect territorial additions more than fertility increases. Even in the Ottoman heartland of Anatolia, population did not expand nearly as dramatically as it did in other lands in early modern times. From 6 million in 1500, the population of Anatolia rose to just 9 million in 1800.

THINKING ABOUT *Traditions*

TRADITIONS IN THE ISLAMIC EMPIRES. Although the Ottoman, Safavid, and Mughal empires each developed in distinctive ways, they nevertheless shared features based on their common origins in central Asian steppe societies and in their experience of Islam. In what ways did these common traditions shape political, economic, social, and cultural institutions in all three realms?

TRADE The Islamic empires ruled lands that had figured prominently in long-distance trade for centuries and participated actively in global trade networks in early modern times. In the Ottoman empire, for example, the early capital at Bursa was also the terminus of a caravan route that brought raw silk from Persia to supply the Italian market. The Ottomans also granted special trading concessions to merchants from England and France to cement alliances against common enemies in Spain and central Europe, and the city of Aleppo became an emporium for foreign merchants engaged primarily in the spice trade.

Shah Abbas promoted Isfahan as a commercial center and extended trading privileges to foreign merchants to help create a favorable environment for trade. European merchants sought Safavid raw silk, carpets, and ceramics. The English East India Company, the French East India Company, and the Dutch VOC all traded actively with the Safavids. To curry favor, the English company even sent military advisors to help introduce gunpowder weapons to Safavid armed forces and provided a navy to help them retake Hormuz in the Persian Gulf from the Portuguese.

The Mughals did not pay as much attention to foreign trade as the Ottomans and the Safavids, partly because of the enormous size and productivity of the domestic Indian economy and partly because the Mughal rulers had little interest in maritime affairs. Nevertheless, the Mughal treasury derived significant income from foreign trade. The Mughals allowed the creation of trading stations and merchant colonies by Portuguese, English, French, and Dutch merchants. Meanwhile, Indian merchants formed trading companies of their own, venturing both overland as far as Russia and by sea to ports all over the Indian Ocean.

Religious Affairs in the Islamic Empires

RELIGIOUS DIVERSITY All the Islamic empires had populations that were religiously and ethnically diverse, and imperial rulers had the daunting challenge of maintaining harmony among different religious communities. The Ottoman empire included large numbers of Christians and Jews in the Balkans, Armenia, Lebanon, and Egypt. The Safavid empire embraced sizable Zoroastrian and Jewish communities as well as many Christian subjects in the Caucasus. The Mughal empire was especially diverse. Most Mughal subjects were Hindus, but large numbers of Muslims lived alongside smaller communities of Jains, Zoroastrians, Christians, and devotees of syncretic faiths such as Sikhism.

AKBAR'S DIVINE FAITH In India, Akbar was especially tolerant of diverse religions and worked to find a religious synthesis that would serve as a cultural foundation for unity in his diverse empire. As part of that effort, he supported the early Sikhs, who combined elements of Hinduism and Islam in a new syncretic faith. He also attempted to elaborate his own "divine faith," which emphasized loyalty to the emperor while borrowing eclectically from different religious traditions. Akbar never explained his ideas systematically, but it is clear that they drew most heavily on Islam. The divine faith was strictly monotheistic, and it reflected the influence of Shiite and Sufi teachings. But it also glorified the emperor: Akbar even referred to himself as the "lord of wisdom," who would guide his subjects to an understanding of god. The divine faith was tolerant of Hinduism, and it even drew inspiration from Zoroastrianism in its effort to bridge the gaps between Mughal India's many cultural and religious communities.

STATUS OF RELIGIOUS MINORITIES The Islamic empires relied on a long-established model to deal with subjects who were not Muslims. They did not require conquered peoples to convert to Islam but extended to them the status of *dhimmi* (a protected people). In return for their loyalty and payment of a special tax known as *jizya,*

Sikhs (SIHKS)
dhimmi (DIHM-mee)
jizya (JIHZ-yuh)

dhimmi communities retained their personal freedom, kept their property, practiced their religion, and handled their own legal affairs. In the Ottoman empire, for example, autonomous religious communities known as *millet* retained their own civil laws, traditions, and languages. *Millet* communities usually also assumed social and administrative functions in matters concerning birth, marriage, death, health, and education.

The situation in the Mughal empire was different, since its large number of religious communities made a *millet* system impractical. Mughal rulers reserved the most powerful military and administrative positions for Muslims, but in the day-to-day management of affairs, Muslims and Hindus cooperated closely. Some Mughal emperors, such as Akbar, worked particularly hard to forge links between religious communities and to integrate Muslim and Hindu elites. Indeed, in an effort to build bridges between the different religious communities of his realm, he abolished the *jizya* and sponsored discussions and debates between Muslims, Hindus, Jains, Zoroastrians, and Christians.

PROMOTION OF ISLAM Policies of religious tolerance were not popular with many Muslims, who worried that toleration might lead to their absorption into Hindu society. They therefore insisted that Mughal rulers create and maintain an Islamic state based on Islamic law. When Aurangzeb reached the Mughal throne in 1659, that policy gained strength. Aurangzeb reinstated the *jizya* and promoted Islam as the official faith of Mughal India. His policy satisfied zealous Muslims but at the cost of deep bitterness among his Hindu subjects. Tension between Hindu and Muslim communities in India persisted throughout the Mughal dynasty and beyond.

Cultural Patronage of the Islamic Emperors

As the empires matured, the Islamic rulers sought to enhance their prestige through public works projects and patronage of scholars. They competed to attract outstanding religious scholars, artists, and architects to their courts and lavished resources on public buildings.

Views of Isfahan
www.mhhe.com/bentleybrief2e

ISTANBUL Capital cities and royal palaces were the most visible expressions of imperial majesty. The Ottomans took particular pride in Istanbul, which quickly revived after conquest and became a bustling, prosperous city of more than a million people. At its heart was the great Topkapi palace, which housed government offices and meeting places for imperial councils. At its core was the sultan's residence with its harem, gardens, pleasure pavilions, and a repository for the most sacred possessions of the empire, including the mantle of the prophet Muhammad. Sultan Süleyman the Magnificent was fortunate to be able to draw on the talents of the architectural genius Sinan Pasha (1489–1588) to create the vast religious complex called the Süleymaniye, which blended Islamic and Byzantine architectural elements. It combined tall, slender minarets with large domed buildings supported by half domes in the style of the Byzantine church Hagia Sofia (which the Ottomans converted into the mosque of Aya Sofya).

The Süleymaniye Mosque. | This massive mosque was built for Sultan Süleyman the Magnificent by the Ottoman architect Sinan Pasha in 1556.

ISFAHAN Shah Abbas made his capital, Isfahan, into one of the most precious jewels of urban architectural development anywhere in the world. Abbas concentrated markets, the palace, and the royal mosque around a vast polo field and public square. Broad, shaded avenues and magnificent bridges linked the central city to its suburbs. Safavid architects made use of monumental entryways, vast arcades, spacious courtyards, and intricate, colorful

Topkapi (TOHP-kah-pih)
Sinan Pasha (sih-NAHN pah-cha)

ISFAHAN ROYAL MOSQUE. | The Royal Mosque of Isfahan, centerpiece of the city as rebuilt by Shah Abbas at the end of the sixteenth century. With its combination of an open space flanked by markets, the palace, and religious structures, Isfahan stands as a unique example of urban planning in Islamic lands.

decoration. Unlike the sprawling Ottoman and Mughal palaces, the Safavid palaces in Isfahan were relatively small and emphasized natural settings with gardens, pools, and large, open verandas. The point was not only to enable the shah to observe outside activities but also to emphasize his visibility and accessibility, qualities long esteemed in the Persian tradition of kingship.

In India, Mughal architects skillfully blended central Asian traditions with elements of Hindu architecture, and they built on a scale that left no doubt about their wealth and resources. They constructed scores of mosques, fortresses, and palaces and sometimes created entire cities.

FATEHPUR SIKRI The best example was Fatehpur Sikri, a city planned and constructed by Akbar that served as his capital from 1569 to 1585. With its mint, records office, treasury, and audience hall, the new city demonstrated Akbar's strength and imperial ambitions. Fatehpur Sikri was also a private residence and retreat for the ruler, reproducing in stone a royal encampment with exquisite pleasure palaces where Akbar indulged his passions for music and conversation with scholars and poets. At yet another level, it was a dramatic display of Mughal piety and devotion, centered on the cathedral mosque and the mausoleum of Akbar's Sufi guru, Shaykh Salim Christi. Despite their intensely Islamic character, many of the buildings consciously incorporated Indian elements, such as verandas supported by columns and decorations of stone elephants. Unfortunately, Akbar had selected a poor site for the city and soon abandoned it because of its bad water supply.

The Red Fortress of Agra
www.mhhe.com/bentleybrief2e

Taj Mahal
www.mhhe.com/bentleybrief2e

THE TAJ MAHAL The most famous of the Mughal monuments—and one of the most prominent of all Islamic edifices—was the Taj Mahal. Shah Jahan had twenty thousand workers toil for eighteen years to erect the exquisite white marble mosque and tomb. He originally planned to build a similar mausoleum out of black marble for himself, but his son Aurangzeb deposed him before he could carry out the project. Shah Jahan spent his last years confined to a small cell with a tiny window, and only with the aid of a mirror was he able to catch the sight of his beloved wife's final resting place.

The Empires in Transition

The Islamic empires underwent dramatic change between the sixteenth and the eighteenth centuries. The Safavid empire disappeared entirely. In 1722 a band of Afghan tribesmen marched all the way to Isfahan, blockaded the city until its starving inhabitants resorted to cannibalism, forced the shah to abdicate, and executed thousands of Safavid officials as well as many members of the royal family. After the death of Aurangzeb in 1707, Mughal India experienced provincial rebellions and foreign invasions. By midcentury the subcontinent was falling under British imperial rule. By 1700 the Ottomans, too, were on the defensive: the sultans lost control over provinces such as Lebanon and Egypt, and throughout the eighteenth and nineteenth centuries European and Russian states placed political, military, and economic pressure on the shrinking Ottoman realm.

The Deterioration of Imperial Leadership

Strong and effective central authority was essential to the Islamic empires, and Muslim political theorists never tired of emphasizing the importance of rulers who were diligent, virtuous, and just. Weak, negligent, and corrupt rulers would allow the social order to

Fatehpur Sikri (fah-teh-poor SIH-kree)
Shaykh Salim Christi (sheyk sah-LEEM KRIS-tee)

break down. The Ottomans were fortunate in having a series of talented sultans for three centuries, and the Safavids and the Mughals produced their share of effective rulers as well.

DYNASTIC DECLINE Eventually, however, all three dynasties had rulers who were incompetent or irresponsible about tending to affairs of state. Moreover, all three dynasties faced difficulties because of suspicion and fighting among competing members of their ruling houses. In the Ottoman empire alone, notorious examples of problem rulers included Süleyman's successor, Selim the Sot (reigned 1566–1574) and Ibrahim the Crazy (reigned 1640–1648), who taxed and spent to such excess that government officials deposed and murdered him. Indeed, after the late seventeenth century, weak rule increasingly provoked mutinies in the army, provincial revolts, political corruption, and insecurity throughout the Ottoman realm.

RELIGIOUS TENSIONS Political troubles often arose from religious tensions. Conservative Muslim clerics had considerable influence in the Islamic empires because of their monopoly on education and their deep involvement in the everyday lives and legal affairs of ordinary subjects. The clerics mistrusted the emperors' interests in unconventional forms of Islam such as Sufism, complained bitterly when women or subjects who were not Muslims played influential political roles, and protested any exercise of royal authority that contradicted Islamic law.

In the Ottoman empire, disaffected religious students often joined the Janissaries in revolt. A particularly serious threat came from the Wahhabi movement in Arabia, which denounced the Ottomans as dangerous religious innovators who were unfit to rule. Conservative Muslims fiercely protested the construction of an astronomical observatory in Istanbul and forced the sultan to demolish it in 1580. In 1742 they also forced the closure of the Ottoman printing press, which they regarded as an impious technology.

In the Safavid empire, rulers fell under the domination of conservative Shiite clerics. Shiite leaders pressured the shahs to persecute Sunnis, non-Muslims, and even the Sufis who had helped establish the dynasty. Religious tensions also afflicted Mughal India. In the mid–eighteenth century, as Aurangzeb struggled to claim the Mughal throne, he drew on conservative Islamic ideas when he required non-Muslims to pay the poll tax and ordered the destruction of Hindu temples. Those measures inflamed tensions between the various Sunni, Shiite, and Sufi branches of Islam and also fueled animosity among Hindus and other Mughal subjects who were not Muslims.

THINKING ABOUT *Encounters*

ENCOUNTERS IN THE ISLAMIC EMPIRES. The Ottoman, Safavid, and Mughal empires were all expansive imperial states that sought to incorporate new territories and new peoples into their realms during the early modern period. At the same time, however, none were particularly interested in world affairs far beyond their territories, and none encouraged their own people to travel or trade extensively in foreign lands. What were the reasons behind this approach to cultural encounters, and what were some of its long-term consequences?

The observatory in Istanbul, 1580
www.mhhe.com/bentleybrief2e

Wahhabi (wuh-HAH-bee)
Sufis (SOO-fees)

FATEHPUR SIKRI. This city was built by Akbar in the 1570s to commemorate the emperor's military conquests and house the tomb of his religious guide. It included a palace, an audience hall where Akbar attended religious and philosophical debates, and a great mosque.

Economic and Military Decline

In the sixteenth century, all the Islamic empires had strong domestic economies and played prominent roles in global trade networks. By the eighteenth century, however, domestic economies were under great stress, and foreign trade had declined dramatically or had fallen under the control of European powers. The Islamic empires were well on their way to becoming marginal lands that depended on goods produced elsewhere.

ECONOMIC DIFFICULTIES The high cost of maintaining an expensive military and administrative apparatus helped to bring about economic decline in the Islamic empires. As long as the empires were expanding, they were able to finance their armies and bureaucracies with fresh resources extracted from newly conquered lands. When expansion slowed, ceased, or reversed, however, they faced the problem of supporting their institutions with limited resources. The long, costly, and unproductive wars fought by the Ottomans with the Habsburgs in central Europe, by the Safavids and Ottomans in Mesopotamia, and by Aurangzeb in southern India exhausted the treasuries of the Islamic empires without making fresh resources available to them.

As expansion slowed and the empires lost control over remote provinces, officials reacted to the loss of revenue by raising taxes, selling public offices, accepting bribes, or resorting to simple extortion. All those measures did long-term economic damage. To make matters worse, the governments viewed foreign trade as just another opportunity to bring in revenue. The Ottomans expanded the privileges enjoyed by foreign merchants, and the Mughals encouraged the establishment of Dutch and English trading outposts and welcomed the expansion of their business in India. In other words, imperial authorities were content to have foreign traders come to them. None made serious efforts to establish commercial stations abroad, although Indian merchants organized their own private trading companies.

MILITARY DECLINE As they lost initiative to western European peoples in economic and commercial affairs, the Islamic empires also did not seek actively to improve their military technologies. During the sixteenth and early seventeenth centuries, the Islamic empires were able to purchase European weapons in large numbers and attract European expertise that kept their armies supplied with powerful gunpowder weapons. By about the mid–seventeenth century, however, European military technology was advancing so rapidly that the Islamic empires could not keep pace. None of the empires had a large armaments industry, so they had to rely on foreign suppliers. They still were able to purchase European weapons and expertise, but their arsenals became increasingly dated, since they depended on technologies that European peoples had already replaced. By the late eighteenth century, even the once-influential Ottoman navy was closing its shipbuilding operations and ordering new military vessels from foreign shipyards.

Cultural Conservatism

While experiencing economic and military decline, the Islamic empires also neglected cultural developments in the larger world. Europeans who visited the Islamic empires attempted to learn as much as possible about the language, religion, social customs, and history of the host countries. They published accounts of their travels that became extremely popular in their homelands, and they advocated serious study of Islamic lands.

PIRI REIS Meanwhile, the Islamic empires expressed only limited interest in world affairs. In the sixteenth century, just as European mariners were scouting Atlantic waters, Ottoman mariners did reconnoiter the Indian Ocean basin from east Africa to Indonesia. Ottoman geographers also manifested great interest in European knowledge of geography, some of which had considerable military value. The Ottoman admiral and cartographer Piri Reis produced several large-scale maps and a major navigational text, the *Book of Seafaring,* which drew on reports and maps from European mariners and explorers. Some of

Piri Reis (pir-ree reys)

Piri Reis's maps included the Atlantic coast of North America and the lands visited by Columbus, which the cartographer probably learned about from Spanish sailors captured in naval conflicts with Ottoman forces.

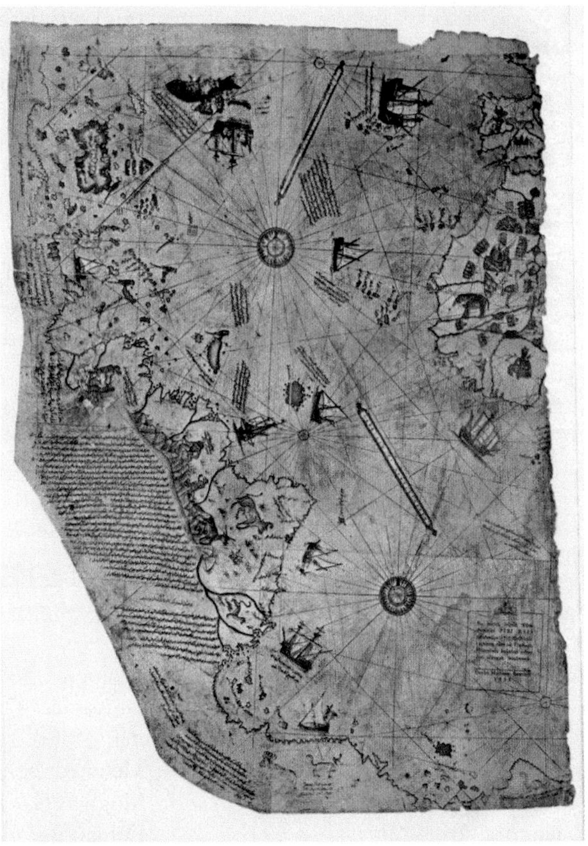

OTTOMAN MAP. | Ottoman cartographer Piri Reis drew on European charts when preparing this map of the Atlantic Ocean basin in 1513. Caribbean and South American coastlines are visible at left, and Iberian and west African coastlines appear in the upper right corner. ***What function might the illustrations of ships and other figures have served on a map such as this?***

CULTURAL CONSERVATISM On the whole, however, few Muslims traveled willingly to the infidel lands of "the Franks." Muslim rulers and their Muslim subjects were confident that they had nothing to learn from Europeans. As a result, most Muslims remained largely oblivious to European cultural and technological developments. Not until 1703 was there an attempt to introduce European scientific instruments such as the telescope into astronomical observatories. Then conservative Muslim clerics soon forced the removal of the foreign implements, which they considered impious and unnecessary.

THE PRINTING PRESS The early experience of the printing press in the Islamic empires illustrates especially well the resistance of conservative religious leaders to cultural imports from western Europe. Jewish refugees from Spain introduced the first printing presses to Anatolia in the late fifteenth century. Ottoman authorities allowed them to operate presses in Istanbul and other major cities as long as they did not print books in the Turkish or Arabic language. Not until 1729 did government authorities lift the ban on the printing of such books. During the next thirteen years, a Turkish press published seventeen books dealing mostly with history, geography, and language before conservative Muslims forced its closure in 1742. Only in 1784 did a new Turkish press open.

Printing also caught on slowly in Mughal India. Jesuit missionaries in Goa published books, including translations of the Bible into Indian and Arabic languages, as early as the 1550s. Yet Mughal rulers displayed little interest in the press, and printing did not become prominent in Indian society until the establishment of British colonial rule in Bengal in the eighteenth century.

To some extent, aesthetic considerations stood in the way of the printing press: particularly in the Ottoman and Safavid empires, scholars and general readers alike preferred elegant handwritten books to cheaply produced printed works. Yet resistance to printing also reflected the concerns of conservative religious leaders that readily available printed books would introduce all manner of new and dangerous ideas to the public.

Thus, like imperial China and Tokugawa Japan, the Islamic empires resisted the introduction of cultural influences from western European societies. Rulers of the Islamic empires readily accepted gunpowder weapons as enhancements to their military and political power, but they and their subjects drew little inspiration from European religion, science, or ideas. Moreover, under the influence of conservative religious leaders, Islamic authorities actively discouraged the circulation of ideas that might pose unsettling challenges to the social and cultural order. Like the Ming, Qing, and Tokugawa rulers, the Ottoman, Safavid, and Mughal emperors preferred political and social stability to the risks that foreign cultural innovations might bring.

SUMMARY

Like China and Japan, the Islamic empires largely retained control of their own affairs throughout the early modern era. Ruling elites of the Ottoman, Safavid, and Mughal empires came from nomadic Turkish stock, and they all drew on steppe traditions in organizing their governments. But the rulers also devised institutions that maintained order over a long term. During the sixteenth and seventeenth centuries, all the Islamic empires enjoyed productive economies that enabled merchants to participate actively in the global trade networks of early modern times. By the early eighteenth century, however, these same empires were experiencing economic difficulties that led to political and military decline. Like the Ming, Qing, and Tokugawa rulers in east Asia, the Islamic emperors mostly sought to limit foreign and especially European influences in their realms. The Islamic emperors ruled lands that were religiously and ethnically diverse, and most of them worried that such influences would threaten political and social stability. They allowed their subjects to practice faiths other than Islam, and a few emperors actively worked to defuse religious tensions in their realms. For the most part, however, rulers of the Islamic empires followed the advice of conservative Muslim clerics, who promoted Islamic values and fought the introduction of foreign cultural imports that might undermine their authority. By the late eighteenth century, the Safavid empire had collapsed, and economic difficulties and cultural insularity had severely weakened the Ottoman and Mughal empires.

STUDY TERMS

Akbar (477)
Aurangzeb (477)
Babur (475)
devshirme (472)
dhimmi (480)
Fatehpur Sikri (482)
ghazi (472)
Hürrem Sultana (478)
Istanbul (473)
Jahangir (478)
Janissaries (473)
jizya (480)
Mehmed the Conqueror (473)
Mughals (476)
Osman Bey (472)
Ottomans (472)
Piri Reis (484)
quizilbash (474)
Safavids (474)
Shah Abbas the Great (475)
Shah Ismail (474)
Süleyman the Magnificent (473)
Süleymaniye mosque (481)
Topkapi Palace (481)
Twelver Shiism (474)

FOR FURTHER READING

Esin Atil. *The Age of Sultan Süleyman the Magnificent.* Washington, 1987. Richly illustrated volume that emphasizes Süleyman's role as a patron of the arts.

Palmira Brummett. *Ottoman Seapower and Levantine Diplomacy in the Age of Discovery.* Albany, 1994. A scholarly study of Ottoman military strategy and diplomacy in the Mediterranean during the sixteenth century.

Stephen Frederic Dale. *Indian Merchants and Eurasian Trade, 1600–1750.* Cambridge, 1994. Examines the workings of an Indian trading community that conducted business in Persia, central Asia, and Russia.

Halil Inalçik. *The Ottoman Empire: The Classical Age, 1300–1600.* New York, 1973. A reliable survey by the foremost historian of the early Ottoman empire.

Çemal Kafadar. *Between Two Worlds: The Construction of the Ottoman State.* Berkeley, 1995. Studies the origins and early development of the Ottoman empire.

Bernard Lewis. *The Muslim Discovery of Europe.* New York, 1982. An important study that charts Muslim interest in European affairs.

Leslie Pierce. *The Imperial Harem: Women and Sovereignty in the Ottoman Empire.* Oxford, 1993. Challenges many stereotypes about the role of women in the imperial Ottoman elite.

John F. Richards. *The Mughal Empire.* Cambridge, 1993. A concise and reliable overview of Mughal history, concentrating on political affairs.

Roger Savory. *Iran under the Safavids.* Cambridge, 1980. A rich and authoritative survey of Safavid history, especially interesting for its views on Safavid origins, culture, and commercial relations.

Bringing It All Together

Part V The Origins of Global Interdependence, 1500–1800

When European mariners made contact with the peoples of the Americas in the late fifteenth century, they initiated a process of interaction and exchange that had profound consequences for the whole world. Indeed, by 1800 few of the world's peoples remained untouched by the transformations wrought by early modern global exchanges in material items such as trade goods, plants, animals, people, and technologies as well as intangible items such as ideas and microbes.

Yet the impact of these exchanges was not uniform around the world. For the Europeans who established trade routes across the earth's oceans, who settled the Americas, and who founded trading posts in both Africa and Asia, the early modern era was one of unprecedented territorial expansion, population increase, and growing political and economic influence in the wider world.

For the peoples of the Americas, however, the establishment of global networks of exchange was nothing short of catastrophic. European diseases such as smallpox and influenza decimated indigenous communities, killing as much as 90 percent of the population. European conquerors then took advantage of weakened populations to claim, conquer, and settle huge tracts of valuable land for their own uses, relegating indigenous peoples to marginal lands or to providing labor for the conquerors. These same global networks of exchange also wreaked havoc on west African communities. Indeed, the labor shortages caused by population loss in the Americas led Europeans to force millions of Africans into crossing the Atlantic to serve as slaves on European plantations.

The new global exchanges of the early modern period also affected east, south, and southwest Asia in important but less dramatic ways. In China, American silver fueled the economy, while American food crops contributed to population growth. In the Islamic empires, European traders gained significant footholds in port cities, while American crops including tobacco became firmly enmeshed in Islamic culture. Yet—unlike the Americas, which had been overwhelmed by Europeans as a result of disease—the states of east, south, and southwest Asia remained strong and powerful in the early modern period.

Nevertheless, by 1800 the world was a different place than it had been in 1500. Contact and conquest in the Americas had created fundamentally new, hybrid societies that blended indigenous, European, and African populations. Moreover, while states in east, south, and southwest Asia remained powerful in this period, Europeans—via their role in connecting the world through trade—had become more prominent in world affairs than ever before.

VI An Age of Revolution, Industry, and Empire, 1750–1914

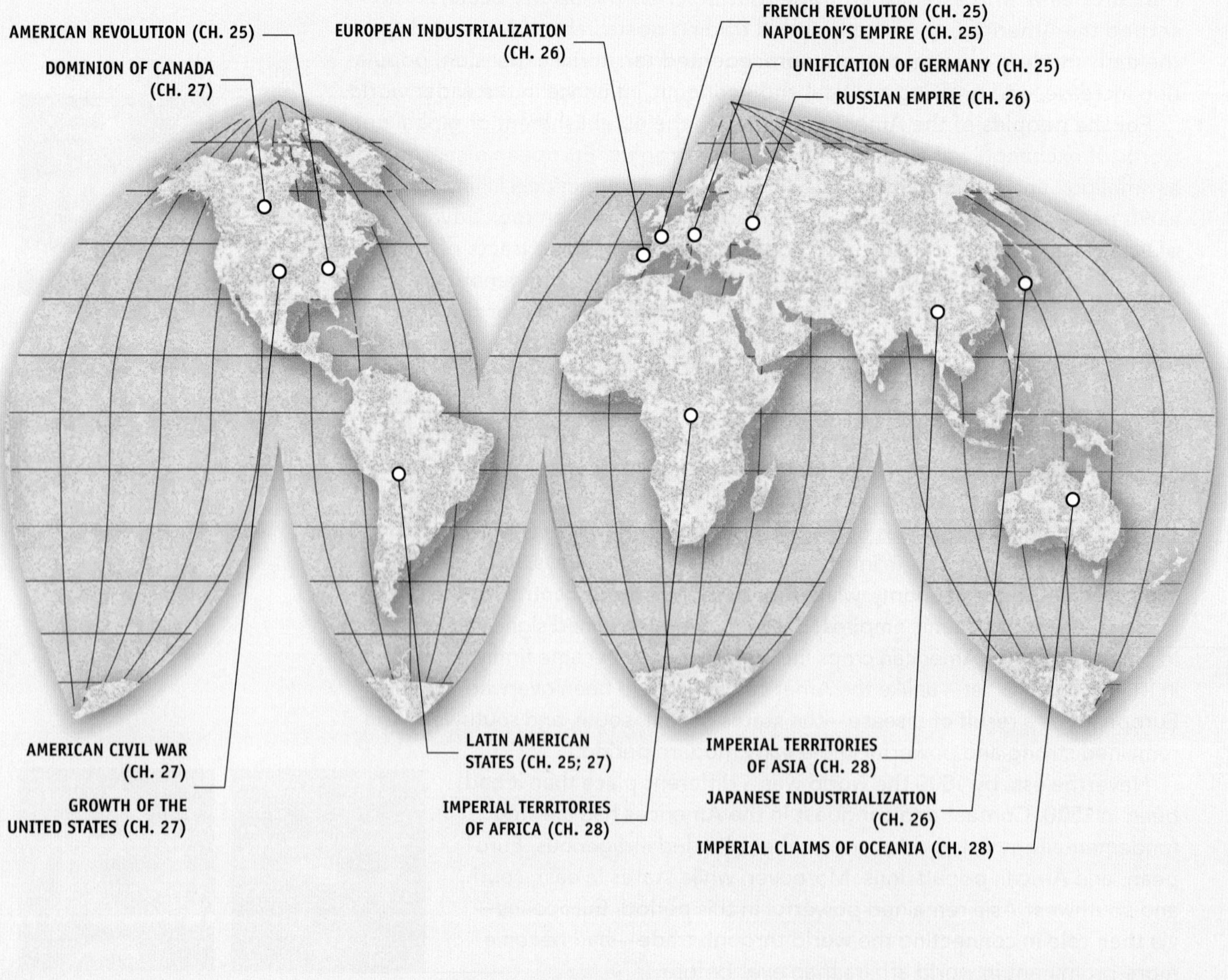

AMERICAN REVOLUTION (CH. 25)
DOMINION OF CANADA (CH. 27)
EUROPEAN INDUSTRIALIZATION (CH. 26)
FRENCH REVOLUTION (CH. 25)
NAPOLEON'S EMPIRE (CH. 25)
UNIFICATION OF GERMANY (CH. 25)
RUSSIAN EMPIRE (CH. 26)
AMERICAN CIVIL WAR (CH. 27)
GROWTH OF THE UNITED STATES (CH. 27)
LATIN AMERICAN STATES (CH. 25; 27)
IMPERIAL TERRITORIES OF AFRICA (CH. 28)
IMPERIAL TERRITORIES OF ASIA (CH. 28)
JAPANESE INDUSTRIALIZATION (CH. 26)
IMPERIAL CLAIMS OF OCEANIA (CH. 28)

During the period from about 1750 to 1914, European peoples parlayed the profits they had gained from early modern trade, as well as their recent and advantageous domination of the Americas, into global hegemony. In stark contrast to the period from 1500 to 1800, by the late nineteenth century European powers controlled affairs in most of Asia and almost all of Africa, and their Euro-American cousins continued to dominate the Americas. Three historical developments—revolution, industrialization, and imperialism—help to explain how European and Euro-American peoples came to dominate so much of the world.

Revolution transformed societies in North America, France, Haiti, and South America during the late eighteenth and early nineteenth centuries. Although the results of each revolution were different, Enlightenment values of freedom, equality, and popular sovereignty played a large role in each. Revolutions also had a profound effect on the organization of societies in the Atlantic Ocean basin. First in Europe and later in the Americas as well, revolutions and the conflicts that followed from them encouraged the formation of national identities.

The idea of organizing states around national communities eventually influenced political development throughout the world. While organizing themselves into national states, western European and North American peoples also embarked on processes of industrialization. Although industrialization initially caused a great deal of discomfort and dislocation for workers, over time industrial societies became economically much stronger than agricultural societies, and industrial production brought about general improvement in material standards of living. After originating in Britain in the late eighteenth century, industrialization spread rapidly to western Europe and North America, and by the late nineteenth century to Russia and Japan as well.

Alongside increased material standards of living, industrialization brought political, military, and economic strength. In western Europe, the United States, and Japan, industrialization helped underwrite processes of imperialism and colonialism. Railroads, steamships, telegraphs, and lethal weapons enabled industrial powers to impose their rule in most of Asia and Africa in the nineteenth century, just as Euro-American settlers relied on industrial technologies to drive the indigenous peoples of North America and South America onto marginal lands.

Revolution, industrialization, and imperialism had effects that were felt around the world. Western European and North American peoples vastly strengthened their position in the world by exercising political or economic influence over other societies. They also inspired sustained resistance among colonized peoples, which eventually led to the organization of anticolonial movements. Indeed, revolution, industry, and empire fueled conflict throughout the world in the nineteenth century, and in combination they forced the world's peoples to deal with one another more systematically than ever before in history.

Revolutions and National States in the Atlantic World

25

arie Gouze was a French butcher's daughter who educated herself by reading books, moved to Paris, and married a junior army officer. Under the name Olympe de Gouges she won some fame as a journalist, actress, and playwright. Gouges was as flamboyant as she was talented, and her well-publicized love affairs scandalized Parisian society.

Gouges was also a revolutionary and a strong advocate of women's rights. She responded enthusiastically when the French revolution broke out in July 1789, and she applauded in August when revolutionary leaders proclaimed freedom and equality for all citizens in the *Declaration of the Rights of Man and the Citizen.* It soon became clear, however, that freedom and equality pertained only to male citizens. Revolutionary leaders welcomed women's contributions to the revolution but refused to grant them political and social rights.

Gouges demanded that women share equal rights in family property and campaigned for equal education. She even appealed to Queen Marie Antoinette to use her influence to advance women's rights. In 1791 Gouges published a *Declaration of the Rights of Woman and the Female Citizen,* which claimed the same rights for women that revolutionary leaders had granted to men in August 1789. She insisted on the rights of women to vote, speak their minds freely, participate in the making of law, and hold public office.

Gouges's declaration attracted a great deal of attention but little support. Revolutionary leaders dismissed her appeal, and in 1793 they executed her because of her affection for Marie Antoinette and her persistent crusade for women's rights. Yet Gouges's campaign illustrated the power of the Enlightenment ideals of freedom and equality. Revolutionary leaders stilled her voice, but once they had proclaimed freedom and equality as universal human rights, they were unable to suppress demands to extend them to new constituencies.

A series of violent revolutions brought dramatic political and social change to lands throughout much of the Atlantic Ocean basin in the late eighteenth and early nineteenth centuries. Revolution broke out first in the British colonies of North America, where colonists founded a new republic. A few years later, revolutionaries abolished the French monarchy and thoroughly reorganized French society. Revolutionary ideas soon spread, prompting Latin American peoples to seek independence from Spanish and Portuguese colonial rule. In Saint-Domingue,

‹ Liberty, personified as a woman, leads the French people in a famous painting by Eugène Delacroix.

Olympe de Gouges (oh-LIM-peh de gouj)

CHRONOLOGY

1632–1704	Life of John Locke
1694–1778	Life of Voltaire
1712–1778	Life of Jean-Jacques Rousseau
1744–1803	Life of Toussaint Louverture
1748–1793	Life of Olympe de Gouges
1753–1811	Life of Miguel de Hidalgo
1769–1821	Life of Napoleon Bonaparte
1774–1793	Reign of King Louis XVI
1775–1781	American Revolution
1783–1830	Life of Simón Bolívar
1789–1799	French revolution
1791–1803	Haitian revolution
1799–1814	Reign of Napoleon
1810–1825	Wars of independence in Latin America
1814–1815	Congress of Vienna

revolution led to the abolition of slavery as well as independence from French rule. By the 1830s, peoples had reorganized political and social structures throughout western Europe and the Americas.

The revolutions of the late eighteenth and early nineteenth centuries had two results of deep global significance. First, they helped to spread a cluster of Enlightenment ideas concerning freedom, equality, and popular sovereignty. Revolutionary leaders argued that political authority arose from the people rather than the rulers and often sought to establish republican forms of government in which the people selected delegates to represent their interests. In fact, early revolutionaries extended political rights only to a privileged group of white men, but they justified their actions in general terms that prompted disenfranchised groups to seek freedom, equality, and a political voice as well. Indeed, such ideas spread globally in the nineteenth and twentieth centuries as social reformers and revolutionaries struggled to make freedom and equality a reality for oppressed groups throughout the world.

Second, while promoting Enlightenment values, revolutions encouraged the consolidation of national states as the principal form of political organization. As peoples defended their states from enemies and sometimes mounted attacks on foreign lands, they developed a powerful sense of identity with their compatriots. During the nineteenth century, strong national identities led to movements to build national states, which in turn profoundly influenced the political experiences of European states. During the late nineteenth and twentieth centuries, efforts to harness nationalist sentiments and form states based on national identity became one of the most powerful and dynamic movements in world history.

Popular Sovereignty and Political Upheaval

Drawing on Enlightenment ideals, revolutionaries of the eighteenth and nineteenth centuries sought to fashion equitable societies by instituting governments that were responsive to the peoples they governed. In justifying their policies, revolutionaries argued for popular sovereignty—the notion that legitimate political authority resides not in kings but, rather, in the people who make up a society. In North America, colonists declared independence from British rule and instituted a new government founded on the principle of popular sovereignty. Soon thereafter, French revolutionaries abolished the monarchy and revamped the social order. Yet revolutionaries in France were unable to devise a stable alternative to the monarchy. In the early nineteenth century, Napoleon Bonaparte imposed military rule on France and helped spread revolutionary ideas to much of western Europe.

Enlightened and Revolutionary Ideas

Throughout history kings or emperors ruled almost all settled agricultural societies. In justifying their rule, they often identified themselves with deities or claimed divine sanction for their authority. In imperial China, for example, dynastic houses claimed to rule in accordance with the "mandate of heaven," and in early modern Europe centralizing monarchs often asserted a "divine right of kings" to rule as absolute monarchs.

POPULAR SOVEREIGNTY During the seventeenth and eighteenth centuries, philosophes and other advocates of Enlightenment ideas (discussed in chapter 20) began to question such notions and argued that kings should be responsible to the people they governed. The English philosopher John Locke (1632–1704), for example, regarded government as a contract between rulers and ruled. In his *Second Treatise of Civil Government,* published in 1690, Locke held that individuals granted political rights to their rulers but retained personal rights to life, liberty, and property. Furthermore, according to Locke, rulers derived their authority from the consent of those they governed. If rulers broke the contract, the people had the right to replace their rulers. In effect, Locke's political thought relocated sovereignty, removing it from rulers as divine agents and vesting it in the people of a society.

INDIVIDUAL FREEDOM Enlightenment thinkers addressed issues of freedom and equality as well as sovereignty. Philosophes such as Voltaire (1694–1778) resented the persecution of religious minorities as well as royal censorship. Philosophes called for religious toleration and freedom to express their views openly. Thus, when censors prohibited the publication of their writings in France, they often published their books in Switzerland or the Netherlands and smuggled them across the border into France.

POLITICAL AND LEGAL EQUALITY Many Enlightenment thinkers also called for equality. They argued that privileged aristocrats made no more contribution to the larger society than peasants, artisans, or workers and recommended the creation of a society in which all individuals would be equal before the law. The most prominent advocate of political equality was the French-Swiss thinker Jean-Jacques Rousseau (1712–1778). In his influential book *The Social Contract* (1762), Rousseau argued that members of a society were collectively the sovereign. In an ideal society all individuals would participate directly in the formulation of policy and the creation of laws.

GLOBAL INFLUENCE OF ENLIGHTENMENT VALUES Most Enlightenment thinkers were of common birth but comfortable means. Though seeking to limit the prerogatives of ruling and aristocratic classes, they did not envision a society in which they would share political rights with women, children, peasants, laborers, or slaves. Nevertheless, Enlightenment thought constituted a serious challenge to long-established notions of political and social order. Although arguments for freedom, equality, and popular sovereignty originally served the interests of relatively privileged European and Euro-American men, many other groups made effective use of them in seeking the extension of political rights.

The American Revolution

In the mid–eighteenth century there was no sign that North America would become a center of revolution. Residents of the thirteen British colonies there regarded themselves as British subjects: they recognized British law, read English-language books, and benefited handsomely from British rule. Trade brought prosperity to the colonies, and British military forces protected colonists' interests. From 1754 to 1763, for example, British forces waged an expensive conflict in North America known as the French and Indian War. That conflict merged with a larger contest for imperial supremacy, the Seven Years' War (1756–1763), in which British and French forces battled each other in Europe and India as well as North America. Victory in the Seven Years' War ensured that Britain would dominate global trade and that British North America would prosper.

The American Revolution
www.mhhe.com/
bentleybrief2e

British and French territories, 1756
www.mhhe.com/
bentleybrief2e

philosophes (fil-uh-sofs)
Voltaire (vohl-TAIR)

TIGHTENED BRITISH CONTROL OF THE COLONIES After the mid-1760s, however, North American colonists became increasingly disenchanted with British imperial rule. Faced with staggering financial difficulties arising from the Seven Years' War, the British parliament expected that the North American colonies would bear a fair share of the cost through new taxes. But new taxes proved extremely unpopular in North America. Colonists especially resented the imposition of taxes on molasses by the Sugar Act (1764), on publications and legal documents by the Stamp Act (1765), on a variety of imported items by the Townshend Act (1767), and on tea by the Tea Act (1773). Colonists also took offense at the Quartering Act (1765), which required them to provide housing and accommodations for British troops.

Colonists argued that they should pay such taxes only if the North American colonies were represented in the British parliament, arguing that there should be "no taxation without representation." They boycotted British products, physically attacked British officials, and mounted protests. They also organized the Continental Congress (1774), which coordinated the colonies' resistance to British policies. By 1775 tensions were so high that British troops and a colonial militia skirmished at the village of Lexington, near Boston. The war of American independence had begun.

THE DECLARATION OF INDEPENDENCE On 4 July 1776 the Continental Congress adopted a document titled "The unanimous Declaration of the thirteen united States of America." This Declaration of Independence drew deep inspiration from

MAP 25.1 | The American revolution. Note the location of both the major towns and cities in the colonies and the location of the major battles that occurred during the revolution. ***Why were both situated so close to the eastern coast?***

THE CONTINENTAL CONGRESS. | In this painting by American artist John Trumbull, authors of the Declaration of Independence, including John Adams, Thomas Jefferson, and Benjamin Franklin, stand before a desk at the Continental Congress in Philadelphia.

Enlightenment political thought in its insistence "that all men are created equal, that they are endowed by their Creator with certain unalienable Rights, that among these are Life, Liberty, and the pursuit of Happiness." It echoed John Locke's contractual theory of government in arguing that governments derive their power and authority from "the consent of the governed." When any government infringes on individuals' rights, the document continued, "it is the Right of the People to alter or abolish it, and to institute new Government." The Declaration of Independence presented a long list of specific abuses charged to the British crown and concluded by proclaiming the colonies "Free and Independent States."

It was one thing to declare independence, but a different matter to make independence a reality. Britain enjoyed many advantages over the rebels: a strong government, the most powerful navy in the world, a competent army, and a sizable population of loyalists in the colonies. But the colonies were far away, and British opponents were many. In addition, many European states were eager to see Britain lose its colonies: France, Spain, the Netherlands, and several German principalities all contributed militarily and economically to the American quest for independence. Moreover, George Washington (1732–1799) provided strong and imaginative military leadership for the colonial army while local militias employed guerrilla tactics effectively against British forces.

By 1780 all combatants were weary of the conflict. In October 1781 British forces surrendered to American and French forces commanded by George Washington at Yorktown, Virginia. In September 1783 diplomats concluded the Peace of Paris, by which the British government formally recognized American independence.

BUILDING AN INDEPENDENT STATE The leaders of the fledgling republic organized a state that reflected Enlightenment principles. In 1787 a constitutional convention drafted the Constitution of the United States, which emphasized the rights of individuals. American leaders based the federal government on popular sovereignty, and they agreed to guarantee individual liberties such as freedom of speech, of the press, and of religion. Full political and social rights, however, were accorded only to men of property: landless men, women, slaves, and indigenous peoples were not included. Over the long term, however, disenfranchised groups claimed and struggled for political and legal rights and helped broaden the implications of the Enlightenment values of freedom and equality as well as popular sovereignty.

The French Revolution

French revolutionaries also drew inspiration from Enlightenment political thought, but the French revolution was a more radical affair than its American counterpart. American revolutionary leaders sought independence from British imperial rule, but they were content to retain British law and much of their British social and cultural heritage. In contrast, French revolutionary leaders repudiated existing society, often referred to as the *ancien régime* ("the old order"), and sought to replace it with new political, social, and cultural structures.

THE ESTATES GENERAL Serious financial, political, and social problems put France on the road to revolution. When Louis XVI (reigned 1774–1793) became king, he inherited an enormous debt from his predecessors, most of which had been incurred during France's many wars in the seventeenth and eighteenth centuries. To make matters worse, the French government had spent large sums of money helping the Americans in their war of independence. As a result, by the 1780s half of the French royal government's revenues went to pay off the national debt, and an additional quarter supported the French armed forces. Although France was a wealthy country in the eighteenth century, it did not have a national banking system to finance loans, and it did not have an efficient system of tax collection. Even if it had, the wealthiest French classes—including the nobility and the clergy—were exempt from most taxes, which meant that nearly all direct taxes had to be levied on the already poor and overburdened French peasantry.

By 1787 King Louis XVI was desperate for money. When he turned to the French nobility and clergy for help, however, they refused. They did so in part to protect their financial status, but they also wanted to demonstrate to the king their ability to act independently. If the king wanted their help, they argued, he was going to have to allow the nobility a larger share of power. This issue of power was one that the king and the nobles had clashed over repeatedly in the past, and it was one over which the king was not willing to compromise. In the hope that Louis would be forced to institute reforms to their liking, then, the nobility demanded that Louis summon the Estates General, an assembly that represented the entire French population through three groups, known as estates. The first estate consisted of about one hundred thousand Roman Catholic clergy, and the second included some four hundred thousand nobles. The third estate embraced the rest of the population—about twenty-four million serfs, free peasants, and urban residents. It had as many delegates as the other two estates combined.

PSI img Versailles www.mhhe.com/bentleybrief2e

THE NATIONAL ASSEMBLY In May 1789 King Louis called the Estates General into session at the royal palace of Versailles in hopes that it would authorize new taxes. But the mood of many of the representatives was grim. People of the third estate, in particular, were extremely dissatisfied with Louis. The middle classes resented the assumption of the best jobs and offices by the nobility and were also influenced by calls for political reforms that were making their way through France and the Atlantic world. The poorer classes, meanwhile, resented the burden of taxation they had to carry and were in any case feeling desperate because of economic hardship brought about by extremely bad harvests in 1788.

PSI img The Bastille www.mhhe.com/bentleybrief2e

It quickly became clear to the members of the third estate that the members of the first and second estates wanted to maintain control by insisting that each estate cast only one vote. Members of the third estate insisted, in contrast, that the estates vote together by head. Disillusioned by weeks of arguing, on 17 June 1789 representatives of the third estate took the dramatic step of seceding from the Estates General and proclaiming themselves to be the National Assembly. Three days later, members of the new Assembly swore

---

ancien régime (ahn-syan rey-ZHEEM)
Louis (LOO-ee)

not to disband until they had provided France with a new constitution. The next month, on 14 July 1789, a Parisian crowd stormed the Bastille, a royal jail and arsenal, in search of weapons to defend themselves from what they feared would be a royal crackdown on supporters of the Assembly. The military garrison protecting the Bastille surrendered to the crowd but only after killing many of the attackers. To vent their rage, members of the crowd hacked the defenders to death. News of the event soon spread, sparking insurrections in cities throughout France. Those insurrections grew even more intense when rumors spread that armed bands organized by nobles were moving through the countryside to restore order. This "Great Fear" prompted the peasantry all over France to burn monasteries, public records offices, and the houses of nobles.

Fearing that the revolution would swing out of their control unless they acted quickly, the National Assembly undertook a broad program of political and social reform. The *Declaration of the Rights of Man and the Citizen,* which the National Assembly promulgated in August 1789, articulated the guiding principles of the program. Reflecting the influence of American revolutionary ideas, the *Declaration of the Rights of Man and the Citizen* proclaimed the equality of all men, declared that sovereignty resided in the people, and asserted individual rights.

LIBERTY, EQUALITY, AND FRATERNITY Between 1789 and 1791 the National Assembly reconfigured French society. Taking the Enlightenment ideals of "liberty, equality, and fraternity" as its goals, the Assembly abolished the old social order. It seized church lands, abolished the first estate, defined clergy as civilians, and required clergy to take an oath of loyalty to the state. It also produced a constitution that left the king in place but deprived him of legislative authority. France became a constitutional monarchy in which men of property—about half the adult male population—had the right to vote in elections to choose legislators.

THE CONVENTION The revolution soon took a radical turn. Many Parisians who were supposed to be represented by the third estate felt that the changes effected by the revolution were not radical enough and favored transforming France into a republic. The desire for a more radical approach was further encouraged by the efforts of the French nobility to ally with foreign powers—especially Austria and Prussia—to help restore the ancien régime. Faced with this threat to the survival of the revolution, the Assembly declared war against Austria and Prussia in April 1792. In the following year, revolutionary leaders declared war on Spain, Britain, and the Netherlands. Fearing military defeat and counterrevolution, revolutionary leaders created the Convention, a new legislative body elected by universal manhood suffrage, which abolished the monarchy and proclaimed France a republic. The Convention rallied the French population by instituting the *levée en masse,* a "mass levy" that drafted people and resources for use in the war against invading forces. The Convention also rooted out enemies at home by making frequent use of the guillotine. In 1793 King Louis XVI and his wife, Queen Marie Antoinette, went to the guillotine when the Convention found them guilty of treason to the principles of the revolution.

Revolutionary chaos reached its peak in 1793 and 1794 when Maximilien Robespierre (1758–1794) and the radical Jacobin party dominated the Convention. A lawyer by training, Robespierre had emerged during the revolution as a ruthless but popular radical known as "the Incorruptible," and he dominated the Committee of Public Safety, the executive authority of the Republic. The Jacobins believed passionately that France needed complete restructuring, and they unleashed a campaign of terror to promote their revolutionary agenda. They sought to eliminate the influence of Christianity in French society by closing churches, forcing priests to take wives, and promoting a new, secular "cult of reason." They reorganized the calendar, replacing seven-day weeks with ten-day units that recognized no day of religious observance. The Jacobins also encouraged citizens to display their revolutionary zeal by wearing working-class clothes and granted increased rights to women by permitting them to inherit property and divorce their husbands. The Jacobins made especially frequent use of the guillotine: in a yearlong "reign of terror" between the summer of 1793 and the summer of 1794, they executed about forty thousand people and imprisoned three hundred thousand others as suspected enemies of the revolution.

SOURCES FROM THE PAST

Declaration of the Rights of Man and the Citizen

While developing their program of reform, members of the National Assembly consulted closely with Thomas Jefferson, the principal author of the American Declaration of Independence, who was the U.S. ambassador to France in 1789. Thus it is not surprising that the Declaration of the Rights of Man and the Citizen *reflects the influence of American revolutionary ideas.*

First Article. Men are born and remain free and equal in rights. Social distinctions may be based only on common utility.

Article 2. The goal of every political association is the preservation of the natural and inalienable rights of man. These rights are liberty, property, security, and resistance to oppression.

Article 3. The principle of all sovereignty resides essentially in the nation. No body and no individual can exercise authority that does not flow directly from the nation.

Article 4. Liberty consists in the freedom to do anything that does not harm another. The exercise of natural rights of each man thus has no limits except those that assure other members of society their enjoyment of the same rights. These limits may be determined only by law.

Article 6. Law is the expression of the general will. All citizens have the right to participate either personally or through their representatives in the making of law. The law must be the same for all, whether it protects or punishes. Being equal in the eyes of the law, all citizens are equally eligible for all public honors, offices, and occupations, according to their abilities, without any distinction other than that of their virtues and talents.

Article 7. No person shall be accused, arrested, or imprisoned except in the cases and according to the forms prescribed by law. Any one soliciting, transmitting, executing, or causing to be executed, any arbitrary order, shall be punished. But any citizen summoned or arrested in virtue of the law shall submit without delay, as resistance constitutes an offense.

Article 9. As all persons are held innocent until they shall have been declared guilty, if arrest shall be deemed indispensable, all harshness not essential to the securing of the prisoner's person shall be severely repressed by law.

Article 11. The free communication of thoughts and opinions is one of the most precious rights of man: every citizen may thus speak, write, and publish freely, but will be responsible for abuse of this freedom in cases decided by the law.

Article 13. For the maintenance of public military force and for the expenses of administration, common taxation is necessary: it must be equally divided among all citizens according to their means.

Article 15. Society has the right to require from every public official an accounting of his administration.

Article 16. Any society in which guarantees of rights are not assured and separation of powers is not defined has no constitution at all.

Article 17. Property is an inviolable and sacred right. No one may be deprived of property except when public necessity, legally determined, clearly requires it, and on condition of just and prearranged compensation.

■ **In what ways do the principles established in the Declaration reflect the political transformations taking place throughout the age of Atlantic revolutions?**

SOURCE: *Déclaration des droits de l'homme et du citoyen.* Translated by Jerry H. Bentley.

THE DIRECTORY Eventually, such political purges undermined confidence in the regime itself. In July 1794 the Convention arrested Robespierre and his allies, convicted them of tyranny, and sent them to the guillotine. A group of conservative men of property then seized power and ruled France under a new institution known as the Directory (1795–1799). However, the Directory was unable to resolve the economic and military problems that plagued revolutionary France. In seeking a middle way between the ancien régime and radical revolution, they lurched from one policy to another, and the Directory faced constant challenges to its authority. It came to an end in November 1799 when a young general named Napoleon Bonaparte staged a coup d'état and seized power.

The Execution of King Louis XVI. | The guillotine was an efficient killing machine. In this contemporary print the executioner displays the just-severed head of King Louis XVI to the crowd assembled to witness his execution.

The Reign of Napoleon

Born to a minor noble family on the Mediterranean island of Corsica, Napoleon Bonaparte (1769–1821) studied at French military schools and became an officer in the army of King Louis XVI. A brilliant military leader, he became a general at age twenty-four. He was a fervent supporter of the revolution and defended the Directory against a popular uprising in 1795. In a campaign of 1796–1797, he drove the Austrian army from northern Italy and established French rule there. In 1798 he mounted an invasion of Egypt, but the campaign ended in a French defeat. Politically ambitious, Napoleon returned to France in 1799 and joined the Directory. When Austria, Russia, and Britain formed a coalition to attack France and end the revolution, he overthrew the Directory, imposed a new constitution, and named himself first consul. In 1802 he became consul for life, and two years later he crowned himself emperor.

Napoleon's empire
www.mhhe.com/bentleybrief2e

NAPOLEONIC FRANCE Napoleon brought political stability to a land torn by revolution and war. He made peace with the Roman Catholic church and reversed the most radical religious policies of the Convention. In 1804 Napoleon promulgated

Napoleon on his imperial throne
www.mhhe.com/bentleybrief2e

Napoleon Bonaparte (nuh-POH-lee-uhn BOH-nuh-pahrt)

the Civil Code, a revised body of civil law, which also helped stabilize French society. The Civil Code affirmed the political and legal equality of all adult men and established a merit-based society in which individuals advanced in education and employment because of talent rather than birth or social standing. The Civil Code confirmed many of the moderate revolutionary policies of the National Assembly but retracted measures passed by the more radical Convention. The code restored patriarchal authority in the family, for example, by making women and children subservient to male heads of households.

Although he approved of the Enlightenment ideal of equality, Napoleon was no champion of intellectual freedom or representative government. He limited free speech and routinely censored newspapers and other publications. He established a secret police force that relied heavily on spies and detained suspected political opponents by the thousands. He made systematic use of propaganda to manipulate public opinion. He ignored elective bodies and founded a dynasty that set his family above the people in whose name they ruled.

Napoleon was exiled to Elba in 1814, but escaped and ruled for 100 more days.

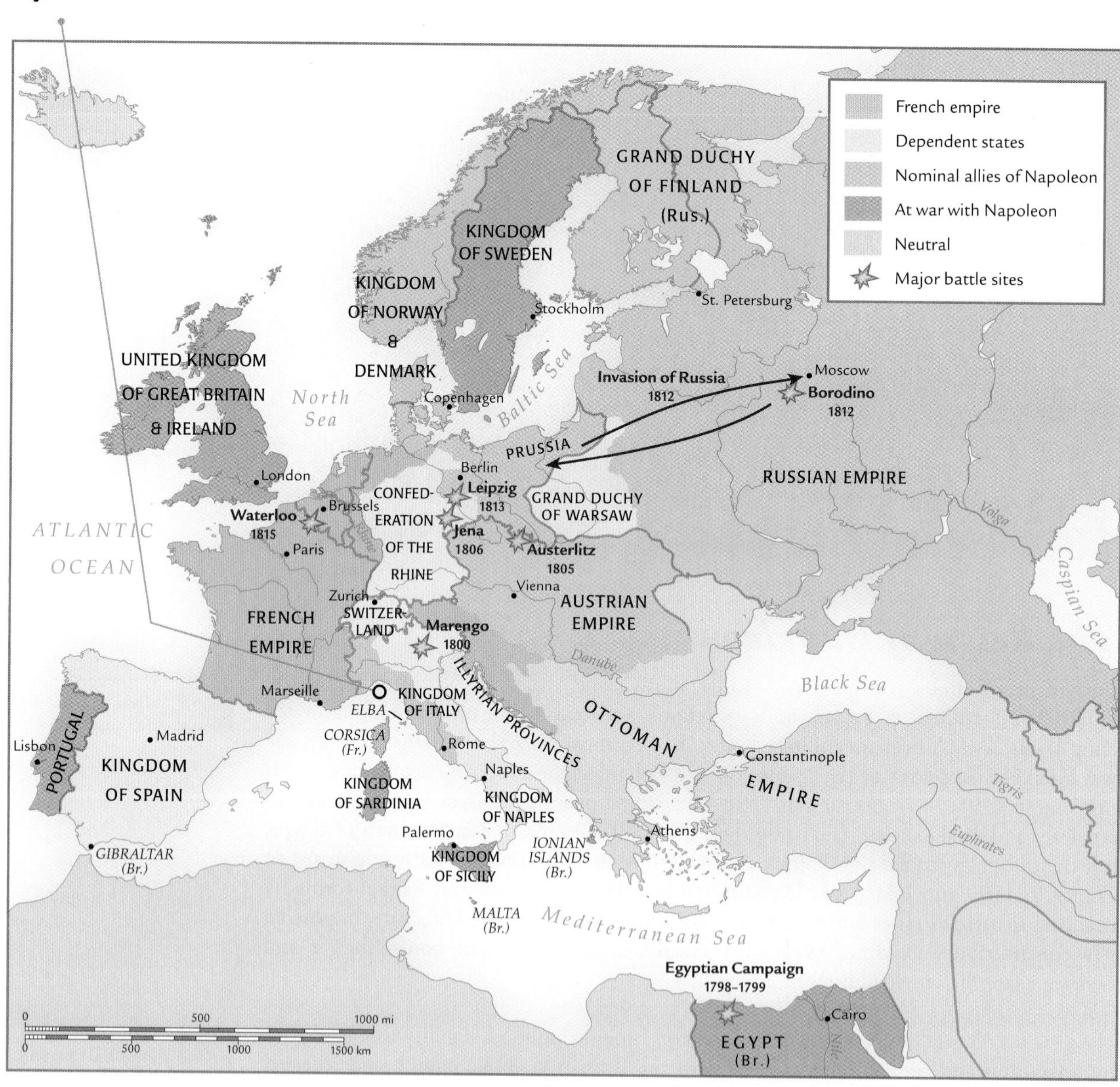

MAP 25.2 | Napoleon's empire in 1812. Observe the number of states dependent on or allied with Napoleon as opposed to those who were at war with him. ***Were there geographical conditions that allowed some states to resist Napoleon's efforts at conquest better than others?***

NAPOLEON'S EMPIRE While working to stabilize France, Napoleon also sought to extend his authority throughout Europe. Napoleon's armies conquered the Iberian and Italian peninsulas, occupied the Netherlands, and inflicted humiliating defeats on Austrian and Prussian forces. Napoleon sent his brothers and other relatives to rule the conquered and occupied lands, and he forced Austria, Prussia, and Russia to ally with him and respect French hegemony in Europe.

Napoleon's empire began to unravel in 1812, when he decided to invade Russia. Convinced that the tsar was conspiring with his British enemies, Napoleon led an army of six hundred thousand soldiers to Moscow. He captured the city, but the tsar withdrew and set Moscow ablaze, leaving Napoleon's vast army without adequate shelter or supplies. Napoleon ordered a retreat, but the bitter Russian winter destroyed his army, and only a battered remnant of thirty thousand soldiers managed to limp back to France.

THE FALL OF NAPOLEON Napoleon's disastrous Russian campaign emboldened his enemies. A coalition of British, Austrian, Prussian, and Russian armies converged on France and forced Napoleon to abdicate his throne in April 1814. The victors restored the French monarchy and exiled Napoleon to the tiny Mediterranean island of Elba. But in March 1815 Napoleon escaped from Elba, returned to France, and ruled France for a hundred days before a British army defeated him at Waterloo in Belgium. This time, European powers banished Napoleon to the remote and isolated island of St. Helena in the South Atlantic Ocean, where he died of natural causes in 1821.

The Influence of Revolution

The Enlightenment ideals promoted by the American and French revolutions appealed to peoples throughout Europe and the Americas. In the Caribbean and Latin America, they inspired revolutionary movements: slaves in the French colony of Saint-Domingue rose against their overlords and established the independent republic of Haiti, and Euro-American leaders mounted independence movements in Mexico, Central America, and South America. The ideals of the American and French revolutions also encouraged social reformers to organize broader programs of liberation for women and slaves of African ancestry.

The Haitian Revolution

The only successful slave revolt in history took place on the Caribbean island of Hispaniola. The Spanish colony of Santo Domingo occupied the eastern part of the island (modern Dominican Republic), and the French colony of Saint-Domingue occupied the western part (modern Haiti). Saint-Domingue was one of the richest of all European colonies in the Caribbean: sugar, coffee, and cotton produced there accounted for almost one-third of France's foreign trade.

SAINT-DOMINGUE SOCIETY In 1790 the population of Saint-Domingue included about forty thousand white French settlers, thirty thousand *gens de couleur* (free people of color), and some five hundred thousand black slaves, most of whom were born in Africa. Led by wealthy planters, white residents stood at the top of society. *Gens de couleur* farmed small plots of land, sometimes with the aid of a few slaves, or worked as artisans in the island's towns. Most of the colony's slaves toiled in the fields under brutal conditions. Many slaves ran away into the mountains to escape such treatment. By the late eighteenth century, Saint-Domingue had many large communities of maroons (escaped slaves).

The American and French revolutions prepared the way for a violent political and social revolution in Saint-Domingue. Because French policy supported North American colonists against British rule, colonial governors in Saint-Domingue sent about five hundred *gens de couleur* to fight in the American war of independence. They returned to Saint-Domingue with the intention of reforming society. When the French revolution broke

of the Mexican empire declared their own independence. They formed a Central American Federation until 1838, then split into the independent states of Guatemala, El Salvador, Honduras, Nicaragua, and Costa Rica.

MIGUEL DE HIDALGO. | Hidalgo was a priest and a leader of the Mexican War of Independence in 1810. This painting shows him celebrating after a victory at the Battle of Monte de las Cruces in 1810. Although he was executed by royalist forces in 1811, in Mexico he is seen as the father of the nation.

SIMÓN BOLÍVAR In South America, creole elites such as Simón Bolívar (1783–1830) led the movement for independence. Born in Caracas (in modern Venezuela), Bolívar was a fervent republican steeped in Enlightenment ideas about popular sovereignty. Inspired by the example of George Washington, he took up arms against Spanish rule in 1811. In 1819, after many reversals, he assembled an army that surprised and crushed the Spanish army in Colombia. Later he campaigned in Venezuela, Ecuador, and Peru, coordinating his efforts with other creole leaders such as José de San Martín (1778–1850) in Argentina and Bernardo O'Higgins (1778–1842) in Chile. By 1825 creole forces had overcome Spanish armies and deposed Spanish rulers throughout South America.

Bolívar's goal was to weld the former Spanish colonies of South America into a confederation like the United States. During the 1820s independent Venezuela, Colombia, and Ecuador formed a republic called Gran Colombia, and Bolívar attempted to bring Peru and Bolivia into the confederation. By 1830, however, strong political and regional differences led to the breakup of Gran Colombia. As the confederation disintegrated, a bitterly disappointed Bolívar—who died shortly afterward—pronounced South America "ungovernable."

BRAZILIAN INDEPENDENCE Independence came to Portuguese Brazil at the same time as to Spanish colonies, but by a different process. When Napoleon invaded Portugal in 1807, the royal court fled Lisbon and established a government-in-exile in Rio de Janeiro. In 1821 the king returned to Portugal, leaving his son Pedro in Brazil as regent. The next year Brazilian creoles called for independence from Portugal, and Pedro agreed to their demands. In 1822 Pedro declared Brazil's independence and accepted appointment as Emperor Pedro I (reigned 1822–1834).

CREOLE DOMINANCE In Brazil as in the former Spanish colonies, creole elites dominated both politics and society. Indeed, independence brought little social change in Latin America: although the *peninsulares* returned to Europe, Latin American society remained stratified and unequal. The newly independent states granted military authority to local strongmen, known as caudillos, allied with creole elites. The new states also allowed the continuation of slavery, confirmed the wealth and authority of the Roman Catholic church, and repressed the lower orders. The principal beneficiaries of independence in Latin America were the creole elites.

The Emergence of Ideologies: Conservatism and Liberalism

While inspiring revolutions and independence movements in other lands, the American and French revolutions also prompted political and social theorists to crystallize the modern ideologies of conservatism and liberalism. An *ideology* is a coherent vision of human nature, human society, and the larger world that proposes some particular form of politi-

caudillos (KAHW-dee-yohs)

MAP 25.3 | Latin America in 1830. Note the dates each state won its independence. ***Since most states became independent in very close succession, what conditions prevented Latin American states from joining together in a federation like that in the United States?***

cal and social organization as ideal. People who promote a given ideology seek to design a political and social order for their communities.

CONSERVATISM The modern ideology of conservatism arose as political and social theorists responded to the challenges of the American and especially the French revolution. Conservatives believed that social change, if necessary at all, must be undertaken gradually and with respect for tradition. The English political philosopher Edmund Burke (1729–1797), for example, condemned radical or revolutionary change, which in his view could only lead to anarchy. Thus Burke approved of the American revolution, which he viewed as a natural and logical change, but he denounced the French revolution as a chaotic and irresponsible assault on society.

LIBERALISM In contrast to conservatives, liberals viewed change as the agent of progress. Conservatism, they argued, was just a means to justify the status quo and maintain the privileges enjoyed by favored classes. For liberals the trick was not to stifle change but, rather, to manage it in the best interests of society. Liberals such as the English political philosopher John Stuart Mill (1806–1873) championed the Enlightenment values of freedom and equality, which they believed would lead to higher standards of morality and increased prosperity for the whole society. They usually favored republican forms of government in which citizens elected representatives to legislative bodies, and they called for written constitutions that guaranteed freedom and equality for all citizens. Although some liberals, such as Mill, advocated universal suffrage (and in Mill's case even women's suffrage), many liberals during the nineteenth century did not go so far: for most, universal suffrage still seemed dangerous because it allowed the uneducated masses to participate in politics.

Testing the Limits of Revolutionary Ideals: Slavery and Women's Rights

The Enlightenment ideals of freedom and equality were watchwords of revolution in the Atlantic Ocean basin. Yet different revolutionaries understood the implications of freedom and equality in very different ways, and the Atlantic revolutions had produced widely varying results. Nevertheless, in the wake of the revolutions, social activists in Europe and the Americas considered the possibility that the ideals of freedom and equality would have further implications as yet unexplored. They turned their attention especially to the issues of slavery and women's rights.

MOVEMENTS TO END THE SLAVE TRADE The campaign to end the slave trade and abolish slavery began in the eighteenth century. Only after the American, French, and Haitian revolutions, however, did the antislavery movement gain momentum. The leading spokesman of the movement was William Wilberforce (1759–1833), a prominent English philanthropist elected in 1780 to a seat in Parliament. There he tirelessly attacked slavery on moral and religious grounds. After the Haitian revolution he attracted supporters who feared that continued reliance on slave labor would result in more and larger slave revolts, and in 1807 Parliament passed Wilberforce's bill to end the slave trade. Under British pressure, other states also banned international commerce in slaves: the United States in 1808, France in 1814, the Netherlands in 1817, and Spain in 1845. The slave trade died slowly, but the British navy, which dominated the North Atlantic Ocean, patrolled the west coast of Africa to ensure compliance with the law.

MOVEMENTS TO ABOLISH SLAVERY The abolition of slavery itself was a much bigger challenge than ending the slave trade because owners had property rights in their slaves and strongly resisted efforts to alter the system. In some places, revolution hastened slavery's end: Haiti abolished the institution in 1801 and Mexico in 1829, and in South America Simón Bolívar freed slaves who joined his forces and provided constitutional guarantees of free status for all residents of Gran Colombia. In other areas slavery was abolished as a result of extensive campaigns by antislavery activists such as Wilberforce. In 1833, one month after Wilberforce's death, Parliament provided twenty million pounds sterling as compensation to slave owners and abolished slavery throughout the British empire. Other states followed the British example: France abolished slavery in 1848, the United States in 1865, Cuba in 1886, and Brazil in 1888.

FREEDOM WITHOUT EQUALITY Abolition brought legal freedom for African and African-American slaves, but it did not bring political equality. In most places, African-American peoples were prevented from voting through property requirements, literacy tests, and campaigns of intimidation. Nor did emancipation bring social and economic improvements for former slaves and their descendants. White creole elites owned most of the property in the Americas, and they kept blacks in subordination by forcing them to accept low-paying work.

ENLIGHTENMENT IDEALS AND WOMEN Meanwhile, women who participated alongside men in the movement to abolish slavery came to believe that women suffered many of the same legal disabilities as slaves: they had little access to education, they could not enter professional occupations that required advanced education, and they were legally deprived of the right to vote. In making the case for their own rights, women drew on Enlightenment ideas about liberty and equality. For example, the English writer Mary Astell (1666–1731) used the political thought of John Locke to suggest that absolute sovereignty was no more appropriate in a family than in a state. Astell also reflected Enlightenment influence in asking why, if all men were born free, all women were born slaves? Mary Wollstonecraft (1759–1797), another British writer, similarly drew on Locke's ideas, especially in her 1792 essay titled *A Vindication of the Rights of Woman.* Like Astell, Wollstonecraft argued that women possessed all the rights that Locke had granted to men. She especially insisted on the right of women to education: it would make them better mothers and wives, she said, and would enable them to contribute to society by preparing them for professional occupations and participation in political life.

WOMEN AND REVOLUTION Women played crucial roles in the revolutions of the late eighteenth and early nineteenth centuries, from making bandages to managing farms to actively taking up arms. Yet even so, they did not win political or social rights. In France, where women did gain rights to property, education, and divorce in the early years of the revolution, they were consistently denied the right to vote or to hold public office. In the later years of the revolution, under the Directory and Napoleon's rule, women lost even the limited rights they had won earlier. In other lands, women never gained as much as they did in revolutionary France. In the United States and the independent states of Latin America, revolution brought legal equality and political rights only for adult white men, who retained patriarchal authority over their wives and families.

WOMEN'S RIGHTS MOVEMENTS Nevertheless, throughout the nineteenth century social reformers pressed for women's rights as well as the abolition of slavery. The American feminist Elizabeth Cady Stanton (1815–1902) was an especially prominent figure in this movement. In 1840 Stanton went to London to attend an antislavery conference but found that the organizers barred women from participation. Infuriated, Stanton returned to the United States and organized a conference of feminists who met at Seneca Falls, New York, in 1848. The conference passed twelve resolutions demanding that lawmakers grant women the right to vote, to attend public schools, to enter professional occupations, and to participate in public affairs. The women's rights movement experienced only limited success in the nineteenth century: some women gained access to education, but nowhere did they win the right to vote. Yet, by seeking to extend the promises of Enlightenment political thought to blacks and women as well as white men, social reformers of the nineteenth century laid a foundation that would lead to large-scale social change in the twentieth century.

THE CONSOLIDATION OF NATIONAL STATES IN EUROPE

The Enlightenment ideals of freedom, equality, and popular sovereignty inspired political revolutions in much of the Atlantic Ocean basin, and the revolutions in turn helped spread Enlightenment values. The wars of the French revolution and the Napoleonic era also inspired the development of a particular type of community identity that had little to do with Enlightenment values—nationalism. Revolutionary wars involved millions of French citizens in the defense of their country against foreign armies and the extension of French influence to neighboring states. Wartime experiences encouraged peoples throughout Europe to think of themselves as members of distinctive national communities. Throughout the nineteenth century, European nationalist leaders worked to fashion states based on national identities and mobilized citizens to work in the interests of their own national communities, sometimes by fostering jealousy and suspicion of other national groups. By the late nineteenth century, national identities were so strong that peoples throughout Europe responded enthusiastically to ideologies of nationalism, which promised glory and prosperity to those who worked in the interests of their national communities.

Nations and Nationalism

One of the most influential concepts of modern political thought is the idea of the nation. At various times and places in history, individuals have associated themselves primarily with families, clans, cities, regions, and religious faiths. Yet, during the nineteenth century, European peoples came to identify strongly with communities they called nations. Members of a nation considered themselves a distinctive people that spoke a common language, observed common customs, inherited common cultural traditions, held common values, and shared common historical experiences.

Intense feelings of national identity fueled ideologies of nationalism. Advocates of nationalism insisted that the nation must be the focus of political loyalty. Zealous nationalist leaders maintained that members of their national communities had a common destiny that they could best advance by organizing independent national states. Ideally, in their view, the boundaries of the national state embraced the territory occupied by the national community, and its government promoted the interests of the national group, sometimes through conflict with other peoples.

CULTURAL NATIONALISM Early nationalist thought often sought to deepen appreciation for the historical experiences of the national community and foster pride in its cultural accomplishments. During the late eighteenth century, for example, Johann Gottfried von Herder (1744–1803) sang the praises of the German *Volk* ("people") and their powerful and expressive language. In reaction to Enlightenment thinkers and their quest for a scientific, universally valid understanding of the world, early cultural nationalists such as Herder emphasized the uniqueness of their societies through the study of history, literature, and song.

POLITICAL NATIONALISM During the nineteenth century, nationalist thought became much more strident. In lands where they were minorities or where they lived under foreign rule, nationalists demanded loyalty and solidarity from the national group and sought to establish independent states. In Italy, for example, the nationalist activist Giuseppe Mazzini (1805–1872) formed a group called Young Italy that promoted independence from Austrian and Spanish rule and the establishment of an Italian national state. Austrian and Spanish authorities forced Mazzini to lead much of his life in exile, but he used the opportunity to encourage the organization of nationalist movements in new lands. By the mid–nineteenth century, Young Italy had inspired the development of nationalist movements in Ireland, Switzerland, and Hungary.

NATIONALISM AND ANTI-SEMITISM While it encouraged political leaders to work toward the establishment of national states for their communities, nationalism also had strong potential to stir up conflict between different groups of people. The more nationalists identified with their own national communities, the more they distinguished themselves both from peoples in other lands and from minority groups within their own societies. This divisive potential of nationalism helps to explain the emergence of Zionism, a political movement that holds that the Jewish people constitute a nation

---

Johann Gottfried von Herder (YOH-hahn GAWT-freet fuhn HER-duhr)
Giuseppe Mazzini (joo-ZEP-pe maht-TSEE-nee)

and have the right to their own national homeland. Unlike Mazzini's Italian compatriots, Jews did not inhabit a well-defined territory but, rather, lived in states throughout Europe. As national communities tightened their bonds, nationalist leaders often became distrustful of minority populations. Suspicion of Jews fueled violent anti-Semitism in many parts of Europe. In Russia and in the Russian-controlled areas of Poland, the persecution of Jews climaxed in a series of anti-Jewish riots called pogroms, which claimed the lives and property of thousands of Jews.

During the late nineteenth and twentieth centuries, millions of Jews migrated to other European lands or to North America to escape persecution and violence. Anti-Semitism was not as severe in France as in central and eastern Europe, but it reached a fever pitch there after a military court convicted Alfred Dreyfus, a Jewish army officer, of spying for Germany in 1894. Although he was innocent of the charges and eventually had the verdict reversed on appeal, Dreyfus was the focus of bitter debates about the trustworthiness of Jews in French society. The trial also became a key event in the evolution of Zionism.

Theodor Herzl
www.mhhe.com/bentleybrief2e

ZIONISM Among the reporters at the Dreyfus trial was a Jewish journalist from Vienna, Theodor Herzl (1860–1904). As Herzl witnessed mobs shouting "Death to the Jews" in the land of enlightenment and liberty, he concluded that anti-Semitism was a persistent feature of human society that assimilation could not solve. In 1896 Herzl published the pamphlet *Judenstaat,* which argued that the only defense against anti-Semitism lay in the mass migration of Jews from all over the world to a land that they could call their own. In the following year, Herzl organized the first Zionist Congress in Basel, Switzerland, which founded the World Zionist Organization. The delegates at Basel formulated the basic platform of the Zionist movement, declaring that "Zionism seeks to establish a home for the Jewish people in Palestine," the location of the ancient kingdom of Israel. During the next half century, Jewish migrants trickled into Palestine, and in 1948 they won recognition for the Jewish state of Israel. Although it arose in response to exclusive nationalism in Europe, Zionism in turn provoked a resentful nationalism among Palestinians displaced by Jewish settlers. Conflicts between Jews and Palestinians continue to the present day.

The Emergence of National Communities

The French revolution and the wars that followed it heightened feelings of national identity throughout Europe. In France the establishment of a republic based on liberty, equality, and fraternity inspired patriotism and encouraged citizens to rally to its defense when foreign armies threatened it. Revolutionary leaders took the tricolored flag as a symbol of the French nation, and they adopted a rousing marching tune, the "Marseillaise," as an anthem that inspired pride and identity with the national community. In Spain, the Netherlands, Austria, Prussia, and Russia, national consciousness surged in reaction to the arrival of revolutionary and Napoleonic armies. Opposition to Napoleon and his imperial designs also inspired national feeling in Britain.

THE CONGRESS OF VIENNA After the fall of Napoleon, conservative political leaders feared that heightened national consciousness and ideas of popular sovereignty would undermine European stability. Meeting as the Congress of Vienna (1814–1815), representatives of Britain, Austria, Prussia, and Russia attempted to restore the prerevolutionary order. Under the guidance of the influential foreign minister of Austria, Prince Klemens von Metternich (1773–1859), the Congress dismantled Napoleon's empire, returned sovereignty to Europe's royal families, restored them to the thrones they had lost during the Napoleonic era, and created a diplomatic order based on a balance of

Theodor Herzl (TEY-aw-dohr HER-tsuhll)
Judenstaat (juh-dehn-STAHT)
Klemens von Metternich (kleh-men fuhn MET-er-nik)

THE CORONATION OF WILHELM I. | Wearing a white jacket, Otto von Bismarck (center) witnesses the crowning of King Wilhelm I of Prussia as German emperor. The coronation followed the victory of Prussia over France in 1871, and it took place in the royal palace at Versailles. ***Why would it have been symbolically significant to stage the Coronation at Versailles?***

power that prevented any one state from dominating the others. A central goal of Metternich himself was to suppress national consciousness, which he viewed as a serious threat to the multicultural Austrian empire. Yet the efforts of the Congress of Vienna to restore the ancien régime had limited success. Although the European balance of power established at Vienna survived for almost a century, it had become impossible to suppress national consciousness and ideas of popular sovereignty.

NATIONALIST REBELLIONS From the 1820s through the 1840s, a wave of rebellions inspired by nationalist sentiments swept through Europe. The first uprising occurred in 1821 in the Balkan Peninsula, where the Greek people sought independence from the Ottoman Turks. With the aid of Britain, France, and Russia, the rebels won formal recognition of Greek independence in 1830. In the same year, liberal revolutionaries in France, Spain, Portugal, and some of the German principalities called for constitutional government based on popular sovereignty. In Belgium, Italy, and Poland, they demanded independence and the formation of national states as well as popular sovereignty. Revolution in Paris drove Charles X from the throne, and uprisings in Belgium resulted in independence from the Netherlands. In 1848 a new round of rebellions shook European states, where they brought down the French monarchy and seriously threatened the Austrian empire. Uprisings also rocked cities in Italy, Prussia, and German states in the Rhineland.

By the summer of 1849, the veteran armies of conservative rulers had put down the last of the rebellions. However, advocates of national independence and popular sovereignty remained active, and the potential of their ideals to mobilize popular support were crucial in the unification of two new European states: Italy by 1870 and Germany by 1871.

The Unifications of Italy and Germany

The most striking demonstration of the power that national sentiments could unleash involved the unifications of Italy and Germany. Since the fall of the Roman empire, Italy and Germany had been disunited lands. A variety of regional kingdoms, city-states, and ecclesiastical states ruled the Italian peninsula for more than a thousand years, and princes divided Germany into more than three hundred semi-autonomous jurisdictions.

CAVOUR AND GARIBALDI The unification of Italy came about when practical political leaders such as Count Camillo di Cavour (1810–1861), prime minister to King Vittore Emmanuele II of Piedmont and Sardinia, combined forces with nationalist advocates of independence. Cavour was a cunning diplomat, and the kingdom of Piedmont and Sardinia was the most powerful of the Italian states. In alliance with France, Cavour expelled Austrian authorities—who had gained control of the region through the Congress of Vienna—from most of northern Italy in 1859. Then he turned his attention to southern Italy, where Giuseppe Garibaldi (1807–1882), a dashing soldier of fortune and a passionate nationalist, led the unification movement. With an army of about one thousand men outfitted in distinctive red shirts, Garibaldi swept through Sicily and southern Italy, outmaneuvering government forces and attracting enthusiastic recruits. In 1860 Garibaldi met King Vittore Emmanuele near Naples. Not ambitious to rule, Garibaldi delivered southern Italy into Vittore Emmanuele's hands, and the kingdom of Piedmont and Sardinia became the kingdom of Italy. During the next decade the new monarchy absorbed several additional territories, including Venice, Rome, and their surrounding regions.

THINKING ABOUT *Encounters*

ENCOUNTERS IN REVOLUTIONS AND NATIONAL STATES IN THE ATLANTIC WORLD. In the late eighteenth and early nineteenth centuries, revolutions based on Enlightenment ideals of freedom and equality swept through Europe and the Americas. How did encounters with the events and ideologies of early revolutions shape the course of events in later revolutions?

Giuseppe Garibaldi (juh-SEP-eh gar-uh-BAWL-dee)
Vittore Emmanuele (vih-tor-reh i-MAHN-yoo-uhl)

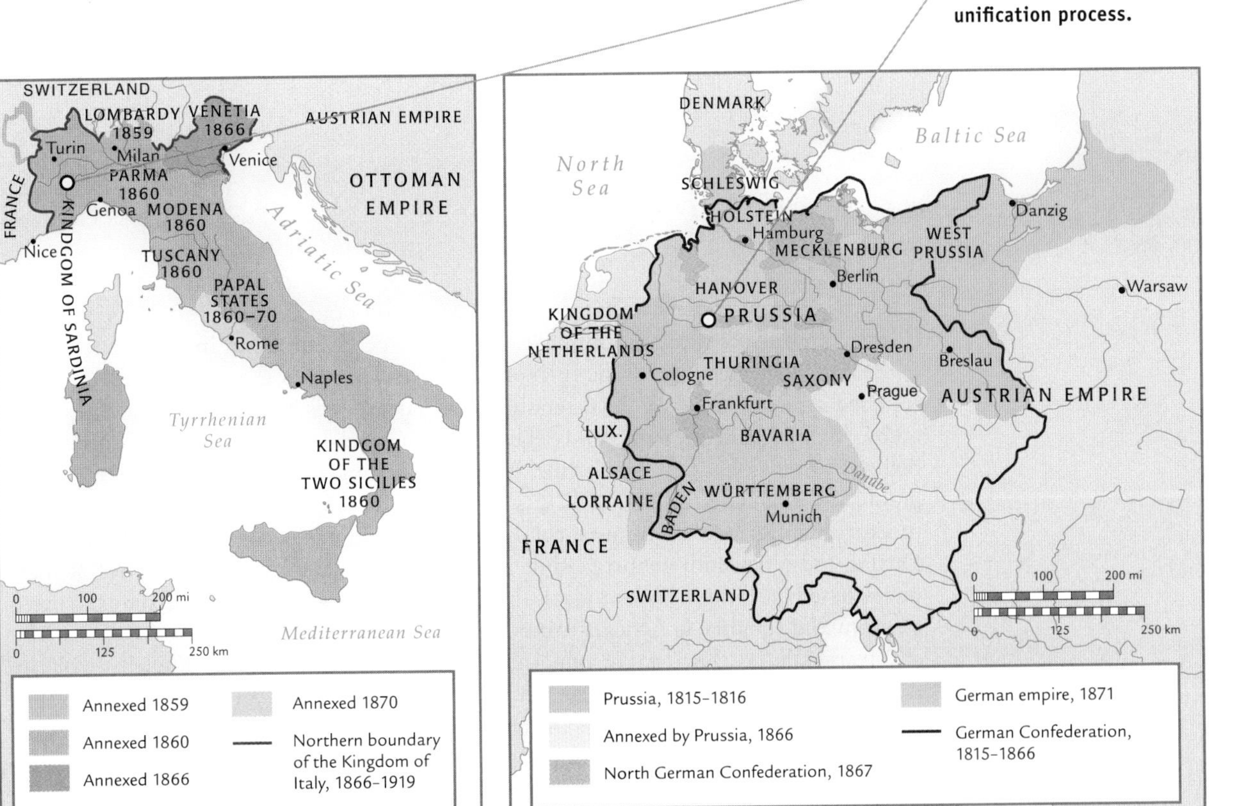

MAP 25.4 | The unifications of Italy and Germany. The unifications of Italy and Germany as national states in the nineteenth century fundamentally altered the balance of power in Europe. ***Why did unification result from diplomacy and war conducted by conservative statesmen rather than popular nationalist action?***

OTTO VON BISMARCK In Germany as in Italy, unification came about when political leaders harnessed nationalist aspirations. The Congress of Vienna created a German Confederation composed of thirty-nine states dominated by Austria. In 1862 King Wilhelm I of Prussia—one of the thirty-nine states—appointed a wealthy landowner, Otto von Bismarck (1815–1898), as his prime minister. Bismarck was a master of realpolitik ("the politics of reality") who argued that "the great questions of the day will not be settled by speeches or majority votes . . . but by blood and iron." It was indeed blood and iron that brought about the unification of Germany. As prime minister, Bismarck reformed and expanded the Prussian army. Between 1864 and 1870 he intentionally provoked three wars—with Denmark, Austria, and France—and whipped up German sentiment against the enemies. In all three conflicts Prussian forces quickly shattered their opponents, swelling German pride. In 1871 the Prussian king proclaimed himself emperor of the Second Reich—meaning the Second German Empire, following the Holy Roman Empire—which embraced almost all German-speaking peoples outside Austria and Switzerland in a powerful and dynamic national state.

The unifications of Italy and Germany made it clear that when coupled with strong political, diplomatic, and military leadership, nationalism had enormous potential to mobilize people who felt a sense of national kinship. Italy, Germany, and other national states went to great lengths to foster a sense of national community. They adopted national flags to serve as symbols of unity, national anthems to inspire patriotism, and national holidays to focus public attention on individuals and events of special importance for the national community. They established bureaucracies that took censuses of national populations and tracked vital national statistics involving birth, marriage, and death. They built schools that instilled patriotic values in students, and they recruited young men into armies that defended national interests and sometimes went on the offensive to enhance national prestige. By the end of the nineteenth century, the national state had proven to be a powerful model of political organization in Europe.

Otto von Bismarck (oht-toh fuhn BIZ-mahrk)

SUMMARY

The Enlightenment ideals of freedom, equality, and popular sovereignty inspired revolutionary movements throughout much of the Atlantic Ocean basin in the late eighteenth and early nineteenth centuries. In North America colonists threw off British rule and founded an independent federal republic. In France revolutionaries abolished the monarchy, established a republic, and refashioned the social order. In Saint-Domingue rebellious slaves threw off French rule, established an independent Haitian republic, and granted freedom and equality to all citizens. In Latin America creole elites led movements to expel Spanish and Portuguese colonial authorities and found independent republics. During the nineteenth century, adult white men were the main beneficiaries of movements based on Enlightenment ideals, but social reformers launched campaigns to extend freedom and equality to African-Americans and women.

Meanwhile, as they fought one another in wars sparked by the French revolution, European peoples developed strong feelings of national identity and worked to establish states that advanced the interests of national communities. Nationalist thought was often divisive: it pitted national groups against one another and fueled tensions, especially in large multicultural states. But nationalism also contributed to state-building movements that had the potential to unite. During the nineteenth and twentieth centuries, peoples throughout the world drew inspiration from Enlightenment ideals and national identities when seeking to build or restructure their societies.

STUDY TERMS

American revolution (493)
ancien regime (496)
anti-Semitism (509)
Civil Code (500)
conservatism (505)
Continental Congress (494)
criollos (503)
Elizabeth Cady Stanton (507)
Estates General (496)
French revolution (496)
gens de couleur (501)
George Washington (495)
German unification (512)
Gran Colombia (504)
Haitian revolution (501)
Italian unification (511)
Jean-Jacques Rousseau (493)
John Locke (493)
liberalism (506)
Mary Wollestonecraft (507)
Maximilien Robespierre (497)
Miguel de Hidalgo (503)
Napoleon Bonaparte (499)
National Assembly (496)
nationalism (508)
peninsulares (503)
reign of terror (497)
Seven Years' War (493)
Simón Bolívar (504)
Toussaint Louverture (502)
Voltaire (493)
Waterloo (501)
William Wilberforce (506)
Young Italy (508)
Zionism (509)

FOR FURTHER READING

Benedict Anderson. *Imagined Communities: Reflections on the Origin and Spread of Nationalism.* Rev. ed. London, 1991. A pioneering work that analyzes the means and the processes by which peoples came to view themselves as members of national communities.

Bernard Bailyn. *The Ideological Origins of the American Revolution.* 2nd ed. Cambridge, Mass., 1992. A fundamental study of pamphlets and other publications that criticized British colonial policy in North America.

Aviva Chomsky and Aldo Lauria-Santiago, eds. *Identity and Struggle at the Margins of the Nation-State: The Laboring Peoples of Central America and the Hispanic Caribbean.* Durham, 1998. Discusses the impact that peasant action had on political and cultural development in different societies.

Linda Colley. *Britons: Forging the Nation, 1707–1837.* New Haven, 1992. A detailed analysis of the emergence of British national identity.

Susan Dunn. *Sister Revolutions: French Lightning, American Light.* New York, 1999. An accessible and stimulating work that traces the different legacies of the American and French revolutions of the eighteenth century.

Carolyn Fick. *The Making of Haiti: The Saint Domingue Revolution from Below.* Knoxville, 1990. A valuable study focusing on the role of slaves in the Haitian revolution.

François Furet. *Revolutionary France, 1770–1880.* Trans. by A. Nevill. Oxford, 1992. An influential interpretation emphasizing the ideological dimension of the French revolution.

Eric Hobsbawm. *Nations and Nationalism since 1780: Programme, Myth, and Reality.* 2nd ed. Cambridge, 1992. A brief interpretation of nationalism in Europe and the larger world.

Lester D. Langley. *The Americas in the Age of Revolution, 1750–1850.* New Haven, 1997. A comparative study of revolutions and wars of independence in the western hemisphere.

David Parker, ed. *Revolutions and the Revolutionary Tradition in the West, 1560–1991.* London and New York, 2000. In this comparative survey of revolutions—from the English revolution of 1649 to the revolutions within eastern Europe and the Soviet Union (1989–1991)—leading historians examine how a wider revolutionary tradition has shaped modern European history.

The Making of Industrial Society

26

n 1827, shortly after marrying at age twenty-three, Betty Harris took a job as a drawer in a coal pit near Manchester, England. A drawer's job involved crawling down narrow mine shafts and hauling loads of coal from the bottom of the pit to the surface. Drawers performed unskilled labor for low wages, but their work was essential for obtaining the coal that fueled the factories and mills of early industrial society.

While working, Harris wore a heavy belt around her waist. Hitched to the belt was a chain that passed between her legs and attached to the coal cart that she pulled through the steep and slippery mine shafts, often on hands and knees. Every workday, even when she was pregnant, Harris strapped on her belt and chain at 6:00 A.M., removing her bindings only at the end of the shift twelve hours later.

Harris reported that drawing coal was "very hard work for a woman," and she did not exaggerate. The belts and chains worn by drawers often chafed their skin raw, and miners contributed to their physical discomfort by beating them for slow or clumsy work. The miners, many of whom worked naked in the hot, oppressive coal pits, also took sexual liberties with the women and girl drawers: Harris personally knew several illegitimate children conceived during forced sexual encounters in the mines.

Betty Harris faced her own sexual problems once she arrived home. Exhausted from twelve hours of work, with only a one-hour break for a lunch consisting of bread and butter, she often tried to discourage her husband's advances. Her husband had little patience, however, and Harris remarked that "my feller has beaten me many a time for not being ready." Harris's work schedule made comfortable family life impossible. A cousin had to care for her two children during the day, and Harris tended to them and her husband at night. At age thirty-seven, after fourteen years in the mines, Harris admitted that "I am not so strong as I was."

❮ This 19th-century photograph of Manchester, England depicts densely packed urban buildings alongside smokestacks, both of which were characteristic of cities during the industrial revolution.

Not all industrial workers worked in such difficult conditions, but Betty Harris's experience nonetheless illustrates some of the deep changes that industrialization wrought in patterns of work and family life. First in Britain, then in western Europe, North America, Russia, and Japan, machines and factories transformed agricultural societies into industrial societies. At the heart of this transformation were technological changes that led to the extensive use of machinery in manufacturing. Industrial machinery transformed economic production by turning out high-quality products quickly, cheaply, and efficiently. The process of industrialization encouraged rapid technological

CHRONOLOGY

1733	John Kay develops the flying shuttle
1765	James Watt patents an improved steam engine
1779	Samuel Crompton develops the spinning mule
1785	Edmund Cartwright develops the power loom
1797	Eli Whitney introduces interchangeable parts to the manufacturing process
1829	George Stephenson's locomotive, the Rocket, attains a speed of 45 kilometers (28 miles) per hour
1848	Karl Marx and Friedrich Engels publish *Manifesto of the Communist Party*
1849–1915	Life of Sergei Witte
1851	Crystal Palace exhibition in London
1853	Arrival of Commodore Perry in Japan
1853–1856	Crimean War
1855–1881	Reign of Tsar Alexander II
1856	Bessemer converter developed
1861	Emancipation of the Russian serfs
1868	Meiji restoration
1913	Henry Ford introduces the assembly line to the manufacture of automobiles

innovation and over the long term raised material standards of living in much of the world.

But the impact of industrialization went beyond economics, generating widespread and often unsettling social change as well. Early industrialists created a new work environment, the factory, which concentrated large numbers of workers under one roof to operate complicated machinery. By moving work outside the home, however, factories drew fathers, mothers, and children in different directions, altered traditional patterns of domestic life, and strained family relations in the industrial era.

Industrialization encouraged rapid urbanization and migration. New cities mushroomed to house workers who left the countryside for jobs in factories. Millions of migrants even crossed the seas in search of opportunities in new lands. Often, however, early industrial workers found themselves living in squalor and laboring under dangerous conditions.

Social critics and reformers worked to alleviate the problems of early industrial society. Despite their appeals, however, capitalism and industrialization flourished and spread rapidly from Britain to continental Europe, North America, and Asia. In some areas, notably western Europe and North America, industrialization was encouraged so that states could gain the economic advantages of industrialization. In other places, including Russia and Japan, industrialization was undertaken as part of a larger program of social, political, and economic reform to avoid domination by western European and American powers. Elsewhere, industrialization created a new international division of labor that made most of Africa, Asia, and Latin America economically dependent on the export of raw materials that supplied the factories and cities of the industrialized world. Thus, although industrialization and its effects spread unevenly and for different reasons, they profoundly influenced social and economic conditions all over the globe.

Patterns of Industrialization

Industrialization refers to a process that transformed agrarian and handicraft-centered economies into economies distinguished by industry and machine manufacture. The principal features of that process were technological and organizational changes that transformed manufacturing and led to increased productivity. Critical to industrialization were technological developments that made it possible to produce goods by machines rather than by hand and that harnessed inanimate sources of energy such as coal and petroleum. Also critical was the development of factory production, wherein workers assembled under one roof to produce goods in mass quantities. The need to invest in expensive factory equipment in turn encouraged the formation of large businesses: by the mid–nineteenth century many giant corporations had joined together to control trade through trusts and cartels.

Foundations of Industrialization

By the mid–eighteenth century, several areas of the world—Great Britain in western Europe, the Yangzi Delta in China, Japan—exhibited dynamic economies that shared many common features. High agricultural productivity resulted in significant population growth, and high population densities encouraged occupational specialization outside of agriculture. Navigable rivers and networks of canals facilitated trade and transport, and cities and towns supported sophisticated banking and financial institutions. At the same time, these sophisticated economies ran up against difficult ecological obstacles—especially soil depletion and deforestation—that threatened continued population growth and consumption levels. Despite their common features, Great Britain was the first to transcend these ecological constraints by exploiting coal deposits fortuitously found at home and natural resources found abroad.

COAL AND COLONIES Until the eighteenth century, wood had served as Great Britain's primary source of fuel for iron production, home heating, and cooking. Such extensive use of wood had resulted in serious wood shortages. However, geographic luck had placed some of western Europe's largest coal deposits in Great Britain, within easy reach of water transport, centers of commerce, and pools of skilled labor. That fortunate conjunction encouraged the substitution of coal for wood, thus creating a promising framework for industrialization. Indeed, without easily accessible coal deposits, it was unlikely that the economy could have supported expanding iron production and the application of steam engines to mining and industry—both crucial to the industrial process in Great Britain. In that respect Britain's experience differed from that of China, because the main coal-producing regions of northwest China were quite distant from the Yangzi Delta, China's most economically promising region for the development of industrialization. Thus, geography conspired against an important early shift from wood to coal in China.

The unique economic relationship between Europe and the Americas gave Great Britain additional ecological relief. The colonized lands of the Americas lifted European land constraints by supplying European societies with a growing volume of primary products. During the eighteenth century slave-based plantations supplied Europe with huge amounts of sugar and cotton; the former increased available food calories, and the latter kept emerging textile industries going. Neither of those products could have been grown in Europe. The significance of valuable American resources grew after 1830, when large amounts of grain, timber, and beef grown on colonial acreage traveled across the Atlantic to European destinations. In addition, American lands served as outlets for European manufactured goods as well as Europe's surplus population. Access to such overseas resources, in addition to coal deposits at home, provided a context—one not available to societies such as China—that increased the odds for an industrial breakthrough.

Industrial expansion in Britain began in the mid–eighteenth century with the textile industry, when consumer demand spurred a transformation of the British cotton industry. During the seventeenth century, English consumers had become fond of calicoes—inexpensive, brightly printed cotton textiles from India. Cotton cloth came into demand because it was lighter and easier to wash than wool, which was the principal fabric of European clothes before the nineteenth century. Although British wool producers tried to protect their industry through a series of laws designed to prohibit imports of cotton cloth in 1720 and 1721, they could not stifle public demand.

MECHANIZATION OF THE COTTON INDUSTRY In fact, demand for cotton was so strong that producers had to speed up spinning and weaving to supply growing markets. To increase production they turned to inventions that rapidly mechanized the cotton textile industry. The first important technological breakthrough came in 1733 when Manchester mechanic John Kay invented the flying shuttle, which sped up the weaving process. Within a few years, inventors created several mechanical spinning devices, the most important of which was Samuel Crompton's spinning "mule," built in 1779. In 1790 the mule was adapted for steam power, and it became the device of choice for spinning cotton. A worker using a steam-driven mule could produce a hundred times more thread than a worker using a manual spinning wheel.

The new spinning machines necessitated new weaving machines so that weavers could keep up with the production of thread. In 1785 Edmund Cartwright, a clergyman without experience in either mechanics or textiles, patented a water-driven power loom. Within two decades steam moved the power loom, and by the 1820s hand weavers were nearly obsolete. A young boy working on two power looms could produce fifteen times more cloth than the fastest hand weaver. Collectively, these technological developments permitted the mass production of inexpensive textile goods. By 1830 half a million people worked in the cotton business, Britain's leading industry, which accounted for 40 percent of exports.

STEAM POWER The most crucial technological breakthrough of the early industrial era was the development of a general-purpose steam engine in 1765 by James Watt, an instrument maker at the University of Glasgow in Scotland. Even before Watt's time, primitive steam engines had powered pumps that drew water out of coal mines, but those devices consumed too much fuel to be useful for other purposes. Watt's version relied on steam to force a piston to turn a wheel, whose rotary motion converted a simple pump into an engine. By 1800 more than a thousand of Watt's steam engines were in use in the British Isles. They were especially prominent in the textile industry, where they allowed greater productivity for manufacturers and cheaper prices for consumers.

PSI img The first iron bridge www.mhhe.com/bentleybrief2e

IRON AND STEEL The iron and steel industries also benefited from technological refinement, and the availability of inexpensive, high-quality iron and steel reinforced the move toward mechanization. After 1709 British smelters began to use coke (a purified form of coal) rather than more expensive charcoal as a fuel to produce iron. As a result, British iron production skyrocketed during the eighteenth century, and prices to consumers fell. Inexpensive iron fittings and parts made industrial machinery stronger, and iron soon became common in bridges, buildings, and ships.

Steel is much harder, stronger, and more resilient than iron, but until the nineteenth century it was very expensive to produce. In 1856, however, Henry Bessemer built a refined blast furnace known as the Bessemer converter that made it possible to produce large quantities of steel cheaply. Steel production rose sharply, and steel quickly began to replace iron in tools, machines, and structures that required high strength.

TRANSPORTATION Steam engineering and metallurgical innovations both contributed to improvements in transportation technology. In 1815 George Stephenson, a self-educated Englishman, built the first steam-powered locomotive. In 1829 his Rocket won a contest by reaching a speed of 45 kilometers (28 miles) per hour. By the mid–nineteenth century, refined steam engines of high efficiency also began to drive steamships.

PSI img Britannia Bridge www.mhhe.com/bentleybrief2e

Because they had the capacity to carry huge cargoes, railroads and steamships dramatically lowered transportation costs. They also contributed to the creation of transportation networks that linked remote interior regions and distant shores more closely than ever before in history. Between 1830 and 1870, British entrepreneurs laid about 20,000 kilometers (13,000 miles) of railroads, which carried some 322 million passengers as well as cargoes of raw materials and manufactured goods. Meanwhile, steamships proved their

WORKING IN THE COAL MINES. | A woman working as a drawer in a British coal mine drags her coal cart with the aid of a belt and chain. Manually produced coal fueled the machines of early industrial society. ***What were the risks associated with this kind of job?***

versatility by advancing up rivers to points that sailboats could not reach because of inconvenient twists or turns.

The Factory System

THE FACTORY The factory system became the characteristic method of production in industrial economies. It emerged in the late eighteenth century, when technological advances transformed the British textile industry, and by the mid–nineteenth century most cotton production took place in factories. Many of the newly developed machines were too large and expensive for home use, so it became necessary to move work to centralized locations. That centralization of production brought together more workers doing specialized tasks than ever before.

THE STEAM LOCOMOTIVE. | George Stephenson's North Star engine of 1837.

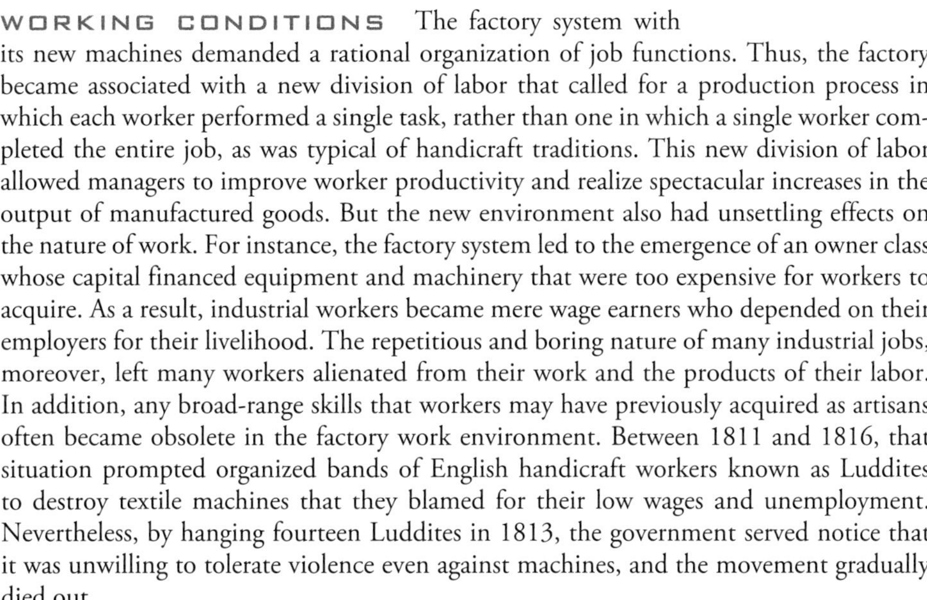

WORKING CONDITIONS The factory system with its new machines demanded a rational organization of job functions. Thus, the factory became associated with a new division of labor that called for a production process in which each worker performed a single task, rather than one in which a single worker completed the entire job, as was typical of handicraft traditions. This new division of labor allowed managers to improve worker productivity and realize spectacular increases in the output of manufactured goods. But the new environment also had unsettling effects on the nature of work. For instance, the factory system led to the emergence of an owner class whose capital financed equipment and machinery that were too expensive for workers to acquire. As a result, industrial workers became mere wage earners who depended on their employers for their livelihood. The repetitious and boring nature of many industrial jobs, moreover, left many workers alienated from their work and the products of their labor. In addition, any broad-range skills that workers may have previously acquired as artisans often became obsolete in the factory work environment. Between 1811 and 1816, that situation prompted organized bands of English handicraft workers known as Luddites to destroy textile machines that they blamed for their low wages and unemployment. Nevertheless, by hanging fourteen Luddites in 1813, the government served notice that it was unwilling to tolerate violence even against machines, and the movement gradually died out.

Equally disturbing was the new work discipline and the pace of work. Those accustomed to rural labor found that the seasons and fluctuations in the weather no longer dictated work routines. Instead, clocks, machines, and shop rules established new rhythms of work. Industrial workers commonly labored six days a week, twelve to fourteen hours a day. The factory whistle sounded the beginning and the end of each working day, and throughout the day workers had to keep pace with the movements of machines. At the same time, they faced strict and immediate supervision. Floor managers pressured men, women, and children to speed up production and punished them when they did not meet expectations. In addition, dangerous work conditions often meant that early industrial workers faced the possibility of maiming or fatal accidents.

The Early Spread of Industrialization

For fifty years industrialization occurred only in Britain. Aware of their head start, British entrepreneurs and government officials forbade the export of machinery, manufacturing techniques, and skilled workers to other lands. Yet Britain's monopoly on industrialization did not last, because enterprising entrepreneurs ignored government regulations and sold machinery and technical know-how abroad. Moreover, European and North American businesspeople did not hesitate to bribe or even kidnap British engineers to learn the secrets of industrialization, and they also smuggled advanced machinery out of the British Isles.

MAP 26.1 | Industrial Europe ca. 1850. Locate the places marked as emerging industrial areas. ***Are there any features those areas have in common? If so, what are they?***

Industrial Europe
www.mhhe.com/bentleybrief2e

INDUSTRIALIZATION IN WESTERN EUROPE As a result, by the mid–nineteenth century industrialization had spread to France, Germany, Belgium, and the United States. The earliest Continental center of industrial production was Belgium, where coal, iron, textile, glass, and armaments production flourished in the early nineteenth century. About the same time, France also moved toward industrialization. By the mid–nineteenth century, French engineers and inventors were devising refinements and innovations that led to greater efficiencies, especially in metallurgical industries. Although German industrialization started off more slowly than in France or Belgium, German coal and iron production soared after the 1840s, and by the 1850s an extensive railroad network was under construction. After unification in 1871, Bismarck's government sponsored rapid industrialization in Germany, especially of heavy industry.

INDUSTRIALIZATION IN NORTH AMERICA Industrialization transformed North America as well as western Europe in the nineteenth century. American industrialization began in the 1820s when entrepreneurs lured British crafts workers to New England and built a cotton textile industry. By midcentury well over a thousand mills were producing fabrics from raw cotton grown in the southern states, and New England had emerged as a site for the industrial production also of shoes, tools, and handguns. In the 1870s heavy iron and steel industries emerged in areas such as western Pennsylvania and central Alabama where there were abundant supplies of iron ore and coal. By 1900 the United States had become an economic powerhouse, and industrialization had begun to spill over into southern Canada.

Industrial Capitalism

MASS PRODUCTION Cotton textiles were the major factory-made products during the early phase of industrialization, but the factory system soon spread to other industries. An important contribution to the evolving factory system came from the American inventor Eli Whitney (1765–1825). Though best remembered as the inventor of the cotton gin (1793), Whitney also developed the technique of using machine tools to produce interchangeable parts in the making of firearms. This method meant that unskilled workers made only a particular part that fit every musket of the same model. Before long, entrepreneurs applied Whitney's method to the manufacture of everything from clocks and sewing machines to uniforms and shoes. By the middle of the nineteenth century, mass production of standardized articles was becoming the hallmark of industrial societies.

In 1913 Henry Ford improved manufacturing techniques further when he introduced the assembly line to automobile production. Instead of organizing production around a series of stations where workers assembled whole cars using standardized parts, Ford designed a conveyor system that allowed each worker to perform a specialized task at a fixed point on the assembly line. With the assembly line, workers churned out a complete chassis every 93 minutes instead of every 728 minutes under the old system. Such huge gains in productivity meant that car prices plummeted, allowing millions of ordinary people to purchase automobiles. The age of the motor car had arrived.

THE CORPORATION As the factory evolved, so too did the organization of business. Industrial machinery and factories were expensive investments, and they encouraged businesses to organize on a large scale. During the 1850s and 1860s, government authorities in Britain and France laid the legal foundations for the modern corporation, which quickly became the most common form of business organization in industrial societies. A corporation was a private business owned by many investors who financed the business through the purchase of stocks representing shares in the company. When a corporation flourished, investors received dividends in proportion to their stake in the company. But if a corporation went bankrupt, laws protected shareholders from liability or financial loss beyond the extent of their investments—which made them extremely attractive to investors. By the late nineteenth century, corporations controlled most businesses requiring large investments in land, labor, or machinery.

MONOPOLIES, TRUSTS, AND CARTELS To protect their investments, some big businesses of the late nineteenth century sought not only to outperform their competitors in the capitalist marketplace but also to eliminate competition. Business firms formed associations to restrict markets or establish monopolies in their industries. Large-scale business organizations formed trusts and cartels, both of which aimed to control the supply of a product and hence its price in the marketplace. Trusts commonly sought control of industries through vertical organization, by which they would dominate all facets of a single industry. John D. Rockefeller's Standard Oil Company and Trust, for example, controlled almost all oil drilling, processing, refining, marketing, and distribution in the United States.

THE CRYSTAL PALACE EXHIBITION. | Exhibitors from around the world displayed fine handicrafts and manufactured goods at the Crystal Palace exhibition of 1851 in London. Industrial products from Britain and the United States particularly attracted the attention of visitors to the enchanting and futuristic exhibition hall.

Cartels, in contrast, tried to eliminate competition by means of horizontal organization, which involved the consolidation or cooperation of independent companies in the same business. Thus cartels sought to ensure the prosperity of their members by absorbing competitors, fixing prices, regulating production, or dividing up markets. By the end of the nineteenth century, some governments outlawed trusts and cartels. However, monopolistic practices continued well into the twentieth century.

INDUSTRIAL SOCIETY

Industrialization brought material benefits in its train: inexpensive manufactured products, rising standards of living, and population growth. Yet industrialization also unleashed dramatic social change. Immense internal and external migrations took place as people moved from the countryside to work in new industrial cities, and as Europeans crossed the Atlantic to seek opportunities in the western hemisphere. Industrialization also encouraged the emergence of new social classes and forced men, women, and children to adjust to distinctly new patterns of family and work life. Reformers sought to alleviate the social and economic problems that accompanied industrialization and worked toward the building of a more equitable and just society.

The Fruits of Industry

Industrialization brought efficiencies in production that flooded markets with affordable manufactured goods. Indeed, industrialization raised material standards of living in many ways. Industrial production led to dramatic reductions in the cost of clothing, for example, so by the early nineteenth century all but the desperately poor could afford several changes of clothes. Industrial factories turned out tools that facilitated agricultural work, and steam-powered locomotives delivered produce quickly and cheaply to distant markets. Consumers in early industrial Europe also filled their homes with more furniture, porcelain, and decorative objects than any but the most wealthy of their ancestors.

POPULATION GROWTH The populations of European and Euro-American peoples rose sharply during the eighteenth and nineteenth centuries, reflecting the rising prosperity and standards of living that came with industrialization. Between 1700 and 1900 the population of Europe increased from 105 to 390 million. Demographic growth in the western hemisphere—fueled by migration from Europe—was even more remarkable. Between 1700 and 1900 the population of North America and South America rose from 13 million to 145 million.

The rapid population growth in Europe and the Americas reflected changing patterns of fertility and mortality. In most preindustrial societies fertility was high, but so was child mortality, which held population growth in check. High birthrates were common also in early industrializing societies, but death rates fell markedly because better diets and improved disease control reduced child mortality. By the late nineteenth century, better diets and improved sanitation led to declining levels of adult as well as child mortality. In combination, these two factors allowed populations to expand rapidly.

THE DEMOGRAPHIC TRANSITION Beginning in the nineteenth century, however, industrializing lands experienced a social change known as the *demographic transition.* As industrialization transformed societies, fertility began a marked decline. In the short run, mortality fell even faster than fertility, so the populations of industrial societies continued to increase. Over time, however, declining birthrates led to lower population growth and relative demographic stability. The principal reason for declining fertility in industrial lands was voluntary birth control through contraception, perhaps because raising children cost more in industrial societies or because more children were likely to survive to adulthood than in the past.

Urbanization and Migration

Industrialization and population growth strongly encouraged migration and urbanization. Within industrial societies, migrants flocked from the countryside to urban centers in search of work. For example, in 1800 about one-fifth of the British population lived in towns and cities of 10,000 or more inhabitants. By 1900 three-fourths of the population worked and lived in cities. That pattern repeated itself elsewhere: by 1900 at least half of the population in industrialized lands lived in towns with populations of 2,000 or more. The increasing size of cities reflected this internal migration. In 1800 there were barely twenty cities in Europe with populations as high as 100,000, and there were none in the western hemisphere. By 1900 there were more than 150 large cities in Europe and North America combined.

THE URBAN ENVIRONMENT With urbanization came intensified environmental pollution. Although cities have always been unsanitary places, the rapid increase in urban populations during the industrial age dramatically increased the magnitude and severity of water and air pollution. The widespread burning of fossil fuels fouled the air with vast quantities of chemicals and particulate matter. This pollution led to occupational diseases in some trades. Chimney sweeps, for instance, contracted cancer of the scrotum from hydrocarbon deposits found in soot. Effluents from factories and mills as well as untreated sewage dirtied virtually every major river. No part of a city was immune to the constant stench coming from air and water pollution. Worse, tainted water supplies and unsanitary living conditions led to periodic epidemics of cholera and typhus. Until the latter part of the nineteenth century, urban environments remained dangerous places in which death rates commonly exceeded birthrates, and only the constant stream of new arrivals from the country kept cities growing.

Income determined the degree of comfort and security offered by city life. The wealthy typically tried to insulate themselves from urban discomforts by retreating to their elegant homes in newly growing suburbs. The working poor, in contrast, occupied overcrowded tenements lacking in comfort and amenities. The cramped spaces in apartments obliged many to share the same bed, increasing the ease of disease transmission. The few open spaces outside the buildings were usually home to herds of pigs living in their own dung or were depositories for pools of stagnant water and human waste.

By the later nineteenth century, though, government authorities were tending to the problems of the early industrial cities. They improved municipal water supplies, expanded sewage systems, and introduced building codes that outlawed the construction of rickety tenements to accommodate poorly paid workers. Those measures made city life safer and

SOURCES FROM THE PAST

Testimony for the Factory Act of 1833: Working Conditions in England

During the 1830s and 1840s, deplorable conditions in England's factories and mines led the British Parliament to conduct a series of investigations on the subject. Investigators asked doctors, workers, and factory owners many questions about working conditions and their effects on laborers. The results of these investigations led to parliamentary legislation designed to protect workers from the worst effects of industrialization, such as the Factory Act of 1833. The following section relates to child labor as presented by John Wright, who was a steward in a silk factory.

Testimony of John Wright.

How long have you been employed in a silk-mill?—More than thirty years.

Did you enter it as a child?—Yes betwixt five and six.

How many hours a day did you work then?—The same thirty years ago as now.

What are those hours?—Eleven hours per day and two over-hours: over-hours are working after six in the evening until eight. The regular hours are from six in the morning to six in the evening, and two others are two over-hours. . . .

Why, then, are those employed in them said to be in such a wretched condition?—In the first place, the great number of hands congregated together, in some rooms forty, in some fifty, in some sixty, and I have known some as many as 100, which must be injurious to both health and growing. In the second place, the privy is in the factory, which frequently emits an unwholesome smell; and it would be worth while to notice in the future erection of mills, that there be betwixt the privy door and the factory wall a kind of a lobby of cage-work. 3dly, The tediousness and the everlasting sameness in the first process preys much on the spirits, and makes the hands spiritless. 4thly, the extravagant number of hours a child is compelled to labour and confinement, which for one week is seventy-six hours. . . . 5thly, About six months in the year we are obliged to use either gas, candles, or lamps, for the longest portion of that time, nearly six hours a day, being obliged to work amid the smoke and soot of the same; and also a large portion of oil and grease is used in the mills.

What are the effects of the present system of labor?—From my earliest recollections, I have found the effects to be awfully detrimental to the well-being of the operative; I have observed frequently children carried to factories, unable to walk, and that entirely owing to excessive labour and confinement. The degradation of the workpeople baffles all description: frequently have two of my sisters been obliged to be assisted to the factory and home again, until by-and-by they could go no longer, being totally crippled in their legs. And in the next place, I remember some ten or twelve years ago working in one of the largest firms in Macclesfield, . . . with about twenty-two men, where they were scarce one half fit for His Majesty's service. Those that are straight in their limbs are stunted in their growth; much inferior to their fathers in point of strength. 3dly, Through excessive labour and confinement there is often a total loss of appetite; a kind of langour steals over the whole frame—enters to the very core—saps the foundation of the best constitution—and lays our strength prostrate in the dust. In the 4th place, by protracted labour there is an alarming increase of cripples in various parts of this town, which has come under my own observation and knowledge.

Are all these cripples made in the silk factories?—Yes, they are, I believe. . . .

■ In Wright's opinion, what aspect of labor in the silk factories is the most damaging for children?

SOURCE: Dennis Sherman et al. *World Civilizations: Sources, Images, and Interpretations,* 3rd ed., Vol. II. Boston: McGraw-Hill, 2002, pp. 119–120.

brought improved sanitation. City authorities also built parks and recreational facilities to make cities more livable.

PSI img Immigration map, 1853 www.mhhe.com/bentleybrief2e

TRANSCONTINENTAL MIGRATION Rapid population growth in Europe also encouraged massive migration to the Americas, especially to the United States. During the nineteenth and early twentieth centuries, about fifty million Europeans migrated to the western hemisphere, which accounts for much of the stunning demographic growth of the Americas. Many of the migrants intended to stay for only a few years and fully expected to return to their homelands with a modest fortune made in the Americas.

URBAN HOUSING. Squalid living conditions, ca. 1885. A group of people live in crowded conditions in one room in New York.

The vast majority, however, remained in the western hemisphere. They and their descendants transformed the Americas into Euro-American lands.

Industry and Society

NEW SOCIAL CLASSES Industrialization radically altered traditional social structures and helped bring new social classes into being. Enterprising businesspeople became fabulously wealthy and powerful enough to overshadow the traditionally privileged classes. Less powerful than this new elite was the middle class, consisting of small business owners, factory managers, engineers, and professionals such as teachers, physicians, and attorneys. A large portion of industrial wealth flowed to the middle class, which benefited greatly from industrialization. Meanwhile, laborers who toiled in factories and mines constituted a new working class. Less skilled than the artisans and crafts workers of earlier times, the new workers tended to machines or provided heavy labor for low wages.

INDUSTRIAL FAMILIES The most basic unit of social organization—the family—also underwent fundamental change during the industrial age. In preindustrial societies the family was the basic productive unit. Whether engaged in agriculture, domestic manufacturing, or commerce, family members worked together and contributed to the welfare of the larger group. Industrialization challenged the family economy and reshaped family life by moving economic production outside the home and introducing a sharp distinction between work and family life. Workers left their homes each day to labor an average of fourteen hours in factories, and family members led increasingly separate lives.

MEN AND THE INDUSTRIAL REVOLUTION Men gained increased stature and responsibility in the industrial age as work dominated public life. Upper-class and middle-class men enjoyed especially increased prestige at home, since they usually were the sole providers who made their families' comfortable existence possible. Working-class men also enjoyed increased prestige because they tended to make wages far in excess of those of working-class women. As a result, their earnings usually constituted the bulk of their families' income.

WOMEN AND THE INDUSTRIAL REVOLUTION Industrialization dramatically changed the terms of work for women. When industry moved production from the home to the factory, married women were unable to work unless they left their homes and children in someone else's care. Millions of working-class women had no choice but to work under such terms, but by the late nineteenth century middle-class society promoted the idea that respectable women should devote themselves to raising children, managing the home, and preserving family values rather than to paid labor.

For middle-class women, then, industrialization brought stringent confinement to the domestic sphere and pressure to conform to new models of behavior revolving around their roles as mothers and wives. Popular books such as *Woman in Her Social and Domestic Character* (1833) insisted that the ideal woman "knows that she is the weaker vessel" and takes pride in her ability to make the home a happy place. Meanwhile, in addition to working in factories, millions of working-class women worked as domestic servants for the growing middle class. In fact, one of every three European women became a domestic servant at some point in her life.

CHILD LABOR Industrialization profoundly influenced the childhood experience. Children in preindustrial societies had always worked in and around the family home. However, industrial work, which took children away from home and parents for long hours with few breaks, made child labor seem especially pitiable and exploitative. Early reports from British textile mills described sensational abuses by overseers who forced children to work from dawn until dark and beat them to keep them awake. In the 1840s the British parliament began to pass laws regulating child labor and ultimately restricted or removed children from the industrial workforce. In the long term, urban industrial societies redefined the role of children. Motivated in part by the recognition that modern society demanded a skilled and educated labor force, governments established the legal requirement that education, and not work for monetary gain, was the principal task of childhood. In England, for instance, education for children ages five to ten became mandatory by 1881.

The Socialist Challenge

Among the most vocal and influential critics of early industrial society were the socialists, who worked to alleviate the social and economic problems generated by capitalism and industrialization. Socialists deplored economic inequalities, as represented by the vast difference in wealth between a captain of industry and a factory laborer, and they condemned the system that permitted the exploitation of laborers, especially women and children. Early socialists sought to expand the Enlightenment understanding of equality: they understood equality to have an economic as well as a political, legal, and social dimension, and they looked to the future establishment of a just and equitable society.

MARX AND ENGELS Most prominent of the nineteenth-century socialists were the German theorists Karl Marx (1818–1883) and Friedrich Engels (1820–1895). Marx and Engels believed that social problems of the nineteenth century were inevitable results of a capitalist economy. They held that capitalism divided people into two main classes, each with its own economic interests and social status: the capitalists, who owned industrial machinery and factories (which Marx and Engels called the means of production), and the proletariat, consisting of wageworkers who had only their labor to sell. Intense competition between capitalists trying to realize a profit resulted in ruthless exploitation of the working class. Moreover, according to Marx and Engels, the state and its coercive institutions, such as police forces and courts of law, functioned to enable capitalists to continue their exploitation of the proletariat. Even music, art, literature, and religion served the purposes of capitalists, according to Marx and Engels, since they amused the working classes and diverted attention from their misery.

THE COMMUNIST MANIFESTO Marx developed those views fully in a long, theoretical work called *Capital.* Together with Engels, Marx also wrote a short, spirited tract titled *Manifesto of the Communist Party* (1848). In the *Manifesto* Marx and

INDUSTRIAL CONFLICT. | Robert Koehler's painting *The Strike* depicts a situation verging on violence as workers mill about in a confrontation with factory owners and one angry laborer crouches to pick up a stone.

Engels aligned themselves with the communists, who worked toward the abolition of private property and the institution of a radically egalitarian society. The *Manifesto* asserted that all human history has been the history of struggle between social classes. It also argued that the future lay with the working class. Crises of overproduction, underconsumption, and diminishing profits would shake the foundations of the capitalist order. Meanwhile, members of the proletariat would come to view the forcible overthrow of the existing system as the only alternative available to them. Marx and Engels believed that a socialist revolution would result in a "dictatorship of the proletariat," which would abolish private property and destroy the capitalist order. After the revolution was secure, the state would wither away. Coercive institutions would also disappear, since there would no longer be an exploiting class. Thus socialism would lead to a fair, just, and egalitarian society infinitely more humane than the capitalist order.

The doctrines of Marx and Engels came to dominate European and international socialism, and socialist parties grew rapidly throughout the nineteenth century. Political parties, trade unions, newspapers, and educational associations all worked to advance the socialist cause. Yet socialists disagreed strongly on the best means to reform society. Revolutionary socialists such as Marx and Engels urged workers to forcibly seize control of the state. In contrast, evolutionary socialists placed their hopes in representative governments and called for the election of legislators who supported socialist reforms.

SOCIAL REFORM Although socialists did not win control of any government until the Russian revolution of 1917, their critiques helped persuade government authorities to attack the abuses of early industrialization and provide more security for the working classes. In Britain, for example, Parliament prohibited underground employment for women and stipulated that children under age nine not work more than nine hours a day. Beginning in 1832, a series of parliamentary acts also expanded the franchise for men by reducing property qualifications, preparing the way for universal male suffrage. In Germany in the 1880s, Otto von Bismarck introduced medical insurance, unemployment compensation, and retirement pensions to provide social security for working people in industrial society.

PSI img IWW demonstration www.mhhe.com/bentleybrief2e

TRADE UNIONS Trade unions also sought to advance the quest for a just and equitable society. As governments regulated businesses and enhanced social security, trade unions struggled to improve workers' lives by seeking higher wages and better working conditions for their members. Through most of the nineteenth century, both employers and governments considered trade unions illegal associations whose purpose was to restrain trade. Yet trade unions persisted, and over the long run they improved the lives of working people and reduced the likelihood that a disgruntled proletariat would mount a revolution to overthrow industrial capitalist society.

GLOBAL EFFECTS OF INDUSTRIALIZATION

Although early industrialization was a British, western European, and North American affair, it had deep global implications. In part this was because industrial powers used their tools, technologies, business organization, financial influence, and transportation networks to obtain raw materials from preindustrial societies around the world. Many lands that possessed natural resources were unable to maintain control over them because representatives of industrial countries dominated the commercial and financial institutions associated with their trade. Other societies, in particular Russia and Japan, saw the writing on the wall and embarked on huge industrialization programs of their own to stave off Euro-American domination.

The International Division of Labor

Industrialization influenced the economic and social development of many societies because it promoted a new international division of labor. Industrial societies needed minerals, agricultural products, and other raw materials to supply their factories, and they frequently obtained them from distant regions of the world.

Although large-scale global trade in agricultural products such as sugar, tea, and cotton was nothing new, industrial society fueled the demand for additional products as industrialists sought the natural resources and agricultural products of Africa, the Americas, Asia, Australia, and eastern Europe. The mechanization of the textile industry, for example, produced a demand for large quantities of raw cotton, which came mostly from India, Egypt, and the southern rim of the United States. Similarly, new industrial technologies increased demand for products such as rubber, the principal ingredient of the belts and tires that were essential to industrial machinery, which came from Brazil, Malaya, and the Congo River basin.

ECONOMIC DEVELOPMENT In some lands specialization in the production and export of primary goods paved the way for economic development and eventual industrialization. That pattern was especially noticeable in lands settled by European colonists, including Canada, Argentina, Uruguay, South Africa, Australia, and New Zealand, each of which experienced economic growth through the export of primary products and the infusion of foreign capital and labor. The same societies had an additional advantage in that they were high-wage economies. High incomes fostered economic development in two ways: they created flourishing markets, and they encouraged entrepreneurs to counteract high wages and labor security by inventing new labor-saving technologies.

ECONOMIC DEPENDENCE In most of Latin America, sub-Saharan Africa, south Asia, and southeast Asia, however, dependence on exporting primary products such as sugar, cotton, and rubber resulted in little or no industrialization. Foreign investors owned and controlled the plantations that produced those crops, and most of the profits generated went abroad, depriving domestic economies of funds that might have contributed to the building of markets and industries. The low wages of plantation workers made the situation worse by dampening demand for manufactured goods. The result was the concentration of wealth in the hands of a small group of people, whether local or foreign, who contributed little to the creation of a domestic market. To compound the problem, both native and foreign financial interests adopted a free-trade policy that permitted unrestricted entry of foreign manufactures, further limiting opportunities for indigenous industrialization. Thus, although industrialization linked all the world's peoples in increasingly complex ways, its benefits and rewards went primarily to those who controlled the tools, capital, and trade rather than to those who provided the raw materials that made production possible.

THINKING ABOUT *Traditions*

TRADITIONS IN THE MAKING OF INDUSTRIAL SOCIETY. Although Russia and Japan both embarked on aggressive programs of industrialization in the late nineteenth and early twentieth centuries, the motivation for mechanization came from government policies rather than the British model of entrepreneurial initiative. In what ways did political traditions in Russia and Japan help to shape their government-driven approaches to industrialization?

The Continuing Spread of Industrialization: Russia and Japan

Industrialization brought great economic and military strength to societies that reconfigured themselves and relied on mechanized production. Their power encouraged other societies to seek their own paths to industrialization. Indeed, by the late nineteenth century it had become clear to leaders in many preindustrial lands that unless they undertook programs of social, political, and economic reform, they would grow progressively weaker in relation to industrial powers. Faced with such a reality, after 1870 both Russia and Japan embarked on campaigns of rapid industrialization to strengthen their societies and enable them to resist military and economic pressures from western Europe and the United States.

Russia in 1870 was a multiethnic, multilingual, multicultural empire that stretched from Poland to the Pacific Ocean. The Romanov tsars ruled their diverse and sprawling realm through an autocratic regime in which all initiative came from the central administration. The tsars enjoyed the support of a powerful class of nobles who owned most of the land and were exempt from taxes and military duty. Peasants made up the vast majority of the population, and most of them were serfs bound to the lands that they cultivated.

Although the Russian army in the nineteenth century was huge, conflict with France and Britain in the Crimean War (1853–1856) clearly revealed the inability of Russian forces—based as they were on an agrarian economy—to compete with the industrial powers of western Europe. Military defeat compelled the tsarist autocracy to reevaluate the Russian social order and undertake an extensive program of reform along western European lines.

EMANCIPATION OF THE SERFS The key to social reform in Russia was emancipation of the serfs (1861), an institution many believed had become an obstacle to economic development. Indeed, Tsar Alexander II (reigned 1855–1881) emancipated the serfs partly with the intention of creating a mobile labor force for emerging industries, and the tsarist government encouraged industrialization as a way of strengthening the Russian empire. Thus, although Russian industrialization took place within a framework of capitalism, it differed from western European industrialization in that the motivation for development was political and military and the driving force was government policy rather than entrepreneurial initiative. Industrialization proceeded slowly at first, but it surged during the last two decades of the nineteenth century.

PSI img Tsar Alexander II www.mhhe.com/bentleybrief2e

RAILROADS In Russia the tsarist government promoted industrialization by encouraging the construction of railroads to link the distant regions of the far-flung empire. In 1860 Russia had fewer than 1,100 kilometers (700 miles) of railroads, but by 1900 there were more than 58,000 kilometers (36,000 miles). Most impressive of the Russian railroads was the trans-Siberian line, constructed between 1891 and 1904, which stretched more than 9,000 kilometers (5,600 miles) and linked Moscow with the port of

Romanov (ROH-muh-nawf)
tsar (zahr)

Vladivostok on the Pacific Ocean. Apart from drawing the regions of the Russian empire together, railroads stimulated the development of coal, iron, and steel industries and enabled Russia to serve as a commercial link between western Europe and east Asia.

THE WITTE SYSTEM Russian industry experienced explosive growth when Count Sergei Witte served as finance minister (1892–1903). Witte oversaw construction of the trans-Siberian railroad, and he worked to push Russian industrialization by reforming commercial law, protecting infant industries, supporting steamship companies, and promoting nautical and engineering schools. He invited foreign investors to bring their capital and expertise to Russia, and he encouraged the establishment of savings banks to raise additional investment funds at home. By 1900 Russia produced half the world's oil, and Russian steel production ranked fourth in the world, behind that of the United States, Germany, and Britain. As a result of Witte's efforts, Russia also had enormous coal and iron industries, and government demand for weapons also supported a huge armaments industry.

INDUSTRIAL DISCONTENT Although Russia successfully began a program of industrialization, such efforts came at a high cost. As in other lands, industrial growth generated an urban working class, which endured miserable working and living conditions. Employers kept wages of overworked and poorly housed workers at the barest minimum. Moreover, economic exploitation and the lack of political freedom made workers increasingly receptive to socialist and revolutionary propaganda, which—when combined

Sergei Witte (SAYR-gay VIHT-tee)

MAP 26.2 | The Russian empire, 1801–1914. Note the sheer size of Russian territory in this period, and that the state included part of Europe, central Asia, and east Asia. ***How would straddling so much space and so many cultures have affected the process of industrialization and nationalism in Russia?***

with further military defeat and political oppression—eventually undermined the Russian state itself in the early twentieth century.

TSAR ALEXANDER II OF RUSSIA. | After signing the Treaty of Paris in 1856, ending the Crimean War, Alexander abolished serfdom in the Russian empire.

FOREIGN PRESSURE In Japan, too, imperial authorities pushed industrialization, although under very different circumstances from those in Russia. Until 1853 Japan had largely closed itself off from interaction with European and American traders. The situation changed abruptly in that year, however, with the arrival of a U.S. naval squadron in Tokyo Bay. The American commander, Commodore Matthew C. Perry, trained his guns on the bakufu capital of Edo (modern Tokyo) and demanded that the shogun open Japan to diplomatic and commercial relations and sign a treaty of friendship. The shogun had no good alternative and so acquiesced to Perry's demands. Representatives of Britain, the Netherlands, and Russia soon won similar rights, all of which opened Japanese ports to foreign commerce, deprived the government of control over tariffs, and granted foreigners extraterritorial rights.

The sudden intrusion of foreign powers precipitated a domestic crisis in Japan that eventually resulted in the collapse of the Tokugawa bakufu and the restoration of imperial rule. After years of conflict and a brief civil war, the boy emperor Mutsuhito—known by his regnal name, Meiji ("Enlightened Rule")—took the reins of power on 3 January 1868.

THE MEIJI RESTORATION The Meiji restoration returned authority to the Japanese emperor and marked the birth of a new Japan. Determined to gain parity with foreign powers, a conservative coalition of daimyo, imperial princes, court nobles, and samurai formed a new government dedicated to the twin goals of prosperity and strength: "rich country, strong army." The Meiji government looked to the industrial lands of Europe and the United States to obtain the knowledge and expertise to strengthen Japan. The Meiji government sent many students and officials abroad to study everything from technology to constitutions, and it also hired foreign experts to facilitate economic development and the creation of indigenous expertise.

ECONOMIC DEVELOPMENT Economic initiatives were critical to the process of Meiji reconstruction. Convinced that a powerful economy was the foundation of national strength, the Meiji government created a modern transportation, communications, and educational infrastructure. The establishment of telegraph, railroad, and steamship lines tied local and regional markets into a national economic network. Aiming to improve literacy rates, the government introduced a system of universal primary and secondary education. Universities provided advanced instruction for the best students, especially in scientific and technical fields. This infrastructure supported rapid industrialization and economic growth. Although most economic enterprises were privately owned, the government controlled military industries and established pilot programs to stimulate industrial development. During the 1880s the government sold most of its enterprises to private investors who had close ties to government officials. The result was a concentration of enormous economic power in the hands of a small group of people, collectively known as *zaibatsu,* or financial cliques. By the early twentieth century, Japan had joined the ranks of the major industrial powers.

THINKING ABOUT *Encounters*

ENCOUNTERS IN THE MAKING OF INDUSTRIAL SOCIETY. Over the course of the nineteenth century, industrialization increasingly linked the world's societies through the dual processes of technology transfer and the exploitation of natural resources. Yet the benefits of industrialization were not uniform throughout the world. Why is it that some societies were able to industrialize on the British model while others were not?

Tokugawa (TOH-koo-GAH-wah)
Mutsuhito (MOO-tsoo-HE-taw)
Meiji (MAY-jee)
daimyo (DEYEM-yoh)
zaibatsu (zeye-BAHT-soo)

JAPANESE INDUSTRIALIZATION. | The Tomioka silk factory, established in the 1870s, was one of the earliest mechanized textile factories in Japan. In this factory, as in many textile mills in Europe and North America, male managers oversaw female factory workers. ***What are most of the women in this drawing doing?***
© Carousel/Laurie Platt Winfrey, Inc.

COSTS OF ECONOMIC DEVELOPMENT As in Russia, economic development came at a price, as the Japanese people bore the social and political costs of rapid industrialization. During this period, hundreds of thousands of rural families lived in destitution, haunted by malnutrition, starvation, and infanticide. In addition, those who took up work in the burgeoning industries learned that working conditions were difficult and that the state did not tolerate labor organizations that promoted the welfare of workers.

Nevertheless, the desire to achieve political and economic equality with Euro-American industrial powers—and to avoid the domination and dependence experienced by preindustrial societies elsewhere—transformed Japan into a powerful industrial society in a single generation. Serving as symbols of Japan's remarkable development were the conclusion of an alliance with Britain as an equal power in 1902 and convincing displays of military prowess in victories over the Chinese empire (1894–1895) and the Russian empire (1904–1905).

SUMMARY

The process of industrialization involved the harnessing of inanimate sources of energy, the replacement of handicraft production with machine-based manufacturing, and the generation of new forms of business and labor organization. Along with industrialization came demographic growth, large-scale migration, and rapid urbanization, which increased the demand for manufactured goods by the masses of working people. Societies that underwent industrialization enjoyed sharp increases in economic productivity: they produced large quantities of high-quality goods at low prices, and their increased productivity translated into higher material standards of living. Yet industrialization brought costs as well as benefits. Family life changed dramatically in the industrial age as men, women, and children increasingly left their homes to work in factories and mines, often under appalling conditions. Socialist critics sought to bring about a more just and equitable society, and government authorities curtailed the worst abuses of the early industrial era. Meanwhile, industrialization increasingly touched the lives of peoples around the world. To avoid being dominated, Russia and Japan followed the lead of Britain, western Europe, and North America into industrialization, whereas many African, Asian, and Latin American lands became dependent on the export of raw materials to industrial societies.

STUDY TERMS

Bessemer converter (518)
cartels (522)
child labor (526)
Commodore Matthew C. Perry (531)
Communist Manifesto (526)
corporations (521)
demographic transition (523)
Eli Whitney (521)
factory system (521)
flying shuttle (517)
Friedrich Engels (526)
George Stephenson (518)
Henry Ford (521)
James Watt (518)
Karl Marx (526)
Luddites (519)
Meiji (531)
middle class (525)
power loom (517)
Sergei Witte (530)
socialism (526)
spinning mule (517)
trade unions (528)
trusts (521)
Tsar Alexander II (529)
working class (525)
zaibatsu (531)

FOR FURTHER READING

William L. Blackwell. *The Industrialization of Russia: An Historical Perspective.* New York, 1982. A useful overview.

Daniel R. Headrick. *The Tentacles of Progress: Technology Transfer in the Age of Imperialism, 1850–1940.* New York, 1988. Concentrates on the political and cultural obstacles that hindered transfer of European technologies to colonial lands.

Marius B. Jansen and Gilbert Rozman, eds. *Japan in Transition: From Tokugawa to Meiji.* Princeton, 1986. Important collection of essays exploring economic and social change during the era of the Meiji restoration.

David S. Landes. *The Wealth and Poverty of Nations: Why Some Are So Rich and Some So Poor.* New York, 1998. A wide-ranging analysis arguing that social and cultural attitudes serve as the foundation of economic development.

Karl Marx and Friedrich Engels. *The Communist Manifesto.* Trans. by Samuel Moore. Harmondsworth, 1967. English translation of the most important tract of nineteenth-century socialism, with an excellent introduction by historian A. J. P. Taylor.

Kenneth Pomeranz. *The Great Divergence: China, Europe, and the Making of the Modern World Economy.* Princeton, 2000. Argues that the fortuitous location of coal deposits and access to the resources of the Americas created a uniquely advantageous framework for English industrialization.

Hans Rogger. *Russia in the Age of Modernisation and Revolution, 1881–1917.* New York, 1983. An important study of Russian social and economic development.

Peter N. Stearns. *The Industrial Revolution in World History.* Boulder, 1993. An excellent overview of industrialization, its European origins, its spread, and its effects in the larger world.

E. P. Thompson. *The Making of the English Working Class.* New York, 1966. A classic work that analyzes the formation of working-class consciousness in England from the 1790s to the 1830s.

Louise A. Tilly. *Industrialization and Gender Inequality.* Washington, D.C., 1993. A brief historiographical survey of debates on gender and industrialization in England, France, Germany, the United States, Japan, and China.

The Americas in the Age of Independence

27

THE BUILDING OF AMERICAN STATES

The United States: Westward Expansion and Civil War

The Canadian Dominion: Independence without War

Latin America: Fragmentation and Political Experimentation

AMERICAN ECONOMIC DEVELOPMENT

Migration to the Americas

Economic Expansion in the United States

Canadian Prosperity

Latin American Dependence

AMERICAN CULTURAL AND SOCIAL DIVERSITY

Multicultural Society in the United States

Canadian Cultural Contrasts

Ethnicity, Identity, and Gender in Latin America

village fish peddler, Fatt Hing Chin often roamed the coast of southern China in search of fish to sell at market. One day at the wharves, he heard a tale of mysterious but enticing mountains of gold beckoning young Chinese to cross the ocean. At age nineteen, Chin longed for the glittering mountains. He learned that he could purchase passage on a foreign ship, and in 1849 he boarded a Spanish ship to sail to California and join the gold rush.

Once at sea, Chin was surprised at the large number of young Chinese men crammed in with him in the ship's vomit-laden hold. Ninety-five difficult days and nights passed before the hills of San Francisco came into view. On arrival the travelers met Chinese veterans of life in the United States who explained the need to stick together if they were to survive and prosper.

Chin hired out as a gold miner, and after two years he accumulated his own little pile of gold. He wrote to his brothers and cousins, urging them to join him, and thus helped fuel the large-scale overseas migration of workers. Having made his fortune, though, Chin decided to return to China. Indeed, California gold provided him with the means to take a wife, build a house, and buy some land in his home country.

Although settled and prosperous, Chin longed for the excitement of California. Leaving his pregnant wife, he sailed for California again after only a year in China. He returned to mining with his brother, but the gold was more difficult to find. Inspired by the luck of another migrant, Tong Ling, who managed to get one dollar for each meal he sold, Chin's cousins in San Francisco decided to open a restaurant. Chin found the city much more comfortable than the mountains. "Let the others go after the gold in the hills," he said. "I'll wait for the gold to come to the city."

Fatt Hing Chin was one of the earliest Chinese migrants to settle in the Americas. His career path—from a miner in search of quick riches to an urban resident committed to a new homeland—was quite typical of Chinese migrants to the United States. Along with millions of others from Europe and Asia, Chinese migrants increased the ethnic diversity of American populations and stimulated political, social, and economic development in the western hemisphere.

During the late eighteenth and early nineteenth centuries, almost all the lands of the western hemisphere won their independence from European colonial powers. American peoples then struggled throughout the nineteenth century to build their own states and societies. The United States built the most powerful state in the western hemisphere and embarked on a westward push that brought most of the temperate regions of North America under U.S. control. Canada built a federal state under British Canadian leadership. The

❮ Chinese immigrants employed to build the California railroads in the 1890s.

CHRONOLOGY

1803	Louisiana Purchase
1804–1806	Lewis and Clark expedition
1812–1814	War of 1812
1838–1839	Trail of Tears
1845–1848	Mexican-American War
1848	Seneca Falls Convention
1849	California gold rush
1850s	*La Reforma* in Mexico
1861–1865	U.S. Civil War
1867	Establishment of the Dominion of Canada
1867	French troops withdraw from Mexico
1867–1877	Reconstruction in the United States
1869	Completion of the transcontinental railroad line in the United States
1876	Battle of Little Big Horn
1876–1911	Rule of Porfirio Díaz in Mexico
1885	Completion of the Canadian Pacific Railroad
1885	Northwest Rebellion
1890	Massacre at Wounded Knee
1911–1920	Mexican revolution

varied lands of Latin America built smaller states that often fell under the sway of local military leaders. One issue that most American peoples wrestled with, regardless of their region, was the legacy of the Enlightenment. The effort to build societies based on freedom, equality, and constitutional government was a monumental challenge that remained only partially realized. Indeed, Asian and European migrants joined freed slaves and native-born workers in labor systems—from plantations and factories to debt peonage—that often betrayed American promises of welcome and freedom.

The age of independence for the United States, Canada, and Latin America was a contentious era characterized by continuous mass migration and explosive economic growth, occasionally followed by deep economic stagnation, and punctuated with civil war, ethnic violence, class conflict, and battles for racial and sexual equality. Goals to build effective states, enjoy economic prosperity, and attain cultural cohesion were elusive throughout the nineteenth century and in many ways remain so even in the present day. Nevertheless, the histories of these first lands to win independence from colonial powers inspired other peoples who later sought freedom from imperial rule.

THE BUILDING OF AMERICAN STATES

After winning independence from Britain, the United States fashioned a government and began to expand rapidly to the west. Yet the United States was an unstable society composed of varied regions with diverse economic and social structures. Differences over slavery and the rights of individual states as opposed to the federal government sparked a bloody civil war in the 1860s. That conflict resulted in the abolition of slavery and the strengthening of the federal state. The experience of Canada was very different from that of the United States. Canada gained independence from Britain without fighting a war, and even though Canada also was a land of great diversity, it avoided falling into a civil war. Canada established a relatively weak federal government, which presided over provinces that had considerable power over local affairs. Latin American lands were even more diverse than their counterparts to the north, and there was never any real possibility that they could join together in a confederation. Throughout the nineteenth century Latin America was a politically fragmented region, and many individual states faced serious problems and divisions within their own societies.

The United States: Westward Expansion and Civil War

After gaining independence the United States faced the need to construct a government. During the 1780s leaders from the rebellious colonies drafted a constitution that entrusted responsibility for general issues to a federal government, reserved authority for local issues for individual states, and provided for the admission of new states and territories to the confederation. Originally, most states limited the vote to men of property, but the Enlightenment ideal of equality encouraged political leaders to extend the franchise: by the mid–nineteenth century almost all adult white men were eligible to vote.

WESTWARD EXPANSION AND MANIFEST DESTINY While working to settle constitutional issues, Americans also began to expand to the west. After the American Revolution, Britain ceded to the new republic all lands between the Appalachian Mountains and the Mississippi River, and the United States doubled in size. In 1803 Napoleon Bonaparte allowed the United States to purchase France's Louisiana Territory, which extended from the Mississippi River to the Rocky Mountains. Overnight the United States doubled in size again. Between 1804 and 1806 a geographic expedition led by Meriwether Lewis and William Clark mapped the territory and surveyed its resources. Settlers soon began to flock west in search of cheap land to cultivate. By the 1840s many Americans spoke of a "manifest destiny" to occupy all of North America from the Atlantic to the Pacific Ocean.

Indian expulsion
www.mhhe.com/
bentleybrief2e

CONFLICT WITH INDIGENOUS PEOPLES Westward expansion brought settlers and government forces into conflict with the indigenous peoples of North America, who resisted efforts to push them from their ancestral lands and hunting grounds. However, U.S. officials and military forces supported Euro-American settlers and gradually forced the continent open to white expansion. With the Indian Removal Act of 1830, the United States government determined to move all Native Americans west of the Mississippi River into "Indian Territory" (Oklahoma). Among the tribes affected by this forced removal from the east were the Cherokees, who suffered a harrowing 800-mile migration from the eastern woodlands to Oklahoma on the Trail of Tears (1838–1839), so known because thousands died from disease, starvation, and the difficulties of relocation.

In 1830, the US government sought to move Native Americans to this territory, which later became Oklahoma.

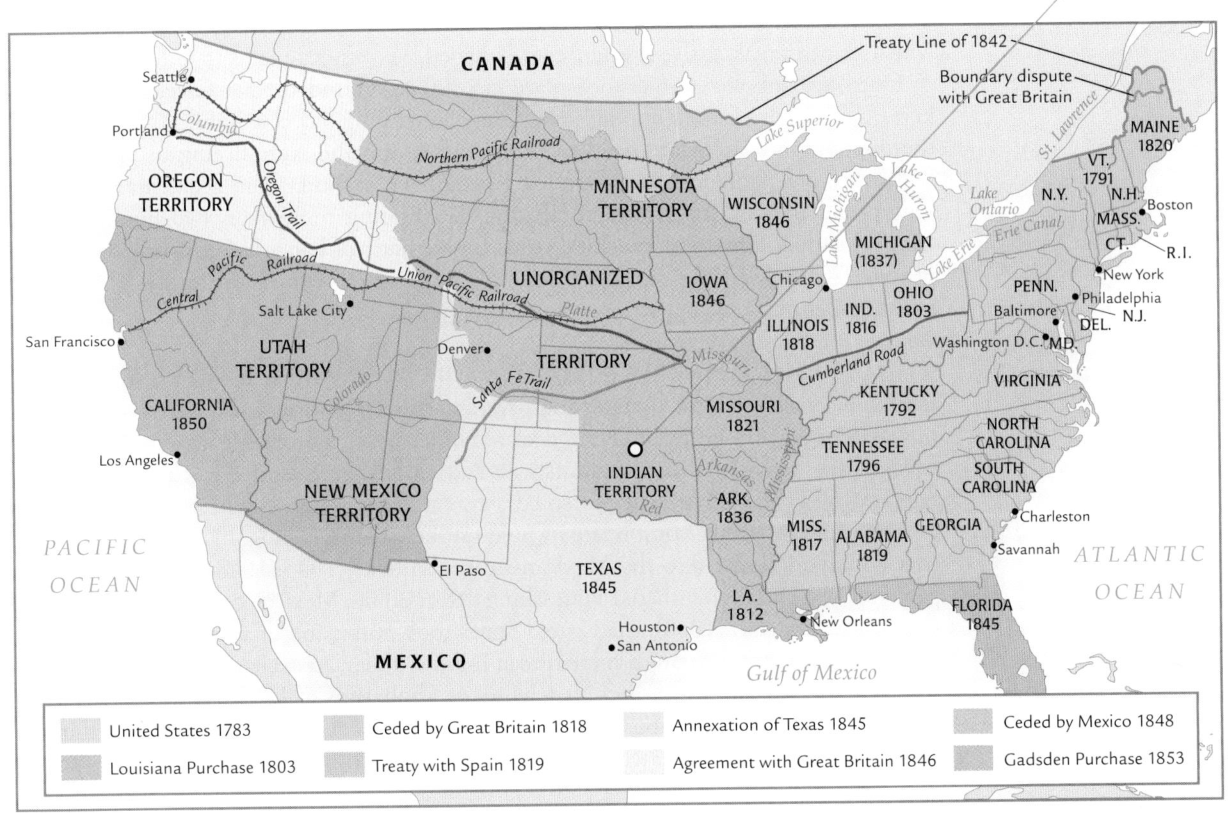

MAP 27.1 | Westward expansion of the United States during the nineteenth century. Note the large land claims ceded by Britain, France, and Mexico. ***Why were there no portions of North America purchased from or ceded by native Americans?***

PLAINS INDIAN CAMP. This photograph from the 1890s in South Dakota offers an idealized, pastoral, and peaceful image of the disappearing indigenous societies in the United States.

After 1840 the site of conflict between Euro-American and indigenous peoples shifted to the plains region west of the Mississippi River. Settlers and ranchers in the trans-Mississippi west encountered peoples such as the Sioux, the Comanche, the Pawnee, and the Apache, who possessed firearms and outstanding equestrian skills. The native peoples of the plains offered effective resistance to encroachment by white settlers and at times won powerful victories over U.S. forces. In 1876, for example, thousands of Lakota Sioux and their allies annihilated an army under the command of Colonel George Armstrong Custer in the battle of Little Big Horn (in southern Montana). Ultimately, however, Native Americans on the plains lost the war against the forces of U.S. expansionism. U.S. forces employed cannons and deadly, rapid-fire Gatling guns against native peoples, which helped break native resistance and opened the western plains to U.S. conquest.

One last symbolic conflict took place in 1890 at Wounded Knee Creek in South Dakota. U.S. cavalry forces, hoping to suppress Sioux religious ceremonies that envisioned the disappearance of white people, chased the Sioux who were fleeing to safety in the South Dakota Badlands. At Wounded Knee Creek, a Sioux man accidentally shot off a gun, and the cavalry overreacted badly, slaughtering more than two hundred men, women, and children with machine guns. Emblematic of harsh U.S. treatment of native peoples, Wounded Knee represented the place where "a people's dream died," as a later native leader put it.

The Mexican-American War
www.mhhe.com/
bentleybrief2e

THE MEXICAN-AMERICAN WAR Westward expansion also generated tension between the United States and Mexico, whose territories included most of what is now the American southwest. Texas declared independence from Mexico in 1836, largely because the many American migrants who had settled there wanted to run their own affairs. In 1845 the United States accepted Texas as a new state—against vigorous Mexican protest—and moved to consolidate its hold on the territory. Those moves led to conflicts that rapidly escalated into the Mexican-American War (1845–1848). U.S. forces instigated the war and then inflicted a punishing defeat on the Mexican army. By the Treaty of Guadalupe Hidalgo (1848), the United States took possession of approximately one-half of Mexico's territory, paying a mere fifteen million dollars in exchange for Texas north of the Rio Grande, California, and New Mexico. Thousands of U.S. and Mexican soldiers died in this conflict, and thousands of Mexican families found themselves stranded in territories annexed by the United States. Some returned to Mexico, while most stayed put

Sioux (soo)

Guadalupe Hidalgo (gwahd-l-OOP hee-DAHL-goh)

The U.S. Civil War. The grotesquely twisted bodies of dead Confederate soldiers lay near a fence outside Antietam, Maryland, in 1862. The Civil War was the most costly in U.S. history in number of lives lost.

and attained U.S. citizenship. This conflict nonetheless fueled Mexican nationalism, as well as Mexican disdain for the United States.

Westward expansion also created problems within the republic by aggravating tensions between regions. The most divisive issue had to do with slavery, which had vexed American politics since independence. The Enlightenment ideal of equality clearly suggested that the appropriate policy was to abolish slavery, but the framers of the Constitution recognized the sanctity of private property, including slaves. American independence initially promoted a surge of antislavery sentiment, and states from Delaware north abolished slavery within their jurisdictions. That move hardened divisions between slave and free states. Westward expansion aggravated tensions further by raising the question of whether settlers could extend slavery to newly acquired territories.

SECTIONAL CONFLICT The election of Abraham Lincoln to the presidency in 1860 was the spark that ignited war between the states (1861–1865). Lincoln was an explicitly sectional candidate who was convinced that slavery was immoral and who was committed to free soil—territories without slavery. Although slavery stood at the center of the conflict, the Civil War also revolved around other important issues: the nature of the Union, states' rights as opposed to the federal government's authority, and the needs of a budding industrial-capitalist system against those of an export-oriented plantation economy.

THE U.S. CIVIL WAR Eleven southern states withdrew from the Union in 1860 and 1861, affirming their right to dissolve the Union and their support for states' rights. Northerners saw the situation differently. They viewed secession as illegal insurrection and an act of betrayal. They fought not only against slavery but also against the concept of a state subject to blackmail by its constituent parts. They also fought for a way of life—their emerging industrial society—and an expansive western agricultural system based on free labor.

Ultimately, the northern states prevailed. They brought considerable resources to the war effort—some 90 percent of the country's industrial capacity and approximately two-thirds of its railroad lines—but still they fought four bitter years against a formidable enemy. The consequences of that victory were enormous, for it ended slavery in the United States. Indeed, once Abraham Lincoln signed the Emancipation Proclamation on 1 January 1863, which made the abolition of slavery an explicit goal of the war, it was clear that a northern victory would entail radical changes in southern life. Moreover, the victory of the northern states ensured that the United States would remain politically united, and it enhanced the authority of the federal government in the American republic. Thus, as European lands were building powerful states on the foundations of revolutionary ideals, liberalism, and nationalism, the United States also forged a strong central government to supervise westward expansion and deal with the political and social issues that divided the American republic.

The Canadian Dominion: Independence without War

AUTONOMY AND DIVISION Canada did not fight a war for independence, and in spite of deep regional divisions, it did not experience bloody internal conflict. Instead, Canadian independence came gradually as Canadians and the British government agreed on general principles of autonomy. The distinctiveness of the two dominant ethnic groups, the British Canadians and the French Canadians, ensured that the process of building an independent society would not be smooth, but intermittent fears about the possibility of a U.S. invasion from the south helped submerge ethnic differences. By the late nineteenth century, Canada was a land in control of its own destiny.

Originally colonized by trappers and settlers from both Britain and France, the colony of New France passed into the British empire after the British victory in the Seven Years' War (1756–1763). Until the late eighteenth century, however, French Canadians outnumbered British Canadians, so imperial officials made large concessions to their subjects of French descent to forestall unnecessary strife. After 1781, however, large numbers of British loyalists fled the newly formed United States and sought refuge in Canada, thus greatly enlarging the size of the English-speaking community there.

THE WAR OF 1812 Ethnic divisions and political differences could easily have splintered Canada, but the War of 1812 stimulated a sense of unity against an external threat. The United States declared war on Britain in retaliation for encroachments on U.S. rights during the Napoleonic wars, and the British colony of Canada formed one of the front lines of the conflict. U.S. military leaders assumed that they could easily invade and conquer Canada to pressure Britain. Despite the greater resources of the United States, however, Canadian forces repelled U.S. incursions. Their victories promoted a sense of Canadian pride, and anti-U.S. sentiments became a means for covering over differences among French and British Canadians.

After the War of 1812, Canada experienced an era of rapid growth. Expanded business opportunities drew English-speaking migrants, who swelled the population. This influx threatened the identity of Quebec, and discontent in Canada reached a critical point in the 1830s. The British imperial governors of Canada did not want a repeat of the American Revolution, so between 1840 and 1867 they defused tensions by expanding home rule in Canada and permitting the provinces to govern their internal affairs.

Dominion of Canada
www.mhhe.com/
bentleybrief2e

DOMINION Fear of U.S. expansion helped stifle internal conflicts among Canadians and prompted Britain to grant independence to Canada. The British North America Act of 1867 joined Quebec, Ontario, Nova Scotia, and New Brunswick and recognized them as the Dominion of Canada. Other provinces joined the Dominion later. Each province had its own seat of government, provincial legislature, and lieutenant governor representing the British crown. The act created a federal government headed by a governor-general, who acted as the British representative. An elected House of Commons and an appointed Senate rounded out the framework of governance. Without waging war, the Dominion of Canada had won control over all Canadian internal affairs, and Britain retained jurisdiction over foreign affairs until 1931.

John A. Macdonald (1815–1891) became the first prime minister of Canada, and he moved to incorporate all of British North America into the Dominion. He negotiated the purchase of the huge Northwest Territories from the Hudson Bay Company in 1869, and he persuaded Manitoba, British Columbia, and Prince Edward Island to join the Dominion. Then, to strengthen the union, he oversaw construction of a transcontinental railroad, completed in 1885. The railroad facilitated transportation and communications throughout Canada and eventually helped bring new provinces into the Dominion: Alberta and Saskatchewan in 1905 and Newfoundland in 1949. Although maintaining ties to Britain and struggling to forge an identity distinct from its powerful neighbor to the south, Canada developed as a culturally diverse yet politically unified society.

MAP 27.2 | The Dominion of Canada in the nineteenth century. Note the provinces that make up the modern state of Canada and the dates in which they were incorporated into the Dominion. ***At what date were eastern and western Canada geographically united?***

The Canadian Pacific Railroad was crucial for connecting eastern and western Canada.

Latin America: Fragmentation and Political Experimentation

Political unity was short-lived in Latin America. Simón Bolívar (1783–1830), hailed as the region's liberator, worked for the establishment of a large confederation that would provide Latin America with the political, military, and economic strength to resist encroachment by foreign powers. The wars of independence that he led encouraged a sense of solidarity in Latin America. But Bolívar once admitted, "I fear peace more than war," and after the defeat of the common colonial enemy, Latin America fragmented into numerous independent states.

CREOLE ELITES AND POLITICAL INSTABILITY Following the example of the United States, creole elites usually established republics with written constitutions for the newly independent states of Latin America. Yet Latin American leaders had less experience with self-government because Spanish and Portuguese colonial regimes were far more autocratic than was the British imperial government in North America. As a result, several Latin American lands lurched from one constitution to another as leaders struggled to create a machinery of government that would lead to political and social stability.

Creole elites also dominated the newly independent states and effectively prevented mass participation in public affairs. Less than 5 percent of the male population was active in Latin American politics in the nineteenth century, and millions of indigenous peoples lived entirely outside the political system. Those disillusioned with the system, then, had little choice beyond rebellion. To make matters worse, elites were divided by vocation—urban merchants versus rural landowners—as well as by ideology, whether liberalism, conservatism, secularism, or Roman Catholicism.

A Chilean hacienda
www.mhhe.com/bentleybrief2e

CONFLICTS WITH INDIGENOUS PEOPLES One thing elites agreed on was the policy of claiming land for agriculture and ranching by pushing aside indigenous peoples. Conflict was most intense on the plains of Argentina and Chile. During the mid–nineteenth century, as the United States was crushing native resistance to western expansion in North America, Argentine and Chilean forces brought modern weapons to bear in their campaign to conquer the indigenous peoples of the South American plains. By the 1870s colonists had pacified the most productive lands and forced indigenous peoples either to assimilate to Euro-American society or to retreat to marginal lands that were unattractive to cultivators and ranchers.

CAUDILLOS Although creole elites agreed on the policy of conquering native peoples, division in the newly independent states helped *caudillos,* or regional military leaders, come to power in much of Latin America. The wars of independence had lasted well over a decade, and they provided Latin America with military rather than civilian heroes. After independence, military leaders took to the political stage by exploiting the discontent of the masses. One of the most notable caudillos was Juan Manuel de Rosas, who from 1835 to 1852 ruled an Argentina badly divided between the cattle-herding society of the pampas (the interior grasslands) and the urban elite of Buenos Aires. Rosas called for regional autonomy in an attempt to reconcile competing interests, but he worked to centralize the government he usurped. He quelled rebellions, but he did so in bloody fashion: one writer counted 22,404 victims murdered under Rosas's rule.

Rosas did what caudillos did best: he restored order. In doing so, however, he made terror a tool of the government, and he ruled as a despot through his own personal army. Yet although caudillo rule limited freedom and undermined republican ideals, it also sometimes gave rise to liberal opposition movements in favor of democratic forms of government.

MEXICO: WAR AND REFORM Independent Mexico was a case in point. The Mexican-American War caused political turmoil in Mexico and helped the caudillo General Antonio López Santa Anna (1797–1876) come to power. After the defeat and disillusion of the war, however, a liberal reform movement attempted to reshape Mexican society. Led by President Benito Juárez (1806–1872), a Mexican of indigenous ancestry, *La Reforma* of the 1850s aimed to limit the power of the military and the Roman Catholic church in Mexican society. The Constitution of 1857 set forth the ideals of *La Reforma.* It curtailed the prerogatives of priests and military elites, and it guaranteed universal male suffrage and other civil liberties, such as freedom of speech.

MEXICO: REVOLUTION *La Reforma* challenged the conservatism of Mexican elites, who led spirited opposition against it. In fact, divisions were so deep that conservatives forced the Juárez government out of Mexico City until 1861. During those difficult times, Juárez chose to suspend loan payments to foreign powers to lessen Mexico's financial woes, and that led to French, British, and Spanish intervention as Europeans sought to protect their investments in Mexico. France's Napoleon III even sent tens of thousands of troops to Mexico and proclaimed a Mexican empire. However, he was forced to withdraw French forces in 1867, and in the same year a Mexican firing squad killed the man he had appointed emperor, the Austrian archduke Maximilian (1832–1867). Juárez managed to restore a semblance of liberal government, but Mexico remained beset by political divisions.

By the early twentieth century, Mexico was a divided land moving toward civil war. The Mexican revolution (1911–1920), a bitter and bloody conflict, broke out when middle-class Mexicans joined with peasants and workers to overthrow the powerful dictator Porfirio Díaz (1830–1915). The revolt, which attempted to topple the grossly unequal system of

caudillos (KAHW-dee-yohs)
Juan Manuel de Rosas (HWAHN mahn-WEL de roh-sahs)
Buenos Aires (BWE-naws AHY-res)
Benito Juárez (beh-nee-toh WAHR-ez)
Porfirio Díaz (pawr-FEER-eeo DEE-ahs)

MAP 27.3 | Latin America in the nineteenth century. Date is year of independence. Note the many states that emerged from the independence movements early in the century. ***Why was it difficult for large, federated republics, such as the Republic of Colombia, founded by Simón Bolívar, to survive?***

landed estates—whereby fully 95 percent of all peasants remained landless—turned increasingly radical as rebels engaged in guerrilla warfare against government forces. The lower classes took up weapons and followed the revolutionary leaders Emiliano Zapata (1879–1919) and Francisco (Pancho) Villa (1878–1923), charismatic agrarian rebels who organized huge armies fighting for *tierra y libertad* (land and liberty). Zapata, the son of a mestizo peasant, and Villa, the son of a field worker, embodied the ideals and aspirations of the indigenous Mexican masses and enjoyed tremendous popular support. They discredited timid governmental efforts at reform and challenged governmental political control; Zapata himself confiscated hacienda lands and began distributing the lands to the peasants, while Villa attacked and killed U.S. citizens in retaliation for U.S. support of Mexican government officials.

Despite the power and popularity enjoyed by Zapata and Villa, they did not command the resources and wealth of the government. The Mexican revolution came to an end soon

Emiliano Zapata (eh-mee-LYAH-no zuh-PAH-tuh)
Francisco Villa (frahn-SEES-kow VEE-uh)

EMILIANO ZAPATA. | Zapata, hailing from the southern state of Morelos, was the very picture of a revolutionary leader, heavily armed and sporting his dashing, trademark moustache. ***In what ways did Zapata's clothing reflect his Mexican identity?***

after government forces ambushed and killed Zapata in 1919. Villa likewise was assassinated, on his ranch in 1923. Government forces regained control over a battered and devastated Mexico: as many as two million Mexicans may have died in the revolution. Although radicals such as Zapata and Villa were ultimately defeated, the Mexican Constitution of 1917 had already addressed some of the concerns of the revolutionaries by providing for land redistribution, universal suffrage, state-supported education, minimum wages and maximum hours for workers, and restrictions on foreign ownership of Mexican land and resources.

In the form of division, rebellion, caudillo rule, and civil war, instability and conflict plagued Latin America throughout the nineteenth century. Many Latin American peoples lacked education, profitable employment, and political representation. Simón Bolívar himself once said that "independence is the only blessing we have gained at the expense of all the rest."

AMERICAN ECONOMIC DEVELOPMENT

During the nineteenth and early twentieth centuries, two principal influences—mass migration and British investment—shaped economic development throughout the Americas. But American states reacted in different ways to migration and foreign investment. The United States and Canada absorbed waves of migrants, exploited British capital, built industrial societies, and established economic independence. The fragmented states of Latin America were unable to follow suit, as they struggled with the legacies of colonialism, slavery, and economic dependence on single export crops. Throughout the Americas, however, life and labor for freed slaves, migrants, or industrial workers often proved arduous and at times heartbreaking, even as these American workers contributed to the economic development of the region.

Migration to the Americas

Underpinning the economic development of the Americas was the mass migration of European and Asian peoples to the United States, Canada, and Latin America. Gold discoveries in California and Canada drew prospectors hoping to make a quick fortune, but outnumbering gold prospectors were millions of European and Asian migrants who made their way to the factories, railroad construction sites, and plantations of the Americas. Following them were others who offered the support services that made life for migrant workers more comfortable and at the same time transformed the ethnic and cultural landscape of the Americas.

PSI img Immigrants arriving by ship www.mhhe.com/bentleybrief2e

INDUSTRIAL MIGRANTS After the mid–nineteenth century, European migrants flocked to North America, where they filled the factories of the growing industrial economy of the United States. Their lack of skills made them attractive to industrialists seeking workers to operate machinery or perform heavy labor at low wages. By keeping labor costs down, migrants helped increase the profitability and fuel the expansion of U.S. industry. In the 1850s alone European migrants to the United States numbered 2.3 million—almost as many as had crossed the Atlantic during the half century from 1800 to 1850—and the volume of migration surged until the early twentieth century. In the first half of the century, migrants came mostly from Ireland, Scotland, Germany, and Scandinavia to escape high rents and indebtedness. By the late nineteenth century, most European migrants came from southern and eastern Europe and included Poles, Russian Jews, Slavs, Italians, Greeks, and Portuguese. Without their labor, the remarkable industrial expansion that the United States experienced in the late nineteenth century would have been inconceivable.

Chinese migration grew rapidly after the 1840s, when British gunboats opened China to foreign influences. Between 1852 and 1875 some two hundred thousand Chinese migrated to California. Some, like Fatt Hing Chin, negotiated their own passage, but most

Immigrants to the United States. These immigrants catch their first glimpse of the Statue of Liberty as they approach New York Harbor. ***What might these immigrants have been thinking as they completed their long journeys?***

traveled on indentured labor contracts that required them to cultivate crops or work on the Central Pacific Railroad. An additional five thousand Chinese entered Canada to search for gold in British Columbia or work on the Canadian Pacific Railroad.

PLANTATION MIGRANTS Whereas migrants to the United States contributed to the development of an industrial society, those who went to Latin American lands mostly worked on agricultural plantations. Some Europeans figured among these migrants. About four million Italians sought opportunities in Argentina in the 1880s and 1890s, for example, and the Brazilian government paid Italian migrants to cross the Atlantic and work for coffee growers after the abolition of slavery there (1888).

Other migrants who worked on plantations in the western hemisphere came from Asia. More than fifteen thousand indentured laborers from China worked in the sugarcane fields of Cuba during the nineteenth century, and Indian migrants traveled to Jamaica, Trinidad, Tobago, and Guyana. Laborers from both China and Japan migrated to Peru, where they worked on cotton plantations, mined guano deposits, and helped build railroad lines. After the middle of the nineteenth century, expanding U.S. influence in the Pacific islands also led to Chinese, Japanese, Filipino, and Korean migrations to Hawai`i, where planters sought indentured laborers to tend sugarcane. About twenty-five thousand Chinese went to Hawai`i during the 1850s and 1860s, and later 180,000 Japanese also made their way to island plantations.

THE RAILROAD. | In this lithograph of Frances F. Palmer's well-known painting *American Express Train* (ca. 1864), the railroad demonstrates its domination of the natural landscape and its role as the harbinger of change and industry.

Economic Expansion in the United States

BRITISH CAPITAL British investment capital in the United States proved crucial to the early stages of industrial development by helping businesspeople establish a textile industry. In the late nineteenth century, it also helped spur a vast expansion of U.S. industry by funding entrepreneurs who opened coal and iron ore mines, built iron and steel factories, and constructed railroad lines. The flow of investment monies was a consequence of Britain's own industrialization, which generated enormous wealth and created a need for investors to find profitable outlets for their funds.

RAILROADS Perhaps the most important economic development of the later nineteenth century was the construction of railroad lines that linked all U.S. regions and helped create an integrated national economy. Because of its enormous size and environmental diversity, the United States offered an abundance of natural resources for industrial exploitation. But vast distances made it difficult to maintain close economic ties between regions until a boom in railroad construction created a dense transportation, communication, and distribution network. Before the Civil War the United States had about 50,000 kilometers (31,000 miles) of railroad lines, most of them short routes east of the Mississippi River. By 1900 there were more than 320,000 kilometers (200,000 miles) of track, and the American rail network stretched from coast to coast.

Railroads decisively influenced American economic development. They provided cheap transportation for agricultural commodities, manufactured goods, and individual travelers. Railroads hauled grain, beef, and hogs from the plains states, cotton and tobacco from the south, lumber from the northwest, iron and steel from Pittsburgh, and finished products from the eastern industrial cities. Quite apart from the transportation services they provided, railroads spurred the development of other industries: they required huge amounts of coal, wood, glass, and rubber, and by the 1880s some 75 percent of U.S. steel went to the railroad industry. Railroads also required the development of new managerial skills to operate large, complicated businesses with multiple employees.

SPACE AND TIME Railroads led to drastic changes in the landscape. Indeed, the westward expansion driven by the railroad led to large-scale land clearing and the extension of farming and mining lands and brought about both human suffering for indigenous peoples and environmental damage through soil erosion and pollution. Railroads even shaped the American sense of time. Until rapid and regular rail transportation became available, communities set their clocks by the sun. As a result, New York time was eleven minutes and forty-five seconds behind Boston time. Those differences in local sun times created scheduling nightmares as well as the potential for train accidents. To simplify matters, in 1883 railroad companies divided the North American continent into four zones in which all railroad clocks read precisely the same time. The general public quickly adopted "railroad time," and in 1918 the U.S. government legally established the four time zones as the national standard.

ECONOMIC GROWTH Led by railroads, the U.S. economy expanded at a blistering pace between 1870 and 1900. Inventors designed new products and brought them to market: electric lights, telephones, typewriters, phonographs, film photography, motion picture cameras, and electric motors all made their appearance during this era. Indeed, by the early twentieth century the United States had emerged as one of the world's major industrial powers.

Canadian Prosperity

British investment deeply influenced the development of the Canadian as well as the U.S. economy in the nineteenth and early twentieth centuries. Canadian leaders, like U.S. leaders, took advantage of British capital to industrialize without allowing their economy to fall under British control.

THE NATIONAL POLICY After the establishment of the Dominion, politicians started a program of economic development known as the National Policy. The idea was to attract migrants, protect nascent industries through tariffs, and build national transportation systems. The centerpiece of the transportation network was the transcontinental Canadian Pacific Railroad, built largely with British investment capital and completed in 1885. The Canadian Pacific Railroad opened the western prairie lands to commerce, stimulated the development of other industries, and promoted the emergence of a Canadian national economy. The National Policy created some violent altercations with indigenous peoples who resisted encroachment on their lands and with trappers who resented disruption of their way of life, but it also promoted economic growth and independence.

As a result of the National Policy, Canada experienced booming agricultural, mineral, and industrial production in the late nineteenth and early twentieth centuries. Canadian population surged as a result of both migration and natural increase. Migrants flocked to Canada's shores from Asia and especially from Europe: between 1903 and 1914 some 2.7 million eastern European migrants settled in Canada. Fueled in part by this population growth, Canadian economic expansion took place on the foundation of rapidly increasing wheat production and the extraction of rich mineral resources, including gold, silver, copper, nickel, and asbestos. Industrialists also tapped Canadian rivers to produce the hydroelectric power necessary for manufacturing.

U.S. INVESTMENT Canada remained wary of its powerful neighbor to the south but did not keep U.S. economic influence entirely at bay. By 1918, Americans owned 30 percent of all Canadian industry, and thereafter the U.S. and Canadian economies became increasingly interdependent. Canada began to undergo rapid industrialization after the early twentieth century, as the province of Ontario benefited from the spillover of U.S. industry in the northeast.

Latin American Dependence

Latin American states did not undergo industrialization or enjoy economic development as did the United States and Canada. Colonial legacies are part of the explanation. Even when Spain and Portugal controlled the trade and investment policies of their American colonies, their home economies were unable to supply sufficient quantities of the manufactured goods that colonial markets demanded. As a result, they opened the colonies to British, French, and German trade, which in turn snuffed out local industries that could not compete with British, French, and German producers of inexpensive manufactured goods. Moreover, both in colonial times and after independence, Latin American elites

THINKING ABOUT *Traditions*

TRADITIONS IN THE AMERICAS IN THE AGE OF INDEPENDENCE. During the nineteenth century, the United States and Canada benefited from foreign financial investment while remaining in control of their economies, while Latin American nations became increasingly dependent on foreign powers as a result of similar investment. In what ways can the traditions established by differing colonial powers prior to independence account for this disparity in the postindependence period?

retained control over local economies. Elites profited handsomely from European trade and investment and thus had little incentive to work toward economic diversification.

BRITISH INVESTMENT Foreign influence in Latin America generally took the form of investment, which brought handsome profits and considerable control over Latin American economic affairs. In Argentina, for example, British investors encouraged the development of cattle and sheep ranching. After the 1860s and the invention of refrigerated cargo ships, meat became Argentina's largest export. British investors controlled the industry and reaped the profits, however, as Argentina became Britain's principal supplier of meat.

ATTEMPTED INDUSTRIALIZATION In a few lands, ruling elites made attempts to encourage industrialization, but with only limited success. The most notable of those efforts came when the dictatorial general Porfirio Díaz ruled Mexico (1876–1911). Díaz represented the interests of large landowners, wealthy merchants, and foreign investors. Under his rule, railroad tracks and telegraph lines connected all parts of Mexico and the production of mineral resources surged. A small steel industry produced railroad track and construction materials, and entrepreneurs also established glass, chemical, and textile industries. The capital, Mexico City, underwent a transformation during the Díaz years: it acquired paved streets, streetcar lines, and electric streetlights. But the profits from Mexican enterprises did not support continuing industrial development. Instead, they went into the pockets of the Mexican oligarchy and foreign investors who supported Díaz while a growing and discontented urban working class seethed with resentment at low wages, long hours, and foreign managers. Even as agriculture, railroad construction, and mining were booming, the standard of living for average Mexicans was declining in the late nineteenth century. Frustration with that state of affairs helps explain the sudden outbreak of violent revolution in 1911.

A coffee hacienda
www.mhhe.com/bentleybrief2e

Despite a large proportion of foreign and especially British control, Latin American economies expanded rapidly in the late nineteenth century. Exports drove this growth: copper and silver from Mexico, bananas from Central America, rubber and coffee from Brazil, beef and wheat from Argentina, copper from Chile, and tobacco and sugar from Cuba. Other areas in the world also developed many of these same products for export, however, and competition for markets tended to drive prices down. As in the United States and Canada, foreign investment in Latin America provided capital for development, but unlike the situation in the northern lands, control over industries and exports remained in foreign hands. Latin American economies were thus subject to decisions made in the interests of foreign investors, and unstable governments could do little in the face of strong foreign intervention. Controlled by the very elites who profited from foreign intervention at the expense of their citizens, Latin American governments helped promote the region's economic dependence, despite growth in industrial and export economies.

American Cultural and Social Diversity

Much of the allure of the Americas derived from their vast spaces and diverse populations. While diversity distinguished the Americas, it also provided abundant fuel for conflicts between ethnic groups, social classes, and those segregated by race or gender. The social and cultural diversity of American societies challenged their ability to achieve cultural cohesion as well as democratically inclusive states. The lingering legacies of European conquest, slavery, migration, and patriarchy highlighted contradictions between the Enlightenment ideals of freedom and equality and the realities of life for native and African-American peoples as well as recent migrants and women. In efforts to maintain their own position and preserve social stability, the dominant political forces in the Americas often repressed demands for recognition by dispossessed groups.

Multicultural Society in the United States

By the late nineteenth century, the United States had become a boisterous multicultural society whose population included indigenous peoples, Euro-American settlers, African-American laborers, and growing numbers of migrants from Europe and Asia. The poet Walt Whitman described the United States as "not merely a nation but a teeming nation of nations." Yet political and economic power rested almost exclusively with white male elites of European ancestry. The United States experienced tension and occasional conflict as members of various constituencies worked for dignity, prosperity, and a voice in society.

NATIVE PEOPLES As they expanded to the west, Euro-American settlers and ranchers pushed indigenous peoples onto reservations. Begrudging Native Americans even those meager lands, the United States embarked in the latter half of the nineteenth century on a policy designed to reduce native autonomy even further through laws and reforms aimed at assimilating tribes to the white way of life. The U.S. government and private citizens acted to undermine or destroy outright the bases of native cultural traditions. For example, government officials removed native children from their families and tribes and enrolled them in white-controlled boarding schools. These schools, such as the Carlisle Indian School and the Toledo Indian School, illustrated the extent to which white society sought to eliminate tribal influences and inculcate Christian, U.S. values. Tribal languages as well as native dress and hair fashions were banned, further distancing the children from their cultures. Native Americans, however, resisted those forms of assimilation, and over the following decades tribes rebuilt and reaffirmed native identities.

FREED SLAVES The Civil War ended slavery, but it did not bring about equality for freed slaves and their African-American descendants. In an effort to establish a place for freed slaves in American society, northern forces sent armies of occupation to the southern states and forced them to undergo a program of social and political reconstruction (1867–1877). They extended civil rights to freed slaves and provided black men with voting rights. People in southern states elected biracial governments for the first time in U.S. history, and freed slaves participated actively in the political affairs of the republic.

After Reconstruction, however, the armies of occupation went home, and a violent backlash soon dismantled the reforms of Reconstruction. By the turn of the century, U.S. blacks faced violence and intimidation when they tried to vote. Southern states fashioned a rigidly segregated society that deprived the African-American population of educational, economic, and political opportunities. Although freedom was better than slavery, it was far different from the hopeful visions of the slaves who had won their emancipation.

WOMEN Even before the Civil War, a small but growing women's movement had emerged in the United States. At the Seneca Falls Convention in 1848, feminists issued a declaration arguing "that all men and women are created equal" and demanding equal political and economic rights. Women fought for equal rights throughout the nineteenth century, and new opportunities for education and employment offered alternatives to marriage and domesticity. Women's colleges, reform activism, and professional industrial jobs allowed some women to pursue careers over marriage. Yet meaningful economic and political opportunities for women awaited the twentieth century.

MIGRANTS Between 1840 and 1914 some twenty-five million European migrants landed on American shores, and in the late nineteenth century most of them hailed from southern and eastern European countries. Migrants introduced new foods, music, dances, holidays, sports, and languages to U.S. society and contributed to the cultural diversity of the western hemisphere. Yet white, native-born citizens of the United States began to feel swamped by the arrival of so many migrants. Indeed, concerns about growing numbers of migrants with different cultural and social traditions eventually led to the exclusion of

Assimilation programs for Native Americans. | The Apache youths at the Carlisle Indian School offer stark faces to the camera, suggesting their discontent with reform efforts directed at assimilation through education.

new arrivals from Asian lands: the U.S. government ordered a complete halt to migration from China in 1882 and Japan in 1908.

Canadian Cultural Contrasts

ETHNIC DIVERSITY British and French settlers each viewed themselves as Canada's founding people. That cleavage, which profoundly influenced Canadian political development, masked much greater cultural and ethnic diversity in Canada. French and British settlers displaced the indigenous peoples, who remain a significant minority of Canada's population today. Slavery likewise left a mark on Canada. Slavery was legal in the British empire until 1833, and many early settlers brought their slaves with them to Canada. After emancipation, blacks in Canada were free but not equal, segregated and isolated from the political and cultural mainstream. Chinese migrants also came to Canada: lured by gold rushes such as the Fraser River rush of 1858 and by opportunities to work on the Canadian Pacific Railway in the 1880s, Chinese migrants lived mostly in segregated Chinatowns in the cities of British Columbia, and like blacks they had little voice in public affairs. Between 1896 and 1914 three million migrants from Britain, the United States, and eastern Europe arrived in Canada, bringing even greater ethnic diversity with them.

Despite the heterogeneity of Canada's population, communities descended from British and French settlers dominated Canadian society, and conflict between the two communities was the most prominent source of ethnic tension throughout the nineteenth and twentieth centuries. After 1867, as British Canadians led the effort to settle the Northwest Territories and incorporate them into the Dominion, frictions between the two groups intensified. Westward expansion brought British Canadian settlers and cultivators into conflict with French Canadian fur traders, lumberjacks, and métis of mixed French and Indian ancestry.

THE MÉTIS AND LOUIS RIEL Indeed, a major outbreak of civil strife took place in the 1870s and 1880s. Native peoples and métis had moved west throughout the nineteenth century to preserve their land and trading rights, but the drive of British Canadians to the west threatened them. Louis Riel (1844–1885), who was himself a métis, emerged as the leader of the métis and indigenous peoples of western Canada. Of particular importance was his leadership in the resistance to the Canadian Pacific Railroad—and the white settlement it promised to bring—during the 1880s. In 1885 he organized a military force of métis and native peoples in the Saskatchewan river country and led an insurrection known as the Northwest Rebellion. Canadian forces quickly subdued the makeshift army, and government authorities executed Riel for treason. Although the Northwest Rebellion never had a chance of success, the execution of Riel nonetheless threatened to undermine the beginnings of Canadian national unity and foreshadowed a long term of cultural conflict between Canadians of British, French, and indigenous ancestry.

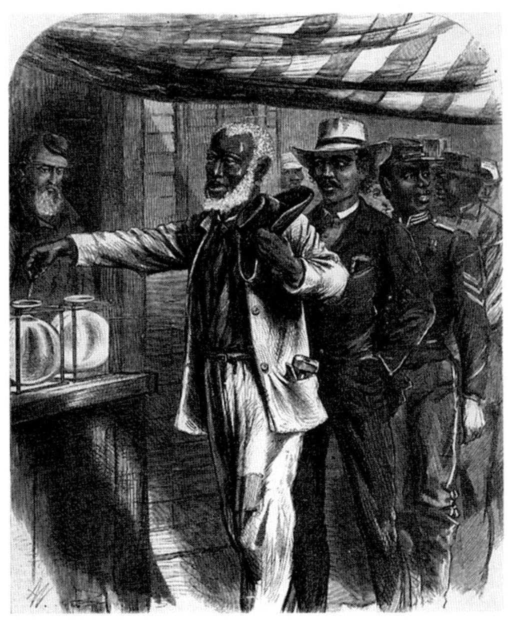

VOTING RIGHTS FOR FREE BLACKS. A lithograph from *Harper's Weekly* after the Civil War. An artisan, a middle-class African-American, and a black Union soldier are in the process of voting, perhaps for the first time in their lives. ***What message might this image have been trying to convey?***

Ethnicity, Identity, and Gender in Latin America

The heritage of Spanish and Portuguese colonialism and the legacy of slavery inclined Latin American societies toward the establishment of hierarchical distinctions based on ethnicity and color. At the top of society stood the creoles, individuals of European ancestry born in the Americas; indigenous peoples, freed slaves, and their black descendants occupied the lowest rungs of the social ladder. In between were various groups of mixed ancestry. Although most Latin American states ended the legal recognition of these groups, the distinctions themselves persisted and limited their opportunities.

MIGRATION AND CULTURAL DIVERSITY Large-scale migration brought cultural diversity to Latin America in the nineteenth century. Indentured laborers who went from Asian lands to Peru, Brazil, Cuba, and other Caribbean destinations carried with them many of their native cultural practices. When their numbers were relatively large, as in the case of Indian migrants to Trinidad and Tobago, they formed distinctive communities in which they observed their inherited cultural and social traditions. Migration of European workers to Argentina brought a lively diversity to the capital of Buenos Aires, which was perhaps the most cosmopolitan city of nineteenth-century Latin America. With its broad avenues, smart boutiques, and handsome buildings graced with wrought iron, Buenos Aires enjoyed a reputation as "the Paris of the Americas."

GAUCHOS One prominent symbol of Latin American identity was Argentina's gauchos (cowboys). Most gauchos were of mixed-race ancestry, but there were also white and black gauchos. In fact, anyone who adopted gaucho ways became a gaucho, and gaucho society acquired an ethnic egalitarianism rarely found elsewhere in Latin America. Gauchos were most prominent in the Argentine pampas, but their cultural practices linked them to the cowboys, or vaqueros, found throughout the Americas. As pastoralists herding cattle and horses on the pampas, gauchos stood apart from both the indigenous peoples and the growing urban and agricultural elites who gradually displaced them with large landholdings and cattle ranches that spread to the pampas.

MALE DOMINATION Even more than in the United States and Canada, male domination was a central characteristic of Latin American society in the nineteenth century. Women could not vote or hold office, nor could they work or manage estates without permission from their male guardians. In rural areas, women were liable to rough treatment

gauchos (GAHW-chohs)
vaqueros (bah-KEH-rohs)

THINKING ABOUT *Encounters*

ENCOUNTERS IN THE AMERICAS IN THE AGE OF INDEPENDENCE. In the nineteenth century, most nations in the Americas were composed of a wide variety of indigenous, European, African, Asian, and mixed-race peoples. Why did encounters between these varied peoples often lead to conflict and tension, and how did ruling elites tend to manage their diverse societies?

SOURCES FROM THE PAST

The Meaning of Freedom for an Ex-Slave

Even before the conclusion of the Civil War brought slavery to an end in the United States, Jourdan Anderson had taken the opportunity to run away and claim his freedom. After the war his former master, Colonel P. H. Anderson, wrote a letter asking him to return to work on his Tennessee plantation. In responding from his new home in Dayton, Ohio, Anderson respectfully referred to the colonel as "my old master" and addressed him as "sir." Yet Anderson's letter makes it clear that his family's freedom and welfare were his principal concerns.

I want to know particularly what the good chance is you propose to give me. I am doing tolerably well here; I get $25 a month, with victuals and clothing; have a comfortable home for Mandy (the folks here call her Mrs. Anderson), and the children, Milly, Jane and Grundy, go to school and are learning well; the teacher says Grundy has a head for a preacher. They go to Sunday-School, and Mandy and me attend church regularly. We are kindly treated; sometimes we overhear others saying, "Them colored people were slaves" down in Tennessee. The children feel hurt when they hear such remarks, but I tell them it was no disgrace in Tennessee to belong to Col. Anderson. Many darkies would have been proud, as I used to was, to call you master. Now, if you will write and say what wages you will give me, I will be better able to decide whether it would be to my advantage to move back again.

As to my freedom, which you say I can have, there is nothing to be gained on that score, as I got my freepapers in 1864 from the Provost-Marshal-General of the Department at Nashville. Mandy says she would be afraid to go back without some proof that you are sincerely disposed to treat us justly and kindly—and we have concluded to test your sincerity by asking you to send us our wages for the time we served you. This will make us forget and forgive old scores, and rely on your justice and friendship in the future. I served you faithfully for thirty-two years and Mandy twenty years. At $25 a month for me, and $2 a week for Mandy, our earnings would amount to $11,680. Add to this the interest for the time our wages has been kept back and deduct what you paid for our clothing and three doctor's visits to me, and pulling a tooth for Mandy, and the balance will show what we are in justice entitled to. Please send the money by Adams Express, in care of V. Winters, esq, Dayton, Ohio. If you fail to pay us for faithful labors in the past we can have little faith in your promises in the future. We trust the good Maker has opened your eyes to the wrongs which you and your fathers have done to me and my fathers, in making us toil for you for generations without recompense. Here I draw my wages every Saturday night, but in Tennessee there was never any pay day for the negroes any more than for the horses and cows. Surely there will be a day of reckoning for those who defraud the laborer of his hire.

In answering this letter please state if there would be any safety for my Milly and Jane, who are now grown up and both good-looking girls. You know how it was with poor Matilda and Catherine. I would rather stay here and starve and die if it comes to that than have my girls brought to shame by the violence and wickedness of their young masters. You will also please state if there has been any schools opened for the colored children in your neighborhood, the great desire of my life now is to give my children an education, and have them form virtuous habits.

■ In what clever ways does Jourdan Anderson test the seriousness of his former owner's offer of employment, and what does his approach say about the meaning of black freedom?

SOURCE: Leon F. Litwack. *Been in the Storm So Long: The Aftermath of Slavery.* New York: Knopf, 1979, pp. 334–35.

and assault by gauchos and other men steeped in the values of *machismo*—a social ethic that honored male strength, courage, aggressiveness, assertiveness, and cunning. Women did carve spaces for themselves outside or alongside the male world of machismo, and this was especially true in the home and in the marketplace, where Latin American women exerted great influence and control. In addition, although Latin American lands did not generate a strong women's movement, they did begin to expand educational opportunities for girls and young women after the mid–nineteenth century. In large cities most girls received some formal schooling, and women usually filled teaching positions in the public schools that proliferated throughout Latin America in the late nineteenth century.

SUMMARY

After gaining independence from European colonial powers, the states of the western hemisphere worked to build stable and prosperous societies. The independent American states faced difficult challenges as they sought to construct viable societies on the Enlightenment principles of freedom, equality, and constitutional government. The United States and Canada built large federal societies in North America, whereas a series of smaller states governed affairs in Latin America. Throughout the hemisphere descendants of European settlers subdued indigenous American peoples and built societies dominated by Euro-American peoples. They established agricultural economies, exploited natural resources, and in some lands launched processes of industrialization. They accepted streams of European and Asian migrants, who contributed to American cultural diversity. All American lands experienced tensions arising from social, economic, cultural, and ethnic differences, which led occasionally to violent civil conflict and often to smoldering resentments and grievances. The making of independent American societies was not a smooth process, but it reflected the increasing interdependence of all the world's peoples.

STUDY TERMS

Abraham Lincoln (539)
Antonio Lopez Santa Anna (542)
Battle of Little Big Horn (538)
Benito Juárez (542)
British North America Act (540)
Canadian Pacific railroad (547)
caudillos (542)
Emancipation Proclamation (539)
Emiliano Zapata (543)
Francisco (Pancho) Villa (543)
gauchos (551)
Indian Removal Act of 1830 (537)
John A. Macdonald (540)
Juan Manuel de Rosas (542)
La Reforma (542)
manifest destiny (537)
massacre at Wounded Knee (538)
Mexican-American War (538)
National Policy (547)
Northwest Rebellion (551)
Porfirio Díaz (542)
railroad time (547)
Reconstruction (549)
Seneca Falls Convention (549)
Trail of Tears (537)
United States Civil War (539)
War of 1812 (541)

FOR FURTHER READING

Victor Bulmer-Thomas, John H. Coatsworth, and Robert Cortés Conde, eds. *The Cambridge Economic History of Latin America. Vol. I: The Colonial Era and the Short Nineteenth Century.* Cambridge, 2006. Scholarly collection of essays that outlines the region's main economic trends and developments.

Colin G. Calloway. *First Peoples: A Documentary Survey of American Indian History.* Boston, 1999. A fine text on native American history, written by a knowledgeable scholar in the field.

William Cronon. *Nature's Metropolis: Chicago and the Great West.* New York, 1991. A valuable study exploring the role of Chicago in the economic development of the American west.

Ellen C. DuBois. *Feminism and Suffrage: The Emergence of an Independent Women's Movement in America, 1848–1869.* Ithaca, 1984. Traces the rise and character of the U.S. women's movement in the nineteenth century.

Tom Holm. *The Great Confusion in Indian Affairs: Native Americans and Whites in the Progressive Era.* Austin, 2005. Study of Native American resistance to the American government's attempts at subjugation.

Patricia Nelson Limerick. *The Legacy of Conquest: The Unbroken Past of the American West.* New York, 1987. A provocative work exploring the influences of race, class, and gender in the conquest of the American west.

Leon F. Litwack. *Been in the Storm So Long: The Aftermath of Slavery.* New York, 1979. The best study of the promises and perils of life for freed slaves after the U.S. Civil War.

J. R. Miller. *Skyscrapers Hide the Heavens: A History of Indian-White Relations in Canada.* Toronto, 1989. An important study of Canadian policies toward indigenous peoples.

Walter Nugent. *Crossings: The Great Transatlantic Migrations, 1870–1914.* Bloomington, 1992. Provides an overview and analysis of the mass migrations to North America in the nineteenth and twentieth centuries.

Ronald Takaki. *A Different Mirror: A History of Multicultural America.* Boston, 1993. A spirited account of the contributions made by peoples of European, African, Asian, and Native American ancestry to the modern American society.

The Building of Global Empires

28

ew Europeans had traveled to south Africa by the mid–nineteenth century, but the discovery of diamonds and rich gold deposits brought European settlers to the region in large numbers. Among the arrivals was Cecil John Rhodes, an eighteen-year-old student at Oxford University, who in 1871 went to south Africa in search of a climate that would relieve his tuberculosis. While there, Rhodes bought claims in the diamond fields, and he bought the rights to others' claims when they looked promising. By 1889, at age thirty-five, he had almost monopolized diamond mining in south Africa, and he controlled 90 percent of the world's diamond production. With ample financial backing, Rhodes also built up a healthy stake in the gold-mining business and entered politics, serving as prime minister (1890–1896) of the British Cape Colony.

Yet Rhodes's ambitions went far beyond business and local politics. In his vision the Cape Colony would serve as a base of operations for the extension of British control to all of Africa. Under Rhodes's guidance, Cape Colony annexed Bechuanaland (modern Botswana) in 1885, and in 1895 it added Rhodesia (modern Zambia and Zimbabwe) to its holdings. But Rhodes's plan did not stop with Africa: he urged the expansion of the British empire until it embraced all the world, including the United States of America. Rhodes considered British imperial expansion as a duty to humankind: "We are the finest race in the world," he said in 1877, "and the more of the world we inhabit, the better it is for the human race." In his sense of superiority to other peoples, his compulsion to expand, and his craving to extract wealth from distant parts of the world, Rhodes represented well the views of European imperialists who carved the world into colonies during the nineteenth century.

From the days of ancient Mesopotamia and Egypt to the present, strong societies have often sought to dominate their weaker neighbors by subjecting them to imperial rule. Yet during the second half of the nineteenth century, a handful of western European states wrote a new chapter in the history of imperialism. Strong nationalist sentiments enabled them to mobilize their populations for purposes of overseas expansion. Industrialization equipped them with the most effective tools and the most lethal weapons available anywhere in the world. Three centuries of experience with maritime trade in Asia, Africa, the Americas, and Oceania provided them with unparalleled knowledge of the world and its peoples. With those

❮ A British husband and wife sit at the breakfast table attended by Indian servants.

Cecil Rhodes (see-sihl rhohdz)
Bechuanaland (bech-oo-AH-nuh-land)

CHRONOLOGY

1805–1848	Reign of Muhammad Ali in Egypt
1808–1839	Reign of Sultan Mahmud II
1809–1882	Life of Charles Darwin
1816–1882	Life of Count Joseph Arthur de Gobineau
1824	Founding of Singapore by Thomas Stamford Raffles
1839–1842	Opium War
1839–1876	Tanzimat era
1850–1864	Taiping rebellion
1853–1902	Life of Cecil Rhodes
1857	Sepoy Rebellion
1859–1869	Construction of the Suez Canal
1860–1864	Land wars in New Zealand
1860–1895	Self-Strengthening Movement
1884–1885	Berlin West Africa Conference
1894–1895	Sino-Japanese War
1897–1901	Term of office of U.S. president William McKinley
1898–1899	Spanish-Cuban-American War
1899–1902	South African War (Boer War)
1901–1909	Term of office of U.S. president Theodore Roosevelt
1904–1905	Russo-Japanese War
1904–1914	Construction of the Panama Canal
1905–1906	Maji-Maji rebellion
1908–1918	Young Turk Era

advantages, western European peoples conquered foreign armies, dominated foreign economies, and imposed their hegemony throughout the world. Toward the end of the century, the United States and Japan joined European states as imperial powers.

The establishment of global empires had far-reaching effects. In many ways, imperialism tightened links between the world's societies. Imperial powers encouraged trade between dominant states and their overseas colonies, for example, and they organized mass migrations of laborers to work in agricultural and industrial ventures. Yet imperialism also fostered divisions between the world's peoples. Powerful tools, deadly weapons, and global hegemony tempted European peoples to consider themselves superior to their subjects throughout the world: modern racism is one of the legacies of imperialism. Another effect of imperialism was the development of both resistance and nationalism in subject lands. Thus, although formal empires almost entirely dissolved in the twentieth century, the influence of global imperialism continues to shape the contemporary world.

FOUNDATIONS OF EMPIRE

In nineteenth-century Europe, proponents of empire advanced a variety of political, economic, and cultural arguments to justify the conquest and control of foreign lands. The imperialist ventures that they promoted enjoyed dramatic success partly because of the increasingly sophisticated technologies developed by European industry.

Motives of Imperialism

MODERN IMPERIALISM The building of empires is an old story in world history. By the nineteenth century, however, European observers recognized that empires of their day were different from those of earlier times. Accordingly, about midcentury they began to speak of *imperialism,* and by the 1880s the recently coined term had made its way into popular speech and writing throughout western Europe. In contemporary usage, imperialism refers to the domination over subject lands in the larger world. Sometimes that domination came through formal imperialism, which involved military conquest and the establishment of political control. Frequently, however, it arose through what is known as informal imperialism: that is, the domination of trade, investment, and business activities that enabled imperial powers to profit from subject societies and influence their affairs without going to the trouble of exercising direct political control.

MODERN COLONIALISM Like the building of empires, the establishment of colonies in foreign lands is a practice dating from ancient times. In modern times, however, colonialism refers not just to the settlement of colonists in new lands but also to the political, social, economic, and cultural

CECIL RHODES. | Here, Rhodes rests in the goldfields of South Africa, about 1897.

structures that enabled imperial powers to dominate subject lands. In some places, such as North America, Chile, Argentina, Australia, New Zealand, and South Africa, European powers established settler colonies populated largely by migrants from the home societies. Yet contemporary scholars also speak of European colonies in India, southeast Asia, and sub-Saharan Africa, even though European migrants did not settle there in large numbers. European agents, officials, and businesspeople effectively turned such places into colonies by controlling their domestic and foreign policies, integrating local economies into the network of global capitalism, and promoting European educational and cultural preferences.

ECONOMIC MOTIVES OF IMPERIALISM During the second half of the nineteenth century, many Europeans came to believe that imperial expansion and colonial domination were crucial for the survival of their societies. A wide range of motives encouraged European peoples to launch campaigns of domination, conquest, and control. Some advocates argued that imperialism was in the economic interests of European societies as well as individuals. They pointed out that overseas colonies could serve as reliable sources of raw materials: rubber, tin, and copper were vital industrial products, for example, and by the late nineteenth century petroleum had also become a crucial industrial resource.

POLITICAL MOTIVES OF IMPERIALISM Geopolitical arguments were also important for justifying imperialism. Even if colonies were not economically beneficial, imperialists held that it was crucial for political and military reasons to maintain them. Some overseas colonies occupied strategic sites on the world's sea-lanes, and others offered harbors or supply stations for commercial and naval ships. Advocates of imperialism sought to gain those advantages for their own states and to deny them to rivals.

Imperialism had its uses also for domestic politics. In an age when socialists and communists directly confronted industrialists, European politicians and national leaders sought to defuse social tension and inspire patriotism by focusing public attention on foreign imperialist ventures. Even spiritual motives fostered imperialism. Like the Jesuits in the early modern era, missionaries flocked to African and Asian lands in search of converts to Christianity, and their spiritual campaigns provided a powerful religious justification for imperialism. Furthermore, missionaries often facilitated communications between imperialists and subject peoples, and they sometimes provided European officials with information they needed to maintain control of overseas colonies.

CULTURAL MOTIVES OF IMPERIALISM While missionaries sought to introduce Christianity to subject peoples, their goals were compatible with those of other Europeans who sought to bring them "civilization" in the form of political order and social and cultural enlightenment. French imperialists routinely invoked the *mission civilisatrice* ("civilizing mission") as justification for their expansion into Africa and Asia, and other European powers routinely justified foreign intervention as their duty to civilize "backward" peoples.

Tools of Empire

Even the strongest motives would not have enabled imperialists to impose their rule throughout the world without the powerful technological advantages of industrialization. During the nineteenth century, industrialists devised effective technologies of transportation, communication, and war that enabled European imperialists to have their way in the larger world.

TRANSPORTATION TECHNOLOGIES The most important innovations in transportation involved steamships and railroads. During the 1830s British naval engineers adapted steam power to military uses and built large, ironclad ships equipped with powerful guns. These steamships traveled much faster than any sailing vessel, and as an additional advantage they could ignore the winds and travel in any direction. Because of that, they could travel much farther upriver than sailboats, which enabled imperialists to project power deep into the interior regions of foreign lands.

PSI img The Panama Canal www.mhhe.com/bentleybrief2e

The construction of new canals enhanced the effectiveness of steamships. Both the Suez Canal (constructed 1859–1869) and the Panama Canal (constructed 1904–1914) facilitated the building and maintenance of empires by enabling naval vessels to travel rapidly between the world's seas and oceans. They also lowered the costs of trade between imperial powers and subject lands.

Once imperialists had gained control of overseas lands, railroads helped them to maintain their hegemony and organize local economies to their own advantage. Rail transportation enabled colonial officials and armies to travel quickly through the colonies. It also facilitated trade in raw materials and the distribution of European manufactured goods in the colonies.

MILITARY TECHNOLOGIES European industrialists also churned out enormous quantities of increasingly powerful weapons. By the middle of the nineteenth century, European armies were using breech-loading firearms with rifled bores that were far more accurate and reliable than any other firearm. By the 1870s Europeans were experimenting with rifled machine guns, and in the 1880s they adopted the Maxim gun, a light and powerful weapon that fired eleven bullets per second.

These firearms provided European armies with an arsenal vastly stronger than any other in the world. Accurate rifles and machine guns devastated opposing overseas forces, enabling European armies to impose colonial rule against far more numerous opponents. In 1898, for example, a British army with twenty machine guns and six gunboats encountered a Sudanese force at Omdurman, near Khartoum on the Nile River. During five hours of fighting, the British force lost 368 men, whereas machine guns and explosive charges fired from gunboats killed some 11,000 Sudanese. The battle of Omdurman opened the door for British colonial rule in Sudan.

PSI img The Suez Canal www.mhhe.com/bentleybrief2e

COMMUNICATIONS TECHNOLOGIES Communications also benefited from industrialization. In the 1830s it took as long as two years for a British correspondent to receive a reply to a letter sent to India by sailing ship. By the 1850s, after the introduction of steamships, correspondence could make the round-trip between London and Bombay in four months. With the opening of the Suez Canal in 1869, steamships traveled from Britain to India in less than two weeks.

mission civilisatrice (mee-see-on sih-vihl-ihs-a-trihs)
Omdurman (om-door-MAHN)
Khartoum (khar-TOOM)

SOURCES FROM THE PAST

Rudyard Kipling on the White Man's Burden

Rudyard Kipling lived in northern India for the first six years of his life. He grew up speaking Hindi, and he mixed easily with Indian subjects of the British empire. After attending a boarding school in England, he returned to India in 1882 and became a journalist and writer. Many of his works express his deep enchantment with India, but he also believed strongly in imperial rule. Indeed, he wrote his famous poem titled "The White Man's Burden" to encourage the United States to impose colonial rule in the Philippines. Although recognizing the unpopularity of foreign rule, Kipling considered it a duty to bring order to colonial lands and to serve subject peoples.

Take up the White Man's burden—
 Send forth the best ye breed—
Go bind your sons to exile
 To serve your captives' need;
To wait in heavy harness,
 On fluttered folk and wild—
Your new-caught, sullen peoples,
 Half-devil and half-child.
Take up the White Man's burden—
 In patience to abide,
To veil the threat of terror
 And check the show of pride;
By open speech and simple,
 An hundred times made plain,
To seek another's profit,
 And work for another's gain.
Take up the White Man's burden—
 The savage wars of peace—
Fill full the mouth of Famine
 And bid the sickness cease;
And when your goal is nearest
 The end for others sought,
Watch Sloth and heathen Folly
 Bring all your hope to nought.
Take up the White Man's burden—
 No tawdry rule of kings,
But toil of serf and sweeper—
 The tale of common things.
The ports ye shall not enter,
 The roads ye shall not tread,
Go make them with your living,
 And mark them with your dead.
Take up the White Man's burden—
 And reap his old reward:
The blame of those ye better,
 The hate of those ye guard—
The cry of hosts ye humor
 (Ah, slowly!) toward the light;—
"Why brought ye us from bondage,
 "Our loved Egyptian night?"
Take up the White Man's burden—
 Ye dare not stoop to less—
Nor call too loud on Freedom
 To cloak your weariness;
By all ye cry or whisper,
 By all ye leave or do,
The silent, sullen peoples
 Shall weigh your Gods and you.
Take up the White Man's burden—
 Have done with childish days—
The lightly proffered laurel,
 The easy, ungrudged praise.
Comes now, to search your manhood
 Through all the thankless years,
Cold, edged with dear-bought wisdom,
 The judgment of your peers!

■ **Compare and contrast the sorts of adjectives Kipling uses to describe native peoples as opposed to Europeans; how does his very language usage convey his sense of white superiority?**

SOURCE: Rudyard Kipling. "The White Man's Burden." *McClure's Magazine* 12, no. 4 (1899): 290–91.

The invention of the telegraph made it possible to exchange messages even faster. By 1870 submarine cables carried messages between Britain and India in about five hours. By 1902 cables linked all parts of the British empire throughout the world, and other European states maintained cables to support communications with their own colonies. Their monopoly on telegraphic communications allowed imperial officials to rapidly mobilize forces to deal with troubles, and the telegraph allowed merchants to respond quickly to developments of economic and commercial significance. Rapid communication was an integral structural element of empire.

European Imperialism

Aided by powerful technologies, European states launched an unprecedented round of empire building in the second half of the nineteenth century. Imperial expansion began with the British conquest of India. Competition between imperial powers led to European intrusion into central Asia, the establishment of colonies in southeast Asia, and interference in the Ottoman and Qing empires in southwest and east Asia. Fearful that rivals might gain control over remaining regions, European states embarked on a campaign of frenzied expansion in the 1880s that brought almost all of Africa and Pacific Ocean territories into their empires.

The British Empire in India

The British empire in south Asia and southeast Asia grew out of the mercantile activities of the English East India Company, which enjoyed a monopoly on English trade with India. The East India Company obtained permission from the Mughal emperors of India to build fortified posts on the coastlines. In the seventeenth century, company merchants traded mostly for Indian pepper and cotton, Chinese silk and porcelain, and spices from southeast Asia. During the eighteenth century, tea and coffee became the most prominent trade items, and European consumers acquired a permanent taste for both beverages.

COMPANY RULE After the death of the emperor Aurangzeb in 1707, the Mughal state entered a period of decline. The East India Company took advantage of Mughal weakness to strengthen and expand its trading posts. In the 1750s company merchants began campaigns of outright conquest in India, largely to protect their commercial interests. From their forts at Calcutta, Madras, and Bombay, the merchants extended their authority inland and won official rights to rule from the Mughal emperors and local authorities. They enforced their rule with armies composed mostly of Indian troops known as sepoys.

In 1857, following widespread campaigns of conquest that left most of the subcontinent under British control, the Indian sepoys of the Bengal army revolted. The Sepoy Rebellion, as it became known, was quickly augmented by civilian peasants and disgruntled elites in north-central India who were deeply dissatisfied with recent British policies regarding taxation and law. To regain control, the British waged a bloody campaign of retribution in which many thousands of Indians—including civilians not directly involved in the rebellion—lost their lives through summary hangings and the destruction of villages. Once order was restored in 1858, the British government abolished the East India Company and assumed direct rule over the subcontinent.

BRITISH IMPERIAL RULE Under the new administration, Queen Victoria (reigned 1837–1901) assigned responsibility for Indian policy to the newly established office of secretary of state for India. A viceroy represented British royal authority and administered the colony through an elite Indian civil service staffed almost exclusively by the English. Indians served in low-level bureaucratic positions, but British officials formulated all domestic and foreign policy in India.

Under both company rule and direct colonial administration, British rule transformed India. To profit from India's enormous size and wealth, British officials cleared forests and encouraged the cultivation of crops, such as tea, coffee, and opium, that were especially valuable trade items. They restructured landholdings and ensured that land taxes

Qing (ching)
Mughal (MOO-guhl)

Sepoy Rebellion of 1857. | Troops loyal to the British hang two participants of the Sepoy Rebellion on a makeshift gallows. During the Rebellion, British forces frequently resorted to summary execution without trial for those they suspected of involvement. ***What kind of message was the placement of such gallows intended to convey?***

financed the costs of British rule. They built extensive railroad and telegraph networks that tightened links between India and the larger global economy. They also constructed new canals, harbors, and irrigation systems to support commerce and agriculture.

Especially after 1857, British colonial authorities made little effort to promote Christianity. They did, however, establish English-style schools for the children of Indian elites, and they suppressed Indian customs that conflicted with European law or values. Most prominent of those customs were sati (the practice of widows burning themselves on their husbands' funeral pyres), infanticide, and slavery.

Sati
www.mhhe.com/bentleybrief2e

Imperialism in Southeast Asia

THE DUTCH EAST INDIES As the East India Company and British colonial agents tightened their grip on India, competition among European states kindled further empire-building efforts. In southeast Asia, Dutch officials tightened their control and extended their authority throughout the Dutch East Indies, the archipelago that makes up the modern state of Indonesia. Along with cash crops of sugar, tea, coffee, and tobacco, exports of rubber and tin made the Dutch East Indies a valuable and productive colony.

BRITISH COLONIES IN SOUTHEAST ASIA In the interests of increasing trade between India, southeast Asia, and China, British imperialists moved in the nineteenth century to establish a presence in southeast Asia. By the 1880s they had established colonial authority in Burma, which became a source of teak, ivory, rubies, and jade. In 1824 Thomas Stamford Raffles founded the port of Singapore, which soon became the busiest center of trade in the Strait of Melaka. Administered by the colonial regime in India, Singapore served as the base for the British conquest of Malaya (modern Malaysia) in the 1870s and 1880s. Besides offering ports that enabled the British navy to control sea-lanes linking the Indian Ocean with the South China Sea, Malaya provided abundant supplies of tin and rubber.

sati (suh-TEE)

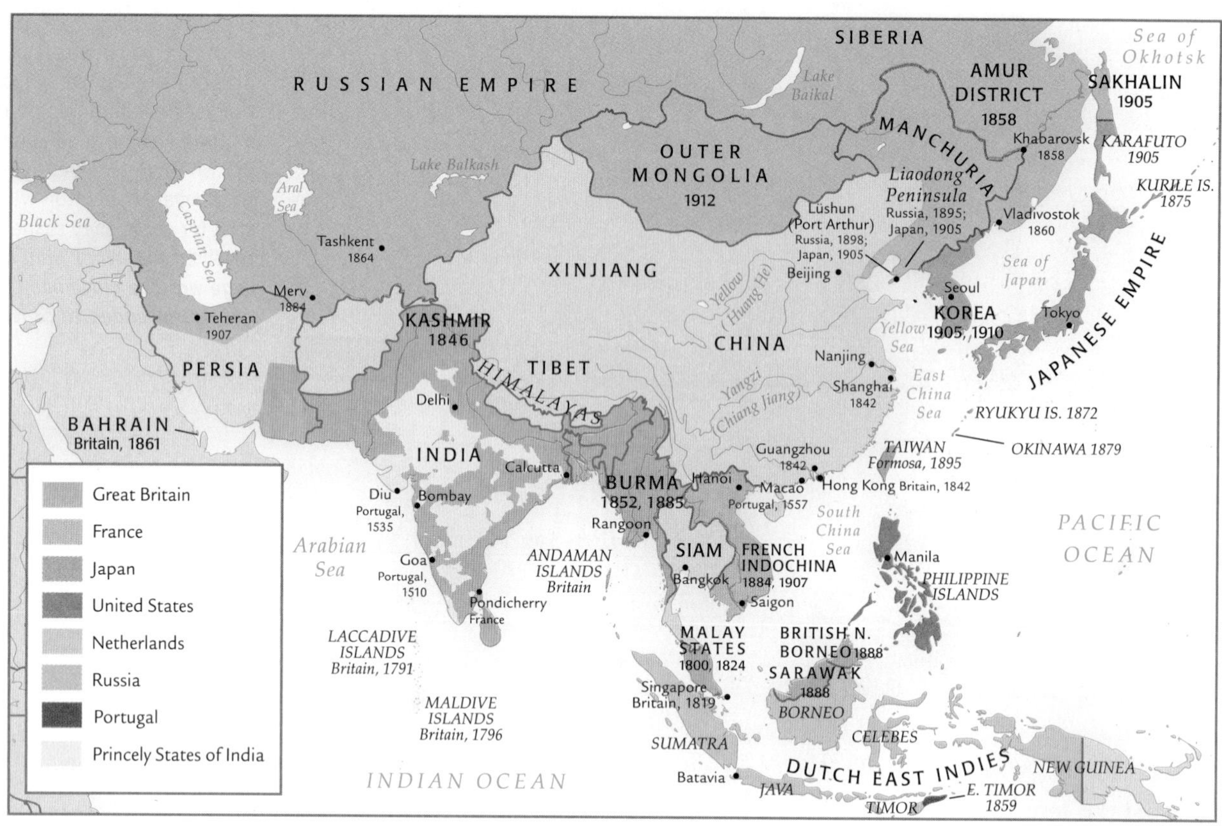

MAP 28.1 | Imperialism in Asia, ca. 1914. Date is year of conquest. Note the claims made by various industrial powers. ***Which territories remained unclaimed, and why? Which power claimed the most imperial territory in Asia?***

FRENCH INDOCHINA French imperialists built the large southeast Asian colony of French Indochina, consisting of the modern states of Vietnam, Cambodia, and Laos, between 1859 and 1893. Like their British counterparts in India, French colonial officials introduced European-style schools and sought to establish close connections with native elites. Unlike their rivals, French officials also encouraged conversion to Christianity, and as a result the Roman Catholic church became prominent throughout French Indochina, especially Vietnam. By century's end, all of southeast Asia had come under European imperial rule except for the kingdom of Siam (modern Thailand), which preserved its independence largely because colonial officials regarded it as a convenient buffer state between British-dominated Burma and French Indochina.

Informal Domination in the Ottoman and Qing Empires

As in India, the Indonesian islands, and Vietnam, European powers in the nineteenth century frequently seized territories outright and ruled them as colonies. More frequently, however, European (and later U.S.) forces used their economic and military power to force concessions out of militarily weak societies. They won rights for businesses to seek opportunities on favorable terms, gained influence in political affairs, and enabled industrial capitalists to realize huge profits without going to the trouble and expense of establishing formal colonies. In the last half of the nineteenth century, two formerly powerful societies—the Ottoman and the Qing empires—increasingly came under such informal domination as each struggled with military weakness and internal problems in contrast to the industrialized and competitive nation-states of Europe. Although reform movements emerged in both lands, the results were inadequate, and by the early twentieth century both empires were still firmly in the grip of foreign domination.

PSI map — The Ottoman empire www.mhhe.com/bentleybrief2e

MILITARY DECLINE By the late seventeenth century, it was already clear that Ottoman forces lagged behind European armies in strategy, tactics, weaponry, and training. Loss of military power translated into declining effectiveness of the central government, which was losing power in the provinces to its own officials. In addition, although the Ottoman government managed to maintain its authority in Anatolia as well as in Iraq, it suffered serious territorial losses in the Caucasus, central Asia, and the Balkan provinces of Greece (independent 1830) and Serbia (independent 1867).

Most significant, however, was the loss of Egypt. In 1798 the ambitious French general Napoleon invaded Egypt in hopes of using it as a springboard for an attack on the British empire in India. His campaign was a miserable failure, but the invasion sparked turmoil in Egypt, as local elites battled to seize power after Napoleon's departure. The ultimate victor was the energetic general Muhammad Ali, who built a powerful army modeled on European forces and ruled Egypt from 1805 to 1848. He also launched a program of industrialization, concentrating on cotton textiles and armaments. Although he remained nominally subordinate to the Ottoman sultan, by 1820 he had established himself as the effective ruler of Egypt, which was the most powerful land in the Muslim world. He even invaded Syria and Anatolia, threatening to capture Istanbul and topple the Ottoman state. Indeed, the Ottoman dynasty survived only because British forces intervened out of fear that Ottoman collapse would result in a sudden and dangerous expansion of Russian influence.

ECONOMIC DIFFICULTIES Meanwhile, European textiles and manufactured goods began to flow into the Ottoman empire in the eighteenth and nineteenth centuries. Because these items were inexpensive and high-quality products, they placed considerable pressure on Ottoman artisans and crafts workers. Gradually, the Ottoman empire moved toward financial dependency on Europe. After the middle of the nineteenth century, economic development in the Ottoman empire depended heavily on foreign loans, as European capital financed the construction of railroads, utilities, and mining enterprises. Interest payments grew to the point that they consumed more than half of the empire's revenues. In 1882 the Ottoman state was unable to pay interest on its loans and had no choice but to accept European administration of its debts.

THE CAPITULATIONS Nothing symbolized foreign influence more than the capitulations, agreements that exempted European visitors from Ottoman law and provided European powers with extraterritoriality—the right to exercise jurisdiction over their own citizens according to their own laws. Capitulations also served as instruments of economic penetration by European businesspeople who established tax-exempt banks and commercial enterprises in the Ottoman empire, and they permitted foreign governments to levy duties on goods sold in Ottoman ports.

THE REFORMS OF MAHMUD II In response to recurring and deepening crises, Ottoman leaders launched a series of reforms designed to strengthen and preserve the state. In the early nineteenth century, a significant period of reform occurred under the leadership of sultan Mahmud II (reigned 1808–1839). Mahmud's program remodeled Ottoman institutions along western European lines, especially in the creation of a more effective army. Before long, Ottoman recruits wore European-style uniforms and studied at military and engineering schools that taught European curricula. Equally important, Mahmud's government created a system of secondary education for boys to facilitate the transition from mosque schools, which provided primary education, to newly established scientific, technical, and military academies. To make his authority more effective, the sultan established European-style ministries, constructed new roads, built telegraph lines, and inaugurated a postal service. By the time of Mahmud's death in 1839, the Ottoman empire had shrunk in size, but it was also more manageable and powerful than it had been since the early seventeenth century.

Caucasus (KAW-kuh-suhs)
Mahmud II (mah-MOOD)

THE TANZIMAT ERA Continuing defeats on the battlefield and the rise of separatist movements among subject peoples, however, prompted the ruling classes to undertake even more radical reforms during the Tanzimat ("reorganization") era (1839–1876). In designing their program, Tanzimat reformers drew considerable inspiration from Enlightenment thought and the constitutional foundations of western European states. One of their primary aims was to make Ottoman law more acceptable to Europeans so they could have the capitulations lifted and recover Ottoman sovereignty. Among the most important Tanzimat reforms were those that guaranteed public trials, rights of privacy, and equality before the law for all Ottoman subjects, whether Muslim or not. By 1869 educational reforms also provided free and compulsory primary education for all children. Yet even though reform and reorganization strengthened Ottoman society, the Tanzimat also provoked spirited opposition. Harsh criticism came from religious conservatives, who argued that reformers posed a threat to the empire's Islamic foundation. Perhaps most dangerously, the Ottoman bureaucracy itself criticized Tanzimat reforms because they believed that too much power was concentrated in the hands of the sultan.

THE YOUNG TURKS The despotic reign of Abdül Hamid II (reigned 1876–1909) only seemed to confirm such criticisms, and a variety of liberal groups grew up to oppose his rule. Among the most articulate were those whose members were familiar with European society, and who believed above all else that Ottoman society was in dire need of a written constitution that defined and limited the sultan's power. The most active dissident organization was the Ottoman Society for Union and Progress, better known as the Young Turk Party. Founded in 1889 by exiled Ottoman subjects living in Paris, the Young Turk Party vigorously called for universal suffrage, equality before the law, freedom of re-

Tanzimat (TAHNZ-ee-MAT)

Istanbul, on the isthmus connecting Europe and west Asia, was the capital of the Ottoman empire until its demise in 1923.

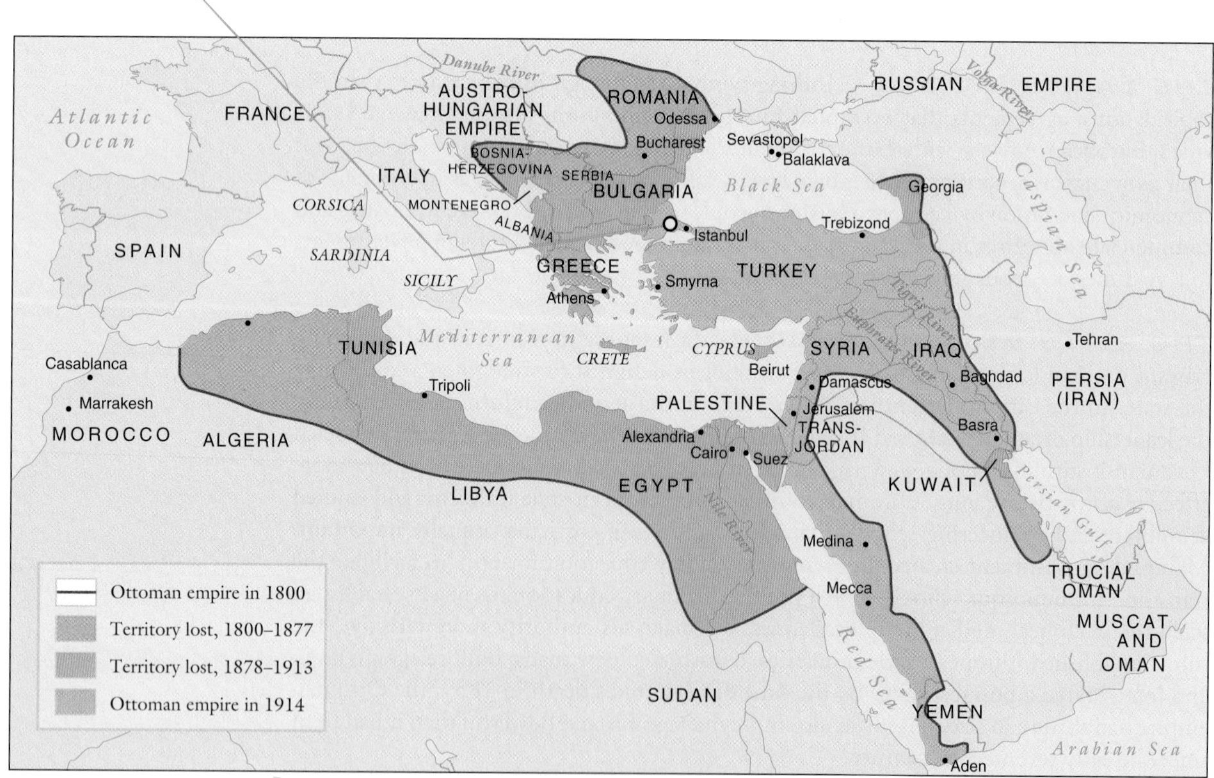

MAP 28.2 | Territorial losses of the Ottoman empire, 1800–1923. Compare the borders of the Ottoman empire in 1800 with what was left of the empire in 1914. ***What might have been the strategic value of the remaining Ottoman territories?***

CHINESE OPIUM SMOKERS. | Chinese efforts to stop opium imports led to a humiliating defeat in the Opium War. ***What do the physical effects of opium seem to have been?***

ligion, free public education, secularization of the state, and the emancipation of women. In 1908 the Young Turks inspired an army coup that forced Abdül Hamid to reinstate a constitution he had abandoned at the start of his reign. In 1909 they dethroned him and established Mehmed V Rashid (reigned 1909–1918) as a puppet sultan. Throughout the Young Turk era (1908–1918), Ottoman sultans reigned but no longer ruled.

Yet in spite of their efforts to shore up the ailing empire, reformers could not turn the tide of decline: Ottoman armies continued to lose wars, and subject peoples continued to seek autonomy or independence. By the early twentieth century, the Ottoman empire survived principally because European diplomats could not agree on how to dispose of the empire without upsetting the European balance of power.

THE OPIUM TRADE The Chinese empire experienced even more difficulties than the Ottoman empire in the nineteenth century. Qing problems became serious in the early nineteenth century when officials of the British East India Company began to trade in opium—rather than silver—in exchange for the Chinese silks, porcelains, and teas so coveted by Europeans. Trade in opium was illegal in China, but it expanded rapidly for decades because Chinese authorities made little effort to enforce the law. By the late 1830s, however, government officials had become aware that China had a trade problem and a drug problem as well. In 1839 the government took active steps to halt the trade, which included the destruction of some twenty thousand chests of opium.

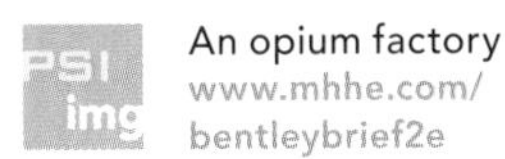

An opium factory
www.mhhe.com/bentleybrief2e

THE OPIUM WAR Outraged, British commercial agents pressed their government into a military retaliation designed to reopen the opium trade. The ensuing conflict, known as the Opium War (1839–1842), made plain the military power differential between Europe and China. The Chinese navy and infantry were no match for their British counterparts, who relied on steam power and modern firearms, and in 1842 the Chinese government sued for peace. China experienced similar military setbacks throughout the second half of the nineteenth century in conflicts with Britain and France (1856–1858), France (1884–1885), and Japan (1894–1895).

UNEQUAL TREATIES In the wake of those confrontations came a series of pacts collectively known in China as unequal treaties, which curtailed China's sovereignty. The Treaty of Nanjing (1842), which ended the British war against the Chinese, ceded Hong

THINKING ABOUT *Traditions*

TRADITIONS IN THE BUILDING OF GLOBAL EMPIRES. Although imperialism connected the world's peoples in unprecedented ways, colonizing peoples often believed in the superiority of their historical traditions and in the inherent superiority of their racial heritage. In what ways did these ideas about historical and racial superiority help both to justify imperialism as well as to unite colonized peoples against it?

Kong Island in perpetuity to Britain, opened five Chinese ports to commerce and residence, compelled the Qing government to extend most-favored-nation status to Britain, and granted extraterritoriality to British subjects. In later years France, Germany, Denmark, the Netherlands, Spain, Belgium, Austria-Hungary, the United States, and Japan concluded similar unequal treaties with China. By 1900 ninety Chinese ports were under the effective control of foreign powers, foreign merchants controlled much of the Chinese economy, Christian missionaries sought converts throughout China, and foreign gunboats patrolled Chinese waters.

To make matters more difficult, China was convulsed by several large-scale rebellions in the nineteenth century, all of which reflected the increasing poverty and discontent of the Chinese peasantry. After 1850, rebellions erupted throughout China: the Nian rebellion (1851–1868) in the northeast, the Muslim rebellion (1855–1873) in the southwest, and the Tungan rebellion (1862–1878) in the northwest. Most danger-

Nian (neen)
Tungan (tuhn-gahn)

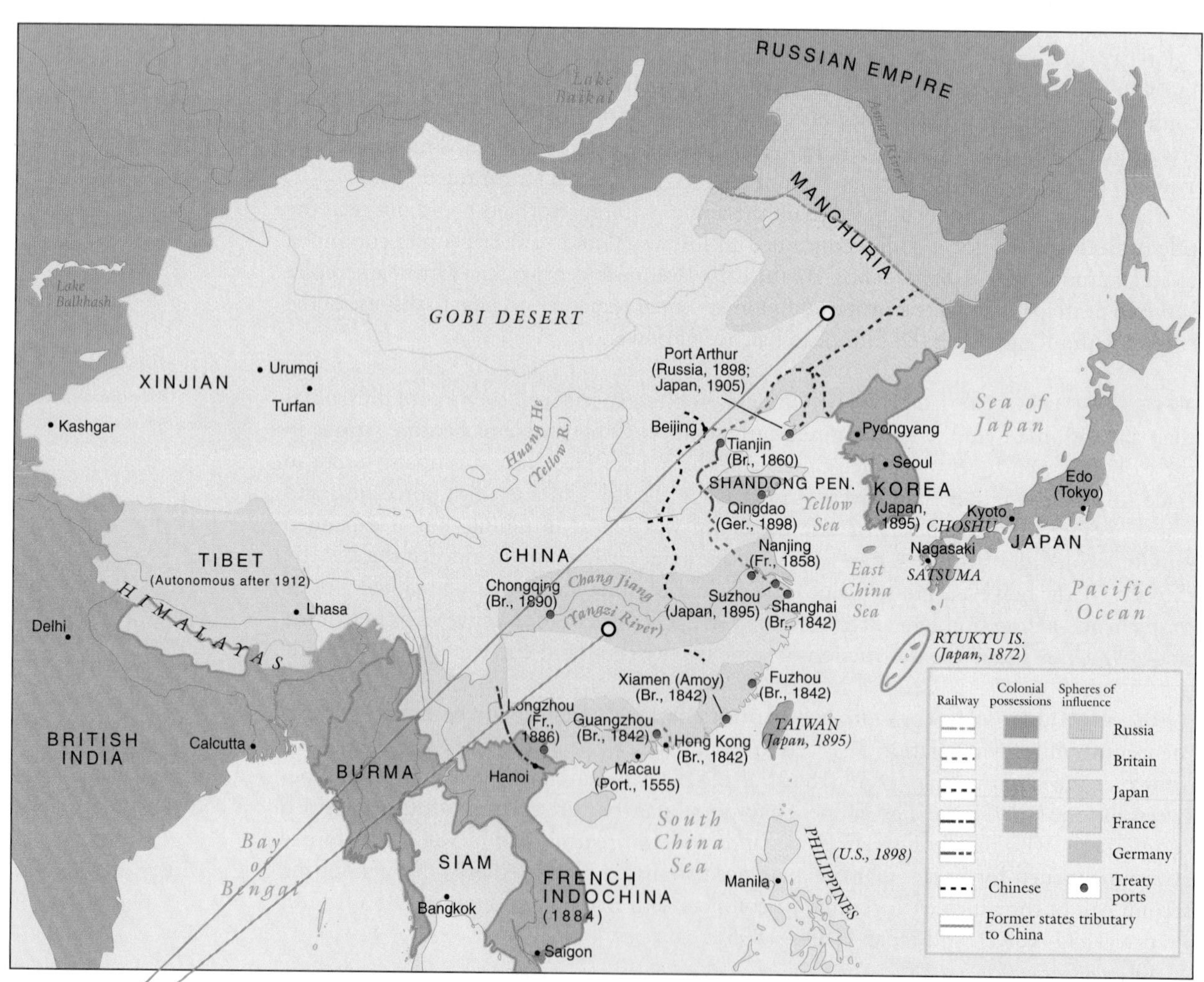

Some of the "spheres of influence" extended far inland, with serious repercussions for Chinese sovereignty.

MAP 28.3 | East Asia in the nineteenth century. Notice the division of China, which technically remained a sovereign nation, into spheres of influence by various European nations and Japan. ***What impact would such spheres of influence have had on the Chinese government in Beijing?***

ous of all was the Taiping rebellion (1850–1864), which raged throughout most of China and brought the Qing dynasty to the brink of collapse.

THE TAIPING REBELLION The village schoolteacher Hong Xiuquan provided both inspiration and leadership for the Taiping rebellion. He called for the destruction of the Qing dynasty and for the radical transformation of Chinese society, including the abolition of private property, the creation of communal wealth to be shared according to needs, the prohibition of foot binding and concubinage, free public education, simplification of the written language, literacy for the masses, and equality of the sexes. After sweeping through southeastern China, Hong and his followers in the Society of God Worshipers took Nanjing in 1853 and made it the capital of their Taiping ("Great Peace") kingdom. In 1855 a million Taipings were poised to attack Beijing, and in 1860 they threatened Shanghai. Although the rebellion was eventually crushed in 1864 with the aid of European advisors and weapons, in all it claimed between twenty and thirty million lives and devastated part of the Chinese countryside.

THE SELF-STRENGTHENING MOVEMENT The Taiping rebellion altered the course of Chinese history. Contending with aggressive foreign powers and lands ravaged by domestic rebellion, Qing rulers recognized that reforms were necessary for the empire to survive. Most imaginative of these programs was the Self-Strengthening Movement (1860–1895). While holding to Confucian values and seeking to reestablish a stable agrarian society, movement leaders built modern shipyards, constructed railroads, established weapons industries, opened steel foundries with blast furnaces, and founded academies to develop scientific expertise.

Yet the Self-Strengthening Movement did not introduce enough industry to bring real military and economic strength to China. It also did not prevent continuing foreign intrusion into Chinese affairs. During the latter part of the nineteenth century, foreign powers began to dismantle the Chinese system of tributary states. In 1885 France incorporated Vietnam into its colonial empire, and in 1886 Great Britain detached Burma from Chinese control. In 1895 Japan forced China to recognize the independence of Korea and cede the island of Taiwan and the Liaodong peninsula in southern Manchuria. By 1898 foreign powers had carved China itself into spheres of economic influence, and only distrust among them prevented the total dismemberment of the Middle Kingdom.

THE HUNDRED DAYS REFORMS These setbacks sparked the ambitious but abortive Hundred Days reforms of 1898, whose purpose was to turn China into a powerful modern industrial society. Impressed by the ideas of reform-minded scholars, the young and open-minded Emperor Guangxu launched a sweeping program to transform China into a constitutional monarchy, guarantee civil liberties, root out corruption, remodel the educational system, modernize military forces, and stimulate economic development. Yet these reform efforts produced a violent reaction from members of the imperial household, from their allies in the gentry, and especially from the young emperor's aunt, the ruthless and powerful empress dowager Cixi. After a period of 103 days, Cixi nullified the reform decrees, imprisoned the emperor in the Forbidden City, and executed six leading reformers.

THE BOXER REBELLION Cixi then threw her support behind an antiforeign uprising known as the Boxer rebellion, a violent movement spearheaded by militia units calling themselves the Society of Righteous and Harmonious Fists. The foreign press referred to the rebels as Boxers. In 1899 the Boxers organized to rid China of "foreign

Imperialism in Asia
www.mhhe.com/
bentleybrief2e

Taiping (TEYE-pihng)
Hong Xiuquan (hoong shee-OH-chew-an)
Liaodong (lyou-dawng)
Guangxu (wang-soo)

devils" and their influences. With the empress dowager's encouragement, the Boxers went on a rampage in northern China, killing foreigners and Chinese who had ties to foreigners. Confident that foreign weapons could not harm them, some 140,000 Boxers besieged foreign embassies in Beijing in the summer of 1900. They were crushed, however, by a heavily armed force of British, French, Russian, U.S., German, and Japanese troops. After the rebellion, the Chinese government was forced to allow foreign powers to station troops at their embassies in Beijing and along the route to the sea. When Cixi died in 1908, anti-Qing revolutionary movements that sought alternative methods to deal with foreign and domestic crises were rife throughout China. Indeed, revolution broke out in the autumn of 1911, and by early 1912 the child Puyi—the last emperor of the Qing dynasty—had abdicated his throne.

The Scramble for Africa

Even as European powers sponsored informal imperialism in the Ottoman and Qing empires in the last half of the nineteenth century, they also embarked on a striking outburst of formal imperialism in Africa. This was all the more remarkable, since as late as 1875 European peoples maintained a limited presence in Africa: their only sizable possessions were the Portuguese colonies of Angola and Mozambique, the French settler colony in northern Algeria, and a cluster of settler colonies populated by British and Dutch migrants in south Africa.

Between 1875 and 1900, however, the relationship between Africa and Europe dramatically changed. Within a quarter century European imperial powers partitioned and colonized almost the entire African continent. Prospects of exploiting African resources and nationalist rivalries between European powers help to explain this frenzied quest for empire, often referred to as the "scramble for Africa."

Physical mutilation in the Belgian Congo. | This 1912 photograph shows a stark portrait of the Belgian king's inhumane treatment of Africans in the Congo. When Africans in the Congo did not collect their allotted quotas of rubber for the state, they or their relatives were liable to have their hands or feet amputated as punishment.

THE BELGIAN CONGO In the 1870s King Leopold II of Belgium (reigned 1865–1909) employed the American journalist Henry Morton Stanley to help develop commercial ventures and establish a colony called the Congo Free State (modern-day Democratic Republic of the Congo) in the basin of the Congo River. To forestall competition from Belgium's much larger and more powerful European neighbors, Leopold announced that the Congo region would be a free-trade zone accessible to merchants and businesspeople from all European lands. In fact, however, he carved out a personal colony with the sole purpose of extracting lucrative rubber using forced labor. Working conditions in the Congo Free State were so brutal, taxes so high, and abuses so many that four to eight million Africans died under Leopold's personal rule. Once those abuses became public, humanitarian pressure induced the Belgian government to take control away from Leopold in 1908 and administer the colony directly.

As Leopold colonized central Africa, Britain established an imperial presence in Egypt. In an effort to build up their army, strengthen the economy, and distance themselves from Ottoman authority, Egypt's leaders had borrowed heavily from European lenders in the mid–nineteenth century. By the 1870s crushing debt forced Egyptian officials to impose high taxes, which provoked popular unrest and a military rebellion. Concerned over the status of their financial interests and the security of the Suez Canal, British forces occupied Egypt in 1882.

THE BERLIN CONFERENCE The British occupation of Egypt intensified tensions between those European powers who were seeking African colonies. To avoid war, delegates from fourteen European states and the United States—not a single African was present—met at the Berlin West Africa Conference (1884–1885) to devise ground rules for the colonization of Africa. According to those rules, any European state could establish African colonies after notifying the others of its intentions and occupying previously unclaimed territory.

During the 1890s European imperialists sent armies to impose colonial rule on the African territories they claimed. Although resistance to colonial rule was often fierce, European cannons and machine guns rarely failed to defeat African forces. By the turn of the century, European colonies embraced all of Africa except for Ethiopia, where native forces fought off Italian efforts at colonization in 1896, and Liberia, a small republic in west Africa that was effectively a dependency of the United States.

DIRECT AND INDIRECT RULE In the wake of rapid conquest, Europeans struggled to identify the most cost-effective and efficient system of rule in Africa. By the early twentieth century, after some experimentation, most European governments sought to establish their own rule, which took the form of either direct rule, typical of French colonies, or indirect rule, characteristic of British colonies. Under direct rule, colonies were headed by European personnel who assumed responsibility for tax collection, labor and military recruitment, and the maintenance of law and order. Administrative boundaries intentionally cut across existing African political and ethnic boundaries to divide and weaken potentially powerful indigenous groups. In contrast, indirect rule sought to exercise control over subject populations through indigenous institutions such as "tribal" authorities and "customary laws." Both methods of government were flawed: under direct rule, imperial powers struggled with a constant shortage of European personnel, which undermined the effectiveness of rule, and indirect rule imposed erroneous and rigid European ideas about what constituted tribal categories and boundaries onto African societies.

SOUTH AFRICA Although already inhabited by Europeans long before the scramble for Africa, still the southern tip of the African continent did not escape conflict at the close of the nineteenth century. In this case, however, the main antagonists were both of European descent: one side was composed of the descendants of Dutch settlers who had founded Cape Town in 1652 (called "Boers" or "Afrikaners"), and the other of British settlers who had taken control of the Cape in 1815. Relations between the two groups had never been good. When the British established themselves at the Cape, they subjected Afrikaners to British language and law—including the abolition of slavery when it became law in 1833. The abolition of slavery was particularly contentious, as Afrikaners believed that God had given them the right to exploit both the people and the resources of the Cape—the results of which left the indigenous Khoikhoi and Xhosa peoples decimated and virtually landless. Chafing under British rule, Afrikaners left their farms in Cape Colony and gradually migrated east in what they called the Great Trek. By the mid–nineteenth century, after fierce conflict with the Ndebele and Zulu peoples indigenous to the interior of the region, the Afrikaners created several independent republics: the Republic of Natal, annexed by the British in 1843; the Orange Free State in 1854; and in 1860 the South African Republic (Transvaal territories).

Boer soldiers
www.mhhe.com/bentleybrief2e

Britain's lenient attitude toward Afrikaner statehood took a drastic turn with the discovery of diamonds (1867) and gold (1886) in Afrikaner territories. The influx of thousands of British miners and prospectors led to tensions between British authorities and Afrikaners, culminating in the South African War (1899–1902; sometimes called the Boer War). Although the brutal conflict pitted whites against whites, it also took a large toll on black Africans, who served both sides as soldiers and laborers. The internment of 100,000 black Africans in British concentration camps, for example, left more than 10,000 dead. The Afrikaners conceded defeat in 1902, and by 1910, the British government had reconstituted

Khoikhoi (KOI-koi)
Xhosa (KOH-suh)
Ndebele (uhn-duh-BEE-lee)

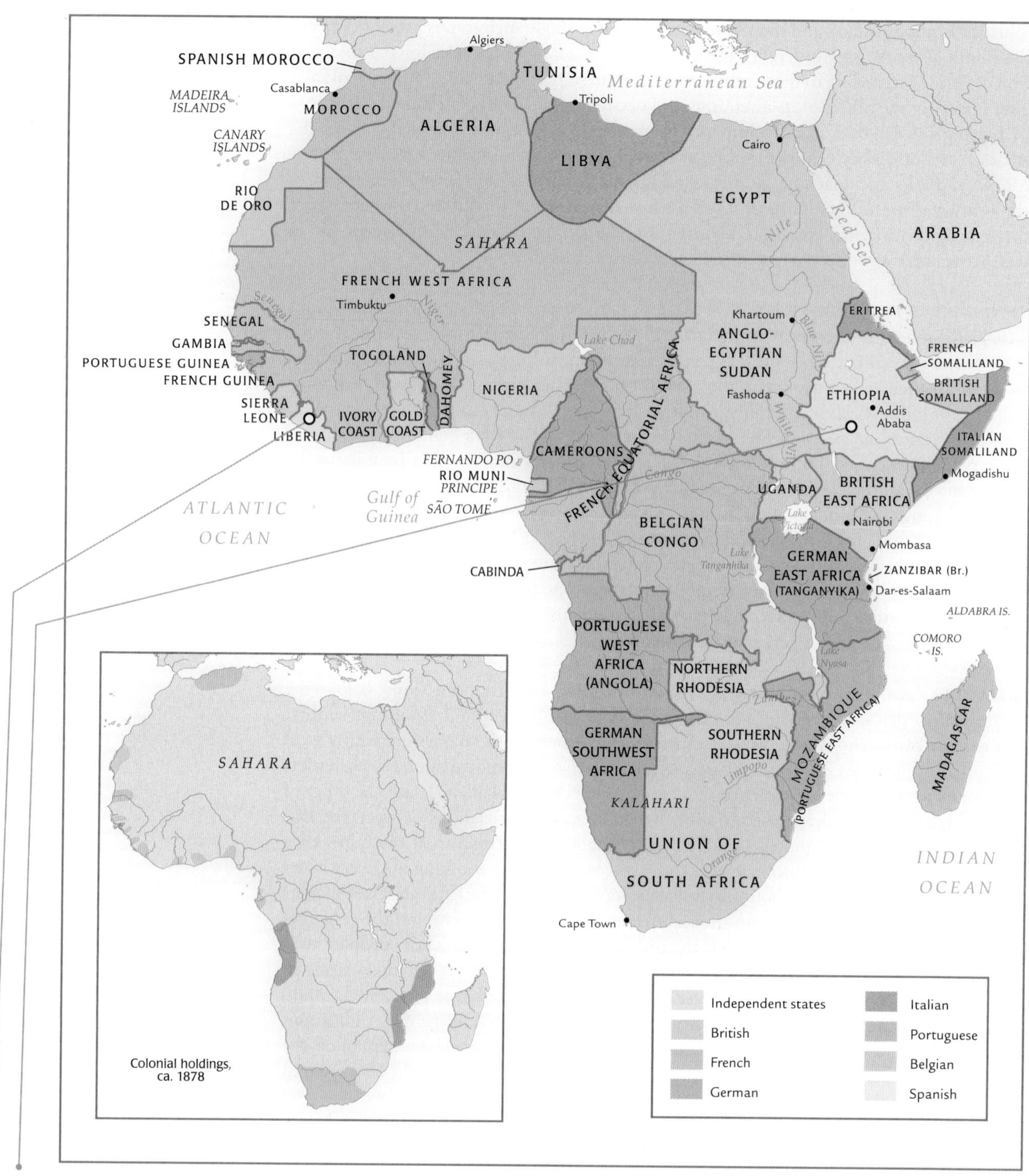

Ethiopia and Liberia were the only two areas that remained independent of European control.

MAP 28.4 | Imperialism in Africa, ca. 1914. Note the dramatic difference between the map of 1878 and the later map. ***How was it possible that Europeans were able to claim so much territory in such a short span of time?***

the four former colonies as provinces in the Union of South Africa, a largely autonomous British dominion. British attempts at improving relations between English speakers and Afrikaners centered on shoring up the privileges of white colonial society and the domination of black Africans.

European Imperialism in the Pacific

While scrambling for Africa, European imperial powers did not overlook opportunities to establish their presence in the Pacific Ocean basin. Imperialism in the Pacific took two main forms. In Australia and New Zealand, European powers established settler colonies and dominant political institutions. In most of the Pacific islands, however, they sought commercial opportunities and reliable bases for their operations but did not wish to go to the trouble or expense of outright colonization. Only in the late nineteenth century did they begin to impose direct colonial rule on the islands.

SETTLER COLONIES IN THE PACIFIC Settlers began to arrive in Australia in 1788, nearly two decades after Captain James Cook reported that the region would be suitable for settlement. In that year, a British fleet with about one thousand settlers, most of them convicted criminals, arrived at Sydney harbor and established the colony of New South Wales. By the 1830s voluntary migrants outnumbered convicts, and the discovery of gold in 1851 brought a surge in migration to Australia. European settlers established communities also in New Zealand, where the islands' fertile soils and abundant stands of timber drew large numbers of migrants.

European migration rocked the societies of Australia and New Zealand. Diseases such as smallpox and measles devastated indigenous peoples at the same time that European migrants flooded into their lands. The aboriginal population of Australia fell from about 650,000 in 1800 to 90,000 in 1900, whereas the European population rose from a few thousand to 3.75 million during the same period. Similarly, the population of indigenous Maori in New Zealand fell from about 200,000 in 1800 to 45,000 a century later, while European numbers climbed to 750,000.

Increasing migration also fueled conflict between European settlers and native populations. Large settler societies pushed indigenous peoples from their lands, often following violent confrontations. Because the nomadic foraging peoples of Australia did not occupy lands permanently, British settlers considered the continent *terra nullius*—"land belonging to no one"—that they could seize and put to their own uses. Despite native resistance, by 1900 the British had succeeded in brutally displacing most indigenous Australians from their traditional lands and dispersing them throughout the continent.

A similarly disruptive process transpired in New Zealand, where Maori leaders organized effective and long-lasting opposition to British attempts to usurp their land and sovereignty. Conflicts over land confiscations and disputed land sales, for example, helped to spark the New Zealand Wars, a series of confrontations between the Maori and the British that flared from the mid- to late nineteenth century. Despite that resistance, by the end of the century the British had managed to force many Maori into poor rural communities separated from European settlements.

IMPERIALISTS IN PARADISE On the smaller Pacific islands, the picture was quite different. Although indigenous peoples were ravaged by European diseases, the imperial powers had little interest in establishing direct colonial rule over the islands. Rather, they were content to use the islands as naval ports, as coaling stations, and sometimes as producers of primary products. The situation changed, however, in the late nineteenth century, as European nationalist rivalries encouraged the imperial powers to stake their claims in the Pacific as they had done in Africa. Thus, although France had established a protectorate in Tahiti, the Society Islands, and the Marquesas as early as 1841, it only imposed direct colonial rule in 1880. Britain made Fiji a crown colony in 1874, and Germany annexed several of the Marshall Islands in 1876 and 1878. At the Berlin Conference, European diplomats agreed on a partition of Oceania as well as Africa, and Britain, France, Germany, and the United States proceeded to claim almost all the Pacific islands. By 1900 only the kingdom of Tonga remained independent, and even Tonga accepted British protection against the possibility of encroachments by other imperial powers.

Maori (MAY-oh-ree)

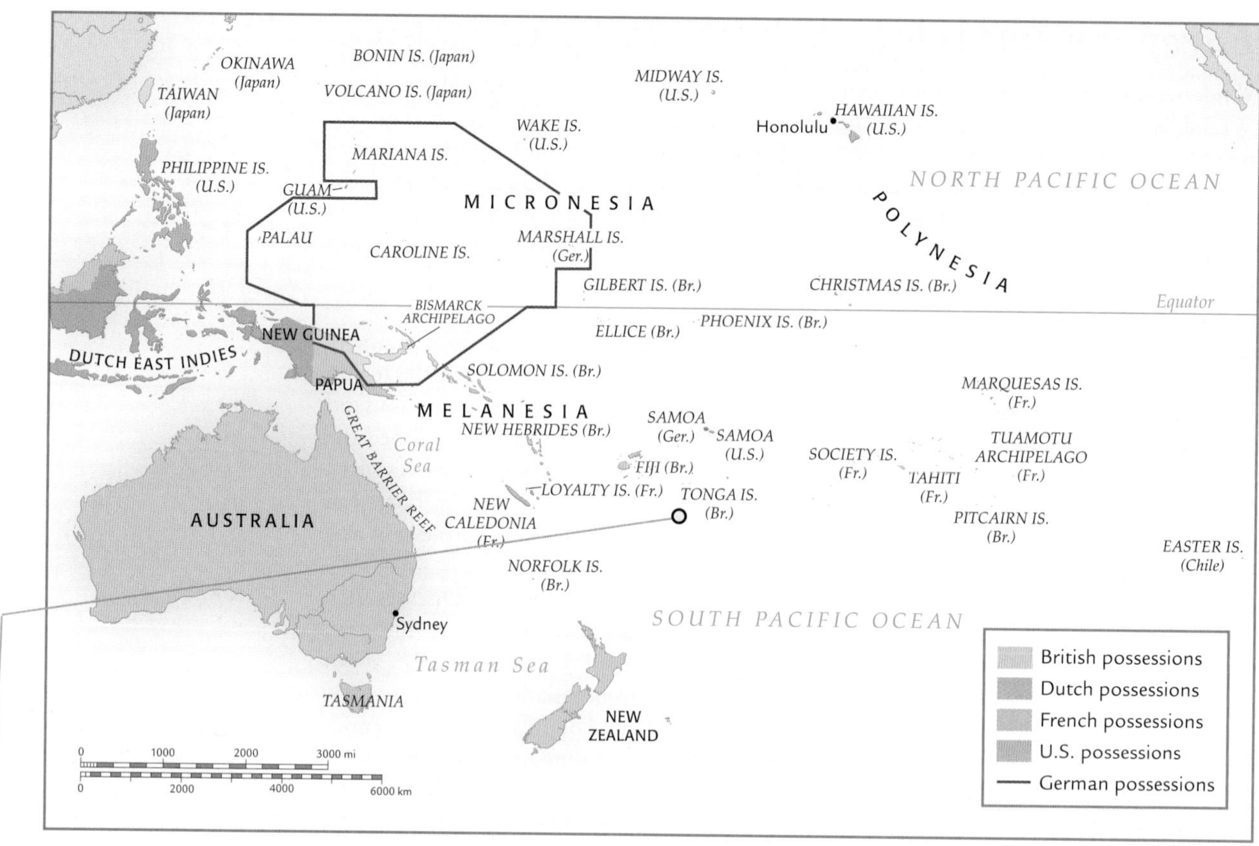

The Tonga Islands were the only Pacific islands to remain independent.

MAP 28.5 | Imperialism in Oceania, ca. 1914. Observe the many small, distant islands of the Pacific. ***Why would imperial powers have thought it so important to claim these islands in the late nineteenth and early twentieth centuries?***

The Emergence of New Imperial Powers

Nineteenth-century imperialism was mostly a European affair until the end of the century. At that point, two new imperial powers appeared on the world stage: the United States and Japan. Both lands experienced rapid industrialization in the late nineteenth century, and both built powerful armed forces. As European imperial powers planted their flags throughout the world, leaders of the United States and Japan decided that they too needed to establish a global imperial presence.

U.S. Imperialism in Latin America and the Pacific

The very existence of the United States was due to European imperialism. After the new republic had won its independence, U.S. leaders brought almost all the temperate regions of North America under their authority. In the process, they pushed indigenous peoples onto marginal lands and reservations. This domination of the North American continent was part of the larger story of European and Euro-American imperialism.

The fledgling United States also tried to wield power outside North America. In 1823 President James Monroe (in office 1817–1825) issued a proclamation that warned European states against imperialist designs in the western hemisphere. The Monroe Doctrine, as it came to be known, later served as a justification for U.S. intervention in hemispheric affairs.

As the United States consolidated its continental holdings, U.S. leaders became interested in acquiring territories beyond the temperate regions of North America. The United States purchased Alaska from Russia in 1867 and in 1875 claimed a protectorate over the islands of Hawai`i, where U.S. entrepreneurs had established highly productive sugarcane plantations. The Hawaiian kingdom survived until 1893, when a group of planters and businesspeople overthrew the last monarch, Queen Lili`uokalani (reigned 1891–1893), and invited the United States to annex the islands. In 1898 the pro-expansion president William McKinley (in office 1897–1901) agreed to acquire the islands.

Queen Lili`uokalani, last monarch of Hawai`i. | In this picture, taken before her deposition in 1893, the queen wears a European dress and sits on a throne covered with a traditional royal cape made of bird feathers.

THE SPANISH-CUBAN-AMERICAN WAR The United States emerged as a major imperial and colonial power after the brief Spanish-Cuban-American War (1898–1899). War broke out as anticolonial tensions mounted in Cuba and Puerto Rico—the last remnants of Spain's American empire—where U.S. business interests had made large investments. In 1898 the U.S. battleship *Maine* exploded and sank in Havana harbor. U.S. leaders claimed sabotage and declared war on Spain. The United States easily defeated Spain and took control and possession of Cuba and Puerto Rico. After the U.S. navy destroyed the Spanish fleet at Manila in a single day, the United States also took possession of Guam and the Philippines to prevent them from falling under German or Japanese control.

The consolidation of U.S. authority in the Philippines was an especially difficult affair. The Spanish-Cuban-American War coincided with a Filipino revolt against Spanish rule, and U.S. forces promised to support independence of the Philippines in exchange for an alliance against Spain. After the victory over Spain, however, President McKinley decided to bring the Philippines under American control instead. In response, Filipino rebels—led by Emilio Aguinaldo—turned their arms against the new intruders. The result was a bitter insurrection that raged until 1902 and claimed the lives of 4,200 American soldiers, 15,000 rebel troops, and some 200,000 Filipino civilians.

Instability and disorder also prompted the United States to intervene in the affairs of Caribbean and Central American lands, even those that were not U.S. possessions, to prevent rebellion and protect American business interests. In the early twentieth century, U.S. military forces occupied Cuba, the Dominican Republic, Nicaragua, Honduras, and Haiti.

THE PANAMA CANAL To facilitate communication and transportation between the Atlantic and the Pacific oceans, the United States sought to build a canal across the Isthmus of Panama in northern Colombia. However, Colombia was unwilling to cede land for the project. Under President Theodore Roosevelt (in office 1901–1909), an enthusiastic champion of imperial expansion, the United States supported a rebellion against Colombia in 1903 and helped rebels establish the breakaway state of Panama. In exchange for that support, the United States won the right to build a canal across Panama and to control the adjacent territory, known as the Panama Canal Zone. Roosevelt then added a corollary to the Monroe Doctrine in 1904, which stated that the United States has the right to intervene in the domestic affairs of nations within the hemisphere if they demonstrate an inability to maintain the security deemed necessary to protect U.S. investments. The Roosevelt Corollary, along with the Panama Canal when it opened in 1914, strengthened U.S. military and economic claims.

Lili`uokalani (lee-lee-oo-oh-kah-lah-nee)
Emilio Aguinaldo (ee-MEE-lyaw AH-gee-NAHL-daw)

THINKING ABOUT *Encounters*

ENCOUNTERS IN THE BUILDING OF GLOBAL EMPIRES. During the nineteenth and twentieth centuries, European, American, and Japanese imperialism helped connect the world's peoples ever more tightly through resource exploitation, trade relationships, and migration patterns. What technologies, ideologies, and institutions made it possible for imperial powers to maintain these connections, even in the face of resistance?

Imperial Japan

Strengthened by the rapid industrialization during the Meiji era, Japan joined the ranks of imperial powers in the late nineteenth century. Indeed, while founding representative political institutions to demonstrate their trustworthiness to American and European diplomats, Japanese leaders also made a bid to stand alongside the world's great powers by launching a campaign of imperial expansion.

EARLY JAPANESE EXPANSION The Japanese drive to empire began in the east Asian islands. During the 1870s Japanese leaders consolidated their hold on Hokkaido and the Kurile Islands to the north, and they encouraged Japanese migrants to populate the islands to forestall Russian expansion there. By 1879 they had also established their hegemony over Okinawa and the Ryukyu Islands to the south.

THE SINO-JAPANESE WAR In 1876 Japan purchased modern warships from Britain, and the newly strengthened Japanese navy immediately began to flex its muscles in Korea. In 1894 conflict erupted between Japan and China over the status of Korea. When an antiforeign rebellion broke out in Korea in 1893, Qing rulers sent an army to restore order and reassert Chinese authority in Korea. However, Japanese businesses had built substantial interests in Korea, and Meiji leaders were unwilling to recognize Chinese control over such an economically important land. Thus in August 1894 they declared war on China. The Japanese navy quickly gained control of the Yellow Sea and demolished the Chinese fleet in a battle lasting a mere five hours. Within a few months the conflict was over. When the combatants made peace in April 1895, Qing authorities recognized the independence of Korea, thus making it essentially a dependency of Japan. They also ceded Taiwan, the Pescadores Islands, and the Liaodong peninsula, which strengthened Japanese control over east Asian waters. Alongside territorial acquisitions, Japan gained unequal treaty rights in China like those enjoyed by European and American powers.

THE RUSSO-JAPANESE WAR The unexpected Japanese victory startled European imperial powers, especially Russia. Tensions between Japan and Russia soon mounted, because both imperial powers had territorial ambitions in the Liaodong peninsula, Korea, and Manchuria. War broke out in 1904, and Japanese forces overran Russian installations before reinforcements could arrive from Europe. The Japanese navy destroyed the Russian Baltic fleet, which had sailed halfway around the world to support the war effort. By 1905 the war was over, and Japan won international recognition of its colonial authority over Korea and the Liaodong peninsula. Furthermore, Russia ceded the southern half of Sakhalin island to Japan, along with a railroad and economic interests in southern Manchuria. Victory in the Russo-Japanese War transformed Japan into a major imperial power.

LEGACIES OF IMPERIALISM

Imperialism and colonialism profoundly influenced the development of world history. In some ways they tightened links between the world's peoples: trade and migration increased dramatically as imperial powers exploited the resources of subject lands and recruited labor forces to work in colonies throughout the world. Yet imperialism and colonialism also brought peoples into conflict and heightened senses of difference between peoples. European, Euro-American, and Japanese imperialists all came to think of themselves as superior to the peoples they overcame. Meanwhile, foreign intrusion stimulated the development of resistance in colonized lands, which over time served as a foundation for anticolonial independence movements.

Empire and Economy

One of the principal motives of imperialism was the desire to gain access to natural resources and agricultural products. As imperial powers consolidated their hold on foreign lands, colonial administrators reorganized subject societies so they would become efficient suppliers of timber, rubber, petroleum, gold, silver, diamonds, cotton, tea, coffee, cacao, and other products. As a result, global trade in those commodities surged during the nineteenth and early twentieth centuries. The advantages of this trade went mostly to the colonial powers, whose policies encouraged subject lands to provide raw materials for processing in the industrialized societies of Europe, North America, and Japan.

THE RUSSO-JAPANESE WAR. | In this painting, Japanese infantry charge into battle. Note the distinctly western uniforms worn by the soldiers.

INTRODUCTION OF NEW CROPS In some cases, colonial rule led to the introduction of new crops that transformed both the landscape and the social order of subject lands. In the early nineteenth century, for example, British colonial officials introduced tea bushes from China to Ceylon and India. The effect on Ceylon was profound. British planters felled trees on much of the island, converted rain forests into tea plantations, and recruited Ceylonese women by the thousands to carry out the labor-intensive work of harvesting mature tea leaves.

Consumption of tea in India and Ceylon was almost negligible, but increased supplies met the growing demand for tea in Europe, where the beverage became accessible to individuals of all social classes. The value of south Asian tea exports rose from about 309,000 pounds sterling in 1866 to 6.1 million pounds sterling in 1900. Malaya and Sumatra underwent a similar social transformation after British colonial agents planted rubber trees there in the 1870s and established plantations to meet the growing global demand for rubber products.

Labor Migrations

Efforts to exploit the natural resources and agricultural products of subject lands led imperial and colonial powers to encourage mass migrations of workers during the nineteenth and early twentieth centuries. Two patterns of labor migration were especially prominent during the imperial and colonial era. European migrants went mostly to temperate lands, where they worked as free cultivators or industrial laborers. In contrast, migrants from Asia, Africa, and the Pacific islands moved largely to tropical and subtropical lands, where they worked as indentured laborers on plantations or manual laborers for mining enterprises or large-scale construction projects.

EUROPEAN MIGRATION Between 1800 and 1914 some fifty million European migrants left their homes and sought opportunities overseas. Most of those migrants left the relatively poor agricultural societies of southern and eastern Europe, especially Italy, Russia, and Poland, although sizable numbers came also from Britain, Ireland, Germany, and Scandinavia. A majority of the migrants—about thirty-two million—went to the United States. Settler colonies in Canada, Argentina, Australia, New Zealand, and south Africa also drew large numbers of European migrants.

INDENTURED LABOR MIGRATION In contrast to their free European counterparts, migrants from Asia, Africa, and the Pacific islands generally traveled as indentured laborers. As the institution of slavery went into decline, planters sought laborers from poor and densely populated lands who could replace slaves. Between 1820 and 1914 about 2.5 million indentured laborers left their homes to work in distant parts of the world. Labor recruiters generally offered workers free passage to their destinations and provided them with food, shelter, clothing, and modest compensation for their services in exchange for a commitment to work for five to seven years.

The majority of the indentured laborers came from India, but sizable numbers also came from China, Japan, Java, Africa, and the Pacific islands. Indentured laborers went mostly to tropical and subtropical lands in the Americas, the Caribbean, Africa, and Oceania. Large numbers of Indian laborers went to work on rubber plantations in Malaya and sugar plantations in south Africa, the Pacific island of Fiji, the Guianas, and the Caribbean islands of Trinidad, Tobago, and Jamaica. After the Opium War, large numbers of Chinese laborers went to sugar plantations in Cuba and Hawai`i, guano mines in Peru, tin mines in Malaya, gold mines in south Africa and Australia, and railroad construction sites in the United States, Canada, and Peru. After the Meiji restoration in Japan, a large contingent of Japanese laborers migrated to Hawai`i to work on sugar plantations, and a smaller group went to work in guano mines in Peru. Indentured laborers from Africa went mostly to sugar plantations in Réunion, the Guianas, and Caribbean islands. Those from Pacific islands went mostly to plantations on other Pacific islands and in Australia.

EMPIRE AND MIGRATION All the large-scale migrations of the nineteenth century reflected the global influence of imperial powers. European migrations were possible only because European and Euro-American peoples had established settler societies in temperate regions around the world. Movements of indentured laborers were possible because colonial officials were able to recruit workers and dispatch them to distant lands where their compatriots had already established plantations or opened mines. In combination the nineteenth-century migrations profoundly influenced societies around the world by depositing large communities of people with distinctive ethnic identities in lands far from their original homes.

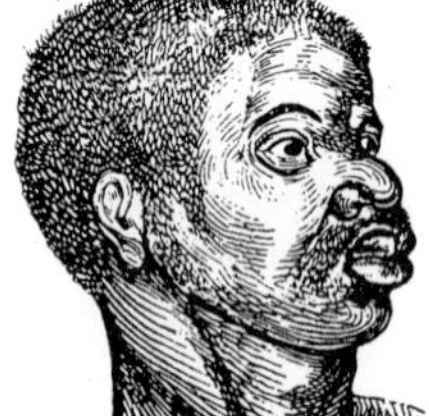

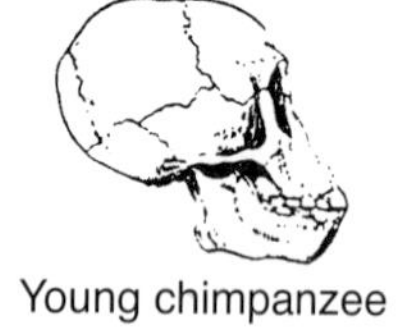

SCIENTIFIC RACISM. | Scientific racists often argued that Europeans had reached a higher stage of evolution than other peoples. An illustration from a popular book by Josiah Clark Nott and G. R. Glidden, *Indigenous Races of the Earth,* deliberately distorted facial and skull features to suggest a close relationship between African peoples and chimpanzees.

Empire and Society

COLONIAL CONFLICT The policies adopted by imperial powers and colonial officials forced peoples of different societies to deal with one another on a regular and systematic basis. Their interactions often led to violent conflicts between colonizers and subject peoples. Indeed, the Sepoy Rebellion was only one among many insurrections organized by discontented Indian subjects between the mid–nineteenth and the mid–twentieth centuries. Colonized lands in southeast Asia and Africa also became hotbeds of resistance, as subject peoples revolted against foreign rule, the tyrannical behavior of colonial officials, the introduction of European schools and curricula, high taxation, and requirements that subject peoples provide compulsory labor for colonists' enterprises.

Many rebellions drew strength from traditional religious beliefs, and priests or prophets often led resistance to colonial rule. In Tanganyika, for example, a local prophet organized the huge Maji-Maji rebellion (1905–1906) to expel German colonial authorities from east Africa. Rebels sprinkled themselves with *maji-maji* ("magic water"), which they believed would protect them from German weapons. Although the rebellion failed and resulted in the deaths of as many as seventy-five thousand insurgents, it testified to the fact that rebellion was a constant threat to colonial rule. Even when subject peoples dared not revolt, they resisted colonial rule by boycotting European goods, organizing political parties and pressure groups, and pursuing anticolonial policies through churches and religious groups.

SCIENTIFIC RACISM Social and cultural differences were the foundation of an academic pursuit known as scientific racism, which became prominent especially after the 1840s. Theorists such as the French nobleman Count Joseph Arthur de Gobineau (1816–1882) took race as the most important index of human potential. In fact, there is no such thing as a biologically pure race, but nineteenth-century theorists assumed that the human species consisted of several distinct racial groups. In his dense, four-volume *Essay on the Inequality of the Human Races* (1853–1855), Gobineau divided humanity into four main racial groups. Gobineau characterized Africans as unintelligent and lazy; Asians as smart but docile; the native peoples of the Americas as dull and arrogant; and Europeans as intelligent, noble, and morally superior to others. Throughout the later nineteenth and early twentieth centuries, racist thinkers sought to identify racial groups on the basis of skin color, bone structure, nose shape, cranial capacity, and other physical characteristics.

After the 1860s scientific racists drew heavily from the writings of Charles Darwin (1809–1882), an English biologist whose book *On the Origin of Species* (1859) argued that all living species had evolved over thousands of years in a ferocious contest for survival. Species that adapted well to their environment survived, reproduced, and flourished, according to Darwin, whereas others declined and went into extinction. The slogan "survival of the fittest" soon became a byword for Darwin's theory of evolution. Theorists known as social Darwinists seized on those ideas, which Darwin had applied exclusively to biological matters, and adapted them to explain the development of human societies. The English philosopher Herbert Spencer (1820–1903) relied on theories of evolution to explain differences between the strong and the weak: successful individuals and races had competed better in the natural world and consequently evolved to higher states than did other, less fit, peoples. On the basis of that reasoning, Spencer and others justified the domination of European imperialists over subject peoples as the inevitable result of natural scientific principles.

Racist views were by no means a monopoly of European imperialists: U.S. and Japanese empire builders also developed a sense of superiority over the peoples they conquered and ruled. U.S. forces in the Philippines disparaged the rebels they fought there as "gooks," and they did not hesitate to torture enemies in a conflict that was supposed to "civilize and Christianize" the Filipinos. In the 1890s Japanese newspapers portrayed Chinese and Korean peoples as dirty, backward, stupid, and cowardly. After their victory in the Russo-Japanese War, political and military leaders came to believe that Japan had an obligation to oversee the affairs of their backward neighbors and help civilize their little Asian brothers.

SUMMARY

The construction of global empires in the nineteenth century noticeably increased the tempo of world integration. Armed with powerful transportation, communication, and military technologies, European peoples imposed their rule on much of Asia and almost all of Africa. They wielded enormous influence throughout the world, even where they did not establish imperial control, because of their wealth and economic power. Toward the end of the nineteenth century, the United States and Japan joined European states as global imperialists. All the imperial powers profoundly influenced the development of the societies they ruled. They shaped the economies and societies of their colonies by pushing them to supply natural resources and agricultural commodities in exchange for manufactured products. They created multicultural societies around the world by facilitating the movement of workers to lands where there was high demand for labor on plantations or in mines. They also provoked subject peoples to resist colonial expansion, which over time led them to develop a sense of national identity. From the early twentieth century forward, much of global history has revolved around issues stemming from the world order of imperialism and colonialism.

STUDY TERMS

Boxer rebellion (567)
capitulations (563)
direct rule (560)
East India Company (565)
formal imperialism (556)
Hundred Days reforms (567)
indentured labor (575)
indirect rule (560)
informal imperialism (556)
King Leopold II (568)
Maji-Maji rebellion (576)
mission civilisatrice (558)
Monroe Doctrine (572)
New Zealand Wars (571)
Opium War (565)
Panama Canal (558)
Roosevelt Corollary (573)
Russo-Japanese War (574)
scientific racism (576)
Self-Strengthening Movement (567)
Sepoy Rebellion (560)
South African War (569)
Spanish-Cuban-American War (573)
Suez Canal (558)
Taiping rebellion (567)
Tanzimat (564)
unequal treaties (565)
Young Turk Party (564)

FOR FURTHER READING

Michael Adas. *Machines as the Measure of Men: Science, Technology, and Ideologies of Western Dominance.* Ithaca, 1988. Argues that European imperialists judged other peoples on the basis of their technological expertise.

W. G. Beasley. *Japanese Imperialism, 1894–1945.* Oxford, 1987. The best study of the topic, emphasizing the relationship between Japanese industrialization and imperialism.

A. Adu Boahen. *African Perspectives on Colonialism.* Baltimore, 1987. A valuable synthetic work that examines African responses to imperial intrusions and colonial regimes.

Philip D. Curtin. *The World and the West: The European Challenge and the Overseas Response in the Age of Empire.* Cambridge and New York, 2000. A work that focuses on cultural change as it examines how various peoples have responded to the establishment of European empires.

John Gallagher. *The Decline, Revival, and Fall of the British Empire.* Ed. by Anil Seal. Cambridge, 1982. A collection of essays that have deeply influenced scholarship on the British empire.

Daniel R. Headrick. *The Tentacles of Progress: Technology Transfer in the Age of Imperialism, 1850–1940.* New York, 1988. Argues that imperial powers reserved the benefits of technological innovation for themselves by limiting the expertise that they shared with subject peoples.

Adam Hochschild. *King Leopold's Ghost: A Story of Greed, Terror, and Heroism in Colonial Africa.* Boston, 1998. A ghastly story of nearly forgotten greed and crime.

Peter Hopkirk. *The Great Game: The Struggle for Empire in Central Asia.* New York, 1992. Exciting account of the contest for power known as the Great Game.

David Northrup. *Indentured Labor in the Age of Imperialism, 1834–1922.* Cambridge, 1995. Careful study of indentured labor migrations and working conditions.

Thomas Pakenham. *The Scramble for Africa, 1876–1912.* New York, 1991. Detailed popular history of empire building in sub-Saharan Africa.

Bringing It All Together

Part VI An Age of Revolution, Industry, and Empire, 1750–1914

Since the end of the fifteenth century, the world's peoples grew increasingly interconnected as a result of transoceanic networks of trade and migration. Indeed, the forces unleashed by multiple revolutions, rapid industrialization, and widespread imperialism in this period radically intensified earlier patterns of intercultural exchange.

The Atlantic revolutions clearly demonstrate the multiple threads that connected people and places across the oceans even at the beginning of this period. The first revolution to occur, in the thirteen North American English colonies, was fed by Enlightenment ideals of liberty and equality that traveled from Europe to the Americas along with trade items and migrants. From there, the success of the American Revolution inspired French thinkers. Both American and French success then inspired Haitian and Latin American revolutionaries to sever their colonial ties. Meanwhile, revolutionaries began to form identities on the basis of nation-states—an idea that, once formed, reverberated around the Atlantic basin and, later, the world.

By the nineteenth century, new technologies produced by industrialization—including the railroad, the steamship, and the telegraph—allowed ideas, trade goods, and people to travel far faster and over far greater distances than in the past. As a result, huge geographical expanses across oceans as well as continents were knitted together into new relationships. Moreover, the global impact of industrialization increased as new states in western Europe, North America, Russia, and Japan undertook their own programs of industrialization. These powers then spread industrial technologies to every continent in the world.

Although the impact of industrial technologies was global by 1914, the world's peoples did not realize the benefits of industrialization equally. Instead, industrial powers—especially Europeans and their North American descendants—used their technological advantages to conquer and dominate vast territories in Asia, Africa, and Oceania. As a result, by the start of the twentieth century the leading industrial powers had carved the world into vast empires—each connected by networks of trade, resource exploitation, and migration.

The global webs of connection forged via industry and empire did not breed harmony. Rather, the growth of nationalism around the world encouraged intense competition for natural resources, strategic ports, and international prestige. In addition, industrial and imperial powers increasingly justified their domination of the world in terms of racial superiority, which bred discontent among the conquered and dominated peoples of the world. Such discontent, when combined with disputes between the great powers, led to explosive conflicts that would make the twentieth century the most violent in the history of humankind.

VII Contemporary Global Realignments

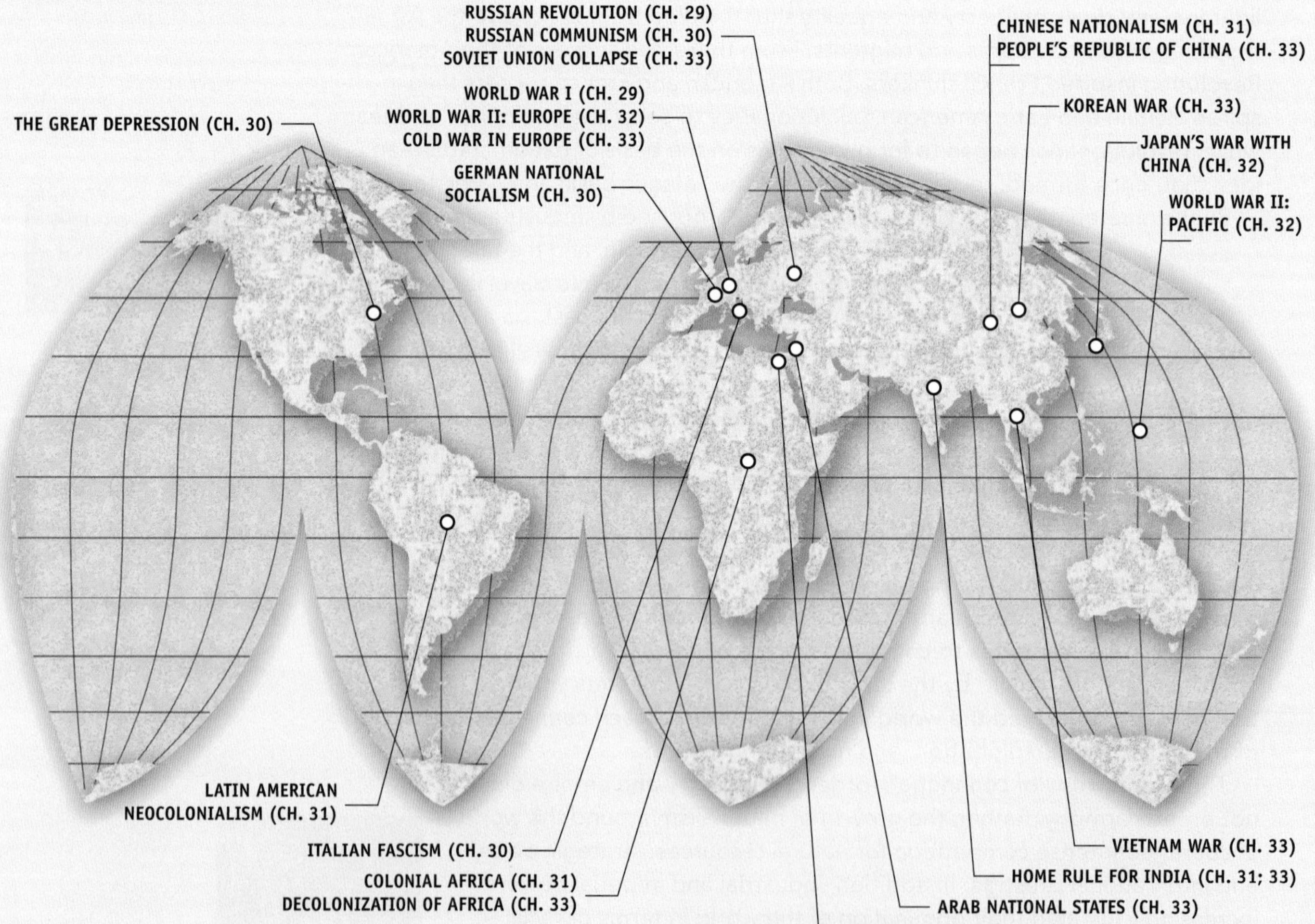

At the time the Great War erupted in 1914, Europeans and their descendants in North America dominated global affairs to an unprecedented extent, exercising political and economic control over peoples and their lands in most of Asia, nearly all of Africa, the Americas, and the Pacific islands. This global dominance was the outcome of three interconnected historical developments that took place between 1750 and 1914: the formation of national states, industrialization, and imperial expansion.

Those same historical developments, which encouraged national rivalries, colonial disputes, and nationalist aspirations, plunged Europe—and then much of the world—into war in 1914. By the time the war ended in 1918, all the major European powers had exhausted much of their economic wealth and global political primacy.

Global interdependence ensured that economic instability after the Great War affected much of the world. This was especially true in the Great Depression, when political turmoil and social misery paved the way to fascist dictatorships in Italy and Germany and to nationalist movements in Asia. Meanwhile, the Soviet Union embarked on a state-sponsored program of rapid industrialization that transformed it into a major international power.

Sparked as a result of the Great War and the Great Depression, World War II began in China in 1931 when Japanese forces established a colonial empire in Manchuria. The conflict spread to Europe in the late 1930s when the Nazi regime embarked on a policy of territorial expansion. By 1941 all the world's major powers had been sucked into a maelstrom of violence and suffering that engulfed most European societies, almost all of Asia and the Pacific, and parts of Africa.

World War II completed the economic and political weakening of European societies and led to the immediate outbreak of the cold war and the dismantling of colonial empires, both of which realigned the world of the late twentieth and twenty-first centuries. The cold war conflict between the forces of capitalism and communism produced a new set of global relationships, shaping the foreign policies, economic systems, and political institutions of nations throughout the world until its abrupt end in the late 1980s.

In the three decades after World War II, an irresistible wave of independence movements swept away colonies and empires and led to the establishment of new nations in Africa and Asia. However, the initial euphoria that accompanied freedom from imperial control was tempered by neocolonial and postcolonial problems such as interference by the superpowers, lack of economic development, and regional and ethnic conflicts.

Other forces that reshaped the twentieth- and twenty-first-century world include globalization, a process that widened the extent and the forms of cross-cultural interaction among the world's peoples. Technological advances dissolved old political, social, and economic barriers. The resulting global integration encouraged similar economic and political preferences and fostered common cultural values, but forces promoting distinct cultural traditions and political identities also arose to challenge the universalizing effects of globalization.

The Great War: The World in Upheaval

29

rchduke Francis Ferdinand (1863–1914) was aware that his first official visit to Sarajevo in 1914 was fraught with danger. That ancient city was the capital of Bosnia-Herzegovina, twin provinces that had been under Ottoman rule since the fifteenth century, then occupied in 1878, and finally annexed by Austria-Hungary in 1908. These provinces became the hotbed of pan-Serbian nationalism. Most Serbian nationalists hated the Austro-Hungarian dynasty and the empire represented by Ferdinand, the heir to the throne.

It was a warm and radiant Sunday morning when Ferdinand's motorcade made its way through the narrow streets of Sarajevo. Waiting for him along the designated route were seven assassins armed with bombs and revolvers, one of whom threw a bomb into the open car. Glancing off Ferdinand's arm, the bomb exploded near another vehicle and injured dozens of spectators.

Undeterred, Ferdinand went on to a reception at city hall; after the reception he instructed his driver to take him to the hospital where those wounded in the earlier attack were being treated. While Ferdinand was on his way to the hospital, a young Bosnian Serb named Gavrilo Princip (1894–1918) lunged at the archduke's car and fired a revolver. The first bullet blew a gaping hole in the side of Ferdinand's neck. A second bullet intended for the governor of Bosnia went wild and entered the stomach of the expectant Duchess Sophie, the wife of the archduke. Turning to his wife, the archduke pleaded: "Sophie, dear! Don't die! Stay alive for our children!" By the time medical aid arrived, however, the archduke and the duchess were dead.

The assassination of the archduke and his wife brought to a head the tensions between the Austro-Hungarian empire and the neighboring kingdom of Serbia. As other European powers took sides, the stakes far outgrew Austro-Serbian conflicts. Nationalist aspirations, international rivalries, and an inflexible alliance system transformed that conflict into a general European war and ultimately into a global struggle involving thirty-two nations. Twenty-eight of those nations, collectively known as the Allies and the Associated Powers, fought the coalition known as the Central Powers, which consisted of Germany, Austria-Hungary, the Ottoman empire, and Bulgaria. The shell-shocked generation that survived the carnage called this clash of arms the Great War. A subsequent generation of survivors renamed the conflict World War I, because it was, sadly, only the first of two wars that engulfed the world in the first half of the twentieth century.

The Great War lasted from August 1914 to November 1918 and ushered in history's most violent century. In geographic

❮ *This painting by C. R. W. Nevinson, called* Harvest of Battle, *testifies to the appalling scale of death and destruction during the battles of WWI. © Detail. Imperial War Museum (IWM Art 1921)*

CHRONOLOGY

1914	Assassination of Archduke Francis Ferdinand
1915	Japan makes twenty-one demands on China
1915	Gallipoli campaign
1916	Battles at Verdun and the Somme
1917	German resumption of unrestricted submarine warfare
1917	United States declaration of war on Germany
1917	Bolshevik Revolution
1918	Treaty of Brest-Litovsk
1918	Armistice suspends hostilities
1919	Paris Peace Conference
1920	First meeting of the League of Nations

extent the conflict surpassed all previous wars, compelling men, women, and children on five continents to participate directly or indirectly in a struggle that many did not understand. The Great War also had the distinction of being the first total war in human history, as governments mobilized every available human and material resource for the conduct of war. Moreover, the industrial nature of the conflict meant that it was the bloodiest in the annals of organized violence. The military casualties passed a threshold beyond previous experience: approximately fifteen million soldiers died, and an additional twenty million combatants suffered injuries.

The war of 1914–1918 did more than destroy individual lives. It seriously damaged national economies, it led to the redrawing of European boundaries, and it caused the demise of four dynasties and their empires—the Ottoman empire, the Russian empire, the Austro-Hungarian empire, and the German empire. The war also helped unleash the Bolshevik Revolution of 1917, which set the stage for an ideological conflict between capitalism and communism that endured to the end of the twentieth century. Finally, the Great War was responsible for an international realignment of power. It undermined the preeminence and prestige of European society, signaling an end to Europe's global primacy.

THE DRIFT TOWARD WAR

Although the catalyst for war was the assassination of Archduke Francis Ferdinand, the assassin's bullets would have had limited effect if there had not been deeper reasons for war. Indeed, the underlying causes for the war of 1914–1918 were many, including intense nationalism, abrasive colonial rivalries, and a general struggle over the balance of power in Europe and in the world at large. Between 1871 and 1914, European governments adopted foreign policies that increased steadily the danger of war. So as to not find themselves alone in a hostile world, national leaders sought alignments with other powers. The establishment and maintenance in Europe of two hostile alliances—the Allies and the Central Powers—helped spread the war from the Balkans.

Nationalist Aspirations

The nationalist fervor that spread throughout most of Europe in the nineteenth century had led many Europeans to rally behind the idea of *self-determination,* or the idea that peoples with the same ethnic origins, language, and political ideals had the right to form sovereign states. In fact, that idea helped inspire the nationalist movements that led to the creation of the new nations of Belgium (1830), Italy (1861), and Germany (1871). Yet at the end of the nineteenth century, the issue of nationalism remained unresolved in other areas of Europe, most notably in eastern Europe and the Balkans. There the nationalist aspirations of subject minorities threatened to tear apart the multinational empires of the Ottoman and Habsburg dynasties and with them the regional balance of power.

The Ottoman empire had controlled the Balkan peninsula since the fifteenth century, but after 1829 the Turkish empire shriveled, largely because of nationalist revolts. Greece was the first to gain independence (in 1830), but within a few decades Serbia, Romania, and Bulgaria followed suit. Austria-Hungary also confronted nationalism within its realms, especially the aspirations of Slavic peoples—Poles, Czechs, Slovaks, Serbs, Croats, and Slovenes. Most menacing and militant were the Serbs, who pressed for unification with the independent kingdom of Serbia. Russia and Germany added fuel to this volatile situation by supporting opposing sides. Russia supported Serbia and the notion of Slavic cultural unity, while Germany backed Austria-Hungary. Thus the stage was set for international conflict.

National Rivalries

Aggressive nationalism was also manifest in economic competition and colonial conflicts, fueling dangerous rivalries among the major European powers. All the industrialized nations of Europe competed for foreign markets and engaged in tariff wars, but the most unsettling economic rivalry involved Great Britain and Germany. By the twentieth century, Germany's rapid industrialization threatened Britain's longstanding economic predominance. Indeed, by 1914 Britain's share of global industrial output had declined to a level roughly equal to Germany's 13 percent. British reluctance to accept the relative decline of British industry vis-à-vis German industry strained relations between the two economic powers.

THINKING ABOUT *Traditions*

TRADITIONS IN THE GREAT WAR. At the beginning of the twentieth century, the force of nationalism had led many European groups who were part of larger state or imperial structures to insist on their right to national self-determination. In what ways did the idea of tradition inform and justify their various calls for separate nationhood?

THE NAVAL RACE An expensive naval race further exacerbated tensions between the two nations. When Germany's political and military leaders announced their program to build a fleet with many large battleships, they seemed to undermine Britain's longtime mastery of the seas. The British government moved to meet the German threat through the construction of super battleships known as *dreadnoughts.* Rather than discouraging the Germans, the British determination to retain naval superiority stimulated the Germans to build their own flotilla of dreadnoughts. As the two nations raced to outdo each other, international hostilities boiled under the surface.

Dreadnought
www.mhhe.com/bentleybrief2e

COLONIAL DISPUTES National rivalries also fomented colonial competition. During the late nineteenth and early twentieth centuries, European nations searched aggressively for new colonies or dependencies to bolster economic performance. In their

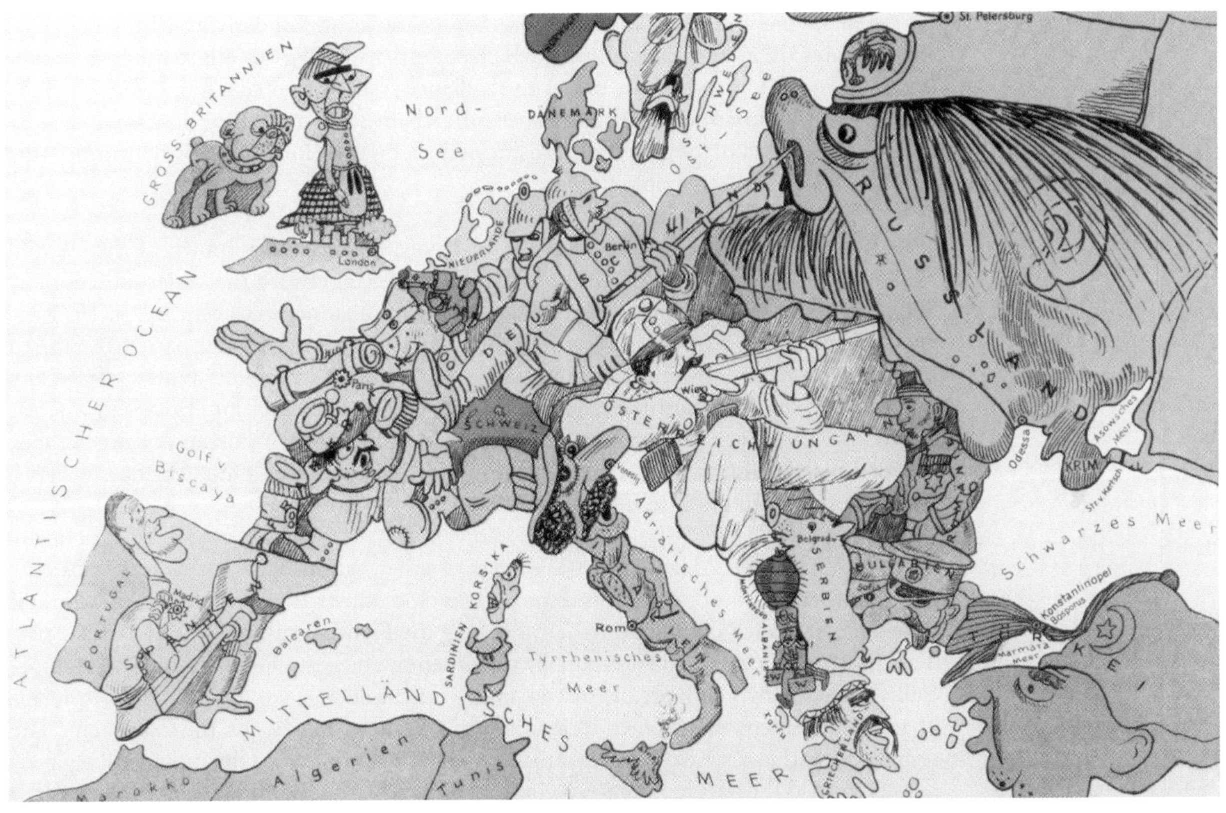

EUROPEAN RIVALRIES AT THE START OF WWI. | This satirical map was created by dissident cartoonist Walter Trier. ***What message was Trier trying to convey with this map?***

haste to conquer and colonize, the imperial powers stumbled over one another, repeatedly clashing in one or another corner of the globe: Britain and Russia faced off in Persia (modern-day Iran) and Afghanistan; Britain and France in Siam (modern-day Thailand) and the Nile valley; Britain and Germany in east and southwest Africa; Germany and France in Morocco and west Africa.

PSI img 1912 Cairo *Punch* cartoon www.mhhe.com/bentleybrief2e

Between 1905 and 1914, a series of international crises and two local wars raised tensions and almost precipitated a general European war. The first crisis resulted from a French-German confrontation over Morocco in 1905. When the German government announced its support of Moroccan independence, which French encroachment endangered, the French responded by threatening war. An international conference in the following year prevented a clash of arms, but similar crises threatened the peace in subsequent years. Contributing to the growing tensions in European affairs were the Balkan wars. Between 1912 and 1913, the states of the Balkan peninsula—including Bulgaria, Greece, Montenegro, Serbia, and Romania—fought two wars for possession of European territories held by the Ottoman empire. The Balkan wars strained European diplomatic relations and helped shape the tense circumstances that led to the outbreak of the Great War.

PUBLIC OPINION Public pressure also contributed to national rivalries. New means of communication—especially cheap, mass-produced newspapers—nourished the public's desire to see their country "come in first," whether in the competition for colonies or in the race to the South Pole. However, public pressure calling for national greatness placed policymakers and diplomats in an awkward situation. Compelled to achieve headline-grabbing foreign policy successes, these leaders ran the risk of paying for short-lived triumphs with long-lasting hostility from other countries.

Understandings and Alliances

In addition to a basic desire for security, escalating national rivalries and nationalist aspirations of subject minorities spawned a system of entangling alliances. The complexity of those obligations could not hide the common characteristic underlying all the alliances: they outlined the circumstances under which countries would go to war to support one another. Intended to preserve the peace, rival alliance systems created a framework whereby even a small international crisis could set off a chain reaction leading to global war. By 1914 Europe's major powers had transformed themselves into two hostile camps—the Triple Alliance and the Triple Entente.

THE CENTRAL POWERS The Triple Alliance, also known as the Central Powers, grew out of the close relationship that developed between the leaders of Germany and Austria-Hungary during the last three decades of the nineteenth century. In 1879 the governments of the two empires formed the Dual Alliance, a defensive pact that ensured reciprocal protection from a Russian attack and neutrality in case of an attack from any other power. Fear of a hostile France motivated Germans to enter into this pact, whereas Austrians viewed it as giving them a free hand in pursuing their Balkan politics without fear of Russian intervention. Italy, fearful of France, joined the Dual Alliance in 1882, thereby transforming it into the Triple Alliance.

THE ALLIES Meanwhile, the leaders of other nations viewed this new constellation of power with suspicion. This response was especially true of French leaders, who still remembered France's humiliating defeat during the Franco-Prussian War of 1870–1871. The tsarist regime of Russia was equally disturbed by the new alignment of powers, especially by Germany's support of Austria, and British leaders were traditionally suspicious of any arrangement that seemed to threaten the balance of power on the Continent. The result was that, in a series of agreements between 1904 and 1914, the most unlikely bedfellows formed the Triple Entente, a combination of nations commonly referred to as the

Triple Entente (ahn-TAHNT)

Allies. The construction of such alliances made it difficult for diplomats to contain what otherwise might have been relatively small international crises.

WAR PLANS The preservation of peace was also difficult because the military staffs of each nation had devised inflexible military plans and timetables to be carried out in the event of war. German war plans in particular played a crucial role in the events leading to the Great War. Germany's fear of encirclement by France and Russia encouraged its military planners to devise a strategy that would avoid a war on two fronts. It was based on a strategy developed in 1905 by General Count Alfred von Schlieffen (1833–1913). The Schlieffen plan called for a swift knockout of France, followed by defensive action against Russia. German planners predicated their strategy on the knowledge that the Russians could not mobilize their soldiers and military supplies as quickly as the French, thus giving German forces a few precious weeks during which they could concentrate their full power on France. However, Germany's military strategy was a serious obstacle to those seeking to preserve the peace. In the event of Russian mobilization, Germany's leaders would feel compelled to stick to their war plans by attacking France first, thereby setting in motion a military conflict of major proportions.

Global War

In the capitals of Europe, people danced in the streets when their governments announced formal declarations of war. When the first contingents of soldiers left for the front, jubilant crowds threw flowers at the feet of departing men, who expected to return victorious after a short time. However, reality crushed any expectations of a short and triumphant war. On most fronts the conflict quickly bogged down and became a war of attrition in which the firepower of modern weapons slaughtered soldiers by the millions. For the first time in history, belligerent nations engaged in total war. Even in democratic societies, governments assumed dictatorial control to marshal the human and material resources required for continuous war. One result was increased participation of women in the labor force. Total war had repercussions that went beyond the borders of Europe.

Imperial ties drew millions of Asians, Africans, and residents of the British dominions into the war to serve as soldiers and laborers. Struggles over far-flung colonies further underlined the global dimension of this war. Last, the war gained a global flavor through the entry of Japan, the United States, and the Ottoman empire, nations whose leaders professed little direct interest in European affairs.

The Guns of August

Serbian ambulance tent
www.mhhe.com/bentleybrief2e

DECLARATIONS OF WAR The shots fired from Gavrilo Princip's revolver on that fateful day of 28 June 1914 set in motion a flurry of diplomatic activity that quickly escalated into war. Austrian leaders in Vienna were determined to teach the unruly Serbs a lesson, and on 23 July the Austrians issued an ultimatum to the government of Serbia. When the Serbian government rejected one of its terms, Austria-Hungary declared war on Serbia. The war had begun. The subsequent sequence of events was largely determined by two factors: complex mobilization plans and the grinding logic of the alliance system. Military planners were convinced that the timing of mobilization orders and adherence to precise timetables were crucial to the successful conduct of war.

On 29 July the Russian government mobilized its troops to defend its Serbian ally and itself from Austria. The tsar of Russia then ordered mobilization against Germany. Nicholas II (1868–1918) took that decisive step reluctantly and only after his military experts had convinced him that a partial mobilization might invite defeat should the Germans enter the war on the side of Austria. His action precipitated a German ultimatum to Russia on 31 July, demanding that the Russian army cease its mobilization immediately. Another

Schlieffen (SHLEE-fn)

ultimatum addressed to France demanded to know what France's intentions were in case Germany and Russia went to war. The Russians replied with a blunt "impossible," and the French never answered. Thus on 1 August the German government declared war on Russia, and France started to mobilize.

On 3 August the Germans declared war on France. On the same day, German troops invaded Belgium in accordance with the Schlieffen plan. Key to this plan was an attack on the weak left flank of the French army by an imposing German force through neutral Belgium. On 4 August the British government sent an ultimatum to Germany demanding that Belgian neutrality be respected. When Germany's wartime leaders refused, the British immediately declared war. A local conflict had become a general European war.

Mutual Butchery

Everyone expected the war to be brief. In the first weeks of August 1914, twenty million young men donned uniforms, took up rifles, and left for the front. Many of them looked forward to heroic charges, rapid promotions, and a quick homecoming. Some dreamed of glory and honor, and they believed that God was on their side. Similar attitudes prevailed among the political and military leaders of the belligerent nations, who were preoccupied by visions of sweeping assaults, envelopments, and, above all, swift triumphs. Their visions could hardly have been more wrong.

THE WESTERN FRONT The initial German thrust toward Paris in August 1914 came to a grinding halt along the river Marne, after which each side tried to outflank the other in a race to the Atlantic coast. For the next three years, the battle lines remained virtually stationary, as both sides dug in and slugged it out in a war of attrition that lasted until the late autumn of 1918. Each belligerent tried to wear down the enemy by inflicting continuous damage and casualties, only to have its own forces suffer heavy losses in return. Trenches on the western front ran from the English Channel to Switzerland. Farther south, Italy left the Triple Alliance to enter the war on the side of the Allies in 1915. Allied hopes that the Italians would pierce Austrian defenses quickly faded. After a disastrous defeat at Caporetto in 1917, Italian forces maintained a defensive line only with the help of the French and the British.

STALEMATE AND NEW WEAPONS The stalemate on the western and southern fronts reflected technological developments that favored defensive tactics. Barbed wire proved highly effective in frustrating the advance of soldiers across "no-man's-land," the deadly territory between opposing trenches. In addition, the rapid and continuous fire of machine guns turned infantry charges across no-man's-land into suicide missions. Both sides developed weapons to break the deadly stalemate and reintroduce movement into the war. Gas often proved lethal, and it caused its victims excruciating pain. Mustard gas, for example, rotted the body from both within and without. After blistering the skin and damaging the eyes, the gas attacked the bronchial tubes, stripping off the mucous membrane. Death could occur in four to five weeks. Yet although both sides suffered heavy casualties, totaling about 800,000 soldiers, gas attacks failed to deliver the promised strategic breakthroughs. Other novel weapons developed during the war included tanks and airplanes. Other weapons systems, such as the submarine, had made earlier appearances in warfare but were most effectively used by the German navy against Allied commercial shipping in the Great War.

NO-MAN'S-LAND The most courageous infantry charges, even when preceded by pulverizing artillery barrages and clouds of poisonous gas, were no match for determined defenders. Shielded by the dirt of their trenches and by barbed wire and gas masks, they unleashed a torrent of lethal metal with their machine guns and repeating rifles. In

Caporetto (kap-uh-RET-oh)

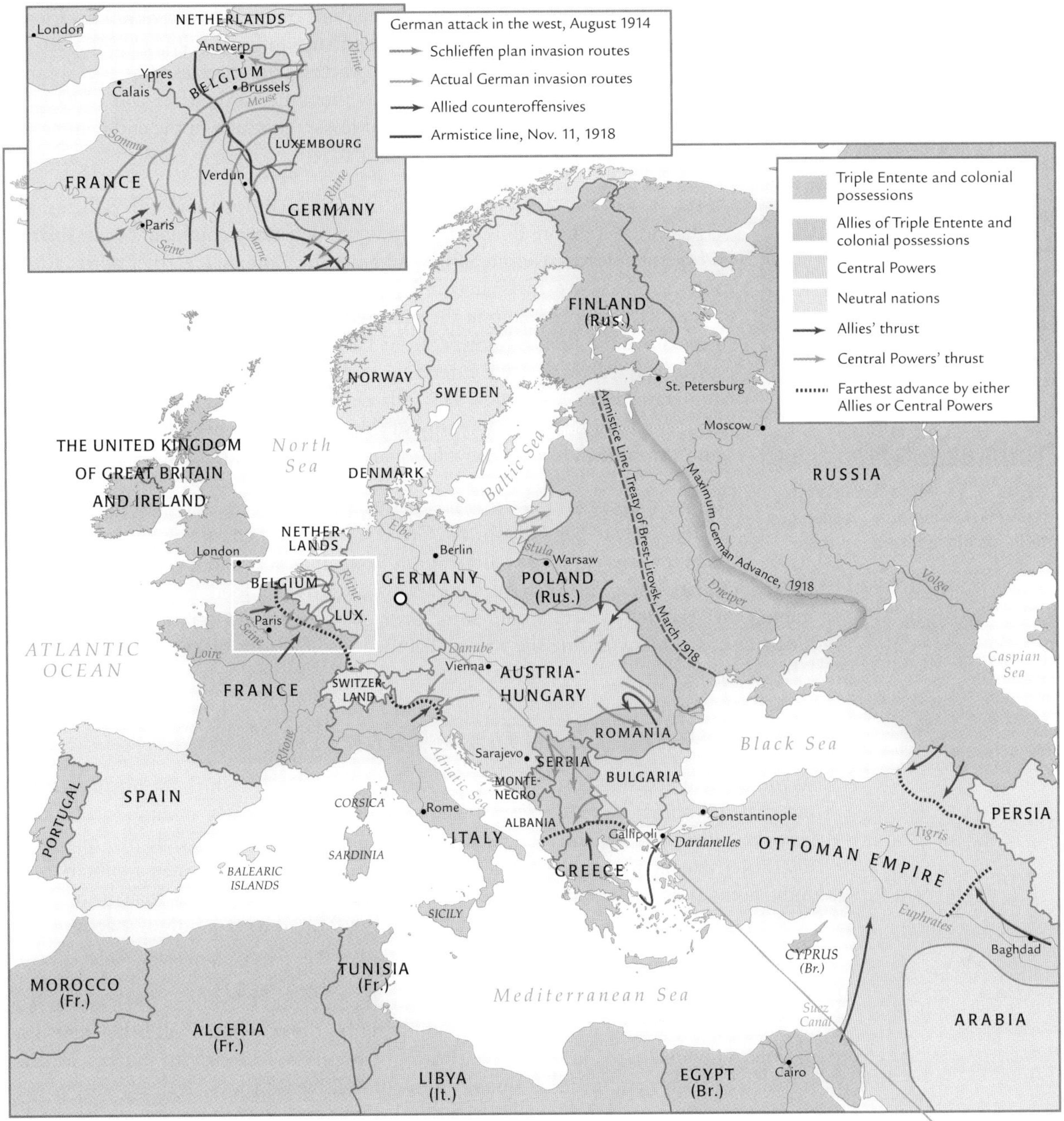

MAP 29.1 | The Great War in Europe and southwest Asia, 1914–1918. Note the locations of both the eastern and the western fronts in Europe during the war. ***Why didn't the same kind of trench warfare immobilize opposing armies on the eastern front the way it did on the western front?***

Germany's position between France and Russia ensured a war on two fronts if hostilities arose between the Triple Entente and the Central Powers.

every sector of the front, those who fought rarely found the glory they sought. Instead, they encountered death. No-man's-land was strewn with shell craters, cadavers, and body parts. The grim realities of trench warfare—the wet, cold, waist-deep mud, gluttonous lice, and corpse-fed rats—contrasted sharply with the ringing phrases of politicians and generals justifying the unrelenting slaughter.

In the trenches at Verdun
www.mhhe.com/bentleybrief2e

BLOODLETTING Many battles took place, but some were so horrific, so devastating, and so futile that their names are synonymous with human slaughter. The casualty figures attested to this bloodletting. In 1916 the Germans tried to break the deadlock with a huge assault on the fortress of Verdun. The French rallying cry was "They shall not

Poison Gas. | Air raid warden in helmet and gas mask, holding a wooden gas attack rattle in his gloved hand.

pass," and they did not—but at a tremendous cost: while the victorious French counted 315,000 dead, the defeated Germans suffered a loss of 280,000. To relieve the pressure on Verdun, British forces counterattacked at the Somme, and by November they had gained a few thousand yards at the cost of 420,000 casualties. The Germans suffered similar losses, although in the end neither side gained any strategic advantage.

THE EASTERN FRONT In eastern Europe and the Balkans, the battle lines were more fluid. After a staunch defense, a combination of Austrian and German forces overran Serbia, Albania, and Romania. Farther north, Russia took the offensive early by invading Prussia in 1914. The Central Powers recovered quickly, however, and in the summer of 1915, combined German-Austrian forces drove the Russian armies out of East Prussia and then out of Poland and established a defensive line extending from the Baltic to the Ukraine. Russian counterattacks in 1916 and 1917 collapsed in a sea of casualties. Those Russian defeats undermined the popularity of the tsar and his government and played a significant role in fostering revolutionary ferment within Russian society.

NEW RULES OF ENGAGEMENT Dying and suffering were not limited solely to combatants: the Great War established rules of engagement that made civilians targets of warfare, both from air attacks and from naval blockades. Indeed, military leaders on both sides used blockades to deny food to whole populations, hoping that starving masses would force their governments to capitulate. The British blockade of Germany during the war contributed to the deaths of an estimated half million Germans.

Total War: The Home Front

As the Great War ground on, it became a conflict of attrition in which the organization of material and human resources was of paramount importance. War became total, fought between entire societies, and total victory was the only acceptable outcome that might justify the terrible sacrifices made by all sides. The nature of total war created a military front and a home front. The term *home front* expressed the important reality that the outcome of the war hinged on how effectively each nation mobilized its economy and activated its noncombatant citizens to support the war effort.

THE HOME FRONT As the war continued beyond Christmas 1914 and as war weariness and a decline in economic capability set in, the response of all belligerents was to limit individual freedoms and give control of society increasingly to military leaders. Initially, ministers and generals shrank from compulsive measures, even conscription of recruits, but they quickly changed their minds. Each belligerent government eventually militarized civilian war production by subordinating private enterprises to governmental control and imposing severe discipline on the labor process.

Economic measures were foremost in the minds of government leaders because the war created unprecedented demands for raw materials and manufactured goods. Planning boards reorganized entire industries, set production quotas and priorities, and determined what would be produced and consumed. Government authorities also established wage and price controls, extended work hours, and in some instances restricted the movement of workers. Because bloody battlefields caused an insatiable appetite for soldiers, nations responded by extending military service. In Germany, for example, men between the ages of sixteen and sixty were eligible to serve at the front. By constantly tapping into the available male population, the war created an increasing demand for workers at home. Unemployment—a persistent feature of all prewar economies—vanished virtually overnight.

WOMEN AT WAR As men marched off to war, women marched off to work. Conscription took men out of the labor force, and wartime leaders exhorted women to fill the gaps in the workforce. A combination of patriotism and high wages drew women into many formerly "male" jobs in a wide variety of industries and public sectors. Perhaps the most crucial work performed by women during the war was the making of shells. Several million women, and sometimes children, put in long, hard hours in munitions factories. That work exposed them to severe dangers, not to mention death, from explosions and poisoning from long-term exposure to TNT.

Although some middle- and upper-class women reported that the war was a liberating experience in regard to personal and economic freedom, most working-class women found little that was liberating in war work. Most of the belligerent governments promised equal pay for equal work, but in most instances that promise remained unfulfilled. Moreover, substantial female employment was a transitory phenomenon. Once the war was over, many women workers—especially those in traditionally male occupations—found themselves forced to concede their jobs to men. Nevertheless, the extension of voting rights to women shortly after the war—in Britain (1918, for women thirty years and older), Germany (1919), and Austria (1919)—was in part due to the role women assumed during the Great War.

War Casualties on the Western Front. | This photograph depicts a mutilated body among barbed wire in no-man's-land.

PROPAGANDA To maintain the spirit of the home front and to counter threats to national unity, governments resorted to the restriction of civil liberties, censorship of bad news, and vilification of the enemy through propaganda campaigns. While some government officials busily censored war news, people who had the temerity to criticize their nation's war effort were prosecuted as traitors. Meanwhile, the propaganda offices of the belligerent nations tried to convince the public that military defeat would mean the destruction of everything worth living for, and to that end they did their utmost to discredit and dehumanize the enemy.

German propaganda depicted Russians as semi-Asiatic barbarians, and French authorities chronicled the atrocities committed by the German "Hun" in Belgium. In 1917 the *Times* of London published a story claiming that Germans converted human corpses into fertilizer and food. In Germany, one widely distributed poster invoked images of bestial black Allied soldiers raping German women to suggest the horrors that would follow if the nation's war effort failed. Most atrocity stories were patently false, and they eventually engendered public skepticism and cynicism. Ironically, public disbelief of wartime propaganda led to an inability to believe in the abominations perpetrated in later wars.

War Propaganda. | "The Heroes of Belgium, 1914." French propaganda poster expresses outrage at the German invasion of Belgium. ***What are these "German" soldiers trampling underfoot?***

Conflict in East Asia and the Pacific

The Great War quickly turned from a European war into a global conflict. There were three reasons for the war's expansion. First, European governments carried their animosities into their colonies, embroiling them—especially African societies—in their war. Second, because Europe's human reserves were not enough to satisfy the appetite of war, the British and the French augmented their ranks by recruiting men from their colonies. Millions of Africans and Asians were drawn into the war. Behind their trenches the French employed laborers from Algeria, China, and French Indochina, and the British did not hesitate to draft Indian and African troops for combat. The British in particular relied on troops furnished by the dominion lands, including Australia, New Zealand, Canada, Newfoundland, and South Africa. Third, the Great War assumed global significance because of the entrance into the war of Japan, the United States, and the Ottoman empire.

SOURCES FROM THE PAST

Dulce et Decorum Est

The Great War produced a wealth of poetry. The poetic response to war covered a range of moods from early romanticism and patriotism to cynicism, resignation, and the angry depiction of horror. Perhaps the greatest of all war poets was Wilfred Owen (1893–1918), whose poems are among the most poignant of the war. Owen, who enlisted for service on the western front in 1915, was injured in March 1917 and sent home. Declared fit for duty in August 1918, he returned to the front. German machine-gun fire killed him on 7 November, four days before the armistice, when he tried to cross the Sambre Canal.

Bent double, like old beggars under sacks,
Knock-kneed, coughing like hags, we cursed through sludge,
Till on the haunting flares we turned our backs
And towards our distant rest began to trudge.
Men marched asleep. Many had lost their boots
But limped on, blood-shod. All went lame; all blind;
Drunk with fatigue; deaf even to the hoots
Of gas-shells dropping softly behind.

Gas! GAS! Quick, boys!—An ecstasy of fumbling,
Fitting the clumsy helmets just in time;
But someone still was yelling out and stumbling
And floundering like a man in fire or lime.—
Dim, through the misty panes and thick green light
As under a green sea, I saw him drowning.
In all my dreams, before my helpless sight,
He plunges at me, guttering, choking, drowning.

If in some smothering dreams you too could pace
Behind the wagon that we flung him in,
And watch the white eyes writhing in his face,
His hanging face, like a devil's sick of sin;
If you could hear, at every jolt, the blood
Come gargling from the froth-corrupted lungs,
Obscene as cancer, bitter as the cud
Of vile, incurable sores on innocent tongues,—
My friend, you would not tell with such high zest
To children ardent for some desperate glory,
The old Lie: Dulce et decorum est
Pro patria mori.*

*Author's note: "Sweet and fitting is it to die for one's country" comes from a line by the Roman poet Horace (65–8 B.C.E.)

■ **How does Owen poetically describe the effects of a gas attack? Is his literary depiction more or less effective than detached descriptions of war's effects?**

SOURCE: Edmund Blunden, ed. *The Poems of Wilfred Owen.* London: Chatto & Windus, 1933, p. 66.

On 15 August 1914 the Japanese government sent an ultimatum to Germany demanding the handover of the German-leased territory of Jiaozhou (northeastern China) to Japanese authorities without compensation. The same note also demanded that the German navy unconditionally withdraw its warships from Japanese and Chinese waters. When the Germans refused to comply, the Japanese entered the war on the side of the Allies on 23 August 1914. Japanese forces then proceeded to seize German territories in China and—aided by forces from New Zealand and Australia—in the Pacific. Next, Japan shrewdly exploited Allied support and European preoccupation to advance its own imperial interests in China. On 18 January 1915 the Japanese presented the Chinese government with twenty-one secret demands. The terms of that ultimatum, if accepted, would have reduced China to a protectorate of Japan. Chinese diplomats leaked the note to the British authorities, who spoke up for China, thus preventing total capitulation. The Twenty-one Demands reflected Japan's determination to dominate east Asia and served as the basis for future Japanese pressure on China.

Jiaozhou (jyou-joh)

Battles in Africa and Southwest Asia

COLONIAL PARTICIPATION IN WWI. An Indian gun crew in the Somme area, 1916.

The geographic extent of the conflict also broadened beyond Europe when the Allies targeted German colonies in Africa. When the war of 1914–1918 erupted in Europe, all of sub-Saharan Africa (except Ethiopia and Liberia) consisted of European colonies, with the Germans controlling four: Togoland, the Cameroons, German Southwest Africa, and German East Africa. Unlike the capture of German colonies in the Pacific, which Allied forces accomplished during the first three months of the war with relative ease, the conquest of German colonies in Africa was difficult. Fighting took place on land and sea; on lakes and rivers; in deserts, jungles, and swamps; and in the air. Indeed, the German flag did not disappear from Africa until after the armistice took effect on 11 November 1918.

The most extensive military operations outside Europe took place in the southwest Asian territories of the Ottoman empire, which was aligned with the Central Powers at the end of 1914. Seeking a way to break the stalemate on the western front, Winston Churchill (1874–1965), first lord of the Admiralty (British navy), suggested that an Allied strike against the Ottomans—a weak ally of the Central Powers—would hurt the Germans. Early in 1915 the British navy conducted an expedition to seize the approach to the Dardanelles Strait in an attempt to open a warm-water supply line to Russia through the Ottoman-controlled strait. The campaign was a disaster. Turkish defenders, ensconced in the cliffs above, quickly pinned down the Allied troops on the beaches. Trapped between the sea and the hills, Allied soldiers dug in and engaged in their own version of trench warfare. The resulting stalemate produced a total of 250,000 casualties on each side. Despite the losses, Allied leaders took nine months to admit that their campaign had failed.

ARMENIAN MASSACRES The war provided the pretext for a campaign of extermination against the Ottoman empire's two million Armenians. Friction between Christian Armenians and Muslim Ottoman authorities went back to the nineteenth century, when distinct nationalist feelings stirred many of the peoples who lived under Ottoman rule.

After 1913, the Ottoman state adopted a new policy of Turkish nationalism intended to shore up the crumbling imperial edifice. The new nationalism stressed Turkish culture and traditions and regarded Christian minorities as obstacles to Turkism. During the Great War, the Ottoman government branded Armenians as traitorous internal enemies. The government then unleashed a murderous campaign against the Armenians, which included mass evacuations that were accompanied by starvation, dehydration, and exposure. Equally deadly were government-organized massacres that claimed victims through mass drowning, incineration, or assaults with blunt instruments.

Best estimates suggest that close to a million Armenians perished between 1915 and 1917 in what has become known as the Armenian genocide. Although it is generally agreed that the Armenian genocide did occur, the Turkish government denies the label of state-sponsored genocide, arguing instead that the deaths occurred as a result of communal warfare, disease, and famine.

THE END OF THE WAR

The war produced strains within all the belligerent nations, but most of them managed, often ruthlessly, to cope with food riots, strikes, and mutinies. In the Russian empire, the war amplified existing stresses to such an extent that the Romanov dynasty was forced to

Romanov (ROH-mah-nahv)

abdicate in favor of a provisional government in the spring of 1917. Eight months later, the provisional government yielded power to Bolshevik revolutionaries, who took Russia out of the war early in 1918. This blow to the Allies was more than offset by the entry of the United States into the conflict in 1917, which turned the tide of war in 1918. The resources of the United States finally compelled the exhausted Central Powers to sue for peace in November 1918.

In 1919 the victorious Allies gathered in Paris to hammer out a peace settlement that turned out to be a compromise that pleased few of the parties involved. The most significant consequence of the war was Europe's diminished role in the world. The war of 1914–1918 undermined Europe's power and simultaneously promoted nationalist aspirations among colonized peoples, who clamored for self-determination and national independence. For the time being, however, the major imperialist powers kept their grip on their overseas holdings.

Revolution in Russia

The Great War had undermined the Russian state. In the spring of 1917, disintegrating armies, mutinies, and food shortages provoked a series of street demonstrations and strikes in Petrograd (St. Petersburg). The inability of police forces to suppress the uprisings, and the subsequent mutiny of troops garrisoned in the capital, persuaded Tsar Nicholas II (reigned 1894–1917) to abdicate the throne.

THE STRUGGLE FOR POWER After its success in Petrograd, this "February Revolution" spread throughout the country, and political power in Russia shifted to two new agencies: the provisional government and the Petrograd soviet of Workers' and Soldiers' Deputies. Soviets, which were revolutionary councils organized by socialists, surfaced all over Russia in 1917, wielding considerable power through their control of factories and segments of the military. The period between February and October witnessed a political struggle between the provisional government and the powerful Petrograd soviet. At first the new government enjoyed considerable public support as it eliminated the repressive institutions of the tsarist state, but it failed to satisfy popular demands for an end to war and for land reform. It claimed that, being provisional, it could not make fundamental changes such as confiscating land and distributing it among peasants. The government also promised to continue the war and to bring it to a victorious conclusion. The Petrograd soviet, in contrast, called for an immediate peace.

LENIN Into this tense political situation stepped Vladimir Ilyich Lenin (1870–1924), a revolutionary Marxist and the leader of the small but radical Bolshevik socialist party. Although Lenin had been living in enforced exile in Switzerland, early in 1917 the German High Command helped him return to Russia in the hope that he would foment revolution and bring about Russia's withdrawal from the war. He did. Already in April 1917 Lenin began calling for the transfer of legal authority to the soviets and advocated uncompromising opposition to the war.

Under Lenin's leadership, the Bolsheviks eventually gained control of the Petrograd soviet. Crucial to this development was the provisional government's insistence on continuing the war, its inability to feed the population, and its refusal to undertake land reform. Workers and peasants became increasingly convinced that their problems could be solved only by the soviets. In September, Lenin persuaded the Central Committee of the Bolshevik party to organize an armed insurrection and seize power in the name of the All-Russian National Congress of Soviets, which was then convening in Petrograd. During the night of 24 October and the following day, armed workers, soldiers, and sailors stormed the Winter Palace, the home of the provisional government. By the afternoon of

Bolshevik (BOHL-shih-vehk)
Vladimir Ilyich Lenin (VLAD-uh-meer IL-yich LEHN-in)

25 October, the virtually bloodless insurrection had run its course, and power passed from the provisional government into the hands of Lenin and the Bolshevik party.

VLADIMIR LENIN. | In this photograph, Lenin makes a speech in Red Square on the first anniversary (1918) of the Bolshevik revolution.

TREATY OF BREST-LITOVSK The Bolshevik rulers then ended Russia's involvement in the Great War by signing the Treaty of Brest-Litovsk with Germany on 3 March 1918. The treaty gave the Germans possession or control of one-third of Russia's territory (the Baltic States, the Caucasus, Finland, Poland, and the Ukraine) and one-quarter of its population. Although the terms of the treaty were harsh and humiliating, taking Russia out of the war gave the new government an opportunity to deal with internal problems. Russia's departure from the war also meant that Germany could concentrate all its resources on the western front.

U.S. Intervention and Collapse of the Central Powers

The year 1917 was crucial for another reason: it marked the entry of the United States into the war on the side of the Allies. In 1914 the American public firmly opposed intervention in a European war. That sentiment soon changed. After the outbreak of the war, the United States pursued a neutrality that favored the Allies, and as the war progressed, the United States became increasingly committed economically to an Allied victory.

AMERICA DECLARES WAR The official factor in the United States' decision to enter the war, however, was Germany's resumption of unrestricted submarine warfare in February 1917—a practice that had aroused American outrage in the early years of the war. Germany's leaders took this decisive step because they were desperate to break the British blockade that threatened to starve the Central Powers and hoped to use their submarines to do so. German military experts calculated that submarine attacks against the ships of Great Britain and all the ships headed to Great Britain would bring about the defeat of Great Britain in six months. By that time, however, both the American public and its leadership were invested in an Allied victory, and thus Germany's decision brought the United States into the war in April 1917.

COLLAPSING FRONTS The corrosive effects of years of bloodletting showed. For the first two years of the conflict, most people supported their governments' war efforts, but the continuing ravages of war took their toll everywhere. The Central Powers suffered from food shortages as a result of the British blockade, and increasing numbers of people took to the streets to demonstrate against declining food rations. Food riots were complemented by strikes as prewar social conflicts reemerged. Governments reacted harshly to these challenges, pouncing on strikers, suppressing demonstrators, and jailing dissidents. Equally dangerous was the breakdown of military discipline on both sides. In France, for example, a mutiny in the spring of 1917 involved 50,000 soldiers, resulting in 23,385 courts-martial and 432 death sentences.

Against that grim background, Germany took the risk of throwing its remaining might at the western front in the spring of 1918. The gamble failed, and as the offensive petered out, the Allies—strengthened by fresh U.S. troops—broke through the front and started pushing the Germans back. By that time Germany had effectively exhausted its human and material means to

PRISONERS OF WAR. | German prisoners taken in France in the fall of 1918.

wage war. Meanwhile, Bulgaria capitulated to the invading Allies on 30 September, the Ottomans concluded an armistice on 30 October, and Austria-Hungary surrendered on 4 November. Finally, the Germans accepted an armistice, which took effect on 11 November 1918. At last the guns went silent.

After the War

The immediate effects of the Great War were all too obvious. Aside from the physical destruction, which was most visible in northern France and Belgium, the war had killed, disabled, orphaned, or rendered homeless millions of people. Conservative estimates suggest that the war killed fifteen million people and wounded twenty million others. In the immediate postwar years, millions more succumbed to the effects of starvation, malnutrition, and epidemic diseases.

THE INFLUENZA PANDEMIC OF 1918 The end of the Great War coincided with the arrival of one of the worst pandemics ever recorded in human history. No one knows its origins or why it vanished in mid-1919, but by the time this virulent influenza disappeared, it had left more than 20 million dead. This exceptionally lethal virus hit young adults—a group usually not severely affected by influenza—with particular ferocity.

The Great War did not cause the flu pandemic of 1918–1919, but wartime traffic on land and sea probably contributed to the spread of the infection. From the remotest villages in Arctic climates and crowded cities in India and the United States to the battlefields of Europe, men and women were struck down by high fever. Within a few days they were dead. In Calcutta, India, the postal service and the legal system ground to a halt. The Pacific Islands suffered worst of all as the flu wiped out up to 25 percent of the entire population. Indeed, the influenza plague did not discriminate between the rich and poor, men and women, or the sick and healthy. Moreover, the presence of doctors and nurses made no difference. There was no cure for the flu of 1918.

Before the costs of the war were assessed fully, world attention shifted to Paris. There, in 1919, the victorious powers convened to arrange a postwar settlement and set terms for the defeated nations. At the outset, people on both sides of the war had high hopes for the settlement, but in the end it left a bitter legacy. Ultimately, Georges Clemenceau (1841–1929), David Lloyd George (1863–1945), and Woodrow Wilson—the representative leaders of France, Great Britain, and the United States—dominated the deliberations. The Allies did not permit representatives of the Central Powers to participate, and the Soviet Union was not invited to the conference. Throughout this time the British blockade of Germany remained in effect, adding a sense of urgency to the proceedings.

PSI doc — Wilson's Fourteen Points
www.mhhe.com/bentleybrief2e

WILSON'S FOURTEEN POINTS One year before the opening of the Paris Peace Conference, in January 1918, U.S. president Woodrow Wilson had forwarded a proposal for a just and enduring postwar peace settlement. Wilson's postwar vision subsequently prompted the defeated Central Powers to announce their acceptance of his so-called Fourteen Points as the basis for the armistice. They also expected the Allies to use them as the foundation for later peace treaties. Key among Wilson's Fourteen Points were the following recommendations: open covenants (agreements) of peace, openly arrived at; absolute freedom of navigation upon the seas in peace and war; the removal of all economic barriers and the establishment of an equality of trade conditions among all nations; adequate guarantees for a reduction in national armaments; adjustments of colonial disputes to give equal weight to the interests of the controlling government and the colonial population; and a call for "a general association of nations."

The idealism expressed in the Fourteen Points gave Wilson a position of moral leadership among the Allies. Those same allies also opposed various points of Wilson's peace formula, because those points compromised the secret wartime agreements by which they

Georges Clemenceau (jawrj klem-uhn-SOH)

had agreed to distribute among themselves territories and possessions of the defeated nations. The defeated powers, in turn, later felt betrayed when they faced the harsh peace treaties that so clearly violated the spirit of the Fourteen Points.

THE PEACE TREATIES The final form of the treaties represented a series of compromises among the victors. The hardest terms originated with the French, who desired the destruction or the permanent weakening of German power. Thus, in addition to requiring Germany to accept sole responsibility and guilt for causing the war, the victors demanded a reduction in the military potential of the former Central Powers. In addition, the Allies prohibited Germany and Austria from entering into any sort of political union. The French and the British agreed that the defeated Central Powers must pay for the cost of the war and required the payment of reparations either in money or in kind.

The Paris Peace Conference resulted in additional treaties with Bulgaria, Austria, Hungary, and the Ottoman empire. Whereas Bulgaria lost only small portions of territory as a result, the Austro-Hungarian empire was destroyed: in separate treaties both Austria and Hungary suffered severe territorial losses. Arrangements between the defeated Ottoman empire and the Allies proved to be a more complicated and protracted affair that involved two treaties. In 1920 the Treaty of Sèvres effectively dissolved the empire, calling for the surrender of Ottoman Balkan and Arab provinces and the occupation of eastern and southern Anatolia by foreign powers. However, Turkish nationalists—led by the war hero Mustafa Kemal—set out to defy those terms. Kemal organized a national army that drove out Allied occupation forces, abolished the sultanate, and replaced it with the Republic of Turkey, with Ankara as its capital. In a great diplomatic victory for Turkish nationalists, the Allied powers officially recognized the Republic of Turkey in a final peace agreement, the Treaty of Lausanne (1923).

THE LEAGUE OF NATIONS Although the war was over, the peace settlement that resulted from it was weak. To be sure, some efforts to avoid future conflicts were made. At the urging of U.S. president Woodrow Wilson, the Covenant of the League of Nations was made an integral part of the peace treaties, and every signatory to a peace treaty had to accept this new world organization. However, the league suffered from fundamental weaknesses that made it unable to enforce its decisions. Over the next two decades, it became clear that the league could not stop the aggression that would lead to World War II, and the institution closed its doors in 1940. Nevertheless, the league did establish the pattern for a permanent international organization and served as a model for its successor, the United Nations.

SELF-DETERMINATION Another weakness of the peace was the uneven way in which key ideas of the peacemaking process—especially the idea of national self-determination—were put into practice around the world. In Europe, the peacemakers in Paris did in fact try to apply the principle of self-determination and nationality to a variety of peoples, such as Slavs, Czechs, and Slovaks, although the results were far from perfect. Yet in other instances peacemakers pushed the principle aside for strategic and security reasons, such as in Austria and Germany, whose peoples were denied the right to form one nation.

THE MANDATE SYSTEM However imperfect the results, the peacemakers at Paris tried to apply the principle of self-determination and nationality throughout Europe. Elsewhere, however, they did not do so. The unwillingness to apply the principle of self-determination became most obvious when the victors confronted the issue of what to do with Germany's former colonies and the Arab territories of the Ottoman empire. Because the United States rejected the establishment of old-fashioned colonies, the European

---

Treaty of Sèvres (SEV-ruh)
Mustafa Kemal (MOOS-tah-fah kuh-MAHL)

Note the many new nations created from the former Austro-Hungarian empire.

MAP 29.2 | Territorial changes in Europe after the Great War. Observe the territories ceded by the Central Powers and the Soviet Union. ***Which power lost the most territory, and why?***

powers came up with the enterprising idea of trusteeship. Article 22 of the Covenant of the League of Nations referred to the colonies and territories of the former Central Powers as areas "inhabited by peoples not yet able to stand by themselves under the strenuous conditions of the modern world." As a result, "The tutelage of such peoples should be entrusted to the advanced nations who . . . can best undertake this responsibility." The administration of the mandates fell to the victorious powers of the Great War.

PSI doc The Balfour Declaration www.mhhe.com/bentleybrief2e

The Germans interpreted the mandate system as a division of colonial booty by the victors, who had conveniently forgotten to apply the tutelage provision to their own colonies. German cynicism was more than matched by Arab outrage. The establishment of mandates in the former territories of the Ottoman empire violated promises (made to Arabs) by French and British leaders during the war. They had promised Arab nationalists independence from the Ottoman empire and had promised Jewish nationalists in Europe a homeland in Palestine. Where the Arabs hoped to form independent states, the

French (in Lebanon and Syria) and the British (in Iraq and Palestine) established mandates. The Allies viewed the mandate system as a reasonable compromise between the reality of imperialism and the ideal of self-determination. To the peoples who were directly affected, the mandate system smacked of continued imperial rule draped in a cloak of respectability.

ENCOUNTERS IN THE GREAT WAR. During the First World War, millions of people from European colonies and dependencies served as soldiers and laborers on the western front. What were the short- and long-term consequences of these wartime encounters and experiences for colonized peoples?

Challenges to European Preeminence

When the war ended, it seemed to most Europeans that their global hegemony was more secure than ever. But the Great War did irreparable damage to European power and prestige and set the stage for a process of decolonization that gathered momentum during and after the Second World War. The decline in European power was closely related to diminished economic stature, a result of the commitment to total war. Nothing was more indicative of Europe's reduced economic might than the reversal of the economic relationship between Europe and the United States. Whereas the United States was a debtor nation before 1914, owing billions of dollars to European investors, by 1919 it was a major creditor.

The war also weakened the European hold over colonial territories. Colonial subjects in Africa, Asia, and the Pacific tended to view the Great War as a civil war among the European nations, a bloody spectacle in which the haughty bearers of an alleged superior society vilified and slaughtered one another. Because Europe seemed weak, divided, and vulnerable, the white overlords no longer appeared destined to rule over colonized subjects. The colonials who returned home from the war in Europe and southwest Asia reinforced those general impressions with their own firsthand observations. In particular, they were less inclined to be obedient imperial subjects.

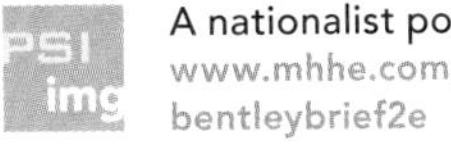
A nationalist poster
www.mhhe.com/bentleybrief2e

The war also helped spread revolutionary ideas to the colonies. The U.S. war aims spelled out in the Fourteen Points raised the hopes of peoples under imperial rule and promoted nationalist aspirations. The peacemakers repeatedly invoked the concept of self-determination, and Wilson publicly proposed that in all colonial questions "the interests of the native populations be given equal weight with the desires of European governments." Nationalists struggling to organize anti-imperialist resistance also sought inspiration from the Soviet Union, whose leaders denounced all forms of imperialism and pledged their support to independence movements. Taken together, those messages were subversive to imperial control and had a great appeal for colonial peoples. Although nationalist movements endured many setbacks, the days of European global dominance were numbered.

SUMMARY

The assassination of the Austrian archduke Francis Ferdinand had a galvanizing effect on a Europe torn by national rivalries, colonial disputes, and demands for self-determination. In the summer of 1914, inflexible war plans and a tangled alliance system transformed a local war between Austria-Hungary and Serbia into a European-wide clash of arms. With the entry of the Ottoman empire, Japan, and the United States, the war of 1914–1918 became a global conflict. Although many belligerents organized their societies for total war and drew on the resources of their overseas empires, the war remained at a bloody stalemate until the United States entered the conflict in 1917. The tide turned, and the combatants signed an armistice in November 1918. The Great War, a brutal encounter between societies and peoples, inflicted ghastly human casualties, severely damaged national economies, and discredited established political and cultural traditions. The war also altered the political landscape of many lands as it destroyed four dynasties and their empires and fostered the creation of several new European nations. In Russia the war served as a backdrop for the world's first successful socialist revolution. In the end the Great War sapped the strength of European colonial powers while it promoted nationalist aspirations among colonized peoples.

STUDY TERMS

Allies (Triple Entente) (586)
Bolshevik revolution (594)
Central Powers (Triple Alliance) (586)
dreadnoughts (585)
February Revolution (594)
Fourteen Points (596)
Francis Ferdinand (583)
home front (590)
League of Nations (597)
mandate system (597)
no-man's-land (588)
Paris Peace Conference (597)
poison gas (588)
Schlieffen plan (587)
self-determination (584)
soviets (594)
total war (590)
Treaty of Brest-Litovsk (595)
Treaty of Lausanne (597)
Twenty-one Demands (592)
unrestricted submarine warfare (595)
Vladimir Lenin (594)
western front (588)
Winston Churchill (593)

FOR FURTHER READING

Joanna Bourke. *Dismembering the Male: Men's Bodies, Britain, and the Great War.* Chicago, 1996. A study that examines the most intimate site of the war—the bodies of the men who fought it.

Belinda Davis. *Home Fires Burning: Food, Politics, and Everyday Life in World War I Berlin.* Chapel Hill, 2000. Effectively covers daily life in wartime and also offers insights into how government policies during the war affected the reconstruction of society following it.

Niall Ferguson. *The Pity of War: Explaining World War I.* New York, 2000. A stimulating example of revisionist history that shifts the blame for the war away from Germany and onto England.

Paul Fussell. *The Great War and Modern Memory.* Oxford, 1975. An original and deeply moving piece of cultural history.

James Joll. *The Origins of the First World War.* 2nd ed. London, 1991. The most lucid and balanced introduction to a complex and controversial subject.

John Keegan. *The First World War.* New York, 1999. A comprehensive and stunningly vivid account of the Great War.

John Maynard Keynes. *The Economic Consequences of the Peace.* New York, 1920. A classic and devastating critique of the Versailles treaty.

John H. Morrow. *The Great War: An Imperial History.* New York, 2003. A global history of the Great War that places the conflict squarely in the context of imperialism.

Richard Pipes. *The Russian Revolution, 1899–1919.* 2nd ed. London, 1992. An up-to-date and well-argued interpretation.

Erich Remarque. *All Quiet on the Western Front.* New York, 1958. A fictional account of trench warfare.

An Age of Anxiety

30

PROBING CULTURAL FRONTIERS

Postwar Pessimism

Revolutions in Physics and Psychology

Experimentation in Art and Architecture

GLOBAL DEPRESSION

The Great Depression

Despair and Government Action

Economic Experimentation

CHALLENGES TO THE LIBERAL ORDER

Communism in Russia

The Fascist Alternative

Italian Fascism

German National Socialism

Born on a lovely spring day in 1889, in a quaint Austrian village, he was the apple of his mother's eye. He basked in Klara's warmth and indulgence as a youth, enjoying the fine life of a middle-class child. As he grew older, however, he sensed a tension between the competing expectations of his parents. Contented with the dreamy indolence allowed by Klara, he bristled at the demands of his father, Alois, who expected him to study hard and enter the Austrian civil service. He had no desire to become a bureaucrat. In fact, he envisioned a completely different life for himself. He wanted to be an artist.

Alois's unexpected death in 1903 freed him from a future as a bureaucrat. He left school in 1905, not at all dissatisfied with having achieved only a ninth-grade education, because now he could pursue an education as an artist. He followed his ambitions to Vienna, only to find bitter disappointment when the Vienna Academy of Fine Arts rejected him as an art student in 1907. His beloved Klara died the following year, and he meandered the city streets of Vienna, admiring the architecture of the city and attending the opera when his funds permitted.

Eventually, he hit bottom and began staying at a homeless shelter. It was interesting, though, to hear the different political points of view spouted by the shelter's other inhabitants. They discussed compelling issues of the day, and he listened intently to those who hailed the supremacy of the Aryan race and the inferiority of the Jews. He came to hate Jews and Marxists, who he thought had formed an evil union with the goal of destroying the world. He also despised liberalism and democracy.

In 1913 he left his Austrian homeland and found refuge in Munich, Germany. In Germany he volunteered for service in the army, which had just embarked on the greatest war ever fought. He discovered in himself a real talent for military service, and he remained in the army for the duration of the war, 1914–1918. Twice wounded and decorated for bravery, he nonetheless found himself in despair at war's end. An impotent rage coursed through him when he learned of Germany's defeat. He knew with all his being that the Jews were responsible for this humiliation, and he also knew that he had to enter the political arena in his chosen fatherland and save the nation. Adolf Hitler had finally found his mission in life.

Hitler (1889–1945) stood as just one personification of Europe's age of anxiety in the early decades of the twentieth century. Embittered by a sense of dislocation and fear stemming from the enormous changes engulfing the society around him, Hitler dedicated himself to discovering a way out of the anxiety for Germany. Ultimately, his solutions brought about more rather than less anxiety, but the novelty and cruelty

❮ *Edvard Munch,* Anxiety, *1896.*

CHRONOLOGY

1905	Einstein publishes special theory of relativity
1907	Picasso paints *Les demoiselles d'Avignon*
1918–1920	Civil war in Russia
1919	Mussolini launches fascist movement in Italy
1921–1928	Lenin's New Economic Policy
1927	Heisenberg establishes "uncertainty principle"
1928–1932	First Soviet Five-Year Plan
1929	U.S. stock market crash
1929	Beginning of Great Depression
1929	Hemingway and Remarque publish antiwar novels
1933–1945	Hitler is ruler in Germany
1935–1938	Stalin's "Great Purge" in the Soviet Union

of his political and military agendas reflected brilliantly the traumatic consequences of the Great War and the Great Depression.

Just as Adolf Hitler changed as a result of his life experiences in the early twentieth century, so too did European society as a whole. Badly shaken by the effects of war, Europeans experienced a shock to their system of values, beliefs, and traditions. Profound scientific and cultural transformations in the postwar decades also contributed to a sense of loss and anxiety. Then, as peoples in Europe and around the world struggled to come to terms with the aftermath of war, an unprecedented economic contraction gripped the international community.

Against the background of the Great Depression, dictators in Russia, Italy, and Germany tried to translate blueprints for utopias into reality. Those political innovations unsettled many Europeans and much of the world, contributing significantly to the anxiety of the age. Moreover, such innovations matched in their radicalness, however strangely, the vast alterations taking place in the intellectual and cultural realms of European society after the Great War.

PROBING CULTURAL FRONTIERS

The Great War discredited established social and political institutions and long-held beliefs about the superiority of European society. Writers, poets, theologians, and other intellectuals lamented the decline and imminent death of their society. While some wrote obituaries, however, others embarked on bold new cultural paths that established the main tendencies of contemporary thought and taste.

The discoveries of physicists undermined the Newtonian universe, in which a set of inexorable natural laws governed events, with a new and disturbing cosmos. Equally discomfiting were the insights of psychoanalysis, which suggested that human behavior was fundamentally irrational. Disquieting trends in the arts paralleled developments in science and psychology. Especially in painting, an aversion to realism and a pronounced preference for abstraction heralded the arrival of new aesthetic standards.

ADOLF HITLER. | This is one of the few known photographic images of a young Hitler, taken in 1923.

Postwar Pessimism

"You are all a lost generation," noted Gertrude Stein (1874–1946) to her fellow American writer Ernest Hemingway (1899–1961). Stein had given a label to the group of American intellectuals and literati who congregated in Paris in the postwar years. This "lost generation" expressed in poetry and fiction the malaise and disillusion that characterized U.S. and European thought after the Great War. The brutal realities of industrialized warfare left no room for heroes or glory, and during the 1920s artists and intellectuals spat out their revulsion in a host of war novels, such as Hemingway's *A Farewell to Arms* (1929) and Erich Maria Remarque's *All Quiet on the Western Front* (1929)—works overflowing with images of meaningless death and suffering. Postwar writers lamented the decline of Western society. A retired German schoolteacher named Oswald Spengler (1880–1936) made headlines when he published *The Decline of the West* (1918–1922). In this work, which might have been seen as an obituary of civilization, Spengler proposed that all societies pass through a life cycle of growth and decay comparable to the biological cycle of living organisms. His analysis of the history of western Europe led him to conclude that European society had entered the final stage of its existence. All that remained was irreversible decline, marked by imperialism and warfare.

Theologians joined the chorus of despair. In 1919 Karl Barth (1886–1968), a notable Christian theologian, published a religious bombshell titled *Epistle to the Romans.* In his work Barth sharply attacked the liberal Christian theology that embraced the idea of progress, that is, the tendency of European thinkers to believe in limitless improvement as the realization of God's purpose. The Augustinian, Lutheran, and Calvinist message of original sin—the depravity of human nature—fell on receptive ears as many Christians refused to accept the idea that contemporary human society was in any way a realization of God's purpose. The Russian orthodox thinker Nikolai Berdiaev (1874–1948) summed up those sentiments: "Man's historical experience has been one of steady failure, and there are no grounds for supposing it will be ever anything else."

The Great War destroyed long-cherished beliefs, such as belief in the universality of human progress. Many idols of nineteenth-century progress came under attack, especially science and technology. The scientists' dream of leading humanity to a beneficial conquest of nature seemed to have gone awry, because scientists had spent the war making poisonous gas and high explosives. Democracy was another fallen idol. The idea that people should have a voice in selecting the leaders of their government enjoyed widespread support in European societies. By the early twentieth century, such sentiments had led to universal male suffrage in most societies, and after the Great War many societies also extended the franchise to women. However, many intellectuals abhorred what they viewed as weak political systems that championed the tyranny of the average person. In Germany, for example, a whole school of conservatives lamented the "rule of inferiors."

Revolutions in Physics and Psychology

The postwar decade witnessed a revolution in physics that transformed the character of science. Albert Einstein (1879–1955) struck the first blow with his theory of special relativity (1905), showing that there is no single spatial and chronological framework in the universe. According to the theory, it no longer makes sense to speak of space and time as absolutes, because the measurement of those two categories always varies with the motion of the observer. That is, space and time are relative to the person measuring them. To the layperson such notions suggested that a commonsense universe had vanished, to be replaced by a radically new one in which reality or truth was merely relative.

ALBERT EINSTEIN. | One of the best-known faces of the twentieth century, Einstein was the symbol of the revolution in physics.

THE UNCERTAINTY PRINCIPLE More disquieting even than Einstein's discoveries was the theory formulated by Werner Heisenberg (1901–1976), who in 1927 established the "uncertainty principle." According to Heisenberg, it is impossible to specify simultaneously the position and the velocity of a subatomic particle. The more accurately one determines the position of an electron, the less precisely one can determine its velocity, and vice versa. In essence, scientists cannot observe the behavior of electrons objectively, because the act of observation interferes with them.

It quickly became evident that the uncertainty principle had important implications beyond physics. Indeed, Heisenberg's theory

Nikolai Berdiaev (nih-koh-LYE ber-dee-ev)
Werner Heisenberg (VER-nuhr HAHY-zuyn-burg)

called into question established notions of truth. Likewise, objectivity as it was understood was no longer a valid concept, because the observer was always part of the process under observation. Accordingly, any observer—an anthropologist studying another society, for instance—had to be alert to the fact that his or her very presence became an integral part of the study.

SIGMUND FREUD. | In this painted portrait, Freud presents a striking figure.

FREUD'S PSYCHOANALYTIC THEORY As equally unsettling as the advances in physics were developments in psychology that challenged established concepts of morality and values. Beginning in 1896, the Austrian medical doctor Sigmund Freud (1856–1939) embarked on research that focused on psychological rather than physiological explanations of mental disorders. Through his clinical observations of patients, Freud identified a conflict between conscious and unconscious mental processes that lay at the root of neurotic behavior. That conflict, moreover, suggested to him the existence of a repressive mechanism that keeps painful memories away from the conscious mind. Freud believed that dreams held the key to the deepest recesses of the human psyche. Using the free associations of patients to guide him in the interpretation of dreams, he identified sexual drives and fantasies as the most important source of repression. For example, Freud claimed to have discovered a so-called Oedipus complex, in which male children develop an erotic attachment to their mother and hostility toward their father.

In the end, Freudian doctrines shaped the psychiatric profession and established a powerful presence in literature and the arts. During the 1920s, novelists, poets, and painters acknowledged Freud's influence as they focused on the inner world of their characters. The creators of imaginative literature used Freud's bold emphasis on sexuality as a tool for the interpretation and understanding of human behavior.

Experimentation in Art and Architecture

The roots of contemporary painting go back to nineteenth-century French avant-garde artists who disdained realism and instead were concerned with freedom of expression. The aversion to visual realism was heightened by the spread of photography. When everyone could create naturalistic landscapes or portraits with a camera, it made little sense for artists to do the same with paint and brush. Thus painters began to think that the purpose of a painting was not to mirror reality but to create it.

At the beginning of the twentieth century, this new aesthetic led to the emergence of a bewildering variety of pictorial schools, all of which promised an entirely new art. Regardless of whether they called themselves expressionists, cubists, abstractionists, dadaists, or surrealists, artists generally agreed on a program "to abolish the sovereignty of appearance." Paintings no longer depicted recognizable objects from the everyday world, and beauty was expressed in pure color or shape. Some painters sought to express feelings and emotions through violent distortion of forms and the use of explosive colors; others, influenced by Freudian psychology, tried to tap the subconscious mind to communicate an inner vision or a dream.

PSI img Edgar Degas, *Absinthe* www.mhhe.com/bentleybrief2e

ARTISTIC INFLUENCES The artistic heritages of Asian, Pacific, and African societies fertilized various strains of contemporary painting. Nineteenth-century Japanese prints, for example, influenced French impressionists such as Edgar Degas (1834–1917).

Sigmund Freud (SIG-muhnd froid)
Edgar Degas (ED-gahr day-GAH)

Pablo Picasso's *Les Demoiselles d'Avignon.* | This painting (1907) was the first of what would be called cubist works. This image had a profound impact on subsequent art.

The deliberate violation of perspective by Japanese painters and their stress on the flat, two-dimensional surface of the picture, their habit of placing figures off center, and their use of primary colors encouraged European artists to take similar liberties with realism. In Germany a group of young artists known as the "Bridge" made a point of regularly visiting the local ethnographic museum to be inspired by the boldness and power of indigenous art. The early works of Pablo Picasso (1881–1973), the leading proponent of cubism, displayed the influence of African art forms.

By the third decade of the twentieth century, it was nearly impossible to generalize about contemporary painting. All artists were acknowledged to have a right to their own reality, and generally accepted standards that distinguished between "good" and "bad" art disappeared.

Global Depression

After the horrors and debilitating upheavals of the Great War, much of the world yearned for a return to normality and prosperity. By the early 1920s the efforts of governments and businesses to rebuild damaged economies seemed to be bearing fruit. Prosperity, however, was short-lived. In 1929 the world plunged into an economic depression that was so long-lasting, so severe, and so global that it has become known as the Great Depression. The old capitalist system of trade and finance collapsed, and until a new system took its place after 1945, a return to worldwide prosperity could not occur.

The Great Depression

By the middle of the 1920s, most countries seemed on the way to economic recovery, and industrial productivity had returned to prewar levels. But that prosperity was fragile, perhaps false, and many serious problems and dislocations remained in the international economy.

ECONOMIC PROBLEMS The economic recovery and well-being of Europe, for example, was tied to a tangled and interdependent financial system. In essence, the governments of Austria and Germany relied on U.S. loans and investment capital to finance reparation payments to France and England. The French and British governments, in turn, depended on those reparation payments to pay off loans taken out in the United States during the Great War. Strain on any one part of the system, then, inevitably strained them all.

There were other problems as well. Improvements in industrial processes reduced worldwide demand for certain raw materials, which had devastating consequences for export-dependent areas. Technological advances in the production of automobile tires, for instance, permitted the use of reclaimed rubber. The resulting glut of natural rubber badly damaged the economies of the Dutch East Indies, Ceylon, and Malaysia, which relied on rubber exports. Similarly, the increased use of oil undermined the coal industry, and the growing adoption of artificial nitrogen virtually ruined the nitrate industry of Chile.

One of the nagging weaknesses of the global economy in the 1920s was the depressed state of agriculture. During the Great War, when Europe's agricultural output declined significantly, farmers in the United States, Canada, Argentina, and Australia expanded their own production. At the end of the war, European farmers resumed their agricultural activity, thereby contributing to worldwide surpluses. As production increased, prices collapsed throughout the world. By 1929 the price of a bushel of wheat was at its lowest level in four hundred years, and farmers everywhere became impoverished. The reduced income of farm families contributed to high inventories of manufactured goods, which in turn caused businesses to cut back production and to dismiss workers.

THE CRASH OF 1929 The United States enjoyed a boom after the Great War, which prompted many people in the United States to invest their earnings and savings in speculative and risky financial ventures, particularly in stocks. By October 1929, warnings from experts that stock prices were overvalued prompted investors to pull out of the market. On Black Thursday (24 October), a wave of panic selling on the New York Stock Exchange caused stock prices to plummet. Investors who had overextended themselves through speculative stock purchases watched in agony. Thousands of people, from poor widows to industrial tycoons, lost their life savings, and by the end of the day eleven financiers had committed suicide. The crisis deepened when lenders called in loans, thereby forcing more investors to sell their securities at any price.

ECONOMIC CONTRACTION SPREADS In the wake of this financial chaos came a drastic decrease in business activity, wages, and employment. When businesses realized that shrinking consumer demand meant they could not sell their inventories, they responded with layoffs. With so many people unemployed, demand plummeted further, causing more business failures and soaring unemployment. In 1930 the slump deepened, and by 1932 industrial production had fallen to half of its 1929 level. National income had dropped by approximately half, and 44 percent of U.S. banks were out of business. Because much of the world's prosperity depended on the export of U.S. capital and the strength of U.S. import markets, the contraction of the U.S. economy created a ripple effect that circled the globe.

Most societies experienced economic difficulties throughout the 1930s. Virtually every industrialized society saw its economy shrivel, but nations that relied on exports of manufactured goods to pay for imported fuel and food—Germany and Japan in particular—suffered the most. The depression also spread to primary producing economies in Latin America, Africa, and Asia. Hardest hit were countries that depended on the export of a few primary products such as coffee, sugar, minerals, ores, and rubber.

U.S. investors, shaken by the collapse of stock prices, tried to raise money by calling in loans and liquidating investments, and Wall Street banks refused to extend short-term loans as they became due. Banking houses in Austria and Germany became vulnerable to collapse, because they had been major recipients of U.S. loans. Devastated by the loss of U.S. capital, the German economy experienced a precipitous economic slide that by 1932 resulted in 35 percent unemployment and a 50 percent decrease in industrial production. As the German economy—which had remained a leading economic power in Europe throughout the postwar years—ground to a virtual halt, the rest of Europe sputtered and stalled with it. Likewise, because of its great dependence on the U.S. market, the Japanese economy felt the depression's effects almost immediately. Unemployment in export-oriented sectors of the economy skyrocketed as companies cut back on production.

The Social Effects of the Great Depression. | This photo by Dorothea Lange, called *Migrant Mother, Nipomo, California* (1936), is one of the most famous images of the period.

ECONOMIC NATIONALISM The Great Depression destroyed the international financial and commercial network of the capitalist economies. As international cooperation broke down, governments turned to their own resources and practiced economic nationalism. By imposing tariff barriers, import quotas, and import prohibitions, politicians hoped to achieve self-sufficiency. Yet economic nationalism invariably backfired. Each new measure designed to restrict imports provoked retaliation by other nations whose interests were affected. After the U.S. Congress passed the Smoot-Hawley Tariff Act in 1930, which raised duties on most manufactured products to prohibitive levels, the governments of dozens of other nations retaliated by raising tariffs on imports of U.S. products. The result was a sharp drop in international trade. Between 1929 and 1932, world production declined by 38 percent and trade dropped by more than 66 percent.

Despair and Government Action

By 1933 unemployment in industrial societies had reached thirty million, more than five times higher than in 1929. Both men and women lost their jobs, and over the course of the depression most governments enacted policies restricting female employment, especially for married women. Indeed, the notion that a woman's place was in the home was widespread, and some—such as the French physician Charles Richet (1850–1935)—even insisted that removing women from the workforce would solve the problem of male unemployment.

The Great Depression caused enormous personal suffering. The stark statistics documenting the failure of economies do not convey the anguish and despair of those who lost their jobs, savings, and homes. For millions of people the struggle for food, clothing, and shelter grew desperate. Shantytowns appeared overnight in urban areas, and breadlines stretched for blocks. Marriage, childbearing, and divorce rates declined, and suicide rates rose. Those simply trying to survive came to despise the wealthy, who, despite their own reduced incomes, remained shielded from the worst impact of the economic downturn. Adolescents completing their schooling faced an almost nonexistent job market.

A depression-era breadline
www.mhhe.com/
bentleybrief2e

"Hoovervilles"
www.mhhe.com/
bentleybrief2e

Economic Experimentation

Classical economic thought held that capitalism was a self-correcting system that operated best when left to its own devices. Thus, in the initial stages of the depression most governments did nothing, hoping that the crisis would resolve itself. Faced with such human misery, however, some governments assumed more active roles, pursuing deflationary

Charles Richet (shawrl ri-SHEY)

HUMAN FACES OF THE GREAT DEPRESSION. | This photograph depicts children bathing in the Ozark Mountains, Missouri, 1940. ***What kinds of items signify the poverty of this family?***

measures by balancing national budgets and curtailing public spending. Rather than lifting national economies out of the doldrums, however, those remedies only worsened the depression's impact. Far from self-correcting, capitalism seemed to be dying. Many people called for a fundamental revision of economic thought.

KEYNES John Maynard Keynes (1883–1946), the most influential economist of the twentieth century, offered a novel solution. In his seminal work, *The General Theory of Employment, Interest, and Money* (1936), he argued that the fundamental cause of the depression was not excessive supply but inadequate demand. Accordingly, he urged governments to stimulate the economy by increasing the money supply, thereby lowering interest rates and encouraging investment. He also advised governments to undertake public works projects to provide jobs and redistribute incomes through tax policy. Such intervention would result in reduced unemployment and increased consumer demand, which would lead to economic revival. These measures were necessary even if they caused governments to run deficits and maintain unbalanced budgets.

THE NEW DEAL Although Keynes's theories did not become influential with policymakers until after World War II, the administration of U.S. president Franklin Delano Roosevelt (1882–1945) anticipated his ideas. Roosevelt took aggressive steps to reinflate the economy and ease the worst of the suffering caused by the depression. His program for dealing with the national calamity—called the New Deal—included legislation designed to prevent the collapse of the banking system, to provide jobs and farm subsidies, to guarantee minimum wages, and to provide social security in old age. Its fundamental premise, that the federal government was justified in protecting the social and economic welfare of the people, represented a major shift in U.S. government policy and started a trend toward social reform legislation that continued long after the depression years.

PSI doc — FDR on the New Deal
www.mhhe.com/bentleybrief2e

CHALLENGES TO THE LIBERAL ORDER

Amid the gloom and despair of the Great Depression, some voices proclaimed the promise of a better tomorrow. Marxists believed that capitalist society was on its deathbed, and they had faith that a new and better system based on rule by the proletariat was being born out of the ashes of the Russian empire. The new rulers of Russia, Vladimir Ilyich Lenin and then Joseph Stalin, transformed the former tsarist empire into the world's first socialist society, the Union of Soviet Socialist Republics (1922). Other people, uncomfortable with socialism, found solace in fascist movements, which seemed to offer revolutionary answers to the economic, social, and political problems of the day. Among these fascist movements, the Italian and German ones figured most prominently.

Lenin giving a speech
www.mhhe.com/bentleybrief2e

Communism in Russia

In 1917 Lenin and his fellow Bolsheviks had taken power in the name of the Russian working class, but socialist victory did not bring peace and stability to the lands of the former Russian empire. After seizing power, Lenin and his supporters had to defend the world's first "dictatorship of the proletariat" against numerous internal and external enemies.

CIVIL WAR Opposition to the Bolshevik Party—by now calling itself the Russian Communist Party—erupted into a civil war that lasted from 1918 to 1920. In response, Lenin's government began a policy of terror in which 200,000 suspected anticommunists (known as Whites) were arrested, tried, and executed. In July 1918 the Bolsheviks executed Tsar Nicholas II, Empress Alexandra, and their five children because they feared that the Romanov family could strengthen counterrevolutionary forces. White terror was often equally as brutal as Red terror. The peasantry, although hostile to the communists, largely supported the Bolsheviks, fearing that a victory by the Whites would result in the return of the monarchy.

Meanwhile, foreign powers in Britain, France, Japan, and the United States, angry over Russia's withdrawal from the Great War and inflamed by anticommunism, supported the Whites and sent a limited number of troops and supplies to aid them. Their efforts failed, however, and in 1920 the Red Army defeated the Whites. The costs of war were devastating: estimates place the number of lives lost in the civil war at ten million, mostly from disease and starvation. Moreover, the political system that emerged from the civil war bore the imprint of political oppression, which played a significant role in the later development of the Soviet state.

WAR COMMUNISM Over the course of the civil war, the new rulers of Russia transformed the economy by embarking on a hasty and unplanned course of nationalization, known as war communism. After officially annulling private property, the Bolshevik government assumed control of banks, industry, and other privately held commercial properties. Landed estates and the holdings of monasteries and churches also became national property. Private trade was abolished, and the party seized crops from peasants to feed people in the cities. This last measure proved especially unpopular and caused peasants to drastically reduce their production. By 1920 industrial production had fallen to about one-tenth of its prewar level and agricultural output to about half its prewar level.

THE NEW ECONOMIC POLICY In 1921, as the Reds consolidated their military victories after the civil war, the Soviet economy was in a shambles. Workers were on strike, cities were depopulated, and factories were destroyed. Faced with economic paralysis, in the spring of 1921 Lenin decided on a radical reversal of war communism. In its place he implemented the New Economic Policy (NEP), which temporarily restored the market economy and some private enterprise in Russia. Large industries and banks remained under state control, but the government returned small-scale industries to private ownership. The government also allowed peasants to sell their surpluses at free-market prices. Other features of the NEP included a vigorous program of electrification and the establishment of technical schools to train technicians and engineers. Lenin did not live to see the success of the NEP. After suffering three paralytic strokes, he died in 1924.

JOSEPH STALIN After a bitter political struggle for power, Joseph Stalin (1879–1953), general secretary of the Communist Party, emerged as the new leader of the Soviet Union in 1928. A Georgian by birth, an Orthodox seminarian by training, and a Russian nationalist by conviction, Stalin indicated his unified resolve to gain power in his surname, which meant "man of steel." His first economic program, which replaced Lenin's NEP, was both ambitious and ruthless. Indeed, Stalin's First Five-Year Plan, implemented in 1929, aimed at nothing less than transforming the Soviet Union from a predominantly agricultural country to a leading industrial power. The First Five-Year Plan set targets for increased productivity in all spheres of the economy but emphasized heavy industry—especially steel and machinery—at the expense of consumer goods. As the rest of the world teetered on the edge of economic collapse, Stalin's plan offered a bold alternative to market capitalism. Stalin repeatedly stressed the urgency of this monumental endeavor, telling his people, "We are 50 to 100 years behind the advanced countries. Either we do it, or we shall go under."

JOSEPH STALIN. | Here, Stalin attends a Soviet congress in 1936.

COLLECTIVIZATION OF AGRICULTURE Integral to the drive for industrialization was the collectivization of agriculture. The Soviet state expropriated privately owned land to create collective, or cooperative, farm units whose profits were shared by all farmers. Stalin and his regime viewed collectivization as a means of increasing the efficiency of agricultural production and ensuring that industrial workers would be fed.

In some places, outraged peasants reacted to the government's program by slaughtering their livestock and burning their crops. Faced with enforced collectivization, millions of farmers left the land and migrated to cities in search of work. Those who stayed behind were often unable to meet production quotas and starved to death on the land they once owned. When Stalin called a halt to collectivization in 1931, half the farms in the Soviet Union had been collectivized. Estimates of the cost in number of peasant lives lost have fluctuated wildly, but even the most cautious place it at three million. Among them, the *kulaks*—relatively wealthy peasants who had risen to prosperity during the NEP—were nearly eliminated.

The Soviet leadership proclaimed the First Five-Year Plan a success after only four years. The Soviet Union industrialized under Stalin even though the emphasis on building heavy industry first and consumer industries later meant that citizens postponed the gratifications of industrialization. However, the scarcity or nonexistence of such consumer goods as refrigerators, radios, and automobiles was to some degree balanced by full employment, low-cost utilities, and cheap housing and food. Set against the economic collapse of the capitalist world, the ability of a centrally planned economy to create more jobs than workers could fill made it appear an attractive alternative.

THE GREAT PURGE Nevertheless, the disaster of collectivization and the ruthlessness with which it was carried out had raised doubts about Stalin's administration. As the Communist Party prepared for its seventeenth congress in 1934, the "Congress of Victors," Stalin learned of a plan to bring more pluralism back into leadership. The Congress of Victors quickly became the "Congress of Victims" as Stalin purged two-thirds of the delegates from the Communist Party. Between 1935 and 1938 Stalin removed from posts of authority all persons suspected of opposition, including more than half the army's high-ranking officers. In 1939 eight million Soviet citizens faced long-term suffering in labor camps, and three million were dead as a result of the "cleansing," as Stalin's supporters termed this process.

The outside world watched the events unfolding within the Soviet Union with a mixture of contempt, fear, and admiration. The establishment of the world's first dictatorship of the proletariat challenged the values and institutions of liberal society all over the world and seemed to demonstrate the viability of communism as a social and political system.

The Fascist Alternative

While socialism was transforming the former Russian empire, another political force swept across Europe after the Great War. Fascism, a political movement and ideology that sought to create a new type of society, developed as a reaction against liberal democracy and the spread of socialism and communism. In 1919 Benito Mussolini founded the first fascist party. Movements comparable to Italian fascism subsequently developed in many European societies, most notably in Germany in the guise of National Socialism (Nazism). Although fascism enjoyed widespread popularity in many European countries, it rarely threatened the political order and overthrew parliamentary systems only in Italy and Germany. Although potential fascist movements sprang up during the 1930s in Japan, China, and South Africa; in Latin American societies such as Brazil and Argentina; and in several Arab lands, fascism nevertheless remained basically a European phenomenon in the era between the two world wars.

> THINKING ABOUT *Traditions*
>
> **TRADITIONS IN AN AGE OF ANXIETY.** In the period between the world wars, fascism arose as an alternative to what appeared to be weak and failing capitalist democracies. In what ways did the fascist states call on national traditions and characteristics in order to legitimate their authoritarian natures?

During the 1920s and 1930s, fascism attracted millions of followers and proved especially attractive to middle classes and rural populations. Those groups became radicalized by economic and social crises and were especially fearful of the perceived threat from the political left. Fascism also proved attractive to nationalists of all classes. Asserting that society faced a profound crisis, fascists sought to create a new national community, which they defined either as a nation-state or as a unique ethnic or racial group. Although each fascist movement had its own unique characteristics, most nevertheless shared certain common features, such as the veneration of the state, a devotion to a strong leader, and an emphasis on ultranationalism, ethnocentrism, and militarism.

Fascist ideology consistently invoked the primacy of the state, which stood at the center of the nation's life and history. Strong and charismatic leaders, such as Benito Mussolini in Italy and Adolf Hitler in Germany, embodied the state and claimed indisputable authority. Consequently, fascists were hostile to liberal democracy, which they viewed as weak and decadent. Fascism was also extremely hostile to socialism and communism. Fascist movements emphasized a belligerent form of nationalism (chauvinism) and a fear of foreign people (xenophobia), which they frequently linked to an exaggerated ethnocentrism. The typical fascist state also embraced militarism, a belief in the rigors and virtues of military life as an individual and national ideal. In practice, militarism meant that fascist regimes maintained large and expensive military establishments, tried to organize much of public life along military lines, and generally showed a fondness for uniforms, parades, and monumental architecture.

Italian Fascism

The first fascist movement grew in Italy after the Great War. Conditions conducive to the rise of fascism included a widespread disillusionment with uninspired political leadership and ineffective government, extensive economic turmoil and social discontent, and a growing fear of socialism. In addition, there was vast disappointment over Italy's skimpy territorial spoils from the peace settlement after the Great War.

BENITO MUSSOLINI The guiding force behind Italian fascism was Benito Mussolini, a former socialist who turned, after the Great War, to a political program that emphasized virulent nationalism, demanded repression of socialists, and called for a strong political leader. In 1919 he established the Fasci Italiani di Combattimento (Italian Combat Veteran League). Mussolini's movement gained widespread support after 1920, and by 1921 his league managed to have thirty-five fascists elected to the Italian parliament. Much of the newly found public support resulted from the effective use of violence against socialists by fascist armed squads known as Blackshirts. In 1922 Mussolini and his followers decided the time was ripe for a fascist seizure of power, and on 28 October they staged a march on Rome. While Mussolini stayed safely in Milan, thousands of his black-shirted troops converged on Rome. Rather than calling on the military to oppose the fascist threat, King Victor Emmanuel III hastily asked Mussolini on 29 October to become prime minister and form a new government. Mussolini inaugurated a fascist regime in 1922.

THE FASCIST STATE Between 1925 and 1931, Italy's fascists consolidated their power through a series of laws that transformed the nation into a one-party dictatorship. In 1926 Mussolini seized total power as dictator and subsequently ruled Italy as Il Duce ("the leader"). The regime moved quickly to eliminate all other political parties, curb the freedom of the press, and outlaw

BENITO MUSSOLINI. | In this photograph, the Italian dictator strikes a dramatic pose on horseback in 1940. ***What message might Mussolini have been trying to convey with such a pose?***

chauvinism (SHOH-vuh-niz-uhm)
xenophobia (zen-uh-FOH-bee-uh)

THINKING ABOUT *Encounters*

ENCOUNTERS IN AN AGE OF ANXIETY. When the United States stock market crashed in 1929, it caused a cascade effect that brought markets all over the world down in its wake. Why were economies as far flung as the Americas, Europe, Asia, and Africa so intricately connected in this period, and how did failure in one set off a chain reaction in the rest?

free speech and association. A Special Tribunal for the Defense of the State, supervised by military officers, silenced political dissent. Marked as antifascist "subversives," thousands of Italians found themselves imprisoned or exiled on remote islands, and some faced capital punishment. Allying himself and his movement with business and landlord interests, Il Duce also crushed labor unions and prohibited strikes. In 1932, on the tenth anniversary of the fascist seizure of power, Mussolini felt confident enough to announce that "the twentieth century will be a century of fascism, the century of Italian power."

Although racism and anti-Semitism were never prominent components of Italian fascism, in 1938 the government suddenly issued a series of anti-Semitic laws. That development may have been occasioned by Mussolini's newly found friendship with fellow dictator Adolf Hitler. In 1936 Mussolini told his followers that from now on, world history would revolve around a Rome-Berlin axis. In May 1939 the leaders of fascist Italy and Nazi Germany formalized their political, military, and ideological alliance by signing a ten-year Pact of Steel.

German National Socialism

PSI img Axis rally www.mhhe.com/bentleybrief2e

HITLER AND THE NAZI PARTY After Adolf Hitler's postwar political awakening, he came into contact with an obscure political party sympathetic to his ideas. In 1921 he became chairman of the party now known as the National Socialist German Workers' Party. National Socialism (the Nazi movement) made its first major appearance in 1923 when party members and Hitler attempted to overthrow the democratic Weimar Republic, which had replaced the German empire in 1919. The revolt was a failure, however, and Hitler was jailed. When Hitler emerged from prison in 1924, he resolved to gain power legally through the ballot box and, once successful, to discard the very instrument of his success.

NAZI PRONATALISM. | "Mother and Child" was the slogan on this poster, idealizing and encouraging motherhood. The background conveys the Nazi predilection for the wholesome country life, a dream that clashed with the urban reality of German society.

THE STRUGGLE FOR POWER National Socialism made rapid gains after 1929 because it had broad appeal. Hitler attracted disillusioned people, many of whom blamed the young German democracy for Germany's misfortunes: a humiliating peace treaty—the Treaty of Versailles—that identified Germany as responsible for the Great War and assigned reparation payments to the Allies; the hyperinflation of the early 1920s that wiped out the savings of the middle class; and the suffering brought on by the Great Depression. Adolf Hitler promised an end to all those misfortunes by creating a new order that would lead to greatness for Germany. By stressing racial doctrines, particularly anti-Semitism, the Nazis added a unique and frightening twist to their ideology. Although the Nazis avoided class divisions by recruiting followers from all strata of society, National Socialism in the main appealed to the members of the lower-middle classes: ruined shopkeepers, impoverished farmers, discharged white-collar workers, and disenchanted students.

As Germany slipped into the Great Depression, the government's inability to find solutions to unemployment and impoverishment radicalized the electorate and caused them to lose faith in the democratic system. Between 1930 and 1932 the Nazi Party became the largest party in parliament, and the reactionary and feeble president, Paul von Hindenburg (1847–1934), decided to offer Hitler the chancellorship. Hitler lost little time in transforming the dying republic into a single-party dictatorship. He promised a German *Reich,* or empire, that would endure for a thousand years.

SOURCES FROM THE PAST

Mein Kampf

Mein Kampf (My Struggle) is the title of a book written by Adolf Hitler in which he presented his political views. Crudely written and turgid in style, it became the bible of the Nazi movement and the blueprint for the Third Reich. Hitler's basic theme was racial. He believed that a titanic struggle between a superior Aryan race and inferior non-Aryan races—including, most notably, Jews—determined the course of history. Originally, the term Aryan *designated a language group, not a mythological breed of people.*

So humans invariably wander about the garden of nature, convinced that they know and understand everything, yet with few exceptions are blind to one of the fundamental principles Nature uses in her work: the intrinsic segregation of the species of every living thing on the earth.

Any cross-breeding between two not completely equal beings will result in a product that is in between the level of the two parents. That means that the offspring will be superior to the parent who is at a biologically lower level of being but inferior to the parent at a higher level. This means the offspring will be overcome in the struggle for existence against those at the higher level. Such matings go against the will of Nature for the higher breeding of life.

As little as nature approves the mating of higher and lower individuals, she approves even less the blending of higher races with lower ones; for indeed otherwise her previous work toward higher development perhaps over hundreds of thousands of years might be rendered useless with one blow. If this were not the case, progressive development would stop and even deterioration might set in. . . . All the great civilizations of the past died out because contamination of their blood caused them to become decadent.

. . . What we see before us today as human culture, all the yields of art, science, and technology, are almost exclusively the creative product of the Aryans. Indeed this fact alone leads to the not unfounded conclusion that the Aryan alone is the founder of the higher type of humanity, and further that he represents the prototype of what we understand by the word: MAN.

The Jew provides the greatest contrast to the Aryan.

Since the Jew—for reasons I will deal with shortly—never had a civilization of his own, others have always provided the foundations of his intellectual labors. His intellect has always developed by the use of those cultural achievements he has found ready at hand around him. Never has it happened the other way around.

He stops at nothing, and his vileness becomes so monstrous that no one should be surprised if among our people the hateful figure of the Jew is taken as the personification of the devil and the symbol of evil.

■ Although he twisted their meaning, the precepts of science were adapted by Hitler to support his racial theories. Why would he take such an approach? Was it particularly effective?

SOURCE: Adolf Hitler. *Mein Kampf.* Boston: Houghton Mifflin, 1939, pp. 390–414.

CONSOLIDATION OF POWER Under the guise of a state of national emergency, the Nazis used all available means to impose their rule. They began by eliminating all working-class and liberal opposition. The Nazis suppressed the German communist and socialist parties and abrogated virtually all constitutional and civil rights. Subsequently, Hitler made the National Socialist Party the only legal party. Between 1933 and 1935 the regime replaced Germany's federal structure with a highly centralized state. The National Socialist state then guided the destruction of trade unions and the elimination of collective bargaining, subsequently prohibiting strikes and lockouts. The Nazis also purged the judiciary and the civil service, took control of all police forces, and removed enemies of the regime—both real and imagined—through incarceration or murder.

Nazi book burning, 1933
www.mhhe.com/bentleybrief2e

THE RACIAL STATE Once securely in power, the Nazi regime translated racist ideology, especially the notions of racial superiority and racial purity, into practice. The leaders of the Third Reich pursued the creation of a race-based national community by introducing eugenic measures designed to improve both the quantity and the "quality" of the German "race." Alarmed by declining birthrates, the Nazis launched a campaign to

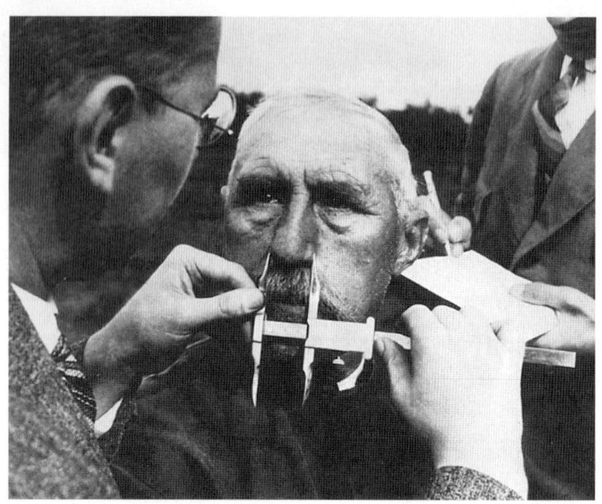

RACISM UNDER THE NAZIS. | A Nazi "racial expert" uses a caliper to measure the racial purity of a German. ***How were the measurements of noses supposed to indicate racial purity?***

increase births of "racially valuable" children. Through tax credits, special child allowances, and marriage loans, the authorities tried to encourage marriage and, they hoped, procreation among young people. At the same time, the regime outlawed abortions, restricted birth control devices, and made it difficult to obtain information about family planning. The Nazis also became enamored of pronatalist (to increase births) propaganda and set in motion a veritable cult of motherhood. Annually on 12 August—the birth date of Hitler's mother—women who bore many children received the Honor Cross of the German Mother in three classes: bronze for those with more than four children, silver for those with more than six, and gold for those with more than eight. By August 1939 three million women carried this prestigious award, which many Germans cynically called the "rabbit decoration." In the long term, however, any efforts by the Nazis to increase the fecundity of German women failed, and the birthrate remained below replacement level.

The quantity of offspring was not the only concern of the new rulers, who were obsessed with "quality." Starting in 1933, the regime initiated a compulsory sterilization program for men and women whom the regime had identified as having "hereditarily determined" sicknesses, including schizophrenia, manic depression, hereditary blindness, hereditary deafness, and serious physical deformities. Between 1934 and 1939 more than thirty thousand men and women underwent compulsory sterilization. The mania for "racial health" culminated in a state-sponsored euthanasia ("mercy killing") program that was responsible for the murder of approximately two hundred thousand women, men, and children. Between 1939 and 1945 the Nazis systematically killed those people judged useless to society, especially the physically and mentally handicapped.

Anti-Semitism, or prejudice against Jews, was a key element in the designs to achieve a new racial order. Immediately after coming to power in 1933, the Nazis initiated systematic measures to suppress Germany's Jewish population. A flood of discriminatory laws and directives designed to humiliate, impoverish, and segregate Jews from the rest of society followed. In 1935 the notorious Nuremberg Laws deprived German Jews of their citizenship and prohibited marriage and sexual intercourse between Jews and other Germans. The Nazi party, in cooperation with government agencies, banks, and businesses, took steps to eliminate Jews from economic life and expropriate their wealth. Party authorities also supervised the liquidation of Jewish-owned businesses or argued for their purchase—at much less than their true value—by companies owned or operated by non-Jews.

The official goal of the Nazi regime was Jewish emigration. Throughout the 1930s thousands of Jews left Germany, depriving the nation of many of its leading intellectuals, scientists, and artists. The exodus gained urgency after what came to be known as "the night of broken glass" *(Kristallnacht).* During the night of 9–10 November 1938, the Nazis arranged for the destruction of thousands of Jewish stores, the burning of most synagogues, and the murder of more than one hundred Jews throughout Germany and Austria. This *pogrom* (a Yiddish term for devastation) was a signal that the position of Jews in Hitler's Reich was about to deteriorate dramatically. Indeed, approximately 250,000 Jews had left Germany by 1938. Those staying behind, especially the poor and the elderly, contemplated an uncertain destiny.

SUMMARY

In the decades after the Great War, European intellectuals questioned and challenged established traditions. While scientists and social thinkers conceived new theories that reshaped human knowledge and perceptions, artists forged a contemporary aesthetic. In an age of global interdependence, the U.S. stock market crash of 1929 ushered in a period of prolonged economic contraction and social misery that engulfed much of the world. As most of the industrialized world reeled under the impact of the Great Depression, the leadership of the Soviet Union embarked on a state-sponsored program of rapid industrialization that, despite causing widespread suffering, transformed the Soviet Union into a major industrial and military power.

Italians under the leadership of Mussolini rebuilt their state through fascist policies and imperial expansion. In Germany the effects of the Great Depression paved the way for the establishment of the Nazi state, which was based on the principle of racial inequality. Although many different peoples suffered under the new regime, Jews were the principal victims of the Nazi racial state. Adolf Hitler's mission in life, envisioned in the wake of the Great War, was coming to a spectacular conclusion that culminated in another world war. That war brought both the fulfillment and the destruction of the goals and dreams he had crafted in an age of anxiety.

STUDY TERMS

Adolf Hitler (603)
agricultural collectivization (612)
Albert Einstein (605)
anti-Semitism (616)
Benito Mussolini (613)
Black Thursday (608)
cubism (606)
Fasci Italiani di Combattimento (613)
fascism (612)
First Five-Year Plan (611)
Franklin Delano Roosevelt (610)
Great Depression (608)
Great Purge (612)
John Maynard Keynes (610)
Joseph Stalin (611)
Karl Barth (605)
Kristallnacht (616)
National Socialism (614)
New Deal (610)
New Economic Policy (611)
Nuremberg Laws (616)
pronatalism (614)
Reich (614)
Sigmund Freud (606)
Smoot-Hawley Tariff Act (609)
war communism (611)
Werner Heisenberg (605)

FOR FURTHER READING

Martin Broszat. *The Hitler State: The Foundation and Development of the Internal Structure of the Third Reich.* New York, 1981. An account that does justice to the complexity of the Nazi movement and its rule.

Robert Conquest. *Stalin: Breaker of Nations.* New York, 1991. A compelling and absorbing biography.

Sheila Fitzpatrick. *The Russian Revolution, 1917–1932.* 2nd ed. New York, 1984. This work stands out for the author's ability to make complex processes accessible to the general reader and still instruct the specialist.

George Gamow. *Thirty Years That Shook Physics.* Garden City, N.Y., 1966. A leading physicist engagingly tells the story of modern physics.

Peter Gay. *Freud: A Life for Our Time.* New York, 1988. A balanced biography of one of the most influential social thinkers of the twentieth century.

George Heard Hamilton. *Painting and Sculpture in Europe, 1880–1940.* 6th ed. New Haven, 1993. A classic that presents a discerning overview of the subject.

Ian Kershaw. *The Nazi Dictatorship: Problems and Perspectives of Interpretation.* 2nd ed. London, 1989. A superb assessment that also provides the best introduction to the enormous literature on the Third Reich.

A. J. H. Latham. *The Depression and the Developing World, 1914–1939.* London, 1981. One of the few works that look beyond the industrialized world to give a global perspective on the subject.

Robert Paxton. *The Anatomy of Fascism.* New York, 2004. A groundbreaking and fascinating history of fascism.

Richard Pipes. *The Russian Revolution.* New York, 1990. When the Communist Party collapsed in 1991, this sweeping study was quickly translated into Russian and became a national best seller.

哈德門

還是他好

HATAMEN
大號
O.N.C.
大號
CIGARETTES
BRITISH CIGARETTE CO. LTD.
10 CIGARETTES

Nationalism and Political Identities in Asia, Africa, and Latin America

31

hanfei lived in politically exciting times. The daughter of a wealthy Chinese landowner, she grew up amid luxury and opportunity. Shanfei, however, matured into a woman who rejected the rich trappings of her youth. Her formative years were marked by the unsettling political and cultural changes that engulfed the globe in the wake of the Great War. The rise of nationalism and communism in China after the revolution of 1911 and the Russian revolution in 1917 guided the transformation of Shanfei—from a girl ruled by tradition and privilege, she became an active revolutionary.

With the exception of Shanfei's father, the members of her family in Hunan province took in the new spirit of the first decades of the twentieth century. Her brothers returned from school with compelling ideas, including some that challenged the subordinate position of women in China. Shanfei's mother, to all appearances a woman who accepted her subservience to her husband, listened quietly to her sons as they discussed new views and then applied them to her daughter. She used every means at her disposal to persuade her husband to educate their daughter. He relented but still insisted that Shanfei receive an old-fashioned education and submit to foot binding and childhood betrothal.

When Shanfei was eleven years old, her father suddenly died. Shanfei's mother took the opportunity to rip the bandages off Shanfei's feet and send her to a modern school. In the lively atmosphere of her school, Shanfei bloomed into an activist. At sixteen she incited a student strike against the administration of her school, transferred to a more modern school, and became famous as a leader in the student movement. She broke tradition in both her personal and her political life. In 1926 Shanfei abandoned her studies to join the Communist Youth, and she gave up her fiancé for a free marriage to the man she loved: a peasant leader in the communist movement.

❮ In this cigarette advertisement from 1935, Chinese women are shown challenging traditions. They are "new women," affected by the radical changes in identity and behavior taking place after the Great War and during the Great Depression.

The twists of fate that altered the destiny of Shanfei had parallels throughout the colonial world after 1914. Two major events, the Great War and the Great Depression, defined much of the turmoil of those years. Disillusion and radical upheaval marked areas in Asia, Africa, and Latin America. In Japan the ravages of the Great Depression prompted militarist leaders to build national strength through imperial expansion. Latin American states worked to alter the economic domination of their

Shanfei (shahn-fahy)

CHRONOLOGY

1912	Taft establishes "dollar diplomacy" as U.S. foreign policy
1914–1918	2.5 million African troops and carriers serve in the Great War
1919	May Fourth movement in China
1920	Non-cooperation movement in India
1921	Rivera returns to Mexico to paint
1928	Socialist Party of Peru is founded
1929	Beginning of Great Depression
1930	Civil disobedience movement in India
1930s–1940s	Vargas's *estado novo* in Brazil
1931	Japanese invasion of Manchuria
1933	Roosevelt begins practice of the Good Neighbor Policy
1934	Long March by Chinese communists
1935	Government of India Act is passed
1938	Cárdenas nationalizes oil industry in Mexico

"good neighbor" to the north, and African peoples suffered a contraction in living standards along with their imperial overlords.

European empires still appeared to dominate global relations, but the Great War opened fissures within the European and American spheres of influence. Beneath colonial surfaces, resistance to foreign rule and a desire for national unity were stronger than ever. This situation was especially true in India and China, but it also pertained to those in Africa and Latin America who struggled against the domination of imperial powers.

ASIAN PATHS TO AUTONOMY

The Paris peace settlement barely altered the prewar colonial holdings of Europeans, yet indirectly the Great War affected relations between Asian peoples and the imperial powers. In the decades following the Great War, nationalism developed into a powerful political force in Asia, especially in India and China. Achieving the twin ideals of independence from foreign powers and national unity became a dream of intellectuals and a goal of new political leaders. In their search for new identities untainted by the dependent past, Asians transformed and adapted European ideologies such as nationalism and socialism to fit indigenous traditions. In that sense, peoples in India and China followed in the footsteps of Japan, which had already adapted European and American economic strategies to its own advantage. Still dissatisfied with its status, Japan used militarism and imperial expansion in the interwar years to enhance its national identity.

Indian, Chinese, and Japanese societies underwent a prolonged period of disorder and struggle until a new order emerged. In India the quest for national identity focused on gaining independence from British rule but was complicated by sectarian differences between Hindus and Muslims. The Chinese path to national identity was fraught with foreign and civil war as two principal groups—the Nationalist and Communist parties—contended for power. Japanese militarists made China's quest for national unity more difficult, because Japan struggled to overcome its domestic problems through conquests that focused on China.

India's Quest for Home Rule

By the beginning of the twentieth century, Indian nationalism threatened the British empire's hold on India. The construction of a vast railway network across India to facilitate the export of raw materials contributed to national unity by bringing the people of the subcontinent within easy reach of one another. Moreover, the British had created an elite of educated Indian administrators to control and administer the vast subcontinent. A European system of education familiarized this elite with the political and social values of European society. Those values, however—democracy, individual freedom, and equality—were the antithesis of empire, and they promoted nationalist movements.

INDIAN NATIONAL CONGRESS Of all the associations dedicated to the struggle against British rule, the most influential was the Indian National Congress, founded in 1885. This organization, which enlisted the support of many prominent Hindus and Muslims, at first stressed collaboration with the British to bring self-rule to India, but after the Great War the congress pursued that goal in opposition to the British.

During the Great War, large numbers of Indians rallied to the British cause, and nationalist movements remained inactive. But as the war led to scarcities of goods and food, social discontent with British rule led to an upsurge in nationalist activity. Indian nationalists also drew encouragement from ideas emanating from Washington, D.C., and St. Petersburg. They read Woodrow Wilson's Fourteen Points, which called for national self-determination, and Lenin's appeal for a united struggle by proletarians and colonized peoples. The British government responded to increased nationalism in this period with a series of repressive measures that precipitated a wave of violence and disorder throughout the Indian subcontinent.

MOHANDAS GANDHI (1869–1949). | This photo, which dates from about 1920, was taken several years after Gandhi's return to India from South Africa. By this time, he was a dominant force in Indian politics.

MOHANDAS K. GANDHI Into this turmoil stepped Mohandas Karamchand Gandhi (1869–1948), one of the most remarkable and charismatic leaders of the twentieth century. Gandhi grew up in a prosperous and pious Hindu household, married at thirteen, and left his hometown in 1888 to study law in London. In 1893 he went to South Africa to accept a position with an Indian firm, and there he quickly became involved in organizing the local Indian community against a system of racial segregation that made Indians second-class citizens. During the twenty-two years he spent in South Africa, Gandhi embraced a moral philosophy of tolerance and nonviolence *(ahimsa)* and developed the technique of passive resistance that he called *satyagraha* ("truth and firmness"). His belief in the virtue of simple living led him to renounce material possessions, dress in the garb of a simple Indian peasant, and become a vegetarian.

Returning to India in 1915, Gandhi became active in Indian politics and succeeded in transforming the Indian National Congress from an elitist institution into a mass organization. Gandhi's unique mixture of spiritual intensity and political activism appealed to a broad section of the Indian population, and in the eyes of many he quickly achieved the stature of a political and spiritual leader, their Mahatma, or "great soul." Although he was himself a member of the merchant caste, Gandhi was determined to eradicate the injustices of the caste system. He fought especially hard to improve the status of the lowest classes of society, the casteless Untouchables, whom he called *harijans* ("children of God").

Under Gandhi's leadership the congress launched two mass movements: the noncooperation movement of 1920–1922 and the civil disobedience movement of 1930. Convinced that economic self-sufficiency was a prerequisite for self-government, Gandhi called on the Indian people to boycott British goods and return to wearing homespun cotton clothing. Gandhi furthermore admonished his people to boycott institutions operated by the British in India, such as schools, offices, and courts. Despite Gandhi's cautions against the use of force, violence often accompanied the protest movement. The British retaliated with arrests. That the British authorities could react brutally was shown in 1919 in the city of Amritsar, where colonial troops fired on an unarmed crowd, killing 379 demonstrators.

Gandhi marches to the sea to make salt
www.mhhe.com/bentleybrief2e

Mohandas Karamchand Gandhi (moh-huhn-DAHS kuhr-uhm-CHUND GAHN-dee)
ahimsa (uh-HIM-sah)
satyagraha (suh-TYA-gruh-hah)
harijan (har-i-jahn)

SOURCES FROM THE PAST

Mohandas Gandhi, *Hind Swaraj (Indian Home Rule)*

After Mohandas Gandhi completed his study of law in England, he moved to British South Africa to serve the colony's large Indian population. While there, he became outraged at British laws that discriminated against Indians. As part of his strategy of resistance to such discrimination, Gandhi developed the idea of satyagraha, *or soul-force.* Satyagraha *sought justice through love rather than violence, and its followers disobeyed unjust laws through nonviolent resistance. In 1908, Gandhi articulated his ideas about* satyagraha *in a pamphlet called* Hind Swaraj (Indian Home Rule), *which took the form of a dialogue between a reader and an editor.*

Chapter XVII: Passive Resistance

Reader: Is there any historical evidence as to the success of what you have called soul-force or truth-force? No instance seems to have happened of any nation having risen through soul-force. I still think that the evil-doers will not cease doing evil without physical punishment.

Editor: . . . The fact that there are so many men still alive in the world shows that it is based not on the force of arms but on the force of truth or love. Therefore the greatest and most unimpeachable evidence of the success of this force is to be found in the fact that, in spite of the wars of the world, it still lives on. . . . History does not and cannot take note of this fact. History is really a record of every interruption of the even working of the force of love or of the soul. . . . Soul-force, being natural, is not noted in history.

Reader: According to what you say, it is plain that instances of the kind of passive resistance are not to be found in history. It is necessary to understand this passive resistance more fully. . . .

Editor: Passive resistance is a method of securing rights by personal suffering; it is the reverse of resistance by arms. When I refuse to do a thing that is repugnant to my conscience, I use soul-force. For instance, the government of the day has passed a law which is applicable to me: I do not like it. If, by using violence, I force the government to repeal the law, I am employing what may be termed body-force. If I do not obey the law and accept the penalty for its breach, I use soul-force. It involves sacrifice of self.

Everybody admits that sacrifice of self is infinitely superior to sacrifice of others. Moreover, if this kind of force is used in a cause that is unjust, only the person using it suffers. He does not make others suffer for his mistakes.

Reader: From what you say, I deduce that passive resistance is a splendid weapon of the weak but that, when they are strong, they may take up arms.

Editor: That is gross ignorance. Passive resistance, that is, soul-force, is matchless. It is superior to the force of arms. How, then, can it be considered only a weapon of the weak? Physical-force men are strangers to the courage that is requisite in a passive resister. . . . A passive resister will say he will not obey a law that is against his conscience, even though he may be blown to pieces at the mouth of a cannon.

What do you think? Wherein is courage required—in blowing others to pieces from behind a cannon or with a smiling face to approach a cannon and to be blown to pieces? Who is the true warrior—he who keeps death always as a bosom-friend or he who controls the death of others? Believe me that a man devoid of courage and manhood can never be a passive resister.

This, however, I will admit: that even a man, weak in body, is capable of offering this resistance. One man can offer it just as well as millions. Both men and women can indulge in it. It does not require the training of an army; it needs no Jiu-jitsu. Control over the mind is alone necessary, and, when that is attained, man is free like the king of the forest, and his very glance withers the enemy.

■ **Why, according to Gandhi, is soul-force stronger than physical force?**

SOURCE: Alfred J. Andrea and James H. Overfield. *The Human Record: Sources of Global History,* 3rd ed., *Vol. II: Since 1500.* Boston and New York: Houghton Mifflin, 1998.

THE INDIA ACT In the face of sustained nationalist opposition and after years of hesitation, the British parliament enacted the Government of India Act, which gave India the institutions of a self-governing state. The legislation allowed for the establishment of autonomous legislative bodies in the provinces of British India, the creation of a bicameral (two-chambered) national legislature, and the formation of an executive arm under the control of the British government. Upon the urging of Gandhi, the majority of Indians approved the measure, which went into effect in 1937.

The India Act proved unworkable, however, because India's six hundred nominally sovereign princes refused to cooperate and because Muslims feared that Hindus would dominate the national legislature. Muslims had reason for concern because they already faced economic control by Hindus, a fact underlined during the Great Depression, which had a severe impact on India. Indeed, since Muslims constituted the majority of indebted tenant farmers, during the Great Depression they found themselves increasingly unable to pay rents and debts to their Hindu landlords. As a result, many Muslims felt that they had been economically exploited by Hindus, which exacerbated tensions between the two groups. Muhammad Ali Jinnah (1876–1948), an eloquent and brilliant lawyer who headed the Muslim League—a separate nationalist organization founded in 1906 that focused on the needs of Indian Muslims—warned that a unified India represented nothing less than a threat to the Muslim faith and its Indian community. In place of one India, he proposed two states, one of which would be the "land of the pure," or Pakistan. Jinnah's proposal reflected an uncomfortable reality that society in India was split by hostility between Hindus and Muslims.

China's Search for Order

As Shanfei's life story suggested, during the first half of the twentieth century China was in a state of almost continual revolutionary upheaval. The conflict's origins dated from the nineteenth century, when the Chinese empire came under relentless pressure from imperialist powers (see chapter 28). As revolutionary and nationalist uprisings gained widespread support, a revolution in 1911 forced the Xuantong emperor, still a child (also known as Puyi), to abdicate. The Qing empire fell with relative ease. Dr. Sun Yatsen (1866–1925), a leading opponent of the old regime, became the first provisional president of what would become the new Chinese republic in 1912.

THE REPUBLIC Yet the revolution of 1911 did not establish a stable government. Indeed, the republic soon plunged into a state of political anarchy and economic disintegration marked by the rule of warlords, who were disaffected generals from the old imperial Chinese army. Although the central government in Beijing ran the post office and a few other services, the warlords established themselves as provincial rulers. Because the warlords were responsible for the neglect of irrigation projects, for the revival of the opium trade, and for the decline of economic investments, they contributed to the deterioration and instability of Chinese society. Yet warlords were just one symbol of the disintegration of the political order. The relationship between native authority and foreign powers was another. Since the nineteenth century, a collection of treaties, known in China as the unequal treaties, had established a network of foreign control over the Chinese economy that permitted foreigners to intervene in Chinese society. Foreigners did not control the state, but through their privileges they impaired its sovereignty.

CHINESE NATIONALISM After the Great War, nationalist sentiment developed rapidly in China. Youths and intellectuals, who had looked to Europe and the United States as models for Chinese reform, eagerly anticipated the results of the 1919 peace conference in Paris. They expected the U.S. government to support the termination of the treaty system and the restoration of full Chinese sovereignty. Instead, the peacemakers approved increasing Japanese interference in China. That decision gave rise to the May Fourth movement. Spearheaded by students and intellectuals in China's urban areas, all classes of Chinese protested against foreign, especially Japanese, interference. In speeches, newspapers, and novels, the movement's leaders—including student leaders such as Shanfei—pledged themselves to rid China of imperialism and reestablish national unity.

Muhammad Ali Jinnah (moo-HAM-id ah-lee JIN-uh)
Xuantong (soo-ahn-tohng)

Disillusioned by the cynical self-interest of the United States and the European powers, some Chinese became interested in Marxist thought and the social and economic experiments under way in the Soviet Union. The anti-imperialist rhetoric of the Soviet leadership prompted the founding of the Chinese Communist Party (CCP) in Shanghai in 1921. Among its early members was Mao Zedong (1893–1976), a former teacher and librarian who viewed a Marxist-inspired social revolution as the cure for China's problems.

SUN YATSEN The most prominent nationalist leader at the time, Sun Yatsen, did not share the communists' enthusiasm for a dictatorship of the proletariat. Rather, Sun's basic ideology called for elimination of special privileges for foreigners, national reunification, economic development, and a democratic republican government based on universal suffrage. To realize those goals, he was determined to bring the entire country under the control of his Nationalist People's Party, or Guomindang. In 1923 members of the small CCP began to augment the ranks of the Guomindang, and by 1926 they made up one-third of the Guomindang's membership. Both organizations availed themselves of the assistance offered

Mao Zedong (mow zuh-doong)
Guomindang (GWOH-mihn-dahng)

MAP 31.1 | The struggle for control in China, 1927–1936. Compare the continental territories controlled by Japan and the Guomindang in 1934. ***How would the size of Japan's territories in Manchuria and Korea influence Chinese abilities to challenge Japanese expansion?***

Nanjing became the capital of the nationalist government, while Mao made his CCP headquarters in Yan'an.

by the Soviet Union, whose advisors helped reorganize the Guomindang and the CCP into effective political organizations. In the process, the Soviets bestowed upon China the basis of a new political system.

CIVIL WAR After the death of Sun Yatsen in 1925, the leadership of the Guomindang fell to Jiang Jieshi (Chiang Kai-shek, 1887–1975), a young general who had been trained in Japan and the Soviet Union. Before long, Jiang Jieshi launched a political and military offensive, known as the Northern Expedition, that aimed to unify the nation and bring China under Guomindang rule. Toward the end of his successful campaign, in 1927, Jiang Jieshi brutally and unexpectedly turned against his former communist allies, bringing the alliance between the Guomindang and the CCP to a bloody end. In the following year, nationalist forces occupied Beijing, set up a central government in Nanjing, and declared the Guomindang the official government of a unified and sovereign Chinese state. Meanwhile, the badly mauled communists retreated to a remote area of southeastern China to reconstitute and reorganize their forces.

The nationalist government had to deal with many concerns, but Chinese leaders evaded one major global crisis—the Great Depression. Foreign trade in such items as tea and silk, which did decline, made up only a small part of China's economy, which was otherwise dominated by its large domestic markets. Although the new government in China generally avoided having to contend with global economic devastation, it did have to confront three major problems during the 1930s. First, the nationalists actually controlled only part of China, leaving the remainder of the country in the hands of warlords. Second, in the early 1930s communist revolution was still a major threat. Third, the Guomindang faced increasing Japanese aggression.

In dealing with those problems, Jiang Jieshi gave priority to eliminating the CCP. No longer able to ward off the relentless attacks of nationalist forces, the communists took flight in October 1934 to avoid annihilation, and some eighty-five thousand troops and auxiliary personnel of the Red Army began the legendary Long March, an epic journey of 10,000 kilometers (6,215 miles). After traveling across difficult terrain and fighting for survival against hunger, disease, and Guomindang forces, those marchers who had not perished arrived in a remote area of Shaanxi province in northwestern China in October

THINKING ABOUT *Traditions*

TRADITIONS IN NATIONALISM AND POLITICAL IDENTITIES IN ASIA, AFRICA, AND LATIN AMERICA. During the 1920s and 1930s, colonized peoples in Asia and Africa created nationalist, anticolonial movements that were partly inspired by Western ideals of freedom and democracy or by revolutionary Marxism. How did Asian and African nationalists modify these Western-inspired ideals with local cultural and political traditions to create unique movements of their own?

Jiang Jieshi (jyahng jeh-she)

JIANG JIESHI AND MAO ZEDONG. | Adversaries in the struggle for power in China: at left, Jiang Jieshi (Chiang Kai-shek); at right, Mao Zedong.

1935 and established headquarters at Yan'an. During the Long March, Mao Zedong emerged as the leader and the principal theoretician of the Chinese communist movement. He came up with a Chinese form of Marxist-Leninism, or Maoism, an ideology grounded in the conviction that peasants rather than urban proletarians were the foundation for a successful revolution in China.

Imperial and Imperialist Japan

After the Great War, Japan achieved great-power status and appeared to accept the international status quo that the major powers fashioned in the aftermath of war. After joining the League of Nations as one of the "big five" powers, in 1922 the Japanese government entered into a series of international agreements whereby Japan agreed to limit naval development, pledged to evacuate Shandong province of China, and guaranteed China's territorial integrity. In 1928 the Japanese government signed the Kellogg-Briand Pact, which renounced war as an instrument of national policy. Concerns about earlier Japanese territorial ambitions in China receded from the minds of the international community.

Japan's limited involvement in the Great War gave a dual boost to its economy. Japanese businesses profited from selling munitions and other goods to the Allies throughout the war, and they gained a bigger foothold in Asia as the war led Europe's trading nations to neglect Asian markets. Economic prosperity was short-lived, however, as the postwar economy of Japan faced a series of recessions that culminated in a giant economic slump caused by the Great Depression.

Economic contraction set the stage for social unrest and radical politics. Public demands for sweeping political and social reforms figured prominently in Japanese domestic politics throughout the 1920s. Yet conservatives blocked any major advances beyond the suffrage law of 1925, which established universal male suffrage. By the early 1930s an increasingly frustrated and disenchanted public blamed its government for the nation's continuing economic problems. Right-wing political groups called for an end to party rule, while xenophobic nationalists argued for the preservation of a unique Japanese culture and the eradication of "Western" influences. A campaign of assassinations, targeting political and business leaders, culminated in the murder of Prime Minister Inukai Tsuyoshi (1855–1932).

Politicians who supported Japan's role in the international industrial-capitalist system faced increasing opposition from those who were inclined toward a militarist vision of a self-sufficient Japan that would dominate east Asia. Indeed, the hardships of the depression only seemed to discredit the internationalist position and make the militarist vision of self-sufficiency more attractive.

Meanwhile, militarists were setting their sights on expansion in China, where political instability made it an inviting target. In 1931 Japan's military forces began their campaign of expansion in Manchuria, which had historically been Chinese territory. The choice of Manchuria was no accident: the Japanese had significant economic interests there by the twentieth century, not least of which was the Manchurian Railroad, which they had built in 1906 and continued to maintain.

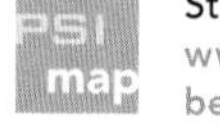

Struggle for control in China
www.mhhe.com/bentleybrief2e

THE MUKDEN INCIDENT On the night of 18 September 1931, Japanese troops used explosives to blow up a few feet of rail on the Japanese-built South Manchuria Railway north of Mukden, then accused the Chinese of attacking their railroad. This "Mukden incident" became the pretext for war between Japanese and Chinese troops. Although the civilian government in Japan tried to halt this military incursion, by 1932 Japanese troops controlled all of Manchuria. The Japanese established a puppet state called Manchukuo, but in reality Japan had absorbed Manchuria into its empire, challenged the international peace system, and begun a war. In response to the Manchurian invasion, the Guomindang (Nationalist Party) leader Jiang Jieshi appealed to the League of Nations

---

Inukai Tsuyoshi (ee-NO-kigh ts-yo-she)

to halt Japanese aggression. The league eventually called for the withdrawal of Japanese forces and for the restoration of Chinese sovereignty. The Japanese responded by leaving the league, and nothing was done to stop the aggression. That reaction set the pattern for future responses to the actions of expansionist nations like Japan. Embarking on conquests in east Asia, Japanese militarists found a sure means of promoting a new militant Japanese national identity. They also helped provoke a new global conflagration.

Africa under Colonial Domination

The Great War and the Great Depression similarly complicated quests for national independence and unity in Africa. The colonial ties that bound African colonies to European powers ensured that Africans became participants in the Great War, willing or not. European states transmitted their respective animosities and their military conflicts to African soil and drew on their colonies for soldiers and carriers. The forced recruitment of military personnel led some Africans to raise arms against their colonial overlords, but Europeans generally prevailed in putting down those uprisings. African contributions to the Great War and the wartime rhetoric of self-determination espoused by U.S. president Woodrow Wilson led some Africans to anticipate a different postwar world. The peacemakers in Paris, however, ignored African pleas for social and political reform.

In the decades following the peace settlement of 1919, colonialism grew stronger on the African continent as European powers focused on the economic exploitation of their colonies. The imposition of a rapacious form of capitalism destroyed the self-sufficiency of many African economies, and African economic life became more thoroughly enmeshed in the global economy. During the decades following the Great War, African intellectuals searched for new national identities and looked forward to the construction of nations devoid of European domination and exploitation.

Africa and the Great War

The Great War had a profound impact on Africa. The conflict of 1914–1918 affected Africans because many belligerents were colonial powers with colonies in Africa. Except for Spanish-controlled territories, which remained neutral, every African colony as well as the two independent states of Ethiopia and Liberia took sides in the war.

WAR IN AFRICA Although Germany had been a latecomer in the race for overseas colonies, German imperialists had managed to carve out an African empire in Togo, Cameroon, German Southwest Africa, and German East Africa. Thus, one immediate consequence of war for Africans in 1914 was that the Allies invaded those German colonies. Badly outnumbered by French and British-led troops, the Germans could not hope to win the war in Africa. Yet, by resorting to guerrilla tactics, some fifteen thousand German troops tied up sixty thousand Allied forces and postponed defeat until the last days of the war.

More than one million African soldiers participated directly in military campaigns, in which they witnessed firsthand the spectacle of white people fighting one another. The colonial powers also encouraged their African subjects in uniforms to kill the enemy "white man," whose life until now had been sacrosanct because of his skin color. Even more men, as well as women and children, served as carriers to support European armies, many of them serving involuntarily. In French colonies, military service became compulsory for all males between the ages of twenty and twenty-eight, and by the end of the war over 480,000 colonial troops had served in the French army. In British colonies, a compulsory service order in 1915 made all men aged eighteen to twenty-five liable for military service. In the Congo, the Belgians impressed more than half a million porters. Ultimately, more than 150,000 African soldiers and carriers lost their lives, and many suffered injury or became disabled.

CHALLENGES TO EUROPEAN AUTHORITY While the world's attention was focused on the slaughter taking place in Europe between 1914 and 1918, Africans mounted bold challenges to European colonial authority. Indeed, opportunities for rebellion and protest increased when the already thin European presence in Africa grew even thinner as commercial and administrative personnel left the colonies in large numbers to serve the war effort. The causes of those revolts varied. In some cases, as in Libya, revolts simply represented continued resistance to European rule. In other instances, religious opposition manifested itself in uprisings. The Mumbo cult in Kenya, for example, targeted Europeans and their Christian religion, declaring that "all Europeans are our enemies, but the time is shortly coming when they will disappear from our country." The major inspiration for most revolts, however, stemmed from the resentment and hatred engendered by the compulsory conscription of soldiers and carriers. No matter the cause, colonial authorities responded ruthlessly to put down the revolts.

The Colonial Economy

The decades following the Great War witnessed a thorough transformation of African economic life. Colonial powers pursued two key economic objectives in Africa: they wanted to make sure that the colonized paid for the institutions—bureaucracies, judiciary, police, and military forces—that kept them in subjugation; and they developed export-oriented economies characterized by the exchange of raw materials or cash crops for manufactured goods from abroad. In pursuit of those goals, colonial authorities imposed economic structures that altered, subordinated, or destroyed African economies by making them increasingly dependent on a European-dominated global economy. One result of this integration was that global economic downturns could spell disaster for African economies. During the Great Depression, for example, as international markets for primary products shrank, prices for African raw materials and cash crops dropped sharply and trade volume often fell by half. This, in turn, wreaked havoc on economies that had been geared almost completely toward the production of a single resource or crop.

INFRASTRUCTURE Part of the process of global economic integration involved investment in infrastructures such as port facilities, roads, railways, and telegraph wires. Efficient transportation and communication networks not only facilitated conquest and rule but also linked the agricultural or mineral wealth of a colony to the outside world. Although Europeans later claimed that they had given Africa its first modern infrastructure, Europeans and their businesses were usually its main beneficiaries. Even though Africans paid for the infrastructure with their labor and taxes, Europeans designed such systems with their own needs, rather than the needs of Africans, in mind.

FARMING AND MINING Colonial taxation was used as an important tool to drive Africans into the labor market. To earn the money to pay colonial taxes, African farmers had to become cash-crop farmers or seek wage labor on plantations and in mines. In most colonies, farmers specialized in one or two crops destined for export to the country governing them, among them peanuts from Senegal and northern Nigeria, cotton from Uganda, cocoa from the Gold Coast, rubber from the Congo, and palm oil from the Ivory Coast and the Niger delta. In areas with extensive white settlement, such as in Kenya, Rhodesia, and South Africa, settlers expropriated African lands and grew cash crops—using African labor—themselves. In British-controlled Kenya, for example, four thousand white farmers seized seven million acres in the Kikuyu highlands, the colony's richest land.

In South Africa, the government reserved 88 percent of all land for whites, who made up just 20 percent of the total population. Colonial mining enterprises geared toward the extraction of copper, gold, and diamonds loomed large in parts of central and southern Africa. These enterprises depended on the labor of African men who were recruited from rural areas and were paid minimal wages. Such recruitment practices set in motion a vast pattern of labor migration that persisted throughout the twentieth century. In many cases,

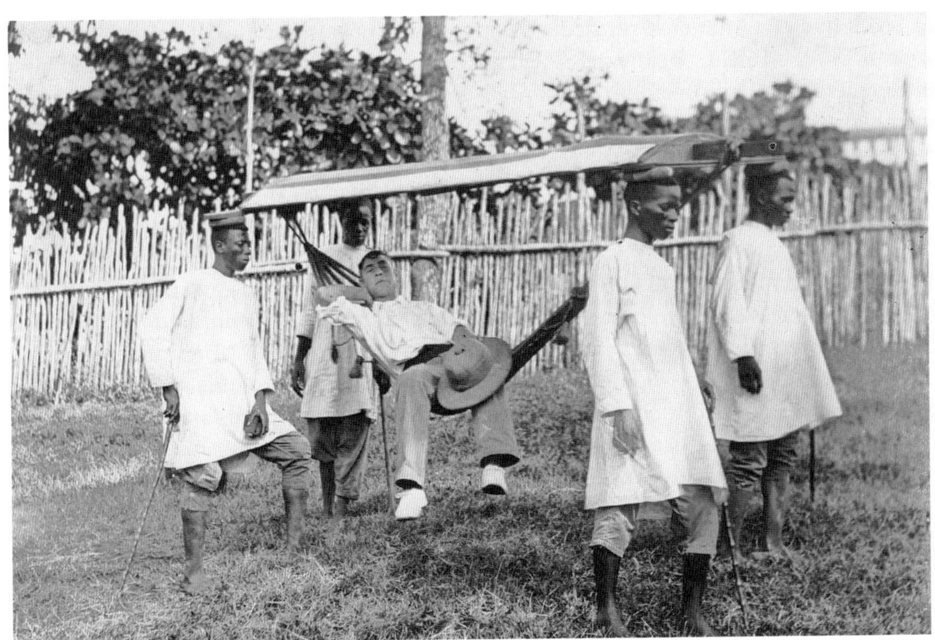

Europeans in Africa. A European colonialist takes advantage of African labor and is "traveling in hammock," as this 1912 photograph's title suggests. ***What does this photograph suggest about European attitudes toward Africans?***

the absence of male labor and the payment of minimal wages had the effect of impoverishing rural areas, where the women left behind could not grow enough food to feed their children and elderly relatives.

PSI img Slaves in the Congo, ca. 1910 www.mhhe.com/bentleybrief2e

LABOR PRACTICES Where taxation failed to create a malleable native labor force, colonial officials resorted to outright forced labor and barely disguised variants of slavery. Indeed, the construction of railways and roads often depended on forced-labor regimes. When the French undertook the construction of the Congo-Ocean railway from Brazzaville to the port at Point-Noir, for example, they rounded up some ten thousand workers annually. Within a few years, between fifteen and twenty thousand African laborers had perished from starvation, disease, and maltreatment. A white settler in Kenya candidly expressed the view held by many colonial administrators: "We have stolen his land. Now we must steal his limbs. Compulsory labor is the corollary to our occupation of the country."

African Nationalism

In the decades following the Great War, many Africans were disappointed that their contributions to that conflict went unrewarded. In place of anticipated social reforms or some degree of greater political participation came an extension and a consolidation of the colonial system. Nevertheless, ideas concerning self-determination, articulated by U.S. president Woodrow Wilson during the war, gained adherents among a group of African nationalists. Those ideas influenced the growth of African nationalism and the development of incipient nationalist movements. An emerging class of native urban intellectuals, frequently educated in Europe, became especially involved in the formation of ideologies that promised freedom from colonialism and promoted new national identities.

AFRICA'S NEW ELITE Colonialism prompted the emergence of a new African social class, sometimes called the "new elite." This elite derived its status from European-style education and employment in the colonial state, in foreign companies, or in Christian missions. The upper echelons of this elite were high-ranking civil servants, physicians, lawyers, and writers who had studied abroad in western Europe or the United States. A case in point was Jomo Kenyatta (1895–1978), who spent almost fifteen years in Europe, during which time he attended various schools, including the London School of Economics. An immensely articulate nationalist, Kenyatta later led Kenya to independence from the British. Below men such as Kenyatta in status stood teachers, clerks, and interpreters who had obtained a European-derived primary or secondary education. All members of the elite, however, spoke and understood the language of the colonizer and outwardly adopted the cultural norms of the colonizer, such as wearing European-style clothes or adopting European names. It was within the ranks of this new elite that ideas concerning African identity and nationhood germinated.

FORMS OF NATIONALISM Because colonialism had introduced Africans to European ideas and ideologies, African nationalists frequently embraced the European concept of the nation as a means of forging unity—as well as colonial resistance—among disparate African groups. Some nationalists looked to the precolonial past for inspiration. There they found identities based on ethnicity, religion, and languages, and they believed that any future nation must reconstitute distinctively African spiritual and political institutions. Race had provided colonial powers with one rationale for conquest and exploitation; hence it was not surprising that some nationalists used the concept of an African race as a foundation for identity, solidarity, and nation building. Indeed, race figured prominently in a strain of African nationalism known as pan-Africanism, which originated in the western hemisphere among the descendants of slaves. Representative of this pan-Africanism was the Jamaican nationalist leader Marcus Garvey (1887–1940), who thought of all Africans as members of a single race and who promoted the unification of all people of African descent into a single African state. Still other nationalists looked for an African identity rooted in geography rather than in race. That approach commonly translated into a desire to build the nation on the basis of borders that defined existing colonial states. Collectively those ideas influenced the development of nationalist movements during the 1930s and 1940s, which, after World War II, translated into demands for independence from colonialism.

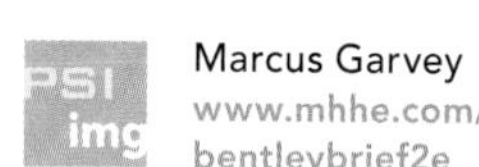

Marcus Garvey
www.mhhe.com/bentleybrief2e

Latin American Struggles with Neocolonialism

The postcolonial history of Latin American states in the early twentieth century offered clues about what the future might hold for those areas in Asia and Africa still seeking independence from colonial rule. Having gained their independence in the nineteenth century, most sovereign nations in Latin America thereafter struggled to achieve political and economic stability in the midst of interference from foreign powers. The era of the Great War and the Great Depression proved crucial to solidifying and exposing to view the neocolonial structures that guided affairs in Latin America. Generally seen as a more subtle form of imperial control, neocolonialism refers to foreign economic domination, as well as military and political intervention, in states that have already achieved independence from colonial rule. In Central and South America, as well as in the Caribbean, this new imperial influence came not from former colonial rulers in Spain and Portugal but, rather, from wealthy, industrial-capitalist powerhouses such as Great Britain and the United States. Neocolonialism impinged on the political and economic development of Latin American states, but it did not fully prevent nationalist leaders from devising strategies to combat the newfound imperialism.

The Impact of the Great War and the Great Depression

The Great War, the Russian revolution, and the Mexican revolution spread radical ideas and the promise of new political possibilities throughout Latin America. The disparate ideals emerging from this time of political ferment found receptive audiences in Latin America, especially during the global economic crisis of the Great Depression. Marxism,

Vladimir Lenin's theories on capitalism and imperialism, and a growing concern for the impoverished Indian masses as well as exploited peasants and workers in Latin American societies informed the outlooks of many disgruntled intellectuals and artists. The Enlightenment-derived liberalism that had shaped independence movements and the political systems of many postindependence nations no longer served as the only form of political legitimacy.

Some of the most radical responses to U.S. economic domination came from Latin American universities, whose students became increasingly politicized in this period. Many took their inspiration from the Mexican and Russian revolutions—both of which were inimical to the ideas of the United States. Indeed, universities became training grounds for future political leaders, including Cuba's Fidel Castro (1926–). In many Latin American countries, radicalism also expressed itself in the formation of political parties that either openly espoused communism or otherwise adopted rebellious agendas for change.

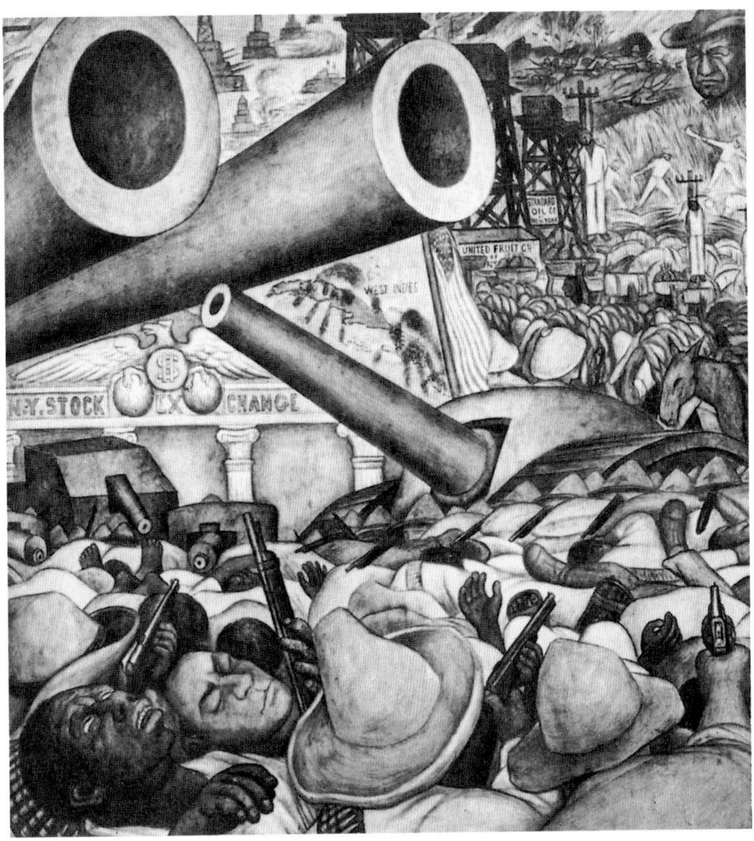

DIEGO RIVERA'S *IMPERIALISM*. | This painting was one in a series on the United States and offered a visual critique of U.S. neocolonialism in Latin America.

DIEGO RIVERA AND RADICAL ARTISTIC VISIONS The ideological transformations apparent in Latin America became stunningly and publicly visible in the murals painted by famed Mexican artist Diego Rivera (1886–1957). Artistically trained in Mexico in his youth, Rivera went to study in Europe in 1907 and did not return to Mexico until 1921. Influenced by indigenous art forms as well as the European Renaissance artists and Cubists, Rivera's paintings reflected the turmoil and shifting political sensibilities taking place during the Great War and its aftermath. He blended his artistic and political visions in vast public murals in Mexico's cities, because he believed that art should be on display for working people.

Fidel Castro
www.mhhe.com/bentleybrief2e

As a political activist, Rivera also used his art to level a pointed critique of the economic dependency and political repressiveness engendered by U.S. neocolonialism in Latin America. In the painting *Imperialism,* for example, Rivera depicted massive guns and tanks extending over the New York Stock Exchange. In the foreground and at the edges of the stock exchange are a variety of Latin American victims of this monied-military oppression. Indeed, Rivera made visible the impact of U.S. imperialism on Latin American societies, and by doing so he helped spread political activism in the Americas.

The Evolution of Economic Imperialism

Latin American states were no strangers to foreign economic domination in the nineteenth and early twentieth centuries. Their export-oriented economies had long been tied to global finances and had been subject to controls imposed by foreign investors, largely those from Great Britain and the United States. The major evolution in economic neocolonialism during this period concerned the growing predominance of the United States in the economic affairs of Latin American nations, which was sealed by the Great War. Between 1924 and 1929, U.S. banks and

THINKING ABOUT *Encounters*

ENCOUNTERS IN NATIONALISM AND POLITICAL IDENTITIES IN ASIA, AFRICA, AND LATIN AMERICA. As a result of physical and intellectual encounters during and after World War I, peoples in Asia, Africa, and Latin America became increasingly aware of their common exploitation by Western powers in Europe and the United States. What encounters were most responsible for this heightened awareness, and how did they encourage the creation of nationalist and anticolonial movements in many parts of the world?

Note that the number of U.S. interventions in Latin America belied the official policy of "dollar diplomacy."

MAP 31.2 | The United States in Latin America, 1895–1941. Note the number of states where U.S. troops intervened in local politics. ***On what basis did U.S. policymakers justify those interventions?***

businesses more than doubled their financial interests in Latin America as investments grew from $1.5 billion to $3.5 billion.

That U.S. neocolonialism was meant to be largely economic became evident in the policies of President William Howard Taft (1857–1931). In his final address to Congress in 1912, Taft argued that the United States should substitute "dollars for bullets" in its foreign policy. He wanted businesses to develop foreign markets through peaceful commerce and believed that expensive military intervention should be avoided as much as possible. This new vision of U.S. expansion abroad, dubbed "dollar diplomacy" by critics, encapsulated the gist of what those in Latin America perceived as "Yankee imperialism."

The economic crisis of the Great Depression demonstrated the extent to which Latin America had become integrated into the world economy. Indeed, the Great Depression halted fifty years of economic growth in Latin America and illustrated the region's susceptibility to global economic crises. For one thing, U.S. capital investments for nascent industries and other financial concerns during the 1920s could not be maintained during this disastrous economic downturn. Moreover, most Latin American states, because they exported agricultural products or raw materials, suffered from plummeting prices. Indeed, the prices of sugar from the Caribbean, coffee from Brazil and Colombia, wheat and beef from Argentina, tin from Bolivia, nitrates from Chile, and many other products fell sharply after 1929. Throughout Latin America unemployment rates increased rapidly. The drastic decline in the price of the region's exports and the drying-up of foreign capital prompted Latin American governments to raise tariffs on foreign products and impose various other restrictions on foreign trade.

Although the weaknesses of export-oriented economies and industrial development financed by foreigners became evident during the Great Depression, the international crisis also allowed Latin American nations to take alternative paths to economic development. Economic policy stressing internal economic development was most visible in Brazil, where dictator-president (1930–1945, 1950–1954) Getúlio Dornelles Vargas (1883–1954) turned his nation into an *estado novo* (new state). Ruling with the backing of the military but without the support of the landowning elite, Vargas and his government during the 1930s and 1940s embarked on a program of industrialization that created new enterprises. Key among them was the iron and steel industry. The Vargas regime also implemented protectionist policies that shielded domestic production from foreign competition, which pleased both industrialists and urban workers. Social welfare initiatives accompanied industrial development, protecting workers with health and safety regulations, minimum wages, limits on working hours, unemployment compensation, and retirement benefits. Thus the Great Depression contributed in many ways to the evolution of both economic neocolonialism and economic experimentation within Latin American states.

Conflicts with a "Good Neighbor"

The U.S. in Latin America
www.mhhe.com/bentleybrief2e

THE "GOOD NEIGHBOR POLICY" The pressures of the Great Depression and the instability of global politics led to a reassessment of U.S. foreign policy in Latin America during the late 1920s and 1930s. U.S. leaders realized the costliness and the ineffectiveness of direct interventions in Latin America, especially when committing U.S. marines as peacekeeping forces. To extricate U.S. military forces and rely more fully on "dollar diplomacy," policymakers instituted certain innovations that nonetheless called into question any true change of heart among U.S. neocolonialists. They approved "sweetheart treaties" that guaranteed U.S. financial control in the Caribbean economies of Haiti and the Dominican Republic, for example, and the U.S. Marines provided training for indigenous police forces to keep the peace and maintain law and order. This revamped U.S. approach to relations with Latin America became known as the "Good Neighbor Policy," and it was most closely associated with the administration of Franklin D. Roosevelt (1882–1945).

Under Roosevelt, the Good Neighbor Policy evolved into a more conciliatory U.S. approach to Latin American relations. The interventionist corollary to the Monroe Doctrine enunciated previously by President Theodore Roosevelt (1859–1919) was formally renounced in December 1933, when Secretary of State Cordell Hull attended the Seventh International Conference of American States in Montevideo, Uruguay. Hull signed the Convention on the Rights and Duties of States, which held that "no state has the right to intervene in the internal or external affairs of another." That proposition faced a severe challenge in March 1938 when Mexican president Lázaro Cárdenas (1895–1970) nationalized the oil industry, much of which was controlled by foreign investors from the United States and Great Britain.

Given the history of tempestuous relations between the United States and Mexico, including multiple U.S. military incursions into Mexico during the revolution, it seemed there was little chance for a peaceful resolution to this provocative move on the part of Cárdenas. The reluctance of U.S. and British oil companies to grant concessions to Mexican oil workers prompted him to this drastic act. Yet despite calls for a strong U.S. and British response, Roosevelt and his administration officials resisted the demands of big businesses and instead called for a cool, calm response and negotiations to end the conflict. This plan prevailed, and the foreign oil companies ultimately had to accept only $24 million in compensation rather than the $260 million that they initially demanded.

Although the nationalization crisis in Mexico ended in a fashion that suggested the strength of the Good Neighbor Policy, a good deal of the impetus for this policy came from economic and political concerns associated with the Great Depression and the deterioration

Getúlio Dornelles Vargas (zhi-TOO-lyoo door-NE-lis VAHR-guhs)

CARMEN MIRANDA. This Hollywood publicity photo of Carmen Miranda features the type of lively costuming that made her a colorful favorite in both the United States and Latin America.

of international relations in the 1930s. The United States wanted to cultivate Latin American markets for its exports, and it wanted to distance itself from the militarist behavior of Asian and European imperial powers. The U.S. government knew it needed to improve relations with Latin America, if only to secure those nations' support in the increasingly likely event of another global war. Widespread Mexican migration to the United States during and after the Great War suggested the attractiveness of the United States for at least some Latin Americans.

Filling the migration void left by Europeans prevented from coming to the United States by the war and by the U.S. immigration restriction laws of the 1920s, Mexican men, women, and children entered the United States in the hundreds of thousands to engage in agricultural and industrial work. The migrants suffered the animosity of some U.S. citizens, who considered them "cheap Mexican labor," but the political power of agribusinesses prevented the government from instituting legal restrictions on Mexican migration. Federal and local officials managed, however, to deport thousands of Mexicans during the Great Depression.

Trying to contribute to the repairing of relations and the promoting of more positive images of Latin American and U.S. relations, Hollywood adopted a Latin American singing and dancing sensation, Carmen Miranda (1909–1955). Born in Portugal but raised from childhood in Brazil, Miranda found fame on a Rio de Janeiro radio station and recorded hundreds of hit songs. In the United States, she gained her greatest visibility in films produced during World War II, such as *Down Argentine Way* (1940). Carmen Miranda appeared as an exotic Latin American woman, usually clothed in sexy, colorful costumes that featured headdresses adorned with the fruits grown in Latin America—such as bananas. She softened representations of Latin Americans for audiences in the United States, providing a less threatening counterpoint to laboring migrants or women guerrilla fighters in Mexico's revolution. She also became a source of pride for Brazilians, who reveled in her Hollywood success. Hollywood's espousal of Roosevelt's Good Neighbor Policy proved a success.

SUMMARY

In the decades after the Great War, and in the midst of the Great Depression, intellectuals and political activists in Asia, Africa, and Latin America challenged the ideological and economic underpinnings of empire and neocolonialism. Often embracing the ideas and theories that were disseminated around the globe as a result of the war, including self-determination, socialism, communism, and anti-imperialism, radicals and nationalists revised understandings of political identity in the colonial and neocolonial worlds.

Japanese and U.S. imperial practices incited military and civil discord within their respective spheres, while European colonial rulers continued to limit, often brutally, the freedom of peoples in India and Africa. Like Shanfei, young intellectuals and older political leaders alike emerged transformed in these years. Their efforts to inspire nationalism and to achieve economic and political autonomy came to fruition later—after another world war had come and gone.

STUDY TERMS

ahimsa (621)
Chinese Communist Party (624)
civil disobedience movement (621)
Diego Rivera (631)
dollar diplomacy (632)
estado novo (633)
Fidel Castro (631)
Good Neighbor Policy (633)
Government of India Act (622)
Guomindang (624)
Indian National Congress (620)
Jiang Jieshi (625)
Jomo Kenyatta (629)
Kellogg-Briand Pact (626)
Long March (625)
Manchukuo (626)
Mao Zedong (624)
Marcus Garvey (630)
May Fourth movement (623)
Mohandas Karamchand Gandhi (621)
Muhammad Ali Jinnah (623)
Mukden incident (626)
Mumbo cult (628)
Muslim League (623)
non-cooperation movement (621)
pan-Africanism (630)
satyagraha (621)
Sun Yatsen (624)

FOR FURTHER READING

A. Adu Boahen, ed. *Africa under Colonial Domination, 1880–1935.* Berkeley, 1985. Part of the ambitious UNESCO General History of Africa (vol. 7), this work reflects how different Africans view their own history.

Victor Bulmer-Thomas, John H. Coatsworth, and Robert Cortés Conde, eds. *The Cambridge Economic History of Latin America, Vol. 2: The Long Twentieth Century.* Cambridge, 2006. Scholarly collection of essays that outlines the region's main economic trends and developments.

Cynthia Enloe. *Bananas, Beaches & Bases: Making Feminist Sense of International Politics.* Berkeley, 1989. A gendered analysis of U.S. and other foreign policies through such categories as tourism and diplomats' spouses.

Robert E. Hannigan. *The New World Power: American Foreign Policy, 1898–1917.* Philadelphia, 2002. A detailed account of U.S. foreign relations that links class, race, and gender influences to policymakers.

John Iliffe. *Africans: The History of a Continent.* New York, 1995. A well-written introductory text that is organized thematically rather than chronologically.

Jim Masselos. *Indian Nationalism: A History.* 3rd ed. Columbia, 1998. A keen work that remains the standard, most readable introduction to Indian leaders and movements.

Michael E. Parish. *Anxious Decades: America in Prosperity and Depression, 1920–1941.* New York, 1992. A detailed portrait of the United States between the world wars, featuring treatments of foreign relations with Latin America.

Jonathan D. Spence. *Mao Zedong.* New York, 1999. Blending history with cultural analysis, this intimate portrait of Mao is informative despite its brevity.

Odd Arne Westad. *Decisive Encounters: The Chinese Civil War, 1946–1950.* Stanford, 2003. An engagingly written work that introduces the reader to the salient political and military events that led to the eventual defeat of the Guomindang.

Louise Young. *Japan's Total Empire: Manchuria and the Culture of Wartime Imperialism.* Berkeley, 1999. An important and penetrating work on the nature of Japanese imperialism.

New Conflagrations: World War II

32

n 6 August 1945, as he listened to the armed services radio on Saipan (a U.S.-controlled island in the North Pacific), U.S. marine Victor Tolley heard the president of the United States announce that a "terrible new weapon" had been deployed against the city of Hiroshima, Japan. Tolley and the other marines rejoiced, realizing that the terrible new weapon—the atomic bomb—might end the war. A few days later Tolley heard that the city of Nagasaki had also been hit with an atomic bomb and that radio announcers suggested it might be decades before either city would be inhabitable.

Imagine Tolley's astonishment when he was assigned to the U.S. occupation forces in Nagasaki just a few weeks after the Japanese surrender. Assured that Nagasaki was "very safe," Tolley lived there for three months, during which he became very familiar with the devastation wrought by the bomb. Tolley also became acquainted with some of the Japanese survivors in Nagasaki, which proved to be an eye-opening experience. After seeing "young children with sores and burns all over," Tolley, having become separated from his unit, befriended a young boy who took Tolley home to meet his surviving family. Tolley recalled that while speaking to the boy's father about his missing son-in-law, "it dawned on me that they suffered the same as we did. They lost sons and daughters and relatives, and they hurt too."

Before his chance meeting with this Japanese family, Tolley had felt nothing except contempt for the Japanese. He pointed out, "We were trained to kill them. They asked for it and now we're gonna give it to 'em. That's how I felt until I met this young boy and his family." But after coming face-to-face with his enemies, Tolley saw only their common humanity, their suffering, and their hurt.

The civility that reemerged at the end of the war was little evident during the war years. The war began and ended with Japan. In 1931 Japan invaded Manchuria, and the United States concluded hostilities by dropping atomic bombs on Hiroshima and Nagasaki. By 1941 World War II was a truly global war. Hostilities spread from east Asia and the Pacific to Europe, north Africa, and the Atlantic. Beyond its immense geographic scope, World War II exceeded even the Great War (1914–1918) in demonstrating the willingness of societies to make enormous sacrifices in lives and other resources to achieve complete victory. Moreover, World War II redefined gender roles and relations between colonial peoples and their colonizers. The cold war and the atomic age that began almost as soon as World War II ended also inaugurated a new global order.

‹ A Japanese child crouches and cries in the rubble of Hiroshima in the aftermath of the atomic bombing, expressing the profound sadness of war and its devastating weapons.

CHRONOLOGY

1937	Invasion of China by Japan
1937	Rape of Nanjing
1938	German *Anschluss* with Austria
1939	Nazi-Soviet pact
1939	Invasion of Poland by Germany
1940	Fall of France, Battle of Britain
1941	German invasion of the Soviet Union
1941	Attack on Pearl Harbor by Japan
1942	U.S. victory at Midway
1943	Soviet victory at Stalingrad
1944	D-Day, Allied invasion at Normandy
1945	Capture of Berlin by Soviet forces
1945	Atomic bombing of Hiroshima and Nagasaki
1945	Establishment of United Nations
1947	Truman Doctrine
1948	Marshall Plan
1949	Establishment of NATO
1955	Establishment of Warsaw Pact

In particular, the United States and the Soviet Union gained geopolitical strength during the early years of the cold war as they competed for global influence.

Origins of World War II

In 1941 two major alliances squared off against each other. Japan, Germany, and Italy, along with their conquered territories, formed the Axis powers. The Allied powers included France and its empire; Great Britain, its empire, and its Commonwealth allies (such as Canada, Australia, and New Zealand); the Soviet Union; China; and the United States and its allies in Latin America. Driven in part by a desire to revise the peace settlements that followed the Great War and compelled by the economic distress of the worldwide depression, Japan, Italy, and Germany engaged in a campaign of territorial expansion that ultimately broke apart the structure of international cooperation that had kept the world from violence in the 1920s. These revisionist powers, so called because they revised or overthrew the terms of the post–Great War peace, confronted nations that were committed to the avoidance of another world war. To expand their global influence, the revisionist nations remilitarized and conquered territories they deemed central to their needs. The Allies acquiesced to the revisionist powers' early aggressive actions, but in the late 1930s and early 1940s they decided to engage the Axis powers in a total war.

Japan's War in China

The global conflict opened with Japan's attacks on China in the 1930s: the conquest of Manchuria between 1931 and 1932 was the first step in the revisionist process of expansionism and aggression. In 1933, after the League of Nations condemned its actions in Manchuria, Japan withdrew from the league and followed an ultranationalist and promilitary policy. Four years later, Japan launched a full-scale invasion of China. Japanese troops first took Beijing and then moved south toward Shanghai and Nanjing, the capital of China. Japanese naval and air forces bombed Shanghai, killing thousands of civilians, and secured it as a landing area for armies bound for Nanjing. By December 1937 Shanghai and Nanjing had fallen, and during the following six months Japanese forces won repeated victories.

Casualties of Japanese attack on Shanghai
www.mhhe.com/bentleybrief2e

THE RAPE OF NANJING China became the first nation to experience the horrors of World War II: brutal warfare against civilians and repressive occupation. Chinese civilians were among the first to feel the effects of aerial bombing of urban centers; the people of Shanghai died by the tens of thousands when Japanese bombers attacked the city. What became known as the Rape of Nanjing demonstrated the brutality of the war as the residents of Nanjing became victims of Japanese troops inflamed by war passion and a sense of racial superiority. Over the course of two months, Japanese soldiers raped seven thousand women, murdered hundreds of thousands of unarmed soldiers and civilians, and burned one-third of the homes in Nanjing. Four hundred thousand Chinese lost their lives as Japanese soldiers used them for bayonet practice and machine-gunned them into open pits.

CHINESE RESISTANCE Despite Japanese military successes, Chinese resistance persisted throughout the war. Japanese aggression aroused feelings of nationalism among the Chinese that continued to grow as the war wore on. By September 1937 nationalists and communists had agreed on a

Japanese Brutalities in China. | In this photograph, Japanese soldiers prepare to execute Chinese prisoners.

"united front" policy against the Japanese, uniting themselves into standing armies of some 1.7 million soldiers. Although Chinese forces failed to defeat the Japanese, who retained naval and air superiority, they tied up half the Japanese army, 750,000 soldiers, by 1941.

Throughout the war, the coalition of nationalists and communists threatened to fall apart as the two groups competed for control of enemy territory and for political control within China. Those clashes rendered Chinese resistance less effective. While the nationalists shied away from direct military confrontation with Japanese forces and kept the Guomindang government alive by moving inland to Chongqing, the Chinese communists carried on guerrilla operations against the Japanese invaders. The guerrillas did not defeat the Japanese, but they captured the loyalty of many Chinese peasants through their resistance to the Japanese and their moderate policies of land reform. At the end of the war, the communists were poised to lead China.

The Japanese invasion of China met with intense international opposition, yet other world powers, distracted by depression and military aggression in Europe, could offer little in the way of an effective response to Japanese actions. The government of Japan aligned itself with the other revisionist nations, Germany and Italy, by signing a ten-year military and economic pact, the Tripartite Pact, in September 1940. Japan also cleared the way for further empire building in Asia and the Pacific basin by concluding a neutrality pact with the Soviet Union in April 1941, thereby precluding hostilities in Manchuria. Japan did not face determined opposition to its expansion until it ran into conflict with the United States in December 1941.

Italian and German Aggression

Italy's expansionism helped destabilize the post–Great War peace. Italians suffered tremendously in World War I. Six hundred thousand Italian soldiers died, and the national economy was badly damaged. Many Italians expected far greater recompense and respect than they received at the conclusion of the Great War.

ITALY Benito Mussolini promised to bring glory to Italy through the acquisition of territories that it had been denied after the Great War. Italy's conquest of Ethiopia in 1935 and 1936, when added to the previously annexed Libya, created an overseas empire. Italy also intervened in the Spanish Civil War (1936–1939) on the side of General Francisco Franco (1892–1975), and it annexed Albania in 1939. The invasion and conquest of Ethiopia in particular infuriated other nations, but as with Japan's invasion of Manchuria, the League of Nations offered little effective opposition.

What angered nonrevisionists about Italy's conquest of Ethiopia was not just the broken peace but also the excessive use of force. Mussolini sent an army of 250,000 soldiers armed with tanks, poison gas, artillery, and aircraft to conquer the Ethiopians, who were entirely unprepared for the assault. The mechanized Italian troops mowed them down. Italy lost 2,000 soldiers, whereas 275,000 Ethiopians lost their lives.

GERMANY Japan and Italy were the first nations to challenge the post–World War I settlements through territorial conquest, but it was Germany that systematically undid the Treaty of Versailles and the fragile peace of the interwar years. Most Germans deeply resented the harsh terms imposed on their nation in 1919. Adolf Hitler (1889–1945) came to power in 1933, riding a wave of public discontent with Germany's postwar powerlessness and the suffering caused by the Great Depression. Hitler referred to the signing of the 1918 armistice as the "November crime" and blamed it on those he viewed as Germany's internal enemies: Jews, communists, and liberals of all sorts. Hitler's scheme for ridding Germany of its enemies and reasserting its power was remilitarization—which was legally denied to Germany under the Versailles Treaty. Hitler's aggressive foreign policy helped relieve the German public's feeling of war shame and depression trauma. After withdrawing Germany from the League of Nations in 1933, his government carried out a large-scale plan to strengthen the German armed forces. Hitler reinstated universal military service in 1935, and in the following year his troops entered the previously demilitarized Rhineland, which bordered France. In 1938 Hitler began the campaign of expansion that ultimately led to the outbreak of World War II in Europe.

Germany's forced *Anschluss* ("union") with Austria took place in March 1938. Hitler justified this annexation as an attempt to reintegrate all Germans into a single homeland. Europe's major powers, France and Britain, did nothing in response, thereby enhancing Hitler's reputation in the German military and deepening his contempt for the democracies. Soon thereafter, using the same rationale, the Nazis attempted to gain control of the Sudetenland, the western portion of Czechoslovakia, which was inhabited largely by ethnic Germans. In September 1938 Hitler demanded the immediate cession of the Sudetenland to the German Reich. Against the desires of the Czechoslovak government, the leaders of France and Britain accommodated Hitler and allowed Germany to annex the Sudetenland. Neither the French nor the British were willing to risk a military confrontation with Germany to defend Czechoslovakian territory.

At the Munich Conference, held in September 1938, European politicians formulated the policy that came to be known as appeasement. In conceding demands to Hitler, or "appeasing" him, the British and French governments extracted a promise that Hitler would cease further efforts to expand German territorial claims. Their goal was to keep peace in Europe, even if it meant making major concessions. Britain's prime minister, Neville Chamberlain (1869–1940), arrived home from Munich to announce that the meeting had achieved "peace for our time." Unprepared for war and distressed by the depression, nations sympathetic to Britain and France also embraced peace as an admirable goal in the face of aggression by the revisionist nations.

Hitler, however, refused to be bound by the Munich agreement, and in the next year German troops occupied most of Czechoslovakia. As Hitler next threatened Poland, it became clear that the policy of appeasement was a failure, which caused Britain and

Anschluss (AHN-shloss)

Sudetenland (soo-DEYT-n-land)

France to abandon it by guaranteeing the security of Poland. By that time Joseph Stalin (1879–1953) was convinced that British and French leaders were conspiring to deflect German aggression toward the Soviet Union, which made him seek an accommodation with the Nazi regime. In August 1939 the foreign ministers of the Soviet Union and Germany signed the Russian-German Treaty of Nonaggression, an agreement that promised neutrality in the event of war with a third party and prevented the possibility of a war on two fronts. Additionally, a secret protocol divided eastern Europe into German and Soviet spheres of influence. Hitler was ready to conquer Europe.

TOTAL WAR: THE WORLD UNDER FIRE

Two months after the United States became embroiled in World War II, President Franklin Roosevelt (1882–1945) delivered one of his famous radio broadcasts, known as fireside chats. In it he explained: "This war is a new kind of war. It is warfare in terms of every continent, every island, every sea, every air lane." There was little exaggeration in FDR's analysis. Before World War II was over, almost every nation had participated in it, and virtually every weapon known to humanity had been used. More so than the Great War, this was a conflict in which entire societies engaged in warfare and mobilized every available material and human resource.

The war between Japan and China had been in progress for eight years when European nations stormed into battle in 1939. By 1941 nations outside Europe had also been drawn into the conflict, including the French and British colonies in Africa and India, as well as Canada, Australia, and New Zealand. As the war dragged on, only eleven countries avoided direct involvement: Afghanistan, Greenland, Iceland, Ireland, Mongolia, Portugal, Spain, Sweden, Switzerland, Tibet, and Yemen.

Nazi rallies in Nuremberg
www.mhhe.com/bentleybrief2e

Blitzkrieg: Germany Conquers Europe

During World War II it became common for aggressor nations to avoid overt declarations of war. Instead, the new armed forces relied on surprise and swiftness for their conquests. Germany demonstrated the advantages of that strategy in Poland, when its air force and *Panzer* ("armored") columns moved into Poland unannounced on 1 September 1939. Within a month they had subdued its western expanses, while the Soviets took the eastern sections in accordance with the Nazi-Soviet pact. The Germans stunned the world with their *Blitzkrieg* ("lightning war") and sudden victory.

THE FALL OF FRANCE With Poland subdued, Germany prepared to break through European defenses. In April 1940 the Germans occupied Denmark and Norway, then launched a full-scale attack on western Europe. Their offensive against Belgium, France, and the Netherlands began in May, and again the Allies were jolted by Blitzkrieg tactics. Belgium and the Netherlands fell first, and the French signed an armistice in June. After the fall of France, Italy's Benito Mussolini entered the conflict in the hopes of reaping any potential benefits his partnership with the Germans might offer.

THE FALL OF FRANCE. | Adolf Hitler proudly walks through conquered Paris in 1940, with the Eiffel Tower as a backdrop. ***Why might it have been important to Hitler to make such a public tour of Parisian monuments?***

Before the battle for France, Hitler had boasted to his staff, "Gentlemen, you are about to witness the most famous victory in history!" Given France's rapid fall, Hitler was not far wrong. In a moment of exquisite triumph, Hitler had the French sign their armistice in the very railroad car in which the Germans had signed the armistice in 1918. Meanwhile, the British, in an attempt to rescue the remaining Allied troops in France, engineered a stunning retreat from Dunkirk across the English Channel, but it could not hide the bleak failure of the Allied troops. Britain now stood alone against the German forces.

THE BATTLE OF BRITAIN Germany therefore launched the Battle of Britain, led by its air force, the Luftwaffe. "The Blitz," as the British called this air war, rained bombs on heavily populated metropolitan areas, especially London, and killed more than forty thousand British civilians. The Royal Air Force staved off defeat, however, forcing Hitler to abandon plans to invade Britain. Yet despite the setback in Britain, Hitler had plenty of reasons to be happy by the summer of 1941, for the swastika-bedecked Nazi flag waved from the streets of Paris to the Acropolis in Athens, and he had succeeded beyond his dreams in his quest to reverse the outcome of World War I.

The German Invasion of the Soviet Union

Flush with victory in the spring of 1941, Hitler turned his sights on the Soviet Union. This land was the ultimate German target, from which Jews, Slavs, and Bolsheviks could be expelled or exterminated to create more *Lebensraum* ("living space") for resettled Germans. Believing firmly in the bankruptcy of the Soviet system, Hitler was confident that in the Soviet Union "you only have to kick in the door, and the whole rotten structure will come crashing down."

Lebensraum (LAY-behnz-rahwm)

THE BATTLE OF STALINGRAD. | In this photograph, taken in 1942, women dig to repair train tracks damaged by German guns. The terrible destruction of the city can be seen on the hill behind them. During the long battle, men, women, and children took part in the defense of the city.

OPERATION BARBAROSSA On 22 June 1941, Adolf Hitler ordered the initiation of Operation Barbarossa, the invasion of the Soviet Union. For that, the German military assembled the largest and most powerful invasion force in history, attacking with 3.6 million soldiers, thirty-seven hundred tanks, twenty-five hundred planes, and thirty divisions from the governments of Hungary, Finland, and Romania. The invasion along a front of 3,000 kilometers (1,900 miles) took Stalin by surprise and caught the Red Army off guard. By December 1941 German troops had reached the gates of Moscow. Germany seemed assured of victory.

However, German Blitzkrieg tactics that had earlier proved so effective in Poland and western Europe failed the Germans in the vast expanses of Russia. Hitler and his military leaders underestimated Soviet personnel reserves and industrial capacity. Within a matter of weeks, for example, the 150 German divisions faced 360 divisions of the Red Army. By the time the German forces reached the outskirts of Moscow, fierce Soviet resistance had produced eight hundred thousand German casualties.

The arrival of winter—the most severe in decades—also helped Soviet military efforts. So sure of an early victory were the Germans that they did not bother to supply their troops with winter clothing and boots. One hundred thousand soldiers suffered frostbite, and two thousand of them underwent amputation. The Red Army, in contrast, prepared for winter and found further comfort in the thirteen million pairs of felt-lined winter boots sent by their new allies in the United States. By early December, Soviet counterattacks along the entire front had stopped German advances.

In the spring of 1942 the Germans briefly regained the military initiative, and by June they were approaching the city of Stalingrad. As the Germans came upon Stalingrad in September, the Russians dug in. "Not a step back," Stalin ordered. The Russians did indeed hold Stalingrad, but only at the price of waging a bloody street-by-street defense of the city until the Red Army could regroup for a counterattack.

Battles in Asia and the Pacific

Before 1941 the United States was inching toward greater involvement in the war. In 1939 it instituted a cash-and-carry policy of supplying the British, in which the British paid cash and carried the materials on their own ships. More significant was the lend-lease program initiated in 1941, in which the United States "lent" destroyers and other war goods to the British in return for the lease of naval bases. The program later extended such aid to the Soviets, the Chinese, and many others.

German victories in 1940 and Great Britain's precarious military position in Europe encouraged the Japanese to project their influence into southeast Asia in their quest for raw materials such as tin, rubber, and petroleum. Between September 1940 and July 1941, and with the blessings of the German-backed Vichy government of France, Japanese forces occupied French Indochina (now Vietnam, Laos, and Cambodia). The government of the United States—supported by Great Britain, the Commonwealth of Nations, and the Dutch East Indies—responded to this situation by freezing Japanese assets in the United States and by imposing a complete embargo on oil. To Japanese militarists faced with the alternative either of succumbing to U.S. demands—which included the withdrawal of Japanese forces from China and southeast Asia—or of engaging the United States in war, war seemed the lesser of two evils.

PEARL HARBOR The Japanese hoped to destroy American naval capacity in the Pacific with an attack at Pearl Harbor. On 7 December 1941, "a date which will live in infamy," as Franklin Roosevelt concluded, more than 350 Japanese bombers, fighters, and torpedo planes struck in two waves, sinking or disabling eighteen ships and destroying more than two hundred. Except for the U.S. aircraft carriers, which were out of the harbor at the time, American naval power in the Pacific was devastated.

FDR's declaration of war
www.mhhe.com/
bentleybrief2e

On 11 December 1941, though not compelled to do so by treaty, Hitler and Mussolini declared war on the United States. That move provided the United States with the only reason it needed to declare war on Germany and Italy. The United States, Great Britain,

PEARL HARBOR. | Flames and smoke flare in the background at the United States Naval Air Station after the Japanese attack on Pearl Harbor on 7 December 1941.

and the Soviet Union came together in a coalition that linked two vast and interconnected theaters of war, the European and Asian-Pacific theaters, and ensured the defeat of Germany and Japan. Winston Churchill (1874–1965), prime minister of Britain, expressed a vast sense of relief when he said: "So we had won after all!"

JAPANESE VICTORIES Yet after Pearl Harbor the Japanese swept on to one victory after another. They coordinated their strike against Pearl Harbor with simultaneous attacks against the Philippines, Guam, Wake Island, Midway Island, Hong Kong, Thailand, and British Malaya. For the next year the Japanese military maintained the initiative in southeast Asia and the Pacific, capturing Borneo, Burma, the Dutch East Indies, and several Aleutian islands off Alaska. Australia and New Zealand were now within striking distance. Moreover, the humiliating surrender of British-held Singapore in February 1942 dealt a blow to British prestige and shattered any myths of European military invincibility.

The slogan under which Japan pursued expansion in Asia was "Asia for Asians," according to which the Japanese would lead Asian peoples to independence from the despised European imperialists. In this struggle for Asian independence, Japan required the region's resources, arguing that this was necessary to build a "Greater East Asia Co-Prosperity Sphere." The appeal to Asian independence at first struck a responsive chord among Asians, but conquest and brutal occupation soon made it obvious to most Asians that the real agenda was "Asia for the Japanese." Proponents of the Greater East Asia Co-Prosperity Sphere advocated Japan's expansion in Asia and the Pacific while cloaking their territorial and economic designs with the idealism of Asian nationalism.

THINKING ABOUT *Traditions*

TRADITIONS IN WORLD WAR II. During World War II, the force of nationalism prompted millions of people on both the Axis and Allied sides to fight for their countries. In what ways did leaders in Japan, Germany, the United States, and Britain emphasize national traditions or characteristics as a way of encouraging active participation in wartime efforts?

Defeat of the Axis Powers

The entry of the Soviet Union and the United States into the war in 1941 was decisive, because personnel reserves and industrial capacity were the keys to the Allied victories in the European and Asian-Pacific

MAP 32.1 | High tide of Axis expansion in Europe and north Africa, 1942–1943. Observe the number of nations occupied by or allied with the Axis powers. ***Given Axis dominance in Europe, what factors finally allowed the Allies to turn the tide of war in their favor?***

Once Germany invaded the Soviet Union in 1941, only Britain opposed the Axis powers in Europe.

theaters. The U.S. automotive industry alone, for instance, produced more than four million armored, combat, and supply vehicles of all kinds during the war. Not until the United States joined the struggle in 1942 did the tide in the battle for the Atlantic turn in favor of the Allies.

ALLIED VICTORY IN EUROPE By 1943 German forces in Russia faced bleak prospects. Moscow never fell, and the battle for Stalingrad, which ended in February 1943, resulted in the first large-scale victory for Soviet forces. The Red Army, drawing on enormous personnel and material reserves, then pushed the German invaders out of Russian territory. By April 1945 the Soviets had reached the suburbs of Berlin. At that point, the Soviets had inflicted more than six million casualties on the German enemy—twice the number of the original German invasion force. The Red Army had broken the back of the German war machine.

With the eastern front disintegrating under the Soviet onslaught, British and U.S. forces attacked the Germans from North Africa and then through Italy. In August 1944 the Allies forced Italy to withdraw from the Axis and to join them. In the meantime, the Germans also prepared for an Allied offensive in the west, where the British and U.S. forces opened a front in France. On D-Day, 6 June 1944, British and U.S. troops landed on the French coast of Normandy and overwhelmed the Germans. With the two fronts collapsing around them and round-the-clock strategic bombing by the United States and

World War II in Europe
www.mhhe.com/bentleybrief2e

D-Day Landing. | Omaha Beach one week after the landing on D-Day. Troops continue to teem into the area from offshore, while ships and dirigibles offer support and protection. ***What kinds of resources did the Allies have to marshal in order to put together such a massive invasion force?***

Britain leveling German cities, German resistance faded. Indeed, the British firebombing raid on Dresden alone killed 135,000 people in February 1945. As Germans and Russians engaged in a brutal street-by-street battle in Berlin and U.S. and British forces advanced through western Germany, the Germans surrendered unconditionally on 8 May 1945. A week earlier, on 30 April, as fighting flared right outside his Berlin bunker, Hitler had committed suicide. He therefore did not live to see the Soviet red flag flying over the Berlin Reichstag, Germany's parliament building.

TURNING THE TIDE IN THE PACIFIC The turning point in the Pacific war came at Midway (4 June 1942), the last U.S.-controlled island in the Pacific. The victory was accomplished by a code-breaking operation known as *Magic,* which enabled a cryptographer to discover the plan to attack Midway. On the morning of 4 June, thirty-six carrier-launched dive-bombers attacked the Japanese fleet, sinking three Japanese carriers in one five-minute strike; a fourth one was sunk later in the day. After Midway, the Allies took the offensive in the Pacific. They adopted an island-hopping strategy, capturing islands from which they could make direct air assaults on Japan. Deadly, tenacious fighting characterized these battles in which the United States and its allies gradually retook islands in the Marianas and the Philippines and then, early in 1945, moved toward areas more threatening to Japan: Iwo Jima and Okinawa.

The fighting on Iwo Jima and Okinawa was savage. On Okinawa the Japanese introduced the kamikaze—pilots who volunteered to fly planes with just enough fuel to reach an Allied ship and dive-bomb into it. In the two-month battle for Okinawa, the Japanese flew nineteen hundred kamikaze missions, sinking dozens of ships and killing more than five thousand U.S. soldiers. The kamikaze, and the defense mounted by Japanese forces and the 110,000 Okinawan civilians who died refusing to surrender, convinced many people in the United States that the Japanese would never capitulate.

kamikaze (kah-mih-KAH-zee)

JAPANESE SURRENDER The fall of Saipan in July 1944 and the subsequent conquest of Iwo Jima and Okinawa brought the Japanese homeland within easy reach of U.S. strategic bombers. The release of napalm firebombs during low-altitude sorties at night met with devastating success. The firebombing of Tokyo in March 1945 destroyed 25 percent of the city's buildings and annihilated approximately one hundred thousand people. The final blows came on 6 and 9 August 1945, when the United States used its revolutionary new weapon, the atomic bomb, against the cities of Hiroshima and Nagasaki. The atomic bombs either instantaneously vaporized or slowly killed by radiation poisoning upward of two hundred thousand people. The Soviet Union declared war on Japan on 8 August 1945, and that new threat, combined with the devastation caused by the bombs, persuaded Emperor Hirohito (1901–1989) to surrender unconditionally on 15 August. On 2 September 1945, the war officially ended.

Mushroom cloud over Nagasaki
www.mhhe.com/bentleybrief2e

The battle of Midway turned the tide of the Pacific war in favor of the Allies.

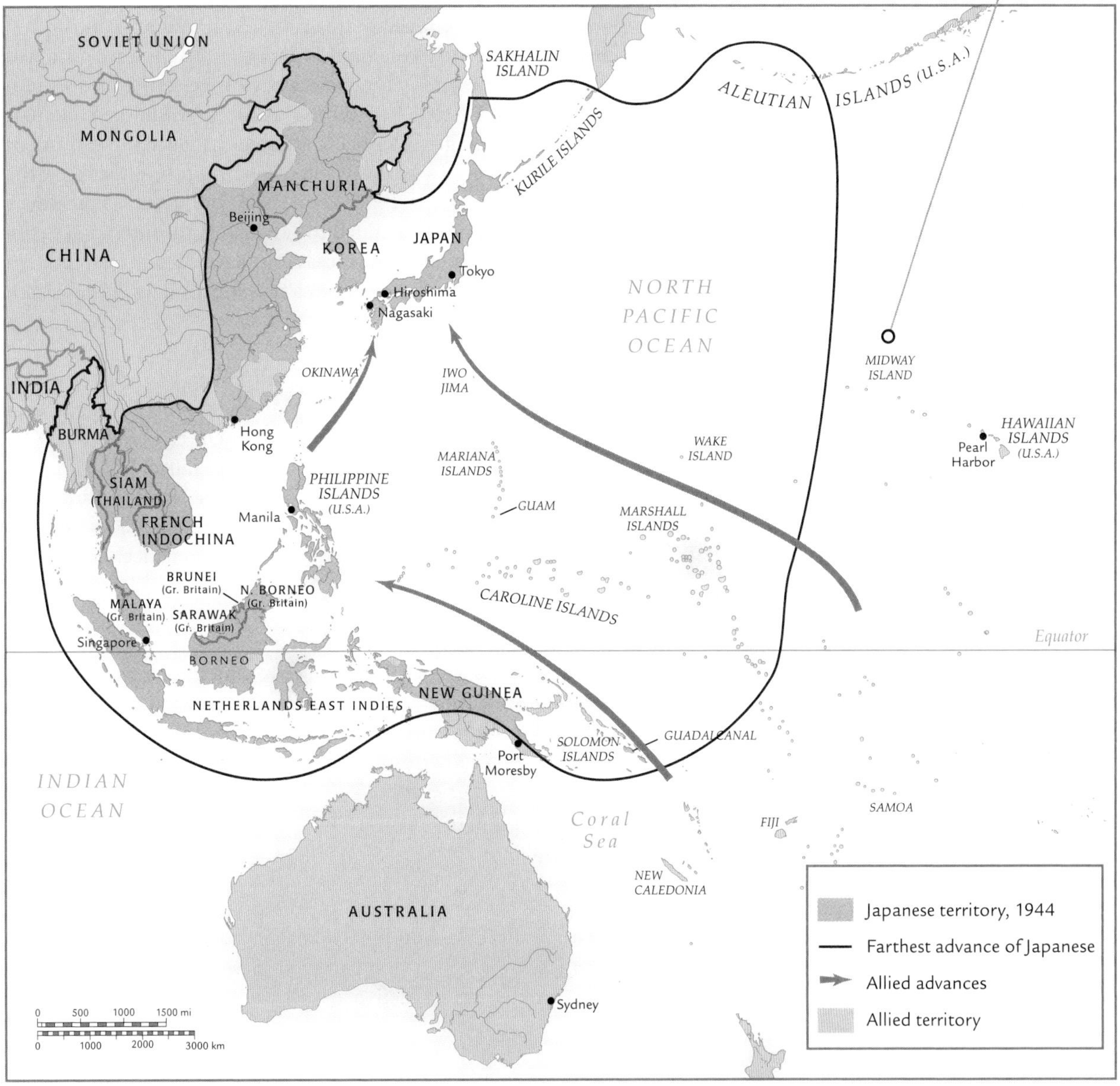

MAP 32.2 | World War II in Asia and the Pacific. Compare the geographical conditions of the Asian-Pacific theater with those of the European theater. ***What kinds of resources were necessary to win in the Asian-Pacific theater as opposed to the European theater?***

Life during Wartime

The widespread bombing of civilian populations during World War II, from its beginning in China to its end in Hiroshima and Nagasaki, meant that there was no safe home front during the war. So too did the arrival of often brutal occupation forces in the wake of Japanese and German conquests in Asia and Europe. In this total war, civilian death tolls far exceeded military casualties. In spite of the war's brutality, however, the human spirit endured, personified in the contributions of resistance groups and mobilized women, and in the survivors of bombings or concentration camps.

Occupation, Collaboration, and Resistance

The administration imposed on conquered territories by Japanese and German forces varied in character. In territories such as Manchukuo, Japanese-controlled China, Burma, and the Philippines, Japanese authorities installed puppet governments. Other conquered territories either were considered too unreliable for "self-rule" or were deemed strategically too important to be left alone. Thus territories such as Indochina, Malaya, the Dutch East Indies, Hong Kong, Singapore, Borneo, and New Guinea came under direct military control.

In Europe, Hitler's racist ideology played a large role in determining how occupied territories were administered. Hitler intended that most areas of western and northern Europe—populated by racially valuable people, according to him—would become part of a Greater Germanic Empire. Accordingly, Denmark retained its elected government and monarchy under German supervision. In Norway and Holland, the Germans left the civilian administration intact. Though northern France and the Atlantic coast came under military rule, the so-called Vichy government remained the civilian authority in the unoccupied southeastern part of the country. In contrast, most conquered territories in eastern Europe and the Balkans came under direct military rule as a prelude for harsh occupation, economic exploitation, and German settlement.

EXPLOITATION Japanese and German authorities administered their respective empires for economic gain and proceeded to ruthlessly exploit the resources of the lands under their control for their own benefit. The most notorious form of economic exploitation involved the use of slave labor. In Poland, the Soviet Union, France, Italy, and the Balkan nations, German occupiers forced millions of people to labor in work camps and war industries, and the Japanese did likewise in China and Korea. These slave laborers worked under horrific conditions and received little in the way of sustenance.

COLLABORATION AND RESISTANCE Reaction to Japanese and German occupation varied from willing collaboration and acquiescence to open resistance. In both Asia and Europe, local notables often joined the governments sponsored by the conquerors because collaboration offered them the means to gain power or because they thought native rule was better than foreign rule. Businesspeople and companies often collaborated because they prospered financially from foreign rule. Still other people assisted occupation forces to get revenge for past grievances.

Nevertheless, occupation and exploitation created an environment for resistance that took various forms. The most dramatic forms of resistance were campaigns of sabotage, armed assaults on occupation forces, and assassinations. Resistance fighters as diverse as Filipino guerrillas and Soviet partisans blew up ammunition dumps and destroyed communication and transportation facilities. More quietly, other resisters gathered intelligence or hid and protected refugees.

Resistance also comprised simple acts of defiance such as scribbling anti-German graffiti or walking out of bars and restaurants when Japanese soldiers entered. German and Japanese citizens faced different decisions about resistance than conquered peoples

Vichy (vee-SHEE)

SOURCES FROM THE PAST

A Hiroshima Maiden's Tale

Yamaoka Michiko, at fifteen years of age, worked as an operator at a telephone exchange in Hiroshima and attended girls' high school. Many young women had been mobilized for work during World War II, and they viewed even civilian work on telephone exchanges as a means of helping to protect Japan during wartime. On the morning of 6 August 1945, when the first U.S. atomic bomb used in battle devastated Hiroshima, Yamaoka Michiko had just started off for work.

That morning I left the house at about seven forty-five. I heard that the B-29s [U.S. bomber planes] had already gone home. Mom told me, "Watch out, the B-29s might come again." My house was one point three kilometers from the hypocenter [the exact point of the atomic bomb's impact]. My place of work was five hundred meters from the hypocenter. I walked toward the hypocenter. . . . I heard the faint sound of planes. . . . The planes were tricky. Sometimes they only pretended to leave. I could still hear the very faint sound of planes. . . . I thought, how strange, so I put my right hand above my eyes and looked up to see if I could spot them. The sun was dazzling.

That was the moment. There was no sound. I felt something strong. It was terribly intense. I felt colors. It wasn't heat. You can't really say it was yellow, and it wasn't blue. At that moment I thought I would be the only one who would die. I said to myself, "Goodbye, Mom."

They say temperatures of seven thousand degrees centigrade hit me. You can't really say it washed over me. It's hard to describe. I simply fainted. I remember my body floating in the air. That was probably the blast, but I don't know how far I was blown. When I came to my senses, my surroundings were silent. There was no wind. I saw a threadlike light, so I felt I must be alive. I was under stones. I couldn't move my body. I heard voices crying, "Help! Water!" It was then I realized I wasn't the only one. . . .

"Fire! Run away! Help! Hurry up!" They weren't voices but moans of agony and despair. "I have to get help and shout," I thought. The person who rescued me was Mom, although she herself had been buried under our collapsed house. Mom knew the route I'd been taking. She came, calling out to me. I heard her voice and cried for help. Our surroundings were already starting to burn. Fires burst out from just the light itself. It didn't really drop. It just flashed. . . .

My clothes were burnt and so was my skin. I was in rags. I had braided my hair, but now it was like a lion's mane. There were people, barely breathing, trying to push their intestines back in. People with their legs wrenched off. Without heads. Or with faces burned and swollen out of shape. The scene I saw was a living hell.

Mom didn't say anything when she saw my face and I didn't feel any pain. She just squeezed my hand and told me to run. She was going to rescue my aunt. Large numbers of people were moving away from the flames. My eyes were still able to see, so I made my way toward the mountain, where there was no fire, toward Hijiyama. . . .

I spent the next year bedridden. All my hair fell out. When we went to relatives' houses later they wouldn't even let me in because they feared they'd catch the disease. There was neither treatment nor assistance for me. . . . It was just my Mom and me. Keloids [thick scar tissue] covered my face, my neck. I couldn't even move my neck. One eye was hanging down. I was unable to control my drooling because my lip had been burned off. . . .

The Japanese government just told us we weren't the only victims of the war. There was no support or treatment. It was probably harder for my Mom. Once she told me she tried to choke me to death. If a girl had terrible scars, a face you couldn't be born with, I understand that even a mother could want to kill her child. People threw stones at me and called me Monster. That was before I had my many operations.

■ What did Yamaoka Michiko's psychological and physical reactions to the atomic bombing of Hiroshima suggest about the nature of these new weapons? Why did friends and relatives treat her as if she were a "monster"?

SOURCE: Yamaoka Michiko. "Eight Hundred Meters from the Hypocenter." In Haruko Taya Cook and Theodore F. Cook. *Japan at War: An Oral History.* New York: The New Press, 1992, pp. 384–87.

did, since they had no antiforeign axe to grind. Moreover, many institutions that might have formed the core of resistance in Japan and Germany, such as political parties, labor unions, and churches, were weak or had been destroyed. As a result, there was little or no opposition to the state and its policies in Japan, while in Germany resistance remained generally sparse and ineffective.

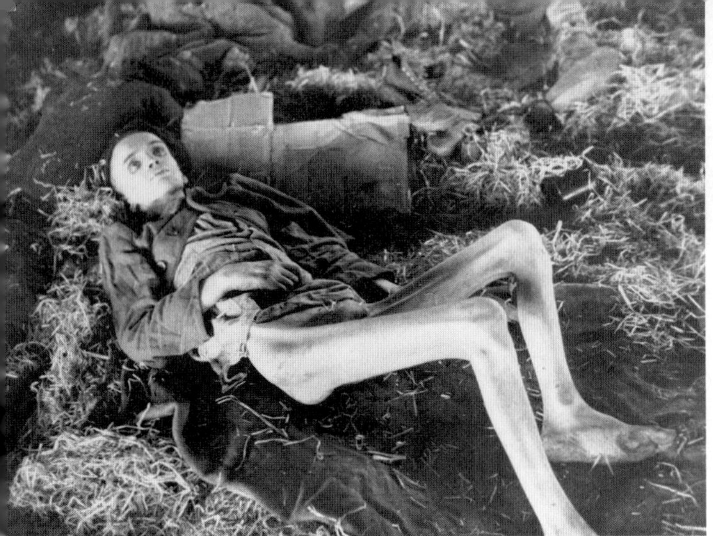

The Holocaust. | Titled "Abyss of Human Horror," this photograph shows a survivor of the concentration camp at Nordhausen, Germany, upon its liberation by Allies in 1945.

ATROCITIES Occupation forces reacted swiftly and brutally to resistance. When in May 1942 members of the Czech resistance assassinated the Nazi official Reinhard Heydrich, the Nazis eliminated the entire village of Lidice as punishment. Likewise, when a group of officers and civilians tried to kill Adolf Hitler in July 1944, many of the conspirators were hanged with piano wire suspended from meat hooks, a process recorded on film for Hitler. The Japanese were equally brutal. When eight hundred Chinese slave laborers were captured after escaping from their camp in the small Japanese town of Hanaoka, at least fifty were beaten and tortured to death as they hung by their thumbs from the ceiling of the town hall. Yet despite such deadly retaliation meted out to people who resisted occupation, widespread resistance movements grew throughout the war.

The Holocaust

By the end of World War II, the Nazi regime and its accomplices had physically annihilated millions of Jews, Slavs, Gypsies, homosexuals, Jehovah's Witnesses, communists, and others targeted as undesirables. Jews were the primary target of Hitler's racially motivated genocidal policies, and the resulting Holocaust nearly wiped out the Jewish population of Europe.

The murder of European Jews was preceded by centuries of anti-Semitism in Europe, where Jews were routinely marked as outsiders. Thus Europeans' passive acceptance of anti-Semitism, combined with Nazi determination to destroy the Jewish population, laid the groundwork for genocide. Initially, the Nazi regime encouraged Jewish emigration. Although tens of thousands of Jews availed themselves of the opportunity to escape from Germany and Austria, many more were unable to do so because most European nations limited the migration of Jewish refugees and because German victories in Europe brought an ever-larger number of Jews under Nazi control. Early in the war, Nazi "racial experts" toyed with the idea of mass deportation of Jews, but that idea proved to be impractical as well as threatening, since the concentration of Jews in one area led to the dangerous possibility of the creation of a separate Jewish state, hardly a solution to the so-called Jewish problem in the Nazi view.

THE FINAL SOLUTION The German occupation of Poland in 1939 and the invasion of the Soviet Union in the summer of 1941 gave Hitler an opportunity to solve what he considered the problem of Jews throughout Europe. When German armies invaded the Soviet Union in June 1941, the Nazis dispatched three thousand troops in mobile detachments known as SS *Einsatzgruppen* ("action squads") to kill entire populations of Jews and Roma (Gypsies), and many non-Jewish Slavs in the newly occupied territories. By the end of 1941, the special units had killed 1.4 million Jews.

PSI doc The Holocaust (film clip) www.mhhe.com/bentleybrief2e

Sometime during 1941 the Nazi leadership committed to the "final solution" of the Jewish question, which entailed the attempted murder of every Jew living in Europe. At the Wannsee Conference, on 20 January 1942, fifteen leading Nazi bureaucrats agreed to evacuate all Jews from Europe to camps in eastern Poland, where they would be worked to death or exterminated. Soon German forces—aided by collaborating authorities in foreign countries—rounded up Jews and deported them by rail to specially constructed concentration camps in occupied Poland. The Jewish victims packed into those suffocating railway cars never knew their destinations, but rumors of mass deportations and mass deaths spread among Jews remaining at large and among the Allied government leaders, who were apparently apathetic to the fate of Jews.

Einsatzgruppen (ain-zats-groopen)

MAP 32.3 | The Holocaust in Europe, 1933–1945. Observe the geographical locations of the concentration and extermination camps. ***Why were there more concentration camps in Germany and more extermination camps in Poland?***

In camps such as Belzec, Treblinka, and Auschwitz, the final solution took on an organized and technologically sophisticated character. Nazi camp personnel subjected victims from all corners of Europe to industrial work, starvation, medical experiments, and outright extermination. The German commandant of Auschwitz—the largest camp, where at least one million Jews perished—explained proudly how his camp became the most efficient at killing Jews: by using the fast-acting crystallized prussic acid Zyklon B as the gassing agent, by enlarging the size of the gas chambers, and by lulling victims into thinking they were going through a delousing process. At Auschwitz and elsewhere, the Germans also constructed large crematories to incinerate the bodies of gassed Jews and hide the evidence of their crimes. Even though Jews put up fierce resistance throughout the war, by 1945 approximately 5.7 million Jews had perished in the Holocaust.

Women and the War

Observing the extent to which British women mobilized for war, the U.S. ambassador to London noted, "This war, more than any other war in history, is a woman's war." While hundreds of thousands of women in Great Britain and the United States joined the armed forces or entered war industries, women around the world were affected by the war in a variety of ways. In some nations, such as the Soviet Union and China, women took up arms. So, too, did female members of resistance groups, who often excelled at resistance work because they were less suspect in the eyes of occupying security forces and less subject to searches. Nazi forces did not discriminate, though, when rounding up Jews for transport and extermination: Jewish women and girls died alongside Jewish men and boys.

Although women's roles changed during the war, often in dramatic ways, those new roles were temporary. After the war, women warriors and workers were expected to return home and assume their traditional roles as wives and mothers. In the meantime, though, women made the most of their opportunities. In Britain, more than half a million women joined British military services, and approximately 350,000 women did the same in the United States.

Women's experiences in war were not always ennobling or empowering. The Japanese army forcibly conscripted as many as three hundred thousand women aged fourteen to twenty to serve in military brothels, called "comfort houses" or "consolation centers." Most of the women came from Japanese colonies such as Korea, Taiwan, and Manchuria and from occupied territories in the Philippines and elsewhere in southeast Asia. Eighty percent of the women came from Korea.

Once forced into this imperial prostitution service, "comfort women" catered to between twenty and thirty men each day. Some were killed by Japanese soldiers, especially if they tried to escape or contracted venereal diseases. At the end of the war, soldiers massacred large numbers of comfort women to cover up the operation. The impetus behind the establishment of comfort houses came from the horrors of Nanjing, where Japanese soldiers had engaged in the mass rape of Chinese women. In trying to avoid such atrocities, however, the Japanese army created another. Comfort women who survived the war experienced deep shame and hid their past or faced shunning by their families. They found little comfort or peace after the war.

WOMEN IN THE ARMED FORCES. An American WAVES (Women Accepted for Volunteer Emergency Service) recruitment poster proclaims "It's A Woman's War Too!"

NEITHER PEACE NOR WAR

The end of World War II produced moving images of peace, including those of Soviet and U.S. soldiers clasping hands in camaraderie at the Elbe River, celebrating their victory over the Germans. Indeed, the Soviet Union and the United States emerged as the two strongest powers after the war, and each played a central role in shaping, influencing, and rebuilding the postwar world. It quickly became clear that both powers sought to create a world in their own image. Initially, the struggle to align postwar nations on one side or the other centered on areas liberated at the end of the war. Ultimately, however, it spread to the whole world.

Postwar Settlements and Cold War

Although the peoples of victorious nations danced in the streets on Victory in Europe (V-E) Day and Victory in Japan (V-J) Day, they also gazed at a world transformed by war. At least sixty million people perished in World War II. The Soviets lost more than twenty million, one-third of whom were soldiers; fifteen million Chinese, mostly civilians, died; Germany and Japan suffered the deaths of four million and two million people, respectively; six million Poles were also dead; in Great Britain four hundred thousand people died; and the United States lost three hundred thousand. The Holocaust claimed the lives of almost six million European Jews. In Europe and Asia tens of millions of displaced persons further contributed to the difficulty of rebuilding areas destroyed by war.

At the same time, the cold war between the Soviet Union and the United States began. That long-drawn-out conflict (1947–1991) divided humans and nations as sympathetic either to the Soviet Union or to the United States. The cold war came to define the postwar era as one of political, ideological, and economic hostility between the two superpowers and affected nations around the globe.

THE ORIGINS OF THE COLD WAR Throughout most of World War II, Hitler had believed that the alliance of the communist Soviet Union, the imperialist Great Britain, and the unwarlike U.S. democracy would break up over ideological differences. Yet Hitler underestimated the extent to which opposition to his regime could unite such unusual allies. Winston Churchill had put it like this: "If Hitler invaded Hell, I would at least make favorable reference to the Devil in the House of Commons."

The necessity of defeating the Axis nations glued the Allies together, although there were tensions among them. Some of those tensions began to surface at the second wartime conference between the Allied leaders, at Yalta (4–11 February 1945), but they became obvious at the third and final wartime conference, at Potsdam (16 July–2 August 1945). By the time of the Yalta Conference, the Soviets were 64 kilometers (40 miles) from Berlin, and they controlled so much territory that Churchill and Roosevelt could do little to alter Stalin's plans for eastern Europe. They attempted to persuade Stalin to allow democracy in Poland, but Stalin's plans for Soviet-occupied nations prevailed. The Soviets suppressed noncommunist political parties and prevented free elections in Poland, Czechoslovakia, Hungary, Romania, and Bulgaria. They also installed a communist government in Poland and took similar steps elsewhere in eastern Europe.

ENCOUNTERS IN WORLD WAR II. As a result of far-flung theaters of combat, peoples from all over Europe, Asia, Africa, the Pacific, and the Americas came into direct contact during World War II. How and why did these encounters promote both greater understanding and greater hostility between peoples?

At Yalta Stalin ensured that the Red Army's presence would dictate the future of states liberated by the Soviets, and at Potsdam Truman initiated the pro-capitalist, pro-democracy stance of the United States. The successful test of the atomic bomb while Truman was at Potsdam stiffened the president's resolve, and tensions over postwar settlements intensified. Having just fought a brutal war to guarantee the survival of their ways of life, neither the United States nor the Soviet Union would easily forgo the chance to remake occupied territories as either capitalist or communist allies.

In the end, all the Allies agreed on was the dismemberment of the Axis states and their possessions. The Soviets took over the eastern sections of Germany, and the United States, Britain, and France occupied the western portions. The capital city of Berlin, deep within the Soviet area, remained under the control of all four powers. In 1946, Churchill proclaimed that an "iron curtain" had come down on Europe, separating the Soviet-controlled nations of eastern Europe from the capitalist nations of western Europe. A somewhat similar division occurred in Asia. Whereas the United States alone occupied Japan, Korea remained occupied half by the Soviets and half by the Americans.

The enunciation of the Truman Doctrine on 12 March 1947 crystallized the new U.S. perception of a world divided between free and enslaved peoples. Articulated partly in response to crises in Greece and Turkey, where communist movements seemed to threaten democracy and U.S. strategic interests, the Truman Doctrine starkly drew the battle lines of the cold war. As Truman explained to the U.S. Congress: "I believe that it must be the policy of the United States to support free peoples who are resisting attempted subjugation by armed minorities or by outside pressures." Thus the United States committed itself to an interventionist foreign policy, dedicated to the "containment" of communism, which meant preventing any further expansion of Soviet influence. As a result, the world was polarized into two armed camps, each led by a superpower that provided economic and military aid to nations within its sphere of influence.

PSI doc Speech outlining the Truman Doctrine www.mhhe.com/bentleybrief2e

Global Reconstruction and the United Nations

THE MARSHALL PLAN As an economic adjunct to the Truman Doctrine, the U.S. government developed a plan to help shore up the destroyed infrastructures of western Europe. The European Recovery Program, commonly called the Marshall Plan after U.S. secretary of state George C. Marshall (1880–1959), proposed to rebuild European economies to forestall Soviet influence in the devastated nations of Europe. Beginning in 1948, the Marshall Plan provided more than $13 billion to reconstruct western Europe.

In response, the Soviet Union countered with a plan for its own satellite nations. The Soviet Union established the Council for Mutual Economic Assistance (COMECON) in

1949, offering increased trade within the Soviet Union and eastern Europe as an alternative to the Marshall Plan.

NATO AND THE WARSAW PACT The creation of the U.S.-sponsored North Atlantic Treaty Organization (NATO) and the Soviet-controlled Warsaw Pact signaled the militarization of the cold war. In 1949 the United States established NATO as a regional military alliance against Soviet aggression. The original members included Belgium, Canada, Denmark, France, Great Britain, Iceland, Italy, Luxembourg, the Netherlands, Norway, Portugal, and the United States. The intent of the alliance was to maintain peace in postwar Europe through collective defense. When NATO admitted West Germany and allowed it to rearm in 1955, the Soviets formed the Warsaw Pact as a countermeasure. A military alliance of seven communist European nations, the Warsaw Pact matched the collective defense policies of NATO.

THE UNITED NATIONS Despite their many differences, the superpowers were among the nations that agreed to the creation of the United Nations (UN), a supranational organization dedicated to keeping world peace. The commitment to establish a new international organization derived from Allied cooperation during the war, and in 1945 the final version of the United Nations charter was hammered out by delegates from fifty nations at the United Nations Conference in San Francisco. The United Nations was dedicated to maintaining international peace and security and promoting friendly relations among the world's nations. It offered an alternative for global reconstruction that was independent of the cold war.

It rapidly became clear, however, that international peace and security eluded both the United Nations and the superpowers. The cold war dominated postwar reconstruction efforts. It remained cold for the most part, characterized by ideological and propaganda campaigns, but it became "hot" in places, such as Korea between 1950 and 1953, and it had the potential to escalate into a war more destructive than World War II. The Soviet Union broke the U.S. monopoly on the atomic bomb in September 1949, and from that point on the world held its collective breath at the possibility of a nuclear war.

SUMMARY

At the end of World War II, it was possible for a U.S. marine to enjoy the hospitality of a Japanese family in Nagasaki, but not for Soviet and U.S. troops to continue embracing in camaraderie. World War II was a total global war that forced violent encounters between peoples and radically altered the political shape of the world. Beginning with Japan and China in 1931, this global conflagration spread to Europe and its empires and to the Pacific Ocean and the rest of Asia. Men, women, and children throughout the world became intimate with war as victims of civilian bombing campaigns, as soldiers and war workers, and as slave laborers and comfort women. When the Allies defeated the Axis powers in 1945, destroying the German and Japanese empires, the world had to rebuild as the cold war began. The cold war helped determine the new shape of the world as nations reconstructed under the auspices of either the United States or the Soviet Union, the two superpowers of the postwar era.

STUDY TERMS

Adolf Hitler (640)
Allied powers (638)
Anschluss (640)
appeasement (640)
Axis powers (638)
Battle of Britain (642)
Benito Mussolini (640)
Blitzkrieg (641)
cold war (652)
COMECON (653)
D-Day (645)
final solution (650)
Greater East Asia Co-Prosperity Sphere (644)
Hiroshima and Nagasaki (647)
Holocaust (650)
Joseph Stalin (641)
kamikaze (646)
Lebensraum (642)
lend-lease (643)
Marshall Plan (653)
NATO (654)
Operation Barbarossa (643)
Pearl Harbor (643)
Rape of Nanjing (638)
Russian-German Treaty of Nonaggression (641)
Tripartite Pact (639)
Truman Doctrine (653)
United Nations (654)
Warsaw Pact (654)
Winston Churchill (644)

FOR FURTHER READING

Ian Buruma. *The Wages of Guilt: Memories of War in Germany and Japan.* New York, 1995. A moving account of how societies deal with the war crimes of World War II.

Haruko Taya Cook and Theodore F. Cook. *Japan at War: An Oral History.* New York, 1992. Views of World War II in the words of the Japanese who witnessed it.

John Dower. *War without Mercy: Race and Power in the Pacific War.* New York, 1986. An insightful and important work on how race influenced the Japanese and U.S. war in the Pacific.

Paul Fussell. *Understanding and Behavior in the Second World War.* Oxford, 1989. A dissection of the culture of war; see the author's similar treatment of World War I.

Margaret Higgonet, Jane Jenson, Sonya Michel, and Margaret Weitz, eds. *Behind the Lines: Gender and the Two World Wars.* New Haven, 1987. A penetrating series of articles on women in both world wars, focusing generally on U.S. and European experiences.

Raul Hilberg. *The Destruction of the European Jews.* New York, 1967. One of the most important works on the Holocaust.

Akira Iriye. *The Origins of the Second World War in Asia and the Pacific.* New York, 1987. An examination of the Asian and Pacific origins of the war by one of the field's leading scholars.

You-Li Sun. *China and the Origins of the Pacific War, 1931–1941.* New York, 1993. An account of the origins of the war in which China takes center stage.

Studs Terkel. *"The Good War": An Oral History of World War II.* New York, 1984. A valuable collection of oral histories on the war from a U.S. perspective.

Gerhard Weinberg. *A World at Arms: A Global History of World War II.* Cambridge, 1994. An exhaustive look at the war from a global perspective.

The Cold War and Decolonization

33

n 16 February 1946, six months after the final end of World War II in Asia, the Vietnamese revolutionary leader Ho Chi Minh wrote a letter to U.S. president Harry Truman. Ho, who had fought for decades against French imperial rule and then against the Japanese occupation of Vietnam, had reason to expect a sympathetic hearing from the American president. After all, during the war the United States had sent its own OSS (Office of Strategic Services) officers to aid Ho's Viet Minh party in their resistance against the Japanese, and the previous president (Franklin Delano Roosevelt) had been hostile to French imperialism in Asia. Thus, when Ho Chi Minh took control of Vietnam from the hated Japanese, he expected American support for his new republic. Indeed, when Ho issued his declaration of independence on 2 September 1945, some of the Vietnamese people in the huge crowd carried homemade pictures of President Harry Truman and waved American flags.

Imagine Ho's surprise when he discovered that Truman would not stand in the way of the French decision to recolonize Vietnam. As French troops landed in Vietnam and began reestablishing French authority in early 1946, Ho penned his letter to the American president, arguing that "this aggression is contrary to all principles of international law and the pledge made by the Allies during World War II. It is a challenge to the noble attitude shown before, during, and after the war by the United States Government and People. . . . [Vietnam's] security and freedom can only be guaranteed by our independence from any colonial power, and our free cooperation with all other powers. It is with this firm conviction that we request of the United States as guardians and champions of World Justice to take a decisive step in support of our independence." In fact, Ho pointed out, the Vietnamese were simply asking for the same kind of independence granted that very year to the Philippines by the United States itself.

Truman never answered Ho's letter of 16 February. Instead, as tensions between the United States and the Soviet Union became increasingly apparent by the end of World War II, the struggle between global capitalism and global communism overshadowed the way both new superpowers regarded the world around them. Although Ho had fought with the Allies in World War II, he was a founder of the French Communist Party, had lived in Moscow, and was committed to socialist ideals. With an enormous Soviet Union set to impose its will on eastern Europe in the immediate aftermath of the war, U.S. policymakers became convinced that any group with communist sympathies represented a serious threat to global security. Thus in spite of its professed anti-imperial attitude, the United States government was induced by the realities of cold war politics not

‹ An American air strike against Viet Cong positions results in the destruction of a Vietnamese village.

CHRONOLOGY

1947	Partition of India
1948	Creation of Israel
1948–1949	Berlin blockade and airlift
1949	Division of Berlin and Germany
1949	Establishment of People's Republic of China
1950–1953	Korean War
1954	French defeat at Dienbienphu
1955	Bandung Conference
1956	Suez crisis
1956	Uprising in Hungary
1957	Ghana gains independence
1958–1961	Great Leap Forward in China
1959	Castro comes to power in Cuba
1961	Bay of Pigs invasion
1961	Construction of Berlin Wall
1962	Cuban missile crisis
1964	Creation of Palestinian Liberation Organization (PLO)
1964	Sino-Soviet rift
1965–1973	U.S. troops to Vietnam
1968	Prague Spring
1973	U.S. defeat in Vietnam
1979	Revolution in Iran
1979	Sandinistas in power in Nicaragua
1989	Soviet withdrawal from Afghanistan
1989	Fall of Berlin Wall
1990	Reunification of Germany
1991	Collapse of Soviet Union
1991	End of cold war

only to aid the French as they tried to reconquer Vietnam, but to take on the project of eradicating communism in Vietnam once French efforts failed in 1954.

As Ho discovered, Vietnam's struggle for independence collided head-on with emerging cold war politics. Vietnam was not alone. Since decolonization and the cold war occurred simultaneously in the decades after World War II, it was almost inevitable that the wave of new nation-states that came into being as empires fell would have to face the two opposing superpowers now dominating global politics. Indeed, decolonization and the cold war were two of the most important processes to emerge out of World War II, and both fundamentally reshaped the late-twentieth-century world—particularly in cases, such as Vietnam, where they intertwined.

The cold war was a strategic struggle that developed after World War II between the United States and its allies on the one hand and the USSR and its allied communist countries on the other. Yet the confrontation was more than an instance of power rivalry; it was also a tense encounter between rival social and economic systems and competing political ideologies. The geopolitical and ideological rivalry between the Soviet Union and the United States lasted almost five decades and affected every corner of the world. The cold war was responsible for the formation of military and political alliances, the creation of client states, and an arms race of unprecedented scope. It engendered diplomatic crises, spawned military conflicts, stimulated social change, and at times brought the world to the brink of nuclear annihilation. It was a contest in which neither side gave way, yet in the end the United States and the Soviet Union always avoided a direct clash of arms, hence the term *cold war.*

Like the cold war, and frequently in conjunction with it, decolonization after World War II contributed significantly to global political transformations. Decolonization, in essence the relinquishing of all colonial possessions by imperial powers, brought the world to its current international standing. Imperial agents lost control, and dozens of new independent states gained autonomy and self-determination. As cold war animosities deepened, however, the leaders of the Soviet Union and the United States often demanded that new nations take sides and choose between capitalism and communism. At times these demands compromised their independence, particularly in new nations deemed strategically important by the superpowers.

Partly as a result of cold war tensions, people in new and developing nations around the world discovered that independence was just the first step on a much longer, and often much more difficult, road to national unity and social and economic stability. Yet despite all the complications of decolonization and its aftermath, colonial peoples fought for freedom and then for security in a bipolar world.

Although both decolonization and the cold war had come to an end by the late twentieth century, from their beginning to end both processes suggested that powerful new global forces were at work in the wake of World War II.

THE FORMATION OF A BIPOLAR WORLD

The cold war's initial arena was war-torn Europe. By the time Germany surrendered in the spring of 1945, the wartime alliance between the Soviet Union and the United States was disintegrating. With the advent of peace, the one-time partners increasingly sacrificed cooperation for their own national interests. The hostility and competition between these new adversaries resulted in a divided Europe, in powerful change within the societies of both superpowers, and ultimately in a divided world.

The Cold War in Europe

Among the first manifestations of the cold war was the division of the European continent into competing political, military, and economic blocs—one dependent on the United States and the other subservient to the USSR—separated by what Winston Churchill called an "iron curtain." In essence, each bloc adopted the political institutions, economic systems, and foreign policies of one of the two superpowers. Thus western European nations that were tied to the United States embraced parliamentary political systems and capitalist economic structures and adjusted their foreign policies to the U.S. vision of the postwar world. On the other hand, under the watchful eyes of Soviet occupation armies, the governments of eastern European states adopted Soviet political and economic institutions and supported Moscow's foreign policy goals.

A DIVIDED GERMANY The fault lines of cold war Europe were first visible in Germany. There in 1948–1949 an international crisis arose when the Soviet Union pressured the western powers to relinquish their jurisdiction over Berlin. After the collapse of Hitler's Third Reich, the forces of the United States, the Soviet Union, Britain, and France occupied Germany and its capital, Berlin, both of which they divided for administrative purposes into four zones. In accordance with agreements made at Yalta, specific travel corridors running through the Soviet occupation zone of Germany gave the French, British, and Americans access from their sectors in Berlin to their respective zones of occupation in western Germany.

BLOCKADE AND AIRLIFT When the western powers decided to merge their occupation zones in Germany—including their sectors in Berlin—into a single economic unit, however, the Soviets saw the move as a threat to their own zone of control. In retaliation, on 24 June 1948 the Soviets announced that the western powers no longer had jurisdiction in Berlin and blockaded road, rail, and water links between Berlin and western Germany. Two days later, in the first serious test of the cold war, the Americans and British responded with an airlift designed to keep the city's inhabitants alive, fed, and warm. For eleven months, American and British aircrews flew around-the-clock missions to supply West Berlin with the necessities of life. Tensions remained high during the airlift, but the cold war did not turn hot. Finally, the Soviet leadership called off the blockade in May 1949, though the airlift continued until September. Also in May of that year, the U.S., British, and French zones of occupation coalesced to form the Federal Republic of Germany (West Germany). The Soviets responded by creating the German Democratic Republic (East Germany) in their own zone. A similar process repeated itself in Berlin, which was deep within the Soviet zone. The Soviet sector formed East Berlin

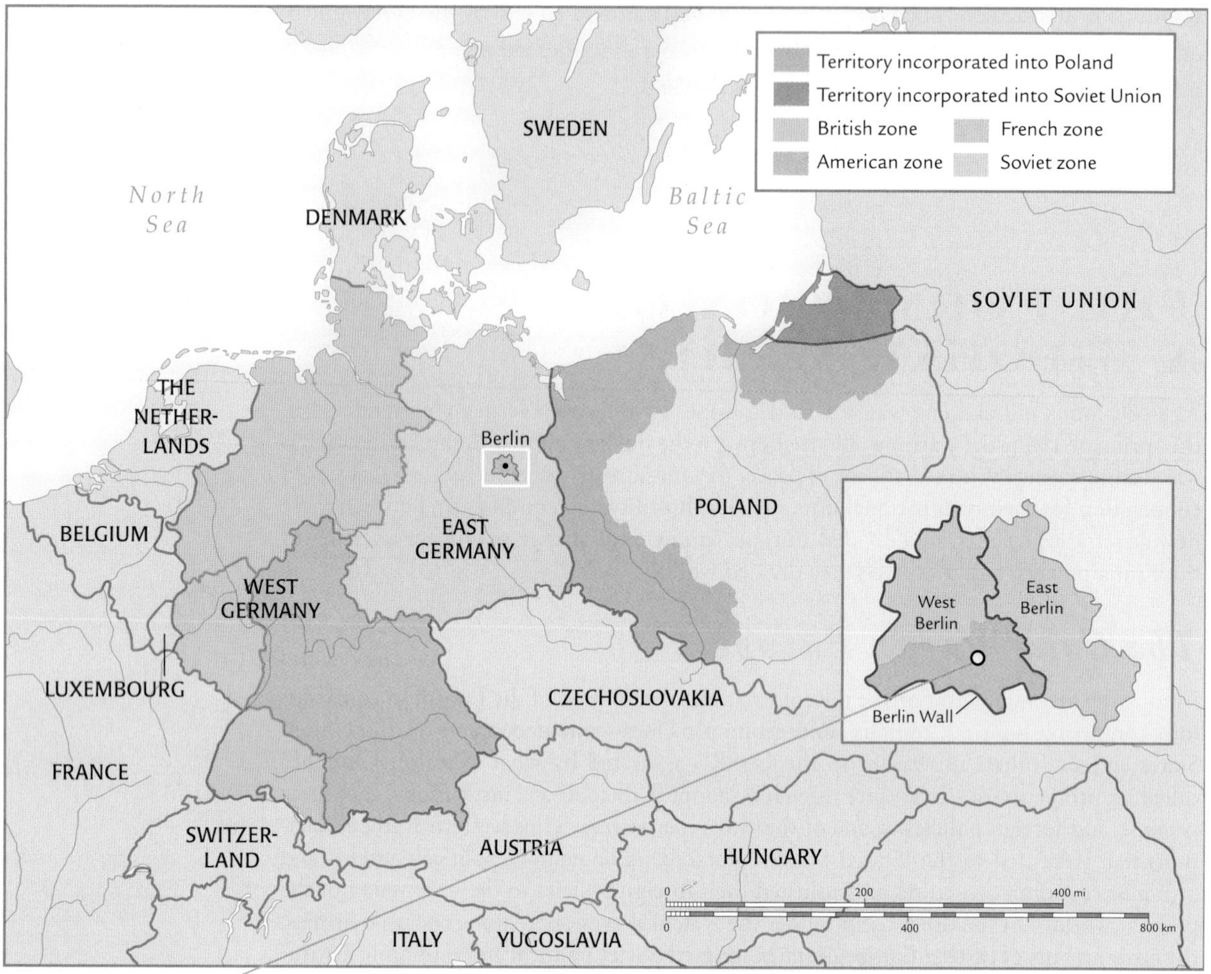

The city of Berlin was divided into zones of power, mimicking the divisions between East and West Germany.

MAP 33.1 | Occupied Germany, 1945–1949. Locate the city of Berlin in Soviet-controlled territory. ***How was it possible for the British, Americans, and French to maintain their zones of control in Berlin, given such geographical distance from western Germany?***

and became the capital of the new East Germany, while the remaining three sectors united to form West Berlin.

BERLIN WALL By 1961 the communist East German state was hemorrhaging from a steady drain of refugees—nearly 3.5 million since 1949—who preferred life in capitalist West Germany. To counter this embarrassing problem, in August 1961 the communists erected a fortified wall—replete with watchtowers, searchlights, and border guards—between East and West Germany. In subsequent years several thousand East Germans escaped to West Germany, and several hundred others died trying. Meanwhile, the Berlin Wall accomplished its purpose of stemming the flow of refugees, though at the cost of openly demonstrating that the regime lacked legitimacy among its own people.

THE NUCLEAR ARMS RACE A central feature of the cold war world was a costly arms race and the terrifying proliferation of nuclear weapons. The struggle between the United States and the Soviet Union led to the creation of two military blocs: the North Atlantic Treaty Organization, or NATO (1949), intended to serve as a military counterweight to the Soviet forces in Europe, and the Warsaw Treaty Organization, or Warsaw Pact (1955), established as a response to the rearming of West Germany. Because the United States was determined to retain military superiority and because the Soviet Union was equally determined to reach parity with the United States, both sides amassed

NATO Treaty
www.mhhe.com/bentleybrief2e

The Berlin Wall. In this 1961 photo from the Schoenholz region of Berlin, West Berliners peer over the brick and barbed-wire fence separating East and West Berlin. ***Why did the Communist regime in East Germany take the drastic step of building such a wall?***

enormous arsenals of thermonuclear weapons and developed a multitude of systems for deploying those weapons. By 1970, both powers had reached parity, which meant that they had acquired the capacity for mutually assured destruction, or MAD. Although the prospect of MAD was terrifying, the balance of terror had the effect of restraining the contestants and stabilizing their relationship.

SPACE RACE During the nuclear arms race, cold war tensions accelerated when it seemed that one superpower gained a critical technological edge over the other. This was certainly the case when the Soviets took the cold war into space by announcing, on 4 October 1957, the launching into space of the first satellite, *Sputnik.* The Soviet head start in this "space race" provoked panic among U.S. citizens and politicians. U.S. panic only intensified in April 1961 when the Soviets rocketed cosmonaut Yuri Gagarin (1934–1968) into space, where he became the first man to orbit Earth. The U.S. responded to Soviet successes in space with its own, launching the satellite *Explorer I* in 1958 and sending astronaut John Glenn (1921–) into orbit in 1962. When John F. Kennedy took office in 1961, he dedicated himself and the National Aeronautics and Space Administration (NASA) to the task of landing a man on the moon. That came to fruition on 20 July 1969 when *Apollo XI* gently set down on the moon's Sea of Tranquility and thereby ensured that Americans were the first to make this "great leap for mankind." During the cold war, critical technological and scientific breakthroughs were achieved on both sides of the iron curtain as a result of intense competition between the superpowers.

Cold War Societies

The forces that split Europe into opposing blocs and created the nuclear arms race also had dramatic effects on the domestic affairs of the United States, the Soviet Union, and their European allies. Postwar social transformations in each demonstrated how domestic policies and international affairs became linked in this period.

DOMESTIC CONTAINMENT In the United States, for example, cold war concerns about the spread of communism reached deeply into the domestic sphere. Politicians, FBI agents, educators, and social commentators warned of communist spies trying to undermine the institutions of U.S. life, and Senator Joseph McCarthy (1909–1957) became infamous in the early 1950s for his unsuccessful quest to expose communists in the U.S. government. Thousands of citizens who supported any radical or liberal cause—especially those who were or once had been members of the Communist Party—lost their jobs and reputations after being deemed risks to their nation's security. Conforming to a socially sanctioned way of life and avoiding suspicion became the norm during the early, most frightening years of the cold war. Some scholars have dubbed this U.S. retreat to the home and family "domestic containment," indicating its similarity to the U.S. foreign policy of the containment of international communism. At the same time, however, people in the United States enjoyed unprecedented prosperity and leisure during the early decades of the cold war. Access to automobiles, Hollywood movies, record albums, and supermarkets therefore lessened some of the pain of atomic anxiety and international insecurity.

SOVIET SOCIETY In the Soviet Union and eastern Europe, cold war ideologies also profoundly influenced domestic realities. After the war, Stalin imposed Soviet economic planning on governments in eastern Europe and expected the peoples of the Soviet Union and eastern Europe to conform to anticapitalist ideological requirements. Rebellious artists and novelists found themselves silenced or denounced in an exaggerated and reversed form of the McCarthyism that affected government workers, writers, and filmmakers in the United States in the same years. After Stalin's death in 1953, this policy of repression relaxed somewhat, as his successor—Nikita Khrushchev—pursued a slightly more liberal path with respect to domestic society. There were limits to this Soviet liberalization, though: Soviet troops cracked down on Hungarian rebels in 1956, and Soviet novelist Boris Pasternak (1890–1960), author of *Dr. Zhivago,* was not allowed to receive his Nobel Prize for Literature in 1958. In addition to political repression, social conditions and material wealth in the Soviet Union and eastern Europe differed dramatically from those in the United States and western Europe. Whereas people in the capitalist bloc enjoyed increased prosperity and access to consumer items, those in the communist bloc did not: dishwashers, automobiles, fashionable clothing, and high-quality manufactured goods remained out of the reach of most ordinary people.

Ironically, despite their intense competition and opposition, societies in the Soviet Union and the United States came to resemble one another in some ways, especially in their domestic censorship policies and their quest for cold war supremacy. There is no doubt that societies on both sides underwent dramatic transformations as a result of the international competition between capitalism and communism. Indeed, the cold war—like the world wars and the Great Depression before it—demonstrated once again that global political events had the power to shape even the day-to-day lives of ordinary people.

Confrontations in Korea and Cuba

As the tensions of the cold war were dividing Europe and spurring change within the societies of the superpowers and their allies, they also spilled out into the global arena. When hostilities broke out on the Korean peninsula in the summer of 1950, the focus of the cold war shifted to east Asia. At the end of World War II, the leaders of the Soviet Union and the United States had partitioned Korea along the thirty-eighth parallel of latitude into a northern Soviet zone and a southern U.S. zone. In 1948 they consented to the establishment of two separate Korean states: in the south, the Republic of Korea, with Seoul as its capital and the conservative anticommunist Syngman Rhee (1875–1965) as its president; in the north, the People's Democratic Republic of Korea, with Pyongyang as its capital and the revolutionary communist Kim Il Sung (1912–1995) as its leader. After arming their respective clients, each of which claimed sovereignty over the entire country, U.S. and Soviet troops withdrew.

THE KOREAN WAR On the early morning of 25 June 1950, the unstable political situation in Korea came to a head. Determined to unify Korea by force, the Pyongyang regime ordered more than one hundred thousand troops across the thirty-eighth parallel in a surprise attack, capturing Seoul on 27 June. Convinced that the USSR had

SOURCES FROM THE PAST

National Security Council Paper Number 68

In 1949, the cold war seemed to be going badly for the United States. The Chinese Communist Party had just taken control of China, and the Soviets had detonated their first atom bomb. President Harry Truman, anxious over these new developments, commissioned the State and Defense departments to draft a statement on the U.S. position toward the Soviet Union and Soviet expansion. The result was National Security Council Paper Number 68, which was completed in the spring of 1950. It remained classified until the 1970s.

. . . During the span of one generation, the international distribution of power has been fundamentally altered. . . . Two complex sets of factors have now basically altered this historical distribution of power. First, the defeat of Germany and Japan and the decline of the British and French Empires have interacted with the development of the United States and Soviet Union in such a way that power has increasingly gravitated to these two centers. Second, the Soviet Union, unlike previous aspirants to hegemony, is animated by a new fanatic faith, antithetical to our own, and seeks to impose its absolute authority over the rest of the world. Conflict has, therefore, become endemic and is waged, on the part of the Soviet Union, by violent or non-violent methods in accordance with the dictates of expediency. . . .

The issues that face us are momentous, involving the fulfillment or destruction not only of this Republic but of Civilization itself. They are issues which will not await our deliberations. With conscience and resolution this Government and the people it represents must now take new and fateful decisions. . . .

Our overall policy at the present time may be described as one designed to foster a world environment in which the American system can survive and flourish. It therefore rejects the concept of isolation and affirms the necessity of our positive participation in the world community. . . .

As for the policy of "containment," it is one which seeks by all means short of war to (1) block further expansion of Soviet power, (2) expose the falsities of Soviet pretensions, (3) induce a retraction of the Kremlin's control and influence and (4) in general, so foster the seeds of destruction within the Soviet system that the Kremlin is brought at least to the point of modifying its behavior to conform to generally accepted international standards.

It was and continues to be cardinal in this policy that we possess superior overall power in ourselves or in dependable combination with other like-minded nations. One of the most important ingredients of power is military strength. . . .

Our position as the center of power in the free world places a heavy responsibility upon the United States for leadership. We must organize and enlist the energies and resources of the free world in a positive program for peace which will frustrate the Kremlin design for world domination by creating a situation in the free world to which the Kremlin will be compelled to adjust. Without such a cooperative effort, led by the United States, we will have to make gradual withdrawals under pressure until we discover one day that we have sacrificed our positions of vital interest. . . .

The whole success of the proposed program hangs ultimately on recognition by this Government, the American people, and all free peoples, that the cold war is in fact a real war in which the survival of the free world is at stake.

■ **According to this document, why was the cold war so important, and how did the United States government see its role in the conflict?**

SOURCE: Alfred J. Andrea and James H. Overfield. *The Human Record: Sources of Global History*, 3rd ed., *Volume II: Since 1500.* Boston and New York: Houghton Mifflin, 1998.

sanctioned the invasion, and armed with UN support, the U.S. military went into action. Within two weeks U.S. forces pushed North Koreans back to the thirty-eighth parallel. However, sensing an opportunity to unify Korea under a pro-U.S. government, they pushed on into North Korea, occupied Pyongyang, and made advances toward the Chinese border. These advances caused the government of the People's Republic of China to issue a warning: the U.S. incursion across the thirty-eighth parallel threatened Chinese national interests and could result in Chinese intervention in the Korean conflict.

When U.S. leaders gave no indication of heeding China's warning, some three hundred thousand Chinese soldiers surged into North Korea. A combined force of Chinese and North Koreans pushed U.S. forces and their allies back into the south, and the war settled

The Korean War. | In August 1950, U.S. troops marched toward North Korea while South Koreans moved in the opposite direction to escape the fighting.

into a protracted stalemate near the original border at the thirty-eighth parallel. After two more years of fighting that resulted in three million deaths—mostly of Korean civilians—both sides finally agreed to a cease-fire in July 1953.

THE GLOBALIZATION OF CONTAINMENT From a strategic and political standpoint, the Korean conflict was important because it was the first test of "containment" outside of Europe. The U.S. leadership had viewed North Korean aggression as part of a larger communist conspiracy to conquer the world and thus felt obligated to act. In 1954 U.S. president Dwight D. Eisenhower (1890–1969) articulated the famous "domino theory," which held that if one country became communist, neighboring countries would collapse to communism the way a row of dominoes falls sequentially. Thereafter, subsequent U.S. administrations extended the policy of containment to the entire world, applying it to local or imagined communist threats in Central and South America, Africa, and Asia.

CUBA: NUCLEAR FLASHPOINT Ironically, the cold war confrontation that came closest to unleashing nuclear war took place not at the expected flashpoints in Europe or Asia but on the island of Cuba. In 1959 a revolutionary movement headed by Fidel Castro Ruz (1926–) overthrew the autocratic Fulgencio Batista y Zaldivar (1901–1973), whose regime had gone to great lengths to maintain the country's traditionally subservient relationship with the United States. Denouncing American imperialism, Castro seized foreign properties and businesses, most of which were U.S. owned. He also accepted assistance from the Soviet Union. The U.S. government promptly retaliated by cutting off Cuban sugar imports to the U.S. market and imposing a severe export embargo of U.S. goods on Cuba. U.S. officials also cut diplomatic relations with Cuba and secretly began planning an invasion of the island.

The severing of ties between Cuba and the United States gave the Soviet Union an unprecedented opportunity to contest the dominant position of the United States in its own hemisphere. Castro's regime accepted a Soviet offer of massive military and economic aid, including an agreement to purchase half of Cuba's sugar production. In return for the Soviet largesse, Castro loudly declared his support for the USSR's foreign policy at the UN General Assembly on 26 September 1960.

THE BAY OF PIGS Cuba's alignment with the Soviet Union spurred newly elected president John F. Kennedy (1917–1963) to approve a plan to invade Cuba and overthrow Castro. In April 1961 a force of 1,500 anti-Castro Cubans trained, armed, and transported by the Central Intelligence Agency (CIA) landed on Cuba at a place called the Bay of Pigs. The invasion, however, was a complete failure and actually strengthened Castro's position in Cuba as well as his commitment to communism. It also likely encouraged Castro to accept and the Soviets to deploy nuclear missiles in Cuba as a deterrent to any future invasion.

PSI img Missile sites in Cuba www.mhhe.com/bentleybrief2e

THE CUBAN MISSILE CRISIS On 22 October 1962 President Kennedy went on national television to inform the public about the U.S. discovery of offensive nuclear missiles and launch sites in Cuba. He told the public that the deployment of nuclear missiles so close to the United States represented an unacceptable threat to U.S. national security. Kennedy also called on the Soviet leadership to withdraw all missiles from Cuba and stop the arrival of additional nuclear armaments. To back up his demand, Kennedy imposed an air and naval quarantine on the island nation that went into effect two days later. The superpowers seemed poised for nuclear confrontation, and for a week the world's peoples held their collective breath.

Understanding the seriousness of a nuclear showdown over Cuba, Nikita Khrushchev agreed to Kennedy's demand that he withdraw the missiles on the condition that the United States pledge not to invade Cuba. He also received a private promise from Kennedy

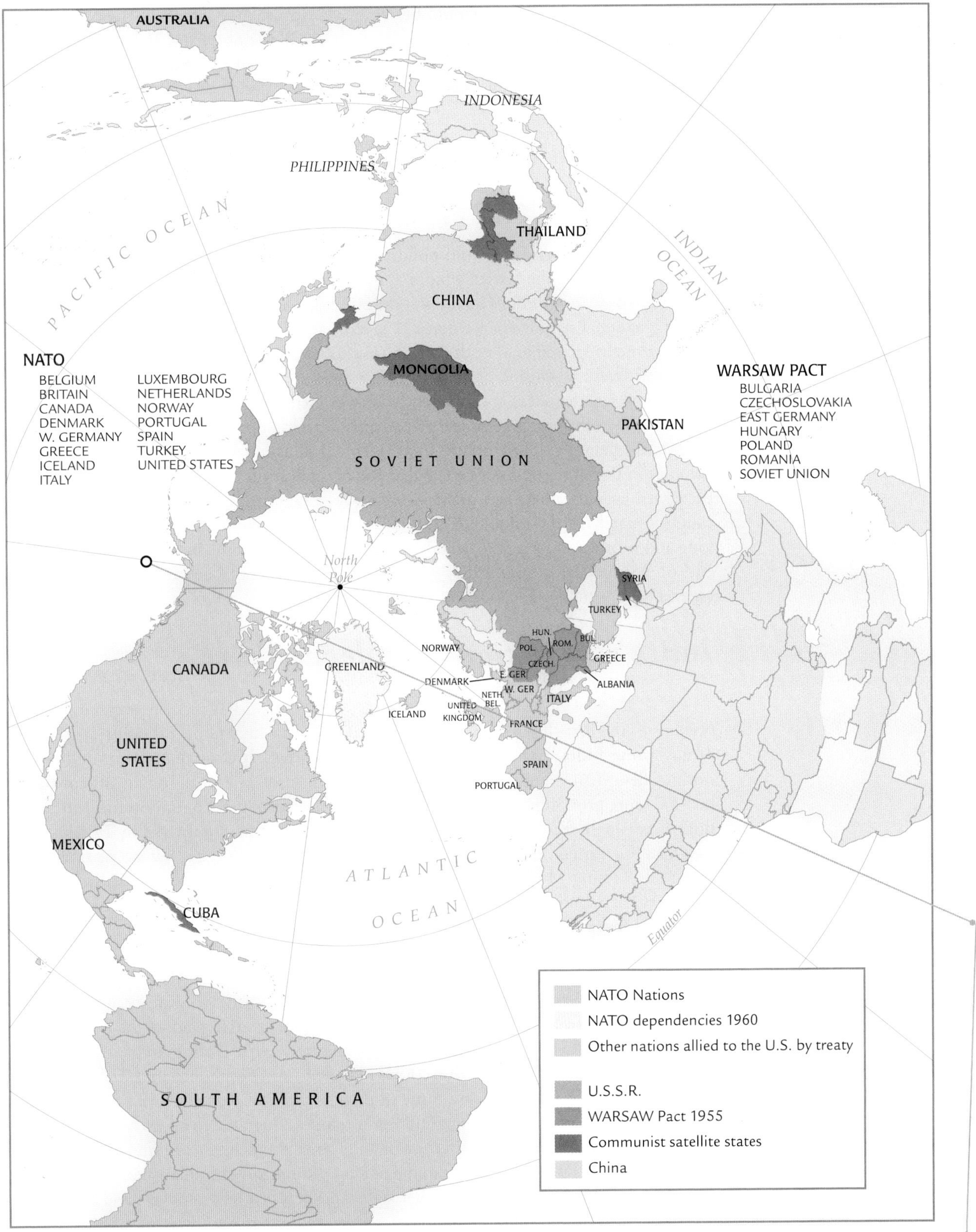

MAP 33.2 | The cold war, 1949–1962. Note the size of the territories and the number of states allied to both sides. ***Were these alliances a source of global stability or global instability?***

Note how many nations had ties to one or the other superpower.

that U.S. missiles in Turkey would be removed. Khrushchev informed the public of the end of the crisis in a worldwide radio broadcast on 28 October, and global tension began to ebb. Nonetheless, the Cuban missile crisis revealed the dangers of the bipolar world—especially the ways in which cold war rivalries so easily drew other areas of the world into their orbit.

Decolonization and the Global Cold War

While the cold war was in the midst of dividing western Europe and the United States from eastern Europe and the Soviet Union, another global process had already begun to transform the postwar world in equally important ways: decolonization. By the end of World War II, nationalist movements devoted to the cause of independence from imperial rule had become irrepressible in both Asia and Africa. Independence came at different times in different places, depending on local circumstances and the attitude of the imperial power. In some places, the course of independence was intricately tied to the politics of the cold war because both new superpowers frequently offered support to nationalist leaders who pledged allegiance to their political and ideological agendas. While most former British colonies in both Asia and Africa avoided the complication of becoming tied up in superpower struggles for influence, others—such as Vietnam and Angola—found that they were caught squarely in the middle of nationalist and cold war politics. Yet despite sometimes long and protracted struggles, more than ninety nations became independent between the end of World War II and 1980, while others that had not been formally controlled—especially in Latin America—also sought to throw off the shackles of foreign influence.

India's Partitioned Independence

THE COMING OF SELF-RULE After World War II, it became painfully obvious to the British government that it could not continue to bear the financial burden of governing India, particularly since nationalists made it clear that they would accept nothing less than complete independence. As the probability of Indian independence became more pronounced, the issue of Muslim separatism grew in importance, and Muslims increasingly feared their minority status in a free India dominated by Hindus. Muhammad Ali Jinnah (1876–1948), leader of the Muslim League, felt no qualms about frankly expressing Muslim concerns and desires for a separate Muslim state. In response, Congress Party leaders like Jawaharlal Nehru (1889–1964) and Gandhi urged all Indians to act and feel as one nation, undivided by what came to be known as communalism—emphasizing religious over national identity.

PSI img Partition of India www.mhhe.com/bentleybrief2e

PARTITION AND VIOLENCE Jinnah had his way, however, and when the British withdrew from India in 1947 two new flags were raised in place of the British Union Jack—with Jinnah leading Pakistan and Jawaharlal Nehru leading India. Gandhi condemned the division as a "vivisection" of his homeland and prophesied that "rivers of blood" would flow in its wake. His vision came true as the terms of partition were announced and hundreds of thousands of Muslim and Hindu refugees migrated to either Muslim Pakistan (divided between parts of Bengal in the east and Punjab in the west) or Hindu India in order to escape religious persecution. By mid-1948 an estimated ten million refugees had made the tortuous journey to one or the other state, and between half a million and one million people had died in the violence that accompanied those massive migrations.

Though mired in violence, Indian independence became a reality with momentous consequences for the process of decolonization. Just as Gandhi's nonviolent resistance to British rule inspired nationalists around the globe before and after World War II, independence in India and Pakistan further encouraged anti-imperial movements throughout Asia and Africa. Moreover, once India left the British empire, there could be little doubt about the fate of Britain's remaining imperial possessions.

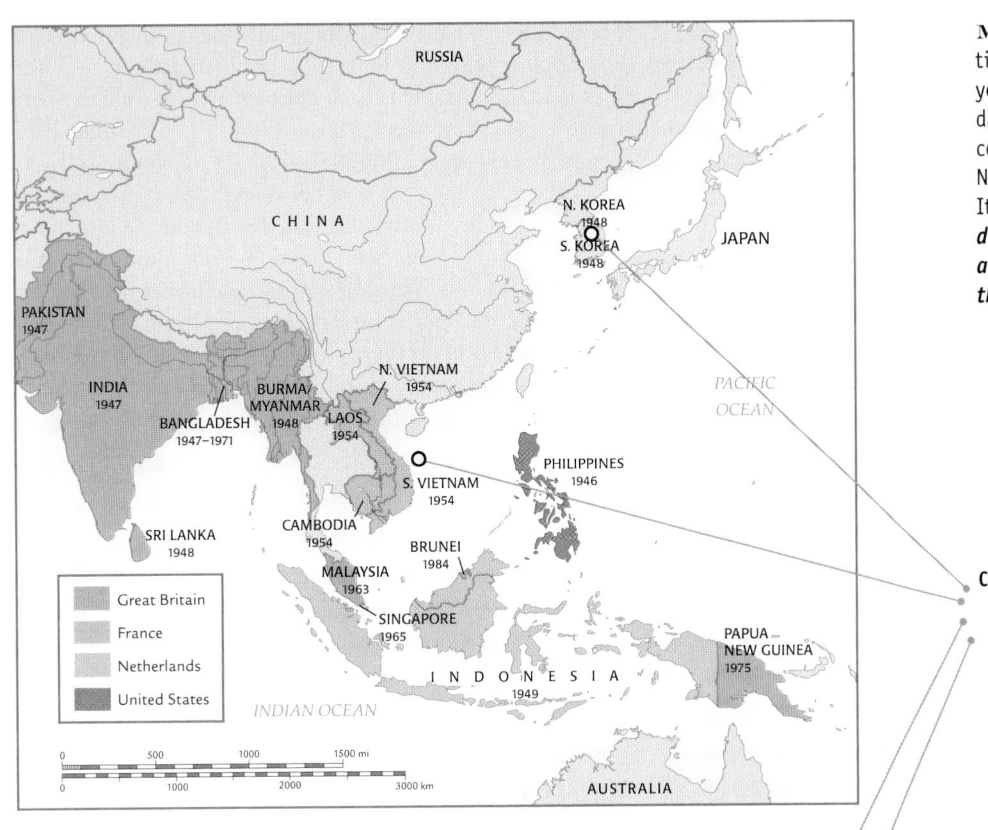

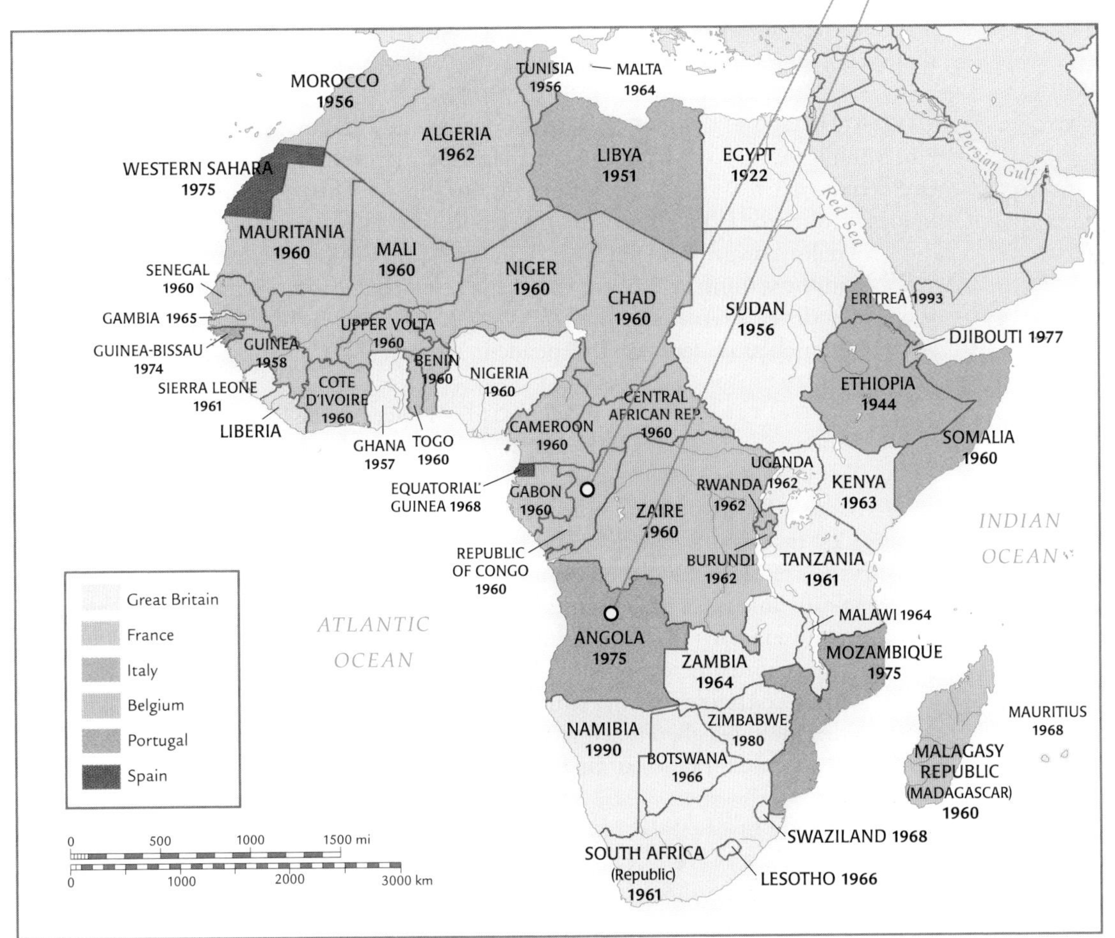

MAP 33.3 | Decolonization in Asia and Africa. Date is year of independence. Note the dates of independence for the colonies of Great Britain, the Netherlands, the United States, Italy, Belgium, and France. ***Why did independence occur in such a short time span for most of these colonies?***

Cold war hot spots.

NONALIGNMENT Another way in which Indian independence inspired other nations was Nehru's strategy for grappling with decolonization in the midst of a cold war. Nehru called his strategy nonalignment, arguing that "each country has not only the right to freedom but also to decide its own policy and way of life." In April 1955 leaders from twenty-three Asian and six African nations—including Nehru—met in Bandung, Indonesia to discuss nonalignment as an alternative to choosing between the United States and the Soviet Union. Besides discussing neutrality in the cold war, the Bandung Conference also stressed the struggle against colonialism and racism. Bandung was the precursor of the broader Nonaligned Movement, which held occasional meetings so that its members could discuss their relations with the United States and the Soviet Union. The movement's primary goal was to maintain formal neutrality. However, although theoretically nonaligned with either cold war superpower, many member states had close ties to one or the other, and this situation caused dissension within the movement. For example, the Philippines and Cuba clearly supported the U.S. and Soviet camps, respectively. Nevertheless, other individual states avoided becoming pawns in the cold war by announcing the policy of nonalignment advocated by Nehru.

Since winning its independence, India has stood out among decolonized nations not just for its advocacy of nonalignment, but also for its ability to maintain its political stability and its democratic system. Indeed, even though India has faced many of the same crises that have shaken other developing nations—ethnic and religious conflict, wars, poverty, political assassinations, and overpopulation—Nehru's heirs have remained committed to free elections and a critical press.

Nationalist Struggles in Vietnam

In contrast to India, Vietnam could not keep its nationalist struggle for independence separate from the complications of the cold war. Rather, Vietnam became deeply enmeshed in the contest between capitalism and communism, which meant that decolonization there was a long and bloody process.

PSI img Ho Chi Minh, 1920 www.mhhe.com/bentleybrief2e

FIGHTING THE JAPANESE Vietnam's nationalist communist leader, Ho Chi Minh (1890–1969), had been struggling for autonomy from French imperialism for two decades when World War II broke out in Europe. Thus the Japanese invasion of his homeland after the fall of France in 1940 seemed to Ho like the replacement of one imperialist power with another. During the war, Ho fought against the Japanese and in the waning days of the war helped oust them from Vietnam altogether. With both the French and the Japanese gone, Ho took the opportunity to establish himself as leader of an independent Vietnam.

HO CHI MINH. | Ho was leader of North Vietnam from 1945 to 1969 and was one of southeast Asia's most influential communist leaders.

FIGHTING THE FRENCH However, the French, humiliated by their country's easy defeat and occupation by the Germans, sought to reclaim their imperial possessions—including Vietnam—as a way of regaining their world-power status. By 1947, they seemed to have secured their power in much of the country. Yet that security proved to be temporary. Much like the Chinese communists in their battles against the Japanese and then against the nationalists in the postwar years, the Vietnamese resistance forces, led by Ho Chi Minh and General Vo Nguyen Giap (1912–), mounted a campaign of guerrilla warfare. The Vietnamese communists increasingly regained control of their country, especially after 1949 when communist China sent aid and arms to the Viet Minh. Thus strengthened, they defeated the French at their fortress in Dienbienphu in 1954. The French had to sue for peace at the conference table.

THE GENEVA CONFERENCE AND PARTIAL INDEPENDENCE The peace conference, held in Geneva in 1954, determined that Vietnam should be temporarily divided at the seventeenth parallel; North Vietnam would be controlled by Ho Chi Minh and the communist forces, and

South Vietnam would remain in the hands of noncommunists. Leaving all of Vietnam in the hands of Ho's communists was unthinkable for the United States, especially after the globalization of the cold war that had accompanied the Korean War. The U.S. had already aided the French in their struggle against Ho—now they did the same with the government of South Vietnam. Violating the terms of the Geneva Agreements, which required elections that would likely have brought Ho to power, South Vietnam's leaders, with U.S. military support, avoided elections and sought to build a government that would prevent the spread of communism in South Vietnam and elsewhere in Asia. However, the leaders of South Vietnam did not have the support of the people, who quickly grew discontented enough to resort to arms.

THINKING ABOUT *Traditions*

TRADITIONS IN THE COLD WAR AND DECOLONIZATION. During the process of decolonization, some emerging nations embraced the cultural traditions of the past in order to form independent national identities, while others rejected traditions in favor of new ideologies. Provide an example of both approaches, and discuss the rationale behind each.

COLD WAR STALEMATE In 1960 South Vietnamese nationalists—with the aid of weapons and troops from the north—formed the National Liberation Front to fight for freedom from South Vietnamese rule and to end U.S. military interference in the area. In North Vietnam, the government received economic and military assistance from the Soviet Union and China, which in turn reinforced the U.S. military commitment in the south. The participation of three major world powers in the Vietnamese conflict ensured that the war would be a long, bloody, and expensive stalemate. Ultimately, United States forces withdrew from this unwinnable war in 1975, and in 1976 North Vietnam conquered the south, united the country, and at long last declared independence.

Although the Vietnamese ultimately did achieve their long-awaited independence, their experience demonstrated the dangers of what could occur when independence movements became entangled with the politics and logic of the cold war.

The People's Republic of China

The birth of a communist China simultaneously ended a long period of imperialist intrusion in China and further transformed the cold war. Although China had not been formally ruled by an imperial power, many countries had impinged on its sovereignty in the nineteenth and early twentieth centuries. During the 1920s, two groups had arisen in China to reassert Chinese control over internal affairs: the nationalists and the communists. When World War II broke out, these two groups had been engaged in a civil war. After the Japanese defeat, it was clear by mid-1948 that the strategic balance favored the communists, who inflicted heavy military defeats on the nationalists throughout 1948 and 1949. With the communist People's Liberation Army controlling most of mainland China, the national government under Jiang Jieshi (Chiang Kai-shek) sought refuge on the island of Taiwan, taking along most of the nation's gold reserves. Although Jiang Jieshi continued to proclaim that the government in Taiwan was the legitimate government of all China, Mao Zedong, the chairman of the Chinese Communist Party, nevertheless proclaimed the establishment of the People's Republic of China on 1 October 1949. That declaration, much to the alarm of the United States, spawned a close relationship between China and the Soviet Union, especially since Mao sought to imitate Soviet socialism.

PSI img Mao speaking
www.mhhe.com/bentleybrief2e

SOCIAL AND ECONOMIC TRANSFORMATIONS The government of the new People's Republic created new political, economic, and social organizations that completely reorganized all aspects of Chinese society. Political power was monopolized by the Communist Party and a politburo chaired by Mao, while opposition was ruthlessly repressed. In 1955 the Chinese introduced their first Five-Year Plan to encourage rapid industrialization and the collectivization of agriculture on the Soviet model. The Five-Year Plan emphasized improvements in infrastructure and the expansion of heavy industry at the expense of consumer goods. A series of agrarian laws confiscated the landholdings of rich peasants and landlords and redistributed them among the people so that virtually every peasant had at least a small plot of land. Quickly, however, state-mandated collective farms replaced private farming. In the wake of economic reforms came social reforms, many of which challenged or eliminated Chinese family traditions. Supporting equal rights for women, Chinese authorities introduced marriage laws that eliminated such practices as child or forced marriages, gave women equal access to divorce, legalized abortion, and outlawed foot binding, a symbol of women's subjugation.

FRATERNAL COOPERATION Moscow and Beijing drew closer during the early years of the cold war, in part because of their common socialism and in part as a result of active efforts by the United States to establish anticommunist bastions throughout Asia. Most disconcerting to Soviet and Chinese leaders was the American-sponsored rehabilitation of their former enemy, Japan, and client states South Korea and Taiwan. The Chinese-Soviet partnership matured during the early 1950s and took on a distinct form when Beijing recognized Moscow's undisputed authority in world communism in exchange for Russian military equipment and economic aid.

CRACKS IN THE ALLIANCE As the Chinese embarked on a crash program of industrialization, the Soviet Union rendered valuable assistance in the form of economic aid and technical advisors. By the mid-1950s the Soviet Union was China's principal trading partner. Before long, however, cracks appeared in the Soviet-Chinese alliance. From the Chinese perspective, Soviet aid programs were far too modest and had too many strings attached. For example, in 1955 the Soviet Union supplied more economic aid to noncommunist countries such as Egypt and India than to China. Another source of friction was the conflict between China and India over Tibet in 1961. The Chinese were furious when the Soviets announced their neutrality in the conflict and then belied the announcement by giving a loan to India that exceeded any similar loan ever granted to China.

By the end of 1964, the rift between the Soviet Union and the People's Republic of China had become embarrassingly public, with both sides engaging in name-calling. In addition, both nations openly competed for influence in Africa and Asia, especially in the nations that had recently gained independence. The fact that the People's Republic had conducted successful nuclear tests in 1964 enhanced its prestige. An unanticipated outcome of the Chinese-Soviet split was that many countries gained an opportunity to pursue a more independent course in the global cold war by playing capitalists against communists and by playing Soviet communists against Chinese communists.

During the 1960s and 1970s, Mao succeeded in transforming European communist ideology into a distinctly Chinese communism. After 1949 he embarked on two programs designed to accelerate development in China and to distinguish Chinese communism from Soviet communism: the Great Leap Forward (1958–1961) and the Great Proletarian Cultural Revolution (1966–1976). Both were far-reaching policies that nevertheless hampered the political and economic development that Mao so urgently sought.

THE GREAT LEAP FORWARD Mao envisioned his Great Leap Forward as a way to overtake the industrial production of more developed nations, and to that end he worked to collectivize all land and to manage all business and industrial enterprises collectively. Private ownership was abolished, and farming and industry became largely rural and communal. The Great Leap Forward—or "Giant Step Backward" as some have dubbed it—failed. Most disastrous was its impact on agricultural production in China: the peasants could not meet quotas, and a series of bad harvests contributed to one of the deadliest famines in history. Between 1959 and 1962 as many as twenty million Chinese may have died of starvation and malnutrition in this crisis.

THE GREAT PROLETARIAN CULTURAL REVOLUTION In 1966 Mao tried again to mobilize the Chinese and reignite the revolutionary spirit with the inauguration of the Great Proletarian Cultural Revolution. Designed to root out foreign, bourgeois, or anticommunist values in Chinese life, the Cultural Revolution subjected millions of people to humiliation, persecution, and death. The elite constituted the major targets of the Red Guards, youthful zealots empowered to cleanse Chinese society of opponents to Mao's rule. Victims were beaten and killed, jailed, or sent to corrective labor camps or to toil in the countryside. The Cultural Revolution, which cost China years of stable development and gutted its educational system, remained undiminished until after Mao's death in 1976. It fell to one of Mao's heirs, Deng Xiaoping, to heal the nation.

DENG'S CHINA Deng came to power in 1981, and the 1980s are often referred to as the years of "Deng's Revolution." Deng moderated Mao's commitment to Chinese self-sufficiency and isolation and engineered China's entry into the international financial and trading system, a move that was facilitated by the normalization of relations between China and the United States in the 1970s. To push the economic development of China, Deng opened the nation to the influences that were so suspect under Mao—foreign, capitalist values. Although Deng did not hesitate to crack down on elements in Chinese society that sought democratic reform—as he did against students in Beijing's Tiananmen Square in 1989—he oversaw impressive economic growth and development by selectively opening Chinese society to global trade. In the twenty-first century, Chinese leaders have managed to maintain massive economic growth without giving up the centralized, communist political control established by Mao in the early years of the cold war.

THE CULTURAL REVOLUTION. | A 1966 poster shows Mao Zedong inspiring the Red Guards to launch the Great Proletarian Cultural Revolution.

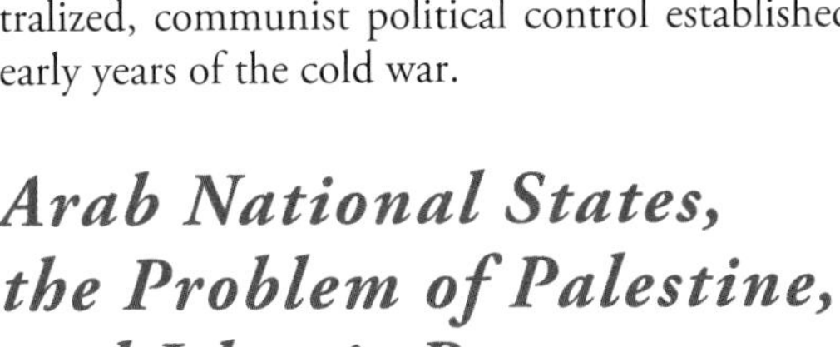

Arab National States, the Problem of Palestine, and Islamic Resurgence

After World War II, the Arab states of southwest Asia—including Syria, Iraq, Lebanon, and Jordan—gained complete independence from the colonial powers of France and Britain. Yet significant vestiges of imperial rule impeded Arab sovereignty. The battle to rid southwest Asia of those remnants of imperialism took some twists and turns as the superpowers interfered in the region, drawn by its vast reserves of oil, the lifeblood of the cold war's military-industrial complexes. Independent states responded in various ways to superpower interference, including a turn to radical fundamentalist interpretations of Islam. Throughout, one ambiguous legacy of imperialism—Palestine—absorbed much of the region's energies and emotions.

PALESTINE Great Britain served as the mandate power in Palestine after the Great War, and before and during its mandate made conflicting promises both to Palestinian Arabs and to Jews who hoped to establish a secure homeland in Palestine. With the Balfour Declaration of 1917, the British government committed itself to the support of a Jewish homeland—a cause strongly advocated by Zionists, who were dedicated to combating anti-Semitism by establishing a national Jewish state. Thus the British were compelled to allow Jewish migration to Palestine under their mandate, but they also had to allay the fears of those in possession of the land—the Palestinian Arabs. The British therefore limited the migration and settlement of Jews and promised to protect the Arabs' political and economic rights.

PSI doc The Balfour Declaration www.mhhe.com/bentleybrief2e

This British attempt to balance the causes of two conflicting groups was unsuccessful, and large-scale violence was prevented only through the use of imperial military forces. The Palestinian Muslims perceived the Jews as alien interlopers in their own land. At the same time, European Jews were dangerously under attack by the Nazis, and Zionists in Palestine armed themselves to protect Jewish settlers against Arab reprisals. At the end of

World War II, a battle brewed. As Arab states around Palestine gained their freedom from imperial rule, they developed a pan-Arab nationalism sparked by support for their fellow Arabs in Palestine and opposition to the possibility of a Jewish state there. The Holocaust, however, intensified the Jewish commitment to build a state capable of defending the world's remaining Jews.

THE CREATION OF ISRAEL While the Arabs in Palestine insisted on complete independence under Arab rule, in 1945 the Jews embarked on a course of violent resistance to the British to compel recognition of Jewish demands for self-rule. The British could not resolve the dispute and in 1947 turned the region over to the newly created United Nations. Before the UN could implement its own plans in the region, in May 1948 the Jews in Palestine announced the creation of the independent state of Israel, claiming territories far larger than those that would have been granted by the UN. In response, the outraged Arab states of Egypt, Jordan, Syria, Lebanon, and Iraq joined Palestinians in a war to destroy the new state.

Arab attacks and campaigns, although boldly fought, were uncoordinated, and the Israelis managed to achieve a stunning victory. A truce went into effect in early 1949 under UN auspices, and the partition of Palestine resulted. Jerusalem and the Jordan River valley were divided between the new Israeli state and the kingdom of Jordan, while Israel controlled the coastal areas of Palestine and the Negev Desert to the Red Sea.

EGYPT AND ARAB NATIONALISM Meanwhile, Egyptian military leaders under the leadership of Gamal Abdel Nasser (1918–1970) committed themselves to opposing Israel and taking command of the Arab world. In July 1952 Nasser and other officers staged a bloodless coup that ended the monarchy of Egypt's King Farouk. In

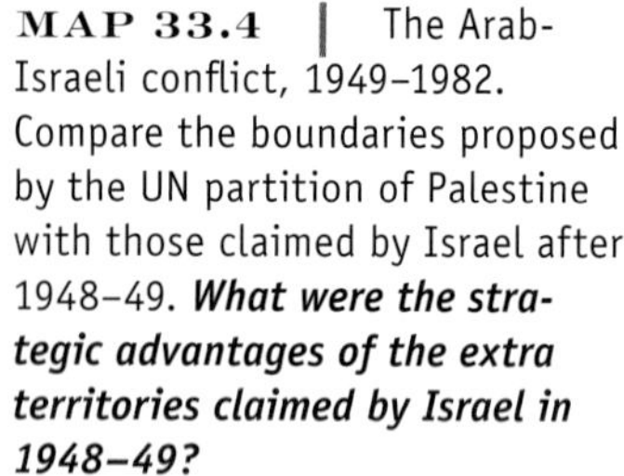

MAP 33.4 | The Arab-Israeli conflict, 1949–1982. Compare the boundaries proposed by the UN partition of Palestine with those claimed by Israel after 1948–49. ***What were the strategic advantages of the extra territories claimed by Israel in 1948–49?***

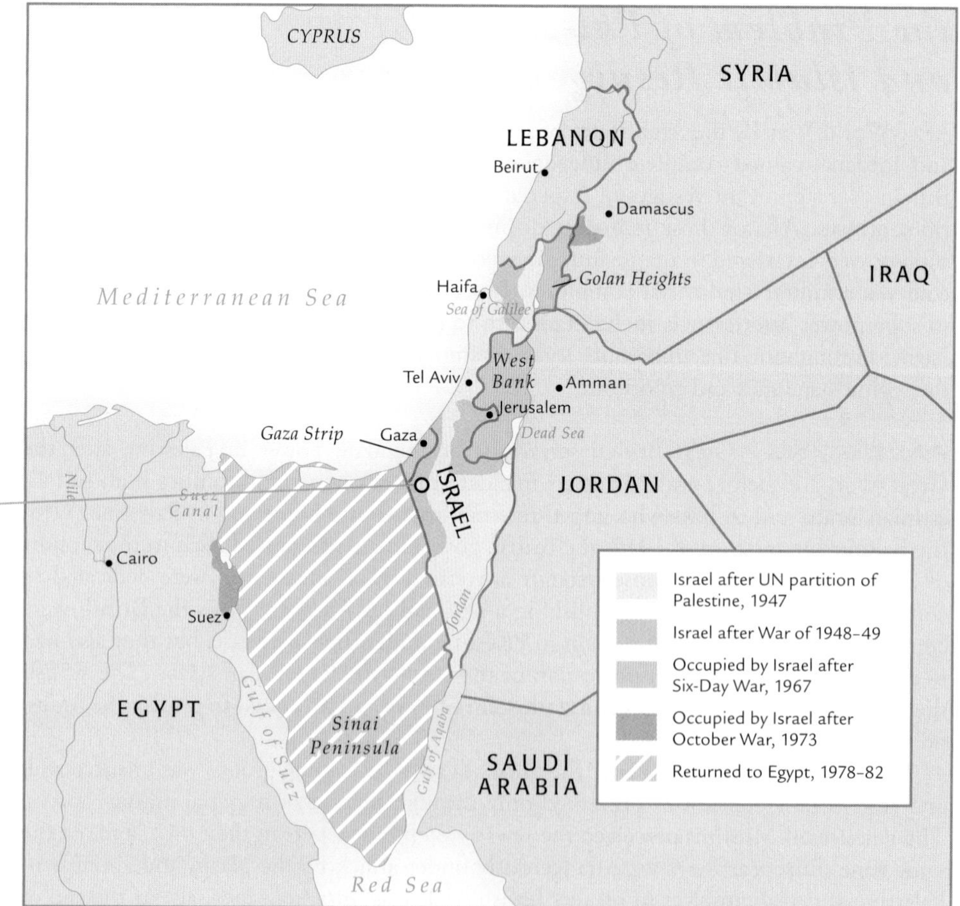

Note the substantially larger territories claimed by Israel after the war of 1948–49.

1954, Nasser named himself prime minister and took control of the government. He then labored assiduously to develop Egypt economically and militarily and make it the fountainhead of pan-Arab nationalism.

THE SUEZ CRISIS Like India's Nehru, Nasser refused to align himself with either the United States or the Soviet Union, because he believed that cold war power politics were a new form of imperialism. In fact, Nasser dedicated himself to ridding Egypt and the Arab world of imperial interference. However, Nasser sealed his reputation during the Suez crisis of 1956, when he decided to nationalize the Suez Canal and use the money for internal Egyptian projects. When he did not bow to international pressure to provide multinational control of the vital Suez Canal, British, French, and Israeli forces combined to wrest control of the canal away from him. Their military campaign was successful, but they failed miserably on the diplomatic level and tore at the fabric of the bipolar world system. They had not consulted with the United States, which strongly condemned the attack and forced them to withdraw. The Soviet Union also objected forcefully, thereby gaining a reputation for being a staunch supporter of Arab nationalism. Nasser gained tremendous prestige, and Egypt solidified its position as leader of the charge against imperial holdovers in southwest Asia and north Africa. Meanwhile, the Suez crisis further tangled cold war power politics because it divided the United States and its allies in western Europe.

Despite Nasser's successes, he did not manage to rid the region of Israel, which was growing stronger with each passing year. More wars were fought in the decades to come, and peace between the Arab states and Israel seemed not only elusive but at times impossible. Indeed, violence between Israelis and Palestinians—under the leadership of Yasser Arafat's (1929–2004) Palestinian Liberation Organization (PLO)—continued into the 1990s and beyond. A brief break in the violence occurred in 1993 and 1995, when Arafat and Israeli prime minister Yitzhak Rabin (1922–1995) signed peace treaties that advanced the notion of limited Palestinian self-rule in Israeli-occupied territories. Yet the assassination of Rabin in 1995 by a Jewish extremist who opposed the peace agreements, as well as other hurdles, blocked the peace process and led to the resumption of violence in the region.

ISLAMISM In southwest Asia, peace seemed a distant prospect given the political turmoil caused by the presence of Israel in the midst of Arab-Islamic states, many of which allied themselves with the Soviet Union as Israel became a staunch ally of the United States. The region could hardly be ignored by either of the superpowers, because the strategic importance of oil dictated that both superpowers vie for favor—and interfere when necessary—in the Arab states. One response to U.S. and Soviet interference in southwest Asia and north Africa was a revival of Muslim traditions, which found expression in Islamism. At the heart of Islamism was the desire for the reassertion of Islamic values in Muslim politics. Many Muslims had become skeptical about European and American models of economic development and political and cultural norms, which they blamed for economic and political failure as well as the breakdown of traditional social and religious values. The solution to the problems faced by Muslim societies lay, according to Islamists, in the revival of Islamic identity, values, and power.

THE IRANIAN REVOLUTION The Iranian revolution of 1979 demonstrated the power of Islam as a means of staving off secular foreign influences. Islamist influences grew in Iran during the lengthy regime of Shah Mohammed Reza Pahlavi (1919–1980), whom the CIA helped bring to power in 1953. Money from Iran's lucrative oil industry helped finance industrialization under the shah, while the United States provided Iran with the necessary military equipment to fight communism in the region. By the late 1970s, however, opposition to the shah's government was coming from many quarters. Shia Muslims despised the shah's secular regime, Iranian small businesses detested the influence of U.S. corporations on the economy, and leftist politicians rejected the shah's repressive policies. The shah fled the country in early 1979, and power was captured by the Islamist movement under the direction of Ayatollah Ruhollah Khomeini (1900–1989).

The revolution took on a strongly anti-U.S. cast, partly because the shah was allowed to travel to the United States for medical treatment. In retaliation, Shia militants captured sixty-nine hostages at the U.S. embassy in Tehran, fifty-five of whom remained captives until 1981. In the meantime, Iranian leaders shut U.S. military bases and confiscated U.S.-owned economic ventures. This Islamic power play against a developed nation like the United States inspired other Muslims to undertake terrorist actions.

Both cold war politics and decolonization complicated events in southwest Asia in the decades following World War II. The existence of Israel—increasingly supported by the capitalist United States—encouraged the wrath of many Arab leaders who supported Palestinian rights. In addition, interference by both superpowers in the region led some Muslims in the region to turn to a fundamentalist interpretation of Islam as an alternate to the capitalist and communist worldviews.

African Nationalism and Independence

PSI map — Imperialism in Africa
www.mhhe.com/bentleybrief2e

In Africa, as in most of Asia, the increase in the superpowers' global influence after World War II complicated the process of decolonization. Also complicating the decolonization process were internal divisions in African societies, which undermined attempts to forge national or pan-African identities. Tribal, ethnic, religious, and linguistic divides within and between state boundaries, all of which colonial rulers had exploited, posed a challenge to African leaders, particularly once independence came and the imperial enemy departed. Given the variety of barriers to African independence, then, it is not astonishing that independence to all the states in Africa came over the course of several decades—from the late 1950s until 1980.

AFRICAN INDEPENDENCE Agitation for independence in Africa took on many forms, peaceful and violent, and decolonization occurred at a different pace in different nations. Ghana became independent in 1957, but independence came much later—and after bloody conflicts—to Algeria (1962), Angola (1975), and Zimbabwe, formerly Southern Rhodesia (1980). In many instances, African nations sealed their severance from imperial control by adopting new names that shunned the memory of European rule and drew from the glory of Africa's past empires. Ghana set the pattern, and the map of Africa soon featured similar references to precolonial African places: Zambia, Malawi, Zimbabwe.

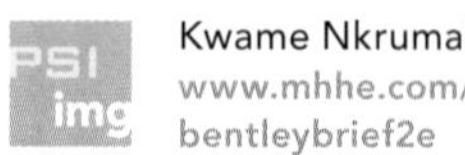

Kwame Nkrumah
www.mhhe.com/bentleybrief2e

GHANA Ghana's success in achieving its freedom from British rule in 1957 served as a hallmark in Africa's end of empire. Under the leadership of Kwame Nkrumah (1909–1972), political parties and strategies for mass action took shape. Although the British initially subjected Nkrumah and other nationalists to jail terms and repressive control, gradually they allowed reforms and negotiated the peaceful transfer of power in their Gold Coast colony. After it became independent in 1957, Ghana emboldened and inspired other African nationalist movements. Nkrumah, as leader of the first sub-Saharan African nation to gain independence from colonial rule, became a persuasive spokesperson for pan-African unity.

ANTICOLONIAL REBELLION IN KENYA The process of attaining independence did not always prove as nonviolent as in Ghana. The battle that took place in the British colony of Kenya in east Africa demonstrated the complexity and difficulty of African decolonization. The situation in Kenya turned tense and violent in a clash between powerful white settlers and nationalists, especially the Kikuyu, one of Kenya's largest ethnic groups. Beginning in 1947, Kikuyu rebels embarked on a violent campaign against Europeans and African collaborators. The settlers who controlled the colonial government in Nairobi refused to see the uprisings as a legitimate expression of discontent with colonial rule. Rather, they branded the Kikuyu tribes as radicals—calling them Mau Mau subversives or communists—bent on a racial struggle for primacy.

Zimbabwe (zihm-BAHB-way)

In reality, Kikuyu radicalism and violence had much more to do with nationalist opposition to British colonial rule, especially land policies in Kenya. In the 1930s and 1940s, white settlers had pushed many Kikuyu off the most fertile highland farm areas and reduced them to the status of wage slaves or relegated them to overcrowded "tribal reserves." Resistance began in the early 1940s with labor strikes and violent direct-action campaigns, but attacks on white settlers and black collaborators escalated in the 1950s. In 1952 the British established a state of emergency to crush the anticolonial guerrilla movement. Unable or unwilling to distinguish violent activism from nonviolent agitation, the British moved to suppress all nationalist groups and jailed Kenya's nationalist leaders, including Jomo Kenyatta (1895–1978) in 1953. Amid growing resistance to colonial rule, the British mounted major military offenses against rebel forces, supporting their army troops with artillery, bombers, and jet fighters. By 1956 the British had effectively crushed all military resistance in a conflict that claimed the lives of tens of thousands of Africans and one hundred Europeans.

The Mau Mau Rebellion. | Rebel suspects in a British internment camp, Nairobi, Kenya.

Despite military defeat, Kikuyu fighters broke British resolve in Kenya and gained increasing international recognition of African grievances. The British resisted the radical white supremacism and political domineering of the settlers in Kenya and instead responded to calls for Kenya's independence. In 1959 the British lifted the state of emergency, and as political parties formed, nationalist leaders like Kenyatta reemerged to lead those parties. By December 1963 Kenya had negotiated its independence.

INTERNAL COLONIALISM IN SOUTH AFRICA As in Kenya, the presence of large numbers of white settlers in South Africa delayed the arrival of black freedom. For decades after World War II, South Africa's majority black population remained dispossessed and disenfranchised. Anticolonial agitation thus was significantly different in South Africa than in the rest of sub-Saharan Africa: it was a struggle against internal colonialism, against an oppressive white regime that denied basic human and civil rights to tens of millions of South Africans.

APARTHEID The ability of whites to resist majority rule had its roots in the South African economy, the strongest on the continent. This strength had two sources: extraction of minerals and industrial development, which received a huge boost during World War II. In 1948, white South Africans—who feared the black activism and political reform that seemed to be stirring in the nation—brought the Afrikaner National Party to power. Under the National Party the government instituted a harsh new set of laws designed to control the restive black population. These new laws constituted the system known as apartheid, or "separateness," which was designed to divide the peoples of South Africa by skin color and ethnicity and to reserve South Africa's resources for whites.

Apartheid, however, generated tremendous resistance to white rule. The African National Congress (ANC), formed in 1912, gained new young leaders like Nelson Mandela (1918–), who inspired direct action campaigns to protest apartheid. Yet because its goals directly challenged white rule, the ANC, along with all other black activists in South Africa, faced severe repression. Indeed, protests against white rule frequently erupted into violence. One notorious incident, for example, occurred in Sharpeville in 1960, when white police killed sixty-nine black demonstrators and wounded almost two hundred others. However, even though government forces captured and imprisoned the leaders of the ANC's military unit in 1963, including Nelson Mandela, protests against the system persisted throughout the 1970s and 1980s.

Whites Telephone Kiosk. | The South African system of apartheid institutionalized racial segregation.

THE END OF APARTHEID Meanwhile, international opposition to oppressive white South African rule grew. Eventually, the combined effects of massive black agitation and a powerful international anti-apartheid boycott led to a growing recognition that if it were to survive, South Africa had to change. Thus, when F. W. de Klerk (1936–) became president of South Africa in 1989, he and the National Party began to dismantle the apartheid system. De Klerk released Mandela from jail in 1990, legalized the ANC, and worked with Mandela and the ANC to negotiate the end of white minority rule. Collaborating and cooperating, the National Party, the ANC, and other African political groups created a new constitution and in April 1994 held elections that were open to people of all races. The ANC won overwhelmingly, and Mandela became the first black president of South Africa. In 1994, as president, he proclaimed his nation "free at last."

THE DEMOCRATIC REPUBLIC OF THE CONGO The experience of some African countries, however, demonstrated the dangers of becoming entangled in cold war politics after World War II. This was the case in the land once known as the Belgian Congo, which was reconfigured as Zaire in 1971 and renamed the Democratic Republic of the Congo in 1997. The region won independence from Belgium in 1960 under the popular leadership of Patrice Lumumba (1925–1961), who was also a Maoist Marxist. The general Mobutu Sese Seko (1930–1997), a contender for power, killed Lumumba the very next year in a military coup supported by the United States. Although Mobutu ruled Zaire as a dictator and devastated the economy in the process of enriching himself, his government continued to receive support from the United States and other European democracies hoping to quell the growth of communism in Africa. Thus the convergence of decolonization with the politics of the cold war helped to undermine the possibilities for lasting stability in an independent Zaire.

Neoimperialism in Latin America

The uneasy path to independence in Asia and Africa also affected states on the other side of the world—states that had gained their freedom from colonial rule more than a century before postwar decolonization but that were still in many ways subject to the grasp of imperialist forces. Indeed, after World War II nations in Central and South America along with Mexico grappled with the conservative legacies of Spanish and Portuguese colonialism, particularly the political and economic power of the landowning elite of European descent. Latin America, moreover, had to deal with neocolonialism, because the United States not only intervened militarily when its interests were threatened but also had long influenced economies through investment and full or part ownership of enterprises like the oil industry.

In addition, during the cold war the establishment of communist and socialist regimes—or the instigation of programs and policies that hinted of anti-Americanism—regularly provoked a response from the United States. To be sure, the United States had insisted on the right to interfere in Latin American affairs since the enunciation of the Monroe Doctrine in 1823, and by the early 1920s Latin America had become the site of fully 40 percent of U.S. foreign investments. Yet after World War II cold war imperatives also shaped many U.S. actions in Latin America.

NICARAGUA A prime example of U.S. intervention based on cold war imperatives was Nicaragua. Anastacio Somoza Garcia (1896–1956) was serving as president of Nicaragua in 1954, just as the CIA was helping Guatemalan rebels overthrow what many believed was a communist-inspired government. During that time, Somoza demonstrated himself to be a staunch U.S. ally by funneling weapons to noncommunist Guatemalan rebels and by outlawing the communist party in Nicaragua. Somoza first grasped power in the 1930s, when members of his Nicaraguan National Guard killed nationalist Augusto Cesar Sandino (1893–1934), who had led a guerrilla movement aimed at ending U.S. interference in Nicaragua. After murdering Sandino, Somoza and his sons controlled Nicaraguan politics for more than forty years, aided by U.S. financial and military support.

IRAN-CONTRA SCANDAL The brutality, corruption, and pro-U.S. policies of the Somoza family alienated other Latin American nations as well as Nicaraguans. In the early 1960s, a few Nicaraguans created the Sandinista Front for National Liberation in honor of the murdered Augusto Sandino. The Sandinistas, as they became known, launched guerrilla operations aimed at overthrowing the Somozas and finally took power in 1979. Although the Sandinistas were recognized by the administration of then president Jimmy Carter, when the staunchly anticommunist Ronald Reagan came to the presidency in 1981 this recognition was reversed. Because Reagan believed that the Sandinistas were helping communist rebels elsewhere in Central America, such as El Salvador, he halted aid to Nicaragua and instituted an economic boycott of the country. Then, in 1983, Reagan offered increasing support—monetary and military—to the Contras, a CIA-trained counterrevolutionary group dedicated to overthrowing the Sandinistas. When a wary U.S. Congress imposed a two-year ban on all military aid to the Contras in 1984, Reagan went outside the law. In 1986, he provided funds for the Contras by using the profits that accrued from secretly selling weapons to Iran—a scandal that became public and highly visible in late 1986 and early 1987. Only with the help of Central American leaders such as Costa Rica's Oscar Arias Sanchez (1940–) and the presence of a UN peacekeeping force, agreed to in 1989, were the Contras effectively disarmed. In the 1990s, new elections made it clear that Sandinista power was weakened but not eliminated despite the extensive interference of the United States.

Both decolonization and the assertion of independence after decolonization were complicated infinitely by the politics and ideologies of the cold war. Indeed, nationalist leaders had to navigate the tricky business of building independent states in the context of an international arena marked by the stark division of the world into capitalist and communist blocs. In areas that attracted the attention of either of the superpowers for strategic reasons, the transition to true independence—whether in Asia, Africa, or Latin America—could be both dangerous and bloody.

From Dissent to Dissolution in the Cold War

Despite the enormous power and influence of the United States and the Soviet Union, their authority was nevertheless challenged on a variety of fronts, both at home and abroad, during the cold war. Yet the desperate competition for military superiority between the two powers ultimately fell more heavily on the shoulders of the Soviet Union, and it struggled with the economic demands such competition imposed. Moreover, decades of oppression within the Soviet bloc led many under its power to desire greater freedom. When these issues converged with the leadership of Mikhail Gorbachev, who sought both economic and political reforms, the Soviet system collapsed with astonishing speed and the cold war came to an abrupt and unexpected end.

Defiance and Intervention in Europe and Beyond

DE-STALINIZATION Some of the most serious challenges to the cold war system came from within the Soviet bloc. This was partly because of Nikita Khrushchev's policy of de-Stalinization, which entailed ending Stalin's reign of terror after his death in 1953 and allowing partial liberalization of Soviet society. Government officials removed portraits of Stalin from public places, renamed localities bearing his name, and commissioned historians to rewrite textbooks to deflate Stalin's reputation. The de-Stalinization period, which lasted from 1956 to 1964, also brought a "thaw" in government control and resulted in the release of millions of political prisoners. With respect to foreign policy,

Khrushchev emphasized the possibility of "peaceful coexistence" between different social systems and the recognition that a nuclear war was more likely to lead to mutual annihilation than to victory. The peaceful coexistence that Khrushchev fostered with the United States appeared to apply to domestic Soviet and eastern European societies also and tempted communist leaders in eastern Europe to experiment with domestic reforms and seek a degree of independence from Soviet domination.

THE HUNGARIAN CHALLENGE The most serious challenge to Soviet control in eastern Europe came in 1956 from nationalist-minded communists in Hungary. When the communist regime in Hungary embraced the process of de-Stalinization, large numbers of Hungarian citizens demanded democracy and the breaking of ties to Moscow and the Warsaw Pact. In the wake of massive street demonstrations joined by the Hungarian armed forces, communist Imre Nagy (1896–1958) gained power and visibility as a nationalist leader who announced Hungary's withdrawal from the Warsaw Pact. Yet there were limits to Soviet tolerance for reform: viewing Hungary's demands as a threat to national security, Soviet officials sent tanks into Budapest and crushed the uprising in the late autumn of 1956.

THE PRAGUE SPRING Twelve years after the Hungarian uprising, Soviets again intervened in eastern Europe, this time in Czechoslovakia. In 1968 the Communist Party leader, Alexander Dubcek (1921–1992), launched a liberal movement known as the "Prague Spring" and promised his fellow citizens "socialism with a human face." But Khrushchev's successor, Leonid Ilyich Brezhnev (1906–1982), fearful that such reforms might undermine Soviet control in eastern Europe, sanctioned military intervention by the Soviet army and brought an end to the Prague Spring. Brezhnev justified the invasion of Czechoslovakia by the doctrine of limited sovereignty, better known as the "Brezhnev doctrine," which reserved the right of the Soviet Union to invade any socialist country that was deemed to be threatened by internal or external elements "hostile to socialism." The destruction of the Prague Spring served to reassert Soviet control over its satellite nations in eastern Europe and led to tightened controls within the Soviet Union.

DETENTE AND COOPERATION In spite of Soviet repression in Europe, by the late 1960s relations between the United States and the Soviet Union had actually improved. Both agreed on a policy of *detente,* or a reduction in hostility, trying to cool the costly arms race and slow their competition in developing countries. Between 1972 and 1974, U.S. and Soviet leaders exchanged visits and signed agreements calling for cooperation in areas such as health research, environmental protection, space ventures, and cultural exchange programs. The spirit of detente was most visible in negotiations designed to reduce the threat posed by strategic nuclear weapons. U.S. and Soviet negotiators concluded their Strategic Arms Limitations Talks (SALT) in 1972 with two agreements and reached another accord in 1979. The two cold war antagonists cooperated despite the tensions caused by the U.S. incursion into Vietnam, Soviet involvement in Angola and other African states, and continued Soviet repression of dissidents in eastern Europe.

THE DEMISE OF DETENTE The spirit of detente deteriorated markedly in the early 1980s, in large part due to Soviet intervention in Afghanistan. In 1978, a pro-Soviet coup in Afghanistan sparked widespread resistance from anticommunist Afghans. By the summer of 1979, antigovernment rebels controlled much of the Afghan countryside and were poised to oust the pro-Soviets from power. At that point the Soviet Union intervened, installing the Marxist Babrak Karmal as president. This Soviet-backed government was highly unpopular, and a national resistance movement spread throughout the country.

For nine years, well-equipped Soviet forces fought a brutal, unsuccessful campaign against Afghan mujahideen, or Islamic warriors, who gradually gained control of most of the countryside. The mujahideen were aided by weapons and money from the United States, Saudi Arabia, Iran, Pakistan, and China—all of whom wished to block Soviet influence in the area. The fact that the United States and the Soviet Union were once again in direct competition for influence—as they had been in Vietnam—crippled relations between the two powers, and U.S. military spending soared under Ronald Reagan in the 1980s. Also as with Vietnam, the participation of the superpowers in the Afghan conflict ensured a long, bloody war that could not be easily won by either side. Finally, in 1986, the Kremlin decided to pull its troops out of the seemingly unwinnable war, having damaged Soviet prestige at huge cost to itself—a cost that it could ill afford if it were to keep up with U.S. military spending. Moreover, the war in Afghanistan increased instability in that country. Five years after the Soviets finally withdrew in 1989, a fundamentalist Islamic group called the Taliban began a campaign to unify Afghanistan. In 1996 they captured the capital of Kabul after an eleven-month siege and proclaimed the Islamic State of Afghanistan.

ENCOUNTERS IN THE COLD WAR AND DECOLONIZATION. Although the United States and the Soviet Union never directly confronted each other in battle during the cold war, the superpowers nevertheless encountered each other—both ideologically and through their proxies in a variety of conflicts—all over the world. In what ways were these encounters shaped by preconceptions each held about the other?

The End of the Cold War

Between 1989 and 1991, the Soviet system in Europe collapsed with stunning speed. This was partly encouraged by U.S. president Ronald Reagan's insistence on massive military spending, which in turn forced the Soviets to spend lavishly on defense when they could least afford it. Yet while Reagan's cold war rhetoric and budgets challenged the Soviet ability to match U.S. spending, internal changes in the Soviet Union and eastern Europe worked most effectively to end communism and the cold war. Between 1989 and 1990, through a series of mostly nonviolent revolutions, the peoples of eastern and central Europe regained their independence, instituted democratic forms of government, and adopted market-based economies.

The downfall of communist regimes in Europe was the direct consequence of interrelated economic and political developments. The economic weakness of the communist regimes in eastern and central Europe and the Soviet Union became so apparent as to require reforms. The policies espoused by Soviet leader Mikhail Gorbachev (1931–), who came to power in 1985, represented an effort to address this economic deterioration, but they also unleashed a tidal wave of revolution that brought down governments from Czechoslovakia to the Soviet Union. As communism unraveled throughout eastern and central Europe, Gorbachev desperately tried to save the Soviet Union from disintegration by restructuring the economy and liberalizing society. Caught between the rising tide of radical reforms and the opposition of entrenched interests, however, there was little he could do except watch as events unfolded beyond his control. By the time the Soviet Union collapsed in 1991, the cold war system of states and alliances had become irrelevant to international relations.

GORBACHEV'S IMPACT When Gorbachev came into office, much of eastern and central Europe was seething with discontent. While early hopes for reform had been dashed in the 1950s and 1960s, Gorbachev's leadership brought new hope to many. Indeed, in light of Soviet economic stagnation and political discontent, Gorbachev had already committed himself to a restructuring of the Soviet Union and to unilateral withdrawal from the cold war. In public interviews he surprised his grim-faced hosts with the announcement that the Brezhnev doctrine was no longer in force and that from then on each country would be responsible for its own destiny. The new Soviet orientation led in rapid succession to the collapse or overthrow of regimes in Poland, Bulgaria, Hungary, Czechoslovakia, Romania, and East Germany.

REVOLUTIONS IN EASTERN EUROPE The end of communism came first in Poland, where Solidarity—a combined trade union and nationalist movement—put pressure on the crumbling rule of the Communist Party. The Polish government legalized the previously banned Solidarity movement and agreed to multiparty elections in 1989 and 1990. The voters favored Solidarity candidates, and Lech Walesa (1943–), the movement's leader, became president of Poland. In Bulgaria popular unrest forced Todor

Lech Walesa (LEHK wah-LEHN-sah)

THE FALL OF THE BERLIN WALL. Berliners climb the wall after it fell on 9 November 1989. ***Why might it have been so symbolically important to stand on the wall?***

Zhivkov (1911–1998), eastern Europe's longest surviving communist dictator, to resign in November 1989. Two months later a national assembly began dismantling the communist state. In 1990 Hungarians also held free elections and launched their nation on the rocky path toward democracy and a market economy.

The disintegration of communism continued elsewhere in eastern Europe. In Czechoslovakia a "velvet revolution"—so called because it entailed little violence—swept communists out of office and restored democracy in 1990. In 1993 disagreements over the time frame for shifting to a market economy led to a "velvet divorce," breaking Czechoslovakia into two new nations, the Czech Republic and Slovakia. In Romania, by contrast, the regime of dictator Nicolae Ceauşescu (1918–1989) savagely repressed demonstrations, setting off a national uprising that ended within four days and left Ceauşescu and his wife dead.

East Germany had long been a staunchly communist Soviet satellite. Its aging leader, Erich Honecker (1912–1994), openly clung to Stalinist policies. It was too late for anything other than radical changes, however. Honecker's own party removed him from power and decided to open the Berlin Wall to intra-German traffic on 9 November 1989. The end to a divided Berlin was in sight, literally, as thousands of East and West Berliners tore down the Berlin Wall in the last weeks of 1989. In 1990 the two Germanies, originally divided by the cold war, formed a united nation.

The Collapse of the Soviet Union

The desire to concentrate attention and resources on urgent matters at home motivated Gorbachev's decision to disengage his nation from the cold war and its military and diplomatic extensions. Although he never intended to abolish the existing political and economic system, it proved impossible to fix parts of the system without undermining the whole.

GORBACHEV'S REFORMS Gorbachev's reform efforts focused on the ailing economy. Antiquated industrial plants and obsolete technologies resulted in shoddy and outmoded products, and in any case the diversion of crucial resources to the military made it impossible to produce enough consumer goods. The failure of state and collective farms to feed the population compelled the Soviet government to import grains from the United States, Canada, and elsewhere. In 1990 the government imposed rationing to cope with the scarcity of essential consumer goods and food. Economic stagnation in turn contributed to the decline of the Soviet standard of living and the disintegration of the state-sponsored health care system. Funding of the educational system dropped precipitously, and pollution threatened to engulf the entire country. Demoralization affected ever larger numbers of Soviet citizens as divorce rates climbed, corruption intensified, and alcoholism became more widespread.

PERESTROIKA AND GLASNOST When it was clear that the old methods of boosting productivity through bureaucratic exhortation and harassment would not work, Gorbachev contemplated different kinds of reform, using the term *perestroika,* or "restructuring," to describe his efforts to decentralize the economy. To make perestroika work, the Soviet leader linked it to *glasnost,* a term that referred to the opening of Soviet society to public criticism and admission of past mistakes.

perestroika (payr-eh-STROY-kuh)
glasnost (GLAHS-nost)

MAP 33.5 | The collapse of the Soviet Union and European communist regimes, 1991. Note the number of states suddenly created by the breakup of the Soviet Union. ***How would this affect the ability of each to survive, both economically and politically?***

The Baltic states of Estonia, Latvia, and Lithuania were the first to declare independence from the Soviet Union.

COLLAPSE By the summer of 1990, it was clear that Gorbachev's reforms could not halt the downward slide of industrial and agricultural production or control skyrocketing inflation. As the Soviet economy disintegrated, many minorities contemplated secession from the Soviet Union. The Baltic peoples—Estonians, Latvians, and Lithuanians—were first into the fray, declaring their independence in August 1991. In the following months the remaining twelve republics of the Soviet Union followed suit. The largest and most prominent of the Soviet republics, the Russian Soviet Federated Socialist Republic, and its recently elected president, Boris N. Yeltsin (1931–), led the drive for independence. Soviet leaders vacillated between threats of repression and promises of better treatment, but neither option could stop the movement for independence. On 25 December 1991 the Soviet flag fluttered for the last time atop the Kremlin, and by the last day of that year the Union of Soviet Socialist Republics had ceased to exist.

In many ways the cold war provided comfort to the world—however cold that comfort seemed at the time. World War II left most of the major imperialist, fascist, and militarist nations in shambles, and the United States and the Soviet Union stepped into what could have been an uncomfortable vacuum in global leadership. Perilous and controlling it may have been, but the cold war that resulted from the ideological contest between the superpowers had ordered and defined the world for almost fifty years. The cold war also shaped how the nations and peoples of the world perceived themselves—as good capitalists fighting evil communists, as progressive socialists battling regressive capitalists, or as nonaligned peoples striving to follow their own paths. Although these perceptions placed constraints on the choices open to them, particularly given the control exerted by the United States and the USSR at the peak of their power, the choices nonetheless were familiar. At the end of the cold war, those easy choices disappeared. Indeed, the end of the cold war suggested the possibility of a radical shift in power relations, a global realignment that marked a new era of world history devoid of the categories embraced during the cold war.

SUMMARY

In the years immediately before and after World War II, a few nations controlled the political and economic destiny of much of the world. The decades following 1945 witnessed the stunning reversal of this state of affairs, as two new superpowers emerged and as European empires fell. The cold war that ensued began first in Europe but quickly spread to the world stage in places as far afield as Cuba, Vietnam, and the Congo. As European empires fell, tens of new nations struggled for independence in the midst of the cold war. While nearly every quest for independence was eventually realized, the cold war both complicated and shaped the course of events in many decolonizing and newly independent states. Yet resistance to superpower dominance occurred in many nations desiring true independence, and also from within the superpower societies themselves. These challenges put enormous strains on the cold war system, which continually demanded enormous expenditures for military defense. In the 1980s, strains within the Soviet bloc caused the sudden and unexpected collapse of the Soviet Union. With its collapse came an end to an alliance system that had dominated world affairs since the end of World War II as well as the reformation, once again, of national boundaries.

STUDY TERMS

Berlin Wall (660)
cold war (659)
containment (664)
Cuban missile crisis (664)
decolonization (666)
de-Stalinization (677)
detente (678)
domestic containment (662)
domino theory (664)
Gamal Abdel Nasser (672)
glasnost (680)
Great Leap Forward (670)
Great Proletarian Cultural Revolution (670)
Ho Chi Minh (668)
Iran-Contra scandal (677)
Iranian revolution (673)
iron curtain (659)
Islamism (673)
Israel (672)
Korean conflict (662)
Kwame Nkrumah (674)
MAD (661)
Mao Zedong (669)
Mau Mau rebellion (674)
Mikhail Gorbachev (679)
NATO (660)
nonalignment (668)
Palestinian Liberation Organization (673)
perestroika (680)
Sandinistas (677)
Sputnik (661)
Suez crisis (673)
velvet revolution (680)
Warsaw Pact (660)

FOR FURTHER READING

Franz Ansprenger. *The Dissolution of the Colonial Empires.* New York, 1989. A discerning and thorough treatment of the dismantling of European empires and colonies.

Michael J. Cohen. *Palestine and the Great Powers 1945–48.* 2nd ed. Princeton, 1992. An evenhanded assessment of the role played by the great powers in the partition of Palestine and the creation of Israel.

Prasenjit Duara, ed. *Decolonization (Rewriting Histories).* New York, 2004. The perspective of the colonized is privileged through a selection of writings by leaders of the colonizing countries.

John Lewis Gaddis. *The Cold War: A New History.* New York, 2005. A fresh and concise history of the cold war by the dean of cold war historians.

Akira Iriye. *The Cold War in Asia: A Historical Introduction.* Englewood Cliffs, N.J., 1974. A leading diplomatic historian provides an excellent introduction to the subject.

Madeline Kalb. *The Congo Cables: The Cold War in Africa—From Eisenhower to Kennedy.* New York, 1982. Proper attention for an often neglected aspect of the cold war.

Bruce Kuniholm. *The Origins of the Cold War in the Near East.* Princeton, 1980. A dissection of great power diplomacy and conflicts that focuses on Greece, Turkey, and Iran.

Robert A. Mortimer. *The Third World Coalition in International Politics.* New York, 1980. Surveys the political evolution of the nonaligned world.

Thomas E. Skidmore and Peter H. Smith. *Modern Latin America.* New York, 1992. Excellent overview covering the region from the 1880s to the 1980s and supported by an extensive bibliography.

Odd Arne Westad. *The Global War: Third World Interventions and the Making of Our Times.* New York, 2005. Integrates the Third World into the history of the cold war by tracing U.S. and Soviet interventions.

A World without Borders

34

n 9 November 1989, Kristina Matschat felt excitement and tension in the night air of Berlin. She had joined thousands of other East Germans at Checkpoint Charlie, one of the most famous crossing points in the Berlin Wall. Anticipating that the wall might come down that night, she also shivered in fear at the proximity of the *Volkspolizei* ("people's police")—the same officers who since 1961 had gunned down East Germans attempting to scale the wall and escape to freedom in West Berlin. She wore running shoes in case she needed to sprint away if shooting broke out.

She remembered that "everybody was full of fear—but also full of hope." Her hope overcame her fears, though, as she chanted with her fellow compatriots, "Tear the wall down! Open the gates!" Just before midnight East German soldiers suddenly began not only opening gates in the wall but also gently helping East Germans cross to the West, often for the first time in their lives. Her near disbelief at the swift downfall of Berlin's decades-old barricade registered in the word she heard shouted over and over again by those passing through the wall: *Wahnsinn* ("craziness").

Kristina Matschat remained at the wall until 3:00 or 4:00 A.M., celebrating with hundreds of thousands of other Berliners. While celebrating the fall of the barbed wire and mortar structure, she became aware of the significance of a world without borders: "Suddenly we were seeing the West for the first time, the forbidden Berlin we had only seen on TV or heard about from friends. When we came home at dawn, I felt free for the first time in my life. I had never been happier." The fall of the Berlin Wall brought down one of the world's most notorious borders and symbolized the breaching of all sorts of boundaries in the contemporary world.

« This stunning digitally crafted photograph, called "Omnipotent Technology" (1999), blurs the boundaries between art and reality. Its composition of an ethnically fluid face from computer chips and hardware suggests how global identity has morphed and how computers have breached borders between humans and machines.

Along with decolonization, the fall of the Berlin Wall, and the end of the cold war, many other forces were at work to create a new, more open world. One pronounced feature of this world was an increased level of economic interaction between countries and a tighter economic integration of the world. The forces driving the world economy in this direction, often referred to as *globalization,* included advances in communication technology, an enormous expansion of international trade, and the emergence of new global enterprises as well as governments and international organizations that favored market-oriented economics. Global economic interaction and integration were

CHRONOLOGY

1947	Establishment of GATT
1948	UN adopts Universal Declaration of Human Rights
1950	World population at 2.5 billion
1960	Introduction of birth control pill
1960	Creation of OPEC
1967	Establishment of ASEAN
1967	Birth of European Community
1981	Identification of AIDS
1992	Beginning of socialist market economy in China
1993	Establishment of NAFTA
1995	WTO supersedes GATT
2000	World population at 6 billion
2001	China joins WTO
2001	Terrorist attacks against the United States
2003	Operation Iraqi Freedom

not new in world history, of course, but the more recent phenomenon of globalization has been different and unprecedented in both scope and speed, and it has the potential to fundamentally transform the world.

Although many formal national borders changed only after decolonization and the end of the cold war, cultural and technological developments since World War II had steadily broken down the distances between countries and peoples. Consumer goods, popular culture, television, computers, and the Internet all spread outward from advanced capitalist and industrialized nations, particularly Europe and the United States, and other societies had to come to terms with this breakdown of cultural and technological barriers.

The world's peoples also underwent changes in a world with fewer barriers. Women struggled to close the divide between the sexes, while both women and men embarked on migrations when their societies could no longer adequately support their growing populations. The populations moving around the globe revealed the diminishing significance of national boundary lines, but they also posed problems that could not be solved by any one state acting alone. International organizations such as the United Nations acknowledged that global problems like epidemic diseases, labor servitude, terrorism, and human rights crossed national boundaries and required global solutions. Indeed, as Kristina Matschat discovered at the fall of the Berlin Wall, by the late twentieth century global interconnectedness made it more difficult to maintain boundaries among the peoples and countries of the world.

THE GLOBAL ECONOMY

The global economy came into sharp focus after the spectacular collapse of communism in 1990. Economists pointed to a new economic order characterized by the expansion of trade between countries, the growth of foreign investments, the unfettered movement of capital, the privatization of former state enterprises, and the emergence of a new breed of corporations. Supporting the new global economy were technological developments in communications that have virtually eliminated geographic distances, causing an ever-faster integration of the market economy. The forces driving the world economy toward increased economic integration have been responsible for a process termed *globalization.*

Economic Globalization

FREE TRADE International trade proved to be a key driving force behind economic globalization. Although trade across long distances has figured prominently as an integrating force in the shaping of human history, the idea of *free trade*—meaning freedom from state-imposed limits and constraints on trade across borders—is of more recent origin. In the aftermath of World War II, leaders from industrialized nations, especially from the United States, took a decisive stand on the issue.

GATT AND WTO U.S. politicians and business leaders wanted to establish an international trading system that suited their interests, and they pushed for the elimination of restrictive trading practices that stood in the way of free trade. At the Bretton Woods Conference in New Hampshire in 1944, they established the International Monetary Fund (IMF) to promote market economies, free trade, and high growth rates. However, the main vehicle for the promotion of unrestricted global trade was the General Agreement on Tariffs and Trade (GATT), which was signed by the representatives of 23 noncommunist nations in 1947. GATT members held a series of negotiations with the intent of removing or loosening barriers to free trade. After the round of negotiations that ended in 1994, the member nations of GATT (now totaling 123) signed an agreement to establish the World Trade Organization (WTO), which took over the activities of GATT in 1995. The WTO has developed into a forum for settling international trade disputes, with the power to enforce its decisions. Since the establishment of GATT, world trade has increased dramatically: world trade grew by 6.6 percent annually between 1948 and 1966 and by 9.2 percent annually between 1966 and 1977. Although trade slowed in the 1980s, by 1990 world trade exceeded six trillion U.S. dollars, roughly double the figure for 1980.

PSI map International organizations www.mhhe.com/bentleybrief2e

GLOBAL CORPORATIONS The emergence of a new breed of corporation played another key role in the development of the new economic order. Global corporations have increasingly replaced the more traditional international or multinational forms of corporate enterprises. Whereas multinational corporations conducted their business in several countries and had to operate within the confines of specific laws and customs of a given society, global corporations rely on a small headquarters staff while dispersing all other corporate functions across the globe in search of the lowest possible operating costs. Global corporations treat the world as a single market and act as if the nation-state no longer exists. Many multinational corporations, such as General Motors, Siemens AG, and Nestlé, have transformed themselves into global enterprises, both benefiting from and contributing to the ongoing process of globalization. Indeed, during the past twenty-five years, the transformation of the corporate landscape has resulted in the birth of some fifty thousand global corporations.

Global corporations have become the symbols of the new economy because they have transformed the political and social landscape of many societies. During the past fifty-five years, multinational corporations throughout the developed world operated under the legal constraints of the nations where they were located, which meant that they were bound by national tax laws, union agreements, and environmental regulations. Highly mobile global corporations that are no longer bound to any particular location have managed, however, to escape those obligations. For example, global corporations have moved jobs from high-wage facilities to foreign locations where wages are low and environmental laws are weak or nonexistent. The implications of this development are serious. For example, U.S. federal tax receipts show that corporations that once paid 30 percent of all federal taxes now pay only 12 percent. This trend is not confined to the United States but is visible throughout the industrialized world. In all instances, declining corporate taxes mean less money for social services and welfare programs.

ECONOMICS IN ART FORM. | This image of a "balanced world economy" (1996) artistically expresses the precariousness of economic globalization.

Economic Growth in Asia

Globalization and the speeding up of worldwide economic integration also benefited from economic developments in east and southeast Asia, where the economies of Japan, China, and the so-called Asian tigers underwent dramatic growth.

JAPAN U.S. policies jump-started Japan's economic revival after its defeat in 1945, and by 1949 the Japanese economy had already attained its prewar level of productivity. Just as western European countries had benefited from the Marshall Plan, so Japan benefited from direct U.S. financial aid ($2 billion), investment, and the timely abandonment of war reparations. In addition, there were no restrictions on the entry of Japanese products into the U.S. market. And, because a 1952 mutual defense treaty stipulated that Japan could never spend more than 1 percent of its gross national product on defense, Japan's postwar leaders channeled the nation's savings into economic development.

Although Japan had lost its overseas empire and was hampered by a large population and a lack of natural resources, its economic planners sidestepped those disadvantages by promoting an economic policy that emphasized export-oriented growth supported by low wages. Low wages in turn gave Japanese employers a competitive edge over international rivals.

Initially, the Japanese economy churned out labor-intensive manufactured goods such as textiles, iron, and steel slated for export to markets with high labor costs, particularly the United States. By the 1970s, however, Japanese corporations were shifting their economic resources toward technology-intensive products such as random-access memory chips, liquid crystal displays, and CD-ROM drives. By that time the label "Made in Japan," once associated with cheap manufactured goods, signified state-of-the-art products of the highest quality. Indeed, by the 1980s Japan seemed poised to overtake the United States as the world's largest economy. Even though the Japanese economy sputtered into a recession that has continued into the twenty-first century, the Japanese success story nevertheless served as an inspiration for other Asian countries.

THE LITTLE TIGERS The earliest and most successful imitators of the Japanese model for economic development were Hong Kong, Singapore, South Korea, and Taiwan. Their remarkable and rapid growth rates earned them the nickname of the "four little tigers," and by the 1980s these newly industrializing countries had become major economic powers.

Like Japan, all four countries lacked natural resources and had to cope with overpopulation. But like Japan a generation earlier, they transformed apparent disadvantages into advantages through a program of export-driven industrialization. By the 1990s the four little tigers were no longer simply imitators of Japan but had become serious competitors. Before long, Indonesia, Thailand, and Malaysia joined the original tigers in their quest for economic development and prosperity.

THE RISE OF CHINA China provides yet another economic success story. In the aftermath of Mao Zedong's disastrous economic policies in the 1960s and 1970s, China's leaders launched economic reforms that reversed some earlier policies and opened Chinese markets to the outside world, encouraged foreign investment, and imported foreign technology. By 1992, it was clear that the planned economic system of the past had given way to a market economy. Besides acting as a major exporter, China benefited from its large pool of cheap labor, and its enormous domestic markets have made the Chinese economy the destination of choice for foreign investment capital. In December 2001 China became a member of the World Trade Organization and moved closer to gaining global economic superpower status.

PERILS OF THE NEW ECONOMY For the supporters of the new global economy, the spectacular economic development of so many Asian societies was proof that globalization could deliver on the promise of unprecedented prosperity. However, a financial crisis that came to a head in 1997 also pointed to the perils of the new global economy. In the preceding twenty years, the developing Asian economies had started to embrace the market, opening their borders to imports and courting foreign investments. After years of generous lending and growing national debts, the international investment community suddenly lost confidence in the booming economies and withdrew support. The crisis began in Thailand in mid-1997, when investments that once easily poured into the country now left it equally quickly, causing the Thai stock market to lose 75 percent of its value and plunging the nation into depression. From there, the financial panic spread to Malaysia, Indonesia, the Philippines, and South Korea. In each instance, the rise and fall of the individual economies resulted from their integration into the new global economy, which rewarded and punished its new participants with equal ease.

EMERGING ECONOMIES IN ASIA AND BEYOND Contrary to all expectations, the nations hit so hard by the financial crisis recovered quickly. Their recovery was matched by other emerging economies, including Brazil, China, India, Mexico, Russia, eastern European nations, and several countries in Africa. In 2005 these emerging economies accounted for over half of global economic output. During the first five years of the twenty-first century, the annual growth rate of emerging economies averaged almost 7 percent—the fastest pace on record. Experts predict that by 2040 the world's ten largest economies will include Brazil, China, India, Mexico, and Russia. In addition, the IMF predicts that China will surpass the United States as the world's largest economy within the next three decades. What all this means is that the rich, developed countries no longer dominate the global economy the way they did during the nineteenth and twentieth centuries. This shift is not as astonishing as it first seems, as some of today's emerging economies—especially China and India—are simply regaining their pre–nineteenth-century preeminence.

Trading Blocs

Accepting free trade and open markets meant acknowledging global economic interdependence; no single economic power could fully control global trade and commerce. In the rapidly changing global economy, groups of nations have therefore entered into economic alliances designed to achieve advantages and greater strength for their partners in the competitive global economy.

EUROPEAN UNION The most famous and most strongly integrated regional bloc is the European Union. In March 1957, representatives of six nations—France, West Germany, Italy, the Netherlands, Belgium, and Luxembourg—established the European Economic Community (renamed the European Community in 1967). At the heart of this new community of nations lay the dismantling of tariffs and other barriers to free trade among member nations. In 1993, the Maastricht Treaty took a further step toward economic and political integration by creating the European Union. Twenty-seven European nations have submerged much of their national sovereignty in the European Union, and since 1999 thirteen members have adopted a common currency. In the future, this tight economic integration is expected to lead to a European Political Union.

OPEC One of the earliest and most successful economic alliances was the Organization of Petroleum Exporting Countries (OPEC), a producer cartel established in 1960 by the oil-producing states of Iran, Iraq, Kuwait, Saudi Arabia, and Venezuela, and later joined by Qatar, Libya, Indonesia, Abu Dhabi, Algeria, Nigeria, Ecuador, and Gabon. The mostly Arab and Muslim member states of OPEC sought to raise the price of oil through cooperation, but OPEC demonstrated during the Arab-Israeli War of 1973 that cooperation had political as well as economic potential. The cartel ordered an embargo on oil shipments to the United States, Israel's ally, and quadrupled the price of oil between 1973 and 1975. The huge increase in the cost of petroleum triggered a global economic downturn, as did a curtailment of oil exports in the later 1970s. OPEC's influence diminished in the 1980s and 1990s as a result of overproduction and dissension among its members over the Iran-Iraq War and the Gulf War.

ASEAN Another well-established economic partnership is the Association of Southeast Asian Nations, or ASEAN. Established in 1967 by the foreign ministers of Thailand, Malaysia, Singapore, Indonesia, and the Philippines, it had as its principal objectives

MAP 34.1 | European Union membership, 2004. In 2007 the European Union celebrated the fiftieth anniversary of its founding as a supranational and intergovernmental organization that encompasses twenty-seven member states. ***What major challenge faced the European Union in the twenty-first century?***

Note that the founding member states were contiguous.

accelerating economic development and promoting political stability in southeast Asia. In 1992 member states agreed to establish a free-trade zone and to cut tariffs on industrial goods over a fifteen-year period.

NAFTA The United States, although still home to the largest national economy in the world, also saw the need to become involved in regional trade groupings. The United States entered its own regional alliance, approving the North American Free Trade Agreement (NAFTA) with Canada and Mexico in 1993. NAFTA, which went into effect in 1994, constitutes the world's second-largest free-trade zone, but it lacks the economic coordination so typical of the European Union. There are plans to expand NAFTA to all noncommunist nations in the Americas, underscoring the increasing commitment to the elimination of tariffs and other barriers to regional and global free trade.

GLOBALIZATION AND ITS CRITICS The global economy is still very much a work in progress, and it is not clear what the long-term effects will be on the economies and societies it touches. Proponents of globalization argue that the new economy is the only way to bring prosperity—the kind previously enjoyed only by industrialized nations—to the developing world. Critics of globalization, in contrast, argue that globalization diminishes the sovereignty of local and national governments and transfers that power to transnational corporations and global institutions such as the IMF and the WTO. Detractors of globalization also claim that the hallmark of globalization—rapid economic development—is responsible for the destruction of the environment, the widening gap between rich and poor societies, and the worldwide homogenization of local, diverse, and indigenous cultures.

Cross-Cultural Exchanges and Global Communications

The demise of European colonial empires, the fall of the Berlin Wall, and the end of the cold war brought down the most obvious political barriers of the post–World War II world. Long before then, however, cultural and technological developments had started a similar process of breaching boundaries. Indeed, cultural practices have become increasingly globalized, thriving on a continuous flow of information, ideas, tastes, and values. At the turn of the twentieth century, local traditions—commonly derived from gender, social class, or religious affiliation—still determined the cultural identity of the vast majority of people. At the end of the twentieth century, thanks in part to advances in technology and communications, information and cultural practices were becoming truly global. Their impact was summarized in a jingle popularized by the Walt Disney corporation during the 1964–1965 World's Fair in New York City: "It's a small world after all."

Consumption and Cultural Interaction

New communications media have tied the world together and have promoted a global cultural integration whose hallmark is consumption. Although the desire to consume is hardly new, the modern consumer culture has become a means of self-expression as well as a source for personal identity and social differentiation. The peculiar shape of this consumer culture resulted from two seemingly contradictory trends: a tendency toward homogenization of cultural products and heightened awareness of local tastes and values.

AMERICANIZATION Critics sometimes refer to the homogenizing aspect of global culture as the "Americanization" or "McDonaldization" of the world. Those terms suggest that the consumer culture that developed in the United States during the mid–twentieth century has been exported throughout the world. Indeed, nothing symbolizes the global marketing of U.S. mass culture more than the spread of its food and beverage products. While Pepsi and Coca-Cola fight battles over the few places on earth that their beverages have not yet dominated, fast-food restaurants such as Burger King, McDonald's, and Starbucks sell their standardized foods throughout the world. So successful has the

GLOBALIZATION. In this photo, the golden arches of McDonald's fast-food restaurant rise against the skyline of Shenzhen, China. ***What effects might the spread of restaurants such as these have on the economies and cultures of distant lands?***

global spread of U.S. mass culture been that it seems to threaten local or indigenous cultures everywhere.

The export of U.S. products and services is not the sole determinant of global cultural practices, however. Because the contemporary consumer culture encourages consumers to make purchase decisions based on brand names designed to evoke particular tastes, fashions, or lifestyles, it also fosters differentiation. Indeed, global marketing often emphasizes the local value of a product. For example, genuinely Australian products, such as Foster's Lager, have become international commodities precisely because they are Australian in origin.

Experiences in Latin America have also indicated that the sharing or imposing of cultural practices is a two-way phenomenon. A trend in Latin America is Music Television (MTV) Latino, which was initially perceived by many critics as another case of foreign cultural intrusion. Yet by the 1990s many critics had relaxed their guard. They saw evidence of increased cultural sharing among Latin societies, noting that MTV and cable television have come to serve as a means of communication and unity by making the nations of Latin America more aware of one another. While the sheer dominance and size of the U.S. entertainment-technology industry keeps cultural sharing lopsided, cultural dominance is also limited by those societies' ability to blend and absorb a variety of foreign and indigenous practices.

The Age of Access

Throughout history technological advances such as in shipbuilding have provided the means to dissolve boundaries between localities and peoples and thus allowed cultural transmission to take place. Today virtually instantaneous electronic communications have dissolved time and space. Contemporary observers have labeled our era "the age of access." Communication by radio, telephone, television, and networked computers has swept away the social, economic, and political isolation of the past. However, because it takes capital to purchase the necessary equipment, maintain and upgrade it, and train people to use it, many societies find it difficult to participate in the communications revolution. The resulting gulf between the connected and the unconnected has the potential therefore to become one border in a world without physical borders.

This new world of global interconnectedness is not without its detractors. Critics have charged, for instance, that mass media are a vehicle for cultural imperialism because most electronic media and the messages they carry emanate from advanced capitalist societies. A specific consequence is that English is becoming the primary language of global communications systems, effectively restricting vernacular languages to a niche status.

ADAPTATIONS OF TECHNOLOGY Yet some societies have managed to adapt European and U.S. technology to meet their needs while opposing cultural interference. Television, for example, has been used to promote state building around the world, since most television industries are state controlled. In Zaire, for example, the first television picture residents saw each day was of Mobutu Sese Seko. He especially liked to materialize in segments that pictured him walking on clouds—a miraculous vision of his unearthly power. Likewise, the revolution in electronic communications has been rigidly controlled in other societies—including Vietnam and Iraq—where authorities limit access to foreign servers on the Internet. They thus harness the power of technology for their own purposes while avoiding cultural interference.

THINKING ABOUT *Traditions*

TRADITIONS IN A WORLD WITHOUT BORDERS. In spite of the pressures of a global market, international consumerism, and the Internet, not all of the world's communities are willing to accept the values and practices of a world without borders. In what ways have some societies used religious, national, or ideological traditions to resist globalization?

GLOBAL PROBLEMS

By the end of the twentieth century, many traditional areas of state responsibility—whether pertaining to population policies, health concerns, or environmental issues—needed to be coordinated on an intergovernmental level. Global problems demanded global solutions, and together they compelled the governments of individual states to surrender some of their sovereignty to larger international organizations such as the United Nations. Issues concerning labor servitude, poverty, epidemic diseases, terrorism, and human rights demanded attention and action on a scale greater than that of the nation-state.

Population Pressures and Environmental Degradation

The past hundred years or so have been accompanied by vast population increases. As the result of advances in agriculture, industry, science, medicine, and social organization, the world experienced a fivefold population increase over a period of three hundred years: from 500 million people in 1650 to 2.5 billion in 1950. By 2005 roughly 6.5 billion people shared the planet, and the population division of the United Nations has estimated that the earth's population will stabilize around 9 billion in 2050.

A large population changes the earth and its environment, raising an important question: How many people can the earth support? The exact carrying capacity of the planet is, of course, a matter of debate, but by many measures the earth seems to strain already to support the current population. Scientists and concerned citizens have become increasingly convinced that human society cannot infinitely expand beyond the physical limits of the earth and its resources. For that reason, many governments have taken action to control fertility. In fact, some eighty countries to date have adopted birth control programs.

ENVIRONMENTAL IMPACT Indeed, the prodigious growth of the human population is at the root of many environmental problems. As people are born, pollution levels increase, more habitats and animal and plant species disappear, and more natural resources are consumed. In recent decades, two environmental issues have taken center stage: biodiversity and global warming. Biodiversity relates to the maintenance of multiple species of plants and animals. The most serious threat to biodiversity emerged from the destruction of natural habitats in the wake of urbanization, extension of agricultural activity, and exploitation of mineral and timber resources. Extinction currently threatens some 4,500 animal species.

Global warming refers to a rise in global temperature, which carries potentially dire consequences for humanity. Atmospheric pollution causes global warming because the emission of greenhouse gases prevents solar heat from escaping from the earth's atmosphere, leading to a rise in global temperatures. Even a seemingly modest rise of 1 to 3 degrees Celsius in

TABLE 34.1 **Population (in Millions) for Major Areas of the World, 1900–2050**

Major Area	1900	1950	1975	2005	2050
Africa	133	224	416	906	1937
Asia	947	1396	2395	3905	5217
Europe	408	547	676	728	653
Latin America	74	167	322	561	783
North America	82	172	243	331	438
Oceania	6	13	21	33	48
World (total)	1650	2519	4074	6465	9076

SOURCE: *World Population Prospects: The 2004 Revision. Highlights.* New York: United Nations, 2005.

the temperature of the atmosphere might have serious consequences, such as a rise in sea levels that would completely inundate low-lying islands and coastal areas on all continents. In the ancient Japanese capital of Kyoto, at a conference dedicated to pressing environmental problems, the delegates of 159 countries agreed in 1997 to cut greenhouse gas emissions blamed for global warming. However, the conference did not require developing countries—some of them major polluters, such as India and China—to reduce their emissions.

DEFORESTATION. | This scene from Pantanal, Brazil, depicts the massive deforestation taking place in the region. In the background, the intact forest contrasts sharply with the denuded areas of the foreground.

Economic Inequities and Labor Servitude

The unequal distribution of resources and income and the resulting poverty have materialized as key concerns of the contemporary world. Several hundred million people, especially in the developing areas of eastern Europe, Africa, Latin America, and Asia, struggle daily for sufficient food, clean water, adequate shelter, and other basic necessities. Malnutrition among the poor has led to starvation and death and is also responsible for stunted growth, poor mental development, and high rates of infection. Because of inadequate shelter, lack of safe running water, and the absence of sewage facilities, the poor have also been exposed disproportionately to bacteria and viruses. Poverty has correlated strongly with higher-than-average infant mortality rates and lower-than-average life expectancies.

GLOBAL HAVES AND HAVE-NOTS The division between rich and poor has been a defining characteristic of all complex societies. Although relative poverty levels within a given society remain a major concern, a worldwide shortage of natural resources as well as the uneven distribution of resources has divided the world's nations into haves and have-nots. In part, the unequal distribution of resources in the world economy has resulted from five hundred years of colonialism, and it is certainly true that pervasive poverty characterizes many former colonies and dependencies. All of these developing societies have tried to raise income levels and eliminate poverty through diversified economic development, but only a few, such as South Korea, Singapore, Malaysia, and Indonesia, have accomplished their aims. In the meantime, economic globalization has generated unprecedented wealth for developed nations, creating an even deeper divide between rich and poor countries.

LABOR SERVITUDE Poor economic conditions have been closely associated with forms of servitude similar to slavery. Although legal slavery no longer exists, forced and bonded labor practices continue to affect millions of poor people in the developing world. Of particular concern is child-labor servitude. Currently, more than 250 million children between ages five and fourteen work around the world, many in conditions that are inherently harmful to their physical health and emotional well-being. Child-labor servitude is most pronounced in south and southeast Asia, affecting an estimated 50 million children in India alone. Most child labor occurs in agriculture, domestic service, family businesses, and the sex trade, making it difficult to enforce existing prohibitions and laws against those practices.

HUMAN TRAFFICKING A growing and related global problem that touches societies on every continent is the trafficking of persons. In this insidious form of modern slavery, one to two million human beings annually are bought and sold across international and within national boundaries. In Russia and the Ukraine, for example, traffickers lure victims with the promise of well-paying jobs abroad. Once the victims arrive in the countries of their destination, they become captives of ruthless traffickers who force them into bonded labor, domestic servitude, or the commercial sex industry through threats and physical brutality. Most of the victims of trafficking are girls and women, which is a reflection of the low social and economic status of women in many countries. In south Asia, for instance, it is common for poverty-stricken parents or other relatives to sell young women to traffickers for the sex trade or forced labor. The trafficking industry is one of the fastest growing and most lucrative criminal enterprises in the world, generating billions of dollars annually in profits.

Global Diseases

HIV/AIDS Since the dawn of history, disease has played a significant role in the development of human communities. Although many advances were made in the fight against epidemic disease in the twentieth century, serious threats remain. The most serious epidemic threat comes from acquired immunodeficiency syndrome (AIDS). This fatal disorder of the immune system is caused by the human immunodeficiency virus (HIV), which slowly attacks and destroys the immune system. AIDS is the last stage of HIV infection. The HIV infection is spread through sexual contact with an infected person, contact with contaminated blood, and transmission from mother to child during pregnancy and breast-feeding.

Medical experts identified AIDS for the first time in 1981 among homosexual men and intravenous drug users in New York and San Francisco. Subsequently, evidence for an epidemic appeared among heterosexual men, women, and children in sub-Saharan Africa, and rather quickly AIDS developed into a worldwide epidemic that affected virtually every nation. At the end of 2005, the number of people living with HIV/AIDS was 38.6 million, and over 20 million AIDS deaths had occurred since the beginning of the epidemic.

AIDS IN AFRICA The AIDS epidemic is a serious public health threat throughout the world, but the disease has struck the developing world hardest, especially sub-Saharan Africa. Indeed, of the 38.6 million people identified with HIV/AIDS worldwide, 24.5 million of them currently live in sub-Saharan Africa. If current trends persist, AIDS deaths and the loss of future population from the demise of women in childbearing ages will lead to a 70-million drop in population by 2010. The AIDS epidemic threatens to overwhelm the social and economic fabric of African societies; the health infrastructure of most African nations cannot cope with the impact of this epidemic. Although sophisticated palliative treatments—not cures—are available, only the wealthy can afford them. When AIDS claims the lives of people in their most productive years, grieving orphans and elders must contend with the sudden loss of financial support, communities must bear the burden of caring for those left behind, and countries must draw on a diminishing number of trained and talented workers.

There are signs that HIV incidence may stabilize in sub-Saharan Africa. So many people in the sexually active population have been affected that only a small pool of people is still able to acquire the infection. In addition, successful prevention programs in a small number of countries, notably Uganda, have reduced infection rates and contributed to a regional downturn of the epidemic.

ADVANCES IN HIV TREATMENT Although no vaccine has yet emerged to prevent or cure HIV infection, some advances have been made. When scientists first identified AIDS, there was no treatment for the disease. By 1995, though, researchers had succeeded in developing a new class of drugs known as protease inhibitors and, in combination with some of the older drugs, they produced what is now known as highly active anti-retroviral therapy, or HAART. In most cases, HAART can prolong life indefinitely. The high cost of these sophisticated drugs initially prevented poor people from sharing in their benefits, but this too is changing. By 2007 over one million people in sub-Saharan Africa routinely received anti-AIDS drugs, and optimistic estimates suggest that by 2010 effective AIDS drugs will be available to all who might benefit from them. Although an effective vaccine remains elusive, vaginal microbicides designed to prevent the virus from entering the body and prophylactic drug regimens that create a hostile environment for any virus hold out great promise.

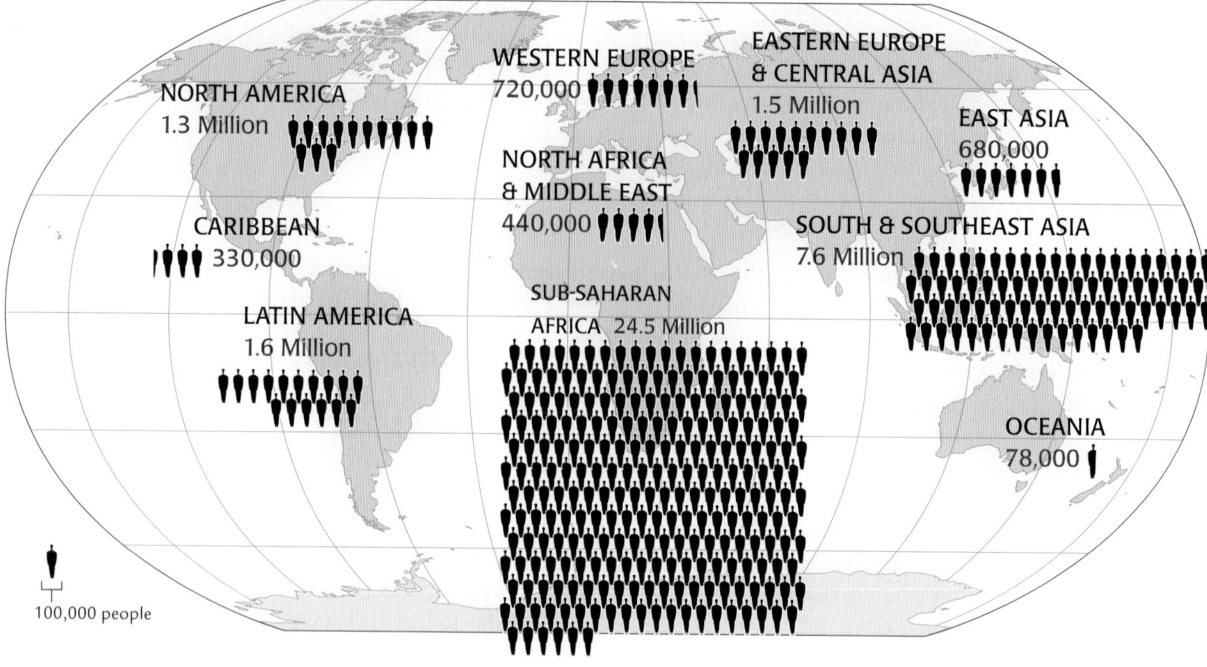

MAP 34.2 | Global estimates of HIV/AIDS. HIV infection in humans is one of the most destructive pandemics in recorded history, having claimed the lives of twenty-five million people since scientists first identified it in 1981. ***What regions of the world have been most affected?***

Global Terrorism

Terrorism has become a persistent feature of the globalized world. Although not a recent phenomenon, terrorism has attained its greatest impact in a world distinguished by rapid technological advances in transportation, communications, and weapons development. No universally agreed-on definition of terrorism exists, a fact underlined by the often-cited glib observation that "one person's terrorist is another person's freedom fighter." Most experts agree, nevertheless, that a key feature of terrorism is the deliberate and systematic use of violence against civilians, with the aim of advancing political, religious, or ideological causes. In contrast to the populations and institutions they fight, terrorists and their organizations are limited in size and resources. During the last decades of the twentieth century and the first decade of the twenty-first century, terrorism increasingly assumed a global character because sustained terror campaigns require sophisticated financial support networks and places of sanctuary. Aside from regional initiatives such as those emanating from the European Union, however, the international community did not respond to the threat of global terrorism in a coherent or unified manner. The thorny issues of what constitutes terrorism and how to respond to it gained renewed attention, however, as a result of the terror attacks against the United States in September 2001.

9/11 On the morning of 11 September 2001, New York City and Washington, D.C., became the targets of a coordinated terrorist attack that was unprecedented in scope, sophistication, and destructiveness. Hijackers seized four passenger jetliners and used them as guided missiles. Two of the planes crashed into the World Trade Center towers, causing the collapse of the two towers and thousands of deaths. Before the morning was over, another plane crashed into the Pentagon, the nerve center of the U.S. military in Washington, D.C., and the fourth jet crashed into a field outside Pittsburgh, Pennsylvania, after passengers stormed the hijackers. As millions around the world watched events unfold on television, the U.S. government identified the Islamic militant Osama

11 September 2001. This photograph shows an aerial view of the Pentagon after terrorists hijacked a commercial airplane and crashed it into the building. The attack was part of a coordinated effort that involved the hijacking of three other airplanes. ***Why did the terrorists choose the Pentagon as a target?***

bin Laden (1957–) as the mastermind behind the attacks. Before the dust of the collapsed World Trade towers had settled, U.S. president George W. Bush (1946–) declared war on Osama bin Laden and global terrorism itself.

WAR IN AFGHANISTAN AND IRAQ Osama bin Laden headed al-Qaeda ("the base"), the core of a global terrorist network. Bin Laden had been a key figure in the U.S.-backed effort to aid mujahideen (Islamic warriors) who fought Soviet forces in Afghanistan, but by the end of the Persian Gulf War (1990–1991), he had begun to regard the United States and its allies with unqualified hatred. The stationing of U.S. troops on the holy soil of Saudi Arabia, the bombing of Iraq, and the support of Israel, bin Laden claimed, were tantamount to a declaration of war against God. Convinced that he was carrying out God's will, bin Laden in 1998 publicly called on every Muslim to kill Americans and their allies "wherever he finds them and whenever he can."

Taliban, think you are safe?
www.mhhe.com/bentleybrief2e

A related radical manifestation of Islam's resurgence was the creation of the Islamic State of Afghanistan in 1996 by the Taliban movement. The Taliban emerged out of the disorder and devastation of the Afghan-Soviet war (1979–1988) and the later civil war (see chapter 33). Dominated by Pashtuns—the majority ethnic group of Afghanistan—the Taliban under its leading mullah (male religious leader), Mohammed Omar, fought a series of holy wars against other ethnic and Muslim groups. At the same time, the Taliban provided sanctuary and training grounds for Islamist fighters in southwest and central Asia, most notably for Osama bin Laden and al-Qaeda.

Afghanistan map
www.mhhe.com/bentleybrief2e

The Taliban espoused a strict brand of Islam that barred women from education and the workplace. In addition, women had to be completely veiled in burkas, while men had to eschew neckties and grow full, untrimmed beards. The Taliban also called for a ban on television, movie theaters, photographs, and most styles of music. A religious police, the Ministry of the Promotion of Virtue and Prevention of Vice, enforced these rules with an extremely harsh code of justice. Meanwhile, the United Nations and most governments in the world withheld recognition of the Taliban as Afghanistan's legitimate government, recognizing instead the Northern Alliance—an opposition force composed of the country's smaller religious and ethnic groups. The Northern Alliance became a crucial ally of the United States in its mission to find and punish those responsible for the 11 September attacks.

When the United States government announced its war against global terrorism it also pointedly targeted governments and states that supported and provided sanctuary for terrorists. The refusal of the Taliban government to surrender Osama bin Laden prompted the United States and its allies on 7 October 2001 to begin military operations against Taliban military positions and terrorist training camps. By November, U.S.-led bombardments permitted Northern Alliance troops to capture Kabul and other key Afghan cities. In a decisive military campaign, the United States' coalition smashed both the Taliban and al-Qaeda.

Another international action against terrorism came in March 2003, when President Bush coordinated what he termed "Operation Iraqi Freedom." A multinational coalition force some three hundred thousand strong, largely made up of U.S. and British troops, carried out an invasion of Iraq designed to wage further war on terrorism by ousting the regime of Saddam Hussein. One special target was Hussein's suspected stockpile of chemical and biological weapons, otherwise termed "weapons of mass destruction," which could presumably be employed by global terrorists to wreak destruction on a scale even greater than that of 11 September 2001. Coalition forces managed to establish their military supremacy in Iraq, but they did not uncover any such cache of weapons nor did they immediately control Hussein. President Bush declared an end to major battle operations on 1 May 2003, and coalition forces since that time have struggled in their efforts to occupy and stabilize Iraq. Hussein was finally caught in December 2003 and executed in 2006, but deadly resistance in Iraq persisted.

The costs of the Iraq war climbed in terms of both casualties and expenditures. Tens of thousands of Iraqi military personnel and civilians had died, as had over 4200 coalition soldiers, by the beginning of 2009. The United States has spent approximately $4 billion per month to maintain troops in Iraq. While President Bush sustained the United States' willingness to pay such a price, some critics in the United States and around the globe balked at the president's aggressive approach to the war on terrorism. Dubbed by some the "Bush Doctrine of Deterrence," his preemptive strike against Iraq—which had not overtly committed a terrorist act or been proven to harbor terrorists—set a troubling precedent in U.S. foreign policy. Moreover, the increased presence of foreign military personnel in Iraq may serve only to intensify the sort of Islamist fervor already fanned by Osama bin Laden.

Coping with Global Problems: International Organizations

Because global economic and cultural interdependence demands that political activity focus on cross-societal concerns and solutions, nations are under pressure to surrender portions of their sovereignty. The widespread recognition that the national state is ill equipped to handle problems of a global magnitude has led to an increase in the number of organizations dedicated to solving global problems through international coordination and action. Often categorized as nongovernmental international organizations and international governmental organizations, these institutions are important because they have the potential to tackle problems that do not respect territorial boundaries.

PSI doc Declaration of Human Rights www.mhhe.com/bentleybrief2e

THE UNITED NATIONS The premier international governmental organization is the United Nations, which superseded the League of Nations (1920–1946). This association of sovereign nations attempts to find solutions to global problems and to deal with virtually any matter of concern to humanity. Under its charter a principal purpose of the UN is "to maintain international peace and security." Cynics are quick to point to the UN's apparent inability to achieve that goal, citing a variety of recent conflicts. Yet however flawed its role as an international peacemaker, the UN has compiled an enviable record with respect to another role defined in its charter, namely, "to achieve international cooperation in solving international problems of an economic, social, cultural, or humanitarian character." Quietly and without attracting attention from the news media, the specialized agencies of the UN have achieved numerous successes. For example, in 1980 the World Health Organization proclaimed the worldwide eradication of smallpox as a result of its thirteen-year global program. On other fronts, UN efforts resulted in a more than 50 percent decrease in both infant and child mortality rates in developing countries between 1960 and 2002.

HUMAN RIGHTS Governmental and nongovernmental organizations have focused much of their attention on the protection of human rights, the notion that all persons are entitled to basic rights. Universal recognition and acceptance of the concept of human rights came in the aftermath of World War II, especially with the exposure of the crimes of the Nazi regime. In the charter establishing the United Nations in 1945, fifty member nations pledged to achieve "universal respect for, and observance of, human rights, and fundamental freedoms." In 1948, the National Assembly of the UN adopted the Universal Declaration of Human Rights, which singled out specific human rights violations such as extrajudicial or summary executions, arbitrary arrest and torture, and slavery or involuntary servitude as well as discrimination on racial, sexual, or religious grounds. By the late 1980s, human rights had emerged as one of the principal themes of global politics.

Given the present level of global interaction, international coordination to solve global problems is a necessity. However, contentious issues have sometimes paralyzed the UN and its affiliated organizations, because societies at different stages of economic development have pursued sometimes conflicting social and political goals. Yet despite the shortcomings of international organizations, for the present they represent the closest thing humanity has to a global system of governance that can help the world's peoples meet the challenges of international problems.

THINKING ABOUT *Encounters*

ENCOUNTERS IN A WORLD WITHOUT BORDERS. The world was more connected across time and space in the late twentieth and early twenty-first centuries than at any other time in history. How have these multiple and rapid encounters shaped identities, practices, and material conditions for the world's peoples?

CROSSING BOUNDARIES

Human populations also underwent radical transformations. Peoples throughout the world challenged gender definitions and embarked on large-scale migrations. Women in Europe, the United States, China, and the Soviet Union gained greater equality with men, even while women in most countries continued to be bound by traditional expectations for their sex. Meanwhile, both women and men also experienced either forced or voluntary migrations and in the process helped to create an increasingly borderless world.

Women's Traditions and Feminist Challenges

The status of women began changing after World War II. Women gained more economic, political, social, and sexual rights in highly industrialized states than in developing nations, but nowhere have they achieved full equality with men. Indeed, while some women have attained high political offices or impressive leadership positions, most do not exert political power commensurate with their numbers. At the same time, the political, legal, social, and cultural rights women in some societies have gained are unprecedented in the history of the world.

Women's liberation march
www.mhhe.com/
bentleybrief2e

Agitation for gender equality is often linked to women's access to employment, and the industrialized nations have the largest percentage of working women. For example, women constitute 40 to 50 percent of the workforce in industrial societies, compared with 20 percent or less in developing countries. In all countries, women work primarily in low-paying jobs such as teaching, service, and clerical positions. In addition, 40 percent of all farmers are women, many at the subsistence level.

FEMINISM AND EQUAL RIGHTS The discrimination that women faced in the workplace was a major stimulus for the feminist movement in industrialized nations. Women in most of those nations had gained the right to vote after the Great War, but they found that political rights did not guarantee economic or sexual equality. After World War II, when more and more women went to work, women started to protest job discrimination, pay differentials between women and men, and their lack of legal equality. In the 1960s those complaints expanded into a feminist movement that criticized all aspects of gender inequality.

Women started to expose the ways in which a biologically determined understanding of gender led to their oppression. In addition to demanding equality in the workplace, women demanded full control over their bodies and their reproductive systems. In the United States, the introduction of the birth control pill in the 1960s and legal protection of abortion in the 1970s provided a measure of sexual freedom for women even as the Civil Rights Act of 1964 prohibited discrimination on the basis of both race and sex.

PSI doc Civil Rights Act
www.mhhe.com/
bentleybrief2e

GENDER EQUALITY IN CHINA Some socialist or communist societies—such as the Soviet Union, Cuba, and China—transformed their legal systems to ensure basic equality. "Women hold up half the sky," Mao Zedong declared, and that eloquent acknowledgment of women's role translated into a commitment to fairness. In 1950 communist leaders passed a marriage law that abolished patriarchal practices such as child betrothal and upheld equal rights for men and women in the areas of work, property ownership, and inheritance.

Critics argue that despite such laws China's women have never gained true equality. Although most women in China have full-time jobs outside the home and are able to enter most professions, they do not receive wages equal to those of men. Long-standing Confucian values continue to degrade the status of women, especially in rural areas. One unintended consequence of China's population policies, which limits couples to one child, is the mysterious statistical disappearance of a half million baby girls every year. Some population experts speculate that a continued strong preference for male children causes parents to send baby girls away for adoption, to be raised secretly, or in some cases to resort to infanticide.

Although girls and women in industrial and communist nations are guaranteed basic if not fully equal legal rights and are educated in roughly the same numbers as boys and men, women in other areas of the world have long been denied access to education. In Arab and Muslim lands, women are twice as likely as men to be illiterate, and in some places nine of ten women are illiterate. In India, female literacy had reached 54 percent by 2001, and yet women remained largely confined to the home. Fewer than one-quarter of women of all ages were engaged in work, while the birthrate remained high even with the greater availability of birth control measures. This condition has ensured a life of domesticity for many Indian women, who are often completely dependent on their husbands' families and can be subject to severe domestic abuse.

Migration

El Paso Second Ward
www.mhhe.com/
bentleybrief2e

Migration, the movement of people from one place to another, is as old as humanity and has shaped the formation and identity of societies throughout the world. The massive influx of outsiders has transformed the ethnic, linguistic, and cultural composition of indigenous populations. With the advent of industrialization during the eighteenth century, population experts distinguished between two types of migration: internal migration and external or international migration. Internal migration describes the flow of people from rural to urban areas within one society, whereas external migration describes the movement of people across long distances and international borders. Both types of migration result from push factors such as population pressure or political persecution, pull factors such as better services and employment, or a combination of both.

INTERNAL MIGRATION The largest human migrations today are rural-to-urban flows. During the last half of the twentieth century, these internal migrations led to rapid urbanization in much of the world. Today the most highly urbanized societies are those of western and northern Europe, Australia, New Zealand, and temperate South America and North America. In these societies the proportion of people living in urban areas exceeds 75 percent; in some countries, such as Germany, it exceeds 85 percent.

URBANIZATION In Latin America, Africa, and south Asia, large numbers of people have migrated to metropolitan areas in search of relief from rural poverty. Once in the cities, though, they often find themselves equally destitute. More than ten million

SOURCES FROM THE PAST

China's Marriage Law, 1949

When the Chinese Communist Party came into power under Mao Zedong in 1949, the new government quickly instituted the "Marriage Law," which made Chinese men and women legal equals in marriage. This was truly revolutionary, since women traditionally held very low status in China's highly patriarchal social structure. Although actual equality was more elusive than legal equality, the Marriage Law marked a significant step toward granting women more rights in Chinese society.

Chapter I. General Principles

Article 1. The arbitrary and compulsory feudal marriage system, which is based on the superiority of man over woman and which ignores the children's interests, shall be abolished.

The new democratic marriage system, which is based on free choice of partners, on monogamy, on equal rights for both sexes, and on protection of the lawful interests of women and children, shall be put into effect.

Article 2. Bigamy, concubinage, child betrothal, interference with the remarriage of widows, and the exaction of money or gifts in connection with marriage shall be prohibited. . . .

Chapter III. Rights and Duties of Husband and Wife

Article 7. Husband and wife are companions living together and shall enjoy equal status in the home.

Article 8. Husband and wife are in duty bound to love, respect, assist, and look after each other, to live in harmony, to engage in production, to care for the children, and to strive jointly for the welfare of the family and for the building up of a new society.

Article 9. Both husband and wife shall have the right to free choice of occupation and free participation in work or in social activities.

Article 10. Both husband and wife shall have equal right in the possession and management of family property.

Article 11. Both husband and wife shall have the right to use his or her own family name.

Article 12. Both husband and wife shall have the right to inherit each other's property.

■ In what ways were these marriage laws similar to or different from the demands for gender equality made by feminists in the United States and western Europe during the 1960s and 1970s?

SOURCE: Dennis Sherman et al. *World Civilizations: Sources, Images, and Interpretations,* 3rd ed., Volume 2. Boston and New York: McGraw-Hill, 2002.

people cram the environs of cities such as Calcutta, Cairo, and Mexico City, straining those cities' resources. The few services originally available to the slum dwellers—potable water, electricity, and medical care—have diminished with the continuous influx of new people, and disease and malnutrition often run rampant.

EXTERNAL MIGRATION The largest migrations in the second half of the twentieth century consisted of refugees fleeing war. For example, the 1947 partition of the Indian subcontinent into two independent states resulted in the exchange of six million Hindus from Pakistan and seven million Muslims from India. More recently, three million to four million refugees fled war-torn Afghanistan during the 1980s. According to UN estimates, at the end of 2003 there were some ten million refugees who lived outside their countries of origin and who could not return because of fear of persecution.

Many of these migrants left their home countries because they wanted to escape the ravages of war, but many others leave their country of birth in search of better jobs and more readily available health care, educational opportunities, and other services. Thus since 1960 some thirteen million "guest workers" from southern Europe, Turkey, and northern Africa have taken up permanent residence in western Europe, and more than ten million permanent migrants—mostly from Mexico—have entered the United States. Worldwide, approximately 130 million people currently live outside their country of citizenship,

TABLE 34.2	World's Urban Areas of 10 Million or More Inhabitants in 1996		
Rank	**Urban Area**	**Country**	**Population (thousands)**
1	Tokyo	Japan	27,242
2	Mexico City	Mexico	16,908
3	São Paulo	Brazil	16,792
4	New York	United States	16,390
5	Bombay	India	15,725
6	Shanghai	China	13,659
7	Los Angeles	United States	12,576
8	Calcutta	India	12,118
9	Buenos Aires	Argentina	11,931
10	Seoul	Republic of Korea	11,768
11	Beijing	China	11,414
12	Lagos	Nigeria	10,878
13	Osaka	Japan	10,618
14	Delhi	India	10,298
15	Rio de Janeiro	Brazil	10,264
16	Karachi	Pakistan	10,119

SOURCE: United Nations, *World Population Prospects: The 1998 Revisions.*

A RIO DE JANEIRO SLUM. | These shanties, built on a hillside in Rio de Janeiro, reflect the poverty of many of the city's inhabitants. ***To what extent would residents be likely to have access to running water, sewers, and electricity here?***

collectively constituting a "nation of migrants" equivalent in size to Japan, the world's eighth most populous nation.

MIGRANT COMMUNITIES International mass migrations have accelerated and broadened the scope of cross-cultural interaction. After their arrival on foreign shores, migrants established cultural and ethnic communities that maintained their social customs and native languages and transformed many cities into multicultural environments. Although the arrival of migrants has enriched societies in many ways, it has also sparked resentment and conflict. People in host countries often believe that foreigners and their ways of life undermine national identity. Beyond that, many citizens of host societies view migrants, who are often willing to work for low wages, as competitors for jobs. As a result, governments in many countries have come under pressure to restrict immigration or even expel foreign residents. Thus, while migrants are reshaping the world outside their home countries, international mass migration poses challenges both to the migrants themselves and to the host society.

SUMMARY

By the late twentieth century, borders created by the bipolar world and European empires had dissolved, reshaping the world's landscape. Another barrier-crushing development that became visible at the end of the century was economic globalization, a process responsible for the unprecedented integration of the global economy. Globalization pointed to the new relevance of international organizations and to the increasing irrelevance of national boundaries; it signified the arrival of a world without borders. Technological and cultural developments likewise combined to break down barriers and create a global village that connected diverse peoples. Although many societies resisted cultural influences from Europe and the United States, the prevalence of communications technology and cultural diffusion made interactions and encounters inevitable. Women's efforts to achieve greater equality with men also collided with cultural traditions, while the global movement of human populations crisscrossed boundaries and contributed—for better and worse—to a more interconnected world than has ever before existed in human history.

STUDY TERMS

age of access (692)
AIDS (695)
al-Qaeda (697)
ASEAN (689)
biodiversity (693)
Bush Doctrine of Deterrence (698)
European Union (689)
feminist movement (699)
free trade (686)
GATT (686)
globalization (686)
global warming (693)
HAART (695)
IMF (687)
little tigers (688)
McDonaldization (691)
NAFTA (690)
Northern Alliance (697)
OPEC (689)
Operation Iraqi Freedom (698)
Osama bin Laden (697)
Saddam Hussein (698)
Taliban (697)
terrorism (696)
United Nations (698)
Universal Declaration of Human Rights (699)
WTO (686)

FOR FURTHER READING

Peter Baldwin. *Disease and Democracy: The Industrialized World Faces AIDS.* Berkeley, 2005. Probing comparative history of the public health policies implemented by Western democracies to contain domestic AIDS epidemics in the 1980s and 1990s.

Jagdish Bhagwati. *In Defense of Globalization.* New York, 2004. A convincing rebuttal to popular fallacies about global economic integration.

Thomas L. Friedman. *The Lexus and the Olive Tree.* New York, 1999. A readable overview that does justice to the complexities of globalization.

Margaret Jean Hay and Sharon Stichter. *African Women South of the Sahara.* Boston, 1984. An analysis of social and economic change and how it affected African women in the twentieth century.

Nikki R. Keddie and Beth Baron, eds. *Women in Middle Eastern History: Shifting Boundaries in Sex and Gender.* New Haven, 1992. A sensitive selection of articles by the leading scholars in the field.

Naomi Klein. *No Logo: Taking Aim at the Brand Bullies.* New York, 2000. Part cultural analysis and part political manifesto, this work makes an angry case against multinational corporations.

Joanna Liddle and Rama Doshi. *Daughters of Independence: Gender, Caste, and Class in India.* New Delhi, 1986. A work on the contemporary women's movement that covers the Indian caste system, British colonial rule, and class structure.

J. R. McNeill. *Something New under the Sun: An Environmental History of the Twentieth-Century World.* New York, 2000. A brilliant but dark tale of the past century's interaction between humans and the environment.

Joseph Stiglitz. *Globalization and Its Discontents.* New York, 2002. A former chief economist at the World Bank and the 2002 Nobel Prize winner takes aim at the institutions that govern globalization, especially the IMF.

Margery Wolfe. *Revolution Postponed: Women in Contemporary China.* New Haven, 1985. Explores one of the more problematic legacies of the Chinese revolution.

Bringing It All Together

Part VII Contemporary Global Realignments

Interactions and encounters between the world's peoples have been a feature of human history since ancient times. Yet in the twentieth and twenty-first centuries, the human ability to conquer space and time with technology has led to massive change at the global level and has intensified economic and cultural trends already set in motion during the industrial revolution.

Some of the most dramatic changes of the twentieth century occurred at the level of global leadership. At the beginning of the twentieth century, the world was dominated by a few major powers—especially Great Britain and France—who had used industrial technologies to conquer large empires in Asia and Africa. By midcentury, after two of the deadliest wars in the history of humankind, the great European empires were fatally weakened. In the four decades after World War II, the United States and the Soviet Union assumed global dominance, using industrial and military might to carve the world into competing capitalist and communist blocs. At the same time, nearly every colony once subject to formal imperial control struggled for and won independence—a process that necessitated the literal redrawing of the world map. Finally, by the last decade of the twentieth century the collapse of the Soviet Union brought an end to the bipolar world system, leaving an uncertain conglomeration of nation-states, regional associations, and international organizations in its place.

In addition to significant changes in global leadership, the tendency toward global economic, technological, and cultural integration accelerated dramatically during the twentieth century. Indeed, markets are now so deeply intertwined that shifts in one national stock market can affect markets in the rest of the world within hours. Global cultural habits are similarly intertwined, as people around the world now have unprecedented access to goods and services produced in distant parts of the world.

Yet while the world is more interconnected than ever before, interconnections do not always breed harmony. Many people resent the economic bullying of international organizations and argue that economic globalization has impoverished underdeveloped areas of the world. Others dislike the cultural homogenization brought about by "McDonaldization" and believe that unique cultural traditions will soon be lost forever. Indeed, the globalized world of today is replete with problems, many of which—including environmental destruction, epidemic disease, and violent conflict—are at least partly the result of accelerated connections between peoples and places. At the same time, organizations like the United Nations, international aid organizations, and regional trade networks have indicated that humans are capable of global cooperation as well. In the twenty-first century and beyond, the world's peoples will be faced with both the problems and the successes of the multiple interconnections forged in the modern world.

GLOSSARY AND PRONUNCIATION GUIDE

A	short *a* sound, as in *asp, fat, parrot*
AH	*a* sound, as in *car, father*
AHW	diphthong *au* in Romance languages, similar to vowel sound in *ouch*
AHY	diphthong *ai* in Romance languages, similar to vowel sound in *die*
AW	diphthong *a* sound, as in *awful, paw, law*
AY	long *a* sound, as in *ape, date, play*
EE	long *e* sound, as in *even, meet, money*
EH	short *e* sound, as in *ten, elf, berry, how, bow*
EHY	diphthong *ei* in Romance languages, similar to "ay" in *day*
EW	diphthong *iu* in Romance languages, similar (but shorter than) *you*
EYE	long *i* sound, as in *ice, high, bite*
IH	short *i* sound, as in *fit, his, mirror*
KH	hard *k* sound
OH	long *o* sound, as in *open, go, tone*
OHI	diphthong *oi* in Romance languages, similar to "oy" in *toy*
OO	long *o* sound, as in *ooze, tool, crew*
'R	tapped *r* like *dd* or *tt* in *latter* and *butter*
RR	trilled *r* (repeated taps)
UH	short *u* sound, as in *up, cut, color*
WA	diphthong *ua* in Romance languages, similar to the "wa" in *want* and *waffle*
WE	diphthong *ui* in Romance languages, similar to the word *we*
Y	like *ll* in *million* or *ny* in *canyon*
YA	diphthong *ia* in Romance languages, similar to "ya" in *yacht*
YE	diphthong *ie* in Romance languages, similar to "ye" in *yet*
YO	diphthong *io* in Romance languages, similar to "yo" in the suffix *yoke*

Note on emphasis: Syllables in capital letters receive the stress. If there is no syllable in capitals, then all syllables get equal stress.

Aachen (AH-kehn) A city in western Germany; formerly Charlemagne's northern capital.

Abbasid (ah-BAH-sihd) Cosmopolitan Arabic dynasty (750–1258) that replaced the Umayyads; founded by Abu al-Abbas and reaching its peak under Harun al-Rashid.

Abolitionism Antislavery movement.

Absolutism Political philosophy that stressed the divine right theory of kingship: the French king Louis XIV was the classic example.

Abu Bakr (ah-BOO BAHK-uhr) First caliph after the death of Muhammad.

Achaemenid empire (ah-KEE-muh-nid) First great Persian empire (558–330 B.C.E.), which began under Cyrus and reached its peak under Darius.

Aegean (ih-JEE-uhn) Bronze Age civilization that flourished near the Aegean Sea.

Aeschylus (ES-kuh-luhs) Greek tragedian, author of the *Oresteia.*

Age of Access Label for contemporary times regarding the ability of communication technologies to change the social, economic, and political solution of the past.

Age grades Bantu concept in which individuals of roughly the same age carried out communal tasks appropriate for that age.

Agricultural transition The gradual transition from a dependence on hunting and gathering for subsistence to a dependence on cultivation and animal husbandry. First evidence of transition is from around 12,000 B.C.E.

Aguinaldo, Emilio (AH-gee-NAHL-daw, ee-MEE-lyaw) Filipino independence leader who fought for independence from Spain and then the United States.

Ahimsa (uh-HIM-suh) A Buddhist, Hindu, and Jainist doctrine that all life is sacred and that violence should be avoided at all costs.

Ahmosis (AH-moh-sis) Egyptian pharaoh (c. 1500 B.C.E.), founder of the New Kingdom.

Ahura Mazda (uh-HOORE-uh MAHZ-duh) Main god of Zoroastrianism who represented truth and goodness and was perceived to be in an eternal struggle with the malign spirit Angra Mainyu.

AIDS Acquired immune deficiency syndrome.

Akhenaton (ahk-eh-NAH-ton) Early ruler of Egypt who created a tradition of sun worship.

Al-Andalus (al-ahn-dah-LOOS) Islamic Spain.

Alboquerque, Afonso d' (AL-buh-kur-kee, al-FAWN-soo d') Portuguese nobleman who established the Portuguese colonial empire in the Indian Ocean.

Aliæi nui Hawaiian class of high chiefs.

Allah (AH-lah) God of the monotheistic religion of Islam.

Al Qaeda A radical Sunni Muslim organization dedicated to the elimination of a Western presence in Arab countries and militantly opposed to Western foreign policy.

Amon-Re (AH-mohn RAY) Egyptian god, combination of the sun god Re and the air god Amon.

Ancestor worship Belief that dead ancestors can influence one's fortunes in this life. People who practice ancestor worship characteristically practice rituals and ceremonies to the memory or remains of their ancestors.

Ancien régime (ahn-syan rey-ZHEEM) The political and social system that existed in France before the French Revolution.

Angkor (AHN-kohr) Southeast Asian Khmer kingdom (889–1432) that was centered around the temple cities of Angkor Thom and Angkor Wat.

Anschluss (AHN-shloss) 1938 annexation of Austria into Greater Germany by the Nazi regime.

Antigonus (an-TIG-uh-nuhs) A general of Alexander the Great and king of Macedonia.

Anti-Semitism Term coined in late nineteenth century that was associated with a prejudice against Jews and the political, social, and economic actions taken against them.

Antonianism African syncretic religion, founded by Doña Beatriz, that taught that Jesus Christ was a black African man and that heaven was for Africans.

Apartheid (ah-PAHR-teyed) South African system of "separateness" that was implemented in 1948 and that maintained the black majority in a position of political, social, and economic subordination.

Appeasement British and French policy in the 1930s that tried to maintain peace in Europe in the face of German aggression by making concessions.

Arianism Early Christian heresy that centered around teaching of Arius (250–336 C.E.) and contained the belief that Jesus was a mortal human being and not coeternal with God; Arianism was the focus of Council of Nicaea.

Aristotle (AHR-ih-stot-uhl) One of the greatest ancient Athenian philosophers and pupil of Plato.

Artha Hindu concept for the pursuit of economic well-being and honest prosperity.

Arthashastra (UHRR-th-sha-strrah) Ancient Indian political treatise from the time of Chandragupta Maurya; its authorship was traditionally ascribed to Kautalya, and it stressed that war was inevitable.

Aryans (AYR-ee-uhns) Indo-European tribes who settled in India after 1500 B.C.E.; their union with indigenous Dravidians formed the basis of Hinduism.

Asante (uh-SAN-tee) Empire that emerged in 1670 in what is now modern Ghana.

Asceticism (uh-SET-uh-siz-uhm) Doctrine that through the renunciation of worldly pleasure one can achieve a high spiritual or intellectual state.

Association of Southeast Asian Nations (ASEAN) Regional alliance established in 1967 by Thailand, Malaysia, Singapore, Indonesia, and the Philippines; the alliance was designed to promote economic progress and political stability; it later became a free-trade zone.

Assyrians (uh-SEER-ee-uhns) Southwest Asian people who built an empire that reached its height during the eighth and seventh centuries B.C.E.; it was known for a powerful army and a well-structured state.

Astrolabe (as-truh-leyb) Navigational instrument for determining latitude.

Atahualpa (ah-tah-WAHL-pah) The last sovereign emperor of the Inca empire, executed by the Spanish.

Aten Monotheistic god of Egyptian pharaoh Akhenaten (r. 1353–1335 B.C.E.) and arguably the world's first example of monotheism.

Audiencias (AW-dee-uhns-cee-ahs) Spanish courts in Latin America.

Australopithecus (ah-strah-loh-PIHTH-uh-kuhs) "Southern ape," oldest known ancestor of humans; it lived from around four million down to around one million years ago, and it could walk on hind legs, freeing up hands for use of simple tools.

Austronesians People who, by as early as 2000 B.C.E., began to explore and settle islands of the Pacific Ocean basin.

Avesta Book that contains the holy writings of Zoroastrianism.

Axum (AHK-soom) Capital of ancient Ethiopian kingdom.

Azores (uh-ZAWRZ) Volcanic islands in the Northern Atlantic belonging to Portugal.

Aztec empire Central American empire constructed by the Mexica and expanded greatly during the fifteenth century during the reigns of Itzcoatl and Motecuzoma I.

Babur (BAH-ber) Founder of the Mughal dynasty in India.

Bakufu (bah-kuh-fuh) Military government under the Japanese shoguns.

Balfour Declaration British declaration from 1917 that supported the creation of a Jewish homeland in Palestine.

Bantu (BAHN-too) African peoples who originally lived in the area of present-day Nigeria; around 2000 B.C.E. they began a centuries-long migration that took them to most of sub-Saharan Africa; the Bantu were very influential, especially linguistically.

Bechuanaland (bech-oo-AH-nuh-land) Protectorate established in 1885 by the British in southern Africa.

Bedouins (BEHD-oh-ihnz) Nomadic Arabic tribespeople.

Belisarius (bel-uh-SAIR-ee-uhs) Byzantine general who fought against the Persians and recovered Roman territories in northern Africa.

Benefice Grant from a lord to a vassal, usually consisting of land, which supported the vassal and signified the relationship between the two.

Benin (beh-NEEN) Large precolonial African state in what is now modern Nigeria.

Berdiaev, Nikolai (ber-dee-ev, nih-koh-LYE) Late nineteenth- and early twentieth-century Russian philosopher.

Berlin Conference Meeting organized by German chancellor Otto von Bismarck in 1884–1885 that provided the justification for European colonization of Africa.

Berlin Wall Wall that separated West Berlin from East Germany.

Bhagavad Gita (BUHG-uh-vuhd GEE-tah) Sacred "song of god" composed in 200 B.C.E. and incorporated into the *Mahabharata,* a Sanskrit epic.

Bhakti (BHUK-tee) Indian movement that attempted to transcend the differences between Hinduism and Islam.

Biodiversity Diversity among and within plant and animal species in an environment.

Black Hand Pre–World War I secret Serbian society; one of its members, Gavrilo Princip, assassinated Austrian archduke Francis Ferdinand and provided the spark for the outbreak of the Great War.

Blitzkrieg German style of rapid attack through the use of armor and air power that was used in Poland, Norway, Denmark, Belgium, the Netherlands, and France in 1939–1940.

Boddhisatvas (BOH-dih-SAT-vuhs) Buddhist concept regarding individuals who had reached enlightenment but who stayed in this world to help people.

Bolshevik (BOHL-shih-vehk) Russian communist party headed by Lenin.

Bourgeoisie Middle class in modern industrial society.

Boyars (BOY-ahrs) Russian nobles.

Brahmins (BRAH-minz) Hindu caste of priests.

Brezhnev Doctrine Policy developed by Leonid Brezhnev (1906–1982) that claimed for the Soviet Union the right to invade any socialist country faced with internal or external enemies; the doctrine was best expressed in the Soviet invasion of Czechoslovakia.

Bubonic plague Epidemic that swept Eurasia, causing devastating population loss and economic disruption. It was known as the Black Death in Europe after around 1350 C.E.

Buddha (BOO-duh) The "enlightened one," the term applied to Siddhartha Gautama after his discoveries that would form the foundation of Buddhism.

Buddhism (BOO-diz'm) Religion, based on Four Noble Truths, associated with Siddhartha Gautama (563–483 B.C.E.), or the Buddha; its adherents desired to eliminate all distracting passion and reach nirvana.

Buenos Aires (BWE-naws AHY-res) Capital and largest city in Argentina.

Bunraku (boon-RAH-koo) A form of traditional Japanese puppet theater.

Bush Doctrine of Deterrence U.S. policy after 9/11 that preemptively attacks any supposed terrorist threat.

Bushido (BOH-shee-DOH) The "way of the warrior," the code of conduct of the Japanese samurai that was based on loyalty and honor.

Byzantine (BIHZ-uhn-teen) Long-lasting empire centered at Constantinople; it grew out of the end of the Roman empire and carried the legacy of Roman greatness and was the only classical society to survive into the early modern age; it reached its early peak during the reign of Justinian (483–565).

Caesaropapism Concept relating to the mixing of political and religious authority, as with the Roman emperors, that was central to the church versus state controversy in medieval Europe.

Cahokia (kuh-HOH-kee-uh) Large structure in modern Illinois that was constructed by the mound-building peoples; it was the third largest structure in the Americas before the arrival of the Europeans.

Caliph (KAH-leef) "deputy," Islamic leader after the death of Muhammad.

Calpulli (kal-po-lee) An organizational unit and geographical area of the Aztec capital Tenochtitlan.

Cambyses (kam-BIE-sees) Son of the Persian leader Cyrus the Great.

Candomblé (kan-duhm-BLEH) African-oriented religion practiced mainly in Brazil.

Capet (KAHP-ay) Surname of the founder of the French dynasty by the same name.

Capetian (cah-PEE-shuhn) Early French dynasty that started with Hugh Capet.

Capitalism An economic system with origins in early modern Europe in which private parties make their goods and services available on a free market.

Capitulation Highly unfavorable trading agreements that the Ottoman Turks signed with the Europeans in the nineteenth century that symbolized the decline of the Ottomans.

Caporetto (kap-uh-RET-oh) 1917 Battle of World War I in which the Italians were defeated by a combined Austro-German force.

Carolingian (kar-uh-LIHN-jee-uhn) Germanic dynasty that was named after its most famous member, Charlemagne.

Carthage (KAHR-thihj) Northern African kingdom, main rival to early Roman expansion, that was defeated by Rome in the Punic Wars.

Caste A social class system with distinctions that are transferred through generations or through occupation. Restrictions are placed on marriage, occupation, handling of food, and other matters, according to caste. Caste usually refers to the social system of India.

Çatal Hüyük (chat-l-hoo-yook) Important Neolithic settlement in Anatolia (7250–6150 B.C.E.).

Cathars Medieval heretics, also known as the Albigensians, who considered the material world evil; their followers renounced wealth and marriage and promoted an ascetic existence.

Catholic Reformation Sixteenth-century Catholic attempt to cure internal ills and confront Protestantism; it was inspired by the reforms of the Council of Trent and the actions of the Jesuits.

Caucasus (KAW-kuh-suhs) Mountain range between the Black and Caspian seas.

Caudillos (kahw-DEE-yohs) Latin American term for nineteenth-century local military leaders.

Central Powers World War I term for the alliance of Germany, Austria-Hungary, and the Ottoman empire.

Ceuta (SYOO-tuh) An autonomous Spanish city situated on the north African side of the Straits of Gibraltar.

Chagatai (chah-guh-TAHY) One of the sons of Chinggis Khan.

Chalcedon (kal-SED-n) An ancient city in northwest Asia Minor on the Bosphorus, opposite Byzantium.

Chaldiran (chahld-ih-rahn) Site of a battle between the Safavids and Ottomans in 1514, where the Safavids were badly defeated.

Chamorro (chuh-MAWR-oh) Indigenous peoples of the Mariana Islands.

Chan Buddhism (CHAHN BOO-diz'm) Most popular branch of Buddhism in China, with an emphasis on intuition and sudden flashes of insight instead of textual study.

Chan Chan (chahn chahn) Capital of the pre-Incan, South American Chimu society that supported a large population of fifty thousand.

Chang'an (chahng-ahn) Ancient capital in China during the Han, Sui, and Tang dynasties.

Charlemagne (SHAHR-leh-mane) King of the Franks and the Holy Roman Emperor.

Charvaka (CHAHR-vah-kuh) Indian philosophy based on philosophical skepticism.

Chauvinism (SHOH-vuh-niz-uhm) Prejudiced belief in the superiority of one's own kind, particularly with respect to nation or biological sex.

Chavín cult Mysterious but very popular South American religion (1000–300 B.C.E.).

Chimu Pre-Incan South American society that fell to the Incas in the fifteenth century.

Chinampas Style of agriculture used by Mexica (Aztecs) in which fertile muck from lake bottoms was dredged and built up into small plots.

Chinggis Khan (CHIHN-gihs kahn) Conqueror of much of Eurasia in the thirteenth century, from China in the east to the Abbasid empire in the west.

Chivalry European medieval concept, a code of conduct for the knights based on loyalty and honor.

Chola Southern Indian Hindu kingdom (850–1267), a tightly centralized state that dominated sea trade.

Christianity Religious doctrine that emerged in southeast Asia in the first century C.E. and then spread through Europe, north Africa, parts of Asia, and eventually to the Americas. Central to the religion is the belief that Jesus was the son of God and sacrificed himself on behalf of humankind.

Chucuito (choo-CWE-toh) Pre-Incan South American society that rose in the twelfth century and fell to the Incas in the fifteenth century.

Cicero (SIHS-ser-oh) Roman senator and bitter enemy of Marc Antony.

City-state Urban areas that controlled surrounding agricultural regions and that were often loosely connected in a broader political structure with other city-states.

Clemenceau, Georges (klem-uhn-SOH, jawrj) French statesman who played a key role in negotiating the Treaty of Versailles.

Coen, Jan Pieterszoon (KOH-uhn, yahn PEE-tuhr-sohn) Governor-general of the Dutch East Indies in the sixteenth century.

Cohong Specially licensed Chinese firms that were under strict government regulation.

Cold War Strategic struggle that developed after World War II between the U.S. and USSR.

Collectivization Process beginning in the late 1920s by which Stalin forced the Russian peasants off their own land and onto huge collective farms run by the state; millions died in the process.

Colombo, Cristoforo (kuh-LUHM-boh, crihs-toh-for-oh) Italian navigator who discovered the Caribbean islands for Europeans while trying to find a western route to China.

Columbian Exchange The trans-Atlantic exchange of plants, animals, and diseases that followed European contact with the Americas at the end of the fifteenth century.

COMECON The Council for Mutual Economic Assistance, which offered increased trade within the Soviet Union and eastern Europe; it was the Soviet alternative to the United States's Marshall Plan.

Communalism A term, usually associated with India, that placed an emphasis on religious rather than national identity.

Communism Philosophy and movement that began in middle of the nineteenth century with the work of Karl Marx; it has the same general goals as socialism, but it includes the belief that violent revolution is necessary to destroy the bourgeois world and institute a new world run by and for the proletariat.

Confucianism (kuhn-FEW-shuhn-iz'm) Philosophy, based on the teachings of the Chinese philosopher Kong Fuzi (551–479 B.C.E.), or Confucius, that emphasizes order, the role of the gentleman, obligation to society, and reciprocity.

Congress of Vienna Gathering of European diplomats in Vienna, Austria, from October 1814 to June 1815. The representatives of the "great powers" that defeated Napoleon—Britain, Austria, Prussia, and Russia—dominated the proceedings, which aimed to restore the prerevolutionary political and social order.

Conquistadores (kohn-kees-tah-DOH-rays) Spanish adventurers like Cortés and Pizarro who conquered Central and South America in the sixteenth century.

Conservatism A political philosophy that emphasizes gradual change, continuity of traditions, and established authority. Although the word has taken on many shades of meaning, nineteenth-century conservatives generally opposed democracy and supported traditional institutions such as the church, monarchy, and nobility.

Constantine (KAHN-stuhn-teen) Emperor of Rome who made Christianity the official religion of the Roman empire in 324.

Constitutionalism Movement in England in the seventeenth century that placed power in Parliament's hands as part of a constitutional monarchy and that increasingly limited the power of the monarch; the movement was highlighted by the English Civil War and the Glorious Revolution.

Containment U.S. policy to block further expansion of Soviet power.

Coromandel (kawr-uh-MAN-dul) Southeastern coast of India.

Corporation A concept that reached mature form in 1860s in England and France; it entailed private business owned by thousands of individual and institutional investors who financed the business through the purchase of stocks.

Corpus iuris civilis (KOR-poos EW-rees sih-VEE-lees) *Body of the Civil Law,* the Byzantine emperor Justinian's attempt to codify all Roman law.

Cortés, Hernán (kawr-TEZ, er-NAHN) Spanish conquistador who defeated the Aztecs and conquered Mexico.

Cossacks (KAW-sacks) Russian "free men" recruited by Ivan III to settle conquered land in return for their freedom; the strategy eventually played a key role in Russian expansion eastward.

Criollos (kree-OH-lohs) The term for Spaniards born in the Americas during the Spanish colonial period.

Croesus (CREE-suhs) The last king of Lydia who died in 546 B.C.E.

Cro-Magnon (CROH MAHG-nohn) *Homo sapiens sapiens,* who appeared forty thousand years ago during the Paleolithic age and were the first human beings of the modern type.

Cross staff Device that sailors used to determine latitude by measuring the angle of the sun or pole star above the horizon.

Ctesiphon (TES-uh-phon) Ancient city of central Iraq on the Tigris River southeast of Baghdad.

Cuneiform Written language of the Sumerians, probably the first written script in the world.

Cuzco (KOOS-koh) A town in the Andes in southern Peru; former capital of the Inca empire.

Cyrus (SIGH-ruhs) King of Persia and founder of the Persian empire.

Dahomey Oyo (dah-HO-meh OH-yoh) Precolonial West African empire in what is now modern Nigeria.

Daimyo (DEYEM-yoh) Powerful territorial lords in early modern Japan.

Dao Key element in Chinese philosophy that means the "way of nature" or the "way of the cosmos."

Daodejing (DOW-DAY-JIHNG) Book that is the fundamental work of Daoism.

Daoism (dow-ism) Chinese philosophical system advocating a simple, honest life and following the natural patterns of the universe.

Dar al-Islam The "house of Islam," a term for the Islamic world.

Declaration of Independence Drafted by Thomas Jefferson in 1776; the document expressed the ideas of John Locke and the Enlightenment, represented the idealism of the American rebels, and influenced other revolutions.

Declaration of the Rights of Man and Citizen Document from the French Revolution (1789) that was influenced by the American Declaration of Independence and in turn influenced other revolutionary movements.

Decolonization Process by which former colonies achieved their independence, as with the newly emerging African nations in the 1950s and 1960s.

Degas, Edgar (day-GAH, ED-gahr) Nineteenth- and early twentieth-century French impressionist painter.

Deism (DEE-iz'm) An Enlightenment view that accepted the existence of a god but denied the supernatural aspects of Christianity; in deism, the universe was an orderly realm maintained by rational and natural laws.

Demographic transition Adjustments in the rate of births and deaths that usually accompany industrialization. The demographic transition is often triggered by improvements in health and nutrition, which result in lower death rates. Birthrates remain high initially, but after a period of rapid population growth, birthrates fall in response to the lower death rates. Eventually, in highly industrialized societies, birthrates and death rates stabilize at low levels.

Descamisados "Shirtless ones," Argentine poor who supported Juan and Eva Perón.

De-Stalinization The policy of ending Stalin's reign of terror after his death in 1953.

Détente A reduction in cold war tension between the United States and the Soviet Union from 1969 to 1973.

Devshirme Ottoman requirement that the Christians in the Balkans provide young boys to be slaves of the sultan.

Dharma (DHUHR-muh) Hindu concept of obedience to religious and moral laws and order.

Dhimmi (DIHM-mee) Islamic concept of a protected people that was symbolic of Islamic toleration during the Mughal and Ottoman empires.

Dhow Indian, Persian, and Arab ships, one hundred to four hundred tons, that sailed and traded throughout the Indian Ocean basin.

Dias, Bartolomeu (dee-as, bahr-tol-uh-MEY-oh) The first European explorer (Portuguese) to sail around the southern tip of Africa.

Diaz, Porfirio (DEE-ahs, pawr-FEER-eeo) Mexican politician who became president of Mexico from 1876 to 1880 and from 1884 to 1911.

Diaspora (dahy-AS-per-uh) The dispersion of peoples outside their homeland.

Diocletian (dah-yuh-KLEE-shuhn) Roman emperor who divided the empire into two parts, east and west, in 286 C.E.

Dionysus Greek god of wine, also known as Bacchus; Greek plays were performed in his honor.

Domestic Containment Concern that Communist spies had infiltrated the United States.

Domino Theory Theory that if one country becomes Communist, neighboring countries will also "collapse" to communism the way dominoes fall.

Dravidian (drah-VIHD-een) A member of one of the aboriginal groups of India.

Dreadnoughts A class of British battleships whose heavy armaments made all other battleships obsolete overnight.

Duma Russian parliament, established after the Revolution of 1905.

Dutch learning European knowledge that reached Tokugawa Japan.

East India Company British joint-stock company that grew to be a state within a state in India; it possessed its own armed forces.

Eastern Orthodox Christianity An eastern branch of Christianity that evolved after the division of the Roman Empire and the subsequent development of the Byzantine Empire in the east and the medieval European society in the west. The Eastern Orthodox Church acknowledged what became known as the Byzantine rite and recognized the primacy of the patriarch of Constantinople.

Eight-legged essay Eight-part essays that an aspiring Chinese civil servant had to compose, mainly based on a knowledge of Confucius and the Zhou classics.

Einsatzgruppen (ain-zats-groopen) Paramilitary group run by the German SS in World War II, whose main task was to annihilate Jews, Gypsies, and Slavs as the German army moved east, invading the Soviet Union.

Encomienda (ehn-koh-MYEN-dah) System that gave the Spanish settlers *(encomenderos)* the right to compel the indigenous peoples of the Americas to work in the mines or fields.

Engenho (ehn-GEN-yo) Portuguese term for a sugar mill and its facilities.

Enlightenment Eighteenth-century philosophical movement that began in France; its emphasis was on the preeminence of reason rather than faith or tradition; it spread concepts from the Scientific Revolution.

Epicureans (ehp-ih-KYOOR-eeuhns) Hellenistic philosophers who taught that pleasure—as in quiet satisfaction—was the greatest good.

Equal-field system Chinese system during the Han dynasty in which the goal was to ensure an equitable distribution of land.

Equiano, Olaudah (ay-kwee-AHN-oh, oh-LAU-duh) An ex-slave who became deeply involved in the fight against slavery and the slave trade.

Erasmus, Desiderius (ih-raz-muhs, des-i-DEER-ee-uhs) Dutch humanist and leading Renaissance scholar in northern Europe.

Essenes Jewish sect that looked for the arrival of a savior; they were similar in some of their core beliefs to the early Christians.

Etruscans (ih-TRUHS-kuhns) Northern Italian society that initially dominated the Romans; the Etruscans helped convey Greek concepts to the expanding Romans.

Eunuch (YOO-nuhk) A castrated man.

European Community (EC) Organization of European states established in 1957; it was originally called the European Economic Community and was renamed the EC in 1967; it promoted economic growth and integration as the basis for a politically united Europe.

European Union Established by the Maastricht Treaty in 1993, a supranational organization for even greater European economic and political integration.

Fascism Political ideology and mass movement that was prominent in many parts of Europe between 1919 and 1945; it sought to regenerate the social, political, and cultural life of societies, especially in contrast to liberal democracy and socialism; fascism began with Mussolini in Italy, and it reached its peak with Hitler in Germany.

Fatehpur Sikri (fah-teh-poor SIH-kree) City built by the Mughal emperor Akbar to serve as the Mughal capital.

Feminist Movement The movement of women in postwar industrialized nations to gain political and economic equality.

Fernando of Aragon (fer-NAWN-doh of ah-ruh-GAWN) Husband of Isabella of Castille, who jointly funded Cristoforo Colombo's expedition to search for a western trade route to China.

Ferreira, Christovao (feh-RAY-rah, chris-STOH-voh) Portuguese Jesuit who renounced his faith in Japan in 1632.

Fief (FEEF) A grant of land from a lord to a vassal.

Five Pillars The foundation of Islam; (1) profession of faith, (2) prayer, (3) fasting during Ramadan, (4) alms, and (5) pilgrimage, or hajj.

Five-year plans First implemented by Stalin in the Soviet Union in 1928; five-year plans were a staple of communist regimes in which every aspect of production was determined in advance for a five-year period; five-year plans were the opposite of the free market concept.

Four Noble Truths The foundation of Buddhist thought: (1) life is pain, (2) pain is caused by desire, (3) elimination of desire will bring an end to pain, (4) living a life based on the Noble Eightfold Path will eliminate desire.

Free trade Economic doctrine, first argued by Adam Smith in the late eighteenth century, of unrestricted trade between nations without protective tariffs or duties. Smith and his followers argue that, through free trade and competition, the forces of supply and demand will ensure that the best product is available at the best price. Free trade has gained wide acceptance since World War II.

Freud, Sigmund (froid, SIG-muhnd) Nineteenth- and early twentieth-century Austrian neurologist who developed psychoanalysis.

Front de Libération Nationale (FLN) The Algerian organization that fought a bloody guerilla war for freedom against France.

Fulani (foo-LAH-nee) Sub-Saharan African people who, beginning in the seventeenth century, began a series of wars designed to impose their own strict interpretation of Islam.

Gandhi, Mohandas Karamchand (GAHN-dee, moh-huhn-DAHS kuhr-uhm-CHUND) Political and spiritual leader of the Indian Independence movement, assassinated by a Hindu extremist in 1948.

Gao (gou) City that served as capital of the Mali Empire in Africa.

Garibaldi, Giuseppe (gar-uh-BAWL-dee, juh-SEP-eh) Nineteenth-century Italian nationalist who led the Italian unification movement.

Gathas (GATH-uhs) Zoroastrian works believed to be compositions by Zarathustra.

GATT General Agreement on Tariffs and Trade, promoted unrestricted free trade.

Gauchos (GAHW-chohs) Argentine cowboys, highly romantic figures.

Gaugamela (GAW-guh-mee-luh) Site, in modern Iraq, of Alexander the Great's final victory over Darius III in 331 B.C.E.

Gaunahani (gwah-nah-nee) The name indigenous peoples called the island Columbus called San Salvador in the Caribbean.

Geechee (GEE-chee) See Gullah.

General Agreement on Tariffs and Trade (GATT) Free trade agreement first signed in 1947; by 1994 it had grown to 123 members and formed the World Trade Organization (WTO).

Ghana (GAH-nuh) Eighth- through eleventh-century empire in West Africa that grew wealthy from the trans-Saharan trade.

Ghazi (GAH-zee) Islamic religious warrior.

Ghaznavids Turkish tribe under Mahmud of Ghazni who moved into northern India in the eleventh century and began a period of greater Islamic influence in India.

Gilgamesh Legendary king of the Mesopotamian city-state of Uruk (ca. 3000 B.C.E.), subject of the *Epic of Gilgamesh,* world's oldest complete epic literary masterpiece.

Glasnost (GLAHS-nohst) Russian term meaning "openness" introduced by Mikhail Gorbachev in 1985 to describe the process of opening Soviet society to dissidents and public criticism.

Global warming The emission of greenhouse gases, which prevents solar heat from escaping the earth's atmosphere and leads to the gradual heating of the earth's environment.

Globalization The breaking down of traditional boundaries in the face of increasingly global financial and cultural trends.

Golden Horde Mongol tribe that controlled Russia from the thirteenth to the fifteenth centuries.

Gorbachev, Mikhail Leader of the USSR in the 1980s, responsible for the opening up of the USSR in social and economic policy.

Gouges, Olympe de (gouj, oh-LIMP de) French playwright and journalist who advocated that women and men should share equal rights during the French Revolution.

Great Game Nineteenth-century competition between Great Britain and Russia for the control of central Asia.

Great Leap Forward The vision by Mao that planned how China could overtake the industrial production of more developed nations.

Great Proletarian Cultural Revolution Attempt by Mao to mobilize the Chinese and reignite revolutionary spirit.

Great Zimbabwe Large sub-Saharan African kingdom in the fifteenth century.

Greater East Asia Co-Prosperity Sphere Japanese plan for consolidating Asia under their control during World War II.

Greenpeace An environmental organization founded in 1970 and dedicated to the preservation of earth's natural resources.

Guadalupe Hidalgo (gwahd-i-LOOP hee-DAHL-goh) Peace treaty that ended the Mexican-American War in 1848.

Guangxu (wang-soo) Tenth Qing emperor who initiated the Hundred Days' Reform in 1898, but was removed from power by the Empress Dowager Cixi.

Guarani (gwahr-uh-NEE) Ethnic group of indigenous people from modern Paraguay and Bolivia, as well as their language.

Guild Organizations whose membership is based on occupation. They often regulate the production and sale of goods and serve as mutual aid societies for their members. They were particularly powerful in medieval European cities.

Gullah (GUHL-uh) Also known as Geechee, the Gullah are African Americans who live in the low country of South Carolina and Georgia. They have preserved much of their syncretic African culture from the days of slavery, including the creole Gullah language.

Guomindang (GWOH-mihn-dahng) Chinese nationalist party founded by Sun Yat-sen (1866–1925) and later led by Jiang Jieshi; it has been centered in Taiwan since the end of the Chinese civil war.

Gupta (GOOP-tah) Indian dynasty (320–550 C.E.) that briefly reunited India after the collapse of the earlier Mauryan dynasty.

HAART The active antiretroviral therapy that treats AIDS.

Hacienda (ah-SYEN-dah) Large Latin American estates.

Hagia Sophia (HAH-yah soh-FEE-uh) Greek orthodox temple constructed by the Byzantine emperor Justinian and later converted into a mosque.

Hajj (HAHJ) Pilgrimage to Mecca.

Hammurabi's Code (hahm-uh-RAH-beez cohd) Sophisticated law code associated with the Babylonian king Hammurabi (r. 1792–1750 B.C.E.).

Han Feizi (hahn fay-zi) Chinese philosopher who developed the doctrine of Legalism.

Han Wudi (hahn woo-dee) Seventh emperor of the Han dynasty who developed a strong, centralized, Confucian state.

Hanseatic (han-see-AT-ik) A commercial and defensive confederation of free cities in northern Germany and surrounding areas in the thirteenth and fourteenth centuries.

Harappan (huh-RUHP-puhn) Early brilliant Indian society centered around Harappa and Mohenjo-Daro.

Harijans (har-i-jahns) Literally meaning the "children of God," very low-status Indian people who are outside the caste system.

Hatshepsut (hat-SHEP-soot) Queen of Egypt (1505 B.C.E.) who shared her throne with her nephew Tuthmosis III.

Hebrews Semitic-speaking nomadic tribe influential for monotheistic belief in Yahweh.

Heian (HAY-ahn) Japanese period (794–1185), a brilliant cultural era notable for the world's first novel, Murasaki Shikibu's *The Tale of Genji.*

Heisenberg, Werner (HAHY-zuyn-burg, VER-nuhr) Twentieth century German theoretical physicist responsible for the development of uncertainty theory.

Hellenic Era First phase in Greek history (ca. 2000–328 B.C.E.), which was highlighted by the Golden Age of Athens in the fifth century B.C.E.

Hellenistic Era Second phase in Greek history (328–146 B.C.E.), from the conquest of Greece by Philip of Macedon until Greece's fall to the Romans; this era was a more cosmopolitan age facilitated by the conquests of Alexander the Great.

Herzl, Theodore (HER-tsuhll, TEY-aw-dohr) Hungarian Jewish journalist and author of the book *Judenstaat,* he is considered by many to be the father of modern Zionism.

Hidalgo, Miguel de (hee-DHAHL-goh, mee-GEL de) Priest and leader of the Mexican War of Independence in 1810–1821.

Hieratic (hahy-uh-RAT-tik) A cursive form of Egyptian hieroglyphics.

Hieroglyphics (heye-ruh-GLIPH-iks) Ancient Egyptian written language.

Hijra (HIHJ-ruh) The migration of Muhammed and his followers to the city of Medina in 622 C.E.

Hinayana (HEE-nah-yah-nuh) Branch of Buddhism known as the "lesser vehicle," also known as Theravada Buddhism; its beliefs include a strict, individual path to enlightenment, and it is popular in south and southeast Asia.

Hinduism Main religion of India, a combination of Dravidian and Aryan concepts; Hinduism's goal is to reach spiritual purity and union with the great world spirit; its important concepts include dharma, karma, and samsara.

Ho Chi Minh Leader of Vietnam during revolution.

Holocaust German attempt in World War II to exterminate the Jews of Europe.

Holy Roman Empire A confederation of states mostly in central and western Europe. It began in 962 C.E. with the crowning of Otto I by the pope.

Home front Term made popular in World War I and World War II for the civilian "front" that was symbolic of the greater demands of total war.

Hominid (HAW-mih-nihd) A creature belonging to the family Hominidae, which includes human and humanlike species.

Homo erectus (HOH-moh ee-REHK-tuhs) "Upright-walking human," which existed from 1.5 million to two hundred thousand years ago; *Homo erectus* used cleavers and hand axes and learned how to control fire.

Homo sapiens (HOH-moh SAY-pyans) "Consciously thinking human," which first appeared around two hundred fifty thousand years ago and used sophisticated tools.

Homo sapiens sapiens (HOH-moh SAY-pyans SAY-pyans) First human being of the modern type, which appeared roughly one hundred thousand years ago; Cro-Magnon falls into this category.

Hong Xiuquan (hoong shee-OH-chew-an) The leader of the nineteenth-century Taiping Rebellion.

Hongwu (hawng-woo) The first Ming emperor, who overthrew the Yuan dynasty in 1368.

Huitzilopochtli (we-tsee-loh-POCK-tlee) Sun god and patron deity of the Aztecs.

Hulegu (Hoo-LAY-goo) Grandson of Chinggis Khan and leader of the Ilkhan khanate, who was responsible for the destruction of Baghdad.

Humanism Cultural movement during the Renaissance that drew inspiration from the humanities, that is, literature, history, philosophy, and the arts. In contrast to medieval theologians, humanists argued that one could live a moral life and still be actively engaged in the affairs of the world.

Hundred Days of Reform Chinese reforms of 1898 led by Kang Youwei and Liang Qichao in their desire to turn China into a modern industrial power.

Hunting/gathering culture Any culture whose primary means of subsistence is through hunting and gathering from the environment. Humans survived this way for millions of years before the agricultural transition, and some hunting/gathering cultures persisted into the twenty-first century C.E.

Hyksos (HICK-sohs) Invaders who seized the Nile delta and helped bring an end to the Egyptian Middle Kingdom.

Ibn Battuta (ih-bun BAH-too-tah) A famous fourteenth-century traveler and historian of Africa and Asia.

Ibn Rushd (IB-uhn RUSHED) A twelfth-century Muslim philosopher, born in Cordoba in modern Spain, whose philosophy influenced European thought.

Iconoclasts (eye-KAHN-oh-klasts) Supporters of the movement, begun by the Byzantine Emperor Leo III (r. 717–741), to destroy religious icons because their veneration was considered sinful.

Ife (EE-fehy) Eighth- to tenth-century kingdom in what is now modern Nigeria.

Ilkhanate (EEL-kahn-ate) Mongol state that ruled Persia after abolition of the Abbasid empire in the thirteenth century.

IMF International Monetary Fund.

Imperialism Term associated with the expansion of European powers and their conquest and colonization of African and Asian societies, mainly from the sixteenth through the nineteenth centuries.

Inca empire Powerful South American empire that would reach its peak in the fifteenth century during the reigns of Pachacuti Inca and Topa Inca.

Indentured labor Labor source in the Americas; wealthy planters would pay the European poor to sell a portion of their working lives, usually seven years, in exchange for passage.

Indo-Europeans Series of tribes from southern Russia who, over a period of millennia, embarked on a series of migrations from India through western Europe; their greatest legacy was the broad distribution of Indo-European languages throughout Eurasia.

Indra Early Indian god associated with the Aryans; Indra was the king of the gods and was associated with warfare and thunderbolts.

Indus (IN-duhs) A river with its source in Tibet that flows southwest through India to the Bay of Bengal.

Intelligentsia Refers to an educated and literate class in Russia that often advocated social and political reform. In the late nineteenth century the Russian intelligentsia became frustrated when reform efforts failed, and many turned to anarchism and violence. Some members of the intelligentsia supported the Bolshevik rise to power in the revolution of 1917.

Inti (ihn-tee) The Inca sun god.

Investiture (ihn-VEHST-tih-tyoor) The granting of church offices by a lay leader; one aspect of the medieval European church versus state controversy.

Iran-Contra Scandal Political scandal over arms for hostages in Iran and funding for Nicaraguan contras.

Iranian Revolution Islamist revolution to throw out the U.S.-backed shah in 1979.

Iron Curtain Dividing line between the two blocs of Europe, with one supported by the USSR and the other by the U.S.

Iroquois (EER-uh-kwah) Eastern American Indian confederation made up of the Mohawk, Oneida, Onondaga, Cayuga, and Seneca tribes.

Isabel of Castile (IHZ-uh-bel of ka-steel) Queen of Castile and Leon and wife of Fernando II of Aragon, who together funded Cristoforo Colombo's expedition to discover a westerly route to China.

Islam Monotheistic religion of the prophet Muhammad (570–632); influenced by Judaism and Christianity, Muhammad was considered the final prophet because the earlier religions had not seen the entire picture; the Quran is the holy book of Islam.

Islamism The reassertion of Islamic values in Muslim politics.

Israel A Jewish state created after World War II.

Istanbul (iss-TAHN-bull) Capital city of the Ottoman Empire, built on the site of the capital city of the Byzantine Empire, Constantinople.

Isthmus of Kra (ihs-muhs of krah) A narrow isthmus linking the Malay peninsula to the Asian mainland.

Itzcoatl (tsee-ko-atl) The name of the fourth emperor of the Aztecs who ruled from 1427 to 1440.

Jainism (JEYEN-iz'm) Indian religion associated with the teacher Vardhamana Mahavira (ca. 540–468 B.C.E.) in which every physical object possessed a soul; Jains believe in complete nonviolence to all living beings.

Jati Indian word for a Hindu subcaste.

Jenne (jehn-neh) City in what is now modern Mali, famous for its role in the trans-Saharan trade and for its mud-brick mosque.

Jiaozhou (jyou-joh) A city in the Shandong province of China.

Jieshi, Jiang (jeh-she, jyahng) Also known as Chiang Kai-shek, Jiang became leader of the Kuomintang party after the death of Sun Yat-sen in 1925. After the communist victory in 1949, Jiang and the Kuomintang retreated to the island of Taiwan.

Jihad Arabic word meaning "struggle." In Islam this word is understood to be one's duty to struggle on behalf of the faith. Although this struggle might be a personal and spiritual effort, it has frequently been a call for holy war against perceived enemies. In recent years, radical Islamists such as al-Qaeda have called for a *jihad* against the United States and other "nonbelievers."

Jizya (JIHZ-yuh) Tax in Islamic empires that was imposed on non-Muslims.

Joint-stock companies Early forerunner of the modern corporation; individuals who invested in a trading or exploring venture could make huge profits while limiting their risk.

Judaism The monotheistic religion of the Jewish people that traces its origins to Abraham (ca. 2000 B.C.E.).

Judenstaat (juh-dehn-STAHT) 1896 book written by Theodore Herzl advocating the creation of a Jewish state.

Junzi (juhn-zee) Confucian idea of the ideal human, who lives according to virtue.

Jurchen (JUHR-chehn) A people who inhabited Manchuria until the seventeenth century.

Ka'ba (KAH-bah) Main shrine in Mecca, goal of Muslims embarking on the hajj.

Kabuki (kah-BOO-kee) Japanese theater in which actors were free to improvise and embellish the words.

Kama Hindu concept of the enjoyment of physical and sexual pleasure.

Kamikaze (KAH-mih-kah-zee) A Japanese term meaning "divine wind" that is related to the storms that destroyed Mongol invasion fleets; the term is symbolic of Japanese isolation and was later taken by suicide pilots in World War II.

Kangxi (kahng shee) The third emperor of the Qing dynasty, famous for his learning and work ethic.

Kanun (KUH-noon) Laws issued by the Ottoman Süleyman the Magnificent, also known as Süleyman Kanuni, "the Lawgiver."

Kapu Hawaiian concept of something being taboo.

Karakorum (kahr-uh-KOR-uhm) Capital of the Mongol empire in the thirteenth century.

Karma (KAHR-mah) Hindu concept that the sum of good and bad in a person's life will determine his or her status in the next life.

Kautalya (KAHT-ahl-yah) A minister of Chandragupta, founder of the Mauryan dynasty in India.

Kebra Nagast (kee-brah NAH-gahst) A book written in the priestly Ethiopian language Ge'ez, that traces the Solomonic origins of the Ethiopian emperors.

Kemal, Mustafa (kuh-MAHL, MOOS-fah) Turkish statesman and World War I hero who abolished the caliphate and established Turkey as a modern secular state.

Khanbaliq (Kahn-bah-LEEK) Name of the capital of the Yuan dynasty in China.

Khartoum (khar-TOOM) The capital of Sudan, located at the confluence of the Blue Nile and the White Nile.

Khoikhoi (KOI-koi) An ethnic group in southern Africa.

Khubilai Khan (KOO-bih-lie kahn) Prominent Mongol ruler in the thirteenth century and founder of the Yuan dynasty.

Kilwa (KILH-wah) A thriving Swahili city-state in east Africa between the twelfth and sixteenth centuries.

Kin-based society A society that governs itself primarily through family and clan relationships; many existed in sub-Saharan Africa throughout history.

Kongo Central African state that began trading with the Portuguese around 1500; although their kings, such as King Afonso I (r. 1506–1543), converted to Christianity, they nevertheless suffered from the slave trade.

Korean Conflict The Korean War between North and South Korea.

Koumbi-Saleh Important trading city along the trans-Saharan trade route from the eleventh to the thirteenth centuries.

Kowtow (kou-tou) A former Chinese custom of bowing the forehead to touch the ground as an act of submission.

Kshatriayas (SHUHT-ree-uhs) Hindu caste of warriors and aristocrats.

Kulaks Land-owning Russian peasants who benefited under Lenin's New Economic Policy and suffered under Stalin's forced collectivization.

Kush (kuhsh) An ancient African state of the Nile River Valley, also known as Nubia.

Lamaist Buddhism (LAH-muh-ihst BOO-diz'm) Branch of Buddhism that was similar to shamanism in its acceptance of magic and supernatural powers.

Lapita (Lah-PEE-tah) The pottery style of an ancient Pacific Ocean culture.

La Reforma Political reform movement of Mexican president Benito Juárez (1806–1872) that called for limiting the power of the military and the Catholic church in Mexican society.

Latifundia (lah-tee-FOON-dya) Huge state-run and slave-worked farms in ancient Rome.

League of Nations Forerunner of the United Nations, the dream of American president Woodrow Wilson, although its potential was severely limited by the refusal of the United States to join.

Lebensraum (LAY-behnz-rahwm) German term meaning "living space"; the term is associated with Hitler and his goal of carving out territory in the east for an expanding Germany.

Legalism Chinese philosophy from the Zhou dynasty that called for harsh suppression of the common people.

Legazpi, Miguel Lopez de (le-GAHS-pee, mee-GEHL LOH-pess de) Spanish conquistador who established one of the first European settlements in the East Indies.

Leif Ericson (leef ER-ik-suhn) A Norse explorer who probably landed in North America in the eleventh century.

Lenin, Vladimir Ilyich (LEHN-in, VLAD-uh-meer IL-yich) Founder of the Bolshevik party, leader of the Russian Revolution, and first leader of the Soviet Union from 1917 to 1924.

Leonardo da Vinci (lee-uh-NAHR-doh duh VIHN-chee) Italian artist and scientist of the Italian Renaissance.

Levée en Masse (leh-VAY ahn MAS) A term signifying universal conscription during the radical phase of the French revolution.

Lex talionis (lehks tah-LYO-nihs) "Law of retaliation," laws in which offenders suffered punishments similar to their crimes; the most famous example is Hammurabi's Laws.

Li (LEE) Confucian concept, a sense of propriety.

Liaodong peninsula (lyou-dawng) A peninsula in northeastern China that extends into the Yellow Sea.

Liberalism A political philosophy inspired by John Locke and the ideals of the Enlightenment that advocated individual liberty, constitutional government, and free trade. Nineteenth-century liberals favored representative government but not necessarily democracy.

Liberation theology The beliefs of Christian thinkers and social activists who emphasize Jesus' role in helping those who were oppressed, a view that gained wide support in Latin America in the late twentieth century. Liberation theologians question the historic role of the church in supporting traditional regimes.

Lil'iuokalani (lee-lee-oo-oh-kah-LAH-nee) The last monarch of Hawaii before it was annexed by the United States.

Linear A Minoan written script.

Linear B Early Mycenaean written script, adapted from the Minoan Linear A.

Little Tigers Asian countries that followed the Japanese model for economic development.

Louis (LOO-ee) French name for many of the Capetian kings.

Luddites Early-nineteenth-century artisans who were opposed to new machinery and industrialization.

Macedon (MAS-ih-don) The ancient kingdom of Alexander the Great in the southeastern Balkans.

Machismo (mah-CHEEZ-moh) Latin American social ethic that honored male strength, courage, aggressiveness, assertiveness, and cunning.

Madeiras (muh-DEER-uhs) A group of islands in the Atlantic Ocean to the west of Morocco.

Madrasas (MAH-drahs-ahs) Islamic institutions of higher education that originated in the tenth century.

Magellan, Ferdinand (muh-JEHL-uhn, FUR-dih-nand) Portuguese navigator who commanded an expedition that was the first to circumnavigate the world.

Magyars (MAH-jahrs) Hungarian invaders who raided towns in Germany, Italy, and France in the ninth and tenth centuries.

Mahabharata (mah-hah-BAH-rah-tah) Massive ancient Indian epic that was developed orally for centuries; it tells of an epic civil war between two family branches.

Mahayana (mah-huh-YAH-nah) The "greater vehicle," a more metaphysical and popular northern branch of Buddhism.

Mahmud of Ghazni (mah-muhd of gahz-nee) Founder of the Ghaznavid empire in what is now Afghanistan.

Mahmud II (mah-MOOD) The thirtieth sultan of the Ottoman Empire, famous for instituting extensive military and legal reforms.

Majapahit (mah-jah-PAH-hit) An Indianized kingdom of eastern Java, powerful from the late thirteenth to the end of the fourteenth century.

Mali (MAH-lee) West African kingdom founded in the thirteenth century by Sundiata; it reached its peak during the reign of Mansa Musa.

Malindi (mah-LIN-dee) East African town on the Indian Ocean.

Malintzin (mal-een-tzeen) Also known as La Malinche, Malintzin was an indigenous woman who acted as interpreter and guide for Hernán Cortés during his conquest of Mexico.

Manchus Manchurians who conquered China, putting an end to the Ming dynasty and founding the Qing dynasty (1644–1911).

Mandate of Heaven Chinese belief that the emperors ruled through the mandate, or approval, of heaven contingent on their ability to look after the welfare of the population.

Mandate system System that developed in the wake of World War I when the former colonies ended up as mandates under European control, a thinly veiled attempt at continuing imperialism.

Manichaeism (man-ih-KEE-iz'm) Religion founded by the prophet Mani in the third century C.E., a syncretic version of Zoroastrian, Christian, and Buddhist elements.

Manifest destiny The idea, popular in the United States in the mid-nineteenth century, that the North American continent was intended by God to be settled by white Americans. This notion helped justify the Mexican war of 1846–1848 and the Indian wars of the 1870s and 1880s.

Manor Large estates of the nobles during the European middle ages, home for the majority of the peasants.

Mansa Musa (MAHN-suh MOO-suh) Emperor of the Kingdom of Mali in Africa who made a famous pilgrimage to Mecca.

Mao Zedong (mow zuh-doong) Revolutionary leader of the Chinese Communist Party, who came to power in 1949 and ruled until 1976.

Maori (MAY-oh-ree) Indigenous peoples of New Zealand.

Marae Polynesian temple structure.

Marathon Battlefield scene of the Athenian victory over the Persians in 490 B.C.E.

Maroons Runaway African slaves.

Marshall Plan U.S. plan, officially called the European Recovery Program, that offered financial and other economic aid to all European states that had suffered from World War II, including Soviet bloc states.

Masulipatam (mahsu-lih-pah-tahm) Ancient port town in east-central India.

Mau Mau revolution Revolution in Kenya, forcing out the British.

Maurya, Chandragupta (MORE-yuh, chuhn-drah-GOOP-tah) Founder of the Indian Mauryan empire.

Mauryan empire Indian dynasty (321–185 B.C.E.) founded by Chandragupta Maurya and reaching its peak under Ashoka.

May Fourth Movement Chinese movement that began 4 May 1919 with a desire to eliminate imperialist influences and promote national unity.

Maya (MY-uh) Brilliant Central American society (300–1100) known for math, astronomy, and a sophisticated written language.

Mazzini, Giuseppe (maht-TSEE-nee, joo-ZEP-pe) Italian nationalist whose writings spurred the movement for a unified Italy in the nineteenth century.

McDonaldization The term for cultural homogenization created by globalization.

Medes (meeds) Indo-European branch that settled in northern Persia and eventually fell to another branch, the Persians, in the sixth century.

Meiji Restoration (MAY-jee) Restoration of imperial rule under Emperor Meiji in 1868 by a coalition led by Fukuzawa Yukichi and Ito Hirobumi; the restoration enacted western reforms to strengthen Japan.

Melaka (may-LAHK-ah) Southeast Asian kingdom that was predominantly Islamic.

Mencius (MEN-shi-us) Chinese philosopher who refined the ideas of Confucius and spread them across China.

Menes (mee-neez) The Egyptian pharoah who unified Egypt in 3100 B.C.E.

Mesoamerica (mez-oh-uh-MER-i-kuh) The region comprising Mexico and Central America.

Mesopotamia Term meaning "between the rivers," in this case the Tigris and Euphrates; Sumer and Akkad are two of the earliest societies.

Mestizo (mehs-TEE-soh) Latin American term for children of Spanish and native parentage.

Metallurgy The process of extracting metal from ores, or purifying metals, and of creating objects from metals.

Métis (may-TEE) Canadian term for individuals of mixed European and indigenous ancestry.

Mexica (meh-SHEE-kah) An indigenous people of the Valley of Mexico who became the rulers of the Aztec Empire.

Michelangelo Buonarotti (mik-uhl-AN-juh-loh baw-nahr-RAW-tee) Famous Italian Renaissance painter, sculptor, and architect.

Millet An autonomous, self-governing community in the Ottoman empire.

Mindanao (min-duh-NAH-oh) Second largest island in the Philippines.

Ming Chinese dynasty (1368–1644) founded by Hongwu and known for its cultural brilliance.

Minoan (mih-NOH-uhn) Society located on the island of Crete (ca. 2000–1100 B.C.E.) that influenced the early Mycenaeans.

Missi dominici (MEE-see doh-mee-NEE-chee) "Envoys of the lord ruler," the noble and church emissaries sent out by Charlemagne.

Mission civilisatrice (mee-see-on sih-vihl-ihs-a-trihs) Belief by French colonial rulers in the duty to bring Western civilization to colonized subjects.

Mithradates (mihth-rah-DAY-teez) Ancient king of Pontus who expanded his kingdom by defeating the Romans.

Mithraism (MIHTH-rah-iz'm) Mystery religion based on worship of the sun god Mithras; it became popular among the Romans because of its promise of salvation.

Mochica (moh-CHEE-kah) Pre-Incan South American society (300–700) known for their brilliant ceramics.

Moksha Hindu concept of the salvation of the soul.

Monotheism (mah-noh-THEE-iz'm) Belief in only one god, a rare concept in the ancient world.

Monroe Doctrine American doctrine issued in 1823 during the presidency of James Monroe that warned Europeans to keep their hands off Latin America, and that expressed growing American strength and also growing American imperialistic views regarding Latin America.

Motecuzoma (mo-tec-oo-ZO-ma) Aztec emperor who ruled when Hernán Cortés conquered Mexico.

Mozambique (moh-zam-BEEK) A country on the southeast coast of Africa that became independent from Portugal in 1975.

Mughals (MOO-guhls) Islamic dynasty that ruled India from the sixteenth through the eighteenth centuries; the construction of the Taj Mahal is representative of their splendor; with the exception of the enlightened reign of Akbar, the increasing conflict between Hindus and Muslims was another of their legacies.

Muhammad (muh-HAHM-mahd) Prophet of Islam (570–632).

Muhammed Ali Jinnah (moo-HAM-id ah-lee JIN-uh) Indian statesman and founder of the state of Pakistan.

Mumtaz Mahal (moom tahz muh-HAHL) Beloved wife of the Mughal emperor Shah Jahan, whose death inspired him to build the Taj Mahal.

Muslim A follower of Islam.

Mutsuhito (MOO-tsoo-HEE-taw) Emperor of Japan who encouraged the modernization of Japan after the Meiji Restoration.

Mycenaean (meye-suh-NEE-uhn) Early Greek society on the Peloponese (1600–1100 B.C.E.) that was influenced by the Minoans; the Mycenaeans' conflict with Troy is immortalized in Homer's *Odyssey*.

Nahuatl (na-watl) Ancient language of the Valley of Mexico, and language of the Aztec empire.

Napoleon Bonaparte (nuh-POH-lee-uhn BOH-nuh-pahrt) French general who became emperor of the French from 1804 until his defeat by enemy European powers in 1815.

Nara era Japanese period (710–794), centered around city of Nara, that was the highest point of Chinese influence.

Nasser, Gamal Abdel Leader of Egypt and founder of pan-Arab nationalism.

National Policy Nineteenth-century Canadian policy designed to attract migrants, protect industries through tariffs, and build national transportation systems.

NATO The North Atlantic Treaty Organization, which was established by the United States in 1949 as a regional military alliance against Soviet expansionism.

Navajo (NAH-vah-ho) Native American group that settled in what is now Arizona, New Mexico, and Utah.

Ndebele (uhn-duh-BEE-lee) A people of South Africa that split from King Shaka of the Zulu in the 1820s.

Ndongo (n'DAWN-goh) Angolan kingdom that reached its peak during the reign of Queen Nzinga (r. 1623–1663).

Neandertal (nee-ANN-duhr-tawl) Early humans (100,000 to 35,000 years ago) who were prevalent during the Paleolithic period.

Nebuchadnezzar (neb-uh-kud-NEZ-er) Chaldean king of Babylon.

Negritude (NEH-grih-tood) "Blackness," a term coined by early African nationalists as a means of celebrating the heritage of black peoples around the world.

Neo-Confucianism (nee-oh-kuhn-FYEW-shuhn-iz'm) Philosophy that attempted to merge certain basic elements of Confucian and Buddhist thought; most important of the early Neo-Confucianists was the Chinese thinker Zhu Xi (1130–1200).

Neolithic (nee-uh-LITH-ik) New Stone Age (10,000–4000 B.C.E.), which was marked by the discovery and mastery of agriculture.

Nestorian (neh-STOHR-eeuhn) Early branch of Christianity, named after the fifth-century Greek theologian Nestorius, that emphasized the human nature of Jesus Christ.

New Economic Policy (NEP) Plan implemented by Lenin that called for minor free market reforms.

Nian (neen) An armed uprising that occurred in China in 1851 contemporaneously with the Taiping rebellion.

Nicaea (nahy-SEE-uh) The first ecumenical council in 325 C.E. that produced the wording of the Nicene Creed and condemned heresy.

Nirvana (ner-VAHN-nah) Hindu belief in the state of having transcended the cycle of reincarnation and ending the human cycle of desire and suffering.

Nkrumah, Kwame The leader of Ghana who gained freedom from Britain for Ghana.

Noble Eightfold Path Final truth of the Buddhist Four Noble Truths that called for leading a life of balance and constant contemplation.

Nonalignment Countries not associated with the two powers in the cold war, the USSR and the U.S.

North American Free Trade Agreement (NAFTA) Regional alliance established in 1993 between the United States, Canada, and Mexico; it formed the world's second largest free-trade zone.

Northern Alliance A multiethnic coalition in Afghanistan opposed to the Taliban.

Nostrum (NAHS-truhm) Latin word for "our."

Nubia (NOO-bee-uh) Area south of Egypt; the kingdom of Kush in Nubia invaded and dominated Egypt from 750 to 664 B.C.E.

Nurhaci (NOOR-hacheh) Founding father of the Manchu state.

Nzinga Mbemba (IN-zinga MEHM-bah) Also called King Afonso I, he was ruler of the kingdom of Kongo in the first half of the sixteenth century.

Oaxaca (wah-hah-kah) A city in southeastern Mexico.

Oceania Term referring to the Pacific Ocean basin and its lands.

Odovacer (AHD-oh-vah-cer) Germanic general and first non-Roman ruler after 476.

Olmecs Early Central American society (1200–100 B.C.E.) that centered around sites at San Lorenzo, La Venta, and Tres Zapotes and that influenced later Maya.

Omdurman (om-door-MAHN) 1898 battle in the Sudan in which a British and Egyptian force defeated the Sudanese.

Operation Iraqi Freedom The Iraq War.

Oprichnina (oh-PREEK-nee-nah) A Russian term meaning the "land apart," Muscovite territory that the Russian Tsar Ivan IV (r. 1533–1584) demanded to control; the tsar created a new class of nobles called the *oprichniki* for this territory.

Oracle bones Chinese Shang dynasty (1766–1122 B.C.E.) means of foretelling the future.

Organization of African Unity (OAU) An organization started in 1963 by thirty-two newly independent African states and designed to prevent conflict that would lead to intervention by former colonial powers.

Organization of Petroleum Exporting Countries (OPEC) An organization begun in 1960 by oil-producing states originally for purely economic reasons but that later had more political influence.

Osama bin Laden Founder of Al Qaeda and terrorist wanted for 9/11 attack on the U.S.

Osiris Ancient Egyptian god that represented the forces of nature.

Osman (oz-MAHN) Founder of the dynasty that ruled the Ottoman Empire from 1289–1923.

Otto von Bismarck (oht-toh fuhn BIZ-mahrk) German statesman under whose leadership Germany was united.

Ottoman empire Powerful Turkish empire that lasted from the conquest of Constantinople (Istanbul) in 1453 until 1918 and reached its peak during the reign of Süleyman the Magnificent (r. 1520–1566).

Pachacuti (pah-cha-KOO-tee) Ruler of Inca society from 1438 to 1471, whose military campaigns greatly extended Inca control.

Paleolithic (pey-lee-oh-LITH-ik) Old Stone Age, a long period of human development before the development of agriculture.

Palestinian Liberation Organization (PLO) Ruling party of the Palestinian territories occupied by Israel.

Paris Peace Accords Agreement reached in 1973 that marked the end of the United States's role in the Vietnam War.

Parsis (pahr-SEES) Indian Zoroastrians.

Parthians Persian dynasty (247 B.C.E.–224 C.E.) that reached its peak under Mithradates I.

Pasargadae (pah-SAR-gah-dee) Capital city of ancient Persia.

Pasion (pahs-ee-on) Fourth-century B.C.E. Athenian slave who eventually became a wealthy Athenian citizen.

Pataliputra (pah-tal-ih-puh-trah) Capital city of the Indian Mauryan and Gupta empires.

Pater familias (PAH-tehrr fah-MEE-lyas) Roman term for the "father of the family," a theoretical implication that gave the male head of the family almost unlimited authority.

Patriarch (PAY-tree-ahrk) Leader of the Greek Orthodox church, which in 1054 officially split with the Pope and the Roman Catholic church.

Patriarchy A system of social organization in which males dominate the family and in which the public institutions and descent and succession are traced through the male line.

Patricians Roman aristocrats and wealthy classes.

Pax Americana "American Peace," a term that compares American domination in the years after World War II with the power of Rome at its peak.

Pax Romana (Pahks roh-MAH-nah) "Roman Peace," a term that relates to the period of political stability, cultural brilliance, and economic prosperity beginning with unification under Augustus and lasting through the first two centuries C.E.

Peloponnesian (pell-uh-puh-NEE-suhn) A large peninsula in southern Greece.

Peloponnesus (pell-uh-puh-NEE-suhs) See Peloponnesian.

Peninsulares (peh-neen-soo-LAH-rehs) Latin American officials from Spain or Portugal.

Perestroika (PAYR-eh-stroy-kuh) Economic policy adopted by the USSR to increase labor efficiency.

Pericles (PEH-rih-kleez) Athenian orator and statesman whose leadership contributed to the political and cultural supremacy of Athens.

Persepolis (per-SEP-uh-lis) Ancient capital of the Persian empire.

Petrarca, Francesco (pe-TRAHRK-a, frahn-CHES-kaw) Fourteenth-century Italian poet famous for his love poems.

Pharaohs (FARE-ohs) Egyptian kings considered to be gods on earth.

Philosophes (fil-uh-sofs) Enlightenment intellectuals who sought to apply the methods of science to the improvement of society.

Phoenicians (fi-NEE-shins) Inhabitants of ancient Phoenicia, a narrow coastal plain north of Palestine between the Mediterranean Sea and the Lebanon Mountains.

Piri Reis (pir-ree reys) An Ottoman Turkish admiral and cartographer famous for his maps and charts.

Plebeians (plih-BEE-uhns) Roman common people.

Polis (POH-lihs) Greek term for the city-state.

Popol Vuh (poh-pohl VOO) Mayan creation epic.

Potosi (paw-taw-SEE) City in what is now Bolivia, where Spanish conquerors discovered one of the richest silver veins in the world in 1545.

Prehistory The period before the invention of writing.

Procopius (proh-KOH-pee-uhs) Roman member of the Constantinian dynasty.

Proletariat Urban working class in a modern industrial society.

Protestant Reformation Sixteenth-century European movement during which Luther, Calvin, Zwingli, and others broke away from the Catholic church.

Ptolemaic (tawl-oh-MAY-ihk) Term used to signify both the Egyptian kingdom founded by Alexander the Great's general Ptolemy and the thought of the philosopher Ptolemy of Alexandria (second century C.E.), who used mathematical formulas in an attempt to prove Aristotle's geocentric theory of the universe.

Pueblo (PWEB-loh) Native American groups native to what is now the southwestern United States, called such because they lived in communal adobe homes called pueblos.

Putting-out system Method of getting around guild control by delivering unfinished materials to rural households for completion.

Qadi (KAH-dee) An Islamic judge.

Qanat (kah-NAHT) Persian underground canal.

Qi (chee) Chinese concept of the basic material that makes up the body and the universe.

Qianlong (chyahn-lawng) The fifth Qing emperor of China who ruled at the end of the eighteenth century and was famous for his erudition.

Qin (chihn) Chinese dynasty (221–207 B.C.E.) that was founded by Qin Shihuangdi and was marked by the first unification of China and the early construction of defensive walls.

Qin Shihuangdi (chin she-huang-dee) Founder of the Qin dynasty.

Qing (chihng) Chinese dynasty (1644–1911) that reached its peak during the reigns of Kangxi and Qianlong.

Qizilbash (gih-ZIHL-bahsh) Term meaning "red heads," Turkish tribes that were important allies of Shah Ismail in the formation of the Safavid empire.

Quanzhou (chwahn-joh) Chinese city-port established during the Tang dynasty.

Quecha (keh-CHUA) South American ethnic group of Peru who were once the ruling people of the Inca Empire.

Quetzalcoatl (keh-tzahl-koh-AHT'l) Aztec god, the "feathered serpent," who was borrowed originally from the Toltecs; Quetzalcoatl was believed to have been defeated by another god and exiled, and he promised to return.

Quiché (keesh-AY) Mayan ethnic group of south-central Guatemala.

Quinto (KEEN-toh) The one-fifth of Mexican and Peruvian silver production that was reserved for the Spanish monarchy.

Quipu (KEE-poo) Incan mnemonic aid comprised of different colored strings and knots that served to record events in the absence of a written text.

Quran (koorr-AHN) Islamic holy book that is believed to contain the divine revelations of Allah as presented to Muhammad.

Raja (RAH-juh) A prince or king in India.

Ramayana (rah-MAHY-yuh-nah) Ancient Indian masterpiece about the hero Rama that symbolized the victory of *dharma* (order) over *adharma* (chaos).

Rape of Nanjing Japanese conquest and destruction of the Chinese city of Nanjing in the 1930s.

Realpolitik (ray-AHL-poh-lih-teek) The Prussian Otto von Bismarck's "politics of reality," the belief that only the willingness to use force would actually bring about change.

Reconquista (ray-kohn-KEES-tah) Crusade, ending in 1492, to drive the Islamic forces out of Spain.

Reconstruction System implemented in the American South (1867–1877) that was designed to bring the Confederate states back into the union and also extend civil rights to freed slaves.

Remus (REE-muhs) Along with his brother Romulus, one of the twin founders of Rome.

Renaissance (ren-uh-SAHNS) A period of European history between the fourteenth and mid-seventeenth century in which culture and the arts experienced a rebirth.

Repartimiento (ray-pahrr-tee-MYEN-toh) Spanish labor system in Latin America, supposed to replace the *encomienda* system, in which native communities were compelled to provide laborers for the farms or mines and the Spanish employers were expected to pay fair wages.

Rhodes, Cecil (rhohdz, see-sihl) British financier and statesman in Southern Africa who made his fortune in gold and diamonds.

Ricci, Matteo (REET-chee, maht-TAY-oh) Italian Jesuit priest famous for his service in China during the sixteenth century.

Richelieu (RISH-uh-loo) French statesman and principal minister to king Louis XIII of France.

Richet, Charles (ri-SHEY, shawrl) French physiologist in the late nineteenth and early twentieth centuries.

Romanov (ROH-muh-nawf) The Russian imperial dynasty that ruled from 1613 to 1917.

Romulus (ROM-yuh-luhs) Along with his brother Remus, one of the twin founders of Rome.

Rosas, Juan Manuel de (roh-sahs, HWAHN mahn-WEL de) A conservative Argentine politician who ruled the country from 1829 to 1852.

Rubaiyat (ROO-beye-aht) "Quatrains," famous poetry of Omar Khayyam that was later translated and transformed by Edward Fitzgerald.

Saddam Hussein President of Iraq before the U.S. operation in 2003.

Safavid (SAH-fah-vihd) Later Persian empire (1501–1722) that was founded by Shah Ismail and that became a center for Shiism; the empire reached its peak under Shah Abbas the Great and was centered around the capital of Isfahan.

Saint-Domingue (san doe-MANG) French colony in the Caribbean in what is now the republic of Haiti.

Sakk Letters of credit that were common in the medieval Islamic banking world.

Saljuqs (sahl-JYOOKS) Turkish tribe that gained control over the Abbasid empire and fought with the Byzantine empire.

Samsara (suhm-SAH-ruh) Hindu term for the concept of transmigration, that is, the soul passing into a new incarnation.

Samurai (SAM-uhr-eye) A Japanese warrior who lived by the code of *bushido.*

Sandinistas A socialist Nicaraguan political party in the 1960s and 1970s looking to overthrow the government.

Sanskrit (SAHN-skriht) An ancient classical language of India.

Santeria (sahn-tuh-REE-uh*)* A syncretic Afro-Caribbean religion.

Sao Jorge de Mina (Sou hor-hay day meena) The first Portuguese trading post built on the Gulf of Guinea, which later became an important site for the Atlantic slave trade.

São Tomé (SOU tuh-MEY) Island in the Atlantic west of Africa's Kongo kingdom, used by the Portuguese beginning in the fifteenth century to produce sugar.

Saramaka (sar-ah-mah-kah) A group of Maroons (runaway slaves) who established themselves in the interior of Suriname.

Sasanids (suh-SAH-nids) Later powerful Persian dynasty (224–651) that would reach its peak under Shapur I and later fall to Arabic expansion.

Sati (suh-TEE) Also known as *suttee,* Indian practice of a widow throwing herself on the funeral pyre of her husband.

Satraps (SAY-traps) Persian administrators, usually members of the royal family, who governed a satrapy.

Satyagraha (suh-TYA-gruh-hah) "Truth and firmness," a term associated with Gandhi's policy of passive resistance.

Schlieffen (SHLEE-fn) Early twentieth century German plan for fighting a continental European war on two fronts.

Scholar-bureaucrats Describes the administrative apparatus of China created by the Ming dynasty (1368–1644) and continued by the Qing dynasty (1644–1911). Under this system, Confucian scholars, chosen through a highly competitive series of examinations, ran the country. This system meant that China was a meritocracy, but a very conservative one.

Scholasticism Medieval attempt of thinkers like St. Thomas Aquinas to merge the beliefs of Christianity with the logical rigor of Greek philosophy.

Scientific racism Nineteenth-century attempt to justify racism by scientific means; an example would be Gobineau's *Essay on the Inequality of the Human Races.*

Sebiumeker (sehb-ih-meh-kur) Ancient Nubian creator god.

Seleucid (sih-LOO-sid) A successor state of Alexander the Great that comprised modern Syria, Iraq, and Iran in the Hellenistic era.

Self-determinism Belief popular in World War I and after that every people should have the right to determine their own political destiny; the belief was often cited but ignored by the Great Powers.

Self-strengthening movement Chinese attempt (1860–1895) to blend Chinese cultural traditions with European industrial technology.

Semitic (suh-MIHT-ihk) A term that relates to the Semites, ancient nomadic herders who spoke Semitic languages; examples of Semites were the Akkadians, Hebrews, Aramaics, and Phoenicians, who often interacted with the more settled societies of Mesopotamia and Egypt.

Sengoku (sehn-goh-koo) Also called the "Warring States" period, a time in Japan of social upheaval and military conflict between the fifteenth and seventeenth centuries.

Sepoys Indian troops who served the British.

Seppuku A Japanese term for ritual suicide committed by the samurai when he had been dishonored.

Serfs Peasants who, while not chattel slaves, were tied to the land and who owed obligation to the lords on whose land they worked.

Shah Ismail (shah IZ-may-el) Founder of the Safavid dynasty that ruled Persia in the sixteenth and seventeenth centuries.

Shah Jahan (shah jah-han) Mughal emperor of India, famous for building the Taj Mahal in memory of his beloved wife.

Shamanism (SHAH-mah-niz'm) Belief in shamans or religious specialists who possessed supernatural powers and who communicated with the gods and the spirits of nature.

Shanfei (shahn-fahy) Twentieth-century communist revolutionary in China.

Sharia (shah-RREE-ah) The Islamic holy law, drawn up by theologians from the Quran, and accounts of Muhammad's life.

Shaykh Salim Christi (sheyk sah-LEEM KRIS-tee) Sufi saint whose correct prophecy to Akbar prompted the Mughal emperor to move his capital to Fatehpur Sikri.

Shia (SHEE-ah) Islamic minority in opposition to the Sunni majority; their belief is that leadership should reside in the line descended from Ali.

Shintoism (SHIHN-toh-iz'm) Indigenous Japanese religion that emphasizes purity, clan loyalty, and the divinity of the emperor.

Shiva (SHIH-vuh) Hindu god associated with both fertility and destruction.

Shogun (SHOH-gun) Japanese military leader who ruled in place of the emperor.

Shudras (SHOO-druhs) Hindu caste of landless peasants and serfs.

Siddhartha Gautama (sih-DHAR-thuh GAHW-tah-mah) Indian *kshatriya* who achieved enlightenment and became known as the Buddha, the founder of Buddhism.

Sikhs (SIHKS) Indian syncretic faith that contains elements of Hinduism and Islam.

Silk roads Ancient trade routes that extended from the Roman empire in the west to China in the east.

Sinan Pasha (sih-NAHN pah-cha) Ottoman military commander who was appointed governor of Egypt in 1569.

Singosari (sihng-oh-sah-ree) Thirteenth-century kingdom in east Java.

Sioux (soo) Native North American tribe that ranged from Lake Michigan to the Rocky Mountains.

Social Darwinism Nineteenth-century philosophy, championed by thinkers such as Herbert Spencer, that attempted to apply Darwinian "survival of the fittest" to the social and political realm; adherents saw the the elimination of weaker nations as part of a natural process and used the philosophy to justify war.

Socialism Political and economic theory of social organization based on the collective ownership of the means of production; its origins were in the early nineteenth century, and it differs from communism by a desire for slow or moderate change compared to the communist call for revolution.

Socrates (SAHK-rah-teez) Ancient Athenian philosopher and teacher of Plato.

Solidarity Polish trade union and nationalist movement in the 1980s that was headed by Lech Walesa.

Song (SOHNG) Chinese dynasty (960–1279) that was marked by an increasingly urbanized and cosmopolitan society.

Song Taizu (sawng tahy-zoo) Founder of the tenth-century Song dynasty in China.

Songhay (song-AHY) Fifteenth- through sixteenth-century empire in west Africa specializing in the gold trade.

Soviets Russian elected councils that originated as strike committees during the 1905 St. Petersburg disorders; they represented a form of local self-government that went on to become the primary unit of government in the Union of Soviet Socialist Republics. The term was also used during the cold war to designate the Soviet Union.

Spanish Inquisition Institution organized in 1478 by Fernando and Isabel of Spain to detect Protestant heresy and the secret practice of Judaism or Islam.

Spartacus (SPAHR-tah-cus) A Roman slave who became the leader of an uprising meant to overthrow the Roman Republic.

Spheres of influence A region dominated by an outside power. Generally refers to the intrusion of western imperial powers into China in the late nineteenth century. China, although technically a sovereign state, was divided into "spheres," each one occupied by a European state that had license to conduct business without any interference.

Sputnik The first manmade satellite to orbit Earth, made by the USSR.

Srivijaya (sree-vih-JUH-yuh) Southeast Asian kingdom (670–1025), based on the island of Sumatra, that used a powerful navy to dominate trade.

Stateless societies Term relating to societies such as those of sub-Saharan Africa after the Bantu migrations that featured decentralized rule through family and kinship groups instead of strongly centralized hierarchies.

Stoicism A Hellenistic philosophy that emphasized strict adherence to duty and personal self-discipline. It became very popular among the Roman upper classes.

Stoics (STOH-ihks) Hellenistic philosophers who encouraged their followers to lead active, virtuous lives and to aid others.

Strabo (STRAH-boh) Greek geographer (first century C.E.).

Strategic Arms Limitations Talk (SALT) Agreement in 1972 between the United States and the Soviet Union.

St. Scholastica (skuh-LAS-tih-kah) The twin sister of St. Benedict of Nursia, the compiler of *The Rule of St. Benedict,* which provided a guide to monastic living based on poverty, obedience, and service. St. Scholastica (480–547 C.E.) is believed to have spread the *Rule* among communities of nuns.

St. Thomas Aquinas (uh-KWAHY-nuhs) Thirteenth-century Italian theologian best remembered for his attempt to reconcile faith and reason in Christian theology.

Stupas (STOO-pahs) Buddhist shrines.

Sudetenland (soo-DEYT-n-land) The name used to describe the western regions of Czechoslovakia inhabited mostly by ethnic Germans.

Suez Crisis When Britain, France, and Israel attacked Egypt in 1956 to regain the Suez Canal.

Sufis (SOO-fees) Islamic mystics who placed more emphasis on emotion and devotion than on strict adherence to rules.

Sui (SWAY) Chinese dynasty (589–618) that constructed Grand Canal, reunified China, and allowed for the splendor of the Tang dynasty that followed.

Sui Yangdi (sway-yahng-dee) Second emperor of the Sui dynasty, famous for completing the Grand Canal and reconstructing the Great Wall in the early seventh century.

Süleyman (SOO-lehy-mahn) Ottoman Turkish ruler Süleyman the Magnificent (r. 1520–1566), who was the most powerful and wealthy ruler of the sixteenth century.

Sumerians (soo-MEHR-ee-uhns) Earliest Mesopotamian society.

Sundiata (soon-JAH-tuh) Founder of the Mali empire (r. 1230–1255), also the inspiration for the *Sundiata,* an African literary and mythological work.

Sunni (SOON-nee) "Traditionalists," the most popular branch of Islam; Sunnis believe in the legitimacy of the early caliphs, compared to the Shiite belief that only a descendent of Ali can lead.

Sunni Ali (soon-ee ah-lee) First great king of the Songhay empire in West Africa.

Surat (soo-RAHT) Port city on India's northwest coast with an important historical role in trade.

Suriname (SOOR-uh-nahm) Former Dutch colony in northeastern South America that achieved independence in 1975.

Suu Kyi, Aung San (SOO KEE, AWNG SAHN) Opposition leader (1945–) in Myanmar; she was elected leader in 1990 but she was not allowed to come to power; she was a Nobel Peace Prize recipient in 1991.

Swahili (swah-HEE-lee) East African city-state society that dominated the coast from Mogadishu to Kilwa and was active in trade.

Taino (tah-EE-noh) A Caribbean tribe who were the first indigenous peoples from the Americas to come into contact with Christopher Columbus.

Taiping rebellion (TEYE-pihng) Rebellion (1850–1864) in Qing China led by Hong Xiuquan, during which twenty to thirty million were killed; the rebellion was symbolic of the decline of China during the nineteenth century.

Taliban A fundamentalist Islamic militia in Afghanistan.

Tang Taizong (TAHNG TEYE-zohng) Chinese emperor (r. 627–649) who founded the Tang dynasty (618–907).

Tanzimat (TAHNZ-ee-MAT) A period of reform in the Ottoman Empire between 1845 and 1876.

Temüjin (TEM-oo-chin) Mongol conqueror (ca. 1167–1227) who later took the name Chinggis Khan, "universal ruler."

Tenochtitlan (teh-noch-tee-TLAHN) Capital of the Aztec empire, later Mexico City.

Teotihuacan (tay-oh-tee-wa-KAHN) Central American society (200 B.C.E.–750 C.E.); its Pyramid of the Sun was the largest structure in Mesoamerica.

Terrorism The use of violence against civilians in order to gain political or religious goals.

Teutonic Knights Crusading European order that was active in the Baltic region.

Texcoco (TEHS-co-co) A major city-state in the Valley of Mexico during the Aztec period, and a member of the Aztec Triple Alliance.

Tezcatlipoca (tehs-cah-tlee-poh-cah) A central deity in the Aztec religion.

Theodosius (thee-uh-DOH-see-uhs) The last emperor of a united Roman Empire. He became a Christian in 391 C.E.

Theravada (thehr-ah-VAH-dah) One of two schools of Buddhism emphasizing personal salvation through one's own efforts.

Third Rome Concept that a new power would rise up to carry the legacy of Roman greatness after the decline of the Second Rome, Constantinople; Moscow was referred to as the Third Rome during the fifteenth century.

Three Principles of the People Philosophy of Chinese Guomindang leader Sun Yat-sen (1866–1925) that emphasized nationalism, democracy, and people's livelihood.

Tian (TEE-ehn) Chinese term for heaven.

Tian Shan (tyahn shahn) A mountain range located in central Asia.

Tikal (tee-KAHL) Maya political center from the fourth through the ninth centuries.

Timbuktu (tim-buhk-TOO) A city in what is now central Mali, famous for its historical role in the gold trade.

Timur-i lang (tee-MOOR-yee LAHNG) "Timur the Lame," known in English as Tamerlane (ca. 1336–1405), who conquered an empire ranging from the Black Sea to Samarkand.

Tlacopan (tee-laaa-co-pawn) A major city-state in the Valley of Mexico during the Aztec period, and a member of the Aztec Triple Alliance.

Tlatelolco (tl-tay-LOL-ko) Once a separate island city in Lake Texcoco, it was later incorporated into the Aztec capital of Tenochtitlan.

Tokugawa (TOH-koo-GAH-wah) Last shogunate in Japanese history (1600–1867); it was founded by Tokugawa Ieyasu who was notable for unifying Japan.

Toltecs Central American society (950–1150) that was centered around the city of Tula.

Topkapi (TOHP-kah-pih) A palace in Istanbul that was the main residence of the Ottoman sultans from 1465 to 1853.

Trail of Tears Forced relocation of the Cherokee from the eastern woodlands to Oklahoma (1837–1838); it was symbolic of U.S. expansion and destruction of indigenous Indian societies.

Treaty of Sevres (SEV-ruh) The peace treaty (1920) between the Ottoman Empire and the Allies after World War I.

Tres Zapotes (TRACE-zah-POE-tace) Ancient Olmec city in what is now Veracruz state in Mexico.

Triangular trade Trade between Europe, Africa, and the Americas that featured finished products from Europe, slaves from Africa, and American products bound for Europe.

Triple Alliance Pre–World War I alliance of Germany, Austria-Hungary, and Italy.

Triple Entente (ahn-TAHNT) Pre–World War I alliance of England, France, and Russia.

Truman Doctrine U.S. policy instituted in 1947 by President Harry Truman in which the United States would follow an interventionist foreign policy to contain communism.

Tsar (ZAHR) Old Russian term for king that is derived from the term *caesar.*

Tsuyoshi, Inukai (ts-yo-she, ee-NO-kigh) Prime Minister of Japan from December 1931 to May 1932.

Tungan (tuhn-gahn) A term used to describe a Muslim people of Chinese origin.

Tuthmosis (tuh-MOE-sis) Egyptian pharaoh from the eighteenth dynasty.

Twelver Shiism (SHEE'i'zm) Branch of Islam that stressed that there were twelve perfect religious leaders after Muhammad and that the twelfth went into hiding and would return someday; Shah Ismail spread this variety through the Safavid empire.

Tyre (tah-yer) A port in what is now southern Lebanon, formerly an important Phoenician city for trade in silk.

Uighurs (WEE-goors) Turkish tribe.

Ukiyo Japanese word for the "floating worlds," a Buddhist term for the insignificance of the world that came to represent the urban centers in Tokugawa Japan.

Ulaanbaatar (OO-lahn-bah-tahr) Mongolian city.

Ulama (oo-lah-MAH) Islamic officials, scholars who shaped public policy in accordance with the Quran and the *sharia.*

Umayyad (oo-MEYE-ahd) Arabic dynasty (661–750), with its capital at Damascus, that was marked by a tremendous period of expansion to Spain in the west and India in the east.

Umma (UM-mah) Islamic term for the "community of the faithful."

United Nations (UN) Successor to the League of Nations, an association of sovereign nations that attempts to find solutions to global problems.

Universal Declaration of Human Rights United Nations bill of rights protecting all human beings.

Upanishads (oo-pan-NIH-shuhds) Indian reflections and dialogues (800–400 B.C.E.) that reflected basic Hindu concepts.

Urdu (OOR-doo) A language that is predominant in Pakistan.

Uruk (OO-rook) Ancient Mesopotamian city from the fourth millennium B.C.E. that was allegedly the home of the fabled Gilgamesh.

Vaishyas (VEYESH-yuhs) Hindu caste of cultivators, artisans, and merchants.

Vaqueros (bah-KEH-rohs) Latin American cowboys, similar to the Argentine gaucho.

Vardhamana (vahr-duh-MAH-duh) Indian sage who developed the central tenets of Jainism.

Vargas, Getúlio Dornelles (VAHR-guhs, zhi-TOO-lyoo door-NE-lis) Twentieth century Brazilian statesman who ruled Brazil as a virtual dictator.

Varna (VUHR-nuh) Hindu word for caste.

Varuna (vuh-ROO-nuh) Early Aryan god who watched over the behavior of mortals and preserved the cosmic order.

Vasco da Gama (VAS-koh duh GAM-uh) Portuguese explorer who was the first to sail directly from Europe to India in 1498.

Vedas (VAY-duhs) "Wisdom," early collections of prayers and hymns that provide information about the Indo-European Aryans who migrated into India around 1500 B.C.E.; *Rig Veda* is most important collection.

Velvet revolution A term that describes the nonviolent transfer of power in Czechoslovakia during the collapse of Soviet rule.

Venta, La (BEHN-tah, lah) Early Olmec center (800–400 B.C.E.).

Venus figurines Small Paleolithic statues of women with exaggerated sexual features.

Vernacular (ver-NA-kyoo-lar) The language of the people; Martin Luther translated the Bible from the Latin of the Catholic church into the vernacular German.

Versailles (vehr-SEYE) Palace of French King Louis XIV.

Vichy (vee-SHEE) A city in France that served as the capital of unoccupied France during World War II.

Viet Minh North Vietnamese nationalist communists under Ho Chi Minh.

Vijayanagar (vih-juh-yuh-NUH-guhr) Southern Indian kingdom (1336–1565) that later fell to the Mughals.

Villa, Francisco (VEE-uh, frahn-SEES-kow) General in the Mexican Revolution, also known as "Pancho Villa."

Viracocha (veer-rah-coh-chah) A deity in the Inca religion believed to have been responsible for the creation of civilization.

Virgin of Guadalupe (gwah-dah-LOO-pay) Iconic image of the Virgin Mary who appeared to a peasant in Mexico in 1531, after which a shrine was built to commemorate the vision. It is an enduring symbol of Mexican national identity.

Vishnu (VIHSH-noo) Hindu god, preserver of the world, who was often incarnated as Krishna.

Volksgeist (FOHLKS-geyest) "People's spirit," a term that was coined by the German philosopher Herder; a nation's volksgeist would not come to maturity unless people studied their own unique culture and traditions.

Volta do mar (VOHL-tah doh MAHR) "Return through the sea," a fifteenth-century Portuguese sea route that took advantage of the prevailing winds and currents.

Voltaire (vohl-TAIR) French writer who embodied the spirit of the eighteenth-century Enlightenment.

Von Herder, Johann Gottfried (fuhn HER-duhr, YOH-hahn GAWT-freet) Eighteenth-century German philosopher who advocated the power of intuition over reason.

Von Metternich, Klemens (fuhn MET-er-nik, kleh-mens) German-Austrian politician who was critical in the negotiations of the Congress of Vienna after the end of the Napoleonic wars.

Voudou (voo-doo) A polytheistic West African religion that traveled with African slaves and was adapted to conditions in the Caribbean, particularly on the island of Haiti.

Wahhabi (wuh-HAH-bee) Orthodox Sunni Muslim sect from Saudi Arabia that rejects any changes in Islam after the third century of its existence.

Waldensians Twelfth-century religious reformers who criticized the Roman Catholic church and who proposed that the laity had the right to preach and administer sacraments; they were declared heretics.

Walesa, Lech (WAH-lehn-sah, LEHK) Leader of the Polish Solidarity movement.

Wanli (wahn-LEE) Chinese Ming emperor (r. 1572–1620) whose refusal to meet with officials hurried the decline of Ming dynasty.

War Communism The Russian policy of nationalizing industry and seizing private land during the civil war.

Warsaw Pact Warsaw Treaty Organization, a military alliance formed by Soviet bloc nations in 1955 in response to rearmament of West Germany and its inclusion in NATO.

Westphalia (west-FEY-lee-uh) Peace treaties that ended the Thirty Years' War.

Wind wheels Prevailing wind patterns in the Atlantic and Pacific Oceans north and south of the equator; their discovery made sailing much safer and quicker.

Witte, Sergei (VIHT-tee, SAYR-gay) Late-nineteenth-century Russian minister of finance who pushed for industrialization.

World Health Organization (WHO) United Nation organization designed to deal with global health issues.

World Trade Organization (WTO) An organization that was established in 1995 with more than 120 nations and whose goal is to loosen barriers to free trade.

Wuwei (woo-WAY) Daoist concept of a disengagement from the affairs of the world.

Xavier, Francis (ZEY-vee-er, fran-sis) Jesuit missionary who introduced Christianity to Japan.

Xenophobia (zen-uh-FOH-bee-uh) A fear of foreigners or strangers.

Xhosa (KOH-suh) An agriculturalist people in southeast South Africa who speak a Bantu language.

Xia (shyah) Early Chinese dynasty (2200–1766 B.C.E.) that is known mainly from legend.

Xi'an (shee-ahn) One of the oldest cities in Chinese history, and one of the capitals of the Zhou, Qin, Han, Sui, and Tang dynasties.

Xianyang (SHYAHN-YAHNG) Capital city of Qin empire.

Xiao (SHAYOH) Confucian concept of respect for one's parents and ancestors.

Xinjiang (shin-jyahng) Western Chinese province.

Xiongnu (SHE-OONG-noo) A nomadic people of Central Asia who frequently invaded Han dynasty China.

Xuantong (soo-ahn-tohng) Also known as Puyi, the twelfth and final Qing emperor to rule China.

Xuanzang (SHWEN-ZAHNG) Seventh-century Chinese monk who made a famous trip to India to collect Buddhist texts.

Xunzi (SHOON-dzuh) Chinese philosopher who lived during the Warring States period, who believed human nature was essentially bad.

Yahweh (YAH-way) God of the monotheistic religion of Judaism that influenced later Christianity and Islam.

Yangshao (YAHNG-shahw) Early Chinese society (2500–2200 B.C.E.).

Yangzi (YAHNG-zuh) River in central China.

Yemelian Pugachev (yehm-eel-ian puh-gah-chehf) Leader of a major Cossack rebellion during the reign of Catherine II in eighteenth-century Russia.

Yongle (YAWNG-leh) Chinese Ming emperor (r. 1403–1424) who pushed for foreign exploration and promoted cultural achievements such as the *Yongle Encyclopedia.*

Young Turks Nineteenth-century Turkish reformers who pushed for changes within the Ottoman empire, such as universal suffrage and freedom of religion.

Yu (yoo) Legendary founder of the Xia dynasty (ca. 2200 B.C.E.).

Yuan (yoo-AHN) Chinese dynasty (1279–1368) that was founded by the Mongol ruler Khubilai Khan.

Yucatan (yoo-kah-TAN) Peninsula in Central America, home of the Maya.

Yurts (yuhrts) Tents used by nomadic Turkish and Mongol tribes.

Zacatecas (sah-kah-TEH-kahs) The capital of the Mexican state of Zacatecas.

Zahir al-Din Muhammad (zah-here ahl-dihn muh-HAHM-mud) Also known as Babur, founder of the Mughal dynasty in India.

Zaibatsu (zeye-BAHT-soo) Japanese term for "wealthy cliques," which are similar to American trusts and cartels but usually organized around one family.

Zambos (SAHM-bohs) Latin American term for individuals born of indigenous and African parents.

Zamudio, Adela (sah-MOO-dyo, ah-DEH-lah) Nineteenth-century Bolivian poet, author of "To Be Born a Man."

Zanj (zahn-jee) Slave revolt led by Ali bin Muhammed in 869 C.E. The rebels successfully captured Basra in Mesopotamia and established a state in the region until they were defeated by the Abbasid Empire fourteen years later.

Zapata, Emiliano (zuh-PAH-tuh, eh-mee-LYAH-no) Revolutionary who was a leading figure in the Mexican Revolution of 1910.

Zarathustra (zar-uh-THOO-struh) Persian prophet (ca. 628–551 B.C.E.) who founded Zoroastrianism.

Zemstvos (ZEHMST-voh) District assemblies elected by Russians in the nineteenth century.

Zen Buddhism Japanese version of Chinese Chan Buddhism, with an emphasis on intuition and sudden flashes of insight instead of textual study.

Zhang Qian (jung-chen) Imperial envoy during the Han dynasty in the second century B.C.E., who was the first to bring reliable information about central Asia back to the Emperor.

Zheng He (jung ha) Chinese eunuch mariner who commanded the famous Seven Voyages from 1405 to 1433.

Zhou (JOH) Chinese dynasty (1122–256 B.C.E.) that was the foundation of Chinese thought formed during this period: Confucianism, Daoism, Zhou Classics.

Zhu Xi (ZHOO-SHEE) Neo-Confucian Chinese philosopher (1130–1200).

Zhuangzi (joo-wong-dz) Fourth-century B.C.E. Chinese philosopher who developed the Hundred Schools of Thought tradition.

Ziggurats (ZIG-uh-rahts) Mesopotamian temples.

Zimbabwe (zihm-BAHB-way) Former colony of Southern Rhodesia that gained independence in 1980.

Zoroastrianism (zohr-oh-ASS-tree-ahn-iz'm) Persian religion based on the teaching of the sixth-century B.C.E. prophet Zarathustra; its emphasis on the duality of good and evil and on the role of individuals in determining their own fate would influence later religions.

CREDITS

PHOTO CREDITS

Chapter 1 Page 4: © Erich Lessing/Art Resource, NY; p. 11: © Georg Gerster/Photo Researchers, Inc.; p. 12: © Réunion des Musées Nationaux/ Art Resource, NY; p. 15: © Nik Wheeler; p. 16: © The Oriental Institute Museum, University of Chicago **Chapter 2** Page 26: © Will & Deni McIntyre/Getty Images/Stone; p. 31: © Erich Lessing/Art Resource, NY; p. 35: © Robert Partridge/The Ancient Egypt Picture Library; p. 36: © The British Museum, London/Bridgeman Art Library; p. 38: © Werner Foreman/Art Resource, NY; p. 40: © The British Museum, London/Bridgeman Art Library **Chapter 3** Page 46: © Scala/Art Resource, NY; p. 51: © MacQuitty International Collection; p. 53: © The British Museum; p. 54: © Los Angeles County Museum of Art, From the Nasli and Alice Heeramaneck Collection, Museum Associates Purchase, Photograph © 2006 Museum Associates/LACMA; p. 59: © Ritual vessel (chia), Chinese, Shang Dynasty, 12th century BC, Bronze, 52.8 × 30.5 cm. Freer Gallery of Art, Smithsonian Institution, Washington, DC: Purchase F1923.1; p. 61: © Werner Foreman/ Art Resource, NY; p. 63: © Keren Su/Corbis **Chapter 4** Page 66: © DOUG STERN/National Geographic Stock; p. 71: © Andrew Rakaczy/ Photo Researchers, Inc.; p. 72: © Richard Steedman; p. 73: © Justin Kerr; p. 75: © Robert Frerck/ Odyssey; p. 78: © Osterreichische National Bibliothek, Vienna. Photo © Bildarchiv, ONB, Wien; p. 80: © The British Library Board. All rights reserved 05/29/2009/ADD. 23921 fol. 20 **Chapter 5** Page 86: © Erich Lessing/Art Resource, NY; p. 90: © The Art Archive/Alfredo Dagli Orti; p. 92: © The Oriental Institute Museum, University of Chicago; p. 93: Courtesy Museum of Fine Arts, Boston. Reproduced with permission. Gift of Mrs. George M. Brett. Photograph © 2010 Museum of Fine Arts, Boston. All rights reserved; p. 94: © The State Hermitage Museum, St. Petersburg, Russia; p. 97: © Fred J. Maroon/Photo Researchers, Inc.; p. 99: © The State Hermitage Museum, St. Petersburg, Russia **Chapter 6** Page 102: © Bibliotheque Nationale, Paris, France/The Bridgeman Art Library; p. 105: © Photo: akg-images, London; p. 108: © Burstein Collection/Corbis; p. 112: © O. Louis Mazzatenta/ NGS Image Collection; p. 116: © The Nelson-Atkins Museum of Art, Kansas City, Missouri, Purchase: William Rockhill Nelson Trust, 33-521.; p. 117: © Erich Lessing/Art Resource, NY **Chapter 7** Page 120: © SEF/Art Resource, NY; p. 124: © Sarnath, Uttar Pradesh, India/ © The Bridgeman Art Library; p. 127: © The Art Archive; p. 128: © Borromeo/Art Resource, NY; p. 129: © The British Museum; p. 131: © Royalty-Free/Corbis; p. 132: © Foto Features; p. 133: © Pakistani (ancient Gandhara), Bodhisattva, 2nd-3rd century, schist, 150.5 × 53.3 × 19 cm, The James W. and Marilynn Alsdorf Collection, 198.1997. © The Art Institute of Chicago. All rights reserved. **Chapter 8** Page 138: © Vanni Archive/Corbis; p. 143: © Réunion des Musées Nationaux/Art Resource, NY; p. 148: © The British Museum; p. 150: © The British Museum; p. 155: © Photos.com/Jupiterimages; p. 157: © Vatican Museum/Robert Harding Picture Library; p. 161: © Robert Frerck/Odyssey **Chapter 9** Page 164: © Werner Foreman/Art Resource, NY; p. 169 left: © The British Museum; p. 169 right: © With permission of the Royal Ontario Museum. © ROM (910.159.644); p. 171: © Photo: akg-images, London; p. 173: © Bildarchiv Preussischer Kulturbesitz/Art Resource, NY; p. 178: © Erich Lessing/Art Resource, NY; p. 181: © Ancient Art & Architecture Collection **Chapter 10** Page 186: © Erich Lessing/Art Resource, NY; p. 191: © Scala/Art Resource, NY; p. 192: © John A. Rizzo/Getty Images; p. 193: © The Granger Collection, New York; p. 195: © Bibliothèque Nationale de France, Paris (RCA12523); p. 202: © Biblioteca Apostolica, atican Library/Index S.A.S. **Chapter 11** Page 204: © Bibliotheque Nationale de France, Paris (Ms Arabe 5847 fol 138); p. 208: © Erich Lessing/Art Resource, NY; p. 212: © photoasia; p. 214: © Bodleian Library, University of Oxford, MS. Pococke 275 folios 3v-4r; p. 215: © Bibliothèque Nationale de France, Paris (Ms Arabe 5847 fol 105); p. 216: © Benjamin Rondel; p. 218: Courtesy of the Arthur M. Sackler Museum, Harvard University Art Museums, Promise gift of Mr. and Mrs. Stuart Cary Welch, Jr. Partially owned by the Metropolitan Museum of Art and the Arthur M. Sackler Museum, Harvard University, 1988. In honor of the students of Harvard University and Radcliffe College (1988.460.3) **Chapter 12** Page 222: © The Nelson-Atkins Museum of Art, Kansas City, Missouri. Purchase: William Rockhill Nelson Trust, 47-71. Photograph by John Lamberton.; p. 227: © Dean Conger/Corbis; p. 230: © Cultural Relics Publishing House, Beijing; p. 232: © Michael Freeman/Corbis; p. 235: © Cultural Relics Publishing House, Beijing; p. 236: © Fujita Museum of Art; p. 238: © V&A Images, London/Art Resource, NY **Chapter 13** Page 242: © The British Museum; p. 247: © DPA/NMK/The Image Works; p. 249: © Abraham Nowitz/National Geographic Stock; p. 253: © V&A Images, London/Art Resource, NY; p. 256: © The British Library Board. All rights reserved 05/29/2009/J-55[3]; p. 258: © Albrecht G. Schaefer/Corbis; p. 259: © Alain Evrard/Photo Researchers, Inc. **Chapter 14** Page 264: © National Palace Museum, Taipei, Taiwan, Republic of China; p. 267: © Topkapi Palace Museum, Istanbul, Turkey/The Bridgeman Art Library; p. 271: © National Palace Museum, Taipei, Taiwan, Republic of China; p. 272: © Bibliothèque Nationale de France, Paris (Ms. Persan Suppl. 1113 f.49); p. 275: © Bibliothèque Nationale de France, Paris (Ms. Persan Suppl. 1113 f.180v); p. 278: © Travel Ink/Getty Images **Chapter 15** Page 282: © Explorer/Photo Researchers, Inc; p. 286:Photograph © 1979 Dirk Bakker; p. 289: © Marc and Evelyne Bernheim/ Woodfin Camp and Associates; p. 290: © Peter Guttman/Corbis; p. 293: © Werner Forman/Art Resource, NY; p. 294: © British Library/HIP/Art Resource, NY; p. 295: © Great Aimbabwe/ Woodfin Camp/Aurora Photos **Chapter 16** Page 298: © Scala/Art Resource, NY; p. 301: © Erich Lessing/Art Resource, NY; p. 306: © British Library/HIP/Art Resource, NY; p. 308: © Bodleian Library, University of Oxford (MS Bodl. 264, fol. 218r); p. 310: © Erich Lessing/Art Resource, NY; p. 313: © The Pierpont Morgan Library/Art Resource, NY; p. 314: © Royalty-Free/Corbis; p. 318: © The Bridgeman Art Library **Chapter 17** Page 322: © Private Collection/ Jean-Pierre Courau/The Bridgeman Art Library; p. 327: © Bodleian Library, University of Oxford (MS Arch. Selden, A.1, fol. 31r); p. 329: © Biblioteca Nazionale Centrale, Florence/ Index S.A.S.; p. 330: © Georg Gerster/Photo Researchers, Inc.; p. 333: © Jim Zuckerman/ Corbis; p. 334: © Collection of the New-York Historical Society, USA/The Bridgeman Art Library; p. 337: © Honolulu Academy of Arts, Gift of George R. Carter, 1927 (5945); p. 338: © Douglas Peebles Photography/Alamy **Chapter 18** Page 342: © National Palace Museum, Taipei, Taiwan, Republic of China; p. 348: © Bibliotheque Nationale, Paris, France/The Bridgeman Art Library; p. 351: © Bibliothèque Nationale de France, Paris (RCC9816); p. 353: © White porcelain with under glaze blue decoration. China Ming dynasty, early 15th century. With permission of the Royal Ontario Museum © ROM (925.25.15a-b); p. 354: © Medioimages/Getty Images; p. 360: © World map engraving, 1532, Typus Comsmographicus Universalis by Münster, Sebastian. With permission of the Royal Ontario Museum © ROM (956.186.2) **Chapter 19** Page 366: © Banco Nacional Ultramarino, Portugal/ Giraudon/The Bridgeman Art Library; p. 369: © Osterreichische National Bibliothek, Vienna. Photo © Bildarchiv, ONB, Wien; p. 376: © National Maritime Museum, Greenwich, London; p. 379: © Maritiem Museum, Rotterdam. P-2161-31; p. 382: © Peabody Museum, Harvard University (2004.24.29636); p. 383: © From the James Ford Bell Library, University of Minnesota **Chapter 20** Page 386: © Erich Lessing/Art Resource, NY; p. 391: © Bildarchiv Preussischer Kulturbesitz/Art Resource, NY; p. 394: © Bibliothèque Nationale de France, Paris; p. 395: © The Granger Collection, New York; p. 397: © Bridgeman-Giraudon/Art Resource, NY; p. 402: © The Granger Collection, New York; p. 404: © Bettmann/Corbis; p. 407: © World History Archive/Alamy **Chapter 21** Page 410: © The Granger Collection, New York; p. 413: © The New York Public Library/Art Resource, NY; p. 414: © Bridgeman-Giraudon/Art Resource, NY; p. 419: Courtesy of Whitehall-Robins Company, Photograph by Don Eiler; p. 420: © Museo Nacional de Historia, Mexico City, Mexico/Giraudon/The Bridgeman Art Library; p. 424: © The New York Public Library/Art Resource, NY; p. 425: © The Bridgeman Art Library **Chapter 22** Page 430: © North Wind Picture Archives; p. 433: © Bibliothèque Nationale de France, Paris (RC C 1619); p. 436: © From Description de l'Afrique by Olifert Dapper, 1686; p. 441: © National Maritime Museum, London, #A1818; p. 443: © The New York Public Library/Art Resource, NY; p. 445: © From Debret, Voyages Pittoresque et Historiques au Bresil, 1816-1831; p. 447: © National Portrait Gallery, Smithsonion Institution/Art Resource, NY **Chapter 23** Page 450: © Erich Lessing/Art Resource, NY; p. 454: © David Noton/Aurora Photos; p. 456: © The Metropolitan Museum of Art, Rogers Fund, 1942. (42.141.2). Photograph © 1980 The Metropolitan Museum of Art; p. 459: © Golestan Palace, Tehran, Iran/© Giraudon/Bridgeman Art Library; p. 460: © The New York Public Library/Art Resource, NY; p. 466: © Carousel/Laurie Platt Winfrey, Inc.; p. 467: © The British Museum **Chapter 24** Page 470: © Andrea Pistolesi/The Image Bank/Getty Images; p. 474: © Bridgeman-Giraudon/Art Resource, NY; p. 475: © The British Library Board. All rights reserved 05/29/2009/OR.3248, f. 55v; p. 478: © V&A Images, London/Art Resource, NY; p. 479: © Private Collection/The Stapleton Collection/The Bridgeman Art Library; p. 481: © Harvey Lloyd; p. 482: © Robert Harding/Robert Harding World Imagery/Corbis; p. 483: © Byron Crader/Ric Ergenbright Photography; p. 485: © Topkapi Palace Museum **Chapter 25** Page 490: © Bridgeman-Giraudon/Art Resource, NY; p. 495: © Yale University Art Gallery, Trumbell Collection; p. 499: © Bibliothèque Nationale de France, Paris (RCC 17519); p. 502: © The Granger Collection, New York; p. 504: © Art Resource, NY; p. 510: Schloss Friedrichsruhe/© The Bridgeman Art Library **Chapter 26** Page 514: © The Art Archive; p. 518: © Bettmann/Corbis; p. 519: Science Museum, London/© The Bridgeman Art Library; p. 522:Guildhall Library, Corporation of London/© The Bridgeman Art Library; p. 525: © Hulton-Deutsch Collection/Corbis; p. 527:Deutsches Historisches Museum, Berlin; p. 531: Library of Congress; p. 532: © Carousel/Laurie Platt Winfrey, Inc. **Chapter 27** Page 534: © Underwood & Underwood/Corbis; p. 538: Library of Congress; p. 539: Library of Congress; p. 544: © Lake County Museum/Corbis; p. 545: © The Mariners' Museum/Corbis; p. 546: © Museum of the City of New York/Corbis; p. 550: © Corbis; p. 551: © Bettmann/Corbis **Chapter 28** Page 554: © Erich Lessing/Art Resource, NY; p. 557: © Baldwin H. Ward & Kathryn C. Ward/Corbis; p. 561: © V&A Images, Victoria and Albert Museum; p. 565: © Historical Picture Archives/Corbis; p. 568: © Anti-Slavery International/Panos; p. 573: © Brown Brothers; p. 575: © Chris Hellier/Corbis **Chapter 29** Page 582: © Detail. Imperial War Museum (IWM ART 1921); p. 585: © Christel Gersetenberg/Corbis; p. 590: © Imperial War Museum, London; p. 591 top: © Photo: akg-images, London; p. 591 bottom: National Archives; p. 593: National Archives; p. 595 top: © Hulton-Deutsch Collection/Corbis; p. 595 bottom: © Imperial War Museum, London **Chapter 30** Page 602: © Scala/Art Resource, NY. © 2006 Artists Rights Society (ARS), New York. © 2006 The Munch Museum/The Munch-Ellingsen Group/Artists Rights Society (ARS), New York; p. 604: © Bettmann/Corbis; p. 605: © Bettmann/Corbis; p. 606: © Bettmann/Corbis; p. 607: © The Museum of Modern Art/Licensed by SCALA/Art Resource, NY + © 2006 Estate of Pablo Picasso/Artists Rights Society (ARS), New York; p. 609: © Dorothea Lange Collection, The Oakland Museum of California. The City of Oakland. Gift of Paul Taylor; p. 610: Library of Congress; p. 611: © Bettmann/Corbis; p. 613: © Hulton-Deutsch Collection/Corbis; p. 614: © Photo: akg-images, London; p. 616: © Henry Guttmann/Getty Images **Chapter 31** Page 618: © Swim Ink/Corbis; p. 621: © Bettmann/Corbis; p. 625 left: © Bettmann/Corbis; p. 625 right: © Bettmann/Corbis; p. 629: © Hulton-Deutsch Collection/Corbis; p. 631: © 2005 Banco de México, Diego Rivera & Frida Kahlo Museums Trust. Av. Cinco de Mayo No. 2, Centro, Del. Cuauhtémoc 06059, Mexico, D.F.; p. 634: Courtesy Everett Collection **Chapter 32** Page 636: © Bettmann/Corbis; p. 639: © Hulton-Deutsch Collection/Corbis; p. 641: © Harwood/Getty Images; p. 642: © Photo by Hulton Archive/Getty Images; p. 644: © Photo by Time Life Pictures/US Navy/Time Life Pictures/Getty Images; p. 646: © Time & Life Pictures/Getty Image; p. 650: © Bettmann/Corbis; p. 652: Library of Congress **Chapter 33** Page 656: © Photo by Larry Burrows/Time Life Pictures/Getty Images; p. 661: © Bettmann/Corbis; p. 664: © Bettmann/Corbis; p. 668: © Baldwin H. Ward & Kathryn C. Ward/Corbis; p. 671: © Sovfoto; p. 675 top: © Bert Hardy/Getty Images; p. 675 bottom: © Martin Jones/Corbis; p. 680: © Tom Stoddart/Katz Pictures/Woodfin Camp and Associates **Chapter 34** Page 684: © Sanford/Agliolo/Corbis; p. 687: © William Whitehurst/Corbis; p. 691: © Michael S. Yamashita/Corbis; p. 694: ©Getty Images/National Geographic Creative; p. 697: © Photo by Mai/Mai/Time Life Pictures/Getty Images; p. 702: © Vittoriano Rastelli/Corbis.

TEXT CREDITS

Chapter 1 "The Flood Story from Epic of Gilgamesh," Thomas Sanders, et al, *Encounters in World History: Sources and Themes from the Global Past,* Vol I, McGraw-Hill, 2006, pp. 40–41. **Chapter 2** Miriam Lichtheim, ed., *Ancient Egyptian Literature,* Three Volumes: Vol. 1. Berkeley: University of California Press, 1973. Copyright © 1973–1980 Regents of the University of California. Pp. 25–27. **Chapter 3** James Legge, trans. *The Chinese Classics,* 5 vols. London: Henry Frowde, 1893, 4:171–72. **Chapter 4** From POPOL VUH by Dennis Tedlock. Copyright © 1985, 1996 by Dennis Tedlock. Pp. 163–65, 167. Reprinted with the permission of Simon & Schuster, Inc., from POPOL VUH: *The Definitive Edition of the Mayan Book of the Dawn of Life* by Dennis Tedlock. Copyright © 1985, 1996, by Dennis Tedlock. All rights reserved. **Chapter 5** D.J. Irani, *The Divine Songs of Zarathustra,* George Allen & Unwin, 1924. **Chapter 6** James Legge, trans. *The Chinese Classics,* 7 vols. Oxford: Clarendon Press, 1893, 1:145, 146, 152, 254, 258–59, 266. **Chapter 7** "The Teachings of the Buddha," Thomas Sanders, et al, *Encounters in World History: Sources and Themes from the Global Past,* Vol I, McGraw-Hill, 2006, pp. 113–114. **Chapter 8** F.J. Church, trans. *The Trial and Death of Socrates,* 2nd ed. London: Macmillan, 1886, pp. 76–78. **Chapter 9** Wilhelm von Hartel, ed. S. *Thasci Caecili Cypriani opera onmia in Corpus scriptorum ecclesiasticorum latinorum.* Vienna: 1868, vol. 3, pp. 305–6. (Translation by Jerry H. Bentley.) **Chapter 10** From THE ALEXIAD OF ANNA COMNENEA translated by E.R.A. Sewter (Penguin Classics, 1969). Copyright © E.R.A. Sewter, 1969. **Chapter 11** *Al-Qur'an: A Contemporary Translation.* Trans. By Ahmed Ali. Princeton: Princeton University Press, 1984, pp. 11, 358, 359, 540, 559. **Chapter 12** Gabriel Ferrand, trans. *Voyage du marchand arage Sulayman en Inde et en Chine.* Paris, 1922, pp. 45, 53-54, 60–61 (Translated into English by Jerry H. Bentley). **Chapter 13** *Cosmas Indicopleustes. The Christian Topography of Cosmas, an Egyptian Monk.* Trans. By J.W. McCrindle. London: Hakluyt Society, 1897, pp. 364–72. **Chapter 14** Marco Polo. *The Book of Ser Marco Polo,* 3rd ed. Trans. and ed. by Henry Yule and Henri Cordier. London: John Murray, 1921, pp. 260–63. **Chapter 15** H.A.R. Gibb, trans. *The Travels of Ibn Battuta,* A.D. 1325–1354. 4 vols., Cambridge: Hakluyt Society, 1958–1994, vol. 2, pp. 374–77. **Chapter 16** *Translations and Reprints from the Original Sources of European History,* vol. 2. Philadelphia: University of Pennsylvania Press, 1900. **Chapter 17** Teuira Henry and others, Dennis Kawaharada, ed., *Voyaging Chiefs of Havai'i.* Copyright 1995. pp. 138–39, 144–46. Kalamaku Press. **Chapter 18** From Said Hamdun and Noel King, *Ibn Battuta in Black Africa.* **Chapter 19** *Diario of Christopher Columbus's First Voyage to America,* 1492–1493, by Christopher Columbus, edited by Oliver C. Dunn and James E. Kelley, Jr. University of

Oklahoma Press, 1989. Used by permission of University of Oklahoma Press. **Chapter 20** "Galileo Galilei, Letter to the Grand Duchess Christina," from Alfred J. Andrea and James H. Overfield, *The Human Record: Sources of Global History,* 3rd ed, Volume II: Since 1500, Houghton Mifflin, 1998. **Chapter 21** Bernardino de Sahagun, Florentine Codex: *General History of the Things of New Spain,* 13 vols. Trans. By Arthur J. O. Anderson and Charles E. Dibble. Salt Lake City: University of Utah Press, 1950–82, 13:19–20. Used by permission of University of Utah Press. **Chapter 22** Basil Davidson, *The African Past,* Little, Brown, 1964, pp. 191–93. Copyright © 1964 by Basil Davidson. Reprinted by permission of Curtis Brown, Ltd. **Chapter 23** J.O.P. Bland, Annals and Memoirs of the Court of Peking. Boston: Houghton Mifflin, 1914, pp. 325–31. **Chapter 24** "Sultan Selim I, Letter to Shah Ismail of Persia," from Alfred J. Andrea and James H. Overfield, *The Human Record: Sources of Global History,* 3rd ed, Volume II: Since 1500, Houghton Mifflin, 1998. **Chapter 25** "Declaration des droits de l'homme et du citoyen." Translated by Jerry H. Bentley. **Chapter 26** "Testimony for the Factory Act of 1833: Working Conditions in England", sourced from Dennis Sherman et al, *World Civilizations: Sources, Images, and Interpretations,* 3rd edition, Volume II, McGraw-Hill, 2002, pp. 119–120. **Chapter 27** From BEEN IN THE STORM SO LONG by Leon F. Litwack, copyright © 1979 by Leon F. Litwack. Used by permission of Alfred A. Knopf, a division of Random House, Inc. **Chapter 28** Rudyard Kiplin, "The White Man's Burden." McClure's Magazine 12, no. 4 (1899): 290–91. **Chapter 29** Edmund Blunden, ed., The Poems of Wilfred Owen. London: Chattus & Windus, 1933, p. 66. **Chapter 30** From MEIN KAMPF by Adolf Hitler, translated by Ralph Manheim. Copyright © 1939, 1943 by Houghton Mifflin Company. Reprinted by permission of Houghton Mifflin Harcourt Publishing Company. All rights reserved. **Chapter 31** Mohandas Gandhi, Hind Swaraj (Indian Home Rule) from Alfred J. Andrea and James H. Overfield, *The Human Record: Sources of Global History,* 3rd ed, Volume II: Since 1500, Houghton Mifflin, 1998. **Chapter 32** Yamaoka Michiko, "Eight Hundred Meters from the Hypocenter," Haruko Taya Cook and Theodore F. Cook, *Japan at War: An Oral History,* The New Press, 1992, pp. 384–87. Copyright © 1992 *Japan at War: An Oral History* by Haruko Taya Cook and Theodore F. Cook. Reprinted by permission of The New Press. www.thenewpress.com. 84–87.

INDEX

Subheadings are arranged under headings chronologically rather than alphabetically. The date ranges of names of people refer to life spans, unless otherwise stated.

The italicized word "map" following page numbers refers to maps, and "source document" refers to primary source material. The italicized abbreviation "illus." following page numbers refers to illustrations, "B.C.E." following dates refers to "Before the Common Era." C.E. following dates refers to "Common Era." Dates without qualifiers are in the Common Era.

Arctic Ocean
Arctic Circle
ALASKA RANGE
ROCKY MOUNTAINS
NORTH AMERICA
CANADIAN SHIELD
Mississippi
APPALACHIAN MTS.
North Pacific Ocean
North Atlantic Ocean
Tropic of Cancer
Equator
SOUTH AMERICA
Amazon
ANDES MOUNTAINS
Tropic of Capricorn
South Pacific Ocean
South Atlantic Ocean
CAPE HORN
EUROPE
ALPS
Danube
Volga
URAL MOUNTAINS
Ob
Yenisey
SAHARA
SYRIAN DESERT
Nile
AFRICA
NAMIB DESERT
KALAHARI DESERT
CAPE OF GOOD HOPE
ASIA
GOBI DESERT
HINDU KUSH
HIMALAYAS
Yangtze
DECCAN PLATEAU
Indian Ocean
Pacific Ocean
GREAT SANDY DESERT
AUSTRALIA
Antarctic Circle
ANTARCTICA
Ice cap
Tundra
Forest
Grassland
Desert
Mountains

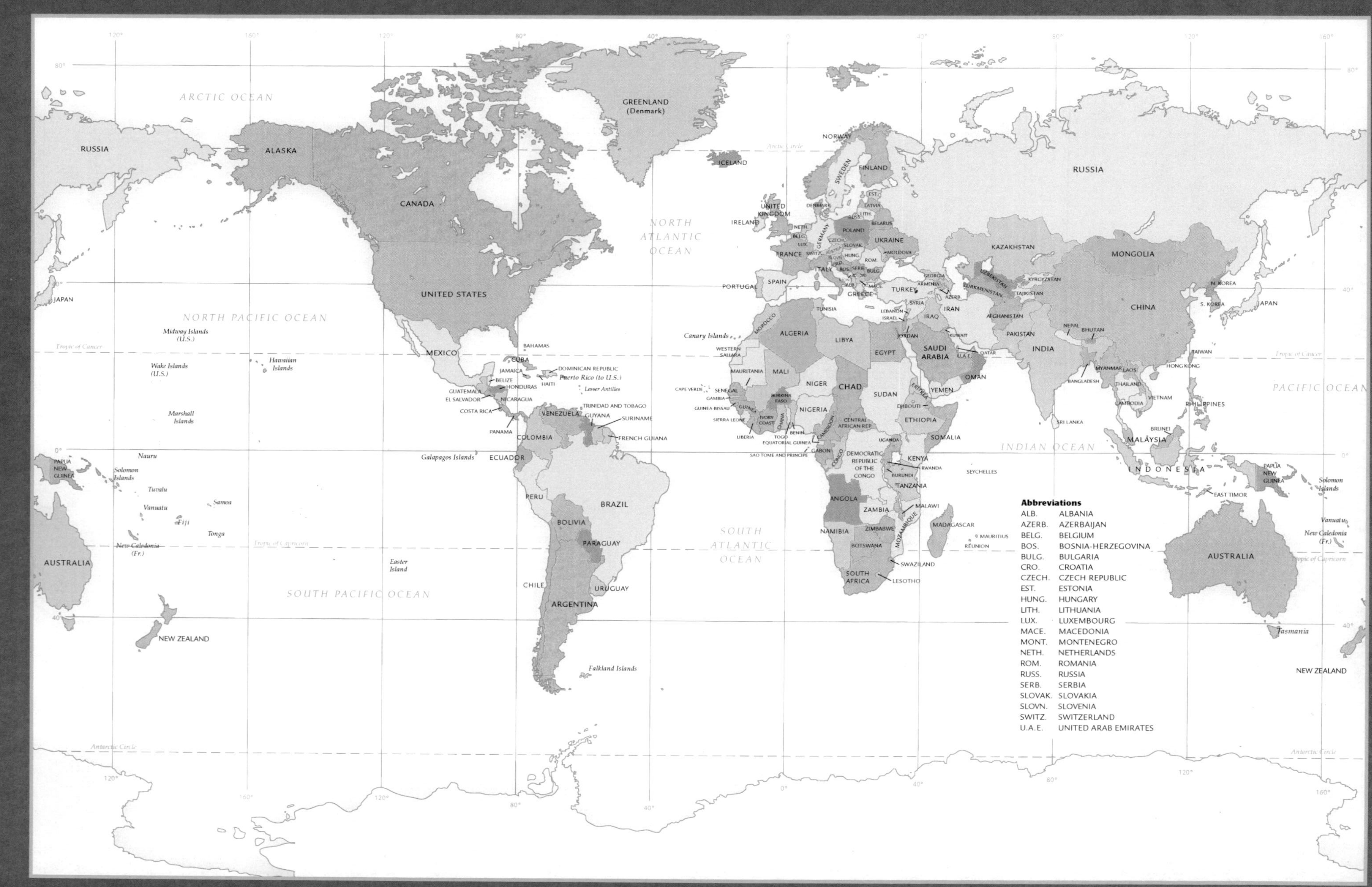

ARCTIC OCEAN
NORTH PACIFIC OCEAN
SOUTH PACIFIC OCEAN
NORTH ATLANTIC OCEAN
SOUTH ATLANTIC OCEAN
INDIAN OCEAN
PACIFIC OCEAN
Arctic Circle
Tropic of Cancer
Tropic of Capricorn
Antarctic Circle
RUSSIA
ALASKA
CANADA
GREENLAND (Denmark)
ICELAND
UNITED STATES
MEXICO
JAPAN
Midway Islands (U.S.)
Wake Islands (U.S.)
Hawaiian Islands
Marshall Islands
Nauru
Solomon Islands
Tuvalu
Vanuatu
Samoa
Fiji
Tonga
New Caledonia (Fr.)
PAPUA NEW GUINEA
AUSTRALIA
NEW ZEALAND
Easter Island
Galapagos Islands
BAHAMAS
CUBA
JAMAICA
BELIZE
HONDURAS
HAITI
DOMINICAN REPUBLIC
Puerto Rico (to U.S.)
Lesser Antilles
GUATEMALA
EL SALVADOR
NICARAGUA
COSTA RICA
PANAMA
TRINIDAD AND TOBAGO
VENEZUELA
GUYANA
SURINAME
FRENCH GUIANA
COLOMBIA
ECUADOR
PERU
BRAZIL
BOLIVIA
PARAGUAY
CHILE
URUGUAY
ARGENTINA
Falkland Islands
NORWAY
SWEDEN
FINLAND
UNITED KINGDOM
IRELAND
DENMARK
NETH.
BELG.
LUX.
GERMANY
POLAND
CZECH.
SLOVAK.
SWITZ.
FRANCE
ITALY
HUNG.
ROM.
SERB.
BOS.
BULG.
MACE.
ALB.
GREECE
EST.
LATVIA
LITH.
BELARUS
UKRAINE
MOLDOVA
PORTUGAL
SPAIN
Canary Islands
MOROCCO
WESTERN SAHARA
ALGERIA
TUNISIA
LIBYA
EGYPT
MAURITANIA
MALI
NIGER
CHAD
SUDAN
CAPE VERDE
SENEGAL
GAMBIA
GUINEA-BISSAU
GUINEA
SIERRA LEONE
LIBERIA
IVORY COAST
BURKINA FASO
GHANA
TOGO
BENIN
NIGERIA
CAMEROON
EQUATORIAL GUINEA
SAO TOME AND PRINCIPE
GABON
CONGO
CENTRAL AFRICAN REP.
DEMOCRATIC REPUBLIC OF THE CONGO
UGANDA
KENYA
RWANDA
BURUNDI
TANZANIA
ERITREA
DJIBOUTI
ETHIOPIA
SOMALIA
ANGOLA
ZAMBIA
MALAWI
MOZAMBIQUE
ZIMBABWE
NAMIBIA
BOTSWANA
SOUTH AFRICA
SWAZILAND
LESOTHO
MADAGASCAR
MAURITIUS
RÉUNION
SEYCHELLES
TURKEY
GEORGIA
ARMENIA
AZERB.
SYRIA
LEBANON
ISRAEL
JORDAN
IRAQ
IRAN
KUWAIT
SAUDI ARABIA
QATAR
U.A.E.
OMAN
YEMEN
KAZAKHSTAN
UZBEKISTAN
TURKMENISTAN
KYRGYZSTAN
TAJIKISTAN
AFGHANISTAN
PAKISTAN
INDIA
NEPAL
BHUTAN
BANGLADESH
SRI LANKA
MONGOLIA
CHINA
N. KOREA
S. KOREA
TAIWAN
HONG KONG
MYANMAR
LAOS
THAILAND
CAMBODIA
VIETNAM
PHILIPPINES
BRUNEI
MALAYSIA
INDONESIA
EAST TIMOR
Tasmania
Abbreviations
ALB. ALBANIA
AZERB. AZERBAIJAN
BELG. BELGIUM
BOS. BOSNIA-HERZEGOVINA
BULG. BULGARIA
CRO. CROATIA
CZECH. CZECH REPUBLIC
EST. ESTONIA
HUNG. HUNGARY
LITH. LITHUANIA
LUX. LUXEMBOURG
MACE. MACEDONIA
MONT. MONTENEGRO
NETH. NETHERLANDS
ROM. ROMANIA
RUSS. RUSSIA
SERB. SERBIA
SLOVAK. SLOVAKIA
SLOVN. SLOVENIA
SWITZ. SWITZERLAND
U.A.E. UNITED ARAB EMIRATES

TAKING SIDES

Clashing Views in

World History

ISSUE 1

Was Sumerian Civilization Exclusively Male Dominated?

YES: Chester G. Starr, from *A History of the Ancient World* (Oxford University Press, 1965)

NO: Samuel Noah Kramer, from "Poet and Psalmists: Goddesses and Theologians: Literary, Religious, and Anthropological Aspects of the Legacy of Sumer," in Denise Schmandt-Besserat, ed., *The Legacy of Sumer: Invited Lectures on the Middle East at the University of Texas at Austin* (Undena Publications, 1976)

ISSUE SUMMARY

YES: Historian Chester G. Starr finds Sumerian society to be male dominated, from the gods to human priests and kings, and he barely acknowledges the status of women in either the heavenly or the earthly realm.

NO: Museum curator Samuel Noah Kramer relies on much of the same data as Starr, but finds powerful goddesses and earthly women to have played prominent roles in both cosmic and everyday Sumerian life.

This issue rests on a difference in interpretation rather than on a clearly stated topic debate. Each writer makes assumptions about what ancient Sumerian society was like and each finds evidence to support those assumptions. As you read the following two selections, notice that both cite remarkably similar findings. The difference is that for Chester G. Starr they are asides, whereas, for Samuel Noah Kramer they are the focus. For centuries the story of life in the Fertile Crescent has been told as if only men were actors in the drama. If royal queens received splendid burials, does it make sense to refer to rulers exclusively as kings? If women in a particular culture exhibited what historians like to call *agency*, acting on their own behalf to shape their own lives, is it accurate to term that culture male dominated? Much will depend on interpretation, on whose perspective seems to you more accurate. Was Inanna a "fertility goddess" as Starr assumes or "Queen of Heaven" and goddess of everything as

Kramer implies? Although Kramer's perspective is gaining acceptance, your textbook may continue to make Starr's assumptions.

Since the sophisticated civilization at Sumer is one of the earliest in human history, it has become a model for our understanding of human behavior. If men have always dominated women, then arguments that this arrangement is "natural" have greater strength. If, on the other hand, women played more active roles, then perhaps our understanding of what is by nature and what is by custom needs to be rethought. Virtually all of Kramer's evidence is present in Starr's essay. Is Starr correct to downplay or ignore most of it in favor of male-centered givens? As you read the first essay, pay particular attention to every mention of women as a group and to particular royal and divine women. When you find these female characters more fully developed in the second essay, ask yourself which viewpoint you question.

One of the dangers that historians must constantly be aware of is called *presentism.* We all have a tendency to judge whatever we read about the past in terms of our present values. If we assume that our ways of doing and being are best, we may judge the past in terms of what makes sense for us. Those who find it proper and even natural for men to dominate social, cultural, and religious life may assume that the past generated this pattern and fit existing evidence into these assumptions. Those who question patriarchal dominance may be inclined to look for and find evidence of strong, contributing, and empowering women. The historian's task is to take the evidence on its own terms and let it tell its own story, whether or not that story meshes with the present one.

In 1970 virtually all world history books would have told the story of Sumer as Professor Starr has done. Thirty years later new understandings have led a growing number of scholars to take a fresh look at all of the past and question its archaeological and literary records, making as few assumptions as possible. Curator Kramer represents this new breed of scholars. He does not assert that women dominated Sumerian society, but he finds areas in which women seem to have held as exalted positions as men and he discovers female deities who refuse to be demoted. Their authority and enduring inspiration suggest that women were not seen as outsiders to power. Indeed, the idea of "sacred marriage" suggests that the vital acts of creation and sustenance flowed from a blending of male and female energies.

Try to set aside your own assumptions about how women and men should behave and your own early-twenty-first-century way of looking at the world. Try to see only the evidence as it has come to us in cylinder seals, burial chambers, and texts. Based purely on what both selection authors agree is there, what conclusions can we draw about Sumerian society? Being able to critically evaluate what we learn permits us to make our own judgments and frees us from dependence on the theories of others.

YES 

Chester G. Starr

The First Civilization of Mesopotamia

The Mesopotamian Outlook

Sumerian civilization. The Sumerians, who were in the forefront of early Mesopotamian progress, are linguistically a puzzle, for their agglutinative, largely monosyllabic speech cannot be connected with any of the major groups of languages. By about 3500 B.C. they had begun to draw conventionalized pictograms (representations of physical objects) on clay tablets, found at Kish and Uruk, and perhaps on other, less enduring materials. Three hundred years later, about 3200, tablets show that the scribes of Sumer took a tremendous step, which we do not know ever to have occurred independently elsewhere; that is, they advanced to a mixture of ideograms (marks representing concepts such as "day") and phonograms (symbols expressing syllabic phonetic values, as we might draw a bee for the sound be). Since some symbols expressed more than 1 phonetic value and, on the other hand, 1 single sound could be expressed by up to 14 different marks, sometimes "determinatives" were prefixes to indicate the class to which the word in question belonged, as deity, bird, and so on. These elements came to be wedge-shaped marks impressed in the clay by a stylus; from the Latin word *cuneus* for wedge the Mesopotamian script is called "cuneiform."

From this stage onward cuneiform script could be employed to set down languages of any type; both Semitic dialects like Akkadian and Indo-European tongues like Hittite and Old Persian were so written. Due to the mixture of ideograms, syllabic phonograms, determinatives, and other complications the number of individual signs was much larger than in an alphabetic form of writing. The earliest Sumerian script had perhaps 2000 symbols, but eventually about 500-600 sufficed. Each of these, though considerably simplified over the years, remained so complicated that only professional scribes commonly wrote in the ancient Near East. Writing was an arcane mystery down to Greek times.

The earliest Sumerian tablets are very difficult to comprehend. Largely, though not entirely, they are temple accounts: "so many sheep, so many goats"; or "to so-and-so, beer and bread for one day." If we place them against the much larger bulk of written documents which had appeared by the end of the third millennium, it is nonetheless possible to gain precious light upon early Sumerian thought. The main characteristics of this outlook appeared very swiftly and were essentially fixed as the main lines of Mesopotamian civilization over the next 2500 years. Yet we can also observe that the structure of this outlook became ever more complicated and advanced. The "black-headed people," as the Sumerians called themselves, affected greatly their Semitic neighbors and followers, reaching on up through the Fertile Crescent, and were in turn influenced from the outside.

To a modern observer the pattern of thought which developed in third millennium Mesopotamia is marked by its formal, outwardly static, and religious qualities. In the Sumerian view their arts and crafts had been "revealed" to them by the gods above and were unchanging. Everything must have its name to assure its place in the universe, and one who knew the true name of something had a power over it. Among the earliest Sumerian documents are lists of stones, animals, plants, and the like, classified on their outward characteristics. Yet these lists, which students probably learned by heart, reflect the fact that men were deliberately analyzing and imposing abstract order upon the materials of nature. We must not make the mistake of underestimating the tremendous achievements of these first civilized thinkers merely because their approach was so different from our own; indeed, they created many of the basic tools of thought and concepts we take for granted.

It was now, for instance, necessary to count and to write down numbers; Mesopotamian arithmetic was based sometimes on units of 10, sometimes on units of 60. The latter style, which through its fractions gives us our division of the hour and of the circle, was eventually used especially in astronomy, where men charted the major constellations still marked on modern sky-charts. By the first millennium Mesopotamian scholars began a tradition of ever more refined, precise, and abstract thinking and evolved a concept of place-value notation which was the root of our number system. Civilization also required the measurement and weighing of quantities of grain and metals; the chief weight, a talent of 60 minas, remained the standard quantity on down through the Greek era. Geometry began in the measurement of fields and the requirements of building. The year was solar but was defined in 12 lunar months, with an intercalary month inserted about every 3 years, to fix the great religious festivals and so to regulate agricultural activity.

The arts also progressed. The use of mudbrick and baked brick produced heavy, massive architecture, in which true arches were developed. To cover the ugly brick walls the Sumerians decorated their temples with bands of colored clay cones rammed into the walls and semi-columns; painted frescoes appeared later.

The gods were now visualized in human shape and were represented in statues which are, as it were, the gods themselves; for any transcendental quality was lacking. In some temples there were placed before the gods statues of the rulers, commemorating their devout piety in an equally straightforward, factual, yet reverent manner. The technical problem that stone was hard to come by forced sculptors often to create seated figures and almost always to exaggerate the size of the head. Although some pieces are sharply conceived, they do not exhibit in general an intense interest in nature or a sense of human individuality. Equally significant are the many cylinder seals of men of property, carved with a representation of gods, imaginary animals, or myths. The demonic or bestial motifs that developed in this field were a rich repertoire of great influence on other Near Eastern and Greek art forms, but a modern rationalist will often feel disturbed by their suggestion that man did not yet recognize the distinctiveness of his own nature.

Early Mesopotamian religion. Man's failure fully to recognize himself is reflected in the religious aspect of the early Mesopotamian outlook. Sumerian civilization had a very strong religious imprint. Only in the confidence born of their common belief in divine support could these men have endured the hardships and unremitting toils necessary to assure a firm foothold in the valley. Their greatest building, the temples, are a mighty testimonial to a human ideal; the priests who clustered about these temples were so important that one may almost call an early Sumerian city-state a theocracy.

The character of this religious system becomes more apparent once there are written copies of Mesopotamian myths and artistic representations of the gods and heroes. To the inhabitants of Mesopotamia the gods were many, for they represented the forces which drove mankind; and in primitive thought these forces were many, distinct in origin. Yet the gods were grouped in a regular pantheon.

Highest was An, the divine force, which could be visualized in the overarching bowl of Heaven; his name meant "sky" or "shining." Then came Enlil, the active force of nature, who at times manifested himself in the raging storms of the plains, and at other times aided men. The goddess of earth was worshiped as Nin-khursag and under other names. Last of the four creator gods came Enki, the god of waters who fertilized the ground, and by extension became the patron of the skills of wisdom. To these were added 50 "great gods" who met in the assembly of the gods, the Annunaki; a host of other deities, demons, and the like also floated in the Mesopotamian spiritual world.

To the Sumerians their physical environment had come into being from a primordial chaos of water, whence the forces Tiamat and Abzu arose and, by processes of procreation, created the gods. Thereafter came the sky, the earth, and finally mankind. In the spring of each year occurred the greatest religious festival of the land, known as the Akitu in later Babylonia. This was the New Year's feast, an 11-day ceremony of gloom and purification and then of joy, which ended as the gods set the lots for mortal men during the coming year. On the fourth day of the festival the priests recited a myth of the creation called from its opening words *enuma elish*:

> When on high the heaven had not been named,
> Firm ground below had not been called by name . . .
> No reed hut had been matted, no marsh land had appeared.

Beside this ritual myth many other tales evolved to explain the nature of life. The underlying scheme of thought expressed therein postulated that the world was the product of conscious divine action for divine purposes; obvious, too, is the feeling that the world was all animate. Throughout ancient times, down to and past the rise of Christianity, mankind could not quite divest itself of the idea that trees, springs, and the like were endowed with human characteristics or were directed by manlike immortals. In Mesopotamia, as elsewhere, religion not only bound together society but also assured to man the fertility of his fields, his flocks, and himself. One of the greatest figures in Mesopotamian myth was the goddess of human fertility, Inanna (later Ishtar), who may in root have gone back to the Neolithic female figurines found in Halafian levels. Her descent to the underworld and then her return symbolized the renewal of agricultural life; her husband Dumuzi (later Tammuz), went permanently to the nether regions as a substitute for her. Each year he was mourned, and his marriage with Inanna was celebrated at the New Year's feast.

To modern men, who approach these early myths from a scientific point of view, the tales of the gods are neither sensible nor logical, and the view of life which they express in their repetitious verse is basically a primitive one of gross action and elemental passions. In explaining the nature of the universe men translated into divine terms their own earthly concepts of personal clash and procreation. Yet in early civilized societies these tales were so satisfying that people all over the Near East accepted them. Mesopotamian stories thus passed into the early chapters of the Book of Genesis, where they continued to answer men's curiosity about the Creation down to the past century.

Place of man. The gods, though human in appearance, paid little attention to mortal men as they drank and made merry, and also wrangled and abused each other in the divine assemblies. Men feared and honored the gods; each city-state was but the earthly domain of certain divine forces on high, for whose ease men toiled throughout their lives. Once dead, men and women could expect only to go to a shadowy, gray land of departed spirits. Such views befitted a land that had recently raised itself to the level of civilization by hard labor, where the climate was severe, where the dangers of flood and sudden disease were ever present, inexplicable, and incurable by human means.

Yet two further reflections may be made. In the first place, the spiritual world of early Mesopotamia was an orderly structure, within which men could operate in a rational fashion; the gods could be propitiated by their human servants through the creation of divine ceremonies. Again, mankind could not quite forget that *it* was the agent that built and tilled, even though human society was far from perfect. In part this hidden realization led to a nagging fear that men might be upsetting an order laid down by the gods. One myth thus depicted the gods, angered by the clamor of men, sending down the Flood; other myths seem akin to the Hebrew story of the Fall of Man from a primitive grace and leisure through his own unwillingness to be passive. In part, however, men were proud of their achievements. A prime reflection of this point of view is the myth of Gilgamesh.

The Gilgamesh epic. The tale of the hero Gilgamesh, two-thirds god in origin, had Sumerian roots but was more fully formulated into a continuous epic about 2000 B.C. Then it spread all over the Near East and long exercised men's imagination; one artistic symbol drawn from it, that of Gilgamesh strangling a lion, was handed down age after age until it appeared on medieval cathedrals in Western Europe.

Unlike the other myths, which were largely theological creations associated with certain rituals, this epic was centered on human figures. Essentially it was a mighty reflection on the nature of man, who strives and creates but in the end must die. Gilgamesh himself was a legendary king of Uruk, who built its great wall but treated his subjects so harshly that the gods created a wild man, Enkidu, to subdue him. Gilgamesh, wily as well as harsh, did not meet Enkidu head-on, but sent out a harlot, who by her arts tamed Enkidu—this taming we may perhaps take as an exemplification of the passage of mankind to civilization. "Become like a man," Enkidu put on clothing and went forth to protect the cattle against lions and wolves. The bulk of the epic then recounts the heroic adventures of Gilgamesh and Enkidu against various inhuman monsters:

> Who, my friends, [says Gilgamesh] is superior to death?
> Only the gods live forever under the sun.
> As for mankind, numbered are their days;
> Whatever they achieve is but the wind!

So, while they lived, let them at least make a name for themselves.

During the course of these exploits Enkidu offended the gods (especially Ishtar), and died after a long death-bed scene of recrimination against divine decrees. Gilgamesh first lamented, then set out to seek the plant of eternal life so that he might bring his friend back to life. Eventually Gilgamesh made his way to Ut-napishtim, the original Noah, who told him the story of the Flood and advised him how to get the miraculous plant under the sea. Although Gilgamesh succeeded in his quest, on his return journey he lost the plant to a snake. The dead, in sum, cannot be brought back to life.

When later we come to Greek civilization we shall meet another half divine hero, Achilles, who fought in the war against Troy and there lost his friend Patroclus; and at that point we shall be able to compare the essential qualities of two different civilizations, the Greek and the Mesopotamian, as reflected in their great epics, the tale of Gilgamesh and the *Iliad*. Here it may be observed that in the earlier tale the story is balder and has less artistic unity; it is more naive, far earthier (especially in the harlot scenes). Monsters are prominent in the plot of Gilgamesh's adventures, and the appeal is rather to emotion and passion than to reason, as is that of the *Iliad*.

In both epics the divine plane determines earthly events, though men have freedom to oppose the gods; but the heroes of the *Iliad* are more strongly characterized and far more optimistic. Mesopotamian pride in human achievements went hand in hand with fear for human audacity. Men must cling closely to their fellow men on earth and must appease the jealous gods carefully. The individualism of Homer's heroes, their ability to accept human fate while yet enjoying life, their passionate curiosity and delight in the physical world—these were qualities which did not exist in early, god-fearing Mesopotamia. Yet in saying so much, in an effort to relate the alien world of Gilgamesh to a world that most of us know far better, we must not depreciate the earlier epic too much. Poetically it was a magnificent creation, and psychologically it reflects a truly civilized meditation upon the qualities of mankind.

The Results of Civilization

Rise of classes (3000-2000 B.C.*).* That the early Mesopotamian outlook had at times a gloomy cast the modern historian can well understand. Not only did the fabrication of civilization itself impose terrific social burdens upon its human creators, but also the subsequent developments during the third millennium resulted in disturbing changes.

This evolution must be considered, if only briefly, in any sketch of early Mesopotamian civilization, for the structure of society had been greatly elaborated by the time of Hammurabi (1700); therewith, inevitably, the outlook of the Mesopotamian world was modified in important particulars. Although the documents available at the present time are not yet adequate to trace the political history of the third millennium in detail, it is amazing—and instructive—to see even dimly the rise of many critical problems which have been enduring issues in all subsequent civilized societies. Social classes, for example, became differentiated. Economic exploitation and social unrest inevitably followed hard upon this differentiation; law developed both to regulate social and economic relationships and to prevent undue oppression. Interstate warfare appeared and led to imperialism, which in turn produced military classes and bureaucratic systems to run the larger states born of conquest.

The first cities seem to have been masses of relatively undifferentiated fellow workers who were tightly grouped in an economic and spiritual unity. Separate classes, however, evolved rather quickly. Toward the top were the priests, who also worked in the early days but tended to become managers on behalf of the gods; the temples grew into powerful economic centers, which owned much of the land and absorbed a large part of the product in rents and temple dues. The records of Baba, divine consort of the main god of Lagash, show that her priests directed about one-sixth of the farm land of the city-state in the Early Dynastic period. Half of this domain was rented out to peasants, who paid their dues at the rate of one-third to one-sixth of the yield and also owed sums in silver, which they obtained by selling other parts of their produce in the city. The second half of her domain was cultivated by the labor of the peasants, organized in guilds under foremen. The goddess also controlled large flocks, shipping craft, fishermen, brewers, bakers, and spinners of wool; the growth in industrial production in Early Dynastic times, which was remarkable, was largely for purposes of cult as well as for military use and for the kings and their henchmen. The raw materials needed from outside Mesopotamia were obtained by merchants, who trafficked by sea, by river, and by land for stone, metals, wood incenses, and jewels.

Beside and above the priests rose the king or *lugal*. In later views kingship "was lowered from heaven by the gods" as a guarantee of earthly order.

Palaces began to appear; the tomb of one queen of Ur, about 2500 B.C., astounded the modern world with its wealth of delicate jewelry, its harps, and the masses of sacrificed servants. To conclude that the kings and priests were simply parasites would be unjust, for these upper elements held together the state, harbored its reserves, and expanded its strength. Yet they did draw profit from their superior position, and the rest of society now fell into a dependent status.

One mark of this situation is the appearance of slavery. Some men were forced to sell themselves or their children into bondage through the workings of debt; others were captives, especially from the hilly country to the east. While the reduction of human beings to the legal level of chattels always has a distorting influence upon social relationships, morals, and general views of human nature, its effects must be assessed soberly. In the present case, the institution of slavery was but the extreme edge of the fact that the leisure of the upper classes and the great monuments of early times rested upon the forced labor of the multitude and otherwise would have been impossible. In other words, civilization was not lightly bought and did not directly benefit all men alike. Most of the labor force, however, in Mesopotamia as in other slave-holding societies of the ancient world consisted of technically free men. Slaves were rarely used in agriculture, the main occupation of mankind throughout the ancient world; rather, slaves lived in cities, where they were domestic servants, concubines, and artisans. As valuable pieces of capital, slaves were usually accorded a minimum standard of human needs, and at times were able to rise again into freedom through hard work. . . .

Conclusion. If we look back, rather than forward, the story of man's advance in Mesopotamia from the first Neolithic villages of the valley down to the age of Hammurabi must strike us as one of the most amazing achievements of mankind. Despite the difficulties of climate and terrain the settlers had harnessed their energies toward a remarkable physical progress, and the compact masses of population which now dotted lower Mesopotamia were far larger than had ever before been possible.

Samuel Noah Kramer

Poets and Psalmists: Goddesses and Theologians

Introductory

Let us now turn . . . to an anthropological inquiry relating to the Sumerian counterpart of one of modern man's more disturbing social ills: the victimization of woman in a male-dominated society. At the *XVIII Rencontre assyriologique internationale* held in Munich in 1970, I read a paper entitled "Modern Social Problems in Ancient Sumer," that presented evidence in support of the thesis that Sumerian society, not unlike our own rather tormented society, had its deplorable failings and distressing shortcomings: it vaunted utopian ideals honored more in the breach than in observance; it yearned for peace but was constantly at war; it preferred such noble virtues as justice, equity and compassion, but abounded in injustice, inequality, and oppression; materialistic and shortsighted, it unbalanced the ecology essential to its economy; it was afflicted by a generation gap between parents and children and between teachers and students; it had its "drop-outs," "cop-outs," hippies and perverts.

This highly competitive, and in some ways hypocritical, unjust, oppressive, genocidal Sumerian society, resembled our own sick society in one other significant aspect—it was male dominated: men ran the government, managed the economy, administered the courts and schools, manipulated theology and ritual. It is not surprising to find therefore, that by and large, women were treated as second-class citizens without power, prestige, and status, although there are some indications that this was predominantly true only of later Sumerian society, from about 2000 B.C. on; in earlier days the Sumerian woman may have been man's equal socially and economically, at least among the ruling class. Moreover, in the religious sphere, the female deity was venerated and worshipped from earliest times to the very end of Sumer's existence; in spite of some manipulative favoritism on the part of the male theologians, God in Sumer never became all-male.

From Samuel Noah Kramer, "Poet and Psalmists: Goddesses and Theologians: Literary, Religious, and Anthropological Aspects of the Legacy of Sumer," in Denise Schmandt-Besserat, ed., *The Legacy of Sumer: Invited Lectures on the Middle East at the University of Texas at Austin* (Undena Publications, 1976).

Woman in Early Sumer

We begin our inquiry with the little that is known about women's rights and status in early Sumer. Some time about 2350 B.C., a king by the name of Urukagina reigned for a brief period in Lagash, one of Sumer's important city-states. Many of his inscriptions were excavated by the French almost a century ago and have since been deciphered and translated. Among them is a "reform" document in which Urukagina purports to depict the evil "of former days," that is, of the times preceding his reign, as well as the measures he introduced to alleviate them. One of these reforms reads as follows: "The women of former days used to take two husbands, but the women of today (when they attempted to do this) were stoned with stones inscribed with their evil intent." To judge from this rather strident boast, women in pre-Urukagina days practiced polyandry, which hardly smacks of a male-dominated society.

Or, take the case of Baranamtarra, the wife of Urukagina's predecessor, Lugalanda. Quite a number of administrative documents concerned with this lady have been uncovered, and these indicate that she managed her own estates, and even sent diplomatic missions to her counterpart in neighboring city-states, without consulting her husband.

Even Urukagina who, because of his uptight reaction to polyandry, might perhaps be stigmatized as the first "sexist" known to history, was not all anti-feminine. His wife Shagshag, for example, like her predecessor Baranamtarra, was the mistress of vast estates, and ran her affairs every bit her husband's equal. In fact Urukagina might well be acclaimed as the first known individual to favor "equal pay for equal work" regardless of sex. One of the remedial measures he proudly records in the above-mentioned reform document, concerns the bureaucratic gouging of the bereaved by officials in charge of a funeral. In pre-Urukagina days, reads the document, when a citizen was brought to rest "among the reeds of Enki," a cemetery that was deemed more desirable than an ordinary burial ground, there were on hand three male officials who received a considerable amount of beer, bread, and barley, as well as a bed and a chair, as compensation for their services. But Urukagina decreed that the food rations of the three male attendants be reduced considerably and that the furniture "bonus" be eliminated altogether. At the same time he ordered that a woman designated as *nin-dingir,* "Lady Divine," who formerly had received no remuneration, be given a headband and a *sila*-jar (about one-fifth of a gallon) of scented ointment as compensation for her services—a payment that compared not unfavorably with that received by her male colleagues.

Enheduanna: The First Woman Poet on Record

Nor was the *nin-dingir* the only priestess who played a significant role in the cult. A more prominent and important lady was the *en,* a Sumerian word that may be rendered "high priestess" as well as "high priest." According to Sumerian religious practice, the main temple in each large city had its *en* who was male if the deity worshipped in that temple was female, and was female if the deity worshipped there was male. Quite a number of these high-priestesses are known to us by name, beginning with about 2300 B.C., a generation or two after the days of Urukagina. The first of these is Enheduanna, the daughter of Sargon the Great, one of the first empire-builders of the ancient world, whom her father appointed to be high-priestess of great moon-god temple in the city of Ur. But not only was she the spiritual head of one of Sumer's largest temples, she was also a poet and author of renown. Quite recently it has been demonstrated that at least three poetic compositions—a collection of temple hymns and two hymnal prayers to the Goddess Inanna, are at least in part, the imaginative literary creation of this Enheduanna. Here, in Sumer, therefore, some 4300 years ago, it was possible for a woman, at least if she was a princess, to hold top rank among the literati of the land, and to be a spiritual leader of paramount importance.

Woman in Later Sumer

From the three centuries following the days of Enheduanna, little is known about Sumerian society and the status of woman. But from about 2000 B.C. there have been recovered legal documents and court decisions of diverse content, and from these we learn that the role of woman had deteriorated considerably, and that on the whole it was the male who ruled the roost. Marriage, for example, was theoretically monogamous, but the husband was permitted one or more concubines, while the wife had to stay faithful to her one and only spouse. To be sure, a married woman could own property and other possessions, could sometimes buy and sell without consulting her husband, and on rare occasions, could even set special conditions in her marriage contract. In case of divorce, however, the husband had very much the upper hand—he could divorce his wife virtually at will, although if he did so without good cause, he had to pay her as much as *mina* (about a pound) of silver, no mean sum in those days.

Female Deities: Victimization and Resentment

But it was not only on the human plane that women had lost some of their rights and prerogatives in the course of the centuries—it also happened on the divine plane. Some of the female deities that held top rank in the Sumerian pantheon, or close to it, were gradually forced down the hierarchical ladder by the male theologians who manipulated the order of the divinities in accordance with what may well have been their chauvinistic predilections. The goddesses, however, were no "pushovers"; more determined and aggressive than their human counterparts, they struggled to hold or regain at least part of their deprived supremacy to the very end of Sumer's existence. What is more, at least one of the goddesses, Inanna, "Queen of Heaven," continued to be predominant and preeminent to the very last, although the theologians ranked her only seventh in the divine hierarchy. The available texts are not explicit on the subject, but with a bit of between-the-lines reading and burrowing, it is possible to follow the struggling career of at least two important female deities, and to trace some of their ups and downs in myth and cult.

Nammu, Goddess of the Primeval Sea

The female deity that seems to have suffered the sharpest decline was Nammu, the goddess of the primeval sea who, according to several texts, was the creator of the universe and the mother of all the gods. By all genealogical rights, therefore, had the theologians played it fair, she should have had top billing in the pantheon. But in the god-lists where the deities are arranged in hierarchical order, she is rarely mentioned, and never at the head of the list. Moreover, her vast powers as goddess of the sea were turned over to the male deity Enki, who was designated by the theologians as the son of Nammu, in an apparent attempt to mitigate and justify this bit of priestly piracy. Even so, the king who founded the Third Dynasty of Ur, and ushered in a political and cultural Sumerian renaissance about 2050 B.C., chose as his royal name *Ur-Nammu*, "Servant of Nammu," which indicates that the goddess was still worshipped and adored by the mighty of the land.

Ki, Mother Earth

But it is Nammu's daughter Ki, "(Mother) Earth," whose gradual decline can be followed almost step by step with the help of the ancient texts. As noted above, the sea-goddess Nammu was conceived as the creator of the universe. Now the Sumerian word for universe is the compound *an-ki*, where *an* means both "heaven," and "(Father) Heaven," and *ki* means both "earth," and "(Mother) earth." It was the sexual union of Father Heaven with Mother Earth, that according to the Sumerian theologians, ushered in the birth of the gods unto their generations. The first to be born of this Heaven-Earth union, was the airgod Enlil, "Lord Air," and it was he who, by making use of his atmospheric power, succeeded in separating Heaven from Earth, thus preparing the way for the creation of vegetation and all living things including man. In view of these theological premises and postulates, the leading deities of the pantheon, once Nammu had been deprived of her supremacy, should have been ranked by the theologians in the order An (Heaven), Ki (Earth), and Enlil (Lord Air), and this may have been so in very early times. But by 2400 B.C., when the relevant inscriptional evidence first becomes available, we find the leading deities of the pantheon usually arranged in the order An (Heaven), Enlil (Lord Air), Ninhursag (Queen of the Mountain), and Enki (Lord of the Earth). What had evidently happened was, that the theologians, uncomfortable and unhappy with a female deity as the ruler of so important a cosmic entity as earth, had taken this power away from her and transferred it to the male deity Enlil who, as one poet puts it, "carried off the earth," after he had separated it from heaven. Moreover, after taking away from the goddess the rulership over the earth, the theologians also deprived her of the name *Ki*, (Mother) Earth," since it no longer accorded with her reduced status. Instead they called her by one of her several epithets, Ninhursag, that means "Queen of the Mountain," and demoted her to third place in the pantheon.

But the worst was yet to come—even third place was deemed too high by male "chauvinistic" theologians, and she was finally reduced to fourth place, third going to Enki, "Lord of the Earth." This god's name was actually a misnomer, since he had charge only of the seas and rivers, and even this power, as noted earlier, he usurped from the Goddess Nammu. But the theologians of Eridu, a city not far from Ur, which was the God's main seat of worship, were consumed with ambition. As the name "Lord of the Earth" indicates, the devotees of this God were really out to topple the God Enlil who had become the ruler of the earth after he had separated it from heaven. To achieve their goal, they went so far as to have their God Enki confound the speech of man and turn it into a "babel" of tongues, in order to break up Enlil's universal sway over mankind that worshipped him "in one tongue." In spite of this, however, they failed to dethrone Enlil from second place, since his bailiwick was Nippur, Sumer's holy city, whose priests were too powerful to overcome. Disappointed and frustrated the Eridu theologians turned upon the female deity Ninhursag (originally named Ki) whose devotees were evidently too weak to prevent her victimization. And so, by 2000 B.C., when the pertinent texts become available once again, the order of the four leading deities of the pantheon is no longer An, Enlil, Ninhursag, Enki, but An, Enlil, Enki, and Ninhursag.

Still, as already noted, the Sumerian goddesses did not take male-domination "lying down," and not infrequently, according to the mythographers, they registered their resentment in no uncertain terms, and showed the male "victors" who was really "boss." As of today, for example, we have two myths in which Ninhursag and Enki are the main protagonists, and in both it is Ninhursag who dominates the action, with Enki "playing second fiddle."

The scene of one of these myths is Dilmun, the Sumerian "Paradise" land, where both Ninhursag and Enki are at home. Here, after considerable maneuvering, Ninhursag contrived to make eight different plants sprout. But when Enki sees them, they tempt his appetite, and he sends his vizier to pluck them and bring them to him. After which, he proceeds to eat them one at a time. This so enrages Ninhursag that she pronounces against him the "curse of death." And mighty male though he was, eight of his organs become sick, one for each of the plants he had eaten without permission from the goddess. The failing Enki would surely have died in due course, had not the goddess finally taken pity on him, and created eight special deities, each of whom healed one of Enki's ailing organs.

In the other available myth, we find Ninhursag and Enki acting as partners in the creation of man from the "clay that is over the Deep." In the course of a banquet of the gods, however, the two deities become tipsy, and the partnership turns into a competition. First Ninhursag fashions six malformed creatures whom Enki dutifully blesses and for whom he even finds useful "jobs" in spite of their handicaps. Then it was Enki's turn. But the creature he fashions displeased Ninhursag who proceeds to rebuke Enki bitterly for his clumsy effort, a reproach that the god accepts as his due, in language that is obsequious and flattering.

Prestigious Female Deities

Nor was Ninhursag the only female deity who, in spite of occasional victimization by the theologians, continued to be revered and adored in the land. There was Nidaba, the patroness of writing, learning, and accounting, whom the theologians provided with a husband by the name of Haia, who seemed to be no more than a shadowy reflection of the goddess. There was the goddess of medicine and healing who was worshipped in Lagash under the name of Bau, and in Isin under the name of Ninisinna. In Lagash, it is true, the theologians did succeed in making her husband Ningirsu paramount in cult and adoration. Even so, there are indications that originally Bau was of higher rank than her spouse. Moreover, when it came to the naming of their children, the people of Lagash preferred by far to include Bau rather than Ningirsu in the chosen theophoric name—clear evidence of the popularity of the goddess, no matter what the theological dogma. As for Ninisinna, it was she who was venerated as the heroic tutelary deity of Isin, while her husband Pabilsag is a far less impressive figure. Most interesting is the case of the Lagashite goddess Nanshe who was acclaimed and adored as Sumer's social conscience, and who was depicted as judging mankind every New Year. Her spouse Nindara, a far less significant figure, did not participate in this solemn and fateful procedure; it was her bailiff, the male deity Hendursagga, who carried out obediently and faithfully the verdict of his deeply revered mistress.

Inanna, "Queen of Heaven"

But the goddess that should be soothing balm to the resentful wounds of liberated women the world over, is the bright, shining Inanna, the brave, crafty, ambitious, aggressive, desirable, loving, hating "Queen of Heaven," whose powers and deeds were glorified and extolled throughout Sumer's existence in myth, epic, and hymn. No one, neither man nor god, dared oppose her, stand in her way, or say her nay. Early in her career, perhaps about 3000 B.C., she virtually took over the divine rulership of the important city, Erech, from the theoretically and theologically all powerful heaven-god An. In an effort to make her city Erech the center of civilized life, she braved a dangerous journey to the *Abzu*, "the Deep," where the cosmic and cultural divine laws were guarded by its King Enki. When this same Enki organized the universe and somehow failed to assign her the insignia and prerogatives she felt were her due, he had to defend himself apologetically and contritely against her angry complaint. When the rebellious highland, Ebih, failed to show her due honor, she virtually destroyed it with her fiery weapons, and brought it to its knees. Raped by the gardener Shukalletuda while sleeping wearily after a long cosmic journey under one of his shade-trees, she pursued him relentlessly and finally caught up with him and put him to death, but was gracious enough to console him with the promise to make his name endure in story and song.

The role that no doubt delighted Inannamost, one that guaranteed her the affection and veneration of every Sumerian heart, was that which she played in the New Year "Sacred Marriage" rite, that celebrated her sexual union with the King of Sumer in order to ensure the fertility of the soil and the fecundity of the womb. The first king whom the goddess selected as her mortal spouse was Dumuzi (Biblical Tammuz), who reigned early in the third millennium B.C. From then on, many, if not most of the rulers of Sumer, celebrated their marriage to the goddess as avatars, or incarnations of Dumuzi. Throughout the "Sacred Marriage" ceremony, it was the goddess who was the active, dominant protagonist; the king was but the passive, ecstatic recipient of the blessings of her womb and breasts, and of just a touch of her immortality. And when—so tell the mythographers—Dumuzi, with typical male arrogance, became weary of being subordinate to the goddess, and, in her absence, began to play high and mighty, she fastened upon him her "eye of death," and had him carried off to the Nether World. There he would have remained forever, had not his loving sister offered herself as his substitute, thus allowing him to return to earth for half the year.

Monotheism: Death-Knell of the Female Deity

So much for the Goddess Inanna, the feared and beloved "Holy Terror" of the ancients. The female deity, as is clear from what was said above, had her ups and downs in Sumerian religion, but she was never really licked or totally eclipsed by her male rivals. Even in much later days, when Sumer had become generally known as Babylonia, and the Sumerian language was superseded by the Semitic Akkadian, the poets continued to compose hymns and psalms to the female deities, and especially to the Goddess Inanna under her Semitic name Ishtar. The death-knell of the female deity in Near Eastern religious worship came with the birth of monotheism, and especially the Jahwistic monotheism propagated by the Hebrew prophets. For them, Jahweh was the one and only, omniscient, omnipotent and all-male—there was no room for any goddess no matter how minimal her power, or how irreproachable her conduct. Still, even in Jahwistic Judaism there are faint echoes of the female divinities of earlier days, and it is not altogether surprising to find that the Hebrew mystics, the Kabbalists, spoke of a feminine element in Jahweh designated as the "Shekinah," opposed to a masculine element designated as the "Holy One, Blessed Be He." And at least one passage in the renowned Kabbalistic book, the Zohar, states that Moses, the son of God, actually had intercourse with the "Shekinah,"—a distant but not so faint reminder of the "Sacred Marriage" between Dumuzi and Inanna, that provides us with one more example of the far, gossamer, reach of the "legacy of Sumer."

POSTSCRIPT

Was Sumerian Civilization Exclusively Male Dominated?

Because humans make assumptions about race and gender and then find evidence to support these assumptions, it is not surprising that Starr and Kramer reach different conclusions. Among Kramer's many books is *Sumerian Mythology: A Study of Spiritual and Literary Achievement in the Third Millennium B.C.* (Peter Smith Publisher, 1980). Sir C. Leonard Woolly discovered and excavated the Royal Cemetery of Ur; his *The Sumerians* (Oxford at the Clarendon Press, 1928, 1929) is a classic in the field. William W. Hallo, who participated with Kramer in the Invited Lectures, which produced the book from which the No-side selection is taken, is a prolific and compelling chronicler of this period. His recent *Origins: The Ancient Near Eastern Background of Some Modern Western Institutions* (E. J. Brill, 1996) contains three chapters concerning women—in law, in public life, and as authors.

Has patriarchy—the rule of society by men—always existed? Or, as historian Gerda Lerner argues in *The Creation of Patriarchy* (Oxford University Press, 1986), was this pattern created as a historical event? Erich Newman's *The Great Mother: An Analysis of the Archetype* (Princeton University Press, 1963) broke new ground in explaining the goddess archetype as did Elizabeth Gould Davis's *The First Sex* (Putnam, 1971); Merlin Stone's *When God Was a Woman* (Dorset Press, 1976); and Marija Gimbutus's *Goddesses and Gods of Old Europe* (University of California Press, 1982). All of these books explore goddess cultures and the earthly women who lived within them. *Engendering Archaeology: Women and Prehistory*, Joan M. Gero and Margaret W. Conkey, eds. (Basil Blackwell, 1991) examines the archaeological record for gender-based approaches and assumptions. In that work, see Susan Pollack's "Women in a Man's World: Images of Sumerian Women." Also see Pollack's book entitled *Ancient Mesopotamia: The Eden That Never Was* (Cambridge University Press, 1999).

For a look at assumptions challenged, students may enjoy Elaine Morgan's anthropological study *The Descent of Woman* (Bantam, 1972). Playing on the title of Charles Darwin's *The Descent of Man*, Morgan assumes that the mother/ child dyad rather than the male/female pair-bond is the basis of evolution. What brought about the worldwide transition to patriarchy? Leonard Shlain's *The Alphabet Versus the Goddess* (Viking/Penguin, 1998) states that the widespread acquisition of alphabet literacy changes the way we perceive the world and rewires the brain. In each world civilization, Shlain finds this transition from image to word leading to the demise of goddess worship, a plunge in women's status, and the advent of harsh patriarchy and misogyny.

Inanna's enduring fascination is captured in two recent books, both based on the poems dedicated to the goddess. Kim Echilin's *Inanna: From the*

Myths of Ancient Sumer (Groundwood, 2003), which credits the priestess Enheduanna mentioned in the No-side selection, explores the amorous and warlike aspects of the goddess and follows her descent into the underworld. In *Inanna: Queen of Heaven and Earth* (Point Foundation, 1992), storyteller and folklorist Diane Wolkstein has taken the goddess's words form "Inanna's scribe" [Samuel Noah Kramer] and, in her own words, "I have sung them as best I can."

ISSUE 2

Does Alexander the Great Deserve His Reputation?

YES: N. G. L. Hammond, from *The Genius of Alexander the Great* (University of North Carolina Press, 1997)

NO: Ian Worthington, from "How 'Great' Was Alexander?" *The Ancient History Bulletin* (April-June 1999)

ISSUE SUMMARY

YES: Professor emeritus of Greek N. G. L. Hammond states that research has proven that Alexander the Great is deserving of his esteemed historical reputation.

NO: Professor Ian Worthington counters that Alexander's actions were self-serving and eventually weakened his Macedonian homeland; therefore, he does not merit the historical reputation he has been given.

From 431–404 B.C.E. Greek city-states (polei) were destroying themselves in a needless but predictable series of wars that have become known as the Peloponnesian Wars. Chronicled by Thucydides (460–400 B.C.), an eyewitness and participant, these wars showed the Greek states at their worst—selfish, contentious, avaricious, and power-hungry. The result was a series of conflicts in which one side, Sparta and its allies, was able to defeat its traditional enemy, Athens and its Delian League allies. Both sides suffered heavy losses and learned no lessons from the prolongued conflict. In their weakened, unenlightened state, they were easy prey to a strong, united Greek kingdom from the north—the Macedonians and their powerful king Philip.

The Macedonians were considered by the Greek city-states of the south to be barbaric. However, they had unification and military prowess on their side, and soon all of Greece was under their control. Philip was deprived of his chance for a more exalted place in history when he was assassinated by a bodyguard while attending a wedding festival in 336 B.C.E. He was succeeded by his son Alexander, then a young man of 19 years.

Alexander seemed to be destined for greatness. At an early age he displayed strong leadership and military skills, and to complement these,

Philip hired the noted Greek philosopher Aristotle as a tutor to help develop Alexander's intellectual side. Although it is difficult to pinpoint specific contributions that Aristotle made to the development of his pupil, some general ones were a passion for Greek culture, a strong affinity for intellectual pursuits, and a keen interest in Greek literature and art.

Given the volatile nature of Macedonian politics and Alexander's lack of experience, accession to his father's crown was not guaranteed. But he did succeed, and within 14 years he conquered most of the then-known world. This earned him a place in history with the sobriquet—Alexander the Great.

Alexander's place in history was created immediately after his death. There were some who spoke of him as a divinity, even while he was alive, and Alexander did nothing to discourage it. This glorification process continued through the next few centuries. The Romans, who featured likenesses of him in many of their art works, saw themselves in him as they began to follow in his footsteps, conquering much of the known world. The apex of his Roman reputation occurred when Plutarch (42–102 C.E.) wrote glowingly of him in his *Lives*, claiming that Alexander was descended from Hercules. A few of the historical figures who engaged in Alexandrine worship included Julius Caesar, Napoleon Bonaparte, and U.S. World War II general George Patton. Alexander's persona has also been featured in literary works by writers too numerous to mention.

What is the basis of Alexander's glowing historical reputation? Obviously, his conquests form its essence—but it is based on more than territorial accumulation. It is the story of the "philosopher-king," the cultured leader who attempted to create a cultural synthesis by fusing the best of the East and the West. It is the saga of an attempt by a man to create a "one world" ideal, a man trying to achieve the "impossible dream" and coming close to it.

For most of recorded history, humankind's story has been told through the words and deeds of its great men, and occasionally, great women. This is known as the "heroic" approach to the study of history. In the first part of the twentieth century, this version of history dominated, and historical figures such as Alexander still received favorable press. But the repetitive violence of the twentieth century influenced people to interpret history in a less militaristic vein, and the positive assessment of Alexander the Great began to change. How much it will change remains to be seen.

N. G. L. Hammond, who has written three books about Alexander, still finds much to admire in him, especially his love of Greek culture and his strong intellectual qualities. To Hammond, Alexander is worthy of his historical appellation. On the other hand, Ian Worthington states that Alexander's historical reputation may be undeserved due to the death and suffering caused by his military campaigns, and how they weakened the Macedonian state at home.

YES  N. G. L. Hammond

The Plans and Personality of Alexander

Arrangements Affecting the Macedonians and Macedonia

After the reconciliation in late summer 324 Alexander [the Great] offered his terms for any Macedonians who might volunteer to go home. They would be paid the normal wage up to their arrival in Macedonia, and each man would receive a gratuity of one talent. They were ordered to leave their Asian wives and children in Asia, where Alexander undertook to bring up the boys "in the Macedonian manner in other respects and in military training"; and he said he would send them thereafter to their fathers in Macedonia. He made provision also for orphans of Macedonian soldiers in Asia. Some 10,000 Macedonians accepted these terms. "He embraced them all, with tears in his eyes and tears in theirs, and they parted company." They were being released from the campaign in Asia, not from military service. In summer 323 they reached Cilicia, where Alexander intended that they should winter. In spring 322 they were to be transported to Macedonia by his newly built fleet. By then Alexander expected to have completed his Arabian campaign and to be in Egypt or Cilicia. He was to be joined there by 10,000 Macedonians "in their prime," who would be replaced in Macedonia by the returning veterans. . . .

Arrangements Affecting the City-States

Alexander respected the sovereignty of the Greek Community in the settlement of affairs after the defeat of Agis and his allies, and he continued to do so, for instance by sending captured works of art to the states in the Greek Community. His conduct in these years indicates that the allegations of exceeding his powers as *Hegemon*, which were made in a speech "On the Treaty with Alexander" in 331, were groundless. Within the Greek Community only one breach of the charter was reported in our sources, the expulsion of the people of Oeniadae from their city by the Aetolians. It happened perhaps in 325; for Alexander said that he himself would punish the Aetolians, presumably on his return to the West. In the years of peace a large number of Greek allies went east to serve in Alexander's army, and no doubt others emigrated to trade or settle in Asia. At Athens Phocion was re-elected general repeatedly as the advocate of compliance with the Charter, and Lycurgus used the prosperity which Athens enjoyed under the peace to complete the construction in stone of the auditorium of the theatre of Dionysus and to improve the naval shipyards.

In June 324, when Alexander was at Susa, one of his financial officers, Harpalus, fled to Greece in order to escape punishment for misconduct. He came to Cape Sunium with 5,000 talents, 6,000 mercenaries and 30 ships, and as an Athenian citizen (for he had been honoured earlier by a grant of citizenship) he proceeded to Athens and asked for asylum and in effect alliance against Alexander. The Assembly rejected his request. He and his forces went on to Taenarum in the Peloponnese, but he returned as a suppliant with a single ship and a large amount of money. The Assembly then granted him asylum as an Athenian citizen. Although he gave bribes freely in Athens, he did not win over the leading politicians. Meanwhile Antipater [general "with full powers"] and Olympias [handler of religious and financial affairs] made the demand that Athens as Macedonia's ally should extradite Harpalus; and envoys from Alexander came from Asia with a similar demand. On the proposal of Demosthenes the Assembly voted to arrest Harpalus, confiscate his money, and hold him and his money "for Alexander." . . .

When his forces were assembled at Susa, Alexander announced to them that all exiles, except those under a curse and those exiled from Thebes, were to be recalled and reinstated. . . . The wording was as follows: "Alexander to the exiles from the Greek cities . . . we shall be responsible for your return . . . we have written to Antipater about this, in order that he may compel any states which are unwilling to restore you." . . . The purpose of Alexander was twofold: to resettle the floating population of exiles (we may call them refugees today), which caused instability and often led to mercenary service; and to reconcile the parties which had fought one another and caused the vicious circle of revolutionary faction.

Such an act of statesmanship was and is unparalleled. It affected almost all Greek city-states to varying degrees, and it hit Athens and Aetolia hardest. For Athens had expelled the population of Samos in 365 and occupied the island herself; and now, forty years later, she would have to restore the island to its proper owners. And Aetolia had to hand back Oeniadae to the Acarnanians she had expelled. At the time Alexander could not be accused of restoring his own partisans; for the bulk of the exiles had been opponents of the pro-Macedonian regimes in power. According to Hieronymus, an objective historian born around 364, "people in general accepted the restoration of the exiles as being made for a good purpose." In many states the restoration had taken place at the time of Alexander's death, but Athens and Aetolia were still making objections. . . .

Alexander's Beliefs and Personal Qualities

Alexander grew up in a kingdom which was continually at war, and he saw it as his duty to lead the Macedonians in war not from a distance but in the forefront of the fighting. He saw the destiny of Macedonia as victory in war, and he and his men made military glory the object of their ambitions. Thus he spoke of the victorious career of Philip [king of Macedonia (359–336 B.C.) and father of Alexander] as conferring "glory" both on him and on "the community of Macedonians." His own pursuit of glory was boundless. As he declared to his Commanders at the Hyphasis, "I myself consider that there is no limit for a man of spirit to his labours, except that those labours should lead to fine achievements." He made the same demand on his Commanders and his men. They had committed themselves to following him when they had sworn the oath of allegiance (*sacramentum pietatis*), to be loyal and have the same friend and enemy as their king. If a man should be killed in his service, Alexander assured them that his death would bring him glory for ever and his place of burial would be famous.

Life was competitive for boys in the School of Pages and for boys being trained for the militia in the cities, and thereafter in civilian affairs and in the services. No Macedonian festival was complete without contests in such arts as dramatic performance, recitation of poetry, proclamation as a herald, and musicianship, and in athletic events which on occasion included armed combat. Alexander was intensely competitive throughout his life. He would be the first to tame Bucephalus [a wild horse], to attack the Theban Sacred Band [an army of the boldest Theban warriors, organized to fight the Spartans in 371 B.C.], to mount a city wall or climb an impregnable rock. He was the inspirer and often the judge of competition in others. He alone promoted soldiers and officers, awarded gifts for acts of courage, bestowed gold crowns on successful Commanders, and decided the order in the hierarchy of military rank up to the position of Senior Friend and Leading Bodyguard. Competitions between military units and between naval crews were a part of training and of battle. Alexander himself believed that he must compete with Philip, Cyrus the Great, Heracles and Dionysus and surpass them all, and as Arrian remarked, "if he had added Europe to Asia, he would have competed with himself in default of any rival."

His belief in the superiority of Greek civilisation was absolute. His most treasured possession was the *Iliad* of Homer, and he had the plays of the three great tragedians sent to him in Asia, together with dithyrambic poems and the history of Philistus. They were his favourite reading. He admired Aristotle as the leading exponent of Greek intellectual enquiry, and he had a natural yearning (*pothos*) for philosophical discussion and understanding. His mind was to some extent cast in the Aristotelian mould; for he too combined a wide-ranging curiosity with close observation and acute reasoning. His belief in the validity of the Greek outlook of his time was not modified by his acquaintance with Egyptian, Babylonian and Indian ideas. One mark of Greek civilisation was the vitality of the city, both in Europe and in Asia, and Alexander believed that the best way to spread Greek culture and civilisation was by founding cities throughout Asia. At the outset the leaders in these cities were the Macedonians and the Greek mercenary soldiers, who conducted the democratic form of self-government to which they were accustomed. At the same time the future leaders were being educated "in Greek letters and in Macedonian weaponry" in the schools which Alexander established. The process was already well under way before Alexander died, as we see from a passage in Plutarch's *Moralia*: "When Alexander was civilising Asia, the reading was Homer and the boys (*paides*) of the Persians, Susianians and Gedrosians used to chant the tragedies of Euripides and Sophocles . . . and thanks to him Bactria and Caucasus revered the Greek gods." Egypt has yielded a teaching manual of the late third century, which was designed to teach Greek as a foreign language and included selections from Homer and the tragedians. The excavations at Ai Khanoum in Afghanistan have revealed Greek temples, theatre and odeum (for music) alongside a very large Asian temple in the late fourth century. Alexander was the standard-bearer of Greek civilisation. His influence in education and so in civilisation has been profound, extending even into our own age.

Faith in the orthodox religion of Macedonia was deeply implanted in Alexander's mind. He sacrificed daily, even in his last illness, on behalf of himself and the Macedonians and on innumerable other occasions. He organised traditional festivals in honour of the gods in the most lavish fashion. He believed as literally as Pindar had done in the presence in our world of the Olympian gods, in the labours of heroes such as Heracles and the exploits of Achilles, both being his ancestors. The deities made their wishes or their warnings manifest to men through natural phenomena and through omens and oracles, which were interpreted and delivered by inspired men and women. It was an advantage of polytheism that the number of gods was not limited, and Alexander could see Zeus in the Libyan Ammon and in the Babylonian Belus, and Heracles in the Tyrian Melkart or the Indian Krishna. His special regard for Ammon was probably due to the prophetic oracles which he received at Siwah and which were evidently fulfilled *in toto* when Alexander reached the outer Ocean. He gave thanks time and again to "the usual gods" (the twelve Olympians) for the salvation of himself and his army, and he must have thought that he owed his charmed life to them. Even in his last illness he believed that his prayers in the course of sacrifices would be heard and that he would live. For he died without arranging for the transition of power.

Of the personal qualities of Alexander the brilliance, the range and the quickness of his intellect are remarkable, especially in his conduct of warfare. At Gaugamela and at the Hydaspes he foresaw precisely the sequence of moves by his own units and the compulsion they would place on his enemies. As Ptolemy, himself a most able commander, observed of the first campaign, "the result was as Alexander inferred that it would be," and after the last campaign "not a one of the operations of war which Alexander undertook was beyond his capability" (*aporon*). In generalship no one has surpassed him. Arrian wrote that Alexander had "the most wonderful power of grasping the right course when the situation was still in obscurity." Thus he knew on his landing in Asia that he must set up his own Kingdom of Asia and obtain the willing cooperation of his subjects. Already at Sardis he began the training of boys who would become soldiers of that kingdom. The orginality of his intellect was apparent in his development of the Indus, the Tigris and the Euphrates as waterways of commerce and his reorganisation of the irrigation of Mesopotamia. The boldness of his calculations was rewarded with success in many engagements and especially in the opening of navigation between the Indus Delta and the Persian Gulf.

His emotions were very strong. His love for his mother was such that one tear of hers would outweigh all the complaints of Antipater. He sent letters and gifts to her constantly, and he said that he would take her alone into his confidence on his return to Macedonia. His loyalty to the friends of his own generation was carried sometimes to a fault, and his passionate grief for Hephaestion [his closest friend from childhood days] was almost beyond reason. He loved his soldiers and they loved him; he and his veterans wept when they parted company; and he and they acknowledged that love in his last moments. When he killed Cleitus [an old-fashioned noble in a drunken brawl], his remorse was desperate. His compassion for the Theban Timoclea and for the family of [Persian ruler] Darius and his love for [wife] Roxane were deeply felt and led to actions which were probably unique in contemporary warfare.

As King of the Macedonians and as King of Asia he had different roles to fill. His way of life was on the same level as that of the Macedonians on campaigns and in leisure. As he said at Opis, his rations were the same as theirs and he shared all their dangers and hardships; and he enjoyed the same festivals and drinking parties as they did. He led them not by fiat but by persuasion, and a crucial element in that persuasion was that he should always tell them the truth, and they should know that he was telling them the truth. Thus he respected the constitutional rights of the Macedonians, and his reward was that he was generally able to convince them in their Assemblies that they should accept his policies. His role as King of Asia was almost the opposite. His court, like that of the Persian King of Kings, was the acme of luxury and extravagance. He gave audience in a huge pavilion which rested on fifty golden columns, and he himself sat on a golden chair, surrounded by so many richly-dressed guardsmen that "no one dared approach him, such was the majesty associated with his person." He accepted obeisance, and he ruled by fiat. The wealth at his command was beyond belief; for he had taken over the accumulated treasure of the Persian monarchy, and he received the fixed tribute which was paid by his subjects over a huge area. His expenditure was extraordinary by Greek standards, for instance on memorials commemorating Hephaestion, but it was in proportion to his wealth as King of Asia. The strength of his personality was such that he was able to keep the two roles separate in his mind and in his behaviour, and Ptolemy and Aristobulus were correct in seeing the real Alexander as Alexander the Macedonian.

Alexander combined his extraordinary practicality with a visionary, spiritual dimension which stemmed from his religious beliefs. As a member of the Temenid house he had a special affinity with his ancestors Heracles and Zeus, and he inherited the obligation to rule in a manner worthy of them and to benefit mankind. His vision went beyond Macedonia and the Greek Community. When he landed on Asian soil, his declaration, "I accept Asia from the gods," and his prayer, that the Asians would accept him willingly as their king, were expressions of a mystical belief that the gods had set him a special task and would enable him to fulfil it. This spiritual dimension in his personality created in him the supreme confidence and the strength of will which overrode the resistance of the Macedonians to his concept of the Kingdom of Asia, and which convinced the Asians of the sincerity of his claim to treat them as equals and partners in the establishment of peace and prosperity. The power of his personality was all-pervading. It engaged the loyalty of Persian commanders and Indian rulers after defeat in battle and the loyalty of Asian troops at all levels in his service. It inspired *The Alexander Romance* in which Asian peoples adopted Alexander as their own king and incorporated his exploits into their own folk-lore. We owe to Plutarch [Greek writer and historian (45 A.D.–125 A.D.)], drawing probably on the words of Aristobulus, an insight into this spiritual dimension in Alexander.

> Believing that he had come from the gods to be a governor and reconciler of the universe, and using force of arms against those whom he did not bring together by the light of reason, he harnessed all resources to one and the same end, mixing as it were in a loving-cup the lives, manners, marriages and customs of men. He ordered them all to regard the inhabited earth (*oikoumene*) as their fatherland and his armed forces as their stronghold and defence.

Ian Worthington

NO

How "Great" Was Alexander?

Why was Alexander III of Macedon called 'Great'? The answer seems relatively straightforward: from an early age he was an achiever, he conquered territories on a superhuman scale, he established an empire until his times unrivalled, and he died young, at the height of his power. Thus, at the youthful age of 20, in 336, he inherited the powerful empire of Macedon, which by then controlled Greece and had already started to make inroads into Asia. In 334 he invaded Persia, and within a decade he had defeated the Persians, subdued Egypt, and pushed on to Iran, Afghanistan and even India. As well as his vast conquests Alexander is credited with the spread of Greek culture and education in his empire, not to mention being responsible for the physical and cultural formation of the hellenistic kingdoms—some would argue that the hellenistic world was Alexander's legacy. He has also been viewed as a philosophical idealist, striving to create a unity of mankind by his so-called fusion of the races policy, in which he attempted to integrate Persians and Orientals into his administration and army. Thus, within a dozen years Alexander's empire stretched from Greece in the west to India in the far east, and he was even worshipped as a god by many of his subjects while still alive. On the basis of his military conquests contemporary historians, and especially those writing in Roman times, who measured success by the number of body-bags used, deemed him great.

However, does a man deserve to be called 'The Great' who was responsible for the deaths of tens of thousands of his own men and for the unnecessary wholesale slaughter of native peoples? How 'great' is a king who prefers constant warfare over consolidating conquered territories and long-term administration? Or who, through his own recklessness, often endangered his own life and the lives of his men? Or whose violent temper on occasion led him to murder his friends and who towards the end of his life was an alcoholic, paranoid, megalomaniac, who believed in his own divinity? These are questions posed by our standards of today of course, but nevertheless they are legitimate questions given the influence which Alexander has exerted throughout history—an influence which will no doubt continue.

The aims of this [selection] are to trace some reasons for questioning the greatness of Alexander as is reflected in his epithet, and to add potential evidence dealing with the attitude of the Macedonians, Alexander's own people,

From Ian Worthington, "How 'Great' Was Alexander?" *The Ancient History Bulletin*, vol. 13, no. 2 (April-June 1999). Notes and references omitted.

in their king's absence. It is important to stress that when evaluating Alexander it is essential to view the 'package' of king as a whole; i.e., as king, commander and statesman. All too often this is not the case. There is no question that Alexander was spectacularly successful in the military field, and had Alexander only been a general his epithet may well have been deserved. But he was not just a general; he was a king too, and hence military exploits form only a percentage of what Alexander did, or did not do—in other words, we must look at the 'package' of him as king as a whole. By its nature this [selection] is impressionistic, and it can only deal rapidly with selected examples from Alexander's reign and discuss points briefly. However, given the unequalled influence Alexander has played in cultures and history from the time of his death to today, it is important to stress that there is a chasm of a difference between the mythical Alexander, which for the most part we have today, and the historical.

Alexander died in 323, and over the course of time the mythical king and his exploits sprang into being. Alexander himself was not above embellishing his own life and achievements. He very likely told the court historian Callisthenes of Olynthus what to say about his victory over Darius III at the battle of Issus in 333, for example. Contemporary Attic oratory also exaggerated his achievements, and so within a generation of his death erroneous stories were already being told.

As time continued we move into the genre of pulp fiction. In the third or second century BC Alexander's exploits formed the plot of the story known as the *Alexander Romance*, which added significantly to the Alexander legend and had such a massive influence on many cultures into the Middle Ages. Given its lifespan, deeds were attributed to Alexander which are unhistorical, such as his encounters with the tribe of headless men, his flying exploits in a basket borne by eagles, and the search for the Water of Life, which ended with his transformation into a mermaid. These stories became illustrative fodder for the various manuscripts of the *Alexander Romance*—one of the most popular episodes is Alexander's ascent to heaven, inspired by the myth of Bellerephon to fly to Mount Olympus on Pegasus, which is found in many Byzantine and later art-works, sculptures and paintings. As a result of the *Romance* Alexander astonishingly appears in the literature of other cultures: in Hebrew literature, for example, he was seen as a preacher and prophet, who even becomes converted to Christianity. In Persian literature he is the hero Sikandar, sent to punish the impure peoples. In the West he appears as a Frank, a Goth, a Russian and a Saxon.

Then there is Plutarch, writing in the late first and second century AD, who has probably done the most damage to our knowing the historical Alexander. In his treatise *On The Fortune or The Virtue of Alexander*, Plutarch was swayed (understandably) by the social background against which he was writing and especially by his own philosophical beliefs, and he portrayed Alexander as both an action man and a philosopher-king, whose mission was to impose Greek civilisation on the 'barbarian' Persians. Plutarch's work is essentially a rhetorical exercise, but as time continued the rhetorical aspects were disregarded in favour of a warrior-king who was more than the stuff legends were made of; this was a warrior who was seen to combine military success with wisdom and unification. And so Alexander emerges as the promoter of the brotherhood of man in Tarn's 1948 biography, which was greatly influenced by what Plutarch wrote.

The Alexander legend was a ready feeding ground for artists throughout the centuries as well. When Alexander invaded Persia in 334 he detoured to Troy to sacrifice at the tomb of his hero Achilles. This was a stirring story, which became a model for heroic piety in the Renaissance and later periods; thus, for example, we have Fontebasso's painting of Alexander's sacrifice at Achilles' tomb in the eighteenth century. In modern Greece Alexander became both an art-work and a symbol, as seen in the painting by Engonopoulos in 1977 of the face-less Alexander standing with his arm around the face-less Pavlos Melas, a modern hero of the struggle for Macedonian independence.

Thus, we can see how the historical Alexander has faded into the invincible general, the great leader, explorer and king, as time continued, especially in the Middle Ages with its world of chivalry, warriors and great battles: a superb context into which to fit Alexander, even if this meant distortion of the truth, and history subsumed to legend. Indeed, during the Middle Ages he was regarded as one of the four great kings of the ancient world. Let us now consider some specific aspects of Alexander's reign in support of this.

In 334 Alexander III left home for Asia, entrusting to Antipater as guardian . . . a stable—for a while—Greece and Macedon. The king also unilaterally made Antipater deputy hegemon in the League of Corinth. Alexander's 'mandate' or prime directive, as inherited from his father Philip II and endorsed by the League of Corinth, was to pursue his father's plan of punishing the Persians for their sacrilegious acts of 150 years ago and to 'liberate' (whatever that meant) the Greek cities of Asia Minor. In other words, a panhellenic mandate. After he had fulfilled it, people quite rightly would have expected him to return home. People were wrong: the king would soon disregard the prime directive for personal reasons, causing discontent amongst the army with him and also, even more ominously, with his countrymen back home.

We have a fair amount of information for events in mainland Greece, especially Athens, during the reign of Alexander, however events in Macedon in this period are undocumented and largely unknown. We certainly cannot say that there was a hiatus in Macedonian history, for Antipater kept Macedon powerful and united while Alexander was absent, so much so that there was economic growth, and education and military training, for example, remained at a high standard. However, appearance is not likely to reflect reality. Macedon in this period may well have been fraught with discontent, and it provides insights into the Macedonians' attitude to their king and he to them. At the same time a consideration of the Macedonian background also lends further weight to questioning the aptness of Alexander's title 'Great'.

Alexander's military successes throughout his reign were spectacular to a very large degree—and certainly manufactured by the king to be great—and we should expect his people back home to feel proud of their king at the head of his panhellenic mission of punishment and liberation, and to proclaim his victories to all and sundry. His deeds and the geographical extent of his conquests were certainly known for we have references to them in contemporary Attic oratory. However, the impression which strikes us about the Macedonians themselves is that Alexander was far from their idea of an ideal king. Why might they feel this way? In addressing this, we can begin with the vexed question of Macedonian manpower. Did Alexander's demands for reinforcements from the mainland seriously deplete the fighting strength of the army under Antipater? Did he make these demands regardless of the pressure under which he was putting Antipater and without regard for the lives of his people and the security of his kingdom from external threat? And if so, how did the people feel and how did they react? . . .

Alexander's generalship and actual military victories may be questioned in several key areas. For example, after the battle of Issus in 333 Darius fled towards Media, but Alexander pressed on to Egypt. He did not pursue Darius, as he surely ought to have done and thus consolidate his gains, especially when so far from home and with the mood of the locals so prone to fluctuation, but left him alone. He was more interested in what lay to the south: the riches of Babylon and then Susa, or as Arrian describes them the 'prizes of the war'. However, a war can hardly be seen as won if the opposing king and commander remains at large and has the potential to regroup. Alexander's action was lucky for Darius, then, as he was able to regroup his forces and bring Alexander to battle again almost two years later, at Gaugamela (331). It was not lucky for Alexander, though, and especially so for those men on both sides who fell needlessly that day in yet another battle.

We have also the various sieges which Alexander undertook and which were often lengthy, costly, and questionable. A case in point is that of Tyre in 332 as Alexander made his way to Egypt after his victory at Issus. In Phoenicia Byblos and Sidon surrendered to Alexander, as did the island town (as it was then) of Tyre until the king expressed his personal desire to sacrifice in the main temple there. Quite rightly considering his demand sacrilegious, the Tyrians resisted him and Alexander, his ego affronted and refusing to back down, laid siege to the town. The siege itself lasted several months, cost the king a fortune in money and manpower, and resulted in the slaughter of the male Tyrians and the selling of the Tyrian women and children into slavery. There is no question that control of Tyre was essential since Alexander could not afford a revolt of the Phoenician cities, given their traditional rivalries, as he pushed on to Egypt. Nor indeed, if we believe his speech at Arrian, could he allow Tyre independence with the Persian navy a threat and the Phoenician fleet the strongest contingent in it. However, there was no guarantee that the destruction of Tyre would result in the Phoencian fleet surrendering to him as he only seems to have *expected* it would. Moreover, laying siege to Tyre was not necessary: he could simply have left a garrison, for example, on the mainland opposite the town to keep it in check. Another option, given that the Tyrians had originally surrendered to him, would have been the diplomatic one: to recognise the impiety of his demand in their eyes and thus relinquish it, thereby continuing on his way speedily and with their goodwill. Ultimately no real gain came from his siege except to Alexander on a purely personal level again: his damaged ego had been repaired; the cost in time, manpower and reputation mattered little.

Alexander's great military victories over his Persian and Indian foes which have so long occupied a place in popular folklore and been much admired throughout the centuries are very likely to have been embellished and nothing like the popular conceptions of them. A case in point is the battle of Issus in 333. Darius threw victory away at that battle and he was, to put it bluntly, a mediocre commander—the battle might have been very different if Alexander had faced a more competent commander such as Memnon, for example. Alexander was lucky, but this does not come in the 'official' account we have of the battle, probably since he told Callisthenes, the court historian, what to write about it.

. . . [W]ord would filter through to the Macedonians back home. Alexander's growing orientalism, as seen in his apparent integration of foreigners into his administration and army, was a cause of great discontent as the traditional Macedonian warrior-king transformed himself into something akin to a sultan. He began to change his appearance, preferring a mixture of Persian and Macedonian clothing, despite the obvious displeasure of his troops, and he had also assumed the upright tiara, the symbol of Persian kingship. Some saw the writing on the wall and duly pandered to the king. Thus, Peucestas, the Macedonian satrap of Persis, was well rewarded by the king for adopting Persian dress and learning the Persian language. However, he was the only Macedonian to do so according to Arrian.

Significant also was Alexander's attempt to adopt the Persian custom of *proskynesis*—genuflection—at his court in Bactra in 327, and his expectation that his men would follow suit. *Proskynesis* was a social act which had long been practised by the Persians and involved prostrating oneself before the person of the king in an act of subservience, and thereby accepting his lordship. The custom however was regarded as tantamount to worship and thus sacrilegious to the Greeks—worship of a god or a dead hero was one thing, but worship of a person while still alive quite another. Callisthenes thwarted Alexander's attempt, something which the king never forgot and which would soon cost Callisthenes his life in sadistic circumstances.

Why Alexander tried to introduce *proskynesis* is unknown. Perhaps he was simply attempting to create a form of social protocol common to Macedonians, Greeks and Persians. However, he would have been well aware of the religious connotations associated with the act and hence its implications for his own being. It was plain stupidity on his part if he thought his men would embrace the custom with relish, and his action clearly shows that he had lost touch with his army and the religious beliefs on which he had been raised. Evidence for this may be seen in the motives for the Pages' Conspiracy, a serious attempt on Alexander's life, which occurred not long after Alexander tried to enforce *proskynesis* on all. A more likely explanation for the attempt to introduce *proskynesis* is that Alexander now thought of himself as divine, and thus *proskynesis* was a logical means of recognising his divine status in public by all men.

Indeed, Alexander's belief that he was divine impacts adversely on any evaluation of him. History is riddled with megalomaniacs who along the way suffered from divine pretensions, and the epithet 'Great' is not attached to them. Regardless of whether his father Philip II was worshipped as a god on his death, Alexander seems not to have been content with merely following in his footsteps but to believe in his own divine status while alive. . . .

Was Alexander using his own people for his own personal ends now? Philip II risked the lives of his men as well, but for his state's hegemonic position in international affairs, not for his own selfish reasons or a *pothos* which might well jeopardise that position of Macedon. Others saw the danger, even from early in his reign. Thus in 335, after the successful termination of the Greek revolt, which broke out on the death of Philip II, Diodorus says that Parmenion and Antipater urged Alexander not to become actively involved in Asia until he had produced a son and heir. Alexander opposed them for personal reasons: he could not procrastinate at home waiting for children to be born when the invasion of Asia had been endorsed by the League of Corinth! In the end, says Diodorus, he won them over. Then in 331 Darius III offered *inter alia* to abandon to Alexander all territories west of the Euphrates and to become the friend and ally of the king. Parmenion thought the Persian king's offer to be in the Macedonians' best interests, but Alexander refused to accept it (in a famous exchange in which Parmenion is alleged to have said that if he were Alexander he would accept the terms, and a displeased Alexander is alleged to have replied that if he were Parmenion he would, but instead he was Alexander). . . .

Alexander's autocratic nature and its adverse impact on his army have been illustrated many times, but it extended beyond the men with him to the Greeks back on the mainland. One example is his Exiles Decree of 324, which ordered all exiles to return to their native cities (excluding those under a religious curse and the Thebans). If any city was unwilling, then Antipater was empowered to use force against it. The context was no doubt to send home the large bands of mercenaries now wandering the empire and which posed no small military or political danger if any ambitious satrap [subordinate official] or general got his hands on them. The decree was technically illegal since it clearly flouted the autonomy of the Greek states, not to mention the principles of the League of Corinth, but Alexander cared little about *polis* autonomy or the feelings of the Greeks. Although the Athenians refused to receive back their exiles, resistance, to coin a phrase, was futile: Alexander was king, the Macedonians controlled Greece, and the final clause of the decree on coercing Greek cities would not be lost on them. The flurry of diplomatic activity to the king over the decree proves this, even though outright rebellion was not planned at that stage. His death altered the situation dramatically, and only one state, Tegea, actually implemented the decree.

There is no need to deal in great detail with the notion which originates in Plutarch's treatise on Alexander, and has found its way into some modern works (such as Tarn's biography), that Alexander pursued an actual policy to promote a unity of mankind. In other words, that Alexander is deserving of the title 'Great' for these ideological reasons. The belief is 'founded' on such factors as his integration of foreigners into his army and administration, the mass mixed marriage at Susa (324), and Alexander's prayer for concord amongst the races after the Opis mutiny (also 324). The belief is quite erroneous, and Alexander, as with everything else, was acting for purely political/military, not ideological, purposes. For one thing, it is important to note that in the army foreigners were not peppered consistently amongst existing units, and when this did happen the instances are very few and far between. Thus, a few Persians are found incorporated in the *agema* [the Royal squadron] of the Companion cavalry, and Persians and Macedonians served together in a phalanx at Babylon, but Alexander's motive in both cases was military.

While Alexander did use Persians and Orientals in his administration it was always Macedonians and Greeks who controlled the army and the treasury. For example, at Babylon Alexander appointed as satrap the Persian Mazaeus, who had been satrap of Syria under Darius and commander of the Persian right at the battle of Gaugamela. However, Apollodorus of Amphipolis and Agathon of Pydna controlled the garrison there and collected the taxes. In a nutshell, the natives had the local knowledge and the linguistic expertise. The conscious policy on the part of Alexander was to have the different races working together in order to make the local administration function as efficiently as possible, and had nothing to do with promoting racial equality.

Then there is the mass wedding at Susa, also in 324, at which Alexander and 91 members of his court married various Persian noble women in an elaborate wedding ceremony (conducted in Persian fashion too), which lasted for five days. The symbolism as far as a fusion of the races is concerned is obvious, but again too much has been made of this marriage: it is important to note that no Persian men were given honours at Alexander's court or in his military and administrative machinery. Moreover, no Macedonian or Greek women were brought out from the mainland to marry Persian noble men, which we would expect as part of a fusion 'policy'. A closer explanation to the truth is probably that Alexander could not afford these noble women to marry their own races and thus provide the potential for revolt, something mixed marriages with his own court might offset. That the marriages were forced onto his men is proved by the fact that all apart from Seleucus seem to have divorced their wives upon the king's death. Once again, however, Alexander seems to have ignored the displeasure of his men, ultimately at great cost to himself and his empire.

Finally, the great reconciliation banquet at Opis in 324 (after the second mutiny), in which Macedonian, Greek, Persian and Iranian sipped from the same cup, and Alexander significantly 'prayed for various blessings and especially that the Macedonians and Persians should enjoy harmony as partners in the government'. Yet, *inter alia* it is important to remember that Alexander had played on the hatred between the Macedonians and the Persians in ending the mutiny, and that the Macedonians were seated closest to him at the banquet, thereby emphasising their racial superiority and power. Moreover, we would expect a prayer to future concord after such a reconciliation since dissension in the ranks was the last thing Alexander needed given his plans for future conquest, which involved the invasion of Arabia in the near future! Thus, we may reject the notion of a 'brotherhood of mankind', and divorce it from any objective evaluation of Alexander.

In conclusion, the 'greatness' of Alexander III must be questioned, and the historical Alexander divorced from the mythical, despite the cost to the legend. There is no question that Alexander was the most powerful individual of his time, and we must recognise that. For sheer distance covered, places subdued, battle strategy, and breadth of vision he deserves praise. In just a decade he conquered the vast Persian empire that had been around for two centuries, and he amassed a fortune so vast that it is virtually impossible to comprehend. Alexander also improved the economy of his state (to an extent) and encouraged trade and commerce, especially by breaking down previously existing frontiers (of major importance in the hellenistic period), and an offshoot of his conquests was the gathering of information on the topography and geography of the regions to which he went, as well as new and exotic flora and fauna. However, at what cost? Was the wastage in human lives, the incalculable damage to foreign peoples, institutions, livelihoods, and lands, not to mention the continuation of the dynasty at home, the security of Macedon, the future of the empire, and the loyalty of the army worth it?

That Alexander did not endear himself to his own people and that they grew discontented with him, has significant implications for his ultimate objectives and how he saw himself. The move to establish a kingdom of Asia with a capital probably at Babylon is significant. Given his disregard of the feelings of his own people (as evidenced by his lack of interest in producing a legal and above-age heir to continue the dynasty and hegemonic position of Macedon), we can only surmise that his belief in his own divinity and his attempts to be recognised as a god while alive—including the attempt at *proskynesis*—are the keys to his actions and motives. As Fredricksmeyer has so persuasively argued, Alexander was out to distance himself as far as possible from the exploits and reputation of Philip II since his attitude to his father had turned from one of admiration and rivalry, from one warrior to another, to resentment. He strove to excel him at all costs and he could not handle praise of Philip. . . . Military conquest was one thing, but simple conquest was not enough: Alexander had to outdo Philip in other areas. Deification while alive was the most obvious way. Everything else became subordinated to Alexander's drive towards self-deification and then his eventual and genuine total belief in it.

Therefore, it is easy to see, on the one hand, why Alexander has been viewed as great, but also, on the other hand, why that greatness—and thus his epithet—must be questioned in the interests of historical accuracy.

POSTSCRIPT

Does Alexander the Great Deserve His Reputation?

Someone once stated, "Pity the nation that has no heroes!" Someone else wryly replied, "Pity the nation that needs them!" To what extent have national desires created the aura of Alexander the Great? How many historical figures were so inspired by his story that they sought to emulate it? And what were the results of such actions? Military historian John Keegan, in *The Mask of Command* (Jonathan Cape, 1987), contends that Alexander's "dreadful legacy was to ennoble savagery in the name of glory and to leave a model of command that far too many men of ambition sought to act out in the centuries to come." But should Alexander be held responsible for the actions of those who have attempted to emulate him?

Also contributing to future analyses of Alexander might be a reaction against the experiences of many in what was the most violent century in the history of the world. The twentieth century saw two world wars and countless smaller ones. Words such as *Holocaust* and *genocide* were created to describe some of the century's barbarities. It saw the names of Hitler, Stalin, and Mao Zedong become infamous for the millions of deaths they have caused, many in their own countries. Noted Holocaust historian Yehuda Bauer sums up the world's propensity for violence and war—and its consequences—in *Rethinking the Holocaust* (Yale University Press, 2001), pp. 40, "Napoleon . . . won the Battle of Austerlitz—but was he there alone? Was he not helped a little bit by a few tens of thousands of soldiers whom he (and others) led into battle? How many soldiers were killed on both sides? . . . And what about the civilians near the roads that the armies traveled on? What about the dead, the wounded, the raped, and the dispossessed? We teach our children about the greatness of the various Napoleons, Palmerstons, and Bismarcks as political or military leaders and thus sanitize history." Should Alexander's name be added to this list?

As one can imagine, books about Alexander are numerous. The late Ulrich Wilcken's classic biography, *Alexander the Great,* first published in 1931, has been reissued in 1997 (W. W. Norton). It contains an insightful chapter entitled, "Introduction to Alexander Studies" by Eugene N. Borza of Pennsylvania State University. Other Alexander biographies that are worth reading are A. B. Bosworth, *Conquest and Empire: The Reign of Alexander the Great* (Cambridge University Press, 1993) and Peter Green, *Alexander of Macedon: A Historical Biography* (University of California Press, 1991). Michael Wood's *In the Footsteps of Alexander the Great* (University of California Press, 1997) is a recent book/television series that is worth recommending. Since the book contains the program narration, rent the videos and get the visual images along with the words. Ian Worthington has made two recent contributions to Alexandrine Scholarship: *Alexander the Great: A Reader* (Routlegde, 2003); and *Alexander the Great: Man and God* (Pearson Longman, 2003).

ISSUE 3

Could the Crusades Be Considered a Christian Holy War?

YES: Arthur Jones, from "Memories of Crusades Live on in Today's War," *National Catholic Reporter* (October 26, 2001)

NO: Jonathan Phillips, from "Who Were the First Crusaders?" *History Today* (March 1997)

ISSUE SUMMARY

YES: Editor-at-large Arthur Jones presents a case for calling the Crusades a Christian holy war and finds resonances of that long-ago conflict in today's Muslim-Christian conflicts.

NO: Lecturer in medieval history Jonathan Phillips finds motivations for the Crusades in religious fervor, the desire for wealth, and a family history of pilgrimage, not in holy war.

Arthur Jones begins his essay with President Bush's inadvertent use of the word "crusade" on September 16, 2001 ("This crusade, this war on terrorism, is going to take a long time)—a word he claims echoed into Muslim memories of centuries of Christian incursions. Point-of-view is pivotal. Christians might view the Crusades as a noble effort to reclaim the central sites of their faith, or as an unfortunate but long-forgotten chapter in world history. Muslims, by contrast, may have fresh memories of "the holy religious war of the Christians" and their own "war against the cross" that began in the eleventh century and continues today.

Christianity began as a persecuted sect in the Roman Empire that took seriously its founder's injunction to "turn the other cheek" and repay evil with good. Early Christians would have no part of war. But by the fourth century, Constantine, the Holy Roman Emperor, had won battles with the cross on his shield and made Christianity the official faith of the Empire. Even against this background, however, papally sanctioned violence was something new, Jones suggests.

Muhammad's revelation from God ignited a fervor on the Arabian Peninsula that swept across north Africa and into Christian Europe, beginning in the seventh century. By 750 it had spread throughout the Byzantine

Empire. At least in part, Jones argues, the Crusades can be viewed as a Christian counteroffensive, designed to take back their conquered territories and reclaim the Holy Land, the site of Jesus's ministry, death, and burial.

Muslims regard both Jews and Christians as People of the Book, praise their prophets—Abraham, Moses, and Jesus—and permit them to worship freely. The higher head tax Jews and Christians had to pay in Muslim-controlled lands was another disincentive to convert them. So, in the Fertile Crescent, Muslims and Christians had lived together for centuries before the First Crusade—in mutual toleration, if not friendship. One key to the ferocity of the First Crusade is its point of origin. Most Frankish knights would have had no contact with Islam. However, their epic poem *The Song of Roland* changed the "enemy" that defeated Charlemagne's rearguard in the Pyrenees from the Basques, who were the actual victors, into the "treacherous" Muslims of Spain.

Jonathan Phillips situates the Crusades within the social, intellectual, religious, economic, and psychological realities of late eleventh-century Europe, which he calls "one of the most guilt-ridden societies in history." People, he argues, would have had many reasons for joining a crusade—the promise of salvation, the lure of wealth, and family traditions of pilgrimage. And, Pope Urban II's original goal was a very specific one—to assist the Byzantine emperor Alexius in his struggle against the Seljuk Turks of Asia Minor. These motivations, Phillips contends, are sufficient to account for the 60,000 who joined the first Crusade. It is not necessary to posit a holy war as motivation.

Fulcher of Chartres, the priest-chaplain of the First Crusade, described "a new path to heaven" and said confidently that those who undertook this "holy war" would experience "forgiveness of sins." Those who quest for God—in the eleventh century of the twenty-first—believe they will be blessed. During the Seventh Crusade, led by St. Louis, King of France, Yves le Breton reported encountering an old woman who wandered the streets with a dish of fire in her right hand and a bowl of water in her left hand. With the fire, she explained, she would burn up Paradise, until there was nothing left of it, And with the water, she would put out the fires of Hell, until nothing remained of them. "Because," she said, "I want no one to do good in order to receive the reward of Paradise, or from fear of Hell; but solely out of love of God."

YES 

Arthur Jones

Memories of Crusades Live on in Today's War

Crusade!

On Sept. 16, the word shot around the Islamic world. And shocked it. President George W. Bush thought he'd used the term innocently enough. On that Sunday, walking from his helicopter to the White House, he said of U.S. retaliation to the Sept. 11 attacks, "this crusade, this war on terrorism, is going to take a long time."

As the Muslim uproar swelled, Bush quickly apologized. But damage had been done. The BBC, for example, in its Persian and Uzbeck broadcast news services, had translated Bush's remark in the way the Islamic world understands it, as "the war of those signed with the cross," and "the holy, religious war of the Christians." (In Islam's many national languages, from Arabic to Farsi to Urdu, the Muslims call their defense against the crusaders, "the war against the cross.")

Only a minority of Muslims actually believe America had declared a "holy war" against them, cautions Paul E. Chevedden of the University of California, Los Angeles. And Georgetown University's Zahid H. Bukhari, speaking of both Muslims and Westerners, said, "Certain lobbies, certain people, do use the word [crusade] to project what is happening because they have their own agendas to present. They like the terminology and can be more effective because of it."

To Muslims, whose memory of historic grievances may be sharper than that of most Christians, the concept of a "holy war" has implications lost in history's mists. To some millions of Muslims within the Islamic world, crusade still means centuries of bloody Western Christian incursions fought over the Holy Land. Those memories are like ghosts dancing to the U.S. drums of war.

NCR talked to historians of religion and those engaged in Muslim-Christian dialogue and, as the globe's sole superpower searches for one man among the rocks and caves of Islamic Afghanistan, learned lessons for today from the history of the medieval crusades. From today's perspective, there are some surprises, some odd similarities and parallels.

Christians did indeed at one time have their "holy wars," accompanied by language that could have come from bin Laden himself.

The historical record tells us that Fulcher of Chartres (1058–1130), priest-chaplain on the First Crusade, wrote in his eyewitness account that this Crusade was a *novum salutis genus*, "a new path to Heaven." Those Christians

From *National Catholic Reporter,* Volume 38, issue 1, October 26, 2001, pp. 1(3).

who followed this "holy war" path would, wrote Fulcher, experience "full and complete satisfaction" and "forgiveness of sins."

A World Bursting Apart

To Chevedden, however, who is an associate at UCLA's Gustav E. von Grunebaum Center for Near Eastern Studies, the Crusades have to be understood as part of tremendous geo-political, socio-economic and religious shifts underway at the time. "The Mediterranean world of the 11th century was changing in a remarkable manner; it was witnessing the birth of a new world. The Crusades were the product of the sudden and all-transforming change that produced Western European civilization. An old world burst apart, and a new one took its place."

Bukhari, director and principal co-investigator for Georgetown's Muslims in the American Public Square project, and Fr. James Fredericks of Loyola Marymount theology department, see similar shifts underway today. Bukhari explained that during a period of great transformation "the Crusades were a clash of religions. In the transformations of modern times, we have a clash of civilizations. To some extent there is the same connotation, the whole West as a symbol of Christianity, the entire Muslim world as the symbol of Islam."

But what must be taken into account, he said, is the evolution underway. One aspect of that, he said, is "the evolving debate within Islam about living according to Islamic beliefs, to divine guidance. The notion of how to do that has been evolving since World War II, which triggered the end of colonialism. Among Muslim countries and the Muslim world (which includes those Muslims who live as minorities in non-Muslim countries), there is a debate over issues of democracy, civil rights, human rights, the role of women and living with people of other faiths."

And that debate, he said, "will be violent in some places, look absurd in others, be serious in others, but evolve ultimately, hopefully, in a positive direction."

Bukhari, a Pakistani who has lived in the West for 17 years, said that when "looked at in the time period of 30 to 40 years, things are going very much in a positive direction. Especially with those Muslims living in Western societies. But we are talking only about 30 to 40 years. What evolution will the next 30 to 40 years bring?"

Fredericks, a priest of the San Francisco archdiocese whose field is comparative religion, comments, "We Americans are so concerned with the violent [Islamic] fringe, we miss what's going on at a deeper level."

To Fredericks, the geo-politic transformations Islam is signaling are enormous. This is a huge, huge topic. First, Christianity and Islam—you cannot say it about Judaism—are religions that have been at the foundations of empires. Further, Christianity and Islam are the bases of entire cultural outlooks.

Christian nations today are, by and large, secular societies, in which Protestantism was able to adjust more quickly than Roman Catholicism. "Christianity has made its peace—an uneasy truce—with secular culture. Christianity," he continued, "has grudgingly yielded its place at the center of culture. It isn't that anymore."

The peace isn't total, and opposition to the peace does not just come from Christian reactionaries, traditionalists and conservatives. "We see opposition," he said, "not just from the new religious right, though in the culture wars they get all the publicity, but in the theology of liberation. The theology of liberation also says that religious voices, religious values, need to be very public realities at the center of culture.

"The other thing—and it's such a complicated picture," he said, "there is something in the very character of Christianity that resists privatization. Christianity wants to be a very public religion. So when Christianity becomes a private religion, it is in a rather anomalous situation."

The same statement, he said, can be made about Islam. "Islam wants to be a very public force, a very public reality." Islam wants of its very character to be the basis of society. It always has.

"From the beginnings of Islam," said Fredericks, "submitting to Islam meant renouncing one culture that was sinful and violent and discriminatory and based on petty racial and ethnic rivalries, and recognizing there is this universal humanity, universal morality. A powerful conversion takes place from an immoral society to a moral society." In fact, he said, submission—submission to Allah—is what Islam means.

For Islam to accept a privatized place within secular society "is very, very difficult. We in the West tend to presume that this is an inevitable process. I think that's naive."

Fredericks argues that because Christians "slowly and begrudgingly, and with a great deal of violence" more or less worked out a modus vivendi with the secular nation, Muslims will not necessarily follow suit.

"Why should we presume that that's normative?" he asked.

"Alternative Modernities"

Speaking to Bukhari's point about Islam in the recent post-colonial period, Fredericks talked of "alternative modernities," of Islamic states developing in unique and non-Western ways.

He uses Indonesia, the largest of all Islamic nations, as an example. "If one allows, and it is controversial to do so, that Indonesia's Sukarno [1949–1967] and Suharto [1967–1998] regimes were aftermaths connected to Dutch colonialism, then what we're hearing from Indonesia's Muslims today is, 'We want to be a nation. We don't want to go back to the Middle Ages. And—the West doesn't get this—we want to be a modern nation. We just don't want to be modern the way you're modern. We think that's sick.'"

Think of such a development, says Fredericks, in terms "of 'religious nationalism' as an alternative to Western secularism. Islam saying our religious nationalism is a way of being a modern, national state: Economically competitive, a state able to provide basic social services to its population. We want to be a success. But secularism—with all the immorality that comes with it—isn't going to cut it for us. We're not that kind of people. We want to be an Islamic state."

What the world may be witnessing, contends Fredericks, is not just a violent fringe but manifestations of religious nationalism that from Egypt to

Iran to Indonesia "may have more in common with the theology of liberation than we've recognized. Both are a critique of Western secular, capitalist, consumerist, materialist, globalist secularism. And that's something we ought to pay attention to and be respectful of." Like Islam, liberation theology seeks to put Christian values, such as a preferential option for the poor, at the center of culture.

Scott Bartchy, director of the Center for the Study of Religion at UCLA, said Americans need to understand that at the deepest level they have been moving away from cultural values built around honor–shame–still the dominant framework for values around much of the world. In contrast, the United States "has an achievement-guilt culture focused almost entirely on the individual," he said.

"Certainly we have very little sense of honor," he said. "Most Americans will say honor is nice, but give me the check instead. And if we had any shame, we wouldn't have had the last 20 years of U.S. politics."

Bartchy said that in Germany in the 1970s, Chancellor Willi Brandt resigned as a matter of honor when an East German mole penetrated West Germany's security services. In Japan, "CEOs or government officers caught in whatever, resign." By contrast, he said, "in America if you get caught out, you back and fill. You don't resign, you just tough it out."

The 80 percent of the world living with honor-shame values have strict gender divisions and roles, systems that generate enormous competition among the males, and a sense of bonding within the family. "Islam," he said, "has created a sense of what anthropologists call 'fictive' and I choose to call 'surrogate' kinship: It goes beyond the family to create a sense of brotherhood. It's no accident that the extremist group in Egypt is the 'Brotherhood.'"

In many ways, said Bartchy, "Islam, for all the way it looks, is still kind of a thin overlay of ancient tribal cultures." For example, nothing in the Quran or the Islamic tradition supports honor killing of women, yet in some countries women are killed if they have been raped, he said. "If the father isn't strong enough, the brothers are supposed to go out there and kill that woman. And if they can kill her in public it's even better, because that at least eliminates the shame from the family."

The only groups in the United States that live up to these strong honor-shame codes, Bartchy said, are inner-city gangs and the Mafia. They cannot allow themselves or their family to be "dissed, or shamed." Every time they step over the threshold, they are in competition with the world outside. "From the time you're 3 years old until you die, you do and say those things that will bring honor back to your family."

Which, in part, said Bartchy, explains Osama bin Laden's popularity in Afghanistan. "Whatever else he was doing," he said, "Osama was accumulating an enormous amount of honor. Spending his own wealth initially on the widows and orphans of the mujahideen–an enormous contrast to what the royal elites back home in Saudi Arabia were doing."

In bin Laden's eyes, said Bartchy, these Saudis were not sharing, and Islam requires it. As bin Laden and those sympathetic to him looked at the United States, "they saw the ever-increasing gap between the elite–the enormously rich—and the Americans at the bottom. Then Osama and his allies looked at the Saudi leadership doing the same and reasoned: 'How did Saudis learn that those values are OK? Because they looked to the West.'" (Bartchy left unanswered the next question: "How did the West learn that those values are OK?")

"Basically," he said, "what Muslims in the Near East want is the same things we want. Even the most conservative bring their kids to the United States to be educated. What they can't understand is how we say we're so strong for democracy and participation and yet we continue to prop up regimes in their part of the world they regard as terribly oppressive and corrupt."

At home what bothers Bartchy is the tone of the American popular response, even among his students. They believe, he said, "the only way to look at us is as the victims. We can do anything we damn well please overseas, and that should never have any effect on what comes down."

What the Peeves Really Are

Bush used the word crusade and apologized. He warned against racism and bigotry, and visited with Muslims at Islamic centers. Sound moves?

If Bush wants support, to prove he's not against Islam "the first place you start is at home," said Yvonne Haddad, professor of the history of Islam and Christian-Muslim relations at Georgetown University. "And his rhetoric—in the speech to Congress, listening to it as an American, I was impressed. Listening with the other ear, as Muslims overseas would hear it, it was awful: he talked about 'us' and 'them,' you're either with us or against us. He showed no reflection on what the issues, the peeves, really are."

And some of those peeves can be seen as related to the Crusades. Israel occupies the same geographic area the Crusades were about, she said. "Therefore anybody who supports Israel's policies is perceived as continuing the Crusades."

And a thousand years after the first one, the Crusades remain a source of contention.

Pressures That Led to an Empire-wide Movement

The Nine Crusades, which took place in the 11th, 12th and 13th centuries, were a counteroffensive by Christians against Muslims occupying the Holy Land.

Was the Islamic threat real? "You betcha," said Professor Paul E. Chevedden. "Islamic conquest had taken from Christendom its choicest province—Syria, Egypt, North Africa and Iberia [Spain and Portugal]."

Islam pushed its way north into Italy until it captured Monte Cassino, St. Benedict's monastery, then moved into eastern Switzerland. On the Great St. Bernard Pass, Muslims even captured the abbot of Cluny, France.

The Crusades, in response, were applications of Roman Catholicism's "just war" tradition, said Chevedden of UCLA's Gustav E. von Grunebaum Center for Near Eastern Studies. Islam had the Holy Land, and the pope wanted it back.

A grave pitfall for today, insists Chevedden, would be to view the Crusades in isolation from the world-transforming events in the Mediterranean and in western Asia at the turn of the second millennium. Those events included pressures from expanding populations, rapidly developing urbanism, intellectual and technological inquiries and advances, plus rising commerce pushing into new areas.

The clash between Christendom and Islam was a 1,000-year struggle, the most protracted conflict in human history. What should not be overlooked, Chevedden said, is that, for the most part, Islam, rather than Christianity, was in the ascendancy.

Scott Bartchy, director of UCLA's Center for the Study of Religion, though well aware of what Islam gave to the West during those 1,000 years, looks at the early heritage of both Christianity and Islam from the perspective of violence/non-violence.

During the first 250 to 300 years of Christianity, it was initially persecuted, then scapegoated through four more tense periods, as it became an empire-wide movement. "Never," emphasized Bartchy, "never once during this period is anybody killed in the name of Jesus. The Christians are not a guerrilla band, they are not social bandits. They stay in the urban environment, gain a reputation not only for helping their own widows and orphans, but others' as well. Not only burying their own dead but—a major deal at that time—other people's as well. They never become violent."

Bartchy called it "remarkable" that Jesus' nonviolence had taken "such a hold" across those early centuries. It was Emperor Constantine's adopting Christianity as the Roman Empire's religion in the fourth century that "wrecked things. He never got it," said Bartchy. "He puts the Chi-Rho symbol on Roman shields, and for the first time Christians start killing people in the name of Jesus."

Bartchy contrasts that Jesus with Islam's Muhammad who, in the early seventh century, "goes into Medina and in effect becomes the civil authority. Functionally he's an innovator, a Jesus of Nazareth and a Constantine, all rolled into one."

Bartchy said Muhammad "never ever renounces violence, and for all the fine things in the Islamic tradition, there's never been any serious commitment to nonviolence. In a war, if you follow the prophet, you shouldn't hurt women or children. Or trees. Quite charming that. And the violence should be defensive."

Bartchy said that after the Crusades the Near Eastern Islamic world felt itself transgressed upon, "and there's a certain victim mentality." Culturally, he said, Muslims saved much from the Greek philosophers that the West later appropriated. Technologically Islam held its own, even into the 16th and 17th centuries. "But then the West got the technological edge in military stuff and began pushing," said Bartchy, "and the Muslims again get into the mentality of being victims."

Consequently, Bartchy summarized, today "some of the more extreme people have given themselves permission to do almost anything in the name of defense. And that's what we see."

The Crusades were religious, political and economic. The First Millennium had just ended, the 11th century was the setting of an enormous spiritual revival. For centuries, with the Holy Land under benign Islamic rule, pilgrims traveled together to Jerusalem under arms to protect themselves from robbers. Confessors in that era regularly gave pilgrimages as a penance, so ensuring the safety of pilgrims was one element of the Crusades.

Other elements included merchants in Italian cities wanting Eastern trading outlets and the ambitions of chivalrous knights—high-born youths looking for action and conquest.

There also was a shift within Islam precipitating the Crusades. The more restrictive Turkish Muslims had taken over the Holy Land, and the pope, disenchanted with the warring European nobles' inability to form a coalition to battle Islam, brought his own unifying authority to bear.

The scene was set, and all the elements combined in the urge to free the Holy Land from Islam. Thus nine Crusades, each generally less successful than the one before it.

Crusaders Went from Victory to Disaster

In box scores, there were nine Crusades between 1095 and 1272. The outcome was Crusaders 2, Muslims 5, plus two negotiated ties. And the Muslims remained in control.

The Crusades (1095–1272) got their name from the crosses Pope Urban II distributed in 1095 after he called on the factious European kings and princes to band together and recover the Holy Sepulcher from the Muslim Seljuk Turks.

They agreed. It would be the first of nine crusades.

Even as the potential First Crusaders were looking into strategy and logistics, peasants in France heard the papal call. Less worried than their leaders about tactics and supplies, several thousand started marching. They resupplied themselves by sacking Belgrade. German peasants set out and financed themselves by attacking Jews.

At Constantinople, what was left of these ragtag bands joined forces, sailed to Jerusalem, dispersed the Turks and declared a victory.

The European nobility finally set off, led by Raymond IV of Toulouse and Bishop Ademar. The First Crusade (1096–99) took Nicea, Antioch and consolidated Western control over what they now called the Latin Kingdom of Jerusalem, with Godfrey of Bouillon as ruler.

The Muslims retaliated. The Second Crusade (1147–49) failed to recapture cities taken by the Turks; the Third Crusade (1189–91) failed to retake Jerusalem, which was back in Muslim hands. But Saladin decreed Christians could have access to the Holy Sepulcher.

The Fourth Crusade (1220–04) got bogged down in the more profitable venture of fighting Venice, sacking Constantinople, crushing the Byzantine Empire and establishing the Latin Empire of Constantinople.

Quite disastrous was the 1202 Children's Crusade, led by two young peasants. Stephen in France and Nicolas in Germany led several thousand children out of their homelands and into starvation and disease, and into the arms of adults who sold them into slavery and other fates worse than death.

The second longest crusade, the Fifth Crusade (1218–21) was an unsuccessful war against Egypt, and the Sixth Crusade (1228–29), which eschewed military arms, was led by Holy Roman Emperor Frederick II who negotiated a degree of Christian control over the holy sites.

France's Louis IX led the next two crusades, the Seventh (1248–50) and Eighth (1270), with no noticeable gains. Louis died in North Africa, and the Eighth Crusade was called off. The English launched the Ninth Crusade (1271–72) under Prince Edward. It changed nothing, though the prince later became King Edward I.

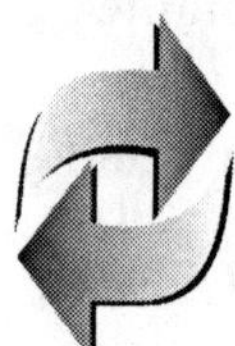

Jonathan Phillips  **NO**

Who Were the First Crusaders?

Who were the people who answered Urban II's call to crusade between 1096 and 1099? Jonathan Phillips investigates their origins and motives.

The canons of the council summarised the offer made by Urban II as he launched the First Crusade:

> Whoever, for devotion alone, not to gain honour or money, goes to Jerusalem to liberate the Church of God can substitute this journey for all penance.

In other words, if people fought God's enemies on earth and completed a pilgrimage to the Holy Land, their actions would receive a spiritual reward of remarkable magnitude. Urban blended the familiar ideas of pilgrimage and penance with the more radical notion of papally-sanctioned violence to produce what a contemporary writer described as "a new means of attaining salvation." He followed the speech at Clermont with an extensive preaching tour through France and by the dispatch of letters and legations elsewhere in Europe.

The response to his appeal was remarkable, and in total almost 60,000 people set out for the Holy Land. The population of Europe at the end of the eleventh century is estimated to have been around 20 million, so clearly the vast majority of people chose to remain in the West. If, however, one adds contact through ties of family and friendship then it is clear that the crusade touched the lives of millions.

Fulcher of Chartres, a participant in the crusade, wrote that people "of any and every occupation" took the cross. He also commented "whoever heard of such a mixture of languages in one army, since there were French, Flemings, Frisians, Gauls, Allobroges [Savoyards], Lotharingians, Allemani [South Germans and Swiss], Bavarians, Normans, English, Scots, Aquitainians, Italians, Danes, Apulians, Iberians, Bretons, Greeks and Armenians." Representatives of the last two groups probably joined the expedition en route, but the remainder had been attracted by Urban's initial call to arms. The crusade therefore appealed to people from almost every level of society right across Christian Europe. The purpose here is to give some insight into who the First Crusaders were, to explain why they took the cross, and to understand the importance of identifying those who took part in the expedition.

From *History Today,* Vol. 47, No. 3, March 1997, pp. 16(7).

The reasons for such a wide-ranging response are complex. Our distance from events and the nature of the surviving evidence mean that we can never achieve a perfect insight into a crusader's mind. We should not necessarily look for a single motive in determining an individual's desire to take the cross, although certain themes emerge more clearly than others. An understanding of the actions of each crusader must be grounded in the cultural, political and economic context of the time.

Spiritual concerns were a prominent factor governing people's lives in the late eleventh century. It was an intensely religious age; pilgrimage and monastic life flourished, and donations to ecclesiastical institutions were increasingly commonplace. Christian Europe was also one of the most guilt-ridden societies in history. Sin was ubiquitous in everyday life and the images of fire and torture so frequently depicted on churches reinforced the fear of eternal damnation. The need for all people—whether rich or poor, nobles or labourers—to atone for their actions helps to explain the level of enthusiasm for the First Crusade and also the crusaders' determination to fulfil their vows by completing the journey to Jerusalem.

The pope's original conception of the crusade was for a compact contingent of knights to assist Emperor Alexius of Byzantium in his struggle against the Seljuk Turks of Asia Minor before marching on to the Holy Land. His appeal was directed, therefore, towards the knightly classes of his native France, a region of weak central authority and endemic lawlessness which was often initiated by the knights themselves. The crusade may have been one way to channel this violence elsewhere as well as giving the knights an opportunity of salvation. The knights responded in large numbers and formed the backbone of the Christian army.

As we have seen, however, Urban's offer was so attractive that almost all elements of society were represented on the crusade. The most notable exception to this was the absence of any kings. Urban regarded the crusade as a papally-directed enterprise and had not explicitly invited the secular monarchs to become involved. In any case, Philip I of France was excommunicated on account of an adulterous relationship with the Countess of Anjou; Henry IV of Germany was the papacy's principal opponent in a bitter struggle concerning the supremacy of lay versus sacral power (known as the Investiture Contest), and William Rufus was too entangled in the government of England to be particularly interested. It was not until the crusade of Sigurd of Norway (1107–10), that a king participated in a campaign in the Holy Land, although it should be noted that the rulers of Spain had long been involved in the Reconquista, their own struggle against the Muslims.

While the non-participation of kings may be regarded as part of Urban's design, the pope had not anticipated that his call would appeal to monks. He wrote "we do not want those who have abandoned the world and vowed themselves to spiritual warfare either to bear arms or to go on this journey; we go so far as to forbid them to do so." Other churchmen such as priests and clerks, were permitted to join as long as they secured the permission of their bishop, and in any case, some religious officials were needed to administer to the crusaders' spiritual needs during the course of the expedition. Urban's message also struck a deep chord with the wider populace, including women, children, the old, the infirm and the poor. Clearly these groups would hinder the progress of an army because they had to be fed and protected. The pope tried to limit their involvement by requiring people to consult their parish priests before taking their vows, but this measure failed and the crusade set out accompanied by many noncombatants. In the course of the crusade the majority of this anonymous mass perished through starvation or disease, deserted, or were enslaved.

It is among the members of the noble and knightly classes that we can begin to pinpoint the individuals who took the cross. In part this is because, as men of standing, their deeds feature in the narrative accounts of the crusade. Some, such as the southern Italian knight, Hugh the Beserk, are mentioned on only one occasion for an act of particular bravery: in this case because Hugh had single-handedly defended a tower for an entire day against Turkish attacks during the siege of Antioch. For the leaders of the major contingents, however, there is a much fuller picture, particularly when their force happens to have included a chronicler. The anonymous author of the Gesta Francorum, for example, was a member of Bohemond of Taranto's army, and Raymond of Aguilers was the chaplain to Raymond of Saint-Gilles, the Count of Toulouse. The latter writer noted "It seems too tiresome to write of each journey . . . so we have taken care to write of the Count of Saint-Gilles without bothering with the others." In the case of Hugh of Vermandois, younger brother of Philip I of France, there is much less information because, as far as we are aware, no member of his contingent wrote an account of the crusade.

While narrative works provide the majority of our material they are not the only source of information for the crusade. In recent years the use of charters has enhanced our understanding of the motivation, financing and family networks of the crusaders. It is the nature of eleventh-century charters which holds the key to this. Charters from later periods tend to convey only a bare minimum of information, such as names, places, dates, and the exact subject of the transaction. Some charters from the time of the First Crusade, however, provide more of a clue to the hopes and fears of individual crusaders, as well as basic factual information.

Crusading was extremely expensive. To equip oneself with chainmail, horses and supplies would cost a great deal—some estimates suggest over four years' annual income. However, the recent experience of the Norman Conquest, for example, would have given people some idea of the resources needed to fight a large-scale and lengthy military expedition. In order to finance the crusade it was often necessary to mortgage or sell lands and rights to the church. The records of these transactions give further indication as to who took part and how they raised money for the journey. Incidentally, the issue of cost is another reason why the old cliche of crusaders being freebooting younger sons is deeply suspect, simply because such men would have been unable to afford to set out in the first instance.

In fact, largely through the use of charters, all sorts of combinations of family members can be found on the crusade. For example, Hugh of Merysur-Seine mortgaged lands at Rosnay to the abbey of Molesme in order to pay for both his own and his brother's journey. Jonathan Riley-Smith has traced the remarkable involvement of the Montlhery clan. One member, Miles of Bray, was accompanied on the First Crusade by his son, Guy, his brother-in-law, Walter of St. Valery, and two of Walter's sons; his nephew, Baldwin (later Baldwin II of Jerusalem), and two other nephews—Humberge of Le Puiset and Everard III of Le Puiset—were amongst members of the network to take the cross in 1095–96.

Some crusader families had an existing tradition of pilgrimage to the Holy Land which may have formed a further reason for their taking the cross. For example, both the great-grandfather and the grandfather of the First Crusader, Adhemar III of Limoges, had been to Jerusalem in the course of the eleventh century. The influence of pilgrimage is a theme more thoroughly explored in the work of Marcus Bull.

Although the religious motivation of the First Crusaders should be emphasised, it would be naive to argue that other interests were absent. When a noble embarked upon the crusade it was inevitable that he would be accompanied by his household retainers. He would have to provide support for his knights, squires and servants. All were an integral part of a medieval army and, because of this, ties of allegiance and loyalty should be advanced as a further reason for taking the cross, even though such a commitment was, in theory, a strictly voluntary exercise. The desire for land was a further motive, but it did not apply to all the crusaders. Many charters contain clauses detailing financial arrangements that would come into force only if the crusader died during the expedition. Such measures suggest that the participants were well aware of the dangers of the crusade, but hoped to return home once the vow was completed. Two brothers, Bernard and Odo, entered into an agreement with the abbey of Cluny:

> For the remission of our sins, setting out with all the others on the journey to Jerusalem, we have made over for 100 solidi . . . a manor known as Busart. We are making this on the condition that if, on the pilgrimage that we are undertaking, we may die, the manor may remain in perpetuity under the control of . . . the monastery of Cluny. But if we may return . . . we may keep it in our lifetime, but after our death it may not come into the possession of our heirs . . . but will pass to Cluny.

The fact that the Crusader States were seriously undermanned throughout their existence also indicates that relatively few crusaders chose to remain in the Levant and become settlers. Some men, however, were explicit in their intention never to return to the West and clearly planned to carve out new territories for themselves in the East. Raymond of Saint-Gilles was rumoured to be one such person. The French knight Achard of Montmerle might also have been planning to stay in the Holy Land. The charter detailing his agreement with the abbey of Cluny includes the clause "if I die, or if I choose to remain in those lands [the Levant] . . ." shows at least an awareness of the possibility of settling in the East, a course of action which would presumably necessitate the taking of land.

The need to repay debts incurred in paying for the expedition, coupled with poor economic conditions—a series of droughts and bad harvests had marked the early 1090s—suggests that the desire for money may have been a priority for the crusaders. Perhaps the search for salvation and the wish for financial gain seem too mutually exclusive in our eyes. One has only to think of TV evangelism to shudder at the potential for abuse in this connection, yet it is not improbable or contradictory that pious men took the cross also hoping to improve their financial and material prospects. There must also have been crusaders for whom the wish to accumulate wealth predominated. The sources indicate that such people must have been gravely disappointed. There is remarkably little evidence of people returning from the crusade with newfound riches. One rare example is reported by Abbot Suger of Saint Denis. He wrote that Count Guy of Rochefort "returned from the expedition to Jerusalem renowned and rich," an ironic reversal of Urban II's injunction against crusaders seeking honour or money.

People certainly brought back relics from the Holy Land. Lord Riou of Loheac, for example, acquired a fragment of the True Cross and bequeathed it to his local church when he died in 1101. But the experience of the First Crusade does not suggest that it was the route to easy profit. None-the-less, the narrative sources contain frequent reports of the crusaders seeking booty. After the siege of Ma'arrat an Nu'man (December 1098) Muslim graves were dug up and the bodies slit open to check if any treasure had been swallowed. Acts of a similarly brutal nature were repeated elsewhere. The most likely explanation for this behaviour is that substantial sums of money were required to keep the expedition going.

The duration and rigour of the campaign exhausted the resources of the vast majority. Crusaders endured terrible suffering during the march across Asia Minor and at the siege of Antioch (October 1097–June 1098). Food prices became grossly inflated and losses of horses and equipment were enormous. It is an important distinction, therefore, that acts of greed were usually initiated in response to the need to survive, rather than the long-term motivation to accumulate treasure. For those interested solely in money, the cost of warfare and the duration of the expedition meant that the depredation of land closer to home had to be a safer option than going on crusade. If some had set out hoping to acquire untold riches it seems that the hardships of the expedition soon deterred them because throughout the course of the crusade a stream of deserters left the main army unable to endure the experience.

News of the expedition to Jerusalem spread rapidly across Northern and Central Europe and also down through Italy and to Sicily. The pope accepted the reality of the situation and began to dispatch letters of instruction and encouragement to these areas. The only region where he actively discouraged recruitment was the Iberian peninsula because he did not want people distracted from the "reconquista," although we know that some Spanish crusaders ignored him and travelled to Jerusalem. When the forces of the First Crusade began to assemble in 1096 the racial mix of the armies is an impressive testimony to the power of Urban's appeal. Another indication of the range of participants involved is provided by Raymond of Aguilers. He relates that in the Provencal contingent alone no less than seven different currencies were in circulation. He mentioned the use of coins from Lucca, Chartres, Le Mans,

Melgueil, Le Puy, Valence and Poitou. Currency from the first five places have been discovered in a single collection at Antioch and tentatively associated with the siege that took place there.

Because almost every region of Latin Christendom was represented on the First Crusade difficulties emerged in communication and leadership. Problems also arose on account of hostility between regional contingents of the army. An episode related by Ralph of Caen—a visitor to the Levant soon after the First Crusade—serves to illustrate the tensions that sometimes broke out in the course of the campaign. As morale sagged during the siege of Antioch, gangs of northern and southern French grouped up on linguistic lines to forage for supplies. They assaulted or freed their captives according to the language they spoke, while those responding in tongues other than Occitan or a northern French dialect were spared as neutrals.

In the course of the crusade and afterwards, the Franks (as they were known collectively) established a series of states in the Levant. During the early years of settlement the polyglot nature of the crusader army was, to some extent, distilled. In some states the origins of the dominant Latin Christian element reflected the ancestry of the particular leader who had based himself there. Bohemond of Taranto's principality of Antioch had a strong contingent of Normans from Southern Italy. Similarly, because it was Raymond of Saint-Gilles who had set up the county of Tripoli, the area had a Provencal influence. The kingdom of Jerusalem, in consequence of its spiritual importance, attracted sellers from a wider number of regions and represented, therefore, a more diverse grouping.

The creation of the Frankish states, each with its own character and links to the West, as well as the over-arching bond of Latin Christianity, meant that strong ties existed between the settlers and their co-religionists in Europe. As the Muslim jihad gathered momentum in the course of the twelfth century, the Franks in the East needed military and financial help. It is interesting to note that traditions of crusading and ties of kinship between those in the Holy Land and the West were two ideas that the settlers emphasised in their attempts to secure support.

Pope Eugenius III drew attention to the concept of crusading ancestory in Quantum Praedecessores his appeal for the Second Crusade (1145–49). He wrote:

> It will be seen as a great token of nobility and uprightness if those things acquired by the efforts of the fathers are vigorously defended by you, their good sons. But if, God forbid, it comes to pass differently, then the bravery of the fathers will have proved to be diminished in the sons. We impress upon you . . . to defend in this way the Eastern Church, which was freed from their [the Muslims'] tyranny, as we have said before by the spilling of your fathers' blood.

In effect this amounted to an appeal to those families with traditions of crusading. The counts of Flanders were a group particularly receptive to such a message. They also had close family ties with the settlers. When Count Thierry took the cross in 1146 he was perpetuating a well-established line of involvement with the Holy Land. His grandfather, Robert I, had mounted a large-scale pilgrimage to Jerusalem in 1087–90. His uncle, Count Robert II, was one of the leading figures on the First Crusade. His cousin, Count Charles the Good, had visited Jerusalem around 1107, and was probably offered the throne of the kingdom of Jerusalem in 1123–24. In 1134 Thierry gained close links with the house of Jerusalem through his marriage to Sibylla of Anjou, a daughter of King Fulk. Thierry had also journeyed to the Holy Land in 1139 and seems to have planned another trip in 1142 only to turn back at an early stage.

An awareness of the identity of the First Crusaders reveals the impact of Pope Urban's call on the people of Europe in 1095–96. But answering the question "Who were the First Crusaders?" can tell us more. We are able to use the answer to start following traditions of crusading and the creation of family ties between the Levant and the West and from this information we have a better understanding of the nature of Latin settlement in the East and the subsequent history of the crusades.

POSTSCRIPT

Could the Crusades Be Considered a Christian Holy War?

With the emergence of Islamic revivalism in the modern world, the historical relationships between the West and the Muslim world have taken center stage. Are the Crusades at the root of this contemporary conflict? The Islamic world has always viewed the Crusades as an invasion of its territory by a foreign power; the west has not shared this perspective. This issue asks: To what extent can the Crusades be viewed as a Christian Holy War? As the West responds to radical Islamic-inspired terrorism today with shock and outrage, is it not possible that a millennium ago, Middle Eastern Muslims responded in the same manner to the European crusaders?

Both struggles spring, at least in part, from religious motivation present. Christian crusaders believed they were fighting a just war in the service of God; securing indulgences for services rendered; and the ultimate prize, gaining the right to eternal salvation. With a slight change in language, we hear the same promises in Islamic revivalism—fighting the infidels in the name of Allah; participating in a fierce struggle between the forces of good and evil; and ultimately acquiring a special place in heaven as martyrs of the faith. Failure to hear these resonances might prevent us from learning a lesson form history.

For sources on the Crusades from a Muslim viewpoint, see: Amin Maalouf, *The Crusades Through Arab Eyes* (Schocken Books, 1985); Francesco Gabrieli, ed., *Arab Historians of the Crusades* (University of California Press, 1984); and Carol Hillenbrand, *The Crusades: Islamic Perspectives* (Routledge, 2000). Karen Armstrong's *Holy War: The Crusades and their Impact on Today's World* (Anchor Books, 2001) is a Western source that speaks of the Crusades in an objective and critical manner, especially their links with contemporary conflicts among Muslims, Christians, and Jews in the Middle East.

As far as general sources on the Crusades are concerned, start with Steven Runciman's three-volume work *A History of the Crusades*, 4th ed. (Cambridge University Press, 1954). Jonathan Riley-Smith's *The First Crusaders*, 1095–1131 (Cambridge University Press, 1997) represents current scholarship. Smith states that the Crusades "drew on the tradition of Pilgrimage to Jerusalem . . . and pious violence" as motivating forces. He also points out that many of the Crusaders from the times he researched came from the same families and clans, and concludes that the sustenance they received from these ties helped make the Crusades possible. A readable, popular account of the Crusades, which features many interesting illustrations and useful maps, is W. B. Bartlett, *God Wills It: An Illustrated History of the Crusades* (Oxford University Press, 1999). Another general source is Thomas F. Madden, *A Concise History of the Crusades* (Roman & Littlefield, 1999).

ISSUE 4

Did China's Worldview Cause the Abrupt End of Its Voyages of Exploration?

YES: Nicholas D. Kristof, from "1492: The Prequel," *The New York Times Magazine* (June 6, 1999)

NO: Bruce Swanson, from *Eighth Voyage of the Dragon: A History of China's Quest for Seapower* (Naval Institute Press, 1982)

ISSUE SUMMARY

YES: Journalist Nicholas D. Kristof states that China's worldview, shaped by centuries of philosophical and cultural conditioning, was responsible for its decision to cease its maritime ventures during the Ming dynasty.

NO: Naval historian Bruce Swanson acknowledges that China's worldview played a role in its decision to cease its maritime programs, but maintains that there were other, more practical considerations that were responsible for that decision.

Few historical figures of the last 500 years can match the name recognition of Christopher Columbus, whose voyages and what resulted from them forever altered the course of history. But what about Zheng He? Does his name have the same evocative power as Columbus's? Probably not, and yet in the same century, Zheng He led more and longer naval expeditions, commanded larger ships and more men, and was within the Asian world as popular and as noteworthy as Columbus. An interesting historical lesson, replete with "what might have beens," can be learned from the life and career of the "Chinese Columbus."

Zheng He's life is in itself an interesting story. Born to Muslim parents living in China, he was a young boy when he was captured by the Chinese army and eventually castrated, a common practice for prisoners of war at that time. Eventually, he came into the service of Chinese royal prince Zhu Di, one of twenty-six sons of the Chinese emperor, whom he served with honor and distinction. As a result of an internal power struggle, Prince Zhu Di seized the royal throne from his nephew and became the Ming dynasty's Emperor Yongle, who would rule China from 1402 to 1424. Zheng He played a significant role in this chain of events and would soon be rewarded for his meritorious service.

China's new emperor was an ambitious man who set out to establish his legacy as one of China's greatest rulers. As ameans to achieve this exalted status, he emphasized the importance of China's need to re-establish its role in the commercial and maritime affairs of Asia. When it was time to select someone to command this project, the new emperor selected Zheng He.

For more than two decades Zheng He ran China's maritime operations for his emperor, and his plan included seven major voyages. In the process, "Admiral Zheng visited 37 countries, traveled around the tip of Africa into the Atlantic Ocean and commanded a single fleet whose numbers surpassed the combined fleets of all of Europe. Between 1405 and 1433, at least 317 ships and 37,000 men were under his command" (Admiral Zheng's Fleet: `www.oceans online.com/zheng.htm`)

China's dominance of Asian waters brought the anticipated fame, wealth, and glory to Emperor Yongle and his eunuch admiral. However, when the former died suddenly in 1424, his successor decided to de-emphasize China's international maritime policies and ordered plans already under way for Zheng He's seventh voyage to be halted. This proved to be only a temporary setback when a new emperor, interested in reviving Yongle's maritime policies, ordered Zheng He's seventh voyage to proceed at once. It would prove to be China's last government-sponsored maritime venture.

Zheng He died in 1433, and soon after China began to lose interest in overseas exploration and eventually scrapped its maritime projects. This would have grave consequences for China when, later in the century, European countries began to send ships into Asian waters. What began as exploration eventually turned into domination, conquest, colonization, and imperialism—with dire consequences for China and the rest of Asia. Much of what follows is historical speculation, but one wonders what would have occurred if those first Western explorers who rounded Africa and headed toward Asia ran into a strong maritime force the size of Admiral Zheng's. And, if China had continued to support its maritime ventures after his death, perhaps history would have had to credit one of his successors with the discovery of the "New World."

There are numerous reasons given for China's retreat from maritime excellence. Some state that a Ming court conflict between eunuchs and Confucian scholars, traditional rivals in court politics, occurred, and the latter eventually won by depicting China's maritime expeditions as costly, eunuch-induced extravagances and not in China's best long-range interests. Others stress a series of other factors, including 1) fear of future Mongol invasions; 2) population shifts away from costal provinces; 3) a desire to promote internal trade efforts; 4) the high cost of supporting the maritime ventures, including the money spent to prevent piracy and the profits lost to it; 5) the corruption which emanated from the costly maritime programs.

In the following selections, Nicholas D. Kristof argues that China gave up on its maritime efforts because these efforts contradicted the worldview that China had cultivated for thousands of years. Navel historian Bruce Swanson counters that this was only one of many factors responsible for China's retreat from naval supremacy.

YES 

Nicholas D. Kristof

1492: The Prequel

For most of the last several thousand years, it would have seemed far likelier that Chinese or Indians, not Europeans, would dominate the world by the year 2000, and that America and Australia would be settled by Chinese rather than by the inhabitants of a backward island called Britain. The reversal of fortunes of East and West strikes me as the biggest news story of the millennium, and one of its most unexpected as well.

As a resident of Asia for most of the past 13 years, I've been searching for an explanation. It has always seemed to me that the turning point came in the early 1400's, when Admiral Zheng He sailed from China to conquer the world. Zheng He (pronounced jung huh) was an improbable commander of a great Chinese fleet, in that he was a Muslim from a rebel family and had been seized by the Chinese Army when he was still a boy. Like many other prisoners of the time, he was castrated—his sexual organs completely hacked off, a process that killed many of those who suffered it. But he was a brilliant and tenacious boy who grew up to be physically imposing. A natural leader, he had the good fortune to be assigned, as a houseboy, to the household of a great prince, Zhu Di.

In time, the prince and Zheng He grew close, and they conspired to overthrow the prince's nephew, the Emperor of China. With Zheng He as one of the prince's military commanders, the revolt succeeded and the prince became China's Yongle Emperor. One of the emperor's first acts (after torturing to death those who had opposed him) was to reward Zheng He with the command of a great fleet that was to sail off and assert China's pre-eminence in the world.

Between 1405 and 1433, Zheng He led seven major expeditions, commanding the largest armada the world would see for the next five centuries. Not until World War I did the West mount anything comparable. Zheng He's fleet included 28,000 sailors on 300 ships, the longest of which were 400 feet. By comparison, Columbus in 1492 had 90 sailors on three ships, the biggest of which was 85 feet long. Zheng He's ships also had advanced design elements that would not be introduced in Europe for another 350 years, including balanced rudders and watertight bulwark compartments.

The sophistication of Zheng He's fleet underscores just how far ahead of the West the East once was. Indeed, except for the period of the Roman

Empire, China had been wealthier, more advanced and more cosmopolitan than any place in Europe for several thousand years. Hangzhou, for example, had a population in excess of a million during the time it was China's capital (in the 12th century), and records suggest that as early as the 7th century, the city of Guangzhou had 200,000 foreign residents: Arabs, Persians, Malays, Indians, Africans and Turks. By contrast, the largest city in Europe in 1400 was probably Paris, with a total population of slightly more than 100,000.

A half-century before Columbus, Zheng He had reached East Africa and learned about Europe from Arab traders. The Chinese could easily have continued around the Cape of Good Hope and established direct trade with Europe. But as they saw it, Europe was a backward region, and China had little interest in the wool, beads and wine Europe had to trade. Africa had what China wanted—ivory, medicines, spices, exotic woods, even specimens of native wildlife.

In Zheng He's time, China and India together accounted for more than half of the world's gross national product, as they have for most of human history. Even as recently as 1820, China accounted for 29 percent of the global economy and India another 16 percent, according to the calculations of Angus Maddison, a leading British economic historian.

Asia's retreat into relative isolation after the expeditions of Zheng He amounted to a catastrophic missed opportunity, one that laid the groundwork for the rise of Europe and, eventually, America. Westerners often attribute their economic advantage today to the intelligence, democratic habits or hard work of their forebears, but a more important reason may well have been the folly of 15th-century Chinese rulers. That is why I came to be fascinated with Zheng He and set out earlier this year to retrace his journeys. I wanted to see what legacy, if any, remained of his achievement, and to figure out why his travels did not remake the world in the way that Columbus's did.

Zheng He lived in Nanjing, the old capital, where I arrived one day in February. Nanjing is a grimy metropolis on the Yangtze River in the heart of China. It has been five centuries since Zheng He's death, and his marks on the city have grown faint. The shipyards that built his fleet are still busy, and the courtyard of what had been his splendid 72-room mansion is now the Zheng He Memorial Park, where children roller-skate and old couples totter around for exercise. But though the park has a small Zheng He museum, it was closed—for renovation, a caretaker told me, though he knew of no plans to reopen it. . . .

The absence of impressive monuments to Zheng He in China today should probably come as no surprise, since his achievement was ultimately renounced. Curiously, it is not in China but in Indonesia where his memory has been most actively kept alive. Zheng He's expeditions led directly to the wave of Chinese immigration to Southeast Asia, and in some countries he is regarded today as a deity. In the Indonesia city of Semarang, for example, there is a large temple honoring Zheng He, located near a cave where he once nursed a sick friend. Indonesians still pray to Zheng He for a cure or good luck.

Not so in his native land. Zheng He was viewed with deep suspicion by China's traditional elite, the Confucian scholars, who made sure to destroy the archives of his journey. Even so, it is possible to learn something about his story from Chinese sources—from imperial archives and even the memoirs of crewmen. The historical record makes clear, for example, that it was not some sudden impulse of extroversion that led to Zheng He's achievement. It grew, rather, out of a long sailing tradition. Chinese accounts suggest that in the fifth century, a Chinese monk sailed to a mysterious "far east country" that sounds very much like Mayan Mexico, and Mayan art at that time suddenly began to include Buddhist symbols. By the 13th century, Chinese ships regularly traveled to India and occasionally to East Africa.

Zheng He's armada was far grander, of course, than anything that came before. His grandest vessels were the "treasure ships," 400 feet long and 160 feet wide, with nine masts raising red silk sails to the wind, as well as multiple decks and luxury cabins with balconies. His armada included supply ships to carry horses, troop transports, warships, patrol boats and as many as 20 tankers to carry fresh water. The full contingent of 28,000 crew members included interpreters for Arabic and other languages, astrologers to forecast the weather, astronomers to study the stars, pharmacologists to collect medicinal plants, ship-repair specialists, doctors and even two protocol officers to help organize official receptions.

In the aftermath of such an incredible undertaking, you somehow expect to find a deeper mark on Chinese history, a greater legacy. But perhaps the faintness of Zheng He's trace in contemporary China is itself a lesson. In the end, an explorer makes history but does not necessarily change it, for his impact depends less on the trail he blazes than on the willingness of others to follow. The daring of a great expedition ultimately is hostage to the national will of those who remain behind. . . .

The disappearance of a great Chinese fleet from a great Indian port symbolized one of history's biggest lost opportunities—Asia's failure to dominate the second half of this millennium. So how did this happen? While Zheng He was crossing the Indian Ocean, the Confucian scholar-officials who dominated the upper echelons of the Chinese Government were at political war with the eunuchs, a group they regarded as corrupt and immoral. The eunuchs' role at court involved looking after the concubines, but they also served as palace administrators, often doling out contracts in exchange for kickbacks. Partly as a result of their legendary greed, they promoted commerce. Unlike the scholars—who owed their position to their mastery of 2,000-year-old texts—the eunuchs, lacking any such roots in a classical past, were sometimes outward-looking and progressive. Indeed, one can argue that it was the virtuous, incorruptible scholars who in the mid-15th century set China on its disastrous course.

After the Yongle Emperor died in 1424, China endured a series of brutal power struggles; a successor emperor died under suspicious circumstances and ultimately the scholars emerged triumphant. They ended the voyages of Zheng He's successors, halted construction of new ships and imposed curbs on private shipping. To prevent any backsliding, they destroyed Zheng He's sailing records and, with the backing of the new emperor, set about dismantling China's navy.

By 1500 the Government had made it a capital offense to build a boat with more than two masts, and in 1525 the Government ordered the destruction of all oceangoing ships. The greatest navy in history, which a century earlier had 3,500 ships (by comparison, the United States Navy today has 324), had been extinguished, and China set a course for itself that would lead to poverty, defeat and decline.

Still, it was not the outcome of a single power struggle in the 1440's that cost China its worldly influence. Historians offer a host of reasons for why Asia eventually lost its way economically and was late to industrialize; two and a half reasons seem most convincing.

The first is that Asia was simply not greedy enough. The dominant social ethos in ancient China was Confucianism and in India it was caste, with the result that the elites in both nations looked down their noses at business. Ancient China cared about many things—prestige, honor, culture, arts, education, ancestors, religion, filial piety—but making money came far down the list. Confucius had specifically declared that it was wrong for a man to make a distant voyage while his parents were alive, and he had condemned profit as the concern of "a little man." As it was, Zheng He's ships were built on such a grand scale and carried such lavish gifts to foreign leaders that the voyages were not the huge money spinners they could have been.

In contrast to Asia, Europe was consumed with greed. Portugal led the age of discovery in the 15th century largely because it wanted spices, a precious commodity; it was the hope of profits that drove its ships steadily farther down the African coast and eventually around the Horn to Asia. The profits of this trade could be vast: Magellan's crew once sold a cargo of 26 tons of cloves for 10,000 times the cost.

A second reason for Asia's economic stagnation is more difficult to articulate but has to do with what might be called a culture of complacency. China and India shared a tendency to look inward, a devotion to past ideals and methods, a respect for authority and a suspicion of new ideas. David S. Landes, a Harvard economist, has written of ancient China's "intellectual xenophobia"; the former Indian Prime Minister Jawaharlal Nehru referred to the "petrification of classes" and the "static nature" of Indian society. These are all different ways of describing the same economic and intellectual complacency.

Chinese elites regarded their country as the "Middle Kingdom" and believed they had nothing to learn from barbarians abroad. India exhibited much of the same self-satisfaction. "Indians didn't go to Portugal not because they couldn't but because they didn't want to," mused M. P. Sridharan, a historian, as we sat talking on the porch of his home in Calicut.

The 15th-century Portuguese were the opposite. Because of its coastline and fishing industry, Portugal always looked to the sea, yet rivalries with Spain and other countries shut it out of the Mediterranean trade. So the only way for Portugal to get at the wealth of the East was by conquering the oceans.

The half reason is simply that China was a single nation while Europe was many. When the Confucian scholars reasserted control in Beijing and banned shipping, their policy mistake condemned all of China. In contrast, European countries committed economic suicide selectively. So when Portugal slipped into a quasi-Chinese mind-set in the 16th century, slaughtering Jews and burning heretics and driving astronomers and scientists abroad, Holland and England were free to take up the slack. . . .

If ancient China had been greedier and more outward-looking, if other traders had followed in Zheng He's wake and then continued on, Asia might well have dominated Africa and even Europe. Chinese might have settled in not only Malaysia and Singapore, but also in East Africa, the Pacific Islands, even in America. Perhaps the Famao [a clan of people who live in Pate, an island off the coast of Africa, and who are rumored to be descendents of Chinese shipwreck survivors from countless generations ago] show us what the mestizos [racially mixed people] of such a world might have looked liked, the children of a hybrid culture that was never born. What I'd glimpsed in Pate was the high-water mark of an Asian push that simply stopped—not for want of ships or know-how, but strictly for want of national will.

All this might seem fanciful, and yet in Zheng He's time the prospect of a New World settled by the Spanish or English would have seemed infinitely more remote than a New World made by the Chinese. How different would history have been had Zheng He continued on to America? The mind rebels; the ramifications are almost too overwhelming to contemplate. So consider just one: this [selection] would have been published in Chinese.

Bruce Swanson

NO

Continental and Maritime Ideologies in Conflict: The Ming Dynasty

In 1405, China's progressive attitude toward exploitation of the sea culminated in a series of naval expeditions into the South China Sea and the Indian Ocean. The latter expeditions included visits to Ceylon, India, the Persian Gulf, and Africa. These spectacular voyages, in fact, proved that China was the supreme world seapower whose shipbuilding techniques and navigational abilities were unmatched by any other nation.

But China's prominence as the world's greatest naval and maritime power was short-lived. The last of seven expeditions ended in 1433; never again were naval expeditions attempted by emperors. As a result, it is tempting to dismiss these voyages as a temporary aberration of the Chinese emperor who sponsored them. To do so, however, would be to ignore the ineluctable influence of the maritime spirit on China, particularly the growing awareness of the potential of seapower to expand and control the tribute system. At the same time, the subsequent cessation of the voyages clearly highlights the equally strong force of continentalism among members of the imperial court as they attempted to steer China away from maritime pursuits.

Early Ming Strategic Considerations

Before discussing the voyages and their itineraries, it is important to examine certain factors that reflected China's continuing struggle between supporters of continentalism on the one hand and the maritime ideology on the other.

The First Ming Emperor

The first Ming emperor, Zhu Yuanzhang, was an orphaned peasant from the riverine area near Nanjing. As a child, he had been taken in by Buddhist monks and educated in a monastery. Upon leaving the monastery, he was unable to gain employment and was soon begging for a living. At the age of twenty-five, the vagrant joined a rebel band that fought government soldiers for over a decade in the central China river valleys. Warfare finally wore down the Mongol-backed local forces and the entire Yangzi Valley came under rebel control. In due course, Zhu assumed leadership of the rebels and defeated the

From Bruce Swanson, *Eighth Voyage of the Dragon: A History of China's Quest for Seapower* (Naval Institute Press, 1982). Notes omitted.

government forces. He then established his capital at Nanjing in 1356. Twelve years later, after taking his rebel army north and capturing Beijing from the Mongols, Zhu founded the Chinese Ming dynasty.

Although Zhu, being from a riverine area, had presumably come into contact with many men who had knowledge of the sea, his initial concerns lay in consolidating Chinese rule and making China's borders and strategic cities safe from Mongol invasion. Accordingly, he took several actions that temporarily stifled maritime activities.

Walls, Canals, and Coastal Defense

With the Mongols only recently defeated, Zhu set about improving city defenses. For example, he directed the construction of a protective wall some 20 miles in length around Nanjing. The barrier was 60 feet high and nearly impenetrable by a force armed with the weapons of the time.

On the coast, Zhu faced the problem of piracy by Japanese and Chinese freebooters, which had increased alarmingly. He ordered that Chinese not be permitted to go overseas—those who violated his edict would be executed as traitors. In 1374 Zhu backed up his decree by abolishing the superintendencies of merchant ships at the ports of Ningbo, Quanzhou, and Guangzhou. Next, he strengthened coastal defenses by constructing forts; in the four-year period from 1383 to 1387, more than one hundred thirty forts were built in the Zhejiang-Fujian coastal zones. In Zhejiang alone, more than fifty-eight thousand troops were conscripted to man the provincial coastal forts.

Zhu also directed the Board of Works to undertake extensive reconstruction of the canal system, which had been damaged by flood and warfare. One of the long-term projects called for enlarging the Grand Canal, which upon completion was to replace the pirate-plagued sea route. The latter route had been reopened earlier when civil strife closed down the canal.

The Tribute System

The first Ming emperor wasted little time before trying to reestablish the tributary system. He ordered missions to proceed to peripheral states such as Japan, Annam, Champa, and Korea, where it was proclaimed that all who wished to enter into relations with China must acknowledge the suzerainty of the new emperor. Very soon some of these states sent reciprocal missions to Peking where Zhu received their kowtows acknowledging him as the Son of Heaven. These missions also served other purposes, such as providing the new Chinese dynasty with information on the current situations in border areas. . . .

The Mongol-Muslim Alliance

The first Ming emperor also had to deal with the continuing threat posed by the retreating Mongols. It took Zhu's armies until 1382 to drive remaining Mongol military units from Yunnan in southwest China. Moreover, during the next twenty years, periodic "mopping-up" operations continued beyond the Great Wall in northeast China and in Korea as well.

For the Ming government, the biggest threat lay westward. A Turkic nomad and Muslim named Timur, or Tamerlane, was conquering the entire central Asian region from Siberia to the Mediterranean and southward to the Indian Ocean. Included in the ranks of his fierce Muslim cavalry were remnants of the retreating Mongol armies.

According to an official Ming history, Zhu was anxious to bring Timur into the tribute system. He sent several small missions on the overland caravan route to seek out the Muslim leader. The Chinese apparently were unaware of just how paltry their offer of suzerainty appeared to the ferocious Timur. The Muslims, in fact, scorned the Chinese. "Because they believe [that] our people [are] wild and boorish, they do not hope for politeness, nor respect, nor honor, nor law from us; and apart from their own realms they do not know of a city [anywhere] in the world."

In 1394, after only a quarter century of Ming rule, an incident occurred that would seriously jeopardize the Chinese dynasty. At that time, Zhu received what he thought was a tribute mission from Timur that delivered a letter acknowledging the Chinese emperor as the ruler of all mankind. The letter, forged by an ambitious merchant or court official, led Zhu to send a return mission to central Asia in appreciation of Timur's vassalage. In 1395, when the Chinese embassy reached Timur and delivered Zhu's note, the Muslim leader became so enraged that he advised his staff to prepare for an invasion of China to bring down the Chinese "infidels." He took the Chinese mission hostage. By 1404 his plans were nearly complete, and he had massed two-hundred thousand Muslim and Mongol cavalrymen in the Pamirs, near modern-day Afghanistan.

Fortunately for the Chinese, Timur died in 1405, following an all-night drinking bout. On his deathbed he reportedly "expressed his regret in having neglected the conquest of such infidel countries as China and drawn his sword against Muslim armies." Two more years passed before the Chinese heard from the freed hostages that Timur had died.

Foreign Policy Under the Second Ming Emperor

While Timur was preparing to invade China, the death of Zhu Yuanzhang in 1398 produced another period of civil war lasting until 1403. Succeeding Zhu was his grandson, a young boy whose court remained in Nanjing. In the north, however, Zhu's fourth son, Chengzu, decided to overthrow his nephew from the southern capital. As the military commander responsible for anti-Mongol operations in the Peking area, he controlled some of the best troops in China. His ultimate success came in 1403, when he defeated the Nanjing forces loyal to his father and assumed the throne with the name Yongle, meaning "perpetual happiness."

Clearly, Yongle's ambition and leadership ability forecast a dynamic reign. As with his father before him, one of Yongle's primary objectives was to establish his sovereignty throughout the tribute system by reinstilling the belief among all foreign states that China was supreme. In order to persuade the tributaries, however, Yongle had to work out a strategy that would both gain respect for Chinese power and enrich the imperial treasuries.

He dealt with Japan first. In 1403 the superintendencies of merchant shipping were reopened and new hostels were built to house Japanese tributary missions coming by sea. A system was devised whereby legitimate Japanese merchants were given trading passports that could be checked by Chinese authorities on each visit. In this way pirates could be identified, while honest Japanese and Chinese businessmen were free to carry on lucrative trade.

In Annam Yongle faced a critical problem. In 1400, while he was fighting to usurp the throne from his nephew, events there were coming to a head. Hanoi had fallen to Champa and the Annamese Tran dynasty was destroyed. The South China Sea was now in the hands of Cham and rebel Annamese pirates, and Chinese merchant shipping, both official and unofficial, was seriously disrupted. In 1406 Yongle decided to attack across the land border in order to pacify the two warring states and then reestablish Annam as a Chinese province. Hanoi was captured in 1406, but the Chinese armies soon bogged down in Annamese cities awaiting reinforcements and supplies. Before long nearly ninety thousand Chinese troops were in Annam attempting to control the countryside through a costly sinicization program.

Problems in inner Asia were developing concurrently with the Annam invasion. Word of the Muslim conquests in central Asia had reached Yongle, but the distance and harsh nature of that western area precluded the dispatch of a large army to confront Timur. Caution got the better of Yongle. He elected to send a small fact-finding mission to Timur in 1402 to inquire why the Muslim leader, since 1395, had failed to pay tribute. In a move that suggested that Yongle would settle for political equality with remote central Asia, he approved the construction of a Muslim mosque in Peking. This may have been done to induce the warring Muslims to keep open the silk route connecting western China with the cities of the Timurid empire (these included Gilgit and Herat, located in modern-day Pakistan and Afghanistan, respectively).

With the silk route used only sporadically, the wealthy classes, the court, and the treasury had become heavily dependent upon southern maritime trade for the import of precious stones, fragrant woods, spices, and rare objects. To ensure the safety of Chinese traders on the sea and the uninterrupted flow of luxury items, it was essential that Yongle build a navy that would convince the ocean states of China's "world supremacy." He devised a forceful plan calling for the aggressive use of seapower to underline Chinese suzerainty over the peripheral southern ocean states. Since the first expedition was to sail all the way to the Muslim states of Aden, Mecca, Djofar, and Hormuz, Yongle likely concluded that the voyages would also be useful in countering Timur's influence in that area.

The Ming Ships and Expeditions

In 1403, a year of momentous decisions, Yongle directed Chinese shipyards in Fujian to undertake an aggressive shipbuilding effort that would result in the construction of more than two thousand large seagoing vessels over the next sixteen years.

The *baochuan*, or treasure ships, were the largest vessels constructed by the Chinese. Their size has been the subject of many arguments among scholars. Ming histories record that the treasure-ships were 440 feet long and 180 feet wide (an unlikely construction ratio of 5:2). At best, this configuration is an exaggeration, for such broad-beamed vessels would be unresponsive even under moderate sea conditions. In fact, acceptance of these figures degrades the reputation of Chinese shipbuilders of the period, who would have recognized that such vessels were impractical to build. Until research proves otherwise, it is this writer's opinion that the largest vessels were shaped much like the three largest junks, of which records are available. These, the Jiangsu trader, the Beizhili trader, and the Fuzhou pole junk, were built on a proportion of about 6.4:1—much closer to the modern naval architecture ratio of 9:1. The former was about 170 feet long and had five masts, while the latter two had lengths of 180 feet with a beam of 28 feet. It may be significant that Fujian shipyards were give the first-order calling for the construction of 137 ships, since these were the yards that probably developed the technique for building the Fuzhou pole junk. . . .

Zheng He

In addition to overseeing the construction of the Ming fleet, Yongle selected the senior officers who were to lead the expeditions. For overall commander the emperor picked a Muslim eunuch named Zheng He, who had been in his service since 1382. As a small boy, Zheng He had been taken prisoner in Yunnan during the final rout of the Mongols.

Following his capture, Zheng He, by custom, was castrated and subsequently made an officer in Yongle's army, where he distinguished himself during the successful usurpation campaign of 1403. For his loyal service, Zheng He, at age thirty-three, was made a grand eunuch and appointed superintendent of the Office of Eunuchs. His military prowess, along with his knowledge of Turku languages and Islam, made Zheng He the ideal choice for senior admiral of the Ming fleet. He was given the name Sanbao Taijian, meaning "three-jewelled eunuch."

During his voyages, Zheng He was accompanied by other Chinese Muslims, including one named Ma Huan, who came from the Hangzhou Bay area. Ma was knowledgeable in matters of the sea and in the Arabic and Persian languages. His chief distinction, however, was the account of three voyages he made with Zheng He.

From Ma Huan we learn that Zheng He's general procedure was to bring the fleet together in late spring near modern-day Shanghai, where a series of briefings and religious ceremonies was conducted. Once prayers had been offered, and the fleet had been organized and briefed, it sailed leisurely on a four- to eight-week "shakedown cruise" to an anchorage at the mouth of the Min River in Fujian Province. There the ships would carry out further intensive training throughout the late summer and early fall. Finally, in December or January, they would set sail during the favorable monsoon.

The Sea Routes

The sea routes followed by Ming naval captains had been known and used for several centuries. Since the Song dynasty, in fact, the routes had been systematized into two major sea lanes: the East Sea Route and the West Sea Route. Each was subdivided into a major and minor route. For example, the major East Sea Route extended to northern Borneo and the Philippines. The minor West Sea

Route encompassed ports in Sumatra and the Malay Peninsula. The major West Sea Route was that route taken to the Indian Ocean via the Malacca Strait.

Following the period of intensive training, the fleet wound its way through the Taiwan Strait and sailed directly into the South China Sea, where land falls were made on Hainan Island and the Xisha Islands (Paracel Islands). From the Xishas the fleet turned westward and made for an anchorage at modern-day Qui Nhon on the Champa (southern Vietnam) coast. The total time of the Fujian-Champa transit was about ten days. Once there, provisions were taken aboard and the crews had "liberty" and "swim call." From Qui Nhon the fleet sailed southward toward the west coast of Borneo, making land falls on the various islands in the southern portion of the South China Sea.

After rounding Borneo, the ships entered the Java Sea and sailed to Sarabaja in Java. At this port Chinese crews were again rested for several months, until about July, when the period of favorable winds occurred. They then sailed through the Malacca Strait via Palembang and thence westward to Sri Lanka. From Sri Lanka the ships made their way to Calicut on the Indian coast, where the fleet was divided into smaller "task forces." Some went to Chittagong in modern-day Bangladesh; others went to Hormuz, Aden, and Jidda; and some visited the African coast near the mouth of the Red Sea. Hormuz usually was reached in January of the first year, and the Chinese returned to Malacca by March. They remained in Malacca only briefly, sailing northward to the Yangzi River by July of the second year. . . .

The Decline of Maritime Spirit in the Ming

During the Ming expeditions, a number of political, military, social, and economic factors acted to slow and then finally halt the policies that had promoted maritime experimentation and growth.

The Grand Canal

One of the first indications of China's impending maritime collapse occurred when the Grand Canal was reopened in 1411, making it again possible to ship grain via the inland route. This event marked another closing of the coastal maritime route, and many personnel of the coastal fleets were reassigned to work on the canal. In 1415 the government officially banned grain transport by sea and authorized the construction of three thousand shallow-draft canal barges. This diversion of manpower and shipbuilding expertise was soon felt in the maritime industries. Ocean-going ship construction lagged and was halted altogether by Yongle's successor in 1436. At the same time, regulations were issued that reassigned the men of the Indian Ocean expeditionary force to canal duties as stevedores.

Population Shifts

Significantly, the conclusion of Ming voyages caused a shift of population away from the sea coast that, from 1437 to 1491, resulted in a loss of eight million people in the three principal coastal provinces of Zhejiang, Fujian, and Guangdong. Meanwhile, inland areas such as Yunnan and Hebei gained four million in population. Many coastal inhabitants also emigrated to southeast Asia.

Warfare and Border Pressure

During the fifteenth century China suffered several serious military setbacks along its land borders that deflected interest in maritime expeditions. In 1418 Annam, tiring of the Chinese presence, launched a war of independence. In a way similar to recent United States efforts, the Chinese tried to carry the fight for some nine years, but Annamese guerrilla tactics eventually prevailed. In 1420 the Ming navy lost a battle on the Red River; in 1427 the Chinese emperor finally grew weary of increased war costs and evacuated nearly one hundred thousand Chinese soldiers from Annam. Chinese suzerainty was maintained, however.

In the north, China faced a graver threat in the form of continued Mongol raids along the entire length of the Great Wall. In 1421, in an effort to counter the resurgent Mongols, Yongle moved the capital from Nanjing to Beijing. Troops were shifted from the seacoast to shore up the northern capital's defenses, which lay less than 100 miles from one of the strategic northern passes that intersected the Great Wall. Despite these precautions, the Chinese emperor was captured in 1449, and the Ming court was forced to resurrect its continental defense strategy completely. These policies did little to diminish the northern nomad threat, however; the critical northern frontier remained under nomad pressure for the next three hundred years. Martial law was periodically imposed, and senior military officials spent their careers defending the north rather than performing naval and coastal defense duties.

Corruption in Government

Politics within the Ming court also began to turn attention away from the sea, as eunuchs and Chinese bureaucrats vied for power. The praise and favors lavished on palace eunuchs in the early Ming period eventually led to their complete domination of governmental affairs. By the middle of the fifteenth century, the first in a series of eunuch strongmen ascended to power. Very quickly they set about sealing their hold over the most important government agencies, taking control of the army, the police, and finance ministries. When opposed, the eunuchs often resorted to terrorist tactics, arresting and executing those that dared question their authority. Many became quite corrupt, employing ships and crews to transport ill-gotten goods and transferring soldiers to palace construction work.

By 1480 the political intrigues had increased to such an extent that when a powerful eunuch initiated a request to prepare another series of maritime expeditions in emulation of Zheng He, he was greeted by fierce opposition within the ranks of government bureaucrats. Jealous officials within the Board of War conspired to have records of the Indian Ocean voyages destroyed, so as to frustrate any attempt to imitate the early Ming expeditions.

Piracy

As officials became more absorbed in intrigues at court, they too tended toward corruption, which carried over to coastal trade. Unscrupulous merchants regained control as the government's monopoly on foreign trade was relinquished, and smuggling and piracy flourished. The Ming histories record that "the powerful families of Fujian and Zhejiang traded with the Japanese pirates. Their associates at court protected them and carried out their bidding. . . . Palace attendants outfitted merchant ships and the criminal elements of the coast abetted them in making profit." In fact, while Zheng He and his companions were conducting their voyages, Japanese pirates successfully carried out five major incursions against the Chinese mainland. In 1419 the northern coastguard fleets were helpless in preventing a sizeable force of several thousand pirates from landing on the Liaodong Peninsula. It required a well-trained force of Chinese army troops to subdue the pirates. As an example of the magnitude of this action, the Chinese army commander captured 857 pirates alive and beheaded another 742.

Although Japanese piracy continued to plague the Chinese, it ceased in 1466 when Japan fell into civil war. By 1523, however, Japanese and Chinese raiders were again launching attacks along the coast. Ningbo was burned in that year, and in 1552 a flotilla sailed up the Yangzi, sacking cities without opposition. Natives of the coast fled further inland to escape the ravages of these attacks. In 1555 Nanjing came under seige and the port of Quanzhou in Fujian was plundered. In an attempt to stop these raids, Ming provincial administrators resorted to the Tang dynasty's practice of constructing beacon stations to give advance warnings of pirates. By 1562, 711 beacon stations lined the coast from Jiangsu to Guangdong. By 1563 the army had to be used to combat the sea rovers, who controlled nearly all of the Fujian coast.

Scholarship and Neo-Confucianism

Finally, a version of neo-Confucianism developed that was markedly idealistic and influenced by Buddhism, resulting in a loss of interest in geomancy and maritime expansion. As early as 1426, a minister memorialized the court, stating the following:

> Arms are the instruments of evil which the sage does not use unless he must. The noble rulers and wise ministers of old did not dissipate the strength of the people by deeds of arm. This was a farsighted policy. . . . Your minister hopes that your majesty . . . would not indulge in military pursuits nor glorify the sending of expeditions to distant countries. Abandon the barren lands abroad and give the people of China a respite so that they could devote themselves to husbandry and to the schools. Thus, there would be no wars and suffering on the frontier and no murmuring in the villages, the commanders would not seek fame and the soldiers would not sacrifice their lives abroad, the people from afar would voluntarily submit and distant lands would come into our fold, and our dynasty would last for ten thousand generations.

Such statements helped check Chinese maritime pursuits and force China to restore continentalist policies. Scholars who devoted their lives to the classics were again revered, while the military class was looked upon with great suspicion by the gentry and officials.

By the early fifteenth century, regulations were again in force that made it a capital offense to build a seagoing junk with more than two masts. By

1525 an imperial edict authorized coastal officials to destroy all ships of this kind and place the crews under arrest.

The timing of Chinese maritime decline could not have been worse, for it coincided with European maritime expansion into Asia. The Portuguese arrived in 1516, and although they were expelled in 1521, their exodus was short-lived. They returned and established settlements in Xiamen in 1544 and Macao in 1535. The Spanish occupied the Philippines in 1564 and established trade relations with China shortly thereafter. Then, in the seventeenth century, the Dutch arrived in Asia just as the Ming dynasty was being conquered by the Manchu cavalry that overran Beijing in 1644. Thus was the stage set for the last foreign imperial rulers in China—the Qing.

POSTSCRIPT

Did China's Worldview Cause the Abrupt End of Its Voyages of Exploration?

In this book's last issue, two historians debate the extent to which the West dominated the modern world through an extension of its power and culture. One is left to wonder whether this western intrusion would have been possible if a strong Chinese naval presence had existed. Perhaps the course of world history would have been altered. No colonialism; no imperialism!

The role of court eunuchs throughout Chinese history has been a turbulent one; sometimes they're portrayed as loyal civil servants, other times as despised outcasts. No one however can question their staying power, as during the reign of Pu Yi (1903–1912), who would be China's last emperor, they were still a troublesome court presence. In Bernardo Bertolucci's Academy Award-winning film, *The Last Emperor,* they are shown as having a corrupting influence on the court and are eventually banned from the "Forbidden City." Although historically they were far from angelic, they have sometimes been blamed for conditions and events that were not of their making. Shih-Shan Henry Tsai attempts to correct the myths and stereotypes regarding eunuchs in his *The Eunuchs in the Ming Dynasty* (State University of New York Press, 1996), which provides a badly needed fresh look at the eunuchs in the period covered by this Issue.

For other works on the subject, see Shi-Shah Henry Tsai, *Perpetual Happiness: The Ming Emperor Yongle* (University of Washington Press, 2001) which provides a fresh look at the man responsible for Ming China's maritime activities; Timothy Brook, *The Confusions of Pleasure: Commerce and Culture in Ming China* (University of California Press, 1999) is more useful for general information on Chinese society during the Ming dynasty than specific information of Zheng He and his voyages. An ancillary work, *Chinese Maps: Images Of 'All Under Heaven'* by Richard J. Smith provides background to China's worldview and its development and displays the advanced Chinese map work completed during its history.

Last year, Gavin Menzies's *1421: The Year China Discovered America* (William Morrow, 2003) was published. It extended the breadth of China's maritime efforts by claiming that it was the Chinese who discovered America during the Ming era. However, most who reviewed the book found it long on claims and short on documentation.

Finally, two important reference works on Ming China, both edited by Frederick W. Mote and Denis Twitchett are: *The Cambridge History of China: The Ming Dynasty, 1368-1644, Part I* (Cambridge University Press, 1988); and *The*

Cambridge History of China: The Ming Dynasty, 1368–1644, Part II (Cambridge University Press, 1998).

The recent publication date on many of these books, and the presence of numerous computer web sites containing information about Zheng He, show the timeliness of the subject and give hope that more information on a neglected figure in Chinese and world history will be forthcoming.

ISSUE 5

Did Christopher Columbus's Voyages Have a Positive Effect on World History?

YES: Robert Royal, from "Columbus and the Beginning of the New World," *First Things: A Monthly Journal of Religion and Public Life* (May 1999)

NO: Gabriel Garcia Marquez, from "For a Country Within Reach of the Children," *Americas* (November/December 1997)

ISSUE SUMMARY

YES: Robert Royal states although there were negatives that emanated from Columbus's New World discoveries, they continue to "remind us of the glorious and ultimately providential destiny on the ongoing global journey that began in the fifteenth century."

NO: Nobel laureate Gabriel Garcia Marquez argues that Columbus's voyages had a negative effect on the Americas, much of which is still felt today.

In October 1998, a *New York Times* article covered a dispute between Hispanic-Americans and Italian-Americans with regard to which ethnic group should play the more important role in the organization of New York's Columbus Day Parade. While both groups had legitimate claims to the Columbus legacy (after all, Columbus was a Genoese Italian, but he did his most important work for the Spanish nation), the dispute must have drawn an ironic response from those who witnessed the revisionist bashing that the "Admiral of the Ocean Sea" had received in recent years.

In the five centuries since "Columbus sailed the ocean blue," his historical reputation and the significance of his accomplishments have undergone a series of metamorphoses. In the distant past, an eclectic collection of Columbus critics would number essayist Michel Montaigne, English writer Samuel Johnson, philosopher Jean-Jacques Rousseau, and French historian and philosopher Abbe Guillaume Reynal, some of whom believed that the world would have been better off without the admiral's discoveries.

It has only been in the last two centuries that Columbus's stock has risen in the theater of public opinion and historical significance. There were many reasons for this change including: (1) the United States acting as a model for democratic government in a 19th/20th-century world living under monarchial/autocratic rule; (2) the part played by the U.S. in the Allied victory during World War I, which ended the German, Austrian, Ottoman, and Russian Empires and brought a greater level of democracy to many parts of Europe; (3) the role assumed by the U.S. in saving Europe and the world from the specter of fascist militarism during World War II. All affected the reversal of Columbus's historical fortunes, as many wondered what the world would have become if the U.S. had not been there to provide inspiration and assistance in these times of need. Thus, some of the credit our nation accrued was passed on to Columbus, whose work had made our nation possible. Samuel Eliot Morison's 1940 book, ADMIRAL OF THE OCEAN SEA, marked the climax of this laudatory view of Columbus and his accomplishments.

Historians and publishers love anniversaries and the publicity they generate, and, next to a millennial celebration, none may be more significant than a quincentennial one. Thus, on the 500th anniversary of Columbus's first voyage, the requisite number of tomes on Columbus and his accomplishments were made ready for an eager market. But the world of 1992 was different than the world of Morison's "Admiral of the Ocean Sea," and the historical profession had changed along with it.

The end-of-the millennium generation of historians treated Columbus differently than had their immediate predecessors. Operating from a different world view, Columbus became to many of them a flawed figure responsible for the horrors of the trans-atlantic slave trade, the annihilation of Native American civilizations through cruelty and disease, and the ecological destruction of a continental paradise.

The recently published books about Christopher Columbus opened a national dialogue on the subject. A national Columbus exhibition in Washington, D.C. was received with skepticism by some and quiet reverence by others. While some participated in the national Columbus Day celebration on October 12, 1992, others declared it a day of mourning in honor of those who lost their lives as a result of Columbus's enterprises. A cultural hornet's nest was unleashed, and any who entered into the Columbus fray had to have the thickest of skin.

Fortunately, as is usually the case, time has a soothing effect, and we will have to wait until the year 2092 for the next major Columbus debate. For now, we have the opportunity—with cooler heads and calmer temperaments—to examine the Columbus legacy.

In this Issue, Robert Royal stresses the positive elements that came from Columbus's discoveries. Gabriel Garcia Marquez emphasizes their negative impact on the New World and its peoples.

YES  **Robert Royal**

Columbus and the Beginning of the New World

. . . The world we know began in the fifteenth century. Not the world of course in the sense of human life or human civilizations, which had already existed for millennia, but the world as a concrete reality in which all parts of the globe had come into contact with one another and begun to recognize themselves as part of a single human race—a process still underway. The spherical globe we had known about since the classical world; in the Middle Ages, readers of Dante took it for granted. Yet it was only because of a small expedition by a few men driven by a mishmash of personal ambition, religious motives, and the desire for profit that an old mathematical calculation was turned into a new human fact. Or as a historian sixty years later accurately characterized the discovery of the New World, it was "the greatest event since the creation of the world (excluding the incarnation and death of Him who created it)."

In our own confused way, we continue to pay homage to that achievement. In 1999, NASA will put a satellite into an orbit a little less than a million miles out into space in what is called L-l, the libration point where the gravity of the earth and the sun exactly balance one another. Equipped with a telescopic lens and video camera, it will provide a twenty-four-hour-a-day image of the surface of the earth. Not surprisingly, one of the enthusiasts behind the project is Al Gore, probably the most environmentally agitated public figure alive. But in spite of the damage that Gore and many others believe we humans have inflicted on the planet since our first large steps in exploring it, and despite the laments of multiculturalists about Europe's rise to world dominance, the new satellite will be called Triana, after Rodrigo de Triana, who first spotted lights on land from the deck of the Pinta during the first voyage of Columbus.

Perhaps the name is only a bow to growing Hispanic influence in the United States; perhaps it hints that we would like to think of ourselves as equally on the verge of another great age of discovery. But whatever our sense of the future, the Columbus discoveries and the European intellectual and religious developments that lay behind them are today at best taken for granted, at worst viewed as the beginning of a sinister Western hegemony over man and nature. The last five centuries, of course, offer the usual human spectacle of great glories mixed with grim atrocities. But we cannot evaluate the voyages of discovery properly—much less the fifteenth-century culture from which they sprang—without gratitude for what they achieved or understanding of their human dimensions. In the fifteenth century, the discoveries were rightly regarded as close to a miracle, especially given the way the century had begun.

The early 1400s were marked by profound religious, political, economic, and even environmental turmoil. At one point in the first decade of the century, there were simultaneously three claimants to the papal throne and three to the crown of the Holy Roman Empire. And the large-scale institutional crises were only a small part of the story. Europe was still suffering from the devastation wrought at the height of the Black Death over half a century earlier and in smaller waves thereafter. Overall, something like 40 percent of the population disappeared in the mid-fourteenth century, in some regions even more. Land lay fallow for lack of workers, villages were deserted, poverty spread. As many modern environmentalists have devoutly wished, nature took its vengeance as human population decreased. Wolves multiplied and returned, even appearing in capital cities. Human predators—in the form of brigands—made travel unsafe over wide areas. The consequences of the retreat of civilization spurred Henry V, fabled victor of Agincourt, to offer rewards for the elimination of both types of pests. Though the beauty of landscapes emerged as never before in contemporary painting and literature, it was not a century that indulged itself in easy sentimentality about the goodness of unimproved nature, human or otherwise. On the contrary, natural hardships spurred the fifteenth century to nearly unparalleled achievements.

But if the internal situation were not enough, Europe was also being squeezed by forces from outside. In 1453, the Ottoman Turks finally succeeded in taking Byzantium. Turkish troops had already been fighting as far into the Balkans as Belgrade a few years earlier. Otranto, in the heel of Italy, fell to them in 1480 for a time. We might have expected the Christian powers to lay aside rivalries momentarily and defend themselves from an alien culture and religion. But the main Atlantic nation-states—England, France, and Spain—were still only beginning to take shape. The rest of Western Europe was broken, despite the theoretical claims of the emperor, into a crazy quilt of competing small powers. So no coordinated effort occurred, though Plus II and other popes called for a crusade. Plus even wrote to Sultan Muhammad II, conqueror of Constantinople, inviting him to convert to Christianity. Whether this letter was intended seriously or as a mere pretext for further action, it failed. Neither "European" nor "Christian" interests were sufficiently united to galvanize the effort. The Pope died in 1464 at the eastern Italian port of Ancona waiting for his people to rally behind him.

A crusade to retake the Holy Land was sometimes a mere pipe dream, sometimes a serious proposal during the course of the century. Ferdinand of Spain listened frequently to such plans, but refrained from doing much. (Machiavelli praises him in The Prince as one of those rulers who shrewdly take pains to appear good without necessarily being so.) Charles VIII of France invaded Italy in 1494 but also had in mind an attempt to retake

Constantinople and restore the Eastern Christian Empire. Earlier, Henry V, on his way to Agincourt, proclaimed his intentions not only to assume the French throne but to "build again the walls of Jerusalem." Western Europe had a persistent if vague sense of responsibility to defend Christianity front Islamic military threats and a deeper need to recover the parts of Christendom lost to Muslim conquest, even if the good intentions were thwarted by intra-European distractions.

Had Islam continued its advance, much of Europe might have then resembled the cultures we now associate with the Middle East. The Americas might have been largely Muslim countries as opposed to largely Christian ones. Islam was more advanced than Europe in 1492, but in the paradoxical ways of culture, its very superiority contributed to its being surpassed. Muslims do not seem to have taken much interest in Western technical developments in navigation, and even well-placed countries like Morocco were never moved to brave the high seas in search of new lands. European technological innovation and military advance may have been born of necessity, given the superiority of outside cultures and the conflicts and rivalries among European nations.

This reminds us of something often overlooked in most contemporary historical surveys. The "Eurocentric" forces, of which we now hear so much criticism, were actually something quite different in the fifteenth century. What we today call "Europeans" thought of themselves as part of Christendom, and a Christendom, as we shall serf, that desperately needed to return to some of its founding truths. Similarly, they did not regard themselves as the bearers of the highest culture. Ancient Greece and Rome, they knew, had lived at a higher level, which is why the Renaissance felt the need to recover and imitate classical models. The fabled wealth of the distant Orient and the clearly superior civilization of nearby Islam did not allow Christendom to think itself culturally advanced or, more significantly, to turn in on itself, as self-satisfied empires of the time such as China did. Contemporary European maps—the ones all the early mariners consulted in the Age of Discovery—bear witness to their central belief: Jerusalem, not Europe, was the center of the world.

But this very sense of threat and inferiority, combined with the unsettled social diversity of Europe at the time, gave Europeans a rich and dynamic restlessness. Not surprisingly, the rise towards a renewed Europe began in the places least affected by the population implosion and, therefore, more prosperous: what we today call the Low Countries and, above all, Northern Italy. Renascences, as Erwin Panofsky demonstrated a few decades ago, had been occurring in Europe since the twelfth century. But the one that took place in Northern Italy in the fifteenth century—the one we call the Renaissance—produced multiple and wide-ranging consequences.

Pius II was in many ways emblematic of the mid-century. A cultivated humanist born in Siena in 1405 with the imposing name Aeneas Sylvius Piccolomini, he initially came under the spell of St. Bernardino, who preached a strictly observant reformed Franciscan life (of which more anon). But he shortly became attracted to the exciting life of the Renaissance Italian humanists, which is to say libertinism and literary pursuits. He shifted parties among papal contenders, pursuing his own ambitions for many years, wrote a popular history (Historia rerum ubique gestarum) that gathered together wide-ranging facts and fictions about foreign lands, and even became imperial poet and secretary to the Holy Roman Emperor Frederick III. But compared with the squabbling popes and anti-popes who preceded him and the colorful escapades of the Borgias, Pius had his virtues. He was learned and hard-working, enjoyed nature, sought reform, and could have made a difference in Europe had his office enjoyed the respect it once had and was to have again later. The religious renaissance, however, like the cultural, scientific, and artistic one with which we are more familiar, had to come from other sources.

Renaissance achievements found multiple and overlapping uses in a Europe in ferment. The geometry developed by the Florentine Paolo Toscanelli allowed Fillippo Brunelleschi, over the objections of a commission of Florentine experts, to dare construction of the unsupported dome that crowns the magnificent Florentine Duomo. Just a few decades later, an intellectually curious Genoese mariner corresponded with Toscanelli in preparation for his attempts to convince another panel of experts in Spain that it was possible to sail west to the Indies (no serious thinker at the time, by the way, believed the earth was flat). His figures were wrong; the distance was greater than he claimed. The experts—and perhaps Columbus himself—knew it. But it was an age when for various reasons people had the faith to attempt things beyond what was previously thought possible. It is worth looking closely at some of those reasons.

Much has recently been written, for example, claiming that the Christian dimension of Columbus' personality was merely a cover for greed and ambition. These alleged traits are then read as a metaphor for a hypocritical European expansion under the cover of religion. Hypocrites certainly existed in the fifteenth century, as they do today. But real history—as opposed to anachronistic morality tales—is always more complex than the simple motives we project back onto figures quite different from ourselves. Like the Italian humanists, who are often wrongly portrayed as modern unbelieving intellectuals, Columbus combined his faith with new knowledge and new interests. But that did not make his faith any less real. He wanted that Renaissance ideal, glory: in this case, that of an unprecedented voyage. He drove hard bargains with Ferdinand and Isabella to secure the financial benefits of his discoveries for himself and his descendants. (The Muslim conquests and consequent monopolies over Eastern trade routes made the European search for alternate routes all the more necessary and profitable.) Yet when all the mundane reasons have been listed, the spiritual dimension of the project remains in ways that are quite unexpected.

In the preface to his Libro de las profecias (Book of Prophecies), an anthology of prophetic texts that he compiled near the end of his life, Columbus relates to Ferdinand and Isabella how, long before he ever approached them, he had become convinced that the westward voyage was not merely possible but his own personal vocation:

> During this time, I searched out and studied all kinds of texts: geographies, histories, chronologies, philosoph[ies], and other subjects. With a hand that could be felt, the Lord opened my mind to the fact that it would be possible to sail from here to the Indies, and He opened my will to desire to

> accomplish this project. This was the fire that burned within me when I came to visit your Highnesses.

Of course, the reading alone suggests we are dealing with an unusual kind of sailor, one who, like the humanists of his day, has engaged in sifting and comparing ancient and modern knowledge for new purposes. There is some irony, then, in the fact that he claims that God intended to produce a milagro ebidentisimo ("highly visible miracle") in this enterprise by using an uneducated man: "For the execution of the journey to the Indies, I was not aided by intelligence, by mathematics, or by maps. It was simply the fulfillment of what Isaiah had prophesied."

Columbus clearly employed considerable intelligence, mathematical skill, and geographical knowledge in planning his route. He also knew from much experience at sea that winds in the Atlantic nearer the equator would carry him west, those to be found more to the north would take him east, back to Europe. And he was alert to other environmental signs. Late in the first voyage he turned south to follow a flock of birds that he rightly assumed were headed towards land. Without this chance or providential fact, he probably would have come ashore somewhere between Virginia and Florida instead of the Caribbean, with doubtless immensely different effects on subsequent world history.

Despite all the knowledge, abstract and practical, that Columbus brought to bear on his task, the religious intuitions he describes may strike us as bordering on delusion, on a par with the equally unexpected mystical speculations of the mathematician Pascal, or Newton's commentaries on the prophecies in the Book of Daniel. But anyone familiar with how prophecies have functioned throughout history knows they often work themselves out in ways their authors never envisioned. In Columbus' case, we may wish to avoid judging too quickly the "hand that could be felt" and other evidence that at times he seems to have heard something like divine locutions. They may have been delusions, intuitions, or something else moving in the depths of human history.

Far from being a later and idealized reinterpretation of his own past, Columbus' remarks are confirmed by a curious source. Recent scholars have discovered notes in Columbus' own hand dated 1481, over a decade before his first voyage, in the back of a copy of Aeneas Sylvius Piccolomini's (the later Pius II) Historia rerum ubique gestarum. There Columbus compiles a shorter list of prophecies from various sources which, it now seems perfectly clear, guided his whole life project. . . .

Much of this real history has been obscured for a long time by persons who found it expedient to use Columbus as a symbolic figure. For most older Americans, he was presented as a heroic proto-American, combating the obscurantism of reactionary Spanish Catholics who thought he would sail off the end of the flat earth. (As we have seen, neither Columbus nor his intellectual critics believed in such absurdities.) In that reading, he became a forerunner of American Protestantism, modern science, and capitalist enterprise. It is no great loss that we have discarded that historical illusion.

Columbus also did service as an ethnic hero for Catholics, mostly Irish and Italian, during the large waves of immigration at the end of the nineteenth and beginning of the twentieth century. There was less harm here, because he was a true hero. Enthusiasm grew so heated that on the four hundredth anniversary of his voyage in 1892 efforts were made to have him canonized. But Leo XIII, fully aware of Columbus' irregular marital situation (for reasons of inheritance he never married the woman he lived with after his wife died), contented himself with praising his human virtues: "For the exploit is in itself the highest and grandest which any age has ever seen accomplished by man; and he who achieved it, for the greatness of mind and heart, can be compared to but few in the history of humanity."

In recent years, of course, Columbus' standing as hero has come under severe assault. He and the culture he represented have been castigated for initiating the modern cultural dominance of Europe and every subsequent world evil: colonialism, slavery, cultural imperialism, environmental damage, and religious bigotry. There is a kernel of truth in these charges, but obviously to equate a single individual or a complex entity like a culture with what are currently judged to be the negative dimensions of the emergence of an interconnected human world is to do great historical injustice to both individuals and ideas.

Europeans, for example, had an ambivalent stance towards the new peoples they encountered. On the one hand, there arose almost instantaneously the beginnings of the "noble savage" myth, which had a varied career in the hands of writers like Thomas More, Montaigne, and Rousseau. On the other hand, actual experience of the new cultures revealed peoples who displayed much savagery and sometimes little nobility.

Columbus himself adhered to one side or the other in this culture war at different times in his life. In one of his first communications with the Spanish monarchs after the discovery, he described the Tainos of the Caribbean in glowing terms:

> I see and know that these people have no religion whatever, nor are they idolaters, but rather they are very meek and know no evil. They do not kill or capture others and are without weapons. They are so timid that a hundred of them flee from one of us, even if we are teasing. They are very trusting; they believe there is a God in Heaven, and they firmly believe that we come from Heaven. They learn very quickly any prayer we tell them to say, and they make the sign of the cross. Therefore Your Highnesses must resolve to make them Christians.

As the self-contradictions of this passage suggest, Columbus was under the spell of one current in European mythology that believed such "uncivilized" peoples to be somehow closer to the conditions of the Garden of Eden than those enmeshed in the conflicts of "civilization."

In fact, the Tainos themselves were enmeshed in the tribal raiding, slavery, and cannibalism that existed in the Caribbean long before any European arrived (the word "cannibal" is a corruption of the native term for the fierce Caribs who eventually gave their name to the whole region). Columbus was for a while on surprisingly good terms with his Tainos, who in turn used the Spaniards to their advantage against their enemies. But the distance between the cultures was great, and, with the arrival of less-than-ideal explorers in subsequent voyages, the situation took a bad turn. Towards the end of his third voyage, Columbus wrote to complain about criticism of his governorship over both natives and Spaniards:

> At home they judge me as a governor sent to Sicily or to a city or two under settled government and where the laws can be fully maintained, without fear of all being lost. . . . I ought to be judged as a captain who went from Spain to the Indies to conquer a people, warlike and numerous, and with customs and beliefs very different from ours.

Columbus had discovered that the Indians were real flesh-and-blood human beings, with the same mix of good and evil that everywhere constitutes the human condition.

Today, the usual way of characterizing the behavior of the Europeans at this early stage is to fault them for not having the kind of sensitivity to the Other that a modern anthropologist or ethnologist would bring to such situations. Overlooked in this condemnation is the fact that it was precisely out of these tumultuous conflicts that the West began to learn how to understand different cultures as objectively as possible in their own terms. Columbus himself astutely noted differences between the various subgroupings of Tainos as well as their distinctiveness from other tribes. And even when he was driven to harsh action—against both Indians and Spaniards—it was not out of mere desire for power. Bartolome de las Casas, the well-known defender of the Indians, notes the "sweetness and benignity" of the admiral's character and, even while condemning what actually occurred, remarks, "Truly I would not dare blame the admiral's intentions, for I knew him well and I know his intentions were good." Las Casas attributes Columbus' shortcomings not to malign intent but to ignorance concerning how to handle an unprecedented situation.

This raises the question of larger intentions and the world impact of fifteenth-century European culture. The atrocities committed by Spain, England, Holland, and other European powers as they spread out over the globe in ensuing centuries are clear enough. No one today defends them. Less known, however, are the currents within that culture that have led to the very universal principles by which, in retrospect, we criticize that behavior today. For instance, not only Las Casas, but a weighty array of other religious thinkers began trying to specify what European moral obligations were to the new peoples.

Las Casas, who was the bishop of Chiapas, Mexico, where relations between mostly native populations and the central government remain dicey even today, bent over backwards to understand local practices. He once even described human sacrifices as reflecting an authentic piety and said that "even if cruel [they] were meticulous, delicate, and exquisite," a view that some of his critics have remarked exhibits a certain coldness towards the victims. Other missionaries learned native languages and recorded native beliefs. The information coming from the New World stimulated Francisco de la Vitoria, a Dominican theologian at the University of Salamanca in Spain, to develop principles of natural law that, in standard histories, are rightly given credit as the origin of modern international law. To read Vitoria on the Indies is to encounter an atmosphere closer to the UN Universal Declaration of Human Rights than to sinister Eurocentrism.

Las Casas and Vitoria influenced Pope Paul III to make a remarkable statement in his 1536 encyclical Sublimis Deus:

> Indians and all other people who may later be discovered by the Christians are by no means to be deprived of their liberty or the possession of their property, even though they be outside the faith of Jesus Christ. . . . Should the contrary happen it shall be null and of no effect. . . . By virtue of our apostolic authority we declare . . . that the said Indians and other peoples should be converted to the faith of Jesus Christ by preaching the word of God and by the example of good and holy living.

The Spanish crown itself had moral qualms about the conquest. Besides passing various laws trying to eliminate atrocities, it took a step unmatched before or since by any expanding empire: it called a halt to the process while theologians examined the question. In the middle of the sixteenth century, Charles V ordered a theological commission to debate the issue at the monastery of Valladolid. Las Casas defended the Indians. Juan Gines de Sepulveda, the greatest authority on Aristotle at the time, argued that Indians were slaves by nature and thus rightly subject to Spanish conquest. Though the commission never arrived at a clear vote and the Spanish settlers were soon back to their old ways, Las Casas' views were clearly superior and eventually prevailed.

Conquest aside, the question of even peaceful evangelizing remains very much with us. Today, most people, even Christians, believe it somehow improper to evangelize. The injunction to preach the gospel to all nations, so dear to Columbus' heart, seems an embarrassment, not least because of the ways the command has been misused. But some of the earlier missionaries tried a kind of inculturation that recognized what was good in the native practices and tried to build a symbolic bridge between them and the Christian faith. The Franciscans in New Spain and the Jesuits in Canada, for example, tried this approach. Not a few of them found martyrdom.

Many contemporary believers do not think that there was much need to evangelize. This usually arises out of the assumption that native religions are valid in their own way. It will not do, however, given the anthropological evidence, to make facile assumptions that all spiritual practices are on an equal plane. The early explorers who encountered them did not think so, and neither should we. For example, the Mexican novelist Carlos Fuentes, no special friend of Christianity or the Spanish conquest, in the very act of admiring the richness of Aztec culture, characterizes the Aztec gods as "a whole pantheon of fear." Fuentes deplores the way that missionaries often collaborated with unjust appropriation of native land, but on a theological level notes the epochal shift in native cultures thanks to Christian influence: "One can only imagine the astonishment of the hundreds and thousands of Indians who asked for baptism as they came to realize that they were being asked to adore a god who sacrificed himself for men instead of asking men to sacrifice themselves to gods, as the Aztec religion demanded."

This Copernican Revolution in religious thought has changed religious practice around the world since it was first proclaimed in Palestine two millennia ago, yet is all but invisible to modern critics of evangelization. Any of us, transported to the Aztec capital Tenochtitlan or to many other places around the world before the influence of Christianity and Europe, would react the way the conquistadors did—with rage and horror. We might not feel much different about some of the ways that Europeans, imitating Islamic practice, evangelized at times by the sword and perpetrated grave injustices around the world. But it is reductionist in the extreme to regard evangelization simply as imperialism. The usual uncritical way in which we are urged to respect the values of other cultures has only the merest grain of truth buried beneath what is otherwise religious indifferentism.

For all our sense of superiority to this now half-millennium-old story, we still face some of the same questions that emerged in the fifteenth century. We still have not found an adequate way to do justice to the claims of both universal principle and particular communities. We have what Vaclav Havel has called a "thin veneer of global civilization" mostly consisting of CNN, Coca Cola, blue jeans, rock music, and perhaps the beginning glimmer of something approaching a global agreement on how we should treat one another and the planet.

But that minimal unity conceals deeper conflicts involving not only resistance to superficiality but the survival of particular communities of meaning. We say, for example, that we have an equal respect for all cultures—until we come up against religious castes and sexism, clitorectomies and deliberate persecution. Then we believe that universal principles may take precedence. But whose universal principles? A Malaysian prime minister has lately instructed us that, contrary to international assumptions, "Western values are Western values: Asian values are universal values." It may take another five hundred years to decide whether that is so, or whether the opposition it assumes between East and West will persist.

All of this may seem a long way from the fifteenth century. But it is not mere historical fantasy to see in that beginning some of the global issues that are now inescapably on the agenda for the new millennium. Christianity and Islam, the two major proselytizing faiths in the world, are still seeking a modus vivendi. The global culture initiated by Columbus will always be inescapably European in origin and, probably, in basic shape. We chose long ago not to stay quietly at home and build the otherwise quite wonderful contraptions called cuckoo clocks. That decision brought (and brings) many challenges, but the very struggle should remind us of the glorious and ultimately providential destiny of the ongoing global journey that began in the fifteenth century.

Gabriel Garcia Marquez  **NO**

For a Country Within Reach of the Children

Christopher Columbus, with the authorization of a letter from the Spanish monarchs to the emperor of China, had discovered this paradise through a geographical error that changed the course of history. On the eve of his arrival, even before he heard the wings of the first birds in the darkness at sea, Columbus detected the scent of flowers on the wind coming off the land, and it seemed the sweetest thing in the world to him. He wrote in his shipboard diary that they were met on the beach by natives as naked as the day they were born, handsome, gentle, and so innocent they traded all they had for strings of colored beads and tin trinkets. But his heart almost burst from his chest when he discovered that their noserings were made of gold, and their bracelets, necklaces, earrings, and anklets; that they had gold bells to play with, and some sheathed their private parts in gold. Those splendid ornaments, and not their human values, condemned the natives to their roles as protagonists in the second Genesis which began that day. Many of them died not knowing where the invaders had come from. Many of the invaders died not knowing where they were. Five centuries later the descendants of both still do not know who we are.

It was a more discovered world than anyone believed at the time. The Incas had a well-organized, legendary state with ten million inhabitants and monumental cities built on the Andean peaks to touch the sun god. To the amazement of European mathematicians, they had masterful systems of numeration and computation, archives and records for general use, and an unremitting veneration for public works, whose masterpiece was the garden of the imperial palace with its life-size trees and animals, all of gold and silver. The Aztecs and Mayas molded their historical consciousness into sacred pyramids among active volcanoes, and they had clairvoyant emperors, celebrated astronomers, and skilled artisans who overlooked the industrial uses of the wheel but utilized it in children's toys.

At the juncture of the two great oceans lay a territory of forty thousand square leagues, barely glimpsed by Columbus on his fourth voyage although today it bears his name: Colombia. For some ten thousand years it had been inhabited by scattered communities with different languages, distinct cultures, and their own well-defined identities. They had no notion of the state or of political cohesion but had discovered the political miracle of living as equals despite their differences. They possessed ancient systems of science and

From *Americas Magazine*, Vol. 49, No. 6, November–December 1997, pp. 28(12).

education, and a rich cosmology linked to brilliant metalwork and inspired pottery. In their creative maturity, they had aspired to incorporate art into daily life—perhaps the supreme destiny of the arts—and achieved their goal with remarkable success, in household utensils as well as in the way they lived. For them, gold and precious gems did not have exchange value but cosmological and artistic power, although the Spaniards viewed them with Western eyes: more than enough gold and gems to leave the alchemists idle and pave the streets of heaven with pieces of four. This was the motive and force behind the Conquest and the Colonization, and the real origin of what we are. A century went by before the Spaniards shaped the colonial state with one name, one language, one god, and the same borders and political division into twelve provinces that it has today. Which gave rise, for the first time, to the notion of a centralized, bureaucratic nation, creating out of colonial lethargy the illusion of national unity. Sheer illusion in a society that was an obscurantist model of racial discrimination and larval violence beneath the cloak of the Holy Office. The cruelty of the conquistadors, and the unknown diseases they brought with them, reduced the three or four million Indians encountered by the Spaniards to no more than a million. But the racial mixing known as mestizaje had already become a demographic force that could not be contained. The thousands of African slaves brought here against their will for barbaric labor in mines and on plantations contributed a third notable element to the criollo crucible, with new rituals of imagination and memory and other, distant gods. But the Laws of the Indies imposed millimetric standards of segregation according to the degree of white blood in each race: several categories of mestizos, black slaves, free blacks, varying classifications of mulattoes. It became possible to distinguish as many as eighteen different degrees of mestizos, and the white Spaniards even set their own children apart, calling them criollo whites. Mestizos were not permitted to fill certain high positions in government, to hold other public offices, or to enroll in secondary schools and seminaries. Blacks lacked everything, even a soul; they did not have the right to enter heaven or hell, and their blood was deemed impure until distilled by four generations of whites. Because of how difficult it was to determine the intricate demarcation lines between races, and given the very nature of the social dynamic that created mestizaje, such laws could not be enforced with too much rigor, yet racial tensions and violence increased. Until just a few years ago the children of unmarried couples were still not admitted to secondary schools in Colombia. Blacks have achieved legal equality but still suffer many forms of discrimination in addition to the ones peculiar to poverty.

The generation that won independence lost the first opportunity to eradicate this deplorable legacy. The group of young romantics inspired by the enlightenment of the French Revolution established a well-intentioned modern republic but could not eliminate these vestiges of colonialism. Even they were not free of its evil influence. At the age of thirty-five, Simon Bolivar ordered the execution of eight hundred Spanish prisoners, even those lying wounded in a hospital. Francisco de Paula Santander was twenty-eight when he gave the order to shoot thirty-eight Spaniards, including their commanding officer, who had been captured at the Battle of Boyaca. In an indirect way, some of the virtuous aims of the republic fostered new social tensions between poor and rich, laborers and artisans, and other marginal groups. The savage civil wars of the nineteenth century were an outgrowth of these inequalities, as were the countless political upheavals that have left a trail of blood throughout our history. Two innate abilities have helped U.S. to elude our calamitous fate, to compensate for the gaps in our cultural and social circumstances and carry on a fumbling search for our identity. One is a talent for creativity, the supreme expression of human intelligence. The other is a fierce commitment to self-improvement. Enhanced by an almost supernatural shrewdness, and as likely to be used for good as for evil, they were a providential resource employed by the Indians against the Spaniards from the very day they landed. To get rid of Columbus they sent him from island to island, always on to the next island, to find a king covered in gold who never existed. They deceived the conquistadors, already beguiled by novels of chivalry, with descriptions of fantastic cities built of pure gold, right there, on the other side of the hill. They led them astray with the tale of a mythical El Dorado who covered his body with gold dust once a year and plunged into his sacred lagoon. Three masterpieces of a national epic, used by the Indians as an instrument of survival. Perhaps another of the pre-Columbian talents that we have inherited is an extraordinary flexibility in adapting without delay to any environment and learning with ease the most dissimilar trades: fakirs in India, camel drivers in the Sahara, English teachers in New York.

On the other hand, a trait that may come from the Spanish side is our congenital status as immigrants with a spirit of adventure that seeks out risks rather than avoiding them. Of the five million or so Colombians who live abroad, the immense majority left to seek their fortune with nothing but their temerity, and today they are everywhere, for good reasons or bad, for better or worse, but never unnoticed. The distinguishing Colombian trait in world folklore is that they never let themselves die of hunger. Even more striking is that the farther away they are from Colombia, the more Colombian they become.

This is true. They have assimilated the customs and languages of others and made them their own but have never been able to shake the ashes of nostalgia from their hearts, and they miss no opportunity to express this with every kind of patriotic ceremony, exalting all that they long for in the distant homeland, even its defects.

In the most unexpected countries you can turn the corner and find a living replica of any spot in Colombia: the square, its dusty trees still hung with paper garlands from the last Friday night party; the little restaurant named for an unforgotten town, with the heartbreaking aromas of Mama's kitchen; the July 20 school next to the August 7 tavern that plays music for crying over the sweetheart who never was.

The paradox is that, like their forebears, these nostalgic conquistadors were born in a country of closed doors. The liberators tried to open them to fresh winds out of England and France—the legal and ethical theories of Bentham, the education of Lancaster, the study of languages, the popularization of arts and sciences—in order to eradicate the vices of a Spain more Catholic than the Pope and still wary after the financial harassment of the Jews and eight hundred years of Muslim occupation. The nineteenth century radicals, and then the Generation of the Centenary, proposed the same idea with policies of massive immigration aimed at enriching the culture of mestizaje, but all of them were frustrated by our almost theological fear of foreign devils. Even today we have no idea how much we depend on the vast world we know nothing about. We are conscious of our ills but have exhausted ourselves struggling against the symptoms while the causes go on forever. An indulgent version of our history, meant to hide more than it clarifies, has been written for us and made official; in its original sins are perpetuated, battles are won that never were fought, and glories we never deserved are sanctified. In short, we indulge ourselves with the delusion that although history may not resemble the Colombia we live in, one day Colombia will resemble her written history.

In similar fashion, our conformist, repressive education seems designed to force children to adapt to a country that never took them into account, rather than placing the country within their reach and allowing them to transform and enlarge it. The same kind of thoughtlessness inhibits their innate creativity and intuition, thwarts their imaginations and precocious insights, their wisdom of the heart, until children forget what they doubtless knew at birth: that reality does not end where textbooks say it does; that their conception of the world is more attuned to nature than any adult's; that life would be longer and happier if all people could do the work they like and only the work they like.

These intersecting destinies have forged a dense, indecipherable nation where improbability is the only measure of reality. Our banner is excess. Excess in everything: in good and evil, in love and hate, in the jubilation of victory and the bitterness of defeat. We are as passionate when we destroy idols as when we create them.

We are intuitive people, immediate and spontaneous autodidacts, and pitiless workers, but the mere idea of easy money drives us wild. In our hearts we harbor equal amounts of political rancor and historical amnesia. In sports a spectacular win or defeat can cost as many lives as a disastrous plane crash. For the same reason we are a sentimental society where action takes precedence over reflection, impulsiveness over reason, human warmth over prudence. We have an almost irrational love of life but kill one another in our passion to live. The perpetrator of the most terrible crimes is betrayed by his sentimentality. In other words, the most heartless Colombian is betrayed by his heart.

For we are two countries: one on paper and the other in reality. We are precursors of the sciences in America but still take a medieval view of scientists as hermetic wizards, although few things in daily life are not scientific miracles. Justice and impunity cohabit inside each of us in the most arbitrary way; we are fanatical legalists but carry in our souls a sharp-witted lawyer skilled at sidestepping laws without breaking them, or breaking them without being caught. We adore dogs, carpet the world with roses, are overwhelmed by love of country, but we ignore the disappearance of six animal species each hour of the day and night because of criminal depredations in the rain forest, and have ourselves destroyed beyond recall one of the planet's great rivers. We grow indignant at the nation's negative image abroad but do not dare admit that often the reality is worse. We are capable of the noblest acts and the most despicable ones, of sublime poems and demented murders, of celebratory funerals and deadly debauchery. Not because some of us are good and others evil, but because all of us share in the two extremes. In the worst case—and may God keep us from it—we are all capable of anything.

Perhaps deeper reflection would allow us to determine to what extent our character comes from our still being essentially the same clannish, formalistic, introverted society that we were in colonial times. Perhaps calmer reflection would allow us to discover that our historical violence is the force left over from our eternal war against adversity. Perhaps we are perverted by a system that encourages us to live as if we were rich while forty percent of the population exists in abject poverty, that fosters in us an elusive, instantaneous notion of happiness: we always want a little more of what we already have, more and more of what once seemed impossible, much more of what the law allows, and we obtain it however we can, even if that means breaking the law. Realizing that no government can satisfy these desires, we have become disbelieving, non-participatory, ungovernable, and characterized by a solitary individualism that leads all of us to think we depend only on ourselves. More than enough reason to go on asking ourselves who we are and by which face we wish to be known in the third millennium.

POSTSCRIPT

Did Christopher Columbus's Voyages Have a Positive Effect on World History?

Pouring through the many Columbus-oriented works which were products of the quincentennial anniversary is likely to leave one bewildered and perplexed. One wonders how many writers can take the same information and come to diametrically opposed conclusions concerning Columbus and his place in history. Of course, as is usual in historical matters, one's experiences and the perspective derived from them are important determinants in drawing conclusions form the historical process.

It is worth noting that when the Columbus "iconography" was established in the West, the perspective on civilization was a Eurocentric one, and many of its potentionally-negative voices were muted or silent. As Western history became more "inclusionary" and a multi-cultural view of history made its way into the public consciousness, these voices began to be heard. They produced an alternative interpretation of Columbus's voyages and their impact on history for different from their predecessors. What the future will hold for the subject remains to be seen.

One important question germane to the Columbus debate is: To what extent can he be held personally responsible for the transatlantic slave trade, the annihilation of Native American populations, the ecological destruction of the Western Hemisphere, and other evils that were committed long after his death? Any assessment of Columbus's role in world history needs to explore answers to this question.

The post-quincentennial Columbus years have produced a large volume of works on the subject. Some of those on the negative side of the admiral's contributions to world history include Basil Davidson, *The search for Africa: History, Culture, Politics* (Random House, 1994)—that contains a chapter entitled "The Curse of Columbus"—which blames him for the horrors of the transatlantic slave trade. David Stannard, *American Holocaust: Columbus and the Conquest of the New World* (oxford University press, 1992) goes so far as to hold Columbus responsible for the genocidal acts committed against Native American populations. Kirkpatrick Sale's *The Conquest of Paradise: Christopher Columbus and the Columbian Legacy* (Penguin Books, 1991) takes a more philosophical approach, but still considers Columbus's legacy to be a negative one, especially as far as the environment is concerned.

Columbus has not been without support. The late Italian historian Paolo Emilio Taviani (1913–2001), in *Columbus: The Great Adventure: His Life, His Times, and His Voyages* (Orion Books, 1991) makes a passionate plea for history to view the positive side of the Columbus legacy. Several articles do the same, including: Robert Royal, "Columbus as a Dead White Male: the Ideological Underpinnings of the Controversy over 1492." *The world and I* (December, 1991); Dinesh D'Sousa, "The Crimes of Christopher Columbus," *First Things* (November, 1995); Michael Marshall, "Columbus and the Age of Exploration," *The World And I* (November, 1999).

ISSUE 6

Was the Scientific Revolution Revolutionary?

YES: Edward Grant, from "When Did Modern Science Begin?" *American Scholar* (Winter 1997)

NO: Steven Shapin, from *The Scientific Revolution* (University of Chicago Press, 1996)

ISSUE SUMMARY

YES: Distinguished professor emeritus of history and philosophy of science Edward Grant argues that there was a revolution in science that took place in the seventeenth century; however, it might have been delayed by centuries if several key developments between 1175 and 1500 had not paved the way for it.

NO: Professor of sociology and historian of science Steven Shapin questions the idea of a Scientific Revolution, suggesting greater continuity with the past and rejecting a single time/space event we might call a Scientific Revolution.

When you open a history textbook, you will find it conveniently divided into chapters and units with titles that mark the major turning points of history. One of those titles in a text on World History or Western Civilization is likely to be The Scientific Revolution. Known as periodization, this tendency of historians to provide interpretive groupings of events has recently been subjected to reappraisal. If "where you stand determines what you see," then the very act of labeling periods of history makes judgments about what is important and valuable.

The assumption behind periodization is that there are moments when the path of history is re-routed, when a sharp break with the past leads to a new kind of experience or a new way of understanding the world. One of the questions historians must ask, therefore, is whether a particular event or series of events represents primarily continuity with the past or discontinuity from it. Traditional periodization has seen the Scientific Revolution as a classic example of discontinuity—as a sharp break with the medieval past and the ushering in of the modern world. Recently, however, historians have taken a fresh look at the late sixteenth and early seventeenth centuries and wondered how scientific and how revolutionary this period actually was.

A danger historians must also remain alert to is called presentism, the tendency to judge and interpret the past by the standards and concerns of the present. From the perspective of the early twenty-first century, for example, we might be tempted to emphasize progress, as the Industrial Revolution replaced backbreaking labor with the power of machines. People who actually lived through these changes, by contrast, might have focused on the breakup of the productive family unit in the home, as individuals left the home to do wage work. Two questions we must ask ourselves are: Did Europeans living in the seventeenth century experience revolutionary changes? and How much of a break with the past did the scientific discoveries of that century represent?

For Edward Grant, there was undoubtedly a Scientific Revolution. He sees the fields of astronomy, cosmology, and physics undergoing "momentous changes" over the sixteenth and seventeenth centuries. However, he also documents a series of events—the translation of Greek and Arabic scientific/philosophical works into Latin, the formation of the medieval university, and the emergence of a class of theologian/natural philosophers—without which the scientific revolution would not have occurred when it did.

Steven Shapin begins with a boldly revisionist declaration: "There was no such thing as the Scientific Revolution." Reflecting a postmodern view of the world, Shapin questions whether or not it is even possible to speak about an "essence" of something called "science." Instead of a single, discrete entity, he sees a wide variety of ways of understanding, explaining, and controlling the natural world. If we list the characteristics of the so-called revolution, Shapin believes we will find that experimental method, mathematical approaches, and even mechanical conceptions of nature were both advocated and rejected by people who thought of themselves as scientists.

Both Grant and Shapin acknowledge continuity with the medieval past rather than a radical break from it. And, both would agree that the past did not become the "modern world" at a single historical moment. Where they differ, is that Grant does see a seventeenth-century turning point—although rooted in a steady forward progression—whereas, Shapin insists that every development we might label revolutionary had "significantly variant contemporary forms" or was criticized by contemporaries whom we also regard as revolutionary "moderns."

YES 

Edward Grant

When Did Modern Science Begin?

Although science has a long history with roots in ancient Egypt and Mesopotamia, it is indisputable that modern science emerged in Western Europe and nowhere else. The reasons for this momentous occurrence must, therefore, be sought in some unique set of circumstances that differentiate Western society from other contemporary and earlier civilizations. The establishment of science as a basic enterprise within a society depends on more than expertise in technical scientific subjects, experiments, and disciplined observations. After all, science can be found in many early societies. In Islam, until approximately 1500, mathematics, astronomy, geometric optics, and medicine were more highly developed than in the West. But science was not institutionalized in Islamic society. Nor was it institutionalized in ancient and medieval China, despite significant achievements. Similar arguments apply to all other societies and civilizations. Science can be found in many of them but was institutionalized and perpetuated in none.

Why did science as we know it today materialize only in Western society? What made it possible for science to acquire prestige and influence and to become a powerful force in Western Europe by the seventeenth century? The answer, I believe, lies in certain fundamental events that occurred in Western Europe during the period from approximately 1175 to 1500. Those events, taken together, should be viewed as forming the foundations of modern science, a judgment that runs counter to prevailing scholarly opinion, which holds that modern science emerged in the seventeenth century by repudiating and abandoning medieval science and natural philosophy, the latter based on the works of Aristotle.

The scientific revolution appeared first in astronomy, cosmology, and physics in the course of the sixteenth and seventeenth centuries. Whether or not the achievements of medieval science exercised any influence on these developments is irrelevant. What must be emphasized, however, is that the momentous changes in the exact sciences of physics and astronomy that epitomized the scientific revolution did not develop from a vacuum. They could not have occurred without certain foundational events that were unique products of the late Middle Ages. To realize this, we must inquire whether a scientific revolution could have occurred in the seventeenth century if the level of science in Western Europe had remained much as it was in the first half of the twelfth century, before the transformation that occurred as a consequence of

Reprinted from *The American Scholar,* Volume 66, No. 1, Winter 1997.

a great wave of translations from the Greek and Arabic languages into Latin that began around 1150 and continued on to the end of the thirteenth century. Could a scientific revolution have occurred in the seventeenth century if the immense translations of Greco-Arabic (or Greco-Islamic) science and natural philosophy into Latin had never taken place? Obviously not. Without those translations many centuries would have been required before Western Europe could have reached the level of Greco-Arabic science. Instead of the scientific revolution of the seventeenth century, our descendants might look back upon a "Scientific Revolution of the Twenty-first Century." But the translations did occur in the twelfth and thirteenth centuries, and so did a scientific revolution in the seventeenth century. It follows that something happened between, say, 1175 and 1500 that paved the way for that scientific revolution. What that "something" was is my subject here.

To describe how the late Middle Ages in Western Europe played a role in producing the scientific revolution in the physical sciences during the seventeenth century; two aspects of science need to be distinguished, the contextual and the substantive. The first—the contextual-involves changes that created an atmosphere conducive to the establishment of science, made it feasible to pursue science and natural philosophy on a permanent basis, and made those pursuits laudable activities within Western society. The second aspect—the substantive—pertains to certain features of medieval science and natural philosophy that were instrumental in bringing about the scientific revolution.

The creation of an environment in the Middle Ages that eventually made a scientific revolution possible involved at least three crucial preconditions. The first of these was the translation of Greco-Arabic science and natural philosophy into Latin during the twelfth and thirteenth centuries. Without this initial, indispensable precondition, the other two might not have occurred. With the transfer of this large body of learning to the Western world, the old science of the early Middle Ages was overwhelmed and superseded. Although modern science might eventually have developed in the West without the introduction of Greco-Arabic science, its advent would have been delayed by centuries.

The second precondition was the formation of the medieval university, with its corporate structure and control over its varied activities. The universities that emerged by the thirteenth century in Paris, Oxford, and Bologna were different from anything the world had ever seen. From these beginnings, the medieval university took root and has endured as an institution for some eight hundred years, being transformed in time into a worldwide phenomenon. Nothing in Islam or China, or India, or in the ancient civilizations of South America is comparable to the medieval university. It is in this remarkable institution, and its unusual activities, that the foundations of modern science must be sought.

The university was possible in the Middle Ages because the evolution of medieval Latin society allowed for the separate existence of church and state, each of which, in turn, recognized the independence of corporate entities, the university among them. The first universities, of Paris, Oxford, and Bologna, were in existence by approximately 1200, shortly after most of the translations had been completed. The translations furnished a ready-made curriculum to the emerging universities, a curriculum that was overwhelmingly composed of the exact sciences, logic, and natural philosophy.

The curriculum of science, logic, and natural philosophy established in the medieval universities of Western Europe was a permanent fixture for approximately 450 to 500 years. It was the curriculum of the arts faculty, which was the largest of the traditional four faculties of a typical major university, the others being medicine, theology, and law. Courses in logic, natural philosophy, geometry, and astronomy formed the core curriculum for the baccalaureate and master of arts degrees and were taught on a regular basis for centuries. These two arts degrees were virtual prerequisites for entry into the higher disciplines of law, medicine, and theology.

For the first time in the history of the world, an institution had been created for teaching science, natural philosophy, and logic. An extensive four-to-six-year course in higher education was based on those subjects, with natural philosophy as the most important component. As universities multiplied during the thirteenth to fifteenth centuries, the same science-natural philosophy-logic curriculum was disseminated throughout Europe, extending as far east as Poland.

The science curriculum could not have been implemented without the explicit approval of church and state. To a remarkable extent, both granted to the universities corporate powers to regulate themselves: universities had the legal right to determine their own curricula, to establish criteria for the degrees of their students, and to determine the teaching fitness of their faculty members.

Despite some difficulties and tensions between natural philosophy and theology—between, essentially, reason and revelation—arts masters and theologians at the universities welcomed the arrival of Aristotle's natural philosophy as evidenced by the central role they gave it in higher education. Why did they do this? Why did a Christian society at the height of the Catholic Church's power readily adopt a pagan natural philosophy as the basis of a four-to-six-year education? Why didn't Christians fear and resist such pagan fare rather than embrace it?

Because Christians had long ago come to terms with pagan thought and were agreed, for the most part, that they had little or nothing to fear from it. The rapprochement between Christianity and pagan literature, especially philosophy, may have been made feasible by the slowness with which Christianity was disseminated. The spread of Christianity beyond the Holy Land and its surrounding region began in earnest after Saint Paul proselytized the Gentile world, especially Greece, during the middle of the first century. In retrospect—and by comparison with the spread of Islam—the pace of the dissemination of Christianity appears quite slow. Not until 300 A.D. was Christianity effectively represented throughout the Roman Empire. And not until 313, in the reign of Constantine, was the Edict of Milan (or Edict of Toleration) issued, which conferred on Christianity full legal equality with all other religions in the Empire. In 392, Christianity was made the state religion of the Roman Empire. In that year, the Emperor Theodosius ordered all pagan temples closed, and also prohibited pagan worship, thereafter classified as treason. Thus it was not until 392 that Christianity became the exclusive religion supported by the state. After almost four centuries of existence, Christianity was triumphant.

By contrast, Islam, following the death of Mohammad in 632, was carried over an enormous geographical area in a remarkably short time. In less than one hundred years, it was the dominant religion from the Arabian peninsula westward to the Straits of Gibraltar, northward to Spain and eastward to Persia, and beyond. But where Islam was largely spread by conquest during its first hundred years, Christianity spread slowly and, with the exception of certain periods of persecution, relatively peacefully. It was this slow percolation of Christianity that enabled it to come to terms with the pagan world and thus prepare itself for a role that could not have been envisioned by its early members.

The time it took before Christianity became the state religion enabled Christianity to adjust to the pagan society around it. In the second half of the third century, Christian apologists concluded that Christianity could profitably utilize pagan Greek philosophy and learning. In a momentous move, Clement of Alexandria (ca. 150–ca. 215) and his disciple Origen of Alexandria (ca. 185–ca. 254) laid down the basic approach that others would follow. Greek philosophy, they argued, was not inherently good or bad, but one or the other depending on how it was used by Christians. Although the Greek poets and philosophers had not received direct revelation from God, they did receive natural reason and were therefore pointed toward truth. Philosophy—and secular learning in general—could thus be used to interpret Christian wisdom, which was the fruit of revelation. They were agreed that philosophy and science could be used as "handmaidens to theology"—that is, as aids to understanding Holy Scripture—an attitude that had already been advocated by Philo Judaeus, a resident of the Jewish community of Alexandria, early in the first century A.D.

The "handmaiden" concept of Greek learning became the standard Christian attitude toward secular learning by the middle of the fourth century. That Christians chose to accept pagan learning within limits was a momentous decision. They might have heeded the words of Tertullian (ca. 150–ca. 225), who asked pointedly: "What indeed has Athens to do with Jerusalem? What concord is there between the Academy and the Church?" With the total triumph of Christianity at the end of the fourth century, the Church might have reacted adversely toward Greek pagan learning in general, and Greek philosophy in particular, since there was much in the latter that was offensive to the Church. They might even have launched a major effort to suppress pagan thought as a danger to the Church and its doctrines. But they did not.

The handmaiden theory was obviously a compromise between the rejection of traditional pagan learning and its full acceptance. By approaching secular learning with caution, Christians could utilize Greek philosophy—especially metaphysics and logic—to better understand and explicate Holy

Scripture and to cope with the difficulties generated by the assumption of the doctrine of the Trinity and other esoteric dogmas. Ordinary daily life also required use of the mundane sciences such as astronomy and mathematics. Christians came to realize that they could not turn away from Greek learning.

When Christians in Western Europe became aware of Greco-Arabic scientific literature and were finally prepared to receive it in the twelfth century, they did so eagerly. They did not view it as a body of subversive knowledge. Despite a degree of resistance that was more intense at some times than at others, Aristotle's works were made the basis of the university curriculum by 1255 in Paris, and long before that at Oxford.

The emergence of a class of theologian-natural philosophers was the third essential precondition for the scientific revolution. Their major contribution was to sanction the introduction and use of Aristotelian natural philosophy in the curriculum of the new universities. Without that approval, natural philosophy and science could not have become the curriculum of the medieval universities. The development of a class of theologian-natural philosophers must be regarded as extraordinary. Not only did most theologians approve of an essentially secular arts curriculum, but they were convinced that natural philosophy was essential for the elucidation of theology. Students entering schools of theology were expected to have achieved a high level of competence in natural philosophy. Since a master of arts degree, or the equivalent thereof, signified a thorough background in Aristotelian natural philosophy, and since a master's degree in the arts was usually a prerequisite for admittance to the higher faculty of theology, almost all theologians can be said to have acquired extensive knowledge of natural philosophy. Many undoubtedly regarded it as worthy of study in itself and not merely because of its traditional role as the handmaiden of theology. . . .

Medieval natural philosophers investigated the "common course of nature," not its uncommon, or miraculous, path. They characterized this approach, admirably, by the phrase "speaking naturally" (loquendo naturaliter)—that is, speaking by means of natural science, and not by means of faith or theology. That such an expression should have emerged, and come into common usage in medieval natural philosophy, is a tribute to the scholars who took as their primary mission the explanation of the structure and operation of the world in purely rational and secular terms.

The widespread assumption of "natural impossibilities" or counterfactuals—or, as they are sometimes called, "thought-experiments"—was a significant aspect of medieval methodology. An occurrence would have been considered naturally impossible" if it was thought inconceivable for it to occur within the accepted framework of Aristotelian physics and cosmology. The frequent use of natural impossibilities derived largely from the powerful medieval concept of God's absolute power, in which it was conceded that God could do anything whatever short of a logical contradiction. In the Middle Ages, such thinking resulted in conclusions that challenged certain aspects of Aristotle's physics. Where Aristotle had shown that other worlds were impossible, medieval scholastics showed not only that the existence of other worlds was possible, but that they would be compatible with our world.

The novel replies that emerged from the physics and cosmology of counterfactuals did not cause the overthrow of the Aristotelian world-view, but they did challenge some of its fundamental principles. They made many aware that things could be quite different from what was dreamt of in Aristotle's philosophy. But they accomplished more than that. Not only did some of the problems and solutions continue to influence scholastic authors in the sixteenth and seventeenth centuries, but this characteristically medieval approach also influenced significant non-scholastics, who reveal an awareness of the topics debated by scholastics.

One of the most fruitful ideas that passed from the Middle Ages to the seventeenth century is the concept of God annihilating matter and leaving behind a vacuum—a concept used effectively by John Locke, Pierre Gassendi, and Thomas Hobbes in their discussions of space.

A famous natural impossibility derived from a proposition condemned in 1277. As a consequence, it was mandatory after 1277 to concede that God could move our spherical world rectilinearly, despite the vacuum that might be left behind. More than an echo of this imaginary manifestation of God's absolute power reverberated through the seventeenth century, when Pierre Gassendi and Samuel Clarke (in his famous dispute with Leibniz) found it useful to appeal to God's movement of the world. In medieval intellectual culture, where observation and experiment played negligible roles, counterfactuals were a powerful tool because they emphasized metaphysics, logic, theology, and the imagination—the very areas in which medieval natural philosophers excelled.

The scientific methodologies described here produced new conceptualizations and assumptions about the world. Ideas about nature's simplicity, its common course, as well as the use of counterfactuals, emphasized new and important ways to think about nature. Galileo and his fellow scientific revolutionaries inherited these attitudes, and most would have subscribed to them.

Another legacy from the Middle Ages to early modern science was an extensive and sophisticated body of terms that formed the basis of later scientific discourse such terms as potential, actual, substance, property, accident, cause, analogy, matter, form, essence, genus, species, relation, quantity, quality, place, vacuum, infinite, and many others. These Aristotelian terms formed a significant component of scholastic natural philosophy. The language of medieval natural philosophy, however, did not consist solely of translated Aristotelian terms. New concepts, terms, and definitions were added in the fourteenth century, most notably in the domains of change and motion. Definitions of uniform motion, uniformly accelerated motion, and instantaneous motion were added to the lexicon of natural philosophy. By the seventeenth century, these terms, concepts, and definitions were embedded in the language and thought of European natural philosophers.

Medieval natural philosophy played another momentous role in the transition to early modern science. It furnished some—if, it is true, not many—of the basic problems that exercised the minds of non-scholastic natural philosophers in the sixteenth and seventeenth centuries. Medieval natural philosophers produced hundreds of specific questions about nature, the answers to which included a vast amount of scientific information. Most of the questions had multiple answers, with no genuine way of choosing between them. In the sixteenth and seventeenth centuries, new solutions were proposed by scholars who found Aristotelian answers unacceptable, or, at best, inadequate. The changes they made, however, were mostly in the answers, not in the questions. The scientific revolution was not the result of new questions put to nature in place of medieval questions. It was, at least initially, more a matter of finding new answers to old questions, answers that came, more and more, to include experiments, which were exceptional occurrences in the Middle Ages. Although the solutions differed, many fundamental problems were common to both groups. Beginning around 1200, medieval natural philosophers, largely located at European universities, exhibited an unprecedented concern for the nature and structure of the physical world. The contributors to the scientific revolution continued the same tradition, because by then these matters had become an integral part of intellectual life in Western society.

The Middle Ages did not just transmit a great deal of significantly modified, traditional, natural philosophy, much of it in the form of questions; it also conveyed a remarkable tradition of relatively free, rational inquiry. The medieval philosophical tradition was fashioned in the faculties of arts of medieval universities. Natural philosophy was their domain, and almost from the outset masters of arts struggled to establish as much academic freedom as possible. They sought to preserve and expand the study of philosophy. Arts masters regarded themselves as the guardians of natural philosophy and fought for the right to apply reason to all problems about the physical world. By virtue of their independent status as a faculty, with numerous rights and privileges, they achieved a surprisingly large degree of freedom during the Middle Ages.

Theology was always a potential obstacle, true, but in practice theologians offered little opposition, largely because they, too, were heavily imbued with natural philosophy. By the end of the thirteenth century, the arts faculty had attained virtual independence from the theological faculty. By then, philosophy and its major subdivision, natural philosophy, had emerged as an independent discipline based in the arts faculties of European universities. True, arts masters were always subject to restraints with regard to religious dogma, but the subject areas where such issues arose were limited. During the thirteenth century, arts masters had learned how to cope with the problematic aspects of Aristotle's thought. They treated those problems hypothetically, or announced that they were merely repeating Aristotle's opinions, even as they offered elaborations of his arguments. During the Middle Ages, natural philosophy remained what Aristotle had made it: an essentially secular and rational discipline. It remained so only because the arts faculty struggled to preserve it. In doing so, they transformed natural philosophy into an independent discipline that embraced as well as glorified the rational investigation of all problems relevant to the physical world. In the 1330s, William of Ockham expressed the sentiments of most arts masters and many theologians when he declared:

> Assertions . . . concerning natural philosophy, which do not pertain to theology, should not be solemnly condemned or forbidden to anyone, since in such matters everyone should be free to say freely whatever he pleases.

Everyone who did natural philosophy in the sixteenth and seventeenth centuries was the beneficiary of these remarkable developments. The spirit of free inquiry nourished by medieval natural philosophers formed part of the intellectual heritage of all who engaged in scientific investigation. Most, of course, were unaware of their legacy and would probably have denied its existence, preferring to heap ridicule and scorn on Aristotelian scholastics and scholasticism. That ridicule was not without justification. It was time to alter the course of medieval natural philosophy.

Some Aristotelian natural philosophers tried to accommodate the new heliocentric astronomy that had emerged from the brilliant efforts of Copernicus, Tycho Brahe, and Galileo. By then, accommodation was no longer sufficient. Medieval natural philosophy was destined to vanish by the end of the seventeenth century. The medieval scholastic legacy, however, remained—namely, the spirit of free inquiry, the emphasis on reason, a variety of approaches to nature, and the core of legitimate problems that would occupy the attention of the new science. Inherited from the Middle Ages, too, was the profound sense that all of these activities were legitimate and important, that discovering the way the world operated was a laudable undertaking. These enormous achievements were accomplished in the late Middle Ages, between 1175 and 1500.

To illustrate how medieval contributions to the new science ought to be viewed, let me draw upon an analogy from the Middle Ages. In the late thirteenth century in Italy, the course of the history of medicine was altered significantly when human dissection was allowed for postmortems and was shortly afterward introduced into medical schools, where it soon became institutionalized as part of the anatomical training of medical students. Except in ancient Egypt, human dissection had been forbidden in the ancient world. By the second century A.D., it was also banned in Egypt. It was never permitted in the Islamic world. Its introduction into the Latin West marked a new beginning, made without serious objection from the Church. It was a momentous event. Dissection of cadavers was used primarily in teaching, albeit irregularly until the end of the fifteenth century. Rarely, if at all, was it employed to enhance scientific knowledge of the human body. The revival of human dissection and its incorporation into medical training throughout the Middle Ages laid a foundation for what was to come.

Without it, we cannot imagine the significant anatomical progress that was made by such keen anatomists as Leonardo da Vinci (1452–1519), Bartolommeo Eustachio (1520–74), Andreas Vesalius (1514–64), and many others.

What human dissection did for medicine, the translations, the universities, the theologian-natural philosophers, and the medieval version of Aristotelian natural philosophy did collectively for the scientific revolution of the seventeenth century. These vital features of medieval science formed a foundation that made possible a continuous, uninterrupted eight hundred years of scientific development, a development that began in Western Europe and spread around the world.

Steven Shapin

NO

The Scientific Revolution

The Scientific Revolution: The History of a Term

There was no such thing as the Scientific Revolution, and this [selection is from] a book about it. Some time ago, when the academic world offered more certainty and more comforts, historians announced the real existence of a coherent, cataclysmic, and climactic event that fundamentally and irrevocably changed what people knew about the natural world and how they secured proper knowledge of that world. It was the moment at which the world was made modern, it was a Good Thing, and it happened sometime during the period from the late sixteenth to the early eighteenth century. In 1943 the French historian Alexandre Koyré celebrated the conceptual changes at the heart of the Scientific Revolution as "the most profound revolution achieved or suffered by the human mind" since Greek antiquity. It was a revolution so profound that human culture "for centuries did not grasp its bearing or meaning; which, even now, is often misvalued and misunderstood." A few years later the English historian Herbert Butterfield famously judged that the Scientific Revolution "outshines everything since the rise of Christianity and reduces the Renaissance and Reformation to the rank of mere episodes. . . . [It is] the real origin both of the modern world and of the modern mentality." It was, moreover, construed as a conceptual revolution, a fundamental reordering of our ways of *thinking* about the natural. In this respect, a story about the Scientific Revolution might be adequately told through an account of radical changes in the fundamental categories of thought. To Butterfield, the mental changes making up the Scientific Revolution were equivalent to "putting on a new pair of spectacles." And to A. Rupert Hall it was nothing less than "an *a priori* redefinition of the objects of philosophical and scientific inquiry."

This conception of the Scientific Revolution is now encrusted with tradition. Few historical episodes present themselves as more substantial or more self-evidently worthy of study. There is an established place for accounts of the Scientific Revolution in the Western liberal curriculum, and this [selection] is an attempt to fill that space economically and to invite further curiosity about the making of early modern science. Nevertheless, like many twentieth-century "traditions," that contained in the notion of the Scientific Revolution is not nearly as old as we might think. The phrase "the Scientific Revolution" was probably coined by Alexandre Koyré in 1939, and it first became a book title in

A. Rupert Hall's *The Scientific Revolution* of 1954. Before that time there was no event to be studied in the liberal curriculum, nor any discrete object of historical inquiry, called the Scientific Revolution. Although many seventeenth-century practitioners expressed their intention of bringing about radical intellectual change, the people who are said to have made the revolution used no such term to refer to what they were doing.

From antiquity through the early modern period, a "revolution" invoked the idea of a periodically recurring cycle. In Copernicus's new astronomy of the mid-sixteenth century, for example, the planets completed their revolutions round the sun, while references to political revolutions gestured at the notion of ebbs and flows or cycles—fortune's wheel—in human affairs. The idea of revolution as a radical and irreversible reordering developed together with linear, unidirectional conceptions of time. In this newer conception revolution was not recurrence but its reverse, the bringing about of a new state of affairs that the world had never witnessed before and might never witness again. Not only this notion of revolution but also the beginnings of an idea of revolution in science date from the eighteenth-century writings of French Enlightenment philosophes who liked to portray themselves, and their disciplines, as radical subverters of ancient régime culture. (Some . . . seventeenth-century writers . . . saw themselves not as bringing about totally new states of affairs but as restoring or purifying old ones.) The notion of a revolution as epochal and irreversible change, it is possible, was first applied in a systematic way to events in science and only later to political events. In just this sense, the first revolutions may have been scientific, and the "American," "French," and "Russian Revolutions" are its progeny.

As our understanding of science in the seventeenth century has changed in recent years, so historians have become increasingly uneasy with the very idea of "the Scientific Revolution." Even the legitimacy of each word making up that phrase has been individually contested. Many historians are now no longer satisfied that there was any singular and discrete event, localized in time and space, that can be pointed to as "the" Scientific Revolution. Such historians now reject even the notion that there was any single coherent cultural entity called "science" in the seventeenth century to undergo revolutionary change. There was, rather, a diverse array of cultural practices aimed at understanding, explaining, and controlling the natural world, each with different characteristics and each experiencing different modes of change. We are now much more dubious of claims that there is anything like "a scientific method"—a coherent, universal, and efficacious set of procedures for making scientific knowledge—and still more skeptical of stories that locate its origin in the seventeenth century, from which time it has been unproblematically passed on to us. And many historians do not now accept that the changes wrought on scientific beliefs and practices during the seventeenth century were as "revolutionary" as has been widely portrayed. The continuity of seventeenth-century natural philosophy with its medieval past is now routinely asserted, while talk of "delayed" eighteenth- and nineteenth-century revolutions in chemistry and biology followed hard upon historians' identification of "the" original Scientific Revolution.

Why Write About the Scientific Revolution?

There are still other reasons for historians' present uneasiness with the category of the Scientific Revolution as it has been customarily construed. First, historians have in recent years become dissatisfied with the traditional manner of treating ideas as if they floated freely in conceptual space. Although previous accounts framed the Scientific Revolution in terms of autonomous ideas or disembodied mentalities, more recent versions have insisted on the importance of situating ideas in their wider cultural and social context. We now hear more than we used to about the relations between the scientific changes of the seventeenth century and changes in religious, political, and economic patterns. More fundamentally, some historians now wish to understand the concrete human *practices* by which ideas or concepts are made. What did people *do* when they made or confirmed an observation, proved a theorem, performed an experiment? An account of the Scientific Revolution as a history of free-floating concepts is a very different animal from a history of concept-making practices. Finally, historians have become much more interested in the "who" of the Scientific Revolution. What kinds of people wrought such changes? Did everyone believe as they did, or only a very few? And if only a very few took part in these changes, in what sense, if at all, can we speak of the Scientific Revolution as effecting massive changes in how "we" view the world, as the moment when modernity was made, for "us"? The cogency of such questions makes for problems in writing as unreflectively as we used to about the Scientific Revolution. Responding to them means that we need an account of changes in early modern science appropriate for our less confident, but perhaps more intellectually curious, times.

Yet despite these legitimate doubts and uncertainties there remains a sense in which it is possible to write about the Scientific Revolution unapologetically and in good faith. There are two major considerations to bear in mind here. The first is that many key figures in the late sixteenth and seventeenth centuries vigorously expressed *their* view that they were proposing some very new and very important changes in knowledge of natural reality and in the practices by which legitimate knowledge was to be secured, assessed, and communicated. They identified *themselves* as "moderns" set against "ancient" modes of thought and practice. Our sense of radical change afoot comes substantially from them (and those who were the object of their attacks), and is not simply the creation of mid-twentieth-century historians. So we can say that the seventeenth century witnessed some self-conscious and large-scale attempts to change belief, and ways of securing belief, about the natural world. And a book about the Scientific Revolution can legitimately tell a story about those attempts, whether or not they succeeded, whether or not they were contested in the local culture, whether or not they were wholly coherent.

But why do we tell *these* stories instead of others? If different sorts of seventeenth-century people believed different things about the world, how do we assemble our cast of characters and associated beliefs? Some "natural philosophers," for example, advocated rational theorizing, while others pushed a program of relatively atheoretical fact collecting and experimentation.

Mathematical physics was, for example, a very different sort of practice from botany. There were importantly different versions of what it was to do astronomy and believe as an astronomer believed; the relations between the "proper sciences" of astronomy and chemistry and the "pseudosciences" of astrology and alchemy were intensely problematic; and even the category of "nature" as the object of inquiry was understood in radically different ways by different sorts of practitioners. This point cannot be stressed too strongly. The cultural practices subsumed in the category of the Scientific Revolution—however it has been construed—are not coextensive with early modern, or seventeenth-century, science. Historians differ about which practices were "central" to the Scientific Revolution, and participants themselves argued about which practices produced genuine knowledge and which had been fundamentally reformed.

More fundamentally for criteria of selection, it ought to be understood that "most people"—even most educated people—in the seventeenth century did not believe what expert scientific practitioners believed, and the sense in which "people's" thought about the world was revolutionized at that time is very limited. There should be no doubt whatever that one could write a convincing history of seventeenth-century thought about nature without even *mentioning* the Scientific Revolution as traditionally construed.

The very idea of the Scientific Revolution, therefore, is at least partly an expression of "our" interest in our ancestors, where "we" are late twentieth century scientists and those for whom what they believe counts as truth about the natural world. And this interest provides the second legitimate justification for writing about the Scientific Revolution. Historians of science have now grown used to condemning "present-oriented" history, rightly saying that it often distorts our understanding of what the past was like in its own terms. Yet there is absolutely no reason we should not want to know how we got from there to here, who the ancestors were, and what the lineage is that connects us to the past. In this sense a story about the seventeenth-century Scientific Revolution can be an account of those changes that we think led on—never directly or simply, to be sure—to certain features of the present in which, for certain purposes, we happen to be interested. To do this would be an expression of just the same sort of legitimate historical interest displayed by Darwinian evolutionists telling stories about those branches of the tree of life that led to human beings—without assuming in any way that such stories are adequate accounts of what life was like hundreds of thousands of years ago. There is nothing at all wrong about telling such stories, though one must always be careful not to claim too much scope for them. Stories about the ancestors as ancestors are not likely to be sensitive accounts of how it was in the past: the lives and thoughts of Galileo, Descartes, or Boyle were hardly typical of seventeenth-century Italians, Frenchmen, or Englishmen, and telling stories about them geared solely to their ancestral role in formulating the currently accepted law of free fall, the optics of the rainbow, or the ideal gas law is not likely to capture very much about the meaning and significance of their own careers and projects in the seventeenth century.

The past is not transformed into the "modern world" at any single moment: we should never be surprised to find that seventeenth-century scientific practitioners often had about them as much of the ancient as the modern; their notions had to be successively transformed and redefined by generations of thinkers to become "ours." And finally, the people, the thoughts, and the practices we tell stories about as "ancestors," or as the beginnings of our lineage, always reflect some present-day interest. That we tell stories about Galileo, Boyle, Descartes, and Newton reflects something about our late twentieth-century scientific beliefs and what we value about those beliefs. For different purposes we could trace aspects of the modern world back to philosophers "vanquished" by Galileo, Boyle, Descartes, and Newton, and to views of nature and knowledge very different from those elaborated by our officially sanctioned scientific ancestors. For still other purposes we could make much of the fact that most seventeenth-century people had never heard of our scientific ancestors and probably entertained beliefs about the natural world very different from those of our chosen forebears. Indeed, the overwhelming majority of seventeenth century people did not live in Europe, did not know that they lived in "the seventeenth century," and were not aware that a Scientific Revolution was happening. The half of the European population that was female was in a position to participate in scientific culture scarcely at all, as was that overwhelming majority—of men and women—who were illiterate or otherwise disqualified from entering the venues of formal learning.

Some Historiographical Issues

I mean this [selection] to be historiographically up to date—drawing on some of the most recent historical, sociological, and philosophical engagements with the Scientific Revolution. On the other hand, I do not mean to trouble readers with repeated references to methodological and conceptual debates among academics. This [selection] is not written for professional specialized scholars. . . . There is no reason to deny that this story about the Scientific Revolution represents a particular point of view, and that, although I help myself freely to the work of many distinguished scholars, its point of view is my own. Other specialists will doubtless disagree with my approach—some vehemently—and a large number of existing accounts do offer a quite different perspective on what is worth telling about the Scientific Revolution. The positions represented here on some recent historiographic issues can be briefly summarized:

1. I *take for granted* that science is a historically situated and social activity and that it is to be understood in relation to the *contexts* in which it occurs. Historians have long argued whether science relates to its historical and social contexts or whether it should be treated in isolation. I shall simply write about seventeenth-century science as if it were a collectively practiced, historically embedded phenomenon, inviting readers to see whether the account is plausible, coherent, and interesting.

2. For a long time, historians' debates over the propriety of a sociological and a historically "contextual" approach to science seemed to divide practitioners between those who drew attention to what were called "intellectual factors"—ideas, concepts, methods, evidence—and those who stressed "social

factors"—forms of organization, political and economic influences on science, and social uses or consequences of science. That now seems to many historians, as it does to me, a rather silly demarcation, and I shall not waste readers' time here in reviewing why those disputes figured so largely in past approaches to the history of early modern science. If science is to be understood as historically situated and in its collective aspect (i.e., sociologically), then that understanding should encompass all aspects of science, its ideas and practices no less than its institutional forms and social uses. Anyone who wants to represent science sociologically cannot simply set aside the body of what the relevant practitioners *knew* and how they went about obtaining that knowledge. Rather, the task for the sociologically minded historian is to display the structure of knowledge making and knowledge holding *as social processes*.

3. A traditional construal of "social factors" (or what is sociological about science) has focused on considerations taken to be "external" to science proper—for example, the use of metaphors from the economy in the development of scientific knowledge or the ideological uses of science in justifying certain sorts of political arrangements. Much fine historical work has been done based on such a construal. However, the identification of what is sociological about science with what is external to science appears to me a curious and a limited way of going on. There is as much "society" inside the scientist's laboratory, and internal to the development of scientific knowledge, as there is "outside." And in fact the very distinction between the social and the political, on the one hand, and "scientific truth," on the other, is partly a cultural product of the period [I discuss]. What is common sensically thought of as science in the late twentieth century is in some measure a product of the historical episodes we want to understand here. Far from matter-of-factly treating the distinction between the social and the scientific as a resource in telling a historical story, I mean to make it into a topic of inquiry. How and why did we come to think that such a distinction is a matter *of course?*

4. I do not consider that there is anything like an "essence" of seventeenth-century science or indeed of seventeenth-century reforms in science. Consequently there is no single coherent story that could possibly capture all the aspects of science or its changes in which we late twentieth-century moderns might happen to be interested. I can think of no feature of early modern science that has been traditionally identified as its revolutionary essence that did not have significantly variant contemporary forms or that was not subjected to contemporary criticism by practitioners who have also been accounted revolutionary "moderns." . . .

The confrontation over Newton's optical work can stand as an emblem of the fragmented knowledge-making legacies of the seventeenth century. A theoretically cautious and experience-based conception of science was here juxtaposed to one that deployed mathematical as well as experimental tools to claim theoretical certainty. Diffidence was opposed to ambition, respect for the concrete particularities of nature to the quest for universally applicable idealizations, the modesty of the fact gatherer to the pride of the abstracted philosopher. Do you want to capture the essence of nature and command assent to representations of its regularities? Do you want to subject yourself to the discipline of describing, and perhaps generalizing about, the behavior of medium-sized objects actually existing in the world?

Both conceptions of science persist in the late twentieth century, and both can trace elements of their formation back to the seventeenth century. The one is not necessarily to be regarded as a failed version of the other, however much partisans may defend the virtues of their preferred practice and condemn the vices of another. These are, so to speak, different games that natural philosophers might wish to play, and decisions about which game is best are different in kind from decisions about what is a sensible move within a given game: an accurate pass from midfield to the winger in soccer is not a bad jump shot in basketball. In the seventeenth century natural philosophers were confronted with differing repertoires of practical and conceptual skills for achieving various philosophical goals and with choices about which ends they might work to achieve. The goal was always some conception of proper philosophical knowledge about the natural world, though descriptions of what that knowledge looked like and how it was to be secured varied greatly.

POSTSCRIPT

Was the Scientific Revolution Revolutionary?

This question is a philosophical as well as a historical one. At issue are how we understand key terms such as "science" and "revolution" as well as how we interpret what philosophers call epistemology or knowledge theory. Both historians agree that key people in the past understood what they were doing as a break with the past. And, both agree that there are continuities as well as discontinuities. Taking apart texts to reveal their hidden meanings has led many to question whether it is ever possible to have a single, universal meaning for a term like "science." What the word may have meant to people practicing it in the seventeenth century may be worlds away from what it means to people practicing it today. And those of us outside the scientific community in either period generally have even less idea what may be at stake.

Thomas Kuhn, whose widely-read 1962 book *The Structure of Scientific Revolutions* (University of Chicago, 1962, 1970) has shed some light on this controversy, combines continuity with discontinuity. Revolutions, Kuhn writes, are occasional, dramatic breaks from periods of what he calls "normal science" when everyone in the scientific community operates from within an accepted paradigm. Revolutions occur when experiments repeatedly do not yield the expected results or when data do not conform to predicted outcomes. Scientists struggle to make the new material fit the old paradigm; those who challenge the paradigm are marginalized or forced to conform. When it becomes clear that the paradigm has broken down, a new paradigm is accepted. Then everything is explained in terms of the new paradigm. Students are educated in the new paradigm; textbooks are written to reflect it; research takes it as its starting point. Has the world changed or only our way of explaining it to ourselves?

Rethinking the Scientific Revolution, Margaret J. Osler, ed. (Cambridge University Press, 2000) is a collection of fifteen essays; the first defends the traditional image of the Scientific Revolution and the other fourteen challenge it in various ways. In *Ingenious Pursuits: Building the Scientific Revolution* (Doubleday, 1999), Lisa Jardine, a Renaissance scholar, provides thumbnail biographies of major and minor natural scientists. As a general introduction to this subject, students might try *Encyclopedia of the Scientific Revolution: From Copernicus to Newton,* Wilbur Applebaum, ed. (Garland, 2000). In 700 pages, this volume chronicles the extraordinary changes in natural philosophy from the beginning of the sixteenth century to the end of the seventeenth century. It includes the political, religious, social, and technological factors that affected developments in science, biographical selections and some short bibliographies.

ISSUE 7

Was China's Boxer Rebellion Caused by Environmental Factors?

YES: Paul A. Cohen, from *History in Three Keys: The Boxers as Event, Experience, and Myth* (Columbia University Press, 1997)

NO: Henrietta Harrison, from "Justice on Behalf of Heaven: The Boxer Movement," *History Today* (September 2000)

ISSUE SUMMARY

YES: Professor Paul A. Cohen contends that while antiforeign and anti-Christian attitudes played a role in the start of the Boxer rebellion, a more immediate cause was a severe drought and its impact on Chinese society.

NO: Historian Henrietta Harrison concedes that while the Boxers were motivated by more than a single factor, opposition to Christian missionary activity was at the core of their rebellion.

Issue 5 of this volume examines the causes of imperialism, by which the West attempted to extend its influence over the peoples of the non-Western world. This issue provides a case study of the opposition that resulted from imperialism in China: the Boxer rebellion (1898–1900).

Western domination of Asia and Africa took different forms. The establishment of colonialism, which brought direct Western rule to much of Asia and Africa, was the most prevalent. In China, however, geographic size and a large population made this impossible. European nations established "spheres of influence," recognized zones of China that were controlled and exploited by various Western nations. In these areas, China's rule was in name only.

Accompanying those coming to Asia for economic gains were missionaries who came to gain converts for evangelical Christianity. In China, with so many souls to save, this missionary zeal was a powerful force, and to many Chinese, a particularly odious one.

What made this domination of China possible was the weakened nature of the Chinese government. The Manchu dynasty and its Empress Dowager Tsu Hsi appeared to be powerless to stop this Western tidal wave sweeping over the country. When the Chinese did fight back, they were soundly defeated.

During the late 1830s the Chinese government made an attempt control the Western commerce within its borders, especially the opium traded by the British. The latter went to war to guarantee their right to sell the drug in China and won. As a result, the Chinese were forced to grant trade concessions, and a pattern of subservience was established. Any Western nation interested in trade with China would now demand the same deal the British received. In 1857 Britain and France went to war to force China to grant further diplomatic and commercial concessions, and once again the Chinese government was made to accede to their demands.

By the turn of the century, a seemingly intolerable situation became worse, made so by more Western nations becoming involved in Chinese affairs, their increasing demands for further concessions from the Chinese, and the large number of Christian missionaries who had entered China since 1860. These conditions were exacerbated by the Sino-Japanese War (1894–1895), which China lost. The war resulted in the signing of another humiliating treaty. The Chinese government not only seemed powerless to stop Western encroachment; it could not stop the encroachment of one of its Asian neighbors. If China's government was powerless, it was reasoned, perhaps some of China's citizens would have to fight to win back control of their country and bring an end to Western imperialism within its borders. The Boxers were a product of such conditions and concerns.

The Boxer rebellion had its roots in the economically depressed Shandong province, made so by a devastating drought that not only caused massive starvation but brought its people to a psychological breaking point. Many young people turned to secret societies to vent their anger and disillusionment. Eventually they coalesced into a group known as the "Fists of Righteous Harmony." Because its members practiced martial arts, the term *Boxer* was applied to the movement by Westerners. It is a misnomer, which has endured to this day.

The movement began with sporadic attacks in the countryside, aimed primarily at Western missionaries and Chinese converts to Christianity. As the movement grew and its influence spread to some of China's urban centers, many wondered what Tsu Hsi would do. She was under intense pressure from Western officials to suppress the insurrection. But she also recognized in the Boxers a useful tool in fighting against Western influences and restoring Manchu hegemony in China. After a period of fence-straddling, she decided to openly support the Boxer cause. Thus, when the rebellion was suppressed by Western forces, she had to bear responsibility for their actions.

What motivated the Boxers to act as they did seems a simple enough question to answer—they were fighting to rid their country of the "foreign devils" who were causing it irreparable damage. However, some recent scholarship on the subject points to the severe drought and its psychological impact on Chinese society as an overriding factor. In the following selections, Paul A. Cohen stresses the latter, while Henrietta Harrison emphasizes the former.

YES 

Paul A. Cohen

Drought and the Foreign Presence

Drought, Anxiety, and the Spread of the Boxer Movement

Prayer, ... even when offered up by the most powerful people in the realm, does not always work. And, as a drought continues and people become more and more desperate, restlessness, anxiety, and ultimately panic easily set in. To imagine how profound the panic can be among impoverished farmers and poor city folk living in a society with little in the way of a "safety net," it is illuminating to look at the reactions of the newly unemployed in California in the early stages of the recession that began in the latter half of 1990. "The hardest thing," observed the part owner of a small marketing company in Huntington Beach that had recently gone out of business, "is to see how panicked people are.... Right now, I don't have a dime. I'm worried about buying things like sugar. I'm that close to losing my home. Now is when the nerve systems are really going." A young film editor from Hollywood, noting the "prevailing air of uncertainty," expressed a lack of confidence "about the future."

Uncertainty about the future governs virtually all phases of human experience. But it does not always produce anxiety. For anxiety to result, the uncertainty must bear on an aspect of life that is of vital importance: a child's safety, one's performance in a play or a sporting event, the fate of a loved one engaged in combat, the time frame of one's own mortality, the security and dependability of one's livelihood. It was the last-named area of uncertainty that was shared by Californians in 1990 and Chinese farmers in North China almost a century earlier. Different societies, however, are differentially susceptible to the effects of natural or social disasters, and in the case of the drought of 1899–1900 in China (or that of 1899 in western India), because of the absence of a well-functioning crisis support system, it was much more a matter of life and death.

A wide range of sources, including gazetteers, diaries, official memorials, oral history accounts, and the reports of foreigners, indicate a direct link between the spread and intensification of the Boxer movement, beginning in late 1899, and growing popular nervousness, anxiety, unemployment, and hunger occasioned by drought. As early as October 1899, Luella Miner [American Board of Commissioners for Foreign Missions] (ABCFM) identified drought as one cause of growing Boxer-related unrest in northwestern Shandong. In the Beijing area, where for many months very little rain had fallen

From Paul A. Cohen, History in Three keys: The Boxers as Event, Experience, and Myth (Columbia University Press 1997). Notes omitted.

and the wheat seedlings had completely withered, popular feeling was described as unsettled and volatile, owing to drought-induced hunger, and from late April 1900 contagious diseases began to break out with increasing frequency and seriousness. In other parts of Zhili it was much the same. American legation secretary W. E. Bainbridge, noting that during the preceding year "there had been insufficient rain" and that "the entire province was on the verge of famine," concluded that conditions were "peculiarly favorable to its [the Boxer uprising's] friendly reception.... As Spring advanced and early Summer approached with no rains to aid the crops, the excitement ... reached a fever heat." From Zhuozhou, just southwest of Beijing, apprehensions were expressed in early June that, if it did not rain soon, it would become increasingly difficult to control the thousands of Boxers who had gathered in the area. A gentry manager of a *baojia* [local level mutual security system] bureau just west of Tianjin reported that in the spring of 1900 young farmers idled by the drought often took up boxing because they had nothing else to do with their time. The relationship among drought, idleness, and augmented Boxer activity found blunt corroboration in the testimony of a former Boxer from the Tianjin area: "*Gengzi* [1900] was a drought year and there was nothing to do, so we began to practice Yihe Boxing."...

Drought conditions in large areas of Shanxi had by summer 1900 become, if anything, even worse than in Zhili. In many places there had been no rain at all since winter. Farmers were without work. The prices of wheat and rice had shot up. Hunger was widespread and popular anxiety at a high pitch. A missionary report stated that the "organization of the Boxer societies spread rapidly throughout the province when so many were idle because of the drouth." The gazetteers of Qinyuan, Quwo, Lin, Jie, Linjin, Xiangning, and Yuci counties all connected the first emergence of the Boxers in mid- or late June to the protracted drought in their areas. Moreover, it was alleged that famine victims regularly joined in when the Boxers stirred up trouble.

I do not at all want to suggest that the expansion of the Boxer movement in the spring and summer of 1900 was due to drought alone. Within a given area, the official stance toward the Boxers, pro (as in Shanxi) or con (as in Shandong), played a role of perhaps equivalent weight. Nevertheless, drought—and the range of emotions associated with it—was a factor of crucial importance. It is significant, in this connection, that in a number of instances when rain fell to interrupt the drought and possibly bring it to an end, Boxers (as well as Big Sword Society members) dropped everything and returned to their fields. Esherick observes that when "a substantial penetrating rain" fell in early April along the Zhili-Shandong border, peasants went home to plant their spring crops, "quieting things down considerably." After being defeated by the foreign forces in Tianjin during a torrential downpour on July 4, fleeing Boxers are reported to have said to one another: "It's raining. We can return home and till the soil. What use is it for us to suffer like this?" The following day, accordingly, most of them dispersed.

Oral history accounts from Shandong tell a similar story. In late June 1900, during the drought in the western part of the province, a Big Sword Society leader from Zhili named Han Guniang (Miss Han) was invited to a Big

Sword gathering at the hemp market at Longgu, just west of the Juye county seat. Rumored to be a Red Lantern with extraordinary magical powers—it was said that, in addition to being able to withstand swords and spears, "when she mounted a bench it turned into a horse, when she straddled a piece of rope it turned into a dragon, and when she sat on a mat it turned into a cloud on which she could fly"—Han Guniang took charge of food distribution. Within a short time, upwards of a thousand people joined her Big Swords. The grain she handed out had been seized from the supplies of rich families. "After two or threedays,"one account continues, "therewas abig downpour. The next day there were no Big Swords anywhere in sight. They were all gone. The reason these people had come in the first place was to get something to eat. As soon as it rained, they all went back to tend their crops."

Lin Dunkui, who has made a special study of the role of natural disasters in the history of the Boxers, concludes that "from the time of the first outbreak of the Big Sword Society right up to the high tide of the Boxer movement, a sizable number of peasants were prompted to take part in these movements mainly by the weather."...

The Boxer Construction of the Drought

What is fascinating is the degree to which contemporary Chinese—non-Boxers as well as Boxers—also viewed everything that happened in the world, including whether it rained or not, as being in the control of Heaven or "the gods." Indeed, although the Chinese construction of reality differed greatly in specifics from that of the missionaries, in a number of broad respects it formed almost a mirror image of the missionaries' construction. Where the missionaries saw themselves as representatives of the Lord, sometimes describing themselves as "God's soldiers" and often believing quite literally that they had been called by Jesus Christ to go to China to labor for that country's salvation, in jingles repeated and notices circulated throughout North China in 1900 the Boxers were often portrayed, in comparably salvific (as well as martial) terms, as "spirit soldiers"(*shenbing*) sent down from Heaven to carry out a divine mission or, which amounted to the same thing, as mortals whose bodies had been possessed by spirits (thereby rendering them divine) for the identical purpose.

Again, where the missionaries constructed the Boxer movement as a satanic force, whose capacity for evil knew no bounds, the Boxers (and, one presumes, millions of Chinese who were not active participants in the movement) saw the missionaries, and by extension all other foreigners (as well, of course, as Chinese Christians and other Chinese who in one way or another had been tainted by foreign contact), as the root source of evil in their world, the immediate reason for the anger of the gods. The explanation of the drought found in Boxer notices was embedded in a full-blown religious structuring of reality; the notices also provided participants in the movement with a clear program of action designed to mollify the gods and restore the cosmic balance. Such notices began to be widely circulated at least as early as the beginning of 1900. (It is doubtful that one would encounter drought-related notices much before this date, as it was probably not until the late months of 1899 that people in North China began to experience the protracted dry weather as a "drought.") In February of this year the Tianjin agent of the American Bible Society reported the following text to have been "posted everywhere" in North China: "On account of the Protestant and Catholic religions the Buddhist gods are oppressed, and our sages thrust into the background. The Law of Buddha is no longer respected, and the Five Relationships are disregarded. The anger of Heaven and Earth has been aroused and the timely rain has consequently been withheld from us. But Heaven is now sending down eight millions of spiritual soldiers to extirpate these foreign religions, and when this has been done there will be a timely rain."...

Boxer Motives: Anti-Imperialism, Antiforeignism, or Anxiety Over Drought?

The crisis remedy proposed by the Boxers in 1900 reveals a close kinship to that described by [Norman] Cohn for the millenarian movement of 1420. In one placard after another, the Chinese people are enjoined to kill off all foreigners and native Chinese contaminated by foreigners or foreign influence. Only after this process of physical elimination of every trace of the foreign from China has been completed will the gods be appeased and permit the rains once again to fall.

What is peculiar here and needs somehow to be accounted for is why at this particular moment in Chinese history there was such an extreme response to the foreign presence. Chinese had often shown a tendency, during times of military or cultural threat, to lapse into a form of racial thinking that categorized outsiders as fundamentally different and called for their expulsion, and this tendency had been greatly magnified in the nineteenth century with the appearance of "physically discontinuous" Westerners, who also happened to be carriers of a symbolic universe that diverged radically from the Chinese and, directly and indirectly, challenged the validity of the Chinese cultural world. From the early 1800s, people who had had contacts of any sort with Westerners were regularly referred to as "Chinese traitors" (*Hanjian*). More specifically, there had been efforts prior to the Boxer era to link natural disasters (as well as the failure of Chinese prayers to relieve them) with the presence of Christians. And of course there had been no end of anti-Christian and antiforeign incidents in China in the decades leading up to 1900. Never before, however, had there been a movement like the Boxers, uncompromisingly dedicated to the stamping out of foreign influence and backed, all the evidence indicates, by the broadest popular support. How do we explain this?

The reasons are without doubt very complex. Chinese historians, insisting upon the "anti-imperialist and patriotic" (*fandi aiguo*) character of the Boxer movement, tend to assign primary responsibility to the intensification of foreign imperialism in the last years of the nineteenth century. My own view is that the vocabulary of anti-imperialism is so deeply colored by twentieth-century Chinese political concerns and agendas that it gets in the way of the search for a more accurate, credible reading of the Boxer experience. This is not to deny that imperialism was a fact of life in China at the turn of the century or that it formed an important part of the setting within which the Boxer movement unfolded. It was only one causal agency among several, however, and its gravity relative to other causal forces varied considerably from place to place and over time. Furthermore, action taken against the more tangible reflections of imperialism—missionaries and Chinese Christians, railways, telegraphs, foreign armies, and the rest—could, when it occurred, derive from a range of possible motives; it need not have been inspired by either "patriotism" or "anti-imperialism." To superimpose this vocabulary on the Boxer movement, therefore, is to risk radical oversimplification of the complicated and diverse motives impelling the Boxers to behave as they did.

...We have hundreds of samples of Boxer writing—handbills, wall notices, charms, slogans, jingles, and the like. And even though most if not all of these may be assumed to have been composed by Boxer leaders or elite Chinese sympathetic to the Boxer cause rather than by rank-and-file participants in the movement, there is, as argued earlier, little doubt that they incorporate values and beliefs widely shared among the Boxers in general, not to mention millions of Chinese who witnessed and often supported, but were not directly engaged in, the activities of the Boxer movement. Still, as crucially important as these materials are in establishing the mindset of the Boxers, they fall well short of supplying the kind of intimate tracking of experience that we get, say, from the memoir literature of participants in the Cultural Revolution or the heresy trial testimony of the sixteenth-century Italian miller Menocchio or the letters, journals, and even poems composed by British soldiers in the trenches in World War I. In fact, it was not until after 1949 that elderly survivors of the Boxer uprising, mainly in western Shandong and Tianjin and other parts of Hebei (Zhili) province, were finally given a chance to describe more or less in their own words their experiences at the turn of the century. As useful as these oral history materials can sometimes be, however, their value is circumscribed by the advanced age of the respondents, the remoteness in time of the events under discussion, the political and ideological constraints built into the environment within which the interviewing was conducted, the specific questions the interviewers posed, and the editorial process by which the resulting responses were structured.

Consequently, in attempting to get at the range of motives that impelled the Boxers to attack foreigners, foreign-made objects, and foreign-influenced Chinese, we are regularly faced with the necessity of inferring these motives from Boxer actions, of reading back, as it were, from behavior to intent. This is one of the more dangerous kinds of business in which historians must unfortunately all too often engage, as it presents us with an open invitation to discern in the experience of the past the values, thought patterns, and psychological orientations that make the greatest sense to us in our own day.

Although on a macrohistorical level we hear much of the intensification of foreign imperialism that took place in China in the years following the Sino-Japanese War of 1894, it is arguable that, unlike drought, a conspicuously growing foreign presence was not, in 1899–1900, the common experience of the vast majority of Chinese inhabiting the North China plain. Whether we train our sights on expanded communities of native Christians or the growth in strength of the Catholic and Protestant missionary bodies or the construction of railways and telegraphs or the intrusion of foreign armies, the experience of direct confrontation with the foreign or foreign-influenced remained, for those living away from large urban centers, a sporadic and highly localized one in these years. Despite a substantial increase in the numbers of Protestant and Catholic converts in China as a whole in the 1890s—from approximately 37,000 Protestants in 1889 to 85,000 in 1900, and from about 500,000 to over 700,000 Catholics between 1890 and 1900—there were still, in 1899–1900, large stretches of North China that had Christian communities of negligible size or none at all. Similarly, in the case of both the Catholic and Protestant missionary efforts in the empire, although impressive growth occurred in the last decade of the century, this growth was far more in evidence in certain areas—the greatly expanded Catholic presence in southern Shandong, for example—than in others. Again, as of 1899–1900, the only railway lines that had been completed in North China were the Beijing-Baoding line, the Beijing-Tianjin line, and the line extending northeastward from Tianjin, through Tangshan, into Manchuria. And, leaving out the military activities of the Russians in Manchuria, foreign troop movements in the Boxer summer were largely confined to Tianjin and Beijing, their immediately surrounding areas, and the corridor connecting these two cities (although in the months following the lifting of the siege of the legations, ... punitive expeditions were carried out in other parts of Zhili and in eastern Shanxi).

In other words, despite an overall expansion in the opportunities for direct contact with foreigners, foreign-influenced Chinese, and foreign technology in the last years of the century, these opportunities were not evenly distributed throughout North China. Furthermore, there is the curious circumstance—curious, at least, if one interprets the behavior of the Boxers as having been guided in significant measure by anti-imperialist impulses—that the areas where the impact of imperialism was greatest often did not coincide with those areas in which the Boxers were most active. This was especially true in Shandong, where the arenas of greatest foreign economic activity—the eastern and southern coasts—were conspicuously free of Boxer involvement and where approximately half of the missionized areas also were left untouched by the Boxers. Mark Elvin, who includes southern Zhili as well as Shandong within his purview, is so struck by the weakness of the link between "Boxerism and the religious and foreign irritant usually supposed to have caused it" that he questions whether it can serve as "a convincing sufficient explanation" of the movement's origins.

I am not particularly concerned here with the origins of the Boxer movement. I do, however, believe that there is room for a fresh understanding of the range of motives that lay behind what was perhaps the Boxers' most distinctive and defining characteristic: their antiforeignism. The reality of Boxer antiforeignism—and the antiforeignism of many millions of Boxer supporters and sympathizers—is not at issue. What is at issue is the underlying meaning of this antiforeignism. Was it a reflection of simple hatred of foreigners owing to their foreignness? Or did it result from anger over specific foreign actions? Or did it spring from fear and anxiety and the need for a credible explanation for the problems—above all, drought—occasioning this fear and anxiety?

My own view is that antiforeignism, in the sense of fear and hatred of outsiders, was there all along in China in latent form, but that it needed some disturbance in the external environment, a rearrangement of the overall balance of forces within a community or a geographical area, to become activated. Chinese antiforeignism thus functioned in much the same way as fear of witchcraft in late seventeenth-century Salem or anti-Semitism in 1930s Germany. In each of these instances outsiders—Westerners in China, people accused of being witches in Salem, Jews in Germany—lived more or less uneventfully within their respective communities when times were "normal." But when something happened to create an "abnormal" situation—economic insecurity in Germany, apprehension concerning the enormous economic and social forces transforming New England in the late 1600s, anxiety over drought in turn-of-the-century North China—and people sought in desperation to address their grievances and allay their insecurities, outsiders became especially vulnerable.

The specific circumstances favoring outbreaks of antiforeignism in North China in 1899–1900 varied from place to place. In Shandong, escalating Boxer anti-Christian activity in late 1899 resulted (under foreign pressure) in the replacement as governor of Yuxian, who had followed a policy of leniency toward the Boxers, with Yuan Shikai, who, after the killing of the British missionary S. M. Brooks on December 31, pursued an increasingly strong policy of suppression. In Zhili province, especially in the Beijing and Tianjin areas and the corridor connecting the two, there was a relatively high level of exposure to the full range of foreign influences and, from the winter of 1899–1900, to rapidly growing numbers of Boxers. In Shanxi, where there were no significant manifestations of foreign influence apart from the missionaries and native Christians, there was a governor (Yuxian having been transferred there in March) who was deeply antiforeign and pro-Boxer.

Although the precise mix of factors was thus variable, the drought was shared in common throughout the North China plain. It was this factor, more than any other, in my judgment, that accounted for the explosive growth both of the Boxer movement and of popular support for it in the spring and summer months of 1900. Missionary reports and oral history accounts occasionally used the term "famine" to describe conditions in North China at the time. This was, for the most part, a loose usage; severe famine did not appear until the early months of 1901, mainly in Shanxi and Shaanxi. The evidence is overwhelming, on the other hand, that *fear* of famine, with all its attendant bewilderment and terror, was extremely widespread. As has often been the case in other agricultural societies, moreover, the uncertainty, anxiety, and increasingly serious food deprivation accompanying the Chinese drought—the *delírio de fome* or "madness of hunger," in the arresting formulation of Nancy Scheper-Hughes—seem to have inclined people to be receptive to extreme explanations and to act in extreme ways. The year 1900 was not a normal one in China. The menace of inopportune death was everywhere. And, as can be seen in the periodic eruptions of mass hysteria and the apparent readiness of many members of society to give credence to the most spectacular religious and magical claims of the Boxers, there was a strong disposition on the part of the population to depart from normal patterns of behavior.

Henrietta Harrison

NO

Justice on Behalf of Heaven

On the fifth day of the seventh month of the twenty-sixth year of the Guangxu Emperor, Liu Dapeng, a tutor and diarist, stood at the door of his family home in the village of Chiqiao in Shanxi province and watched an army of a thousand Boxers pass through. Liu was a brave man; some forty years later during the Second World War he was to stand on the roof of that same house watching the bombs falling from Japanese planes on his neighbours' houses. When the Boxers passed through, most of the other villagers had fled to the hills or were hiding behind the locked doors of their houses in fear that the Boxer forces would loot and extort money and goods. Liu himself had taken leave from his job as a private tutor in a grand house some twenty or thirty miles away and come home to look after his mother, wife and children because of the crisis. At the head of the Boxers came a young man known as Third Prince, who Liu guessed was less than twenty years old. Two banners before him proclaimed 'Bring justice on behalf of Heaven!' and 'Support the Qing! Destroy the foreign!' Then came rank after rank of men marching down the narrow street that ran through the centre of the village. There were men of all ages, but Liu reckoned that at least two-thirds were not yet adults. All of them wore red belts and red cloths tied around their heads. They marched in an orderly fashion, divided into companies and brigades, and did not, after all, do any damage in the village.

Liu's attitude to the Boxers was divided. On the one hand he approved of their loyalty to the Qing dynasty and their opposition to the expansion of foreign power in China. He was particularly supportive of their campaign against the local Catholics, whom he perceived as having sold out to the foreigners. On the other hand, he was dubious about the movement's religious elements and particularly concerned about the threat they posed to law and order. While he approved of the provincial governor's efforts to force Catholics to renounce their religion, he found it hard to condone the murder of travellers suspected of poisoning wells, let alone pitched battles between Catholic villages and Boxer forces. Liu's feelings, in this respect, were typical of the time and were shared across a wide social spectrum. Indeed, it was just such conflicting attitudes at court that allowed the Boxer movement to spread on such a wide scale. Although events in the northern coastal province of Shandong where the Boxer movement originated are better known, some of the worst violence in the uprising took place in the adjoining Shanxi province, witnessed by Liu.

The Boxers' opposition in the foreign powers and especially to Christianity struck a chord with many Chinese and drew widespread support. China's defeat by Japan in the war over Korea in 1894 was a turning point in perceptions of the foreign threat. The country's perception of itself as the Middle Kingdom, a central realm of civilisation surrounded by tributary states, and by savages and barbarians beyond that, had been affirmed by Korea, which had conducted an elaborate tributary relationship with China. The loss of Korea, moreover, brought with it humiliating defeat by the Japanese, hitherto often dismissively referred to as 'dwarf pirates'. In the Treaty of Shimonoseki, which concluded the war, China not only agreed to Korean independence, but ceded Taiwan to Japan and gave the Japanese the same treaty rights as those of Westerners. These were the events that roused Sun Yatsen, later China's first President, to plan his first revolutionary uprising. But it was not only members of China's tiny reformist elite who were concerned at this outcome. The news was carried across the country and was talked about by the farmers in Chiqiao village, all of whom, Liu reported, opposed the terms of the treaty. Li Hongzhang, who had been the chief negotiator on the Chinese side, became extremely unpopular, with rumours circulating in the countryside that he had married his son to the daughter of the Japanese emperor, and satirical rhymes attacking him for selling his country. It is important to remember that, though often condemned as ignorant, superstitious and xenophobic, the Boxers were acting in an environment where China's changing international situation was widely known and resented.

Popular opposition to foreign power was confirmed in Shanxi when news came through in the summer of 1900 that the government had declared war on the foreign powers. Liu heard that governors had been ordered to kill collaborators, that is to say Christians, and to arrest any foreigners and execute them if they planned to make trouble or plotted with the Christians. Shanxi's governor, Yu Xian, was said to be delighted at the news and immediately sent soldiers to round up those foreigners residing in the province and bring them to the provincial capital. Less than a month later some forty unfortunate foreigners were formally executed outside the provincial government building. The Chinese leaders of the Catholic community were ordered to renounce their faith and one who refused was executed. It was thus clear that the government declaration of war on the foreign powers included not only foreign civilians but also Catholic villagers. When the Boxers marched through the countryside carrying banners that said 'Restore the Qing! Destroy the foreign!' their claims that they were loyal forces obeying the orders of the dynasty were hard to deny.

Catholics were seen as potential collaborators in a war with the foreign powers because Christianity had been introduced into China by foreign missionaries. Indeed the right for Christian missionaries to reside in the interior had repeatedly been the object of treaty negotiations between the Qing dynasty and the foreign powers. In Shanxi, the Protestant missionaries had only a handful of converts, but Catholicism was firmly rooted in many rural areas and had been widespread since the eighteenth century. The heart of the problem lay in the contradictions between Christianity and the belief system that underlay the structures of the state. In the villages–where the Boxers operated–the problems of integrating Christianity in the imperial state were focused around the issue of temple festivals and opera performances. Temple festivals were funded by contributions from all members of the local community. In addition to a market they included sacrifices to the deity in whose honour the festival was held and often theatrical performances on a stage facing the temple. Wealthy villages would hire a travelling opera company who would perform for three to five days. Poorer villages might only have a puppet theatre for a single day. The festival performances were intended for the deity but were also a source of entertainment. Friends and relations came from miles around to see the operas, meet and chat, while the market drew large crowds. The funds raised to pay for the opera, meanwhile, also provided a working budget for such village level local government as existed. They might, for example, be used to pay for the dredging of dikes for a communal irrigation system or a law suit against a neighbouring village. Christians, however, refused to pay the levies on the grounds that they would be used to support idolatrous practices.

By refusing to contribute to the festivals, Shanxi Catholics were excluding themselves from the local community. At the same time locals were aware that allowing Christians to opt out of paying taxes made Christianity, which was generally seen as a heterodox religion, a financially advantageous option for the poor, who often turned out to enjoy the festivities even if they had not helped to pay for them. As a result, the 1890s saw an increasing number of legal cases being brought by village leaders against recalcitrant Catholics. The Catholics were able to fight these suits because the foreign consuls, backed by the threat of arms, negotiated with the central government for the right of Christians not to pay for religious practices in which they did not believe. Both the village leaders and the magistrates, however, saw the cases as resting on matters of loyalty and obedience to the state rather than on religious toleration. An extract (translated by Roger Thompson) from one magistrate's interrogation of a Catholic named Yang accused of refusing to pay village levies gives a sense of the way in which Christians were seen as alienating themselves from the state:

Magistrate: You are a person of what country?

Yang: I am a person of the Qing.

Magistrate: If you are a person of the Qing dynasty then why are you following the foreign devils and their seditious religion? You didn't pay your opera money when requested by the village and you were beaten. But how can you dare to bring a suit? Don't you know why Zuo Zongtang went to Beijing? In order to kill–to exterminate–the foreign devils. You certainly ought to pay the opera subscription. If you don't you won't be allowed to live in the land of the Qing. You'll have to leave for a foreign country.

Liu Dapeng, watching the Boxers pass his front door on their way to join an attack on Catholic villages, shared this view. In his opinion:

> When the foreign barbarians preach their religion, they say they are urging men to do good, but in fact they are disrupting our government, creating turmoil in our system, destroying our customs, and deceiving our people; that is to say that they want to turn the people of China into barbarians.

The issue of Catholic refusal to participate in the religious practices of the local community became particularly powerful and problematic in the summer of 1900 because of the fear of drought. Drought was a constant threat to the North China Plain, where farmers rely on rain falling at precisely the right times of year. In Shanxi many remembered with fear the great famine of the 1870s when in Chiqiao one in ten of the population died, and in parts of the south of the province the death toll was worse still. Drought like this was widely seen as divine punishment for immorality and people reacted with ritual and prayer. In Chiqiao men went with bare heads and bare feet to a spring high up in the mountains to pray for rain. The villages through which they passed set up altars in front of their homes laid out with candles, cakes, branches of willow and dragons' heads carved from gourds. As the procession passed through the village the men would repeat the words 'Amitabha Buddha' and the onlookers knelt and used the willow branches to scatter water on them. For three days the men stayed at the temple beside the spring, eating only thin gruel and praying constantly for rain. Such rituals were commonplace throughout northern China in times of drought and were believed to require the sincere participation of the whole community in order to be effective. Catholic refusal to participate in the rituals needed to save the local community from famine accentuated an already problematic relationship.

The conflict between Catholics and villagers meant that the Boxers could be seen as representing and embodying the community even as they attacked and burned their neighbours' homes. With their banners 'Bring justice on behalf of Heaven!' and 'Support the Qing! Destroy the foreign!', they claimed to uphold the moral and social order where the dynasty, because of foreign pressure, was unable to do so. As Liu Dapeng put it, 'the court could not kill the Christians and the officials dared not kill them, so the Boxers killed them.'

However, the people of Chiqiao village, which had no Catholic families at all, nevertheless fled in panic when they heard the Boxers were approaching the village. Doubts lingered about the beliefs and rituals of the Boxers, and about their violence. People expected that boxing, or martial arts, techniques would be learned from a teacher over many years, but these were mostly young boys with hardly any training. Liu Dapeng went to see them practising at a large temple near Chiqiao. They set up sticks of incense and kowtowed to them. Then they stood facing southeast, put their hands in a certain position and recited an invocation to several deities. Immediately they fell on the floor, as if asleep. Then, as the crowds of spectators gathered, their hands and feet began to move and slowly they stood up and began a kind of dance sometimes with weapons, all the time keeping their eyes closed. Although their expressions were terrifying, they somehow looked as if they were drunk. After keeping up these strange movements for a while they fell to the ground again, and eventually awoke. Later they said that they did not remember what they had done while they were in the trance. When one of the onlookers asked what would happen if they had to face guns, they replied that Heaven was angry and had sent them as soldiers to warn the people. This was the 'spirit possession' that was central to the Boxer movement. Spirit possession by semi-professional mediums is a feature of Chinese folk-religious practice, but mass spirit possession of this sort was, as Liu commented, very strange indeed.

But the strangeness of Boxer claims was not limited to spirit possession. As at other times when drought threatened, bizarre rumours were rife. In Shanxi it was said that the wives of the foreign missionaries stood naked on the roofs of their houses fanning back the winds that would have brought rain. Other rumours concerned the Catholics, who were said to be poisoning village water supplies. Western power, and particularly science, was considered to border on black magic in the eyes of much of the population. The same black magic was also attributed to the Chinese Catholics. Rumours spread through Shanxi that Catholics had painted blood on doorways, and where they had done this the entire family would go mad within seven days. The Boxers claimed to have the power to oppose this Catholic magic and Liu saw people washing the blood off their doors with urine as the Boxers instructed. Strange stories told of full-scale battles between the Catholic and the Boxer magic. In a large town near Chiqiao there was a panic one night that the Catholics had come and many of the townspeople went to guard the city walls. When they were there they heard a huge noise like tens of thousands of people attacking and then suddenly a green hand as big as a cartwheel appeared in the air. The local Boxer leader pointed at it and there was a crash of thunder and rain began to fall. He explained that the green hand had been a form of Catholic magic and he had destroyed it. Outside the city wall the villagers saw the lights, heard strange noises and fled from their homes in panic to hide in the fields. It is clear that such stories were widely believed at the time, and yet there was always an underlying distrust. The next morning, when the villagers cautiously emerged from their hiding places, they realised that there had been no Catholic army and no battle. The fear of drought inevitably gave rise to rumours, but many, including Liu, were not wholly convinced by the magical claims of the Boxers.

Distrust of the Boxers' spiritual powers was increased by a growing realisation of the threat they posed to law and order. This began with the murder of people accused of poisoning wells. Most of these were not even Catholics, but were accused of being in their pay. Magistrates, unsure of how to respond to the movement, failed to investigate the crimes and Boxer confidence grew. Large groups of men assembled and began to fight their Catholic neighbours. The army of men that Liu saw marching through his village had gone out to a nearby village which had a sizable Catholic population. The Catholics had hired men from another province to protect them and had withdrawn to their solidly-built stone church. The Boxers besieged the church and the battle lasted for six days. More than thirty of the mercenaries were killed before the church fell. A few of the Catholics survived the seige and escaped, but the rest were massacred and the church burned.

Magistrates' failure to act in the face of such disorder was due to the weakness and indecision of the central government, which vacillated between support for the Boxers and fear of the foreign powers. For more than fifty years the foreign threat had been at the centre of factional divisions within the court. At the heart of this debate was the question of whether a modern, well-equipped army or popular feeling should be more important in withstanding the foreign powers. The leaders of the bureaucracy were examined and trained in Confucian thought and for many of them it was an article of faith that victory in battle would bethe result of thepeople'ssupport.Onthe othersidestood afaction, many of whom were drawn from the Manchu ruling ethnic group, who had accepted the strength of the European powers and believed that it was necessary to approach them cautiously until such time as China had built up the technical expertise to face them. The radical Confucians saw the growth of the Boxer movement as a sign that the people were at last aroused to fight the foreigners. Putting their trust in this, they were prepared to overlook the folk-religious aspects of the movement, which were clearly at odds with Confucian rationalism, and also the inevitable threat to law and order that would arise if the people were allowed to bear arms outside state control. With the support of the ruling Empress Dowager the court declared war on the foreign powers. However, the more cautious modernisers, many of whom had power bases in the southern provinces, believed that China was still unable to defeat the foreign powers; the governors general of the southern provinces refused to enter the war. Instead they drew up private agreements with the foreign powers, giving protection to foreigners and Christians in return for a promise that the foreigners would not invade. Although the Confucian radicals had won at court the central government was not strong enough to control the regions. The result was indecision and a series of conflicting orders. The Qing army never really engaged with the foreign troops, but country magistrates dared not arrest the Boxers, and thus appeared to be encouraging the movement to spread.

The debate over whether the Boxers should be seen as loyal and patriotic enforcers of the moral order or superstitious and xenophobic peasants has remained at the heart of Chinese perceptions of the uprising. In the early years of the twentieth century the modernisers, who had added a desire for the adoption of Western culture to their Qing predecessors' perception of the need for Western technology, continued to criticise the movement. Indeed, for this group in the 1910s and 20s, the failure of the uprising to solve China's problems by driving out the foreigners was symbolic of the failure of China's encounters with the West. The Boxers embodied what the modernisers saw as the very national characteristics that had led to China's international weakness. They were depicted as ignorant and conservative, a group whose folly and credulous belief that they could be saved from bullets by reciting magic rhymes had ultimately led to the imposition of the huge Boxer Indemnity that sunk the nation in the burden of debt.

However, from the 1920s onwards, a new generation of historians and politicians began to rewrite history in terms of China's resistance to Western imperialism, rather than of its development towards modernity. The events of

1900 came to be known, as they are in China today, not as the Boxer Uprising but as the invasion of the Eight Allied Armies, thus shifting the focus from the Boxers themselves to the foreign response. In addition, the Communists took over the mantle of the radical Confucians in their belief in the centrality of mass popular movements as the foundation of resistance to foreign powers. During the Cultural Revolution in the 1960s the Boxers were depicted as heroic, anti-imperialist fighters while the threat they posed to law and order was reconstructed as rebellious opposition to the forces of feudalism. The mass spirit possession and other elements of folk religion at the centre of the movement were completely ignored. The story of the Boxers was rewritten as one of peasant rebellion against foreign imperialism.

Since the 1980s there has been renewed interest in the Boxers. Chinese social historians are beginning to integrate popular folk religion and mass spirit possession into their interpretations of the movement. However, the ambivalence between interpretations of the Boxers as patriots or a superstitious and disorderly rabble has continued to form the framework of the argument. The ambivalence of contemporaries who observed the Boxers and which in many ways created the movement as a national phenomenon has continued to inform Chinese interpretations of the uprising.

POSTSCRIPT

Was China's Boxer Rebellion Caused by Environmental Factors?

Many problems arise when current interpretations of the Boxer uprising as a historical movement are attempted. One concerns motivation, the subject covered in this issue. Another concerns how the Boxers themselves should be viewed. Were they, as Harrison expresses it, "loyal and patriotic enforcers of the moral order or superstitious and xenophobic peasants"? Finally, as Cohen points out, an important question is, How do we separate Boxer myth from Boxer reality? All of these questions form the basis of all historical inquiry and answers to them must be sought.

Complicating matters is China's status today as a communist nation, adhering to a strict Marxist interpretation of history. There is strong pressure in such a society to fit historical events into this predetermined historical theory, and sometimes the truth can be lost within that process. But even as China's needs change, so does its history. According to Harrison, during the cultural revolution of the 1960s, "The story of the Boxers was rewritten as one of peasant rebellion against foreign imperialism," different from previous Chinese interpretations of the movement. See Hu Sheng's *From the Opium War to the May Fourth Movement*, 2 vols. (Foreign Language Press, 1991) for an analysis of the major events in Chinese history from 1840 to 1920 from a Marxist perspective.

Joseph W. Eshrick's *The Origins of the Boxer Uprising* (University of California Press, 1987) was an important modern work that encouraged others to pursue the Boxers-as-history movement. Cohen's *History in Three Keys: The Boxers as Event, Experience, and Myth* (Columbia University Press, 1997) is an interesting companion, and when combined with Sheng's work mentioned earlier, provides the reader with three different points of view on the Boxer uprising.

The centenary anniversary of the Boxer uprising has produced a number of interesting articles on the subject. R. G. Tiedemann's "Baptism of Fire: China's Christians and the Boxer Uprising of 1900," *International Bulletin of Missionary Research* (January 2000) views the rebellion as a "tragic anomaly" in China's relationship with Christian missionaries. Robert Bickers, in "Chinese Burns Britain in China, 1842–1900," *History Today* (August 2000), places the blame for the Boxer rebellion squarely on the shoulders of British and European imperialism.

Finally, for a more popularly written account of the Boxer uprising, see Diane Preston, *The Boxer Rebellion: The Dramatic Story of China's War on Foreigners That Shook the World in the Summer of 1900* (Walker & Company, 2000).

ISSUE 8

Did the Bolshevik Revolution Improve the Lives of Soviet Women?

YES: Richard Stites, from "Women and the Revolutionary Process in Russia," in Renate Bridenthal, Claudia Koontz, and Susan M. Stuard, eds., *Becoming Visible: Women in European History,* 2nd ed. (Houghton Mifflin, 1987)

NO: Lesley A. Rimmel, from "The Baba and the Comrade: Gender and Politics in Revolutionary Russia," *The Women's Review of Books* (September 1998)

ISSUE SUMMARY

YES: History professor Richard Stites argues that, in the early years of the Bolshevik Revolution, the Zhenotdel, or Women's Department, helped many working women take the first steps toward emancipation.

NO: Russian scholar Lesley A. Rimmel finds that the Russian Revolution remains unfinished for women, who were mobilized as producers and reproducers for a male political agenda.

Compared with life under the czars, life for women after the Bolshevik Revolution was characterized by greater variety and freedom. The Romanov dynasty had ruled Russia for 300 years and the Orthodox Church had been entrenched for a much longer period. Both had reinforced a world of patriarchal authority, class structure, and patterns of deference. Although the revolution overthrew the power of both church and monarch, the new communist state had a power and authority of its own. Between 1917 and 1920, Soviet women received equal rights in education and marriage, including the choice to change or keep their own names and the opportunity to own property; the rights to vote and hold public office; access to no-fault divorce, common-law marriage, and maternity benefits; workplace protection; and access to unrestricted abortion. They were the first women to gain these rights—ahead of women in France, England, and the United States—but the question is whether or not these legal rights translated into improvements in their day-to-day lives.

A feminist movement had developed in urban areas as early as the 1905 workers' revolution, and women joined men in leading strikes and protest demonstrations. By the time of the Bolshevik Revolution in 1917, however, the goals of the leadership were primarily economic, and feminism was dismissed as bourgeois or middle class. In a workers' revolution, women and men were to be equal. Housework and childcare were to be provided collectively, and the family, like the monarchy, was to be replaced with something new. In theory, women would become workers and gain access to economic independence, which would provide them the basis for equality within marriage.

German philosopher Karl Marx had argued that the family reflects the economic system in society. Under capitalism, the bourgeois family exists to reproduce workers and consumers; it exploits women by unfairly burdening them with full responsibility for housework and childcare. If similarly exploited workers—what Marx called the proletariat—overthrew the capitalist system that allowed factory owners to grow rich from their workers' labor, Marx believed that the family would undergo an equally dramatic transformation. In this scenario, no one would be "owned" by anyone else. Prostitution would disappear, and, as the state took responsibility for childrearing and education, women would be free to work and become economically self-sufficient. People would then be free to marry for love or sexual attraction rather than for economic considerations.

V.I. Lenin, who emerged as leader and architect of the new order, was committed to women's rights. First and foremost, however, he was committed to a socialist revolution. When the struggle to make abstract legal changes "real" in women's lives came into conflict with the goals of the revolution, there was no question in Lenin's mind about which would have to be sacrificed. In this early period, a fascinating group of women briefly held highly visible leadership positions and had the chance to put their ideas into practice, at least during the first decade. Alexandra Kollontai was one of the most articulate and effective leaders of the Zhenotdel, or Women's Department of the Communist Party, whose purpose between 1919 and 1930 was to educate and mobilize the women of the Soviet state to participate fully in the revolution.

In the following selections, Richard Stites focuses on what he calls the "idealistic foreground" of the Revolution—the part that is so often overlooked. Although poverty, cynicism, bureaucratic resistance, rural superstition, and urban blight ultimately thwarted many early dreams of reformers such as Alexandra Kollontai; bold efforts undertaken by the Zhenotdel and experiments in sexual equality raised the consciousness of women and men. A brief glimpse of what might be possible in a stable society kept the dreams and experiments alive—at least for a time, Stites concludes.

Lesley A. Rimmel uses the contrasting images of the baba—an ignorant peasant women—and the comrade—a full-fledged human and citizen—to describe how Russian women were targeted as workers in a class revolution while gender roles remained firmly in place. Rimmel sees the long-delayed gender goals, articulated during the Russian Revolution, including the right of women to define comradeship on their own terms, as, finally, being addressed in contemporary Russia.

YES 

Richard Stites

Women and the Revolutionary Process in Russia

Before the Revolution

Russian society before 1917 was a world of patriarchal power, deferential ritual, clear authority patterns, and visible hierarchy with stratified social classes or estates. At the pinnacle of the state, the tsar-emperor (called *batyushka* or little father by the common folk), considered Russia as a family estate or patrimony and his subjects as children—virtuous, obedient, and loyal. The imperial bureaucratic order of ranks, chanceries, uniforms, and rigidly ordered parades constituted a visual celebration of authoritarianism. To subjects of all classes of the empire, every official building—with its geography of guarded entrances, pass booths, waiting areas, office gates—represented authority, inequality, and the demand for deference. Far from the capital and the towns, in the vastness of rural Russia, a simpler absolutism prevailed in the village cabins where the male head of household wielded domestic power that contrasted sharply with the more or less egalitarian land distribution customs of the village community. The Russian Orthodox Church reinforced values of obedience and subordination at every level in its liturgical idiom, its symbols, its organization, and its political ethos of support for a conservative order. The women dwelling within this ancient authoritarian world felt the additional weight of male power and suffered from the sexual division of labor and open inequality between the sexes....

Women who chose not to challenge the regime and its entire patriarchal structure but who nonetheless wished to improve the lot of women organized the Russian feminist movement (ca. 1860–1917). Feminist women shared the class background (largely gentry) of the nihilists and radicals, but did not call for the destruction of the existing social system. They worked for women's rights—not for the rights of peasants or workers, and not on behalf of a socialist vision. In the four decades or so after 1860 feminists agitated, with considerable success, for permission to form legal societies, engage in charity work, and open university level and medical courses for women. These courses produced impressive numbers of physicians, teachers, lawyers, and engineers. At the dawn of the twentieth century, feminists turned their attention to the national suffrage issue and continued to press for and win reforms in the

From Richard Stites, "Women and the Revolutionary Process in Russia," in Renate Bridenthal, Claudia Koonz, and Susan M. Stuard, eds., *Becoming Visible: Women in European History,* 2d ed. (Houghton Mifflin, 1987). Notes omitted.

status of women in the realm of property rights, divorce, freedom of movement, and other matters that primarily affected women of the gentry and the professional classes of Russia. From 1905 to 1917, no fewer than four feminist parties struggled unsuccessfully in the political arena. Thus all women (and millions of men) remained without representation in the central government. Russian feminism, in the words of its most eloquent historian, was "a movement for women's civil and political equality, whose supporters trusted that a better world could be created without resort to violence, and a constitutional solution be found to Russia's ills." ...

Political Parties

The political parties of the late imperial Russia reacted to the question of women's rights in much the same way as their counterparts in Western Europe—their views on this issue being a litmus test for their outlook on social change and mass interests. Those on the right displayed outright hostility to any kind of feminist platform, identifying legitimate politics with the male sex and proclaiming as their program Faith, Tsar, and Fatherland. The liberal parties in the center—the Kadets, or Constitutional Democrats, most prominent among them—initially wavered on the question of votes for women in the Duma but by 1906 supported the more moderate of the feminist parties. The socialists—like the Populists earlier and like their counterparts in Western Europe—proclaimed support for women's equality, including political equality, maternity protection, and equal economic rights.

The socialist parties also included women activists at many levels, some of whom would become prominent political figures during the Revolution of 1917. Of the three major socialist parties—Socialist Revolutionary, Social Democrat-Menshevik, and Social Democrat-Bolshevik—the first eventually became the largest and most variegated. Heirs to the Populist tradition of the nineteenth century, the Socialist Revolutionaries continued to focus on peasant agrarian socialism and an alliance of the "social trinity": peasant, worker, and intelligentsia. Loose in organization and weak in theory, the Socialist Revolutionary party periodically fell back upon terror as its main weapon. Its best-known women were Ekaterina Breshko-Breshkovskaya (1844–1934), a veteran Populist of the 1870s who tried in the 1905 period to promote a theory of "agrarian terror" that included assaults on landlords in the countryside; and Maria Spiridonova (1886–?), a young schoolteacher who achieved fame first by her assassination of a general in 1906 and then in 1917 as the leader of the Left Socialist Revolutionary party. The Socialist Revolutionaries—like the Anarchist groups—could deploy a large number of female terrorists, but women played a minimal role in the organizational and theoretical work of the party.

The Marxists (Social Democrats) had split into Mensheviks and Bolsheviks in 1903. Both enrolled large numbers of women but in neither did many women rise to leadership positions. Among the Mensheviks, Vera Zasulich was the best-known woman (her fame arose from an attempted assassination she had performed in the 1870s) but her political influence remained strictly secondary. The most important activist women among the Bolsheviks—Roza Zemlyachka and Elena Stasova—were tough organizers, but not leaders or theoreticians. In all the socialist parties the leadership remained in the hands of men, men who spent most of the years from 1905 to 1917 in the émigré centers of Western Europe. Two of the best-known Bolshevik women, Nadezhda Krupskaya (Lenin's wife) and Inessa Armand (their friend), made their mark as loyal assistants of the party leader, Lenin, in the emigration years.

The presence of women in the major socialist parties did not advance the cause of women's rights in Russia. Less than ten percent of the delegates to Socialist Revolutionary conferences in the peak years from 1905 to 1908 were women; the percentages were even lower in Marxist and Social Democratic parties. Even if more women had risen to the top of these organizations, however, the picture would not have changed. Women constituted one-third of the Executive Committee of the People's Will of the 1870s, for example, yet those women displayed almost no interest in the issue of women's rights as such. The same mood prevailed in the generation of 1905; revolutionary women put what they called the "common cause" above what they saw as lesser issues. Vera Zasulich, when asked to help in forming a women workers' club, refused.

The most notable exception, Alexandra Kollontai, had to fight on many fronts when she set about combining the advocacy of women's rights with socialism: against her feminist competitors, against indifference in her own party (she was at first a Menshevik and later a Bolshevik), and against the prevailing opinion of the conservative society. Kollontai, a general's daughter, had come to a feminist consciousness through personal experience—the conflict of work and family. Like many European socialist women, particularly Clara Zetkin, Kollontai believed that women had special problems that Marxist programs did not sufficiently address. She opposed the feminists as bourgeois; she believed that women workers should rally to the proletarian banner; but she also insisted that working women needed their own self-awareness—as workers and as women. Out of this set of beliefs arose the Proletarian Women's Movement.

In the years from 1905 to 1908 Kollontai fought to create a socialist-feminist movement in order to win away proletarian women of St. Petersburg from the feminists who were trying to organize them into an "all-women's" movement. For three years, Kollontai and a few associates agitated among the factory women, taught them Marxism, and attempted to show them that their principal enemy was the bourgeoisie, not men. In this struggle, Kollontai opposed the bourgeois (as she perceived it) program of the feminists with her own vision of socialist feminism—a combination of gender and class awareness, a recognition of the double exploitation of working-class women (as workers and as women), and an honest facing of the issue of abusive proletarian husbands and insensitive socialist males. Although Kollontai exaggerated the selfish class character of Russian feminists, she did in fact go beyond them and beyond her own comrades in the socialist movement in trying to draw attention to these issues. Police harassment in 1908 forced her to leave the country, and during her years in Western Europe Kollontai deepened her understanding of the woman question through study and personal experience.

The Eve of Revolution

On the eve of war and revolution, the woman question in tsarist society remained a public issue. Thousands of women graduates of universities had entered professional life; hundreds languished in jail or in Siberia for their chosen profession as revolutionaries. The female terrorist was the Russian counterpart to the British suffragette—but far more violent. Organized feminists continued to agitate for important reforms in the status of women and won considerable legislative victories in legal, educational, and property rights—though mainly for women of the middle and upper classes. The female work force continued to grow and to feel the rigors of industrial life and of relative neglect by the rest of society. With the revival of the militant labor movement around 1912, Mensheviks and Bolsheviks alike reactivated their efforts to organize women workers. International Women's Day, established in Europe in 1910, was celebrated by adherents of both factions for the first time on Russian soil in 1913, and a newspaper, *The Woman Worker*, was established in 1914. During World War I much of the machinery for organizing women workers was smashed by the authorities and many leaders were arrested before the monarchy itself fell a victim to the same war.

The Revolutionary Era

After three winters of bitter fighting, bloody losses, and patent mismanagement of the war, widespread discontent and hatred of the regime found a focus. In February 1917, cold and hungry women of the capital (renamed Petrograd) rioted, beginning an uprising that led to the collapse of the Romanov dynasty within a week. With the men at the front and the women left behind as workers, breadwinners, and heads of households, the women of the lower classes perceived food shortages and related deprivations as a menace to their very existence and to their roles as women. They struck, demonstrated, rioted, and appealed to the class solidarity of garrison troops to persuade the troops not to fire upon them. When the tsar abdicated, the revolutionary parties linked up with the masses of women. A band of energetic Bolshevik women organizers—including Kollontai—created a network of agitation that was effective in spite of tactical squabbles and the enormous problems of communication in the midst of a major revolt. This network produced mass female demonstrations on behalf of Bolshevik issues, organized women in factories, and enlisted others in political, paramedical, and paramilitary work. Bolshevik leadership and dynamism in this arena proved vastly superior to that of the other radical parties, and Bolshevik hostility to the now-revived feminist movement was active and unambiguous. Out of this year of struggle and organization in many cities emerged the symbolically important "presence" of women in the October Revolution as well as the foundations of a post-revolutionary women's movement.

The Bolsheviks took power on October 25 (November 7 in the modern calendar), 1917, and established a Soviet socialist regime; in 1918 they moved the capital to Moscow, issued a constitution that was the framework for the world's first socialist state, and made peace with Germany. The first years of the new regime were marked by ruthless political struggle on all sides, a bloody and cruel civil war, intervention in that war by foreign troops on behalf of the anti-Bolshevik forces, and a deepening of the extraordinary economic hardship set off by war and revolution and made inevitable by the very backwardness of the country.

How, in this time of dreadful calamity, did the Bolshevik regime perceive the issue—historically always seen as marginal by all governments—of the emancipation of women? What did they do about it? The answers are very complicated; any assessment of their response depends upon how one views revolution in general and the Bolshevik Revolution in particular, and upon one's expectations from an insurgent, culture-changing government that sets out to remake the face of one of the largest countries in the world.

The men and women in the Bolshevik party displayed the contradictions inherent in all forceful agents of social and cultural change: practicality combined with vision, the imperatives of survival combined with the dream of transformation. The party's leader, V. I. Lenin, as both a Marxist and a Russian revolutionary, committed himself and his party to the educational, economic, legal, and political liberation of women; to the interchangeability of gender roles in a future under communism; and to special protection for woman as childbearer and nurturing mother. In addition, Lenin possessed an almost compulsive hatred of the domestic enslavement of women to mindless household work which he called "barbarously unproductive, petty, nerve-wracking, stultifying and crushing drudgery." Lenin's male and female colleagues shared his opinions on these major issues and framed their laws and policies accordingly. Most important, they endorsed the creation of a special women's organization to oversee the realization of these programs in Soviet society. Women did not play a major role in the upper reaches of the party hierarchy; and indeed hostility toward the expenditure of time on women's issues persisted in the party at various levels. This was an inheritance of the twenty years of underground life of party struggle, of the military mentality of Bolshevism that hardened during the Civil War, and of the upsurge within the party of people holding "traditional" patriarchal views of the female sex. In spite of these obvious weaknesses, it is astonishing what the Bolshevik regime proclaimed and actually carried out in the early years of Soviet power.

In a series of decrees, codes, electoral laws, and land reforms, the Bolsheviks proclaimed an across-the-board equality of the sexes—the first regime in history ever to do so. All institutions of learning were opened to women and girls. Women attained equal status in marriage—including the right to change or retain their own names—divorce, family, and inheritance and equal rights in litigation and the ownership of property. By separating church and state, the Bolsheviks legally invalidated all canonical and theological restrictions on the role of women in modern life—a sweeping and drastic measure in a land wrapped in the constraining meshes of traditional faiths, particularly Russian Orthodoxy and Islam. In 1920 the Bolsheviks legalized abortion. On the other hand, prostitution (legally licensed under the old regime) was made illegal. Taken together, these measures offered a structure for equality between the sexes unprecedented in history. The Bolsheviks offered a process as well: the organizations that helped overthrow the old order would help to erect the new one; art, culture, symbol, and mythic vision would reinforce the values of sexual equality.

The organizational form of women's liberation in the first decade of the Bolshevik (now renamed Communist) regime was the Women's Department of the Communist Party (1919–1930), known by its Russian abbreviation Zhenotdel. Founded as an arm of the party rather than as an independent feminist organization, Zhenotdel—led by Inessa Armand and Alexandra Kollontai in the early years—worked to transform the new revolutionary laws into reality through education, mobilization, and social work. Understaffed and hampered by a small budget, Zhenotdel went into the factory neighborhoods, the villages, and the remote provinces of the new Soviet state to bring the message of the Revolution to the female population. Instructors and trainees from among workers and peasant women addressed the practical concerns of women. In the towns they monitored factory conditions and fought against female unemployment and prostitution. In the countryside they opened literacy classes and explained the new laws. In the Muslim regions they opposed humiliating customs and attitudes. Everywhere they counselled women about divorce and women's rights—and tied all such lessons to political instruction about the values and aims of the regime. Activated by Zhenotdel, women virtually untouched by political culture entered into the local administrative process. Most crucial of all, the activists of Zhenotdel learned the rudiments of organizing and modernizing and taught themselves the meaning of social revolution.

Bolshevism contained vision as well as social policy. In societies wracked by poverty and dislocation, social vision—utopian or otherwise—plays a key role in capturing the sentiment of people, particularly the literate and the already engaged. Speculation about the future of sexual relations often helped to reinforce the process of working for improving such relations in the present. The most active and articulate Bolshevik woman activist, Kollontai, gave special attention to a program of communist sexual relations and communal "family" life. In regard to the first, Kollontai vigorously defended woman's need for independence and a separate income. This in turn would give her the dignity and strength needed for an equal and open love-sex relationship and would enhance the pleasure and quality of sexual intercourse. As to the second, she believed in a "marriage" unfettered by economic dependence or responsibility for children. The latter were to be cared for in communal facilities to which parents had easy access. Kollontai believed in parenthood—her ideal in fact for all humans—and in regular contact between parents and children. The material life of the children, however, was to be the responsibility of the local "collective" of work or residence. Housekeeping was to be no more than an "industrial" task like any other, handled by specialists—never the domain of a wife (or husband) alone.

Some of the more daring aspects of Kollontai's sexual theories fell victim to misinterpretation in the 1920s. Hers was an overall vision of equality in life, work, and love that matched the utopian visions of the science fiction writers and revolutionary town planners and architects who were the major futuristic thinkers in this decade of experiment. In the 1920s about 200 science fiction titles appeared, many of them outlining a future world of perfection characterized by social justice and ultramodern technology. Such utopian pictures almost invariably revealed a unified, urbanized globe bathed in peace, harmony, and affluent communist civilization inhabited by a near-androgynous population with genderless names and unisex costumes. Sexual tensions no longer tormented the human race, women worked as equals to men in a machine-run economy of universal participation and communist distribution, and healthy children thrived in colonies.

Architects and town planners of the 1920s and early 1930s designed living spaces as "social condensers"—communal buildings that would shape the collective consciousness of their inhabitants. Although the projects varied in scope, size, and density, almost all of the architectural planning of that period provided for private rooms for single persons and couples, easy divorce by changing rooms, communal care for children, communal cooking and dining, and an environment of male-female cooperation in household tasks. Some of these communal homes actually were built; others remained in the blueprint stage. As a whole, visionary architecture and town planning of that period attested to the central importance of woman's new role as an independent and equal member of society.

The ultimate experiments in sexual equality—the rural and urban communes of the 1920s—put communalism (the complete and equal sharing of lives, partly inspired by [Nicholas] Chernyshevsky) into practice wherever space could be found. Thousands in the countryside and hundreds in the cities joined to share goods, money, books, land, and property of every sort. Members of these collectives rotated work, apportioned income equally, and pooled all resources. Sexual equality worked better in the workers' and student communes of the cities than in the countryside, where the sexual division of labor often prevailed: women took over the big communal kitchens while men labored together in the fields. In the town communes, students and workers made sexual equality a mandatory condition. In these "living utopias," males learned how to cook and iron and wash floors under the guidance of women so that all could take their turns at housework on a strictly rotational basis. In some of the more rigorous communes, love and friendship were declared indivisible—cliques and romantic pairing were outlawed as violations of the collective principle. Tensions and flaring tempers beset many of these communes all through the 1920s; but they persisted as "laboratories of revolution" where communism could be practiced and lived day to day.

This part of the picture of women's liberation—the idealistic foreground—deserves emphasis because it is so often overlooked in assessments of the Revolution. Endemic misery and material poverty hampered these experiments, and cynicism and indifference made mockeries of the dreams, but the experiments and dreams persisted. Life for women—and men—was very difficult in the early years after the Revolution. The rural world presented a vast terrain of disease and superstition, suspicious peasants, archaic tools, and ancient agronomical technique. Towns were filled with unemployed women, deserted and abandoned children, criminals and organized gangs, and conspicuously wealthy businessmen. These last comprised a class created by the introduction of Lenin's New Economic Policy in 1921, which allowed a mixed economy, a limited arena of capitalism and hired labor with enclaves of privileged specialists, government leaders, and foreigners. Women were hit very hard by all of this. About 70 percent of the initial job cutbacks that occurred periodically during this period affected women. Between 70,000 and 100,000 women in de facto marriages with men possessed none of the financial security or legal protection that might have vouchsafed them with registered marriage.

Lesley A. Rimmel

NO

The Baba and the Comrade: Gender and Politics in Revolutionary Russia

During the nearly two years that I lived in Palo Alto, California, I translated several grant proposals from Russian into English for the Global Fund for Women, based nearby. As a long-time student of the USSR and Russia, I was fascinated to see how even in the farthest reaches of the former Soviet Union, women had organized on their own behalf and were writing to this explicitly feminist foundation for support. While all of the groups understandably focused on the need to counter the detrimental effects of recent economic changes on women, how they understood "feminism," and women's "nature" and role in society, varied considerably. This is not surprising, as the idea of gender is contentious in most societies. But what is most encouraging is that in Russia and the Newly Independent States, the issue of gender itself is being seriously grappled with for the first time. As these ... books ... indicate, women in Soviet times were defined as "the same as" or "different from" men according to the current needs of the regime, with gender-specific or gender-neutral policies then applied as the particular situation (war, peace, labor shortages) warranted. Only recently have post-Soviet women begun the difficult but necessary work of claiming agency and making themselves their own first priority.

These ... books— ... written or edited by scholars of distinction—diverge in their approaches and intended audiences. The one that addresses the earliest period of Communist Russia, Elizabeth A. Wood's long-awaited and richly documented *The Baba and the Comrade*, is also the most explicitly scholarly. Nonscholars should not be put off, however, for the book is clearly written and organized, and mostly free of jargon.

The Baba and the Comrade takes as its central theme the question that confronted Bolshevik (after 1918, Communist) activists: were women and men the same or different? Could a baba, generally defined as an ignorant peasant woman, become a comrade, a full-fledged human and citizen? Wood notes how reluctant the Bolsheviks were to target women separately in their propaganda and organizing efforts; only the competition with feminist groups and other socialist parties forced them to do so in the last years before the February and October 1917 revolutions and for several years thereafter.

The dilemma for the Communists was that their revolution was to be class-based, and "any special efforts on behalf of women threatened [the revolution's] class nature." Nadezhda Krupskaia, partner and wife of Bolshevik leader Lenin and usually a stalwart defender of women's interests, illustrated this reluctance (and some typical Communist condescension) in a draft editorial for the party paper Rabotnitsa ("Woman Worker") in 1913:

> The "woman question" for male and female workers is a question [of] how to draw the backward masses of women workers into organization, how best to explain to them their interests, how best to make them into comrades in the general struggle. Solidarity among the male and female workers, a general cause, general goals, a general path to that goal—that is the solution to the "woman" question in the workingclass environment.... The journal Rabotnitsa will strive to explain to unconscious women workers their interests, to show them the commonality of their interests with the interests of the whole working class.

Yet, for practical and historical reasons, women, who were less literate than men and who were charged with all household and childcare duties, in addition to whatever work they might have outside the home, could not be reached by Communist activists as easily as men. Many women could not or would not attend meetings with men, nor would they speak out with men present. But the Communists needed to appeal to women in order to mobilize their support (especially during the crucial years of the civil war, from 1918 to 1920). And if the backward baba was not made to support the new regime, then she might hinder the revolution and even become a source of counter-revolution (defined in practice as any opposition to Bolshevik policy). And as women would be raising the next generation, it was critical that they understand and support the new order. The spectre of the baba who would harm the revolution if not won over became the justification for focusing activism on women separately.

Wood concentrates on the period from 1918 to 1923, when woman-centered activism was most pronounced, but she begins by placing Communist ideas and stereotypes about women and reform in their Russian historical perspective. Beginning in the late [seventeenth] century under Tsar Peter I, who attempted to orient Russia to the West, women were viewed as surrogates for the backwardness of Russia; integrating them into male society would be a step toward "civilizing" Russia and turning women into human beings. The Bolshe-viks basically continued in this vein, giving the tsarist interpretation a Marxist gloss. On the one hand, the Communist regime enacted legislation mandating sexual equality, with the only "special treatment" being pregnancy and maternity leaves for women in the workplace. On the other hand, the culture's traditional gender essentialism remained, to be resurrected when needed.

This dialectic of gender became evident during the civil war, when the Communists appealed to women's supposedly inherent traits as caregivers and homemakers to take on work as nurses and inspectors, to use their "sharp eyes and tender hearts" to care for wounded soldiers and root out any corruption or misdeeds. At the same time, local women's sections of the Communist Party were established, as well as a national organization, the Women's Department of the Party, the Zhenotdel.

Theoretically, the women's sections were to be "transmission belts" (a favorite Bolshevik metaphor) for bringing party policy to ordinary women. They did indeed function this way. However, as the civil war gave way to the era of the New Economic Policy, a time of some economic privatization with greater political centralization (somewhat like the situation of China today, and economically similar to present-day Russia), many women lost their jobs and their health benefits, and the women's sections began lobbying the government on women's behalf. Labor and enterprise leaders, seeing women more as mothers than as workers, were unsympathetic, and the state continued to curtail its "social programs." Zhenotdel activists countered by bringing out the threat of the baba: the NEP was forcing women into "domestic slavery" or prostitution in order to survive (a not untrue contention), and in their regression from comrade to baba, they would take men down with them.

If there was any regression, however, it was on the part of the government in general and men in particular, who by 1923–24 feared not that women would be a drag on the revolution, but that the housework would not get done. Women's section activists, whose political and material support from authorities was being cut, strove to assure men of the party that female comrades would not desert their posts—at the stove. Thus Bolshevik backlash against gender transformation began long before Stalinist family values became institutionalized in the 1930 and 1940s—a time often referred to as the "Great Retreat."

Wood's convincing work is a welcome addition to the growing literature on the gender-role traditionalism the Communists reinstitutionalized with their revolution. Women's opportunities—and workload—may have increased after 1917, but the culture's scepticism about women's "essential nature" did not. For those of us who for years have attempted to point this out (and were vilified, by some on both the Right and the Left, for doing so), Wood's readable narrative and copious examples bring further validation.

How did women in the Soviet Union negotiate their country's contradictory gender expectations? Mostly, it seems, they ignored them and concentrated on survival. Historian Barbara Alpern Engel and demographer and feminist activist Anastasia Posadskaya-Vanderbeck have collected eight interviews with women whose only commonality was (with one exception) that they were born before the Bolshevik Revolution, and survived to see the USSR's demise. The title of their book, *A Revolution of Their Own*, is [somewhat misleading], since it seems to imply that women actually got "their" revolution. In fact, as their stories indicate, most of these women did not benefit from the revolution, and for many the Soviet experience was a largely negative one.

Most interesting, however, is that neither the women's experiences nor their attitudes can be predicted from their backgrounds—a clear retort to the Communists' near obsession with people's "social origins." The interviews took place not just in Moscow but in Siberia and in Ekaterinburg in the Urals; the women themselves were born in a variety of places. While the eight are not a representative sample demographically, their experiences are varied enough to make for a rich and provocative portrait of a generation that lived through one of history's greatest dramas.

Each chapter consists of a thorough introduction to the woman being interviewed, complete with a description of the physical setting, followed by a portion of the interview (edited for length and variety), including abbreviated versions of Posadskaya's questions. The latter reveal Posadskaya's ability to prod the woman being interviewed—for example, on their views on abortion, which was not a topic these women normally discussed. (One area where Posadskaya did not prod was that of lesbian rights, which may have been an issue for one of the women.) Sometimes the questions illuminate more about Posadskaya and her generation's concerns than about her interviewees': when she asks Anna Dubova about who decided how the family income would be spent in the 1930s, Dubova responds, almost with surprise, "we had so little money, there was nothing to decide."

Neither family background nor individual efforts can totally explain each woman's fate or her orientation toward the Communist regime. Among those interviewed, the women with peasant backgrounds shared little except unpromising beginnings. Elena Ponomarenko was the youngest of seventeen siblings (from the same mother), and could rarely attend school because she did not have shoes and had to work. But joining the party gave her life structure and helped her to get a start in journalism, for which she repaid the regime with her consistent loyalty, even to the point of defending the Terror and leaving her dying mother to go on an assignment. Irina Kniazeva, on the other hand, knew nothing but hardship in her peasant life, from the father and husbands who mistreated her, the constant hard labor that was never rewarded, and even the burden of "sin" she carried for years for having stolen a handful of grain to feed her children during the famine of the early 1930s. Reading this woman's words, and seeing her careworn face (each interview includes pictures of the women, usually at various stages of their lives), I was moved to tears.

All the stories are dramatic and even novelistic—Communist activist Sofia Pavlova's nighttime escapes on horseback during the civil war, Ponomarenko fighting off wolves in her travels, Vera Malakhova's experience as a front line doctor during World War Two—and it's no wonder that they can be disdainful of today's younger generation and its seeming worship of luxury. Nearly all the women had difficult family lives—drunken and abusive husbands, wonderful but brief relationships with lovers or second husbands who suddenly disappeared in one of the convulsions of the Stalin era, and long periods of single motherhood in conditions of extreme poverty.

In fact, as Engel and Posadskaya observe, "the 'new Soviet family' essentially consisted of a mother who 'saved the children,' [...] raising one or two by herself, often with the help of her own mother or a nurse but with no evident support, financial or otherwise, from the government." (At the end of World War Two there were 26 million more women than men in the Soviet Union.) Some of these women had to renounce their families of origin in order merely to survive, while others found it necessary to marry men of "correct" backgrounds so as to "lose" their pasts—or even just to gain a place to live. But no amount of "family values" legislation, which the Stalin regime provided in abundance during the 1930s and 1940s, could overcome the problems of hunger, crowded housing, fatigue and policies that separated people from their loved ones and mined "family" happiness for so many.

What did give meaning to most of these women's lives was a love of work. Only a few of them, when prodded, complained about limited opportunities for women; but even party loyalist Pavlova had to admit that women could not get any farther than she had, as head of a department of the Communist Party's Central Committee (its second-highest decision-making body): "There was a ceiling. It's the tenacity of tradition, and unfortunately, to this day, we haven't broken its hold. I don't know how long it will take to overcome it." Under the personal, economic and political conditions that these women lived through, however, their survival and the survival of (most of) their children seems nothing short of miraculous—they were truly "heroes of their own lives," to use Linda Gordon's phrase.

> That these women tend to downplay any long-suppressed resentment at limitations they experienced because of their sex—the overt discrimination and the practical obstacles engendered by single motherhood and poverty—is probably because class-based discrimination affected them more deeply, for better or for worse....

Russian history is full of ironies, and nothing is more ironic than the fact that women's freedom to discuss and protest their situation arrived in the late 1980s and early 1990s, just as most women's lives really began to worsen. The contradictions of gender essentialism that were never really addressed by the Soviet Union bore fruit. Because, for example, parental leave and childcare had been associated with women only, women were and are the ones most likely to be fired as workplaces have to cut costs. With gender roles at home never questioned, and with housework being so extraordinarily time-consuming in Russia (which does not have enough well-supplied, conveniently located shops or labor-saving devices), women, with no more "reserved seats" (few as they were) in government bodies, are at a disadvantage in trying to compete as political players. Old-fashioned male chauvinism also plays a part in keeping women out of politics, and out of business as well.

Not all of this is new; the Communist Party and other powerful institutions had long been affirmative action programs for sons of party leaders. But along with the new opportunities of the post-Soviet era have come new obstacles for Russian women.

Yet the women in this book seem equal to the challenge. The larger groups they founded or reorganized all have Soviet roots, in some cases quite strong ones. One of the best-known is the Center for Gender Studies, the Soviet Union's first center for research on women, and its sister umbrella group, the Independent Women's Forum, which organized the first countrywide, independent gathering for women's groups. The Center and the Forum have been very successful in publicizing their critiques of Russian society. They are less involved in politicking to get women into positions of power, although their members often serve as consultants to government bodies. Although the Center is associated with the venerable Academy of Sciences, it has been outspoken in its feminism, as has its founding director, Anastasia Posadskaya-Vanderbeck.

Posadskaya early on found the Soviet system to be sexist and hypocritical, once she saw underqualified but well-connected men getting into academic programs for which she was rejected although she had passed the exams. She comes across in this book as less comfortable being interviewed than being the interviewer; she calls herself a "reluctant activist," saying she would have preferred to be a full-time scholar, but felt impelled to fight for women to "have their own voice, to speak independently, to speak not from a position of class or of one-half the population, which has been rescued by somebody else, but to set up their own agenda."...

What, then, has women's activism accomplished? There is not a lot of information here on specific achievements, and those interested will have to do further research elsewhere. What clearly has been achieved, however, has been a revolution of consciousness. Although Women's Activism leaves us with questions about the future of feminism in Russia—indeed, the future of Russia itself is always a big question—it also leaves us with hope. While some women have chosen to become active in far-left or far-right splinter groups in the belief that resurrecting the old Stalinism or traditional patriarchalism will restore some imagined women's paradise (although it should be noted that it was the post-Soviet Communists who first organized around women's disproportionate unemployment), there is no going back for Russian women. Too many now know their history, or are being forced to acknowledge it.

The challenges are truly daunting, especially with regard to women's economic situation, to which the growth in sex trafficking of Russian and other women from the Newly Independent States provides eloquent testimony. But activists won't get fooled again; there will be no more "mobiliz[ing] women's support for men's political agendas," for women to be only "producers and reproducers" for the state. There may be few babas left, but "comradeship" will be defined on women's terms. And then women will truly have a revolution of their own....

POSTSCRIPT

Did the Bolshevik Revolution Improve the Lives of Soviet Women?

It is one of history's ironies that, with the stroke of a pen, Soviet women were granted all the legal and political rights that women in Britain and the United States were struggling to achieve. Having won the rights to vote and hold public office, Soviet women struggled to translate those paper rights into improved lives for themselves and their children. It has been a conviction of Western feminism that legal and political equality pave the way for full emancipation of women. The Soviet case raises interesting questions about the confusion that arises when there are conflicting revolutions. Real political power belongs to those who can assure that the goals of their revolution receive first priority. It was the socialist revolution, not women's emancipation, that the party leadership worked to achieve.

Popular accounts of the Russian Revolution may be found in John Reed's *Ten Days That Shook the World* (Penguin, 1977) and Louise Bryant's *Mirrors of Moscow* (Hyperion Press, 1973). The story of Reed and Bryant, two Americans who find themselves eyewitnesses to the Bolshevik Revolution, is captured in the film "Reds." Another film covering the same period is "Doctor Zhivago," which is based on the book of the same title by Boris Pasternak (1958). For Lenin's views on women, one of the best sources is his book *The Emancipation of Women* (International Publishers, 1972). *The Unknown Lenin: From the Secret Archives*, edited by the eminent Russian historian Richard Pipes (Yale University Press, 1996) dips into the secret archives and brands Lenin a ruthless and manipulative leader. Robert McNeal's *Bride of the Revolution* (University of Michigan Press, 1972) focuses on the fascinating marriage and revolutionary relationship between Lenin and Bolshevik propagandist Nadezhda Krupskaya. And Sheila Fitzpatrick, in *The Russian Revolution* (Oxford University Press, 1982) surveys the critical 1917–1932 period with special emphasis on the work of Zhenotdel. For essays on the lives of women during this period, students may want to see *Women in Soviet Society,* edited by Gail Lapidus (University of California Press, 1978) and *Women in Russia,* edited by D. Atkinson, A. Dallin, and G. Lapidus (Stanford University Press, 1977), which grew out of a 1975 conference that was held at Stanford University titled "Women in Russia." The fascinating character Alexandra Kollontai, who died at 80, may be explored through her own writings in *Selected Writings* (W.W. Norton, 1972), *The Autobiography of a Sexually Emancipated Communist Woman* (Schocken Books, 1975), *Red Love* (Hyperion Press, 1990), and *Love of Worker Bees* (Academy of Chicago Press, 1978). Books about Kollontai include *Bolshevik Feminist* by Barbara Clements (Indiana University Press,

1979). Some recent scholarship on Bolshevik women includes: Elizabeth A. Wood's *The Baba and the Comrade: Gender and Politics in Revolutionary Russia* (Indiana Universtiy Press, 1997); Barbara Evans Clements's *Bolshevik Women* (Cambridge University Press, 1997); Anna Hillyar and Jane McDermid's *Revolutionary Women in Russia, 1870-1917: A Study in Collective Biography* (Manchester University Press, 2000); and Choi Chatterjee's *Celebrating Women: Gender, Festival Culture, and Bolshevik Ideology, 1910-1939* (University of Pittsburgh Press, 2002).

ISSUE 9

Have Afghan Women Been Liberated From Oppression?

YES: Sima Wali, from "Afghan Women: Recovering, Rebuilding," *Carnegie Council on Ethics & International Affairs* (October 2002)

NO: Noy Thrupkaew, from "What Do Afghan Women Want?" *The American Prospect* (August 26, 2002)

ISSUE SUMMARY

YES: International Afghan advocate for refugee women Sima Wali documents the pivotal roles Afghan women have played in rebuilding their communities, praises their courage in denouncing warlords, and calls for their full participation in the newly formed constitutional government.

NO: Journalist Noy Thrupkaew argues that dissension among women's groups in Afghanistan and the high profile of the Western-backed Revolutionary Association of the Women of Afghanistan (RAWA) are hampering progress; a more unified and moderate approach is needed.

The modern history of Afghanistan began in 1979, with the Soviet invasion and subsequent occupation. The powerful jihad that ultimately expelled the Soviets also fortified indigenous tribal codes that treat women as property and encouraged the fundamentalism that brought the Taliban to power in 1996. During the 1990s, Western journalists began reporting on the draconian measures decreed by the Taliban that barred women from education, health care, work, and freedom of movement. In this oppressive environment, RAWA (Revolutionary Association of the Women of Afghanistan) opened clandestine schools and hospitals for Afghan women and girls, provided international journalists with secret film footage of Taliban atrocities (including public executions of women for adultery), and offered ferociously anti-fundamentalist rhetoric that was repeated in news media around the world.

Likening the situation of rigid separation of the sexes in Afghanistan to rigid separation of the races in South Africa, human rights organizations in the West began to use the term "gender apartheid" to describe the plight of Afghan women. Following the September 11, 2001 attacks, the United States launched a bombing campaign targeting Taliban and Al-Qaeda bases in Afghanistan.

After the Taliban regime fell, the United Nations held peace talks in Bonn, Germany, that brought various political parties together in conversation and sketched out the parameters of an interim government with Hamid Karzai, a unifying political figure, as president. In January 2002, interim President Karzai signed a Declaration of Essential Rights of Afghan Women, which guaranteed legal equality between women and men, equal protection under the law, equal rights to both education and political participation, and the freedoms of movement, speech, and dress (to wear or not wear the burqa or any form of head covering). The following June a loya jirga, or grand assembly, met to elect a transitional goverment; women delegates participated.

Months of intense negotiations led to a constitution that was agreed to in January 2004 by a *loya jirga* of regional representatives. Karzai, president of the transitional government, signed the constitution later that month. In 12 chapters and 161 articles, the Afghan constitution mandates a strong presidency and provides for upper and lower legislative houses, secures equal legal rights for women and men, and establishes Islam as the country's sacred religion, but guarantees protection for other faiths. Women have been guaranteed a percentage of the seats in both upper and lower legislative houses. On October 9, 2004, the first presidential election was held in Afghanistan, with extraordinarily high turnout, including large numbers of women who stood in line for hours. Although Karzai was elected in a landslide, Massouda Jalal, a female physician, was also a candidate for president. She gave campaign speeches inside mosques and rallies in villages where women still needed their husband's permission to register to vote. Many women, in fact, were instructed by their husbands how to vote. In preparation for parliamentary elections on September 18, 2005, a census—the first since 1979—was conducted in spring 2005. The lower house will have 249 seats, with provinces sharing them on the basis of population, very much like the U.S. House of Representatives.

There are clear signs of hope. Roads and schools have been rebuilt, and women will have a voice in the government. The first woman-managed radio station in Kabul came on the air November 13, 2001, with the words, "The Taliban are gone," and Voice of Afghan Women recently received the first Reflections of Hope Award from Oklahoma City, on the tenth anniversary of the bombing of the Murrah Federal Building. But, the Taliban are resurgent, people do not feel safe, narcotic trafficking and the flow of arms continue unabated, and warlord-ism and violence against women persist. In the villages far from the capital city of Kabul, women are not allowed to speak with men outside their immediate families, and fathers can still force their daughters into arranged marriages, even treating them as commodities to settle debts. Once married, a woman has no protection from an abusive husband. If a woman runs away from her husband (threatening his honor and dignity), she can be beaten or even jailed and prosecuted. A woman who is kidnapped or raped brings shame upon her household and, typically, will not be accepted back. An increasing number opt for suicide. Throughout Afghanistan, maternal and infant mortality ratios are the highest in the world, 300,000 children die each year from preventable diseases, and 85 percent of women are illiterate. Clearly, some Afghan women have been liberated from oppression, but others have not.

YES 

Sima Wali

Afghan Women: Recovering, Rebuilding

The United States' foreign policy in Afghanistan has a long history of misguided plans and misplaced trust—a fact that has contributed to the destruction of the social and physical infrastructure of Afghan society. Afghans contend that after having fought as U.S. allies against the Soviet Union—with the price of more than two million dead—the United States swiftly walked away at the end of that bloody, twenty-three-year conflict. The toll of the war on Afghan society reflected in current statistics is so staggering as to be practically unimaginable: 12 million women living in abject poverty, 1 million people handicapped from land mine explosions, an average life expectancy of forty years (lower for women), a mortality rate of 25.7 percent for children under five years old, and an illiteracy rate of 64 percent. These horrific indicators place Afghanistan among the most destitute countries in the world in terms of human development.

In 1996 the Taliban walked into this breach, immediately issuing edicts banning Afghan women from the public domain. The harshness of the terms of segregation evoked comparisons with South Africa's apartheid regime—leading human rights organizations in the West to call it "gender apartheid." Women were prohibited from working outside their homes, attending school, or appearing in public without a close male relative. They were forced to ride on "women only" public buses, were forbidden to wear brightly colored clothes, and had to have the windows in their houses painted so that they could not be seen from outside. Initially, they could only be treated by female doctors; later, they could be examined—but not seen or touched—by male doctors, in the presence of a male relative. The standard punishment for theft and adultery was public stoning, or even execution; yet a woman had no right to petition a court directly.

These ultraconservative policies and the hardships they imposed are by now quite well known—thanks in part to work done before the war in Afghanistan by women's groups in the United States. In 1998, for example, an alliance of women's rights groups protested the U.S. oil company Unocal's collaboration with the Taliban regime in a project to build a natural gas pipeline through Afghanistan. This grassroots campaign, much like the 1980s anti-apartheid movement for South Africa, publicized the plight of Afghan women and provided a new set of interlocutors in U.S. foreign policy. In essence, the message of this movement was that the conditions of life for Afghan women symbolized the total devastation of Afghan society.

From *Ethics & International Affairs*, vol. 16, issue 2, October 2002, pp. 15-20. Notes omitted.

The Status Of Women

From the beginning of the war, the status of women denied even the most basic human rights under the Taliban regime was a significant part of the moral justification for the antiterrorism campaign in Afghanistan. The Taliban's introduction of draconian measures against Afghan women left them exceedingly poor, unhealthy, and uneducated. In Afghan society, women constitute the most underprivileged group: the vast majority of the 22 million Afghans who rely on international assistance for survival have been women. Globally, they represent the most extreme example of what is known as the "feminization of poverty": for years their health care and nutritional needs have been ignored; their labor has gone unrecognized and unpaid; they have lacked access to education; they have been denied land ownership or inheritance rights; and they have had no decision-making power in the community. That is, they have had none of the resources they would need to escape the cycle of poverty.

Contributing to this near-total lack of capabilities women in particular have to adequately take care of themselves and their families is the fact that the Afghan crisis is currently the most serious and complex human emergency in the world. There are 1.1 million internally displaced people in Afghanistan and almost 3.6 million living in neighboring countries. The majority of them are women. Because of the disproportionate death toll in men during the war against the Soviet Union, it is women who are now charged with taking care of the approximately one million orphaned children, the elderly, and the handicapped—though they are, themselves, traumatized, malnourished, and undersupported.

How can the status of women in Afghanistan improve given these daunting challenges? The first thing to realize is that despite these appalling statistics, Afghan women are resources for development, not just victims. I can testify to their resilience and courage and to the contributions they have made in the past two decades of war. While men took up arms, Afghan women and their male supporters were busy rebuilding their communities by providing critically needed human services. Thus the success of rapid development schemes hinges on the formal rehabilitation and active protection of women's equal status in Afghan society.

The implications of gender inequality for the future of Afghanistan are significant given that women represent more than half of the population. Without their participation in political and economic life, it will be impossible for the country to develop and integrate successfully into a global society. What is needed to start the process is an up-to-date, accurate analysis of gender inequality. Reliable basic data—such as the percentage of women in the total population, family size, the number of households headed by women—and human development indicators for health, education, and income were last published in 1996.

Only after the appropriate data is collected can the government create responsible policies for gender mainstreaming—that is, for alleviating the segregation of women and their effective social, economic, and political marginalization. Women must be integrated into all sectors of Afghan society, including public life as paid government employees. For gender inequality to be addressed seriously, women need to participate more proportionately in government (currently, they hold only 11 percent of seats in the loya jirga council). They should also hold posts in all ministries, not just in the Ministry of Women's Affairs.

The War On Terrorism And Its Aftermath

Following a long lapse in U.S. interest in Afghanistan, this war-ravaged nation stood at the epicenter of world attention almost immediately after the September 11 attacks on U.S. soil. Afghanistan, which had been denied the credit it was due for having helped free the world of communism, now grabbed headlines for all the wrong reasons. Suddenly made famous as the homeland of the Taliban and host to Osama bin Laden and his mercenaries, Afghanistan was excoriated as a country that waged war against its women. The Western world did not need any more justifications than these to launch its offensive. For the first time in world history, a major war was being linked—however tenuously—to the freedom of women.

Initially, the people of Afghanistan—and women in particular—welcomed U.S. and international forces, publicly rejoicing in the streets of Kabul. As the euphoria wore off, however, the burqa-clad women were increasingly unwilling to emerge from their shroud-like coverings, alleging a lack of security, rampant rape, ethnic witch-hunting campaigns against the Pashtun tribe, generalized violence, and widespread abuse by various factions of the Northern Alliance forces. Women in refugee camps spoke of becoming the targets of recently disarmed men—whose new weapons were harassment and rape. Without the protection of security forces, refugee and internally displaced women from neighboring countries who had fled the war fear returning to their home areas in Afghanistan, while others fear leaving their homes to participate in public life as teachers, health workers, entrepreneurs, and government officials.

Given these dangers, women demonstrated remarkable courage during the recent loya jirga—the council that met in Kabul June 10–16 to elect a transitional government by articulating their long-held grievances against warlords and their armed supporters. Giving testimony was not without its risks, particularly for those who came from outside Kabul and whose safe return to their provinces and respectful treatment by local warlords could not be assured. As the campaign to bring down al-Qaeda progressed, both Afghan women and men had to be wary of the increased power of these warlords, whom the U.S.-led forces hoped to win over to the war on terrorism through gifts of weapons and money. Indeed, Afghan women cite this empowerment of warlords as one of the gravest threats to the establishment and the maintenance of a secure environment. For these reasons, multinational peacekeeping forces must be expanded beyond Kabul to provide security for women and all Afghans, and to train Afghan security forces which should themselves accept women recruits.

In addition to serious questions about basic security for women, there are deep socioeconomic issues for all Afghans such as the lack of adequate employment, education, income, and housing—coupled with a new nepotism among certain forces in power. Under these circumstances, the needs of Afghan women have once again been deferred. However, as the cases of intimidation against Sima Samar, the former minister of women's affairs, and other female loya jirga delegates indicate, women's issues concern everyone—not just women. Samar was alleged to have said that she did not believe in sharia (Islamic law), and was charged in court with blasphemy. Warlords invoked the allegation to threaten her repeatedly, and it became the basis for the Supreme Court chief justice's claim that she was not fit to hold a government office. It took the intervention of then-Chairman Karzai to abolish all charges against her and subsequently reassign her to head the Human Rights Commission. By undermining the legitimate representation of all Afghan people, gender-inspired threats to current or former government officials directly imperil the prospects for Afghanistan's success in building a state governed by the rule of law and the respect for human rights.

It is thus important that international nongovernmental organizations and other interlocutors pressure national governments to place conditionalities on reconstruction aid that are predicated on gender sensitivity. As soon as the transitional government gains access to the funds promised but as yet unreleased—at the International Conference for Reconstruction Assistance to Afghanistan in Tokyo last January, the international community will give its first attention to rebuilding political institutions and physical infrastructure, and to making provisions for security forces. Only a fraction of the funds may be used to address the social and civil institutions ravaged by the war. It is here, then, that the international community should reorient some of its priorities toward these latter institutions, and thereby show its commitment to helping build a peaceful, tolerant, and democratic Afghan society.

Looking Ahead

The era when states might commit grave human rights abuses against their own citizens with impunity is past. The U.S. public has, as a result of September 11, broad access to images of and news stories about human beings who are experiencing inordinate suffering. Will they reach out to help? That depends. First, Americans should reconsider the origins of the war in Afghanistan, and come to terms with the United States' own role in it. Second—and consequentially—they should understand that events in Afghanistan directly affect their lives in the United States.

As tragic as the attacks on September 11 were, one of their unintended outcomes was to produce renewed thinking about the need to address the inhumane conditions to which the Afghan people have long been subject. The most striking aspect of this effect is that rhetoric decrying the indecency and criminality of Taliban treatment of Afghan women actually passed from rhetoric to action. This may have simply been a by-product of the U.S.-led war on terrorism, but it should not distract us from accepting and building on these opportunities for the Afghan people and, especially, for Afghan women.

Noy Thrupkaew

NO

What Do Afghan Women Want?

The unveiling took place amid the giddy whirl of a $1,000 ticket, all-star production of Eve Ensler's *The Vagina Monologues* on Feb. 10, 2001. Raucous merriment had come and gone: Ensler conducted a chorus of ecstatically groaning celebrities, Glenn Close urged the audience to reclaim the c-word by yelling it at the top of its lungs. Then Oprah Winfrey recited Ensler's latest monologue, "Under the *Burqa*," and a hush fell over the crowd as Oprah exhorted its members to "imagine a huge dark piece of cloth / hung over your entire body / like you were a shameful statue." As the piece wound to a close, a figure in a *burqa* ascended to the stage. Oprah turned and lifted the head-to-toe shroud.

Voila! There stood Zoya, a young representative of the Revolutionary Association of the Women of Afghanistan (RAWA), the group of 2,000 Afghan women who had seized the West's imagination with ferociously anti-fundamentalist rhetoric, secret footage of Taliban atrocities and clandestine schools and hospitals for Afghan girls and women. Center stage, Zoya delivered a fiery speech about the oppression of Afghan women and RAWA's ongoing resistance to the Taliban regime. Eighteen thousand people leaped to their feet, and New York City's Madi-son Square Garden rang with cheers.

RAWA has always had a flair for the dramatic, and this appearance was no exception. It was pure, delicious theater: the stark words, the ominous, oppressive *burqa* and the "hey presto" transformation of suffering into strength with the flick of a hem. The unveiling also captured part of RAWA's appeal to American feminists, as it let the audience appreciate the friction between the image of silenced Afghan women and the brand of outspoken feminism that RAWA espouses.

Although the Pakistan- and Afghanistan-based group was founded in Kabul in 1977, RAWA didn't receive worldwide recognition until U.S. feminist campaigns for Afghan women's rights hit their stride in the late 1990s. After September 11, the attention only intensified. Hundreds of articles and two books chronicled RAWA's struggle, the group's *burqa*-clad members spoke across the United States and, at one point, a flashing banner reading "Welcome, Oprah viewers!" greeted visitors to RAWA's Web site.

But is a group that is inspirational in the United States effective in Afghani-stan? With its confrontational, no-holds-barred language and allegiance to a secular society, RAWA reflects much of the Western feminist community's own values— a fact that has earned RAWA strong support in the West but few friends in a strongly Muslim country weary of political battles and bloodshed. Similarly, part of RAWA's allure, for Ensler at least, has been its militant, radical, "uncompromising" nature, as Ensler told Salon.com in November 2001. But this quality has a dark side. RAWA has denounced numerous other Afghan women's groups as insuf-ficientlly critical of fundamentalism. It has also publicly attacked prominent Afghan women activists—some of whom have in turn raised questions about RAWA's own political connections. As a result, Afghan women's nongovernmental organizations and Afghan feminist expatriates have expressed concern about a radical, lone-wolf organization garnering so much Western attention. In Afghani-stan's slow, painful shift from war to nation building, they say, perhaps the country needs stronger support for voices of coalition building rather than for those advocating solitary revolution.

To understand the nature of RAWA's partnership with Western feminists, it helps to return to the starting point for U.S. feminist activism on Afghan women's rights: the Feminist Majority's "Campaign to Stop Gender Apartheid in Afghanistan." Although the campaign has come under fire for a few alleged missteps—some critics have charged it with focusing too much on the *burqa* as a symbol of victimhood—the Feminist Majority's project has earned widespread praise for mobilizing grass-roots support and scoring significant U.S. political victories for Afghan women's rights.

After the Taliban militia seized control of Afghanistan in 1996, the Feminist Majority's staff began noticing "one-inch Associated Press clips that women couldn't go out unattended, couldn't gather, wear noisy shoes, white socks," according to Eleanor Smeal, the Feminist Majority's executive director. Shocked by these reports and by news that the Taliban had denied countless women access to work, health care and education, Feminist Majority staff consulted with the U.S. State Department and Afghan women activists in the United States before launching their campaign in 1997. Through a series of petitions, protests, celebrity fundraisers and political negotiations, the Feminist Majority played a significant role in the 1998 refusal by the United Nations and the United States to grant formal recognition to the Taliban. Its next pressure campaign helped push U.S. energy company Unocal out of a $3 billion venture to put a pipeline through Afghanistan, which would have provided the Taliban with $100 million in royalties. Within three years of launching the campaign, the Feminist Majority and its allies had also improved U.S. refugee policy toward Afghanistan, set up support for Afghan schools for girls and pushed through increases in emergency aid.

RAWA was only one of about 240 U.S. and Afghan women's groups the Feminist Majority contacted over the course of its campaign. But when the Feminist Majority invited RAWA to its Feminist Expo 2000, the campaign helped catapult the Afghan group into the spotlight. Dispatches from the exposition, a conference of 7,000 feminists from around the world, invariably mentioned the RAWA delegates' powerful speeches and passionate conviction. RAWA had officially caught the eye of the feminist world.

Ensler, too, played a vital role in bringing RAWA to the U.S. public's attention. After seeing RAWA's Pakistan-based orphanages and schools, where little girls were "being brought up as revolutionaries," Ensler became "completely smitten by [RAWA]" and decided to help, she told Salon.com. "V-Day," Ensler's worldwide campaign to eradicate violence against women through performances of The Vagina Monologues, awarded RAWA $120,000 in 2001 and a similar grant in 2002.

Nothing, however, drew attention to the plight of Afghan women like the aftermath of September 11. The Feminist Majority and RAWA were soon deluged with calls from the media. Smeal was quoted in countless articles; RAWA was so overwhelmed that members had to decline interview requests. RAWA's secret footage of public hangings and shootings, captured on video cameras hidden under its members' *burqas*, aired over and over on Saira Shah's *Beneath the Veil* documentary, which was in heavy rotation on CNN. Oprah viewers sent more digital cameras than RAWA could use, while poems from Western women imagining themselves under the *burqa* choked the group's Web site. The site also featured numerous songs, including one about RAWA's martyred founder written by the women's rock band Star Vomit. In short, RAWA became "the darling of the media and the feminists," recalls Illinois State University women's studies director Valentine M. Moghadam.

September 11 brought both the Feminist Majority and RAWA new momentum. The Feminist Majority purchased *Ms. Magazine* and published a special insert on its Afghanistan campaign to introduce itself to *Ms.* readers. Along with coalition partners Equality Now, the National Organization for Women and Ensler, the project, renamed the Campaign to Help Afghan Women and Girls, pushed for an expansion of security forces beyond Kabul and an increase in funding to the interim government and women-led NGOs. RAWA continued to raise funds for its schools and hospitals and went on speaking tours around the world. Both organizations were busy but productive, blessed with a resurgence of public interest and largely positive media attention. And then came the letter.

On April 20, 2002, a U.S.-based RAWA supporter posted an open letter to *Ms.* on RAWA's listserv. It would later appear all over the Internet—on Middle Eastern studies' listservs and feminist online communities. Written by Elizabeth Miller from Cincinnati, the letter called Ms. Magazine the "mouthpiece of hegemonic, U.S.-centric, ego driven, corporate feminism." Miller proceeded to take the Feminist Majority to task for failing to mention the work of RAWA in its *Ms. Magazine* insert; it also charged the organization with ignoring the atrocities Afghan women suffered under the current U.S. allies in Afghanistan, the Northern Alliance. Even worse, the letter continued, was the Feminist Majority's support for the work of Sima Samar, then Afghanistan's interim minister of women's affairs. Miller claimed that Samar was "a member of the leadership council of one of the most notorious fundamentalist factions Hezb-e Wahdat [the Islamic Unity Party of Afghanistan]."

Asked about the letter, Smeal chuckles, then sighs. "The idea [behind the insert] was to introduce us by one of our campaigns," she says. Part of the insert's role was to tell "the pre-September 11, U.S. feminist story behind the campaign," according to Jennifer Jackman, the Feminist Majority's director of research. That story necessarily highlighted the unsung work of UN feminists, the two women appointed to the interim Afghan government and Afghan expatriate activist Sima Wali. The omission of RAWA was not political, Smeal insists. "We felt everyone knew RAWA," she said.

As for the letter's allegation that the Feminist Majority had not spoken out against the Northern Alliance, Smeal's own words to the media discount that. "The Northern Alliance is better than the Taliban toward women, but they are still not good," Smeal told me shortly after September 11. "We have to think beyond wartime, and we can't call some crowd 'freedom fighters' if they're not."

But the allegation against Samar was the most disturbing and difficult to dismiss. Human Rights Watch has charged Hezb-e Wahdat, a largely Hazara group, with taking part in reprisals against Pashtun civilians in northern Afghani-stan. Some probing, however, finds little evidence that Samar has anything to do with Hezb-e Wahdat. Rather, what comes to light is a pattern of RAWA-led smear campaigns against other Afghan women who rise to prominence.

A strongly outspoken advocate for women's rights and a former RAWA member herself, Samar seems an unlikely member of Hezb-e Wahdat, although she is Hazara. Samar is renowned for her nonprofit group Shuhada, which operates hospitals and schools for girls throughout Pakistan and Afghanistan. In light of her women's work, the allegation of Samar's affiliation with a fundamentalist group is "baseless," says Jackman, especially considering the recent ultraconservative attacks that effectively prevented Samar from being reappointed to her position as women's affairs minister.

The Hezb-e Wahdat allegation surfaced throughout RAWA's interviews with the press, and also in a series of e-mails that a RAWA supporter named Sarah Kamal sent to Afghan expatriate activist Zieba Shorish-Shamley and the International Centre for Human Rights and Democratic Development, a Canadian organization that planned to award Samar a human-rights award in 2001. (The e-mails also included attacks against Fatana Gailani, executive director of the Afghanistan Women's Council and a four-time humanitarian-aid award winner for her work on behalf of Afghan refugees.) After conducting an investigation, the president of the organization wrote a letter dismissing the charges and lauding Samar's humanitarian work. Backed by Amnesty International research, the Canadian group found that Samar had set up schools and hospitals in Hazarajat, a Hezb-e-Wahdat-controlled area, and it concluded that "it would have been inevitable for Dr. Samar to be in touch with leaders of this party to facilitate her work. Contact with party officials is a common feature of humanitarian activity throughout Afghanistan but does not amount to taking up the membership of the party." Bolstered by references from organizations including the UN and the U.S.-based Afghan Refugee Information Network, the jury panel granted Samar the award.

As for Shorish-Shamley, she says she was initially supportive of RAWA but that her feelings changed when she saw the "vicious" nature of the accusations against Samar and Gailani. Shorish-Shamley shared an e-mail that she said RAWA wrote to Samar:

> While our beloved land is being reduced for more than a decade to a pulp in the filthy claws of a handful of fundamentalist executioners ... and RAWA, as the sole anti-fundamentalists organization, is at a tough strife with the insane Taliban and Jehadi gangs, it sounds really illogical to discuss the 'fighting with each other' but we are committed to expose it, for you are no longer 'ours,' as it is long ago you have aligned yourself to the rank of the most traitorous enemies of our people. We, thereby, treat you as a leader of the fundamentalists' party; alas it is as a part of our struggle against fundamentalism.

After continuing on for eight more vitriolic pages ("... persons like Sima Samar enjoy the favor of the fundamentalist slaughterers") the letter ends with an absurdly polite postscript: "As I was busy with many other preoccupations, sorry that it took time to reply [to] your letter."

Not surprisingly, RAWA's letter offensives and the distrustful atmosphere in Afghanistan have fueled rumors about the group's own political ties. Azadi Afghan Radio has reported that RAWA is "alleged to be run by men who belong to the former Afghan Maoist (pro-Chinese Shohla Communist Party) group." Other rumors include RAWA's alleged connection to Pakistani intelligence or Mujahideen-e Khalq, a group the U.S. State Department deemed a terrorist organization in 1999. RAWA member Saba denies all accusations, saying, "When women ... are leading a movement, it is difficult for people to tolerate. They think politics is only something for men."

The allegations haven't slowed RAWA down much. As the only Afghan feminist organization with significant Western support, media access and an Internet presence, RAWA has remained productive and resilient. Nor have RAWA's accusers chosen tactics likely to scorch the earth. The Azadi Afghan Radio, which has ties to the Northern Alliance, was careful to praise RAWA's "courage," and it advised Western supporters to speak to Afghans and NGOs about RAWA before making up their minds about the group. Afghan expatriate activists Wali and Shorish-Shamley have fielded many complaints from Afghan NGOs about RAWA, but both women were initially reluctant to air the grievances they heard.

Many of RAWA's Western backers, in turn, remain unfazed by rumors of unsavory political connections. Ensler has denied RAWA's alleged Maoist ties, telling Salon.com, "I may not be the most thorough investigator—that's why

I'm not a journalist." Nonetheless, she said in the same interview, "I've become RAWA's greatest defender."

The Feminist Majority, however, was none too pleased with RAWA's role in lobbing accusations at other groups. "We really have problems with groups attacking each other," says Jackman. "There needs to be solidarity among women's organizations." The Feminist Majority has refuted RAWA's attacks, but not as a matter of "public debate" because "we have not wanted to engage in debate other than over what strategies are most effective. It's not our role to be passing judgment on groups," Jackman says.

Now that the Feminist Majority is focusing on nation building rather than on fighting the Taliban's oppression of women, RAWA has ceased in any case to represent the strategy in greatest demand. "They're not involved in the [push for] security, women's participation, reconstruction, working with a lot of different groups," says Jackman. Some Afghan and Afghan-expatriate feminists put a finer point on this concern. The ability to work with others, build coalitions and use tactics that are in keeping with the more moderate "Afghan norm," says Wali, are all crucial skills for making the transition from resistance to reconstruction—and they are skills that RAWA seems to lack.

Navigating the factionalism and distrust of post-war Afghanistan would be a challenge for any political group, but the ground is clearly most fertile for one that is moderate and inclusive. Civil war, drought and interference from neighboring states have contributed to an atmosphere of mutual suspicion among Afghans, according to Neamat Nojumi, a Central and South Asian specialist and former *mujahideen* unit commander in the Soviet-Afghan war who is currently a United States Agency for International Development consultant. After years of Soviet occupation and wars among factions with extreme agendas, intimations of Maoist, Marxist or any overtly political agenda are terrifying for many Afghans, he says.

In this fragile environment, RAWA's perceived strengths—the uncompromising, radically feminist quality that Ensler recognizes as that of a "kindred spirit"—seem more like liabilities. As Ensler's quote attests, for many Western feminists, RAWA reflects a familiar yet glorified self-image: the fiery words, the clenched fists and protest signs, the type of guerilla feminism that seems unflinchingly brave. But to many Afghan women, RAWA's tactics look altogether too dangerous. Says Sayed Sahibzada, an Afghan United Nations Development Programme officer who has worked with more than 40 Afghan women-led NGOs, "I have not heard one group that goes along with RAWA. They say, 'If there is a RAWA participant [in a training], we are not going to participate.'" New York City's large Afghan-American population is similarly conflicted about the group. Masuda Sultan of Women for Afghan Women lauds RAWA's "long and committed history" of bravery. But she notes that "most Afghan women don't feel that RAWA represents them," because of the group's revolutionary rhetoric and alleged ties to Maoism.

RAWA has done little to build bridges. In addition to the campaign against Samar and Gailani, it has often shunned other women's groups. RAWA member Saba took issue with all the prominent Afghan and Afghan-American women I mentioned, saying that they had been part of the Northern Alliance, or the Soviet regime, or hadn't taken a strong stand against fundamentalism. This stance hasn't won over many Afghans: One activist calls RAWA the "Talibabes" because of its fiercely judgmental attitude.

But to effectively counter RAWA's perceived intolerance, opposing feminist groups need to build coalitions themselves. "I'm not trying to bring [RAWA] down. We have to work across political boundaries and viewpoints," says Wali. "They are one of the diverse voices of Afghan women." But RAWA's radical language and tactics, along with the strategies of some Western feminists—such as Ensler, who brought *The Vagina Monologues* to Pakistan and Afghanistan—"backfire on people like us," says Wali. "We are trying to influence the men, many of whom still have Taliban ideology, and they say, 'You are part of these extremists.' It's not time yet. We can't do something extreme and leave Afghan women to deal with it. [RAWA has] a very Westernized radical approach. They are revolutionary. The Afghan people are saying we don't need a revolution, we need a democracy."

Afghanistan may be closer now than ever to a day when voices such as RAWA's won't seem dangerously radical. But in the meantime, Western feminists need to support, fund and take their cues from the other "moderate ... diverse voices of Afghan women," and keep the pressure on their own governments, says Wali. This is something that even RAWA fan Ensler is beginning to do by working with Samar and by contributing to other groups. The Feminist Majority has nurtured connections with Samar's Shuhada group, which kept open numerous clinics, hospitals and schools in the central part of Afghanistan despite the Taliban's restrictions, as well as with the Pakistan-based Afghan Women's Resource Center, among many other Afghan NGOs.

In their own way, these Afghan groups are themselves "revolutionary," says Jackman. "This is a place where giving a girl a book and a pencil is revolutionary." Equally revolutionary is the dedication "to sharing the same agenda," adds Jackman. Even women who were formerly "arch rivals" are working together, says Wali, and their willingness to reach across ethnic and political divides is an important step toward forging trust in the strife-torn country. "There are so many non-partisan Afghan community organizers and leaders," says Wali, "but no one hears them because they are trying to mend society. RAWA has a place in that society, but we need to sit down together—especially with the dissenting, far-fetched voices—and realize that we have a common agenda....We are waging a jihad of social justice and peace. We need to transcend our differences and work together—that is the key to rebuilding Afghanistan."

POSTSCRIPT

Have Afghan Women Been Liberated From Oppression?

Afghanistan has been eclipsed by Iraq as the focus for international media attention. Even when a story is reported from inside Afghanistan, however, it almost always reflects life in the capital city of Kabul. President Hamid Karzai lives and works in a heavily fortified area in Kabul and rarely ventures outside the capital. For most women (and men) in Afghanistan, village life proceeds as it always has. A good place to begin exploring this issue might be with the Amnesty International Report *Afghanistan: Women Under Attack.* Published in May 2005, the report compiled by Nazia Hussein reflects interviews she conducted with women across the country. It details the persistence of feudal customs, in which men treat women as property with no fear of punishment or social disapproval. Afghan women, the report concludes, are murdered, raped, and imprisoned with impunity.

Women for Afghan Women, Sunita Mehta, ed., (Palgrave Macmillan, 2002) is a collection of essays, poems, and photographs from the organization named in the title. An introduction by Sima Wali, author of the "Yes" side of this issue, defines the Afghan people as historically and ethnically distinct from both Arabs and Iranians, describes the languages they speak—chiefly Dari and Pashto—and strongly asserts their lack of connection with Osama bin Laden and Al-Qaeda. Essays dispel the stereotype of Afghan men as "women-haters" and explore both the *loya jirga* and United Nations policies as they affect Afghan women. Cheryl Benard's *Veiled Courage: Inside the Afghan Women's Resistance* (Broadway Books, 2002) explores the resistance of Afghan women to oppression. She provides a history of RAWA (Revolutionary Association of the Women of Afghanistan), beginning with its founding in the late 1970s by a charismatic woman known as Meena, who was killed by Pakistani police with ties to the Afghan secret police. Her courageous leadership continues to inspire RAWA members today, especially the 11 elected women who comprise leadership. RAWA members serve as role models for others who face demoralizing conditions and engage both supporters and challengers in dialogue. Resisting the current project of nation building that accepts ethnic identity as the most important factor, RAWA seeks to alter the culture of female inferiority by altering patterns of male socialization and ideals of masculinity.

My Forbidden Face: Growing Up Under the Taliban, a Young Woman's Story by Latifa (Talk Miramax, 2002) offers a true account of Kabul life from 1996–2001, by a young author using a pseudonym. Educated during the Soviet occupation and ready to begin her university education as a journalist in

1996, "Latifa" describes how her life was "confiscated" by the Taliban. Her narrative concludes as the American bombing begins in October 2001: "... who speaks for Afghanistan? I don't know anymore." *Prisoners of Hope: The Story of Our Captivity and Freedom in Afghanistan* (Doubleday, 2002), by Dayna Curry and Heather Mercer, describes the imprisonment, trial by the Taliban, and rescue by U.S. Special Forces of two Christian missionaries from Waco, Texas. And *Behind the Burqa: Our Life in Afghanistan and How We Escaped to Freedom* by "Sulima" and "Hala" as told to Batya Swift Yasgur (John Wiley & Sons, 2002), is the story of two sisters, 16 years apart in age. "Sulima," the elder, fled the Communist regime in 1979 and "Hala," the younger, fled persecution by the Taliban in 1997. Both were working to educate women. Finally, the first novel in English about Afghanistan is *The Kite Runner* (Penguin, 2003) by Khaled Hosseini, a physician now living in the United States. It is especially helpful in illustrating the power of tribal differences (majority Pashtun and minority Hazara) as well as sectarian ones (majority Sunni and minority Shi'a). It evokes life before the Soviet invasion and confronts the repressive Taliban regime as well.